THE OXFORD HAND

NORTH AMER
ARCHAEOLOGY

THE OXFORD HANDBOOK OF

NORTH AMERICAN ARCHAEOLOGY

TIMOTHY R. PAUKETAT

OXFORD
UNIVERSITY PRESS

Oxford University Press is a department of the University of Oxford.
It furthers the University's objective of excellence in research, scholarship,
and education by publishing worldwide.

Oxford   New York
Auckland   Cape Town   Dar es Salaam   Hong Kong   Karachi
Kuala Lumpur   Madrid   Melbourne   Mexico City   Nairobi
New Delhi   Shanghai   Taipei   Toronto

With offices in
Argentina   Austria   Brazil   Chile   Czech Republic   France   Greece
Guatemala   Hungary   Italy   Japan   Poland   Portugal   Singapore
South Korea   Switzerland   Thailand   Turkey   Ukraine   Vietnam

Oxford is a registered trade mark of Oxford University Press
in the UK and certain other countries.

Published in the United States of America by
Oxford University Press
198 Madison Avenue, New York, NY 10016

© Oxford University Press 2012

First issued as an Oxford University Press paperback, 2015.

All rights reserved. No part of this publication may be reproduced, stored in a
retrieval system, or transmitted, in any form or by any means, without the prior
permission in writing of Oxford University Press, or as expressly permitted by law,
by license, or under terms agreed with the appropriate reproduction rights organization.
Inquiries concerning reproduction outside the scope of the above should be sent to the Rights
Department, Oxford University Press, at the address above.

You must not circulate this work in any other form
and you must impose this same condition on any acquirer.

Library of Congress Cataloging-in-Publication Data
The Oxford handbook of North American archaeology /edited by Timothy R. Pauketat.
p.   cm.
ISBN 978-0-19-538011-8 (hardcover); 978-0-19-024109-4 (paperback)
1. Indians of North America—Antiquities—Handbooks, manuals, etc. 2. Archaeology—North
America—Handbooks, manuals, etc. 3. North America—Antiquities—Handbooks,
manuals, etc. I. Pauketat, Timothy R.
E77.9.O94   2011
970.004'97—dc22   2011009268

1 3 5 7 9 8 6 4 2

Printed in the United States of America
on acid-free paper

This book is dedicated to the public archaeologists and governmental officials of the United States, Canada, and Mexico whose job it is to ensure that the continent's heritage is understood and preserved for posterity.

Preface

This volume was conceived as more than simply a comprehensive overview of the archaeology of North America. The goal from the outset was twofold. On the one hand, the book needed to track the big cultural-historical patterns of past North American people through time. Doing so provides a foundation on which researchers, students, and laypeople might build in the future. On the other hand, I wanted the book to do more, to engage some of the key theoretical issues of relevance to constructing a general understanding of human experience on earth. Specific chapters do this by investigating historical moments, places, and people that enable an understanding of why the past happened the way that it did.

The twofold purpose of this volume is achieved in three sections. The first section is short, comprising three papers that lay out some of the theoretical and ethical issues of North American archaeology today. The second section is longer, made up of six chapters that examine issues understandable only at a pan-continental scale. These range from a consideration of transcontinental historical processes during the Spanish mission period (D. H. Thomas) to attempts to clarify Mesoamerica's relationship to the people of North America (R. Hall, P. Peregrine, and S. Lekson), to a synthetic statement about indigenous plant foods (D. Pearsall), to explanations of how Paleolithic native people came to inhabit the continent (N. Waguespack and D. Anderson). As a set, they reveal how development of regions and localities must always be undergirded by larger considerations.

Regional studies are featured in the book's third section, by far the largest. Each of the 44 articles in this third part of the volume focuses on one of the continent's cultural and physiographic areas: the Arctic, Subarctic, Northwest Coast, Interior Plateau, Great Basin, California, Southwest/Northern Mexico, Great Plains, and Eastern Woodlands (further subdivided into the Northeast, Midwest, Midsouth, and Southeast). For present purposes, the cultural and physiographic areas are combined to produce six subsections. Each of the areal subdivisions is opened by a paper (by R. Park, J. Erlandson and T. Braje, C. Chapdelaine, G. Gibbon, G. Milner, and B. Mills) that in some way presages the subsequent chapter discussions of that areal subdivision.

The physiographic and cultural divisions used to carve up section 3 are, of course, somewhat arbitrary, the result of a century and a half of archaeological study (1) constrained by international borders, (2) influenced by old-fashioned notions of culture, and (3) informed by research that is intensive in some areas and scant to none existent in others. Not everything that should be included in a book such as this has been covered. Indeed, much of the archaeology currently under way in

North America is of historic period peoples other than Native North Americans. However, for practical reasons this book is limited to the indigenous past beginning in the far north and stopping just south of the Mexican border. Other Oxford handbooks are dedicated to Mesoamerica and northern Mexico and the Arctic, among other world areas and theoretical topics, including general volumes on world archaeology and material-culture studies.

Timothy R. Pauketat

Acknowledgments

There are many to acknowledge in a volume as large and comprehensive as this, beginning with the 61 other contributing authors. They complied with my scheduling, formatting, and content demands during the two and a half years that this book was in preparation, and I appreciate their diligence and staying power. I also wish to acknowledge Stefan Vranka at Oxford University Press, who commissioned this volume and saw it through to completion with the patience of Job. He, Sarah Pirovitz, and Brian Hurley at Oxford facilitated and prodded in equal measure, and I thank them for their invaluable assistance.

Of course, this book would not be possible without public support, primarily in the form of the universities, colleges, firms, institutes, museums, and state or provincial and federal agencies that employ the authors of this volume or that obtain funds to conduct archaeological research through grants and contracts as required by public laws. In addition, public interest in archaeology—and for learned understandings of history generally—is the real moral support without which the necessary laws and funds would evaporate. For instance, at the national and state levels, my own research and preservation efforts have been supported, facilitated, or promoted by the National Science Foundation, National Endowment for the Humanities, U.S. Army Corps of Engineers, Archaeological Conservancy, Archaeological Institute of America, National Geographic Society, Illinois Department of Transportation, Illinois State Museum, Illinois Historic Preservation Agency, Illinois Humanities Council, Wenner-Gren Foundation, and Universities of Illinois, Buffalo, and Oklahoma. Graduate crew members, undergraduate field school students, and volunteers have shared in much of this work. I am most grateful to all.

Contents

List of Figures   xvii

List of Contributors   xxiii

SECTION I. HISTORIES, PERSPECTIVES, AND DEFINITIONS

1. Questioning the Past in North America   3
   Timothy R. Pauketat

2. Hunter-Gatherer Theory in North American Archaeology   18
   Kenneth E. Sassaman and Asa R. Randall

3. Bone Lickers, Grave Diggers, and Other Unsavory Characters: Archaeologists, Archaeological Cultures, and the Disconnect from Native Peoples   28
   Joe Watkins

SECTION II. PAN-AMERICAN CONNECTIONS, MIGRATIONS, AND ENCOUNTERS

4. Historical Archaeology and Native Agency Across the Spanish Borderlands   39
   David Hurst Thomas

5. Some Commonalities Linking North America and Mesoamerica   52
   Robert L. Hall

6. The North American *Oikoumene*   64
   Peter N. Peregrine and Stephen H. Lekson

7. People, Plants, and Culinary Traditions   73
   Deborah M. Pearsall

8. Early Paleoindians, from Colonization to Folsom   86
   Nicole Waguespack

9. Pleistocene Settlement in the East   96
   David G. Anderson

SECTION III. ARCHAEOLOGICAL HISTORIES AND CULTURAL PROCESSES

I. Arctic and Subarctic

10. Adapting to a Frozen Coastal Environment   113
    Robert W. Park

11. Rethinking Eastern Subarctic History   124
    Donald H. Holly, Jr., and Moira McCaffrey

12. Archaeology of the North Pacific   135
    Herbert D. G. Maschner

II. The West

13. Foundations for the Far West: Paleoindian Cultures on the Western Fringe of North America   149
    Jon Erlandson and Todd J. Braje

14. Archaeology of the Northwest Coast   160
    Herbert D. G. Maschner

15. The Winter Village Pattern on the Plateau of Northwestern North America   173
    Anna Marie Prentiss

16. Great Basin Foraging Strategies   185
    Christopher Morgan and Robert L. Bettinger

17. The Evolution of Social Organization, Settlement Patterns, and Population Densities in Prehistoric Owens Valley   199
    Jelmer W. Eerkens

18. Mound Building by California Hunter-Gatherers   212
    Kent G. Lightfoot and Edward M. Luby

19. Diversity, Exchange, and Complexity in the California Bight 224
    Jennifer E. Perry

20. Archaeologies of Colonial Reduction and Cultural Production in Native Northern California 235
    Stephen W. Silliman

III. Northeast and Mid-Atlantic Seaboard

21. Overview of the St. Lawrence Archaic Through Woodland 249
    Claude Chapdelaine

22. New England Algonquians: Navigating "Backwaters" and Typological Boundaries 262
    Elizabeth S. Chilton

23. What Will Be Has Always Been: The Past and Present of Northern Iroquoians 273
    Ronald F. Williamson

24. Regional Ritual Organization in the Northern Great Lakes, AD 1200–1600 285
    Meghan C. L. Howey

25. Villagers and Farmers of the Middle and Upper Ohio River Valley, 11th to 17th Centuries AD: The Fort Ancient and Monongahela Traditions 297
    Bernard K. Means

26. Native History in the Chesapeake: The Powhatan Chiefdom and Beyond 310
    Martin Gallivan

IV. Plains and Upper Midwest

27. Lifeways Through Time in the Upper Mississippi River Valley and Northeastern Plains 325
    Guy Gibbon

28. The Archaeological Imprint of Oral Traditions on the Landscape of Northern Plains Hunter-Gatherers 336
    Gerald A. Oetelaar

29. Situating (Proto) History on the Northwestern Plains and Rocky Mountains   347
Laura L. Scheiber and Judson Byrd Finley

30. The Origins and Development of Farming Villages in the Northern Great Plains   359
Mark D. Mitchell

31. Planting the Plains: The Development and Extent of Plains Village Agriculturalists in the Southern and Central Plains   373
Richard R. Drass

32. Women on the Edge: Looking at Protohistoric Plains-Pueblo Interaction from a Feminist Perspective   386
Judith A. Habicht-Mauche

33. Cahokia Interaction and Ethnogenesis in the Northern Midcontinent   398
Thomas E. Emerson

34. The Effigy Mound to Oneota Revolution in the Upper Mississippi River Valley   410
Robert F. Boszhardt

35. Post-Contact Cultural Dynamics in the Upper Great Lakes Region   422
Vergil E. Noble

V. Midsouth and Southeast

36. Mound-Building Societies of the Southern Midwest and Southeast   437
George R. Milner

37. Reenvisioning Eastern Woodlands Archaic Origins   448
Dale L. McElrath and Thomas E. Emerson

38. Poverty Point   460
Tristram R. Kidder

39. Origins of the Hopewell Phenomenon   471
Douglas K. Charles

40. Monumental Landscape and Community in the Southern Lower Mississippi Valley During the Late Woodland and Mississippi Periods   483
    Mark A. Rees

41. Making Mississippian at Cahokia   497
    Susan M. Alt

42. Mississippian in the Deep South: Common Themes in Varied Histories   509
    Adam King

43. Living with War: The Impact of Chronic Violence in the Mississippian-Period Central Illinois River Valley   523
    Gregory D. Wilson

44. Moundville in the Mississippian World   534
    John H. Blitz

    VI. Greater Southwest and Northern Mexico

45. The Archaeology of the Greater Southwest: Migration, Inequality, and Religious Transformations   547
    Barbara J. Mills

46. Diversity in First-Millennium AD Southwestern Farming Communities   561
    Lisa Young

47. Hohokam Society and Water Management   571
    Suzanne K. Fish and Paul R. Fish

48. Terraced Lives: *Cerros de Trincheras* in the Northwest/Southwest   585
    Bridget M. Zavala

49. Chaco's Hinterlands   597
    Stephen H. Lekson

50. The Mesa Verde Region   608
    Mark D. Varien, Timothy A. Kohler, and Scott G. Ortman

51. Warfare and Conflict in the Late Pre-Columbian Pueblo World   620
    James E. Snead

52. The Pueblo Village in an Age of Reformation (AD 1300–1600)   631
    Severin Fowles

53. Casas Grandes Phenomenon   645
    Christine S. VanPool and Todd L. VanPool

Index   659

List of Figures

1.1 Select Archaeological Sites and Cultural Landmarks Mentioned in Text   4
1.2 Chart of the Historical Periods of Indigenous North America to 1600 AD   5
1.3 Examples of Embodied Historical Relationships   10
1.4 Map of Traditional Culture Areas of North America   11
5.1 Tethered Warriors in Mexico and the Great Plains   55
5.2 Representations of Fire Drilling Kits   57
5.3 Victims with Splayed Postures on Pole Frames   58
5.4 Bisected Circle or Atlatl Grip Motif and Its Transformations in Mexico and North America   59
7.1 Papago Woman Gathering Cactus Fruit   75
7.2 Coast Pomo Woman Using a Seed Beater to Gather Seeds into a Burden Basket   77
7.3 Timucan Farmers Planting Corn Field   79
7.4 Apache Woman Hoeing Corn with an Infant in Cradleboard   80
8.1 Locations of Likely Entry Routes of North American Colonizers, Pleistocene Ice Sheets, and Key Clovis and Related Sites   88
8.2 Early Paleoindian Technology   90
8.3 Location and Spatial Extent of Key Folsom Sites   93
9.1 Occurrence of Fluted Projectile Points in Eastern North America   97
9.2 Diagnostic Paleoindian Projectile Point Forms in Eastern North America   98
9.3 Paleoindian Site Locations in Eastern North America   100
10.1 Map Showing Locations Mentioned in the Text   114
10.2 Diagram Summarizing the Culture History of the North American Arctic   116
10.3 Thule Tradition Semisubterranean Winter House in the Canadian High Arctic, Gridded for Excavation   118
10.4 Arctic Material Culture from the Canadian Arctic   120
11.1 Map of the Eastern Subarctic   125
11.2 Cache of Meadowood-Type Blades Dating to About 2700 BP   128
11.3 Sample of Recent Period Projectile Points from the Mistassini Region of West-Central Québec   130
12.1 Map of the North Pacific Showing Key Sites   136
12.2 Examples of Harpoons and Figurines from the Western Alaska Peninsula   139

13.1 Stemmed Points 155
13.2 Small Channel Island Barbed Points and Two Crescents 156
13.3 Long-Stemmed, "Tanged" Incipient Jomon Points from Japan 157
14.1 Map of the Northwest Coast Showing Key Sites 161
14.2 Northwest Coast Chronology Chart 163
15.1 Regional Map Showing Approximate Locations of Major Plateau Villages 174
15.2 Map of the Core Village Area of the Keatley Creek Site 178
15.3 Maps Illustrating Growth of the Bridge River Village over Time 181
16.1 The Hydrographic Great Basin, Major Mountain Ranges, and Modern Distribution of Numic-Speaking Peoples 186
16.2 Photograph of Winnemucca Valley, Nevada, Western Great Basin from Inside Rockshelter 187
16.3 Location of Studies Mentioned in the Text 189
16.4 Graphic Representation of the Behavioral Ecology of Logistical versus Residential Foraging 192
17.1 Regional Map with Obsidian Sources and Key Sites 200
17.2 Frequency of Radiocarbon-Dated Structures and Other Archaeological Materials over Time 204
17.3 House Size Plotted by Radiocarbon Date, Showing General Decrease in House Size After 650 BP 207
18.1 Map of Central California Showing the San Francisco Bay Area and Central Valley Regions 214
18.2 Large Mounded Site, Recorded as Mound No. 262 by Nels Nelson During His Pioneering Survey of the San Francisco Bay Area from 1906 to 1908 215
18.3 Excavations at the Ellis Landing Shell Mound 215
18.4 Illustration of a Mounded Site Along a Slough in the Delta Area Near the Modern Town of Stockton 216
18.5 Example of a Sand Dune Mound from Bradford Island in the Delta Area 218
19.1 Historic Chumash Villages in the Santa Barbara Channel Region 226
19.2 Olivella Callus Cup Bead-Making Kit 227
19.3 Tomol Constructed in 1912 by Fernando Librado 228
19.4 Chumash Rock Art in the San Emigdio Area 229
20.1 Map of Northern California in the Early 19th Century 237
20.2 Photograph of Petaluma Adobe, Centerpiece of the Rancho Petaluma, in the Late 20th Century 238
20.3 Photograph of Fort Ross with Native Alaskan and Californian Living Areas in the Foreground 239
21.1 Multidisciplinary Framework for the St. Lawrence Valley 250
21.2 Map of Study Area with Sites Mentioned in the Text 251
21.3 Laurentian Archaic Artifacts 254
21.4 Early Woodland Meadowood Cache Blades Made of Onondaga Chert and Bifaces of the Middlesex Complex 256

LIST OF FIGURES

21.5 Early and Late Middle Woodland Pottery   257
21.6 St. Lawrence Iroquoian Pottery   258
22.1 Map of New England   263
22.2 Map of the Late Pleistocene Glacial Lakes in New England   265
22.3 Arrow Points from the Late Woodland Period, AD 1000–1600   268
22.4 Ceramics from the Late Woodland Period, AD 1000–1600   270
23.1 The Great Lakes Region, Showing Locations of Aboriginal Nations Mentioned in Text   274
23.2 An 18th-Century Depiction of the Feast of the Dead at the Huron Ossuary of Ossossané, Witnessed by the Jesuit Priest Father Jean de Brébeuf in the Year 1636   279
23.3 Mantle Site Plan   280
23.4 Ceramic Vessel Effigy Thought to Be a Mythical Cornhusk Person Associated with Horticultural Crops   281
24.1 The Northern Great Lakes Region   288
24.2 Series of Late Precontact (ca. AD 1200–1600) Circular Earthwork Enclosures   293
24.3 Side-by-Side Comparison of the Ethnohistoric Diagram of Bear's Travels with the Midé Pack and the Schematic of the Missaukee Earthworks Ritual Precinct Layout   294
25.1 Maximum Extent of the Fort Ancient and Monongahela Traditions, Showing Locations of SunWatch and Peck 2–2   298
25.2 Monongahela House with Attached Storage Pit   301
25.3 Schematic Map of Peck 2–2   303
25.4 Schematic Map of SunWatch   304
25.5 Floor Plan of SunWatch's Wall Trench Structure   306
26.1 John Smith's Map of Virginia   313
26.2 Powhatan's Mantle   314
26.3 Excavations at Werowocomoco   317
27.1 Wilber's Four Quadrants Perspective   326
27.2 The Upper Mississippi River-Northeastern Plains Region   328
27.3 Kramer and Turkey Tail Points, with Minnesota Points to the Right   331
27.4 Pre-Emergence and Post-Emergence Pottery Vessels   334
28.1 Map of Northern Plains Showing Places in Blackfoot Homeland   337
28.2 Photographs of Swan's Bill, Crow's Nest, Chief, and Bear's Tooth   340
28.3 Map of Southern Alberta Showing Old North Trail and Trails to Sun Dance Grounds   342
29.1 Map of the Northwestern Plains and Middle Rocky Mountains   349
29.2 Stone Circle at Two Eagle Site, Bighorn Canyon   353
29.3 Sheep Traps of the Absaroka Mountains   355
30.1 Map Showing Distribution of Western and Eastern Initial Middle Missouri Villages on the Plains-Prairie Border   361
30.2 Plan View of an Initial Middle Missouri House from the Langdeau Site   362

30.3 Map Showing Distribution of Initial Coalescent and Extended Middle Missouri Villages   366
30.4 Plan View of an Extended Coalescent House from the La Roche Site   368
31.1 Map of Central and Southern Plains, with Archeological Complexes   375
31.2 Plains Villager Pottery   378
31.3 Bone Digging Tools from Plains Sites   379
32.1 Location of Protohistoric Complexes on the Southern Plains Discussed in the Chapter   389
33.1 Distribution of Regional Mississippian Societies   399
33.2 Langford Phase Vessel   404
33.3 Fisher Phase Vessel   405
33.4 Reconstruction of Fisher Phase Pit House   406
33.5 Plan Map of Partial Huber Phase Longhouse   407
34.1 The Upper Mississippi River Valley and Unglaciated Driftless Area   411
34.2 Photograph of Bird-Shaped Effigy Mound Along the Lower Wisconsin River in the Driftless Area   412
34.3 Overlap of Distribution of Effigy Mounds in Southern Wisconsin, Including the Entire Driftless Area   413
34.4 Locations of Various Clustered Oneota Village Localities in the Upper Midwest   415
35.1 Michigan State University Excavations at the Marquette Mission Site, 1986   425
35.2 Rock Island Site II Excavation Unit Profile Showing Occupation Zone Strata   426
35.3 Carved Catlinite Articles of Adornment from the Lasanen Site   429
35.4 Burial 50, Fletcher Site   431
36.1 The Largest Mound at Poverty Point, Louisiana   438
36.2 Part of the Embankment Surrounding a Hilltop at Fort Ancient, Ohio   439
36.3 The Largest Mound in the United States is Monks Mound, at Cahokia, Illinois   442
37.1 Dalton Period Diagnostics   454
38.1 Map of the Poverty Point Site Locality in Northeast Louisiana   461
38.2 Topographic Map of Poverty Point   462
38.3 Topographic Map of Poverty Point Mound A   463
39.1 Core Area of the Hopewell Phenomenon, ca. 1800 BP   472
39.2 Hypothetical Expressions of Hopewell Material Practice at 100-Year Intervals   473
39.3 Distribution of Hopewell Sites in Ohio and Indiana as They Relate to Different Ecoregions   478
40.1 Map of the Southern Lower Mississippi Valley, Showing Major Geographic Regions and Sites Mentioned in the Text   484
40.2 Plan View of the Troyville Site and Cross-Section Reconstruction of the Great Mound   488

LIST OF FIGURES

40.3 Plan Views of Selected Mound Sites in the Southern LMV, ca. AD 700—1700   491
40.4 Plan View of the Marksville and Greenhouse Sites   493
41.1 Plan View of the Cahokia Site   498
41.2 Chronology of Cahokia Compared to the Lower Ohio and Western Wisconsin Regions   499
41.3 Cahokian Hoe Blade   501
41.4 Cahokia-Style Notched Projectile Points from Pfeffer Site, Richland Complex, St. Clair County, Illinois   502
41.5 Cahokia-Style Chunkey Stone   502
41.6 Ramey Incised Rim Sherd-Showing Variant of the Ramey Scroll Motif, Olszewski Site, St. Clair County, Illinois   503
42.1 Location of Case Study Areas   510
42.2 Mound Towns on the Middle Savannah River   511
42.3 Plan Maps of Lawton, Red Lake, and Spring Lake   513
42.4 Mound Towns in the Etowah River Valley from AD 1000 to 1350   517
42.5 The Etowah Site from AD 1000 to 1350   518
43.1 Locations of Regions Discussed in Text   524
43.2 Locations of Selected Sites in the Central Illinois River Valley   525
44.1 Schematic Map of the Moundville Site   535
44.2 Location of Moundville (Triangle) and Single-Mound Sites in the Black Warrior River Valley, Alabama   535
45.1 Select Sites of the Greater Southwest   548
46.1 Map of Southwestern United States with Areas Where Large and Numerous Sites Were Found Dating to the ninth century AD   564
46.2 Comparison of village Layout from the Sonoran Desert and on the Colorado Plateau   565
46.3 Comparison of the Public Architecture from the Sonoran Desert and the Colorado Plateau   566
47.1 Hohokam Mainline Canals   572
47.2 Map of Major Hohokam Sites and Canal Systems on the Salt River in the 1920s   573
47.3 Large Ceramic Male and Female Figurines are Part of a Set Dating to AD 750–900   574
47.4 Map of Hohokam Ball Court and Platform Mound Distributions in Arizona   575
47.5 Settlement and Agriculture Zones of the Classic Period Marana Community in the Northern Tucson Basin   578
48.1 Distribution of *Cerros de Trincheras* in Northwest Mexico and U.S. Southwest   586
48.2 The Site of Cerro de Trincheras in Sonora, Mexico   589
48.3 The View from a Terrace at Cerro Juanaqueña in Chihuahua, Mexico   590
48.4 Visibility of and from *Cerros de Trincheras* in the Magdalena Valley, Sonora, During the Early Ceramic Period   592

48.5 Visibility of and from *Cerros de Trincheras* in the Magdalena Valley, Sonora, During the El Cerro Period   593
48.6 Location of Cerro Buchunamichi in the Rio Sonora Valley, Sonora   593
49.1 Map of the Southwest's Regional Systems   600
49.2 Pueblo del Arroyo, Chaco Canyon, New Mexico   602
49.3 Aztec Ruins, Aztec, New Mexico   605
50.1 Map of the Mesa Region Showing the Western, Central, and Eastern Subdivisions, the Village Ecodynamics Project Study Area, and Key Sites Mentioned in the Text   609
50.2 Graph Showing Population Estimates from the Village Ecodynamics Project   612
50.3 Photograph of Cliff Palace at Mesa Verde National Park   616
50.4 Photograph of Mesa Verde Pottery   617
51.1 Views of Burnt Corn Pueblo in 2005   626
52.1 Map of the American Southwest Showing Pueblo IV Village Sites Having More Than 50 Rooms   635
52.2 Examples of Pueblo IV Villages from Across the Southwest   637
53.1 Map of the Casas Grandes Region   646
53.2 Schematic Plan Map of Paquimé   650
53.3 Casas Grandes Horned/Plumed Serpent   652
53.4 Casas Grandes Supernatural Realm   653

List of Contributors

SUSAN M. ALT, Assistant Professor of Anthropology, Indiana University, Bloomington

DAVID G. ANDERSON, Professor of Anthropology, University of Tennessee, Knoxville

ROBERT L. BETTINGER, Professor of Anthropology, University of California, Davis,

JOHN H. BLITZ, Associate Professor of Anthropology, University of Alabama, Tuscaloosa

ROBERT F. BOSZHARDT, Independent Researcher, Madison, Wisconsin

TODD J. BRAJE, Assistant Professor of Anthropology, San Diego State University, San Diego, California, USA

CLAUDE CHAPDELAINE, Professor of Prehistoric Archeology, University of Montreal, Québec, Canada

DOUGLAS K. CHARLES, Professor of Anthropology, Wesleyan University, Middletown, Connecticut

ELIZABETH S. CHILTON, Associate Professor of Anthropology, Director of the Center for Heritage and Society, University of Massachusetts, Amherst

RICHARD R. DRASS, Archeologist III, Oklahoma Archeological Survey, University of Oklahoma, Norman

JELMER EERKENS, Professor of Anthropology, University of California, Davis

THOMAS E. EMERSON, Director, Illinois State Archaeological Survey, University of Illinois, Urbana

JON ERLANDSON, Professor of Anthropology, University of Oregon, Eugene

JUDSON BYRD FINLEY, Assistant Professor of Earth Sciences, University of Memphis, Memphis, Tennessee

PAUL R. FISH, Professor of Anthropology, University of Arizona, Curator of Archaeology, Arizona State Museum, Tucson

SUZANNE K. FISH, Professor of Anthropology, University of Arizona, Curator of Archaeology, Arizona State Museum, Tucson

SEVERIN FOWLES, Assistant Professor of Anthropology, Barnard College, Columbia University, New York

MARTIN GALLIVAN, Associate Professor of Anthropology, College of William and Mary, Williamsburg, Virginia

GUY GIBBON, Professor of Anthropology, University of Minnesota, St. Paul

JUDITH A. HABICHT-MAUCHE, Professor of Anthropology, University of California, Santa Cruz

ROBERT L. HALL, Professor Emeritus, University of Illinois, Chicago

DONALD H. HOLLY, JR., Associate Professor of Anthropology, Eastern Illinois University, Charleston

MEGHAN C. L. HOWEY, Assistant Professor of Archaeology, University of New Hampshire, Durham

TRISTRAM R. KIDDER, Professor of Anthropology and Environmental Studies, Washington University, St. Louis, Missouri

ADAM KING, Research Associate Professor, South Carolina Institute of Archaeology and Anthropology, University of South Carolina, Columbia

TIMOTHY A. KOHLER, Professor of Anthropology, Washington State University, Pullman

STEPHEN H. LEKSON, Professor and Curator of Anthropology, University of Colorado, Boulder

KENT G. LIGHTFOOT, Professor of Anthropology, University of California, Berkeley

EDWARD M. LUBY, Professor of Museum Studies, San Francisco State University

HERBERT D. G. MASCHNER, Anthropology Research Professor and Director of the Idaho State University Center for Archaeology, Materials, and Applied Spectroscopy, University of Idaho, Pocatello

MOIRA MCCAFFREY, Vice-President, Research and Collections, Canadian Museum of Civilization, Gatineau, Québec, Canada

DALE L. MCELRATH, Statewide Survey Coordinator, Illinois State Archaeological Survey, University of Illinois, Urbana

BERNARD K. MEANS, Instructor of Anthropology, Virginia Commonwealth University, Richmond

BARBARA J. MILLS, Professor of Anthropology, University of Arizona, Tucson

GEORGE R. MILNER, Professor of Anthropology, Pennsylvania State University, State College

MARK D. MITCHELL, Researcher, Paleocultural Research Group, Arvada, Colorado

CHRISTOPHER MORGAN, Assistant Professor of Anthropology, Utah State University, Logan

VERGIL E. NOBLE, Archeologist, Midwest Archeological Center, National Park Service, and Adjunct Professor of Anthropology, University of Nebraska, Lincoln

LIST OF CONTRIBUTORS

GERALD A. OETELAAR, Associate Professor of Archaeology, University of Calgary, Alberta, Canada

SCOTT G. ORTMAN, Director of Research, Crow Canyon Archaeological Center, Cortez, Colorado

ROBERT W. PARK, Professor of Anthropology, University of Waterloo, Ontario, Canada

TIMOTHY R. PAUKETAT, Professor of Anthropology, University of Illinois, Urbana

DEBORAH M. PEARSALL, Professor of Anthropology, University of Missouri, Columbia

PETER N. PEREGRINE, Professor of Anthropology, Lawrence University, Appleton, Wisconsin

JENNIFER E. PERRY, Associate Professor of Anthropology, Pomona College, Claremont, California

ANNA MARIE PRENTISS, Professor of Anthropology, University of Montana, Missoula

ASA R. RANDALL, Assistant Professor of Anthropology, University of Oklahoma, Norman

MARK A. REES, Associate Professor of Anthropology, University of Louisiana, Lafayette

KENNETH E. SASSAMAN, Professor of Anthropology, University of Florida, Gainesville

LAURA L. SCHEIBER, Associate Professor of Anthropology, Indiana University, Bloomington

STEPHEN W. SILLIMAN, Associate Professor of Anthropology, University of Massachusetts, Boston

JAMES E. SNEAD, Professor of Anthropology, George Mason University, Fairfax, Virginia

DAVID HURST THOMAS, Curator of Anthropology, American Museum of Natural History, and Adjunct Professor of Anthropology, Columbia University, New York

CHRISTINE S. VANPOOL, Assistant Professor of Anthropology, University of Missouri, Columbia

TODD L. VANPOOL, Assistant Professor of Anthropology, University of Missouri, Columbia

MARK D. VARIEN, Research and Education Chair, Crow Canyon Archaeological Center, Cortez, Colorado

NICOLE WAGUESPACK, Associate Professor of Anthropology, University of Wyoming, Laramie

JOE WATKINS, Director of Native American Studies, University of Oklahoma, Norman

RONALD F. WILLIAMSON, Chief Archaeologist, Archaeological Services Inc., Toronto, Ontario, Canada

GREGORY D. WILSON, Associate Professor of Anthropology, University of California, Santa Barbara

LISA YOUNG, Lecturer in the Department of Anthropology and Assistant Research Scientist in the Museum of Anthropology, University of Michigan, Ann Arbor

BRIDGET M. ZAVALA, Researcher at the Institute of Historical Research, University Juarez, Durango, Mexico

SECTION I

HISTORIES, PERSPECTIVES, AND DEFINITIONS

CHAPTER 1

QUESTIONING THE PAST IN NORTH AMERICA

TIMOTHY R. PAUKETAT

All but the last five centuries of some 15 millennia of American history are entirely indigenous. This book focuses on that indigenous history, beginning with the initial Paleolithic settlement of the continent and ending with the beginnings of the European invasion. In the process, we will travel from the Arctic in the north to northern Mexico in the south, and from the west coast to the east, ending at about AD 1600 (Figures 1.1 and 1.2).[1] In the process, the authors will review the broad developmental trends of human society on the continent and, from time to time, focus on the specific people, places, and things that defined those trends.

Tacking between patterns and details in this manner should help reveal the relevance of North American archaeology, which can help us answer questions about why things happen the way they do. That is, this book is also a study of contemporary relevance of North America's deep, pre-Columbian, and early-colonial-era history. That relevance hinges on recognizing indigenous history as a lived and not a written history. It also hinges, of course, on one's perspective. There are multiple points of view in North American archaeology that inform how one tells the stories of the continent.

Most of these varied perspectives may be grouped into two sorts of approaches to understanding the past. These (what I will call the just-the-facts and big-picture approaches) were on display recently during my visit to two archaeological excavations. One was being run by a middle-aged, just-the-facts researcher, and the other was overseen by an older, big-picture thinker. The first site, exemplifying my just-the-facts approach, was a village hidden away on a hill in the woods and had little public-relations potential. The second site, my big-picture example, was a major ceremonial center and, today, a state park. I walked away from the day thinking about the reasons North American archaeology should matter to the contemporary world today.

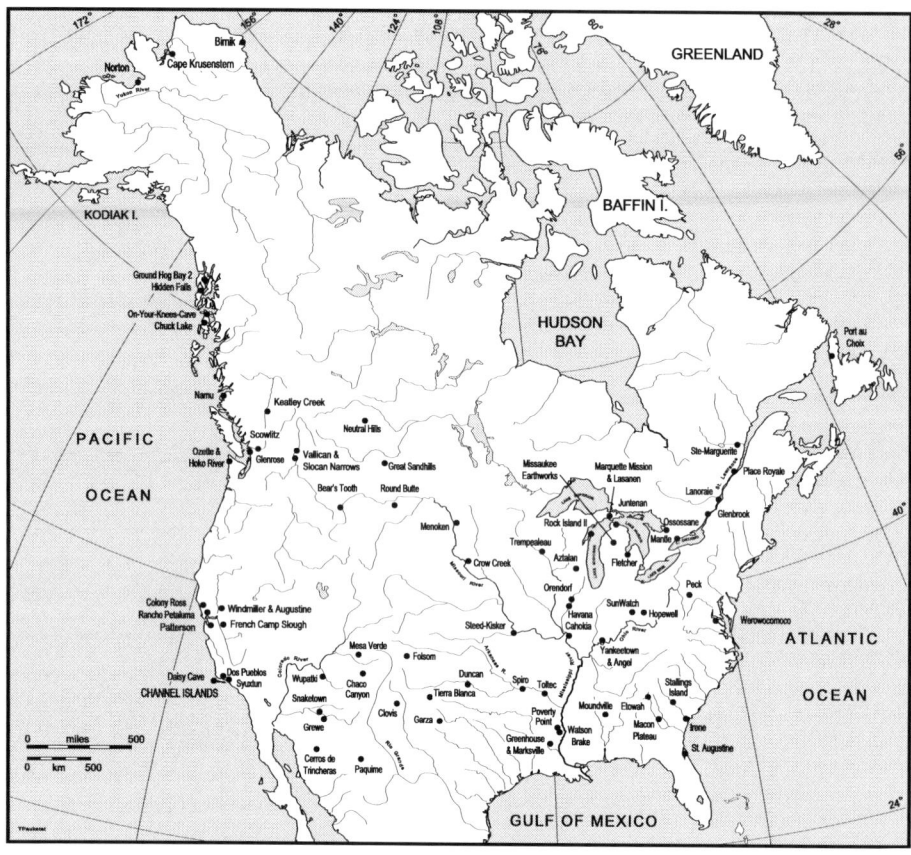

Figure 1.1 Select archaeological sites and cultural landmarks mentioned in text.

Those reasons should become apparent in these opening pages through an interrogation of precisely what archaeology in North America is, who has the right to do it, and how it should be done in the future. Here, I first introduce such questions and then outline some of the theories and important historical developments that make North American archaeology distinct. The Native past here, on one of the earth's eight continents, was unique in many ways. Yet in its specificities, we may gain insight into the general relationships among people, places, and things—or the embodied, spatial, temporal, and material dimensions—of history that are critical in understanding all of human experience on earth.

Opening Questions

Excavating in the debris of the first site, the just-the-facts researcher avoided answering my questions about the big picture.

Q: Who were these people?
A: Unable to say.

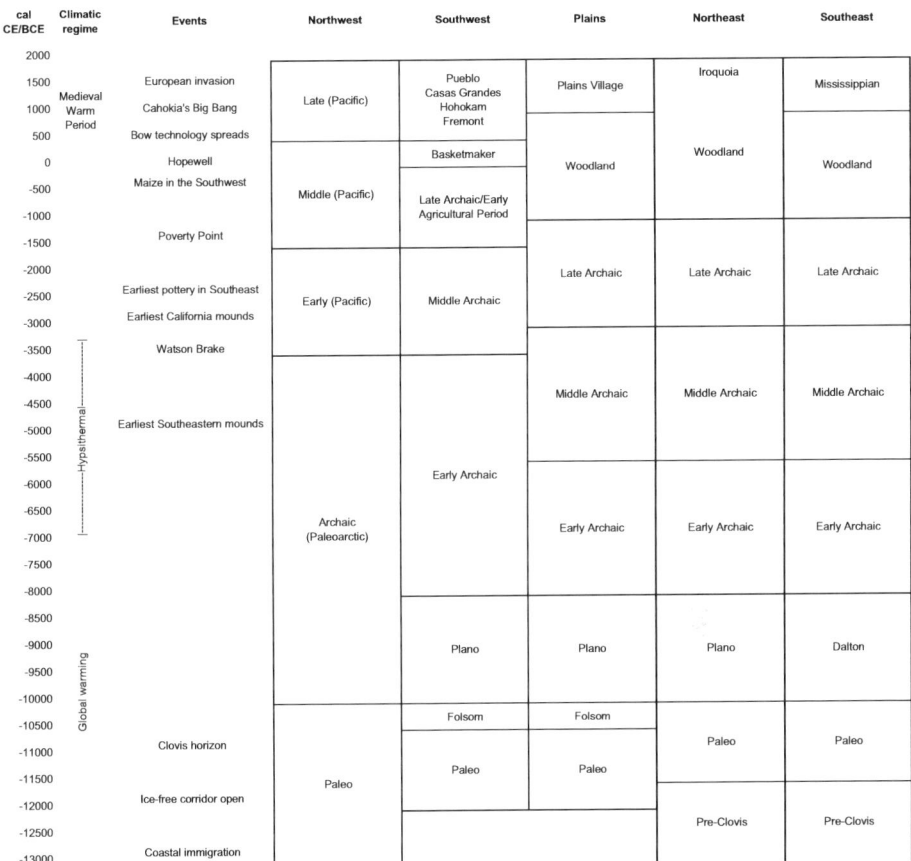

Figure 1.2 Chart of the Historical Periods of Indigenous North America to 1600 AD.

Q: What became of them?
A: We can't know that yet.
Q: Did you find any arrowheads?
A: We won't know if what we suspect may be arrowheads are arrowheads until we've done a full microscopic edge-wear analysis.

Asked to fit his known facts into a larger regional interpretation, he demurred. I still do not understand what motivated this archaeologist, save some pride in doing science in a way that, he presumably believed, would eventually provide answers to some questions, whatever those might be.

By contrast, the older big-picture archaeologist in charge of the second site was all narrative. She had honed her speech repeatedly during many public lectures and site tours. We learned not only who the residents of her site were but what they had been eating, where they had come from, where they went later, and how and why they did it. A couple of the graduate students who were with me were uneasy with her pat story. They appealed to me: surely we can't know all of that. Were there alternative stories? I didn't answer.

The first archaeologist had no overarching story. His research bordered on the pointless and uninteresting. He was seeking truths but didn't know or wasn't willing to tell us exactly which ones. The second archaeologist, on the other hand, was all narrative and really interesting, if unable to demonstrate the validity of (and hence change) her story. Each approach has its problems, but together the two approaches reveal a fundamental truth.

Questions of Truths

Let us begin with a fundamental truth: scientific theories and models—especially large-scale models—are themselves narratives or stories that inform our smaller-scale explanations and practices (Hodder 1999). Unfortunately, many North American archaeologists, like our just-the-facts character, overlook this truth from the get-go. They associate science not with theorizing or storytelling (which a few might identify as "interpretive" or "humanistic" approaches) but only with testing hypotheses. These people mistakenly believe that they are thus less biased and more able to see truths (at some future point in their careers). As it turns out, their hypotheses are also rooted in bigger stories, but they tend not to expose or critically reexamine such stories. They should, because narratives, theories, and scientific models are always constructed in the present to serve the explanatory needs of the present.

One might even argue that the purpose of all archaeologies (and histories more generally) is to understand ourselves in our present relative to our past, the presents and pasts of others, and the wider world wherein the presents and pasts are constructed. This does not mean that archaeologists should always talk about the present-day implications or relevance of doing archaeology. Nor does it mean that every obscure fact from some excavation has immediate relevance to the present. The archaeologist's primary job is to tell the stories of the past in a scientific manner. But we cannot afford to forget that explanations of the past have great relevance in the present.

This is because, without the sort of historical hindsight afforded by archaeology (among other disciplines), it is surely impossible for anyone anywhere at any time to place himself or herself in context. What we are, do, or become can only be understood historically, with reference to a past. Well over 95 percent of past human experience on earth is unwritten. Indeed, most of the living that happens today—the everyday experience of the masses of the world's burgeoning population—is also unwritten. But all people have and will continue to routinely draw on history to live their lives. For to live life is to constantly—if largely unconsciously—make reference to, or analogies with, what is past (your own or that of others). Because of this human quality, we are all in some way archaeologists, all of the time (albeit not in the sense of an established professional practice).

Thus, although most professional archaeologists might agree on the value of figuring out how and why things happened in the past, it would be a mistake to assume that there is only one way to know the past, or that there was only one past to discover (see Gibbon, this volume). My own approach would be to recognize that, broadly speaking, all efforts at knowledge production that use logic and evidence are to a variable degree scientific, including many non-Western, indigenous understandings of the past. Certainly, there were ancient indigenous scientists: astronomers, architects, healers, and learned men and women who produced cosmic, geometric, pharmacological, and even archaeological knowledge of their pasts based on observations, experimentation, logic, and reason (e.g., Pauketat 2008; Romain 2000).

Questions of Rights

This is where North American archaeology begins today, with people assuming positions about who has the authority to interpret the past and all that such an interpretive authority entails (Watkins, this volume). Of course, the decision should always be open, and subject to negotiation. This is because negotiation ensures that multiple voices will be heard, thereby precluding rogue or idiosyncratic claims and inhibiting overly political moves in the interests of one stakeholder over another. Negotiation does not undercut scientific principles since it does not entail that all positions and points of view are equally valid. They are not. Some of what passes as cultural advocacy might be religious zealotry in disguise. Religious freedom and cultural pluralism should not be construed such that one position might silence another position—whether of creationists seeking to eliminate the teaching of biological evolution in public schools or of an activist attempting to control the funerary remains of someone else's ancestors.

We all have an equal right to put the past into perspective even if, in the past, Anglo, masculine, and elite points of view took precedence over indigenous, feminine, and working- or lower-class ones. In the practice of North American archaeology, the struggle over native versus nonnative rights has taken center stage, with focus placed squarely on the reclamation of ancestral remains. The struggle exists to a large extent owing to divergent cultural predispositions. Many nonnative archaeologists see the issue as one of control of the physical remains of people; many indigenous people see the issue as one of ensuring the spiritual integrity of themselves and their ancestors. In theory, there should be no controversy here (but see Thomas 2000). Nevertheless, controversies do play out, and usually in local venues.

As it turns out, resolving questions of indigenous rights vis-à-vis archaeology has seldom turned on nonmortuary sites, and yet this is one area where professional archaeological practice and indigenous interests should perfectly overlap. So much of the North American landscape is being radically altered by developers and corporations whose concerns are antithetical to any and all heritage interests: natural gas drillers, mining operations, and subdivision builders whose seas of housing subdivisions and strip malls are often preceded by the bulldozing of the material traces of ancient Native Americans. We need concerted political action to save what is left simply to allow the archaeologists of the future, native and nonnative alike, to interrogate the past. The big-picture researcher at the second, public site knows this all too well. Allowing archaeological landscapes to be erased inhibits our ability to understand ourselves and chart our collective futures. It is a global concern (http://www.globalheritagefund.org/).

Questions of History

To some extent, appreciating the concern for saving the archaeological heritage of North America is contingent on understanding what and where the continent's history is in the first place. For many years, professional archaeologists have distinguished historic from prehistoric archaeology. Ostensibly, the former describes the postcontact era from which written records exist, and the latter pertains to the precontact (pre-Columbian, pre-Hispanic, precolonial) era where there are no written records. Such a distinction is still made, for instance, by the Society for American Archaeology as a means of organizing presentations at its annual meeting (http://www.saa.org/).

Although not all in this volume would agree, maintaining a distinction between history and prehistory has several unfortunate side effects. According to Kent Lightfoot (1995:200), "the current separation of prehistoric and historical archaeology detracts greatly from the study of long-term culture change, especially in multiethnic contexts." Having worked in both precontact and historic eras, Lightfoot (1995:208) concluded that "the present trend to divide prehistoric and historical archaeology into distinct sub-fields is not conducive to comparative analyses of archaeological materials from different aged contexts." Worse, the separation of history from prehistory often inadvertently privileges the arrival of European literacy as if it were a sea change in Native American society. The diverse multiethnic peoples of the historic era—Europeans or Europeanized—are allowed, in effect, to have history. They are understood to have shaped the contours of their presents in ways that the indigenous people of a more distant past supposedly did not.

The processes of change in the historic era, that is, were presumed to be historic, complete with individuals and events that changed the course of human development. The processes of change in the prehistoric era were said to be evolutionary; human beings and events were not the cause of history but were merely pulled along by it (but see Thomas, this volume). Certainly, major tears in the social fabric of Native America attended the European invasion. But did the precontact Americans become active players in their own history only after the Spanish, French, English and Russians arrived?

Questions of Approach

From the point of view of the narrative-rich, historicized understandings that I advocate here, all people of the past created histories that we need to understand in their own terms. They also wrote this history into the landscapes in which they lived, just as we live and write our history into the landscape today (or erase that history, as developers and corporations know full well). It makes little sense to rigidly separate such landscapes from narratives, or to separate oral histories from material ones (Basso 1996). Navajo basket maker Mary Holiday Black recounted her views as follows: "Each ceremonial basket has a story. There are many basket stories. If we stop making the baskets, we lose the stories" (exhibit at the Sam Noble Oklahoma Museum of Natural History, 2008: see http://www.snomnh.ou.edu/ and http://www.twinrocks.com/).

So it was also with medicine bundles of the traditional peoples of the American Midwest and Plains. Even today, when a medicine bundle, or a packet of sacred or historical objects, is ceremonially unwrapped, the bundle keeper or priest recounts in turn the history attached to each thing in the bundle (see also Zedeño 2008). This is said to be oral history, but note that it is also a material history. Bundled history, like all human history, is inscribed with and through things in the bundles and then in the sacred spaces wherein they are opened.

Of course, history can vary, in its tempo and kind or dimensionality, between historical epochs and world areas (Robb and Pauketat n.d.). That is, human experience might have involved moving through, for example, diffuse social or relational fields of open, wild landscapes and clear night skies as opposed to, say, dense cityscapes thick with layers of past human experiences. The obvious difference between such experiential fields would have held divergent implications for the sorts and scales of narratives that people constructed through things, practices, performances, and experiences. The course of human history turns on such differences.

In this volume, Kenneth Sassaman and Asa Randall (Chapter 2) call such approaches "alternative" to those that typified North American archaeology at the end of the 20th century. These approaches stress human experience as a process involving the living of stories that have a distinctive materiality, spatiality, and the like. These also contrast greatly with traditional materialist and idealist approaches that begin by asserting the preexistence of some organization (household, community, or polity) or cultural/behavioral structure (belief system, key metaphor, strategy), which in turn caused subsequent social, political, and economic developments. As opposed to these, archaeological explanations in newer alternative modes make fewer assumptions and thus demand greater empirical content, often entailing precise measures of what happened where, when, how, and to and by what or whom (Pauketat and Meskell 2010). They also increasingly involve recognizing that the agents of change in the complicated historical webs of experience can be human and nonhuman, the latter including the forces of the earth, sky, and plant and animal worlds (e.g., Ingold 2007).

Big Problems of North American Archaeology

The biggest problems of North American archaeology involve historical relationships that played out simultaneously on large and small scales (Figure 1.3). Such relationships undergird how we might partition the continent (Figure 1.4). The effects

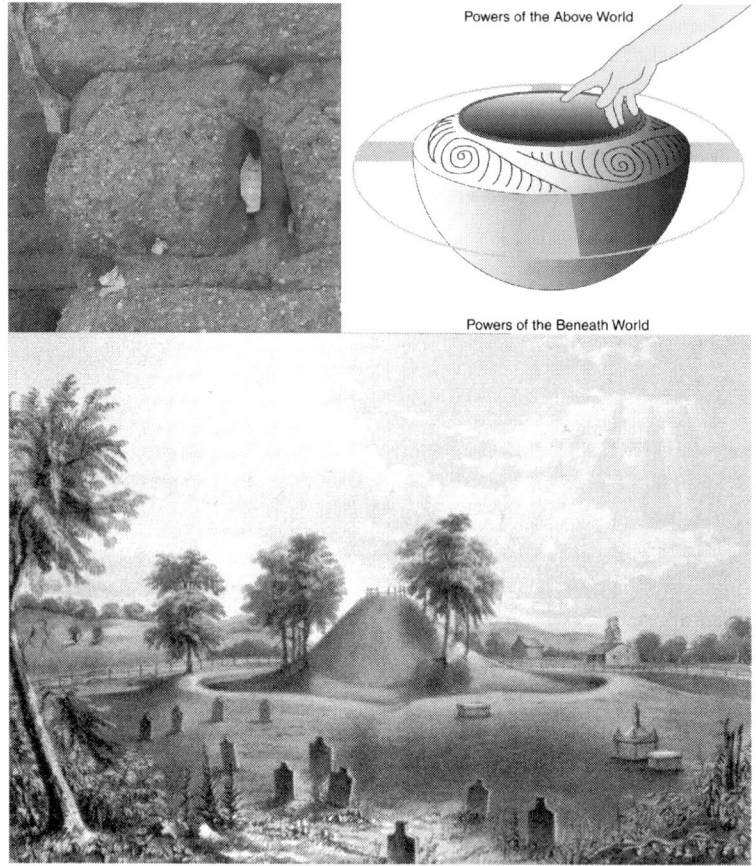

Figure 1.3 Examples of Embodied Historical Relationships: top left, handwritten note left in a wall of El tiradito (the Wishing Shrine), Tucson, Arizona in 2008; top right, Ramey Incised jar from Cahokia instantiates the cosmos; lower, Hopewell-period earthen mound surrounded by vulviform earthen embankment that demarcated sacred interior space (from Squier and Davis 1848).

of particular places, practices, encounters, events, and people on local history always matter, but the extent to which they affect large-scale networks, change global climate, or reach a mass audience clearly makes them even more significant historically, if not also relevant to understanding historical changes in other parts of the world. With this in mind, I identify several overlapping research foci emphasized more or less by authors in this volume that will define North American archaeology into the future.

Climate Change, Demography, Landscape

In decades past, Native American cultures were assumed to have mapped onto geographic regions and climatic regimes, causing populations to grow and adapt to fit their environment. Of course, today fewer archaeologists think in such

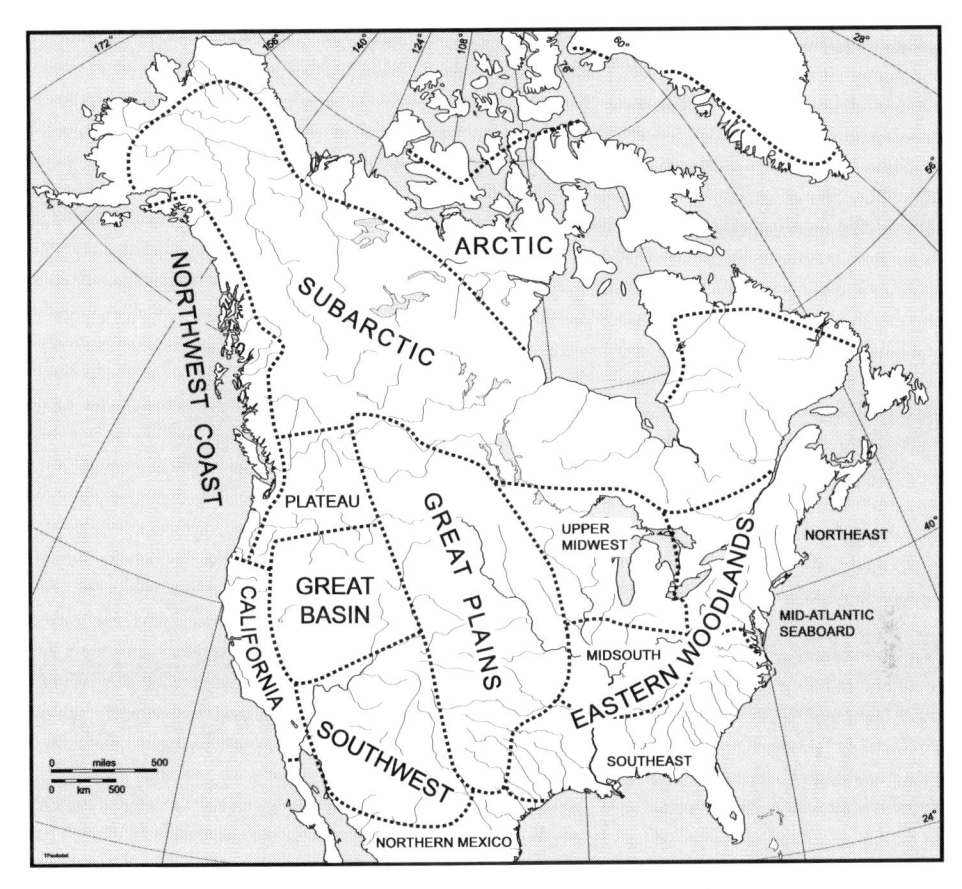

Figure 1.4 Map of Traditional Culture Areas of North America.

deterministic terms. Indigenous Americans were no more conformist—living in static, homogeneous cultures adapted to their natural environments—than anybody else in the world. But climate and demography are related importantly to historical development. Both are aspects of fields of human experience that afford certain relationships and happenings, making some things possible and others unlikely. Obviously, that is, life is lived out in the open, on the land, with people's practices and narratives constrained by the physicality of experience (in the spirit of Ingold 2007).

Conversely, the specificities of that experience also defined landscapes in a recursive manner, minimally at the scale of one's immediate environs and sometimes, these days, at global scales. Big questions remain concerning the extent to which people and their cultural relationships were involved with or responded to climatic shifts (Anderson et al. 2007). Considerable work remains to be done. In pursuing that work, leads are being taken from landscape theories, which recognize spaces and places to be part and parcel of meaningful relational fields that in turn preconditioned history to unfold in locally and regionally distinctive ways (Bowser and Zedeño 2009).

Emplacement

Given those theoretical moves, it may seem especially odd that an older generation of North American archaeologists, in pursuing archaeology as just-the-facts researchers, underdeveloped the big narratives that guide research and thus thoughtlessly lived out a role as the "handmaiden" of history and ethnology (see Thomas, this volume). Such archaeologists have routinely overlooked the historical significance of places and place making (Bowser and Zedeño 2009; Cobb 2005). Too many archaeologists still characterize American Indian cultures as if they were placeless shared traditions, inert expressions of some cultural principles or abstract processes that happened regardless of how they lived their lives on the ground.

Places, especially great centers, caused—not resulted from—cultural developments and social organizations. And cultures were not free-floating abstract knowledges that mysteriously continued on their own for centuries. They would have been made real by, among other practices, emplacing them in the landscape. Large-scale performances and theatrical spectacles at such places as Poverty Point, Chaco, Cahokia, Moundville, Hopewell, Werowocomoco, Paquimé, and other great centers in North America educated people's bodies and channeled their memories, but in a continuous recursive manner (e.g., Sassaman 2005; Van Dyke 2007). Even cosmologies, religious ideologies, and the like were grounded experiences tethered to the real, experiential beings and forces of the earth and sky. Aligned ritual spaces, for instance, were a means whereby people's bodies might move in harmony with the cosmos, thereby establishing cosmic order on earth (e.g., Romain 2000).

A more traditional 20th-century archaeology has called those orders-on-earth "complex societies" (chiefdoms, states, nations, etc.). But seen as lived histories rather than political structures, these are continuously reconfigured orders of moving human and nonhuman bodies on the landscape. Explanations of complexity must become explanations of emplacement (see Alt 2010).

Extended Identities

Archaeologists who look to agency theories are increasingly incorporating this notion of moving human and nonhuman bodies, including cultural objects, the elements, landscape features, and weather conditions in their explanations of local histories. Likewise, an emerging "indigenous archaeology" begins with an understanding that ancient Native American realities were underwritten by more fluid, animistic life forces that extended agency if not personhood to some people, places, and things seen and unseen (Hall 1997; Watkins 2001; Zedeño 2008). Old notions of social status, roles, and prestige goods used by archaeologists to pigeonhole agents, genders, wealth items, etc., are not always well suited to explanations in such veins. Likewise, kinship systems, residence patterns, or political structures imagined by an older generation of anthropologists to derive from such categories may not be useful. Rather, people and things are seen as malleable, moveable, and divisible. Many American Indians recognized multiple genders, souls, and beings, and the implications of this recognition played out over the long run as collective senses of personhood, hybrid communities, and incorporative polities where, say, captives and others might be adopted and integrated into composite personal, political, or ethnic identities (Alt 2008).

Migrations and Encounters

As described above, archaeologists are increasingly shifting their focus from specific individuals, organizations, or cultural structures to the relationships that defined those things. Relationships in turn are facilitated by movements, engagements, or encounters that repeatedly bring people, places, and things into juxtaposition. The identities of mobile hunters and gatherers, for instance, are not based in a kind of kinship system or hunting strategy but are instantiated through the lifelong experiences and commemorations of regional space (Oetelaar, this volume). Similarly, the identities of migrants are formed through the migration process, one where unfamiliar landmarks, peoples, practices, and arrays of things of a new homeland are rearticulated to self, community, place, etc. (Alt, this volume).

Of course, these are the same processes involved in the culture contacts and creolizations that characterized the European colonization of North America (Noble, Silliman, this volume). The point is that such encounters with "others" and their associated ethnogenetic implications, of variable scales and kinds, are common to all people in all times (e.g., Sassaman 2010). Some might have been diffuse, affected through repeated small-scale contacts along border zones. Others might have been large in scale or effect, for example through a great religious revival or establishment of a distant outpost that converted multitudes of people to new or syncretized ways of being.

Movements and Violence

Social and religious movements, missions, and colonial outposts were commonplace during the historic era (ca. AD 1500–present), but they also were found among indigenous peoples centuries if not millennia ago (e.g., Glowacki and Van Keuren 2011; Mooney 1973). Such movements might help to explain the development of political territories in California, the Southwest, or the Eastern Woodlands. Similar movements at a larger transregional scale may account for the development of the great cultural horizons that aligned and oriented the histories of people for centuries thereafter, for instance Poverty Point culture, *pax* Chaco, *pax* Hopewell, and *pax* Cahokiana (see Alt, Charles, Kidder, Lekson, this volume).

Great movements probably were ushered in as periods of peace and thus need to be considered relative to studies of warfare. Of course, such movements may have mitigated warfare, but they did not necessarily eliminate violence, which can take other forms seldom analyzed by archaeologists (Cameron 2008). Likewise, warfare has seldom been analyzed historically. Not only should our explanations address the causes of warfare, they should account for the consequences of warring. The causes and consequences of organized aggression and other forms of violence remain central problems of North American archaeology (Snead, Wilson, this volume). But researchers are increasingly realizing that warfare is not simply a condition of a certain chronological period or societal type (e.g., Mississippian period chiefdoms). Warring and violence generally are discontinuous and unevenly distributed, and they may need to be understood as a fundamental dimension or potentiality of lived experience in some places at some times. As such, they reconstituted relationships and changed history, whatever their proximate and ultimate causes.

Food Production, Technologies, and Traditions

Food production and storage are also fundamental aspects of what it means to be human that, not incidentally, would have been affected by landscapes of violence or peace and by the scale and character of social and religious movements (among other things). Certain plant or animal food productions, for instance, might have been intensified to the detriment of others contingent on the dangers or freedoms of movement to and from gardens, fields, forests, and bodies of water. Explaining the relationships between cause and effect remains especially critical in cases of rapid, transregional, or pan-continental diffusions of these (if not all) knowledge sets and technologies.

Crops or domesticated animals might have been adopted to fill an open social or culinary niche. That they did so in rapid, large-scale fashion—corn in the ancient world, watermelons and horses in the historic era—says something profound about cultural traditions. To wit, these were not sets of norms, customs, and worldviews passively reproduced and shared uniformly by people, although the materiality of certain practices might make them durable mediators of future relationships (Robb 2007). Some American Indian traditions, for instance, might be characterized as future-oriented and made up of fields of objects, places, and peoples that were anything but conservative.

This is an important starting position that might help explain any number of cultural breakouts, bottlenecks, and pan-continental developments along with their effects. These would include the rapid spread of the bow across great portions of the continent after AD 500, the transregional spread of team sports (the ballgame among the Hohokam, or chunkey among the Mississippians), the pioneer Thule movement eastward across the Arctic, the mimicking of architectural forms between regions, or the adoption and intensification of maize. And all of these—the bow, the ballgame, Thule culture, architecture, and maize—did not simply diffuse across the continent (see Hall, Park, Pearsall, and Peregrine and Lekson, this volume). Local cultural rhythms and practices—how human bodies moved through days, seasons, years, and lives—were fundamentally altered in process. There were big, long-term effects that need to be explained.

Closing Questions

The big problems of North American archaeology are being defined by those who seek to understand the contingent and causal relationships among natural forces, cultural constructions, identities, places, technologies, and movements and encounters of all kinds. Increasingly, they recognize that people, places, and things (material and immaterial entities) are all generative of culture (a dynamic, ever-changing set of relationships) and history. In other words, these historical processes are not external to people, causing us to exist in certain social configurations (e.g., Pauketat and Meskell 2010; Sassaman 2010; Snead 2008). Rather, they are relational and are located in what we do and how we do it relative to all of the other forces of life that might be experienced.

Those who are defining and redefining the big problems of North American archaeology are part big-picture and part just-the-facts archaeologists. The former's narratives are obviously an essential aspect of engaging the public, but they might also stifle research if they are too pat (see Erlandson and Braje, this volume). Alternative or hybrid approaches in archaeology, particularly indigenous and subaltern archaeologies, acknowledge the relevance of the questions researchers ask but also require a good deal more empirical content. On the one hand, without such an awareness of relevance, we find ourselves reduced to a naïve, just-the-facts approach that, intentionally or inadvertently, assumes that the problems of archaeology are self-evident and that theorizing or storytelling is not scientific. On the other hand, too much narrative at the expense of historical detail can lead to ossified storylines that inhibit younger generations of archaeologists from seeking better explanations.

The best North American archaeology begins with explicit narratives, some covering the continent (see Section 2). Such stories and theories allow us to envision the scales and complexities of relationships and agencies that define history. Big narratives permit us all to grapple with specific historical processes in regions or at specific sites (see Section 3). Why did people think what they thought or do what they did in the past? How did people accommodate the disparate, if not divergent, political interests of others? Why did they support or resist social movements, adopt or reject new technologies, move to an unfamiliar area, or convert to a new religion? What happened as a consequence of such thought, doing, accommodation, movement, adoption, or conversion? A North American archaeology that asks such questions on the one hand and considers their basis in truths, rights, history, and approach on the other is more than a handmaiden to history and ethnology. It is an essential part of a human understanding of the world and of our humanity that can help us meet the novel challenges and persistent problems of the 21st century.

NOTE

1. In this volume, years are sometimes reported as BP (before present) or RCYBP (radiocarbon years before present). AD (anno domini) and BC (before Christ) are designations used as well, which are the equivalent of CE (common era) and BCE (before common era), respectively. Some authors prefer to work with dates that have been calibrated or adjusted relative to actual tree rings; these are reported herein as cal AD, cal BC, cal BP, or cal RCYBP.

REFERENCES

Alt, S. M. 2008. Unwilling Immigrants: Culture, Change, and the "Other" in Mississippian Societies. In *Invisible Citizens: Slavery in Ancient Pre-State Societies*, edited by C.M. Cameron, pp. 205–222. University of Utah Press, Salt Lake City.

———. 2010. *Ancient Complexities: New Perspectives in Precolumbian North America*. University of Utah Press, Salt Lake City.

Anderson, D. G., K. A. Maasch, and D. H. Sandweiss (editors). 2007. *Climate Change and Cultural Dynamics: A Global Perspective on Mid-Holocene Transitions*. Elsevier/Academic, London.

Basso, K. H. 1996. *Wisdom Sits in Places: Landscape and Language among the Western Apache*. University of New Mexico Press, Albuquerque.

Bowser, B. J., and M. N. Zedeño (editors). 2009. *The Archaeology of Meaningful Places*. University of Utah Press, Salt Lake City.

Cameron, C. M. (editor). 2008. *Invisible Citizens: Slavery in Ancient Pre-State Societies*. University of Utah Press, Salt Lake City.

Cobb, C. R. 2005. Archaeology and the "Savage Slot": Displacement and Emplacement in the Premodern World. *American Anthropologist* 107:563–574.

Glowacki, D. M., and S. Van Keuren (editors). 2011. *Religious Transformation in the Late Prehispanic Pueblo World*. University of Arizona Press, Tuscon.

Hall, R. L. 1997. *An Archaeology of the Soul: Native American Indian Belief and Ritual*. University of Illinois Press, Urbana.

Hodder, I. 1999. *The Archaeological Process: An Introduction*. Blackwell, Oxford.

Ingold, T. 2007. Earth, Sky, Wind, and Weather. *Journal of the Royal Anthropological Institute*, 13:S19–S38.

Lightfoot, K. G. 1995. Culture Contact Studies: Redefining the Relationship Between Prehistoric and Historical Archaeology. *American Antiquity* 60:199–217.

Mooney, J. 1973. *The Ghost-Dance Religion and Wounded Knee*. Dover Publications, New York.

Pauketat, T. R. 2008. Founders' Cults and the Archaeology of Wa-kan-da. In *Memory Work: Archaeologies of Material Practices*, edited by B. Mills and W. H. Walker, pp. 61–79. School for Advanced Research Press, Santa Fe, NM.

———, and L. Meskell. 2010. Changing Theoretical Directions in American Archaeology. In *Voices in American Archaeology*, edited by W. Ashmore, D. Lippert, and B. J. Mills, pp. 193–219. Society for American Archaeology Press, Washington, DC.

Robb, J. 2007. *The Early Mediterranean Village: Agency, Material Culture, and Social Change in Neolithic Italy*. Cambridge University Press, Cambridge.

Robb, J. E., and T. R. Pauketat. n.d. From Moments to Millennia: Theorizing Scale and Change in Human History. In *Big Histories, Human Lives: Tackling Problems of Scale in Archaeology*, edited by J. E. Robb and T. R. Pauketat. Submitted to School for Advanced Research Press, Santa Fe, NM.

Romain, W. F. 2000. *Mysteries of the Hopewell: Astronomers, Geometers, and Magicians of the Eastern Woodlands*. University of Akron Press, Akron, OH.

Sassaman, K. E. 2005. Poverty Point as Structure, Event, Process. *Journal of Archaeological Method and Theory* 12:335–364.

———. 2010. *The Eastern Archaic: Historicized*. AltaMira Press, Lanham, MD.

Snead, J. E. 2008. *Ancestral Landscapes of the Pueblo World*. University of Arizona Press, Tucson.

Squier, E. G., and E. G. Davis. 1848. *Ancient Monuments of the Mississippi Valley*. Smithsonian Institution Contributions to Knowledge, Vol. 1, Washington, DC.

Thomas, D. H. 2000. *Skull Wars: Kennewick Man, Archaeology, and the Battle for Native American Identity*. 1st ed. Basic Books, New York.

Van Dyke, R. M. 2007. *The Chaco Experience: Landscape and Ideology at the Center Place*. School for Advanced Research Press, Santa Fe, NM.

Watkins, J. 2001. *Indigenous Archaeology*. AltaMira, Walnut Creek, CA.

Zedeño, M. N. 2008. Bundled Worlds: The Roles and Interactions of Complex Objects from the North American Plains. *Journal of Archaeological Method and Theory* 15:362–378.

CHAPTER 2

HUNTER-GATHERER THEORY IN NORTH AMERICAN ARCHAEOLOGY

KENNETH E. SASSAMAN AND
ASA R. RANDALL

THAT the study of hunter-gatherers tracks and even informs broader theoretical developments in anthropology (Bettinger 1991; Kelly 1995) holds true for North American archaeology in general. It was in North America that one of the most influential anthropological theories was formulated through the exemplar of foragers. Cultural ecology, under the lead of Julian Steward, owed its mid-20th-century genesis to observations of hunter-gatherers of the Great Basin. Its progeny in contemporary ecological anthropology continue to inflect the study of foragers worldwide. Alternative theory—much of it of a humanistic bent and developed mostly outside of North America—has gained currency in recent decades, bringing greater emphasis to the generative qualities of culture in small-scale societies. This short paper reviews both approaches.

Throughout its 14,000-plus-year human history, North America was dominated by people who made their living completely or predominantly by collecting and capturing natural resources. Variation in subsistence pursuits in North America, both regionally and through time, was highly marked, and some regional populations since about 4,000 years ago depended to some extent on domesticated plants. Agriculture became a major economic pursuit in middle to lower latitudes eventually, but for the longest time after North American foragers adopted tropical cultigens from Mexico or developed their own strain of cultigens from native species, the level of production was low (Smith 2001) and cultigens likely served primarily ritual purposes in some contexts. Thus many gardening and farming communities continued to make a living from collecting, hunting, and gathering wild resources until European contact.

Hunting and gathering, or foraging, describes literally how people acquire food, but it has also connoted, under many theoretical guises, an entire way of life. Mobile settlement, simple and portable technology, and egalitarian social relations are among the features attributed to hunter-gatherers in a variety of theories. More than a few of these approaches also view hunting and gathering as an "original" or "natural" condition, and by extension the evolutionary foil for so-called complex societies whose existence was predicated on production of surplus, a settled life, and ranked or stratified society. Remarkably, archaeology has had less to do with establishment of data on "primitive" societies than has ethnography. Through the comparative method, ethnographers characterized modern-day foragers more by what they lacked than what they had, and they concluded in the middle part of the last century that hunter-gatherers living in remote parts of the world were sound analogs for ancient people because they were relatively unaffected by the developments of food-producing societies. We now know that this is wrong.

Like archaeologists elsewhere, North American archaeologists have relied on the observations and generalizations of research on ethnographic hunter-gatherers. Uniformitarian principles borrowed from geology justify the analogical method of this approach, and it is consistent with efforts to derive generalizable knowledge about hunter-gatherers in the interest of theory building and testing (Binford 2001). Emphasis in recent years has been to seek generalizable knowledge about the relationships between material conditions and behavior that account for *diversity* in hunter-gatherer lifeways (Kelly 1995). This approach has supplanted those of the middle to late 20th century that sought generalizations about the *essence* of hunter-gatherers, be it ecological, structural Marxist, or cognitive. All approaches one could lump together as "materialist" rely on the fundamental assumption that explanation for variation is found in the articulation of human behavior with the physical and energetic conditions of environmental contexts.

There has been a backlash in recent years to longstanding research programs that seek explanation for hunter-gatherers in strictly materialist and evolutionary terms, and in the context of this critique one might wonder if the term *hunter-gatherer* remains a useful heuristic device. Many anthropologists would agree that the concept carries so much theoretical baggage that it biases investigation toward attributes believed to be ancestral and thus "primitive." The concept of hunter-gatherer in this sense is both rhetorical (contrasted with ourselves) and historical (precedence for ourselves). In its lineal logic, Western historicism requires an ancestral human condition, and Enlightenment philosophy insisted that this condition be somehow more primitive than what followed. Archaeologists who study societies traditionally classified as "complex" are as prone to this bias as are hunter-gatherer specialists because the concept of "primitive" provides the basis for recognizing derived attributes, such as institutions of politics, society, and religion, believed to be absent among foragers. Trenchant criticism of the concepts of "chiefdoms" and "states" has exposed the pitfalls of such thinking, but it continues to relegate hunter-gatherers to a societal form that must have either preceded or existed outside the reach of complex society (Pauketat 2007; Yoffee 2005).

The oftentimes scant record of hunter-gatherer experiences in North America exacerbates these conceptual biases. North America has more than its share of lithic scatters in evidence of small-scale, mobile people like those of the ethnographic present, a record that challenges the imagination beyond matters of subsistence, technology, and land-use patterns. However, North America also offers evidence for developments thought patently nonforager, including agriculture enabled by irrigation technology (Mabry 2005), planned communities that were reoccupied and that grew over many generations (Prentiss et al. 2008), pottery and elaborate storage technologies (Sassaman 1993), monumental constructions (Saunders et al. 2005), exchange networks spanning half a continent (Gibson 2001), and institutions of inherited leadership (Arnold 2004). So great is the variation among societies that hunted, gathered, and collected their food that many archaeologists have turned to more relativistic theories that privilege actual and particular human experiences and social interactions over those of human-land relationships.

In the paragraphs to follow, we review briefly the contours of theories applied now and in the recent past to the study of hunter-gatherers in North America. We begin with what have been arguably the dominant theories of the past 50 years, namely those that can be glossed as "ecological" approaches. We then review alternatives to ecological theory that bend interpretation toward social reproduction, symbolic action, and the generative nature of culture. We emphasize here that these are not mutually exclusive bodies of theory, as some recent efforts to historicize ecological perspectives verge on the humanistic approaches of alternative theory.

Ecological Theory

Ecological approaches are not exclusive to the study of hunter-gatherers, although they were developed for anthropology from observations of societies so classified, and they certainly persist as dominant themes in North American archaeology. The foundation of ecological inquiry traces back to classical philosophy, but its gestation in Americanist anthropology was strongly influenced by the work of Julian Steward.

In reaction to early-20th-century theory that culture was self-generative, Steward (1955) focused study on the relationship among society, technology, and environment. Giving primacy in explanation to biological imperatives, Steward developed the notion that "core" aspects of culture were directly related to extraction of energy from the environment. Other aspects of culture, such as social organization and belief systems, were certainly shaped by the core, but those less directly related to successful use of the environment were subject to independent, historical factors such as migration and diffusion. For hunter-gatherers in general, the core consisted primarily of subsistence technology. Being apart from the sorts of historical process that connected them with "others"—an assumption thoroughly debunked in the later part of the last century—hunter-gatherers were, for an emerging cultural ecology, nothing but a core, thus most directly explained by environmental factors. Neoevolutionary models of the mid-20th century—those that draw on evolutionary theory to explain variation in societal forms (e.g., bands, tribes, chiefdoms)—enshrined this reductionist stance in the typologies that placed band-level societies (i.e., most of the world's hunter-gatherers) at the lowest level of sociocultural complexity.

The influence of Steward's theory can be seen in the archaeology of North American foragers conducted a few decades ago. However, most archaeological practice during the mid-20th century was centered on construction of culture history, an enterprise that too often led to normative categories and essentialized particular cultures through identification of a few material attributes. This approach was consistent with the "culture area" theory that Steward eschewed, as it served the need to attribute a given set of cultural features to particular ecological features. Through the urging of Walter Taylor, Lewis Binford, and others, archaeologists began to develop more sophisticated methods drawn from systems theory to model ecological relationships. This too suffered the dilemma of essentializing culture by viewing entire systems as self-regulating and adaptive. Adaptations were considered to be local, direct, and static. Variation within cultures was never a factor, certainly not among individuals in societies believed to be egalitarian and thus like-minded. Critics of cultural ecology approaches to hunter-gatherer archaeology would eventually point out that the regional scale of interactions among most hunter-gatherers is situated in a political economy that cultivates contradictions within constituent societies (Bender 1985). Although strongly influential in ethnographic work, political economic approaches—those that attempt to understand how power relationships within and between societies affect economic activity—had limited impact in archaeological studies of North American hunter-gatherers.

The infusion of Darwinian evolutionary theory into cultural ecology had a more robust and enduring effect on the practice of hunter-gatherer archaeology in North America. Through the mechanism of selection borrowed from Darwinian theory, behavioral or evolutionary ecology had at its disposal a mechanism of change. Selection, as process, is predicated on the existence of variation within any population. Sources of variation in biology are many, and theorists have long debated the degree to which social and cultural variations trace to biology. No matter the source of variation, differential reproductive success, the outcome of selection, results in changing frequencies of variants over time in the context of changing ecological circumstances. Unlike cultural ecology, the unit of analysis in Darwinian-influenced theory is the individual (or even the gene), not the society or system, so variation among individuals in any given population is necessary for change to ensue.

Despite the centrality of individual variation in behavioral and evolutionary ecology, a fatal bias in archaeological applications has been to assume that ancient hunter-gatherers were free from conditions engendering cultural variations within a particular group, apart from those associated with biology (age and sex). This is most apparent in the optimization studies that were popular in the latter decades of the 20th century. Implicitly assuming a quality to hunter-gatherer culture not much different from Steward's core, optimization theory presumes its subjects were motivated to make decisions that optimized returns on energy investments, or that at least, through long-term selection, trended toward more optimal choices over time. For behavioral ecologists, optimization is usually measured in the relative costs and benefits of subsistence pursuits (optimal foraging theory), arguably a universal imperative. Because this theory was developed to model the behavior of nonhuman organisms, it was not equipped to account for cultural dispositions that inflected subsistence choices beyond those of biological need. Without variation in behavior among members of a group, behavioral change could only come from change in "external" conditions.

Most applications of optimal foraging theory in North American archaeology have either been synchronic (e.g., Keene 1982), essentially describing a particular set of choices as optimal or suboptimal, or, if they confronted change, found the ultimate cause in changing material conditions, notably the unforeseen, long-term consequences of foraging optimally (e.g., Broughton 1999). The results have always been the same, namely, that choices of subsistence and changes in those choices were structured by processes that ensured biological survival. The reductionist qualities of much of this work, for lack of better historical context, were further flawed by its underlying tautology (i.e., behavioral variants are adaptive if they persist because adaptive behaviors are those that persist).

Contemporary archaeological research that is broadly defined as ecological or evolutionary has benefited from criticisms of optimal foraging theory and its cognates in behavioral ecology. The intellectual roots of cultural ecology have now blossomed into a series of "new ecologies" that continue in pursuit of understanding the relationship between humans and nature but are now free from the normative, systems-serving, and ahistorical biases of earlier genres (Biersak 1999). Among the new ecologies are those that emphasize the influence of power relations on land use and resource allocation (political ecology); those that emphasize the cultural construction of "nature" (symbolic ecology); and those that emphasize the long-term, mutually constitutive relationships between culture and nature (historical ecology). Of these, only historical ecology has made significant inroads in North American archaeology, and even then with a bias toward unforeseen anthropogenic impacts to environment, as opposed to the generative outcomes of human experience in structuring behavior. Under the purview of evolutionary theory, North American archaeologists have invited an expanded role for lateral or horizontal transmission of knowledge, practice, and material culture in accounting for variation and change, and they have adapted for use generalizing models, such as resiliency theory, to account for variations within cultural traditions. Developments in macroevolutionary theory have an express purpose in explaining cultural change in multidimensional and multiscalar terms (Prentiss et al. 2010).

Alternative Theory

The majority of archaeological literature produced on North American hunter-gatherers over the past 50 years traces its ontological rationale to ecological theory and the evolutionary processes that account for relationships, including cognitive, between humans and nature. However, an increasing number of specialists have become disenchanted with the reductionism in ecological and evolutionary approaches that separate subject matter from its historical and cultural contexts (Sassaman and Holly 2011). Incorporated under the rubric of "alternative approaches" are studies of classic small-scale and highly mobile populations—the "primitives" of cultural evolutionism—who creatively integrated exchange networks, landscape features, and "others" into ordered networks of meaning, as well as those with the labor organization and worldview to construct massive facilities rivaling the intensity and scale of nonforager societies. These alternatives span a variety of theoretical paradigms, some of which, as we noted above, are infiltrating ecological and evolutionary theory to bring greater explanatory weight to the cultural construction of nature through situated human experience. There is thus great promise that theories posed as alternatives to certain strands or assumptions of ecology will continue to offer synergies for a more holistic and multidimensional perspective on hunter-gatherers in general.

The degree to which specific alternative theoretical sources are directly cited by hunter-gatherer specialists varies significantly. We argue that if there is one thread that defines this body of thought, it is analytical foregrounding of traditions enacted through practices, landscape inhabitation, worldviews, and commemorative strategies. Broadly labeled as "practice" or "agency," such approaches hold the promise of transcending social typologies and breaking down long-held dichotomies by investigating traditions as irreducible, contingent, and constitutive of ongoing social reproduction and transformation (Pauketat, this volume). Several theoretical developments outside of North America provide inspiration. Most notable are Bourdieu's practice theory and Giddens's structuration theory, which resituate the actions of individuals and communities in a historically contingent framework. We would add that Actor-Network-Theory, developed by Latour, Law, and others, has significant promise to further interanimate hunter-gatherers, animals, and objects as historical production. Each supplies a model of human agency in which individuals are knowledgeable and strategic, but whose rationality or worldview references systems of meaning framed by experience. Just as these systems of knowledge and sociality are reproduced in practice, they can be transformed or transposed when deployed in novel scenarios. Practice in this sense emerges as history, not only as a source of biographical narratives but as a past that can be politicized and asserted as tradition, and "written" in social memories through oral tradition or landscape alterations traditionally glossed as either subsistence pursuit or "ritual" (see also Holly and McCaffrey, this volume).

A related thread of theoretical insight is derived from recent treatments of place and landscape. Central in this body of thought are de Certeau's work on spatial tactics and Heidegger's notion of dwelling (see Ingold 2000). All practices are by definition spatial, and it is through enactment of daily and commemorative strategies in places and across regions that biographies and histories have significance. By extension, the significance of places emerges through practice (including deposition of materials and objects), through naming conventions, by retelling cosmogonic narratives, and by associating place with ancestors and other nonhuman beings. Places and landscapes are relational, just like objects, persons, and communities; they attain significance through the temporality and situatedness of actions that reference or occur at them. Not only do they constitute a frame of reference for constructing social identities but they have biographies, histories, and agencies of their own. Landscape use is thus an act of objectification and appropriation. Like nonforagers, hunter-gatherer social identities emerge in subsistence practices and social interactions that involve movement through, engagement with, or modification of places. Viewed in this way, hunter-gatherers escape the divisive Western tropes of "culture" and "nature" by constructing practical and experiential networks that link ecologies, social relationships, histories, objects, and others through traditions in place.

Practice-based approaches are a critical venue in which to problematize the historical relationships among subsistence, mobility, environmental structure, and social organization and transformation that are routinely treated as givens. Yet accepting hunter-gatherers with history has several implications for how specialists approach interpretation. For example, recent treatments by Oetelaar (this volume), Wilson (2005), and Riddington (1999) of mobility practices among present and historically documented indigenous groups demonstrate conclusively that acts of movement through landscapes were engaged not out of biological necessity but as a means of reproducing the cosmos on earth; renewing relationships among communities, ancestors, other ancestral beings; and interpreting unusual events. In discourse these actions emerge as narratives, but these are themselves remembered and materialized through the particulars of settlement arrangements, animal butchery and disposal, and the like.

Understanding the complexity of hunter-gatherer histories requires deep context and multiple scales, the full sweep of which may be revealed only through incorporation of indigenous knowledge. Fortunately for archaeologists, practices have a material dimension and can be readily explored through traditional archaeological methods and datasets. Take for example those societies of the Subarctic that have long been held as exemplars of environmental overdetermination in harsh or unpredictable climates. As discussed by Holly and McCaffrey, however, extensive networks between communities emerged and were transformed through time.

These networks are visible now as the distributions of stone raw material at a regional scale, and as structured deposits within settlements. Even though exchange may have facilitated negotiations between communities, the relationships to place implied by material acquisition and circulation may at times preclude integration of communities and lead to their ultimate demise in the face of environmental change.

The examples above highlight how hunter-gatherers reproduced materially subtle yet fundamental associations in place. Yet an emerging body of evidence indicates that hunter-gatherer communities also engaged in monumental constructions, in a variety of times and social contexts (Howey; Lightfoot and Luby; Milner, this volume). Foremost among these traditions is the Archaic-aged Poverty Point, the second-largest indigenous earth work in North America. Poverty Point can be explained only through the histories that were created and subverted through its construction (Kidder, this volume). Although monuments such as Poverty Point were eventlike in their construction, other more gradually accumulating monuments were no less important in hunter-gatherer communities, and no less subject to being the source of discursive acts. This is made evident through reexamination of the long-lived (ca. 7300–3500 cal BP) and now massive Archaic shell mounds of the St. Johns River in Northeast Florida (Randall 2008). In traditional thought, the gradual accumulation of apparently mundane shellfish in places represented deep social continuity, while the significance of shell mounds was reduced to nothing more than refuse heaps in places of habitation. Consideration of the contexts and scales of deposition indicate that shell mounds emerged through the creative acts of regional communities asserting old and new histories in place. Some were indeed places of habitation. Yet such settlements also served as models or literal foundations for mortuary mounds in which individuals and objects with diverse biographies were interred and integrated. In this sense, collection and deposition of shellfish and other materials were the medium through which community histories were literally written on the landscape. Yet in times of change, such as hydrologic perturbation or culture contact, shell mounds were an arena through which different histories could be manifested, politicized, neglected, or asserted.

Conclusion

Hunter-gatherers have long fed, and defied, anthropological theorizing. Despite advances of late in theories identified as ecological or evolutionary, hunter-gatherers persist as an idealized societal type if for no other reason than a lack of an alternative. Meanwhile, applications of alternative theory give pause to the efficacy of a concept that has been, and continues to be, nothing more empirically valid than a description of subsistence. In this sense hunter-gatherer theorizing has come full circle. Just as 19th-century social scientists incorporated recently documented hunter-gatherers into progressive schemes against which to judge "progress," today's specialists are demonstrating how very undifferent hunter-gatherers truly are.

REFERENCES CITED

Arnold, J. E. (editor). 2004. *Foundations of Chumash Complexity*. Cotsen Institute of Archaeology Press, University of California, Los Angeles.

Bender, B. 1985. Emergent Tribal Formations in the American Midcontinent. *American Antiquity* 50:52–62.

Bettinger, R. L. 1991. *Hunter-Gatherers: Archaeological and Evolutionary Theory*. Plenum Press, New York.

Biersack, A. 1999. From the "New Ecology" to the New Ecologies. *American Anthropologist* 101:5–18.

Binford, L. R. 2001. *Constructing Frames of Reference: An Analytical Method for Archaeological Theory Building Using Ethnographic and Environmental Data Sets*. University of California Press, Berkeley.

Broughton, J. M. 1999. *Resource Depression and Intensification During the Late Holocene, San Francisco Bay: Evidence from the Emeryville Shellmound Vertebrate Fauna*. Anthropological Records 32. University of California, Berkeley.

Gibson, J. L. 2001. *The Ancient Mounds of Poverty Point: Place of Rings*. University Press of Florida, Gainesville.

Ingold, T. 2000. *The Perception of the Environment: Essays on Livelihood, Dwelling & Skill*. Routledge, New York.

Keene, A. S. 1982. *Prehistoric Foraging in a Temperate Forest: A Linear Programming Model*. Academic Press, New York.

Kelly, R. L. 1995. *The Foraging Spectrum: Diversity in Hunter-Gatherer Lifeways*. Smithsonian Institution Press, Washington DC.

Mabry, J. B. 2005. Changing Knowledge and Ideas About the First Farmers in Southeastern Arizona. In *The Late Archaic Across the Borderlands: From Foraging to Farming*, edited by B. J. Vierra, pp. 41–83. University of Texas Press, Austin.

Pauketat, T. R. 2007. *Chiefdoms and Other Archaeological Delusions*. AltaMira Press, Lanham, MD.

Prentiss, A. M., G. Cross, T. A. Foor, D. Markle, M. Hogan, and D. S. Clarke. 2008. Evolution of a Late Prehistoric Winter Village on the Interior Plateau of British Columbia: Geophysical Investigations, Radiocarbon Dating, and Spatial Analysis of the Bridge River Site. *American Antiquity* 73:59–82.

Prentiss, A. M., I. Kuijt, and J. C. Chatters (editors). 2010. *Macroevolution in Human Prehistory: Evolutionary Theory and Processual Archaeology*. Springer, New York.

Randall, A. R. 2008. Archaic Shell Mounds of the St. Johns River, Florida. *SAA Archaeological Record* 8:13–17.

Riddington, R. 1999. Dogs, Snares, and Cartridge Belts: The Poetics of Northern Athapaskan Narrative Technology. In *The Social Dynamics of Technology: Practice, Politics, and World Views*, edited by M.-A. Dobres and C. R. Hoffman, pp. 167–185. Smithsonian Institution Press, Washington DC.

Sassaman, K. E. 1993. *Early Pottery in the Southeast: Tradition and Innovation in Cooking Technology*. University of Alabama Press, Tuscaloosa.

———, and D. H. Holly, Jr. (editors). 2011 *Hunter-Gatherer Archaeology as Historical Process*. University of Arizona Press, Tucson.

Saunders, J. W., R. D. Mandel, C. G. Sampson, C. M. Allen, E. T. Allen, D. A. Bush, J. K. Feathers, K. J. Gremillion, C. T. Hallmark, H. E. Jackson, J. K. Johnson, R. Jones, R. T. Saucier, G. L. Stringer, and M. F. Vidrine. 2005. Watson Brake, a Middle Archaic Mound Complex in Northeast Louisiana. *American Antiquity* 70:631–668.

Smith, B. D. 2001. Low-Level Food Production. *Journal of Archaeological Research* 9:1–43.

Steward, J. H. 1955. *Theories of Culture Change: The Methodology of Multilinear Evolution*. University of Illinois Press, Urbana.

Wilson, M. C. 2005. The "Placing" of Identity in Nomadic Societies: Aboriginal Landscapes of the Northwestern Plains of North America. *Material History Review* 62:7–19.

Yoffee, N. 2005. *Myths of the Archaic State: Evolution of the Earliest Cities, States, and Civilizations*. Cambridge University Press, Cambridge.

CHAPTER 3

BONE LICKERS, GRAVE DIGGERS, AND OTHER UNSAVORY CHARACTERS: ARCHAEOLOGISTS, ARCHAEOLOGICAL CULTURES, AND THE DISCONNECT FROM NATIVE PEOPLES

JOE WATKINS

"The audience fell totally silent as Robert [Cruz] began to discuss 'bone lickers,' common terminology for archaeologists, used by the Papago and other Indian peoples from Arizona. The term, never meant to be an insult, was the result of Indians observing archaeologists in the arid deserts of the South West using saliva in the normal course of their work during excavations" (Hammil, as quoted in Ucko 1987:167).

In spite of its close contact with the material culture of native North Americans, archaeology in North America has historically been divorced from the living inhabitants of the continent. This relationship has been strained from the beginning, but especially so during the 1970s when "Red Power" injected itself into the archaeological process. There is still an uneasy "truce" between American Indians and archaeologists, but the relationship seems to be growing stronger in general. This chapter explores some of the issues facing American Indians and archaeologists as each group explores archaeology's relevance, validity, and value.

It becomes difficult to point out the *exact* time when the relationship between archaeologists and Native Americans became contentious, but publication of excerpts of Deloria's *Custer Died for Your Sins* in the August 1969 issue of *Playboy* magazine seems to have given some impetus to call the one-sided relationship into question. American Indian newspapers reprinted articles published originally in mainstream newspapers that dealt with American Indian issues, especially articles detailing archaeological excavations, but they soon stopped reporting such information "objectively." With comments such as "HOW LONG WILL YOU ALLOW THIS KIND OF SACRILEGE TO CONTINUE—your grandmother" handwritten in the margins between stories gleaned from other sources[1], the newspapers pointedly brought attention to American Indian perspectives to such excavations. Editions of the same newspaper during 1971 chronicled disruption of archaeological excavations by members of the American Indian Movement, drew attention to protests over museum displays of American Indian human remains, and generally equated archaeological and anthropological study of American Indians with civil rights issues.

American archaeology has been intertwined with the concept of the "disappearing Native" since the early 19th century, when the advancing frontier and missionizing on the part of religious groups threatened to convert American Indians into farmers and "red brethren" (see Prucha 1964:143–149 for discussion of the impact of Christian reformers on U.S. federal Indian policy). The goal of many early ethnographic and archaeological studies of the Indian was to gather as much information as possible before tribal groups were gone forever. Ethnologists, epitomized by Franz Boas (Rohner 1969) and his students such as Robert Lowie and Alfred Kroeber, scurried to collect information on populations they felt were faced with extinction, while archaeologists were faced with the need to develop broad structures on which to hang the chronologies of the North American inhabitants (Gladwin and Gladwin 1934).

Archaeologists compiled trait lists of material excavated from archaeological remains and then compared their lists to the material remains of other archaeological sites. Those sites that shared similar (or similar enough) traits were grouped together to create regional histories (see Willey and Phillips 1958:11–21). These regional histories could then be interwoven to create an "American history" that was used to place America within international chronologies. The regional histories were based on generalized similarities within the material culture encountered in excavations of archaeological sites over broad geographic ranges.

One such means of classifying regional manifestations during this time of early archaeological development was the McKern system. Developed initially by W. C. McKern, it was based on biological classification systems as a means of grouping these manifestations into larger and larger groups of shared similarities.

This smallest unit within the classification system was the *locus*, the most local unit showing a practical identity of cultural detail. The *component* (the manifestation of a given focus at a site) was next in the system, followed by the *aspect* (containing one or more *foci*), *phases* (containing one or more *aspects*), and finally the *pattern* (one or more *phases*). Archaeologists used such classification systems to create "archaeological cultures" (either temporally or geographically distinct from each other) defined by characteristics indicated within the material culture that were deemed to display adjustments of peoples to their immediate environment. By implication, these cultures were thought to be ethnically or socially distinctive groups that could be distinguished from one another by their characteristic artifacts. Variations in the nonfunctional aspects of artifacts are taken as an expression of variations in cultural conventions. The poor chronological control of that time ultimately negated the utility of this system and led to its demise, but the concept of "archaeological culture" continues to underlie contemporary explanations of the archaeological record.

Though not used today to the extent it was used in the past, perhaps in some ways the tyranny of the archaeological culture concept within archaeology continues to plague the relationships between archaeologists and contemporary American Indian groups. As Dongoske et al. (1997:602) note, many archaeologists "conceive of archaeological cultures in essentially ethnographic terms, considering them to be tribal groups that are synonymous with ethnically distinct groups of people." In this manner, the past the archaeologist attempts to explain is one drawn from the imagination of anthropologists, comprising groupings of material culture traits, assumed to reflect the mental make-up or cultural norms of the people who made them, but also lacking some unquantifiable number of traits no longer (or ever) preserved within the archaeological record itself. Many younger archaeologists may not have taken into consideration the unintended implications of indiscriminate use of archaeological cultures on contemporary Indigenous populations.

Archaeology needs a better mechanism by which to explicate the past; archaeological cultures are so deeply infused within the discipline that it might not be possible to stop speaking of "Clovis Culture" or "Epi-Jomon cultures." We describe general patterns of existence that we translate into scientific shorthand, but we must continue to try to make it understood that the "cultures" we discuss are false creations proceeding from a necessity of brevity, something that is not explained in publications but is taken as general knowledge.

Unfortunately, because of the way that archaeological cultures are bandied about in academic and public texts, they can create walls that act to separate contemporary people (and their cultures) from their archaeological heritage. Even though archaeologists understand the sets of assumptions that go into describing and using the concepts of archaeological cultures, policy makers and others whose actions influence contemporary Indigenous communities often do not understand the difference between actual cultures of the past and those created by archaeologists, sometimes with unintended results.

Searching for Relevance

It is within this background, which archaeology made for itself, that the discipline continues to search for a place of relevance among American Indians. To the general public, archaeology can represent adventurous escapades and exciting finds; to others it can represent the quest for esoteric knowledge inherent in tiny stone chips or pieces of pottery. But regardless of the things the general public finds important or exciting about archaeology, many American Indians still find it an intrusion, a hindrance, or an unwarranted cooption of tribal histories. Archaeology proposes to tell the history of the past peoples of North America, but many American Indians do not necessarily believe that the story the archaeologists piece together is the only acceptable one. Since most tribal groups maintain stories of tribal creation, migration, and resilience, the conflict between scientific and cultural explanations can often be an emotional one. The conflict that erupted over the Kennewick and Spirit Cave Man skeletons illustrates situations whereby scientific hypotheses about early populations created widespread conflict between Indigenous populations and archaeologists.

One archaeologist in the Kennewick Man case, for example, called American Indian efforts to rebury the human remains "a major effort to block scientific inquiry into the study of American origins" (Bonnichsen, as quoted in O'Hagan 1998:8). Armand Minthorn of the Umatilla Tribe, writing about the situation in 1996, drew attention to the idea that *scientific history* is not as important to them as it might seem to others, noting that "From our oral histories, we know that our people have been part of this land since the beginning of time." To some archaeologists, the "scientific" story of the past—the one that can be "discovered" by archaeology—is more important than the cultural ones that exist, even though the cultural stories have played an integral role in cultural maintenance. Yet in spite of some of the issues identified by scientists and American Indians as problematic, other archaeologists (e.g., Dongoske et al. 2000; Whiteley 2002) continue to try to bridge the gap between the scientific presentation and tribal perspectives on that same past even as some archaeologists believe it unsound (cf. Mason 2000; McGhee 2008). And although even some American Indian authors offer suggestions on how to reconcile scientific and tribal perspectives (Echo-Hawk 2000; Lippert 1997), it seems there is a long way to go to create a truly compatible program including both perspectives in a mix that is acceptable to most parties involved.

Searching for Validity

To many people who identify with dominant cultures, archaeology offers a glimpse of how past human groups interacted with their environment and other cultures to survive and flourish. These scientific stories often instill wonder in the minds of readers and exhibit goers and remind present-day cultures of the hardships and successes past groups endured and accomplished. A survey conducted by the Society for American Archaeology by Harris Interactive in 2000 indicated that roughly 60 percent of those who responded that they felt archaeology was important to today's society indicated it was due to their interest in the past and the value of archaeological research and education. Basically, being interested in the past and seeing the value of archaeology in learning about the past to improve the future are key factors that influence the public's view about the importance of archaeology. This seems to indicate that the general public sees value in archaeology and archaeological sites—something archaeologists find supportive.

While archaeology continues to maintain public interest, American Indians are less likely to accept archaeological value as trumping American Indian values. As noted above, many American Indians believe their perspectives are as valid as scientific ones, and when there is a conflict between scientific and tribal perspectives tribal ones should be weighed equally or higher than scientific ones.

Searching for Value

Not all tribal groups reject archaeology, however. As of the writing of this chapter, 81 tribes had taken over the functions of the state historic preservation officers within the National Historic Preservation Act as a portion of the National Park Service's Tribal Preservation program (2009). Tribal groups have taken over the functions of the State Historic Preservation Offices on the lands they control as a means of managing their cultural heritage. They also recognize that the extant federal historic preservation system requires governmental intervention to protect historic and other types of sites from being negatively affected by federally funded projects. Tribal archaeology programs might mirror mainstream archaeology programs in some ways, but the control the tribe exerts over the process allows the tribe to determine not only how impacts are lessened but also the processes through which the "significance" of the sites is determined. Archaeologists are an integral part of these offices, but their voice is just one of many and does not necessarily trump the others. As Don Sampson, a former board of trustees chairman for the Confederated Tribes of the Umatilla Indian Reservation, in a position paper for the tribes stated that "we have anthropologists and other scientists on staff, and we use science every day to help in protecting our people and the land." He went on to note, however, that the tribe does not believe "science is the answer to everything and therefore it should take precedence over the religious rights and beliefs" of tribal groups (Sampson 1997 http://www.umatilla.nsn.us/kman2.html).

Contemporary Archaeological Relationships

Two books published in 1997 offered a glimpse of the relationship between the discipline and the Indigenous groups of North America. *At a Crossroads* (Nicholas and Andrews 1997) offered a glimpse of the situation between archaeologists and First Nations in Canada, while Dongoske et al. (2000) and Mihesuah (2000) offered positive and negative aspects of the relationships between archaeologists and American Indians. More recently, volumes by Colwell-Chanthaphonh and Ferguson (2008) and Silliman (2008) help chronicle the state of the relationships as they exist today. There has been progress, most definitely, but there still remains an area where more work is needed, on the part of both the discipline of archaeology and the American Indian/First Nations groups who are involved with archaeology.

Dongoske, Aldenderfer, and Doehner's compilation of articles published by the Society for American Archaeology (2000) is itself somewhat of a reflection of the changing times. Drawn from articles prepared by archaeologists and American Indian authors for the "Working Together" column of the *Archaeological Record* between 1993 and 1999, the volume gives perspectives on the relationship between various archaeologists and Indigenous groups. Most of the articles chronicle the positive directions the discipline has taken to become more inclusive of alternate perspectives, but not all were so.

Mihesuah (2000), however, does not paint as positive a relationship. Her *Repatriation Reader* examines one of the major sources of friction in the relationships between archaeologists and American Indians. Within it, she calls into focus a different perspective, noting that in the opinion of many Native Americans "the only difference between an illegal ransacking of a burial ground and a scientific one is the time element, sun screen, little whisk brooms, and the neatness of the area when finished" (2000:99). Armand Minthorn, writing about the Kennewick situation, noted that excavation of human remains for scientific study violated Umatilla tribal beliefs: "Scientists have dug up and studied American Indians for decades. We view this practice as desecration of the body and a violation of our most deeply held religious beliefs" (Minthorn 1996).

Alice Beck Kehoe (1998) argued that archaeology treats American Indians as belonging outside of science, and that scientists act as if only they have the ability to understand the processes that led to development of American Indian culture and prehistory, essentially precluding American Indians from their own past. But things are apparently getting better, and relationships stronger. Colwell-Chanthaphonh and Ferguson's edited volume (2008) presents examples of ways in which archaeologists and American Indian groups are actively collaborating to build stronger relationships. In it, archaeologists discuss actively increasing (and including) descendant communities in the process and the product of archaeology. Silliman's volume (2008), on the other hand, offers examples of how archaeological field schools can be used to strengthen overall relationships as well as provide broad-based educational opportunities for archaeology students and American Indian communities.

BRIDGING TROUBLED WATERS

Dongoske et al. (1997:606) believe that "to make archaeology more useful to Native American tribes and to infuse the discipline with a new vitality, archaeologists need to focus on the variation in the archaeological record rather than the reduction of that variation to define units of archaeological cultures." In some sense, this might be seen to go against the grain of a science that purports to create general laws based on individual observations, but there is a point where oversimplification dilutes the information that can be used. As archaeologists continue to discuss archaeological cultures as if they were real, the people who created those cultures lose their identity and their humanity.

NOTE

1. *Akwesasne Notes.* 1970, 2(6):12.

REFERENCES

Colwell-Chanthaphonh, C., and T. J. Ferguson (editors). 2008. *Collaboration in Archaeological Practice: Engaging Descendant Communities.* AltaMira Press, Lanham, MD.

Dongoske, K. E., M. Aldenderfer, and K. Doehner (editors). 2000. Working Together: Native Americans and Archaeologists. *Society for American Archaeology*, Washington, DC.

Dongoske, K. E., M. Yeatts, R. Anyon, and T. J. Ferguson. 1997. Archaeological Cultures and Cultural Affiliation: Hopi and Zuni Perspectives in the American Southwest. *American Antiquity* 62(4): 600–608.

Echo-Hawk, R. 2000. Ancient History in the New World: Integrating Oral Traditions and the Archaeological Record in Deep Time. *American Antiquity* 65(2): 267–290.

Gladwin, W., and H. S. Gladwin. 1934. A Method for the Designation of Cultures and Their Variations. Medallion Papers 15, Globe, pp. 1–10.

Kehoe, A. B. 1998. *The Land of Prehistory: A Critical History of American Archaeology.* Routledge, London.

Lippert, D. 1997. In Front of the Mirror: Native Americans and Academic Archaeology. In *Native Americans and Archaeologists: Stepping Stones to Common Ground,* edited by Swidler et al., pp. 120–127. AltaMira Press, Walnut Creek, CA.

Mason, R. J. 2000. Archaeology and Native North American Oral Traditions. *American Antiquity* 65(2): 239–266.

McGhee, R. 2008. Aboriginalism and the Problems of Indigenous Archaeology. *American Antiquity* 73(4): 579–597.

Mihesuah, D. A. 2000. American Indians, Anthropologists, Pothunters, and Repatriation: Ethical, Religious, and Political Differences. In *Repatriation Reader: Who Owns American Indian Remains?* edited by D. A. Mihesuah, pp. 95–105. University of Nebraska Press, Lincoln.

Minthorn, A. 1996. Human Remains Should Be Reburied. http://www.umatilla.nsn.us/kman1.html (accessed October 2, 2009).

National Park Service. 2009. Tribal Historic Preservation Officers. http://grants.cr.nps.gov/THPO_Review/index.cfm (accessed 14 July 2011).

Nicholas, G., and T. D. Andrews (editors). 1997. *At a Crossroads: Archaeology and First Peoples in Canada*. Simon Fraser University Press, Burnaby, BC, Canada.

O'Hagan, M. 1998. Bones of Contention: The Agendas That Have Brought a 9,300-Year Old Skeleton to Life. *Willamette Week*, April 22. http://wweek.com/___ALL_OLD_HTML/cover042298.html (accessed 14 July 2011).

Prucha, F. P. 1964. American Indian Policy in Crisis: Christian Reformers and the Indian, 1865–1900. University of Oklahoma Press, Norman.

Rohner, R. P. (editor). 1969. *The Ethnography of Franz Boas: Letters and Diaries of Franz Boas Written on the Northwest Coast from 1886 to 1931*. Translated by H. Parker. University of Chicago Press, Chicago.

Sampson, D. 1997. (Former) Tribal Chair Questions Scientists' Motives and Credibility. http://www.umatilla.nsn.us/kman2.html. Last accessed October 2, 2009.

Silliman, S.W. (editor). 2008. *Collaborating at the Trowel's Edge: Teaching and Learning in Indigenous Archaeology*. American Studies in Archaeology. University of Arizona Press, Tucson.

Ucko, P. 1987. *Academic Freedom and Apartheid: The Story of the World Archaeological Congress*. Duckworth, London.

Whiteley, P. 2002. Archaeology and Oral Tradition: The Scientific Importance of Dialogue. *American Antiquity* 67(3):405–415.

Willey, G. R., and P. Phillips. 1958. *Method and Theory in American Archaeology*. University of Chicago Press, Chicago.

SUGGESTED READINGS

Biolsi, T., and L. J. Zimmerman (editors). 1997. *Indians and Anthropologists: Vine Deloria, Jr., and the Critique of Anthropology*. University of Arizona Press, Tucson.

Deloria, V., Jr. 1969. *Custer Died for Your Sins: An Indian Manifesto*. Macmillan, London.

Kerber, J. (editor). 2006. *Cultural Collaboration: Native Americans and Archaeology in the Northeastern United States*. University of Nebraska Press, Omaha.

Swidler, N., K. E. Dongoske, R. Anyon, and A. S. Downer (editors). 1997. *Native Americans and Archaeologists: Stepping Stones to Common Ground*. AltaMira Press, Walnut Creek, CA.

Watkins, J. 2000. *Indigenous Archaeology: American Indian Values and Scientific Practice*. AltaMira Press, Walnut Creek, CA.

SECTION II

PAN-AMERICAN CONNECTIONS, MIGRATIONS, AND ENCOUNTERS

CHAPTER 4

HISTORICAL ARCHAEOLOGY AND NATIVE AGENCY ACROSS THE SPANISH BORDERLANDS

DAVID HURST THOMAS

From San Francisco, California to St. Augustine, Florida, the Franciscan mission system of the 16th–19th centuries was the primary locus of protracted contact between Native Americans and Hispanic newcomers. This chapter examines how our perception of the archaeological record—specifically with respect to Indian agency—has long varied across the Spanish Borderlands, reflecting biases and misperceptions constructed in academic historiography and popular regional culture.

Historiography of the Spanish Borderlands

Herbert Eugene Bolton and his legion of students championed the early historiography of the Spanish Borderlands. Eager to dislodge prevailing Euro-American-biased interpretations of U.S. history—a national narrative viewed through

Anglo-colored glasses—Bolton was inextricably drawn to the most positive aspects of Spanish colonial policy (Weber 1987:336). Bolton's Borderlands historiography stressed Hispanic goals and objectives, which were "equaled in humanitarian principles by that of no other country, perhaps, looked to the preservation of the natives, and their elevation to at least a limited citizenship" (Bolton 1917:52). The Boltonians contrasted starkly Hispanic colonial strategies with the Manifest Destiny imperative of British colonizers: "On the frontiers in British North America . . . few Europeans could ever really imagine or work toward a world with Indians meaningfully included . . . the demise of Indians was welcomed as progress hastened" (Hackel 2005:122).

For decades, Borderlands historians framed the Spanish missions as entirely religious in nature, eradicating heathen traditions and populated by obedient Christian native neophytes dependent on kindly Franciscans to safeguard "the welfare of their converts with the rights and dignity of the missions [tantamount to the] rights and dignity of the native peoples" (Gannon 1990:457; see also Bushnell 1994:24). The inescapable byproduct of such Borderlands hyperbole was the specious perception of Native Americans as unwitting pawns in the process. So defined, American Indians became only peripheral participants in the colonial experience, discredited and dismissed as "untamed savages" (Bolton 1915:19), "erstwhile barbarians" (Bolton 1917:58), eternally "unsociable" and little more than "children" (Bolton 1921:200). For decades, the Boltonians degraded American Indian culture, suggesting that resistance to Spanish encroachment should be read as a character flaw (Bannon 1955:142). Fr. Zephrin Englehardt observed that "all accounts agree in representing the natives of California as among the most stupid, brutish, filthy, lazy and improvident of all the aborigines of America" (1930:245); Francis Guest echoed similar sentiments, calling native Californian lifeways "haphazard, irresponsible, brutish, benighted, and barbaric" (Guest 1966:206–207; see also Geiger 1940). This barefaced Hispanophilic bias was perhaps most succinctly summarized by John Francis Bannon, who perpetuated this "Christophilic, triumphalist bias" (Weber 1987:338) into the modern era. To Bannon, the Spanish mission was such "a conspicuous feature of Spain's frontiering genius" (1964:211) that he lumped all American Indians into his opprobrious catchall category of "Borderland Irritants" (1974: chapter 8).

To the modern eye, such Borderlands historiography comes across as mostly misguided and not a little racist. "Just as historians retold the friars' story of their own success, so too did historians emulate Franciscans by not lingering over disturbing questions about the morality of evangelism" (Weber 1990:430). There remains today a vestigial tendency to accept documentary evidence of Spanish-Native interactions at face value—as "eyewitness accounts" establishing the degree of dominance and control exerted by the Europeans living in the Spanish Borderlands (Ivey and Thomas 2005).

More refreshing directions in mission historiography have emerged in the trans-Borderlands writings of David Weber (1990, 1992), in California from Stephen Hackel (1997, 2005) and James Sandos (1994, 2005), from Gary Clayton Anderson (2005) in Texas, by John Kessell (1976, 1980, 2002) in the American Southwest, and from Amy Bushnell (1981, 1994), John Worth (1995, 1998, 2002, 2004), and John Michael Francis (Francis and Kole 2011) in Spanish Florida. Although focusing on local events that transpired at a particular mission, these ethnohistorians neatly dovetail their writings with anthropologists, archaeologists, demographers, and native scholars, transcending the ideological defense or attack on missionaries to consider the perspectives of those being missionized. So viewed, the missions were populated with native people attempting to preserve, or at least reconstitute, their own communities in the face of colonialism, develop ways to participate in and profit from the colonial economy, and adopt new religious symbols into a matrix of indigenous belief systems.

Spanish mission archaeology likewise demonstrates the fallacy of the rigid and misleading Borderlands historiography on European-American Indian interactions. While engaging the archaeology of Mission Santa Catalina de Guale (GA), I suggested a broader-based "cubist" approach to the Spanish Borderlands, to seek "multiple, simultaneous views of the subject" (Thomas 1989:7). Since that time, we can see the degree to which archaeology can indeed constitute a critically important window to "democratize" the past and frame new perspectives on minority populations and their experiences with dominant colonial cultures (Deagan 1982; Lightfoot 2005: 17). Today, such interactive inquiries are typically folded into the language and methodologies of the "Postcolonial Critique," which challenges traditional colonialist epistemologies and questions those colonial and imperial representations of the "other" being colonized. Postcolonial theorists emphasize the importance of native agency and investigate the hybrid, novel forms of culture that develop during colonial experiences (e.g., Gosden 2001; Lightfoot 2005:17; Leibman 2008:2; Patterson 2008:31–32).

Spanish Missions of Alta California

More than a century ago, Californians spun for themselves a romanticized Hispanic past (Thomas 1991). Drawing liberally from Helen Hunt Jackson's Victorian novel *Ramona* (1884), rootless Anglo immigrants identified with the region's earliest European settlers, generating a comforting sense of continuity, tradition, pride, and regional identity. Life in Ramonaland became an antiquarian odyssey, a sentimental passage through the relics and ruins of a dimly remembered past. Both real and imaginary, the 18th- and 19th-century Hispanic sites of California became places of pilgrimage and, for some, chum to lure easterners westward. But the sacred sites were falling apart, and hordes of tourists expedited matters by chipping away tons of adobe remembrances. The architectural manifestations of the *Ramona* myth— the imaginatively "restored" missions and assorted derivatives in the copycat Mission Revival style—underscore the truism that an appropriate past springs from a present need and interpretation.

During *Ramona*'s first half-century, impartial scholarship in California lagged far behind. "Mission archaeology" was little more than a diversion for acquisitive friars and church bureaucrats, pot-hunters, and curious (if archaeologically innocent) historians. Aside from the stellar work at Mission La Purísima Concepción, California saw no significant mission archaeology for decades (Bennyhoff and Elsasser 1954). Heizer and McCown noted dismally "California's record of historic archaeology cannot be called outstanding. [Merely] a bare beginning on an extensive program has been made" (1954:i). Only in the 1960s did the first archaeologist working in California explicitly identify with the field of historical archaeology: James Deetz, whose renewed efforts at Mission La Purísima set a new and lofty standard and motivated a generation to continue in his footsteps (Chartkoff and Chartkoff 1984:304). Since then, important long-term excavation programs have taken place at numerous California mission sites (e.g., Costello and Hornbeck 1989:322–323; Farnsworth 1989; Lightfoot 2005; Silliman 2001).

Unfortunately, as Lightfoot (2005:235) recently observed, "Writers of most colonial histories continue to portray their subjects from a European perspective drawn largely from archival documents . . . although native oral histories and native oral traditions are beginning to receive some attention, the findings of hundreds of archaeological projects across the state remain largely ignored." It is difficult to overemphasize the lingering role of *Ramona* in retarding the progress of mission archaeology in California. Although the missions helped give birth to a Californio identity, the *archaeology* of those mission sites never really mattered much (but see Silliman, this volume). For decades, the mythical *Ramona* seemed to furnish the tools necessary to encounter California's Hispanic past—a perspective that became "fact" when the reconstructed missions generated a reality recapitulated in Mission Revival architecture.

Spanish Missions of the American Southwest

Most archaeologists seem to view the Spanish colonial period in the Southwest as relatively well understood and well investigated. But Ivey and Thomas (2005) question this assumption, especially as regards mission archaeology, where only a dozen or so 17th-century missions have been "excavated" or even minimally "tested." And viewed critically, the details of this research come across as hasty, outdated, and poorly reported. A priori and unwarranted assumptions continue to distort our understanding of missions as Borderlands institutions. Beyond doubt, more enlightened archaeological investigations could shed significant new light on Hispanic-Pueblo interactions (e.g., Preucel and Agoyo 2007; Wilcox 2009).

The Spanish Borderlands perspective in the American Southwest can be attributed, in large measure, to the lasting influence of historian France Scholes (1937,

1942), who tended to accept Franciscan statements at face value—particularly with regard to the level of dominance and control exerted by the Spanish in New Mexico. Scholes read Spanish colonial history as a nearly complete disruption of Puebloan society—with virtually all Pueblo Indians becoming Christians and wholly subjugated by Franciscans (except, of course, for a handful of rebels and troublemakers, who continued to protest the Spanish culture that had absorbed them).

This perspective translated directly into the interpretation of most archaeological evidence from mission sites (Ivey and Thomas 2005; see also Cordell 1989): "Archaeologists see what they expect to see, and most archaeologists thought of missions as poverty-stricken places; their quick, rough excavations confirmed these expectations" (Ivey 1988:xv). These archaeologists included Adolph Bandelier, Nels Nelson, Alfred Kidder, Edgar Lee Hewett, and many others, clearing debris from several mission sites in Arizona and New Mexico and drafting some simple structural outlines (Hewett and Fisher 1943). But shockingly little useful information resulted from such "excavations." The truth is that only two Southwestern mission sites have been thoroughly investigated using the best-available scientific techniques of the day. Frederick Hodge directed the Museum of the American Indian's Hendricks-Hodge expedition at Hawikuh from 1917 to 1923 (reported in Smith, Woodbury, and Woodbury 1966); and John Otis Brew and his team from the Peabody Museum excavated at Awatovi from 1935 to 1939 (Montgomery, Smith, and Brew 1949:xix; see also Elliot 1995:78–101, 162–187).

Considerably more energy was expended in preserving (rather than excavating) the Southwestern missions. During the early 20th century, California and the American Southwest shared quite similar goals of historical preservation, but the pathways soon diverged. The differences between California and the Southwest can be attributed, at least in part, to the lingering power of the *Ramona* myth. California's late-19th-century destiny was defined by gold and real estate, and the flood of Anglos quickly submerged all but the most selective, promotional aspects of Hispanic culture. Because the missions were integral to the mythical Californio identity, they were restored to appropriate heroic proportions. But to late-19th-century Anglo-America, the Southwest was little more than a vast, virtually vacant desert between Texas and California. The major Anglo demographic influx into Arizona and New Mexico was postponed for several decades, and the vastly outnumbered Anglos who did percolate into turn-of-the-century Southwestern territory found Hispanic and Native American populations still very much in residence. Although some of these erstwhile preservationists would live in highly romantic, even visionary, dwellings of the "Santa Fe Revival" style, they did surely conserve the missions.

For decades, the twin excavations at Awatovi and Hawikuh set the archaeological baseline for understanding 17th-century life in the Southwestern missions. Most archaeologists working in mission sites were interested primarily in Pueblo culture—not Spanish culture—and these investigators tended to confirm the long-standing (if usually tacit) assumption that the Spanish missions and civil settlements in New Mexico were second-rate and substandard relative to comparable institutions elsewhere.

Spanish Missions of the American Southeast

Borderlands historiography reached Florida and Georgia as *The Debatable Land*, published by Herbert Bolton and Mary Ross in 1925. Lauded as "constructive" and "brave," the Franciscan Friars of La Florida were framed as the "pioneers of Georgia . . . devout, gentle, zealous, tireless . . . [engaging] a crusade against heathendom" (Bolton and Ross 1925:20). They mistakenly identified the numerous tabby ruins as the archaeological remnants of Spanish missions, a myth that was not corrected until archaeologist James A. Ford excavated at Elizafield (Glynn County, Georgia). Since the 1960s, a host of historical archaeologists have engaged in extensive mission-period archaeology throughout Spanish Florida (e.g., Thomas 1990; McEwan 1993, 2001; Milanich 1999). Ethnohistorians have likewise transcended Bolton's Borderlands framework, recognizing the extent to which the Florida Franciscans depended on Native America for their very survival (Bushnell 1994:28; Worth 1995, 1998, 2002, 2004).

Spanish colonists typically self-characterized La Florida as a place of poverty, neglect, and ruin. But ethnohistoric and archaeological investigations now demonstrate that this self-evaluation is only partially valid. Because Spanish Florida lacked the gold, silver, and other valuables found in many other colonies, the value of St. Augustine was strictly strategic: to guard the treasure-laden Fleet of the Indies through the Bahamanian channel on the way to Spain (Bushnell 1981:4; 1994:20). External supply was difficult during the 16th and 17th centuries, meaning that the citizenry of St. Augustine was forced to rely heavily on the human and natural riches of La Florida.

The economy of Spanish Florida evolved into an exchange network through which native populations channeled their surplus food (primarily maize) and labor into colonial St. Augustine (Bushnell 1994:15). Spanish authorities dealt directly with traditional indigenous chiefs—cementing the alliances with diplomatic gifts—as a mechanism for "achieving the voluntary assimilation of such societies into the expanding colonial system" (Worth 2009:10). Analysis of food remains from Spanish towns and Franciscan missions highlights the dynamic negotiations between natives and immigrants that resulted in new, hybrid subsistence patterns (Reitz et al. 2010; Thomas 1987). Beyond doubt, the Guale of the Georgia coast supplied foods to Spaniards in great quantities, augmenting and expanding the Spanish menu to look more like traditional, precontact Guale diets. In fact, the residents of Mission Santa Catalina de Guale, on St. Catherines Island, likely enjoyed a much higher standard of living than either Franciscan friars dining in the Convento de San Francisco or Spanish citizens living elsewhere in contemporary St. Augustine.

Willingly or not, Europeans living in 16th- and 17th-century Spanish Florida were drawn into the local dynamics of indigenous chiefdoms, bolstering and reinforcing the political power of traditional Indian leaders. Hereditary chiefs retained considerable internal autonomy over secular matters and ruled using traditional lines of authority (Weber 1990:439; Bushnell 1994:28). By pledging allegiance and obedience to Spanish officials, indigenous Timucua, Mocama, and Guale chiefs also annexed a powerful military ally in the Spanish garrison at St. Augustine: "It seems no surprise that most aboriginal chiefs struggled to gain entry into the mission system, and remained there for so long" (Worth 1998:126–214; 2002:58; see also Francis and Kole 2011).

In the process, the paramount chiefs of Spanish Florida not only created a new market for their agricultural surplus but also gained access to new tools and technologies to improve their yield. The *caciques* converted their surpluses into Spanish goods (cloth, tools, beads, and the like) and received tribute from both the Spanish and their own people. Long considered the breadbasket of St. Augustine, Mission Santa Catalina yielded the bulk of the corn used to supply that presidio, as clearly reflected in the extensive array of trade goods recovered archaeologically (Blair et al. 2009; Bushnell 1994:147; Thomas 1990:379; Worth 1998:173–184; 2002:55). Mission-period chiefdoms of the Georgia Bight engaged in an extensive and lucrative exchange system throughout the reach of legitimate Spanish interests, and likely far beyond.

Archaeologists have also demonstrated the persistence of Native American culture during the mission period and explored the degree to which Hispanic authorities vacillated over whether certain native practices were compatible with Christianity or not (e.g., Blair et al. 2009; Ivey and Thomas 2005; Milanich 1999:148–149; Thomas 1988; Worth 1998). At Mission Santa Catalina de Guale, we found considerable variance from idealized Franciscan mortuary patterns (Thomas 1988). Virtually all Guale neophytes were interred inside the church in characteristic "Christian" burial posture: in unmarked graves beneath the church floor, head oriented toward the south, with arms crossed on the chest. Although Franciscan dogma prohibited grave goods and embellishments, native St. Catherines Islanders had for millennia included grave goods as afterlife necessities for the now-dead, and they continued this practice during the mission period. The 400–450 Guale Indian graves within the church at Mission Santa Catalina contained a truly astounding array of funerary furniture, demonstrating the degree to which the Guale had negotiated their own belief system into mission mortuary practices.

Similar negotiations conditioned the layout and architecture of the Southeastern missions. At Mission San Luis de Talimali (Florida), archaeologists discovered a huge council house measuring 120 feet across and capable of seating 2,000–3,000 people inside (Shapiro and Hann 1990). Long a mainstay of Indian villages in La Florida, the council house functioned year-round as the seat of native government, a meeting place for villagers, the locus for interacting with Spanish authorities, and an inn to house scalps. The council house at San Luis fronted the main mission plaza, symbolizing in architecture the ongoing negotiations between native and Franciscan belief systems. As the most powerful symbol of the native community, the council house survived in the Franciscan missions of Spanish Florida.

So did the ballgame, a centuries-old custom played between competing villages (with 50 to 100 participants to a side). During the late 17th century, debate raged among Franciscans about whether or not the indigenous ballgame was compatible with Christianity. Hereditary native leaders initially convinced the Franciscans to "baptize" this seemingly "pagan" custom because the ballgame complex promoted sedentism among neophytes (translating directly into increased participation in the Mass). But the friars eventually reversed this position altogether, after several "converted" Apalachee chiefs insisted that such non-Christian practices should not be permitted among Christianized Indian people (Bushnell 1978; Ivey and Thomas 2005).

The colonial Spanish system also reinforced internal chiefly power by establishing a tributary exchange system in which the Mississippian-style paramount chiefs continued to employ ostentatious displays of wealth and status items as a way to reinforce their hereditary status (cf. Blitz, King, Rees, Wilson, this volume): "In effect, Spanish Florida became a sort of modified paramount chiefdom through which the chiefly matrilineages of destabilized chiefdoms bolstered their own internal power by subordinating themselves to the Spanish crown" (Worth 2002:46). Francis and Kole (2011) have recently published documentary research that radically changes our thinking about the nature and implications of the so-called Juanillo Revolt of 1597. Borderlands historiography has long been unanimous in interpreting this event—in which five Franciscans were martyred—as a bloody indigenous revolt against Spanish rule. Francis and Kole find instead that the root cause of unrest lay within the underlying tensions and competition between indigenous chiefdoms. They question any simplistic juxtaposition of supposed indigenous and Hispanic interests and underscore the serious limitations and sometimes tenuous footing of Spanish rule in Florida.

Conclusion

More than a century of triumphalism and boosterism has masked the power of archaeological research in mission sites across the Spanish Borderlands. Because the *Ramona* myth already told us what happened at the California missions, few thought it worthwhile to dig into the Hispanic past. Mission archaeology was considered largely irrelevant in the Southwest because the native and Hispanic principals remained and standing missions dotted the landscape. The near-invisibility of mission sites in the American Southeast kept archaeologists at bay for decades.

But today, historical archaeologists and ethnohistorians are working in concert to listen to native voices, and the results are extraordinary—if sometimes controversial. Historical archaeology has come a long way since Ivor Noël Hume (1964) famously defined its purpose as being merely a "handmaiden to history." Having transcended an early fascination with the "oldest," "largest," and "most historically significant" sites, many historical archaeologists are today pursuing the goals so clearly articulated by Kathleen Deagan (1982:170–171):

> The unique potential of historical archaeology lies not only in its ability to answer questions of archaeological and anthropological interest, but also in its ability to provide historical data not available through documentation or any other source. Correcting the inadequate treatment of disenfranchised groups in America's past, excluded from historical sources because of race, religion, isolation, or poverty is an important function of contemporary historical archaeology and one that cannot be ignored.

The archaeological record clearly demonstrates a significant give-and-take in the power relationships between native and Hispanic authorities throughout the mission system. In California, excavations in the neophyte quarters and associated social spaces document Indian self-identification. Lightfoot finds "little evidence to support the assertion that the coastal Indians of California had become culturally extinct or entirely 'Hispanicized' as a consequence of their colonial experiences" (2005:96–97, 236–237). In the American Southeast, the Franciscans friars targeted the influence of their limited resources on the most fundamental and visible sacraments of the church—especially baptism, the practice of monogamy, participation in the Mass, and Christian burial. But beyond these religious "necessities," the friars were forced to negotiate extensively for even nominal conversion.

ACKNOWLEDGMENTS

The author thanks Lorann S. A. Pendleton and Chelsea Graham for editorial assistance in preparing this manuscript.

REFERENCES

Anderson, G. C. 2005. *The Conquest of Texas: Ethnic Cleansing in the Promised Land, 1820–1875*. University of Oklahoma Press, Norman.

Bannon, J. F. 1955. *The Mission Frontier in Sonora, 1620–1687*. U.S. Catholic Society, New York.

——— (editor). 1964. *Bolton and the Spanish Borderlands*. University of Oklahoma Press, Norman.

———. 1974. *The Spanish Borderlands Frontier, 1513–1821*. University of New Mexico Press, Albuquerque.

Bennyhoff, J. A., and A. Elsasser. 1954. *Sonoma Mission: An Historical and Archaeological Study of Primary Constructions, 1823–1913*. University of California Archaeological Survey Reports 27. Berkeley.

Blair, E. H., L. S. A. Pendleton, and P. Francis. 2009. *The Beads of St. Catherines Island.* Anthropological Papers of the American Museum of Natural History 89. http://hdl.handle.net/2246/5956.

Bolton, H. E. 1915. *Texas in the Middle Eighteenth Century: Studies in Spanish Colonial History and Administration.* University of California Press, Berkeley.

———. 1917. The Mission as a Frontier Institution in the Spanish-American Colonies. *American Historical Review* 23:42–61.

———. 1921. *The Spanish Borderlands: A Chronicle of Old Florida and the Southwest.* Yale University Press, New Haven, CT.

———, and M. Ross. 1925. *The Debatable Land.* University of California Press, Berkeley.

Bushnell, A.T. 1978. "That Demonic Game": The Campaign to Stop Indian Pelota Playing in Spanish Florida, 1675–1684. *The Americas* 35:1–19.

———. 1981. *The King's Coffer: Proprietors of the Spanish Florida Treasury, 1565–1702.* University of Florida Press, Gainesville.

———. 1994. *Situado and Sabana: Spain's Support System of the Presidio and Mission Provinces of Florida.* Anthropological Papers of the American Museum of Natural History 74:1–249. http://hdl.handle.net/2246/269.

Castillo, E. D. 1989. The Native Response to Colonization in Alta California. In *Columbian Consequences*, vol. 1, *Archaeological and Historical Perspectives on the Spanish Borderlands West,* edited by D. H. Thomas, pp. 377–394. Smithsonian Institution Press, Washington DC.

Chartkoff, J. L., and K. K. Chartkoff. 1984. *The Archaeology of California.* Stanford University Press, Palo Alto, CA.

Cordell, L. S. 1989. Durango to Durango: An Overview of the Southwestern Heartland. In *Columbian Consequences*, vol. 1, *Archaeological and Historical Perspectives on the Spanish Borderlands West,* edited by D. H. Thomas, pp. 17–40. Smithsonian Institution Press, Washington DC.

Costello, J. G., and D. Hornbeck. 1989. Alta California: An Overview. In *Columbian Consequences*, vol. 1, *Archaeological and Historical Perspectives on the Spanish Borderlands West,* edited by David Hurst Thomas, pp. 303–331. Smithsonian Institution Press, Washington DC.

Deagan, K. 1982. Avenues of Inquiry in Historical Archaeology. In *Advances in Archaeological Method and Theory* 5, edited by M. B. Schiffer, pp. 151–177. Academic Press, New York.

Elliot, M. 1995. *Great Excavations: Tales of Early Southwestern Archaeology, 1888–1939.* School of American Research Press, Santa Fe, NM.

Englehardt, Z. 1930. *The Missions and Missionaries of California,* 2nd ed., vol. 2, pt.1, *Upper California.* Published by the author, Old Mission, Santa Barbara, CA.

Farnsworth, P. 1989. The Economics of Acculturation in the Spanish Missions of Alta California. *Research in Economic Anthropology* 11:217–249.

Francis, J. M., and K. M. Kole. 2011. *Murder and Martyrdom in Spanish Florida: Don Juan and the Guale Uprising of 1597.* Anthropological Papers of the American Museum of Natural History 95:1–154.

Gannon, M. V. 1990. Defense of Native American and Franciscan Rights in the Florida Missions. In *Columbian Consequences,* vol. 2: *Archaeological and Historical Perspectives on the Spanish Borderlands East,* edited by David Hurst Thomas, pp. 449–457. Smithsonian Institution Press, Washington DC.

Geiger, M. 1940. *Biographical Dictionary of Franciscans in Spanish Florida and Cuba, 1528–1841.* Franciscan Studies, vol. 21. St. Anthony Guild Press, Patterson, NJ.

Gosden, C. 2001. Postcolonial Archaeology: Issues of Culture, Identity, and Knowledge. In *Archaeological Theory Today*, edited by I. Hodder, pp. 241–261. Blackwell, London.

Guest, F. F. 1966. The Indian Policy Under Fermín Francisco de Lasuén, California's Second Father President. *California Historical Society Quarterly* 45:195–224.

Hackel, S. W. 1997. Land, Labor and Production: The Colonial Economy of Spanish and Mexican California. *California History* 76(2 and 3):111–146.

———. 2005. *Children of Coyote, Missionaries of Saint Francis: Indian-Spanish Relations in Colonial California, 1769–1850*. University of North Carolina Press, Chapel Hill.

Heizer, R. F., and T. D. McCown. 1954. Preface to Sonoma Mission: An Historical and Archaeological Study of Primary Constructions, 1823–1913. University of California Archaeological Survey Reports 27, pp. i–ii. Berkeley.

Hewett, E. L., and R. G. Fisher. 1943. *Mission Monuments of New Mexico*. Handbooks of Archaeological History, edited by E. L. Hewett. University of New Mexico Press, Albuquerque.

Hume, I. Noël. 1964. Handmaiden to History. *North Carolina Historical Review* 41(2):215–225.

Ivey, J. E. 1988. *In The Midst of a Loneliness: The Architectural History of the Salinas Missions*. Salinas Pueblo Missions National Structure Report. Southwest Cultural Resources Center Professional Papers 15. National Park Service, U.S. Department of the Interior, Santa Fe, NM.

———, and D. H. Thomas. 2005. "The Feeling of Working Completely in the Dark": The Uncertain Foundations of Southwestern Mission Archaeology. In *Southwest Archaeology in the Twentieth Century*, edited by L. S. Cordell and D. D. Fowler, pp. 204–219. University of Utah Press, Salt Lake City.

Jackson, H. H. 1884. *Ramona*. Roberts Brothers, Boston.

Kessell, J. 1976. *Friars, Soldiers, and Reformers: Hispanic Arizona and the Sonoran Mission Frontier, 1767–1856*. University of Arizona Press, Tucson.

———. 1980. *The Missions of New Mexico, Since 1776*. University of New Mexico Press, Albuquerque.

———. 2002. *Spain in the Southwest: A Narrative History of Colonial New Mexico, Arizona, Texas, and California*. University of Oklahoma Press, Norman.

Leibman, M. 2008. Introduction: The Intersections of Archaeology and Postcolonial Studies. In *Archaeology and the Postcolonial Critique*, edited by M. Leibman and U. Z. Rizvi, pp. 1–20. AltaMira Press, Lanham, MD.

Lightfoot, K. G. 2005. *Indians, Missionaries, and Merchants: The Legacy of Colonial Encounters on the California Frontiers*. University of California Press, Berkeley.

McEwan, B. G. 1993. *The Spanish Missions of La Florida*. University Press of Florida, Gainesville.

———. 2001. The Spiritual Conquest of La Florida. *American Anthropologist* 103(3):633–644.

Milanich, J. T. 1999. *Laboring in the Fields of the Lord: Spanish Missions and Southeastern Indians*. Smithsonian Institution Press, Washington DC.

Montgomery, R. G., W. Smith, and J. O. Brew. 1949. *Franciscan Awatovi: The Excavation and Conjectural Reconstruction of a 17th-Century Spanish Mission Established at a Hopi Indian Town in Northeastern Arizona*. Papers of the Peabody Museum of American Archaeology and Ethnology, Vol. 36. Harvard University, Cambridge, MA.

Patterson, T. C. 2008. A Brief History of Postcolonial Theory and Implications for Archaeology. In *Archaeology and The Postcolonial Critique*, edited by M. Leibman and U. Z. Rizvi, pp. 21–34. AltaMira Press, Lanham, MD.

Preucel, R. W., and H. Agoyo (editors). 2007. *Archaeologies of the Pueblo Revolt: Identity, Meaning, and Renewal in the Pueblo World*. University of New Mexico Press, Albuquerque.

Reitz, E. J., B. Pavao-Zuckerman, D. C. Weinand, and G. A. Duncan. 2010. *Mission and Pueblo of Santa Catalina de Guale, St. Catherines Island, Georgia: A Comparative Zooarchaeological Analysis*. Anthropological Papers of the American Museum of Natural History 91:1–273.

Sandos, J. A. 1994. From "Boltonlands" to "Weberlands," the Borderlands Enter American History. *American Quarterly* 46:595–604. (December 1994).

———. 2005. *Converting California: Indians and Franciscans in the Missions*. Yale University Press, New Haven, CT.

Scholes, F. V. 1937. *Church and State in New Mexico, 1610–1650*. Historical Society of New Mexico, Publications in History 7. Historical Society of New Mexico, Albuquerque.

———. 1942. *Troublous Times in New Mexico, 1659–1670*. Historical Society of New Mexico, Publications in History 11. Historical Society of New Mexico, Albuquerque.

Shapiro, G. N., and J. H. Hann. 1990. The Documentary Image of the Council Houses of Spanish Florida Tested by Excavations at the Mission of San Luis de Talimali. In *Columbian Consequences*, vol. 2, *Archaeological and Historical Perspectives on the Spanish Borderlands East*, edited by David Hurst Thomas, pp. 511–526. Smithsonian Institution Press, Washington, DC.

Silliman, S. W. 2001. Theoretical Perspectives on Labor and Colonialism: Reconsidering the California Missions. *Journal of Anthropological Anthropology* 20:379–407.

Smith, W., R. B. Woodbury, and N. F. S. Woodbury. 1966. *The Excavation of Hawikuh by Frederick Webb Hodge: Report of the Hendricks-Hodge Expedition, 1917–1923*. Contribution from the Museum of the American Indian 20, New York.

Thomas, D. H. 1987. *The Archaeology of Mission Santa Catalina de Guale: 1. Search and Discovery*. Anthropological Papers of the American Museum of Natural History 63(2):47–161. http://hdl.handle.net/2246/251.

———. 1988. Saints and Soldiers at Santa Catalina: Hispanic Design for Colonial America. In *The Recovery of Meaning: Historical Archaeology in the Eastern United States*, edited by M. Leone and M. Parker Potter, pp. 73–140. Smithsonian Institution Press, Washington DC.

———. 1989. Columbian Consequences: The Spanish Borderlands in Cubist Perspective. In *Columbian Consequences*, vol. 1, *Archaeological and Historical Perspectives on the Spanish Borderlands West*, edited by David Hurst Thomas, pp. 1–14. Smithsonian Institution Press, Washington DC.

———. 1990. The Spanish Missions of La Florida: An Overview. In *Columbian Consequences*, vol. 2, *Archaeological and Historical Perspectives on the Spanish Borderlands East*, edited by David Hurst Thomas, pp. 357–397. Smithsonian Institution Press, Washington DC.

———. 1991 Harvesting Ramona's Garden: Life in California's Mythical Mission Past. In *Columbian Consequences*, vol. 3,: *The Spanish Borderlands in Pan-American Perspective*, edited by David Hurst Thomas, pp. 119–160. Smithsonian Institution Press, Washington DC.

Weber, D. J. (editor). 1987. J. Francis Bannon and the Historiography of the Spanish Borderlands. *Journal of the Southwest* 29(4):331–363.

———. 1990. Blood of Martyrs, Blood of Indians: Toward a More Balanced View of Spanish Missions in Seventeenth-Century North America. In *Columbian Consequences*, vol. 2, *Archaeological and Historical Perspectives on the Spanish Borderlands East*, edited by David Hurst Thomas, pp. 429–448. Smithsonian Institution Press, Washington DC.

———. 1992. *The Spanish Frontier in North America*. Yale University Press, New Haven, CT.

Wilcox, M. 2009. *The Pueblo Revolt and the Mythology of Conquest: An Indigenous Archaeology of Contact*. University of California Press, Berkeley.

Worth, J. E. 1995. The Struggle for the Georgia Coast: An Eighteenth-Century Spanish Retrospective on Guale and Mocama. *Anthropological Papers of the American Museum of Natural History* 75:1–222. http://hdl.handle.net/2246/270.

———. 1998. *The Timucuan Chiefdoms of Spanish Florida:* vol. 1, *Assimilation*. University Press of Florida, Gainesville.

———. 2002. Spanish Missions and the Persistence of Chiefly Power. In *The Transformation of the Southeastern Indians: 1540–1760*, edited by R. Ethridge and C. Hudson, pp. 39–64. University Press of Mississippi, Jackson.

———. 2004. Guale. In *Handbook of North American Indians,* vol. 14, *Southeast*, edited by R. D. Fogelson, pp. 238–244. Smithsonian Institution Press, Washington DC.

———. 2009. Inventing Florida: Constructing a Colonial Society in an Indigenous Landscape. Paper presented at the 74th Annual Meeting of the Society for American Archaeology, Atlanta, GA.

CHAPTER 5

SOME COMMONALITIES LINKING NORTH AMERICA AND MESOAMERICA

ROBERT L. HALL

INTEREST in prehistoric commonalities between Mesoamerica and North America has typically examined the role that Mesoamerican civilizations may have had in influencing the development of high cultures in North America's Puebloan Southwest and Southeast of Adena-Hopewellian and Mississippian times (Ekholm 1940; Griffin 1966; Kehoe 2005; Kelley 1966; Phillips 1940; Riley 2005; White and Weinstein 2008). For the Southwest, this was a logical pursuit. There is undisputed evidence of some continuities of language (Utonahuan or Uto-Aztecan family); unquestioned evidence of trade relations in turquoise, copper bells, and macaw feathers; and some shared technologies not found in North America outside of the Southwest, the true loom with heddle and the spinning of cotton for example. For the Mississippian Southeast, there were town plans featuring plazas flanked by house and temple mounds of truncated pyramid form, whose builders practiced new fire rituals and human sacrifice and created art styles with themes reminiscent of Mesoamerica. Underlying both Southwestern and Mississippian developments, as they came into prominence and climaxed, was an economy based on cultigens introduced from Mesoamerica, most importantly maize.

More difficult to document in the ground have been the commonalities of belief and custom deeply rooted in time that underlay the course toward social complexity in both North America and Mesoamerica. Among these commonalities were certain ideas relating to conception, life, death, and mourning; to the renewal of life in the human and natural worlds; and to perceptions of those worlds. These ideas formed a psychological infrastructure that could be drawn on in creating cosmologies or legitimizing human actions through mythical precedent. Attention to a few such commonalities follows, allowing consideration of how peoples in North America and Mesoamerica charted the particular courses they did toward civilization, beginning from comparable bases in the material and nonmaterial worlds.

The Sweat Bath

The sweat bath was and still is associated, among Native peoples from Alaska and Labrador to Guatemala, variously with birth, renewal, and spiritual cleansing. Nowhere, however, was the sweat bath elevated to such prominence as at the Maya site of Palenque in Chiapas, Mexico. There, sweat baths were created in stone on the vaulted summits of three pyramids and assigned duty as the symbolic birthplaces of a triad of Maya deities (Houston 1996). The humble domestic sweat bath experience became a metaphor of gestation, the model for the phenomenon of divine birth in the cosmology of a major civilization.

Competitive Sports

The concept of a cultural North American Southwest can be expanded slightly southward to include the Casas Grandes or Paquimé site and area of adjacent northwestern Mexico. This location is still well outside of Mesoamerica as formally defined, but trade routes northward from Casas Grandes are believed to have been major conduits of Mesoamerican influences into the southwestern United States. Ball courts found at Casas Grandes were Mesoamerican in outline and sometimes contained adult human remains as apparent sacrificial offerings. Ball courts were also made by the Hohokam people in Arizona but were oval and not of the classic Mesoamerican I shape.

The Southeast also shared with Mesoamerica the idea of team sports, but typically of a different sort. In playing lacrosse the Cherokees, Creeks, and others use racquets for catching and tossing the ball, a practice not found in the familiar Mesoamerican ball game. Natchez ball players propelled the ball with blows from the palm of the hand.

It is possible the Southeastern ritual sport of chunkey diffused southward. Certain flat, round, ground-stone objects found in San Luis Potosí state, Mexico, recall the biconcave, discoidal chunkey stones used in the sport of that name in the north (Dávila 2005). Chunkey was a regional variation on the hoop-and-pole game found throughout North America, sometimes with explicit fertility symbolism (earth and lightning, buffalo cow and buffalo bull).

Mourning and Sacrifice

Mourning rites were universal and sometimes included ritual dramatization of events in mythical history, such as the Creation. In North America, mourning rites were normally limited to services for death by natural attrition or in combat. In Mesoamerica, however, some mourning events were preempted for state use. In the Aztec Great Feast of the Dead, multiple deaths were scheduled for the occasion of a horrifying furnace sacrifice; a mourning event was transformed into a demonstration of authority and intimidating state power (Durán 1971:212–213; Sahagún 1971:59, 111). In eastern North America, mourning rites evolved in complexity through the Woodland and later periods but were adapted to the need for establishing and maintaining peaceful relationships within and between egalitarian polities (Hall 1997).

Both the Aztec Great Feast of the Dead and an Algonquian version of the Great Lakes region Feast of the Dead featured pole-climbing contests (Durán 1971:208; Hall 1997:36–40). These contests probably originated as a means to simulate, and through sympathetic magic to aid or hasten, the ascent of spirits into the afterworld. The ideas underlying ritual pole climbing and the relationship of poles as World Tree and Spirit Trail metaphors to mourning are deeply rooted in North America and Mesoamerica and do not require recent diffusion as an explanation for their distribution (e.g., Hall 1998, 2005). Competitive pole climbing was a feature of the Kutumit or Notish mourning ritual of the Luiseño Indians of Southern California (Du Bois 1908).

In historic times, Aztecs and some northern Mississippi valley tribes shared the practice of performing blood autosacrifice by running peeled wooden skewers specifically through slits in their left arms and depositing them at the base of a mourning pole symbolizing the Path of Souls, in the case of the United States, or at the base of an idol of the sun, in the case of the Aztecs (Durán: 1971 [1574–1579]:191; Hall 2006b). The practice was part of an act to aid the shade of the deceased in its travel along the Spirit Trail. This was relevant to worship of the sun because in Aztec belief the sun died every evening, traveled through the underworld, and was reborn in the morning. Blood offered in sacrifice nourished the Aztec sun for its travels. For the Mayas, a related practice is attested on the tomb of the king Pacal by the imagery of a blood-letting tool deposited at the base of the World Tree symbolizing the path of Pacal's soul entering the Maya afterworld (Schele et al. 1999:113). Blood autosacrifice of this kind in North America—depositing bloodied skewers at the base of the mourning pole of an important figure—was possibly of Mesoamerican derivation because it was limited to tribes believed to have once lived at or in close contact with ancient Cahokia.

Plains Dog Soldiers corresponded in some respects to Aztec no-retreat warriors. Under certain circumstances, a member of a Plains Dog Soldier society might tether himself with a sash to a crook-shaped staff stuck in the ground, pledging no retreat, and defending himself with only a wooden-handled quirt (Figure 5.1a, c). The no-retreat stance of Dog Soldiers paralleled the Aztec gladiatorial sacrifice in which a slave or captive was tethered in place with a cord and obliged to defend himself with only a wooden club (Figure 5.1b; Sahagún 1971:74–77, 154–155).

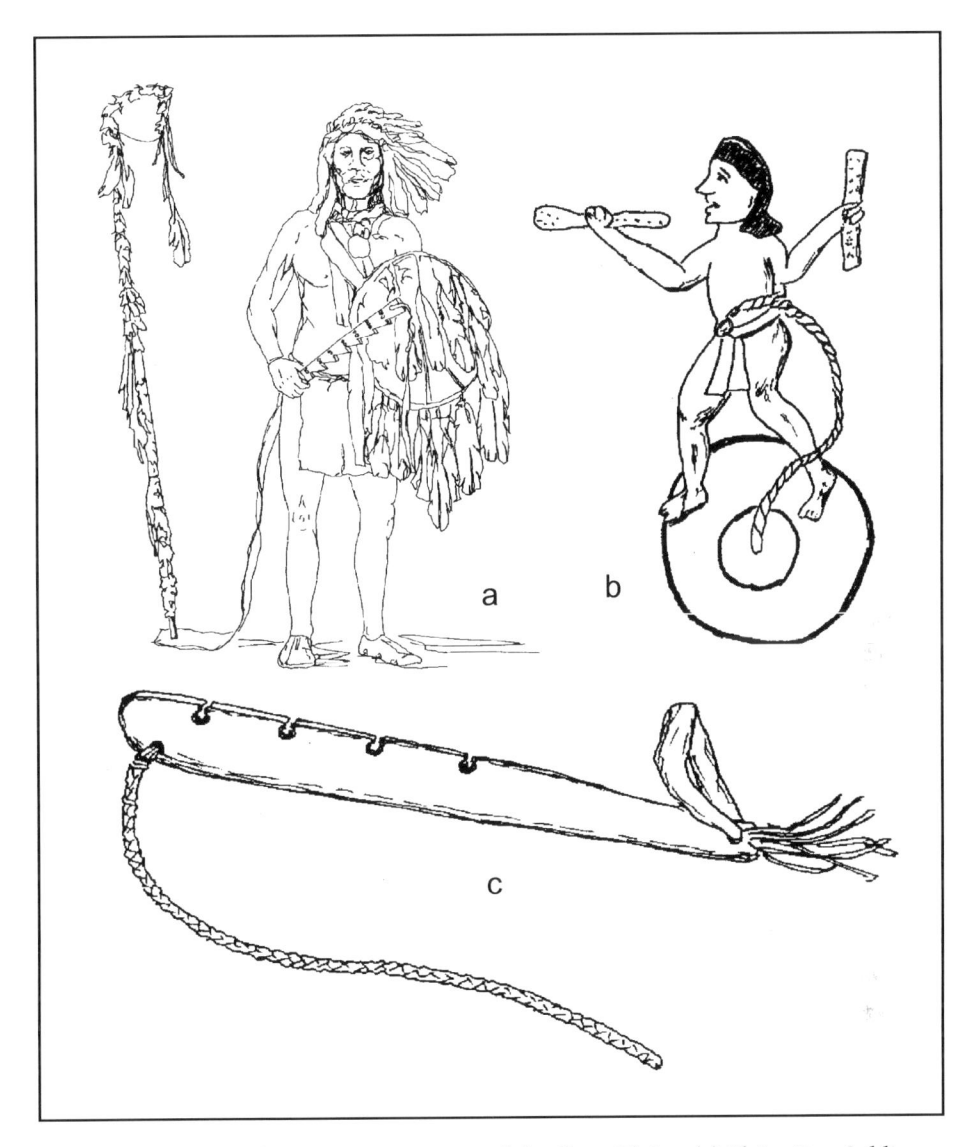

Figure 5.1 Tethered warriors in Mexico and the Great Plains: (a) Plains Dog Soldier tethered to a crook lance and holding a wooden quirt, from Hall (1997: fig. 19.5a), after Mails (1973:48); (b) tethered warrior in the Aztec gladiatorial sacrifice, after Berlin et al. (1947: pl. 15m–n); (c) Comanche quirt in the form of the hearthboard of a fire drilling set, from Hall (1997: fig. 19.5b, after Rollings 1989:47).

The Aztec sacrificial victim was flayed after death and his skin worn by a warrior impersonating the Flayed God Xipe Totec. This was a literal interpretation of the metaphor of reincarnation or rebirth as skin shedding, a metaphor attested to also for the Winnebago in North America and the Amazonian Barasana (Hall 1997:163). Symbolic reincarnation was a major element of the mourning ritual known as Spirit Adoption in eastern North America. In the case of the captive killed in the Aztec gladiatorial sacrifice, the person who provided him was said to have acted like a father to his captive, calling him "son" and simulating mourning of his death (Sahagún 1971:77–78).

The prototypical Calumet ceremony in midcontinental North America contained a simulated, balletlike combat and death followed by symbolic reincarnation of the deceased in the person of a mourner. When the mourner was additionally given an identity with the earth, the symbolic reincarnation amounted also to a world renewal ceremony (Hall 1997:53–57, 2006b:211). The usual explanation for the flaying and "reclothing" in the Aztec gladiatorial sacrifice is that it represents the renewal of the earth in the spring. It would thus seem that from an ancient shared base in mourning behavior a ritual drama of death and reincarnation in the human and natural worlds moved in Mesoamerica away from figurative expression in the direction of stark reality.

In pre-horse and pre-bow-and-arrow days, the Dog Soldier quirt (see above) may have been an atlatl dart fending stick in the form of the hearthboard or lower board of a set of fire drilling sticks (Figure 5.2d–e). In Indian belief, the power of shields (and presumably, once, fending sticks) to protect lay in their power, enhanced magically by their shape or decoration, to attract and thus intercept or deflect missiles. The hearthboard is the female half of a set of operating fire sticks when viewed as a metaphor for human procreation and renewal.

The practice of Aztec warriors to burn spots on their wrist in the pattern of their Fire Sticks constellation (Nahuatl *mamalhuaztli*), probably only the three stars of Orion's "belt" asterism (Figure 5.2a–b), has a parallel in northern Plains ethnoastronomy, where these three stars form the wrist within Orion as the Hand Star constellation (Figure 5.2c; Hall 1998:61–62, 77–78). An Orion constellation association for Aztec fire sticks complements certain Dipper (*Ursa major*) associations of Dog Soldiers (Hall 2005:119, fig. 3). In each area, scarification in this manner was related to beliefs regarding the passage of spirits into the afterworld (Hall 1998; see also Figure 5.2c).

Certain iconographic themes appear in the Southwest by AD 1350 that in Mesoamerica were associated with the rain god Tlaloc and in the Southwest arguably with the cult of Kachina rain spirits. In the Southwest and Southeast feathered, horned, or antlered serpents appear in art between AD 1000 and 1300 that have prompted comparisons to the Mesoamerican Feathered Serpent deity Quetzalcoatl and to his wind god avatar Ehecatl.

Human sacrifice had arrived in the Cahokia area of Illinois by the 11th century AD, possibly even earlier, sometimes in forms duplicating Mesoamerican rites to promote fertility in maize agriculture (Fowler et al. 1999:77; Hall 2000). The arrival of these rites coincided with the opening phase of the Mississippian development at what became the first and largest community of Mississippian temple towns and population aggregations north of Mexico. Human sacrifice approaching the Mesoamerican scale and model—161 sacrificial victims in one small mound—survived three centuries or less at Cahokia itself. A version of the Mesoamerican scaffold sacrifice by arrows did, however, survive into the 20th century among the Skiri band of Pawnees on the Plains and, long enough to be actually witnessed (without the fatal climax) by anthropologists

Figure 5.2 Representations of fire drilling kits: (a) belt and sword asterism within the Orion constellation; (b) Aztec *mamalhuaztli* (fire sticks) constellation, after Sahagún (1953: fig. 21); (c) Lakota Hand Star constellation, from Lankford (2007: fig. 9-3b); (d) *mamalhuaztli* glyph, after Starr (1920); (e) drilling fire, Mexico, after Berlin et al. (1947: pl. XXII-8).

and described in detail (Figures 5.3a, 5.4c; Hall 1997:86–94). Compatible elements of these Mesoamerican introductions were pervasive in influence and are recognizably incorporated into the Pawnee Hako ceremony, the Ponca version of the Plains Sun Dance, and elsewhere (Hall 1989, 1997, 1998, 2006b). The Pawnee scaffold sacrifice and the Ponca Sun Dance recognizably included dramatizations of the five-sun creation story found in the iconography of the Aztec Sun Stone.

Clowning, Contraries, and Reverse Behavior

Ritual humor and use of contrary or reverse behavior or language is known historically and still practiced locally today, in varying degrees, in both Mesoamerica and North America. Contrary behavior originates in the belief that actions are reversed in the

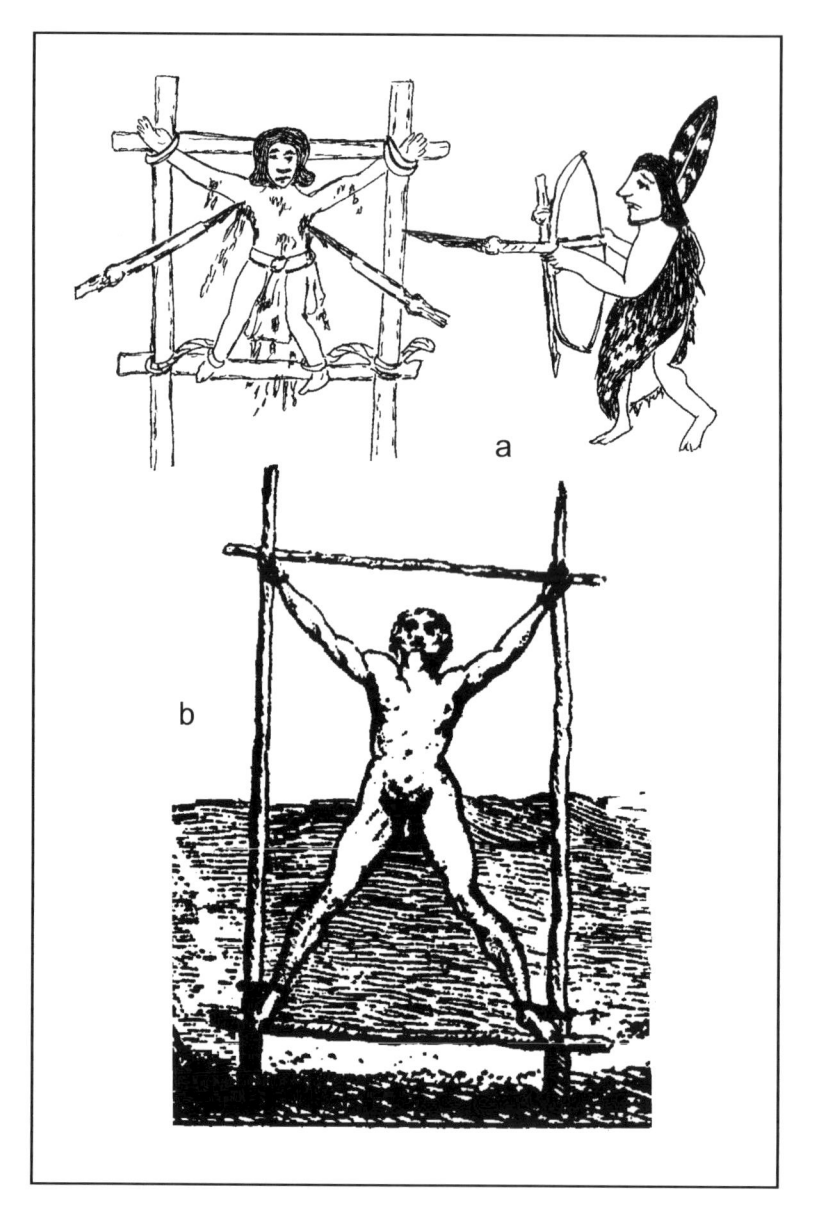

Figure 5.3 Victims with splayed postures on pole frames: (a) Mexican scaffold sacrifice, after Berlin et al. (1947: pl. 15i); (b) Natchez captive, early eighteenth century, from Le Page du Pratz (1972 [1774]:355).

underworld and in the night sky, which is seen as the equivalent of the underworld. Contrary behavior is thus associated also with the dead, with the night sun in the underworld, with plant germination, and with the fertility of animals whose spirits abide in the underworld until their time to be incarnated. Contrary behavior may be associated with institutionalized clowning and ritual humor, as in the case of the Hopi Koshares and other clown societies of the Pueblo area, or used merely to indicate a symbolic presence in an ancestral homeland, as among the Huichol of western Mexico

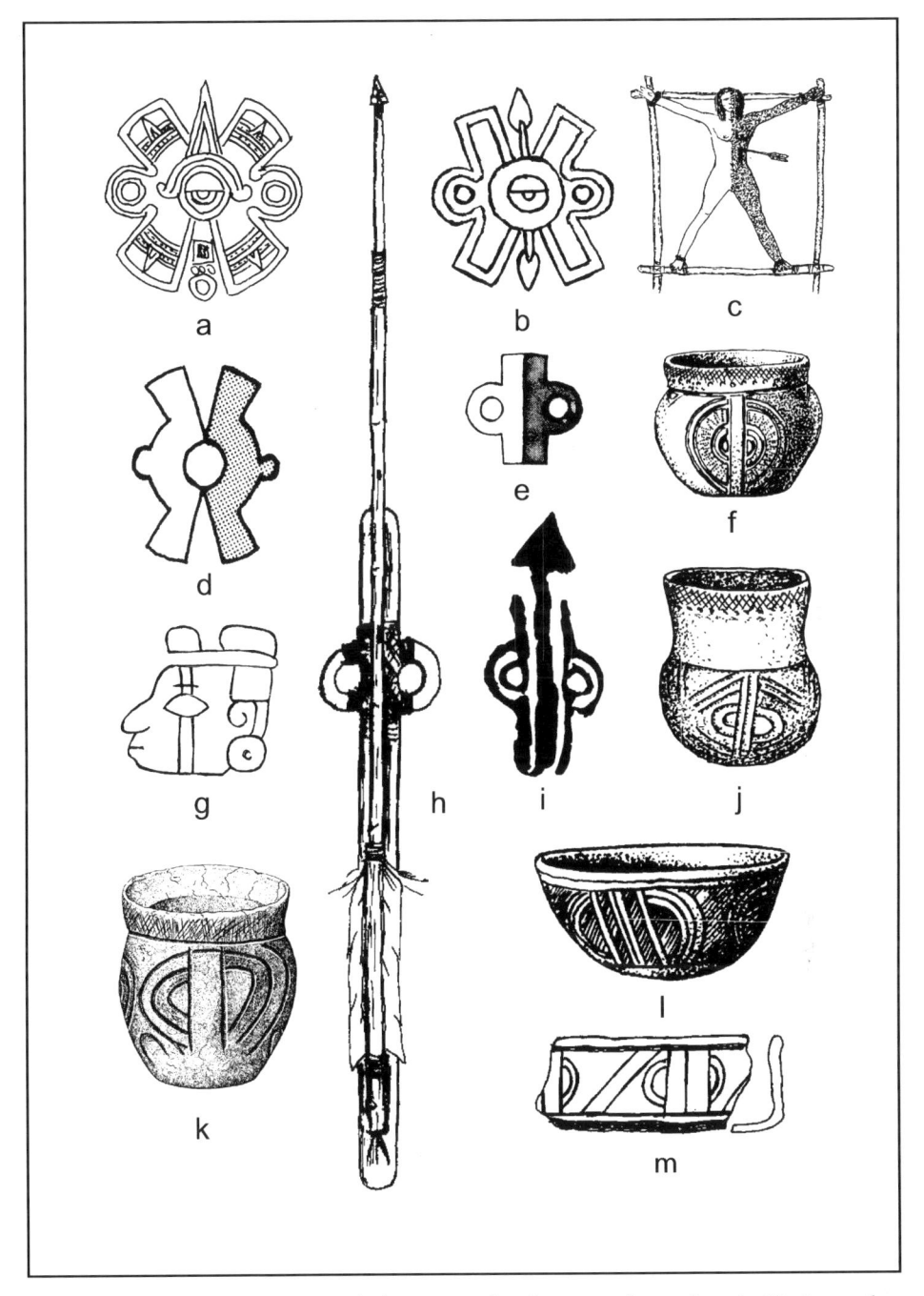

COMMONALITIES LINKING NORTH AMERICA AND MESOAMERICA 59

Figure 5.4 Bisected circle or atlatl grip motif and its transformations in Mexico and North America: (a–b) Aztec day sign Ollin or Motion; (c) splayed posture of victim in Pawnee arrow sacrifice; (d–e) Mixtec day sign Motion; (f) Hopewell jar, Louisiana, from Ford (1952: fig. 23); (g) Glyph P, Zapotec; (h) generic atlatl and dart; (i) atlatl and dart motif from a Preclassic pottery stamp, Tlatilco site, Mexico, after Field (1967: fig. 29); (j) Hopewell jar, Illinois, after Henriksen (1965: fig. 30a); (k) Hopewell jar, Louisiana, from Ford and Willey (1940: fig. 32d); (l) Caddoan jar, Arkansas, from Ford (1952: fig. 23); (m) Preclassic bowl, Veracruz, after García Payón (1950: pl. 12, no. 4).

and Skiri Pawnee of the Plains, especially when that homeland existed in the night sky (e.g., Hall 1997:133, 189 n10).

Clowning in North America is widely associated with fire handling and disdain for heat and fire. Because such disdain is known, in California, to have been associated with persons representing ghosts of the cremated dead, there is an implication that this feature of clowning could have roots deep in a time when cremation was an important feature of mortuary ritual. Contrary behavior is difficult to document archaeologically, especially relating to language. There are, even so, unexplained but possibly related instances of Mayan hieroglyphic texts written in reverse (e.g., Houston 1998).

One class of sacred clowns in the Southwest typically have bodies painted white with black stripes and black circles around their eyes and mouth; the practice compares as well with the preparation in Mexico of certain 16th-century Huexotzincans and Tlaxcalans who participated in an annual ritual animal drive and hunt there. The bodies of these men were painted with white stripes, and they had similar black rings around the eyes and mouth. In the northern Plains, Cheyenne Contraries too participated in ritual animal drives, though of a symbolic nature with the animals only impersonated. The bodies, arms, and legs of these clowns were painted white.

New fire, important in the Busk and an important part of the Huexotzincan and Tlaxcalan ritual hunt as well, honored Camaxtli aka Mixcoatl, the hunting god who was the first to drill fire (Durán 1971). Witthoff (1949) believed that the green corn ritual (the Busk) in the Southeast was a modification of preexisting hunting ceremonialism to accommodate the increasing importance of corn. Some important tropical American influences appear to have begun within a more ancient Gulf- Caribbean theater of interaction that must have once extended from Central America into eastern North America (Hall 2006a).

Discussion

Native societies of the Southwest followed their own road toward climax with the Chaco phenomenon followed by its own decline and diaspora (Lekson, this volume). Mesoamerican influences began with the northward spread of some technologies and cultigens during the first millennium AD, with infusions only much later of religious ideas and organizing principles that mark recognizable changes of course in the trajectory of southwestern development. Mesoamerican influence survived visibly into the present in the Puebloan Southwest in the form of ceremonies by societies of Kachinas, ritual dancers who represented returning spirits. Beliefs in a relationship of spirits of the dead to rain clouds became the organizing principle behind Mesoamerican-inspired sodalities of Kachinas who conducted community-wide ceremonies integrating multiclan pueblos.

This contrasts with eastern North America, where some religious ideas and practices appear to have been shared with tropical America by 1000 BC, or not long afterward, and to have been reinforced through the centuries by periodic contacts from the same direction (Hall 1997: fig. 14.6, 119; 2006a). Such contacts might have involved linguistic exchanges, producing the seemingly cognate relationship of the Cherokee words *selu* and Selu for corn and Corn Mother with the Nahuatl root *xilo-* (phonetically *šilo-*) as in *xilotl* "green corn ear" and Xilonen, Green Corn Goddess (Hall 2000). Such exchanges could also have involved only semantic sets, such as the equation of "earth" and "motion" in ritual references to the Evening Star in certain Pawnee songs (e.g., Hall 1997:96). In the Skiri Pawnee scaffold sacrifice, diffused from Mexico, the victim personating Evening Star assumed the splayed posture of the Aztec day sign Ollin or motion, whose Maya equivalent was Caban earth (Figures 5.3a, cf. 5.3b, 5.4a–c).

The Ollin glyph is a version of the bisected circle motif derived from the imagery of an atlatl handle or grip and atlatl dart that symbolize the earth, sky, and path of the sun (Figure 5.4h; Hall 1997: fig. 11.3). In Mexico this imagery is as old as the Middle Preclassic period (1250–400 BC) but is more evident in later times (Figure 5.4a–b, d–e, g, m). In North America the bisected circle has been found on ceramics of Hopewellian age (100 BC–AD 400) in the upper and lower Mississippi valleys with a late survival in the Caddo area (Figure 5.4f–l; Griffin 1966). This use of an atlatl grip as a cosmogram is, however, preceded by more than 500 years in eastern North America with the widespread use of atlatl handles in the form of a composite bird-crocodilian creature logically representing earth, sky, and water in the manner of such later-period Mesoamerican deities as Cipactli and Itzamna (Hall 1997: fig. 14.5; 2006a).

It appears easier to perceive some commonality of thought in the matter of cosmology between Mesoamerican and eastern North American Indian minds during Hopewellian and earlier times than is possible between Hopewellians and the centuries more recent though regionally proximate Mississippians. Even so, it can be no coincidence that the explosion of development around Cahokia was accompanied at its inception by the sudden appearance there of human sacrifice on a scale until then not known in the Americas north of Mexico. This was a development that arguably involved contacts with a state-level Mesoamerican society of a pre-Aztec time level (see also Alt, and Peregrine and Lekson, this volume).

Unlike Teotihuacan and Tula, Cahokia disappeared, leaving neither myth nor history. What is known of Cahokia is known only from archaeology and from what can be inferred from the ethnographies of tribes believed to have once lived at Cahokia or in its environs or sphere of influence. These would be, principally, the Siouan-speaking Omaha, Ponca, Osage, and Kansa; secondarily, the Siouan-speaking Iowa, Ho-Chunk (Winnebago), Missouri, and Oto; and third, the Pawnees and other Caddoan-speaking nations farther to the west and southwest (Hall 2004:100–103). These ethnographies contain tantalizing details that beg to be placed in broader context (Hall 1998, 2005).

REFERENCES

Berlin, H., S. Rendón, and P. Kirchoff. 1947. *Historia Tolteca Chichimeca: Anales de Quauhtinchan*. Antigua Librería Robredo de José Porrúa e Hijos, México.

Dávila Cabrera, P. 2005. Mound Builders Along the Coast of the Gulf of Mexico and the Eastern United States. In *Gulf Coast Archaeology: The Southeastern United States and Mexico*, edited by N. M. White, pp. 87–107. University Press of Florida, Gainesville.

Du Bois, C. (Goddard). 1908. The Religion of the Luiseño and Diegueño Indians of Southern California. *University of California Publications in American Archaeology and Ethnology* 8(3):69–186. Berkeley.

Durán, D. 1971 [1574–1579]. *Book of the Gods and Rites and the Ancient Calendar*. Translated (from Mexican edition of 1880) and edited by F. Horcasitas and D. Heyden. University of Oklahoma Press, Norman.

Ekholm, G. F. 1940. The Archaeology of Northern and Western Mexico. In *The Maya and Their Neighbors*, edited by C. L. Hay, R. Linton, S. K. Lothrop, H. L. Shapiro, and G. C. Vaillant, pp. 320–330. Appleton-Century, New York.

Field, F. V. 1967. *Thoughts on the Meaning and Use of Pre-Hispanic Mexican Sellos*. Studies in Precolumbian Art and Archaeology 3. Dumbarton Oaks, Washington, DC.

Ford, J. A. 1952. *Measurements of Some Prehistoric Design Elements in the Southeastern United States*. Anthropological Papers, vol. 44, pt. 3. American Museum of Natural History, New York.

———, and G. Willey. 1940. *Crooks Site, a Marksville Period Burial Mound in La Salle Parish, Louisiana*. Department of Conservation, Louisiana Geological Survey, New Orleans.

Fowler, M. L., J. Rose, B. Vander Leest, and S. R. Ahler. 1999. *The Mound 72 Area: Dedicated and Sacred Space in Early Cahokia*. Reports of Investigation 54. Illinois State Museum, Springfield.

García Payón, J. 1950. Restos de una cultura prehistórica encontrados en la región de Zempoala, Ver. *Uni-Ver*, Año II, Tomo II, Número 15, pp. 90–130. Universidad Veracruzana, Jalapa, Ver., México.

Griffin, J. B. 1966. Mesoamerica and the Eastern United States in Prehistoric Times. In *Handbook of Middle American Indians*, vol. 4, *Archaeological Frontiers and External Connections*, edited by G. F. Ekholm and G. R. Willey, pp. 111–131. University of Texas Press, Austin.

Hall, R. L. 1989. The Cultural Background of Mississippian Symbolism. In *The Southeastern Ceremonial Complex: Artifacts and Analysis; The Cottonlandia Conference*, edited by P. Galloway, pp. 239–278. University of Nebraska Press, Lincoln.

———. 1997. *An Archaeology of the Soul: North American Indian Belief and Ritual*. University of Illinois Press, Urbana.

———. 1998. A Comparison of Some North American and Mesoamerican Cosmologies and Their Ritual Expressions. In *Explorations in American Archaeology: Essays in Honor of Wesley R. Hurt*, edited by M. G. Plew, pp. 55–88. University Press of America, Lanham, MD.

———. 2000. Sacrificed Foursomes and Green Corn Ceremonialism. In *Scientific Papers*, vol. 48, *Mounds, Modoc, and Mesoamerica: Papers in Honor of Melvin L. Fowler*, edited by S. R. Ahler, pp. 245–253. Illinois State Museum, Springfield.

———. 2004. The Cahokia Site and Its People. In *Hero, Hawk, and Open Hand: Ancient Indian Art of the Woodlands*, edited by R. F. Townsend and R. V. Sharp, pp. 92–103. Yale University Press, New Haven, CT.

———. 2005. Contradictions as a Source of Historical Perspective: Examples from the Symbolism of Camp Circles and Sacred Poles. *Ontario Archaeology: Journal of the Ontario Archaeological Society*, no. 79/80:115–126.

———. 2006a. The Enigmatic Copper Cutout from Bedford Mound 8. In *Recreating Hopewell*, edited by D. K. Charles and J. E. Buikstra, pp. 464–474. University Press of Florida, Gainesville.

———. 2006b. Exploring the Mississippian Big Bang at Cahokia. In *A Pre-Columbian World*, edited by J. Quilter and M. Miller, pp. 187–229. Harvard University Press, Cambridge, MA.

Henriksen, H. 1965. Utica Hopewell, a Study of Early Hopewell Occupation in the Illinois River Valley. In Illinois Archaeological Survey Bulletin, vol. 5, *Middle Woodland Sites in Illinois*, edited by E. B. Herold, pp. 1–67. Urbana.

Houston, S. 1996. Symbolic Sweatbaths of the Maya: Architectural Meaning in the Cross Group at Palenque, Mexico. *American Antiquity* 7(2):132–151.

———. 1998. Classic Maya Depictions of the Built Environment. In *Function and Meaning in Classic Maya Architecture*, edited by S. D. Houston, pp. 333–372. Dumbarton Oaks, Washington, DC.

Kehoe, A. B. 2005. Wind Jewels and Paddling Gods. In *Gulf Coast Archaeology: The Southeastern United States and Mexico*, edited by N. M. White, pp. 260–280. University Press of Florida, Gainesville.

Kelley, J. C. 1966. Mesoamerica and the Southwestern United States. *Handbook of Middle American Indians*, vol. 4, *Archaeological Frontiers and External Connections*, edited by G. F. Ekholm and G. R. Willey, pp. 95–130. University of Texas Press, Austin.

Lankford, G. 2007. *Reachable Stars: Patterns in the Ethnoastronomy of Eastern North America*. University of Alabama Press, Tuscaloosa.

Le Page du Pratz, A. S. 1972. *The History of Louisiana*. Reprint of 1774 London edition. Claitor's Publishing Division, Baton Rouge, LA.

Mails, T. E. 1973. *Dog Soldiers, Bear Men and Buffalo Women: A Study of the Societies and Cults of the Plains Indians*. Prentice Hall, Englewood Cliffs, NJ.

Phillips, P. 1940. Middle American Influences on the Archaeology of the Southeastern United States. In *The Maya and Their Neighbors*, edited by C. L. Hay, R. Linton, S. K. Lothrop, H. L. Shapiro, and G. C. Vaillant, pp. 349–367. Appleton-Century, New York.

Riley, C. L. 2005. *Becoming Aztlan: Mesoamerican Influence in the Greater Southwest, AD 1200–1500*. University of Utah Press, Salt Lake City.

Rollings, W. H. 1989. *The Comanche*. Chelsea House, New York.

Sahagún, B. 1953. *Florentine Codex, pt. 8 of 13, General History of the Things of New Spain, Book 7: The Sun, Moon, and Stars, and the Binding of the Years*, translated and edited by A. O. Anderson and C. Dibble. Monographs of the School of American Research 14. University of Utah Press, Salt Lake City.

———. 1971. *A History of Ancient Mexico*. Translated by F. R. Bandelier from the edition of Carlos María de Bustamante. Blain Ethridge, Detroit. Reprint of the 1932 Fisk University Press edition, Nashville, TN.

Schele, L., P. Mathews, J. Kerr, and M. Everton. 1999. *The Code of Kings: The Language of Seven Sacred Maya Temples and Tombs*. Simon and Schuster, New York.

Starr, F. 1920. *Aztec Place-Names*. 2nd ed., rev. Privately printed, Chicago.

White, N. M., and R. A. Weinstein. 2008. The Mexican Connection and the Far West of the U.S. Southeast. *American Antiquity* 73(2):227–277.

Witthoff, J. 1949. *Green Corn Ceremonialism in the Eastern Woodlands*. Occasional Contributions from the Museum of Anthropology of the University of Michigan 13. University of Michigan Press, Ann Arbor.

CHAPTER 6

THE NORTH AMERICAN *OIKOUMENE*

PETER N. PEREGRINE AND STEPHEN H. LEKSON

THE title of this paper employs the term *oikoumene*, meaning the inhabited or known world. Among European archaeologists, it has long been assumed that by at least the Bronze Age local populations were in regular contact with one another, forming an *oikoumene* within which processes or events in one region might have an impact on processes or events in another, perhaps distant, region (e.g., Kristiansen and Larsson 2005). In this paper, we explore the value of a continental perspective for North American archaeology, one assuming that populations in North America, like those in Europe, existed within an *oikoumene* of mutually known polities.

We know from historic documents that native peoples living in Eastern North America were well aware of peoples and polities outside of their local area. For example, in 1670 the Jesuit priest Claude Allouez visited a village of Miami Indians near Green Bay, Wisconsin. He asked about the region to the south and was told about the Mississippi River and the peoples living along it who

> are all obliged to burn peat and animal excrement dried in the Sun,—until we come within twenty leagues of the sea, when forests begin to appear again. Some warriors of this country who tell us they have made their way thither, declare that they saw there men resembling the French, who were splitting trees with long knives; and that some of them had their houses on the water,—for thus they expressed themselves in speaking of sawed boards and of Ships (Thwaites 55:209).

Thus in 1670, two years before its "discovery" by Marquette and Joliet, Allouez was told about the Mississippi River and its inhabitants as far south as the Gulf of Mexico, by native peoples who had allegedly traveled the entire length of the river and back.

Not only were native peoples well aware of others far distant from them, events at far distances had a profound effect on their lives. Allouez, for example, came to northeastern Wisconsin because it had become a haven for refugee populations "driven by their fear of the Iroquois from their own territories" (Thwaites 55:183) including Huronia, more than 500 miles to the east. These people apparently lived in fear of the Iroquois, despite the fact that raids had largely ceased almost a decade earlier and the closest the Iroquois had ever come was about 200 miles (raids resumed in the 1680s but were still well to the south). Fear of Iroquois raiders led people to consolidate into large palisaded villages (some with more than 3,000 residents), often multiethnic in composition, and apparently having formal political leaders despite the diverse cultural and linguistic backgrounds of their inhabitants (e.g., Kinietz 1965:179–182, 309–314).

To understand the lives, motivations, and actions of the peoples of northeastern Wisconsin in 1670, then, one must consider both local and supralocal processes. Certainly, local activities and relations were of vital concern (particularly conflict, which by the early to mid-1700s had erupted into regular hostilities; see Hickerson 1970) and must be understood. But the multiethnic composition of villages, and their compact, palisaded forms, can be fully understood only with recognition of events unfolding hundreds of miles away, and by the 1670s decades earlier. If understanding society in a northeastern Wisconsin community in 1670 benefits from a continental perspective, then it may benefit the study of other time periods as well.

Similarly, Native societies of the greater Southwest were densely connected within their region, and beyond. In 1540, Indians at the mouth of the Colorado River knew of Coronado's inland invasion and reported it to the Spanish fleet moving up the Gulf of California—500 kilometers distant from the army they were supposed to support (Flint and Flint 2005:186: "About two months after the vanguard of the Coronado expedition arrived at Cibola . . . linguistically unrelated people more than 350 miles away already had detailed and quite accurate descriptions of the Europeans"). Later, native guides led Coronado east across the Plains, almost certainly toward the indigenous cities and towns of the Mississippi Valley (Kehoe 2002:155, 165; Lekson 2009:25–26). And the peoples of the Southwest and Mesoamerica clearly knew each other: ten years before Coronado, an Indian called Tejo offered to guide conquistador Nuño de Guzman's army north to Southwestern cities that Tejo's father had serviced as a trader (Lekson 2009:25). Guzman's expedition misfired, but the lesson is clear: Native peoples had continental connections, sufficiently detailed to launch and lead Spanish armies.

Southeast-Southwest-Mexico

Regional-scale analysis of Southwest-Mexico interaction has a long history. Until 1846, the U.S. Southwest was, in fact, part of Mexico. More important, a great many artifacts and objects of undeniable Mexican origin have been found in the Southwest:

more than 600 copper bells, more than 400 scarlet macaws, chocolate, and literally tons of shell from as far south on the Mexican Coast as the Bay of Banderas, to name a few. The flow of material was not one-way: considerable quantities of turquoise found in Mexico came from the Southwest, much of it having been processed in Chaco Canyon (an 11th-century center in northwest New Mexico) and the later, even more cosmopolitan Casas Grandes (a 14th-century city in northern Chihuahua).

Chaco Canyon was the first near-urban center in Pueblo prehistory; Casas Grandes was the last. The presence of many Mexican objects and even a few architectural elements suggested to many archaeologists that Mexico played a role in Chaco's emergence. Indeed, primary researchers at Chaco in the 1970s concluded that Chaco was the result of direct Mesoamerican intervention, summarized by Alden Hayes (1981:63): "There is no place to look for the source [of Chaco] except ultimately in Mexico." Despite a marked retreat from this position over the last 20 years (see Mills 2002:95), there still remain an impressive number of Mexican objects at Chaco, and an extraordinary canyonwide industry of turquoise bead and tesserae production. Mexico may not be needed as a source for Chaco, but Mexico remains an essential context.

Casas Grandes (also known as Paquimé) was Chaco's successor—temporally, of course, but perhaps politically as well (Lekson 1999). Even more than Chaco, Casas Grandes embraced Mesoamerica; there are scores of west Mexican copper objects, hundreds of scarlet macaws from southeast Mexico, and two *I*-shaped ball courts, unquestionably Mesoamerican in inspiration. The site's excavator originally concluded that Casas Grandes was founded by Mesoamericans (Di Peso 1974); more recent scholarship sees the city as Southwestern, but with significant Mesoamerican entanglements (Lekson 1999, 2009; Whalen and Minnis 2003). Indeed, the Southwest's engagement with Mexico apparently increased from 11th-century Chaco through Casas Grandes and the Pueblos of the 14th and 15th centuries (Riley 2005)—although actual Mesoamerican artifacts and objects were notably clustered in political centers, specifically Chaco and Casas Grandes.

Although few items of Mexican manufacture have been found in the Southeast, the ties between the two areas may well have been deep and enduring (White 2005; White and Weinstein 2008). Iconographic forms such as birdmen and long-nosed gods, unique manufactures such as engraved shell and ceramic effigy forms (e.g., head pots, hunchbacks), and rituals such as arrow sacrifice suggest deep connections between Mexico and the Southeast (Hall 1997; and Hall, this volume). More concrete examples of the Southeast's connection to Mexico can be found in the triumvirate of corn, beans, and squash. These domesticates moved consistently, and perhaps repeatedly, into the Southeast, and they must have been accompanied by knowledge of sowing, harvesting, storing, and processing (Pearsall, this volume). We might well ask what other information accompanied corn, beans, and squash: means to reckon planting and harvest times? fertility rituals? knowledge of associated supernatural beings such as Tlaloc or Quetzalcoatl (Kehoe 2005)?

No less significant are the pyramidal mounds and plazas that form the core of Mississippian centers. Though based on patterns of settlement organization reaching back at least to Hopewell times (and perhaps well before), Mississippian communities show striking parallels to some Classic and Postclassic Mexican ones (Dávila Cabrera 2005). Flat-topped mounds elevate temples and elite residences above the surrounding community and are arranged around a plaza where public rituals and feasts are held. Plaza and mound groups are often isolated from the rest of the community either spatially or by walls; they are also are aligned to cardinal points or in some cases to celestial objects, suggesting that astronomical observations were an important part of Mississippian polity and ideology (this seems especially true at Cahokia, where the presence of a "wood-henge" observatory highlights the important role of astronomy), just as they were in many Mexican ones.

Cahokia and its environs formed the preeminent Mississippian center, and the largest pre-Columbian settlement north of Mexico. Cahokia appeared suddenly out of a landscape of small villages around AD 1050 (Alt, this volume). Its peak came about AD 1150, after which it declined dramatically, disappearing altogether by about AD 1350. At its height, Cahokia's population may have reached 10,000 or more. It is a unique urban center in a landscape of smaller centers and even smaller villages. Explaining Cahokia's rise and fall has been an exercise for generations of Mississippian archaeologists (Emerson, this volume). The presence of what appear to be clear Mexican parallels in the architecture and iconography led many early researchers to seek a Mexican source for Cahokia. Indeed, one prominent excavator suggested that Cahokia may have been established as a market center for *pochteca* traders from highland Mexico (Porter 1977). But not a single artifact of Mexican origin has been found at Cahokia (however, see Milner and Larsen 1991, and also Barker et al. 2002), and over time the idea that Mexico had any connection at all with Cahokia became anathema.

Does the lack of Mexican-derived material at Cahokia mean that Mexican-derived ideas were not present? Are pyramidal mounds arranged around plazas, birdman iconography, and other parallels between Mexico and Cahokia all independent inventions, or might we more usefully look at them as part of a larger landscape with a deep history—a North American *oikoumene*? For example, clear evidence of significant interactions between the Huasteca and Caddoan regions has been recognized since the 1920s, and Mexican archaeologists continue to explore the nature and extent of these interactions (e.g., Zaragoza Ocaña 2005). Given the importance of these regions to highland Mexico and the Southeast, respectively, it seems implausible to argue that there was no influence or interaction beyond them. Rather, it seems more realistic to assume that polities in both Southeast and highland Mexico were aware of, and perhaps even in contact with, peer polities in distant regions of the Postclassic world (White and Weinstein 2008).

Why are there Mexican sumptuary goods at Chaco and Casas Grandes, but not at Cahokia? We suggest the answer may lie not in Mexico but in the Chacoan and

Cahokian polities themselves. Mississippian polities built upon millennia-deep traditions of monumentality, exotic materials, and their meanings (Reilly and Garber 2007; Townsend and Sharpe 2004). Southwestern polities, such as Chaco, were "start-ups," creating political symbolism on the run. They looked to Mexico for "ready-made" symbols of power. Fledgling Southwestern hierarchies needed legitimation from Mexico; Mississippian lords did not. Mississippian lords could use and manipulate continental-scale traditions that can usefully be considered as something like "Mesoamerica in the Woodlands" without the need for Mexican fripperies. The Southwest's Mesoamerica was distant West Mexico, separated by the spectacular mountains and gorges of the Sierra Madre Occidental; the Southeast's Mesoamerica was of far easier access, along the Gulf Coast to the Huasteca. Thus the great presence of Mexican objects, birds, and artifacts in the Southwest and their (apparent) absence in the Southeast may be misleading; the Southwest was perhaps less culturally integrated with its Mexico (West Mexico) than the Mississippian realm reflected the world and worldviews of its Mexico (Huasteca).

Framing these ideas in more familiar terms, we would argue that Chaco and the Pueblo world were a periphery of Mexico. Chacoan leaders used Mexico as a source of distant power; imported objects and ideologies supported emerging political hierarchies. In contrast, we would argue that Cahokia and the Mississippian world were a center in their own right, essentially equal to Mexican polities. Cahokia was the northernmost city within a landscape of historically deep traditions that stretched from Guatemala to Wisconsin. Mississippian leaders adapted deep internal histories of monument building and intraregional exotic exchange to symbolize new and complex political arrangements. They may have found inspiration in Mexican polities, but Mississippian leaders did not need Mexican objects to demonstrate their power; they were already lords in the North American *oikoumene*. Cahokia's symbolism of power was at once a part of that larger *oikoumene*—especially the rarified world of elites—and the product of long, local histories along the Mississippi.

NORTHEAST-NORTHWEST-CANADA

Although interactions across the Mexican border seem difficult for North American archaeologists to accept and investigate, interactions across the Canadian border seem much more accepted and have not been a major barrier to research. One obvious factor behind this difference is language; the language of scholarship on both sides of the border is English, while a major language barrier separates scholars in Mexico from the United States. It is unfortunate that a modern barrier apparently influences our understanding of the past, but this indeed seems to be the case (Wilcox et al. 2008). There is, however, greater environmental continuity between Canada and the United States than between Mexico and the United States. Where boreal forests, lakes, plains, and mountain ranges permit uninterrupted movement between Canada and the United States, the Rio Grande, the Chihuahuan desert, and the coastal desert of Tamaulipas form a distinct environmental fissure between Mexico and the United States. Thus the linguistic barrier only emphasizes an already existing environmental barrier between the two nations.

Early explorers describe North American native peoples having knowledge of other peoples and places across a vast expanse of the northern United States and Canada. For example, when the Hudson's Bay Company explorer Samuel Hearne first penetrated into the interior of Canada from the west coast of Hudson's Bay in 1771, he took with him native peoples who already had a good knowledge of his destination: the Coppermine River some 2,000 kilometers away (Hearne 1796). Not only did his Chipewyan companions apparently know the peoples who lived at that great distance, but they wanted to kill them. A key incentive for their accompanying Hearne was, apparently, to murder Inuit, perhaps in revenge for an earlier attack, though the reasons were never understood by Hearne (1796:115). What is clear, however, is that the peoples of the Subarctic knew one another across great expanses—knew one another well enough to carefully plan attacks at a great distance.

Interactions across the U.S.-Canadian border are also obvious in the archaeological record. For example, trade in dentalium shells (among other items, including copper, stone bowls, and foodstuffs) has at least a thousand-year history along the Northwest coast, stretching from southern Alaska through western British Columbia and into Washington and Oregon (see, e.g., Hayden and Schulting 1997). Similarly, along the Atlantic coast the peoples of the Maritime Archaic tradition (ca. 3000 to 1800 BC) shared a unique set of artifacts (slender ground slate bayonets) and burial customs (of "the Red Paint People") from southern Maine to Labrador (see Bourque 2001; Chapdelaine, this volume). Archaeologists have had no difficulty identifying and examining cultural interactions across the U.S.-Canadian border, and it is unfortunate that the U.S.-Mexican border appears so impermeable in comparison.

It is an interesting fact that political complexity increased dramatically in the southern California Chumash societies at the same time as Chaco and Cahokia (Arnold 2004; Gamble 2008). Analysis of cause, effect, and coincidence at that scale are beyond the scope of this paper. But certainly, the Southwest knew the Pacific Coast and vice versa; traffic in Pacific shell was less, perhaps, than shell from the Gulf of California and the coastal Mexico, but still quantities of California shell were considerable and Southwestern pottery is found in southern California (Ruby and Blackburn 1964). Closing the loop: a remarkable quantity of California shell found its way to Spiro, the great 14th- and 15th-century Mississippian center on the South Plains (Kozuch 2002)—probably via Pueblo trading centers such as Pecos—and lesser quantities of turquoise (Bell 1947:182).

A Continental Perspective

Cultures are open systems of shared symbols and information. New symbols and new information enter cultural systems all the time, and they can have profound impact. New symbols and new information may come from neighbors, but also from far away. As Mary Helms (1979) described for ancient Panamanian chiefs, distant sources of information can be used to great political effect, particularly in smaller-scale societies like those that covered North America prehistorically (see also Helms 1988). A continental perspective on North American prehistory, then, allows us to look to distant places for sources of symbols, information, and ultimately power. It allows us to explore relationships between cultures that may not leave abundant material traces but that may have had profound cultural impact nonetheless.

Today there is increased interest in ecological disruptions and how they may have influenced ancient cultures (e.g., Redman 1999). We know that in the recent past ecological disasters in one area could have a profound impact on other areas, and we suspect the same might have been true in the distant past. A continental perspective allows us to take such ecological disruptions seriously, and consider how environmental degradation, climate fluctuations, diseases, and the like might affect societies far from the locality of the disruption (Chew 2007). In this way, social transformations that took place across large areas of ancient North America (e.g., the nearly simultaneous consolidation of populations at Chaco and Cahokia and their fragmentation some 200 years later) might make sense in an ecological model even if ecological disruption happened in only one location.

This brings us back to the start of this paper, for it is only in a continental perspective that the impact of colonialism on indigenous societies really makes sense. By understanding cultures as interacting across broad areas, we can understand and explain the dramatic impact of disease on native peoples far in advance of direct contact with Europeans (Ramenofsky 1987). We can explain why conflict on the East Coast might have bred conflict in the far distant "tribal zone" of the Great Plains and Midwest (Ferguson and Whitehead 1992), creating multiethnic palisaded villages in Wisconsin, and even spurring the emergence of an entirely new pattern of horse-based, nomadic bison hunting (Moore 1996). Such understandings of complex interrelationships among populations, polities, and environments are possible only with a continental perspective on North American prehistory.

REFERENCES

Arnold, J. E. (editor). 2004. *Foundations of Chumash Complexity*. Perspectives in California Archaeology 7. Cotsen Institute of Archaeology, Los Angeles.

Barker, A., C. Skinner, M. Shackley, M. Glascock, and J. Rogers. 2002. Mesoamerican Origin for an Obsidian Scraper from the Precolumbian Southeastern United States. *American Antiquity* 67(1):103–108.

Bell, R. E. 1947. Trade Materials at Spiro Mound as Indicated by Artifacts. *American Antiquity* 12(3):181–184.

Bourque, B. 2001. *Twelve Thousand Years: American Indians in Maine*. University of Nebraska Press, Lincoln.

Chew, S. 2007. *The Recurring Dark Ages: Ecological Stress, Climate Change, and System Transformation*. AltaMira, Lanham, MD.

Dávila Cabrera, P. 2005. Mound Builders Along the Coast of the Gulf of Mexico and the Eastern United States. In *Gulf Coast Archaeology*, edited by N. White, pp. 87–107. University Press of Florida, Gainesville.

DiPeso, C. C. 1974. *Casas Grandes: A Fallen Trading Center of the Gran Chichimeca*, vols. 1–3. Amerind Foundation, Dragoon, AZ.

Ferguson, R. B., and N. Whitehead (editors). 1992. *War in the Tribal Zone: Expanding States and Indigenous Warfare*. School of American Research, Santa Fe, NM.

Flint, R., and S. Cushing Flint (editors). 2005. *Documents of the Coronado Expedition, 1539–1542*. Southern Methodist University Press, Dallas.

Gamble, L. H. 2008. *The Chumash World at European Contact: Power, Trade and Feasting Among Complex Hunter-Gatherers*. University of California Press, Berkeley.

Hall, R. 1997. *An Archaeology of the Soul: North American Indian Belief and Ritual*. University of Illinois Press, Urbana.

Hayden, B., and R. Schulting. 1997. The Plateau Interaction Sphere and Late Prehistoric Cultural Complexity. *American Antiquity* 62:51–85.

Hayes, A. C. 1981. A Survey of Chaco Canyon Archaeology. In *Archaeological Surveys of Chaco Canyon, New Mexico*, edited by A. C. Hayes, D. M. Brugge, and W. J. Judge, pp. 1–68. Publications in Archaeology 18A. National Park Service, Washington, DC.

Hearne, S. 1796. *A Journey from Prince of Wale's Fort, in Hudson's Bay, to the Northern Ocean*. Byrne and Rice, Dublin.

Helms, M. W. 1979. *Ancient Panama: Chiefs in Search of Power*. University of Texas Press, Austin.

———. 1988. *Ulysses' Sail: An Ethnographic Odyssey of Power, Knowledge, and Geographical Distance*. Princeton University Press, Princeton, NJ.

Hickerson, H. 1970. *The Chippewa and Their Neighbors*. Holt, Rinehart, Winston, New York.

Kehoe, A. B. 2002. *America Before the European Invasions*. Longman, London.

———. 2005. Wind Jewels and Paddling Gods: The Mississippian Southeast and the Postclassic Mesoamerican World. In *Gulf Coast Archaeology*, edited by Nancy White, pp. 260–280. University Press of Florida, Gainesville.

Kinietz, V. 1965. *The Indians of the Western Great Lakes, 1615–1760*. University of Michigan Press, Ann Arbor.

Kozuch, L. 2002. Olivella Beads from Spiro and the Plains. *American Antiquity* 67:697–709.

Kristiansen, K., and T. Larsson. 2005. *The Rise of Bronze Age Society*. Cambridge University Press, Cambridge.

Lekson, S. H. 1999. *Chaco Meridian: Centers of Political Power in the Ancient Southwest*. AltaMira Press, Walnut Creek, CA.

———. 2009. *A History of the Ancient Southwest*. SAR Press, Santa Fe, NM.

Mills, B. 2002. Recent Research on Chaco: Changing Views on Economy, Ritual, and Society. *Journal of Archaeological Research* 10(1):65–117.

Milner, G., and C. S. Larsen. 1991. Teeth as Artifacts of Human Behavior: Intentional Mutilation and Accidental Modification. In *Advances in Dental Anthropology*, edited by M. A. Kelly and C. S. Larsen, pp. 357–378. Wiley-Liss, New York.

Moore, J. H. 1996. *The Cheyenne*. Blackwell, Cambridge, MA.

Porter, J. W. 1977. The Mitchell Site and Prehistoric Exchange Systems at Cahokia: AD 1000±300. Illinois Archaeological Survey, bulletin 7, *Explorations into Cahokia Archaeology*, edited by M. Fowler, pp. 137–164. Illinois Archaeological Survey, Urbana.

Ramenofsky, A. 1987. *Vectors of Death: The Archaeology of European Contact*. University of New Mexico Press, Albuquerque.

Redmond, C. 1999. *Human Impact on Ancient Environments*. University of Arizona Press, Tucson.

Reilly, F. K., and J. F. Garber (editors). 2007. *Ancient Objects and Sacred Realms: Interpretations of Mississippian Iconography*. University of Texas Press, Austin.

Riley, C. L. 2005. *Becoming Aztlan: Mesoamerican Influences in the Greater Southwest, AD 1200–1500*. University of Utah Press, Salt Lake City.

Ruby, J., and T. Blackburn. 1964. Occurrence of Southwestern Pottery in Los Angeles County, California. *American Antiquity* 30(2):209–210.

Thwaites, R. G. (translator, editor). 1896–1901. *Jesuit Relations and Allied Documents*. Burrows Brothers, Cleveland.

Townsend, R., and R.V. Sharpe (editors). 2004. *Hero, Hawk and Open Hand: American Indian Art of the Ancient Midwest and South*. Yale University Press, New Haven, CT.

Whalen, M. E., and P. E. Minnis. 2003. The Local and the Distant in the Origin of Casas Grandes, Chihuahua, Mexico. *American Antiquity* 68:314–332.

White, N. 2005. Prehistoric Connections Around the Gulf Coast. In *Gulf Coast Archaeology*, edited by N. White, pp. 1–55. University Press of Florida, Gainesville.

White, N., and R. Weinstein. 2008. The Mexican Connection and the Far West of the U.S. Southeast. *American Antiquity* 73(2):227–277.

Wilcox, D. R., P. C. Weigand, J. S. Wood, and J. B. Howard. 2008. Ancient Cultural Interplay of the American Southwest and the Mexican Northwest. *Journal of the Southwest* 50(2):103–135.

Zaragoza Ocaña, D. 2005. Characteristic Elements Shared by Northeastern Mexico and the Southeastern United States. In *Gulf Coast Archaeology*, edited by N. White, pp. 245–259. University Press of Florida, Gainesville.

CHAPTER 7

PEOPLE, PLANTS, AND CULINARY TRADITIONS

DEBORAH M. PEARSALL

CULINARY traditions of Native North Americans at European Contact were diverse, from salmon fishers of the Northwest and root diggers of the Great Basin to maize (corn) agriculturalists of the Eastern Woodlands (see Figure 1.4). Some practices and foods were millennia old; others coalesced late in prehistory, and some disappeared before Contact. The story of people, plants, and culinary traditions is informed by the practices of descendant populations (ethnobotanical observations) and through the study of archaeological plant remains (paleoethnobotany).

This review begins with Western culinary traditions not based on field agriculture, and then looks at traditions in which people relied on maize, beans, and squash, crops that in some cases were accepted by populations already growing native domesticates. There is no strict dichotomy of agriculturally-nonagriculturally based cuisine, but rather a range of people-plant interrelationships in diverse environmental settings, with many commonalities across the continent and through time in plants and plant parts used, processing and cooking techniques, and cultivation and management practices employed.[1]

Several themes emerge from this review. Ethnobotanical observations paint a picture of greater plant food diversity than is documented in paleoethnobotanical records. Although we may never recover remains of foods that did not contact fire (not cooked, dried for storage, or burnt in trash), when water flotation or fine sieving is routinely applied a more complete sample of charred plant parts is recovered, and this difference in diversity narrows.

Of course, root foods are underrepresented archaeologically. In Northwestern North America, for example, more than 25 species are described ethnobotanically, but only four or so are documented archaeologically. These foods are cooked; long cooking times are needed to render unpalatable roots such as balsamroot into a nutritious food (Peacock 2008). Charred pieces of underground organs are challenging to identify, however, or fragile and prone to destruction. Starch grains and phytoliths (plant opal silica bodies) preserved on artifacts used for food processing (grinders, pounders, griddles, cooking pots) have documented "missing" root foods in other regions, and Zarillo and Kooyman (2006) report likely prairie turnip starch on grinding stones from the northern Plains. More food residue studies are needed to understand the development of root food traditions among foragers, as well as the role of root foods prior to and during the transition to food production in the Southwest, Eastern Woodlands, and Great Plains.

Ethnobotany documents commonalities in the kinds of wild plants targeted as foods (small seeds, succulent fruits and berries, nuts, root foods, greens) and how they were prepared for consumption and storage, but it also demonstrates that differences existed in the importance of various foods. Typically the same kinds of wild resources were used regardless of whether native or introduced crops were grown; cultural practices surrounding wild, managed, cultivated, and domesticated resources were often similar.

Paleoethnobotany reveals a similar mix of food kinds (except "missing" roots and greens), but it is more difficult to determine which foods were important, and to identify cultural practices. Food residue studies can provide insight into the latter: Hart et al. (2007) documented pottery cooking of maize and squash (see also Boyd et al. 2008, and Reber and Evershed 2004 for maize) and Zarrillo and Kooyman (2006) found that berries, roots, and maize were ground on the same tools. Thoms (2009) demonstrated how studying fire-cracked rock assemblages can reveal hot-rock cookery practices (i.e., earth ovens, pit steaming, cook stone grilling, stone boiling; see also Peacock 2008). Plant resource management on the landscape scale (burning, altering plant concentrations or ranges) can be investigated through archaeological and paleoenvironmental records.

Western Culinary Traditions

Most Native populations of the Great Basin, California, and the Pacific Northwest did not practice field agriculture in the past. One exception is the agricultural Fremont culture (ca. AD 400–1300) of Utah and adjoining Nevada, Colorado, Idaho, and Wyoming; corn, bean, and squash agriculture was introduced into the Mojave and Sonoran Deserts in late pre-Hispanic if not historic times. There is great environmental diversity in Western North America, but there are also commonalities in the ethnobotany of Western Native peoples.

Plant gathering typically took place in a seasonal round; that is, resources were gathered as they became available in different plant communities and at different elevations. In the dry Great Basin, groups moved seasonally between summer and winter camps as water became available and foods ripened (Chamberlin 1911; Steward 1938). In a typical yearly round, greens were used in early spring as winter stores were depleted; seeds dominated in early summer, roots and berries later in summer, pine nuts in fall. Common plant foods of the Canadian or transitional zone included grass seeds and berries (gooseberry, currant, elderberry, serviceberry, chokecherry, rose, elder, raspberry, strawberry), while the Upper Sonoran zone yielded piñon nuts and sagebrush seeds and the Lower Sonoran joshua tree, mesquite, screw bean, cacti, and yucca (Figure 7.1). Moister high-elevation prairies abounded in camass root, bitter root, yampa, sego lily, wild onions, spring beauty, and wheat grass (Chamberlin 1911; Steward 1938). The Cahuilla of interior southern California followed a similar seasonal round that incorporated the Lower and Upper Sonoran, Transitional, and Canadian-Hudsonian life zones. Agave and stored foods were used in winter; in spring, fruits and buds of yucca, onion, cactus, goosefoot, catsclaw, and ocotillo; mesquite, screwbean were harvested in large quantities in summer, with berries, yucca, and cactus; in fall, grass seeds, chia, saltbush, piñon, palm, thimbleberry, raspberry, blackberry, juniper berry, chokecherry; in late fall, acorns (Bean and Saubel 1972).

The Douglas fir, western hemlock, and mountain hemlock vegetation zones of the coastal Northwest yield many foods, among them fruits (especially berries), green vegetables (sprouts, leaves, seaweeds), underground parts (roots, bulbs,

Figure 7.1 Papago woman gathering cactus fruit (Edward S. Curtis collection, Library of Congress Prints and Photographs Division, Washington, DC, Curtis no. 2298–07, Reproduction no. LC-USZ62–111283).

tubers, rhizomes), and cambium and inner tree bark (Turner 1995). In some areas carbohydrates were replaced with animal fats and oils, especially "grease" (rendered from eulachon fish). A typical seasonal round began in spring with roots (lupines, sea milkwort, wild carrot, springbank clover), the eulachon run, green vegetables (salmonberry, thimbleberry sprouts, nettles, fireweed shoots, seaweed), and cambium; in early summer, berries and fruits (in succession, salmonberries, strawberries, huckleberries, blueberries, blackberries, saskatoon, soapberries, gooseberries, currants, elderberries, raspberries, blackcaps, thimbleberries, salal); in late summer, most bulbs (blue camas, onions, Indian rice or *Fritillaria*); in fall, more of the earlier-ripening roots and late-ripening fruits (hazelnuts, crabapples, cranberries, kinnikinnick berries, rose hips, evergreen huckleberries; Turner 1995). Interior Northwest groups, including the Thompson of British Columbia (Turner et al. 1990) and Sahaptin-speakers of the Columbia Plateau (Hunn 1990), lived in substantial winter villages and intensively used salmon and root foods. Fruits, nuts, seeds, inner bark, mushrooms, and fungi were also eaten.

Species of these kinds of food (i.e., small seeds, succulent fruits and berries, nuts, root foods, and greens) were consumed or processed for storage in similar ways among Western Native groups. Root foods (unearthed with a digging stick) were often dried or cooked (by roasting, boiling, or steaming) in quantities for winter storage. Among the Great Basin Gosiute, sego lily was the most important root, eaten seasonally and dried for winter (cooked with meat as stew); other roots included *Fritillaria pudica*, *Camassia*, wild onions, spring beauty, and yamp, which was roasted in pits and cached for winter (Chamberlin 1911). Lily bulbs were roasted in earth ovens by the Karok of inland northern California (Schenck and Gifford 1952). Among coastal and interior Northwest groups, root foods were cleaned, sorted, and dried on mats, and then placed in fiber bags or cedar boxes; they were boiled in bent-wood boxes with hot stones, or steamed in earth ovens (Turner 1995).

Succulent fruits and berries were also commonly preserved for winter. Serviceberry, the most important succulent fruit among the Gosiute, was preserved by mashing and sun-drying, and then placed in grass-lined pits; dried cakes were broken up and boiled with or without meat, often with seed meals (Chamberlin 1911). Serviceberry and manzanita were dried and stored, and madroño berries stored after steaming, by the Karok (Schenck and Gifford 1952). In the Northwest, berries of all kinds were sorted, de-stemmed, mashed, and cooked with hot stones; the mash was then poured into wooden frames, dried into cakes, and stored in wooden boxes. To use, cakes were soaked in water, mashed, and mixed with other berries and sometimes grease (Turner 1995). A typical dish among interior groups would be dried berries, pounded salmon, and salmon oil (Hunn 1990).

In the Great Basin and California, nuts were another important stored food. Pine nut processing involved gathering the cones, partially charring them, which roasted the nuts, and then beating out the nuts. Pine nuts were eaten after shelling or ground into meal (Chamberlin 1911). Cooked pine nuts stored one to two years (Steward 1938). Acorns were important for some groups; they were shelled, dried over fire, and stored until needed, when they were pounded into meal, leached to remove tannins, and cooked in water (Schenck and Gifford 1952).

Small seeds were an important food among Great Basin and Californian groups (Figure 7.2). Seeds were knocked into baskets or seed heads cut. Processing included threshing, winnowing, parching, grinding, and sometimes boiling (Steward 1938). *Bromus hordeaceus* was an important grain among the Karok; it was harvested by beating, winnowed with coals and shaken to parch it, pounded, and eaten without further cooking (Schenck and Gifford 1952).

Many Western Native peoples managed "wild" plant resources. Throughout the Northwest, for example, people engaged in plant cultivation activities (fertilizing, mulching, tilling, weeding, selective root harvesting, and replanting) and prescribed burning (Lepofsky 2004). The Owens Valley Northern Paiute irrigated certain wild-seed patches; other groups sowed wild seeds (Steward 1938).

Archaeological plant remains document the antiquity of Western culinary traditions. Diverse wild plant and animal resources from terrestrial, riverine, and marine habitats were used in California; among the plants recovered archaeologically throughout the state are pine nuts, acorns, and small seeds of pigweed, goosefoot, mustards, nightshade, legumes, composites, sedges, and grasses. Manzanilla berries are commonly recovered except in deserts; elderberries except in the Sierra Nevada. Seeds of sage, phacelia, and fiddlenecks are often documented. Yucca was

Figure 7.2 Coast Pomo woman using a seed beater to gather seeds into a burden basket (Edward S. Curtis collection, Library of Congress Prints and Photographs Division, Washington, DC, Curtis no. 3997. Reproduction no. LC-USZ62-116525).

widely used in southern California; redmaids seeds were common along the coast. The extent to which native plants were manipulated or managed is an area of active research; increased seed size is documented in archaeological wild goosefoot and redmaids (Hammett and Lawlor 2004). The Great Basin record documents a mix of grasses, other small seeds (suaeda, sedge, goosefoot and cheno-am, knotweed, saltsage), roots (biscuit root, yampah, camas, wild onion, sego lily), juniper, wild cherry, rose, cactus, and piñon, among others (Cummings 2004).

The importance of various wild plant foods was not static through time. In California, plant remains and plant grinders have been recovered from the Early period (3000–2000 BC). There was a change in technology in some regions during the Middle period (1000 BC–0); fewer grinders and more mortars and baked-clay balls (for boiling) are interpreted as decreased reliance on small seeds and increased acorn use. Beginning in the Middle period and culminating in the Late (beginning AD 500–1000), populations were increasingly sedentary, relying on storable foods such as acorns, other nuts, wild cherry, small seeds, and marine and terrestrial animals. Salmon was important in northwestern California (Hammett and Lawlor 2004).

More than 100 plant taxa have been identified from sites in the coastal Northwest. The Early Holocene (pre-3000 BC) record is sparse: seeds of legume, cherry, hazelnut, *Vaccinium* (blueberry or huckleberry), and elderberry. The condition of a charred *Vaccinium* fruit suggests it was dried before being charred. Indirect evidence includes edge-ground cobbles possibly used for plant processing. Berry and fruit seeds are the most common remains at Late Holocene (post-3000 BC) villages, including salal, *Vaccinium*, red elderberry, and *Rubus* (raspberries and related) in quantities and contexts that suggest immediate use and processing for storage. Found in smaller amounts: bitter cherry, rose, red osier dogwood, crabapple, Oregon grape, strawberry, acorn, and hazelnuts. Evidence of root foods is sparse but includes camas and possible wapato *(Sagittaria latifolia)* from rock ovens, onions, and unidentified roots and parenchymous tissues (sometimes in abundance). Plants recovered from short-term camps are similar. Evidence of plant processing includes hundreds of thousands of charred lily-of-the-valley seeds, likely the residues from producing a seedless sauce, and berry-drying features with *Vaccinium* seeds and fruits. Indirect evidence for plant food harvesting and use includes manos, grinding/pounding slabs, mortars, pestles, antler digging stick handles, and digging sticks (Lepofsky 2004).

Evidence is also sparse for the Plateau for the Early Holocene (pre-2000 BC): camas bulbs from 5,500-year-old earth ovens, saskatoon and hawthorn seeds, and possible *Lomatium*. Indirect evidence includes grinding stones, manos, and edge-ground cobbles dating 11000–8000 BP, with mortars and pestles more common later, suggesting increased use of root foods requiring pounding. Food plants recovered from late Holocene pithouses (post-2000 BC) include berries, especially saskatoons; hazelnut, pine nuts and cones; root foods, including Lomatium, camas, balsamroot, possible allium, and unidentified root tissues. Short-term camps document root roasting in earth ovens (Lepofsky 2004).

Domestication and Agriculture in North America

The Mesoamerican domesticate maize became the major component of cuisine centuries before European Contact throughout the Eastern Woodlands and the river valleys of the Great Plains, and nearly two millennia earlier in the Southwest (Figures 7.3–7.4). The antiquity of its introduction and the importance and role of maize in cuisine vis-à-vis native crops and wild plants varied regionally. This is documented in ethnobotanical observations (e.g., Castetter and Bell 1942; Cushing 1920/1974; Densmore 1926–27/1974; Gilmore 1919/1977; Hill 1938; Parker 1910/1968; Swanton 1946; Vestal 1952; Waugh 1916; Whiting 1939; Wilson 1917/1987) and the paleoethnobotanical record.

There are some commonalities of Native American maize practices, as documented ethnobotanically:

1. Maize was grown in carefully spaced hills with introduced beans (common bean in the East; also tepary, lima bean in the Southwest) and squashes or pumpkin, often interplanted with native gourd and squash, sunflower, and tobacco.
2. Maize, beans, and squash were used in different growth stages. An example for maize from the Navajo (Hill 1938): boiled thinnings as greens; roasted young stalks; boiled smut; in silk stage chopped ears and boiled as soup; at

Figure 7.3 Timucan farmers planting corn field (Theodor de Bry engraving, 1591).

Figure 7.4 Apache woman hoeing corn with an infant in cradleboard (Edward S. Curtis collection, Library of Congress Prints and Photographs Division, Washington, DC, Curtis no. 1890–06. Reproduction no. LC-USZ62-46945).

tender kernel stage removed kernels, mashed and boiled or ground and made into bread cooked on a corn leaf, or roasted on cob; harder kernels used to make stiffer bread; mature kernels used in bread, mush, dumplings, fried cakes.

3. All groups processed maize and other crops for storage and winter use; drying (in the sun or over heat) was the primary process. Examples from the Plains-dwelling Hidatsa (Wilson 1917/1987): cut heads of sunflower, dried them, threshed seeds out, stored in skin sacks; dried green corn, boiled on ear until half cooked, shelled, dried, winnowed, put in sacks for winter; main harvest of corn, husked, dried, shelled, winnowed, stored in cache pit; squash cut in slices, spit on willow rods to dry for three days, transferred from spits to strings, dried in sun, stored in cache pit and in parfleche bags; beans picked when pods were dried, threshed.

4. Wild plant and animal foods were eaten with maize, in mixed dishes, as seasonal complements, and in times of scarcity. The northeastern Iroquois (Parker 1910/1968), for example, grew corn on a large scale, with beans, squashes, pumpkin, sunflower, and tobacco, but consumed many wild foods: leaves and stalks of numerous wild plants were cooked with fat meat; mushrooms, puffballs, and lichens were boiled or fried; fruits (crab apple, thorn apple, wild cherry, chokecherry, grape, pawpaw, mandrake, plum) and berries (about 20 species) were eaten in season and dried; nuts (acorns, beechnut, black walnut, butternut, chestnut, bitter hickory, hickory, hazel) were important when crops failed, and nut meat oil was used with corn

bread and puddings and crushed meats mixed with corn mash; sap and bark foods (maple sugar, pine, elm, basswood); wild root foods (Jerusalem artichokes, ground nuts, wild onions, wild leek, yellow pond lily, cattail, arrowhead, Indian turnip, milkweed, Solomon's seal, skink cabbage) were mostly used in times of scarcity.

5. There are many recipes for cooking maize, beans, and squash, but a limited number of core techniques. For maize these included roasting, baking, or steaming immature maize ears in the husk (on fire or in earth oven); boiling immature corn shelled or on the cob (alone, with other plant foods, meat, fish); grinding dried or parched kernels (meal or flour used alone or with other ground seeds, roots, and fruits to make mushes, breads, cakes, and dumplings by boiling, baking, and steaming); and hominy (kernels boiled in water with hardwood ashes; often eaten with beans). Beans and squash were also boiled and baked or steamed. Vegetable oil (sunflower, nuts) and fat meat or grease were common additions to maize-based dishes, as were wild plant flavorings.

Maize was introduced into the Southwest by 1600 BC or somewhat earlier, just prior to the Late Archaic or Early Agricultural Period (1500 BC to AD 0–500). It is found at sites in both high and low elevations at about the same time, indicating rapid spread (Huckell 2006). By 400 BC, maize had transformed foodways that were based on native plants; isotope studies from the northern Southwest show heavy dependence on maize (Coltrain et al. 2007). With widespread adoption of maize came substantial habitations with storage features (Huckell and Toll 2004).

During the Early-Middle Archaic (prior to 1500 BC) in the Southwest annuals such as chenopod/amaranth, grasses (ricegrass, dropseed, wild rye, bentgrass, lovegrass), purslane, mustard, beeweed, wild sunflower, sumpweed, and knotweed were used (Huckell and Toll 2004). Cultivation of native annuals has not been definitively demonstrated, but their ubiquitous occurrence suggests management (Doolittle and Mabry 2006). Other documented resources include juniper, piñon, mesquite, yucca, walnut, acorn, cacti, hackberry, onion, and bullrush. Most early sites are small, short-term, or seasonal occupations (Huckell and Toll 2004). Late in prehistory or during historic times, native panic grass, little barley, and devil's claw were likely cultivated (Fish 2004). Maize, beans (common and tepary), and *pepo* squash form the core of Southwestern agriculture, with cotton and bottle gourd also introduced early, and other beans and squashes later arrivals. Although maize became the central component of diet relatively quickly, wild plants were important through the Pueblo IV/Classic period; among the Anasazi, for example, ricegrass, chenopod/amaranth, piñon, mustards, sunflower, prickly pear, groundcherry, beeweed, and grasses have high archaeological ubiquity (Fish 2004; Huckell and Toll 2004).

In the Eastern Woodlands, maize was incorporated into indigenous crop husbandry based on small-seeded annuals, native squash, and sunflower beginning around 300 BC. For the better part of a millennium, maize was one food in a broad diet, until its transformation into a staple crop between AD 800–900 and AD 1200. Directly dated maize macroremains and cooking residues place the crop in the Midwest and Northeast at about the same time (Hart et al. 2007).

Paleoindian sites in the Northeast document nuts (acorn, walnut, hickory), and seeds and fruits (blackgum, hackberry, buckbean, chenopod, *Rubus*, bunchberry, grape, groundcherry, spikenard; Crawford and Smith 2003). Archaic period (8000–1000 BC) foragers in the East relied on game and native plants, including nuts (hickory, pecan, walnut, hazelnut, acorn, chestnut, chinquapin, beechnut), fleshy fruits (persimmon, plum, pawpaw, raspberry, strawberry, plum, maypop, hawthorn, grape, elderberry, crabapple, blueberry, blackberry), grains and oil seeds (chenopod, knotweed, amaranth, maygrass, little barley, wild rice, wild gourd, sunflower, sumpweed, ragweed), and legumes (wild beans, vetch, peavine). Root foods and greens were undoubtedly used, but archaeological evidence is largely lacking (Scarry 2003). During the Archaic and Early/Middle Woodland, evidence of wild plant use also expands in the Northeast (Crawford and Smith 2003).

Between 3200 and 1785 cal BC, native squash, chenopod, marshelder, and sunflower were domesticated in the East, and maygrass, erect knotweed, little barley, and giant ragweed were grown and moved outside their native ranges. Variation exists on the relative importance of native crops and wild plants, with American Bottom (Mississippi floodplain near St. Louis) populations producing the largest quantities of native crops over the longest time period. Acorn use was often higher in regions with less reliance on native crops (Scarry 2003). The small-seeded native crops (chenopod, knotweed, maygrass, little barley) were likely broadcast-sown in dense single-crop stands or in maslins (combinations of similarly ripening crops), with larger-seeded sunflower, marshelder, and squash dibbled in hills or planted on field edges (Scarry 2008).

There was a shift to greater reliance on food production in the East during the Middle Woodland (500–200 BC to AD 200). Maize was introduced, followed around AD 1000–1200 by common bean (Smith and Cowan 2003). North American domesticated chenopod, *pepo* squash, and sunflower are closely related to Mesoamerican domesticates. DNA analysis of wild sunflowers supports separate origins for North American and Mesoamerican lineages (Harter et al. 2004), and there are also two separate lineages of domesticated *pepo* squashes (Smith and Cowan 2003). Agriculture spread into the Northeast from the south. Crops included squash, sunflower, maize, tobacco, and common bean. There were regional differences in the impact of these introductions, and in the importance of chenopod, erect knotweed, little barley, and marshelder. Between AD 450 and 1000 economic systems characterized by high plant diversity developed, with intensification of food production based on maize after AD 1000. Wild rice collecting occurred throughout the Northeast and adjoining regions, and it had a significant presence after 50 BC (Crawford and Smith 2003; Hart et al. 2007).

In the Great Plains, Paleoindians (8500–3500 BC) hunted large mammals, including mammoth and bison, and limited small animals. Plant foods (prickly pear, goosefoot, sedge, sunflower, pine nut, chokecherry) were recovered from the Barton

Gulch site in Montana, in features dated to 7460 BC. Ground stone artifacts are widespread in Plano-period occupations in Wyoming and Colorado, and seeds of sunflower, prickly pear, pine, juniper, pigweed, and chokecherry have been recovered (Adair 2003). Differences existed in tool technology and subsistence between western mountain-foothill groups and eastern plains groups during the Archaic (3500–500 BC). Archaic foods included native annuals (goosefoot, sedge, dock, smartweed, sunflower, wild bean, marshelder), fruits (chokecherry, buffalo berry, rose, *Prunus*, wolfberry, grape, strawberry, hackberry), nuts (pine nut, walnut, hickory), roots (wild onion), and grasses. By late in the period chenopod was perhaps cultivated. The earliest directly dated domesticates are squash (2218–2142 cal. BC), marshelder (628–609 cal. BC), and maize (AD 813–878), which was likely introduced around AD 1–400 (Adair 2003). Woodland (500 BC to AD 800–900) populations were more sedentary, ceramics were introduced, and cultivated plants were increasingly used. The maize-based Plains Village tradition (AD 900–1600) developed out of this foundation (Adair 2003). Maize was also a widespread component of diet between AD 700 and 1600 in the eastern Canadian prairies and adjacent boreal forests (Boyd et al. 2008).

NOTE

1. Ethnobotanical and paleoethnobotanical resources on the topic of this chapter are vast; only a small selection could be used in this essay. Common names are used to convey the kinds of plants used; consult the sources cited for details. Dates are uncalibrated unless noted.

REFERENCES

Adair, M. J. 2003. Great Plains Paleoethnobotany. In *People and Plants in Ancient Eastern North America*, edited by P. E. Minnis, pp. 258–346. Smithsonian Books, Washington DC.

Bean, L. J., and K. Siva Saubel. 1972. *Temalpakh: Cahuilla Indian Knowledge and Usage of Plants*. Malki Museum, Banning, CA.

Boyd, M., T. Varney, C. Surette, and J. Surette. 2008. Reassessing the Northern Limit of Maize Consumption in North America: Stable Isotope, Plant Microfossil, and Trace Element Content of Carbonized Food Residue. *Journal of Archaeological Science* 35:2545–2556.

Castetter, E. F., and W. H. Bell. 1942. *Pima and Papago Indian Agriculture*. University of New Mexico Press, Albuquerque.

Chamberlin, R. V. 1907–1915. *The Ethno-Botany of the Gosiute Indians of Utah*. Memoirs of the American Anthropological Association 2, pp. 329–405. Lancaster, PA.

Coltrain, J. B., J. C. Janetski, and S. W. Carlyle. 2007. The Stable- and Radio-Isotope Chemistry of Western Basketmaker Burials: Implications for Early Puebloan Diets and Origins. *American Antiquity* 72:301–321.

Crawford, G. W., and D. G. Smith. 2003. Paleoethnobotany in the Northeast. In *People and Plants in Ancient Eastern North America*, edited by P. E. Minnis, pp. 172–257. Smithsonian Books, Washington DC.

Cummings, L. S. 2004. Great Basin Paleoethnobotany. In *People and Plants in Ancient Western North America*, edited by P. E. Minnis, pp. 205–277. Smithsonian Books, Washington DC.

Cushing, F. H. 1920/1974. *Zuni Breadstuff.* Indian Notes and Monographs 8. Museum of the American Indian Heye Foundation, New York.

Densmore, F. 1928/1974. *How Indians Use Wild Plants for Food, Medicine, and Crafts: Uses of Plants by the Chippewa Indians.* Dover, New York.

Doolittle, W. E., and J. B. Mabry. 2006. Environmental Mosaics, Agricultural Diversity, and the Evolutionary Adoption of Maize in the American Southwest. In *Histories of Maize*, edited by J. E. Staller, R. H. Tykot, and B. F. Benz, pp. 109–121. Academic Press, San Diego.

Fish, S. K. 2004. Corn, Crops, and Cultivation in the North American Southwest. In *People and Plants in Ancient Western North America*, edited by P. E. Minnis, pp. 115–166. Smithsonian Books, Washington DC.

Gillmore, M. R. 1919/1977. *Uses of Plants by the Indians of the Missouri River Region.* University of Nebraska Press, Lincoln.

Hammett, J. E., and E. J. Lawlor. 2004. Paleoethnobotany in California. In *People and Plants in Ancient Western North America*, edited by P. E. Minnis, pp. 278–366. Smithsonian Books, Washington DC.

Hart, J. P., H. J. Brumbach, and R. Lusteck. 2007. Extending the Phytolith Evidence for Early Maize (*Zea mays* ssp. *mays*) and Squash (*Cucurbita* sp.) in Central New York. *American Antiquity* 72:563–583.

Harter, A. V., K. A. Gardner, D. Falush, D. L. Lentz, R. A. Bye, and L. H. Rieseberg. 2004. Origin of Extant Domesticated Sunflowers in Eastern North America. *Nature* 430(8): 201–205.

Hill, W. W. 1938. *The Agricultural and Hunting Methods of the Navaho Indians.* Yale University Publications in Anthropology 18. New Haven, CT.

Huckell, L. W. 2006. Ancient Maize in the American Southwest: What Does It Look Like and What Can It Tell Us? In *Histories of Maize*, edited by J. E. Staller, R. H. Tykot, and B. F. Benz, pp. 97–107. Academic Press, San Diego.

Huckell, L. W., and M. S. Toll. 2004. Wild Plant Use in the North American Southwest. In *People and Plants in Ancient Western North America*, edited by P. E. Minnis, pp. 37–114. Smithsonian Books, Washington DC.

Hunn, E. S., with J. Selam and Family. 1990. *Nch'i-Wána "The Big River." Mid-Columbia Indians and Their Land.* University of Washington Press, Seattle.

Lepofsky, D. 2004. Paleoethnobotany in the Northwest. In *People and Plants in Ancient Western North America*, edited by P. E. Minnis, pp. 367–464. Smithsonian Books, Washington DC.

Minnis, P. E. 2004. Southwest Overview: History, Archaeology, and Environment. In *People and Plants in Ancient Western North America*, edited by P. E. Minnis, pp. 17–36. Smithsonian Books, Washington DC.

Parker, A. C. 1910/1968. *Parker on the Iroquois: Iroquois Uses of Maize and Other Food Plants; the Code of Handsome Lake, the Seneca Prophet; the Constitution of the Five*

Nations, edited with an introduction by W. N. Fenton. Syracuse University Press, Syracuse, NY.

Peacock, S. L. 2008. From Complex to Simple: Balsamroot, Inulin, and the Chemistry of Traditional Interior Salish Pit-Cooking Technology. *Botany* 86:116–128.

Reber, E. A., and R. P. Evershed. 2004. How Did Mississippians Prepare Maize? The Application of Compound-Specific Carbon Isotope Analysis to Absorbed Pottery Residues from Several Mississippi Valley Sites. *Archaeometry* 46:19–33.

Scarry, C. M. 2003. Patterns of Wild Plant Utilization in the Prehistoric Eastern Woodlands. In *People and Plants in Ancient Eastern North America*, edited by P. E. Minnis, pp. 50–104. Smithsonian Books, Washington DC.

———. 2008. Crop Husbandry Practices in North America's Eastern Woodlands. In *Case Studies in Environmental Archaeology*, 2nd ed., edited by E. J. Reitz, C. M. Scarry, and S. J. Scudder, pp. 391–404. Springer, New York.

Schenck, S. M., and E. W. Gifford. 1952. Karok Ethnobotany. *Anthropological Records* 13(6):377–392.

Smith, B. D., and C. W. Cowan. 2003. Domesticated Crop Plants and the Evolution of Food Production Economies in Eastern North America. In *People and Plants in Ancient Eastern North America*, edited by P. E. Minnis, pp. 105–125. Smithsonian Books, Washington DC.

Steward, J. H. 1938. *Basin-Plateau Aboriginal Sociopolitical Groups*. Smithsonian Institution Bureau of American Ethnology, bulletin 120. Washington DC.

Swanton, J. R. 1946. *The Indians of the Southeastern United States*. Smithsonian Institution Bureau of American Ethnology, bulletin 137. Washington DC.

Thoms, A. V. 2009. Rocks of Ages: Propagation of Hot-Rock Cookery in Western North America. *Journal of Archaeological Science* 36:573–591.

Turner, N. J. 1995. *Food Plants of Coastal First Peoples*. University of British Columbia Press, Vancouver.

Turner, N. J., L. C. Thompson, M. T. Thompson, and A. Z. York. 1990. *Thompson Ethnobotany: Knowledge and Usage of Plants by the Thompson Indians of British Columbia*. Royal British Columbia Museum, memoir no. 3, Victoria.

Vestal, P. A. 1952. Ethnobotany of the Ramah Navaho. *Peabody Museum of American Archaeology and Ethnology Papers*, vol. 40, no. 4 (entire).

Waugh, F. W. 1916. *Iroquis Foods and Food Preparation*. Canada Department of Mines, Geological Survey, memoir 86, no. 12, Anthropological Series, Ottawa.

Whiting, A. F. 1939. *Ethnobotany of the Hopi*. Museum of Northern Arizona, bulletin 15. Flagstaff.

Wilson, G. L. 1917/1987. *Buffalo Bird Woman's Garden: Agriculture of the Hidatsa Indians*. Minnesota Historical Society Press, St. Paul.

Zarillo, S., and B. Kooyman. 2006. Evidence for Berry and Maize Processing on the Canadian Plains from Starch Grain Analysis. *American Antiquity* 71:473–499.

CHAPTER 8

EARLY PALEOINDIANS, FROM COLONIZATION TO FOLSOM

NICOLE WAGUESPACK

The initial human colonization of North America presents a nagging archaeological mystery. The various issues of who, when, and how the process unfolded have been "solved" countless times, only to be refuted and discounted by the discovery of new sites, new dates, and theoretical developments. As a process, the peopling of a continent can perhaps be expected to leave a distinct archaeological signature. A population of incipient colonizers, a trajectory of movement, and an entrance and dispersal into new territories ideally result in a clear trail of sites, artifacts, dates, and genes with clear affinities. However, from currently available archaeological evidence, such is not the case. The earliest dates, sites, and recovered artifacts provide no clear spatiotemporal indications of the timing, route of entry, or dispersal patterns of the initial colonizers. Clovis undoubtedly represents the first continuous occupation of many North American regions, but it remains unclear if Clovis reveals the rise and spread of an in-situ cultural development by an existing North American population (or populations) or if Clovis peoples were truly the first to colonize the continent.

Identifying definitive evidence of the "first" peoples in the Americas, much like finding the first of any temporally distant phenomenon, is a difficult task. Because colonization is a process involving the spread, occupation, and growth of a population, multiple firsts must be identified. The earliest site, date, or artifact offers evidence merely of a human presence on a continent—but it does not necessarily indicate colonization. It is possible, if not probable, that multiple human groups ventured into North America without establishing a permanent presence. The archaeological signature of colonization then may not open an easily navigable spatiotemporal trail of artifacts but could involve a more complex record of human explorations prior to, concurrent with, and postdating actual colonization. Consequently, Early Paleoindian archaeology is fraught with contentious claims, debates, and theories regarding the expectations and interpretations of evidence concerning the timing of human presence versus colonization.

Scientific investigation of Early Paleoindian archaeology began with the 1927 discovery of the Folsom site in New Mexico. The first widely recognized evidence of artifacts in association with extinct Pleistocene bison, the Folsom site unequivocally established the Pleistocene presence of humans in North America (Meltzer 2006). Five years later, the discovery of artifacts associated with mammoth remains at the Dent site, followed by discoveries at Blackwater Draw, began to solidify the antiquity of human occupation and establish a uniquely American past typified by fluted projectile points. However, as important as these sites were and continue to be, many researchers immediately began to question the emerging view of Pleistocene history; concerns were raised regarding the possibility of erroneous dates, fortuitous associations between artifacts and extinct fauna, and claims of far greater antiquity. The original Folsom and Clovis site finds are rightfully accredited as establishing Paleoindian archaeology as a temporally and technologically distinct arena of study, but these sites also established an enduring legacy of debate. Though 80 years have passed since their discovery, a Pleistocene human presence in the America's remains the single point of agreement among contemporary researchers. Two associated assertions, an Asian origin and entry via Beringia, also remain tenable. Countless new sites have been found, analyzed, and described as well, but the accumulation of data has not substantially altered the key issues of debate sparked by these initial Pleistocene-age finds.

What Is Clovis?

Named after the town of Clovis, New Mexico, where extinct Pleistocene fauna were found in association with distinctive lanceolate projectile points at the Blackwater Draw site (Boldurian and Cotter 1999), Clovis became synonymous with North American colonizers by the 1940s. The repeated occurrence of Clovis projectile points and megafauna (most commonly mammoth) at sites across North America suggested rapid human dispersal. The unique morphology of Clovis points, characterized by basal thinning flakes removed from each surface of the bifacial projectile point base (referred to as "channel flakes" or "flutes"; see Anderson, this volume) further suggested that colonizers quickly established a technologically distinct toolkit for predation of megafauna during the Late Pleistocene. The Clovis archaeological record, coupled with longstanding geologic evidence of a Pleistocene land bridge (i.e., Beringia) connecting Asia to Alaska and the presence of an unglaciated corridor cutting a swath through the Canadian plains, presented a cohesive, albeit simplistic, colonization scenario (Figure 8.1). The makers of Clovis points were thought to have crossed the land bridge, traversed the ice-free corridor, and spread throughout the continent. Early on in this process, Clovis points emerged as the primary weapon and were deposited throughout unglaciated North America. In this view, Clovis populations are thought to have undergone rapid population growth as they spread across a previously unpopulated continent.

Beringia, enabling terrestrial passage from Siberia into Alaska, resulted from the drop in sea level during glacial episodes. The land bridge was exposed numerous times throughout the Pleistocene, but it was not until after the Last Glacial Maximum (LGM), the height of glacial conditions, ca. 18000 cal BP, that a stable human presence in Siberia meant likely populations for dispersal into North America (Goebel et al. 2008). On arrival in North America, colonists would have been confronted with enormous ice masses. During the LGM two of them, the Laurentide and the Cordilleran, coalesced, covering much of present-day Alaska and Canada. As glacial conditions ameliorated, the ice mass diverged into two large ice sheets, the Cordilleran to the west and the Laurentide to the east. Cosmogenic dating of

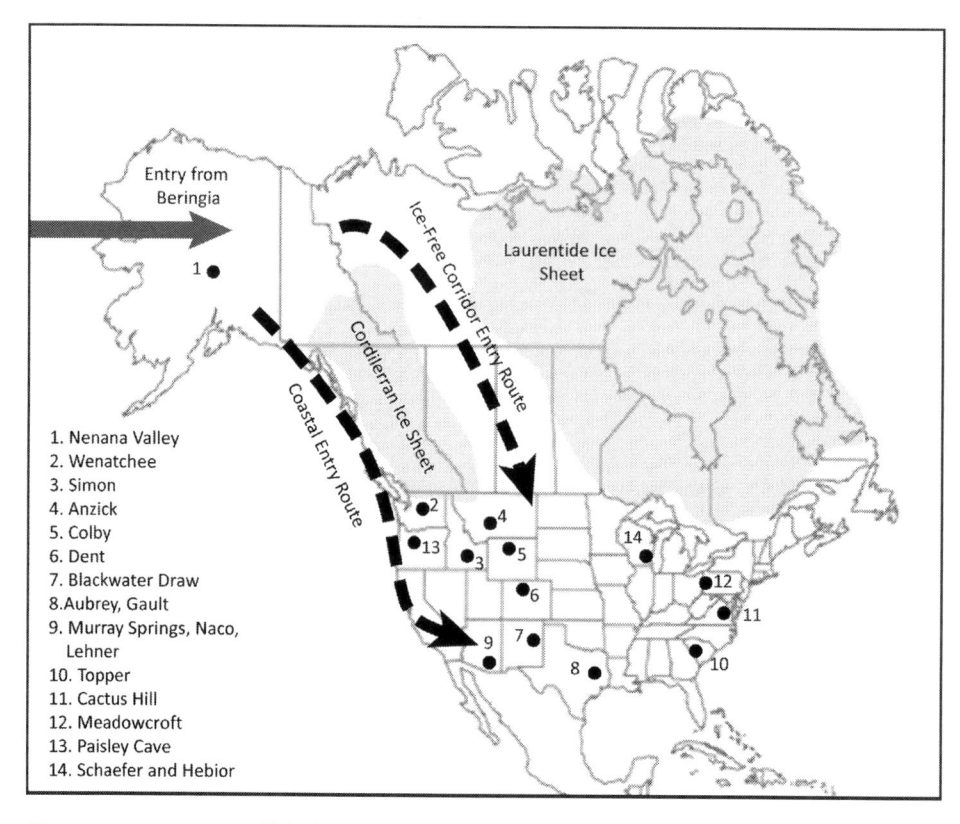

Figure 8.1 Locations of likely entry routes of North American colonizers, Pleistocene ice sheets, and key Clovis and related sites.

glacial erratics and other geologic evidence indicate that an ice-free corridor located in the Yukon and McKenzie River Valleys, separating the two ice masses, was not accessible until after 14000 cal BP (Jackson and Wilson 2004; Figure 8.1). On the basis of the opening of Beringia and subsequently the ice-free corridor, many archaeologists believe that colonization necessarily postdates 14000 cal BP. Passage through the corridor implies that it afforded a suitable habitat for human occupation, or viable enough, in minimally ecological terms, to allow humans to traverse it. How viable a human habitat the corridor presented remains debated, and no sites have been identified within the corridor that predate 13000 cal BP. Because the ice-free corridor was a transient feature resulting from glacial retreat, it temporally limits the earliest possible colonization date. Therefore proponents of the route interpret colonization as an extremely rapid event.

After crossing Beringia, an alternate route into the unglaciated regions of North America is along the Pacific coastline. Coastal models have been favored by some researchers since the 1960s (Mandryke et al. 2001), and they present a cogent alternative to the ice-free corridor. The outermost regions of the northwestern coastline of North America accumulated ice intermittently throughout the Pleistocene but were likely relatively ice-free by at least 15000 cal BP. It is suggested that the initial colonizers followed the coast from an initial Beringian entry into North America all the way down into South America. Movement inland occurred only after significant population growth and dispersion along coastal habitats. This scenario implies that coastally adapted foragers colonized both North and South America and that this was followed by an eventual migration inland. The coastal option permits greater temporal flexibility for a colonization date since the coasts were ice-free long prior to the emergence of the ice-free corridor. Unfortunately, when the ice masses melted at the onset of the Holocene and sea level rose, much of the continental shelf exposed during the Pleistocene was inundated with water. The sites potentially situated on them are now submerged, and no sites predating 13000 cal BP have been found on the North American Pacific coast (an important South American exception is the Monte Verde site). So even though an inland route, in contrast to a coastal entry route, should be detectable from the location and dates of early sites, differential preservation of coastal sites may obscure the record.

Dated Clovis deposits are thus congruent with both an ice-free corridor entry and a coastal entry. For much of the 20th century, Clovis was not thought to be any older than approximately 12000 cal BP. As radiocarbon calibration curves have become more accurate, Clovis materials are now known to date between approximately 13340 and 12830 cal BP (for reference, the Pleistocene-Holocene boundary dates to approximately 11500 BP; Fiedel 2002). Persisting for approximately 600 years, Clovis projectile points have been found from Canada to Mexico (see Anderson, this volume). Clovis sites are generally open-air and often associated with water sources such as springs, streams, and lakes. Clovis technology includes large bifaces; finely retouched flake tools such as scrapers, gravers, and knives; and beveled bone and ivory rods. Nonbifacial tools are frequently manufactured on flakes derived through core reduction and, particularly in the Southern Plains states of the United States, on large prismatic blades derived from conical blade cores (Collins 1999). Fluted Clovis projectile points, and to a limited extent blade production and bone or ivory rods, are the only diagnostic artifacts associated with Clovis (Figure 8.2). Cylindrical bone and ivory rods are often beveled at one or both ends, and their function remains unknown.

Clovis "kill sites" are the most widely known in western North America. Sites such as Blackwater Draw, Colby, Dent, and Naco, where Clovis points are found in direct association with extinct Pleistocene megafauna, have been identified throughout the American Plains. These sites most commonly contain mammoth or mastodon skeletal material with small assemblages of projectile points and butchery tools. Residential sites, such as Aubrey, Gault, and Murray Springs, generally contain more diverse technological and faunal assemblages and are often situated near lithic raw material or kill sites. Clovis caches—small, discrete deposits of Clovis tools—have also been found. Caches may represent implements truly "cached" for later retrieval, ritual offerings, or burials (e.g., the Anzick site in Montana). Well-known caches such as Wenatchee and Simon contain a mix of finished and unfinished tools and often yield extremely large bifaces (bifacial Clovis points are

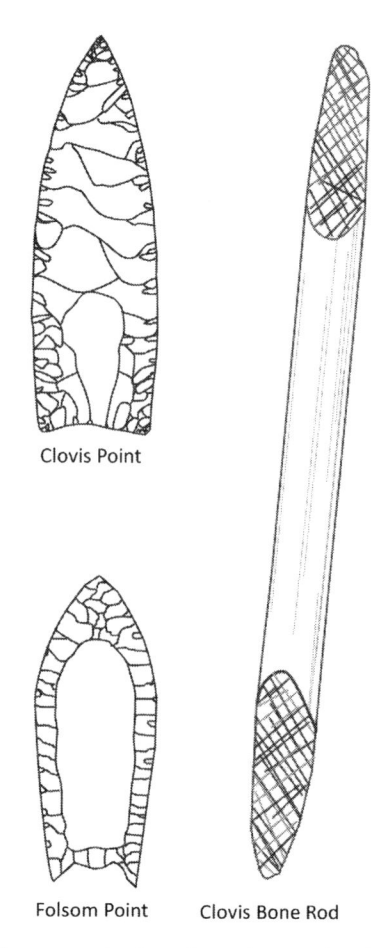

Figure 8.2 Early Paleoindian technology.

generally about 10 cm long; cached Clovis bifaces are upwards of 20 cm long; Dixon 1999). Lithic raw materials from Clovis assemblages indicate that high-quality cryptocrystalline cherts were frequently used and transported great distances. Clovis technology, site distribution, and associated faunal records are interpreted to represent a highly mobile population of foragers living in small groups and subsisting primarily on terrestrial prey (Kelly and Todd 1988). The extent to which Pleistocene megafauna contributed to the Clovis diet remains contested. Some archaeologists argue that Clovis megafauna sites are highly visible components of the record but that species such as mammoth and mastodon contributed only minimally to the everyday diet of Clovis peoples (Grayson and Meltzer 2002). Others interpret Clovis peoples as specialized hunters of Pleistocene prey (Waguespack and Surovell 2003) whose efforts likely contributed to megafauna extinction (Haynes 2002).

Whereas regionally distinct variants of Clovis point morphology are known (Morrow and Morrow 1999), the Clovis point and its associated toolkit undeniably constitutes the first widespread, technologically consistent, material cultural record present in unglaciated regions of North America. However, the relationship between Clovis technology and the earliest assemblages from Alaska is not straightforward. If colonists entered the Americas through Beringia, the Pleistocene archaeological record of Alaska should be the oldest and display the strongest cultural affinities to contemporaneous Siberian populations. Fluted points have been found in Alaska. They are primarily surface finds and comparatively rare and younger than Clovis points from the continental United States (Bever 2001). The Nenana complex, the oldest known lithic tradition from Alaska, may date to as early as 13400–13900 BP (most Nenana sites are coeval with, if not younger than, Clovis). Known from sites in the Nenana and Tanana valleys, the Nenana complex is predominantly characterized as a flake and blade industry. Large bifacial knives, retouched blade tools, endscrapers, pièces esquilles, and diagnostic teardrop-to-triangular-shaped projectile points (i.e., Chindadn points) are characteristic of the complex. It has been argued that the nonpoint components of Nenana and Clovis assemblages, particularly blade and scraper morphology, share distinct morphological attributes (Goebel 2004). Similarities between Clovis and Nenana can then be construed as reflecting an ancestral relationship, implying a general trend of increasing reliance on bifacial reduction as colonists dispersed, which culminated in Clovis projectile point technology. This trend may have its origins in the blade-dominated industries of Upper Paleolithic Siberia; but the relationship between Clovis and Nenana remains tentative.

The Pre-Clovis Archaeological Record

Proponents of the "pre-Clovis" position of New World colonization believe not only that human populations were present in the Americas prior to 13500 cal BP but that colonization occurred, or at least a significant human population was present, prior to Clovis. In this view, Clovis is not representative of the initial colonization event but of a later cultural development or adaptation. Many claims of pre-Clovis-aged sites lack chronological control, are found in disturbed contexts, contain equivocal artifacts, and have struggled to gain widespread professional acceptance. However, with the discovery of the Monte Verde site in Chile, pre-Clovis occupation gained considerable support if not outright acceptance by many archaeologists. Monte Verde component II, dated to between 14650 and 15600 cal BP, remains controversial, but it has supplied the first distinct non-Clovis evidence of human occupation in the Americas (Dillehay 1997). Its location in South America, well over a thousand miles from Beringia, has led many to speculate that colonization necessarily occurred hundreds if not thousands of years prior to Clovis. Sites such as Meadowcroft, Cactus Hill, and Topper all contain potentially pre-Clovis-aged artifacts (Bonnichsen et al. 2006; Figure 8.1).

Meadowcroft, long a debated "contender" for pre-Clovis evidence, is a multi-component rockshelter in Pennsylvania where non-Clovis artifacts in its lower levels potentially predate 14000 cal BP. The Cactus Hill site in Virginia contains a lithic assemblage found below a Clovis component in a dune adjacent to the Nottaway River and may date to 15000 cal BP. At the Topper site, an assemblage of more than a thousand small flakes and microblades has been excavated in a terrace of the Savannah River in Georgia. Like Cactus Hill, the early material was found below a Clovis occupation level, and tentative estimates suggest the material may be as old as (or older than) 16000 cal BP. Pre-Clovis-aged dates have also been obtained on human coprolites at Paisley Cave and are associated with butchered mammoths at Schaefer and Hebior (Overstreet and Kolb 2003). It is unclear what these sites may represent. Found in diverse geographic contexts with disparate artifacts and dates, the pre-Clovis record currently presents no clear interpretation of when and how colonization unfolded. Assuming the dates are accurate, pre-Clovis-aged deposits could record an initial human dispersal event of a population antecedent to Clovis, or an initial human dispersal unrelated to Clovis, or they may be wholly unrelated to colonization and reflect transient excursions into the Americas. If colonization proceeded considerably prior to 14000 cal BP, then the ice-free corridor was not an available option for entry. Consequently, researchers favoring a pre-Clovis colonization date generally favor a Pacific coastal route.

Folsom

Immediately following Clovis throughout the longitudinal center of North America is Folsom. First identified near the town of Folsom, New Mexico, in 1927 the complex is best known for its distinctive projectile points and association with an extinct bison species, *Bison antiquus*. Sites are mainly located in the Rocky Mountains and Great Plains that were prime grassland habitat for bison (Figure 8.3). Dated from ca. 12800 to

11900 cal BP, the Folsom period corresponds with the Younger Dryas, a 1,200-year-long climatic event marking the return to glacial conditions across the Northern Hemisphere. Folsom technology is known for a unique style of projectile point that is notoriously difficult to manufacture. Akin to Clovis points, Folsom points are fluted; however, the resulting flake scar channels often extend along the entire length of the point (Figure 8.2). The removal of such long channel flakes requires extensive platform preparation and a high degree of knapping skill. Unfinished Folsom points (called performs), channel flakes, and finished points are diagnostic artifacts of the period. Ultrathin bifaces (with width-to-thickness ratios of 10:1 or greater), a wide array of unifacially retouched flake tools, and morphologically distinct spurred endscrapers and delicate gravers (Amick 1999) are also common in Folsom assemblages.

Folsom peoples are interpreted to have led highly nomadic lives. Lithic raw materials in Folsom assemblages are often diverse and derived from sources hundreds of kilometers away. *Bison antiquus*, an extinct species larger than modern bison, were the focus of the subsistence economy. Folsom bison kill sites, such as Folsom and Cooper, involve small numbers of animals (usually 15 or fewer). In contrast to Archaic and later-aged bison kills, where large numbers were seasonally killed and processed for eventual consumption, Folsom hunters are thought to have made multiple small bison kills, often lightly butchering their prey, throughout the year. Residential sites are frequently associated with bison kills or located in close proximity to lithic raw material

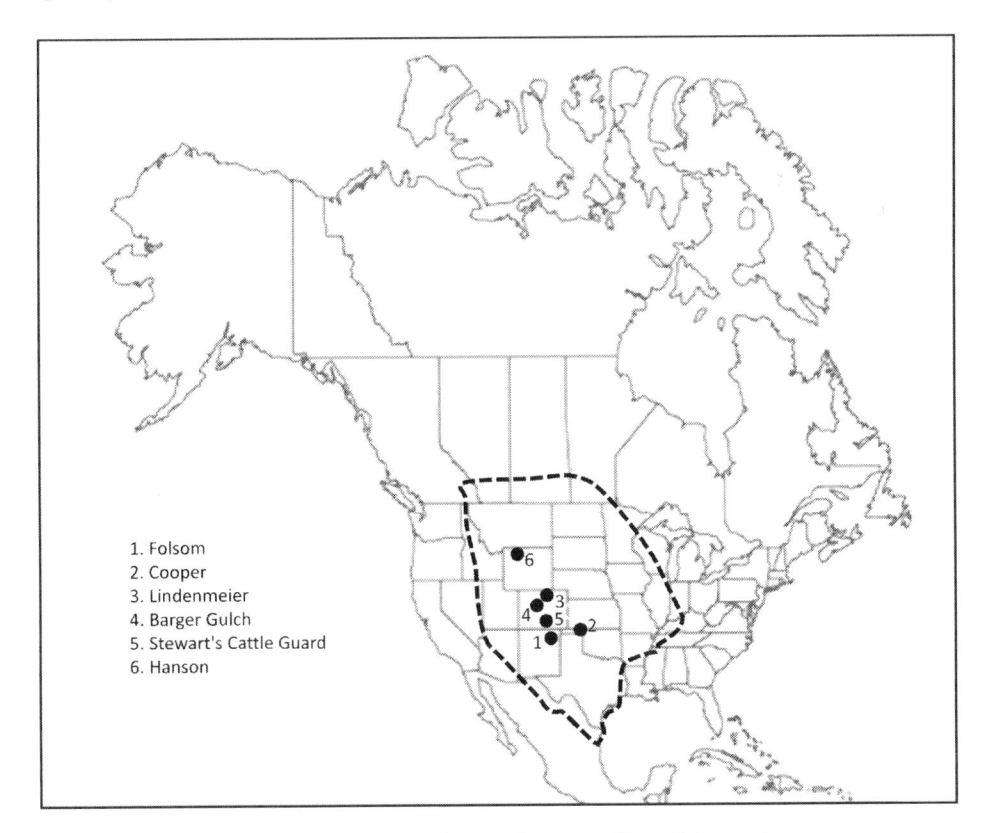

Figure 8.3 Location and spatial extent of key Folsom sites.

sources (e.g., the Hanson Site). A few residential sites with a large number of artifacts (more than a thousand) such as Lindenmeier, Stewarts Cattle Guard, and Barger Gulch preserve nonchipped stone tools such as bone needles and small sandstone abraders.

EARLY PALEOINDIANS

Collectively, Clovis and Folsom represent a widespread cultural phenomenon during the Late Pleistocene of North America. Continuities between Clovis and Folsom include fluting of projectile points, a process exclusive to Early Paleoindians, and a highly nomadic lifestyle associated with pursuit of terrestrial prey. The distribution of Folsom sites is circumscribed by that of Clovis, and Clovis is often immediately preceded by Folsom in multicomponent sites.

Possibly intermediate between Clovis and Folsom, or at least coeval with Folsom, is Goshen. Goshen points resemble unfluted Folsom points and have been found at a handful of sites in the Northern Plains (e.g., the Mill Iron site; Frison 1996). The difficulty of establishing how colonization proceeded highlights the dichotomy between the current empirical record and the increasingly complex expectations of colonization that are theoretically derived.

For instance, which components of Clovis technology (if any) were imported into the Americas as part of the initial dispersal event and which represent unique technological adaptations to Pleistocene North America is difficult to discern. Depending on which sites and dates one accepts, colonization may have occurred quickly or slowly, via the ice-free corridor or the coast, and be associated with or distinct from Clovis. Since any single site or artifact cannot elucidate the cultural and demographic process of colonization, our understanding of the process is likely to become even more contentious and uncertain as the complex relationships among migration of people, culture, and biology are refined and as archaeological evidence is found. An ever more accurate portrayal of the Pleistocene occupation of the Americas is sure to emerge, but it will necessarily require greater understanding of how humans colonized new lands.

REFERENCES

Amick, D. S. (editor). 1999. *Folsom Lithic Technology: Explorations in Structure and Variation*. International Monographs in Prehistory, Ann Arbor.

Bever, M. R. 2001. An Overview of Alaskan Late Pleistocene Archaeology: Historical Themes and Current Perspectives. *Journal of World Prehistory* 15:125–191.

Boldurian, A. T., and J. L. Cotter. 1999. *Clovis Revisited: New Perspectives on Paleoindian Adaptations from Blackwater Draw, New Mexico*. University of Pennsylvania Museum Publication, Philadelphia.

Bonnichsen, R., B. T. Lepper, D. Stanford, and M. R. Waters (editors). 2006. *Paleoamerican Origins: Beyond Clovis*. Texas A&M University Press, College Station.

Collins, M. B. 1999. *Clovis Blade Technology*. University of Texas Press, Austin.

Dillehay, T. D. 1997. *Monte Verde: A Late Pleistocene Settlement in Chile, Vol. 2*. Smithsonian Institution Press, Washington DC.

Dixon, E. J. 1999. *Bones, Boats, & Bison: Archaeology and the First Colonization of Western North America*. University of New Mexico Press, Albuquerque.

Fiedel, S. J. 2002. Initial Human Colonization of the Americas: An Overview of the Issues and the Evidence. *Radiocarbon* 44(2):407–436.

Frison, George C. (editor). 1996. *The Mill Iron Site*. University of New Mexico Press, Albuquerque.

Goebel, T. 2004. The search for a Clovis progenitor in Siberia. In D. Madsen (ed.), *Entering America: Northeast Asia and Beringia Before the Last Glacial Maximum* (pp. 311–358). University of Utah Press, Salt Lake City.

———, M. R. Waters, and D. H. O'Rourke. 2008. The Late Pleistocene Dispersal of Modern Humans in the Americas. *Science* 319(5869):1497–1502.

Grayson, D. K., and D. J. Meltzer. 2002. Clovis Hunting and Large Mammal Extinction: A Critical Review of the Evidence. *Journal of World Prehistory* 16(4):313–359.

Haynes, G. 2002. The Catastrophic Extinction of North American Mammoths and Mastadonts. *World Archaeology* 33(3):391–413.

Jackson, L. E., and M. C. Wilson. 2004. The Ice-Free Corridor Revisited. *Geotimes* 49:16–19.

Kelly, R. L., and L. C. Todd. 1988. Coming into the Country: Early Paleoindian Hunting and Mobility. *American Antiquity* 53(2):23–244.

Mandryke, C., H. Josenhans, D. W. Fedje, and R. W. Mathewes. 2001. Late Quaternary Paleoenvironments of Northwestern America: Implications for Inland Versus Coastal Migration Routes. *Quaternary Science Reviews* 20:301–314.

Meltzer, D. J. 2006. *Folsom: New Archaeological Investigations of a Classic Paleoindian Bison Kill*. University of California Press, Berkeley.

Morrow, J. E., and T. A. Morrow. 1999. Geographic Variation in Fluted Projectile Points: A Hemispheric Perspective. *American Antiquity* 64:215–231.

Overstreet, D. F., and M. F. Kolb. 2003. Pleistocene Archaeological Sites with Human-Modified Woolly Mammoth Remains in Southeastern Wisconsin, U.S.A. *Geoarchaeology* 18:91–114.

Waguespack, N. M., and T. A. Surovell. 2003. Clovis Hunting Strategies, or How to Make Out on Plentiful Resources. *American Antiquity* 68(2):333–352.

FURTHER READING

Barton, C. M., G. A. Clark, D. R. Yesner, and G. A. Pearson. 2004. *The Settlement of the American Continents: A Multidisciplinary Approach to Human Biogeography*. University of Arizona Press, Tucson.

Haynes, C. V., and B. B. Huckell. 2007. *Murray Springs: A Clovis Site with Multiple Activity Areas in the San Pedro Valley, Arizona*. University of Arizona Press, Tucson.

Waters, M. R., and T. W. Stafford. 2007. Redefining the Age of Clovis: Implications for the Peopling of the Americas. *Science* 315(5815):1122–1126.

CHAPTER 9

PLEISTOCENE SETTLEMENT IN THE EAST

DAVID G. ANDERSON

EXACTLY when people first entered eastern North America is currently unknown, but settlement is assumed to have occurred during the Late Pleistocene, around or more likely after the Last Glacial Maximum, which dates from ca. 18000 to 21000 cal BP. Widespread human presence is evident by ca. 13000 to 12000 cal BP and is documented by the occurrence of Clovis and a number of successor fluted projectile point types in all parts of Eastern North America away from areas covered by ice sheets or periglacial lakes or seas (Figure 9.1). Fluting, the removal of large channel or thinning flakes from the base of these points, is a uniquely Paleoindian phenomenon, never duplicated again in prehistory in the Americas, or indeed anywhere else in the world before or since. North American archaeologists are fortunate in this regard because the occurrence of fluting technology, which occurred for a period of no more than about 1,500 years, provides an unambiguous marker of these early occupations.

Diagnostics from possible pre-Clovis occupations, in contrast, are currently somewhat equivocal in nature, although appreciable effort has been devoted to finding early assemblages and artifacts. Several likely sites have been identified, including Cactus Hill in Virginia and Meadowcroft Rockshelter in Pennsylvania, where small, unfluted, triangular or lanceolate point forms are found. Possibly related forms have also been noted at several locations in Florida, such as at the Page-Ladson site, suggesting it is only a matter of time before pre-Clovis diagnostics are securely established and dated in the east (Adovasio et al. 1999; Dunbar and Hemmings 2004; Goodyear 2005; McAvoy and McAvoy 1997; Webb 2006). Although the origins of eastern Paleoindian populations were likely from further to the west, and ultimately from northeast Asia, some researchers have recently suggested

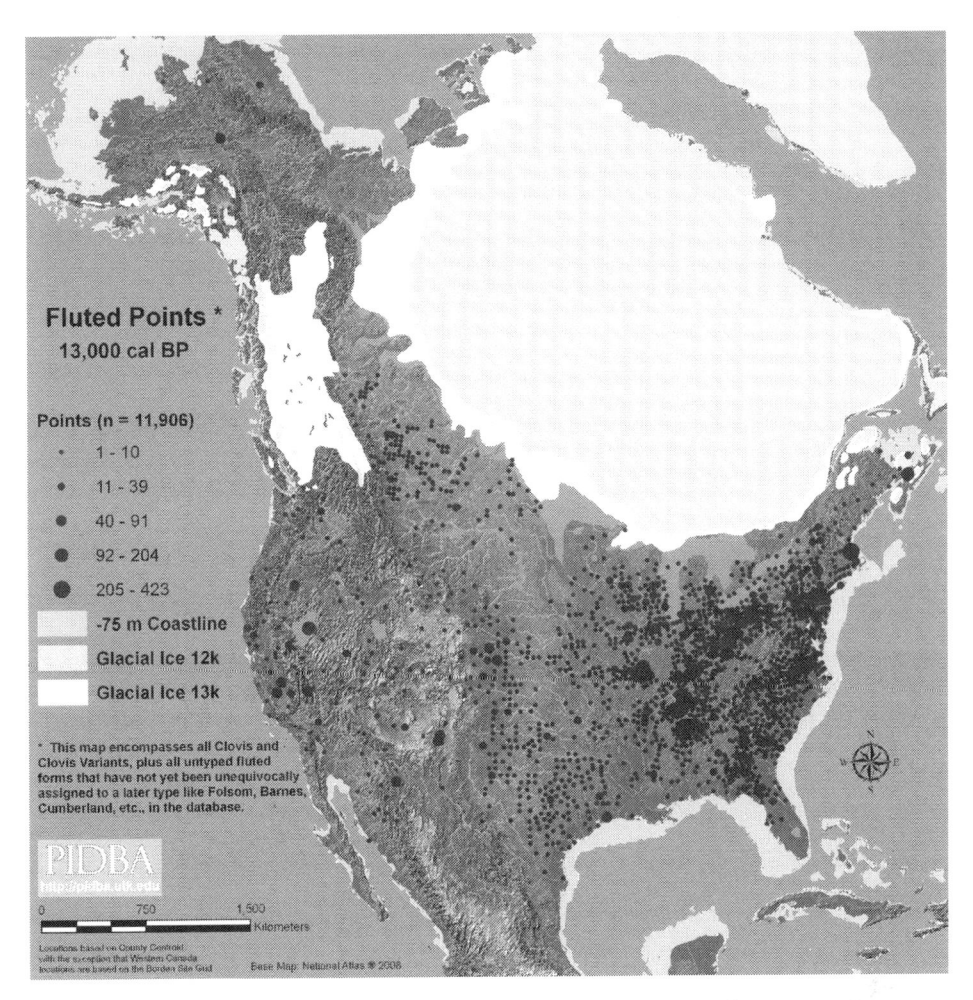

Figure 9.1 Occurrence of fluted projectile points in eastern North America. Image courtesy PIDBA (Paleoindian Database of the Americas, http://pidba.utk.edu/).

movement across the north Atlantic also occurred, although the idea is highly contentious (cf. Stanford and Bradley 2002; Strauss et al. 2005).

Early fluted Clovis points are characterized by short and narrow flutes rarely extending more than a third to half way up the blade (Figure 9.2:a, b). They have been radiocarbon dated at a number of locations, mostly in the western United States, to between ca. 13150 and 12850 cal BP (Waters and Stafford 2007), during the warmer Allerød period and before the onset of the much colder and more variable Younger Dryas period, which occurred from ca. 12850 to 11650 cal BP (Fiedel 1999; Hughen et al. 2000). Later fluted point forms in Eastern North America, of the Folsom, Cumberland, Barnes, Vail-Debert, Bull Brook-West Athens Hill; Michaud-Neponset, and Redstone types (e.g., Figure 9.2:c–g), in contrast tend to be characterized by broad flakes that frequently extend much or all of the way up the blade to or near the tip, forming a "full fluted" horizon dating to the early centuries of the Younger Dryas (Anderson et al. 2010; Bradley et al. 2008; Goodyear 2010).

Many of these later fluted point forms are also characterized by deeply indented, concave bases, particularly in the Northeastern and upper Midwestern parts of the region, where fluting continues to as late as the Pleistocene-Holocene boundary at ca. 11500 cal BP. In areas further to the south, in contrast, "full" fluted forms are apparently replaced within a few centuries by unfluted lanceolate and waisted forms such as the Suwannee, Simpson, Quad, Beaver Lake and, somewhat later, Dalton and Cormier-Nicholas types (Figure 9.2:h–n, q), by ca. 12000 cal BP if not before (see McElrath and Emerson, this volume). Successive side- and corner-notched forms follow, and in the northern and western parts of the region lanceolate points

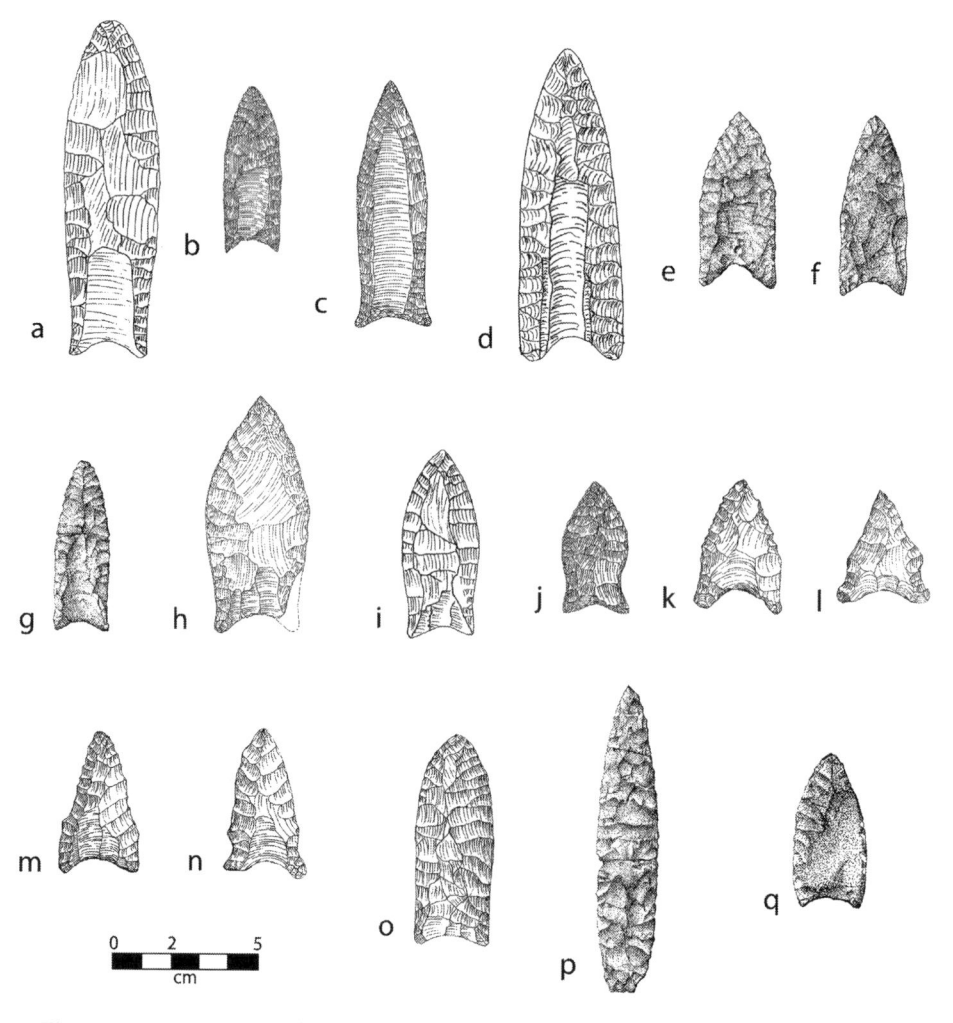

Figure 9.2 Diagnostic Paleoindian projectile point forms in eastern North America: (a–b) Clovis; (c) Cumberland; (d) Redstone; (e) Vail-Debert; (f) Bull Brook-West Athens Hill; (g) Michaud-Neponset; (h–i) Suwannee/Simpson; (j) Beaver Lake; (k) fluted Dalton; (l) Hardaway Dalton; (m–n) Dalton; (o) unfluted lanceolate; (p) Ste. Anne-Varney; (q) Cormier-Nicholas (images drawn by R. Jerald Ledbetter and William Burgess, used by permission of the artists and the Maine Archaeological Society).

resembling Plains types like Agate Basin, Scottsbluff, and Angostura are also found in some incidence, such as the Ste. Anne-Varney type (Figure 9.2:p) (Anderson and Sassaman 1996; Bradley et al. 2008; Johnson 1989). The occurrence and restricted distribution of these differing point forms, at least compared to the preceding Clovis type, is thought to reflect the emergence of local adaptations and cultures, and perhaps population movements between major physiographic regions such as the Plains and the eastern woodlands. Morphological variation, stratigraphic relationships, and the temporal range of many of these forms remains to be better documented, and particularly during the earlier part of the Younger Dryas from ca. 12850 to ca. 12000 cal BP, an interval for which few excavated or dated sites are currently known in the east.

Pre-Clovis sites in eastern North America include Big Eddy in Missouri, Cactus Hill and Saltville in Virginia, Little Salt Springs and Page-Ladson in Florida, Meadowcroft Rockshelter in Pennsylvania, Topper in South Carolina, and Schaefer and Hebior in Wisconsin (Goodyear 1999, 2005; Meltzer 2009; Overstreet 2005; Figure 9.3). Though some doubt remains as to whether all are Pre-Clovis in age, their occurrence suggests small numbers of people, thin on the landscape and hence nearly archaeologically invisible, were present in the east for as much as several thousand years prior to Clovis. Clovis sites, in contrast, are far more common, with several thousand locations currently known that have yielded one or more diagnostic points, some associated with dense quantities of stone tools and debitage (Anderson and Faught 1998, Anderson et al. 2005, 2010; Haynes 2002). Many of these are surface finds exposed and disturbed by plowing or timber harvesting, but dense Clovis assemblages have also been reported in subsurface context at a number of sites, among them at Topper in South Carolina; Cactus Hill, Williamson, and Thunderbird in Virginia; Carson-Conn-Short in Tennessee, and Shoop in Pennsylvania. Many of these are associated with prominent physiographic features or major outcrops of high-quality knappable stone, leading some scholars to suggest that Clovis populations were tethered to quarries; that is, their mobility was shaped, to an unknown but presumably significant amount, by the need to periodically revisit these sources and replenish their supply of toolstone (e.g., Gardner 1989; Goodyear 1979). Easily located places on the landscape, such as falls or fords in rivers, or mountain peaks or unusual geological formations such as monadnocks or craters (i.e., such as the Eagle Hill, Louisiana; Wells Creek Crater, Tennessee; and Stone Mountain, Georgia, Paleoindian sites), would have been ideal places to rendezvous with other groups to maintain interaction and mating networks. Some highly productive locations may have been staging areas, where populations could have settled for a time and grown, and groups radiating away from them would have been able to relocate should problems arise (Anderson 1990, 1995). Archaeologists examining paleosubsistence remains, specifically the plant and animal remains found in these sites—from extinct fauna such as mammoth or mastodon to forms that survived the late Pleistocene such as white-tailed deer, migratory waterfowl, and acorn or hickory nuts—have argued that the foraging behavior and mobility strategies of Paleoindian groups were also strongly shaped by division of labor, notably the seasonal availability of resources that would have likely been obtained and processed by men as opposed to women and children (Hollenbach 2009; Surovell 2000; Walker 2007; Walker and Driskell 2007). Consideration of gender roles is increasingly being considered by Paleoindian researchers, particularly since the presumed rapid population growth sometimes associated with Clovis and post-Clovis occupations would have required a lifestyle facilitating fertility and the survival of children.

Even though surface finds of presumably immediate post-Clovis full-fluted points and associated artifacts are fairly common throughout the southeastern part of North America, few have been found or dated in an excavation context. Their occurrence corresponds to the initial centuries of the Younger Dryas, a major cold

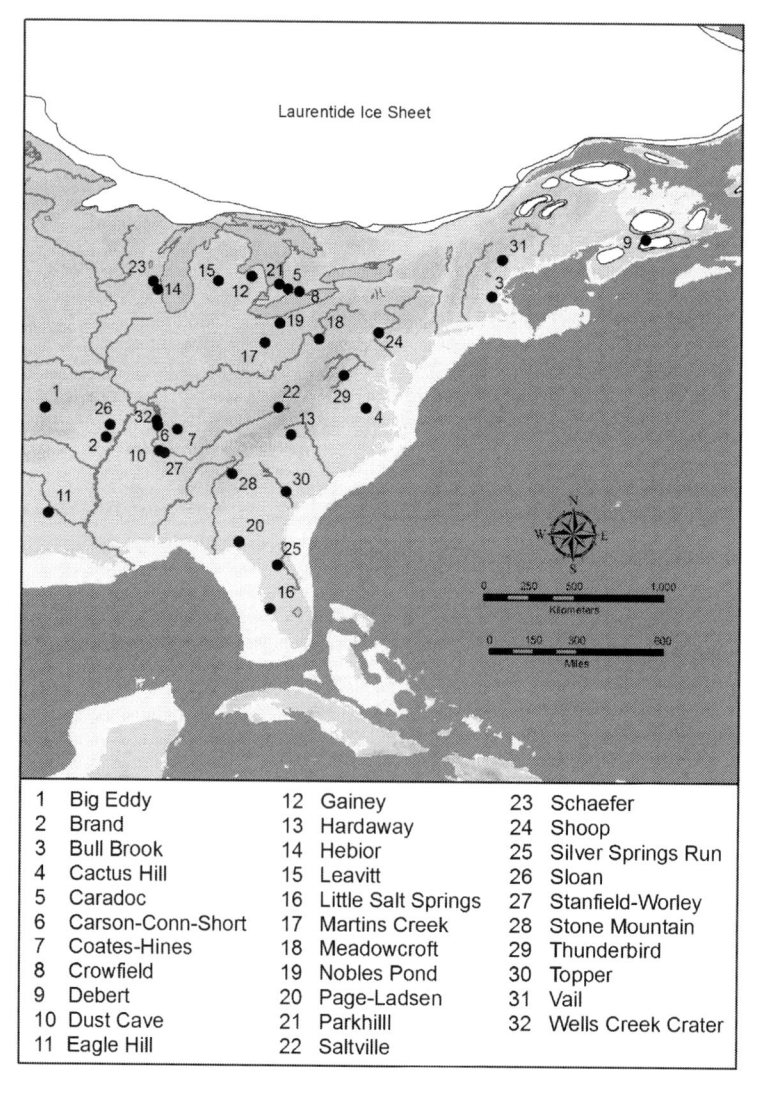

1	Big Eddy	12	Gainey	23	Schaefer
2	Brand	13	Hardaway	24	Shoop
3	Bull Brook	14	Hebior	25	Silver Springs Run
4	Cactus Hill	15	Leavitt	26	Sloan
5	Caradoc	16	Little Salt Springs	27	Stanfield-Worley
6	Carson-Conn-Short	17	Martins Creek	28	Stone Mountain
7	Coates-Hines	18	Meadowcroft	29	Thunderbird
8	Crowfield	19	Nobles Pond	30	Topper
9	Debert	20	Page-Ladsen	31	Vail
10	Dust Cave	21	Parkhilll	32	Wells Creek Crater
11	Eagle Hill	22	Saltville		

Figure 9.3 Paleoindian site locations in eastern North America.

reversal, and perhaps not coincidentally when the last of the Pleistocene megafaunal extinctions is thought to have occurred. There is a decided drop in site and artifact incidence compared to Clovis, suggesting a population decline or a change in settlement patterning, perhaps in response to the dramatic climate change. In the upper Midwest and northeast, in contrast, a great many presumably post-Clovis fluted point sites have been found and a number extensively excavated, including Nobles Pond in Ohio, Gainey and Leavitt in Michigan, Bull Brook in Massachusetts, Vail in Maine, and Debert in Nova Scotia, as well as a number of sites in Ontario, namely Caradoc, Crowfield, and Parkhill (Anderson et al. 2004; Ellis and Dellar 1997). Many of the northern sites are thought to be associated with caribou hunting, and some appear to have been used repeatedly, as at Nobles Pond and Debert, or alternatively to have involved both reuse as well as gatherings of a fairly large number of people, perhaps multiple bands, as suggested at Bull Brook (Robinson et al. 2009). At a few of these northern sites, evidence for ritual behavior is indicated, including the intentional burning of a large number of functional tools and performs at the Crowfield site (Deller et al. 2009). Paleoindian caches, of stone and bone or ivory tools and raw materials, though reported at a number of locations in the western United States, are uncommon in the east, at least until Dalton times, when clusters of tools are sometimes found with burials, as at the Sloan site in Arkansas (Morse 1997; McElrath and Emerson, this volume). The difference in the occurrence of caches between the two regions is puzzling, and their presence in the west is interpreted as a response to greater long-distance mobility, and hence the need to place stores of raw material on the landscape (e.g., Kilby 2008; Meltzer 2002, 2009). Some of the western caches include large and elaborately worked items that are clearly not utilitarian but instead appear to have served some religious or ceremonial purpose. Paleoindian use of stone thus encompassed both ceremonial as well as functional considerations. Indeed, the use of elaborate, carefully manufactured and curated tool forms continued for several thousand years past Clovis times, well into the early Holocene, suggesting this was a very important and conservative cultural tradition.

The last centuries of the Pleistocene, from ca. 12000 to 11500 cal BP, saw the Younger Dryas come to an end and the disappearance of fluting in most areas save in the extreme north near the retreating ice sheets. Terminal Pleistocene sites are recognized by points ranging from lanceolate to side- and corner-notched types, described using many local names and each stylistically somewhat unique. Most of these later point forms were extensively resharpened, apparently from use as multipurpose tools and a need to process numerous animals. Major Dalton sites that have been excavated are Brand and Sloan in Arkansas, Dust Cave and the Stanfield-Worley Bluff Shelter in Alabama, and Hardaway in North Carolina (Daniel 1998; DeJarnette et al. 1962; Goodyear 1974; Hollenbach 2009; Morse 1997). The Sloan site was apparently a marked cemetery, the earliest currently known in the Americas, with more than 20 discrete clusters of human remains and hypertrophic as well as normal-sized Dalton points and tools (Morse 1997). A complex interaction network or social-ceremonial complex is inferred to have been present in the Central Mississippi Valley during Dalton times, an early and precocious organizational development that soon ended, with similar phenomena not noted again in the region until the Mid-Holocene, when hypertrophic Benton points circulated widely in the Midsouth (Sassaman 2005; Walthall and Koldehoff 1998).

Paleoindian lifeways, particularly aspects of subsistence and perishable material culture, are poorly documented over much of eastern North America until fairly late in the period. Part of the reason is preservation. With the exception of a number of submerged sites in Florida such as Page Ladson or Little Salt Spring, and a few rock shelters such as Meadowcroft, Clovis, and pre-Clovis, assemblages are almost exclusively found in open-air settings, where the preservation of organic remains is typically very poor. Not until after ca. 12000 cal BP, during the latter part of the Younger Dryas in Dalton times (and after, in fact), is much evidence found for human use of caves and rock shelters anywhere in the region—something that has been attributed to a decrease in range mobility (Walthall 1998). Several of these sites have yielded well-preserved paleosubsistence remains, as at Dust Cave, Alabama; Modoc Rock Shelter in Illinois; and Rodgers Shelter in Missouri (Hollenbach 2009; Walker and Driskell 2007). Generalized adaptations characterized by an array of wild plant and animal resources are well documented for these terminal Pleistocene occupations, with an apparent emphasis on caribou in the north and a wider range of species in the south: birds, fish, and plant foods, as well as larger mammals such as deer. Generalized subsistence adaptations are also thought to apply to Clovis and presumed earlier occupants of the region (Meltzer 2009), but there is little direct evidence available to test this inference. Perishable textiles have also been found in early Holocene cave and rock shelter deposits, a form of material culture often overlooked by archaeologists emphasizing the surviving stone and bone industries of the Paleoindian era (Adovasio et al. 2004). The oldest textile impressions known from eastern North America, in fact, come from presumed Clovis-age deposits at the Hiscock site in New York (Adovasio et al. 2003).

Whether, and how regularly, Pleistocene megafauna were hunted in the east is currently the subject of some debate. Megafaunal kill sites are rare in the east, unlike the situation in the west, where numerous bison, mammoth, and mastodon kills are known (Grayson and Meltzer 2002). Even so, kill sites from the margins of the region—such as at Kimmswick in Missouri, where mastodon were taken—certainly indicate that these and other large animals could have been hunted further to the east. A number of possible human-proboscidean associations have, in fact, been reported elsewhere in eastern North America, including at the Hebior and Schaefer sites in Wisconsin, the Martins Creek site in Ohio, Coates-Hines in Tennessee, and Silver Springs Run and Page Ladson in Florida (Lepper and Funk 2006; Overstreet 2005; Webb 2006). More telling, tools of bone and ivory from mammoth, horse, and other extinct Pleistocene species that were worked green or fresh are found in large numbers in the rivers and sinks of Florida, indicating a clear association of humans and megafauna, if not direct exploitation (Hemmings et al. 2004). One probable kill site is in Florida, a *Bison antiquus* with a projectile point fragment embedded in the skull in an unhealed wound, meaning the animal died soon after (Webb et al. 1984).

Changes in Late Pleistocene climate, such as the Younger Dryas (ca. 12850–11650 cal BP), appear to have strongly shaped the location and character of early occupations throughout the east. Certainly the rise and fall of sea level and expansion and contraction of ice sheets and periglacial water bodies influenced where on the landscape people could live, while the ongoing extinction of megafauna and shifting of plant and animal ranges over the landscape would have affected the kinds of subsistence resources available to them. Belief systems were also likely influenced. It is suggested, for example, that adoption of an elaborate and highly predictable stone tool industry during Clovis and slightly later times was a reaction, in part, to the uncertainty in the world around them (e.g., Goodyear 1979; Kelly and Todd 1988; Meltzer 2002, 2009). The reason fluting technology was not readopted later in prehistory was it was difficult to accomplish. Yet this same challenge may have helped promote a sense of cultural identity between widely dispersed populations. Possessing exceptional flint-knapping skills, which also helped foster amicable relations among differing groups, would have certainly enhanced the survival of human populations ranging far from raw material sources and needing to conserve toolstone as much as possible.

The disappearance of large Pleistocene megafauna, if previously taken with any regularity, would have likely forced an expansion in breadth of diet, to include smaller package sizes, and experimentation with resources that might not have been considered previously, such as seeds, roots, and greens. Greater use of local, relatively immobile, or minimally ranging resources could have lessened the need for long-distance movement. A pronounced diversification in stone tool assemblages, particularly among projectile points, is noted later in the Pleistocene occupation of the east, particularly following the onset of the Younger Dryas. No point forms are found spanning the entire region, and many are restricted to fairly small areas, on the order of a few hundred kilometers in extent at most. Range restriction is indicated, with human populations assumed to have become increasingly localized and isolated from one another—something that may also reflect the weakening or disappearance of a shared belief system centered around elaborate stone tool manufacture and possibly the hunting of large animals. Adoption of a generalized subsistence economy capable of maximizing the potential of postglacial era biotic resources was once thought to have developed slowly in the east, over the thousands of years of the Archaic period, from ca. 11500 to 3200 cal BP, but it now appears likely that many of these changes were accomplished by Paleoindian peoples.

By the onset of the Holocene about 11500 cal BP, an essentially modern biotic and climatic regime was in place, although sea level would continue to rise and vegetational communities shift over large areas for several thousand more years, in reaction to the northward melting of the continental icesheets and changes in insolation and atmospheric circulation. Conditions were nonetheless stabler, compared to the preceding Pleistocene era, and numerous archaeological sites are found across eastern North America. No uniform way of life was present, however, either then or during the earlier Pleistocene human occupation of the region. Instead, the nature and scale of interaction, group range, social organization, technology, and ceremony appear to have varied greatly and changed over time. The Pleistocene human occupation of eastern North America resulted in a rich, yet still all too incomplete and only minimally examined, archaeological record. Whether Clovis technology arose here remains unknown, but it is certainly plausible given the dense assemblages that occur in greater incidence than in other parts of the Americas. During the Paleoindian period, traditions were established that shaped behavior for millennia to come in the east, such as emphasis on elaborate and hypertrophic stone tools, use of key spots on the landscape to facilitate rendezvous and perhaps ritual, and a highly diversified and generalized approach to subsistence.

REFERENCES

Adovasio, J. M., D. C. Hyland, and O. Soffer. 2004. Perishable Fiber Artifacts and the First Americans: New Implications. In *New Perspectives on the First Americans*, edited by B. T. Lepper and R. Bonnichsen, pp. 157–164. Center for the Study of the First Americans, Texas A&M University Press, College Station.

Adovasio, J. M., R. S. Laub, J. S. Illingworth, J. H. McAndrews, and D. C. Hyland. 2003. Perishable Technology from the Hiscock Site. Bulletin of the Buffalo Society of Natural Sciences 37, *The Hiscock Site: Late Pleistocene and Holocene Paleoecology and Archaeology of Western New York State*, edited by R. S. Laub, pp. 272–280. Buffalo Society of Natural Sciences, Buffalo, NY.

Adovasio, J. M., D. Pedler, J. Donahue, and R. Stuckenrath. 1999. No Vestiges of a Beginning Nor Prospect for an End: Two Decades of Debate on Meadowcroft Rockshelter. In *Ice Age Peoples of North America*, edited by R. Bonnichsen and K. Turnmire, pp. 416–431. Center for the Study of the First Americans, Corvallis, OR.

Anderson, D. G. 1990. The Paleoindian Colonization of Eastern North America: A View from the Southeastern United States. Research in Economic Anthropology, Supplement 5, *Early Paleoindian Economies of Eastern North America*, edited by K. B. Tankersley and B. L. Isaac, pp. 163–216. JAI, Greenwich, CT.

———. 1995. Paleoindian Interaction Networks in the Eastern Woodlands. In *Native American Interaction: Multiscalar Analyses and Interpretations in the Eastern Woodlands*, edited by M. S. Nassaney and K. E. Sassaman, pp. 1–26. University of Tennessee, Knoxville.

———, D. S. Brose, D. F. Dincauze, R. S. Grumet, E. K. Martin-Seibert, M. J. Shott, and R. C. Waldbauer. 2004. *The Earliest Americans Theme Study for the Eastern United States: National Historic Landmark Multiple Property Documentation Form*. National Park Service, National Historic Landmarks Survey National Register of Historic Places, E. K. Martin-Seibert, compiler and editor. National Park Service, Department of the Interior, Washington, DC.

Anderson, D. G., and M. K. Faught. 1998. The Distribution of Fluted Paleoindian Projectile Points: Update 1998. *Archaeology of Eastern North America* 26:163–188.

Anderson, D. G., D. S. Miller, S. J. Yerka, and M. K. Faught. 2005. Paleoindian Database of the Americas: Update 2005. *Current Research in the Pleistocene* 22:91–92.

Anderson, D. G., D. S. Miller, S. J. Yerka, J. C. Gillam, E. N. Johanson, D. T. Anderson, A. C. Goodyear, and A. M. Smallwood. 2010. PIDBA (Paleoindian Database of the Americas) 2010: Current Status and Findings. *Archaeology of Eastern North America* 38:63–90.

Anderson, D. G., and K. E. Sassaman (editors). 1996. *The Paleoindian and Early Archaic Southeast*. University of Alabama Press, Tuscaloosa.

Bradley, J. W., A. E. Spiess, R. A. Boisvert, and J. Boudreau. 2008. What's the Point: Model Forms and Attributes of Paleoindian Bifaces in the New England-Maritimes Region. *Archaeology of Eastern North America* 36:119–172.

Daniel, I. R. 1998. *Hardaway Revisited: Early Archaic Settlement in the Southeast*. University of Alabama, Tuscaloosa.

DeJarnette, D. L., E. Kurjack, and J. Cambron. 1962. Excavations at the Stanfield-Worley Bluff Shelter. *Journal of Alabama Archaeology* 8(1–2):1–124.

Deller, D. B., C. J. Ellis, and J. R. Keron. 2009. Understanding Cache Variability: A Deliberately Burned Early Paleoindian Tool Assemblage from the Crowfield Site, Southeastern Ontario. *American Antiquity* 74:371–397.

Dunbar, J. S., and C. A. Hemmings. 2004. Florida Paleoindian Points and Knives. In *New Perspectives on the First Americans*, edited by B. T. Lepper and R. Bonnichsen, pp. 65–72. Center for the Study of the First Americans, Texas A&M University Press, College Station.

Ellis, C. J., and D. B. Deller. 1997. Variability in the Archaeological Record of Northeastern Early Paleoindians: A View from Southern Ontario. *Archaeology of Eastern North America* 25:1–30.

Fiedel, S. J. 1999. Older Than We Thought: Implications of Corrected Dates for Paleoindians. *American Antiquity* 64:95–116.

Gardner, W. M. 1989. An Examination of Cultural Change in the Late Pleistocene and Early Holocene (circa 9200 to 6800 B.C.). Special Publication 19, *Paleoindian Research in Virginia: A Synthesis*, edited by J. M. Wittkofski and T. R. Reinhart, pp. 5–51. Archeological Society of Virginia, Richmond.

Goodyear, A. C. 1974. *The Brand Site: A Techno-Functional Study of a Dalton Site in Northeast Arkansas*. Research Series 7, Arkansas Archaeological Survey, Fayetteville.

———. 1979. *A Hypothesis for the Use of Cryptocrystalline Raw Materials Among Paleoindian Groups of North America*. Research Manuscript Series 156, South Carolina Institute of Archaeology and Anthropology. University of South Carolina, Columbia.

———. 1999. The Early Holocene Occupation of the Southeastern United States: A Geoarchaeological Summary. In *Ice Age Peoples of North America*, edited by R. Bonnichsen and K. Turnmire, pp. 432–481. Center for the Study of the First Americans, Corvallis, OR.

———. 2005. Evidence for Pre-Clovis Sites in the Eastern United States. In *Paleoamerican Origins: Beyond Clovis*, edited by R. Bonnichsen, B. T. Lepper, D. Stanford, and M. R. Waters, pp. 103–112. Center for the Study of the First Americans, Texas A&M University Press, College Station.

———. 2010. Instrument-Assisted Fluting as a Technochronological Marker Among North American Paleoindian Points. *Current Research in the Pleistocene* 27:86–88.

Grayson, D. K., and D. J. Meltzer. 2002. Clovis Hunting and Large Mammal Extinction: A Critical Review of the Evidence. *Journal of World Prehistory* 16:313–359.

Haynes, G. 2002. *The Early Settlement of North America: The Clovis Era*. Cambridge University Press, Cambridge.

Hemmings, C. A., J. S. Dunbar, and S. D. Webb. 2004. Florida's Early-Paleoindian Bone and Ivory Tools. In *New Perspectives on the First Americans*, edited by B. T. Lepper and R. Bonnichsen, pp. 87–92. Center for the Study of the First Americans, Texas A&M University Press, College Station.

Hollenbach, K. D. 2009. *Foraging in the Tennessee River Valley 12,500 to 8,000 Years Ago*. University of Alabama Press, Tuscaloosa.

Hughen, K. A., J. R. Southon, S. J. Lehman, and J. T. Overpeck. 2000. Synchronous Radiocarbon and Climate Shifts During the Last Deglaciation. *Science* 290: 1951–1954.

Johnson, L., Jr. 1989. *Great Plains Interlopers in the Eastern Woodlands During Late Paleoindian Times.* Report 36. Office of the State Archaeologist, Texas Historical Commission, Austin.

Kelly, R. L., and L. C. Todd. 1988. Coming into the Country: Early Paleoindian Hunting and Mobility. *American Antiquity* 53(2):231–244.

Kilby, J. D. 2008. *An Investigation of Clovis Caches: Content, Function, and Technological Organization.* Doctoral dissertation, Department of Anthropology, University of New Mexico, Albuquerque.

Lepper, B. T., and R. E. Funk. 2006. Paleo-Indian: East. In *Handbook of North American Indians*, vol. 3, *Environment, Origins, and Population*, edited by D. H. Ubelaker, pp. 171–193. Smithsonian Institution, Washington, DC.

McAvoy, J. M., and L. D. McAvoy. 1997. *Archaeological Investigations of Site 44SX202, Cactus Hill, Sussex County, Virginia.* Virginia Department of Historic Resources, Research Report Series No. 8, Richmond.

Meltzer, D. J. 2002. What Do You Do When No One's Been There Before? Thoughts on the Exploration and Colonization of New Lands. Memoir of the California Academy of Sciences 27, In *The First Americans: The Pleistocene Colonization of the New World*, edited by N. G. Jablonski, pp. 27–58. California Academy of Sciences, San Francisco.

———. 2009. *First Peoples in a New World: Colonizing Ice Age America.* University of California Press, Berkeley.

Morse, D. F. 1997. *Sloan: A Paleoindian Dalton Cemetery in Arkansas.* Smithsonian Institution, Washington, DC.

Overstreet, D. F. 2005. Late-Glacial Ice-Marginal Adaptation in Southeastern Wisconsin. In *Paleoamerican Origins: Beyond Clovis*, edited by R. Bonnichsen, B. T. Lepper, D. Stanford, and M. R. Waters, pp. 183–195. Center for the Study of the First Americans, Texas A&M University Press, College Station.

Robinson, B. S., J. C. Ort, W. A. Eldridge, A. L. Burke, and B. G. Pelletier. 2009. Paleoindian Aggregation and Social Context at Bull Brook. *American Antiquity* 74:424–447.

Sassaman, K. E. 2005. Structure and Practice in the Archaic Southeast. In *North American Archaeology*, edited by T. R. Pauketat and D. DiPaolo Loren, pp. 79–107. Blackwell, Malden, MA.

Stanford, D. J., and B. Bradley. 2002. Ocean Trails and Prairie Paths? Thoughts About Clovis Origins. In Memoir of the California Academy of Sciences 27, *The First Americans: The Pleistocene Colonization of the New World*, edited by N. G. Jablonski, pp. 255–271. California Academy of Sciences, San Francisco.

Straus, L. G., D. J. Meltzer, and T. Goebel. 2005. Ice Age Atlantis: Exploring the Solutrean-Clovis "Connection." *World Archaeology* 37:507–532.

Surovell, T. A. 2000. Early Paleoindian Women, Children, Mobility, and Fertility. *American Antiquity* 65:493–509.

Walker, R. B. 2007. Hunting in the Late Paleoindian Period: Faunal Remains from Dust Cave. In *Foragers of the Terminal Pleistocene in North America*, edited by R. B. Walker and B. N. Driskell, pp. 99–115. University of Nebraska Press, Lincoln.

———, and B. N. Driskell (editors). 2007. *Foragers of the Terminal Pleistocene in North America.* University of Nebraska Press, Lincoln.

Walthall, J. A. 1998. Rockshelters and Hunter-Gatherer Adaptation to the Pleistocene/Holocene Transition. *American Antiquity* 63:223–238.

———, and B. Koldehoff. 1998. Hunter-Gatherer Interaction and Alliance Formation: Dalton and the Cult of the Long Blade. *Plains Anthropologist* 43:257–273.

Waters, M. R., and T. W. Stafford, Jr. 2007. Redefining the Age of Clovis: Implications for the Peopling of the Americas. *Science* 315:1122–1126.

Webb, S. D. 2006. *First Floridians and Last Mastodons: The Page Ladson Site in the Aucilla River.* Springer, Dordrecht, Netherlands.

———, J. T. Milanich, R. Alexon, and J. S. Dunbar. 1984. A *Bison antiquus* Kill Site, Wacissa River, Jefferson County, Florida. *American Antiquity* 49:384–392.

SECTION III

ARCHAEOLOGICAL HISTORIES AND CULTURAL PROCESSES

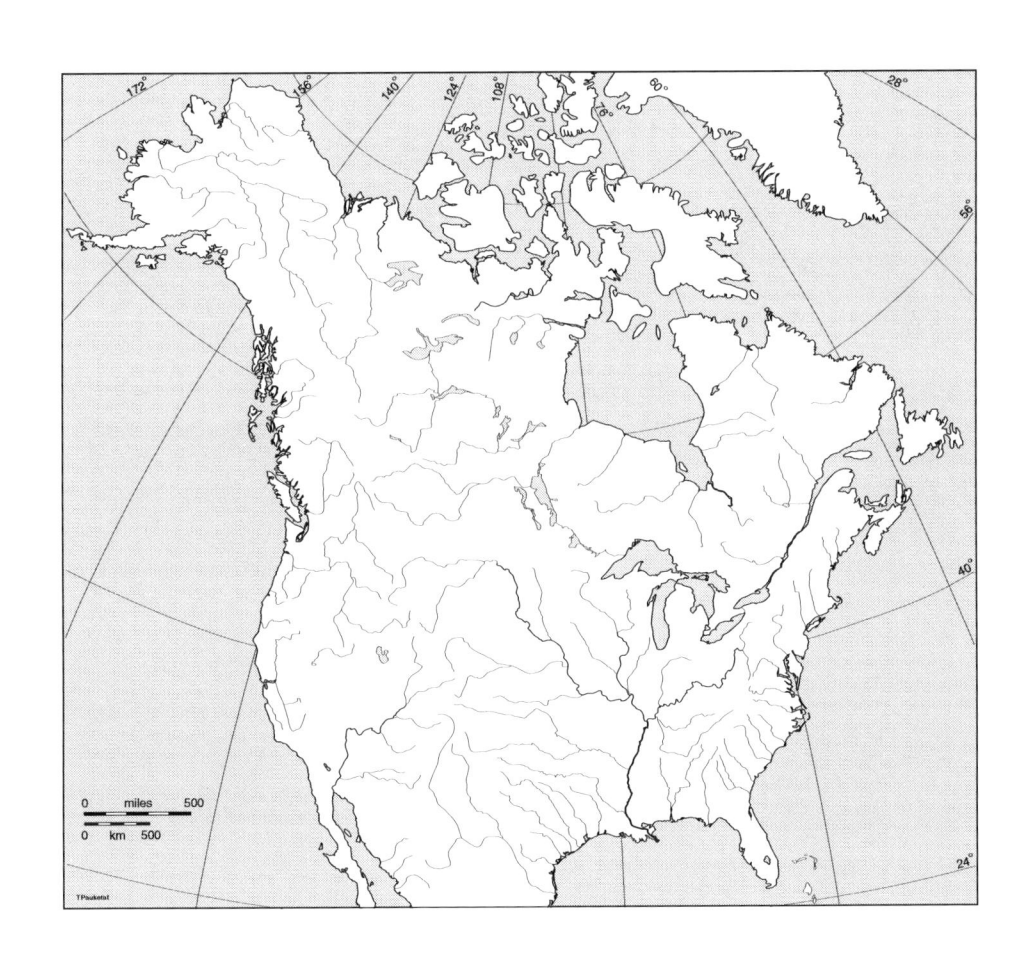

I. Arctic and Subarctic

CHAPTER 10

ADAPTING TO A FROZEN COASTAL ENVIRONMENT

ROBERT W. PARK

In the Arctic, people experience some of the profoundest seasonal changes anywhere on earth: the temperature and amount of daylight differ tremendously between summer and winter, the nature and extent of the usable landscape varies enormously with the annual formation and dissolution of the sea ice, and the composition and abundance of the fauna changes dramatically due to most species' annual migrations. Moreover, because the sea ice environment melts every summer, all direct traces of human use of that landscape are lost annually. Therefore, to a greater extent than in most archaeological situations, our understanding of the history of human use of the sea ice part of the coastal environment must be inferential.

Environmental and Ethnographic Background

The Arctic lies beyond the treeline, the northern limit of continuous forest (Figure 10.1). It is characterized by tundra, which is associated with permafrost: subsurface deposits that remain frozen year-round. Above the permafrost only a thin "active layer" at the surface of the ground thaws every summer. The amount and nature of tundra vegetation varies, but little of it is edible by humans, apart from some berry species. Important terrestrial resources include large land mammals, which provide food, skins for clothing and shelter, and raw materials such as bone, antler, and sinew for manufacture of implements. The most important large land mammal species is caribou, although musk ox is significant in some regions.

The sea forms an important part of the Arctic environment. However, Arctic seas are ice-free for only a relatively small portion of the year. For the rest of the time, they are covered by a thick layer of ice that is recreated annually sometime during the early autumn and then disappears sometime during the summer. Within the channels separating the islands of the Canadian Arctic Archipelago, the sea freezes in almost unbroken expanses. On coasts facing the open ocean, a wide strip of "landfast" ice forms during the winter. The edge of the landfast ice, where it meets the open ocean, is known as the floe edge. The sea ice is an extremely dynamic environment, broken by leads (linear stretches of open water that are created when cracks in the ice are forced open by wind or currents) and polynyas (local patches of permanently or semipermanently open water that are kept that way by fast-moving currents).

For the indigenous people of the Arctic, sea mammals furnished food and skins, but they were vital in the wood-poor regions because they also permitted heating and cooking with fuel in the form of blubber. Important sea mammal species included ringed, harp, harbor, and bearded seals; sea lions; walrus; and narwhal, beluga, and bowhead whales. Ringed seals were especially important in many regions because they are nonmigratory and thus available year round; the other species are migratory to varying degrees and therefore less available or unavailable during the winter.

At the time of European Contact, Inuit adaptations to Arctic coastal landscapes were both complex and diverse. The capsule ethnographic sketch given here most closely reflects the traditional annual round of the Central Inuit of the Canadian Arctic.

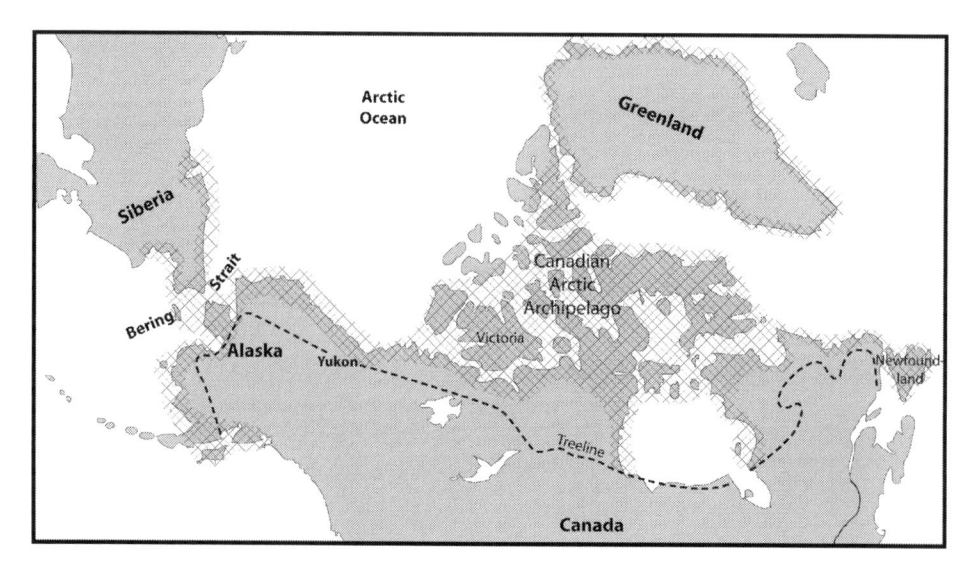

Figure 10.1 Map showing locations mentioned in the text (cross-hatched area encompasses the regions occupied by prehistoric Arctic populations).

Starting at the time the sea ice broke up, many groups would be camping in sites along the coast, hunting seals or fishing from the remaining ice edge or from the shore, or using skin boats to hunt sea mammals. Later in the summer and into the autumn, some people would move inland to hunt caribou. At that time, people would also use weirs to obtain fish such as Arctic char as they returned from the ocean to overwinter in lakes. By early winter, everyone would have returned to the coast to await the sea ice becoming strong enough for travel. In regions where the floe edge was not too distant, people might continue to camp at the coast throughout the winter, traveling to the floe edge for hunting. In regions where the ocean froze completely, they had to rely on hunting ringed seals at their breathing holes. This necessitated moving out onto the sea ice and living in snow houses, moving camp every 10 days to two weeks throughout the winter as the majority of the seals in the immediate vicinity of each campsite were killed. By the early summer, the snow on the ice was melting and the ringed seals emerged from their breathing holes to bask on the ice, where they could be hunted. As the time of breakup approached, groups that were camped out on the sea ice would move to locations on the coast, to begin the cycle again.

Variations from this ethnographic sketch were great, but the pattern of exploiting the resources of both the land and the sea was a common theme in most societies. Understanding the origins of that pattern is one of the main goals of Arctic archaeology.

Archaeological Sequence

The summary given here of the archaeological sequence (also presented schematically in Figure 10.2) draws heavily on the major summaries in Dumond (1987, 2000), Maxwell (1985), and McGhee (1996). The earliest sites in the North American Arctic following the drowning of Beringia are collectively assigned to the "Paleo-Arctic tradition" and date to approximately 11000 to 8500 BP. These sites are found in the unglaciated parts of Alaska and Yukon. Most interpretations emphasize the similarities between the Paleo-Arctic tradition and earlier cultural manifestations of the Asian Upper Paleolithic, suggesting cultural continuity from them. However, on chronological and stylistic grounds it is unclear whether there is also cultural continuity from the Paleo-Arctic to later cultures in the North American Arctic. It is followed in Alaska by the "Northern Archaic tradition," which is known from 6000 to 4000 BP. Stylistic similarities suggest that it has a very close connection to the other "Archaic" populations found throughout much of North America, so the Northern Archaic probably represents a northward expansion of those populations to occupy the expanding Boreal forests of the interior. Thus the Northern Archaic peoples do not appear to be related culturally or biologically to the later coastal populations of these regions.

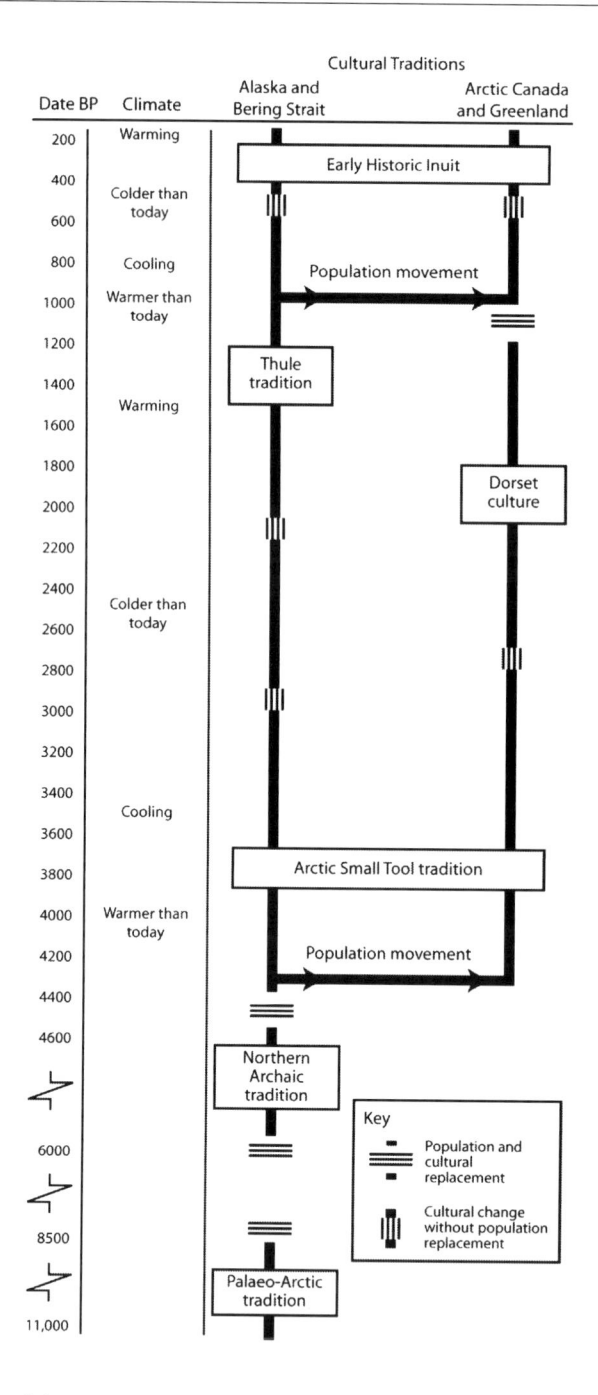

Figure 10.2 Diagram summarizing the culture history of the North American Arctic.

The "Arctic Small Tool tradition" is the collective name given to a distinctive group of cultures that date from approximately 4300 to 2700 BP and that are found from Western Alaska all the way to Greenland. The earliest sites are found in Alaska, and the tradition's later widespread distribution appears to have resulted from one of the most geographically dramatic population expansions in recent human history: the initial colonization of the Canadian Arctic and Greenland. On the basis of results from radiocarbon dating, one can project that their expansion from Alaska all the way to northern Greenland was extremely rapid, taking no more than a few centuries.

In Arctic Canada and Greenland, the way of life and technology of the descendants of the Arctic Small Tool tradition had become sufficiently transformed by 2700 BP that archaeologists give them a new name: Dorset culture. Dorset sites are found from Victoria Island in the west to Greenland in the northeast and to Newfoundland in the southeast. Dorset culture persisted until at least 1200 BP, but at around that time Dorset populations appear to have undergone a dramatic decline; by 1000 BP they had completely disappeared from most parts of their Arctic homeland.

During the centuries when cultures of the Arctic Small Tool tradition and then the Dorset culture flourished in Arctic Canada and Greenland, cultural developments among the Arctic Small Tool tradition descendants living on the Siberian and Alaskan sides of the Bering Strait eventually led to the emergence of what is known as the "Thule tradition," approximately 2100 BP. The cultures of this tradition developed a new form of economic and social adaptation that centered on open-water hunting of large sea mammals from skin boats, in particular the largest of the Arctic whales, bowheads, which can reach 20 meters in length. Sometime between 1100 and 800 BP (there is currently disagreement as to the precise date), small groups of Thule pioneers appear to have begun moving eastward from Alaska into the Canadian Arctic and Greenland and colonizing that entire region (Figure 10.3).

The exact degree and nature of interaction between the earliest Thule immigrants and the last of the Dorset is not clear. Most or perhaps all of the Dorset likely had disappeared prior to the arrival of the Thule. At any rate, from Alaska to Greenland the diverse Inuit groups who greeted Europeans when the latter eventually entered those regions appear to have been the direct biological and cultural descendants of the Thule people (Park 1993, 2008).

The Development of a Frozen Coast Adaptation

Neither the date nor the precise nature of the earliest adaptation to a frozen coast environment is yet completely understood, in part because the evidence for ancient human use of the sea ice melts away annually. However, it seems probable that the earliest populations inhabiting the North American Arctic had a primarily inland

Figure 10.3 Thule tradition semisubterranean winter house in the Canadian High Arctic, gridded for excavation (the bowhead whale bones are the remains of the roof framework).

adaptation and took a considerable length of time to develop the knowledge and skills needed to exploit the frozen coastal environment year-round. Five components together make up the complete adaptation to this environment, and their identification in the archaeological record forms the basis of this analysis: (1) inhabiting Arctic coastal areas; (2) hunting small sea mammals; (3) hunting large sea mammals in the open water, especially from boats; (4) hunting seals at their breathing holes; and (5) living out on the sea ice.

Inhabiting Coastal Areas

All known Paleo-Arctic sites would have been located far inland from contemporary coastlines and so represent terrestrial, noncoastal adaptations. The earliest good evidence for the habitation of a frozen coast environment comes from the Arctic Small Tool tradition, whose earliest sites are found in both interior and coastal parts of western and northwestern Alaska. The houses at the interior sites are substantial semisubterranean structures that are interpreted as winter dwellings. They contrast with the light tent rings of coastal sites, which, judging from the limited organic artifactual and faunal data, are interpreted as having been occupied only during the spring or summer. Thus it seems possible that the tradition's use of the coast was not year-round, but only seasonal (Anderson 1984; Dumond 1987; Giddings 1967).

However, the earliest Arctic Small Tool tradition sites in the Canadian Arctic and Greenland tend all to be located on or near the coast; there is no evidence for winter occupation sites inland. This may be because, in contrast to the situation in western and northern Alaska, in the Canadian Arctic Archipelago the inland areas are not game-rich and there was no incentive to retreat from the coast in the winter. But a winter focus on terrestrial rather than marine species is still evident in the earliest Arctic Small Tool tradition sites in the Eastern Arctic, and current interpretations suggest that these populations survived through the winter largely on stored musk ox meat (Maxwell 1985; McGhee 1996).

Hunting Sea Mammals

The primary benefit of inhabiting coastal areas would have been to take advantage of marine resources, especially small sea mammals. Apart from their bones, archaeologically visible evidence for the hunting of sea mammals comes primarily from the initial appearance of harpoon parts, which are good evidence of open-water hunting, at least from shore or from the floe edge, or as the animals basked at their breathing holes in the late spring and early summer. Harpoon heads are known from the very earliest archaeological sites of the Arctic Small Tool tradition in the Canadian Arctic and Greenland, and the faunal remains from some sites include sea mammals. Organic preservation at Arctic Small Tool sites in Alaska is generally poor, so harpoon parts do not survive; but undoubtedly they were in use there too. Harpoon heads of a wide variety of styles (Figure 10.4a–f, h–k), along with other harpoon parts, are extremely common finds from all subsequent cultures inhabiting the frozen coast regions of Arctic North America and Greenland (Dumond 1987; Park and Stenton 1998).

Hunting Sea Mammals from Boats

Hunting sea mammals from boats, especially larger sea mammals such as whales, requires both boats and additional technology beyond harpoons. There are of course the boats themselves, but the simple transference of shore- or floe-edge-based harpooning to a boat presents a problem because the sudden pull on the line of the harpooned and panicking animal might damage or overturn the fragile boat. To solve this problem, the hunter, instead of holding on to the line or attaching it to the boat, attaches it to a separate "drag float" made from an inflated sealskin. Towing the drag float tires the animal and prevents it from escaping the pursuing hunter. Drag floats themselves almost never survive in identifiable form in the archaeological record, but small bone or ivory nozzles sewn into the floats to facilitate inflating them do survive. These drag float inflator nozzles are very distinctive, and their appearance in the archaeological record is thought to mark the advent of open-water hunting of larger sea mammals from boats.

 A very few finds from Greenland and elsewhere do make it clear that the peoples of the Arctic Small Tool tradition possessed small boats (Grønnow 1994; Maxwell 1985). However, it is not clear how important boat-based hunting was in their

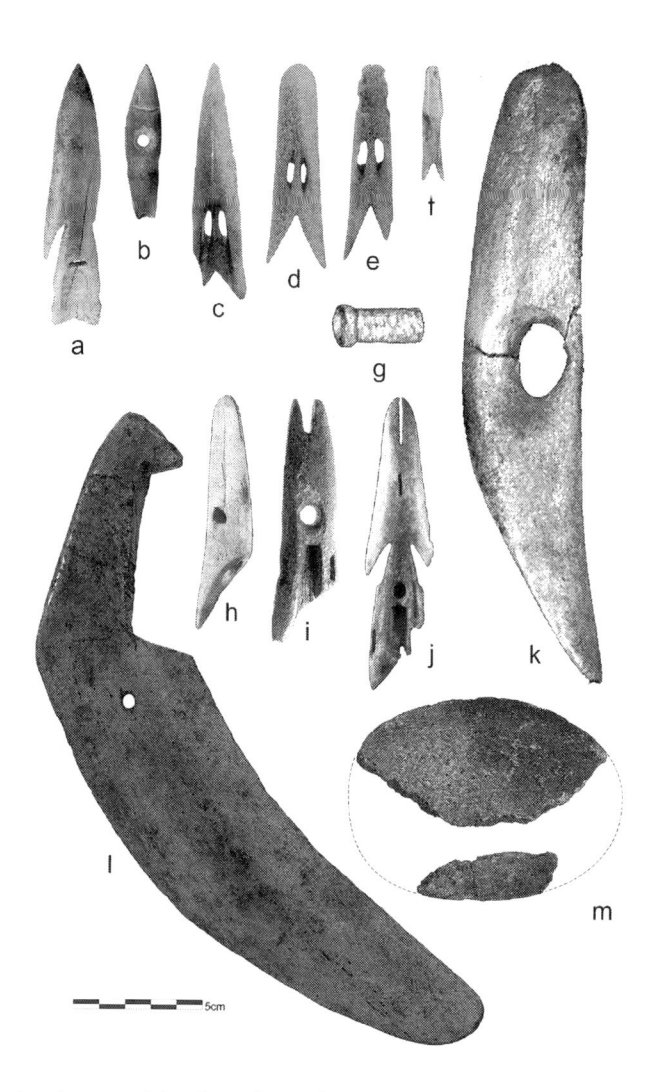

Figure 10.4 Arctic material culture from the Canadian Arctic: (a–b) Arctic Small Tool tradition harpoon heads; (c–f) Dorset culture harpoon heads; (g) Thule tradition drag float inflator nozzle; (h–j) Thule tradition harpoon heads; (k) Thule tradition whaling harpoon head; (l) Thule tradition snow knife; (m) fragments of an Arctic Small Tool tradition stone lamp.

economy. In at least one region, it has been observed that their sites are concentrated in areas where sea ice would have formed relatively early in the autumn and broken up relatively late in the summer, which contrasts with the site distribution of later cultures known to have relied heavily on hunting from boats (McGhee 1979, 1981). This may indicate that pedestrian hunting of seals at the floe edge or basking on the ice was more important than hunting sea mammals from boats, and that during the season when the ocean was free of ice the people lived inland, hunting terrestrial species or fishing. Similarly, there is no evidence that the Dorset people made extensive use of skin boats; in fact, there is reason to believe that pedestrian hunting on the sea ice was even more important for them than for their predecessors of the Arctic Small Tool tradition. It is in the cultures of the Thule tradition that we first see the appearance of drag float inflator nozzles (Figure 10.4g) and abundant faunal remains from large whales, showing that the technology necessary for hunting very large sea mammals had been perfected (Dumond 1987).

Breathing-Hole Sealing

Hunting ringed seals at their breathing holes requires even more complex technology. In many areas, the breathing holes are covered in snow and practically invisible, so dogs were used to locate them by scent. The air hole itself is too small for the hunter to see when a seal has arrived, so the solution to this problem, especially with snow-covered breathing holes, is to use some sort of indicator that informs the hunter when the seal is rising in the hole. Ethnographically, indicators could take the form of a piece of down, fluttering as air was expelled from the breathing hole by the rising seal; or a long and thin bone pin whose bottom end rests on the thin layer of ice that forms on the water's surface within the breathing hole, while its top end protrudes from the hole. When the seal rose in the breathing hole the ice would shift and then break, causing the pin to move up and down.

Both indicator types alerted the hunter to the arrival of a seal, at which he would plunge his harpoon down into the center of the breathing hole in order to harpoon it (Balikci 1970). Unfortunately, both indicators are unlikely to survive archaeologically in a form that would be recognizable. In the absence of unambiguously diagnostic artifactual evidence for breathing-hole sealing, archaeologists are often forced to draw on more inferential arguments. The time of year in which a seal was killed can be determined from the analysis of thin sections of its teeth. If midwinter-killed seals are found at an archaeological site located distant from areas where there was likely open water at that time of year, such as the floe edge, then the likelihood of open-water hunting techniques being used at that location would have been low and breathing-hole sealing can be inferred.

As noted above, in Alaska the coastal sites of the Arctic Small Tool tradition peoples are presumed to have been occupied during the spring or summer only, so on this basis one concludes they probably did not practice breathing-hole sealing. Early sites of the Arctic Small Tool tradition in the High Arctic that are believed to have been occupied during the winter are located near the coast, but the faunal remains suggest that stored food was the core of the midwinter diet. There is somewhat more reason to infer that the Dorset culture practiced breathing-hole sealing, largely from evidence suggesting that using the sea ice environment was an extremely important activity for them. However, the Dorset appear to have lacked one important part of the technology that was an important feature of breathing-hole sealing as practiced in historic times in areas where the ocean freezes completely and the breathing holes become snow-covered: dogs. If breathing-hole sealing in such regions was important for the Dorset, then they must have had some other means of locating the breathing holes beneath the snow.

It is assumed that the Thule people in the Canadian Arctic and Greenland practiced breathing-hole sealing in midwinter as a supplement to the stored food they had accumulated during the open water season, because some sites located far from the floe edge contain winter-killed seals. However, opinion varies on when and how the Thule developed the technique. Some archaeologists have speculated that they learned it from encounters with the Dorset, but even setting aside the chronological problems with this scenario, it seems improbable.

The one aspect of hunting ringed seals at their breathing holes with which the Thule arriving from Alaska might have been unfamiliar—locating breathing holes beneath snow-covered expanses of ice—was something their descendants would do with dogs. Since the Dorset didn't have dogs, it is difficult to imagine the Thule learning the technique from them. Instead, it is likely that the Thule simply elaborated on a hunting technique with which they had already become familiar back in Alaska (Park 1993).

Living on the Sea Ice

The most demanding component of adaptation to the frozen coastal environment in the winter is the ability to actually live out on the sea ice for extended periods of time. In addition to the technology required for breathing-hole sealing, two additional items of technology would seem to be necessary: snow houses (igloos), and lamps. Snow houses and campsites on the sea ice obviously do not survive archaeologically, but one diagnostic implement necessary to construct a snow house does: the snow knife. Snow knives were used to cut the blocks of snow, and their appearance in the archaeological record shows that snow houses were being used. Lamps are perhaps the most important item of technology necessary for living in snow houses because they use a fuel resource that was available out on the sea ice—blubber from seals—and allow very fine control of the amount of heat generated.

No snow knives have been identified from Arctic Small Tool tradition sites, and lamps are infrequent finds (Figure 10.4m). One conclusion that can be drawn from these facts is that snow houses either were not used or were used quite rarely. Stone lamps do become more common in the Dorset culture along with the very first snow knives, consistent with at least occasional use of snow houses (Maxwell 1985).

Despite their demonstrated ability to accumulate large quantities of meat and blubber prior to the winter by hunting large sea mammals on the open ocean, the Thule appear to have made extensive use of the sea ice environment. Evidence for this comes from common occurrence in Thule archaeological assemblages of snow knives and lamps (Figure 10.4l). Seal bones from winter and spring-killed seals are also evidence that the Thule made extensive use of the sea ice environment, despite living in their large winter houses on the coast for much or all of the winter (Park 1999).

Conclusion

Possession of such skills by the Thule clearly set the stage for their Inuit descendants in the central part of the Canadian Arctic. These descendants adopted a settlement pattern that involved spending almost the entire winter out on the sea ice. During that time, they relied almost exclusively on breathing-hole sealing. Through increasingly complex technology, these ancestors of the Inuit developed a successful adaptation to frozen coastal regions, reliably exploiting the resources of this complex and dynamic environment.

References

Anderson, D. D. 1984. Prehistory of North Alaska. In *Handbook of North American Indians*, vol. 5, *Arctic*, edited by D. Damas, pp. 80–93. Smithsonian Institution, Washington, DC.

Balikci, A. 1970. *The Netsilik Eskimo*. Natural History Press, Garden City.

Dumond, D. E. 1987. *The Eskimos and Aleuts*. 2nd ed. Thames and Hudson, London.

———. 2000. The Norton Tradition. *Arctic Anthropology* 37(2):1–22.

Giddings, J. L. 1967. *Ancient Men of the Arctic*. Knopf, New York.

Grønnow, B. 1994. Qeqertasussuk—The Archaeology of a Frozen Saqqaq Site in Disko Bugt, West Greenland. In Mercury Series Paper 149, *Threads of Arctic Prehistory: Papers in Honour of William E. Taylor, Jr.*, edited by D. A. Morrison and J.-L. Pilon, pp. 197–238. Canadian Museum of Civilization, Archaeological Survey of Canada, Hull.

Maxwell, M. S. 1985. *Prehistory of the Eastern Arctic*. Academic Press, Orlando.

McGhee, R. 1979. *The Paleoeskimo Occupations at Port Refuge, High Arctic Canada*. Mercury Series Paper 92. Canadian Museum of Civilization, Archaeological Survey of Canada, Ottawa.

———. 1981. *The Dorset Occupations in the Vicinity of Port Refuge, High Arctic Canada*. Mercury Series Paper 105. Canadian Museum of Civilization, Archaeological Survey of Canada, Ottawa.

———. 1996. *Ancient People of the Arctic*. UBC Press, Vancouver.

Park, R. W. 1993. The Dorset-Thule Succession in Arctic North America: Assessing Claims for Culture Contact. *American Antiquity* 58(2):203–234.

———. 1999. Seal Use and Storage in the Thule Culture of Arctic North America. *Revista de Arqueología Americana /Journal of American Archaeology /Revue d'Archéologie Américaine* 16:77–97.

———. 2008. Contact Between the Norse Vikings and the Dorset Culture in Arctic Canada. *Antiquity* 82:189–198.

Park, R. W., and D. R. Stenton. 1998. *Ancient Harpoon Heads of Nunavut: An Illustrated Guide*. Parks Canada, Department of Canadian Heritage, Government of Canada, Pangnirtung.

CHAPTER 11

RETHINKING EASTERN SUBARCTIC HISTORY

DONALD H. HOLLY, JR., AND MOIRA McCAFFREY

IF an area is perceived as marginal, it is often assumed that the history is too (Abel 1993:265). Such has been the general assessment of the rocky and sparsely forested country of the eastern Subarctic. For a long time, scholars projected a rather dismal reading of this landscape into the past, with the effect that history was imagined as a struggle for survival, but otherwise uneventful (Holly 2002). As a result, culture became adaptation and adaptation became history.

It is difficult to reconcile this perspective with the archaeological record as it is now understood. Over the past few decades, an increasingly rich and complex picture has emerged from archaeological research in subarctic Québec and Labrador, and on the island of Newfoundland. It suggests that history here—rather than being the simple culmination of an environmentally appropriate calculus—was willed and crafted by people who were responding to changing social relations and social phenomena. With this in mind, our brief sketch of eastern Subarctic history aims to highlight the dynamic nature of social interactions through time.

ARCHAIC PERIOD

Nine thousand years ago Amerindian peoples, otherwise known as American Indians, began to press north and east out of the Canadian Maritimes and northern New England, reaching the Strait of Belle Isle by 8000 BP, northern Labrador around 6500 BP, and the island of Newfoundland after 5000 BP (Figure 11.1). A maritime people at first, they stayed close to the shoreline, pursuing seals, walruses, and other coastal resources. The adjacent interior, with its wandering caribou and productive fishing sites, was not ignored but seems to have been visited seasonally at first. Because of their coastal focus, it was proposed that these people belonged to what has come to be called the Maritime Archaic Tradition (Tuck 1976).

In the coastal mountains of northern Labrador, Maritime Archaic groups discovered the source of Ramah chert, a distinctive translucent stone. It would prove to be a significant event in eastern Subarctic history. The stone would soon become the preferred raw material for fashioning tools and social relations over a vast area (Loring 2002).

The earliest dwellings of the Maritime Archaic people consisted of small pit houses and oval and rectangular structures, but over time the size of their dwellings increased, as did their aspirations. By 4500 BP they were extracting Ramah chert for groups living far to the south and inhabiting long, linearly arranged tent structures or longhouses. Most longhouses average 50 meters in length, but some are nearly twice that size and may have housed close to 100 people each (Hood 1995). The appearance of these structures may signal the emergence of competitive corporate groups with a stake in social and lithic exchange networks that stretched all the way to New England. Presumably, successful groups were those able to organize and

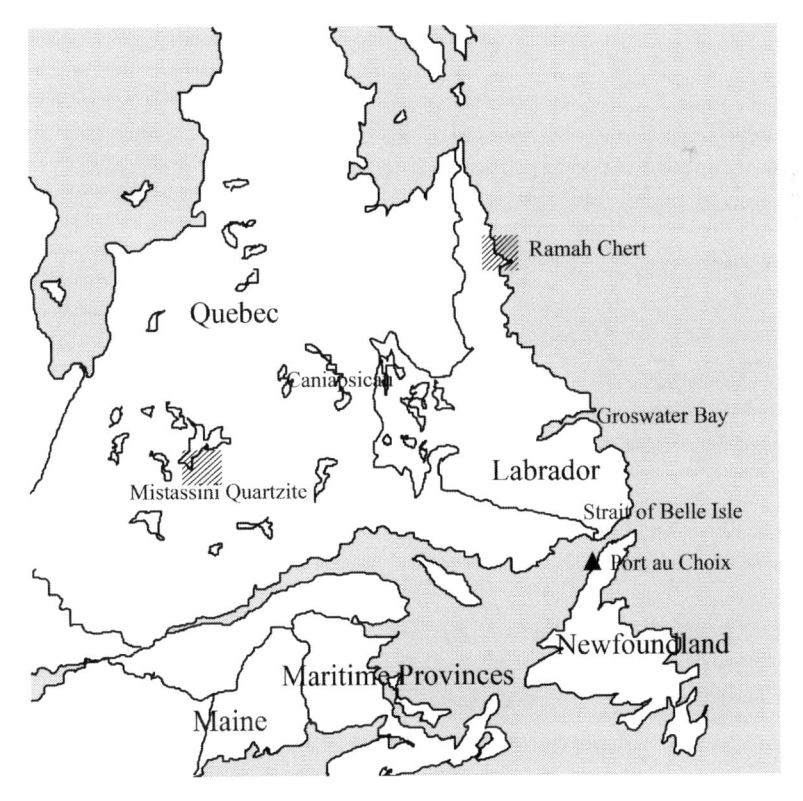

Figure 11.1 Map of the eastern Subarctic.

engage in long-distance expeditions for Ramah chert, and cultivate trading relationships with far-flung partners (Fitzhugh 2006:64).

Perhaps not coincidentally, formal cemeteries appear after 4500 BP. The best known of these, at Port au Choix on the island of Newfoundland, contained the remains of more than 100 people, interred with an elaborate array of bone tools and charms, including great auk bills and animal effigies, as well as ground stone adzes and bayonets (Tuck 1976). Such cemeteries may have served as monuments to corporate groups (Fitzhugh 2006:62; Hood 1995:97), while the individuals buried within them indicate that social ties often dovetailed with the exchange networks in which they were invested. Mitochondrial DNA analysis has shown, for example, that the females interred at Port au Choix were not indigenous to the area (Jelsma 2006) but may have been incorporated into the local group to solidify social and economic ties with others.

Social networks in the Late Archaic (4200–3500 BP) were extensive. Throughout the Far Northeast people shared a proclivity for particular social and ceremonial practices (cf. Chapdelaine, this volume). They covered their dead with red ochre and interred them in cemeteries with exquisitely crafted stone artifacts, animal remains, and zoomorphic objects; and they exchanged raw materials over incredible distances. In this way, social interactions appear to have played a pivotal role in the formation of Late Archaic societies. But if social relations helped constitute such societies, they may also account for their transformation and demise.

Around 4000 BP, Paleoeskimos, peoples who entered the North American Arctic from eastern Siberia prior to the migration of modern Inuit-related groups, start to trickle south into northern Labrador. At about the same time (3800 BP), ideas, and probably people, representing the Susquehanna tradition begin to penetrate north into Maine and the Maritimes. Both encounters likely undermined the tenor of traditional networks and relations across the region and, together with environmental changes and perhaps even epidemics, contributed to cultural collapse in some areas. In northern Labrador, for instance, the arrival of Paleoeskimo peoples appears to have played a part in the erosion of Maritime Archaic societies by 3500 BP (Hood 2008:319–346). Likewise, the Susquehanna advance seems to have precipitated the decline of Archaic societies in Maine and the Maritimes (Sanger 2006:241–244). But nowhere did the Archaic end more abruptly than on the island of Newfoundland, which was completely abandoned by 3200 BP.

Increased activity in the interior of Québec and Labrador may also have undermined traditional social relations. The oldest sites in the far interior date to between 5000 and 3500 BP (David Denton, personal communication 2009; McCaffrey 2006; Rousseau 2007). In general, they are small, with assemblages that are dominated by locally available quartz. Nevertheless, numerous sites contain lithics from distant sources, including Ramah chert and Mistassini quartzite, a distinctive white stone from the boreal forest (Denton 1998). Some sites may represent interior incursions by Maritime Archaic groups from the Labrador and Québec coast; but others suggest affinities with both Laurentian and Maritime Archaic traditions (Denton 1988; McCaffrey 2006). These latter sites, along with the growing significance of interior raw materials, imply more frequent encounters between southern, eastern, and western peoples in the interior (McCaffrey 2006:177–179) and perhaps the ethnogenesis of interior groups. Plausibly, these developments could have led to formation of new social relations that weakened ties with groups to the east, and contributed to the decline of late Maritime Archaic societies on the Québec North Shore and Labrador coast.

Intermediate Period

The period that follows the Archaic is one of radical transformation, particularly for Amerindians; ground stone tools disappear, as do longhouses and cemeteries. Ceremonialism is muted, settlements are dispersed and amorphous, and once-vast social networks seem severed or curtailed. Accordingly, the overall impression of the Intermediate period (3500 to 2000 BP) is one of deflation from the previous era. Indeed, it is difficult to escape the conclusion that something quite dramatic happened at the end of the Archaic. Both on the coast and in the interior, the presence of Amerindians during the Intermediate period is ephemeral in many places and nonexistent in others. The island of Newfoundland is abandoned and remains unoccupied by Amerindian peoples throughout the Intermediate period, and there are significant gaps in the archaeological record on the mainland at this time (McCaffrey 2006:170–172; Nagel 1978:125).

Low visibility could merely suggest a highly mobile lifestyle, but the actual number of known sites declines sharply too. A similar trend has been documented in the Maritime Provinces (Sanger 2006:244) and throughout the Northeast. Fiedel (2001) posits a broad and rapid depopulation, with signs of an apocalypse indicated in a reduction in sites and artifact assemblages, the near invisibility of habitation sites, and the sharp contraction of exchange networks. He suggests environmental change may be to blame, with two severe cooling episodes serving to undermine traditional subsistence economies and cause population decline throughout the Northeast (Fiedel 2001).

Despite such evidence, some places retained a strong Amerindian presence, as in the Hamilton Inlet region of the central Labrador coast (Neilsen 2006). On the Québec Lower North Shore, numerous large sites have been identified, indicating that marine resources continued to play an important, if seasonal, role in the economy (Pintal 1998:70–84).

Lithic assemblages on Intermediate period sites generally reflect a local character; nevertheless, there is evidence for the penetration of ideas and materials from far to the west and south. Meadowood style cache blades, points and drills, made of Onondaga chert from Ontario or local materials, have been recovered from a number of sites. At Vincelotte Lake in northwestern Québec, archaeologists found a cache of Meadowood-type blades made of Nastapoka chert from the Hudson Bay coast (Figure 11.2). Dating to about 2700 BP, the blades had been burnt in what may have been a ceremonial event (Cérane 1995:371–378). This occurrence and other tantalizing indices hint at the formation of new social relations at a time of significant demographic, environmental, and social change.

Paleoeskimos appear to have fared better. During this time a new and successful complex emerges, called Groswater. Appearing first in Labrador around 3000 BP, the complex is soon all along the coast—from the Québec Lower North Shore to the island of Newfoundland. The success of Groswater groups may be due in part to their flexibility. They exploited a wide array of resource environments—including forays into the interior—and they were highly mobile and opportunistic. Yet by all indications, Intermediate peoples were flexible too. Accordingly, the key variable in the Paleoeskimos' success at this time may not have been adaptation but numbers. It is possible that Amerindian populations collapsed to the point that Paleoeskimos were able to prosper at their expense. This certainly seems to have been the case on the island of Newfoundland, where Groswater peoples pioneered an empty landscape marked only by the ruins of the Maritime Archaic. If Intermediate groups were as numerous as Paleoeskimos, it stands to reason that they would have laid claim to the island sometime during the previous 400 years, when it lay vacant, or in the subsequent 800 years, when Groswater peoples lived there; but they did not. Thus the overall impression is that Groswater Paleoeskimos dominated both demographically and geographically at this time, with Amerindians groups confined to the interior and pockets along the coast.

Figure 11.2 Cache of Meadowood-type blades dating to about 2700 BP, made of local Nastapoka chert, found near Vincelotte Lake in west-central Québec (photo by M. McCaffrey, courtesy of the Ministère de la Culture, des Communications et de la Condition féminine, Québec).

Of course, this begs the question of how Paleoeskimos managed to avoid the same fate as Amerindians. One possibility is that Paleoeskimos transmitted new, Asian-derived diseases to Amerindian populations (Fiedel 2001:125–128). Another is that these groups responded differently to changing environmental and social conditions. Hood (2008), for instance, attributes the relative success of Early Paleoeskimos over resident late Archaic populations in northern Labrador to the latter's rigid commitment to particular places, large-scale social aggregations, and long-distance exchange networks.

Recent Period

The past 2,000 years of Amerindian occupation in the eastern Subarctic, referred to as the Recent period or Late pre-Contact period, represents another era of significant social transformation. In northern Québec and Labrador, a case can be made for cultural continuity, but there is also some evidence to suggest the influx of new peoples into the eastern Subarctic from points south and west. On the island of Newfoundland, there is a clear break in Amerindian occupation (during the Intermediate period), followed by an episode of resettlement. From this period forward, archaeologists speak confidently of these peoples as the ancestors of today's Cree, Innu, and Naskapi, and in Newfoundland, the Beothuk.

A general Amerindian resurgence at this time may be attributed in part to the arrival of new groups and synergy from such interactions. Many linguists date the divergence of Proto-Algonquian languages to around 3000 BP in the Great Lakes region (Foster 1996:99–100) and posit that Eastern Algonquian speakers arrived in the greater Northeast sometime between 2500 BP and 1300 BP (Fiedel 1991). If correct, the arrival of Algonquian speakers in the eastern Subarctic would have occurred at a time—the end of the Intermediate period—when Amerindian population density was low and people were widely scattered across the landscape. There is also evidence to suggest that bow and arrow technology and ceramics appear at this time, two items associated with expansion of Proto-Algonquian speakers (Fiedel 1991).

Bow and arrow technology may date to the Archaic period, but recent analysis of projectile points indicates that it appeared on the island of Newfoundland just centuries prior to 1000 BP (Erwin et al. 2005). Given that nearby Québec and Labrador share a similar developmental sequence of projectile point styles, the technology may have been adopted throughout the entire region at this time. Ceramics appear somewhat earlier, around 1600 BP. On the Labrador coast, the Lower North Shore of Québec, and the island of Newfoundland, they are a rare and short-lived phenomenon (Hartery 2007; Pintal 1998). In the western half of northern Québec, however, pottery occurs with some regularity. These early ceramics resemble styles from southern Ontario, the St. Lawrence Valley, and the Maritimes. Later ceramics, which date from 500 BP to the Contact period, include Huron and Iroquois styles from south of the region (Cérane 1995:422–427).

In the vast interior of Labrador and Québec there is a marked increase in the number of sites, evidence for territorial expansion, and invigoration of long-distance lithic exchange networks after 2000 BP (McCaffrey 2011; McCaffrey and Dumais 1989; Figure 11.3). Similar processes are also evident on the coast, as indicated by resettlement of the island of Newfoundland by Amerindian peoples after a nearly 1,200 year hiatus, and the revival of long-distance Ramah exchange networks (Loring 1992; Stopp 2008).

Long-linear hearth features appear at this time too (Denton 1989:61–65), becoming common throughout the region by 1300 BP and widespread by 700 BP. Usually associated with *shaputuans*—elongated dwellings used by the Cree, Innu, and Naskapi—linear hearths may reflect the cooperation of multifamily groups who gathered to process and preserve meat, hides, fur, and bone. Some may also be the remains of *makushans*, ritual feasts to honor important animals such as caribou, beaver, and geese. But their appearance during an era of Amerindian expansion, technological innovation (Samson 1993:82), and social change cannot be coincidental; it suggests that they played an important role in these transformations.

Paleoeskimo societies also undergo significant change. On the Labrador coast, where Paleoeskimo peoples still dominated the landscape, a new tradition emerges after 2500 BP, through absorption or replacement of Groswater or in-situ development. These new Paleoeskimos are called the Dorset, and by 1900 BP they are entrenched along the coast of Labrador and establishing a presence on the island of Newfoundland, and to a lesser extent on the Québec Lower North Shore (Pintal 1994:145–146).

Figure 11.3 Sample of Recent period projectile points from the Mistassini region of west-central Québec; the lithic materials are predominantly Mistassini quartzite and Ramah chert (photo by M. McCaffrey, courtesy of D. Denton).

The Dorset way of life represents quite an elaboration from Groswater. Whereas Groswater sites suggest high mobility, a broad maritime focus, and flexibility, the Dorset seem content to settle in on the coast and focus on seals, resulting in large settlements that were occupied for long periods (see Park, this volume). The Dorset may have benefited from a cool and stable climate that ensured predictable access to harp seals over the course of several centuries (Renouf 1993), but the resurgence of Amerindians in the region may have also had a part to play in the constitution of Dorset lifeways. On the island of Newfoundland, for instance, Dorset subsistence intensification and aggregation may reflect an effort to survive on an increasingly crowded landscape and to ensure some measure of security in the face of a growing Amerindian presence (Holly 2005).

Whatever the case might be, it was unsuccessful. By 1000 BP the Dorset are all but gone on the island of Newfoundland—the victims of a warming trend that denied them access to harp seals (Bell and Renouf 2008; Renouf 1993) or of Amerindian peoples who limited their access to critical food resources and allies (Erwin et al. 2005:60–62). The Dorset retreat would continue north along the Labrador coast, where it would be accompanied by a near-feverish production of animal and anthropomorphic carvings. It must have been a desperate time. To the south, Amerindian groups were expanding into areas they formerly occupied (Renouf 2003), while to the north the Dorset faced an incursion of Thule peoples pressing south.

Contact Period and Conclusions

Beginning around 1400 AD the social landscape of the eastern Subarctic changed yet again. The Thule, ancestors of the contemporary Inuit, reached the northern coast of Labrador. As they continued south, the Dorset disappeared (Loring 1992:13–14). During the 16th century, the arrival of European fishing and whaling vessels along the Labrador and Newfoundland coast brought about further change. Lured onward by the prospects for trading and raiding, Thule groups were eventually able to exercise control over nearly the entire coast.

Amerindian groups were forced to make social and economic adjustments. The low archaeological visibility of Amerindian peoples on the Labrador coast and Lower North Shore during the early contact period suggests they turned toward the interior. Nevertheless, historic accounts indicate that these people continued to make occasional forays to the coast, and skirmishes with Europeans are recorded in oral traditions (Mailhot 1997:7). In the late 1530s, French and Spanish Basques began fishing and hunting whales in the Strait of Belle Isle and eventually along the North Shore of Québec. Their presence, combined with that of the Thule, ruptured a long-established pattern of interaction between Amerindian peoples on the mainland and the island of Newfoundland.

In the interior, some contact period sites are large and complex, suggesting aggregation locales involving many groups. At one such site in the Caniapsicau region of north-central Québec, an enormous *shaputuan* measuring 32 meters was found to contain lithic materials from across the eastern Subarctic, as well as pottery from the St. Lawrence Valley and European trade goods (Denton 1989:62). Introduced diseases and cultural dislocation would soon ensue, however. On the island of Newfoundland, the Beothuk would suffer the most. As a consequence of hostile relations with Europeans, they were compelled to retreat into the interior of the island, where they disappeared.

There is no doubt that the arrival of European peoples fundamentally changed the course of eastern Subarctic history, yet the process was not so different from earlier times. The archaeological record of the region suggests a complex history marked by both continuity and disruption, informed by the arrival, departure, and emergence of different "peoples," and shaped by changing social relations. As such, the European appetite for fish, furs, and souls (and the relations it spawned) may have parallels in the exchange of raw materials and adoption of new beliefs and ceremonial practices that date back to the Archaic. Likewise, the displacement and devastation wrought by Europeans was not an entirely a new phenomenon either, as is evident from the demise of earlier Archaic and Dorset societies. This is not to downplay the effects of European contact, so much as to suggest that the dichotomy between the ancient past and recent history is a false one. Eastern Subarctic history was never narrowly determined by nature or governed by mere necessity; it has always been crafted by the people who live there.

REFERENCES

Abel, K. 1993. *Drum Songs: Glimpses of Dene History*. McGill-Queen's University Press, Montreal.

Bell, T., and M. A. P. Renouf. 2008. The Domino Effect: Culture Change and Environmental Change in Newfoundland, 1500–1100 cal BP. *Northern Review* 28(Winter):72–94.

Cérane 1995. *Contribution à l'histoire des Cris de l'Est: la région de Laforge-1. Rapport synthèse*. 3 vols. Submitted to Société d'énergie de la Baie James, Montreal.

Denton, D. 1988. Long Term Land Use Patterns in the Caniapiscau Area, Nouveau-Québec. Occasional Publication 6, In *Boreal Forest and Sub-arctic Archaeology*, edited by C. S. "Paddy" Reid, pp. 146–156. London Chapter, Ontario Archaeological Society, London.

———. 1989. La période préhistorique récente dans la région de Caniapiscau. *Recherches amérindiennes au Québec* 19(2–3):59–75.

———. 1998. From the Source, to the Margins and Back: Notes on Mistassini Quartzite and Archaeology in the Area of the Colline Blanche. In *L'éveilleur et l'ambassadeur: Essais archéologiques et ethnohistoriques en hommage à Charles A. Martijn*, edited by R. Tremblay, pp. 17–32. Paléo-Québec 27, Recherches amérindiennes au Québec, Montreal.

Erwin, J. C., D. H. Holly, Jr., S. H. Hull, and T. L. Rast. 2005. Form and Function of Projectile Points and the Trajectory of Newfoundland Prehistory. *Canadian Journal of Archaeology* 29(1):46–67.

Fiedel, S. 1991. Correlating Archaeology and Linguistics: The Algonquian Case. *Man in the Northeast* 41(Spring):9–32.

———. 2001. What Happened in the Early Woodland? *Archaeology of Eastern North America* 29:101–142.

Fitzhugh, W. W. 2006. Settlement, Social and Ceremonial Change in the Labrador Maritime Archaic. In *The Archaic of the Far Northeast*, edited by David Sanger and M. A. P. Renouf, pp. 47–81. University of Maine Press, Orono.

Foster, M. K. 1996. Language and the Culture History of North America. In *Handbook of North American Indians*, vol. 17, *Languages*, edited by I. Goddard, pp. 64–116. Smithsonian Institution, Washington, DC.

Hartery, L. 2007. *The Cow Head Complex and the Recent Indian Period in Newfoundland, Labrador and the Québec Lower North Shore*. Occasional Papers in Northeastern Archaeology 17. Copetown Press, St. John's, NL.

Holly, D. H., Jr. 2002. Subarctic "Prehistory" in the Anthropological Imagination. *Arctic Anthropology* 39(1–2):10–26.

———. 2005. The Place of "Others" in Hunter-Gatherer Intensification. *American Anthropologist* 107(2):207–220.

Hood, B. 1995. Circumpolar Comparison Revisited: Hunter-Gatherer Complexity in the Northern Norwegian Stone Age and the Labrador Maritime Archaic. *Arctic Anthropology* 32(2):75–105.

———. 2008. *Towards an Archaeology of the Nain Region, Labrador*. Contributions to Circumpolar Anthropology 7. Arctic Studies Center, National Museum of Natural History, Smithsonian Institution, Washington, DC.

Jelsma, J. 2006. Three Social Status Groups at Port au Choix: Maritime Archaic Mortuary Practices and Social Structure. In *The Archaic of the Far Northeast*, edited by D. Sanger and M. A. P. Renouf, pp. 83–103. University of Maine Press, Orono.

Loring, S. 1992. *Princes and Princesses of Ragged Fame: Innu Archaeology and Ethnohistory in Labrador*. Unpublished Ph.D. dissertation, University of Massachusetts, Amherst.

———. 2002. "And They Took Away the Stones from Ramah": Lithic Raw Material Sourcing and Eastern Arctic Archaeology. Contributions to Circumpolar Anthropology 2, In *Honoring Our Elders: A History of Eastern Arctic Archaeology*, edited by W. W. Fitzhugh, S. Loring, and D. Odess, pp. 163–185. Arctic Studies Center, National Museum of Natural History, Smithsonian Institution, Washington, DC.

Mailhot, J. 1997. The People of Sheshatshit: In the Land of the Innu. *Social and Economic Studies, 58*, ISER, Memorial University of Newfoundland, St. John's, Newfoundland.

McCaffrey, M. T. 2006. Archaic Period Occupation in Subarctic Quebec: A Review of the Evidence. In *The Archaic of the Far Northeast*, edited by D. Sanger and M. A. P. Renouf, pp. 161–190. University of Maine Press, Orono.

———. 2011. Ancient Social Landscapes in the Eastern Subarctic. In *Hunter Gatherer Archaeology as Historical Process*, edited by K. E. Sassaman and D. H. Holly, Jr., pp. 143–166. Amerind Studies in Archaeology, University of Arizona Press, Tucson.

———, and P. Dumais (editors). 1989. *En marche entre deux mondes: Préhistoire récente au Québec, au Labrador et à Terre Neuve*. Recherches amérindiennes au Québec XIX (2–3).

Nagel, C. 1978. Indian Occupations of the Intermediate Period of the Central Labrador Coast: A Preliminary Synthesis. *Arctic Anthropology* 15(2):119–145.

Neilsen, S. W. 2006. Intermediate Indians: The View from Ushpitun 2 and Pmiusiku 1. Master's thesis, Memorial University of Newfoundland, St. John's.

Pintal, J.-Y. 1994. A Groswater Site at Blanc-Sablon, Québec. Mercury Series 149. In *Threads of Arctic Prehistory: Papers in Honour of William E. Taylor*, Jr., edited by D. Morrison and J.-L. Pilon, pp. 145–164. Canadian Museum of Civilization, Hull.

———. 1998. *Aux frontières de la mer: La préhistoire de Blanc-Sablon*. Municipalité de Blanc-Sablon, Collection Patrimoines, Dossiers, 102, Les Publications du Québec.

Renouf, M. A. P. 1993. Palaeoeskimo Seal Hunters at Port au Choix, Northwestern Newfoundland. *Newfoundland Studies* 9(2):185–212.

———. 2003. Hunter-Gatherer Interactions: Mutualism and Resource Partitioning on the Island of Newfoundland. *Before Farming* 1(4):1–16.

Rousseau, G. 2007. L'archéologie de l'Eastmain-1: Deux sites associés à des paléosols enfouis dans des alluvions. *Archéologiques* 20:1–15.

Samson, G. 1993. La préhistoire récente et la période de contact au Mushuau Nipi, Nouveau-Québec: un temps de renouveau culturel. *ArchéoLogiques* 7:70–84.

Sanger, D. 2006. An Introduction to the Archaic of the Maritime Peninsula: The View from Central Maine. In *The Archaic of the Far Northeast*, edited by D. Sanger and M. A. P. Renouf, pp. 221–252. University of Maine Press, Orono.

Stopp, M. P. 2008. FbAx-01: A Daniel Rattle Hearth in Southern Labrador. *Canadian Journal of Archaeology* 32(1):96–127.

Tuck, J. A. 1976. *Ancient People of Port au Choix*. Newfoundland Social and Economic Studies 17. Memorial University of Newfoundland, St. John's.

CHAPTER 12

ARCHAEOLOGY OF THE NORTH PACIFIC

HERBERT D. G. MASCHNER

From Prince William Sound west to the Kenai Peninsula, the Kodiak Archipelago, the Alaska Peninsula, and the Aleutian Archipelago are 3,000 linear kilometers of the most productive marine environment ever to have existed on the planet (Figure 12.1). Home to the world's last great fisheries, a bastion of sea mammal populations, and bird numbers in the millions, this region—covering about the same distance as between Dublin and Istanbul or San Francisco and Chicago—witnessed the rise of the proto-Aleut and their descendants, who would become known as the Unangan (Aleut), Yupik, Chugach, and Alutiiq in the south, and further north would become the Inupiaq of northern Alaska and the Inuit of the high Arctic.

The Russian, British, and American explorers, traders, and priests who entered this region after AD 1740 (see, e.g., Veniaminov 1984) found nearly 50,000 inhabitants expressing an immense amount of cultural variability, given two languages and 10 dialects of Aleut, and at least two Pacific Eskimo (Alutiiq) dialects. But these same explorers found a level of regional interaction manifested in warfare, trade, and marriage alliances seldom seen among foraging peoples, interactions facilitated by the ocean-going kayak. These early ethnohistoric records provide key observations into the lives of these peoples and how they were adapted to living in one of the harshest weather regimes in the modern world, a landscape where these people still hunt, fish, and participate in the 21st-century economy (Crowell 2001; Maschner and Reedy-Maschner 2005; Reedy-Maschner 2010).

The archaeological record of the north Pacific supplies details of the development and histories of these peoples (Dumond 1987a, 1987b). This past is continuous, though disrupted by catastrophic environmental changes (earthquakes, tsunami, glaciations), migrations, climate change, and other factors demonstrating clearly

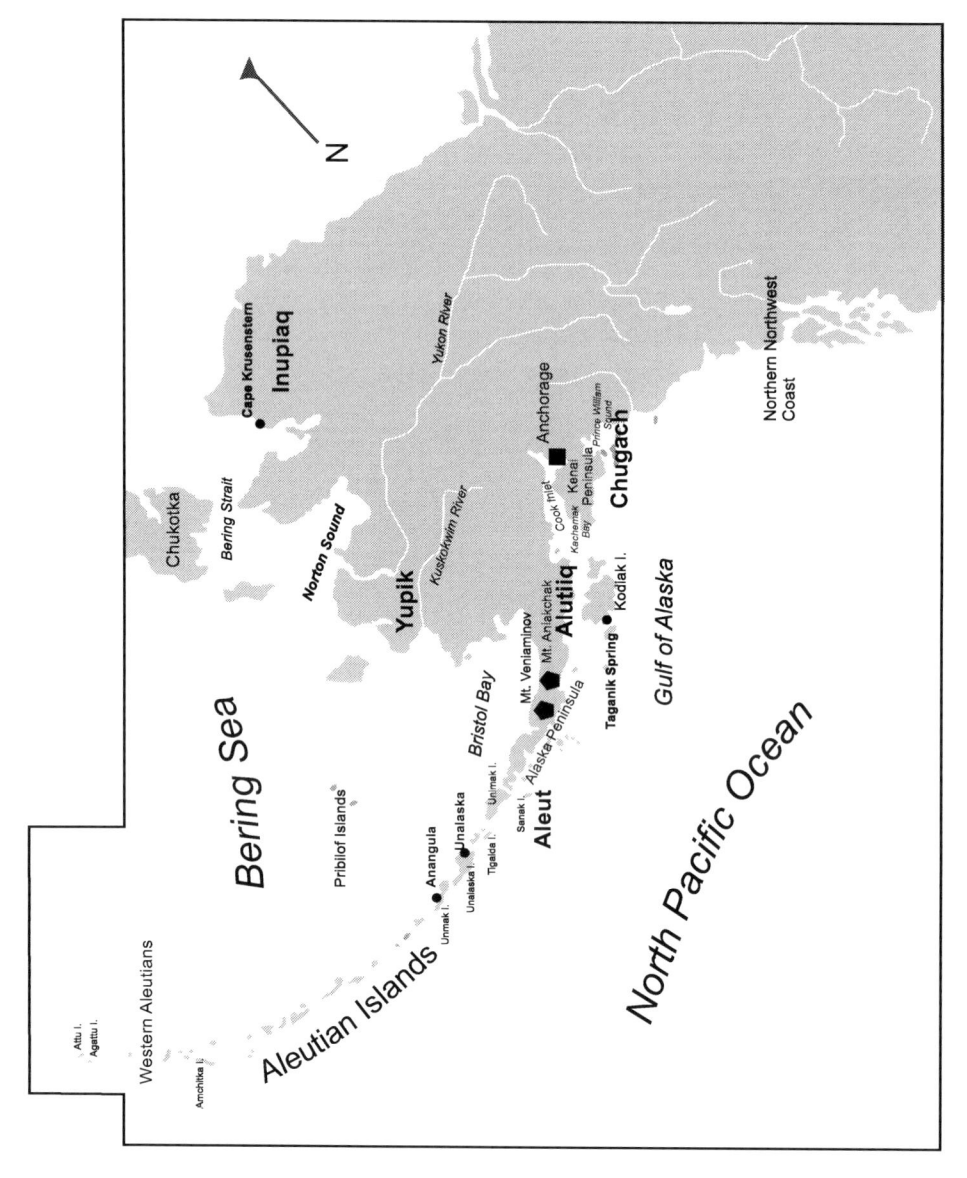

Figure 12.1 Map of the North Pacific showing key sites (dots).

that any ethnographic patterns are a recent snapshot of a very convoluted past, and that regional identities of today are a product of events that cross-cut material and ethnic boundaries. Although the archaeological record of the region shows many macroregional trends as a product of broad degrees of interaction and the common ethnogenesis of these peoples, there is considerable spatial heterogeneity, primarily because of substantial variations in marine productivity and the effects of climate on marine resources (Trites et al. 2007).

This marine productivity led to some of the highest forager population densities ever recorded by anthropologists, and many will be surprised to find that the archaeological record of the region shows a level of hunter-gatherer complexity that rivals the Northwest Coast. For example, when early explorers reached the southern Northwest Coast to find Kwakwaka'wakw (Kwakiutl) and Nuu-Chah-Nulth (Nootka) villages of a few hundred people who were living in plank houses (Ames and Maschner 1999), some Aleut and Alutiiq communities had more than a thousand individuals living in small towns of nobles, commoners, and slaves, and with forager population density rivaled only by the Chumash of the southern California coast. This short review outlines an ancient history of the north Pacific in the context of changing climate regimes, changing sociopolitical dynamics, and regional interactions.

The Earliest Inhabitants

The north Pacific landscape forms the southern margin of the Late Pleistocene Beringian landmass (Hoffecker and Elias 2007). The mountainous Alaska Peninsula portion of this region was glaciated until after 13,000 years ago, but the southern margin of this landscape, a broad coastal plain now submerged, appears to have been deglaciated as early as 17,000 years ago (Misarti 2007). This would have yielded, given the probability of driftwood for fires and boats, a landscape suitable for the migrations of the first peoples into North America. Unfortunately, despite extensive surveys of late Pleistocene landforms in areas not submerged under the modern ocean, there is no evidence of such migrants. In fact, the first archaeological evidence of peoples along the north Pacific occurs after 10,000 years ago, when the sea level first stabilizes in the region.

When we do find the first archaeological remains, it is not some remnant population of Ice Age foragers but rather a fully established group of villagers living on a landscape that required complete maritime adaptation (Aigner 1976, 1978; Laughlin 1975, 1980). The Anangula Village site is the most spectacular example of this early culture, with related sites spread across at least three major islands of the eastern Aleutian archipelago. These sites have evidence of a unifacial core and blade technology established in a village setting, with many functional classes of specialized tools dating about 9,000 years ago (all dates are calibrated). Perhaps equally interesting to the existence of the Anangula Tradition is its sudden demise after approximately a thousand years. There might even have been a catastrophic end to the Anangula Tradition; some of the sites are under massive pyroclastic flows, while others simply disappear during this period of intense volcanic activity approximately 8,000 years ago (Mason 2001).

At this point there is a gap in the Aleutian Island sequence of more than 500 years, but far to the east, this begins the Kodiak Island chronological record, almost as if the remnants of the Anangula Tradition, fleeing the volcanism of the eastern Aleutians, traveled eastward and colonized the Kodiak Archipelago. In fact, the earliest occupations of the Kodiak region have many Anangula characteristics, including red ochre floors and a unifacial core and blade industry, but a bifacial end blade technology has been added to the assemblage and the excavations at Tanginak Spring are perhaps the best documented (Fitzhugh 2004). These early sites begin what is referred to as the "Ocean Bay I Tradition" (Clark 1979), with small villages of red-ochre-covered floors, open-water and near-shore marine adaptation (Kopperl 2003), development of polished slate industries (as Ocean Bay II), and interactions with other archaeological traditions around the region (Steffian and Saltonstall 2005).

The period between 8000 and 6000 BP in the Aleutian Islands is poorly known, and there is little, if any, archaeological evidence. But the Kodiak Island Ocean Bay Tradition was so successful that by 5,800 years ago it expanded off the Kodiak Archipelago back to the Alaska Peninsula, the eastern Aleutian Islands, and northward into the southern Bering Sea, effectively colonizing the entire north Pacific and southern Bering Sea landscape (Dumond 1970; Dumond and Bland 1995; Maschner et al. 2010). These were small groups of foragers living in semipermanent households with a diversity of subsistence practices determined by region and resource availability. After colonization, there was less interaction, and a number of regional variants in stone tool technologies arose (Maschner 2008; Maschner et al. 2010).

But between 5000 and 4000 BP, again there appears to have been a contraction of populations across the north Pacific, only to expand again after 3,800 years ago (although the Kodiak region is a bit out of sequence with the rest of the north Pacific). Indeed, at approximately 3800 BP, the Alaska Peninsula and Aleutian Islands witnessed a substantial population increase, with dozens of fully sedentary village sites showing evidence of off-shore fishing for cod; hunting of large sea mammals such as sea lions, fur seals, and perhaps small whales (see Figure 12.2); and mass harvesting of salmon on the Alaska Peninsula (Corbett et al. 1997, 2001; Maschner 1999a, 1999b; Maschner and Jordan 2001).

Why was there village formation and population expansion at 8500, 5500, and 3800 BP, and population contraction between these eras? Recent research has shown that marine productivity was strongly conditioned by changing climatic conditions, which were driven by the position of the Aleutian low pressure system. It has recently been shown that shifts in historic abundance of salmon, cod, sea lions, and other species were strongly influenced by marine productivity as regulated by changing climate conditions (Finney et al. 2002; Maschner, Betts, Reedy-Maschner,

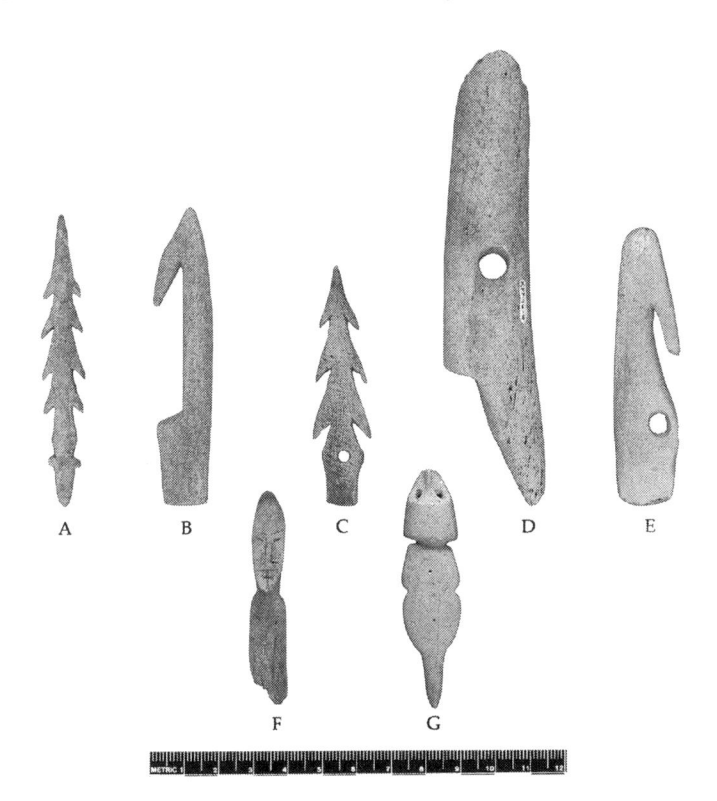

Figure 12.2 Examples of harpoons and figurines from the western Alaska Peninsula: (a) type of harpoon with a cruciform line attachment shelf, common before 4000 BP; (b) type with offset shelf line attachment, common 4000–3600 BP; (c) type with center line hole common 2600–1600 BP; (d) large toggling harpoon for seal mammals and whales 2300–1800 BP; (e) type with offset line hole common after 700 BP; (f) anthropomorphic figures (found before 2600 BP); (g) zoomorphic figures (common after 2600 BP).

and Trites 2008; Maschner, Betts, Cornell, et al. 2009; Maschner, Finney, et al. 2009; Trites et al. 2007). It is also shown that cooler water temperatures tended to lead to higher productivity at all trophic levels, and warmer temperatures tended to lead to lower primary productivity (Misarti 2007; Misarti et al. 2009). All three periods of early village formation, population expansion, and regional cultural development occurred in well-documented colder and wetter periods (Alley and Ágústsdóttir 2005; Calkin et al. 2001; Magny and Haas 2004).

Developments 3,800 to 900 Years Ago

After 3,800 years ago, we see the rise of regional traditions. It is at this time that there was a substantial split between the sequences of the eastern Gulf of Alaska, dominated by Kodiak Island and the Kenai Peninsula, and the western Gulf of

Alaska and the Aleutian Islands. In the east, the Kachemak Tradition arose slowly, with some connection to the preceding Ocean Bay II tradition and rapid development of villages with a diverse array of adaptations, from riverine fishermen to coastal harvesters (Clark 1984, 2008). During this time, a mortuary tradition developed that involved defleshing, disarticulating, and then rearticulating skeletal human remains, perhaps for display in the large pithouses that are inhabited by the Kachemak people (Simon and Steffian 1994; Workman 1992). There was extensive use of labrets and other forms of body ornamentation. The Kachemak tradition was widely distributed to the east, with variations on this tradition across the Kodiak Archipelago and the Alaska mainland coast from Cook Inlet to Prince William Sound (Workman 1980).

Further to the west, the Early and Middle Aleutian traditions develop during a time of village expansion; increased whaling; burgeoning large, corporate households; and the invention of one of the few established traditions of mummification, paralleling mortuary traditions in the Kodiak regions (Laughlin 1980; McCartney 1984). Sometime around 3,000 years ago, strong shamanic belief systems arose, with figurines and bone masks (Maschner 2004a, 2008) in conjunction with large villages and construction of stone-walled multiroom houses in some regions (Knecht and Davis 2001, 2008). By 2,300 years ago, some of these villages were huge, with populations reaching 500 to 1,000 people (Maschner and Jordan 2008). Labrets, zoomorphic and anthropomorphic figures, and other forms of ornamentation were common after 3,500 years ago (Figure 12.2).

Perhaps the most interesting event in this time period was the separation of the archaeological sequences of the western Alaska Peninsula and Aleutian Islands from those of the Kodiak region and eastward. It has been argued that the catastrophic caldera-forming eruptions of the Aniakchak and Veniaminov volcanoes between 3,500 and 3,800 years ago created a dead zone several hundred kilometers in length that cut off the eastern north Pacific from the western region. In fact, there is growing evidence that these eruptions caused a split in regional interactions of such severity that it created the Aleut of the west and the beginnings of the Eskimo-related genetic and linguistic lineages in the east (VanderHoek 2008).

During this 2,800-year interval, there were a number of other events that involved broad, western Arctic interactions. There is some evidence, for example, that the Alaska Peninsula region contributed to development of the Choris Tradition in the Bering Straits (Anderson 1984) about 2,800 years ago (Maschner 2008). There is also evidence that the Kachemak Tradition influenced the rise of the Norton Tradition (early Eskimo-related) of the western Alaska lowlands after 2,500 years ago, based on chronology and house form, but the relationship is not clear (Dumond 1988, 2008). About 1,500 years ago, the Kachemak peoples abandoned the Alaska mainland, which was reoccupied by Dene speakers a few hundred years later (Workman and Workman 1988). By 1,200 years ago, warfare was a focus of north Pacific society, with defensive fortifications found across the region (Maschner 2000; Maschner and Reedy-Maschner 1998). By 900 years ago, we see the first formation of multiroom corporate households (Maschner 2004b; Maschner and Bentley 2003; Maschner and Hoffman 2003; Steffian et al. 2006).

After 900 Years Ago

The period between 900 and 700 years ago was not good for north Pacific peoples. Many areas had a substantial decrease in human population, with village sizes falling from hundreds of people to a few dozen (Maschner 2004b; Maschner, Betts, Cornell, et al. 2009; Maschner et al 2010). This time interval is roughly coterminous with the Medieval Climatic Anomaly and if the relationship between marine productivity and climate is expanded to the negative effects of perhaps warmer sea surface temperatures, then the population decline may have followed a decline in the marine ecosystem.

As evidence, with the cooling of the Little Ice Age about 600 years ago, the converse is true. Across the north Pacific there was an unprecedented population increase. In one area of the western Alaska Peninsula alone, there were over a dozen village sites, each with a population of 300 to 1,000 people (Hoffman 2002; Maschner 1999a, 1999b;). Similar expansions were seen in the Kodiak Archipelago and the eastern Aleutian Islands (Fitzhugh 2003). The relationship between these climate events and human behavior are circumstantial, but the regional impacts are clearly seen (Maschner, Betts, Cornell, et al. 2009a; Maschner, Finney, et al. 2009).

The Late Aleutian Tradition of the western regions and the Koniag Tradition of the eastern regions (including the southern coast of Alaska to Prince William Sound) are quite different archaeologically, and these differences are reflected in the modern peoples who descended from these sequences. Their cultural genesis might be quite different as well, and there is considerable discussion as to the linearity of these developments (Fitzhugh 2003; Maschner, Finney, et al. 2009; Steffian et al. 2006). But one thing is clear: the level of regional interaction across the entire region was strong and largely a product of the kayak, a boat that could withstand substantial storminess in open ocean regions. When exactly the kayak was developed in its ethnographically documented form is unknown, but considering the rapid adaptive and demographic changes of the few hundred years before contact, it must have been a late phenomenon.

Yet this regional interaction, measured in evidence for warfare, migration, and shifting ethnic boundaries, also created strong territories and ethnic markers as well. All Aleut houses had roof entries; all Eskimo houses of the eastern region had side or tunnel entries. Most Koniag Eskimo lithic technologies were of polished slate, but all Aleut lithic technologies were chipped stone industries, even flaking the edges of polished items that entered the Aleut region from the east. There were ceramics on Kodiak, none in the Aleutians. There are many more examples as well, but one note is certain: that these two populations used a suite of material markers to distinguish themselves regardless of (or because of) their high level of interaction.

At historic contact, the peoples of the greater north Pacific region fit every definition of complex hunter-gatherers (Ames and Maschner 1999; Price and Brown 1985; Townsend 1980) and rivaled, or perhaps exceeded, the notable Northwest Coast in many aspects of sociopolitical development. The fundamental difference between the north Pacific and the Northwest Coast is resources. Although the Northwest Coast had huge numbers of salmon, the offshore fisheries, as well as offshore hunting of large sea mammals, was underdeveloped (Moss 1998), probably because open boats were not as successful in rough seas. Many areas of the north Pacific, but especially the south Alaska mainland, the Kodiak archipelago, and the Alaska Peninsula, had huge runs of salmon as well. But the critical difference is that the fully enclosed kayak made the world's largest populations of sea mammals, cod, halibut, and herring fully accessible during most of the year, even during periods of storminess. The demographic impacts of this simple difference in technology and thus adaptive focus were substantial. At present there is still much to learn about the archaeology of the north Pacific. But there is perhaps no place where the interaction among climate, resources, adaptive capability, human demography, and cultural development is more intertwined.

REFERENCES

Aigner, J. S. 1976. Early Holocene Evidence for the Aleut Maritime Adaptation. *Arctic Anthropology* 13(2):32–45.

Aigner, J. S. 1978. The Lithic Remains from Anangula, an 8500 Year Old Aleut Coastal Village. *Urgeschichtliche Materialhefte* 3. Institut fur Urgeschichte, Universität Tübingen.

Alley, R. B., and A. M. Ágústsdóttir. 2005. The 8k Event: Cause and Consequences of a Major Holocene Abrupt Climate Change. *Quaternary Science Reviews* 24(10–11): 1123–1149.

Ames, K., and H. Maschner. 1999. *Peoples of the Northwest Coast: Their Archaeology and Prehistory*. Thames and Hudson, London.

Anderson, D. D. 1984. Prehistory of North Alaska. In *Handbook of North American Indians*, vol. 5, *Arctic*, edited by D. Damas, pp. 81–93. Smithsonian Institution, Washington, DC.

Calkin, P. E., G. C. Wiles, and D. J. Barclay. 2001. Holocene Coastal Glaciation of Alaska: *Quaternary Science Reviews*. Vol. 20, pp. 449–461.

Clark, D. W. 1979. *Ocean Bay: An Early North Pacific Maritime Culture*. National Museum of Man Mercury Series. Archaeological Survey of Canada, Ottawa.

———. 1984. Prehistory of the Pacific Eskimo Region. In *Handbook of North American Indians*, vol. 5, *Arctic*, edited by D. Damas, pp. 136–148. Smithsonian Institution, Washington, DC.

———. 2008. Five Seasons with the Late Kachemak. *Alaska Journal of Anthropology*. 6(1 & 2):185–197.

Corbett, D. G., C. Lefèvre, T. J. Corbett, D. West, and D. Siegel-Causey. 1997. Excavations at KIS-008, Buldir Island: Evaluation and Potential. *Arctic Anthropology* 34:110–117.

Corbett, D. G., D. West, and C. Lefèvre. 2001. Prehistoric Village Organization in the Western Aleutians. In *Archaeology in the Aleut Zone of Alaska: Some Recent Research*, edited by D. Dumond, pp. 251–266. University of Oregon, Ashland.

Crowell, Aron. 2001. *Looking Both Ways: Heritage & Identity of the Alutiiq People*. University of Alaska Press, Fairbanks.

Dumond, D. E. 1970. Eskimos and Aleuts. In *Proceedings of the Eighth International Congress of Anthropological and Ethnological Sciences*, Tokyo and Kyoto, 1968, vol. 3:102–107.

———. 1987a. *Eskimos and Aleuts*. Thames and Hudson, London.

———. 1987b. A Reexamination of the Eskimo-Aleut Prehistory. *American Anthropologist* 89(1):32–56.

———. 1988. The Alaska Peninsula as Superhighway: A Comment. Aurora Monograph Series 4, In *Late Prehistoric Development of Alaska's Native Peoples*, edited by R. Shaw, R. Harritt, and D. Dumond, pp. 379–388,. Alaska Anthropological Association, Anchorage.

———. 2008. Tales of the North Pacific. *Alaska Journal of Anthropology* 6(1 & 2):151–162.

———, and R. L. Bland. 1995. Holocene Prehistory of the Northernmost North Pacific. *Journal of World Prehistory* 9(4):401–451.

Finney, B. P., I. Gregory-Eaves, M. S. V. Douglas, and J. P. Smol. 2002. Fisheries Productivity in the Northeastern Pacific Ocean over the Past 2,200 Years. *Nature* 416:729–733.

Fitzhugh, J. B. 2003. *The Evolution of Complex Hunter-Gatherers: Archaeological Evidence from the North Pacific*. Kluwer Academic/Plenum, New York and Boston.

———. 2004. Colonizing the Kodiak Archipelago: Trends in Raw Material Use and Lithic Technologies at the Tanginak Spring Site. *Arctic Anthropology* 41:14–40.

Hoffecker, J. F., and S. A. Elias. 2007. *Human Ecology of Beringia*. Columbia University Press, New York.

Hoffman, B. W. 2002. The Organization of Complexity: A Study of Late Prehistoric Village Organization in the Eastern Aleutian Region. Ph.D. dissertation, University of Wisconsin, Madison.

Knecht, R. A., and R. S. Davis. 2001. A Prehistoric Sequence for the Eastern Aleutians. In University of Oregon Anthropological Papers No. 58, *Archaeology in the Aleut Zone of Alaska: Some Recent Research*, edited by D. E. Dumond, 269–288, Eugene.

———. 2008. The Amaknak Bridge Site: Cultural Change and the Neoglacial in the Eastern Aleutians. *Arctic Anthropology* 45(1):61–78.

Kopperl, R. E. 2003. *Prehistoric Resource Depletion and Intensification on Kodiak Island, Alaska*. Unpublished Ph.D. dissertation, University of Washington, Seattle.

Laughlin, W. S. 1975. Aleuts: Ecosystem, Holocene History, and Siberian Origins. *Science* 189(4202):507–515.

———. 1980. *Aleuts: Survivors of the Bering Land Bridge*. Holt, Rinehart, and Winston, New York.

Magny, M., and J. N. Haas. 2004. A Major Widespread Climatic Change Around 5300 Cal. Yr BP at the Time of the Alpine Iceman. *Journal of Quaternary Science* 19(5):423–430.

Maschner, H. D. G. 1999a. Prologue to the Prehistory of the Lower Alaska Peninsula. *Arctic Anthropology* 36(1–2):84–102.

———. 1999b. Sedentism, Settlement and Village Organization on the Lower Alaska Peninsula: A Preliminary Assessment. In *Settlement Pattern Studies in the Americas:*

Fifty Years Since Viru, edited by B. Billman and G. Feinman, pp. 56–76. Smithsonian Institution, Washington, DC.

———. 2000. Catastrophic Change and Regional Interaction: The Southern Bering Sea in a Dynamic World System. In *Identities and Cultural Contacts in the Arctic. Proceedings from a Conference at the Danish National Museum, Copenhagen, November 30–December 2, 1999,* edited by M. Appelt, J. Berglund, and H. C. Gulløv, pp. 252–265. Danish National Museum and Danish Polar Center, Copenhagen.

———. 2004a. Redating the Hot Springs Village Site in Port Moller, Alaska. *Alaska Journal of Anthropology* 2(1–2): 100–116.

———. 2004b. Traditions Past and Present: Allen McCartney and the Izembeck Phase of the Western Alaska Peninsula. *Arctic Anthropology* 41(2):98–111.

———. 2008. Fishtails, Ancestors, and Old Islanders: Chirikof Island, the Alaska Peninsula, and the Dynamics of Western Alaska Prehistory. *Alaska Journal of Anthropology* 6(1 & 2):173–185.

———, B. Benson, G. Knudsen, and N. Misarti. 2010. *Archaeology of the Sapsuk River, Alaska*. Monographs of the Archaeology Branch, Alaska Region, Bureau of Indian Affairs. Anchorage, AK.

Maschner, H. D. G., and R. A. Bentley. 2003. The Power Law of Rank and Household on the North Pacific. In *Complex Systems and Archaeology: Empirical and Theoretical Applications*, edited by R. A. Bentley and H. D. G. Maschner, pp. 47–60. University of Utah Press, Salt Lake City.

Maschner, H. D. G., M. W. Betts, J. Cornell, B. Finney, N. Huntly, J. W. Jordan, N. Misarti, K. L. Reedy-Maschner, R. Russell, A. Tews, S. Wood, and B. Benson. 2009. An Introduction to the Biocomplexity of Sanak Island, Western Gulf of Alaska. *Pacific Science* 63(4):673–709.

Maschner, H. D. G., M. W. Betts, K. L. Reedy-Maschner, and A. W. Trites. 2008. A 4500 Year Time Series of Pacific Cod (*Gadus macrocephalus*): Archaeology, Regime Shifts, and Sustainable Fisheries. *Fishery Bulletin* 106:386–394.

Maschner, H. D. G., B. Finney, J. Jordan, N. Misarti, A. Tews, and G. Knudsen. 2009. Did the North Pacific Ecosystem Collapse in AD 1000? In *The Northern World AD 900–1400*, edited by H. Maschner, O. Mason, and R. McGhee, pp. 33–57. University of Utah Press, Salt Lake City.

Maschner, H. D. G., and B. W. Hoffman. 2003. The Development of Large Corporate Households Along the North Pacific Rim. *Alaska Journal of Anthropology* (1)2:41–63.

Maschner, H. D. G., and J. W. Jordan. 2001. The Russell Creek Manifestation of the Arctic Small Tool Tradition on the Western Alaska Peninsula. University of Oregon Anthropological Papers No. 58, *Archaeology in the Aleut Zone of Alaska: Some Recent Research*, edited by D. E. Dumond, pp 151–172. Eugene.

———. 2008. Catastrophic Events and Punctuated Culture Change: The Southern Bering Sea and North Pacific in a Dynamic Global System. In *Time and Change: Archaeological and Anthropological Perspectives on the Long Term*, edited by D. Papagianni, H. Maschner, and R. H. Layton, pp. 95–113. Oxbow Press.

Maschner, H. D. G., and K. L. Reedy-Maschner. 1998. Raid, Retreat, Defend (Repeat): The Archaeology and Ethnohistory of Warfare on the North Pacific. *Journal of Anthropological Archaeology* 17:19–51.

———. 2005. Aleuts and the Sea. *Archaeology* March/April:63–70.

Mason, O. K. 2001. Catastrophic Environmental Change and the Middle Holocene Transition in the Aleutian Islands. In Anthropological Papers, University of Oregon No. 58, *Archaeology in the Aleut Zone: Some Recent Research*, edited by D. E. Dumond, pp. 105–121.

McCartney, A. P. 1984. Prehistory of the Aleutian Region. In *Handbook of North American Indians*, vol. 5, *Arctic*, edited by D. Damas, pp. 119–135. Smithsonian Institution, Washington, DC.

Misarti, N. 2007. *Six Thousand Years of Change in the Northeast Pacific: An Interdisciplinary View of Maritime Ecosystems*. University of Alaska, Fairbanks.

Misarti N., B. P. Finney, H. D. G. Maschner, and M. Wooller. 2009. Changes in Northeast Pacific Marine Ecosystems over 4,500 Years: Evidence from Stable Isotope Analysis of Bone Collagen from Archaeological Middens. *Holocene* 19(8): 1139–1151.

Moss, M. 1998. Northern Northwest Coast Regional Overview. *Arctic Anthropology* 35(1):88–111.

Price, T. D., and J. A. Brown (editors). 1985. *Prehistoric Hunter-Gatherers: The Emergence of Cultural Complexity*. Academic Press, Orlando.

Reedy-Maschner, K. L. 2010. *Aleut Identities: Tradition and Modernity in an Indigenous Fishery*. McGill-Queen's University Press, Montreal.

Simon, J., and Steffian A. 1994. Cannibalism or Complex Mortuary Behavior? In *Reckoning with the Dead*, edited by T. Bray and T. Killion, pp. 75–100. Smithsonian Institution, Washington, DC.

Steffian A., and P. Saltonstall. 2005. Tools But Not Toolkits: Traces of the Arctic Small Tool Tradition in the Kodiak Archipelago. *Alaska Journal of Anthropology* 3(2):17–49.

Steffian, A., P. Saltonstall, and R. Kopperl. 2006. Expanding the Kachemak: Surplus Production and the Development of Multi-Season Storage in Alaska's Kodiak Archipelago. *Arctic Anthropology* 43(2): 93–129.

Townsend, J. B. 1980. Ranked Societies of the Alaskan Pacific Rim. *Senri Ethnological Studies* 4:123–156.

Trites, A. W., A. J. Miller, H. D. G. Maschner, M. A. Alexander, S. J. Bograd, J. A. Calder, A. Capotondi, K. O. Coyle, E. D. Lorenzo, B. P. Finney, E. J. Gregr, C. E. Grosch, S. R. Hare, G. L. Hunt, J. Jahncke, N. B. Kachel, H.-J. Kim, C. Ladd, N. J. Mantua, C. Marzban, W. Maslowski, R. Mendelssohn, D. J. Neilson, S. R. Okkonen, J. E. Overland, K. L. Reedy-Maschner, T. C. Royer, F. B. Schwing, J. X. L. Wang, and A. J. Winship. 2007. Bottom-Up Forcing and the Decline of Steller Sea Lions (*Eumetopias jubatus*) in Alaska: Assessing the Ocean Climate Hypothesis. *Fisheries Oceanography* 16:46–67.

VanderHoek, R. 2008. Cultural Implications of 4th Millennium BP Eruptions on the Central Alaska Peninsula. Paper presented at the Annual Meeting of the Alaska Anthropological Association, Anchorage.

Veniaminov, I., 1984. *Notes on the Islands of the Unalaska District* (translated by L. T. Black and R. H. Goeghegan, and edited by R. A. Pierce). Alaska History 27. Limestone Press, Kingston, ON.

Workman, K. W. and W. B. Workman. 1988. The Last 1300 Years of Prehistory in Kachemak Bay: Where Later Is Less. In Aurora Monograph Series no. 4, *Late Prehistoric Development of Alaska's Native Peoples,* edited by R. Shaw, R. Harritt, and D. Dumond, pp. 339–354. Alaska Anthropological Association, Anchorage.

Workman, W. B. 1980. Continuity and Change in the Prehistoric Record from Southern Alaska. Senri Ethnological Studies No. 4, In *Alaska Native Culture and History*, edited by Y. Kotani and W. B. Workman, pp. 49–102, National Museum of Ethnology, Suita, Osaka.

———. 1992. Life and Death in a First Millennium AD Gulf of Alaska Culture: The Kachemak Tradition Ceremonial Complex. In *Ancient Images, Ancient Thought: The Archaeology of Ideology. Proceedings of the 23rd Annual Chacmool Conference*, pp. 19–25. Calgary.

II. The West

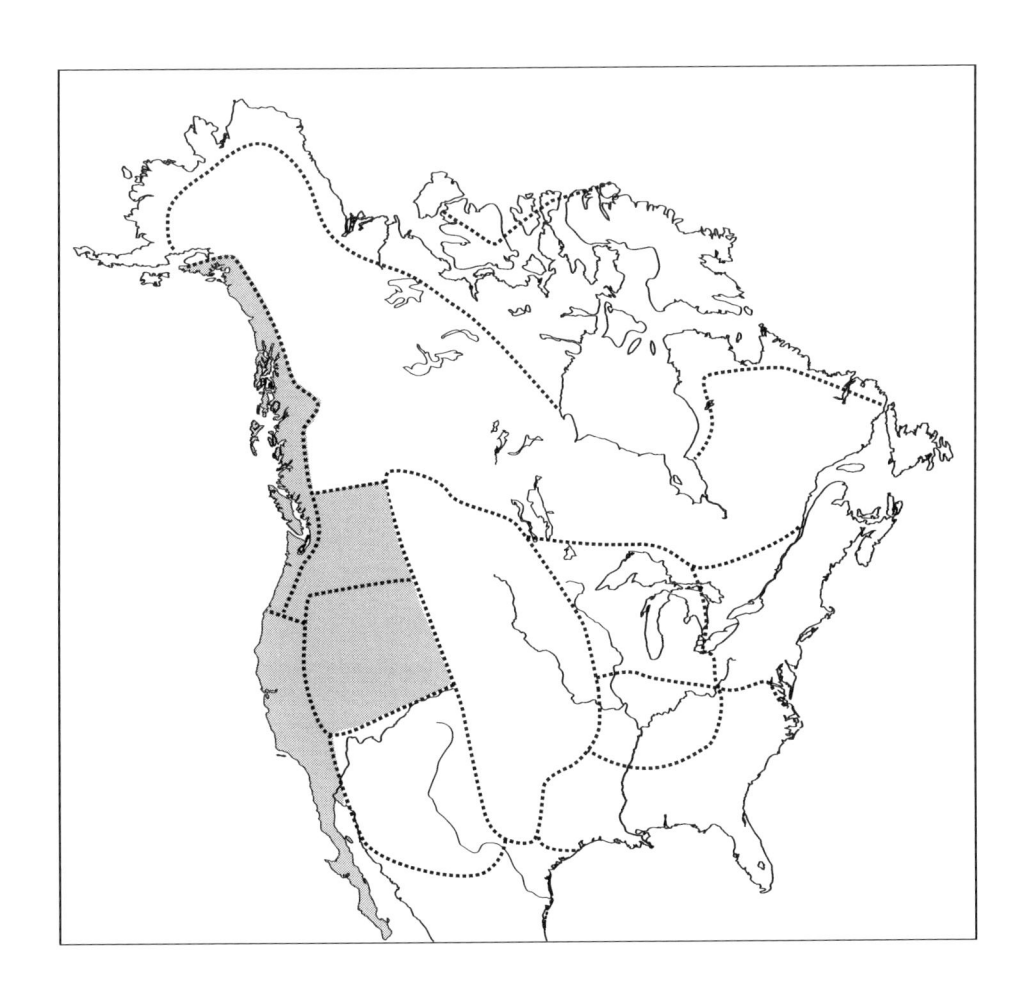

CHAPTER 13

FOUNDATIONS FOR THE FAR WEST: PALEOINDIAN CULTURES ON THE WESTERN FRINGE OF NORTH AMERICA

JON ERLANDSON AND TODD J. BRAJE

LITTLE more than a decade ago, most American archaeologists thought they knew when and how the Americas were first settled. Today, there are more questions than answers about the origins of the First Americans, a situation that has stimulated new ideas and reinvigorated theories once considered to be marginal. Much has yet to be resolved about when humans first arrived in the New World, how many discrete migrations took place, and precisely where these founding populations came from. Our reading of current archaeological evidence suggests, however, that the Americas probably were first settled roughly 15,000 years ago, plus or minus 500. A coastal migration of maritime peoples around the Pacific Rim seems increasingly likely to have contributed significantly to the initial colonization of the Far West and the broader Americas.

For most of the 20th century, American archaeologists were taught that virtually every ancient cultural tradition in the New World was derived from a Clovis mother-culture. This scenario was supported by Greenberg et al. (1986), who synthesized linguistic, dental, genetic, and archaeological data to argue that three waves of migration led to the settling of the Americas. There was a first wave related to and descended from Clovis that extended throughout the Americas, a later Na-Dene migration limited mostly to northwestern North America, and a movement of Arctic Aleut-Eskimo peoples across the northern reaches of North America. In this scenario, most Native American cultures of western North America were descended from Clovis ancestors, terrestrial hunting peoples who migrated from northeast Asia through Beringia and into the Americas via a long, narrow, ice-free corridor. Once they reached the American heartland, these big-game hunters depended heavily on large Pleistocene megafauna (mammoths, mastodons, horses, camels, etc.), spreading rapidly through the continent until they reached the Atlantic, Gulf, and Pacific coasts, where they slowly adapted to life by the sea. For decades, therefore, the Pacific Coast was marginal to theories about the early settlement of the Far West and the Americas, an afterthought that led to some curious and exceptional cases of complex hunter-gatherers living along the coasts of California and the Pacific Northwest.

A good scientific story, especially if it grows from hypothesis to received wisdom, can stifle archaeological research into alternative scenarios for decades. The Clovis First hypothesis did exactly that, marginalizing those who proposed alternative scenarios and the research needed to explore them. For decades most scholars dismissed evidence presented by Luther Cressman of the University of Oregon, for instance, that the Northern Great Basin was occupied by Late Pleistocene peoples—including a pre-Clovis date of 13000 RYBP (~14500 cal BP) for charcoal from a hearth at Fort Rock Cave in central Oregon. Recent research at nearby Paisley Caves confirms that humans occupied the area at least 14,300 years ago (Gilbert et al. 2008), however, suggesting that Cressman was right. With current geological evidence indicating that the ice-free corridor did not open until about 14,000 years ago, the pre-Clovis occupations of Paisley Caves—along with a few other sites such as the 14,000 year old Monte Verde II near the Pacific Coast of central Chile (Dillehay et al. 2008; Erlandson, et al. 2008a)—leaves the Clovis First model in ruins and the terrestrial roots of the First Americans in question.

The demise of the model that dominated 20th-century American archaeology has reinvigorated research related to the initial peopling of the Americas, including the long-marginalized Coastal Migration Theory. In this paper, we discuss the implications of recent research along the Pacific Coast of North America—which has pushed the antiquity of maritime adaptations in Canada, the United States, and Mexico back into the terminal Pleistocene—for understanding the origins of Paleoindian peoples in North America's Far West. Our focus is primarily on technological evidence for the peopling of western North America, in the form of distinctive stemmed projectile points found in early sites around the Pacific Rim, a projectile technology quite different from the fluted points of the Clovis and Folsom traditions. Our results suggest that the Pacific Coast was at the epicenter of Paleoindian origins and may link the initial colonization of the Americas to one of the most significant maritime migrations in human history.

Ecological and Cultural Background

North America's Far West stretches from Alaska to Mexico and from the Pacific Coast to the Rocky Mountains. This vast and rugged region is tectonically active, mountainous, and ecologically diverse. The Far West includes areas as diverse as the Sonoran Desert of Mexico; the cool maritime rainforests of the Pacific Northwest; the giant kelp forests and Channel Islands off the chaparral-clad southern California Coast; the deserts, lakes, and marshes of the Great Basin; the snow-covered peaks of the High Sierras, Cascades, Rockies, and other mountain ranges; and much more. In an area so geographically diverse, all known to have been inhabited by Paleoindians, we should expect a great deal of variation among Paleoindian cultures and adaptations, as well as those of their descendants.

Despite continuing questions about the timing and routes involved in the initial human colonization of the Americas, an overwhelming body of archaeological, genetic, anthropological, and other scientific evidence still supports the theory that the First Americans came from Northeast Asia, traversing Beringia to reach the New World. Two primary migration pathways have been proposed for the early stages of this colonization process. The interior and terrestrial Ice-Free Corridor route dominated archaeological thought about the peopling of the Americas throughout the 20th century, but the coastal migration theory has gained many adherents during the past decade. Near the end of the Pleistocene, these routes would have posed fundamentally different challenges to Beringian peoples spreading out of Northeast Asia into the Americas.

The interior "ice-free corridor" formed as the Laurentide and Cordilleran ice sheets separated roughly 14,000 years ago (Mandryk et al. 2001), a long and sinuous corridor leading from eastern Beringia (Alaska), through the Yukon and British Columbia, to the western Plains of North America. To settle the Americas, the terrestrial ecosystems Paleoindians would have encountered traveling through an interior migration route range from frozen tundra and periglacial lakes to northern boreal and coniferous forests, grasslands, deserts, and tropical forests. The nature of the ice-free corridor route remains relatively obscure. Some have argued that such periglacial habitats would have been relatively sterile and difficult for early Americans to migrate through for a millennium or so after opening. But Fiedel (2007) proposed that the ice-free corridor may have been rich in migrating waterfowl, large flocks of which may have drawn migrants southward into warmer and more diverse ecosystems.

The shorelines of the Pacific Rim provided another route that maritime peoples may have followed from Northeast Asia into the Americas (Fladmark 1979), and the Pacific Flyway may have been even richer in migrating waterfowl and other resources. The shorelines of lowland Beringia during the late glacial period may have contained hundreds of islands along a coast riddled with bays and inlets, providing diverse and highly productive resources for coastal hunter-gatherers. Although it may have been covered with sea ice for six to nine months of the year, the south coast of Beringia probably afforded rich habitat for waterfowl, whales, seals, walruses, fish, seabirds, and other marine organisms.

During the Late Pleistocene, the major barrier preventing maritime peoples from moving southward from Beringia down the Pacific Coast of North America was long considered to be the heavily glaciated coast of the Alaska Peninsula and the northern Northwest Coast. The outer coast in these areas now appears to have been largely deglaciated by about 16,000 years ago, however, and it supported a relatively diverse and productive array of marine and terrestrial resources, including the omnivorous brown (grizzly) bear and other terrestrial mammals. The combination of terrestrial and marine resources available in coastal ecosystems permits a broader economic base for human hunter-gatherers and often results in higher population densities, which may have helped fuel a relatively rapid spread of people around the Pacific Rim.

Similar to the ice-free corridor, a coastal route would have led through a variety of terrestrial ecosystems, but nearshore marine habitats would have offered a similar range of resources along a route entirely at sea level. Recognizing that maritime peoples had adapted to the relatively cool waters around Japan during the last glacial, Erlandson et al. (2007) suggested that the widespread distribution of nearshore kelp forests (which can survive seasonal sea-ice cover) around the margins of the North Pacific may have constituted a "kelp highway" for maritime peoples, offering a similar suite of marine resources, reduced wave energy, and holdfasts for boats. From northern Japan, through the Kurile and Aleutian island chains, and down the Pacific Coast of North America as far as the western Baja California Peninsula, productive kelp forests yielded three-dimensional habitat for a rich assemblage of similar organisms, including seals and sea otters, seabirds, a variety of fish and shellfish, seaweeds, etc. The linear nature of the coastal route and the presence of the same or similar species in kelp forest and estuarine habitats would have posed little ecological resistance to the spread of early maritime peoples of the North Pacific Rim.

Along the Pacific Coast of North America, a series of large rivers (the Yukon, Fraser, Columbia, Klamath, Sacramento, etc.) also supported huge runs of salmon and other anadromous fish, offering a wealth of resources that may have led coastal migrants deep into the interior from marine and estuarine habitats to riverine, lake, and marsh ecosystems. The Columbia River and its tributaries (e.g., the Willamette, John Day, and Snake rivers), for instance, would have been linear migration corridors that Paleoindians traveling in boats or on foot could have followed into the Columbia Plateau region of Washington, Oregon, and Idaho, as well as deep into the vast network of lakes and marshes of the Great Basin region in Oregon, Nevada, Utah, and California. In these transitional aquatic habitats of the Far West, they would have had access to a wide variety of waterfowl, fish, shellfish, and plant foods, as well as land animals of all sizes, including remnants of a Pleistocene megafauna that went extinct about 13,000 years ago.

A significant problem in evaluating the archaeological evidence for the coastal migration theory is the fact that global sea levels have risen nearly 400 feet (approximately 120 meters) since the end of the Last Glacial Maximum about 20,000 years ago. This marine transgression flooded a vast landscape that includes the shorelines and coastal lowlands through which early maritime migrants would have passed, including a huge area of south-central Beringia. Rising seas have less effect on coastal archaeological records in areas where the offshore bathymetry is steep, and research focused on offshore islands and steep coasts has identified a growing number of early archaeological sites along the Pacific Coast (Erlandson et al. 2008b, 2011). Other than the Monte Verde II site in central Chile, none of these early sites predates the Clovis era, but the oldest sites are the most likely to have been lost to rising seas. Some archaeologists have criticized proponents of the coastal route for reliance on such "negative evidence," ignoring the fact that no pre-Clovis or Clovis-age sites have been identified within the 1,500 kilometer-long ice-free corridor either.

Stemmed vs. Fluted Points: Two Paleoindian Traditions of the Far West

What do the stone tool technologies of Paleoindian sites in western North America tell us about the peopling of the Americas? Archaeologists have debated the relative antiquity of fluted versus stemmed point traditions in western North America for decades (see Beck and Jones 2010). The Clovis First model proposed that the distinctive fluted Clovis points were the oldest (around 13250–12750 cal BP), with stemmed point traditions developing later from Clovis precursors. Clovis-like points are found from coast to coast in North America and also extend from Mexico to Alaska, but the chronology of Clovis outside its core areas in the Southeast, the Great Plains, and some sites in the Southwest is not well established. Clovis-like points in Alaska appear to be younger than classic Clovis, for instance, and none of the Clovis points found in California, Oregon, or Washington have come from well-dated contexts. Another problematic issue is that Clovis has no clear precursors in Northeast Asia or Beringia, appearing to be a strictly North American invention. Considering that Clovis peoples no longer appear to have been the initial occupants of the Far West and the broader Americas, where did Clovis come from (see also Anderson, Waguespack, this volume)?

Beck and Jones (2010) proposed an alternative to the Clovis First model in the Far West, suggesting that two great technological traditions may have met and mingled in the area: Clovis peoples with fluted point technologies who moved westward from the Central Plains of North America and Western Pluvial Lakes Tradition (WPLT) peoples armed with stemmed points and crescents who moved eastward from the Pacific Coast into the Columbia Plateau and Great Basin regions. This argument has deep roots, harkening back to a longstanding debate about the relative antiquity of fluted versus stemmed points in the Far West.

Beck and Jones's idea that the stemmed point tradition of western North America might be related to a coastal migration into the Americas is not completely new, as others have proposed technological and cultural relationships between stemmed points found at Ushki Lake on the Kamchatka Peninsula (Figure 13.1a) and at sites in the Pacific Northwest such as Marmes Rockshelter in Washington state, markers of a Late Pleistocene migration from northeast Asia into North America. The Ushki 7 component containing stemmed points was once thought to be about 16,000 years old but has been redated to about 13,000 years ago—roughly the same age as Clovis (Goebel et al. 2003). A stemmed point similar to those from Ushki Lake was found associated with the Buhl Burial in Idaho, dated to about 10700 RCYBP, or about 12700 cal BP (Figure 13.1b). The discovery of a stemmed point in the basal layers at Paisley Caves in south-central Oregon, dated to about 14,300 years ago (see Gilbert et al. 2008), now suggests that stemmed points may be older than Clovis in western North America.

Recent research has also identified delicate, finely made, long-stemmed and barbed or serrated points on California's Northern Channel Islands (Figure 13.2), where they have been dated between at least 12000 and 8400 cal BP (Erlandson et al. 2008b, 2011). These Channel Island Barbed points (Justice 2002) have been found in several sites that also produced chipped stone crescents, similar to early associations of stemmed points (e.g., Lake Mojave points) and crescents found across much of the Far West (see Tadlock 1966). These terminal Pleistocene and Early Holocene technologies suggest that a direct cultural-historical link may exist between Paleocoastal peoples of the California Coast and those of the WPLT in the interior regions of the Far West. What remains to be seen is whether the coastal or interior variant is older.

Although more speculative, Channel Island Barbed points may also support a link between stemmed points and a coastal migration around the North Pacific Rim. California's Northern Channel Islands, occupied by humans for at least 13,000 years (Erlandson et al. 2008b), were not connected to the adjacent mainland during the Quaternary, and it would have required seaworthy boats for humans to colonize them. At the same time that Clovis peoples were hunting down some of the last of the large North American megafauna, therefore, maritime Paleoindians were exploring islands off the California Coast. No diagnostic technologies are associated with the earliest known human occupation of the islands, but no fluted points have been found on the islands where stemmed points were used at least 12,000 years ago. Faunal remains from several Channel Island sites dated between about 12,000 and 11,500 years ago demonstrate that these Paleocoastal peoples were collecting shellfish, fishing, and hunting sea mammals, seabirds, and waterfowl (Erlandson 2007; Erlandson et al. 2011).

Intriguingly, the general morphology of Channel Island Barbed points is quite similar to stemmed and "tanged" points found in many Incipient Jomon sites in Japan dated between about 15500 and 13800 cal BP (Nagai 2007; see Figure 13.3). There are large geographic gaps between Incipient Jomon sites known from Japan and Sakhalin Island, and the stemmed points from Kamchatka, the Channel Islands,

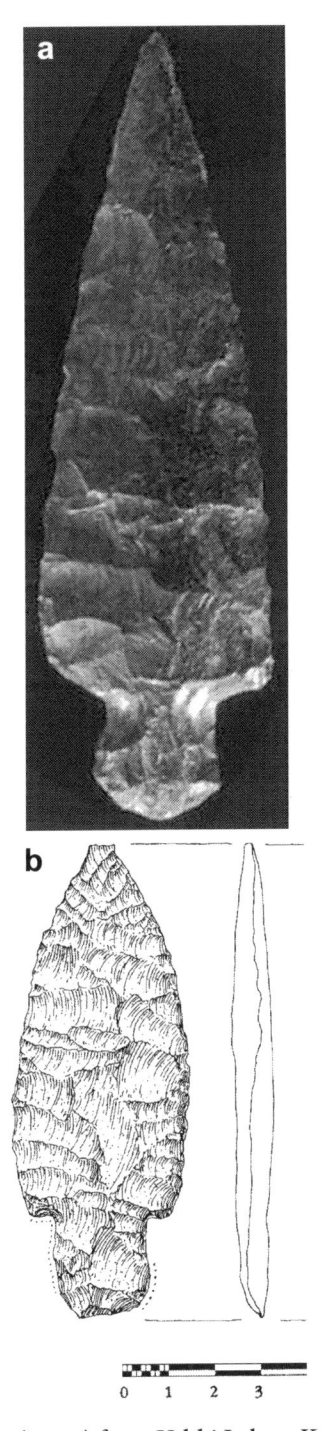

Figure 13.1 Stemmed points: (a, top) from Ushki Lake 7, Kamchatka; (b, bottom) from the Buhl Burial, Idaho.

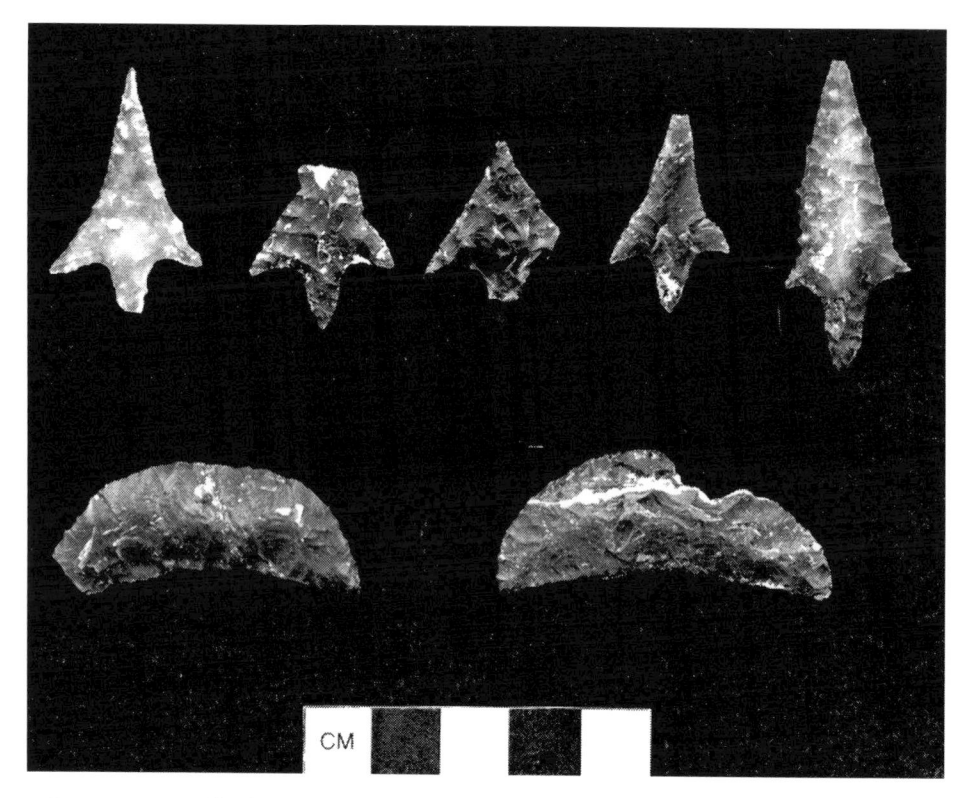

Figure 13.2 Small Channel Island Barbed points (upper row) and two crescents (lower row) from a 12,000-year-old site on Santa Rosa Island (image by J. Erlandson).

and the continental Far West, but if maritime peoples carrying stemmed points settled the Americas approximately 15,000 years ago, much of the evidence would now be submerged on the continental shelves of southern Beringia and western North America. One of the biggest gaps in the distribution of early stemmed points around the North Pacific corresponds to a stretch of southern Beringia more than 1,000 kilometers wide, where the late Pleistocene coastlines and a vast expanse of lowland habitat were lost to postglacial sea level rise.

We note here that early stemmed point traditions are also found along the west coast of South America and into the Amazon Basin (see Roosevelt et al. 2002). Their geographic distribution suggests the possibility that migrating coastal or maritime peoples crossed the narrow Isthmus of Panama, from which they could have spread both northward into the Gulf of Mexico and southward along the Atlantic Coast of South America. Since some of the stemmed fishtail points in South America also have basal fluting, it is worth considering the possibility that the stemmed point traditions found throughout the Far West are markers of a coastal migration from Northeast Asia into the Americas, and that the Clovis technology in North America might be derived from an older stemmed point tradition. Ultimately, only further careful research—at stratified sites with well-dated Paleoindian assemblages—will resolve such issues.

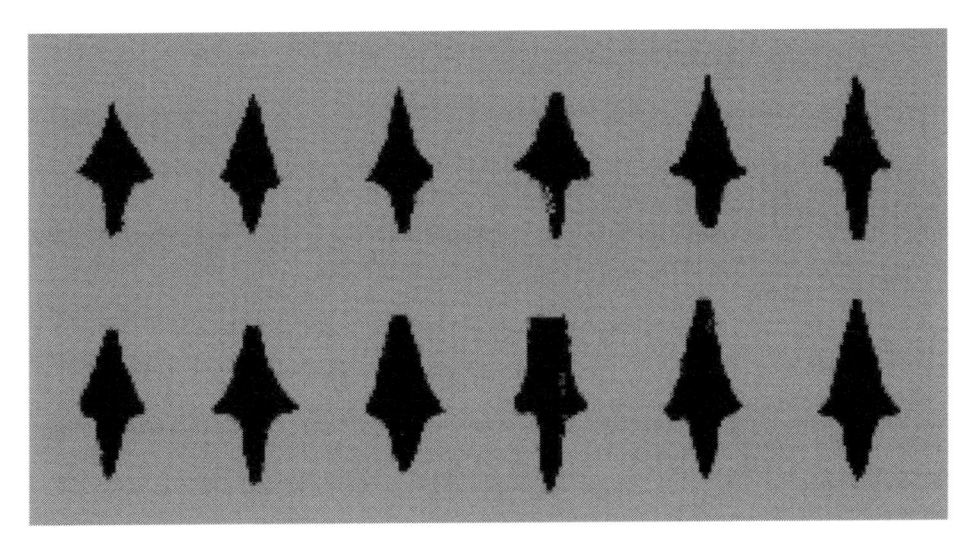

Figure 13.3 Long-stemmed, "tanged" Incipient Jomon points from Japan, dated to about 14,500 cal BP (adapted from Nagai 2007).

Conclusion

It now seems likely that both coastal and interior routes contributed to Pleistocene colonization of the Americas by humans. After a century dominated by Clovis First models, our understanding of human colonization of the Americas is being illuminated by new archaeological, genetic, ecological, and other evidence. A small number of widely accepted pre-Clovis sites in North and South America dated between about 15,000 and 14,000 years ago has led to reassessment of traditional models, and to new theories and interpretations that suggest human colonization of the Americas was a more complex process than once thought. General acceptance of the pre-Clovis Monte Verde II site altered the landscape of Paleoindian studies, especially since the interior ice-free corridor does not appear to have opened in time to account for a presence in coastal Chile at this early date.

Stemmed points as old as or older than Clovis in the Far West may alter the nature of debate similarly. The knowledge that Upper Paleolithic peoples in the western Pacific were colonizing islands and making substantial sea voyages between 50,000 and 25,000 years ago (see Erlandson 2002) also contributed to growing acceptance of the coastal migration theory. Finally, the discovery of terminal Pleistocene sites along the Pacific Coast of North and South America, including several on islands off the California Coast that required seaworthy boats for colonization, also supports the coastal migration theory.

If such a Pleistocene coastal migration occurred, it may be marked by a discontinuous trail of stemmed projectile points from Japan and Kamchatka to the Pacific coasts of North and South America, and deep into the river drainages, lakes, and marshes of the Far West. The Paleoamericans who left these stemmed points, along with chipped stone crescents found throughout the Far West, may have mingled with the descendants of Clovis peoples moving westward out of the continental interior—although they may also have been closely related. Their descendants, along with later migrants from Northeast Asia, ultimately gave rise to the diverse array of Native American cultures and languages characteristic of later archaeological, historical, and ethnographic times in western North America.

As the continent filled with people who increasingly "settled in" to these diverse and dynamic postglacial environments, a series of distinctive archaeological traditions developed in the Far West through cultural processes shaped by environmental variation, demographic expansion, competition, and regional interaction. There is still much to be learned about the cultural foundations of human occupations in North America's Far West, including when the area was first settled, by whom, and from where. Recent research suggests, however, that Clovis is not the first culture or technological tradition present in much of the Far West, that the peopling of the area was more complex than once believed and probably involved multiple waves of migration, that the Pacific Coast of North America was much more central to the migration process than traditional models suggest, that marine and aquatic adaptations were older and more significant than previously believed, and that there was even greater diversity in Paleoindian subsistence and lifeways than many recent models have suggested.

ACKNOWLEDGMENTS

Unless identified as radiocarbon years (RCYBP), all dates referred to are in calendar years before present (cal BP). We thank Tim Pauketat and the editorial staff of Oxford University Press for their assistance in the editing and production of this manuscript. We are also grateful to Charlotte Beck, Loren Davis, Mike Glassow, Ted Goebel, Dennis Jenkins, George Jones, Torben Rick, Jack Watts, and Phillip Walker, who freely shared knowledge and data that contributed this paper.

REFERENCES

Beck, C., and G. T. Jones. 2010. Clovis and Western Stemmed: Population Migration and the Meeting of Two Technologies in the Intermountain West. *American Antiquity* 75(1):81–116.

Dillehay, T. D., C. Ramírez, M. Pino, M. B. Collins, J. Rossen, and J. D. Pino-Navarro. 2008. Monte Verde: Seaweed, Food, Medicine, and the Peopling of South America. *Science* 320:784–786.

Erlandson, J. M. 2002. Anatomically Modern Humans, Maritime Voyaging, and the Pleistocene Colonization of the Americas. In *The First Americans: The Pleistocene*

Colonization of the New World, edited by N. Jablonski, pp. 59–92. University of California Press, Berkeley.

———. 2007. Sea Change: The Paleocoastal Occupations of Daisy Cave. In *Seeking Our Past: An Introduction to North American Archaeology*, by S. W. Neusius and G. T. Gross, pp. 135–143. Oxford University Press, Oxford.

Erlandson, J. M., T. J. Braje, and M. H. Graham. 2008a. How Old Is MVII? Seaweeds, Shorelines, and Chronology at Monte Verde, Chile. *Journal of Island and Coastal Archaeology* 3:277–281.

Erlandson, J. M., M. H. Graham, B. J. Bourque, D. Corbett, J. A. Estes, and R. S. Steneck. 2007. The Kelp Highway Hypothesis: Marine Ecology, the Coastal Migration Theory, and the Peopling of the Americas. *Journal of Island and Coastal Archaeology* 2:161–174.

Erlandson, J. M., M. L. Moss, and M. Des Lauriers. 2008b. Living on the Edge: Early Maritime Cultures of the Pacific Coast of North America. *Quaternary Science Reviews* 27:2232–2245.

Erlandson, J. M., T. C. Rick, T. J. Braje, M. Casperson, B. Culleton, B. Fulfrost, T. Garcia, D. A. Guthrie, N. Jew, D. J. Kennett, M. L. Moss, L. Reeder, C. Skinner, J. Watts, and L. Willis. 2011. Paleoindian Seafaring, Maritime Technologies, and Coastal Foraging on California's Channel Islands. *Science* 331:1181–1185.

Fiedel, S. J. 2007. Quacks in the Ice: Waterfowl, Paleoindians, and the Discovery of America. In *Foragers of the Terminal Pleistocene in North America*, edited by R. B. Walker and B. N. Driskell, pp. 1–14. University of Nebraska Press, Lincoln.

Fladmark, K. R. 1979. Routes: Alternate Migration Corridors for Early Man in North America. *American Antiquity* 44:55–69.

Gilbert, M. T. P., D. L. Jenkins, A. Götherstrom, N. Naveran, J. J. Sanchez, M. Hofreiter, P. F. Thomsen, J. Binladen, T. F. G. Higham, R. M. Yohe II, R. Parr, L. S. Cummings, and E. Willerslev. 2008. DNA from Pre-Clovis Human Coprolites in Oregon, North America. *Science* 320(5877):786–789.

Goebel, T., M. R. Waters, and M. Dikova. 2003. The Archaeology of Ushki Lake, Kamchatka, and the Pleistocene Peopling of the Americas. *Science* 301:501–505.

Greenberg, J. H., C. G. Turner II, and S. L. Zegura. 1986. The Settlement of the Americas: A Comparison of the Linguistic, Dental, and Genetic Evidence. *Current Anthropology* 27(5): 477–497.

Justice, N. D. 2002. *Stone Age Spear and Arrow Points of California and the Great Basin*. Indiana University Press, Bloomington.

Mandryk, C. A. S., H. Josenhans, D. W. Fedje, and R. W. Mathewes. 2001. Late Quaternary Paleoenvironments of Northwestern North America: Implications for Inland Versus Coastal Migration Routes. *Quaternary Science Reviews* 20:301–314.

Nagai, K. 2007. Flake Scar Patterns of Japanese Tanged Points: Toward an Understanding of Technological Variability During the Incipient Jomon. *Anthropological Science* 115:223–226.

Roosevelt, A. C., J. Douglas, and L. Brown. 2002. The Migrations and Adaptations of the First Americans: Clovis and Pre-Clovis Viewed from South America. In *The First Americans: The Pleistocene Colonization of the New World*, edited by N. Jablonski, pp.159–235. University of California Press, Berkeley.

Tadlock, W. L. 1966. Certain Crescentic Stone Objects as a Time Marker in the Western United States. *American Antiquity* 31(5):662–675.

CHAPTER 14

ARCHAEOLOGY OF THE NORTHWEST COAST

HERBERT D. G. MASCHNER

COMPLEX hunters and gatherers have been a major research focus for anthropologists and archaeologists throughout the world (Arnold 2005; Kennett 2005; Prentiss and Chatters 2003; Price and Brown 1985; Price and Feinman 1995; Sassaman 2004; Sassaman and Randall, this volume). From the deserts of the Natufian Middle East and the bogs of Mesolithic Denmark to the fjords of the Northwest Coast of North America, we have theorized as to the evolutionary processes that might have generated sedentary, socially ranked, hunting and gathering societies. The Northwest Coast of North America (Figure 14.1) has been the anthropological hallmark for complexity and the center of this debate because it is one of the few places where politically complex hunters and gatherers evolved and then survived to historic contact, to be recorded by explorers, missionaries, and photographers (Ames and Maschner 1999).

These societies were indeed spectacular. A formalized lineage and clan structure included hereditary nobility, a middle rank related to the nobility, a lower rank without family or property, and a class of slaves outside of the rank system. Lineages and clans owned and maintained territory and resources, supported occasional craft specialists, maintained defense and organized wars, and participated in a suite of status maintenance activities ranging from specific marriage rules to the famous potlatch feasts (Emmons 1991; Rosman and Rubel 1971; chapters in Suttles 1990). Symbols of status were made from elements of the Northwest Coast natural landscape and included mountain goat hair Chilkat blankets from the northern Northwest Coast, copper plates and shields cold pounded from nuggets coming in from central Alaska, elaborately carved spoons made of mountain sheep horn, and items of body ornamentation ranging from special hats and cloaks to labrets and earrings

ARCHAEOLOGY OF THE NORTHWEST COAST 161

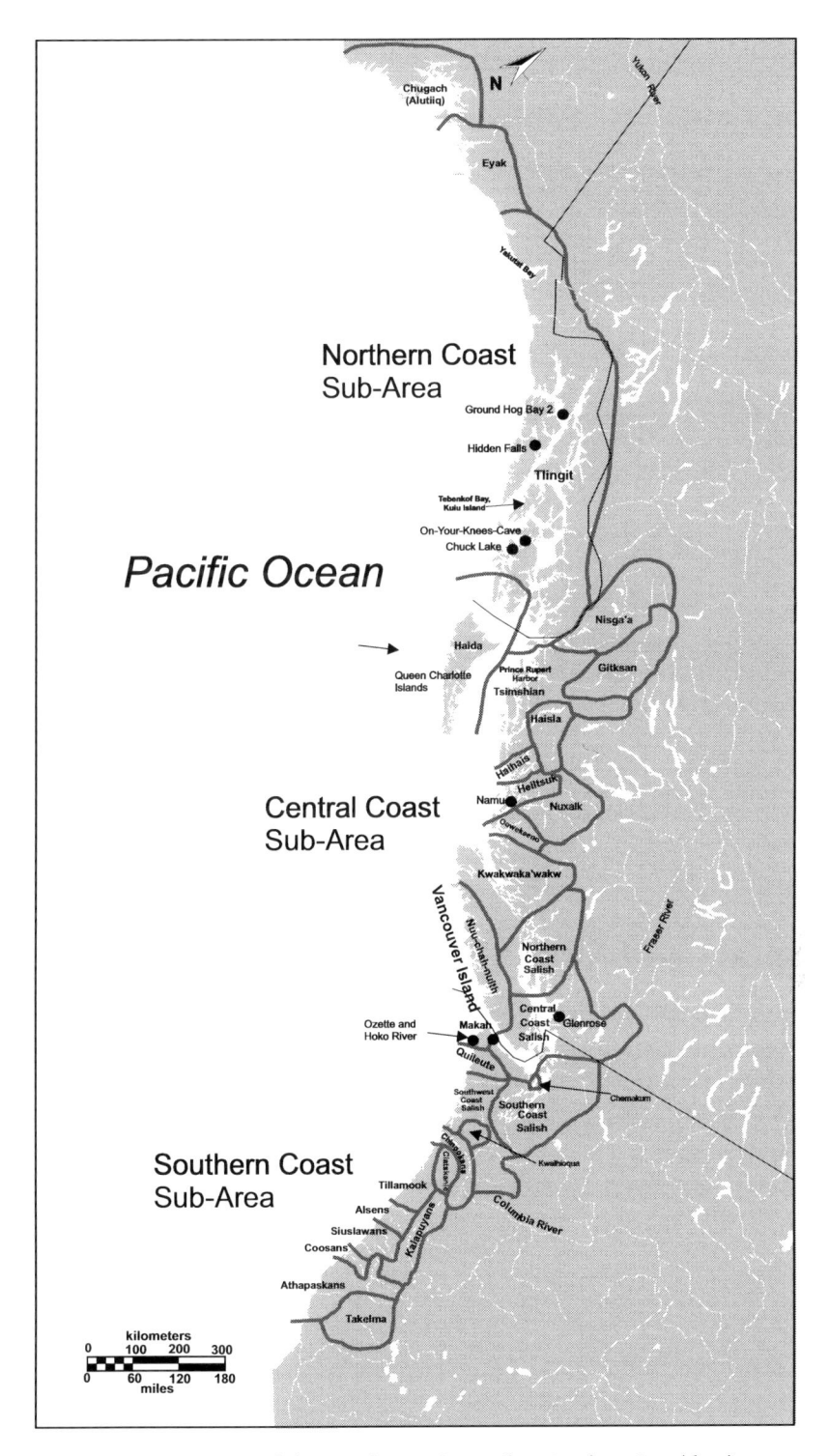

Figure 14.1 Map of the Northwest Coast showing key sites (dots).

(Ames and Maschner 1999). Perhaps the most visually enduring symbols of rank and status were the massive carvings and paintings on housefronts, on poles, boats, or boxes—none of which would have existed had not red cedar been a dominant species on the regional landscape.

If the Northwest Coast had not been part of the historically known societies at the time of European contact, I would argue that the entire concept of cultural complexity among hunters and gatherers would not, in its present form, exist. The result is that most of the models developed for the evolution of complexity among hunters and gatherers have been based, often uncritically, on Northwest Coast ethnography. Considerable research effort has been devoted to the evolution of complexity on the Northwest Coast largely because archaeologists and anthropologists have generally accepted historically recorded behaviors as the prehistoric pattern (e.g., Carlson 1983; for a review see Ames, 1991, 1994; Ames and Maschner 1999). Yet precontact complex hunter-gatherers on the Northwest Coast have been remarkably hard to find. As is outlined below, except for a few items of body ornamentation, burial, and some rather spectacular art finds, the material culture of complexity is almost archaeologically invisible, at least until very late in the archaeological record. This has led archaeologists to put more emphasis on the social aspects of status differentiation, such as warfare, burials, and corporate group size. In hindsight, this author believes this was a good approach, since it has taught us (unlike nearly all other studies around the world where economic and political complexity are obvious in architecture, materials, or economics) that "social" complexity actually arises prior to any representations in economic or political complexity.

After the Ice Age

The ancient history of the region begins with the first colonization of the Americas (Figure 14.2). It is well known that during the peak of the last ice age, sea levels throughout the world were as much as 120 meters lower than today because so much of the earth's water was locked in ice. We also now know that much of the Northwest Coast was an ice-free refugia; that is, it was never glaciated. This region supported diverse ice-age flora and fauna and was probably quite abundant in sea mammals and other marine resources (Heaton 2002). Because it is assumed that they traveled along the shore, and because the shoreline of 14,000 years ago is now under more than 100 meters of ocean, it has been nearly impossible to find traces of these early colonists. But early Holocene submarine sites have recently been identified and important work looking for submerge traces of these early migrants along the shores of British Columbia is ongoing (Fedje 2003; Fedje and Josenhans 2000).

It is not until after the ice sheets melted and sea levels rose to approximately their modern position that we find more extensive traces of the earliest inhabitants along shorelines. This period, from about 10,000 to 5,000 years ago (calibrated

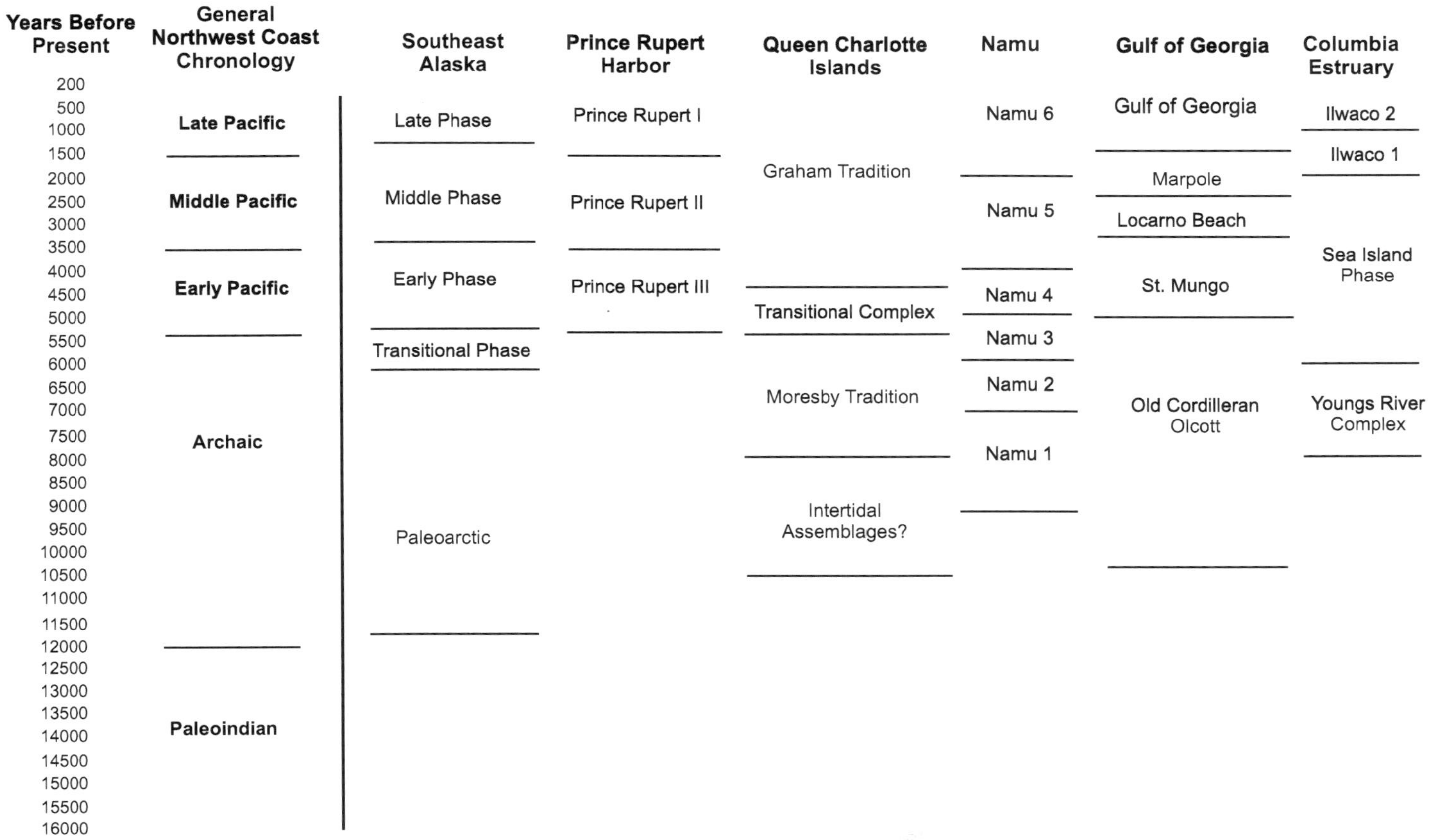

ARCHAEOLOGY OF THE NORTHWEST COAST

Years Before Present	General Northwest Coast Chronology	Southeast Alaska	Prince Rupert Harbor	Queen Charlotte Islands	Namu	Gulf of Georgia	Columbia Estuary
200	Late Pacific	Late Phase	Prince Rupert I	Graham Tradition	Namu 6	Gulf of Georgia	Ilwaco 2
500							
1000							Ilwaco 1
1500						Marpole	
2000	Middle Pacific	Middle Phase	Prince Rupert II		Namu 5	Locarno Beach	
2500							
3000							Sea Island Phase
3500						St. Mungo	
4000	Early Pacific	Early Phase	Prince Rupert III	Transitional Complex	Namu 4		
4500					Namu 3		
5000		Transitional Phase					
5500				Moresby Tradition	Namu 2	Old Cordilleran Olcott	Youngs River Complex
6000							
6500	Archaic				Namu 1		
7000							
7500		Paleoarctic		Intertidal Assemblages?			
8000							
8500							
9000							
9500							
10000							
10500							
11000							
11500							
12000	Paleoindian						
12500							
13000							
13500							
14000							
14500							
15000							
15500							
16000							

Figure 14.2 Northwest Coast chronology chart.

dates), has been referred to as the Archaic Period (Ames and Maschner 1999). One of the earliest dated archaeological sites in southeast Alaska is the Ground Hog Bay 2 site on Icy Strait (Ackerman 1968; Ackerman et al., 1979). Dating to just before 9,500 years ago, it is represented by only a few stone tools. There are a number of other early campsites that date between 5,000 and 10,000 years ago, and one of the most important is the Chuck Lake site on Hecata Island. This site is notable not only for the types of tools found there but more importantly because of preserved subsistence remains. Dating to approximately 8,500 years ago, numerous species of shellfish, halibut, cod, salmon, seals, sea lions, beaver, deer or caribou, and several species of birds were found in the Chuck Lake assemblage, demonstrating that subsistence 8,500 years ago, much like the early occupation of Namu on the British Columbia coast, was not much different from that of the historic period (Ackerman et al. 1985; Cannon 1991). Artifacts include microblade cores of obsidian, argillite, chert, and quartz crystals; scraping, cutting, and engraving tools; fragments of tools of bone; and other items indicating the presence of a diverse toolkit. Microblades are a specialized form of technology indicative of a mobile settlement strategy that required a flexible and generalized toolkit, one in which tools had several functions. One of the more interesting recent finds from the early Holocene is the skeleton in On-Your-Knees Cave on Prince of Wales Island in central southeast Alaska. This early burial, dating to more than 9,000 years ago, is early evidence of a coastal adaptation as chemical analyses of bone samples from this individual indicate his diet was based primarily on marine resources (Dixon 1999; Dixon et al. 1997), corroborating the archaeological midden evidence from the Chuck Lake site, Namu, and elsewhere.

Archaeological sites in this time period are rare, small, and ephemeral. Archaeologists generally interpret these finds as evidence of small, mobile groups of hunters and gatherers with low population density. There is little evidence of any of the cultural characteristics we most often associate with Northwest Coast peoples, but it is significant to note that the basic economic system employed by historically known groups was already in place nearly 9,000 years ago, and probably earlier.

Sometime around 5,000 years ago, a number of remarkable changes occur in the archaeological record of the region. This is the Pacific Period, the time when we begin to see the rise of most of the characteristics we generally associate with the historic Northwest Coast peoples. The Pacific Period is divided into three parts. The Early Pacific dates from about 5,000 to 3,500 years ago, the Middle Pacific 3,500 to about 1,800 years ago, and the Late Pacific 1,800 years ago to the arrival of the first Europeans in the region. These three periods organize the remainder of this discussion.

The most significant changes in the Early Pacific include development of much more permanent communities, greater emphasis on shellfish gathering, and a change in technology. None of these would be visible if the increasing use of shellfish did not also result in formation of shell middens and other garbage at villages and campsites. Some of these shell midden sites are large, covering hundreds of square meters. Mixed in with the shellfish remains are the bones of fish, sea mammals, birds, and ungulates, alongside the remains of fire hearths, food processing areas, and other activity zones. Little remains of houses or other structures in Early Pacific sites, indicating that these peoples were still mobile for at least part of the year, which is supported by intensive use of caves and rock shelters as temporary camps during this period. But conversely, the presence of formal cemeteries on the Queen Charlotte Islands indicates increasing territoriality and village permanence (e.g., Fladmark et al. 1990; Severs [Sutherland] 1974a, 1974b).

The tool technology at this time changes from the chipped-stone industries of the Archaic Period to an emphasis on tools of polished slate, ground stone, antler, and bone, although chipped stone tools are still made, as are microblades in some areas (Fladmark 1986). At the Hidden Falls site in southeast Alaska, Early Pacific deposits include ground slate points, small adzes, labrets, beads, barbed bone harpoon fragments, and other tools (Davis 1990). Further south in British Columbia, contemporary deposits have artifacts with artistic motifs clearly related to historic styles (Ames and Maschner 1999).

Beginning approximately 3,500 years ago, a number of major changes occur in the prehistory of the region once again. Villages become much larger and more permanent, there is more intensive harvesting of offshore fish such as herring and cod, and there are regionwide changes in social and political organization. But two other changes are perhaps even more important. The first is intensive harvesting of salmon and simultaneous development of fish traps and weirs, which are constructed of wooden stakes and are found in streams the length of the Northwest Coast during the Middle Pacific (Maschner 1997b; Moss et al., 1990). The second is development of large cemeteries with many burials. One of the most important southeast Alaska sites is the Coffman Cove site on the northeast side of Prince of Wales Island, where burials, numerous ground slate tools, and extensive shell midden deposits were recovered. In Tebenkof Bay on Kuiu Island, the important Step Island Village site revealed a subsistence economy emphasizing cod, herring, harbor seals, sea otters, porpoise, shellfish, and salmon (Maschner 1991, 1992). Square plank houses, organized into rows, also become more common, such as those on the Skeena River (Coupland 1988).

The Boardwalk site in Prince Rupert Harbor on the northern British Columbia Coast was intensively investigated in the 1970s by Canadian and American archaeologists (Ames 2005b). Here the remains of small plank-walled Middle Pacific houses were found. Near the houses was a cemetery with numerous burials, some with offerings of rare and exotic goods and body adornments indicating that differences in formal status were developing at this time. Most of the male burials showed evidence of violent trauma such as skull fractures, parrying fractures to the arm, and other injuries most often associated with violent conflict. Artistic styles are now in the modern form. Tools are much the same as in the Early Pacific, but there are many more heavy woodworking tools, the type that would be used for splitting large house planks and carving the massive canoes that were so important historically (Ames 1994; Ames and Maschner 1999; Cybulski 1992; Fladmark et al., 1990).

On the southern Northwest coast, the Marpole Phase shows extensive evidence of status differences, especially in regard to cranial deformation and the wealth of grave goods. High-status grave goods include dentalium beads, copper artifacts, carvings, shell rattles, and large spear points (Burley and Knüsel 1989). Surprisingly though, these social, political, and economic changes around the Gulf of Georgia in southern British Columbia, and also found in Prince Rupert Harbor, do not appear to be widespread in the region, with the most complex communities concentrated in the most highly productive regions, while elsewhere there are no large houses, few burials, little evidence of status differences, and far more scattered populations. Most of the largest villages disappear by approximately 2,000 years ago, indicating that this early experiment with large villages did not extend directly into the Late Pacific Period.

The Late Pacific witnesses technology, settlements, social behavior, and economy directly comparable with most historic groups. The most obvious is the rise of large villages composed of numerous plank houses that become dominant after 1,800 years ago and are clearly organized in the Northwest Coast pattern (Ames and Maschner 1999; Cybulski 2001; Matson and Coupland 1995; Matson et al. 2003; Sobel et al. 2006). Defensive fortifications located on inaccessible bluffs and islands, villages with palisades, and a war technology are also developed at this time, implying that there is a relationship between development of these villages and intensification of conflicts in the region (Maschner 1992, 1997a, 1997b; Mitchell 1984, 1990; Moss 1989; Moss and Erlandson 1992). In fact, fortifications are one of the most prominent types of archaeological sites during the Late Pacific. The burial traditions that are so important in the Middle Pacific Period disappear, perhaps replaced by burial in trees or on platforms and totems, but these have not been preserved. Evidence for status differences is seen in the size of social groups, as measured in house size. There is extensive historic evidence that the largest houses had the highest status because they had the most political power, and the earliest Late Pacific villages have clearly different house sizes (Maschner and Patton 1996; Maschner and Bentley 2003).

Artifactual remains from Late Pacific sites bear a striking resemblance to the ethnographic period, with heavy emphasis on ground or polished bone and stone (Ames and Maschner 1999). Bone tools include sea mammal bone harpoons and other barbed projectiles, terrestrial mammal bone points and an array of awls, pins, and other tools. The stone technology includes ground slate blades, spear and arrow points, heavy pecked and ground hammers, chisels, and ground adzes. The extensive woodworking toolkit is a measure of how important the manufacture of houses, poles, boxes, canoes, and other wood items became at this time (Fladmark 1986). The spectacular finds at a number of water saturated sites such as Hoko River and Ozette (Croes 1995; see also the extensive Ozette report series), demonstrate that much of Northwest Coast technology was perishable, and stone tools give us little understanding of the range of technologies present at any one time in the region. Art objects and designs parallel those seen by the earliest explorers in the region. The subsistence economy remains much as it was in the Middle Pacific Period, but there appears to be much greater emphasis on salmon, as found by bones in middens, though less construction of fish weirs on salmon streams, indicating changes in harvesting and storage strategies.

The Late Pacific Period is not stable for its 1,500-year duration. Populations peak about 850 years ago, about the same time there is a peak in construction of villages and defensive fortifications. In some areas of the Northwest Coast, there is a shift from the diverse subsistence economy of the previous 4,000 years to one specialized on salmon and deer (e.g., Maschner 1997b). It is unclear why this occurs, but the specialized diet and intensive warfare do not last long. Within 200 years, some regions are abandoned, and others show a marked decrease in human population, only to be reoccupied in the last 200–300 years before European exploration of the region. This disruption in settlement and demography between 800 and 600 years ago is visible in the archaeological record from southeast Alaska southward to the Gulf of Georgia, where the Coast Salish Pattern develops after this time.

When the first European explorers arrived on the Northwest Coast, many of the characteristics present for the previous 1,500 years were witnessed firsthand. Large sedentary villages, massive houses, intensive warfare, systems of rank and prestige, formal artistic styles, extensive trade networks, craft specialization, and a marine subsistence economy were hallmarks of some of the world's most complex hunting and fishing societies. Some might argue that the continuities in certain categories of Northwest culture indicate there has been little change for the last few thousand years and a linear trajectory leading to the modern peoples, but here we have seen that this is not the case. Although it is clear that the same types of peoples have been in the region for a considerable time, there is also evidence of considerable changes in culture, demography, settlement, and every other aspect of life.

The Archaeology of Rank

At the Glenrose cannery site along the shores of the lower Fraser River in southern British Columbia, a small knife handle with a human figure wearing a top-knot hat and indications of ear ornamentation was found (Ames and Maschner 1999:228). Hats with a top knot were a symbol of rank when the first explorers arrive among the Nuu-Chah-Nulth (Nootka), and some believe that this 4,000-year-old figure is among the earliest evidence for symbols of rank on the Northwest coast. Nearly 1,500 years later, Ames finds differential labret use, as seen in burials at the Boardwalk site, to be a potential measure of rank (Ames and Maschner 1999). We could also look at the burials themselves, and occasionally find evidence for high-status individuals, children with extraordinary grave goods (references in Ames and Maschner), or specialized burial monuments (Lepofsky et al. 2000). One could also look at more structural attributes, such as population size (Croes and Hackenberger 1988), warfare (Maschner 1997a), resource intensification (Ames 2005a; Butler and Campbell 2004; Coupland 1998; Matson 1983), house size variation (Coupland 1988; Maschner 1991; Maschner and Patton 1996; Maschner and Bentley 2003), sedentism (Matson 1985), slavery (Ames 2008; Donald 1983; Mitchell and Donald 1985), or even the organization of households (Ames 1996; Sobel et al. 2006). We have speculated as to the impacts of these attributes on complexity as a cultural adaptation (Keeley 1988), as a means of organizing labor (Ames 1985, 2001), or even the production of feasts such as the potlatch (Hayden 1997, 2001). But as Ames and Maschner (1999) have discussed (perhaps better summarized by Sassaman 2004), there are no origins of complexity on the Northwest Coast. Rather, most of the basic features of complexity are present in the region throughout prehistory. By extension, we might argue that all of the basic features of complex hunter-gatherers are present among all foraging peoples, but there are historical, evolutionary, and structural changes that create the package we refer to as complex hunter-gatherers. What are they?

There appear to be four critical events that can occur simultaneously or individually over thousands of years. The first is sedentism. There are no complex foraging societies that are also highly mobile in the traditional expectation of foragers. Second, there must be a condition that keeps individual kin groups in the same village, such as the location of a critical resource, or for defense, or for something else. Regardless, there must be a reason to maintain a village and for groups to not regularly fission away from the village. The third is population; there must be the environmental productivity needed to provide for large and dense human populations. Ranked societies never develop in regions where small mobile groups are the only possibility because rank is valuable only when expressed with nonkinsmen. If everyone in your village is related to you, expressions of rank become irrelevant. Finally, there must be a means of generating differential kin-group size, and thus social power. As found almost unilaterally around the world in village-based societies, the head person of the largest kin group is most often the head person of the village. Thus, when sedentary populations living in a productive environment are circumscribed into large, multikin-group villages and some of these kin groups are larger than others, cultural complexity—in this case strong social hierarchies—appears in almost every case. This scenario reduces all other factors such as feasting, labor control, territoriality, warfare, trade and exchange for valuables, intensification and storage, and anything else to a symptom of cultural complexity. Conversely, it also implies that the basic tenets of complexity are present in all humans and that the traditional forager models founded in mobility and egalitarian ideals described for southern Africa, the Arctic, Australia, or the Great Basin (Lee and Devore 1966; Kelly 1995) are in fact extremely complex adaptations to very marginal environments.

REFERENCES

Ackerman, R. 1968. Archaeology of the Glacier Bay Region, Southeastern Alaska. *Washington State University. Laboratory of Anthropology. Report of Investigations* 44, Pullman.

Ackerman, R. E., T. D. Hamilton, and R. Stuckenrath. 1979. Early Culture Complexes on the Northern Northwest Coast. *Canadian Journal of Archaeology* 3:195–209.

Ackerman, R. E., K. C. Reid, J. D. Gallison, and M. E. Roe. 1985. *Archaeology of Heceta Island: A Survey of 16 Timber Harvest Units in the Tongass National Forest, Southeastern Alaska*. Washington State University. Center for Northwest Anthropology. Project Reports 3, Pullman.

Ames, K. M. 1985. Hierarchies, Stress, and Logistical Strategies Among Hunter-Gatherers in Northwest North America. In *Prehistoric Hunter-Gatherers: The Emergence of Cultural Complexity*, edited by T. D. Price and J. A. Brown, pp. 155–180. Academic Press, New York.

———. 1991. The Archaeology of the Longue Durée: Temporal and Spatial Scale in the Evolution of Social Complexity on the Southern Northwest Coast. *Antiquity* 65:935–945.

———. 1994. The Northwest Coast: Complex Hunter-Gatherers, Ecology, and Social Evolution. *Annual Review of Anthropology* 23:209–229.

———. 1996. Life in the Big House: Household Labor and Dwelling Size on the Northwest Coast. In *People Who Lived in Big Houses: Archaeological Perspectives on Large Domestic Structures*, edited by C. Coupland and E. B. Banning, pp. 178–200. Prehistory Press, Madison, WI.

———. 2001. Slaves, Chiefs and Labour on the Northern Northwest Coast. *World Archaeology* 33(1):1–17.

———. 2005a. Intensification of Food Production on the Northwest Coast, the Columbia Plateau, and Elsewhere. In *The Northwest Coast, Foragers or Farmers?* edited by D. Duer and N. Turner, pp. 64–94. University of Washington Press, Seattle.

———. 2005b. *The North Coast Prehistory Project Excavations in Prince Rupert Harbour, British Columbia: The Artifacts*. British Archaeological Reports: International Series 1342. John and Erica Hedges, Oxford.

———. 2008. Slavery, Household Production and Demography on the Southern Northwest Coast: Cables, Tacking and Ropewalks. In *Invisible Citizens: Captives and Their Consequences*, edited by C. Cameron, pp 138–158. University of Utah Press, Salt Lake City.

———, and H. Maschner. 1999. *Peoples of the Northwest Coast: Their Archaeology and Prehistory*. Thames and Hudson, London.

Arnold, J. E. 2004. *Foundations of Chumash Complexity*. Cotsen Institute of Archaeology Press, UCLA, Los Angeles.

Burley, D. V., and C. Knüsel. 1989. Burial Patterns and Archaeological Interpretation: Problems in the Recognition of Ranked Society in the Coast Salish Region. In *Preprint Proceedings, Circumpacific Prehistory Conference, Seattle*, vol. III, part 2, unpaginated.

Butler, V. L., and S. K. Campbell. 2004. Resource Intensification and Resource Depression in the Pacific Northwest of North America: A Zooarchaeological Review. *Journal of World Prehistory* 18(4):327–405.

Cannon, A. 1991. *The Economic Prehistory of Namu*. Archaeology Press, Simon Fraser University, Burnaby, report no. 19.

Carlson, R. I. (editor). 1983. *Indian Art Traditions of the Northwest Coast*. Simon Fraser University Press, Burnaby, British Columbia.

Coupland, G. 1988. *Prehistoric Cultural Change at Kitselas Canyon*. Canadian Museum of Civilization, National Museums of Canada, Ottawa.

———. 1998. Maritime Adaptation and Evolution of the Developed Northwest Coast Pattern on the Central Northwest Coast. *Arctic Anthropology* 35:36–56.

Croes, D. L. 1995. *The Hoko River Archaeological Site Complex*, Washington State University Press, Pullman.

———, and Hackenberger, S. 1988. Hoko River Archaeological Complex: Modeling Prehistoric Northwest Coast Economic Evolution. In *Prehistoric Economies of the Pacific Northwest Coast*, edited by B. L. Isaac, pp. 19–85. JAI Press, Greenwich, CT.

Cybulski, J. S. 1992. *A Greenville Burial Ground, Human Remains and Mortuary Elements in British Columbia Coast Prehistory*. Mercury Series Paper No. 146, Archaeological Survey of Canada, Canadian Museum of Civilization, Hull, Quebec.

——— (editor). 2001. *Perspectives on Northern Northwest Coast Prehistory*. Mercury Series, Archaeological Survey of Canada, Paper 160. Canadian Museum of Civilization, Hull, Quebec.

Davis, S. D. 1990. Prehistory of Southeast Alaska. In *Handbook of North American Indians, Vol. 7: Northwest Coast*, edited by W. Suttles, pp. 197–202. Smithsonian Institution, Washington, DC.

Dixon, E. J. 1999. *Bones, Boats and Bison: Archaeology of the First Colonization of Western North America*. University of New Mexico Press, Albuquerque.

———, Heaton, T. H., Fifield, T. E., Hamilton, T. D., Putnam, D. E., and Grady, F. 1997. Late Quaternary Regional Geoarchaeology of Southeast Alaska Karst: A Progress Report. *Geoarchaeology* 12:689–712.

Donald, L. 1983. "Was Nuu-chah-nulth-aht Nootka Society Based on Slave Labor?" In *The Development of Political Organization in Native North America*, edited by E. Tooker, pp. 108–119. Proceedings of the American Ethnological Society, 1979. Washington DC.

Emmons, G. 1991. *The Tlingit Indians*. University of Washington Press, Seattle.

Fedje, D. W. 2003 Ancient Landscapes and Archaeology in Haida Gwaii and Hecate Strait. In *Archaeology of Coastal British Columbia: Essays in Honour of Professor Philip M. Hobler*, edited by R. L. Carlson, pp. 29–38. Archaeology Press, Burnaby, British Columbia.

———, and Josenhans, H. W. 2000. Drowned Forests and Archaeology on the Continental Shelf of British Columbia, Canada. *Geology* 28:99–102.

Fladmark, K. 1986. *British Columbia Prehistory*. Archaeological Survey of Canada, National Museum of Man, National Museums of Canada, Ottawa.

———, K. M. Ames, and P. D. Sutherland. 1990. Prehistory of the Northern Coast of British Columbia. In *Handbook of North American Indians, Vol. 7: Northwest Coast*, edited by W. Suttles, pp. 229–239. Smithsonian Press, Washington DC.

Hayden, B. 1997. *The Pithouses of Keatley Creek*. Harcourt Brace College, Forth Worth, TX.

———. 2001. Fabulous Feasts: A Prolegomenon to the Importance of Feasting. In *Feasts: Archaeological and Ethnographic Perspectives on Food, Politics, and Power*, edited by M. Dietler and B. Hayden, pp. 23–64. Smithsonian Institution Press, Washington, DC.

Heaton, T. H. 2002. Late Quaternary Vertebrate Fossils from the Outer Islands of Southern Southeast Alaska. *Current Research in the Pleistocene* 19:102–104.

Keeley, L. H. 1988. Hunter-gatherer Economic Complexity and "Population Pressure": A Crosscultural Analysis. *Journal of Anthropological Archaeology* 7:373–411.

Kelly, R. L. 1995. *The Foraging Spectrum: Diversity in Hunter-Gatherer/Lifeways*. Smithsonian Institution Press, Washington, DC.

Kennett, D. J. 2005. *The Island Chumash: Behavioral Ecology of a Maritime Society*. University of California Press, Berkeley.

Lee, R. B., and I. DeVore (editors). 1968. *Man the Hunter*. New York: Aldine de Gruyter.

Lepofsky, D., M. Blake, D. Brown, S. Morrison, N. Oakes, and N. Lyons. 2000. The Archaeology of the Scowlitz Site, SW British Columbia. *Journal of Field Archaeology* 27(4):391–416.

Maschner, H. D. G. 1991. The Emergence of Cultural Complexity on the Northern Northwest Coast. *Antiquity* 65:924–934.

———. 1992. *The Origins of Hunter and Gatherer Sedentism and Political Complexity: A Case Study from the Northern Northwest Coast.* Unpublished Ph.D. dissertation, University of California, Santa Barbara.

———. 1997a. The Evolution of Northwest Coast Warfare. In *Troubled Times: Violence and Warfare in the Past,* edited by D. Martin and D. Frayer, pp. 267–302. Gordon and Breach, Amsterdam.

———. 1997b. Settlement and Subsistence in the Later Prehistory of Tebenkof Bay, Kuiu Island. *Arctic Anthropology* 34:74–99.

———. and R. A. Bentley. 2003. The Power Law of Rank and Household on the North Pacific. In *Complex Systems and Archaeology: Empirical and Theoretical Applications,* edited by R. A. Bentley and H. D. G. Maschner, pp 47–60. University of Utah Press, Salt Lake City.

Maschner, H. D. G., and J. Q. Patton. 1996. Kin Selection and the Origins of Hereditary Social Inequality: A Case Study from the Northern Northwest Coast. In *Darwinian Archaeologies,* edited by H. D. G. Maschner, pp. 89–107. Plenum Press, New York.

Matson, R. G. 1983. Intensification and the Development of Cultural Complexity: The Northwest Versus the Northeast Coast. In *The Evolution of Maritime Cultures on the Northeast and the Northwest Coasts of America,* edited by R. J. Nash, pp. 125–148. Simon Fraser University, Publication 11. Burnaby, BC, Canada.

———. 1985. The Relationship Between Sedentism and Status Inequalities Among Hunter Gatherers. In *Status, Structure, and Stratification: Current Archaeological Reconstructions,* edited by M. Thompson, M. T. Garcia, and F. J. Kense, pp. 245–252. Archaeological Association of the University of Calgary, Calgary.

———, and G. Coupland. 1995. *The Prehistory of the Northwest Coast.* Academic Press, New York.

———, and Q. Mackie. 2003. *Emerging from the Mist: Studies in Northwest Coast Culture History.* UBC Press, Vancouver.

Mitchell, D. 1984. Predatory Warfare, Social Status, and the North Pacific Slave Trade. *Ethnology* 231:39–48.

———. 1990. Prehistory of the Coasts of Southern British Columbia and Northern Washington. In *Handbook of North American Indians,* Vol. 7: *Northwest Coast,* edited by W. Suttles, pp. 340–358. Smithsonian Press, Washington, DC.

———, and L. Donald. 1985. Some Economic Aspects of Tlingit, Haida, and Tsimshian Slavery. In *Research of Economic Anthropology,* edited by B. L. Isaac, vol. 7, pp. 19–35. JAI, Greenwich, CT.

Moss, M. 1989 *Archaeology and Cultural Ecology of the Prehistoric Angoon Tlingit.* Ph.D. dissertation. Department of Anthropology, University of California, Santa Barbara.

———, and J. Erlandson. 1992. Forts, Refuge Rocks, and Defensive Sites: The Antiquity of Warfare Along the North Pacific Coast of North America. *Arctic Anthropology* 29:73–90.

Moss, M., J. Erlandson, and R. Stuckenrath. 1990. Wood Stake Weirs and Salmon Fishing on the Northwest Coast: Evidence from Southeast Alaska. *Canadian Journal of Archaeology* 14:143–158.

Prentiss, W., and J. C. Chatters. 2003. The Evolution of Collector Systems on the Pacific Coast of Northwest North America. In *Hunter-Gatherers of the North Pacific Rim,* edited by J. Habu, J. M. Savelle, S. Koyama, and H. Hongo, pp. 49–80. Senri Ethnological Studies No. 63, National Museum of Ethnology, Osaka.

Price, T. D., and J. A. Brown (editors). 1985. *Prehistoric Hunter-Gatherers: The Emergence of Cultural Complexity.* Academic Press, New York.

Price, T. D., and G. M. Feinman (editors). 1995. *Foundations of Social Inequality*. Plenum, New York.

Rosman, A., and P. G. Rubel. 1971. *Feasting with Mine Enemy*. Columbia University Press, New York.

Sassaman, K. E. 2004. Complex Hunter-Gatherers in Evolution and History: A North American Perspective. *Journal of Archaeological Research* 12(3):227–280.

Severs [Sutherland], P. D. S. 1974a. A Review of Island Prehistory: Archaeological Investigations at Blue Jackets Creek 1972–1973. *The Charlottes, A Journal of the Queen Charlotte Islands* 3:2–12.

———. 1974b. Archaeological Investigations at Blue Jackets Creek, FlUa 4, Queen Charlotte Islands, British Columbia. *Bulletin of the Canadian Archaeological Association* 6:163–205.

Sobel, E., A. Trieu, and K. Ames (editors). 2006. *Household Archaeology on the Northwest Coast. Archaeological Series 16*, International Monographs in Archaeology, Ann Arbor, MI.

Suttles, W. (editor). 1990. *Handbook of North American Indians, Vol. 7: Northwest Coast*. Smithsonian Press, Washington DC.

CHAPTER 15

THE WINTER VILLAGE PATTERN ON THE PLATEAU OF NORTHWESTERN NORTH AMERICA

ANNA MARIE PRENTISS

AT the time of European contact, the Plateau region of North America's Pacific Northwest featured a more diverse array of societies than any of its surrounding regions (Figure 15.1). More mobile and egalitarian societies inhabited the portions of the eastern boundary and adjacent Rocky Mountains. Affluent villagers could be found in many sections of the middle to upper Columbia and Thompson River systems. Truly complex societies, rivaling those of the Northwest Coast, inhabited portions of the Lower Columbia River and Middle to Lower Fraser Canyon. Communities throughout the region interacted through extensive exchange networks, moving a wide array of goods that included subsistence items such as dried fish and roots, but also prestige markers such as obsidian eccentrics, nephrite jade adzes, and copper jewelry (Hayden and Schulting 1997; Rousseau 2004).

Plateau societies also connected with groups from surrounding regions; influential persons and groups within so-called gateway communities acted as go-betweens for producers of shell beads on the coast and bison products on the Plains (Hayden et al. 1985). Yet not all Plateau interactions were peaceful. It is now well known that Plateau people participated in violent conflicts, which at times grew so severe that entire villages were built on islands and mesa tops to avoid attack (Chatters 2004).

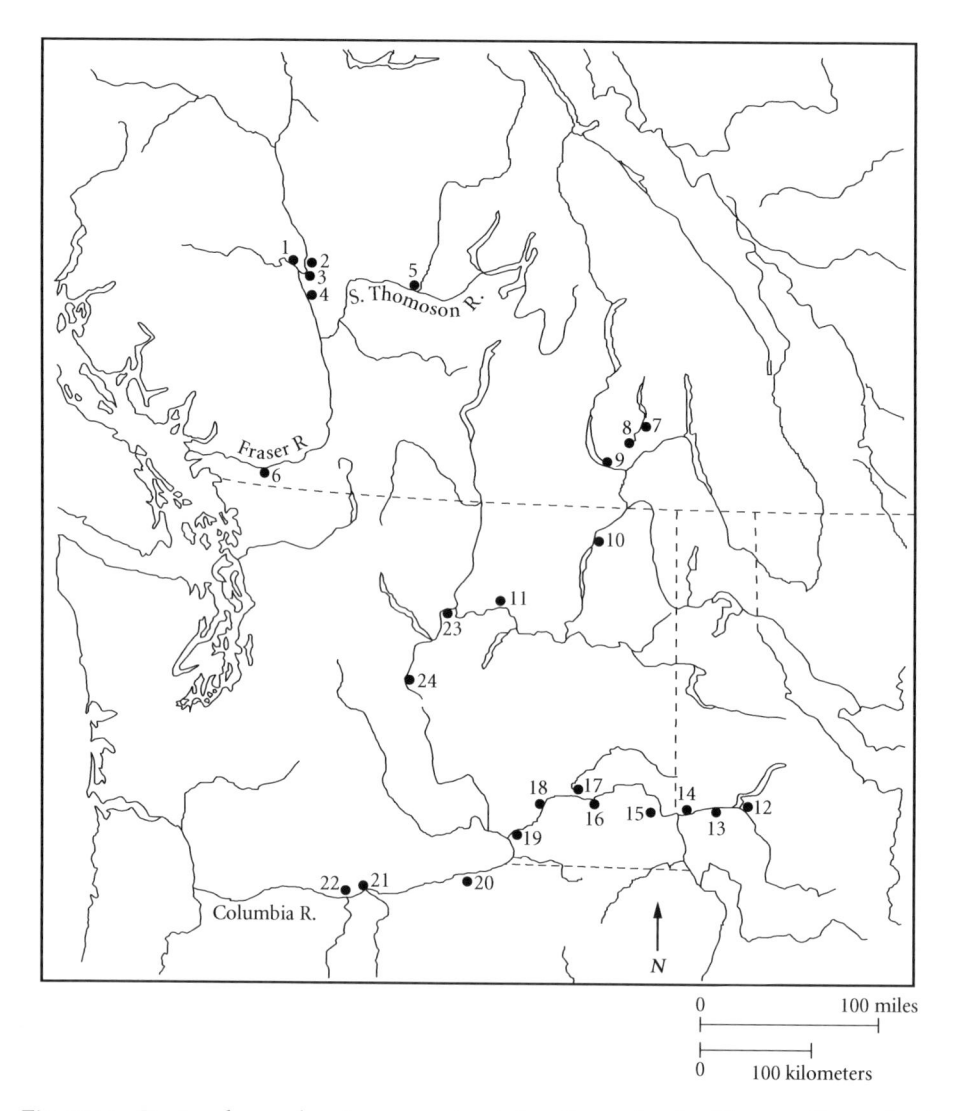

Figure 15.1 Regional map showing approximate locations of major Plateau villages: (1–4) Middle Fraser Canyon villages, including Bridge River, Keatley Creek, Bell, and Lochnore-Nesikep; (5) Kamloops locality villages; (6) Lower Fraser Valley sites (e.g., Scowlitz); (7–10) Upper Columbia Villages, including Slocan Narrows and Vallican; (11, 23–24) Mid-Columbia Villages; (12–19) Lower Snake River Villages; (20–22) Lower Columbia Villages.

We have a long way to go before the ancient history of the Plateau villages can be fully written. However, drawing from Andrefsky (2004), Chatters and Pokotylo (1998), Goodale et al. (2004), Prentiss et al. (2005), and Rousseau (2004), it is possible at this time to outline a basic framework and consider possible explanations for change in some areas. Plateau villages over the past 5,000 years were organized as variable clusters of semisubterranean structures or pithouses. These ranged in scale from small hamlets with a limited number of houses (Chatters 1995) to larger aggregation sites associated with optimal fishing places, such as the Five Mile Rapids and associated locales of the Lower Columbia, temporarily occupied defensive villages placed in inaccessible locales such as Strawberry Island (Chatters 2004), and large winter villages sometimes featuring a high number of simultaneously occupied houses as at the Bridge River site (Prentiss et al. 2008). Pithouses on the Plateau were constructed in a variety of ways, ranging from smaller structures based in shallow depressions, topped by ephemeral superstructures (tipilike arrangements of timbers covered by mats), to the far more labor-intensive permanent winter houses of the Middle Fraser Canyon. Middle Fraser houses could exceed 20 meters in diameter and 2 meters in depth. Superstructures were engineering masterpieces of post, joist, and beam construction, topped by mats and clay or sod (Hayden 1997; Teit 1900).

Development of the historic Plateau cultures is not one of gradual *in situ* change across the millennia of the Holocene. Rather, recent evidence (Chatters 1995; Prentiss and Chatters 2003; Prentiss et al. 2005) suggests a far more complex history involving local change, cultural extinctions, and major intra- and extraregional population expansions and contractions. In this discussion, I offer a short overview of major trends in this history and consider a range of explanatory arguments, particularly focusing on the evolution of variation in Plateau villages. More specifically, I argue that Plateau archaeologists need to draw a distinction between socioeconomically "complex" communities and those designated as "sociopolitically" complex because different processes affected their respective evolution (i.e., the process of historical development that excludes any teleological assumptions).

Plateau Culture History

The very large villages of the Plateau were a relatively late development following centuries of experimentation with pithouse living. The earliest communities appeared shortly after 5000 cal BP and were organized quite differently from the later villages. Early pithouse communities of the Pithouse I period in the Columbia Basin consisted of small hamlets of houses 5–7 meters in diameter, placed in ecotones optimal to a range of resources. There is little to suggest that these people employed storage and delayed consumption to any significant degree, despite the fact that the highly diverse fauna within these sites imply multiseasonal occupation (Chatters 1995). Artifact styles are little different from those of the more mobile foragers of the earlier Cascade phase, suggesting that Pithouse I likely developed within the Columbia Basin (Chatters and Prentiss 2005). The Pithouse I pattern is reflected only at the Baker site on the Canadian Plateau to the north, where it appears to be the result of a brief incursion of southern peoples (Prentiss and Kuijt 2004).

The sedentary foragers (foragers meaning those favoring immediate-return subsistence and limited use of logistical mobility) of Pithouse I emerged at a time of regional diversification in socioeconomic strategies. Elsewhere in the Pacific Northwest, some groups persisted in the more residentially mobile forager pattern, whereas others explored serial specialist and collectorlike (collectors meaning those favoring storage-based subsistence and extensive logistical mobility) strategies (Prentiss and Chatters 2003). By ca. 4100 BP this period came to a relatively sudden end as temperatures dropped and resource structure was severely altered during the early Neoglacial period (Chatters 1995). Immediate-return subsistence strategies associated with sedentary and mobile foraging groups proved maladaptive under the new conditions of longer, colder, and wetter winters. Groups in the interior were apparently unable to rearrange their economies in time to stave off subsistence catastrophe and demographic collapse or regional abandonment. Multiple datasets support our contention that the Plateau was substantially vacated ca. 4100–3600 BP (Chatters 1995; Goodale et al. 2004; Prentiss and Kuijt 2004).

It is not clear where in the greater Pacific Northwest the delayed-consumption collector strategy first developed. Current data suggest that it likely first emerged somewhere on the outer Northwest Coast, perhaps the Queen Charlotte Islands or Haida Gwaii. Regardless of its place of origin, the strategy was well designed for the more seasonal conditions of the Neoglacial and subsequently spread rapidly after ca. 4000 BP, arriving on the Plateau by ca. 3500–3600 BP as Pithouse II in the Columbia Basin and the Shuswap horizon on the Canadian Plateau. Early Plateau collectors placed small pithouse hamlets in positions optimal to specific resources and relied on logistical mobility for acquisition of more distant foods (Chatters 1995). Winter village sedentism was facilitated by intensive harvest and storage of select resources, particularly salmon and roots (Chatters 1995; Thoms 1989). No signs of large permanent social aggregates or inequality are recognizable prior to about 2200 BP.

Today's native peoples of the Plateau (e.g., Upper Lillooet, Wasco, Wishram, and Umatilla) recognize two particularly important fishing places, the Five Mile rapids of the Lower Columbia and the Six Mile Rapids of the Middle Fraser Canyon. Interestingly, the largest early fishing-associated village aggregations probably did not occur at either place, but at the juncture of the North and South Thompson Rivers in what is now Kamloops, British Columbia (Rousseau 2004). A very large number of small housepits with thin floors and shallow rim middens suggests repeated short-lived visits to this locality. A similar process was developing on the Lower Columbia and in the Upper Columbia-Slocan area, though clearly not on the scale of that associated with the Thompson drainage at ca. 1500–2200 BP.

Probably the most dramatic development in Canadian Plateau prehistory was the rapid appearance and apparent expansion of the Lillooet phenomenon (Hayden and Ryder 1991; Matson and Magne 2007; Prentiss et al. 2005). Shortly after 2000 BP, villages made up of unusually large housepits (some span more than 20 meters in diameter) appeared and spread throughout the Middle Fraser Canyon area. Recent surveys suggest the distribution may extend from the vicinity of Kanaka Bar, south of Lytton, British Columbia, all the way to the mouth of the Chilcotin River about 160 kilometers to the north. Villages are consistently large, ranging from 20 to more than 100 housepits placed on terraces within the Fraser Canyon and adjacent drainages, optimal to fishing access (Figure 15.2). Intensive research at the Bell, Bridge River, and Keatley Creek sites indicates that during the period of ca. 1800–800 BP some of these communities developed large populations (estimated at more than 700 in some places) and during the final centuries of occupation also featured indicators of significant social inequality (Prentiss et al. 2007, 2008). The historical origin of the Lillooet village pattern is at this time not clear. Some argue from in situ development associated with rich resources and competitive groups (Hayden 1994). I suggest that the Lillooet phenomenon could alternatively reflect a complex collector socioeconomic strategy that rapidly dispersed, by some combination of demic expansion and cultural transmission, possibly from a single point of origin likely to the south in the Lower Fraser Valley or its associated drainages (Prentiss et al. 2005).

The Lillooet phenomenon ended by ca. 800 BP. Hayden and Rider (1991) sought to explain abandonment of the Middle Fraser villages by virtue of a geological catastrophe that dammed the Fraser River and prevented salmon migrations. However, it is clear that this could not have been the case given problems in dating the event and establishing its effects (Kuijt 2001). Further, not all villages in the Middle Fraser area were abandoned at one time; the Bridge River village was vacated by 1100 BP, possibly up to two centuries before that of nearby Keatley Creek. Finally, it is now known that villages across a much larger area were abandoned in the 700–900 BP range, including many downstream from the purported slump event and even more in other drainages such as the Upper Columbia. Goodale et al. (2004) recognize the rise and decline of large housepit villages in the Upper Columbia, Slocan, and Lower Kutenai River valleys as coinciding very closely to those of the Fraser system. Village abandonments and other signs of cultural disturbance are recognized on the central Northwest Coast in this time frame as well. The rate of interpersonal violence apparently rose throughout the interior and adjacent coastal regions after ca. 1200 BP (Chatters 2004). Consequently, I suggest that a more likely scenario involves subsistence impacts on aggregated village populations (e.g., Prentiss et al. 2007) throughout the region, associated with productivity decline in anadromous fish populations brought on by climatic conditions of the Medieval Warm Period (Chatters et al. 1995; Tunnicliffe et al. 2001).

Villages throughout many portions of the Plateau region reaggregated after ca. 500 BP, resulting in the distribution of ethnographic cultures recognized by early European explorers. Some of the Middle Fraser villages were repopulated, particularly in the Lillooet area, likely by descendants of the original occupants. A similar phenomenon may have occurred in the Upper Columbia area that also included construction of large-scale earthworks, including defensive walls and house platforms (Goodale et al. 2004; Prentiss et al. 2005). Island settlements persisted in portions of the Lower Snake and Columbia drainages (Chatters 2004). Chinookan groups (e.g., ancestors of today's Wasco and Wishram) moved up river into the Dalles area of the Lower Columbia, bringing with them an extremely complex society originally developed closer to the coast (Ames et al. 1998).

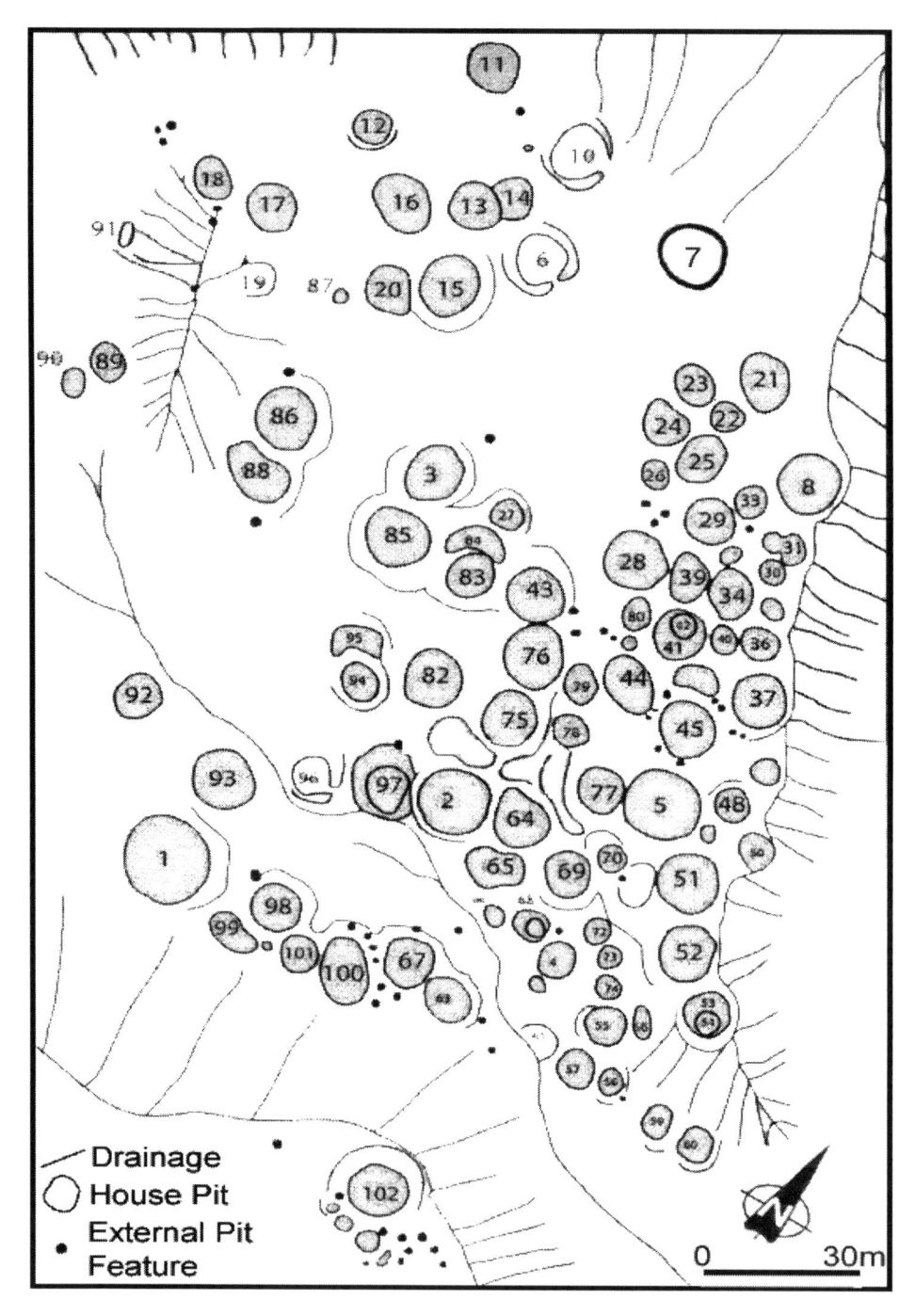

Figure 15.2 Map of the core village area of the Keatley Creek Site.

Complex Hunter-Gatherers on the Plateau

The Lillooet phenomenon of the Middle Fraser Canyon currently provides the best insight into the histories of complex hunter-gatherers on the Plateau. In this context, it appears likely that the pattern, defined in particular by clusters of very large housepits, large-scale storage facilities, and extensive numbers of extramural roasting pits, developed initially as a socioeconomic strategy. The pattern of sociopolitical complexity, centered on interhousehold and possibly interindividual ranking, as described by Hayden (1997), does not appear to have come until somewhat later.

Socioeconomically complex hunter-gatherers (per Prentiss et al. 2005) appeared at ca. 2500 BP in the Fraser Valley between the mouth of the Harrison River and the base of the Fraser Canyon at sites such as Scowlitz (*Qithyil*) and Katz (*Sxwóxwiymelh*) (Lepofsky et al. 2000, 2009). These villages featured a variety of houses, including pithouses in some contexts and large above-ground structures elsewhere, often arranged in rows lining terraces above the nearby rivers. These structures featured multifamily residential patterns, storage facilities, and exchange of goods stretching from the coast to the interior east of the Coast Range (Lepofsky et al. 2000, 2005, 2009). It is very clear that such villages were placed in positions that permitted the inhabitants to protect access to the critical salmon resource while maintaining access to a wider array of resource patches and exchange networks (Lepofsky et al. 2005). However, there are, to date, no conclusive indicators of interhousehold status differentiation. Some of the major Fraser Valley villages were substantially abandoned as residential sites by ca. 1800–2000 BP, during a period of apparent drought and likely weakness in the salmon fishery (Prentiss et al. 2005).

There are a number of critical similarities between the early Fraser Valley villages (e.g., Scowlitz and Katz) and those of the Middle Fraser after 1800 BP. The Middle Fraser Villages featured large multifamily houses, storage features, and production of goods for exchange, very similar to those of the nearby Fraser Valley. Some villages, such as Bridge River, even had a ground slate knife and scraper technology resembling that of the Fraser Valley peoples. At 1800–2000 BP, the Middle Fraser area was only sparsely populated and may have been attractive to groups able to aggregate to control key points while maintaining access to a wider range of resources. This could have been accomplished by large co-residential groups as had already developed in the Fraser Valley. Alternatively, core elements of the Lower Fraser socioeconomic strategy could have been transmitted into the Middle Fraser by social interaction between groups. Regardless, the rapid spread and growth of such villages throughout the 160 kilometers of the Middle Fraser area may reflect the high cultural (and possibly biological) fitness associated with this strategy.

A range of paleoecological and oceanographic studies indicate cooler temperatures and high productivity in eastern Pacific fisheries between ca. 1600 and 1100 BP

(Hay et al. 2007; Reyes and Clague 2004; Tunnicliffe et al. 2001). The apparent rise in Pacific productivity correlates with village growth in the Middle Fraser context as measured at the Bridge River site (Figure 15.3), where populations expanded by as much as 300 percent (Prentiss et al. 2005, 2008). It is possible, though as yet undocumented, that multivillage polities (e.g., Hayden and Ryder 1991) may have developed during peak population times. The Middle Fraser abandonments came as fisheries productivity apparently declined. Since not all villages were abandoned at once, it is likely that those in a slightly better economic position were able to take advantage of the early losers to help prevent demographic collapse in their own houses and communities. One effect of this may have been installment of inherited rights to corporeal and noncorporeal property as older, more established families accepted kin and nonkin into their households but denied them the same rights passed on to their direct kin (Prentiss et al. 2007).

Conclusion

Plateau prehistory offers a variety of implications for understanding the long-term histories of hunter-gatherer societies. Probably the most critical and obvious of these concerns the distinction between emergent socioeconomic strategies and development of sociopolitical complexity featuring inequality. Rapid emergence of the Lillooet phenomenon and its subsequent spread throughout much of the Fraser Canyon was the result of socioeconomic and demographic adjustments made by collectors, originally organized in much smaller, and probably somewhat more mobile, groups, during the period ca. 2000–3000 BP. Although we are not yet able to state the details of the process, it is clear that once fully in place, and given an opportunity for expansion, the strategy spread rapidly, perhaps emerging as the Marpole Phase on the central Northwest Coast and the Lillooet phenomenon in the Middle Fraser Canyon.

In contrast, sociopolitical complexity, as indicated by interhousehold ranking at sites such as Bridge River and Keatley Creek, was not an adaptive strategy but rather a cultural phenomenon that initially developed on a local level, though it is possible that the cultural rules of ranking could still spread via cultural transmission, as indicated by its adoption by the Canyon Division Shuswap during the early historic period (Teit 1909). In the Middle Fraser context and likely elsewhere (e.g., Early to Middle Marpole times on the Central Coast), incipient inequality may have evolved simply through the practice of building large houses. Within this framework, variability in house size was associated with differential house-group size and capacity for surplus production, despite formal operation under relatively egalitarian rules. Subsistence stress, brought on by regional environmental fluctuations and also indigenous subsistence practices (e.g., Kuijt and Prentiss 2004), produced heightened tensions between house groups and favored more overt competition for viability,

THE WINTER VILLAGE PATTERN ON THE PLATEAU

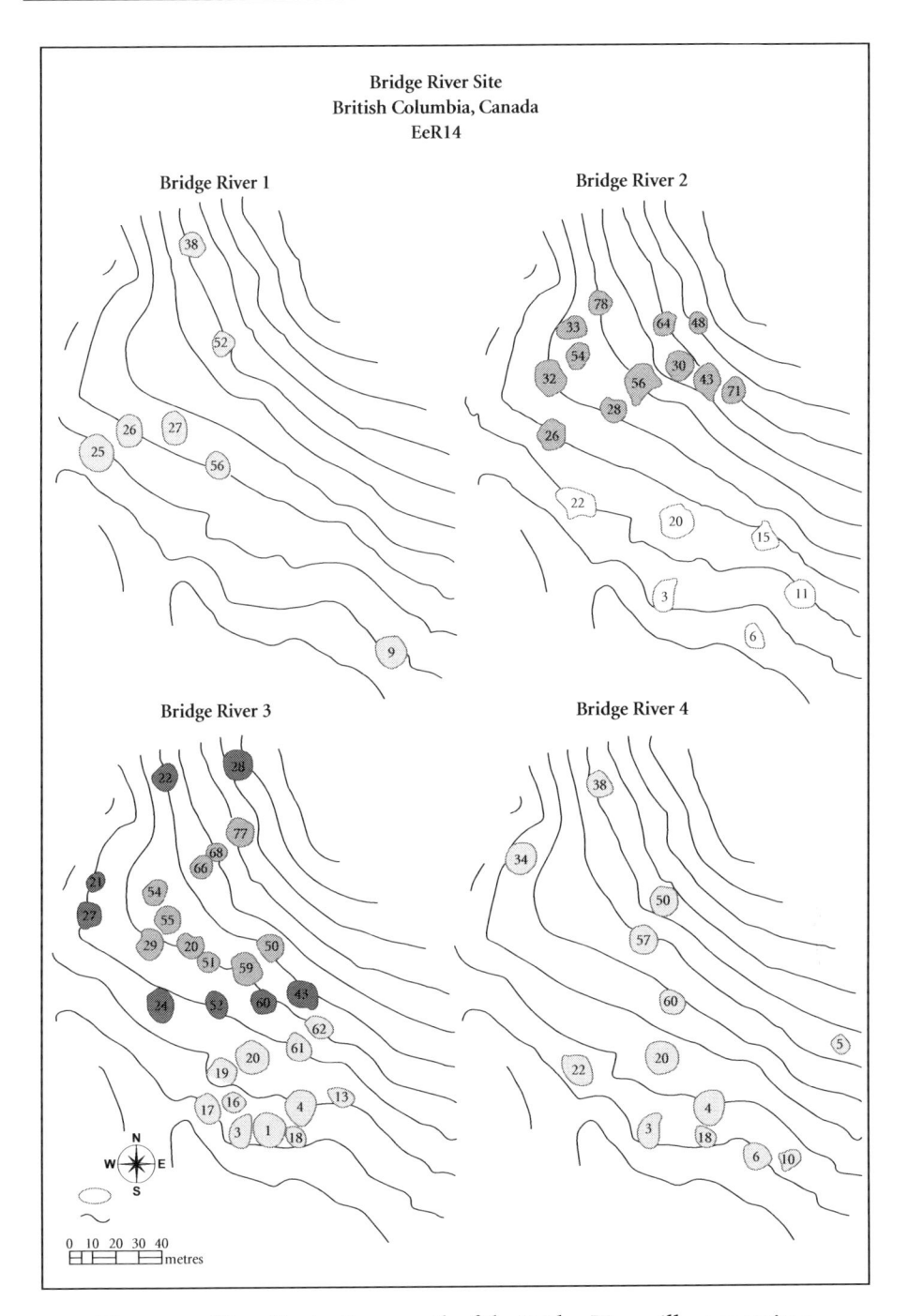

Figure 15.3 Maps illustrating growth of the Bridge River village over time.

which ultimately became status competition. Village scale abandonments may have been, at least in part, driven by excessive demands of aggrandizing individuals and corporate groups in run-away competitive cycles (Prentiss et al. 2007).

The Plateau remains fertile ground for studying hunter-gatherers and development of sedentary and socially complex groups. Contemporary thinking on these subjects suggests that a range of variables—among them natural resource fluctuations, population growth, foraging strategies, social group formation, and competitive feasting—need to be considered in developing explanatory models for early social complexity. Future researchers will require sophisticated models of history and evolutionary process to understand the ancient history of the Plateau.

REFERENCES

Ames, K. M., D. E. Dumond, J. R. Galm, and R. Minor. 1998. Prehistory of the Southern Plateau. In *Handbook of North American Indians, Vol. 12, Plateau*, edited by D. E. Walker, pp. 103–119. Smithsonian Institution Press, Washington DC.

Andrefsky, W., Jr. 2004. Materials and Contexts for a Culture History of the Plateau. In *Complex Hunter-Gatherers: Evolution and Organization of Prehistoric Communities on the Plateau of Northwestern North America*, edited by W. C. Prentiss and I. Kuijt, pp. 23–35. University of Utah Press, Salt Lake City.

Chatters, J. C. 1995. Population Growth, Climatic Cooling, and the Development of Collector Strategies on the Southern Plateau, Western North America. *Journal of World Prehistory* 9:341–400.

———. 2004. Safety in Numbers: Conflict and Village Settlement on the Plateau. In *Complex Hunter-Gatherers: Evolution and Organization of Prehistoric Communities on the Plateau of Northwestern North America*, edited by W. C. Prentiss and I. Kuijt, pp. 67–83. University of Utah Press, Salt Lake City.

Chatters, J. C., V. L. Butler, M. J. Scott, D. M. Anderson, and D. A. Neitzel. 1995. A Paleoscience Approach to Estimating the Effects of Climatic Warming on Salmonid Fisheries of the Columbia Basin. *Canadian Special Publication in Fisheries and Aquatic Sciences* 21:489–496.

Chatters, J. C., and D. L. Pokotylo. 1998. Prehistory: Introduction. In *Handbook of North American Indians, Vol. 12, Plateau*, edited by D. E. Walker, pp. 73–80. Smithsonian Institution Press, Washington DC.

Chatters, J. C., and W. C. Prentiss. 2005. A Darwinian Macro-Evolutionary Perspective on the Development of Hunter-Gatherer Systems in Northwestern North America. *World Archaeology* 37:45–65.

Goodale, N. B., W. C. Prentiss, and I. Kuijt. 2004. Cultural Complexity: A New Chronology of the Upper Columbia Drainage Area. In *Complex Hunter-Gatherers: Evolution and Organization of Prehistoric Communities on the Plateau of Northwestern North America*, edited by W. C. Prentiss and I. Kuijt, pp.36–48. University of Utah Press, Salt Lake City.

Hay, M. B., A. Dallimore, R. E. Thomson, S. E. Calvert, and R. Pienitz. 2007. Siliceous Microfossil Record of Late Holocene Oceanography and Climate Along the West Coast of Vancouver Island, British Columbia (Canada). *Quaternary Research* 67:33–49.

Hayden, B. 1994. Competition, Labor, and Complex Hunter-Gatherers. In *Key Issues in Hunter-Gatherer Research*, edited by E. S. Burch Jr. and L. J. Ellana, pp. 223–242. Berg, Oxford.

———. 1997. *The Pithouses of Keatley Creek*. Harcourt Brace College, Fort Worth, TX.

———, M. Eldredge, A. Eldredge, and A. Cannon. 1985. Complex Hunter-Gatherers of Interior British Columbia. In *Prehistoric Hunter-Gatherers: The Emergence of Cultural Complexity*, edited by T. D. Price and J. A. Brown, pp. 181–199. Academic Press, New York.

Hayden, B., and J. Ryder. 1991. Prehistoric Cultural Collapse in the Lillooet Area. *American Antiquity* 56:50–65.

Hayden, B., and R. Schulting. 1997. The Plateau Interaction Sphere and Late Prehistoric Cultural Complexity. *American Antiquity* 62:51–85.

Kuijt, I. 2001. Reconsidering the Cause of Cultural Collapse in the Lillooet Area of British Columbia: A Geoarchaeological Perspective. *American Antiquity* 66:692–703.

———, and W. C. Prentiss. 2004. Villages on the Edge: Pithouses, Cultural Change, and the Abandonment of Aggregate Pithouse Villages. In *Complex Hunter-Gatherers: Evolution and Organization of Prehistoric Communities on the Plateau of Northwestern North America*, edited by W. C. Prentiss and I. Kuijt, pp. 155–170. University of Utah Press, Salt Lake City.

Lepofsky, D., M. Blake, D. Brown, S. Morrison, N. Oakes, and N. Lyons. 2000. The Archaeology of the Scowlitz Site, SW British Columbia. *Journal of Field Archaeology* 27:391–416.

Lepofsky, D., D. Hallett, K. P. Lertzman, and R. Mathewes. 2005. Climate Change and Culture Change on the Southern Coast of British Columbia 2400–1200 Cal. B.P.: An Hypothesis. *American Antiquity* 70:267–294.

Lepofsky, D., D. M. Schaepe, A. P. Graesch, M. Lenert, P. Ormerod, K. T. Carlson, J. E. Arnold, M. Blake, P. Moore, and J. J. Clague. 2009. Exploring Stó:Lō-Coast Salish Interaction and Identity in Ancient Houses and Settlements in the Fraser Valley, British Columbia. *American Antiquity* 74:595–626.

Matson, R. G., and M. P. R. Magne. 2007. *Athapaskan Migrations: The Archaeology of Eagle Lake, British Columbia*. University of Arizona Press, Tucson.

Prentiss, A. M., G. Cross, T. A. Foor, D. Markle, M. Hogan, and D. S. Clarke. 2008. Evolution of a Late Prehistoric Winter Village on the Interior Plateau of British Columbia: Geophysical Investigations, Radiocarbon Dating, and Spatial Analysis of the Bridge River Site. *American Antiquity* 73:59–82.

Prentiss, A. M., N. Lyons, L. E. Harris, M. R. Burns, and T. M. Godin. 2007. The Emergence of Status Inequality in Intermediate Scale Societies: A Demographic and Socio-Economic History of the Keatley Creek Site, British Columbia. *Journal of Anthropological Archaeology* 26:299–327.

Prentiss, W. C., and J. C. Chatters. 2003. Cultural Diversification and Decimation in the Prehistoric Record. *Current Anthropology* 44:33–58.

Prentiss, W. C., J. C. Chatters, M. Lenert, D. S. Clarke, and R. C. O'Boyle. 2005. The Archaeology of the Plateau of Northwestern North America During the Late Prehistoric Period (3500–200 B.P.): Evolution of Hunting and Gathering Societies. *Journal of World Prehistory* 19:47–118.

Prentiss, W. C., and I. Kuijt. 2004. The Evolution of Collector Systems on the Canadian Plateau. In *Complex Hunter-Gatherers: Evolution and Organization of Prehistoric Communities on the Plateau of Northwestern North America*, edited by W. C. Prentiss and I. Kuijt, pp. 49–66. University of Utah Press, Salt Lake City.

Reyes, A. V., and J. J. Clague. 2000. Stratigraphic Evidence for Multiple Advances of Lillooet Glacier, Southern Coast Mountains, British Columbia. *Canadian Journal of Earth Science* 41:903–918.

Rousseau, M. K. 2004. Culture Historic Synthesis and Changes in Human Mobility, Sedentism, Subsistence, Settlement, and Population on the Canadian Plateau. In *Complex Hunter-Gatherers: Evolution and Organization of Prehistoric Communities on the Plateau of Northwestern North America*, edited by W. C. Prentiss and I. Kuijt, pp. 3–22. University of Utah Press, Salt Lake City.

Teit, J. 1900. *The Thompson Indians of British Columbia.* Memoirs of the American Museum of Natural History 2 (Part IV). American Museum of Natural History, New York.

———, 1909. *The Shuswap.* Memoirs of the American Museum of Natural History 4 (Part VII). American Museum of Natural History, New York.

Thoms, A.V. 1989. *The Northern Roots of Hunter-Gatherer Intensification: Camas and the Pacific Northwest.* Ph.D. dissertation, Washington State University, Pullman.

Tunnicliffe, V., J. M. O'Connell, and M. R. McQuoid. 2001. A Holocene Record of Marine Fish Remains from the Northeastern Pacific. *Marine Geology* 174:197–210.

CHAPTER 16

GREAT BASIN FORAGING STRATEGIES

CHRISTOPHER MORGAN AND ROBERT L. BETTINGER

The whole of nature . . . is a conjugation of the verb to eat, in the active and the passive.
—William Ralph Inge (1922)

CONCEPTUALIZING foraging strategies dominates the study of pre-Columbian human behavior in the Great Basin. The reason for this is that since at least the early 20th century Great Basin anthropological thinking has been predominantly "gastric"—guided by the idea that subsistence concerns have driven most regional cultural developments and thus explain things like technology, social structure, settlement, and even ideology (Zeanah and Simms 1999). So asking (and answering) questions about how and why foraging strategies evolved in the Great Basin is really a matter of explaining how and why foragers behave the way they do, particularly in the high-desert steppes of intermountain western North America. These questions hinge on a dialectic of competing hypotheses and resulting syntheses that describe foraging strategies, model foraging behaviors, and explain foraging variability across space and through time in the Great Basin. These descriptions, models, and explanations inform, as much as they reflect, the development of hunter-gatherer theory through the 20th and 21st centuries.

The Great Basin has been defined many ways—physiographically, hydrologically, floristically, and ethnographically—but generally entails the region between the Sierra Nevada and Cascade ranges to the west, the Rocky Mountains to the east, the deserts

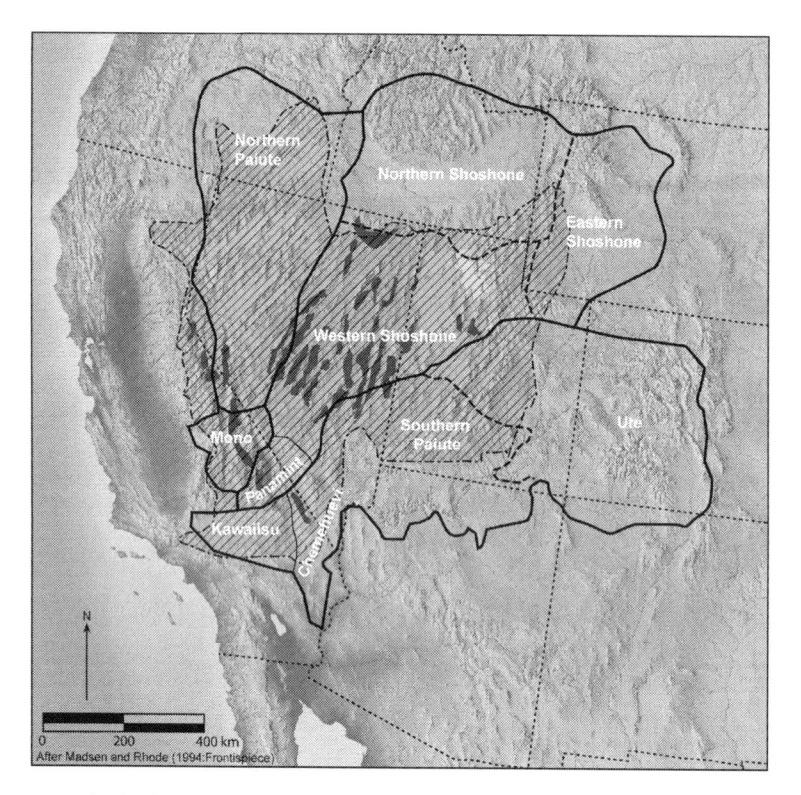

Figure 16.1 The hydrographic Great Basin (hatched), major mountain ranges (shaded), and modern distribution of Numic-speaking peoples.

of the Colorado Plateau and American Southwest to the south, and the Columbia Plateau and the Snake River Plain to the north (Figure 16.1). The region is arid, internally drained, and characterized by a series of high, steep, generally northwest-southeast-trending, fault-block mountain ranges. These ranges are interspersed with high valleys oftentimes containing desiccated lakes (called *playas*) and sometimes perennial streams and marshes, especially on the eastern and western margins of the Basin (Figure 16.2). Ethnographically, the region was inhabited by small, mobile bands of Ute, Paiute, and Shoshone hunter-gatherers who subsisted on a wide variety of plants and animals such as wild grass seeds, roots, rabbit, deer, bighorn sheep, insects, and especially piñon nut gathered in the fall. All spoke Numic languages derived from the greater Uto-Aztecan linguistic stock found throughout most of the arid and highland regions of the American Southwest and Mexico; for this they are sometimes referred to as the Numa.

Social Evolution and Culture History

The origin of the Great Basin foraging dialectic is usually attributed to the groundbreaking work of Julian Steward, but hints of it hark to late-19th and early-20th centuries, the first formal anthropology in the region, and the

Figure 16.2 Photograph of Winnemucca Valley, Nevada, Western Great Basin from inside rockshelter (note flat, sage-covered valley bottom, wetlands in the midground on the valley bottom, and parallel mountain ranges to the west [left] and east [right]; photo by C. T. Morgan).

theoretical juxtaposition between progressive social evolution and historical particularism. Evolutionists such as John Wesley Powell, founder of the American Bureau of Ethnology and one of the first to perform ethnographic and linguistic work among the Numa, saw (with some reservations) Great Basin indigenous populations as representing a basal level of cultural evolution: "primitive" and incapable of variability, except toward more advanced cultural stages. In contrast, particularists such as Clark Wissler and Alfred Kroeber allowed for culture change. To them, Great Basin cultures resulted from historical trajectories, the effect of which was relegation of the Great Basin to a periphery developing out of such ostensible "core" culture areas as California and the American Southwest (see also Sassaman and Randall, this volume). Both perspectives, however, anticipated the ecological bias in the Basin by explaining Numic foraging lifeways as resulting from impoverished environmental circumstances (evolutionists such as Powell) or reliance on wild seeds (particularists such as Wissler). In other words, the simple lifeway of the Numa was determined by a harsh environment and broad-spectrum diet, both ideas prefiguring later ones emphasizing the role of environment and diet in determining Great Basin lifeways. They also entailed another dichotomy and conundrum: what determines lifeway—environment or historical trajectories?

Cultural Ecology and Testing the Desert Culture Hypothesis

The synthetic solution to this problem came with the work of Steward and the theory of cultural ecology. Steward argued that historical trajectories resulted in the technologies available to exploit the types of resources found in the environment. In other words, technology (via history) determined what and how different aspects of the environment could be exploited. It was Steward who coined the term *gastric* to explain Great Basin foraging, and by default culture, arguing that it was the patchy and unpredictable productivity of Great Basin biota (especially a staple, piñon nut), coupled with a mostly simple hunting technology but fairly sophisticated woven plant gathering and groundstone plant processing technologies, that resulted in the Numic "culture core" (those attributes of culture empirically linked to the subsistence economy). This core consisted of small, mobile family bands who fused into larger communities subsisting on stored piñon nut in the winter and dispersed in spring, summer, and fall to exploit a broad spectrum of gathered and hunted resources (Steward 1938).

Steward's synthesis not only solved the dilemma posed by the conflict between determinism and particularism, it also set the stage for the next Great Basin foraging controversy. This is why: if the Numic culture core was an adaptation to Great Basin environments and these environments had been more or less stable since the close of the Pleistocene, it held that ethnographic Great Basin foraging strategies should describe Great Basin behaviors through the Holocene, and that Steward's cultural ecology explained these behaviors through time and across space in the region. This synthesis resulted in the next Great Basin dialectical juxtaposition: stasis or variability in Great Basin foraging strategies?

Taking the former position was Jesse Jennings. Mostly on the basis of his excavation of deep, stratified cave sites such as Danger Cave on the western edge of the Salt Lake Desert (Figure 16.3), Jennings argued that there had not been significant lifeway change in the Great Basin since the close of the Pleistocene (Jennings [1957] 1970). Though criticized, Jennings claimed that lack of significant variation in material assemblages indicated Great Basin people had been generalized foragers who intensively exploited a broad array of food sources throughout the Holocene and were thus well adapted to coping with the arid, limiting environment of the Great Basin. In essence, he implied not only that Steward's ethnographies described Great Basin foraging societies through the Holocene but that cultural ecology and the Numic culture core explained Great Basin adaptations through time. He termed this adaptation the Desert Culture, later renamed the Desert Archaic in accord with continentwide evolutionary schemes.

The opposite view was taken by archaeologists such as Robert Heizer. Heizer and his colleagues, basing their conclusions on a series of cave excavations in the western Great Basin (e.g., Lovelock Cave), argued that large parts of the region

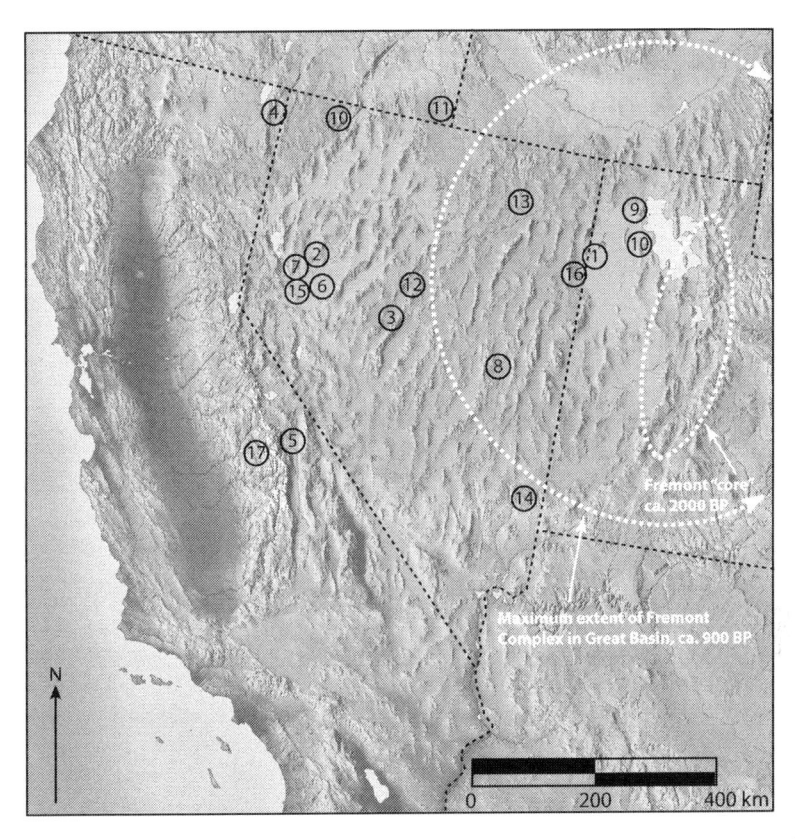

Figure 16.3 Location of studies mentioned in the text: (1) Danger Cave; (2) Lovelock Cave; (3) Reese River Valley; (4) Surprise Valley; (5) Owens Valley; (6) Carson Sink; (7) Sadmat Site; (8) Giroux Wash; (9) Hogup Cave; (10) Last Supper Cave; (11) Dirty Shame Rockshelter; (12) Gatecliff Rockshelter; (13) Pie Creek Shelter; (14) O'Malley Shelter; (15) Stillwater Marsh; (16) Bonneville Estates Rockshelter; (17) Western Mono.

(particularly its relatively well-watered western margin) produced enough resources to result in relatively sedentary, or "limnosedentary," foraging strategies focused on marshes and lakes (Heizer 1956). Subsistence focused on a narrower range of abundant resources such as waterfowl, shadscale, and piñon nut. Heizer and others also proposed that substantial climatic changes, especially a warm and dry interval during the middle Holocene, had a major impact on human adaptations, in particular by forcing abandonment of large portions of a markedly arid mid-Holocene Great Basin.

Resolving whether or not diet was uniformly narrow or broad, the degree to which people were mobile or sedentary, and ultimately whether foraging lifeways varied over time and space drove most of the archaeology in the Great Basin in the late 1960s and 1970s. For example, in the Reese River Valley in the central Great Basin, Thomas (1973) identified an essentially Numic (broad-spectrum, mobile) pattern extending back some 4,500 years. In Surprise Valley in the northwestern Basin, O'Connell and Hayward (1972) documented a shift from narrow-spectrum diets and relatively sedentary behaviors to broad-spectrum and more mobile behaviors around 4500 BP. Likewise, in Owens Valley in the western Great Basin, Bettinger (1977) identified increasingly intensive resource exploitation and fundamental settlement pattern variation through the Holocene, with very intensive exploitation strategies focused on piñon nut and grass seeds developing after 1350 BP. Explanations for this adaptive variability ran the gamut from the environmental, exemplified by O'Connell's argument that climate change drove the diachronic differences he saw in Surprise Valley, to the demographic, with Bettinger arguing monotonic population increase drove the changes he saw in Owens Valley. Ultimately, what this era of research pointed to was a new dilemma hinted at by the differences in explanation between O'Connell and Bettinger: how to best characterize foraging diversity in the Great Basin and how to explain the causes of this diversity.

Behavioral and Evolutionary Approaches to Understanding Human Foraging Ecology

Like many attempts to understand foraging variability in the 1980s, Great Basin researchers initially turned to Binford's forager-collector continuum (1980) to understand how environment conditioned mobility, settlement, storage, and other foraging strategies. Binford's model argued that degrees of hunter-gatherer sociocultural complexity were based mainly on environment, with small groups of mobile *foragers* moving camp often as they mapped on to food resources in mainly low-latitude, aseasonal settings. *Collectors*, on the other hand, sustained larger, more sedentary winter populations by organizing their labor to effect bulk storage of abundant, seasonally available resources common to midlatitudes. Examples of the variability along the forager-collector continuum were soon found with Thomas (1981), for example, ranking Great Basin foragers and collectors mainly on the basis of resource structure. Although making a substantial contribution by pointing to the need for more intensive paleoecological research to understand past resource distributions and their effect on human foraging strategies, this normative approach, like Steward's cultural ecology before it, was found wanting. The approach was criticized mainly because it resulted in "just so," neofunctionalist explanations linking environment and technology with behavior. What was needed, it was argued, was a method for producing testable, middle-range archaeological hypotheses that linked theory with data (Bettinger 1980; O'Connell et al. 1982).

The solution to this problem was nearly wholesale adoption of optimal foraging theory from behavioral and evolutionary ecologies, an approach that drives most Great Basin foraging research to this day. Its basic perspective is that modeling the relative efficiency of foraging decisions (e.g., what to eat, where to camp, when to move, etc.) using microeconomic cost-benefit models generates archaeologically testable predictions without relying on ethnographic analogy or normative ecological generalizations. In evolutionary ecology, optimal or most efficient solutions (i.e., those that return the greatest reward, usually measured in calories relative to labor input) are most adapted and selected for at either the individual or the group level. These behaviors are then passed on through one or more forms of cultural transmission (see Boyd and Richerson 1985).

This modern solution to the weaknesses of descriptive cultural ecology and the forager-collector model has resulted in a multitude of studies in the Great Basin. Most of them use simple cost-benefit equations such as diet breadth and patch choice models, the marginal value theorem, and central place foraging theory. The diet breadth (Schoener 1971) and patch choice models (MacArthur and Pianka 1966) predict that low-ranked resources and resource patches (i.e., those that have comparatively high handling costs relative to caloric benefit—usually seeds, tubers, and nuts) should be included in the diet only when search times for high-ranked resources (usually large-bodied animal prey) are long, a measure of their abundance relative to human foragers. For example, O'Connell et al. (1982) used this model to explain the switch to eating seeds in the early Archaic (ca. 8500 BP). They argued that declining encounter rates with large game drove the transition to eating lower-ranked seed resources, a hypothesis theoretically supported by later work on Great Basin resource return rates (Simms 1987).

The marginal value theorem (Charnov 1976) predicts that a forager should stay in a resource patch only as long as resource return rates (which diminish the longer a forager is in patch) are higher than those available in the environment as a whole. Kelly (1990) used this model to explain decreased mobility in the Carson Sink wetlands after 1500 BP. He argued that deleterious climate change reduced overall return rates of the greater western Great Basin, thereby making the Carson Sink "patch," where return rates were not as affected, more attractive.

Applications of central place foraging theory (Orians and Pearson 1979) in the Great Basin mainly focus on determining optimal logistical foraging radii around central places. They model when it is more efficient (and thus expected) to either move camp (i.e., be residentially mobile) or process food items in the field. The microeconomic bases for these decisions rest on transport costs and caloric content of key resources, which researchers such as Jones and Madsen (1989) and Barlow and Metcalfe (1996) argue determine the distance at which it becomes inefficient (i.e., where transport costs outweigh caloric benefit) to move resources back to camp. At this point (essentially a maximum foraging radius), foragers should either move residence or field process resources to remove low-return bulk, thereby increasing load utility (Figure 16.4). Ultimately, these types of models predict optimal solutions for balancing residential and logistical mobility and such intensive, long-range logistical behaviors as field dressing and processing. They thus speak directly to the economic foundations of foraging behavior variability.

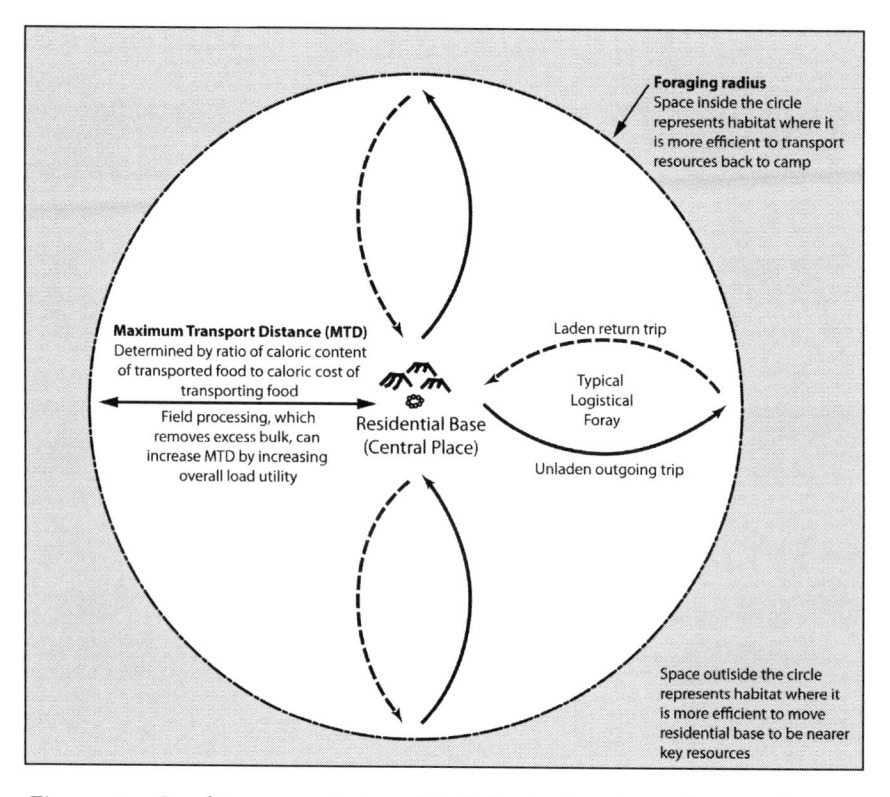

Figure 16.4 Graphic representation of the behavioral ecology of logistical versus residential foraging.

In each of these optimal foraging examples, forager decision making is contingent on quantifying environmental characteristics, prey abundance, and human population. Use of these models thus makes ecologically oriented, quantifiable prediction and analysis of foraging strategies possible; for this they have become the regional research norm. Though nearly universally accepted by Great Basin archaeologists, applications of optimal foraging theory and evolutionary ecology have resulted in at least five new controversies driving the current Great Basin foraging dialectic. The next subsections, by no means exhaustive, summarize these controversies, presented in a sequence roughly corresponding to regional culture chronologies.

Paleoindian or Paleoarchaic? (13000–8500 BP)

This first controversy centers on whether there were fundamental changes in diet breadth and mobility between Paleoindian and Archaic periods. Several Great Basin researchers argue that terminal Pleistocene–early Holocene foraging strategies were broad-spectrum enough and so focused on remnant pluvial wetland resources as to be better classified as an Archaic, rather than a more traditional narrow-spectrum, highly mobile, large-game-focused Paleoindian lifeway.

Numerous lithic procurement and sourcing studies such as those at the Sadmat Site and Giroux Wash, however, point to rather pronounced mobility during this time, with exotic toolstones transported hundreds of kilometers from their sources (Jones et al. 2003). Diet breadth is a bit more contentious. At Danger Cave, for instance, Rhode and Louderback (2007) find very little evidence for intensive seed use, an Archaic hallmark, prior to about 9500 BP. At Bonneville Estates Rockshelter, however, Hockett (2007) identifies a broad Paleoindian diet of small and large fauna as well as seeds. This issue remains unresolved. Part of the problem results from the fact that so much of the Paleoindian record in the Great Basin comes from surface, rather than stratified contexts, meaning organic preservation is generally absent, radiocarbon dates are rare, and artifact associations are oftentimes tenuous. But the controversy is also semantic, as Paleoindian research outside the Basin has also identified broader-spectrum (i.e., not necessarily megafauna-focused) Paleoindian strategies (Haynes 2002). A novel hypothesis that might explain some of this variability is the idea that stemmed points represent an older, wetland-focused adaptation and fluted traditions a later, hunting-focused migrant from the Plains (Beck and Jones 2007). If true, this points to the possibility that foraging diversity developed quite early and that there are deep historical antecedents to Great Basin hunter-gatherer lifeway variability.

Middle Archaic Hunting (4500–1000 BP)

Quite the opposite situation developed during the Middle Archaic. Faunal data from numerous cave and rockshelter sites (Hogup, Last Supper, and Danger caves; Dirty Shame Rockshelter; and Gatecliff, Pie Creek, and O'Malley shelters) point to increased hunting of large artiodactyls such as mule deer, pronghorn, and bighorn sheep. Employing the diet breadth model, Byers and Broughton (2004) argue that post mid-Holocene environmental ameliorization increased artiodactyl abundance. This reduced prey search times to the point that small seed and other low-return items were excluded from the diet, effectively narrowing diet breadth. Alternatively, McGuire and Hildebrandt (2005) argue it was men's focus on garnering prestige through "show-off," long-range logistical hunting that drove increased hunting, an economic pursuit where net returns on labor are often negative but may increase practitioner's social status and mating opportunities. Both hypotheses draw on faunal data and evolutionary anthropological theory, yet it remains unclear the degree to which diet breadth actually narrowed (hunting may have increased at the same time that reliance on small fauna and plant resources intensified) and the extent to which prestige hunting could have contributed to Middle Archaic faunal assemblages. In any event, that similar intensive hunting and foraging patterns appear to have developed continentwide at about the same time begs the question of what effect larger phenomena such as climate change and population pressure may have had on the development of these strategies.

Fremont Adaptive Diversity (2100–500 BP)

The role foraging strategies played in the Fremont phenomenon is of paramount importance to understanding how foraging can give rise to, support, and even hinder agricultural intensification. Though defining *Fremont* is exceedingly contentious, current wisdom holds that the term describes a multifaceted adaptation characterized by a few shared cultural traits (e.g., one-rod-and-bundle basketry) endemic to people who sometimes farmed maize introduced (and possibly brought by migrants) from the Southwest, but who also spent a considerable amount of time foraging (Madsen and Simms 1998). The phenomenon began along the well-watered eastern margin of the Great Basin and developed by about 1000 BP to include most of Utah and parts of eastern Nevada, southern Idaho, southeastern Wyoming, and northeastern Colorado (Figure 16.2), only to disappear some 500 years later. Originally considered a northern variant of Ancestral Puebloan cultures, Fremont is now perceived as a mostly *in-situ* transition from Late Archaic foraging to mixed horticulture/foraging, and then back to a foraging lifeway. This trajectory not only begs comparison to worldwide transitions from foraging to food production but also provides one of the few clear examples where the transition ultimately failed. An interesting hypothesis here is the idea that foraging and farming represent two adaptive peaks, the latter ultimately reliant on a reconfiguration of social norms to recognize private property (i.e., stored agricultural surplus; Bettinger 2001). It might thus be argued that experimenting with farming for more than 1,500 years without fully adopting the rest of the cultural package required for farming (though the Fremont were certainly prodigious storers) may have been a good way of coping with diverse Great Basin environments and pronounced Late Holocene climatic variability in the short run, but it was ultimately an evolutionary cul-de-sac eliciting replacement by, or adoption of, broad-spectrum Numic foraging strategies.

Numic Spread (ca. 1000 BP)

The term "Numic spread" refers to the linguistic hypothesis that ethnographic Numic populations are recent migrants to the area, rapidly migrating north and east from a homeland somewhere in southeastern California in the last thousand years or so. This rapid migration hypothetically accounts for the linguistic similarities between the various Numic languages and their "fan-shaped" distribution across the Great Basin (Lamb 1958; Figure 16.1). Though ultimately a historical question, this extremely contentious hypothesis has resulted in some profound thinking about how migration might be understood from the perspective of evolutionary ecology. As initially modeled (Bettinger and Baumhoff 1982), the Numa were *processors*, exploiting a broad spectrum of abundant but costly-to-process resources such as small seeds and piñon nut, but also high-return items such as deer, and bighorn sheep. The people they displaced were more mobile *travelers* who exploited a narrower spectrum of high-return resources such as large game. Because the Numa exploited larger resource bases, they could net more calories from any given habitat and thus support larger populations than pre-Numic travelers. Ultimately they outcompeted travelers simply by outeating and outreproducing them, the result of which was rapid, wholesale population replacement. Archaeological evidence for the replacement is spotty, and linguistic estimates of the timing of the replacement have been revised to allow for its possibly greater time depth (perhaps 2,000 to 3,000 years). The issue of identifying the presence, absence, and nature of the migration remains, but the competitive foraging model developed to explain the migration retains its theoretical utility regardless of the outcome of the debate because it shows how the economic basis of different hunter-gatherer adaptations can condition the evolution, adoption, and replacement of behavioral strategies.

Foraging Goal Variability (Terminal Pleistocene–Holocene)

Recent Great Basin foraging research has recognized variability, and the implications of variability, in foraging goals. Hints of this variability were initially revealed by osteological analysis of burials recovered from Stillwater Marsh, in the western Basin. Analysis revealed contrasting patterns of osteoarthritis between men and women: men had trauma in the feet, hip, and shoulder, and females more in the spine and hand, suggesting men did a lot of walking and women a lot of sitting and processing near camp (Larson and Kelly 1995). This led to a realization of the obvious: that hunter-gatherers usually divide labor by sex, with females focused on household provisioning and males often on long-range logistical hunting. Optimal foraging analyses subsequently indicated that residential locations should be situated so as to maximize women's foraging returns while also facilitating men's long-range hunting (Zeanah 2004). They also indicated that women's foraging radii ought to be configured in such a way as to all but guarantee net gains on foraging labor due to the uncertain returns affiliated with men's hunting. This is the situation McGuire and Hildebrandt (2005) claim developed during the Middle Archaic as a way of underwriting men's prestige hunting. In later prehistory on the mountainous California-Great Basin frontier, Morgan (2008) argues that this type of labor division developed as a way for Western Mono men to garner prestige more through trade than hunting and thus reflects a similar pattern where women's foraging labor, in essence, paid for development of "big man" status distinctions and even ascribed chieftainships. In any event, research on the division of foraging labor holds promise for understanding foraging strategies such as settlement and diet breadth and also the political economy of various types of foraging societies.

Conclusion

The preceding, of course, elicits more questions than answers. What was the diet breadth of, and how mobile were, the Great Basin's terminal Pleistocene–Early Holocene inhabitants? Was foraging diversity already developing in the early

Holocene? What strategies dominated during the Middle Holocene, and how do they relate to preceding and succeeding patterns? How broad-spectrum were Middle Archaic diets? How did Fremont people manage the trade-off between foraging and farming, if both are evolutionarily exclusive in the long run? Did the Numic Spread really happen, and if so, what explains the counterintuitive link between broad-spectrum foraging strategies and low population densities? Equally important, how did a Numic pattern replace the relatively large populations of the Middle Archaic as well as those of the Fremont Complex? Finally, when did gendered foraging goal variability develop, and what was its effect on regional cultural evolution?

In the end, controversies over Great Basin foraging strategies hinge on a fundamental ecological dialectic that behavior is conditioned mainly by environment and population density, with historically derived social conventions and differential cultural transmission guiding the adoption, persistence, and demise of various behaviors. For example, Late Holocene climatic ameliorization may have altered high-ranking resource abundance, narrowing diet breadth. Monotonic Holocene population increase may have decreased encounter rates with large game, forcing foraging intensification and exploitation of new habitats. Mechanisms of cultural transmission defined which behaviors and technologies persisted in light of both their efficiency and their relationship to social norms. Beyond empirical questions of who ate what when and how they managed to do so, answering these questions will ultimately fall on modeling environmental and behavioral variability and the ultimate causes of the latter. Because variability entails the potential for nonnormative returns (e.g., even one anomalous low-return year can be devastating to a hunter-gatherer), future Great Basin foraging research may be forced to embrace corresponding nonnormative models (e.g., Winterhalder et al. 1999), accounting for risk and uncertainty when coping with things like climatic and environmental change, population density, and cultural dynamics, a possible synthetic solution to some of the limitations of single-currency optimal foraging models.

REFERENCES

Barlow, K. R., and D. Metcalfe. 1996. Plant Utility Indices: Two Great Basin Examples. *Journal of Archaeological Science* 23:351–371.

Beck, C., and G. T. Jones. 2007. Early Paleoarchaic Point Morphology and Chronology. In *Paleoindian or Paleoarchaic? Great Basin Human Ecology at the Pleistocene/Holocene Transition*, edited by K. E. Graf and D. N. Schmitt, pp. 3–22. University of Utah Press, Salt Lake City.

Bettinger, R. L. 1977. Aboriginal Human Ecology in Owens Valley: Prehistoric Change in the Great Basin. *American Antiquity* 42(1):3–17.

———. 1980. Explanatory/Predictive Models of Hunter-Gatherer Adaptation. *Advances in Archaeological Method and Theory* 3:189–245.

———. 2001. Holocene Hunter-Gatherers. In *Archaeology at the Millennium*, edited by G. Feinman and T. D. Price, pp. 137–195. Kluwer/Plenum, New York.

Bettinger, R. L., and M. A. Baumhoff. 1982. The Numic Spread: Great Basin Cultures in Competition. *American Antiquity* 47:485–503.

Binford, L. R. 1980. Willow Smoke and Dog's Tails: Hunter-Gatherer Settlement Systems and Archaeological Site Formation. *American Antiquity* 45(1):4–20.

Boyd, R., and P. J. Richerson. 1985. *Culture and Evolutionary Process*. University of Chicago Press, Chicago.

Byers, D. A., and J. M. Broughton. 2004. Holocene Environmental Change, Artiodactyl Abundances, and Human Hunting Strategies in the Great Basin. *American Antiquity* 69(2):235–255.

Charnov, E. L. 1976. Optimal Foraging: The Marginal Value Theorem. *Theoretical Population Biology* 9:129–136.

Haynes, C. V., Jr. 2002. *The Early Settlement of North America: The Clovis Era*. Cambridge University Press, Cambridge.

Heizer, R. F. 1956. Recent Cave Explorations in the Lower Humboldt Valley, Nevada. *University of California Archaeological Survey Reports* 33:50–57.

Hockett, B. S. 2007. Nutritional Ecology of Late Pleistocene to Middle Holocene Subsistence in the Great Basin: Zooarchaeological Evidence from Bonneville Estates Rockshelter. In *Paleoindian or Paleoarchaic? Great Basin Human Ecology at the Pleistocene/Holocene Transition*, edited by K. E. Graf and D. N. Schmitt, pp. 204–230. University of Utah Press, Salt Lake City.

Inge, W. R. 1922. Confessio Fidei. In *Outspoken Essays: Second Series*. Longmans, London.

Jennings, J. [1957] 1970. *Danger Cave*. Reprint, University of Utah Press, Salt Lake City.

Jones, G. T., C. Beck, E. E. Jones, and R. E. Hughes. 2003. Lithic Source Use and Paleoarchaic Foraging Territories in the Great Basin. *American Antiquity* 68(1):5–38.

Jones, K. T., and D. B. Madsen. 1989. Calculating the Cost of Resource Transportation: A Great Basin Example. *Current Anthropology* 30(4):529–534.

Kelly, R. L. 1990. Marshes and Mobility in the Western Great Basin. Museum of Peoples and Cultures Occasional Papers 1, *Wetland Adaptations in the Great Basin*, edited by J. C. Janetski and D. B. Madsen. Brigham Young University, Provo, UT.

Lamb, S. M. 1958. Linguistic Prehistory in the Great Basin. *International Journal of American Linguistics* 24(2):95–100.

Larson, C. S., and R. L. Kelly. 1995. *Bioarchaeology of the Stillwater Marsh: Prehistoric Human Adaptation in the Western Great Basin*. Anthropological Papers of the American Museum of Natural History 77. American Museum of Natural History, New York.

MacArthur, R. H., and E. R. Pianka. 1966. An Optimal Use of a Patchy Environment. *American Naturalist* 100:603–609.

Madsen, D. B., and S. R. Simms. 1998. The Fremont Complex: A Behavioral Perspective. *Journal of World Prehistory* 12(3):255–336.

McGuire, K. R., and W.,R. Hildebrandt. 2005. Re-Thinking Great Basin Foragers, Prestige Hunting and Costly Signaling During the Middle Archaic Period. *American Antiquity* 70(4):695–712.

Morgan, C. 2008. Reconstructing Prehistoric Hunter-Gatherer Foraging Radii: A Case Study from California's Southern Sierra Nevada. *Journal of Archaeological Science* 35(2):247–258.

O'Connell, J. F., and P. S. Hayward. 1972. Altithermal and Medithermal Adaptations in Surprise Valley, Northeast California. In Desert Research Institute Publications in the

Social Sciences 8. *Great Basin Cultural Ecology: A Symposium*, edited by D. D. Fowler, pp. 25–41. University of Nevada, Reno.

O'Connell, J. F., K. T. Jones, and S. R. Simms. 1982. Some Thoughts on Prehistoric Archaeology in the Great Basin. In SAA Papers 2, *Man and the Environment in the Great Basin*, edited by D. B. Madsen and J. F. O'Connell, pp. 227–241. Society for American Archaeology, Washington, DC.

Orians, G. H., and N. E. Pearson. 1979. On the Theory of Central Place Foraging. In *Analysis of Ecological Systems*, edited by D. J. Horn, G. R. Stairs, and R. D. Mitchell, pp. 155–177. Ohio State University, Columbus.

Rhode, D., and L. A. Louderback. 2007. Dietary Plant Use in the Bonneville Basin During the Terminal Pleistocene/Early Holocene Transition. In *Paleoindian or Paleoarchaic? Great Basin Human Ecology at the Pleistocene/Holocene Transition*, edited by K. E. Graf and D. N. Schmitt, pp. 231–250. University of Utah Press, Salt Lake City.

Schoener, T. W. 1971. Theory of Feeding Strategies. *Annual Review of Ecology and Systematics* 2:369–404.

Simms, S. R. 1987. *Behavioral Ecology and Hunter-Gatherer Foraging, an Example from the Great Basin*. British Archaeological Reports, International Series 381. Archaeopress, Oxford.

Steward, J. H. 1938. *Basin Plateau Aboriginal Sociopolitical Groups*. Bureau of American Ethnology Bulletin 120. Government Printing Office, Washington, DC.

Thomas, D. H. 1973. An Empirical Test for Steward's Model of Great Basin Settlement Patterns. *American Antiquity* 38(2):155–176.

———. 1981. Complexity Among Great Basin Shoshoneans: The World's Least Affluent Hunter-Gatherers? In Senri Ethnological Studies 9, *Affluent Foragers: Pacific Coasts East and West*, edited by S. Koyama and D. H. Thomas, pp. 19–52. National Museum of Ethnology, Osaka, Japan.

Winterhalder, B., F. Lu, and B. Tucker. 1999. Risk-Sensitive Adaptive Tactics: Models and Evidence from Subsistence Studies in Biology and Anthropology. *Journal of Archaeological Research* 7(4):301–348.

Zeanah, D. W. 2004. Sexual Division of Labor and Central Place Foraging: A Model for the Carson Desert of Western Nevada. *Journal of Anthropological Archaeology* 23:1–32.

———, and S. R. Simms. 1999. Modeling the Gastric: Great Basin Subsistence Studies Since 1982 and the Evolution of General Theory. In *Models for the Millennium, Great Basin Anthropology Today*, edited by C. Beck, pp. 118–140. University of Utah Press, Salt Lake City.

CHAPTER 17

THE EVOLUTION OF SOCIAL ORGANIZATION, SETTLEMENT PATTERNS, AND POPULATION DENSITIES IN PREHISTORIC OWENS VALLEY

JELMER W. EERKENS

Many will know Owens Valley for its role in the "water wars" of the early 1900s, as the city of Los Angeles bought up water rights, built an aqueduct, and turned Owens Lake into a dry lakebed (or playa). Others will know Owens Valley for its role in the motion picture industry, especially its role as a backdrop for many Western movies (again owing to its proximity to Los Angeles and Hollywood). Among anthropologists, Owens Valley has equally prominent status; this was the location where Julian Steward cut his teeth as an early scholar, the foundation for his ideas about cultural ecology.

Within smaller circles, the archaeology of Owens Valley is also well known and has received considerable attention. Relative to other regions in California and the Great Basin, much research, both academic and resource-management-focused, has been undertaken. Indeed, several of the "type sites" for projectile point forms recognized across the west, forms that have been used to define the basic culture-historical sequence in many areas, are found in or adjacent to Owens Valley

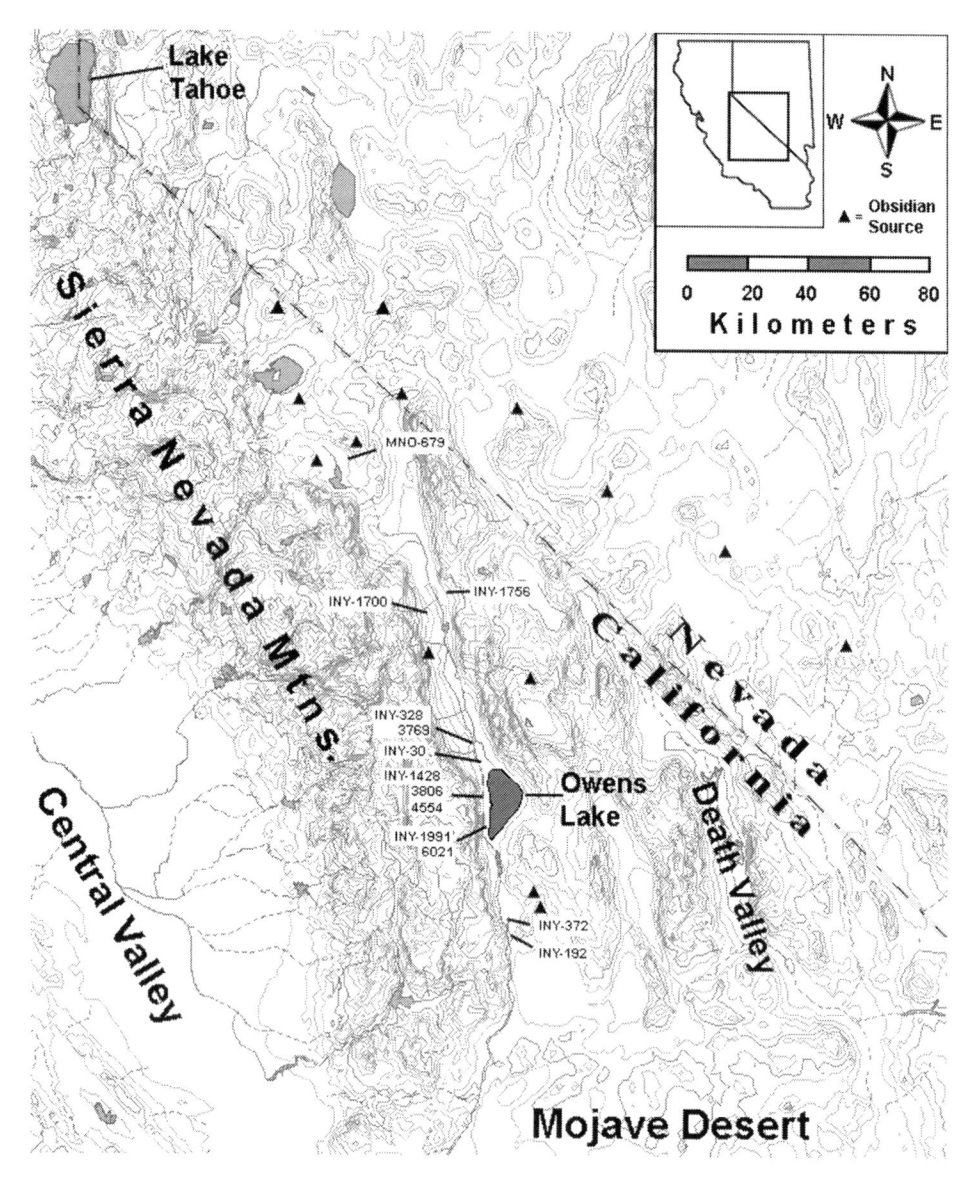

Figure 17.1 Regional map with obsidian sources and key sites.

(e.g., Cottonwood, Rose Springs, Little Lake). As a result, prehistoric lifeways, and diachronic changes therein, are relatively well understood for this area.

Owens Valley lies at the intersection of two geographical regions, cis-montane California to the west and the Great Basin to the east (see Figure 17.1). Technically part of the arid Great Basin, considerable runoff from the Sierra Nevada mountains ensures a dependable source of water to residents of the valley (that is, it did so prior to diversions in the early 1900s). Away from water courses, vegetation conforms to the sagebrush scrub typical of the Great Basin. Along water courses, dense stands of willow, cattail, rush, bulrush, and other wetland plants abound, and in them at least four species of fish and freshwater mussel are found, all of which were exploited by Native American inhabitants. At higher elevations, stands of oaks and piñon pine can be found.

The eastern Sierran region contains a number of important obsidian sources that were exploited from the earliest periods of human occupation. Although most sources fall outside Owens Valley proper, some are adjacent to the valley, and raw materials were moved into the valley proper in large amounts. More than 80–90 percent of the flaked stone material at most sites is obsidian. Not surprisingly, due to its propensity for geochemical provenance analysis and dating by hydration means, obsidian has figured prominently in archaeological research.

Culture History

Archaeological research in Owens Valley does not have a long history. The first reported excavations are from the 1940s and 1950s (Riddell 1951; Riddell and Riddell 1956). As in most of California, much of this early history was focused on establishing the basic culture historical sequence. Taking inspiration from the Southwest, but lacking decorated pottery, archaeologists turned to projectile point seriation as a means to establish local sequences and date sites. The basic sequence of projectile point change was established by the 1970s (Lanning 1963; Bettinger and Taylor 1974) and, augmented by hydration and radiocarbon dating, continues to form the chronological backbone of much research.

Research in the 1960s to 1980s (e.g., Basgall and McGuire 1988; Bettinger 1976, 1989; Hall 1983) focused mainly on sorting out how basic subsistence-settlement patterns had changed over time in the region. These studies included large-scale survey and excavation at a number of key sites, and they brought a rigorous and quantitative approach to artifact and site distribution analysis. Since that time, several large-scale CRM excavation projects, especially those associated with expansion of U.S. Highway 395, which runs down the center of the valley, have contributed a huge corpus of data and greatly expanded our understanding of regional prehistory. Results from these projects are summarized here.

The oldest excavated and dated sites in the Owens Valley region date to the Early Holocene (ca. 9000–7000 BP) and include INY-328, INY-1991, INY-4554, and MNO-679. These sites tend to be small in size, sparse with artifacts, and widely distributed in different environmental contexts. Several are concentrated in the southern section of the valley near the shores of Owens Lake and contain faunal evidence indicating a strong reliance on aquatic resources, including waterfowl and fish, especially the larger Owens Valley sucker (*Catostomus* sp.; see Butler and Delacorte 2004). Evidence hints at small groups of residentially mobile foragers who made short stops at particularly attractive locations to extract various resources (Bettinger 1999a).

Sites dating to the ensuing Middle Holocene (ca. 7000–3500 BP) are comparatively rare (Eerkens et al. 2007b). Most sites contain only surface materials and indicate significant behavioral continuity with the Early Holocene. However, at least one, the Stahl Site (INY-192), contains evidence for more habitual use of space and repeated occupation, as indicated by the presence of hearths, burials, and a possible residential structure (Harrington 1957; Schroth 1994). This site may indicate the beginnings of a transition to more residentially sedentary lifeways in the region. As well, millingstones are more common in sites dating to this period, attesting to increasing use of plant resources in the diet (Bettinger 1989; Gilreath and Hildebrandt 1997; Harrington 1957; Warren 1984).

Relative to the Early and Middle Holocene, Late Holocene sites are well represented in survey and excavation work. The Late Holocene has generally been divided into three culture historical periods, defined by the presence of distinctive projectile point styles. The Newberry period (ca. 3500–1500 BP), marked by Elko series dart points, is the first of these periods. Several sites, including INY-30, INY-3769, and INY-6021, date to the end of this period (ca. 2100–1500 BP) and contain large residential structures with significant accumulations of lithic, faunal, and paleobotanical debris. Such evidence indicates either decreasing residential mobility or repeated use of the same location during seasonal movements. A mixed subsistence economy was in place, including a range of seeds, nuts, roots, and small and large animals.

The Haiwee period (ca. 1500–700 BP) of the Late Holocene is marked by the appearance of smaller corner-notched points that represent the beginnings of bow and arrow technology (Lanning 1963; Yohe 1998). Important sites include INY-372, INY-1428, INY-1700 (Crater Middens), and INY-3806. Outside of the bow and arrow, Haiwee-period material culture suggests much continuity with Newberry populations. However, many lines of evidence point to greatly restricted mobility patterns. Small-bodied animals, especially lagomorphs and waterfowl, are especially prominent in faunal assemblages of these sites. Small seeds and millingstones are present, but not in great amounts.

By contrast, the Marana period (ca. 700 BP–Contact) is marked by introduction of significantly smaller "Desert Series" projectile points (including desert side-notched and cottonwood triangular) and brownware ceramic cooking pots. This record is particularly visible on the desert surface, and a large percentage of artifact debris in the valley dates to this period. Important sites include INY-2, INY-30, INY-1756, and INY-3769. Immense concentrations of charred small seeds, groundstone implements, and scores of potsherds from ceramic cooking vessels all testify to the increasing importance of small seeds in the local diet. Increasing geochemical diversity in exotic obsidian and steatite, and large numbers of marine-shell beads form a stark contrast to Haiwee patterns and indicate higher importance of trade and interregional connections. Faunal remains indicate continued focus on small-bodied animals, and for the first time small shell dumps containing freshwater mussels appear in the record. These trends all hint at a widening diet breadth and a focus on more spatially predictable (i.e., nonmobile) and labor-intensive foods.

This pattern of increasing investment in labor-intensive subsistence strategies is highlighted by documentation, in historical times, of irrigation canal systems in

Owens Valley that were used to feed small patches of land where bulb- and seed-bearing plants were grown (Lawton et al. 1976; Steward 1930, 1933, 1938). Construction, maintenance, and operation of these canals was overseen by a head irrigator, and the Paiute used a number of nonborrowed linguistic terms to describe various aspects and attributes of this practice. Some scholars have referred to this practice this as "proto-agriculture" because of the absence of tilling and minimal investment in fields, while others simply call this agriculture. Regardless of nomenclature, such systems represent a high degree of investment in landscape modification and plant-focused subsistence. Strangely, although these canal systems are still visible in parts of the Owens Valley today, they have not been the subject of much archaeological investigation. Thus, although they are generally thought to be either protohistoric or late pre-Contact, archaeologists actually know little about the antiquity of these practices.

Population Levels

Having outlined the general culture history, I turn in the following sections to examining changes over time in how people in Owens Valley organized themselves and made a living. I believe many of these trends hold in other parts of the Western Great Basin where scientific excavation and survey has been less intense.

Estimating population levels in nonliterate ancient societies is difficult, at best. A number of methods have been used in previous studies, each with its advantages and disadvantages. Here, the focus is on tabulating radiocarbon dates and dated structures as a means of estimating past population, with the understanding that such information *tends to* highlight deposition of hearths and other charcoal-rich features. This is particularly true in studies predating the 1980s, when accelerator mass spectrometry (AMS) was not widely available and dating required large amounts of charcoal. As well, attrition of sites from the archaeological record is expected over time due to erosion or deep burial under alluvium, leading to some overestimation of more recent activities (Surovell and Brantingham 2007). However, I believe such attrition is relatively minor over the last 3,000 years in Owens Valley, the period when major behavioral change is most evident in the record. There are no major erosional, and only minor depositional, events known, such as volcanic ash deposits.

A database of radiocarbon dates recently assembled by Meyer et al. (2009) is borrowed here to assess changes in population activity (see also Basgall 2008). To that database, I added 20 still unpublished dates from my own work and a small number of reports not included in their study. Together, the data tabulate more than 200 radiocarbon dates from sites in Owens Valley. I have broken down this database further into habitation structures versus dates from nonstructural features and general midden. "Modern" (post-1950) dates have been omitted.

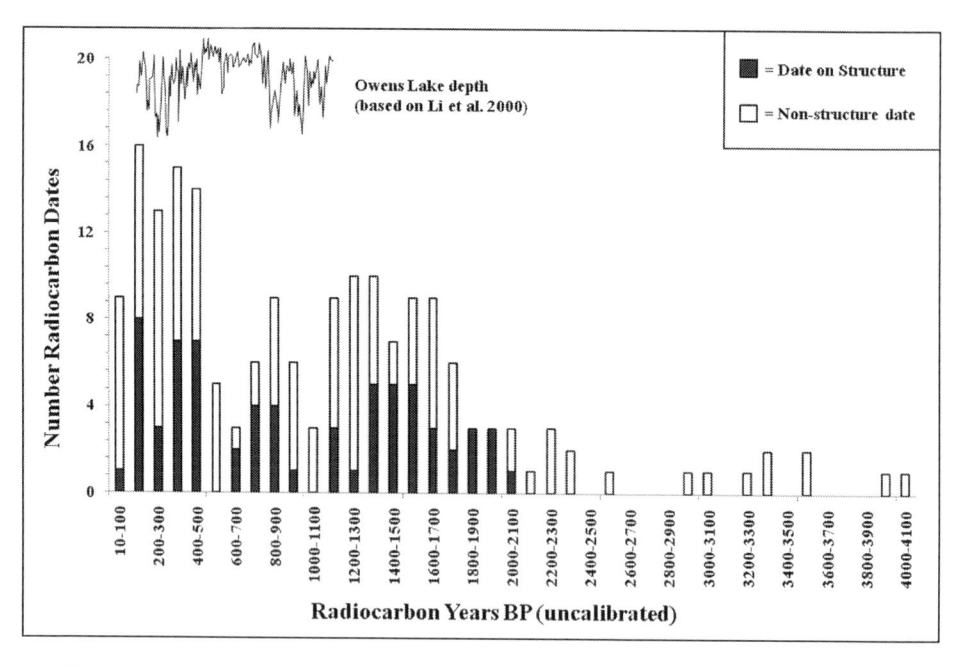

Figure 17.2 Frequency of radiocarbon-dated structures and other archaeological materials over time. Upper part of graph also shows reconstructed depth of Owens Lake based on sediment core, where higher values indicate a deeper lake.

Figure 17.2 summarizes the database in histogram form (by century), with dated structures representing the darkened bottom of each bar. Only the post-4000 BP data are shown because fewer than 15 dates predate this age. As the figure shows, the raw number of radiocarbon dates and structures increases over time, with notable "dips" between 1100 and 900 BP and again from 800 to 500 BP. If radiocarbon dates or structures indicate something about population level, then it can be inferred that populations were steadily increasing within the valley with two short reversals.

Figure 17.2 also plots recently collected high-resolution paleoenvironmental data from Owens Lake, plotting the approximate relative lake level (Li et al. 2000). The line plots parts per million concentrations of lithium in varved lake sediments, with elevated levels interpreted as representing deeper-lake conditions. The first of the two population reversals is roughly coeval with the Medieval Climatic Anomaly (MCA; see Jones et al. 1999), suggesting some degree of disruption in local settlement patterns and behaviors that led to deposition of charcoal and structures. However, the second reversal occurs during a period when the lake is relatively (and consistently) deep, and climatic conditions were presumably wetter. Overall, the figure shows that during the last 1,000 years of prehistory, at least, there is no simple or obvious correlation between population level and climatic conditions, such as wet = growth and dry = decline. Nor is there an obvious correlation between the degree of environmental stability, as measured by the frequency and amplitude of lake level fluctuations, and population level. If analogous high-resolution data from tree rings in the White Mountains (Ababneh 2008) were plotted a similar pattern would have emerged, where no simple correlation between reconstructed climate and population estimates would obtain.

In sum, population does not simply covary with estimates of paleoclimate. I attribute fluctuations in population level, as best it can be reconstructed, largely to changes in three related factors: social organization, organization of labor, and material technologies.

Settlement Patterns

Archaeologists in the Great Basin, including Owens Valley, have relied heavily on detailed analyses of lithic assemblages, especially obsidian, to help reconstruct the extent of ancient mobility patterns (Basgall 1989; Beck et al. 2002; Bettinger 1999a; Eerkens et al. 2008). Because numerous spatially restricted sources are available in the region and because each source has a distinctive geochemical signature, obsidian can act as a geographic tracer of where people have been. However, care must be taken to differentiate trade from embedded procurement and curation, where goods are acquired directly rather than through trade (see Binford 1979). To do so, archaeologists rely on comparison of source diversity within artifact types, especially curated tools, cores, and large (representing primary production) versus small (representing tool maintenance) debitage (Eerkens et al. 2007a).

Because many of the Early and Middle Holocene sites represent brief occupations, obsidian patterns at any particular site usually indicate more about the recent settlement pattern of the individual group that occupied the site. It is only by assembling larger datasets, composed of many sites and a broad range of tool types, that more general notions about settlement patterns can be reconstructed. This has been accomplished only during the last 20 years, primarily as a result of numerous large-scale cultural resource management (CRM) projects.

Together, the data indicate dramatic shifts in settlement patterns over time. For example, Early and Middle Holocene patterns indicate regular access to and conveyance of obsidian materials from a range of locations (Basgall 1989; Delacorte 1999). These patterns extended from the Mojave Desert all the way into the Mono Basin and western Nevada, more than 150 kilometers in extent, and are generally thought to be part of highly residentially mobile settlement systems. Although mainly north-south, east-west movements were also part of this strategy. The general lack of residential structures in the archaeological record (that is, significant investment in domiciles) supports these interpretations of highly mobile groups that spent a short time exploiting various resource patches.

During the Newberry period (3500–1500) of the Late Holocene, settlement patterns constricted geographically and were more limited along the north-south axis. Knappers still had ready access to distant obsidian sources and moved rapidly over long distances (ca. 100 kilometers or more; Eerkens et al. 2008), yet the evenness and diversity of sources is not as large, indicating a focus on movement in certain targeted directions. It is unclear if such movements represent logistical forays on the part of certain segments of society, for example young males accessing distant hunting grounds (Hildebrandt and McGuire 2002), or whether entire groups made such treks (Delacorte 1999; Bettinger 1999a). However, the presence of residential structures with significant investment of time and labor suggests the former.

Beginning around 1,500 years ago (Haiwee period), settlement patterns appear to have shifted again, greatly constricting in extent. Geochemical data indicate a focus on exploiting only the most locally available toolstone sources (Basgall 1989; Eerkens 2003; Eerkens and Spurling 2008). Combined with the presence of large semisubterranean structures, some with more than 20 square meters of covered floor area, these data hint at a semi- or completely sedentary residential mobility pattern. Lithic analyses suggest limited logistical mobility as well. Likewise, most of the plant and animal resources that appear in domestic contexts were available in areas directly adjacent to these settlements, again suggesting a low level of logistical mobility.

Many of these aspects of settlement continue after 700 years ago, with some evidence indicating greater logistical exploitation of more distant resources. What does appear to change is access to exotic goods, such as obsidian, steatite, and marine shell beads, with greater quantities of these items appearing in Marana contexts. However, this appears to be the result of more organized exchange patterns, rather than residential mobility.

Household Organization

At the same time that overall population seems to have been increasing and residential mobility decreasing, detailed excavation data indicate a significant reorganization in social structure. Several trends highlight this shift. First, as shown in Figure 17.3, average house size decreased significantly between about 1200 BP and 700 BP, from an average of about 17 square meters to 11, a nearly 40 percent reduction in area. If house area is correlated to the number of individuals within a household, and the household represents the basic economic unit of production, as is commonly thought, then this shift indicates a focus on smaller family units. In comparison to ethnographic examples of hunter-gatherers (e.g., Cook and Heizer 1968; Naroll 1962), this change is consistent with a shift from extended families to nuclear families as the basic unit of economic production.

Second, with the shift to smaller household size, there is further evidence for less interhousehold sharing and increasing household independence. For example, studies by Eerkens and Spurling (2008) indicate great redundancy in the types and geographic sources of artifacts present on house floors prior to 700 BP. After this time, the density, the range, and especially the geographic source of artifacts are

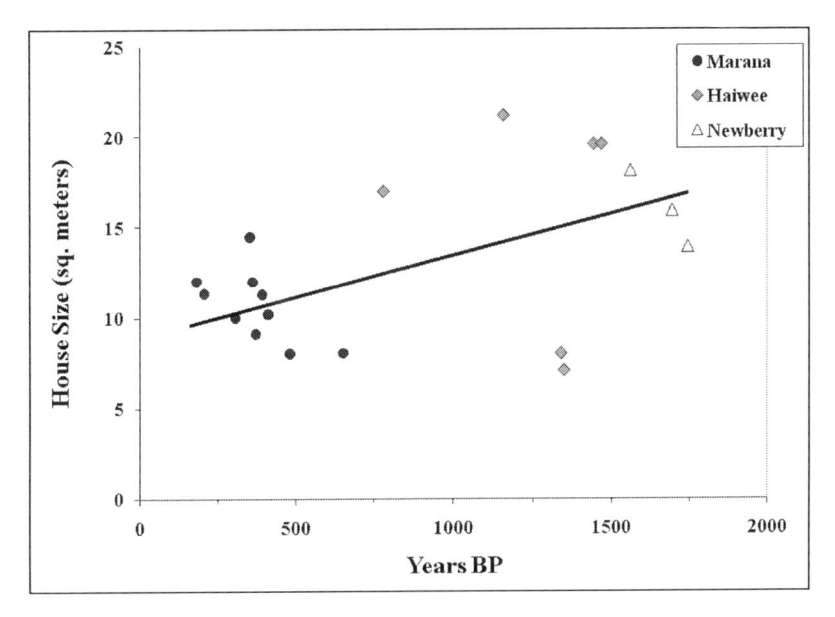

Figure 17.3 House size plotted by radiocarbon date, showing general decrease in house size after 650 BP.

much more variable between household units. These patterns are consistent with a reduction in household size, indicating renewed focus on nuclear families and little intracommunity redistribution of goods.

Third, ongoing research (much of it in progress) on intrahousehold patterning, for example with artifacts, pH, and stable carbon and nitrogen values, indicates increasing domestic activity within households after 700 BP (Eerkens 2003, 2004; Santy and Eerkens 2010). Thus, despite decreasing household size, there is evidence that internal space was more regularly partitioned and that an increasing range of these activities were undertaken within domiciles, especially those leaving organic residues behind. These patterns are consistent with the notion that food preparation and storage moved inside domiciles, where they were less visible to other households (Eerkens 2004). Again, this is indicative of a switch from a more open community with greater public ownership and sharing, to a more closed one with a focus on privately owned goods and less sharing (Wiessner 1982).

Conclusion

As suggested, the connection between paleoenvironmental processes and societal evolution in Owens Valley is not simple. Wetter conditions did not automatically bring about increases in population density or decreases in mobility. Elsewhere in California, archaeologists have implicated environment as an important driving force in shaping human behavior (Jones et al. 1999; Arnold 1992). Others have questioned this role and cite population increase or technology as an important factor (Basgall 2008; Bettinger and Baumhoff 1982; Bouey 1979) while still others (Hildebrandt and McGuire 2002) implicate internal social factors, in particular costly signaling, as equally important forces in fostering evolutionary change (for debate, see Broughton and Bayham 2003). If there are causal relations in Owens Valley between paleoclimate and the various social processes discussed above, they are subtler and more complex. Sorting out these issues will require more detailed analyses.

Regardless of the role of climate, several marked and related diachronic patterns are evident that suggest fundamental changes in lifeways. First, there is a clear trend toward decreasing residential mobility over time, culminating in semi- to completely sedentary residential patterns around 1500 BP. Communities at this time appear to have been fairly "open," with a high degree of redundancy between household units. Presumably, these household units were widely interacting and sharing within a public goods system.

Sometime between 1,000 and 700 years ago, there was a "closing" of villages in the Owens Valley. Households began to act more independently of one another, focusing efforts on different kinds of activities and moving many of these activities indoors. These patterns mimic those at the regional level of increasing territoriality discussed by Bettinger (1982, 1999b), though he places the shift slightly earlier in time (ca. 1500 BP).

What drove these changes? Eerkens (2004) suggests that increasing population densities around 500 BP no longer made an open system feasible. In particular, with more and more people, the average degree of relatedness between any two individuals within a community would have decreased. If kinship played a role in reciprocal altruism, these changes may have altered the costs and benefits of freeloading within a community. In other words, with fewer kin relations it would have been easier for individuals to freeload off the work of others, with lessened repercussions for such behavior. He further hypothesizes that a result of this process was renewed focus on resources that could be individually (rather than communally) procured, processed, and stored, in particular small seeds. As well, settlement shifted away from community-centered activities to ones based in the nuclear family.

These processes set the stage for changes witnessed in the protohistoric and early historic periods. As goods were no longer redistributed, differences developed between household units. As notions of territoriality increased in concert with privatization, some household units may have been able to gain access to more productive resources patches or accumulate material wealth. These differences appear to have also extended to trading networks (Eerkens and Spurling 2008). At some point, likely at the most recent protohistoric period, small-scale leaders emerged from this process. These inherited leadership positions are described in detail in the ethnographic literature (Steward 1933). Leaders were able to organize members within a community toward various ends, such as coordinating feasts, rabbit drives, and construction and maintenance of irrigation systems. This indicates a reemergence of community-level activities, though this time organized by particular individuals who may have accrued social or material benefits from these activities.

Of great interest, then, is exactly when such community-level activities reemerged. Was it immediately around 600–500 BP, or only following contact with Anglo-Americans? Some activities, such as community feasts, may be difficult to detect and date archaeologically. Others, however, such as irrigation systems, should be easier to investigate and date. Yet as mentioned, irrigation systems have not been the focus of much archaeological investigation. In any case, future work should seek to tease apart the timing of such events.

REFERENCES

Ababneh, L. 2008. Bristlecone Pine Paleoclimatic Model for Archeological Patterns in the White Mountains of California. *Quaternary International* 188:59–78.

Arnold, J. E. 1992. Complex Hunter-Gatherer-Fishers of Prehistoric California: Chiefs, Specialists, and Maritime Adaptations of the Channel Islands. *American Antiquity* 57:60–84.

Basgall, M. E. 1989. Obsidian Acquisition and Use in Prehistoric Central-Eastern California. Contributions of the University of California Archaeological Research Facility 45, *Current Directions in California Obsidian Studies*, edited by R. E. Hughes, pp. 111–126. University of California, Berkeley.

———. 2008. An Archaeological Assessment of Late-Holocene Environmental Change in the Southwestern Great Basin. In *From Avocados to Millingstones: Papers in Honor of Delbert L. True*, edited by M. E. Basgall and G. Waugh, pp. 137–153. Archaeological Research Center, California State University, Sacramento.

———, and K. McGuire. 1988. *The Archaeology of CA-INY-30: Prehistoric Culture Change in the Southern Owens Valley, California*. Report submitted to California Department of Transportation, District 9, Bishop, CA.

Beck, C., A. K. Taylor, G. T. Jones, C. M. Fadem, C. R. Cook, and S. A. Millward. 2002. Rocks Are Heavy: Transport Costs and Paleoarchaic Quarry Behavior in the Great Basin. *Journal of Anthropological Archaeology* 21:481–507.

Bettinger, R. L. 1976. The Development of Pinyon Exploitation in Central Eastern California. *Journal of California Anthropology* 3:81–95.

———. 1982. Aboriginal Exchange and Territoriality in Owens Valley, California. In *Contexts for Prehistoric Exchange*, edited by J. E. Ericson and T. K. Earle, pp. 103–128. Academic Press, New York.

———. 1989. *The Archaeology of Pinyon House, Two Eagles, and Crater Middens: Three Residential Sites in Owens Valley, Eastern California*. Anthropological Papers of the American Museum of Natural History 67. American Museum of Natural History, New York.

———. 1999a. From Traveler to Processor: Regional Trajectories of Hunter-Gatherer Sedentism in the Inyo-Mono Region, California. In *Settlement Pattern Studies in the Americas: Fifty Years Since Viru*, edited by B. R. Billman and G. M. Feinman, pp. 39–55. Smithsonian Institution, Washington, DC.

———. 1999b. What Happened in the Medithermal. In *Models for the Millennium*, edited by C. Beck, pp. 62–74. University of Utah Press, Salt Lake City.

———, and M. A. Baumhoff. 1982. The Numic Spread: Great Basin Cultures in Competition. *American Antiquity* 47:485–503.

Bettinger, R. L., and R. E. Taylor. 1974. Suggested Revisions in Archaeological Sequences of the Great Basin in Interior California. *Nevada Archaeological Survey Research Paper* 5:1–26.

Binford, L. R. 1979. Organization and Formation Processes: Looking at Curated Technologies. *Journal of Anthropological Research* 35:255–273.

Bouey, P. D. 1979. Population Pressure and Agriculture in Owens Valley. *Journal of California and Great Basin Anthropology* 1:162–170.

Broughton, J. M., and F. E. Bayham. 2003. Showing Off, Foraging Models, and the Ascendance of Large-Game Hunting in the California Middle Archaic. *American Antiquity* 68:783–789.

Butler, V. L., and M. G. Delacorte. 2004. Doing Zooarchaeology as If It Mattered: Use of Faunal Data to Address Current Issues in Fish Conservation Biology in Owens Valley, California. In *Zooarchaeology and Conservation Biology*, edited by R. Lyman and K. Cannon, pp. 25–44. University of Utah Press, Salt Lake City.

Cook, S., and R. F. Heizer. 1968. Relationships Among Houses, Settlement Areas, and Population in Aboriginal California. In *Settlement Archaeology*, edited by K. C. Chang, pp. 79–116. National Press Books, Palo Alto, CA.

Delacorte, M. G. 1999. *The Changing Role of Riverine Environments in the Prehistory of the Central-Western Great Basin: Data Recovery Excavations at Six Prehistoric Sites in Owens Valley, California.* Report submitted to California Department of Transportation, District 9, Bishop, CA.

Eerkens, J. W. 2003. Sedentism, Storage, and the Intensification of Small Seeds: Prehistoric Developments in Owens Valley, California. *North American Archaeologist* 24:281–309.

———. 2004. Privatization, Small-Seed Intensification, and the Origins of Pottery in the Western Great Basin. *American Antiquity* 69:653–670.

———, W., J. R. Ferguson, M. D. Glascock, C. E. Skinner, and S. A. Waechter. 2007a. Reduction Strategies and Geochemical Characterization of Lithic Assemblages: A Comparison of Three Case Studies from Western North America. *American Antiquity* 72:585–597.

Eerkens, J. W., J. S. Rosenthal, D. C. Young, and J. King. 2007b. Early Holocene Landscape Archaeology in the Coso Basin, Northwestern Mojave Desert, California. *North American Archaeologist* 28:87–112.

Eerkens, J. W., and A. M. Spurling. 2008. Obsidian Acquisition and Exchange Networks: A Diachronic Perspective of Households in Owens Valley. *Journal of California and Great Basin Anthropology* 28:111–126.

———, and M. A. Gras. 2008. Measuring Prehistoric Mobility Strategies Based on Obsidian Geochemical and Technological Signatures in the Owens Valley, California. *Journal of Archaeological Science* 35(3):668–680.

Gilreath, A. J., and W. R. Hildebrandt. 1997. *Prehistoric Use of the Coso Volcanic Field.* Contributions of the University of California Archaeological Research Facility. University of California, Berkeley.

Hall, M. C. 1983. *Late Holocene Hunter-Gatherers and Volcanism in the Long Valley-Mono Basin Region: Prehistoric Culture Change in the Eastern Sierra Nevada.* University Microfilms, Ann Arbor, MI.

Harrington, M. R. 1957. A Pinto Site at Little Lake, California. *Southwest Museum Papers* 17. Southwest Museum, Highland Park, CA.

Hildebrandt, W. R., and K. R. McGuire. 2002. The Ascendance of Hunting During the California Middle Archaic: An Evolutionary Perspective. *American Antiquity* 67:231–256.

Jones, T. L., G. Brown, L. M. Raab, J. McVicar, W. G. Spaulding, D. J. Kennett, A. York, and P. L. Walker. 1999. Environmental Imperatives Reconsidered: Demographic Crises in Western North America During the Medieval Climatic Anomaly. *Current Anthropology* 40:137–156.

Lanning, E. P. 1963. Archaeology of the Rose Spring Site INY-372. *University of California Publications American Archaeology and Ethnology* 49(3):237–336.

Lawton, H. W., P. J. Wilke, M. DeDecker, and W. M. Mason. 1976. Agriculture Among the Paiute of Owens Valley. *Journal of California Anthropology* 3:13–50.

Li, H.-C., J. L. Bischoff, T.-L. Ku, S. P. Lund, and L. D. Stott. 2000. Climate Variability in East-Central California During the Past 1000 Years Reflected by High-Resolution Geochemical and Isotopic Records from Owens Lake Sediments. *Quaternary Research* 54:187–197.

Meyer, J., D. C. Young, and J. Rosenthal. 2009. Geoarchaeological Overview and Assessment of Caltrans Districts 6 and 9. Report by Far Western Anthropological Research Group, submitted to the California Department of Transportation, District 6, Fresno, CA.

Naroll, R. 1962. Floor Area and Settlement Population. *American Antiquity* 27:587–589.

Riddell, H. S. 1951. The Archaeology of a Paiute Village Site in Owens Valley. *Reports of the University of California Archaeological Survey* 12:1–28.

———, and F. A. Riddell. 1956. The Current Status of Archaeological Investigations in Owens Valley, California. *Reports of the University of California Archaeological Survey* 33:28–33.

Santy, J., and J.W. Eerkens. 2010. *The Organization of Domestic Space in Late Prehistoric Owens Valley Households*. Society for California Archaeology Proceedings, vol. 24. http://www.scahome.org/publications/proceedings/Proceedings.24Santy.pdf.

Schroth, A. B. 1994. *The Pinto Controversy in the Western United States*. University Microfilms, Ann Arbor, MI.

Steward, J. H. 1930. Irrigation Without Agriculture. *Papers of the Michigan Academy of Sciences, Arts, and Letters* 12:149–156.

———. 1933. *Ethnography of the Owens Valley Paiute*. University of California Publications in American Archaeology and Ethnology, vol. 33, no. 3. University of California Press, Berkeley.

———. 1938. *Basin-Plateau Aboriginal Sociopolitical Groups*. Smithsonian Institution Bureau of American Ethnology. Bulletin 120. United States Government Printing Office. Washington, D.C.

Surovell, T. A., and P. J. Brantingham. 2007. A Note on the Use of Temporal Frequency Distributions in Studies of Prehistoric Demography. *Journal of Archaeological Science* 34:1868–1877.

Warren, C. N. 1984. The Desert Region. In *California Archaeology*, edited by M. J. Moratto. Academic Press, Orlando, FL.

Wiessner, P. 1982. Beyond Willow Smoke and Dogs' Tails: A Comment on Binford's Analysis of Hunter-Gatherer Settlement Systems. *American Antiquity* 47:171–178.

Yohe, R. M., II. 1998. The Introduction of the Bow and Arrow and Lithic Resource Use at Rose Spring (CA-INY-372). *Journal of California and Great Basin Anthropology* 20(1):72–87.

CHAPTER 18

MOUND BUILDING BY CALIFORNIA HUNTER-GATHERERS

KENT G. LIGHTFOOT AND EDWARD M. LUBY

ONE of the most significant recent developments in North American archaeology is the recognition that hunter-gatherer communities constructed complex and extensive mounded landscapes many thousands of years ago. Twenty years ago, most archaeologists believed indigenous mound building was almost exclusively the domain of complex societies boasting sedentary towns and villages, powerful elite classes, and prolific agrarian economies, as epitomized by the Woodland, Mississippian, and Hohokam peoples of the Eastern Woodlands and American Southwest, who built platform mounds, burial monuments, and effigy earthworks in late prehistoric times (see also Milner, and Sassaman and Randall, this volume).

There is now excellent evidence for much earlier mound construction by non-agrarian groups who fabricated a diverse range of landscape features, including shell mounds, earthen mounds, sand mounds, and concentric or semiconcentric shell rings, dating 7,000 to 3,000 years ago in the American Midwest, American Southeast, and California. The mounded landscapes produced by hunter-gatherers in North America varied tremendously in their scale, architectural features, spatial layouts, methods, and timing of construction, as well as their associated cultural remains (some contain burials or midden deposits, while others are relatively sterile).

The purposes of this chapter are twofold. One is to synthesize briefly archaeological findings of hundreds of mounded sites in California used by local hunter-gatherer groups beginning about 5,000 years ago and spanning to historic times.

The other is to explore how these earthworks compare to those constructed by hunter-gatherers elsewhere in North America.

MOUNDED LANDSCAPES IN CALIFORNIA

One of the most striking features of the archaeological record in California is the pervasive presence of mounds in coastal, estuary, and riverine areas of the state, from the shores of the Pacific Ocean near San Francisco, south through the central and southern coast out to the Channel Islands, up from the shores of the San Francisco Bay through to the Sacramento-San Joaquin Delta region, and into the great Central Valley, with its many rivers and tributaries. Despite many years of investigation and a long-standing interest in these mounded sites (some of which are the size of a football field and up to several meters deep), a comprehensive synthesis of California's mounded landscapes has yet to be presented. Significantly, many questions about the mounds remain unresolved. Are these mounded sites the accumulated result of food debris? Were they used as places of habitation, or as cemeteries? Were some of the California mounds purposefully constructed, as in other areas of North America? Were they villages, ceremonial centers, resource processing places, or all of the above? How might the thousands of mounds in this landscape have varied across time and space?

To begin to characterize the mounded landscapes of California, the archaeological record of two key, adjacent regions in the state, the San Francisco Bay area (SFBA) and the Central Valley region (with specific emphasis on the Delta area), are explored here (Figure 18.1). Mounds in both the SFBA and the Delta make their appearance in the Middle Archaic Period (ca. 7500 to 2500 BP) and continue throughout subsequent periods, including the Upper Archaic (2500 to 850 BP) and Emergent (850 BP to Historic).

San Francisco Bay Area Mounds

Draining nearly 40 percent of California's landmass, the SFBA comprises the largest estuarine system in the state, with an incredible expanse of tidal marshlands and freshwater habitats that support a multitude of plants and animals. Archaeologists have documented hundreds of large and small mounds made up of shellfish remains (clam, mussel, oyster, etc.), dirt, ash, and rocks along the bay shore of San Francisco Bay, San Pablo Bay, the Carquinez Strait, and Suisun Bay of Central California (Figure 18.2). Since the early 1900s, archaeologists have recorded a variety of shell-associated sites (using labels such as shell mounds, shell middens, shell scatters, and shell heaps), in addition to some earthen mounds. Most of these sites would be characterized as "midden mounds" in the Midwest and Southeast, as the matrix of the sites typically contains diverse assemblages of artifacts, mammals,

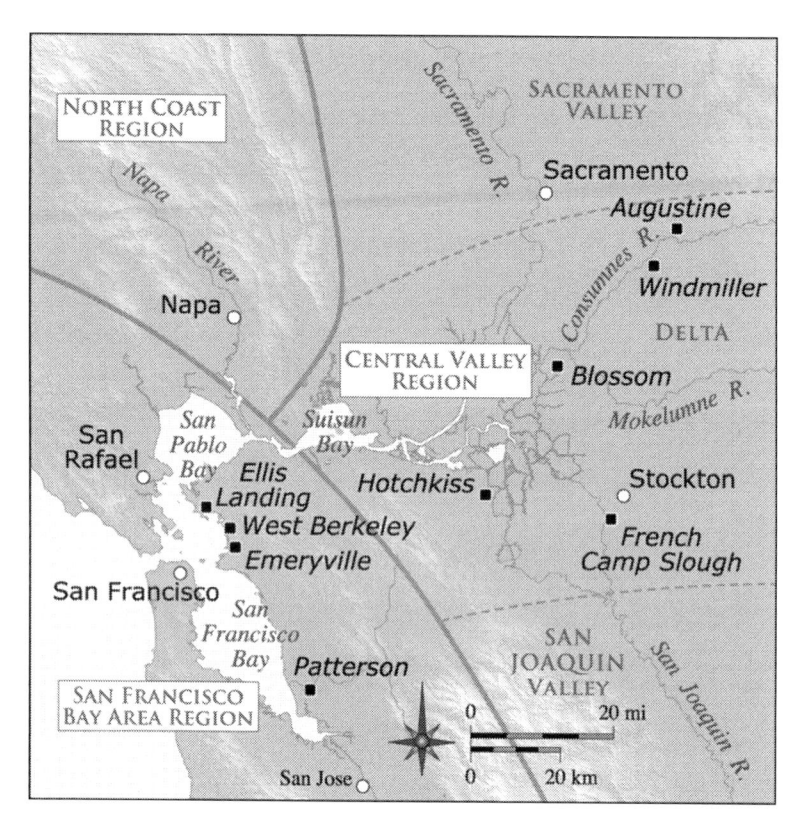

Figure 18.1 Map of central California showing the San Francisco Bay Area and Central Valley regions. The Delta is found in the latter region, at the confluence of the Sacramento and San Joaquin Rivers. Major archaeological sites are illustrated by solid squares; modern towns are depicted by open circles.

birds, and fish, in addition to human and nonhuman burials (e.g., dogs, raptors). Some of the largest mounds, among them Ellis Landing, Emeryville, and West Berkeley (Figure 18.3), rose five to 10 or more meters above the land surface, extending across the equivalent of a couple of football fields and containing hundreds to several thousand human burials (Lightfoot 1997; Luby et al. 2006).

Chronological investigations indicate that some of these mounded places were repeatedly used over hundreds or thousands of years. The earliest dated basal deposits range between 5,000 and 3,000 years ago along the bay shore, when the greater San Francisco estuarine system was stabilizing from rapid sea level rise in post-Pleistocene times. However, many of the dated deposits for large mounds are distributed in the time span of 2000 to 1050 BP, what we have referred to elsewhere as the "golden age" of shell mounds in the SFBA (Lightfoot and Luby 2002). Recent findings indicate that some mounds with intact upper deposits may date to the time of Spanish intrusion into the region in the late AD 1700s and early 1800s.

Most mounds are found in clusters of three to 14 sites distributed along the bay shore or adjacent freshwater streams. These site clusters may be composed of both large and small shell-bearing sites, an occasional earth mound, and petroglyphs;

bedrock milling stations; lithic scatters; and nonmounded cemeteries (Luby et al. 2006). Two kinds of site clusters have been recently identified: "contained" (or "tight") clusters of sites grouped into geographically compact areas and "open" (or "dispersed") clusters in which associated sites are spread relatively far apart from one another, though at a larger scale they still possess spatial unity. Open clusters often span the

Figure 18.2 Large mounded site, recorded as mound no. 262 by Nels Nelson during his pioneering survey of the San Francisco Bay Area from 1906 to 1908. It is located one mile east of the modern town of Pinole. Note the man sitting on the apex of the mound (copyright © Phoebe A. Hearst Museum of Anthropology and the Regents of the University of California, photo probably by Nels Nelson, Catalogue No. 15–5211).

Figure 18.3 Excavations at the Ellis Landing Shell Mound. This photograph shows the 108-foot-long trench excavated by Nels Nelson and his crew in 1906 (copyright © Phoebe A. Hearst Museum and the Regents of the University of California, Photography by Nels Nelson, Catalogue No. 15–5243).

shores of the bay, or reach across several drainages in the nearby hills, and tend to be arranged in a more linear fashion than sites associated with compact clusters.

There are also differences in the kinds of mounded sites found across the SFBA. In general, Native people produced primarily shell-associated mounds in the northern SFBA, including massive shell mounds, while hunter-gatherer groups in the central and southern SFBA tended to employ less shell and more earth in constructing mounds. Currently, there is no consensus among archaeologists about how and why these mounded landscapes were produced by local hunter-gatherer communities. Explanations for the building of the mounds range from their use as refuse dumps and ceremonial centers to specialized burial sites and mounded villages (Luby 2004; Luby and Gruber 1999; Luby et al. 2006).

Delta Mounds

Situated where the Sacramento River and the San Joaquin River merge in the Great Central Valley of California, the topographically flat Delta was once a highly productive wetland environment, particularly rich in fish, bird life, and a variety of plant foods. Similar to the SFBA, mounded sites in the Delta have been documented by archaeologists for more than a century (Figure 18.4). The most recent, comprehensive analyses of the Delta's archaeology by Moratto (1984) and Rosenthal et al. (2007) offer historical overviews and the current status of ongoing research. Traditional areas of concern include explaining the relationship of SFBA cultures to the

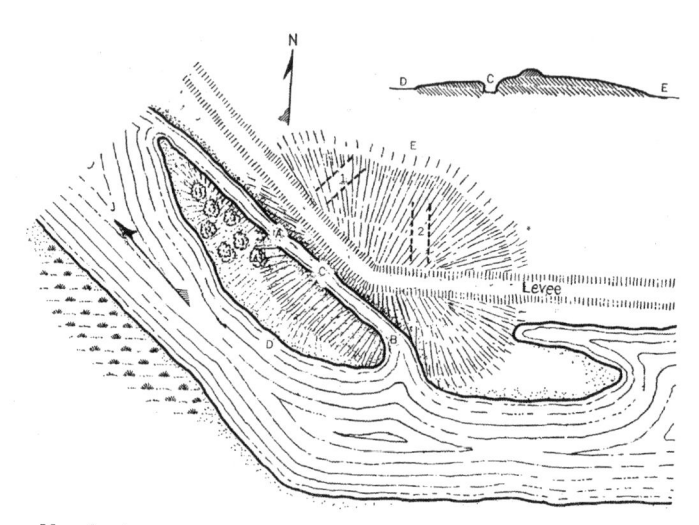

Map showing mound no. 4, Stockton, with relation to slough, levee, cutting, trenches, etc.; also section through mound.

Figure 18.4 Illustration of a mounded site along a slough in the Delta area near the modern town of Stockton (in P. M. Jones, 1923, "Mounded Excavations Near Stockton," in the *University of California Publications in American Archaeology and Ethnology*, vol. 20, no. 7, p. 117).

broader Delta over time, constructing and refining cultural chronologies and trait lists, explaining movements of people through time, and understanding economic and cultural patterns across time. More recent analyses have emphasized issues surrounding resource exploitation, optimal foraging, and resource intensification. What is lacking are synthetic investigations on how and why hunter-gatherer populations constructed the mounded landscapes and what kinds of social, political, and ritual organizations may have characterized these groups.

The predominant site type in the Delta is often described as a "low mound" composed of earth or midden, rising a meter or more above ground level, with the mound atop some kind of natural rise above the surrounding ground level. Sites are also characterized as consisting primarily of mound deposits atop low knolls or hills, often with multiple components from different time periods, though single component sites are also recorded. Mounded sites almost always appear to be associated with burials; tend to be found adjacent to rivers, streams, or wetlands; and even in the most recent literature are sometimes described as "villages."

The best known early mounds in the Delta are defined as part of the Windmiller complex, dating mostly between 3800 and 2700 BP, during the late Middle Archaic Period (Rosenthal et al. 2007). Mortuary deposits are the salient characteristic of Windmiller mounds, with burials consistently positioned and oriented in the same direction, and associated with specific kinds of grave goods. Because the Delta is subject to alluvial deposition, Windmiller components are sometimes found well beneath the ground surface, making it difficult to assess overall site dimensions and shapes. In some cases, these sites appear to be composed of midden containing burials atop low clay knolls, suggesting that they were places of habitation; in other cases, they are apparently composed of burials placed into small elevations of natural deposits, suggesting more of a cemetery (Heizer 1949). In fact, Meighan (1987) argues that Windmiller sites were used exclusively for mortuary activities and that the evidence for habitation is weak, such that the sites could actually represent artificial burial mounds, comparable to those in eastern North America.

During the Upper Archaic and Emergent periods, the evidence for large mounded sites in the Delta is clearer. Beardsley (1954:64) characterizes sites in the Delta at this time as "permanent villages," where "domestic refuse, whole, broken, and unfinished artifacts, house remains and burials of the dead" indicate that these sites are "full communities, with traces of all important community activities." More specifically, Beardsley (77) emphasizes that sites from these periods are midden-accumulated mounds, consisting of "bird and animal bone, fragmented stones, and river shells, ash or charcoal residues and greasy texture of the soil." He further notes that deposits range from about 30 centimeters (especially atop stratified sites) to more than 3.5 meters deep.

Cook and Elsasser (1956:26) also describe low "sand mounds" that may have occurred naturally, in part through wind modification, used for burial in the Upper Archaic and then later as midden deposits in the Emergent period (Figure 18.5). Both chronological components were not commonly found at the same site; only two of the 16 sites they described possessed both middens and burials. In other

Figure 18.5 Example of a sand dune mound from Bradford Island in the Delta area (copyright © Phoebe A. Hearst Museum of Anthropology and the Regents of the University of California. Catalogue No. 15-5199).

words, most sites have either midden deposits found directly *atop* the compacted sand mounds or burials placed directly *within* the sand mounds.

In comparing the mounded landscapes of the SFBA and Delta, there are important similarities: most mounds contain burials, many are associated with midden deposits, many appear to be reused over many centuries or even thousands of years, and all are found near wetland habitats. There are also some significant differences. Delta mounds tend to be earthen, apparently built atop raised natural features from their inception. In SFBA, the sometimes massive mounds, which were associated with shell in numerous cases, were created through accretion or perhaps even active earth or shell moving. Mounds in the SFBA, therefore, did not routinely take advantage of natural features in the landscape, but rather accumulated to their full size through various anthropogenic processes. Delta mounds are also shallower, even though they were occupied for comparably long periods of time, but they often appear analogous in length and width, raising interesting questions about how the sites may have been used differently.

Although some of the Windmiller and sand dune sites may have been used exclusively for mortuary purposes, the majority of the mounded places in the Delta have been interpreted as villages with associated burials. Future comparisons between the Delta and SFBA mounded landscapes will be useful in considering the predominant idea that the large but shallower Delta mounds from later periods were built up from the refuse of hunter-gatherer domestic life, or whether is it possible that for some periods a mortuary or feasting function outweighed other uses. In any event, it is striking that over many time periods and across wide expanses of space, Native peoples of the Delta and SFBA consistently chose mounded sites for the burial of their dead. Whether or not mounded sites were created or were associated with natural deposits, and whether or not mounded areas were used for the first time or accessed after many years, mounded behavior is perhaps the most salient, though underappreciated, aspect of the overall archaeological landscape of Central California.

Archaic Mounds of the American Midwest and Southeast

Much can be learned about early mound building in North America by comparing the mounded landscapes of California with those built by hunter-gatherers in other regions, specifically the Midwest and Southeast. A continental perspective underscores great variation in the methods, materials, and timing of mound construction; the spatial layout of mound complexes; and mound functions—all indications that the histories and meanings of mounded places probably diverged considerably among hunter-gatherers. How California mounds stack up against other mounded places is explored below for several key areas dating to the Middle Archaic (ca. 7000–5000 BP) and Late Archaic (ca. 5000–3000 BP).

Lower Mississippi River Valley

Documentation of more than 30 mound complexes dating to the Middle Archaic, notably Watson Brake, Frenchman's Bend, and Monte Sano, denotes some broad commonalities: multiple earthen mounds with little evidence of burials, artifact caches, or house or temple floors (Sassaman 2004; Saunders 2004). Current interpretations suggest that hunter-gatherer groups intentionally constructed some of the mound complexes to a common plan based on geometric regularities and standard units of measure (Sassaman and Heckenberger 2004). Excavations suggest they were built either in one rapid construction episode or in a few pulses of construction. Although the Middle Archaic earthen mounds were constructed at least 1,500 years before the incredible Late Archaic manifestations at Poverty Point (see Kidder, this volume), there are some common threads. The Poverty Point construction incorporated some components of earlier earthworks into its design, the builders employed a measurement system similar to those of earlier mound builders, and at least some Poverty Point mounds were built very rapidly, such as the imposing Mound A, which appears to have been erected over a few months by a substantial number of people (Kidder 2011).

There is considerable debate about the specific functions and meanings of Archaic mounds in the lower Mississippi River Valley, but most researchers agree they were intentionally built for some kind of communal ceremonies that brought people together for periodic social gatherings. These earthen mounds diverge from California sites in several significant ways: they lack burials, tend to be free of midden deposits (which may or may not be located nearby, as in the ridge features at Poverty Point), and were built in one or a few rapidly occurring episodes. In contrast, the majority of the shell and earth mounds in California (with the exception of some Windmiller and sand dune burial mounds in the Delta) are accretional midden deposits built up over hundreds and even thousands of years. Unlike the builders of the Mississippi mounds, Native Californians continued to use and build up incrementally the same mounded places over many generations. It remains to be seen if mound clusters in California were built to some kind of predetermined plan using standard units of measure, but our preliminary findings suggest that this is not the case.

Shell Rings of the South Atlantic Coast and Gulf Coast

Distinctive sites of circular and semicircular deposits of shell (mostly oyster), animal bones, artifacts, and soil are well documented for coastal South Carolina, Georgia, and Florida during the period of 4500 to 3000 BP. The northern sites tend to be smaller, with shells mounded a few meters wide and one to three meters high in a circular shape, their diameters measuring about 22 to 83 meters; the larger Florida sites (one to four meters high, 150–250 meters in diameter) are open ended in a U- or C-shaped configuration and more architecturally complex, with attached small ringlets and associated shell rings, shell mounds, shell ridges, and sheet midden deposits (Russo and Heide 2001; Thomas 2008). Excavations within and under the mounded deposits have yielded postmolds and other features (such as earth ovens), while units placed in the interior have unearthed ambiguous pit features and relatively limited archaeological materials. Trinkley's pioneering work (1985) suggests that the shell rings were produced from domestic refuse built up over time from houses arranged in a circle around an open communal area. More recent interpretations argue that shell rings may have been produced primarily during social gatherings involving feasting practices. Russo (2004) proposes that the volume of food debris distributed around shell rings may reflect the differential statuses of individuals and families in the broader hunter-gatherer community.

No shell rings have yet been documented for California, and their distribution may be fairly restricted in North America. However, recent debates about how and why the shell rings were created, which range from their accumulation through routine residential and subsistence activities to their use as venues for periodic competitive feasting or even creation as monumental architecture (see Thomas and Sanger 2010; Marquardt 2010), are also interpretations currently being explored in the study of shell and earthen mounds in California.

Archaic Shell Mounds of the Lower Midwest and Southeast

The core area of the so-called Archaic Shell Mound, extending along the Green River in central Kentucky and the Tennessee River of Tennessee and northern Alabama, is defined by extensive mounds of freshwater shellfish, artifacts, some soil, and various kinds of features that date between 7000 and 3000 BP (Sassaman 2004:255). Some of these sites, such as Indian Knoll, contain hundreds or even thousands of human burials, along with many dog burials. The mounded sites appear to be places where shellfish gathering, fishing, and other related tasks took place intermittently among hunter-gatherer groups over some period of time. Shell mounds produced by hunter-gatherers are also well documented from other areas. For example, White (2004) describes shell mounds for northwest Florida composed of freshwater and estuarine (oyster) shell and domestic refuse, but relatively few human burials. Archaic shell mounds and shell ridges, often containing specific burial areas, are also well documented along the St. Johns River of northeast Florida.

Interestingly, archaeological interpretations of the eastern shell mounds are almost identical to those proposed for California mounded sites. The most popular is that these sites are incidental manifestations built up through time by dumping refuse from the repetitive harvesting and processing of shellfish, fish, and other wild foods in specific locations along rich riverine or estuarine locations. It is argued that hunter-gatherers would tend to reuse these high points in lowland wetland environments that frequently flooded (White 2004). Another interpretation is that shell mounds with burials served as specialized ceremonial places where mortuary feasting and other activities took place (Claassen 1996).

Conclusion

The archaeology of mounded landscapes produced by hunter-gatherers shares some commonalities across North America. In all of the regions reviewed, mounded sites have been significantly affected by agriculture, urban expansion, looting, and mining for shell and organically rich soils. Consequently, the archaeology of hunter-gatherer mounds often involves study of previous excavations and extant museum collections in concert with careful sampling of intact deposits that have been preserved in federal, state, and regional parklands. Mounded places are almost universally located near productive wetland habitats, be they rivers, bays, or estuaries. North American archaeologists tend to distinguish two basic types of hunter-gatherer mounds: earthen mounds, which were intentionally constructed by Native peoples for ceremonial purposes; and the so-called midden mounds made up of shell, soil, and domestic refuse, which are believed to be the incidental consequence of hunting-gatherers repeatedly using specific wetland places for shellfish gathering, fishing, and other tasks.

We believe it is time to reevaluate this dichotomous perspective of early mounds because it tends to portray hunter-gatherers as single-minded and inflexible in how they constructed and used mounded places across multiple generations (see also Sassaman and Randall, this volume). We suspect that diverse fisher, hunter, and gatherer groups used and contributed to mounded landscapes over time for many reasons. Our current research on California mounds is exploring how mound uses, construction methods, and meanings changed across generations as distinctive hunter-gatherer communities with their own traditions and histories occupied these places over many centuries.

REFERENCES

Beardsley, R. K. 1954. Temporal and Areal Relationships in Central California Archaeology. *University of California Archaeological Survey Reports* 25:63–131.

Claassen, C. P. 1996. A Consideration of the Social Organization of the Shell Mound Archaic. In *Archaeology of the Mid-Holocene Southeast*, edited by K. E. Sassaman and D. G. Anderson, pp. 235–258. University Press of Florida, Gainesville.

Cook, S. F., and A. B. Elsasser. 1956. Burials in Sand Mounds of the Delta Region of the Sacramento–San Joaquin River System. *University of California Archaeological Survey Reports* 35:26–46.

Heizer, R. F. 1949. The Archaeology of Central California I, the Early Horizon. *Anthropological Records*, vol. 12, no. 1. University of California Press, Berkeley.

Kidder, T. R. 2011. Transforming Hunter-Gatherer History at Poverty Point. In *Hunter-Gatherer Archaeology as Historical Process*, edited by K. E. Sassaman and D. H. Holly, pp. 95–119. University of Arizona Press, Tucson.

Lightfoot, K. G. 1997. Cultural Construction of Coastal Landscapes: A Middle Holocene Perspective from San Francisco Bay. In *Archaeology of the California Coast During the Middle Holocene*, edited by J. Erlandson and M. Glassow, pp. 129–141. UCLA Institute of Archaeology, Los Angeles.

———, and E. M. Luby. 2002. Late Holocene in the Greater San Francisco Bay Area: Temporal Trends in the Use and Abandonment of Shell Mounds in the East Bay. In *Catalysts to Complexity: The Late Holocene on the California Coast*, edited by J. Erlandson and T. Jones, pp. 263–281. Costen Institute of Archaeology, University of California, Los Angeles.

Luby, E. M. 2004. Shell Mound and Mortuary Behavior in the San Francisco Bay Area. *North American Archaeologist* 25(1):1–33.

———, C. D. Drescher, and K. G. Lightfoot. 2006. Shell Mounds and Mounded Landscapes in the San Francisco Bay Area: An Integrated Approach. *Journal of Island and Coastal Archaeology* 1:191–214.

Luby, E. M., and M. F. Gruber. 1999. The Dead Must Be Fed: Symbolic Meanings of the Shellmounds of the San Francisco Bay Area. *Cambridge Archaeological Journal* 9(1):95–108.

Marquardt, W. H. 2010. Shell Mounds in the Southeast: Monuments, Temple Mounds, Rings or Works? *American Antiquity* 75(3):551–570.

Meighan, C. W. 1987. Reexamination of the Early Central California Culture. *American Antiquity*, 52(1):28–36.

Moratto, M. J. 1984. *California Archaeology*. Academic Press, New York.

Rosenthal, J. S., G. G. White, and M. Q. Sutton. 2007. The Central Valley: A View from the Catbird's Seat, in *California Prehistory: Colonization, Culture, and Complexity*, edited by T. L. Jones and K. A. Klar, pp. 147–163. AltaMira Press, Lanham, MD.

Russo, M. 2004. Measuring Shell Rings for Social Inequality. In *Signs of Power: The Rise of Cultural Complexity in the Southeast*, edited by J. L. Gibson and P. J. Carr, pp. 26–70. University of Alabama Press, Tuscaloosa.

———, and G. Heide. 2001. Shell Rings of the Southeast US. *Antiquity* 75(289):491–492.

Sassaman, K. E. 2004. Complex Hunter-Gatherers in Evolution and History: A North American Perspective. *Journal of Archaeological Research* 12(3):227–280.

———, and M. J. Heckenberger. 2004. Crossing the Symbolic Rubicon in the Southeast. In *Signs of Power: The Rise of Cultural Complexity in the Southeast*, edited by J. L. Gibson and P. J. Carr, pp. 214–233. University of Alabama Press, Tuscaloosa.

Saunders, J. 2004. Are We Fixing to Make the Same Mistake Again? In *Signs of Power: The Rise of Cultural Complexity in the Southeast*, edited by J. L. Gibson and P. J. Carr, pp. 146–161. University of Alabama Press, Tuscaloosa.

Thomas, D. H. 2008. Synthesis: The Aboriginal Landscape of St. Catherines Island. In Anthropological Papers 88, *Native American Landscapes of St. Catherines Island, Georgia*, vol. 3, *Synthesis and Interpretations*, edited by D. H. Thomas, pp. 990–1045. American Museum of Natural History, New York.

———, and M. C. Sanger (editors). 2010. *Trend, Tradition, and Turmoil: What Happened to the Southeastern Archaic?* Anthropological Papers 90. American Museum of Natural History, New York.

Trinkley, M. B. 1985. The Form and Function of South Carolina's Early Woodland Shell Rings. In *Structure and Process in Southeastern Archaeology*, edited by R. S. Dickens, pp. 102–118. University of Alabama Press, Tuscaloosa.

White, N. M. 2004. Late Archaic Fisher-Foragers in the Apalachicola–Lower Chattahoochee Valley, Northwest Florida–South Georgia/Alabama. In *Signs of Power: The Rise of Cultural Complexity in the Southeast*, edited by J. L. Gibson and P. J. Carr, pp. 10–25. University of Alabama Press, Tuscaloosa.

CHAPTER 19

DIVERSITY, EXCHANGE, AND COMPLEXITY IN THE CALIFORNIA BIGHT

JENNIFER E. PERRY

THROUGHOUT the Holocene, the coastlines of the continental United States have been characterized by comparatively high population density, rich cultural diversity, and regional exchange networks. Whereas some coastal groups relied extensively on agriculture, as in New England, other regions were inhabited by complex societies that depended exclusively on a combination of hunting, gathering, and fishing through historic times (see Chilton, Maschner, and Sassaman and Randall, this volume). Dispersed along the coasts of the Pacific Northwest, Florida, and California, hunter-gatherer-fisher societies stand apart from their interior counterparts with respect to their complex organization, seen in occupational specialization, ascribed status, and formalized leadership, as well as associated technologies such as ocean-going watercraft and shell bead currencies (Arnold 2001).

Resembling its natural diversity, California was and continues to be culturally, linguistically, and genetically diverse. Inhabiting the northern part of the California Bight, the Chumash are among the most well known of native Californian societies because of the antiquity, continuity, and complexity of human occupation in this region. Regional scholars have focused on questions relating to its earliest colonization, cultural continuity during the Holocene, and the development of ascribed status and political complexity (Arnold 1992, 1995, 2001; Arnold et al. 1997; Erlandson and Rick 2002; Gamble 2005, 2008; Gamble et al. 2001; Johnson 2000; Kennett 2005; Kennett and Kennett 2000; King 1990). As a coastal society with high population densities, sophisticated watercraft, and permanent chiefs, the Chumash offer unique perspectives into the roles of environmental variability, craft specialization, and trade in major cultural developments among complex societies throughout North America.

The Chumash as Complex Hunter-Gatherer-Fishers

The Chumash people occupied an extensive strip of southern California from Malibu to Paso Robles within the northern California Bight and neighboring interiors (Figure 19.1). The California Bight stretches northward from Baja to Point Conception, a prominent point defining the coastal topography of the state and a major transition between warmer and cooler climatic regimes. Just south of Point Conception, warmer ocean waters from the south intersect with cooler waters from the north, resulting in nutrient upwelling that feeds the rich marine life of the Santa Barbara Channel. The protected south-facing shorelines of the mainland offer a diverse and productive mix of marine and terrestrial resources. Four of the eight Channel Islands form the offshore boundary of this region: San Miguel, Santa Rosa, Santa Cruz, and Anacapa Islands. Once making up a large island known as *Santarosae* (at the end of the Pleistocene due to lower sea levels), today these islands vary with respect to their biogeography, ranging from cool to warm, small to large, arid to well-watered, and relatively flat to topographically variable. Combined with pollen samples and tree ring data, high-resolution sediment cores from the Santa Barbara Channel provide a paleoenvironmental record through which to evaluate relationships among fluctuating sea surface temperatures (SSTs), precipitation levels, and subsistence-settlement strategies during the past 13,000 years of human occupation (Kennett 2005; Kennett and Kennett 2000).

The environmental diversity of the northern California Bight is reflective of the cultural diversity of the Chumash, who were never organized as a singular political entity (Johnson 2000). Instead, as many as eight groups speaking mutually unintelligible Chumashan dialects have been recognized ethnographically. The term *Chumash* is relevant nonetheless because of shared material culture and ritual organization. Although population estimates vary, the consensus is that the Chumash numbered around 15,000 to 20,000 at time of European Contact, which represents among the highest densities recorded for hunter-gatherer populations in the world. In contrast to groups in the interior and north of Point Conception, the highest population densities and largest communities of 500 to 1,000 people occurred along the Santa Barbara coast. The demography and complexity of the Chumash, and the persistence of their hunter-gatherer lifeways, relate to the resource abundance and diversity that characterizes the Santa Barbara Channel region. Comparable to plant-oriented economies throughout California, the Chumash targeted a wide range of terrestrial resources, including acorns, island cherries, and other seeds and bulbs (Timbrook

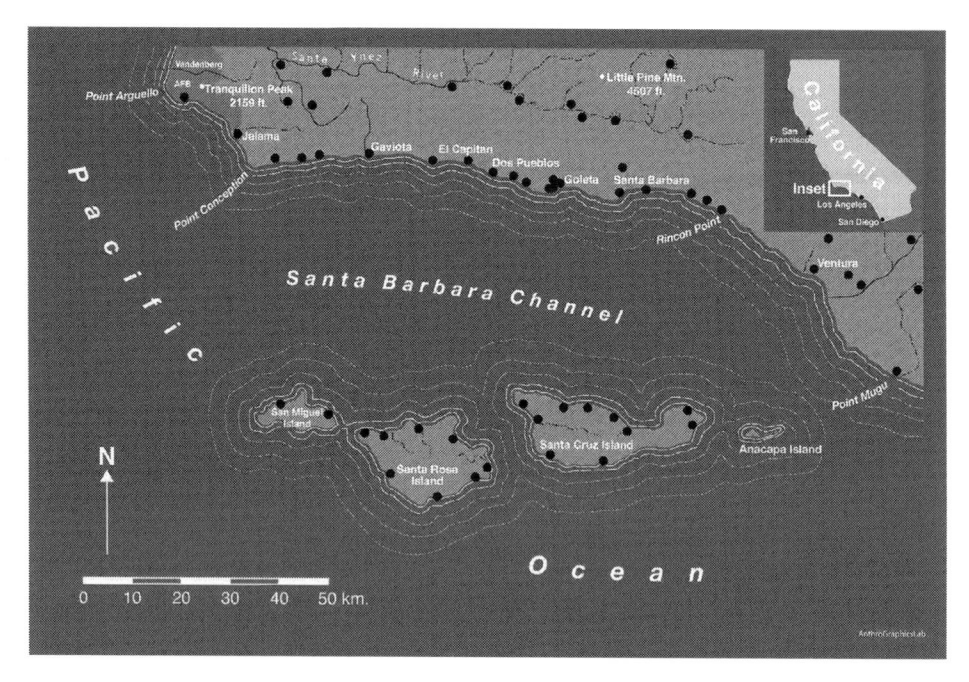

Figure 19.1 Historic Chumash villages in the Santa Barbara Channel region (map adapted from Johnson 2000:303).

2007); rabbits, deer, and other fauna; as well as abundant local and migratory marine life, including shellfish, fish, and sea mammals.

Despite such abundance, the Santa Barbara Channel region was not always the Garden of Eden that has been portrayed by explorers and archaeologists. Spatial heterogeneity and temporal variability, including droughts and El Niño-Southern Oscillation (ENSO) events, rendered resources unreliable and limited (Arnold 1992; Arnold et al. 1997; Jones et al. 1999; Kennett 2005; Kennett and Kennett 2000; Raab and Larson 1997). In fact, central to Chumash cosmology was a way of explaining climatic fluctuations in terms of the annual playing of a gambling game, *peon*, by supernatural beings (Johnson 2000:306). If Sky Coyote won, then the next year would be filled with resource abundance and well-being; if he lost, then the Sun was able to draw closer to the Earth, getting his choice of humans to consume by causing drought and suffering (Blackburn 1975:37). It was the responsibility of shamans to predict the game's outcome and to determine the appropriate strategies for the upcoming seasons, of which winter solstice ceremonies were an important part (Hudson et al. 1977; Hudson and Underhay 1978).

Resource shortfalls were buffered through diversified subsistence activities, storage and surplus, and exchange networks (Arnold 1992, 2001; Johnson 2000; Kennett 2005; King 1990). The significance of trade among the Chumash is best exemplified by the variety of products transported between the mainland and islands. Among them, shell beads, dried fish, and groundstone were exported from the islands, whereas acorns, basketry, deer bone, and obsidian were obtained from the mainland. The most well-known of these is the shell bead currency that was

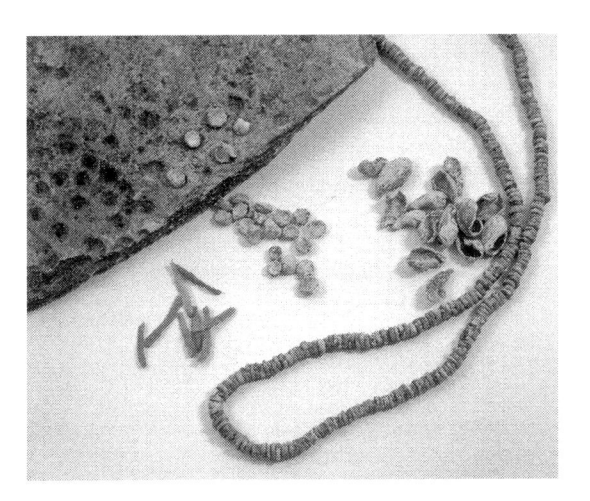

Figure 19.2 Olivella callus cup bead-making kit (photo courtesy of the Santa Barbara Museum of Natural History).

manufactured on Channel Islands (Figure 19.2; Arnold 1992, 2001). Small chert drills, obtained primarily from eastern Santa Cruz Island, were used to make a specific kind of callus cup bead from the purple olive shell (*Olivella biplicata*), which was the source of a variety of beads throughout the Holocene. Much like the dentalium beads of the Pacific Northwest and the clamshell disk variety of the San Francisco area (Gamble 2008), callus cup beads were circulated throughout southern California.

Facilitating trade and interaction between coastal communities of the mainland and islands were the plank canoes, or tomols, and their antecedents (Arnold 1995; Arnold and Bernard 2005; Gamble 2002; Hudson et al. 1978). Stitching and gluing planks of redwood and pine together, the Chumash assembled sophisticated ocean-going watercraft that were used for trade, transportation, and offshore fishing (Figure 19.3). Tomols required greater labor investment than other boat technologies in North America; each one entailed approximately six months of effort by an experienced group of boat makers, as well as large quantities of driftwood, cordage, asphaltum, pine pitch, and chert drills. Their construction was the responsibility of the "Brotherhood of the Tomol," an occupational guild that controlled access to the technical knowledge, tools, and rituals required to make and use plank canoes (Hudson et al. 1978). In contrast to the Pacific Northwest, where boat use was common and widespread, there were far fewer boats per Chumash village, and fewer people controlled their use. Instead, there is a strong correlation between boat owners and people of high political status; all chiefs had boats, but not all boat owners were chiefs (Arnold 1995).

Permeating Chumash society were achieved and ascribed roles based on gender, age, and family affiliation. Individual households specialized in the manufacture of beads, cordage, leather, baskets, nets, bows and arrows, and stone tools, among other items (Arnold 2001; Blackburn 1975; Gamble 2008). In addition to economic specialization, other positions discussed in ethnohistoric accounts included political ones such as chiefs and messengers, and ritual ones such as ceremonial leaders,

Figure 19.3 Tomol constructed in 1912 by Fernando Librado, shown at far right (photo courtesy of the Santa Barbara Museum of Natural History).

astronomers and astrologers, undertakers, dancers, singers, and shamans (Hudson and Underhay 1978). Construction and use of shrines, as well as making rock art, reflect some of the shamanic responsibilities for which there are archaeological correlates. In particular, Chumash petroglyphs are among the most elaborate in North America because of their polychrome cosmological motifs (Figure 19.4).

Villages were connected through the 'antap ritual organization, which was responsible for conducting winter solstice ceremonies (Hudson et al. 1977; Hudson and Underhay 1978). Although specific villages were bound together through ceremonial obligations, marriages, and alliances, most operated independently from one another with respect to subsistence activities, political authority, and social identity. Chumash society is most commonly characterized as a simple chiefdom organized at the village level, with a few examples of paramount chiefs who exerted regional influence (Arnold 2001; Blackburn 1975; Gamble 2008; Kennett 2005). In her discussion of the differences between affluent and complex hunter-gatherer societies, Arnold (2001:3) argues that the Chumash were complex, on the basis of their ascribed status, hierarchical structure, and specifically the "formalization and centralization of political power in the hands of hereditary leaders."

According to Johnson's analysis (2000) of mission records and ethnographic accounts, each village represented an amalgamation of different rules of social organization depending on inherited status. Whereas most Chumash people were monogamous and practiced matrilocal residence after marriage, chiefs tended to be polygamous and patrilocal, intermarrying into the elite families of other villages.

Figure 19.4 Chumash rock art in the San Emigdio area (photo by Rick Bury).

Johnson (2000:305) has argued that the overriding practice of matrilocality relates to the high level of male mortality due to incessant intervillage warfare and lethal violence during the Late Holocene (Lambert and Walker 1991). In response to environmental variability and climatic instability, the Chumash engaged in alternate strategies that mirrored the celestial *peon* game, navigating through cycles of resource abundance and stress through intervillage exchange, interaction, and warfare.

Chronology and Characteristics of Complexity

For decades, archaeologists of the northern California Bight have debated the development of complexity among the Chumash with respect to its chronology and particular manifestations. Most researchers acknowledge the connections between temporal and spatial variability in resource availability, or heterogeneity, to storage, exchange, and nodes of power. The relationship among environmental variability, demography, and human action has been commonly interpreted through the lenses of human behavioral ecology and agency-based theories. Models of diet breadth and patch choice, central place foraging, and game theory, among others, have been commonly employed to interpret faunal data from shell middens throughout the region (Braje 2010; Erlandson 1994, 1997; Erlandson and Rick 2002; Glassow 1993, 1997; Glassow et al. 2007, 2008; Kennett 2005; Rick 2007).

In addition to the environmental factors influencing human decision making, some scholars have considered the organizational strategies and power dynamics surrounding those decisions, particularly as they relate to trade and conflict. As a vocal proponent of agency-based models, Arnold (1992, 1995, 2001) has discussed how differing modes and nodes of resource production and distribution may have facilitated opportunities for ascribed status and political hierarchy among hunter-gatherers. Great attention has also been given to the specific context in which specialization and trade were intensified, which coincides with evidence for climatic instability, poorer health, and lethal violence (Johnson 2000; Jones et al. 1999; Kennett 2005; Lambert and Walker 1991; Raab and Larson 1997).

On the basis of diverse strands of evidence, there are several major periods of environmental, technological, and organizational change during the Middle and Late Holocene. The relative emphasis placed on these time frames relates to different viewpoints regarding the chronology of complexity. Regardless of the proximate causes, a number of researchers have focused on models of climatic instability and punctuated cultural change during the past 1,500 years (Arnold 1992, 2001; Arnold et al. 1997; Johnson 2000; Jones et al. 1999; Kennett 2005; Kennett and Kennett 2000; Raab and Larson 1997). In contrast, King (1990) and Gamble (2005) have advocated gradualist perspectives in which status differentiation originated much earlier in contexts of resource abundance, arguing that "the Chumash developed a multitude of adaptive strategies that allowed them to cope with periodic droughts, El Niño events, and other environmental perturbations" (Glassow et al. 2007:205).

Supporting gradualist perspectives of complexity is evidence for continuity in Chumash material culture over the past 5,000 years (Erlandson and Rick 2002; Glassow et al. 2007). Major technological developments associated with resource diversification and intensification first appear during the Middle Holocene (6500–3500 BP; Erlandson 1997; Glassow 1997; Kennett 2005). Mortars and pestles are among these innovations, which were used to process a variety of pulpy plant foods as well as small animals. Others indicate changes in terrestrial hunting, marine fishing, and water storage, including contracting stem points, stone net weights, circular shell fishhooks, and increased use of asphaltum for sealing baskets, hafting, and other purposes. The broad-spectrum diet that characterizes the Middle Holocene promoted a range of strategies and technologies through which residents capitalized on the region's environmental diversity.

Concurrent with these technological innovations is evidence of intensified marine subsistence, increased coastal sedentism, and cultural elaboration (Erlandson and Rick 2002; Glassow et al. 2007; Kennett 2005; King 1990; Lambert and Walker 1991). The best documented subsistence trend is the shift from resource diversification to intensification from the Middle to Late Holocene. Intensification of fishing, storage, and trade relates to a combination of increased marine productivity, higher population density, increased coastal sedentism, and nonegalitarian social organization (Kennett and Kennett 2000). Evidence of achieved status includes unequal distribution of mortuary items, which were historically associated with high-status individuals (Erlandson and Rick 2002). Shells beads and ornaments are found in a variety of styles, suggesting significant changes in manifestations of social identity. In addition, formal cemeteries, ceremonial enclosures, rock art, and a variety of ethnographically documented ritual items suggest transformations in ceremonialism.

Against the backdrop of cultural elaboration during the Middle Holocene is evidence of punctuated change in the Late Holocene, including the emergence of ascribed status. Most explanations revolve around human response to climatic perturbation, particularly ENSO events and drought, during the past 1,500 years. Arnold (1992) was one of the first to draw attention to episodes of punctuated resource stress. Specifically, she considered the role of ENSO events in adversely affecting marine productivity, and associated opportunities for increased status and power, during the transition from the Middle to Late Period from 800–650 BP. Since her initial argument, however, paleoenvironmental and archaeological evidence has been mounting for long-term drought and high marine productivity in southern California during the Medieval Climatic Anomaly (Jones et al. 1999; Kennett 2005; Kennett and Kennett 2000; Raab and Larson 1997). In the context of high population density and circumscription, fishing would have been one of the few options available to maximize resource yields, storage, and surplus.

Coinciding with the beginning of a series of long-term droughts in southern California around 1500 BP were dramatic changes in technology, coastal settlement, and social organization. Bows and arrows appeared in the Santa Barbara Channel region for the first time, which is strongly correlated with increased conflict and lethal violence (Lambert and Walker 1991; Raab and Larson 1997). Around the same time, plank canoes facilitated expansion of fishing efforts, as well as presumably larger and more consistent shipments of goods. Ownership of plank canoes and the control afforded over exchange networks has been cited as one of the major avenues of economic and political power, despite no one knowing what preceded it. On the basis of ethnohistoric descriptions and indirect material evidence such as redwood plank fragments, asphaltum, and pelagic fishing, there is some consensus that tomols were developed locally around 1500 BP, although others think there is precedence for this technology in wood-working traditions much earlier in time (Arnold 1995; Arnold and Bernard 2005; Cassidy et al. 2004; Gamble 2002, 2008).

The date of 1500 BP fits well not only with evidence of deep sea fishing but also with respect to a major reorientation in coastal settlements around intensified exchange. Coastal sites occupied throughout the Holocene were abandoned around 1,000 to 1,500 years ago, despite being located near productive zones of ecotone convergence (Glassow et al. 2008). Rather, newly established villages were positioned along sandy beaches that were ideal for boat use and along travel routes between settlements. Some of them served as centers of distribution, presumed from the archaeological diversity and abundance of imported and luxury items, estimated site size and density (based on baptismal records and house depressions), number of canoe owners, and analyses of geographic centrality (Gamble 2008; Kennett 2005; Johnson 2000). On the mainland, Dos Pueblos, Syuxtun (Santa Barbara), and Muwu were among the largest and most powerful villages, with paramount chiefs extending their political influence through strategic control of exchange networks that connected the islands and the mainland interior.

Although the chronology of ascribed status, craft specialization, and hierarchical political organization continues to be debated, most archaeologists would agree that they were in place no than later 800 BP (Arnold 2001; Kennett 2005). King (1990) and others think they extend further back in time; Gamble et al. (2001) interpret lineage-based social ranking as being present around 1300 BP, on the basis of mortuary data. From Johnson's perspective (2000), village positioning within the regional exchange network constituted the basis for opportunities to increase one's status and power. Arnold (1992, 2001) complements this with evidence of intensive local and middle-distance trade between Chumash villages in a number of resource zones. She argues that the economic interdependence evidenced between historic villages, such as chert drill manufacturers on eastern Santa Cruz Island and shell bead makers on western Santa Cruz Island, required some degree of coordination on the part of elites. Intercommunity interaction was facilitated by marriage alliances, communal feasting, and the 'antap organization, with particular individuals and communities being situated at the center of intervillage interactions (Johnson 2000).

From continuities in material culture, Erlandson and Rick (2002) and Kennett (2005) have argued that key features of historic Chumash society are rooted in technological innovations, resource diversification, and status differentiation that arose during the Middle Holocene (Erlandson 1997; Glassow 1997; Glassow et al. 2007). At the same time, it is also the case that dramatic changes in technology, demography, and organization began around 1500 BP in association with periods of climatic instability. Whereas the transition from the Middle to the Late Holocene may be described in terms of the gradual emergence of an affluent hunter-gatherer society, it is within the past 1,500 years that elements of Chumash identity and complexity appear to have emerged in contexts of resource stress.

As these interpretations reflect, the prehistory of the northern California Bight encapsulates a range of archaeological perspectives relating to hunter-gatherers and complexity, including gradualism and punctuated equilibrium, cooperation and conflict, and models of human behavioral ecology and agency. Building on thousands of years of technological and organizational changes, the Chumash had a large repertoire of strategies to employ in response to changing climatic and demographic circumstances. During the Medieval Climatic Anomaly, when people of the American Southwest were abandoning their pueblos and dispersing into smaller, mobile groups, the Chumash were transforming into a chiefdom-level society. The environmental variability of the Santa Barbara Channel region, and how people decided to interact with it (particularly in trade), ultimately paved the way to political hierarchy, including chiefs who controlled sedentary villages. As more paleoenvironmental and archaeological data are obtained from the northern

California Bight, the prehistory of the Chumash and their ancestors will to continue to offer insights into broader questions of antiquity, cultural continuity, and complexity in North America.

REFERENCES

Arnold, J. E. 1992. Complex Hunter-Gatherer-Fishers of Prehistoric California: Chiefs, Specialists, and Maritime Adaptations. *American Antiquity* 57:60–84.
———. 1995. Transportation Innovation and Social Complexity Among Maritime Hunter-Gatherer Societies. *American Anthropologist* 97:733–747.
———. 2001. *The Origins of a Pacific Coast Chiefdom: The Chumash of the Channel Islands*, University of Utah Press, Salt Lake City.
———, and J. Bernard. 2005. Negotiating the Coasts: Status and the Evolution of Boat Technology. *World Archaeology* 37:109–131.
Arnold, J. E., R. H. Colten, and S. Pletka. 1997. Contexts of Cultural Change in Insular California. *American Antiquity* 62:300–318.
Blackburn, T. C. (editor). 1975. *December's Child: A Book of Chumash Oral Narratives*, collected by J. P. Harrington. University of California Press, Berkeley.
Braje, T. J. 2010. *Modern Oceans, Ancient Sites: Archaeology and Marine Conservation on San Miguel Island, California*. University of Utah Press, Salt Lake City.
Cassidy, J., L. M. Raab, and N. v A. Kononenko. 2004. Boats, Bones, and Biface Bias: The Early Holocene Mariners of Eel Point, San Clemente Island, California. *American Antiquity* 69:109–130.
Erlandson, J. M. 1994. *Early Hunter-Gatherers of the California Coast*. Plenum Press, New York.
———. 1997. The Middle Holocene on the Western Santa Barbara Coast. In Perspectives in California Archaeology 4, *Archaeology of the California Coast During the Middle Holocene*, edited by J. M. Erlandson and M. A. Glassow, pp. 91–110. Cotsen Institute of Archaeology, University of California, Los Angeles.
———, and T. C. Rick. 2002. Late Holocene Cultural Development Along the Santa Barbara Coast. In Perspectives in California Archaeology 6, *Catalysts to Complexity: Late Holocene Societies of the California Coast*, edited by J. M. Erlandson and T. L. Jones, pp. 166–182.Cotsen Institute of Archaeology, University of California, Los Angeles.
Gamble, L. H. 2002. Archaeological Evidence for the Origin of the Plank Canoe in North America. *American Antiquity* 67(2):301–315.
———. 2005. Culture and Climate: Reconsidering the Effect of Paleoclimatic Variability Among Southern California Hunter-Gatherer Societies. *World Archaeology* 37(1):92–108.
———. 2008. *The Chumash World at European Contact: Power, Trade, and Feasting Among Complex Hunter Gatherers*. University of California Press, Berkeley.
———, P. L. Walker, and G. S. Russell. 2001. An Integrative Approach to Mortuary Analysis: Social and Symbolic Dimensions of Chumash Burial Practices. *American Antiquity* 66(2):185–212.
Glassow, M. A. 1993. Changes in Subsistence on Marine Resources Through 7,000 Years of Prehistory on Santa Cruz Island. In Coyote Press Archives of California Prehistory 34, *Archaeology on the Northern Channel Islands of California*, edited by M. A. Glassow, pp. 75–90. Coyote Press, Salinas, CA.

———. 1997. Middle Holocene Cultural Development in the Central Santa Barbara Channel Region. Perspectives in California Archaeology 4, *Archaeology of the California Coast During the Middle Holocene*, edited by J. M. Erlandson and M. A. Glassow, pp. 73–90. Institute of Archaeology, University of California, Los Angeles.

———, L. H. Gamble, J. E. Perry, and G. S. Russell. 2007. Prehistory of the Northern California Bight and the Adjacent Transverse Ranges. In *California Prehistory: Colonization, Culture, and Complexity*, edited by T. L. Jones and K. Klar, pp. 191–213. AltaMira Press, Lanham, MD.

Glassow, M. A., J. E. Perry, and P. F. Paige. 2008. *The Punta Arena Site: Early and Middle Holocene Cultural Development*. Santa Barbara Museum of Natural History, Santa Barbara, CA.

Hudson, D. T., T. Blackburn, R. Curletti, and J. Timbrook. 1977. *The Eye of the Flute: Chumash Traditional History and Ritual as Told by Fernando Librado Kitsepawit to John P. Harrington*. Malki Museum Press, Banning, CA.

Hudson, D. T., J. Timbrook, and M. Rempe. 1978. *Tomol: Chumash Watercraft as Described in the Ethnographic Notes of John P. Harrington*. Anthropological Papers 9, edited by L. J. Bean and T. C. Blackburn. Ballena Press, Socorro, NM.

Hudson, D. T., and E. Underhay, 1978. *Crystals in the Sky: An Intellectual Odyssey Involving Chumash Astronomy, Cosmology, and Rock Art*. Ballena Press Anthropological Papers No. 10, edited by L. J. Bean and T. C. Blackburn. Ballena Press, Socorro, NM.

Johnson, J. R. 2000. Social Responses to Climate Change Among the Chumash Indians of South-Central California. In *The Way the Wind Blows: Climate, History, and Human Action*, edited by R. J. McIntosh, J. A. Tainter, and S. Keech McIntosh, pp. 301–327. Columbia University Press, New York.

Jones, T. L., G. M. Brown, J. McVicar, M. Raab, D. J. Kennett, W. G. Spaulding, and A. York. 1999. Environmental Imperatives Reconsidered: Demographic Crises in Western North America During the Medieval Climatic Anomaly. *Current Anthropology* 40(2):137–170.

Kennett, D. J. 2005. *The Island Chumash: Behavioral Ecology of a Maritime Society*. University of California Press, Berkeley.

———, and J. P. Kennett. 2000. Competitive and Cooperative Responses to Climatic Instability in Coastal Southern California. *American Antiquity* 65(2):379–395.

King, C. D. 1990. *The Evolution of Chumash Society: A Comparative Study of Artifacts Used in Social System Maintenance in the Santa Barbara Channel Region Before A.D. 1804*. Garland, New York.

Lambert, P. M., and P. L. Walker. 1991. Physical Anthropological Evidence for the Evolution of Social Complexity in Coastal Southern California. *Antiquity* 65:963–973.

Raab, L. M., and D. O. Larson. 1997. Medieval Climatic Anomaly and Punctuated Cultural Evolution in Coastal Southern California. *American Antiquity* 62(2):319–326.

Rick, T. C. 2007. *The Archaeology and Historical Ecology of Late Holocene San Miguel Island*. Perspectives in California Archaeology 8, edited by J. E. Arnold. Cotsen Institute of Archaeology, University of California, Los Angeles.

Timbrook, J. 2007. *Chumash Ethnobotany: Plant Knowledge Among the Chumash People of Southern California*. Santa Barbara Museum of Natural History, Santa Barbara, CA.

CHAPTER 20

ARCHAEOLOGIES OF COLONIAL REDUCTION AND CULTURAL PRODUCTION IN NATIVE NORTHERN CALIFORNIA

STEPHEN W. SILLIMAN

IN 1769, the course of history in Native California took a significant turn when Gaspar de Portola galloped into the region from Mexico as part of a larger colonization effort by the Spanish Crown. This marked only the beginning of colonial infiltrations; Russians and Americans would follow suit about 40 years later after Spain had established settlements along much of California's coastline. California's indigenous peoples, almost exclusively hunting and gathering in their economies and ranging in sociopolitical organization from small bands to ranked chiefdoms, had confronted vectors of change for millennia before, whether climatic, linguistic, social, demographic, or environmental; but these newcomers brought a host of diseases, foods, technologies, institutions, and intentions that posed significant challenges. Many of these challenges proved to be hardships, as thousands of residents succumbed to fatal infections, experienced violent attacks by soldiers and settlers, had their religious beliefs undermined by padres and pathogens alike, and saw their landscapes overrun by livestock, weeds, and settlers in adobe and wooden buildings. Simultaneously, though, some of these challenges became avenues—albeit foisted on indigenous residents and negotiated alongside longer cultural traditions—for survival and cultural persistence for Californian Indians. These outcomes are attested to not only by archival documents, oral histories, and archaeological information but by the presence of numerous indigenous communities across the region today who lived through these difficult centuries.

This chapter makes no attempt to synthesize the entirety and diversity of that multicentury process; readers can consult extended recent treatments (in particular Lightfoot 2004, but also Lightfoot 2006; Silliman 2004; Voss 2008; see also Thomas, this volume). Instead, the specific objective is to outline themes of research in Native northern California, specifically under Spanish/Mexican and Russian control, in order to highlight key issues in North American archaeology that manifest uniquely and informatively on the West Coast. I restrict this discussion to northern California since this region has produced to date some of the most detailed and theoretically rich insights into Native American histories and cultures in colonial California.

A fundamental issue in the archaeology of Native Americans during colonial periods is the question of change and continuity (Silliman 2009). The answers frequently rely on dichotomous categories of colonizer and colonized, or European and Native American, and rarely delve into the intersection of material culture, space, social memory, and labor to answer these difficult questions. We can never lose sight of the devastation and destruction wrought by colonialism, but we must simultaneously consider these sites of colonization, multiethnic interaction, labor, and exchange as places of cultural *production*, not just reduction. Otherwise, how do we account for persistence—that is, the survival of Native American cultures and communities—through these moments? Culture is not just passively retained; it must be actively and repetitively renewed—temporally (over months, years, lifetimes, and generations), spatially (in homes, across regions, through networks, and around the globe, at least in the last few centuries), and materially (through bodies, with things, in texts). Archaeologically, these retentions and renewals have been documented with some detail at the Russian colony of Ross and the Mexican-Californian establishment of Rancho Petaluma (Figure 20.1).

Background

The main thrust of Spanish and later Mexican colonization and settlement in California was a quartet of institutions: missions, presidios, pueblos, and ranchos (Costello and Hornbeck 1989). This was the first European effort to colonize the region and the first sustained colonial contact with Native American groups outside of a few coastal landfalls in prior centuries. Franciscan missions attempted to convert indigenous residents into vassals of the Spanish Crown and to use their labors to sustain the colonization effort, while presidios supplied the military backing for colonization and nexus for new *Californio* identities and multiethnic families. Pueblos served as secular towns and models of "proper" citizenship, and ranchos

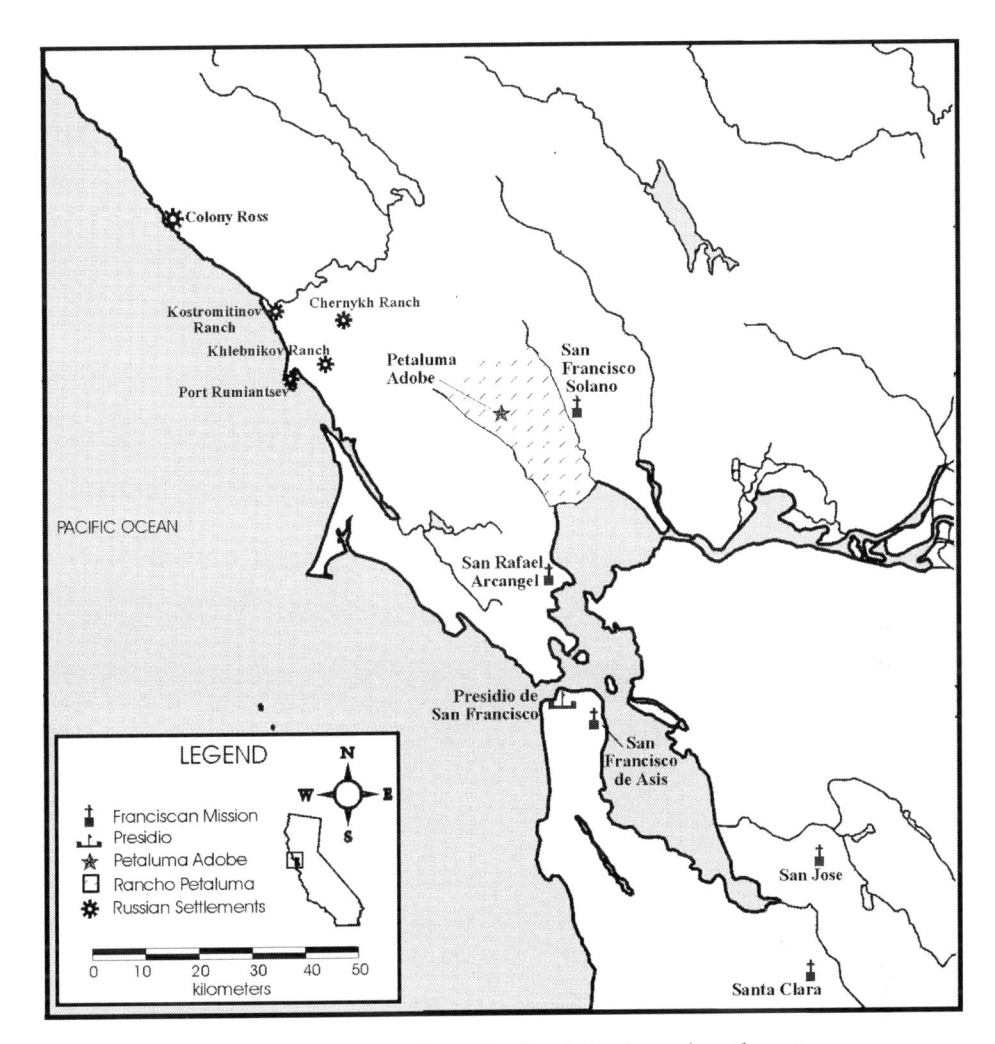

Figure 20.1 Map of Northern California in the early 19th century.

provided ecclesiastical and then often extensive private land grants for generating economic ventures and for staking out additional settlements on the landscape.

The 21 Franciscan missions offered focal points of colonialism, from the first one established in San Diego in 1769 until their final dissolution in 1834, only 11 years after the last mission had been founded on the northern edge of that frontier in Sonoma. These Franciscan missions have been the primary focus of California historical archaeologists and historians for the last half-century, as illustrated by a continued spate of studies in the last decade (Dartt-Newton and Erlandson 2006; Graesch 2001; Hackel 2005; Lightfoot 2004; Sandos 2004; Silliman 2001b; Wade 2008). The four presidios, eight original pueblos, and numerous ranchos have received far less attention from archaeologists and historians, but research has begun to examine some of the same issues of gender, material culture, identity, labor, and other elements, particularly at ranchos (Greenwood 1989; Silliman 2001a, 2004) and presidios (Voss 2005, 2008).

An example is Rancho Petaluma, established in 1834 north of San Francisco Bay by Mariano G. Vallejo as a private tract of land granted by the provincial California government (Silliman 2004). This active military officer also secularized the two northernmost Franciscan missions, which meant dismantling ecclesiastical control and "freeing" Native neophytes from mission obligations and oversight. He waged a series of military campaigns against Native American groups to the north and east of this edge of empire, and mobilized—by economic dealing, alliance, and force—several thousand California Indians to work on his rancho of more than 66,000 acres. Here, indigenous people toiled as cooks, weavers, craftspeople, butchers, herders, supervisors, and other occupations. Sometimes these were ways of navigating a colonial presence by accessing goods, food, and military alliance, but other times they burdened people released from missions who had no families or territories to return to, or who had been captured during raids and forced into labor. The core of the rancho was the Petaluma Adobe, a large two-story adobe building that served as a production center and housed the Vallejo family intermittently, an overseer, and perhaps a few domestic workers (Figure 20.2).

The Russians joined the colonization effort on the West Coast in the early years of the 19th century with a colony, or counter, at Ross (Figure 20.3). This colony involved a fur-trade outpost, small ranches and farms on or near the coast, and a hunting artel on an offshore island, all just north and west of the San Francisco Bay, where the Spanish had held control since the 1770s (Lightfoot 2004; Lightfoot et al. 1993, 1998). The proximity was no accident; the Spanish feared the southward move of the Russian American Company from its bases in the Pacific Northwest and Alaska and subsequently developed missions and ranchos northward from San Francisco (or what they called Yerba Buena) to stem that expansion. Following the

Figure 20.2 Photograph of Petaluma Adobe, centerpiece of the Rancho Petaluma, in the late 20th century. (Photo courtesy of Library of Congress, Historic American Buildings Survey, HABS CAL.49-PET.V, 1–19; cropped slightly by S. Silliman).

Mexican revolution in 1821, the *Californios* (see Voss 2005, 2008 for excellent discussions of this ethnogenesis) materialized this worry with establishment of the Rancho Petaluma and its neighbors in the 1830s and 1840s. The Russians departed in 1841, leaving the region in the control of the *Californios* for only a few short years until 1848, when the United States took over the region and annexed it as a territory before making it a full state in 1850. This precipitated the collapse and subsequent sale of Vallejo's Rancho Petaluma in the 1850s.

The Russian American Company created a unique multiethnic community on the north coast of California for the purpose of supplying sea mammal pelts and food to the broader Russian colonial enterprise and continental homeland (Lightfoot 2003, 2004; Lightfoot et al. 1993, 1997, 1998). Russians brought a variety of Native Alaskan male hunters to this remote outpost for the harvesting of primarily sea otter furs, but these hunters settled among and interacted regularly with local Kashaya Pomo, Coast Miwok, and other indigenous peoples. Three kinds of social relations predominated: trade between colonists and local people, intermarriage between Native Alaskan men and Native Californian women, and conscription of local labor for agricultural and other tasks. These social and cultural intersections produced a variety of outcomes visible archaeologically. It also stands as one of the rare cases in which intermarriage plays a critical role not as a union of colonizer and colonized but rather as a point of negotiation between two indigenous communities in a colonial context.

The Russian footprint in California was significantly smaller than the Spanish/Mexican one. Russians and their mercantile presence held much less land, implanted far fewer institutions, had little aspiration to change indigenous cultures, and spent several decades less time in the region. Yet, as different as the Russians were from the Spanish and Mexican-Californians in origins, purposes for colonization, and concerns about religion and economy, they had one thing in common

Figure 20.3 Photograph of Fort Ross with Native Alaskan and Californian living areas in the foreground (Photo courtesy of Daniel Murley; cropped slightly by S. Silliman).

that renders their intersection a useful one for a volume on North American archaeology. They settled in the same indigenous territories and often interacted with the same people (if not actual individuals), introduced new materials and foods, and put in place a variety of labor regimes that had an impact on both Native change and continuity during the colonial period.

Archaeological Axes of Culture and History

The Rancho Petaluma and Colony Ross case studies represent sites of cultural destruction, reduction, and production that can be examined through the key issues of gender, space, materiality, food practices, and labor. It is difficult to parse out these dimensions for individual analysis, so I opt here to consider them in a larger narrative, much as they would have likely been articulated in the lives of those past people. A central organizing theme in the intersection of my rendering here is history, practice, and identity.

One of the most significant archaeological discoveries at Ross and Petaluma concerns gender and cultural identity. By paying attention to the interethnic gender differences at the Russian colony (that is, Native men from the north brought to a new indigenous territory where they formed sexual, family, and personal unions with local residents) and the long-term cultural trajectories of these intersecting Native groups, researchers have been able to discern the dynamics of gender and culture change and continuity (Lightfoot et al. 1997, 1998). Archaeological research detected Native Alaskan sensibilities in spatial configurations in a linear house arrangement and site location on the coastal terrace outside the Russian stockade, and refuse patterns, household cleanliness, and cooking practices that were decidedly Native Californian. This negotiation of culture and gender in such a multiethnic community had to be reworked in the mundane, everyday practices of household life, and the material remains indicate some habitual and perhaps strategic links to homelands and cultural history. Since the Russian managers permitted significant leeway in how and where Native residents lived (Lightfoot 2004:133–134), this indicates strong Alaskan and Californian preferences.

Not everything played out with obvious separation, though. Household goods showed few things directly linked to Native Alaskan heritages in the far north, save those practices used in maintaining marine hunting tools; but they included a collection of chipped and flaked stone tools (of Native Californian origin) and used and recycled ceramics, glass, and metal objects from European and Asian sources. For Native Alaskan men, their labor for the colony meshed strongly with their cultural labor of hunting, a dual material link that likely contributed to buttressing cultural identities that suggested continuity rather than breaks from their own traditions. For Native Californians, the link was not so strong. Local workers may have worked occasionally of their own accord because of economic or personal connections to the colony, but many were conscripted with considerable force and sometimes taken hostage from their villages without their own household objects (Lightfoot 2004:139). They also were not permitted any social mobility to become supervisors, unlike labor arrangements in the Hispanic missions and ranchos to the south (141). Yet some did enter and leave willingly from personal unions with those Native Alaskan hunters.

The situation at Rancho Petaluma offered a contrast (Silliman 2001a, 2004). This economic powerhouse had Native American men and women employed in a variety of assigned tasks. Regardless of indigenous ideas about gendered worked before the advent of colonial labor, men were directed to livestock; women to weaving, cooking, and other domestic and productive realms; and both men and women to agricultural fields. Food production, rather than food gathering, was novel to people traditionally living by hunting, gathering, and fishing. A hierarchy of labor tasks infused Rancho Petaluma, much as it did the Franciscan missions, with "Christianized" Indians serving as overseers (or *alcaldes*) and skilled craftspeople while nonmissionized Native Americans worked in relatively unskilled tasks (Silliman 2004).

The archaeological record at the rancho revealed gendered differences in the approach to their assigned labor (Silliman 2004). Artifacts associated with women's colonial work, such as scissors and thimbles, appeared in Native household debris, signaling the perceived usefulness of these items in Native households and perhaps a stronger link forged by Native women between their identities and their labors. Artifacts associated with Native men's labors—which might include objects related to riding horses, corralling livestock, butchering animals, and working fields, such as knives, cleavers, spurs, and more—did not appear in those same deposits. Although these items were more likely monitored by overseers, it is still surprising that none made their way into household routine. It is hard to imagine that knives and cleavers could be deemed any less useful than scissors and thimbles, which suggests that, at least at the household level, Native men articulated their identities and strategies not through their connections to colonial labor but through other means. The prevalence of obsidian tools and their sources well away from the rancho may have been that link, given prior strong associations between California Indian men and lithic production and use.

Whether strongly gendered or not, lithic technology offers another window into negotiation of places, things, and histories. At Petaluma, Native American residents in the 19th century actively held on to their practices of lithic production (Silliman 2003, 2005b). One might render this evidence of cultural continuity as a kind of retention of so-called traditional ways, but it had more complexity. For one, accessing the obsidian raw material that made up the majority of lithic tools, cores, and debitage at Rancho Petaluma required mobility and connections to the landscape well outside the rancho. Native people tethered there kept up ties to their networks many kilometers away, or had the flexibility to procure directly or trade for these raw materials while doing their rancho work or taking breaks from it, or managed—if working somewhat by choice as part of a seasonal round in a complexly colonial region—to rotate into the rancho and then out of it again for more traditional activities. Equally important, the use of lithic material does not just register actions of staying the same. It represents both changing and staying the same; familiarity with lithic tools has to be set within the context of now having choices to use either metal or stone tools or both (see Silliman 2001a).

The context of lithic technology at Colony Ross revealed a different engagement. Native Alaskans, who focused more on ground stone and bone tools in their homelands, found the Native Californians masters of chipped stone tool manufacture, frequently using the raw material of obsidian like their cousins at Petaluma. Such technologies made their way into the multiethnic households of Alaskans and Californians at Ross. These same material techniques also transferred to bottle and window glass, as Native residents at the fort and even in the small villages outside of it made arrow points, scrapers, and other items with that imported material (Lightfoot et al. 1997, 1998).

Added to the daily tasks of lithics and labor are food practices, and how they represented locally specific negotiations of history and agency. Both Colony Ross and Rancho Petaluma showed interesting mixtures of new and old, domestic and wild in the food practices of Native residents. The addition of livestock to a hunting economy and cultigens to a wild food diet requires some adjustment of household labor and cultural outlook. Rancho Petaluma overseers provisioned laborers from the stores of beef, pork, wheat, barley, and corn, but these did not serve as the sole sources of nourishment (Silliman 2004). Native workers actively sought wild birds, fish, deer, other mammals, acorns, bay laurel nuts, manzanita berries, and grass seeds to supplement the provisioned diet. This likely required considerable effort during an otherwise full work day, or these workers in the fields and with the herds embedded their subsistence routine within the work one. Either way, some of these wild foods—particularly acorns and berries—would have been harvested at the peak of food availability on the rancho during the *matanza* (or large annual slaughter of cattle for hides and tallow) and after the harvesting of crops. Acquisition of wild foods when one could have eaten plenty on the rancho speaks to active efforts to uphold traditional foods in the colonial context.

At Colony Ross, preparation and consumption of meat reveal other cultural engagements with context and history. Meats included sea mammals, fish, and invertebrates more common to Native Alaskan diets (particularly pinniped flippers), local terrestrial game such as deer more in line with California culinary preferences, and sheep and cattle raised and provided by the Russian colony. This diversity reveals the intersection of novelty, access, and tradition in an environment that was new to all but capable of sustaining dietary comforts. However, preparation of all of this followed Native Californian practices, again a realm likely in the purview of local women (Lightfoot et al. 1997, 1998:212–213).

Conclusion

In both cases, archaeological research has demonstrated the variable cultural strategies and practices undertaken by indigenous individuals or at least small collectives of men and women, workers and spouses, missionized and unmissionized. This nuances our archaeological narratives, which usually tend to focus only on monolithic cultures in contact, by repositioning daily practice with social agents. These results also show how individuals can draw on deep cultural histories *and* can forge more proximate connections to their social context. For example, Native Alaskan men at Colony Ross reproduced their ancestral ways in a new environment with new people several thousand kilometers from their homeland, whereas Native American women at Rancho Petaluma actively forged a dual connection to their new laboring requirements and to their old foraging practices while otherwise having access to provisioned foods from the Petaluma Adobe.

Acknowledging multiple relations between people gives new insights into the archaeological record (see also Thomas, this volume). Intermarriage, a process that can be rendered as change by producing bicultural offspring, must also be seen as a mechanism of cultural continuity, particularly for Native mothers who raised their children in their local networks. This process characterized Colony Ross (Martinez 1998), as well as other colonial contexts across the American West (Tveskov 2007), and even back into the more deeply colonized East Coast when Native men left homes to serve in militias, merchant ships, and whaling ventures. Labor provided another nexus of interaction, frequently being one of the primary ways that many Native Americans interacted with colonists and settlers (Silliman 2001b). It had an impact on scheduling, bodies, material access, and food availability, and it became a context for social mobility and inequality that set some Native people at odds with others. However, like interethnic marriage, labor became a context for survival and practice, not just dilution and diminution.

People who lived in these 19th-century contexts left a material record that reveals how they negotiated their own histories, identities, and labors. Although these events happened well after most of the Native histories covered in this volume, they furnish critical links in cultural memory of Native communities who continue today despite and through those historical moments. They shorten the gaps between the deep histories of ancient California, stretching back millennia, and the recent ethnographies of 19th- and 20th-century anthropologists. Archaeologists hopefully will turn more attention to these middle periods between "first contact" and the ethnographies of the last century, particularly since the general public tends to forget how much Native history, survival, and persistence happened therein.

REFERENCES

Costello, J., and D. Hornbeck. 1989. Alta California: An Overview. In *Columbian Consequences*, vol. 1, *Archaeological and Historical Perspectives on the Spanish Borderlands West*, edited by D. H. Thomas, pp. 303–332. Smithsonian Institution, Washington, DC.

Dartt-Newton, D., and J. M. Erlandson. 2006. Little Choice for the Chumash: Colonialism, Cattle, and Coercion in Mission Period California. *American Indian Quarterly* 30:416–430.

Graesch, A. P. 2001. Culture Contact on the Channel Islands: Historic-Era Production and Exchange Systems. In *The Origins of a Pacific Coast Chiefdom: The Chumash of the Channel Islands*, edited by J. E. Arnold, pp. 261–286. University of Utah Press, Salt Lake City.

Greenwood, R. S. 1989. The California Ranchero: Fact and Fancy. In *Columbian Consequences*, vol. 1, *Archaeological and Historical Perspectives on the Spanish Borderlands West*, edited by D. H. Thomas, pp. 451–465. Smithsonian Institution, Washington, DC.

Hackel, S. W. 2005. *Children of Coyote, Missionaries of Saint Francis: Indian-Spanish Relations in Colonial California, 1769–1850*. University of North Carolina Press, Chapel Hill.

Lightfoot, K. G. 2003. Russian Colonization: The Implications of Mercantile Colonial Practice in the North Pacific. *Historical Archaeology* 37(4):14–28.

———. 2004. *Indians, Missionaries, and Merchants: The Legacy of Colonial Encounters on the California Frontiers*. University of California Press, Berkeley.

———. 2006. Missions, Furs, Gold, and Manifest Destiny: Rethinking an Archaeology of Colonialism for Western North America. In *Historical Archaeology*, edited by M. Hall and S. W. Silliman, pp. 272–292. Blackwell Publishing, Malden, MA.

———, A. Martinez, and A. M. Schiff. 1998. Daily Practice and Material Culture in Pluralistic Social Settings: An Archaeological Study of Culture Change and Persistence from Fort Ross, California. *American Antiquity* 63(2):199–222.

Lightfoot, K. G., A. M. Schiff, and T. A. Wake (editors). 1997. *The Archaeology and Ethnohistory of Fort Ross, California*, vol. 2, *The Native Alaskan Neighborhood, A Multiethnic Community at Colony Ross*. Contributions of the University of California Archaeological Research Facility 55. Archaeological Research Facility, Berkeley.

Lightfoot, K. G., T. A. Wake, and A. M. Schiff. 1993. Native Responses to the Russian Mercantile Colony of Fort Ross, Northern California. *Journal of Field Archaeology* 20:159–175.

Martinez, A. M. 1998. *An Archaeological Study of Change and Continuity in the Material Remains, Practices, and Cultural Identities of Native Californian Women in a Nineteenth Century Pluralistic Context*. Ph.D. dissertation, University of California, Berkeley.

Sandos, J. A. 2004. *Converting California: Indians and Franciscans in the Missions*. Yale University Press, New Haven, CT.

Silliman, S. W. 2001a. Agency, Practical Politics, and the Archaeology of Culture Contact. *Journal of Social Archaeology* 1(2):184–204.

———. 2001b. Theoretical Perspectives on Labor and Colonialism: Reconsidering the California Missions. *Journal of Anthropological Archaeology* 20(4):379–407.

———. 2003. Using a Rock in a Hard Place: Native American Lithic Practices in Colonial California. In *Stone Tool Traditions in the Contact Era*, edited by C. Cobb, pp. 127–150. University of Alabama Press, Tuscaloosa.

———. 2004. *Lost Laborers in Colonial California: Native Americans and the Archaeology of Rancho Petaluma*. University of Arizona Press, Tucson.

———. 2005. Obsidian Studies and the Archaeology of Nineteenth-Century California. *Journal of Field Archaeology* 30(1):75–94.

———. 2009. Change and Continuity, Practice and Memory: Native American Persistence in Colonial New England. *American Antiquity* 74(2):211–230.

Tveskov, M. 2007. Social Identity and Culture Change on the Southern Northwest Coast. *American Anthropologist* 109(3):431–441.

Voss, B. L. 2005. From *Casta* to *Californio*: Social Identity and the Archaeology of Culture Contact. *American Anthropologist* 107(3):461–474.

———. 2008. *The Archaeology of Ethnogenesis: Race and Sexuality in Colonial San Francisco.* University of California Press, Berkeley.

Wade, M. F. 2008. *Missions, Missionaries, and Native Americans: Long-Term Processes and Daily Practices.* University Press of Florida, Gainesville.

III. Northeast and Mid-Atlantic Seaboard

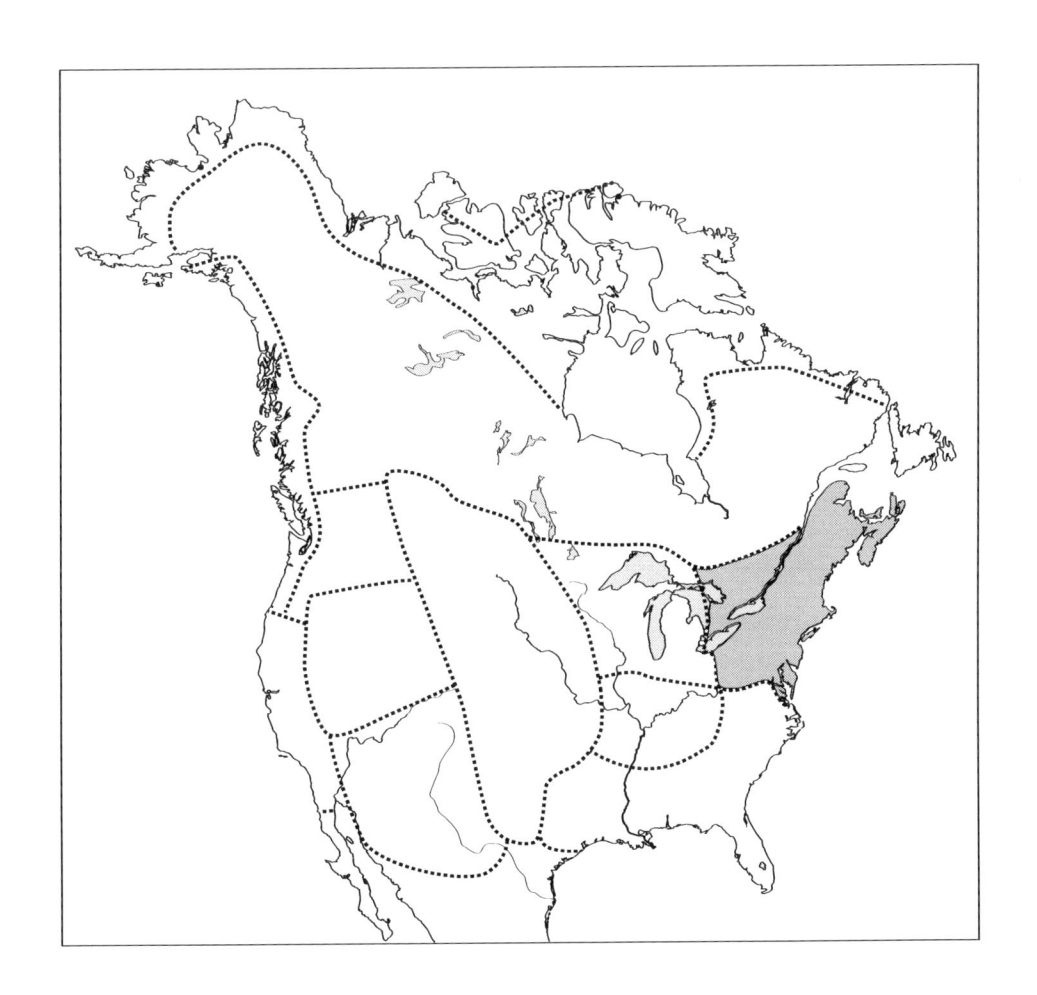

CHAPTER 21

OVERVIEW OF THE ST. LAWRENCE ARCHAIC THROUGH WOODLAND

CLAUDE CHAPDELAINE

The St. Lawrence Valley, with the geographically connected Great Lakes to the West and the Atlantic Seaboard to the East, has been a center of archaeological attention for most the 20th century. During the last 20 years, a major change occurred in the practice of archaeology, shifting from universities and museum-based studies to consulting work carried out by professional archaeologists. In the Northeast, this change resulted the former institutions found it impossible to cope with the unprecedented growth of mitigation projects, something that is not unique in North America.

The cultural sequence of the St. Lawrence Lowlands was first elaborated for New York state. This was then followed by Ontario, and later Quebec and the Maritimes and Newfoundland. Each region has since developed a more detailed regional sequence, giving a local flavor to archaeological systematics, but it remains possible to construct a general framework for the entire St. Lawrence and adjacent regions (Figure 21.1) probably because this major artery exercised a strong homogenizing factor, facilitating exchanges between distant groups (Chapdelaine and Lasalle 1995).

The purpose of this article is to present the major cultural achievements that took place along the St. Lawrence Valley, corresponding geographically to the Laurentian Lowlands, extending west to east from Lake Ontario to the Gulf of St. Lawrence. The order of presentation is chronological.

Date calBP	Period	Tradition	Point Type	Geological Events	Vegetation	
500	Contact	Euro / Native		Little Ice Age	Colder than today	
1000	Late Woodland	St. Lawrence Iroquoian	Levanna			
	Late Middle Woodland	Melocheville	Jack's Reef Corner Notched		Warmer than today	
2000	Early Middle Woodland	Point Peninsula	Small side-notched	Tide movements east of Québec City		
		Middlesex				
3000	Early Woodland	Meadowood				
4000	Terminal Archaic	Susquehanna Narrow Stemmed Lamoka	Orient Fishtail Susquehanna Genesee Lamoka			
5000	Late	Laurentian	Brewerton	Tide movements	Approximate actual vegetation	H Y P S I T H E R M A L
		&	Otter Creek points	Approximate present level configuration		
6000	Archaic	Maritime	ground slate points gouges		Biotic Climax hemlock maximum	
7000	Middle	Gulf of Maine	Regional types	Low water level east of Québec City	(SW) (NE) Oak	
8000	Archaic		Stark Neville		Maple / Birch	
				Proto St. Lawrence R.	Fir / Birch	
9000	Early	Bifurcate base	Swanton Kanahwa			
10000	Archaic Late Paleo-Indian	Cody Plano	Eden Kirk Hell Gap Agate Basin	Lake Lampsilis	Spruce / Pine / Fir Spruce	
11000					Tundra / Taiga	
12000	Early Paleo-Indian	Michaud/Neponset Intermediate phase		Champlain and Goldthwait Seas	Tundra	

Figure 21.1 Multidisciplinary framework for the St. Lawrence Valley (modified and adapted from Chapdelaine and Lasalle 1995:116).

THE PEOPLING OF OUR STUDY AREA

Current evidence indicates that the first human incursion into the St. Lawrence Valley dates to the Late Paleo-Indian Period (Figure 21.2). An eastern variant of Plano culture, defined by projectile points exhibiting parallel retouch flaking, has been identified in the Upper St. Lawrence and along the north coast of the Gaspé Peninsula (see also Anderson, this volume). This incursion is not well dated, but most scholars assign this culture to the early Holocene, with estimated dates ranging between 11300 and 8800 cal BP. The direction of this human expansion is eastward, occurring along a northern corridor corresponding to a cold ecological niche characterized by an

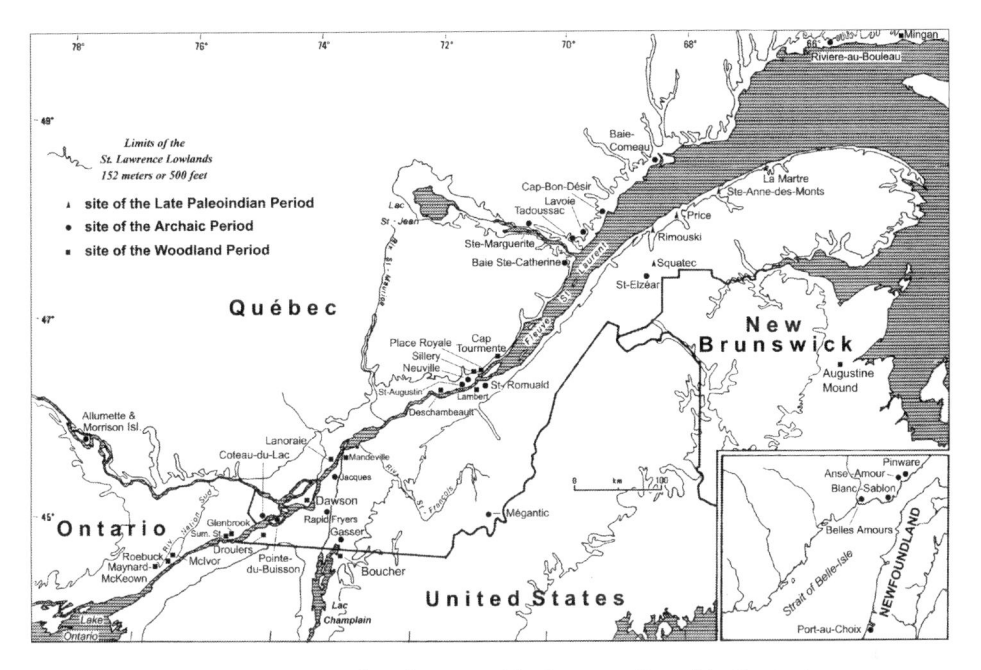

Figure 21.2 Map of study area with sites mentioned in the text.

open forest, the equivalent of a taiga; caribou was probably the dominant seasonally hunted species, complemented by exploitation of marine resources. This incursion seems to have taken place in an area with no prior human occupation, which is more probable if we accept peopling through an early phase related to the Agate Basin type of projectile point and dated between 11300 and 10000 cal BP.

Sites located on the north Gaspé Peninsula seem to be younger; the few available radiocarbon dates indicate that this cultural group lingered there between 10000 and 8800 cal BP. They appear to represent a second wave of migration with a Sainte-Anne/Varney point similar to the western Eden type of projectile point. This Late Paleo-Indian occupation of the north Gaspé Peninsula is coeval with new cultural groups of the Early Archaic that were responsible for extensive settlement of the entire St. Lawrence Valley and adjacent regions.

The Early Archaic Period: 11000 to 8800 or 8300 cal BP

Accepting the fact that Eastern Plano groups were late newcomers (after 11000 cal BP) along the St. Lawrence Lowlands and that they were not descended from Early Paleo-Indian groups, the extensive occupation of a forested environment is the achievement of different Early Archaic groups scattered in diverse settings, such as the St. Lawrence Lower North Shore (Pintal 2006, 1998), the Tadoussac Area, the Québec City area, in adjacent Maine, and up to Lake Ontario (Figure 21.2). The time interval for this period could be between 11000 and 8800 or 8300 cal BP (7,500 uncalibrated radiocarbon years in some areas).

The Saint-Elzéar site, located in a remote mountainous area of the Témiscouata region, has revealed an interesting collection of 36 stone tools associated with red ochre (Chalifoux et al. 1998). The stone tools include a chipped and polished adze, a very large biface, 10 end scrapers resembling the Rimouski site sample, and two limaces associated elsewhere with the Early Archaic Tradition. This Early Archaic unique assemblage shows relationships to the Eastern Plano Tradition of the north Gaspé Peninsula, which transformed itself locally into a regional Archaic occupying the lower terraces made available by the receding St. Lawrence Estuary. The lithic sources used by the Saint-Elzéar occupants indicate an extensive raw material acquisition network with rhyolite from central Maine, chalcedony from Scott's Bay (Nova Scotia), and radiolarian cherts that should come from local sources.

Along the St. Lawrence River, sites on Lower North Shore, around Tadoussac and Québec City, have provided us with the earliest presence of Archaic groups. Radiocarbon dates are few but average between 10000 and 8800 cal BP. A continuous occupation of the Blanc Sablon area during the time interval between 9000 and 7800 cal BP argues for an extensive occupation with no outside influence. Local adaptation to lithic sources (with an emphasis on quartz in the Québec City and Tadoussac areas) is characterized by distinctive typologies and poor representation of projectile points in these assemblages—a problem similar to the one encountered in New England (Robinson et al. 1992; Sanger 1996). Small end scrapers and wedges made of quartz are characteristic tools of the end of the Early Archaic Period at the Cap de Bon Désir site near Tadoussac (Plourde 2006) and in the Québec City area at Saint-Romuald. The oldest radiocarbon date comes from the unpublished CeEv-5 site at Neuville, occupying an old marine terrace 110 meters above sea level and three kilometers north of the actual St. Lawrence River. The lithic assemblage is dominated by rough quartz implements; the calibrated date gives an interval between 10,190 and 9,780 calendar years.

Very few diagnostic projectile points associated elsewhere to the Early Archaic Period have been identified as isolated finds along the St. Lawrence Valley. Finds of bifurcate base points are recorded at Coteau-du-Lac and in the Mégantic Lake area (Chapdelaine 2009). These Early Archaic groups are certainly transitional to the Middle Archaic Period, which is the least visible in the archaeological record.

The Middle Archaic Period: 8800 or 8300 to 6800 cal BP

This period corresponds to an approximate time interval between 8800 and 6800 cal BP, although it is poorly known along the St. Lawrence Lowlands (Figure 21.2). The difficulty of identifying components of this period remains its awkward characteristic, but this does not mean the territory had been abandoned. To the contrary, regional sequences have been established in the Québec City, Tadoussac, Lower North Shore and Coastal Labrador, and north Gaspé Peninsula regions. Linking them into a single cultural unit creates a false cultural homogeneity.

Again, few diagnostic projectile points, associated elsewhere with the Middle Archaic Period, have been identified along the St. Lawrence Valley. Isolated finds of Neville or Stark points are recorded at Sainte-Marguerite in the Lower Saguenay River (Langevin 2004), Baie-Comeau (Pintal 2006), Coteau-du-Lac and in the Mégantic Lake area (Chapdelaine 2009). These Middle Archaic groups likely transformed into Late Archaic Period traditions, which are the most visible in the archaeological record.

THE LATE ARCHAIC PERIOD: 6800 TO 4500 CAL BP

This period is definitely the richest in terms of sites (Figure 21.2). The time interval between 6800 and 5800 cal BP is poor in sites, while the period extending from 5800 to 4500 cal BP is much better documented. It is thus true to say that about 5,000 years ago the St. Lawrence Valley and its adjacent regions were extensively and intensively occupied. This climax is associated with the Hypsithermal, a climatic period extending from 9000 to 4000 cal BP, where ecological conditions were stable and warmer than the conditions described by the first explorers in the 16th and 17th centuries. The archaeological record is characterized by small components of hunter-gatherer groups, very often found mixed with later cultural components.

The Pointe-du-Buisson complex of 16 sites is a good example of a mixed site, with Late Archaic, Terminal Archaic, and Woodland occupations all mixed up within 25 centimeters of soil (Clermont and Chapdelaine 1982). For the first time, the general Northeast typology of projectile points could be applied to our study area. It is conventional to divide Late Archaic groups following three environmental zones: Laurentian, Maritime, and Shield. Only the first two are relevant here, and their respective origins are to be found in Middle Archaic times, which is especially true for the Maritime groups.

The Coteau-du-Lac site claims the only excavated and published burials of the Laurentian Tradition along the St. Lawrence River (Marois 1987). It is complemented by two exceptional sites of the Ottawa Valley, Morrison's Island-6 and Allumettes Island-1 (Figure 21.3), where the Laurentian Archaic buried their dead, optimized eel harvests during fall occupations, and participated in various trade networks, including one related to native copper from sources to the west and another that saw Onondaga chert come to the Ottawa Valley from the south (Chapdelaine and Clermont 2006). Other sites of importance are Rapid Fryers and Jacques along the Richelieu River; Gasser along the Pike River, which flows into Lake

Figure 21.3 Laurentian Archaic artifacts.

Champlain; Saint-Augustin in the Québec City area; and several sites in the Saguenay/Tadoussac area including the Lavoie site, which was considered a Laurentian component with a maritime adaptation.

The Blanc Sablon (Pintal 1998) and Coastal Labrador cultural sequences (Fitzhugh 2006) illustrate well the emergence and evolution of the Maritime Tradition, while Port-au-Choix on the opposite shore in Newfoundland is certainly a major site (Renouf and Bell 2006). The burial of a teenaged boy at l'Anse Amour on the Labrador coast, which is the oldest known burial so far, shows close resemblance between some lithic offerings and typical Maritime Archaic Tradition tools.

Rivière-au-Bouleau near the mouth of the Moisie River, in the Middle St. Lawrence North Shore (Chevrier 1977), could be assigned to the Shield Archaic, which is mostly an interior cultural manifestation.

THE TERMINAL ARCHAIC PERIOD: 4500 TO 3000 CAL BP

This time period is certainly affected by such radical changes as the disappearance of the Laurentian Tradition before 4500 cal BP and the decline of the Maritime Tradition between 4000 and 3500 cal BP. These changes are caused by the arrival of new Archaic groups from the South, a late migration associated with the Narrow small-stem tradition that will take on many regional names. These new groups used local lithic sources and are culturally affiliated with the Lamoka culture of New York state, and later to the Susquehanna Tradition. Radiocarbon dates obtained on Station no. 4 of Pointe-du-Buisson range between 5000 and 3000 cal BP, suggesting that the proposed migration took place while Laurentian groups may still have been hunting and fishing in the St. Lawrence Lowlands.

THE EARLY WOODLAND PERIOD: 3000 TO 2400 CAL BP

Around 3,000 years ago, the biggest change was not the appearance of ceramics (even if archaeologists do often use this new technological element to distinguish the Archaic and Woodland periods). Rather, the major revolution is the rapid establishment of a large network known as the Meadowood Interaction Sphere. Several sites, including cemetery and habitation sites, have been found throughout the St. Lawrence Lowlands (Taché 2008). A ritual with 200 cache blades made of Onondaga chert has been documented at the Lambert site near Québec City, indicating without a doubt the ideological strength of the Meadowood Interaction Sphere with its extensive circulation of exotic goods (Figure 21.4). The earliest pottery, which exhibited cord-markings on vessels interior and exterior walls (named Vinette 1 in our area), was introduced gradually in the domestic activities.

The Middlesex funerary complex is still problematical, culturally and chronologically. Few cemeteries or isolated burials have been found along the St. Lawrence River, but they are highly distinctive, with some elements resembling the Adena culture of the southern Great Lakes region (Figure 21.4). Burials at Sillery and near Mingan in the St. Lawrence Estuary are good examples (Clermont 1990), and the most impressive sites are Boucher near Lake Champlain in Vermont and Augustine Mound in New Brunswick (Figure 21.2). There are some indications that the Middlesex funerary complex started in the Early Woodland Period and continued into the next.

Figure 21.4 Early Woodland Meadowood cache blades made of Onondaga chert and bifaces of the Middlesex Complex.

The Middle Woodland Period: 2400 to 1000 cal BP

Around 2400 cal BP, the cultural groups of this period very rapidly replaced the Meadowood network, and especially the circulation of the distinctive stone tools made of Onondaga chert. We also see the beginning of decorated pottery. Gradually, these fragile containers increase to become the major class of recovery on most sites. This growth correlates with a reduction of the groups' mobility in the St. Lawrence Lowlands, yet the way of life remained nomadic. This period is usually divided into two long phases, on the basis of ceramic decoration and shape.

This pottery may be distinguished in terms of Early and Late Middle Woodland styles. Early Middle Woodland pottery is characterized by pseudo scallop shell impressions produced by dentate tools, and used with two other techniques: rocker stamping, and push-pull or stab-and-drag (Figure 21.5). Several components of this time period are known along the St. Lawrence River, but

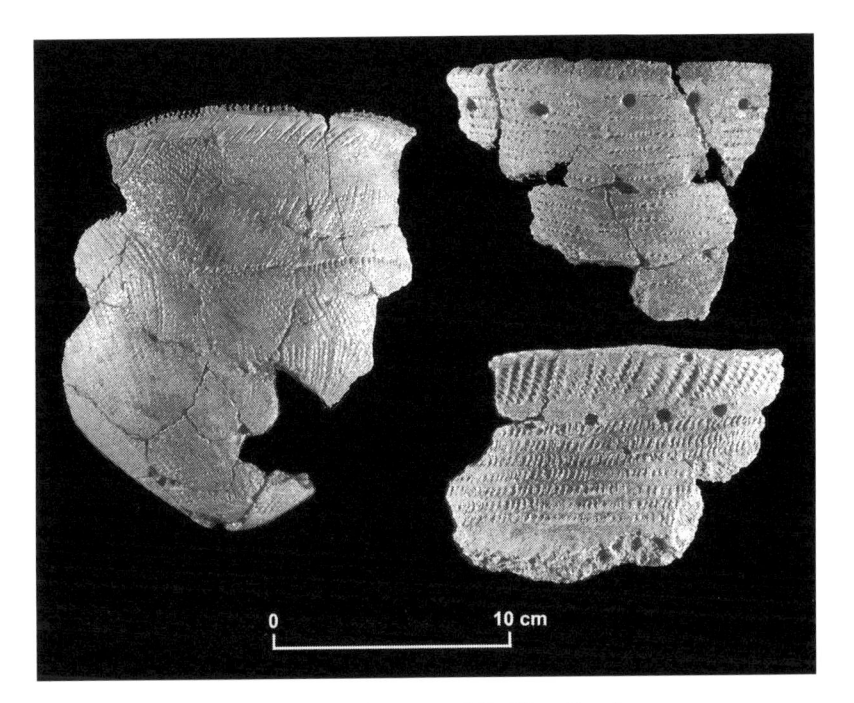

Figure 21.5 Early and Late Middle Woodland pottery.

they are mostly part of multicomponent sites. No clear seriation has been achieved, and this pseudo scallop shell horizon lasted 900 years. A rare, single component site has been excavated in the Cap Tourmente area. Late Middle Woodland pottery is characterized by simultaneous use of dentate and cord-wrapped stick tools on low collared vessels with a row of punctates producing interior bosses on the neck (Figure 21.5). This regional tradition, known as Melocheville, lasted approximately 500 years, with very few changes (Gates-Saint-Pierre 2006).

The late Middle Woodland period is a key time interval to understand the transformation of local groups into food producers, assuming within this scenario that they became the historic St. Lawrence Iroquoians. The major sites for this period are numerous island sites of the Upper St. Lawrence River (Wright 2004a), the Pointe-du-Buisson site complex and the Place Royale site in downtown Québec City (Clermont and Chapdelaine 1992). A zooarchaeological study (Cossette 1996) has revealed no stresses during this time interval, which preceded adoption of cultigens and a new settlement pattern. The major subtle change seems to reside in exploitation of fish during the warm season, permitting staying longer at the summer base camp. Cultigens appeared early in southwestern Ontario, around 550 cal BP, and were exchanged along the St. Lawrence River. However, tasting corn did not make people radically change their habits. It took time to move from a system based on predation to one centered on production.

THE LATE WOODLAND PERIOD: 1000 TO 400 CAL BP

The expected, earliest settled village life and use of cultigens are not yet supported by archaeological data during the first three centuries. Summer camps, occupied during several months, were predominant as well as fishing camps. The first evidence of cultigens appeared during this time period. Slow development of the new mode of production was replaced by a rapid and effective change during the 14th century. The Lanoraie site, with its excavated longhouse, is the best example of this complete revolution.

The inhabitants of Lanoraie were definitely St. Lawrence Iroquoians, producing the distinctive style of pottery that is the key identity marker at major village sites such as Roebuck, Maynard-McKeown, McIvor, Summerstown Station, Glenbrook, Droulers, Mandeville, Dawson, and Deschambault (Figure 21.2). This pottery is basically a medium-sized collared vessel with numerous castellations, decorated with incisions to make complex geometric motifs embellished with circles (annular punctates) made with a hollow implement, and notches (Figure 21.6). This St. Lawrence Iroquoian cultural episode covered most of our study area, about 700 kilometers long starting from eastern Lake Ontario, in Jefferson and St. Lawrence Counties of New York, to reach Québec City and an extension toward the St. Lawrence Estuary.

Following the pioneer work of James Pendergast, who studied the St. Lawrence Iroquoians in the Upper St. Lawrence Valley, a new cluster of villages was found in the Saint-Anicet area. A settlement pattern was emerging for this area, with Droulers

Figure 21.6 St. Lawrence Iroquoian pottery.

being a major settlement almost 7 kilometers away from the St. Lawrence River. The variability of the St. Lawrence Iroquoians, in particular to the east of Montreal, supports the idea of several related tribes living along the St. Lawrence. The exact number of tribes is still a debated issue, but there is agreement that as many as seven regional groups may have had some political autonomy. The Jefferson and St. Lawrence Counties Iroquoians may have constituted more than just one tribe, and the newly defined Lake Champlain cluster (Petersen et al. 2004) may correspond to a short-lived relocation of one existing tribe during the 16th century dislocation and disappearance of all St. Lawrence Iroquoians (Tremblay and Chapdelaine 2006).

The eastern group, living around modern Québec City, was engaged in long-distance travel in order to exploit marine resources in the middle St. Lawrence Estuary, especially seals and belugas. The Iroquoians from the Québec City area, although sharing the same material culture as the other tribes of the St. Lawrence Iroquoian Confederacy, can no longer be considered sedentary horticulturalists but rather semi-sedentary groups with a strong emphasis on exploitation of salt-water resources of the St. Lawrence Estuary. They developed symbiotic relations with Algonquian neighbors.

Unfortunately, there is no clear evidence of European trade items in good stratigraphic context on St. Lawrence Iroquoian sites, except for a single item found on the Maynard-McKeown village site (Wright 2004b:1281–1282). The disappearance of St. Lawrence Iroquoians remains a very popular subject of Canadian history, but new discoveries are needed before we can reconstruct the complex sequence of events. It is thus very difficult to discuss the Contact Period for the 16th century. Several archaeological projects have recently been dedicated to the Basques presence in the St. Lawrence Estuary, but their impact on the Natives remains to be fully discussed.

Conclusion

In summary, three key achievements characterize the St. Lawrence Valley up to European contact. First, the peopling of the St. Lawrence Valley may have been carried out by either Eastern Plano or Early Archaic groups. Early Paleo-Indian hunters, with their distinctive fluted points, were within sight of the vast Champlain Sea when they settled at the Potts site overlooking modern Lake Ontario, but it seems they never ventured east. Second, the Archaic Period in general has not received enough attention, but it is clear that the St. Lawrence River started to act as a highway, permitting circulation of ideas, objects, and groups, and conferring on its inhabitants a relative cultural homogeneity and participation in large networks reaching the scale of the Northeast. Third, the Woodland Period is the richest in terms of the number of sites, and the theoretical paradigm is still *in situ* development of Iroquoian groups starting in Early Woodland times, and perhaps as early as the Late or Terminal Archaic. A majority of scholars also accept that there was cultural continuity between late Middle Woodland and early Late Woodland populations in the St. Lawrence Lowlands.

REFERENCES

Chalifoux, E., A. Burke, and C. Chapdelaine. 1998. *La paléohistoire du Témiscouata.* Collection Paléo-Québec 26. Recherches amérindiennes au Québec, Montréal.

Chapdelaine, C. 2009. A Twelve Thousand Year Archaeological Sequence for the Megantic Lake Area. Mercury Series, Archaeology Paper 170, *Painting the Past with a Broad Brush: Papers in Honour of James Vallière Wright*, edited by D. L. Keenlyside and J.-L. Pilon, pp. 143–173. Canadian Museum of Civilization, Gatineau, Québec.

———, and N. Clermont. 2006. Adaptation, Continuity and Change in the Middle Ottawa Valley: A View from the Morrison and Allumettes Island Late Archaic Sites. In *Archaic of the Far Northeast*, edited by D. Sanger and P. Renouf, pp. 191–219. University of Maine Press, Orono.

Chapdelaine, C. and P. Lasalle. 1995. Physical Environments and Cultural Systems in the Saint Lawrence Valley, 8 to 3 ka: A Multidisciplinary Framework. Special Paper 297, *Archaeological Geology of the Archaic Period in North America*, edited by A. E. Bettis III, pp. 115–129. Geological Society of America, Boulder, CO.

Chevrier, D. 1977. *Préhistoire de la Moisie.* Cahiers du Patrimoine 5. Ministère des Affaires culturelles du Québec.

Clermont, N. 1990. Le Sylvicole inférieur au Québec. *Recherches amérindiennes au Québec* 20(1):5–19.

Clermont, N., and C. Chapdelaine. 1982. *Pointe-du-Buisson 4: quarante siècles d'archives oubliées.* Recherches amérindiennes au Québec, Montréal.

———. 1992. Au pied du cap Diamant: L'occupation préhistorique de la Pointe de Québec. Dossiers 76, *L'occupation historique et préhistorique de la Place Royale*, edited by N. Clermont, C. Chapdelaine, and J. Guimont, pp. 1–279. Ministère des Affaires culturelles du Québec.

Cossette, E. 1996. Pêcheurs et chasseurs à l'aube d'une transformation: les stratégies de subsistance entre 500 et 1000 ap. J.-C. *Recherches amérindiennes au Québec* 26(3–4):115–127.

Fitzhugh, W. 2006. Settlement, Social and Ceremonial change in the Labrador Maritime Archaic. In *Archaic of the Far Northeast*, edited by D. Sanger and P. Renouf, pp. 47–81. University of Maine Press, Orono.

Gates-St-Pierre, C. 2006. *Potières du Buisson: la céramique de tradition Melocheville sur le site Hector Trudel.* Mercury Series, Archaeology Paper 168. Canadian Museum of Civilisation, Gatineau, QC.

Langevin, E. 2004. Écologie humaine à l'embouchure de la rivière Sainte-Marguerite. Collection Paléo-Québec 31, *Un traducteur du passé: Mélanges anthropologiques en l'honneur de Norman Clermont*, edited by C. Chapdelaine and P. Corbeil, pp. 177–202. Recherches amérindiennes au Québec, Montréal.

Marois, R. 1987. Souvenirs d'antan: les sépultures archaïques de Coteau-du-Lac, Québec. *Recherches amérindiennes au Québec* 17(1–2):7–35.

Petersen, J. B., J. G. Crock, E. R. Cowie, R. A. Boisvert, J. R. Toney, and G. Mandel. 2004. St. Lawrence Iroquoians in Northern New England: Pendergast was "Right" and More. Mercury Series, Archaeological Paper 164, *A Passion for the Past: Papers in Honour of James F. Pendergast*, edited by J. V. Wright and J.-L. Pilon, pp. 87–123. Canadian Museum of Civilisation, Gatineau, QC.

Pintal, J.-Y. 1998. *Aux frontières de la mer: la préhistoire de Blanc-Sablon.* Dossiers 102. Ministère de la culture et des communications du Québec.

———. 2006. The Archaic Sequence of the St. Lawrence Lower North Shore, Québec. In *Archaic of the Far Northeast*, edited by D. Sanger and P. Renouf, pp. 105–138. University of Maine Press, Orono.

Plourde, M. 2006. The Cap de Bon-Désir Site: A New Regional Variation of the Gulf of Maine Archaic Tradition. In *Archaic of the Far Northeast*, edited by D. Sanger and P. Renouf, pp. 139–159. University of Maine Press, Orono.

Renouf, P., and T. Bell. 2006. Maritime Archaic Site Locations on the Island of Newfoundland. In *Archaic of the Far Northeast*, edited by D. Sanger and P. Renouf, pp. 1–46. University of Maine Press, Orono.

Robinson, B. S., J. B. Petersen, and A. K. Robinson (editors). 1992. *Early Holocene Occupation in Northern New England*. Occasional Publications in Maine Archaeology 9, Augusta.

Sanger, D. 1996. Gilman Falls Site: Implications for Early and Middle Archaic of the Maritime Peninsula. *Canadian Journal of Archaeology* 20:7–28.

Taché, K. 2008. *Structure and Regional Diversity of the Meadowood Interaction Sphere*. Ph.D. dissertation, Simon Fraser University.

Tremblay, R., and C. Chapdelaine. 2006. La fin d'une ère, le début d'un mystère: rencontres, disparition et hypothèses/End of an Era, Beginning of a Mystery. In *Les Iroquoiens du Saint-Laurent, peuple du maïs/The St. Lawrence Iroquoians, Corn People*, edited by R. Tremblay, pp. 99–130. Éditions de l'Homme, Montréal.

Wright, J. V. 2004a. The Gordon Island North Site and Cultural Settlement Distribution Along the Upper St. Lawrence River Valley. Mercury Series, Archaeology Paper 164, *A Passion for the Past: Papers in Honour of James F. Pendergast*, edited by J. V. Wright and J.-L. Pilon, pp. 321–393. Canadian Museum of Civilization, Gatineau, Québec.

———. 2004b. *A History of the Native People of Canada*, vol. 3, part 1 (A.D. 500–European Contact). Mercury Series, Archaeology Paper 152. Canadian Museum of Civilization, Gatineau, QC.

CHAPTER 22

NEW ENGLAND ALGONQUIANS: NAVIGATING "BACKWATERS" AND TYPOLOGICAL BOUNDARIES

ELIZABETH S. CHILTON

NORTHEASTERN North America, with its glacially formed landscape, broad rivers, rich coastal zones, seasonal variation, and diverse and easily assessable bedrock formations, has long been attractive to human settlement (Figure 22.1). However, the history of American archaeology has relegated the region to the backwater of cultural evolution. In particular, because Algonquians of the Northeast—particularly those in New England—did not at any point in their precolonial history develop sedentary settlements, permanent architecture, craft specialization, or strict social hierarchy, the region's prehistory has attracted less attention from both archaeologists and the general public. Further, many of the social evolutionary models used either explicitly or implicitly by archaeologists are based on typological categories (e.g., "hunter-gatherer," "horticulturalist," or "complex") that leave no room for New England's "mobile farmers."

In this chapter, I argue that New England Algonquians offer us an important historical example of great social and ecological stability—as well as social complexity—over more than 10 millennia. The archaeological record in New

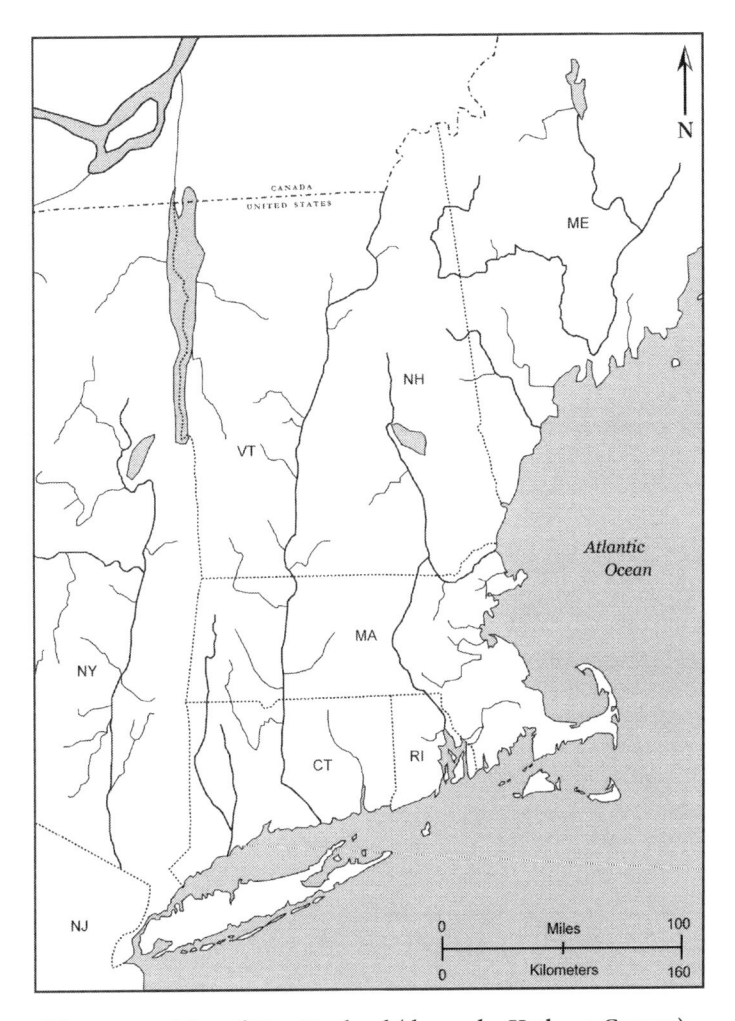

Figure 22.1 Map of New England (drawn by Kathryn Curran).

England allows us to question causal relationships among subsistence, sedentism, and social complexity, and to explore alternative pathways in human history. In this sense, I am challenging directional models of cultural evolution and am, instead, arguing for the importance of historical contingency in human adaptation. I first review the archaeological evidence for the Paleo-Indian and Archaic periods as a backdrop for a full discussion of New England's mobile farmers.

Colonial New England

When the first people came to "New England," or the region North and East of what is now New York City, they encountered a landscape that was just beginning to recover from recent glaciation. Long Island, Cape Cod, Martha's Vineyard, and

Nantucket were all formed from glacial debris deposited at the southernmost point of a continent-sized glacier, which retreated from the area 18,000 years ago. As the glacier retreated, it left behind large amounts of sand, gravel, debris, and water. The glacial scouring and sediment dumping in the retreat left behind exposed bedrock for making stone tools; flat, well-drained sandy shorelines and terraces for habitation; and extensive wetlands and rocky coves for collecting hundreds of species of plants and animals to feed, clothe, and otherwise comfort their families.

When people entered this newly deglaciated landscape around 10000 BC, the environment and its plant and animal resources were still recovering from the Pleistocene, and the Connecticut River Valley was bouncing back after the draining of Glacial Lake Hitchcock (Figure 22.2). They found a forest of northern conifer species, including white pine, spruce, and fir, as well as temperate deciduous trees (McWeeney 2003). Food resources included caribou, giant beaver, wild grapes, hawthorn seeds, migratory birds, and probably many others (Chilton 2004; Dincauze and Jacobsen 2001). New England was—and is—an ideal environment for hunter-gatherers. They subsist on a diverse array of wild plants and animals collected from the local area; they typically shift settlements seasonally to have greater access to the available plants and animals. New England, with its strong seasonal contrasts, affords year-round, diverse, and plentiful resources for hunter-gatherers. Early on, from the Paleo-Indian period to the beginning of the Middle Archaic (10000–7000 BC), the environment was still bouncing back from glaciation, the weather was generally colder and drier, the seasonal contrasts were more severe, and sea level was rising dramatically (see Anderson, Chapdelaine, this volume). Plant and animals resources were somewhat less predictable and changing within perhaps a lifetime. Thus, these early settlers to the region were likely flexible generalists and not focused on one or two staple resources (such as big-game hunting). Likewise, settlements would have had to be flexible to adapt to a drastically changing (and new) environment.

By 7000 BC, at the start of what is called the Middle Archaic, shorelines had stabilized somewhat, and sea level was close to the modern shoreline. Offshore coastal islands such as Martha's Vineyard and Nantucket became cut off from the mainland and supported their own year-round residents. Shellfish beds also formed because of this shoreline stabilization, and offshore seasonal fishing became more reliable. Likewise, inland riverbeds stabilized, allowing establishment of freshwater shellfish beds and substantial freshwater fish. Another consequence of the warming climate and slow recovery of the vegetation from glaciation is that by about 4000 BC (just after the start of the Late Archaic period), New England supported a large deciduous forest with a variety of highly productive and reliable nut-bearing trees, including oak and hickory (Foster and Zebryk 1993). The archaeological record indicates a sharp rise in production of groundstone axes woodworking tools during the Late Archaic. These were likely used to make dugout canoes and lodging, and for chopping firewood.

Thus, from 10000 to 1000 BC New England peoples can be considered classic hunter-gatherers from the perspective of anthropology. They modified and managed their environment through controlled burning and clearing (McWeeney 2003) and were strategic about seasonal movements. By 7000 BC and perhaps even earlier they

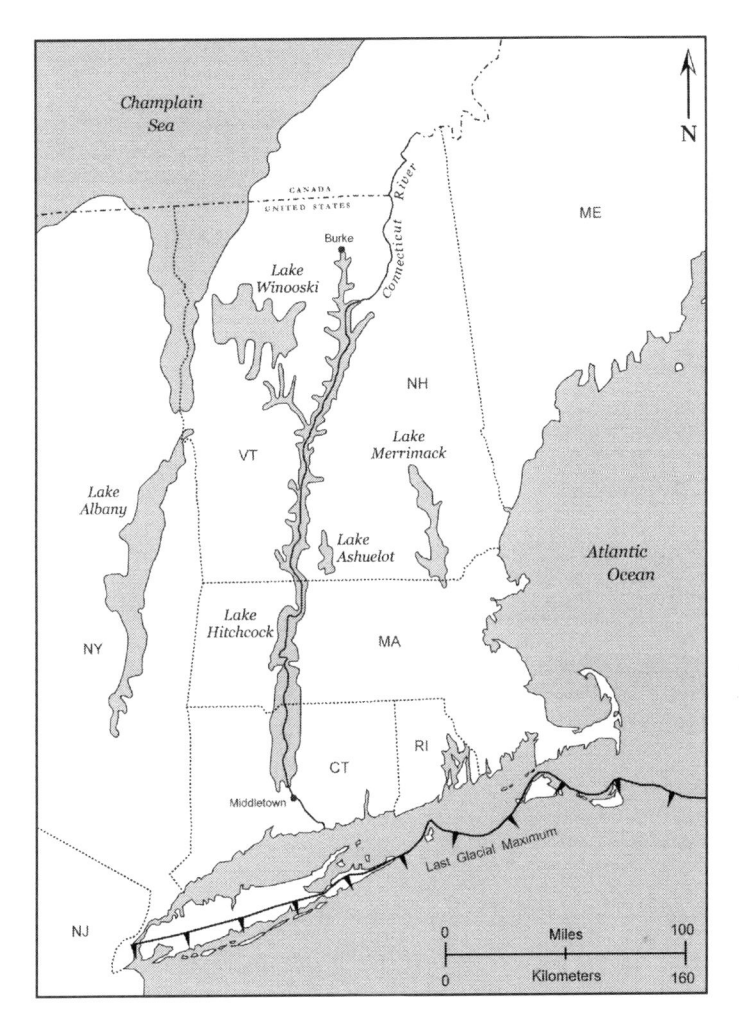

Figure 22.2 Map of the Late Pleistocene Glacial Lakes in New England (drawn by Kathryn Curran).

had formed traditional homelands and returned to certain seasonal sites throughout the year: coming together for spring fish runs, splitting apart for summer berry collecting or hunting, reuniting for fall nut collecting and processing, and perhaps congregating during the winter to share resources, firelight, warmth, and friendship.

Life began to change somewhat toward the end of the Late Archaic (2000–1000 BC). Archaeological evidence suggests that population had reached new heights, second only to that of the Late Woodland period (AD 1000–1600). Also, perhaps because of the stabilization of the shorelines and floodplains—and the ground disturbance caused by establishment of homelands and seasonal rounds—certain weedy plants came to be more widely available and intensively used, particularly goosefoot (*Chenopodium berlandieri*), sumpweed (*Iva annu*), and sunflower (*Helianthus annuus*; Smith 1992). Goosefoot and sumpweed are oily, protein-rich, starchy seeds that were boiled into a porridge or stew for consumption. There is evidence in the Midwest that these seeds were so intensively collected, stored, and propagated that they became domesticated (that is, genetically modified to be more productive and more easily processed; Smith 1992, Pearsall, this volume).

In New England, there is only weak evidence for domestication (George and Dewar 1999), but it is clear that these plants were intensively collected, stored, and perhaps most importantly cooked. Goosefoot and sumpweed require a great deal of boiling to make them both palatable and digestible. Not coincidentally, beginning around 1,500 BC Native peoples began to create and use stone bowls (of soapstone or steatite) for cooking. Native Americans obviously had bowls before that, but they were likely made of wood or other perishable materials and have not survived in the archaeological record. Before the invention or adoption of soapstone bowls, foods were likely roasted over a fire or boiled in a wooden bowl by heating stones and dropping them into the stew or water to be boiled. Soapstone is an excellent heat conductor, a soft rock than can be easily carved and set directly into a fire without cracking. Thus it permitted cooking starchy, oily seeds over a hot fire for a long period.

This new technology would have then opened up the range of food available for consumption for these hunter-gatherers. Interestingly, what appear to be subterranean food storage pits are also prevalent around this time. Food storage is a not a typical activity of hunter-gatherers, since they typically fit their demand to their supply instead of the other way around. Thus, intensive exploitation of what can only be considered third-choice foods for hunter-gatherers, combined with adoption of new technologies to exploit these foods and introduction of food storage behavior, indicate either some kind of population or food stress or another major societal change.

Because soapstone is available only in a few locations in New England, and because it is rather heavy and difficult to transport, Native peoples fairly quickly (within 500 years or so) moved toward creating ceramic vessels made from fired local clays, though it is clear that use of soapstone and ceramics overlapped for quite some time (Hoffman 1998). Clay is available across New England, and fired pottery vessels are also great heat conductors and even more malleable than soapstone. Clay vessels—like their soapstone counterparts—were first used elsewhere in North American before appearing in New England, but they were adopted in each region only when these technologies were needed to solve a particular technological problem or need. David Braun's article "Pots as Tools" (1983) underscores this point nicely: people do not blindly invest in a new technology unless there is a good push or pull toward solving a societal problem.

WOODLAND PERIOD

When Native peoples began to make ceramic—or fired clay—vessels, this marks the beginning of the Woodland Period (1000 BC–AD 1600). Because of the change in cooking technology, it is clear that people were expanding their subsistence base.

Thus both their impact on the landscape and their overall social organization and cultural traditions were also likely changing.

Early ceramic vessels were rather coarse-tempered and thick-walled. But by AD 500 this new technology was familiar enough that users began to experiment with new temper materials (crushed rock or other substances added to the clay), surface treatments (decorations or other markings on the surface of the clay), and design motifs. Strangely, there are fewer archaeological sites dating to the Early and Middle Woodland periods than to the Late Archaic period (see Keegan and Keegan 1999). One explanation for this is that the Late Archaic period is 3,000 years long (4000–1000 BC), while the Early and Middle Woodland periods are each 1,000 years long (1000 BC–AD 1, and AD 1–1000, respectively). Nevertheless, even if one accounts for these differences in duration, it is clear that there are still significantly more Late Archaic sites. Once explanation is that population actually decreased, or at least dispersed, following the Late Archaic.

There is some evidence for social strife during the Late Archaic period (interpersonal and perhaps group-on-group conflict; see Sassaman 2010). And toward the end of the Late Archaic burial ceremonialism and related ritual flourish, which may indicate both territorial marking (with cemeteries) and social tensions (increased ritual). With introduction of a new cooking technology, which then opened up a wider variety of subsistence choices, it is possible that there was population dispersal away from the large, clustered, seasonal sites of the Late Archaic. This is a hypothesis that requires further testing, but it is a possible explanation for the change in overall site density.

Certainly by the Middle Woodland period, populations began to cluster again, and archaeological sites from this period are more visible than for the Early Woodland period. During the Middle Woodland, around AD 700, another new technology was adopted in the region: the bow and arrow. This was likely first adopted in the Arctic between 9000 and 6000 BC through contact with peoples from Northeast Asia; it then spread southward through North and South America, with rapid adoption after AD 500 (Thomas 1999:58). Evidence for this technology in New England is in the adoption of a new projectile point form: a small, lightweight, triangular projectile, which is often thought to be associated with the bow and arrow (Figure 22.3). The significance of bow and arrow technology is that it would have increased hunting efficiency, and was (later) extremely effective as a weapon of war. However, there is no evidence in New England for use of the bow and arrow in warfare until after European colonization.

Maize Horticulture

At the same time that the bow and arrow came to be used in New England, another new technology was being gradually adopted by the region's people: maize horticulture (see Pearsall, this volume). Recent research on pottery vessels from New York

Figure 22.3 Arrow points from the Late Woodland period, AD 1000–1600.

State indicates the presence of maize in charred residues that date back to 2,000 years ago (Hart et al. 2007). Residue analysis indicates the presence or absence of certain plants or animals, but it does not allow us to determine the prevalence of that foodstuff in any quantifiable way. Stable isotopes of human remains from New York and Ontario indicate that maize did not become a dietary staple until about AD 1000 (Katzenberg et al. 1995; Schwartz et al. 1985). Thus, maize was clearly being grown and consumed in the greater Northeast for at least a thousand years before it became a significant food crop for anyone in the region.

Given that there was established trade of materials and new technologies between what is now New York State and New England going back to at least the Late Archaic, maize was almost certainly following these same communication pathways. It is likely—though this remains untested—that ceramic residues from New England vessels would reveal the presence of maize horticulture going back nearly 2,000 years. The earliest maize kernels found archaeologically in New England date to about 1000 AD, with an increase in visibility for sites dating to AD 1300–1500 (Chilton 2006). The fact that the number of Late Woodland period (AD 1000–1600) archaeological sites rises fairly sharply—and outnumbers sites of any other time period if one standardizes for period duration (see Keegan and Keegan 1999 for Connecticut)—suggests that maize horticulture correlated with a rise in population size. Since this is the most recent pre-Contact period, it could also be partly explained by better preservation or visibility; more recent sites are both closer to the surface in some cases as well as less disturbed by time. Of course, correlation does not equal causation, and it is impossible to say whether this new food was the cause or the effect of population increase.

So what was the overall effect on New England Algonquians of adopting maize horticulture? This is where the region's people begin to fall through the evolutionary and typological cracks. Elsewhere in North America, particularly for the New York Iroquois, adoption of maize horticulture is associated with several important societal changes: population increase, population density (i.e., formation of "villages"), multiyear sedentism, and a rise (or even the origin) of warfare and associated defensive features on sites (such as palisades; Fenton 1978; Snow 1994; Tuck 1978).

Archaeological evidence for these particular societal changes is nearly absent in New England. People had been living on that coast year round (or nearly so) since the Late Archaic; the reliable maritime resources of the coast provided ample food for fairly large populations, and substantial base camps show great continuity over generations (Bernstein 1999; Gwynne 1982). Maize horticulture was certainly adopted on the coast, and it was apparently added to the large sweep of plant and animal resources exploited throughout the year. However, it does not seem to have caused a change in settlement location on the coast, though it certainly may have led to growth in population and potentially the density of habitation as well (Duranleau 2009).

For the New England interior, the story is quite different. Prior to adoption of maize horticulture, as discussed earlier, people in the interior lived as hunter-gatherers, coming together for social gatherings as well as for seasonal fishing, hunting, and plant collecting. Related groups would split apart and come back together annually within well-established homelands. Maize horticulture does not seem to have had much effect on this long-held tradition in the New England interior (Chilton 1999). Instead, maize seems to have been tacked on as an additional plant resource. It did not become a staple food until after European colonization, when seasonal movements became severely constricted and prohibited in some cases (Chilton 2002). Archaeological evidence for the Late Woodland period suggests that in the interior people continued their seasonal rounds and diverse diet. Although there is evidence for maize on many sites dating to the Late Woodland period, they all show a diverse array of food resources, including nuts, small and large mammals, fish, birds, reptiles, and berries (Chilton 2008). Maize was planted in the spring, and then some families may have dispersed for the summer, to get together again in the fall for the maize harvest. Thus, I have termed the New England Algonquians of the interior "mobile farmers" (Graham 1994), a cultural category that anthropologists and archaeologists have generally failed to acknowledge or explore.

Archaeological evidence for this "mobile farming" in the New England interior during the Late Woodland period includes (1) continued seasonal use of sites, and lack of year-round (or even strong) evidence for multiseason settlement; (2) continuing diverse subsistence, based on a variety of plants and animal remains; (3) no evidence for sites being located in defensive locations or with defensive structures; and (4) ceramic traditions indicating fluid social boundaries within well established homelands (Figure 22.4; Chilton 2008). Maize, and later beans and squash, certainly had social, ideological, and dietary importance for New England peoples; there is no doubt that farming on any significant level would have had an effect on a hunting and gathering lifestyle. However, people had been collecting (and perhaps even domesticating) several seed crops for a few thousand years. The type of corn that was adopted by Northeastern peoples—Northern Flint or a similar eight-row variety—was similar to goosefoot and sumpweed in that it needed to be cooked for a long period over a hot fire. Thus adoption of maize was not as substantial a dietary

Vessel Lot 9

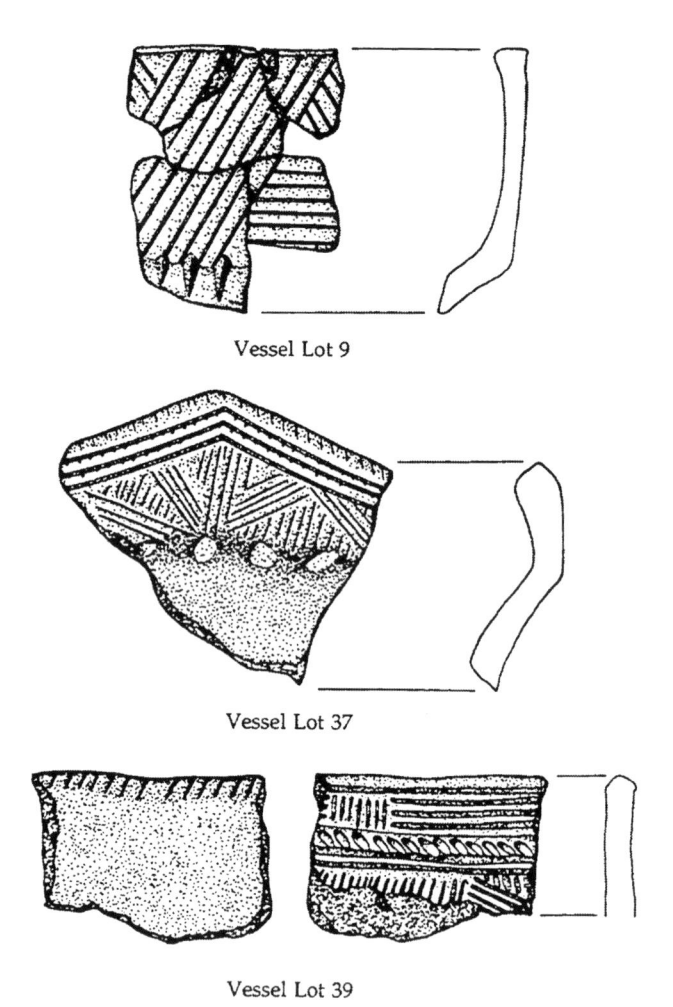

Vessel Lot 37

Vessel Lot 39

Figure 22.4 Ceramics from the Late Woodland period, AD 1000–1600.

change as was once thought. Native peoples had the cooking technology, and knowledge of the environment and its plentiful resources; they were able to use maize, beans, and squash as dietary supplements in ways that did not lead them to reject or significantly move away from their seasonal rounds, fluid social boundaries, and well-established homelands.

European Colonization

The mobile farmers of New England, with their relatively light footprint (at least to the European eye) on the landscape and their fluid territorial boundaries, were in some ways a conundrum to the Europeans who began to colonize the region in the

17th century. Europeans expected—and in fact promoted—strict territorial boundaries, social hierarchy, sedentism, and warfare. These all had a profound effect on New England Algonquians. Their lack of precolonial sedentism has been an impediment to federal recognition, land claims, repatriation of human remains, and general social recognition and respect (Chilton 2005). The mobility of the pre-Contact era was in part a survival tactic, as many Native people sought to "hide in plain sight" (Bruchac 1999), especially after King Philip's War, when it was not at all advantageous to be clearly Native American.

In sum, it is important to uncover the rich, ancient, and colorful history of New England peoples as it transpired before the English, because their history offers us deeper and richer understanding of (1) the importance of individual and group choices and agency in human cultural evolution, (2) the great diversity in the pathways taken in the human story, and (3) the historical unpinning of contemporary Native issues in the United States.

REFERENCES

Bernstein, D. J. 1999. Prehistoric Use of Plant Foods on Long Island and Block Island Sounds. In New York State Museum Bulletin 494, *Current Northeast Paleoethnobotany*, edited by J. P. Hart, pp. 101–120. New York State Museum, Albany.

Braun, D. 1983. Pots as Tools. In *Archaeological Hammers and Theories*, edited by J. A. Moore and A. S. Keene, pp. 107–134. Academic Press, New York.

Bruchac, M. M. 1999. Hiding in Plain Sight: Native Adaptation and Survival in New England. Paper presented at the New England Native American Institute, Worcester Historical Museum, Worcester, MA.

Chilton, E. S. 1999. Mobile Farmers of Pre-contact Southern New England: The Archaeological and Ethnohistorical Evidence. New York State Museum Bulletin 494, *Current Northeast Ethnobotany*, edited by J. P. Hart, pp. 157–176. New York State Museum, Albany.

———. 2002. "Towns They Have None": Diverse Subsistence and Settlement Strategies in Native New England. In New York State Museum Bulletin No. 496, *Northeast Subsistence-Settlement Change: A. D. 700–1300*, edited by J. P. Hart and C. B. Rieth, pp. 265–288. New York State Museum, Albany.

———. 2004. Beyond "Big": Gender, Age, and Subsistence Diversity in Paleo-Indian Societies. In *The Settlement of the American Continents: A Multidisciplinary Approach to Human Biogeography*, edited by C. M. Barton, G. A. Clark, D. Yesner, and G. Pearson, pp. 162–172. University of Arizona Press, Tucson.

———. 2005. Farming and Social Complexity in the Northeast. In *North American Archaeology*, edited by T. Pauketat and D. D. Loren, pp. 138–160. Blackwell Studies in Global Archaeology, Malden, MA.

———. 2006. The Origin and Spread of Maize (Zea Mayz) in New England. In *Histories of Maize: Multidisciplinary Approaches to the Prehistory, Biogeography, Domestication, and Evolution of Maize*, edited by J. Staller, R. Tykot, and B. Benz, pp. 539–547. Elsevier, Burlington, MA.

———. 2008. So Little Maize, So Much Time: Understanding Maize Adoption in New England. In *Current Northeast Ethnobotany II*, edited by J. P. Hart, pp. 53–58. New York State Museum, Albany.

Dincauze, D. F., and V. Jacobson. 2001. The Birds of Summer: Lakeside Routes into Late Pleistocene New England. *Canadian Journal of Archaeology* 25:121–126.

Duranleau, D. L. 2009. Subsistence and Settlement Patterns of the Late Archaic and Late Woodland Periods for Coastal New England and New York: A Regional Survey. Ph.D. dissertation, Harvard University.

Fenton, W. N. 1978. Northern Iroquoian Culture Patterns. In *Handbook of the North American Indians,* vol. 15, *Northeast,* edited by B. G. Trigger, pp. 296–321. Smithsonian Institution, Washington, DC.

Foster, D. R., and T. M. Zebryk. 1993. Long-Term Vegetation Dynamics and Disturbance History of a *Tsuga*-Dominated Forest in New England. *Ecology* 74:982–998.

George, D., and R. E. Dewar. 1999. Chenopodium in Connecticut Prehistory: Wild, Weedy, Cultivated, or Domesticated? In New York State Museum Bulletin No. 494, *Current Northeast Ethnobotany,* edited by John P. Hart, pp. 121–132. New York State Museum, Albany.

Graham, M. 1994. *Mobile Farmers: An Ethnoarchaeological Approach to Settlement Organization Among the Rarámuri of Northwestern Mexico.* International Monographs in Prehistory 3. University of Michigan, Ann Arbor.

Gwynne, M. A. 1982. *The Late Archaic Archaeology of Mount Sinai Harbor, New York: Human Ecology, Economy and Residence Patterns on the Southern New England Coast.* Ph.D. dissertation, State University of New York, Stony Brook.

Hart, J. P., H. J. Brumbach, and R. Lusteck. 2007. Extending the Phytolith Evidence for Early Maize (*Zea mays* ssp. *mays*) and Squash (*Cucurbita* sp.) in Central New York. *American Antiquity* 72:563–583.

Hoffman, C. 1988. Radiocarbon Dates from Massachusetts: An Annotated Listing. *Bulletin of the Massachusetts Archaeological Society*, 49(1):21–39.

Katzenberg, M. A., H. P. Schwartz, M. Knyf, and F. J. Melbye. 1995. Stable Isotope Evidence for Maize Horticulture and Paleodiet in Southern Ontario. *American Antiquity* 60(2):335–350.

Keegan, W. F. and K. N. Keegan (editors). 1999. *The Archaeology of Connecticut: The Human Era: 11,000 Years Ago to the Present.* Bibliopola Press, Storrs, CT.

McWeeney, L. 2003. Cultural and Ecological Continuities and Discontinuities in Coastal New England: Landscape Manipulation. *Northeast Anthropology* 64:75–84.

Sassaman, K. E. 2010. *The Eastern Archaic, Historicized.* AltaMira, Lanham, MD.

Schwartz, H. P., F. J. Melbye, M. A. Katzenberg, and M. Khye. 1985. Stable Isotopes in Human Skeletons of Southern Ontario: Reconstructing Paleodiet. *Journal of Archaeological Science* 12:187–206.

Smith, B. D. 1992. *Rivers of Change: Essays on Early Agriculture in Eastern North America.* Smithsonian Institution, Washington, DC.

Snow, D. R. 1994. *The Iroquois.* Blackwell, Cambridge, MA.

Thomas, D. H. 1999. *Exploring Ancient Native America.* Routledge, New York.

Tuck, J. A. 1978. Northern Iroquoian Prehistory. In *Handbook of North American Indians,* vol. 15, *Northeast,* edited by B. G. Trigger, pp. 322–333. Smithsonian Institution, Washington, DC.

CHAPTER 23

WHAT WILL BE HAS ALWAYS BEEN: THE PAST AND PRESENT OF NORTHERN IROQUOIANS

RONALD F. WILLIAMSON

The region occupied by Northern Iroquoians constitutes most of what is now known as southern Ontario, southwestern Quebec, New York State, and northern Pennsylvania (Figure 23.1). The Iroquoian languages of the people who inhabited this area are distantly related to Cherokee, spoken in the southern Appalachians; and to Tuscarora, spoken near the mid-Atlantic coast. The term *Iroquoian* therefore should not be confused with "Iroquois," an Algonquian word used by Europeans to refer to the Five Nations Confederacy of New York State.

The Huron (Wendat) were the northernmost of the Iroquoians, inhabiting historically the land between Georgian Bay on Lake Huron and Lake Simcoe. The relatively small Tionontaté (Petun) nation lived immediately to the southwest and resembled the Wendat in most linguistic and cultural respects. Their combined population prior to the onset of European-introduced epidemics in the 1630s has been estimated at approximately 30,000 (Warrick 2008:146).

The tribes of the Neutral Confederacy (called Attiwandaron by the Wendat) lived farther to the south between the lower Grand River Valley and the Niagara River. Despite their European name, given by the French to signify the peace between the Attiwandaron and the Wendat and the Attiwandaron's refusal to participate in the long-standing feud between the Wendat and the Iroquois, they were certainly engaged in blood feuds with Algonquians to the west. In 1641, the

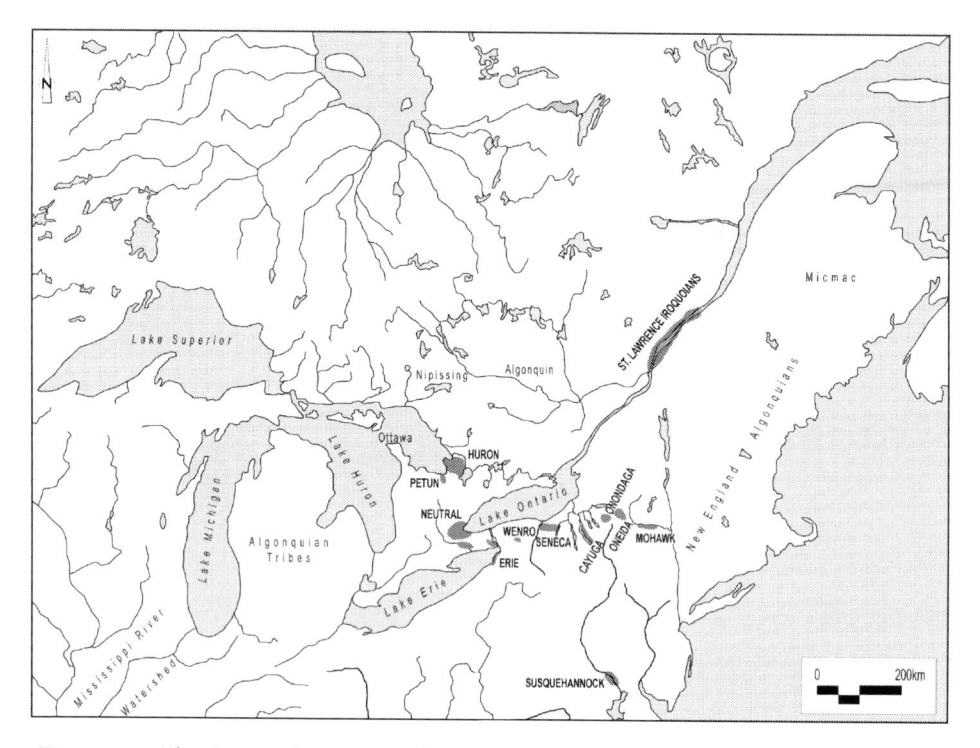

Figure 23.1 The Great Lakes region, showing locations of aboriginal nations mentioned in text.

Jesuits estimated the Attiwandaron population at approximately 12,000 people, although prior to the epidemics their population was significantly higher (Trigger 1985:235).

The Erie were a group relatively unknown to early European visitors, inhabiting the area of the southeastern end of Lake Erie. Even less is known about the Wenro (Oneronon), also a small group who lived farther east. They are reported to have been allies of the Attiwandaron, and at least some of them appear to have joined with the Wendat in 1639.

During the early 17th century, the five tribes of the Iroquois Confederacy lived in tribal clusters across upper New York state. These tribes were culturally distinctive because of their long, separate developments as reflected in differences in language and material culture as well as clan organization, kinship terms, and mortuary patterns. It is likely that the Iroquois were more populous than the Wendat prior to the epidemics (Trigger 1985:236). The Susquehannock lived to the south of the Iroquois, on the lower Susquehanna River. Their linguistic relationship to the other Northern Iroquoian languages is unclear.

There were also Iroquoian-speaking communities living in the St. Lawrence Valley west of Quebec City in the 16th century. Encountered by Jacques Cartier in his 1534 and 1535 visits to eastern Canada, they had moved elsewhere by the time of Samuel de Champlain's visit of 1603. Although their absence 70 years later was at one time considered one of the most compelling mysteries of eastern Canadian history, relocations of that nature were a long-standing option for Iroquoian decision makers when faced with newly emerging social and political challenges.

General characteristics defining the cultural pattern of Northern Iroquoians included primary reliance on horticulture for subsistence; a similar division of labor, whereby men engaged in land clearing, hunting, fishing, building houses, trading, and defending the community while women cared for their young children, manufactured many items such as bone tools and ceramic vessels, and planted, tended, and harvested the crops; habitation in often-fortified villages containing bark-covered longhouses shared usually by matrilineally related extended families; matrilineally defined membership in clans that extended beyond each village to other communities, thereby integrating villages within tribes and confederacies; separate organizations for civil and military functions; a set of common religious beliefs and practices, and similar creation myths, deities, and celebrations; a set of shared social values and attitudes, expressed in careful attention to internal and external social relations; and frequently noted participation in ritualized warfare, trophy taking, and prisoner sacrifice (Trigger 1976:91–104).

There is also a rich 17th-century ethnohistoric record of the lives of Northern Iroquoians. The three principal sources are the works of Samuel de Champlain, an experienced soldier and explorer who recorded his observations of a winter spent with the Wendat in 1615–16 (Biggar 1922–1936); the account of Gabriel Sagard, a Recollet friar who spent the winter of 1623–24 with the Wendat (Wrong 1939); and the annual accounts of the Jesuit priests who lived among the Wendat from 1634 until 1650 and among the Iroquois from 1654 to 1667 (Thwaites 1896–1901).

Perhaps one of the most interesting historical circumstances of northern Iroquoians is the appearance by historic times of an "island" of Iroquoian speakers in the middle of a "sea" of Algonquian speakers. Their origins in the lower Great Lakes region, therefore, have always been of interest to anthropologists but are also of critical concern for northern Iroquoian descendant communities in regard to still contested lands and rights in eastern Canada and the northeastern United States. The ability of anthropologists to recognize ethnicity in the archaeological record and to outline their histories and that of their neighbors is now evaluated regularly in the courts.

Origins

Early anthropological accounts of Iroquoian origins focused on migration (Parker 1916; Griffin 1944) precluding study of significant economic and sociopolitical evolution in Iroquoian society. Later researchers supported an *in situ* theory of Iroquoian cultural development and described the transition from the previous hunting and gathering pattern to the Iroquoian horticultural one as rapid and essentially complete by the end of the first millennium AD (Ritchie 1944; MacNeish

1952). William Ritchie (1969) and J. V. Wright (1966) traced Iroquoian cultural development from ancestral hunter-gatherers through several phases into fully formed Iroquois culture, recognizing two discrete centers for Iroquoian development, one in upper New York state and the other in Ontario.

More recently, Dean Snow (1995, 1996) reintroduced a migrationist hypothesis suggesting that Iroquoians entered the lower Great Lakes region in the sixth century, bringing with them maize agriculture, palisaded settlements with longhouses, matrilineal descent, matrilocal residence patterns, and technologically more sophisticated ceramic vessel manufacturing traditions. Snow's hypothesis has been rejected by many Great Lakes archaeologists (e.g., Crawford and Smith 1996; Engelbrecht 2003; Ferris 1999; Hart 2001;Warrick 2000, 2008); instead, there is agreement that the full expression of Iroquoian culture is not recognizable archaeologically until the turn of the 14th century (e.g., Engelbrecht 2003; Kapches 1995; Warrick 2000, 2008).

It is also clear that maize was introduced centuries before Snow's hypothesized migration of Iroquoian speakers in the sixth century. In New York State, John Hart and his colleagues have employed microscopic phytolith analysis and AMS dating of carbonized food remains to demonstrate that maize was being cooked in central New York by around 2,000 years ago (Hart et al. 2003). Cultigens therefore appeared in the lower Great Lakes well before the Iroquoian cultural pattern crystallized, and perhaps even prior to introduction of a proto-Iroquoian language.

Yet there is linguistic evidence for the migration of an Iroquoian-speaking population into the lower Great Lakes region. Stuart Fiedel (1999), for example, has argued that a Proto-Algonquian language emerged in the Great Lakes region by 1200 BC, after which there was an expansion and divergence of Proto-Algonquian languages during the period between 500 BC and AD 900. In that the Iroquoian language family is "totally unlike" Algonquian languages in vocabulary, phonology, and grammar, Fiedel suggested that the two language families were relatively recent neighbors in the region, the Iroquoian presence having resulted from a more recent migration, ca. AD 500–1000. He suggested the divergence of the Iroquoian languages occurred during this period as well.

This general outline for the antiquity of Algonquian populations in the region has been underscored by recent genetic research in which mtDNA was studied from the skeletal remains of a number of northeastern pre-Contact sites in comparison with several contemporary, potentially descendant Native American populations including Algonquian and Iroquoian-speaking groups (Shook and Smith 2008). The study demonstrated there was genetic homogeneity across language barriers as well as close similarity between ancient populations in the Mississippian drainage and southern Ontario. This suggests sufficient gene flow among geographically distant populations to maintain regional continuities in populations for at least 3,000 years. They suggest that populations were expanding between 2,000 and 4,000 years ago, perhaps associated with expansion of Proto-Algonquian languages or introduction of maize horticulture into the region. This seems to have involved introduction of new genes without replacing existing populations.

It is likely, therefore, that a small number of Iroquoian speakers introduced the language to resident Algonquian-speaking Great Lakes populations, after which the language, perhaps in association with maize subsistence technology, gradually gained widespread acceptance. Engelbrecht (2003:112–114) argues for an "ethnogenetic" perspective on Iroquoian origins because it can accommodate population movements, acculturation, diffusion of ideas, and continuity, allowing a more realistic and complex view of Iroquoian development than simplistic arguments set in a migrationist or diffusionist framework. Peter Ramsden (2006) has even suggested that eastern Iroquoians, consisting of St Lawrence Iroquois, Mohawk, Onondaga, and those Wendats who derive from the eastern part of their territory, have *in situ* origins that differ from the remaining western Iroquoian groups who were influenced by more recent arrivals, perhaps from the Mississippian empire. Ramsden argues the western groups brought the Iroquoian language to their eastern neighbors.

Regardless of the mechanisms by which the Iroquoian language came to the region, introduction of maize ultimately played the leading role in initiating the transition to food production and reducing traditional reliance on naturally occurring resources. Also, possible links with Mississippian populations to the south can be found in the agricultural complex of Iroquoians, especially in the role of bloodshed in promoting agricultural fertility, specifically similarities to the ritual systems of Mesoamerica and the Mississippian valley (i.e., the Arrow Sacrifice ceremony, dog sacrifice, platform torture and sacrifice of victims to the sun, decapitation, and scalping of prisoners; Engelbrecht 2003:37–46; Hall, this volume; Trigger 1976:73–75).

Coalescence and the Path to Confederacies

Maize appears to have become an important dietary component by the end of the first millennium AD, as is evident in studies of stable isotope chemistry in bone apatite and collagen for pre-Contact southern Ontario populations (Harrison and Katzenberg 2003:241). Yet it is also clear that economic security continued to be sought through diversity for the next few centuries (see also Chilton, this volume). Early Iroquoian semisedentary base settlements or "villages" tended to be small, palisaded compounds with longhouses occupied by either nuclear or, with increasing frequency, extended families. Around these sites, camps and hamlets were occupied both seasonally and annually, serving as places from which to collect wild plants or hunt game. There is no evidence that the appearance of early villages marked the end of the transition to matrilocal residence, matrilineality, and formal village organization. On the contrary, residence and descent patterns may have remained largely unchanged from previous hunter-gatherer times (Hart 2001; Williamson 1990:312–313).

Toward the end of the 13th century, small communities amalgamated to form larger villages of approximately 1.5 hectares (three acres) in extent, with twice the population of the earlier base settlements. With this development came widespread similarities in pottery and smoking pipe styles that point to an increasing level of intercommunity communication and integration. There were also shifts in economic strategies, although the degree and nature of such change varied among individual Iroquoian communities. The hamlets and camps of the previous centuries were to a large degree replaced by agricultural cabin sites, which were situated within the vast agricultural fields that surrounded the major villages. These changes in settlement-subsistence patterns probably related to the need to produce more maize for more people in one place. The more elaborate sociopolitical systems inferred from the archaeological record and the building infrastructure that resulted are for the first time recognizably "Iroquoian," conforming to early European descriptions of their life.

This is also when maize consumption peaked, at least in some localities. Detailed isotope analysis of human remains from the ca. AD 1300 ancestral Wendat Moatfield ossuary, located approximately five kilometers north of Lake Ontario in the city of Toronto, indicates that for at least one generation maize comprised 70 percent of the diet. Such intensified cultivation may have been a necessary, temporary response to increased population concentration within a newly amalgamated settlement (van der Merwe et al. 2003). Analysis of remains from later-14th- and 15th-century sites suggest that maize typically made up approximately half the diet of Iroquoians (Schwarcz et al. 1985).

Population growth during the subsequent 14th century occurred at an extraordinary rate (Warrick 2008:181), which necessitated complex political means for regulating village affairs and ceremonial mechanisms for linking separate communities. One such mechanism, ossuary burial, occurred mainly among the Wendat and represents features in which the remains of numerous individuals, who were formerly interred within a village, were disinterred at the time of village relocation and redeposited into one or two mass graves and their remains commingled. Ossuary burial likely began as a family-oriented rite, but by the late 13th century it had become a communitywide event, and within a century it likely involved participation of more than one community and reinterment of 500 or more individuals at a time (Williamson and Steiss 2003; Figure 23.2).

Another integrative mechanism that appears in 14th-through-mid-15th-century Wendat and Attiwandaron villages is the use of semisubterranean sweat lodges. These are a communal feature likely used for ritual, curative, or sociopolitical purposes (MacDonald 1988, 1992). The frequency with which these structures occur within longhouses on Ontario Iroquoian settlements after ca. AD 1300 suggests that their role may have been a fundamental aspect of daily life in an Iroquoian household, especially if they functioned as a socially unifying institution within the emergent tribal systems of the 14th and early-15th centuries (MacDonald and Williamson 2001:66–72). Too few sites that date to between AD 1300 and 1450 have been excavated in sufficient detail to comment on their occurrence at New York Iroquois sites, but they have been documented on sites in the upper Susquehanna Valley of northeastern Pennsylvania.

Figure 23.2 An 18th-century depiction of the Feast of the Dead at the Huron ossuary of Ossossané, witnessed by the Jesuit priest Father Jean de Brébeuf in the year 1636.

Prior to the mid-15th century, the autonomous, multilineage village likely represented the maximal political unit, although many neighboring villages may have participated in loosely formed social and political networks (Engelbrecht 2003:113). It is at the level of such networks, between regional clusters of villages, that the processes that ultimately led to emergence of larger communities and nations operated. Indeed, by the end of the century, amalgamation of a number of these neighboring villages (see, e.g., Finlayson 1985) resulted in very large, well-planned and heavily fortified communities. Although it has traditionally been assumed that the endemic conflict characterizing Late Iroquoian society played out over long distances, as between the geographically disparate Wendat and Iroquois, feuding was also taking place, in some regions, between neighboring communities or tribal systems (Engelbrecht 2003:180–181; Robertson and Williamson 1998:148). Given the likelihood that both alliance formation and conflict between individual communities was highly dynamic, it may be expected that both occurred on varying scales.

This coalescence of multiple households and communities resulted in domestic settings considerably more complex than those during the preceding two generations and almost certainly involved drastic transformations in social relationships and use of domestic spaces. These new social environments would have required considerable negotiation to access resources and public spaces, and it is likely that identities based on clan membership became as significant as those based on lineages. Structuring social relations through the clan system rather than strictly on lines of descent likely aided social integration within coalescent communities and dampened tensions between emerging tribal nations across the wider region (Birch 2008).

These new and larger communities also required significant civic planning. The ancestral Wendat early-16th-century Mantle site, for example, situated northeast of Toronto, encompassed an area of more than 4.2 hectares (nine acres; Figure 23.3). The settlement was enclosed by a three-row palisade that contracted on at least two occasions, although the first contraction does not seem to have involved substantial

Figure 23.3 Mantle site plan: one of the largest and the most complex ancestral Huron site yet to be excavated, on the north shore of Lake Ontario.

population realignment. The site was found to contain more than 90 longhouses, of which approximately 50 seem to have been occupied at one time. The fact that the site may have been occupied initially by approximately 1,500 people belies the considerable complexity with which the Wendat site planners would have been confronted. The community required more than 60,000 even-aged saplings to construct houses and palisade walls, and the agricultural field system would have been hundreds, if not thousands, of hectares in extent. Such field clearance and construction programs would have necessitated months or years of advance planning. During most of the occupation of the site, it would appear that refuse was directed out of the interior of the village into a borrow trench situated on the outside of the palisade—thereby representing one of the first organic and inorganic waste stream management systems known in the northeast.

As is typical of many of the sites of this period, the ceramic assemblage of Mantle includes vessels that are generally considered to be "exotic," including those reminiscent of St. Lawrence Iroquoian, New York Iroquois, or Attiwandaron types. Certain vessels with modeled human faces under their castellations have been previously found only on Oneida and Seneca sites (Figure 23.4). Anthony Wonderley (2002) relates such figures to cornhusk people, "mythical humanlike horticulturalists associated with food crops," and considers them a visual form of thanks for the three sisters: corn, beans, and squash. Many of the "exotic" vessels may have been imported from other communities, but some will have been manufactured locally. Whatever the form of interaction, their presence attests to the cosmopolitan contacts, relationships, or origins of the people who occupied these settlements.

Figure 23.4 Ceramic vessel effigy thought to be a mythical cornhusk person associated with horticultural crops.

Seventeenth-Century Realignment

The final shift and consolidation of communities into the confederacies subsequently encountered by the European explorers and missionaries occurred in the late 16th and early 17th century. In the same way that contacts between communities led to formation of individual nations, contacts between nations (presumably to conclude political alliances) led to confederacies.

Within 20 to 30 years, however, direct contact with Europeans had drastic consequences. Extensive decline in population in excess of 50 percent occurred among all northern Iroquoian groups, due to European-introduced diseases (Warrick 2008). New technologies and economic strategies certainly altered Iroquoian lifestyles, but European colonial expansionist agendas and the resultant intensified pan-regional conflicts, along with religious factionalism, created heightened social and political tensions, which resulted in substantial realignment involving all of the nations living in the Great Lakes region. Intertribal warfare between the Wendat-Tionontaté and Attiwandaron and the Five Nations Iroquois during the 17th century, for example, resulted in dispersal of the three Ontario Iroquoian confederacies and many of their Algonquian-speaking allies of the southern Canadian Shield by circa 1650. Although many of the communities that made up these nations migrated to Quebec, Michigan, Ohio (and ultimately Kansas and Oklahoma), many others were adopted into the New York Iroquois populations.

The Wendat-Tionontaté and Iroquois thereafter survived four centuries of colonial oppression and attempts at assimilation. The enduring arts, crafts, traditions, and ceremonies of all these people stress their future, not their past, and archaeological research continues to play an important role in continuing efforts to assert their rights and interests in their former homelands.

Acknowledgments

I would like to thank William Engelbrecht and Andrew Stewart for their comments on an initial draft of this paper.

References

Biggar, H. P. (editor). 1922–1936. *The Works of Samuel de Champlain*. 6 vols. Champlain Society, Toronto.

Birch, J. 2008. Rethinking the Archaeological Application of Iroquoian Kinship. *Canadian Journal of Archaeology* 32:194–213.

Crawford, G., and D. Smith. 1996. Migration in Prehistory: Princess Point and the Northern Iroquoian Case. *American Antiquity* 61(4):782-790.
Engelbrecht, W. 2003. *Iroquoia: The Development of a Native World.* Syracuse University Press, Syracuse, NY.
Ferris, N. 1999. Telling Tales: Interpretive Trends in Southern Ontario Late Woodland Archaeology. *Ontario Archaeology* 68:1-62.
Fiedel, S. J. 1999. Algonquians and Iroquoians: Taxonomy, Chronology and Archaeological Implications. In *Taming the Taxonomy: Toward a New Understanding of Great Lakes Archaeology*, edited by R. F. Williamson and C. M. Watts, pp. 193-204. Eastend Books, Toronto.
Finlayson, W. 1985. *The 1975 and 1978 Rescue Excavations at the Draper Site: Introduction and Settlement Pattern.* Archaeological Survey of Canada, Mercury Series Paper 130. National Museum of Man, Ottawa.
Griffin, J. B. 1944. The Iroquois in American Prehistory. *Papers of the Michigan Academy of Science, Arts and Letters* 29:357-374.
Harrison, R. G., and M. A. Katzenberg. 2003. Paleodiet Studies Using Stable Carbon Isotopes from Bone Apatite and Collagen: Examples from Southern Ontario and San Nicolas Island, California. *Journal of Anthropological Archaeology* 22:227-244.
Hart, J. 2001. Maize, Matrilocality, Migration, and Northern Iroquoian Evolution. *Journal of Archaeological Method and Theory* 8(2):151-181.
——, R. Thompson, and H. J. Brumbach. 2003. Phytolith Evidence for Early Maize (Zea Mays) in the Northern Fingers Lake Region of New York. *American Antiquity* 68:619-640.
Kapches, M. 1995. Chaos Theory and Social Movements: A Theoretical View of the Formation of the Northern Iroquoian Longhouse Cultural Pattern. In *Origins of the People of the Longhouse: Proceedings of the 21st Annual Symposium of the Ontario Archaeological Society Inc.*, edited by A. Beckerman and G. Warrick. Ontario Archaeological Society, Toronto.
MacDonald, R. 1988. Ontario Iroquoian Sweat Lodges. *Ontario Archaeology* 47:17-26.
——. 1992. Ontario Iroquoian Semi-subterranean Sweat Lodges. In *Ancient Images, Ancient Thought: The Archaeology of Ideology: Proceedings of the 23rd Annual Chacmool Conference*, edited by A. S. Goldsmith, S. Garvie, D. Selin, and J. Smith, pp. 323-330. University of Calgary, Calgary.
——, and R. F. Williamson. 2001. Sweat Lodges and Solidarity: The Archaeology of the Hubbert Site. *Ontario Archaeology* 71:29-78.
MacNeish, R. S. 1952. *Ontario Iroquois Pottery Types.* National Museum of Canada Bulletin 124. Department of Resources and Development, Ottawa.
Parker, A. 1916. The Origins of the Iroquois as Suggested by Their Archaeology. *American Anthropologist, n.s.* 18:479-507.
Ramsden, P. 2006. But Once the Twain Did Meet: A Speculation About Iroquoian Origins. BAR International Series 1507, *From the Arctic to Avalon: Papers in Honour of Jim Tuck*, pp. 27-32. edited by L. Rankin and P. Ramsden. John and Erica Hedges, Oxford.
Ritchie, W. 1944. *Iroquoian Occupations of New York State.* Rochester Museum Memoir 1. Rochester Museum of Arts and Sciences, Rochester, NY.
——. 1969. *The Archaeology of New York State.* Natural History Press, New York.
Robertson, D., and R. F. Williamson. 1998. The Archaeology of the Parsons Site: Summary and Conclusions. In Ontario Archaeology, Special Volume 65/66, *The Archaeology of the Parsons Site: A Fifty Year Perspective*, edited by R. F. Williamson and D. A. Robertson, pp. 146-150. Ontario Archaeological Society, Toronto.

Schwarcz, H., F. J. Melbye, M. A. Katzenberg, and M. Knyf. 1985. Stable Isotopes in Human Skeletons of Southern Ontario: Reconstructing Paleodiet. *Journal of Archaeological Science* 12:187–206.

Shook, B. A., and D. G. Smith. 2008. Using Ancient mtDNA to Reconstruct the Population History of Northeastern North America. *American Journal of Physical Anthropology* 137:14–29.

Snow, D. 1995. Migration in Prehistory: The Northern Iroquoian Case. *American Antiquity* 60:59–79.

———. 1996. More on Migration in Prehistory: Accommodating the New Evidence in the Northern Iroquoian Case. *American Antiquity* 61:791–796.

Thwaites, R. G. 1896–1901. *The Jesuit Relations and Allied Documents*. 73 vols. Burrows Brothers, Cleveland.

Trigger, B. G. 1976. *Children of Aataentsic: A History of Huron People to 1660*. 2 vols. McGill-Queens University Press, Montreal.

———. 1985. *Natives and Newcomers: Canada's "Heroic Age" Reconsidered*. McGill-Queens University Press, Montreal.

van der Merwe, N., R. F. Williamson, S. Pfeiffer, S. C. Thomas, and K. Oakberg Allegretto. 2003. The Moatfield Ossuary: Isotopic Dietary Analysis of an Iroquoian Community, Using Dental Tissue. *Journal of Anthropological Archaeology* 22:245–261.

Warrick, G. 2000. Precontact Iroquoian Occupation of Southern Ontario. *Journal of World Prehistory* 14(4):415–466.

———. 2008. *A Population History of the Huron-Petun, AD 500–1650*. Cambridge University Press, Cambridge, UK.

Williamson, R. F. 1990. The Early Iroquoian Period of Southern Ontario. In Occasional Publication of the London Chapter, Ontario Archaeological Society 5, *The Archaeology of Southern Ontario to AD 1650*, edited by C. Ellis and N. Ferris. pp. 291–320. Ontario Archaeological Society, London.

———, and D. A. Steiss. 2003. A History of Iroquoian Multiple Burial Practice. In Archaeological Survey of Canada, Mercury Series Paper 163, *Bones of the Ancestors: The Archaeology and Osteobiography of the Moatfield Ossuary*, edited by Ronald F. Williamson and Susan Pfeiffer, pp. 89–132. Canadian Museum of Civilization, Hull, Quebec.

Wonderley, A. 2002. Oneida Ceramic Effigies: A Question of Meaning. *Northeast Anthropology* 63:23–48.

Wright, J. V. 1966. *The Ontario Iroquois Tradition*. National Museum of Canada Bulletin 210. National Museums of Canada, Ottawa.

Wrong, G. M. (editor). 1939. *The Long Journey to the Country of the Hurons*. Champlain Society, Toronto.

CHAPTER 24

REGIONAL RITUAL ORGANIZATION IN THE NORTHERN GREAT LAKES, AD 1200–1600

MEGHAN C. L. HOWEY

The North American continent was teeming with diverse populations long before Europeans arrived. These populations represent the full spectrum of human complexity, people who maintained widespread interactions contributing to that social, ideological, political, and economic complexity. The Great Lakes region was a vital part of this extensive interaction sphere. It was a place where diverse Algonquian and Haudenosaunee (Iroquoian) communities had forged interdependent connections over millennia by linking people and goods in networks of waterways and pathways.

The concept of the "common pot" or resource sharing was deeply rooted in the early traditions of the Northeast and Great Lakes; it was epitomized by these intimate connections that ensured sustainability and interdependency, both vital to social stability and physical health (Brooks 2008:5). Brooks (3–4) explains this deeply rooted concept as follows:

> The common pot is that which feeds and nourishes. It is the wigwam that feeds the family, the village that feeds the community, the networks that sustain the village. Women are the creators of these vessels; all people come from them, and with their hands and minds they transform the bodies of their animal and plant relatives into nourishment for their families. The pot is made from the flesh of birch trees or the clay of the earth. It can carry or hold; it can be carried or reconstructed; it can withstand fire and water, and, in fact, it uses these elements to transform that which it contains. The pot is Sky Woman's body, the network of relations that must nourish and reproduce itself.

Inherent in the concept of the common pot is sharing. Whatever "was given from the larger network of inhabitants had to be shared with the human community" (Brooks 2008:5). After contact, Europeans were incorporated into the common pot, whether they knew it or not, and we know from the centuries following contact that they had brought with them ideas, behaviors, and materials that eventually broke the pot.

This essay is not, however, concerned with these post-Contact events but instead focuses on the less studied dynamics of the common pot in the centuries immediately preceding European arrival. To understand the pre-Contact populations, we have to turn to the material remains that form the archaeological record. Through detailed study of these nonperishable items, we gain insight into the lives of the people who produced them and come to better understand exactly what it was that European contact disrupted, the extent and the impact of this contact, and the diversity and complexity that survived the process of culture contact and persist in living tribal communities today.

This essay explores what archaeologists call the "late Late Woodland/Late Prehistoric period," the era from AD 1200 to1600, in the Northern Great Lakes. The essay explores the dynamic choices Anishinaabeg communities made in that era, during the last 400 years before contact was made with Europeans. The Algonquian speakers in the Northern Great Lakes referred to themselves collectively as Anishinaabeg. Ojibway Historian William Warren offers the definition of this term as "Spontaneous People," spontaneous meaning indigenous, natural, always human beings (Warren 1984 [1885]:56). Although there are differing interpretations of specific developments among the Anishinaabeg during this era in the Northern Great Lakes, it is widely agreed that a dramatic shift occurred after AD 1000–1100 that brought an end to a long-established socioeconomic system featuring high mobility, fluid social boundaries, and ready procurement of items across resource zones. New evidence indicates tribal communities crafted a regional network based on multiple scales of interaction that were sanctified and maintained by ritual practices at ceremonial centers to respond to the major changes of this time. As we explore this specific regional system, it is important to keep in mind that the indigenous peoples of the Great Lakes were always part of something even larger: that common pot, Sky Woman's body, a complex and widespread network of relations across vast amounts of Native North America.

The Northern Great Lakes Environmental and Archaeological Setting

Native Americans living in the Northern Great Lakes developed their socioeconomic strategies and cultural practices within the context of the region's beautiful yet often harsh and unpredictable environmental setting (Figure 24.1). The region is distinguished by its complex glaciated landscape, which was sculpted most notably by the last continental ice sheet, the Wisconsinan Glaciation. This last ice advance of the Pleistocene Epoch began in Canada 85,000 years ago and reached as far south as the Ohio River. Around 20,000 years ago, the glacier began to retreat, and this ice age ended around 10,000 years ago with the beginning of the Holocene. The ice retreated in stages, leaving a variety of glacial landforms in its wake, including terminal moraines, recessional moraines, drumlins, eskers, kames, and glacial outwash plains. Michigan might be almost flat without these hilly landforms.

The Initial Populations

The first humans to inhabit the Great Lakes arrived at the end of the Pleistocene between 12,000 and 10,000 years ago (see Anderson, this volume). As the last glacial advance retreated and the Holocene began, large game such as mastodons went extinct and others, such as caribou, elk, and moose, retreated north of Michigan. So too began the emergence of the modern landscape, which included formation of the notable landmarks and features of the Great Lakes region. In fact, the five Great Lakes were formed by the pooling of glacial meltwater at the rim of receding glaciers.

The Great Lakes have been at their current levels for about 4,000 years. Three of the lakes surround the Lower Peninsula of Michigan—Lake Erie, Lake Huron, and Lake Michigan. Lake Michigan, Lake Huron, and Lake Superior form the Upper Peninsula of Michigan (Figure 24.1). Surrounded by Great Lakes, the state of Michigan has 3,200 miles of coastline, more than any other state in the United States except Alaska (Keen 1993:7).

In addition to these major lakes, numerous inland lakes formed in the glacial landscape, and today there are 11,037 inland lakes spread throughout Michigan (Fitting 1970; Figure 24.1). Swamps and marshes emerged as vegetation colonized shallow depressions left by the retreating glacier. Over time, rivers began to crosscut the glacially formed landscape, depositing fluvial sediments in some places and eroding glacial deposits in others.

The environmental changes at the end of the glacial period and the emergence of the modern environment meant the inhabitants of the Great Lakes region, no longer able to rely on large game, had to shift to subsistence practices that took advantage of a new set of opportunities in the emerging modern environment. Early communities across the region formed around a hunting and gathering economy, which involved diverse strategies to procure resources and maximize returns from seasonally available foods. This broad-spectrum foraging system involved exploitation of a wider variety of foods, including wild game, fish, nuts, berries, aquatic tubers, and other resources (Lovis et al. 2005; Lovis 1985). The start of the Holocene and this reliance on seasonal foods mark the period archaeologists call the Archaic (ca. 8000–800 BC), which is traditionally divided into Early (ca. 8000–6000 BC), Middle (ca. 6000–3000 BC), and Late (ca. 3000–800 BC) phases.

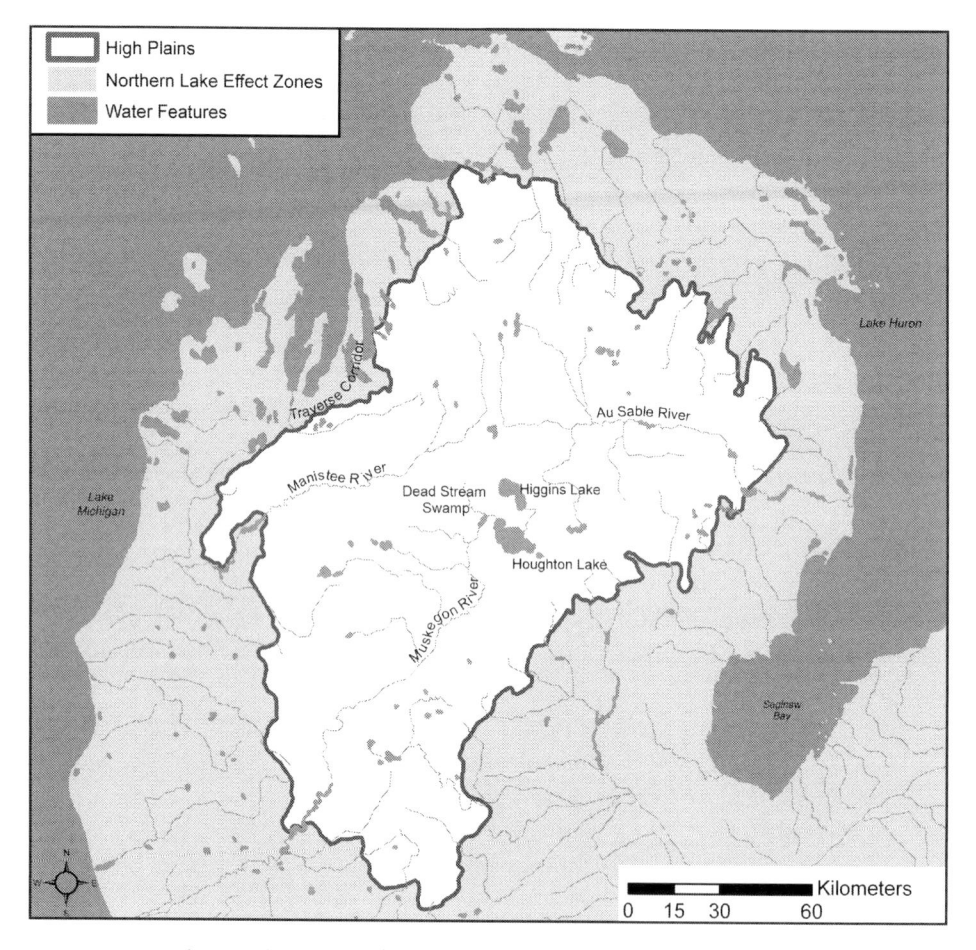

Figure 24.1 The Northern Great Lakes Region, featuring the Great Lakes "lake-effect" resource zones and the inland resource zones.

This widespread social and economic system was fully developed throughout Michigan by the Late Archaic. Its success depended on groups (1) freely moving between resource zones, (2) having widespread kin networks, (3) developing extensive social connections, (4) conducting visits over great distances, and (5) engaging in a generally high level of cooperation and intergroup tolerance. This system was so successful that people maintained it in the Northern Great Lakes for millennia, and it changed notably only after ca. AD 1000–1100.

Woodland Traditions

The first use of ceramics in the Great Lakes region marks the beginning of the Early Woodland period from ca. 800 BC to AD 1. It created small, but significant, changes in subsistence practices. Nuts and starchy seeds were increasingly used as people successfully worked out ways to process them, and to extract oil by simmering them in a pot over a fire (Ozker 1982:77). In general, however, the Early Woodland period just saw additional subsistence strategies augmenting the repertoire of Archaic strategies.

During the Middle Woodland (ca. AD 1–400 or 500), significant cultural developments occurred throughout the Midwest. These developments, known as the Hopewellian Complex, influenced communities in southern Michigan. In southwestern Michigan, at ca. 10 BC, there was a sudden, abrupt, and seemingly complete adoption of Hopewellian mortuary, ceremonial, and technological traits, including engaging in regional trade, building large burial mounds, and adopting elaborate Hopewellian mortuary practices, ceramic styles, and lithic technology (Kingsley 1999:151). Meanwhile, in the Saginaw Valley communities adopted several (but not all) Hopewellian traits. In contrast, Hopewellian traditions were never adopted in Northern Michigan. Groups here continued to practice the socioeconomic strategies they had followed in the Late Archaic (O'Shea 2003).

The transition from the Middle Woodland to the Late Woodland period is not well understood, but we do know early Late Woodland systems (ca. AD 500–1000) developed locally in both Southern and Northern Michigan (Fitting 1970). Ceramic stylistic analysis has demonstrated that during the early Late Woodland social boundaries were relatively permeable, group membership was flexible, and territories were weakly defined (Brashler 1981). Regional cultivation of maize began around AD 500–600, but it did not become a significant crop until around AD 1000 or 1100. The diffuse socioeconomic strategy so effective since the Late Archaic, including generalized reliance on an array of wild foods from many resource zones, remained effective in the early Late Woodland.

Specialized Economies, Exclusive Territories, and Regional Ritual Gatherings in the Northern Great Lakes, AD 1200–1600

This overview of earlier periods shows that communities throughout Northern Michigan had been practicing a broad-spectrum, generalized strategy of foraging in which groups could move easily between resource zones on the shorelines of the Great Lakes and on inland lakes and rivers for millennia. A dramatic shift after AD 1000–1100 transformed the region from this long-established system to a more bounded territorial system. The Northern Great Lakes was hardly the only area seeing changes, and at this moment the broader Midcontinent was marked by dramatic transformations of extant social orders, one of the most notable being the rise of Cahokia in the Mississippi Valley (Alt, this volume). The specific shifts in the Northern Great Lakes mark the start of the period commonly referred to by archaeologists as the late Late Woodland/Late Prehistoric period (AD 1200–1600; referred to hereafter as Late Precontact) and it included an increase in community size, emergence of strong territorial systems with less permeable boundaries, formalization of decision making, and development of stronger group identity (Cleland 1982, 1992; Holman and Lovis 2008; O'Shea and Milner 2002).

Social boundaries and stronger group identities were signaled through distinct ceramic styles in coastal areas of the Great Lakes. These Late Precontact styles included Juntunen wares in northeastern Michigan; Traverse wares in northwestern Michigan; Younge wares in southeastern Michigan; Oneota ceramics in southwestern Michigan, Indiana, and areas to the west; Wisconsin Lake Phase pottery northwest of Lake Michigan; and Iroquois ceramic styles east of Lake Huron (Milner 1998:105–6).

Evidence indicates these significant developments of Late Precontact (AD 1200–1600) were largely related to resource transformations. After ca. AD 1200, communities living along Lake Michigan and Lake Huron developed more specialized subsistence economies that involved a marked increase in maize horticulture as well as targeted exploitation of fall-spawning Great Lakes fish species.

In terms of fishing, emergence of the Inland Shore Fishery was critical to regional development in the northern Great Lakes during this period. This fishing strategy was based on use of the gill net in deep water to capture fall-spawning anadromous fish, particularly whitefish and lake trout, along the shores of the northern Great Lakes (Cleland 1982).

The other notable specialized resource transformation was dispersal of maize agriculture along the coasts of the Great Lakes (Howey and O'Shea 2006; O'Shea and Milner 2002; O'Shea 2003). "Lake effect" is a term used around the Great Lakes area to describe the environmental influence these large lakes have on growing season and duration. As the spring growing season begins, the lakes' cooling effect protects plants until the spring frost season is over. The lakes store daytime heat as the growing season continues. The effect of the warm water lessens the variation between day and night temperatures, lengthening the growing season as much as four weeks along the shorelines compared to inland areas (Figure 24.1). As summer draws to an end, the stored warmth of the lake waters delays frost that might damage fall crops. In summary, this lake effect produced a growing season that was longer in areas adjacent to the Great Lakes than areas inland (Figure 24.1); thus with enough frost-free days, people living adjacent to the Great Lakes had an opportunity to plant and harvest maize, while people living well inland had to rely on those shoreline populations if they wanted any maize.

Although maize (*Zea mays*) began to be cultivated in a limited manner ca. AD 500–600 (Crawford et al. 1997:116), it was after AD 1000–1100 that maize was widely adopted by established forager communities along the shorelines and coasts of the Great Lakes (see also Chilton, Pearsall, this volume). Maize quickly came to play a dominant role in the diet of many coastal Native American communities in the Great Lakes, and by ca. AD 1350 evidence suggests some communities even consumed fewer wild animals because they were relying more and more on maize (Katzenberg et al. 1995:335).

Both of these specialized economic activities—maize cultivation and fall fishing—benefited from an increasing focus on Great Lakes shoreline settlements. Increasing sedentism improved prospects for successful maize horticulture in the highly variable climate of the region (O'Shea 2003) and likewise allowed groups to secure access to key fall-spawning fishing locations (Holman and Lovis 2008).

This decrease in mobility resulted in more intensive interactions between local groups and led people to make stronger territorial claims to resource zones. As spatial proximity became increasingly important in the new socioeconomic setting, coastal horticulturalists settled into more permanent villages on the coasts of Lake Michigan and Huron. They also developed corporate social identities, demarcated exclusive territories, and barred others from these socioeconomic advances. The emergence of those distinctive new ceramic styles along the shores of the Great Lakes during the Late Precontact period reflects this process of coastal group identity formation. Inland groups, living outside of the lake-effect coastal farming and fishing zones, were confined to the interior and lacked access to the developments that had emerged in the lakeshore communities (Figure 24.1). Inland communities found their access to coastal resources progressively limited by alliances that excluded them.

With increasing territorialism and heightening social alterity between the coasts and inland, the long-established foraging and freely mobile system was no longer sustainable in the Northern Great Lakes. The milieu of Late Precontact (AD 1200–1600) demanded creative and new social, economic, and ideological strategies from regional communities. The outcome was a multifaceted regional ritual system that operated for hundreds of years before it was interrupted by European Contact ca. AD 1600.

Local Inland Economic Response

At the local level, inland communities developed a more intensive and territorially restricted forager strategy of mobile rounds of seasonal subsistence activities focused on the most productive inland resources to compensate for reduced access to the coastal zone. These inland resource zones included Michigan's largest inland lake system, Houghton and Higgins; the Dead Stream Swamp; and the headwaters of the Muskegon, Manistee, and Au Sable rivers (Figure 24.1). This foraging strategy was complementary to the intensifying horticultural economy along the coasts of the Great Lakes.

Broader Connections Through Gatherings at Ceremonial Monuments

Although most activities occurred at the household level, intracommunity and intersocietal interaction offered critical economic and social advantages in the exclusive setting of Late Precontact. Recent research indicates communities relied on social relationships and ritual events at two types of ceremonial monuments to ensure these levels of interaction. Burial mounds formed intracommunity ceremonial centers, and earthwork enclosures were constructed to serve as intersocietal aggregation centers between coastal and inland groups.

Intracommunity Ceremonial Monuments

When territorialism was becoming pronounced in the region during Late Precontact, inland and coastal groups both began marking their previously unmarked local resource zones with burial mounds. They were built in the Great Lakes since the Middle Woodland (ca. AD 1–400 or 500), but during Late Precontact they were built in a new fashion, with an outline of the mound laid out like a map for construction. Burial mounds were transformed in Late Precontact, built in this new fashion for distinct use as intracommunity ceremonial monument centers. Through these burial mound constructions, Late Precontact groups benefited from numerous accomplishments: (1) they marked critical resource zones as theirs, (2) they protected the resources at these places against outsiders, and (3) they created nexi or aggregation centers where people from throughout the local area could come together for ritual (and associated economic) renewal.

Intersocietal Ritual Gatherings Between Inland and Coastal Groups

While using these intracommunity ceremonial monuments to increase internal cohesion, inland and coastal communities also invested substantial time, energy, labor, and resources into planning, design, construction, and maintenance of multiple monumental ceremonial precincts for large-scale intersocietal ritual events (Figure 24.2). Both inland and coastal groups occupied environmental settings riddled with risk and uncertainty, making interaction and access to outside resources very important. Periodic aggregations of groups from these different settings would have provided important opportunities for resource pooling and exchange, as well as for establishing social contacts with (and gaining access to the resources of) the social systems outside one's own resource zone.

A series of Late Precontact (ca. AD 1200–1600) circular earthwork enclosures runs east-west across north central Michigan (Figure 24.2). Despite the fact that these circular ditch and embankment structures were built on a larger and more elaborate scale than any other sites, limited excavations over the years have not resulted in strong conclusions about their function. Earlier scholars interpreted them as fortifications. However, the extant data from this cluster of enclosures does not support this interpretation, as all have breaches through their embankments, not all (none conclusively) have palisades, and habitation debris is light.

Recent research focused on this cluster of enclosures shows that rather than being fortifications, they were constructed as ritual precincts for intersocietal events, to draw together inland foragers and coastal horticulturalists (Howey and O'Shea 2006). All the circular enclosures are paired, and repetition of these pairs

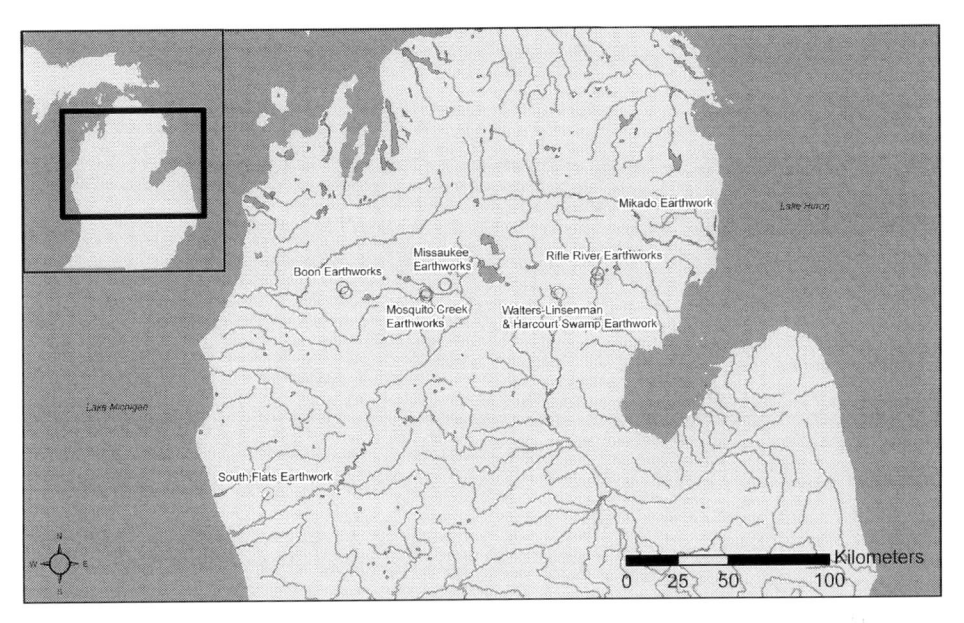

Figure 24.2 The series of Late Precontact (ca. AD 1200–1600) circular earthwork enclosures that anchored the region's ritual system by serving as monumental ceremonial precincts for large-scale intersocietal ritual gatherings between coastal and inland communities.

across the landscape indicates their common origin and the spreading importance of this ritual practice in Late Precontact (Figure 24.2).

We can infer from the known layout of the ritual precinct at one pair in this cluster, the Missaukee Earthworks (Figure 24.2), that these ritual centers involved spatially distinct activity-specific stations outside the earthworks that were repeatedly used, as well as large clusters of cache pits for storage of trade goods or provisioning during ritual events. The open space inside the earthworks was the locus of distinct ritual action.

The material culture found at these enclosures indicates a mixture of inland and coastal presence at all of them. Again, this makes sense because social and economic exchange between these groups would have been mutually beneficial; each lived in an environmental zone with considerable subsistence risk. Embedding this intersocietal interaction in such a highly ritualized setting ensured it would occur regularly and without marked hostility between these increasingly territorially distinct groups.

An "ethnohistoric convergence" bolsters understanding of these enclosures as specifically planned and coherently constructed ritual precincts (detailed in Howey and O'Shea 2006; Figure 24.3). The Midéwiwin (the Grand Medicine Society) is a ceremonial complex whose importance among the Algonquin people of the Great Lakes Region was noted frequently throughout the historical era (cf. Landes 1968; Warren 1984 [1885]). The telling of a version of the origin of the Midéwiwin was

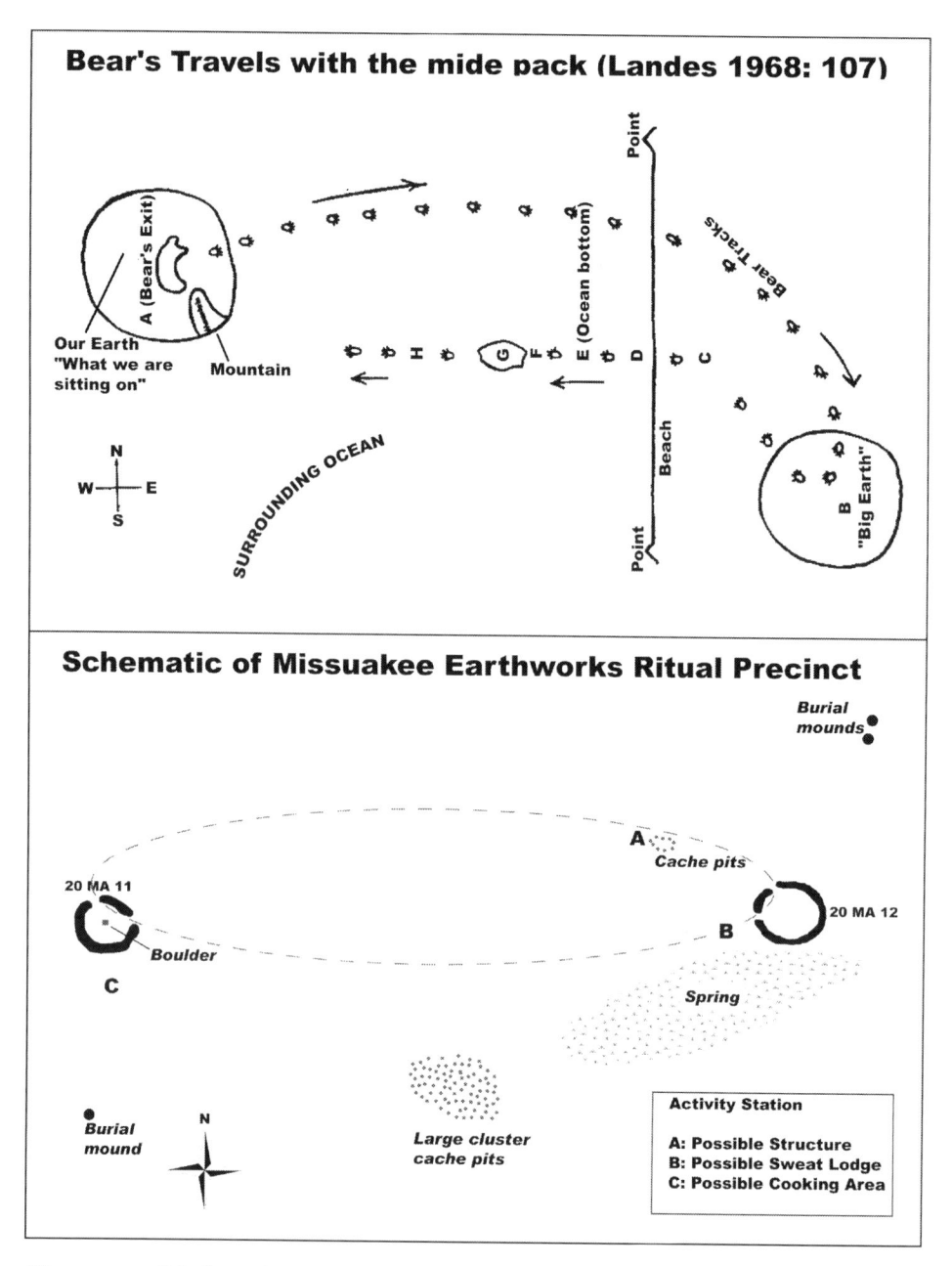

Figure 24.3 Side-by-side comparison of the ethnohistoric diagram of Bear's travels with the midé pack (Landes 1968:107) and the schematic of the Missaukee Earthworks Ritual Precinct Layout. Both figures are oriented north-south. To facilitate reading, the original labeling has been deleted and retyped verbatim (reproduced from Howey and O'Shea 2006).

required at every such ceremony. A common account details Bear as the servant who delivered the great mystery of the Midéwiwin to the Anishinaabeg.

When one compares the physical layout of the Missaukee Earthworks site to the Bear origin narrative and the associated sketch of Bear's travels with the midé pack (Landes 1968:107), as is done in Figure 24.3, the similarities are remarkable. With a cursory glance it is clear that the respective size and location of the two earths and the enclosure circles, the location of water, the topographic setting, and even the directional orientation of the features all match. Along Bear's pathway between the two earths there are even specific stops, matching the prescribed use of the space outside the enclosures found in archaeological survey at Missaukee. The correspondences between the major components of the Missaukee Earthworks site and the diagram of Bear's Journey demonstrate that the Missaukee Earthworks site was constructed as a monumental rendition of Bear's Journey with the midé pack.

These enclosures were monumentally constructed and designed ritual centers for coastal-inland interaction, and together they anchored the regional ritual network that ordered social relationships, economic activities, and ideology in Northern Michigan from the changes that began ca. AD 1200 until European Contact (ca. AD 1600). This ritual system was so important, so foundational in ordering the world during this time, that we see elements of it have shaped the historic and modern Midéwiwin ceremonial.

During Late Precontact in the Northern Great Lakes region, formation of strong group identities helped both coastal and inland peoples specialize, but it was only with ritual and ceremonial gatherings that they could mutually benefit from development of their respective economic specializations. The Northern Great Lakes was a land occupied by dynamic peoples who called themselves the "Spontaneous People" and who developed a complicated and foundational regional ritual system in the centuries before contact. These people were part of a vast and fascinating world playing out across North America for millennia before the first Europeans ever arrived.

REFERENCES

Brashler, J. G. 1981. *Early Late Woodland Boundaries and Interaction: Indian Ceramics of Southern Lower Michigan*. Michigan State University Museum, East Lansing.

Brooks, L. 2008. *The Common Pot: The Recovery of Native Space in the Northeast*. University of Minnesota Press, Minneapolis.

Cleland, C. E. 1982. The Inland Shore Fishery of the Northern Great Lakes: Its Development and Importance in Prehistory. *American Antiquity* 47(4):761–784.

———. 1992. *Rites of Conquest: The History and Culture of Michigan's Native Americans*. University of Michigan Press, Ann Arbor.

Crawford, G. W., D. G. Smith, and V. E. Bowyer. 1997. Dating the Entry of Corn (Zea mays) into the Lower Great Lakes Region. *American Antiquity* 62(1):112–119.

Fitting, J. E. 1970. *Archaeology of Michigan: A Guide to the Prehistory of the Great Lakes Region*. Natural History Press, New York.

Holman, M. B., and W. A. Lovis. 2008. The Social and Environmental Constraints on Mobility in the Late Prehistoric Upper Great Lakes Region. Cotsen Advanced Seminars 4, *The Archaeology of Mobility: Old and New World Nomadism*, edited by H. Barnard and W. Wendrich, pp. 280–306. Cotsen Institute of Archaeology, University of California, Los Angeles.

Howey, M. C. L., and J. M. O'Shea. 2006. Bear's Journey and the Study of Ritual in Archaeology. *American Antiquity* 71(2):261–282.

Katzenberg, M. A., H. Schwarcz, M. Knyf, and F. J. Melbye. 1995. Stable Isotope Evidence for Maize Horticulture and Paleodiet in Southern Ontario, Canada. *American Antiquity* 60(2):335–350.

Keen, R. A. 1993. *Michigan Weather*. American and World Geographic, Helena, MT.

Kingsley, R. 1999. The Middle Woodland Period in Southern Michigan. In *Retrieving Michigan's Buried Past: The Archaeology of the Great Lakes State*, edited by J. R. Halsey, pp. 148–172. Cranbrook Institute of Science, Bloomfield Hills, MI.

Landes, R. G. 1968. *Ojibwa Religion and the Midéwiwin*. University of Wisconsin Press, Madison.

Lovis, W. A. 1985. Seasonal Settlement Dynamics and the Role of the Fletcher Site in the Woodland Adaptations of the Saginaw Drainage Basin. *Arctic Anthropology* 22(2):153–170.

———, R. E. Donahue, and M. B. Holman. 2005. Long-Distance Logistic Mobility as an Organizing Principle Among Northern Hunter-Gatherers: A Great Lakes Holocene Settlement System. *American Antiquity* 70(4):669–693.

Milner, C. M. 1998. *Ceramic Style, Social Differentiation, and Resource Uncertainty in the Late Prehistoric Upper Great Lakes*. Ph.D. dissertation, University of Michigan.

O'Shea, J. M. 2003. Inland Foragers and the Adoption of Maize Agriculture in the Upper Great Lakes of North America. *Before Farming: The Archaeology of Old-World Hunter-Gatherers* 2(3):1–21.

———, and C. McHale Milner. 2002. Material Indicators of Territory, Identity, and Interaction in a Prehistoric Tribal System. In *The Archaeology of Tribal Societies*, edited by W. A. Parkinson, pp. 200–226. International Monographs in Prehistory, Ann Arbor.

Ozker, D. 1982. *An Early Woodland Community at the Schultz Site 20SA2 in the Saginaw Valley and the Nature of the Early Woodland Adaptation in the Great Lakes Region*. University of Michigan Museum of Anthropology, Ann Arbor.

Warren, W. W. 1984 [1885]. *History of the Ojibway People*. Minnesota Historical Society Press, St. Paul, MN.

CHAPTER 25

VILLAGERS AND FARMERS OF THE MIDDLE AND UPPER OHIO RIVER VALLEY, 11TH TO 17TH CENTURIES AD: THE FORT ANCIENT AND MONONGAHELA TRADITIONS

BERNARD K. MEANS

AMERICAN Indians who lived in the Middle and Upper Ohio Valley during the 11th–17th centuries AD are assigned by archaeologists to the Fort Ancient (Middle Ohio Valley) and Monongahela (Upper Ohio Valley) Traditions (Figure 25.1; see Drooker 1997; Means 2007). What these American Indians called themselves is not now known and may never be determined with certainty. The Fort Ancient and Monongahela Tradition peoples left scant traces in the documents of early European explorers and traders, and their connections to historically known American Indian groups are poorly understood and frequently debated (Drooker 1997; Johnson and Means in press). Our understanding of these people who grew maize and squash—adding beans to the mix during or after the 13th century AD (Hart and Scarry 1999)—relies on the ephemeral traces of their lives preserved in the archaeological record.

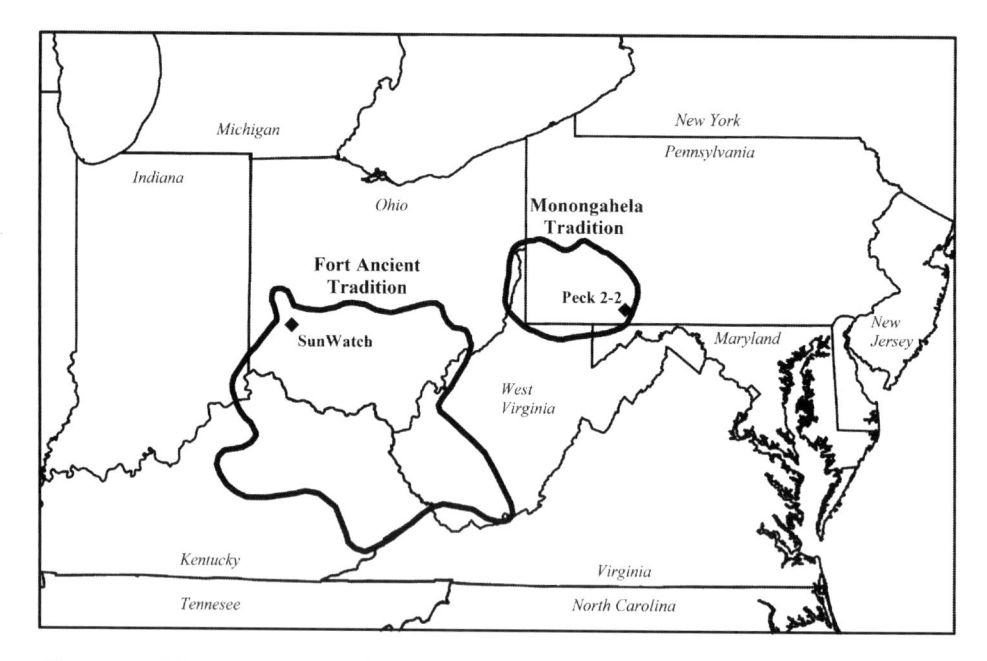

Figure 25.1 Maximum extent of the Fort Ancient and Monongahela Traditions, showing locations of SunWatch and Peck 2-2.

Much of the Fort Ancient and Monongahela Tradition literature consists of *material culture* (artifact) studies, focusing on defining ceramic types. These types were used to construct regional chronologies that persist to this day, resisting decades-old implementation of radiocarbon dating. The two most recent books on the Fort Ancient and Monongahela Traditions have emphasized that material culture studies are insufficient for understanding these American Indians, and that one must look at how they organized their communities when they chose to live together in multifamily settlements (Cook 2008; Means 2007).

Fort Ancient and Monongahela Tradition villagers often placed their dwellings in circles around plazas (Cook 2008; Means 2007). However, relatively few village sites from either tradition have seen broad exposure of their community patterns. Fort Ancient and Monongahela circular villages were designed according to geometric models used to spatially organize both elements of the built environment (architecture and spaces defined by architecture) and village social organizations (Means 2007).

I focus this discussion on village sites because how people organized themselves in village settlements is revealing of the social ties that held their communities together. I examine whether the superficially similar layouts of Fort Ancient and Monongahela Tradition village sites reflected similar or markedly distinct village social organizations. Following a brief overview of the two traditions, I examine a single site associated with each tradition: Peck 2-2, a Monongahela village site; and SunWatch, a Fort Ancient village site. Peck 2-2 is on the eastern edge of the Monongahela culture area; SunWatch is on the western edge of the Fort Ancient culture area. These two sites do not necessarily represent archetypal Monongahela and Fort Ancient villages, but they were sufficiently excavated that we can say something meaningful about how the inhabitants of the Middle and Upper Ohio Valley organized themselves in communities whose members regularly interacted with one another.

Overview of the Fort Ancient and Monongahela Traditions

The Fort Ancient and Monongahela Traditions are archaeological constructs developed largely within the "culture-historical paradigm" to broadly organize sites—especially villages—and items of material culture created by these maize-focused horticulturalists (Drooker and Cowan 2001; Hart et al. 2005). The term *Fort Ancient* was first used in the early 20th century to describe archaeological sites in the southern part of Ohio but was later expanded to include sites in Indiana, Kentucky, and West Virginia (Griffin 1966; Maslowski and Drooker in press). Butler (1939) defined the Monongahela Woodland Culture on the basis of three sites excavated during the New Deal in Somerset County, Pennsylvania, an area now viewed as being on the eastern periphery of the Monongahela Tradition's maximum distribution. Mayer-Oakes (1955) refined the definition of the Monongahela Tradition and created a ceramic seriation that served as the basis for a pre-radiocarbon dating chronology still widely used today (Means 2003).

Major developments and transformations within each tradition are sometimes couched in terms of direct (Fort Ancient) or indirect (Monongahela via Fort Ancient) "Mississippian" influences (Cook 2008; Mayer-Oakes 1955). Mayer-Oakes (1955) considered the Monongahela Tradition to have been Mississippian in character because of the presence of palisaded villages, plazas, and especially shell-tempered pottery (cf. Emerson, Milner, this volume). The practice of tempering pottery with shell is often interpreted as having been introduced to the Monongahela from Fort Ancient groups, who themselves supposedly adopted this technology and other traits directly from Mississippian groups (Cook 2008; Johnson 2001).

The Fort Ancient chronological framework assigns sites to three broad temporal periods: Early (AD 1000/1050 to 1200/1250), Middle (AD 1200/1250 to 1400/1450), and Late Fort Ancient or the Madisonville horizon (AD 1400/1450 to 1650/1750). Some syntheses of Fort Ancient culture simply make a distinction between Early and Middle Fort Ancient sites versus Late Fort Ancient sites (Maslowski and Drooker in press). The Monongahela developmental sequence has traditionally been divided into Early (AD 1050/1100 to 1250), Middle (AD 1250 to 1580/1590), and Late or Protohistoric Monongahela (AD 1580/1590 to 1635) (Johnson 2001).

Village Spatial Layouts

Most Fort Ancient village sites apparently consisted of circular villages with square or rectangular dwellings organized around central plazas (Drooker 1997:48; Drooker and Cowan 2001:91). However, many Fort Ancient sites have been insufficiently excavated to know with confidence their actual settlement plans (Drooker 1997:48). Some villages may have had houses arrayed in a line or an arc, or some combination of the two, creating a D-shaped plan (Maslowski and Drooker in press). Although most Monongahela villages were circular in layout, not all had clearly recognizable central plazas. One village site in Somerset County, Pennsylvania, had a circular component with a plaza that was superimposed atop a slightly earlier component lacking a plaza but created by the same village community or their immediate ancestors (Means 2007). Apparent arc- and linear-shaped villages have also been documented (Johnson and Means in press; Means 2009).

Late Fort Ancient or Madisonville horizon village sites show panregional similarities with the material culture documented at the Madisonville site (Drooker and Cowan 2001:87). During all time periods, village sites exhibited no evidence for a settlement hierarchy, even when presumably increased or sustained interaction led to the greater material culture similarities shared by sites during the Madisonville horizon (Henderson and Pollack 2001:175). Fort Ancient villages were more widely distributed prior to AD 1400/1450 (Maslowski and Drooker in press), and the same is said to be true of the Monongahela Tradition (Johnson 2001).

Houses and Features

House patterns and construction techniques can prove to be the key to identifying distinct cultural traditions (Maslowski and Drooker in press). Fort Ancient dwellings generally had rectilinear floor plans (Henderson and Pollack 2001:174, 177), although five sites in Ohio had circular or oval structures (Maslowski and Drooker in press). At some Fort Ancient sites, unusually large structures have been documented within or adjacent to their plazas, possibly functioning as council or headmen's houses (Drooker 1997:88) or perhaps sodality buildings.

Dwellings at Monongahela sites primarily exhibited curvilinear floor plans throughout the Monongahela sequence (Johnson and Means in press; Means 2007). Some Monongahela houses had attached roofed pits that were presumably used for storage (Figure 25.2; Hart 1995:42). Unusually large structures are documented at a number of Monongahela village sites (Hart 1993; Means 2007). During the late Middle Monongahela and Late Monongahela/Protohistoric periods, unique structures with multiple attached post-enclosed features appeared at a few Monongahela village sites (Anderson 2002; Hart 1995). In plan view, these "petal houses" resemble a child's drawing of a flower, with each petal represented by a

Figure 25.2 Monongahela house with attached storage pit (courtesy of Laura J. Galke).

substantial architectural element in the form of an attached, usually quite narrow, storage pit. Some, but not all, of these structures were unusually large. With as many as two dozen petals on a single structure, these buildings were likely used for ceremonial or council functions in addition to their potential use as communal storage facilities (Hart 1995; Johnson and Means in press). Petal houses may have been symbolically linked to domestic residences with attached storage pits, much in the way that Puebloan kivas, ritual structures used throughout the American Southwest, are symbolically linked to earlier pit houses (Johnson and Means in press; Young, this volume).

Mortuary Behavior

A number of Early to Middle Fort Ancient village sites had burial mounds located near the plaza. After the Middle Fort Ancient period, burial mounds were no longer present at Fort Ancient villages. Late Fort Ancient graves were primarily located either near or within dwellings (Drooker and Cowan 2001:92; Henderson and Pollack 2001:175). Some aspects of Fort Ancient village social organizations were reflected in their mortuary programs. At the Madisonville village site, clusters of graves were associated with dwellings and probably represented family or lineage cemetery areas (Drooker 1997:199).

Burial mounds are not associated with Monongahela village sites, and interments tended to be dispersed throughout the domestic areas of villages, with graves sometimes grouped into apparent lineage cemetery areas (Means 2007). The low number of graves at some village sites could indicate undiscovered cemeteries outside of village settlements (Means 1999). Structures with multiple interments, interpreted as charnel houses, have been encountered at a number of later Monongahela village sites. Even at sites with charnel houses, graves were most frequently distributed throughout the dwelling ring (Johnson 2001).

Village Social Organizations and Village Spatial Layouts

The nuclear family is thought to have been the basic unit of Fort Ancient village social organization, perhaps generating lineages, clans, or moieties—dual social organizations concerned with regulating marriage (Henderson and Pollack 2001:177). However, few researchers have attempted to directly identify such social divisions at Fort Ancient sites (Drooker 1997:89). Monongahela villages were likely composed of similar social groups organized in varying configurations, depending on the individual village community (Hart 1993; Means 2007; Nass 1995).

At least some Fort Ancient and Monongahela villagers projected their village social organizations onto the spatial layouts of their circular villages. As I have discussed elsewhere (Means 2007), circular villages represent a special case of a settlement form built according to cognitive geometric models that can spatially order major social groups within a settlement, as well as their various activities. Patterning in circular villages conforms primarily to two broad categories: concentric and circumferential. One or more rings of dwellings around a central plaza are the most obvious form of concentric patterning in circular villages. Circumferential patterning refers to division of features and dwellings in the domestic zone into segments, often of varying sizes.

PECK 2-2: A MONONGAHELA TRADITION VILLAGE SITE

In exploring the connection between village spatial layouts and village social organizations, I first consider a Monongahela village site. Excavated as a New Deal work relief project in the 1930s, Peck 2-2 is the latest confirmed Monongahela Tradition village in Pennsylvania's Allegheny Mountains, dating to the early 16th century AD (Figure 25.3). This palisaded village site has the most complex community pattern in the region as well (Means 1998, 2007). A small, possible sodality structure is located along the eastern margin of the village's plaza. Notable at Peck 2-2 are two unusually large dwellings located on opposite sides of its plaza. These buildings might have represented communal structures (Hart 1993) or had other functions significant to the community. Both structures began as noticeably smaller dwellings, indicating that their function within village society changed during the occupation of the village. The easternmost unusually large dwelling was located adjacent to the village's entrance and had a potentially privileged position that could have controlled formal access into the village community. A possible village leader was interred in a grave just outside this structure (Means 2007).

The westernmost unusually large dwelling was part of a discrete segment of the dwelling ring that included a small open space—a courtyard—to which other members of the village community had restricted access. The greatest number of

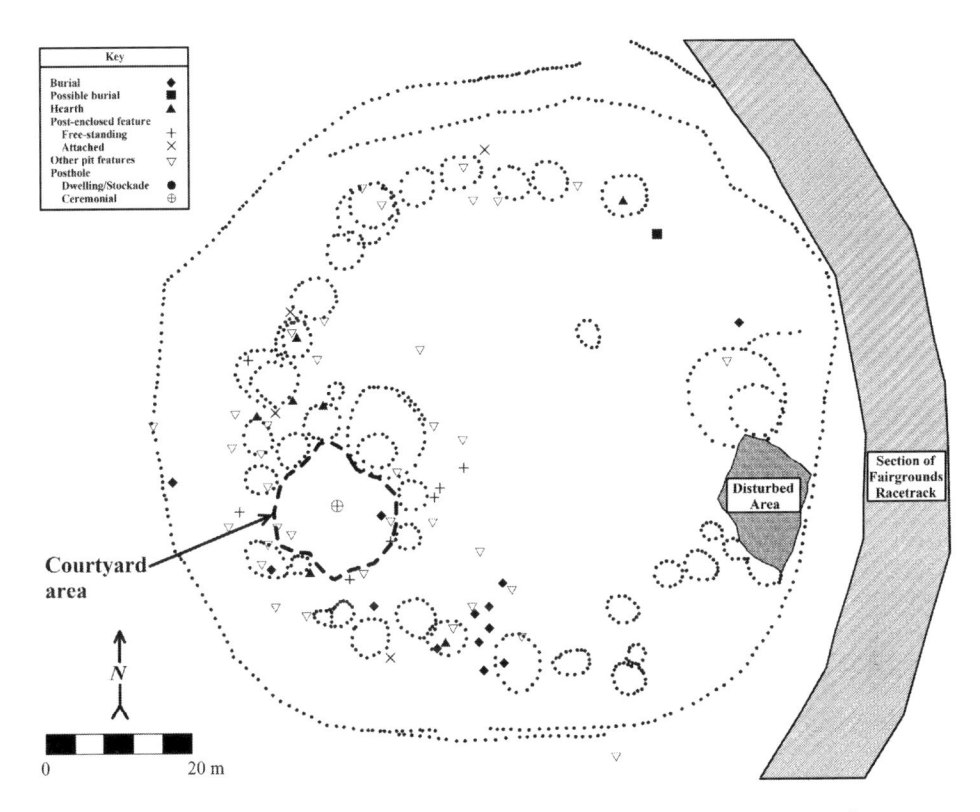

Figure 25.3 Schematic map of Peck 2-2 (adapted from Means 2007:117).

storage features at Peck 2-2 is associated with the courtyard group. No large post or hearth feature (e.g., an *axis mundi*) was found in the center of Peck 2-2's plaza, which could have served as the focus of community-level rituals, but one such post was present in the center of the courtyard. This larger-than-average post could have served as the location of rituals whose access was limited to members of the courtyard group and invited guests (Means 2007). If true, members of Peck 2-2's courtyard group leveraged their enhanced standing in the community to greatly expand a normal-sized dwelling into a much larger structure. This structure was intrusive into the community's plaza and a clear violation of geometric models used to plan and otherwise maintain the entire community (Means 2007). Concentric geometric models at Peck 2-2 therefore operated on two levels that influenced the village's spatial layout and the configuration of village social organizations. One concentric model operated at the level of the entire village community, and the other concentric model pertained only to the courtyard group—"a village within a village."

The courtyard group's existence supports the presence of circumferential patterning at Peck 2-2 as well. This village within a village represented one segment of the dwelling ring; there were at least two major dwelling clusters on either side of the courtyard group. The three dwelling clusters were large enough to represent a lineage, clan, or "house," in Lévi-Straussian parlance, with the clusters on either side of the courtyard group composed of two or three multifamily households each (Means 2007). Thus for Peck 2-2 there is strong spatial evidence that the households were formally linked at more than one level, and that the courtyard group had a higher social standing relative to other village social groups.

Sun Watch: A Fort Ancient Tradition Village

SunWatch is one of the most thoroughly and extensively excavated Fort Ancient villages (Cook 2008). This site consisted of concentric rings of dwellings and features around a central plaza; all were encircled by a palisade (Figure 25.4). Clear radial patterning is evident at the site. A ring of graves is nearest to the plaza's outer edge and separated from dwellings by a ring of storage and trash pits (Means 2007). A wall trench house, more substantially constructed than the other buildings at the site, intruded further into the plaza (Cook 2008). Located in the center of the village plaza are traces of a red cedar pole, which likely functioned as the site's *axis mundi*, apparently used to create alignments to astronomical phenomena (Cook 2008).

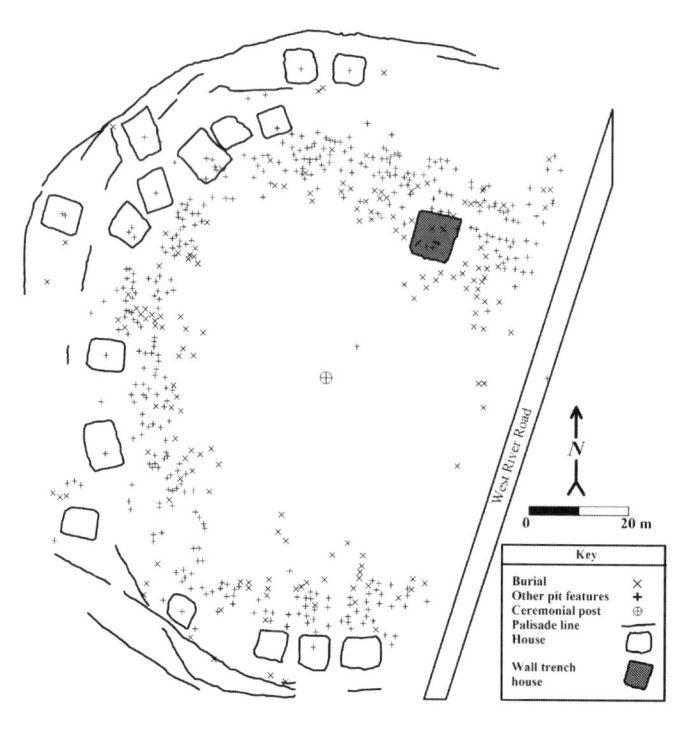

Figure 25.4 Schematic map of SunWatch (adapted from Cook 2008:12).

The SunWatch site exhibited not only radial patterning in the distribution of features, but circumferential patterning as well (Means 2007). The excavated portion of the site was divided into four "ceramic style zones" that are thought to have represented discrete households, lineages, or clans, depending on the researcher's perspective (Cook 2008; Drooker 1997:89; Nass 1989:5). Graves also formed clusters within the ring of grave features, possibly reflecting the deceased's membership in discrete social groups (Cook 2008).

Cook (2008) recently presented a detailed examination of SunWatch's community patterns, viewing changes within the site's layout as resulting from interactions with Mississippian groups further to the south. Arguing that elements of the site's community pattern provided subtle evidence of an intrusive Mississippian presence at SunWatch, he concluded that significant aspects of the SunWatch village social organization and village spatial layout formed as a direct result of interaction with Mississippian societies (19). Specific elements that he asserted were Mississippian in origin are large, uniquely built structures close to site centers; central postholes in circular village layouts; and astronomical alignments incorporated into the built environment (142).

Integral to Cook's argument that there was direct Mississippian influence at SunWatch is the presence of the site's wall trench structure (Figure 25.5). This type of structure is reminiscent of ordinary houses built in other Mississippian regions to the west and south (see Alt, Blitz, King, this volume). Its presence at SunWatch was therefore seen as reflecting an intrusive Mississippian group, and one that may have established leadership over the inhabitants of SunWatch (Cook 2008). But do wall trenches make a structure Mississippian? Or do they represent the technological requirements for a structure that differed meaningfully from other dwellings at the site? For consideration of this issue, see discussions presented in Lacquement (2007). Schroeder (2009) suggested that special structures within some communities had visually distinct roofs and would have required different building techniques from residential structures. Certainly, the wall trench structure at SunWatch was a unique building, given its construction and placement within the community.

The other key element of Cook's argument that the SunWatch community pattern was derived from Mississippian influences is its central post, a feature also present on some Mississippian sites. Astronomical alignments have been documented at Mississippian sites—Cahokia being a notable example—and the central post at SunWatch was apparently part of solar alignments incorporated into the site's layout. Therefore, according to Cook (2008:26) SunWatch's inhabitants must have directly imported aspects of their settlement structure (and even actual residents) from the Mississippian world. However, cross-cultural research shows that circular settlements across the world often have a central feature—sometimes a large post, hearth, or roasting pit—that villagers use to link the layout of their settlement directly to their conception of the cosmos. Central posts and astronomical alignments are not uniquely Mississippian traits (Means 2007).

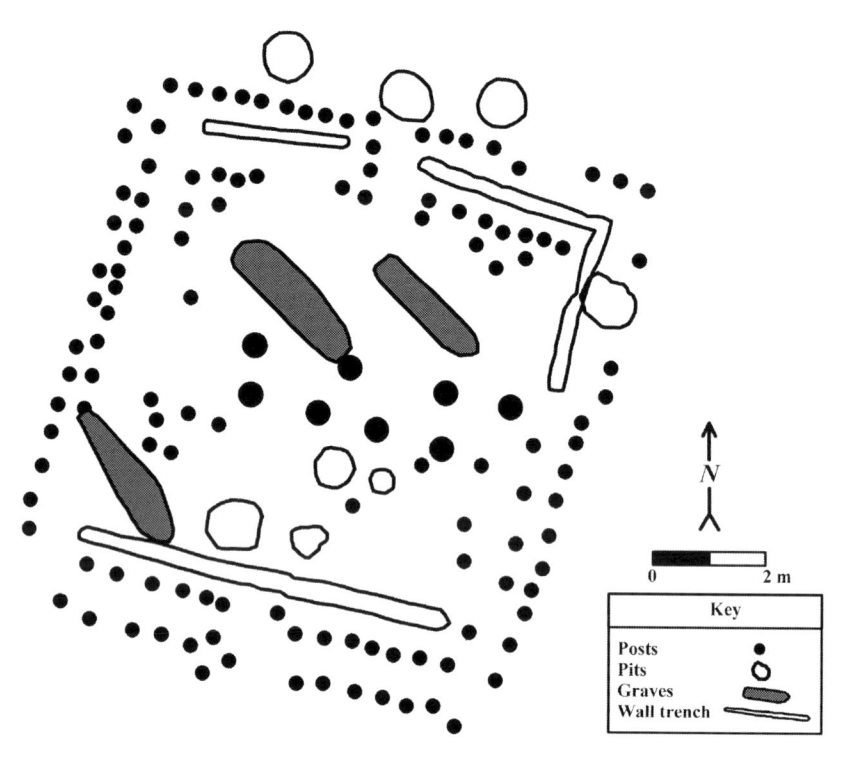

Figure 25.5 Floor plan of SunWatch's wall trench structure (adapted from Cook 2008:12).

Discussion

Ceremonies held around features located in the center of villages reinforce the social identities of villagers and strengthen the bonds linking village social organizations (Means 2007). Alignments of village features to celestial events can serve a similar function of reinforcing village social organizations, perhaps by rooting them spatially in creation myths (Means 2007, 2009). By incorporating celestial alignments into their overall village plans, the inhabitants of SunWatch and other villages could have reactivated on select occasions a link to the cosmos through the layouts of their villages, which represented microcosms or reflections of larger "realities." This process would have helped ensure that the distribution of social groupings and activities adhered to the cosmologically derived geometric models that influenced the initial layout of these village sites (Means 2007).

Cook (2008) established that broad similarities sometimes exist between Fort Ancient and Mississippian village settlement layouts. Does this mean that Fort Ancient village structure was primarily a byproduct of interactions with Mississippian groups? I think not. Broad parallels in settlement layouts simply cannot be seen as evidence of direct connections and influences between two coeval groups—even if they were geographically adjacent. These parallels point toward more general structural issues that occur when comparatively large groups of individuals cohabit the same location and manipulate this space to emphasize those aspects of social organization that strengthen the notion of community while combating the centripetal forces that would tear community members apart (Means 2007).

Within their broadly similar settlement layouts, there are some important differences between Peck 2-2 and SunWatch. SunWatch is larger overall and had square houses as opposed to the round houses seen at Peck 2-2; graves at SunWatch formed a clear ring around the central plaza, while graves were not patterned in this fashion at Peck 2-2. Individual dwellings were generally larger at SunWatch, although the two unusually large structures at Peck 2-2 were more substantial than the biggest structure at SunWatch. Nonetheless, total roofed area was nearly the same between the two sites. SunWatch's larger size relative to Peck 2-2 owes much to its sizeable plaza area (Means 2009). Whether the specific differences in overall village size, total roofed area, and the ratio of plaza area to total settlement area are significant differences between Fort Ancient and Monongahela Tradition villages, or simply noticeable differences between Peck 2-2 and SunWatch, awaits an ongoing analysis of village sites assigned to the two traditions.

Conclusion

New excavations, a revisiting of old sites and collections, and refinement of chronological frameworks suggest that the Fort Ancient and Monongahela Traditions subsume considerable regional variability in village spatial layouts. Therefore, I have focused my discussion not on SunWatch as a Fort Ancient village, nor on Peck 2-2 as a Monongahela village, but rather on what closer attention to their community patterns tells us about the people who designed and lived in these settlements. Social change was fostered by the tensions generated through attempts to impose and maintain geometric order on the arrangement of various elements in a village's layout, beginning at initial establishment. These geometric models were balanced against the reality of multiple families with competing interests residing within a single, dynamic community. Simply assigning a site to one tradition or the other is clearly insufficient for understanding the transformations that occurred after independent Fort Ancient or Monongahela Tradition households joined together to live within villages (Means 2007).

References

Anderson, D. A. 2002. Elites Among the Monongahela? Evidence for Social Complexity in the Late Prehistoric-Protohistoric Period of Southwestern Pennsylvania. *Archaeology of Eastern North America* 30:121–136.

Butler, M. 1939. *Three Archaeological Sites in Somerset County, Pennsylvania*. Pennsylvania Historical Commission Bulletin 753. Pennsylvania Historical Commission, Harrisburg.

Cook, R. A. 2008. *SunWatch: Fort Ancient Development in the Mississippian World.* University of Alabama Press, Tuscaloosa.

Drooker, P. B. 1997. *The View from Madisonville: Protohistoric Fort Ancient Interaction Patterns.* Memoirs of the Museum of Anthropology, University of Michigan 31. Museum of Anthropology, University of Michigan, Ann Arbor.

———, and C. W. Cowan. 2001. Transformation of the Fort Ancient Cultures of the Central Ohio Valley. In *Societies in Eclipse: Archaeology of the Eastern Woodlands Indians, A.D. 1400–1700,* edited by D. S. Brose, C. Wesley Cowan, and R. C. Mainfort, Jr., pp. 83–106. Smithsonian Institution, Washington, DC.

Griffin, J. B. 1966. *The Fort Ancient Aspect: Its Cultural and Chronological Position in Mississippi Valley Archaeology.* University of Michigan, Museum of Anthropology Anthropological Papers 28. Museum of Anthropology, University of Michigan, Ann Arbor.

Hart, J. 1993. Monongahela Subsistence-Settlement Change: The Late Prehistoric Period in the Lower Upper Ohio Valley. *Journal of World Prehistory* 7:71–120.

———. 1995. Storage and Monongahela Subsistence-Settlement Change. *Archaeology of Eastern North America* 23:41–56.

———, J. P. Nass, and B. K. Means. 2005. Monongahela Subsistence-Settlement Change? *Midcontinental Journal of Archaeology* 30(2):327–365.

Hart, J., and C. M. Scarry. 1999. The Age of Common Beans (*Phaseolus vulgaris*) in the Northeastern United States. *American Antiquity* 64(4):653–658.

Henderson, A. G., and D. Pollack. 2001. Fort Ancient. In *Encyclopedia of Prehistory,* vol. 6, *North America,* edited by P. N. Peregrine and M. Ember, pp. 174–194. Kluwer Academic/Plenum, New York.

Johnson, W. C. 2001. The Late Prehistoric and Protohistoric Period Monongahela Culture and the Case for an Iroquoian Connection. In *Societies in Eclipse: Eastern North America at the Dawn of Colonization,* edited by C. W. Cowan, pp. 67–82. Smithsonian Institution, Washington, DC.

———, and B. K. Means. In press. The Monongahela Tradition of the Late Prehistoric and Protohistoric Periods, 12th to 17th Centuries A.D., in the Lower Upper Ohio River Valley. In *A Synthesis of Pennsylvania Prehistoric Archaeology.* Pennsylvania Historical and Museum Commission, Harrisburg.

Lacquement, C. H. (editor). 2007. *Architectural Variability in the Southeast.* University of Alabama Press, Tuscaloosa.

Maslowski, R. F., and P. B. Drooker. In press. Fort Ancient Adaptations in the Mid Ohio Valley. *Quarterly Bulletin of the Archaeological Society of Virginia.* In press.

Mayer-Oakes, W. J. 1955. *Prehistory of the Upper Ohio Valley: An Introductory Archeological Study.* Anthropological Series 2, Annals of Carnegie Museum 34. Carnegie Museum of Natural History, Pittsburgh, PA.

Means, B. K. 1998. Archaeological Past and Present: Field Methodology from 1930s Relief Excavations in Somerset County, Pennsylvania and Its Relevance to Modern Archaeological Interpretations. *Journal of Middle Atlantic Archaeology* 14:39–63.

———. 1999. Monongahela Mortuary Practices in Somerset County, Pennsylvania: Observations and Implications. *Pennsylvania Archaeologist* 69(2):15–44.

———. 2003. Deliver Me from Mononga-Hell: Thinking Beyond the Culture History Paradigm to Examine the Temporal and Spatial Parameters of Somerset Monongahela Village Settlements. *Journal of Middle Atlantic Archaeology* 19:37–58.

———. 2007. *Circular Villages of the Monongahela Tradition.* University of Alabama Press, Tuscaloosa.

———. 2009. Village Peoples: Monongahela and Fort Ancient Communities of the Middle and Upper Ohio River Valley 11th to 17th Centuries A. D. Poster presented at the 74th Annual meeting of the Society for American Archaeology, April 24, Atlanta, GA.

Nass, J., Jr. 1989. Household Archaeology and Functional Analysis as Procedures for Studying Fort Ancient Communities in the Ohio Valley. *Pennsylvania Archaeologist* 59(1):1–13.

———. 1995. An Examination of Social, Economic, and Political Organization at the Throckmorton Site, a Monongahela Community in Greene County, Pennsylvania. *Archaeology of Eastern North America* 23:81–93.

Schroeder, S. 2009. The Ordinary and the Extraordinary: Identifying the Origins of Variation in Mississippian Perishable Architecture at Jonathan Creek. Paper presented at the 74th Annual Meeting of the Society for American Archaeology, April 25, Atlanta, GA.

CHAPTER 26

NATIVE HISTORY IN THE CHESAPEAKE: THE POWHATAN CHIEFDOM AND BEYOND

MARTIN GALLIVAN

As home to the Powhatan chiefdom, the Jamestown colony, and colonial interaction involving a number of recognizable figures of 17th-century history, the Chesapeake region has played a prominent role in American origins mythology. To take an example, colonist John Smith's captivity narrative (1986d:43–59) foregrounds the tale of his wily negotiations with the Algonquian leader Wahunsenacawh (or Powhatan) in the town of Werowocomoco and his rescue from execution by Wahunsenacawh's daughter Pocahontas. Smith's accounts launched a cottage industry of Powhatan studies and assumed iconic status for some as a sign of forthcoming English colonial success and Native societies' retreat. Much of the historiography and archaeology that are focused on James Fort has emphasized such event-driven history, understood as reflecting the roots of American democracy.

By contrast, recent archaeological and ethnohistoric studies focused on Native history in the Chesapeake have explored a different set of questions along a broader range of temporal and geographic scales, including those spanning historical archaeology and "prehistory" that are designed to track links between pre-Contact social processes and colonial-era events. Due in part to the influence of descendant communities seeking to reclaim their past and influence its investigation, such scholarship has shifted in recent years away from primary reliance on an English colonial perspective and on the environmental, demographic, and economic variables prominent in processual archaeology (see also Thomas, this volume). Rather, archaeologists, ethnohistorians, and historians have begun to broaden the scope of their research and foreground regional social ties, material meanings, religious practices, and cultural landscapes that structured diverse social traditions before and beyond the Powhatan chiefdom. Along with this turn, studies of the late prehistoric and early colonial Chesapeake highlight themes with broad significance for North American archaeology:

- Cyclical emergence and dissipation of centralized political structures
- Population movements that introduced new traditions amidst a diverse pre-Contact setting
- Persistent places that became centers of exchange, ritual, and social ranking
- Forms of Native leadership that do not fit easily into existing models of chiefly power

The Cultural Landscapes of Native Societies in the 17th-Century Chesapeake

The Jamestown colony was established in 1607 when about 100 Englishmen began to construct fortifications on an island located 40 miles upstream from the mouth of the Powhatan River, now known as the James. Accounts of this early history written by colonists John Smith (1986a, 1986b, 1986c, 1986d), William Strachey (1953), and Henry Spelman (1998) form the basis of most interpretations of the Tidewater Native communities known to the English as the Powhatans (e.g., Mooney 1907; Feest 1990; Rountree 1989; Gleach 1997; Kupperman 2007; Axtell 2001; Rountree and Turner 2002). In the northern Virginia Coastal Plain, Native groups speaking Algonquian dialects, including the Piscataways and Patawomecks, adopted a shifted set of political relations with the Powhatans, including alliance and hostility (Potter 1993). The Monacans, probably Siouan speakers, resided in the Virginia interior west of the fall line, reportedly invading the Coastal plain during the fall (Hantman 1990, 1993). To the south of the Powhatans were Iroquoian-speaking Nottoway and Meherrin communities along the rivers still named for these groups, as well as the coastal Algonquians encountered by Roanoke colonists decades earlier (Binford 1964; Ward and Davis 1999).

John Smith's *Map of Virginia* (1986a), which includes both a map and a brief ethnographic description of the Powhatans, represents the typical point of departure for characterizations of this social landscape. As depicted on the *Map*, the Virginia Tidewater political landscape consisted of "kings' howses," where local commanders or *weroances* resided, and "ordinary howses" lacking such political leaders. Tribute flowed from commoners to *weroances* and from *weroances* to Wahunsenacawh, the paramount chief (Strachey 1953:87). *Weroances* dominated exchange networks through which these materials moved; they constituted material expression of chiefly social status. The *Map* depicts a fundamentally Native world as perceived through an English colonialist lens (Figure 26.1).

An alternative representation of the Powhatan domain, arguably channeling the perspective of Wahunsenacawh himself, comes to us from "Powhatan's Mantle" (Figure 26.2). The mantle, dating to the opening years of the Jamestown colony, consists of two deerskins sewn together with marginella beadwork depicting a human figure flanked by two animals and surrounded by 32 round discs. E. Randolph Turner (1976:133) has noted that the mantle can be read as a topological map of the Chesapeake and a Native rendition of the Powhatan domain, including the roughly 32 districts claimed by Wahunsenacawh. Seen in this light, the mantle advances a "claim to broader hegemony over a core area plus an incompletely consolidated periphery" (Waselkov 2006:308). Colonial sources document Wahunsenacawh's use of military force, or threat of same, on several occasions to expand his influence within the Tidewater region. Wahunsenacawh labeled this region Tsenacomacoh, emphasizing his conviction that all those residing within (Native and newcomer alike) were "Powhatans" (Smith 1986d:67).

Algonquian communities within Tsenacomacoh practiced maize-based horticulture complemented by a diverse array of wild foods that were hunted, gathered, and fished within rich estuarine and riverine settings. By the Late Woodland period (AD 900–1600), riverfront villages represented the focal point of social life for all but the winter months. In the lower portions of the estuary, settlements were typically located in embayed areas flanked by wetlands. Most settlements were dispersed along floodplain terraces and consisted of fewer than 100 residents. Palisaded communities were rare in the Virginia Tidewater, with most located along Tsenacomacoh's frontiers to the south, west, and north (Turner 1993).

Historical Processes of the Late Pre-Contact Chesapeake

Drawing heavily from English accounts of the Powhatan world and colonial-era cartographic sources, archaeologists and ethnohistorians have constructed models for the Powhatan chiefdom's emergence and organization. The archaeology of hierarchical societies in the Chesapeake—including the Powhatan, Monacan, Piscataway, and Patawomeck—has generally emphasized explanations whereby Middle Woodland (500 BC–AD 900) "harvesters of the Chesapeake" increased in population, developed circumscribed social networks, and became Late Woodland village horticulturalists (Potter 1993:139; Binford 1964; Turner 1976). Lewis Binford's seminal dissertation (1964) opened the way for such interpretations by emphasizing ecological parameters, settlement patterns, and the ethnohistory of the Powhatans

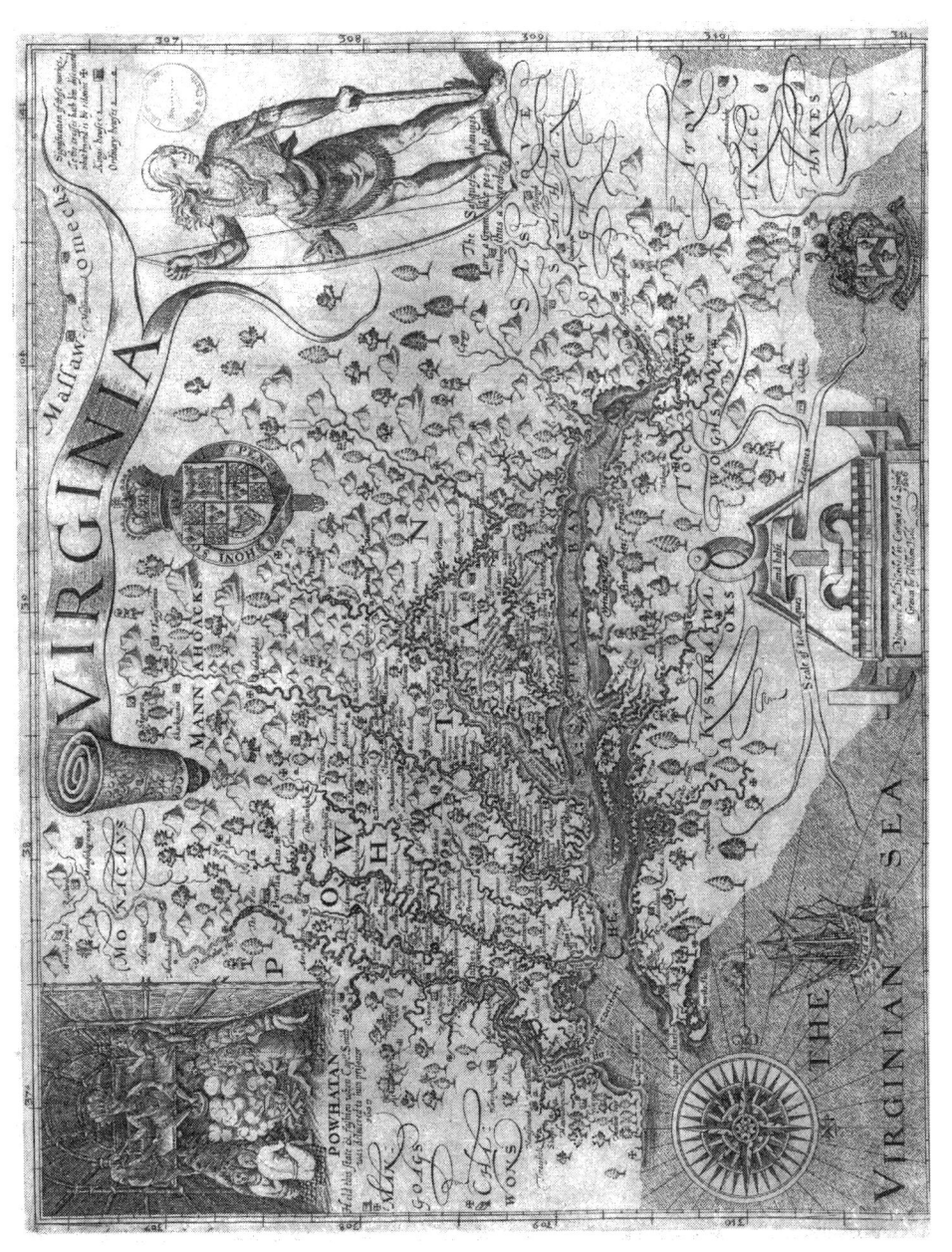

Figure 26.1 John Smith's Map of Virginia.

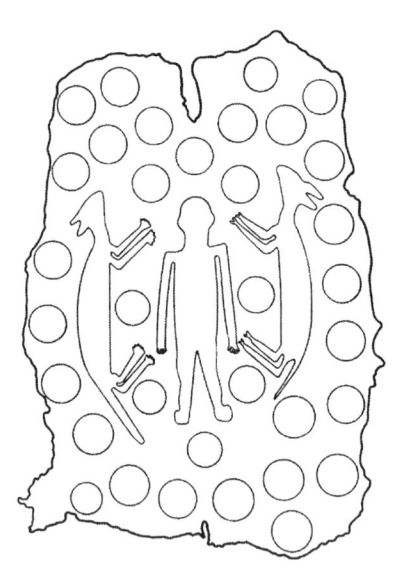

Figure 26.2 Powhatan's Mantle.

and related groups. Stephen Potter's studies of Algonquian cultural development in the Potomac (1982, 1993) have offered a richly textured local context for tracing the history of a Native group. Turner (1976) has linked Tidewater archaeology to Powhatan ethnohistory by focusing on the environmental productivity and demographic profile of the Coastal Plain interior, the area where the Powhatan chiefdom and other powerful polities originated. Helen Rountree's detailed reconstruction of the Powhatan ethnographic present (1989) and colonial-era history (1990) has laid the foundation for the historical anthropology of Tidewater Algonquians.

These accounts of the Powhatan chiefdom emphasize that it represented a classic paramount chiefdom, emerging as a social response to material and demographic circumstances that arose in the centuries prior to contact. Complicating application of neoevolutionary models in the Chesapeake, though, several of the expected attributes of North American chiefly societies—a high volume of prestige goods exchange, much surplus production, high-status mortuary practices, site-size hierarchies—are absent (or nearly so) from the Late Woodland Chesapeake (Turner 1986). Subsequent efforts to shift attention toward the historical processes specific to the Chesapeake have identified changes in domestic production, community organization, and regional exchange that coincided with establishment of large and permanent village communities between AD 1200 and 1500 (e.g., Gallivan 2003). During these centuries the archaeology of domestic spaces suggests that some households increased dramatically in size and began to exercise greater control over storage. Some communities across the drainage erected palisades and began to use large roasting pits for multicommunity feasts. Ceramic styles reflected social networks that were considerably more bounded after AD 1200.

Such changes resulting in powerful lineages, impressive regional centers, and sharp social boundaries produced a Chesapeake landscape more susceptible to the rise of hierarchical political structures that included the Powhatan chiefdom. Drawing the focus back from the specific circumstances giving rise to Late Woodland-era polities in the Chesapeake reveals that their emergence and collapse was part of a broader and longer set of historical processes across the Middle Atlantic. In fact, the region may be characterized, from as early as 1200 BC, by a long-term, cyclical pattern whereby competition for rank "was defined by the ability to access nonlocal prestige goods and distinctive mortuary ritual" (Hantman and Gold 2000:289).

Hantman and Gold have traced these dynamics, which produced locally specific forms of political and ceremonial centralization, through Early Woodland exchange networks involving steatite bowls (Klein 1997), Middle Woodland hunter-forager sites showing signs of seasonal aggregation and feasting (Stewart 1998), and Late Woodland mortuary practices that imply democratization of practices designed to venerate ancestors and mark important places (Dunham 1999). With a similarly wide vista on Middle Atlantic prehistory, Custer (1994:347) noted sporadic signs of increased social complexity, or "flashes in the pan," from the Late Archaic through Contact periods that failed to accord in any simple way with environmental parameters.

Linguistic and archaeological research pointing to the importance of population movements has opened new possibilities for tracing social traditions and historical processes in the prehistoric Chesapeake. On the basis of studies of glottochronology and protolexicon reconstruction, Fiedel (1999) argues that Algonquian populations moved into the Chesapeake during the latter stages of the Middle Woodland period (500 BC–AD 900), disrupting the archaeological record and setting the stage for development of the diverse traditions encountered at contact. Shared terms for town, chief, ceremonial attendant, and fellow clan member also occur across Algonquian languages, implying that traditional social structures included large villages, totemic clans, ranked lineages, and hereditary chiefs. Such reconstructions of Proto-Algonquian and use of glottochronology are by no means universally accepted. As in most places, material traditions and cultural practices frequently crossed social and linguistic boundaries within the Chesapeake, making it difficult to isolate evidence of migration in the archaeological record. Nonetheless, Fiedel's linguistic analysis offers an intriguing line of evidence with which to consider the spread, circa AD 200, of shell-tempered ceramics and the subsequent appearance of ceremonial centers, earthwork enclosures, and chiefly lineages in the Chesapeake.

Nuanced archaeological approaches to the study of population movements in the Chesapeake are still rare, but those that draw from detailed sequences show considerable promise (e.g., Blanton et al. 1999). For example, extensive excavations at the Potomac Creek site in the Potomac River Coastal Plain have traced a history of this unusual settlement, which consisted of a series of concentric ditch features, palisade enclosures, and communal ossuaries. Dennis Blanton and colleagues (1999:92) interpret this evidence as recording the 14th century arrival of "uncomfortable immigrants" from Iroquoian-speaking communities north of the Chesapeake who constructed a fortified settlement. During the 15th century, the immigrants created a "flourishing Tidewater culture"; the palisades were no longer maintained and ancestors were interred in collective ossuaries (Blanton et al. 1999:96). By the 16th century, the settlement was no longer occupied, as residents moved to the nearby town of Patawomeck. The original settlement was never completely forgotten or abandoned, though; the archaeological record suggests periodic events at the location as late as the 17th century. In this way, Potomac Creek represents "persistent place" and a location of continued importance across more than three centuries. The Potomac Creek site location remained significant even after the population had moved on and its importance was defined by memories of past events.

Similarly important persistent places appear in other parts of the Chesapeake region, particularly during the final Late Woodland centuries. Perhaps the most prominent of these was Werowocomoco (Gallivan et al. 2005; Gallivan 2007). Referenced above as the scene of events understood as fundamental to the success of English colonial expansion, Werowocomoco was also a place of periodic social gathering and deep Tidewater Algonquian history. Contemporaneous with 13th-century establishment of an agricultural village at the site, a series of concentric ditches and embankments were constructed within the interior of the settlement, marking spaces distinct from the residential core lining the riverfront (Figure 26.3). Artifacts and features located behind the ditches differed from those identified in the residential core along the riverfront. The interior area contained a high percentage of nonlocal ceramics and serving vessels. The one structure identified in this area is significantly larger than those found on the riverfront. Radiocarbon-dated to the early 17th century, the structure was surrounded by several pieces of copper originating from Jamestown. Werowocomoco appears to be a carefully structured landscape that included spaces associated with Wahunsenacawh during the early colonial era. My colleagues and I have suggested that Werowocomoco was redefined as a ritualized and politicized node within a landscape of similar such places constructed by Algonquian communities across the Chesapeake after AD 1200 (Gallivan 2007). The process of "place making" at Werowocomoco and deep memories of its importance likely played a role in the Late Woodland negotiation of social ranking in the Chesapeake and in the 16th-century origins of the Powhatan chiefdom.

THE HISTORICAL ANTHROPOLOGY OF THE EARLY COLONIAL CHESAPEAKE

Efforts to develop a historical anthropology of Native societies in the early colonial Chesapeake have begun to emphasize how Native actions during the early colonial era accorded with deeply rooted cultural structures. Studies of exchange patterns before and after Contact have emphasized that copper played a powerful role in the

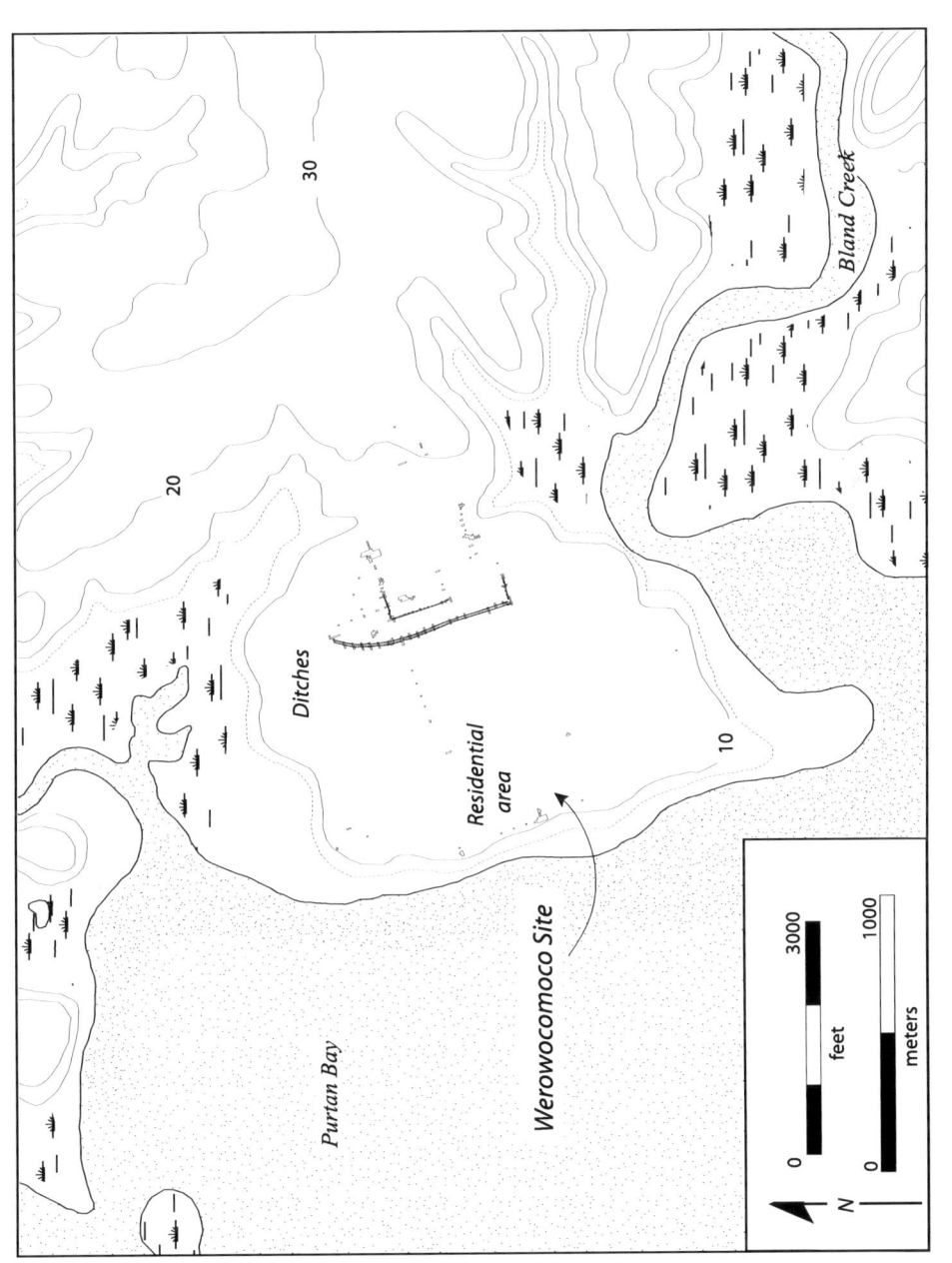

Figure 26.3 Excavations at Werowocomoco.

Native political economy (Hantman 1990; Potter 2006). Recovery of scrap copper at Jamestown (Kelso 2006:179) and of Jamestown copper in Native village sites (see, e.g., Fleming and Swann 1994) opens a window into colonial-era interaction and Native systems of meaning. As a symbol and source of power that circulated through ritualized exchange spheres, copper played a fundamental role in Native religious and political dynamics (Hantman 1990).

Drawing the focus away from the Tidewater area to the Piedmont, Hantman demonstrates that a panregional political economy involving movement of copper from interior sources existed prior to the colonial encounter, only to be transformed and reoriented eastward with the arrival of the Jamestown colonists. Analysis of exchange among Native societies and Jamestown colonists, an earlier Spanish mission, and the Roanoke colony indicates that Europeans repeatedly violated indigenous gift-exchange rules and provoked Native hostilities (Mallios 2006). Eventually, the inundation of copper in the Chesapeake following Wahunsenacawh's 1609 departure from Werowocomoco undermined these Native political structures and contributed to Contact-period social disruptions within Native communities (Potter 2006).

In another reinterpretation of Powhatan history, Gleach's reconstruction of the Powhatan worldview (1997) recognizes a division within Tidewater Algonquian society between internal and external affairs and between peace and war leaders, a pattern paralleled in a number of Native societies in the Southeast. By the early 17th century Wahunsenacawh was acting primarily as a peace chief in this reading, at times constrained by the war chief Opechancanough. Williamson's analysis of Powhatan society likewise demonstrates how ritual and cosmology framed Algonquian notions of leadership (Williamson 2003). In her interpretation, Powhatan society was defined by a dual sovereignty that separated authority (the right to say what will be done) and power (the ability to execute what is authorized; Williamson 2003:14). The Powhatan dual sovereignty was manifest in the distinction between priests' religious authority and the political power exercised by *weroances*. Gleach and Williamson's complementary interpretations offer a number of insights into events of the early colonial encounter. Each also represents an effective effort to reach beyond the presentist mind-set that pervades much Powhatan scholarship, presupposing the inevitability of the European domination (Waselkov 1998:150).

Conclusion

The archaeology and ethnohistory of Native societies in the Chesapeake are significant in different ways to different audiences. Colonial accounts of Powhatan social and political organization offer a basis for considering the comparative archaeology of political complexity and of Native responses to colonialism. Where historians often construct colonial narratives from Contact-period events and personalities, historical anthropologists have highlighted the cultural structures that framed Native experiences of these events. By panning back from a focus on events surrounding Jamestown in 1607, researchers have come to recognize political cycling in the Middle Atlantic, population movements that shaped pre-Contact history, persistent places remembered long after Native communities stopped dwelling there, and forms of Native leadership that were lost on early English chroniclers.

Within recent decades, descendant communities of Virginia Indians have begun to insist that they be included in conversations about their ancestors' past, and this recent development will no doubt play a role in future scholarship. Virginia has eleven state-recognized tribes, among them the Pamunkey and Mattaponi, who have remained on reservations since the 17th century (Moretti-Lanholtz 1998; Rountree 1990). Maryland has at least 12 Native descendant communities, none officially recognized as an indigenous tribe (Hughes and Henry 2006). Native scholars and consultants have become involved with several archaeological projects in the Chesapeake, notably those performed in a cultural resource management context (e.g., Blume 2006; Petraglia and Cunningham 2006) and those conducted under the auspices of university-based research (e.g., Hantman 2004; Gallivan and Moretti-Langholtz 2007). Although the movement toward an indigenous archaeology of the Chesapeake is in a preliminary stage, there are already hints that it will have a notable impact. Native archaeologists played a role in the successful effort to halt construction of the King William Reservoir, located close to the Mattaponi and Pamunkey reservations (Atkins 2009). A partnership between archaeologists at the University of Virginia and the Monacan community of central Virginia represents an example of sustained collaboration in the region. University archaeologists have joined Monacan scholars in an effort to write a seamless Monacan history linking "prehistory" to the recent Monacan past (Hantman et al. 2000).

In coastal Virginia, the Werowocomoco Research Group has developed a framework for consultation and collaboration with six tribes descended from the Powhatans (Gallivan et al. 2005). Several Virginia Indians have joined the project as field and laboratory technicians and received training in fieldwork, laboratory analysis, and interpretation. The effort to recover a biography of place at Werowocomoco that reaches well beyond the colonial-era events is influenced in part by the questions and priorities of these colleagues. More broadly, the growing body of archaeological expertise within Native communities of the Chesapeake will no doubt influence the direction of scholarship on Native history in years to come.

REFERENCES

Atkins, A. L. 2009. *Collaborative Archaeology and Virginia Indian Perspectives*. Paper presented at the Middle Atlantic Archaeological Conference, Ocean City, MD.
Axtell, J. 2001. *Natives and Newcomers: The Cultural Origins of North America*. Oxford University Press, New York.

Binford, L. R. 1964. *Archaeological and Ethnohistorical Investigation of Cultural Diversity and Progressive Development Among Aboriginal Cultures of Coastal Virginia and North Carolina.* Ph.D. dissertation, University of Michigan, Ann Arbor.

Blanton, D. B., S. C. Pullins, and V. L. Deitrick. 1999. *The Potomac Creek Site (44ST2) Revisited.* Virginia Department of Historic Resources Research Report Series 10. Virginia Department of Historic Resources, Richmond.

Blume, C. L. 2006. Working Together: Developing Partnerships with American Indians in New Jersey and Delaware. In *Cross-Cultural Collaboration: Native Peoples and Archaeology in the Northeastern United States*, edited by J. E. Kerber, pp. 197–212. University of Nebraska Press, Lincoln.

Custer, J. F. 1994. Current Archaeological Research in the Middle Atlantic Region of the Eastern United States. *Journal of Archaeological Research* 2(4):329–360.

Dunham, G. H. 1999. Marking Territory, Making Territory: Burial Mounds in Interior Virginia. In *Material Symbols: Culture and Economy in Prehistory*, edited by J. E. Robb, pp. 112–134. Center for Archaeological Investigations, Southern Illinois University, Carbondale.

Feest, C. F. 1990. *The Powhatan Tribes.* Chelsea House, New York.

Fiedel, S. J. 1999. Algonquians and Iroquoians: Taxonomy, Chronology, and Archaeological Implications. In *Taming the Taxonomy: Toward a New Understanding of Great Lakes Archaeology*, edited by R. F. Williamson and C. M. Watts, pp. 193–204. Eastend Books, Toronto.

Fleming, S., and C. Swann. 1994. Technical Analysis of Copper-Base Artifacts. In *Paspahegh Archaeology: Data Recovery Investigations of Site 44JC308 at the Governor's Land at Two Rivers, James City County, Virginia*, edited by N. M. Lucketti, pp. 244–257. Prepared for the Governor's Land Associates by the James River Institute for Archaeology, Williamsburg, VA.

Gallivan, M. D. 2003. *James River Chiefdoms: The Rise of Social Inequality in the Chesapeake.* University of Nebraska Press, Lincoln.

———. 2007. Powhatan's Werowocomoco: Constructing Place, Polity, and Personhood in the Chesapeake, C. E. 1200–C. E. 1609. *American Anthropologist* 109(1):85–100.

———, T. Harpole, D. A. Brown, D. Moretti-Langholtz, and I. E. Randolph Turner. 2005. *The Werowocomoco Research Project: Background and 2003 Archaeological Field Season Results.* Virginia Department of Historic Resources Research Report Series 15. Virginia Department of Historic Resources, Richmond, VA.

Gallivan, M. D., and D. Moretti-Langholtz. 2007. Civic Engagement at Werowocomoco: Reasserting Native Narratives from a Powhatan Place of Power. In *Archaeology as a Tool of Civic Engagement*, edited by B. J. Little and P. A. Shackel, pp. 47–66. AltaMira Press, Lanham, MD.

Gleach, F. W. 1997. *Powhatan's World and Colonial Virginia: A Conflict of Cultures.* University of Nebraska Press, Lincoln.

Hantman, J. L. 1990. Between Powhatan and Quirank: Reconstructing Monacan Culture and History in the Context of Jamestown. *American Anthropologist* 92(3):676–690.

———. 1993. Relations Between Powhatan and the Piedmont Monacans. In *Powhatan Foreign Relations*, edited by H. C. Rountree, pp. 94–111. University Press of Virginia, Charlottesville.

———. 2004. Monacan Meditation: Regional and Individual Archaeologies in the Contemporary Politics of Indian Identity. In *Places in Mind: Archaeology and Communities*, edited by P. Shackel and E. Chambers. Routledge Press, New York.

———, and D. Gold. 2000. The Woodland in the Middle Atlantic: Ranking and Dynamic Political Stability. In *The Woodland Southeast*, edited by D. G. Anderson and R. C. Mainfort, pp. 270–291. University of Alabama Press, Tuscaloosa.

Hantman, J. L., K. Wood, and D. Shields. 2000. Writing Collaborative History: How the Monacan Nation and Archaeologists Worked Together to Enrich our Understanding of Virginia's Native Peoples. *Archaeology* 53(5):56–59.

Hughes, R. B., and D. L. Henry. 2006. Forging New Partnerships: Archaeologists and the Native People of Maryland. In *Cross-Cultural Collaboration: Native Peoples and Archaeology in the Northeastern United States*, edited by J. E. Kerber, pp. 112–128. University of Nebraska Press, Lincoln.

Kelso, W. M. 2006. *Jamestown, the Buried Truth*. University of Virginia Press, Charlottesville.

Klein, M. J. 1997. The Transition from Soapstone Bowls to Marcey Creek Ceramics in the Middle Atlantic Region: Vessel Technology, Ethnographic Data, and Regional Exchange. *Archaeology of Eastern North America* 25:143–158.

Kupperman, K. O. 2007. *The Jamestown Project*. Belknap Press of Harvard University Press, Cambridge, MA.

Mallios, S. 2006. *The Deadly Politics of Giving: Exchange and Violence at Ajacan, Roanoke, and Jamestown*. University of Alabama Press, Tuscaloosa.

Mooney, J. 1907. The Powhatan Confederacy, Past and Present. *American Anthropologist* 9(1):129–152.

Moretti-Langholtz, D. 1998. *Other Names I Have Been Called: Political Resurgence Among Virginia Indians in the Twentieth Century*. Ph.D. dissertation, University of Oklahoma, Norman.

Petraglia, M. D., and K. Cunningham. 2006. Native American Archaeology in the Delmarva: New Meanings and an Expanded Approach to Delaware Archaeology. In *Cross-Cultural Collaboration: Native Peoples and Archaeology in the Northeastern United States*, edited by J. E. Kerber, pp. 213–229. University of Nebraska Press, Lincoln.

Potter, S. R. 1982. *An Analysis of Chicacoan Settlement Patterns*. Ph.D. dissertation, University of North Carolina, Chapel Hill.

———. 1993. *Commoners, Tribute, and Chiefs: The Development of Algonquian Culture in the Potomac Valley*. University Press of Virginia, Charlottesville.

———. 2006. Early English Effects on Virginia Algonquian Exchange and Tribute in the Tidewater Potomac. In *Powhatan's Mantle: Indians in the Colonial Southeast*, edited by G. A. Waselkov, P. H. Wood, and T. Hatley, pp. 215–242. University of Nebraska Press, Lincoln.

Rountree, H. C. 1989. *The Powhatan Indians of Virginia: Their Traditional Culture*. 1st ed. University of Oklahoma Press, Norman.

———. 1990. *Pocahontas's People: The Powhatan Indians of Virginia Through Four Centuries*. 1st ed. University of Oklahoma Press, Norman.

———, and E. R. Turner. 2002. *Before and After Jamestown: Virginia's Powhatans and their Predecessors*. University Press of Florida, Gainesville.

Smith, J. 1986a. Generall Historie of Virginia. In *The Complete Works of Captain John Smith (1580–1631)*, vol. 2, edited by P. L. Barbour, pp. 5–475. 3 vols. University of North Carolina Press, Chapel Hill.

———. 1986b. A Map of Virginia. In *The Complete Works of Captain John Smith (1580–1631)*, vol. 1, edited by P. L. Barbour, pp. 119–189. 3 vols. University of North Carolina Press, Chapel Hill.

———. 1986c. The Proceedings. In *The Complete Works of Captain John Smith (1580–1631)*, vol. 2, edited by P. L. Barbour, pp. 191–279. 3 vols. University of North Carolina Press, Chapel Hill.

———. 1986d. A True Relation. In *The Complete Works of Captain John Smith (1580–1631)*, vol. 1, edited by P. L. Barbour, pp. 5–117. 3 vols. University of North Carolina Press, Chapel Hill.

Spelman, H. 1998. Relation of Virginia. In *Jamestown Narratives: Eyewitness Accounts of the Virginia Colony*, edited by E. W. Haile, pp. 497–519. Roundhouse, Champlain, VA.

Stewart, R. M. 1998. Unraveling the Mystery of Zoned Decorated Pottery: Implications for Middle Woodland Society in the Middle Atlantic Region. *Journal of Middle Atlantic Archaeology* 14:161–182.

Strachey, W. 1953 [1612]. *The Historie of Travell into Virginia Britania*. Printed for the Hakluyt Society, London.

Turner, E. R. 1976. *An Archaeological and Ethnohistorical Study of the Evolution of Rank Societies in the Virginia Coastal Plain*. Ph.D. dissertation, Pennsylvania State University, State College.

———. 1986. Difficulties in the Archaeological Identification of Chiefdoms as Seen in the Virginia Coastal Plain During the Late Woodland and Early Historic Periods. In *Late Woodland Cultures of the Middle Atlantic Region*, edited by J. F. Custer, pp. 19–28. University of Delaware Press, Newark.

———. 1993. Native American Protohistoric Interactions in the Powhatan Core Area. In *Powhatan Foreign Relations, 1500–1722*, edited by H. Rountree, pp. 76–93. University of Virginia Press, Charlottesville.

Ward, H. T., and R. P. S. Davis. 1999. *Time Before History: The Archaeology of North Carolina*. University of North Carolina Press, Chapel Hill.

Waselkov, G. A. 1998. Review of Powhatan's World and Colonial Virginia: A Conflict of Cultures. *William and Mary Quarterly* 55(1):148–150.

———. 2006. Indian Maps of the Colonial Southeast. In *Powhatan's Mantle: Indians in the Colonial Southeast*, edited by G. A. Waselkov, P. H. Wood, and T. Hatley, pp. 435–502. University of Nebraska Press, Lincoln.

Williamson, M. H. 2003. *Powhatan Lords of Life and Death: Command and Consent in Seventeenth-Century Virginia*. University of Nebraska Press, Lincoln.

IV. Plains and Upper Midwest

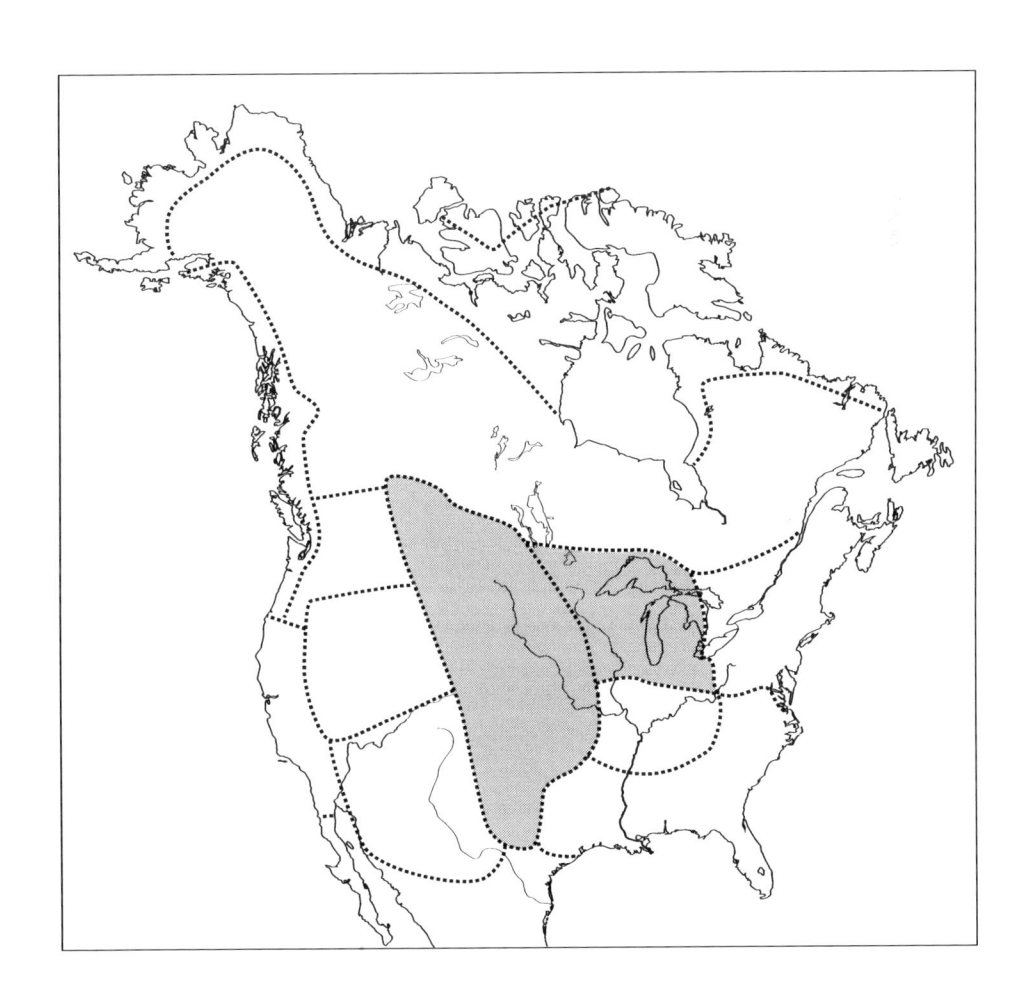

CHAPTER 27

LIFEWAYS THROUGH TIME IN THE UPPER MISSISSIPPI RIVER VALLEY AND NORTHEASTERN PLAINS

GUY GIBBON

A principle of an emerging post-postmodern archaeology is that there is no given past-in-itself, but rather many pasts that come into being with different ways of seeing. To assume otherwise—that is, to assume that there is only one past to be seen—is to commit the epistemic fallacy of the Myth of the Given. As such, archaeologists are obligated to clarify and explicitly lay out their ways of seeing. This conception of the archaeological enterprise is more playful and exploratory, and more uncertain, than one based on naïve empiricism in which a received way of seeing is considered a given. Besides affording diverse perspectives on the past, varied ways of seeing generate models that, if fruitful, lead to new research agendas and discovery of new patterning in the archaeological record.

In this chapter, I illustrate the approach by summarizing an ongoing study of changing lifeways in the Upper Mississippi River–Northeastern Plains region of north central North America. It is divided into four sections: tools for studying past lifeways, the study area, lifeways through time, and pattern in the past.

Tools for Studying Past Lifeways

Archaeologists use taxonomic systems, such as phase and archaeological culture, to impose order on the many thousands of artifacts and features that make up the archaeological record in a region. Since that record is the result of many sociocultural and natural formation processes, they create research programs (or ways of seeing) to get at pattern and at what the pattern means. The working assumptions of the research program adopted here are based on ideas developed by Lewis Binford (2001), John Bodley (2005), Morton Fried (1975), Marshall Sahlins (1968, 2004), Elman Service (1979), and Ken Wilber (2000).

A tool for helping us understand the relationships between past sociocultural systems and the archaeological record, as well as the tasks and problems of archaeological analysis, is Wilber's four quadrant or integral approach (2000) to understanding human beings and their constructed sociocultural systems. As Figure 27.1 illustrates, the upper left quadrant is composed of the interior thoughts and experiences of individual human beings, the lower left quadrant of the

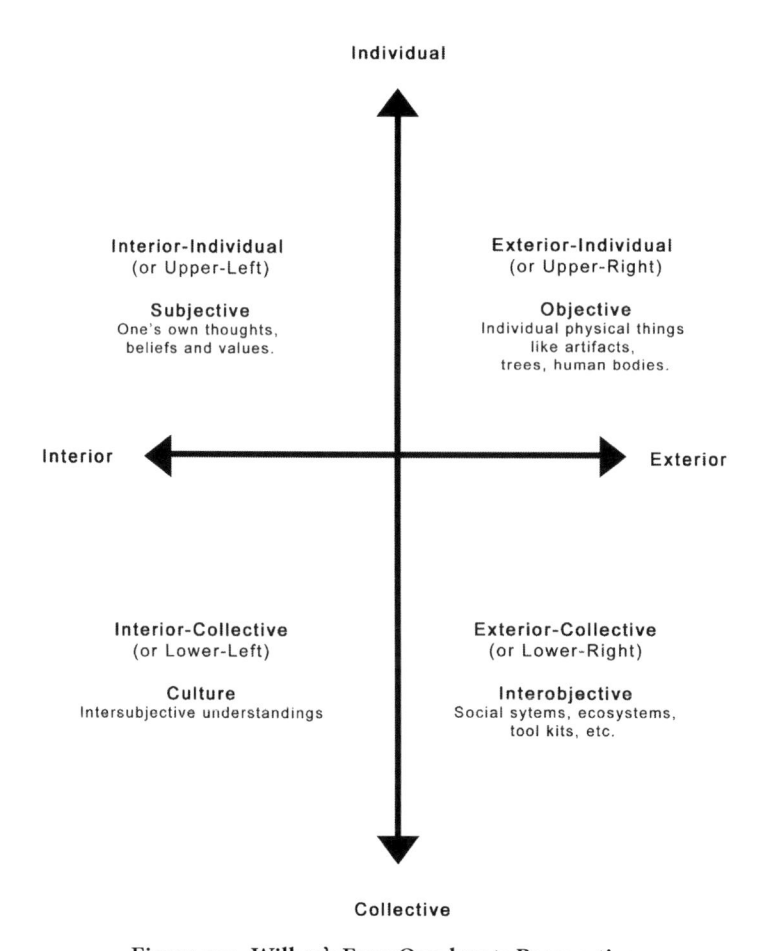

Figure 27.1 Wilber's Four Quadrants Perspective.

intersubjective understandings or culture of groups of people, the lower right of the exterior of social systems (including the system's interconnected material culture), and the upper right of the exterior of individuals and things, including individual artifacts and their constituent elements. Although a fully integral study of a human community is the study of all four of these dimensions (quadrants), I concentrate here on the lower right quadrant, which is the realm of visible systems of social organization—the basic structure of a society (e.g., band, tribe, chiefdom), and the size of its social units, primary economic activity (foraging, horticulture, agrarian), and political sources of social power, among other features.

One tool we use in studying the exterior of the social systems of prehistoric people in our region of study is Bodley's concept of scale of culture (2005:25–28). The scale of culture of a community is based on how people in that community organize *social power*, which he (Bodley 2005:524) defines as an "individual's ability to get what he or she wants, even when others might object." All of the study area's social systems fall within his domestic scale of culture, which Bodley defines as characterized "by small, kinship-based societies, often with only 500 people, in which households organize production and distribution" (25).

Since the study area's prehistoric social systems were all at a domestic scale of culture, I use four strategies to differentiate, examine, and think about them. The first is the familiar division of domestic-scale societies into band-based and tribal-based societies as described by Service (1979) and Sahlin (1968, 2004). I believe this is an important, empirically supported distinction in the study region. In brief, bands tend to be foragers, in Binford's terminology, who capture and gatherer wild foods using residential mobility as a major subsistence strategy (see Morgan and Bettinger, Prentiss, this volume). They are typically small, egalitarian, kin-based groups with a material culture that is simple and meager due in large part to their mobility. Tribes tend to be collectors who live in small, sedentary villages from which task groups venture out to gather resources. Their diet is typically domesticated foods supplemented by hunted and gathered wild foods.

The second strategy is Fried's notion (1975) that a tribe is a mode of social organization forced into existence when band-level groups interact with hostile (or at least competitive) groups having larger-scale social organizations. The third is Binford's "frames of reference" approach (2001) in which population size and density, social organization, subsistence orientation, stepped reaction to social circumscription, expected range size, and many other characteristics of hunter-gatherer groups in an area are approximated using a small number of environmental parameters. The fourth strategy is a series of first-step adaptive ecosystem types that summarize and simplify presentation of the conclusions of this study for a general audience.

The research program used here is very much in the tradition of the *longue durée* approach to the study of history in that its focus is on long-term patterns of change in sociocultural systems in a region. I believe this emphasis is of primary importance in archaeological research today, for the details of lifeways at various scales can be more informatively filled in once this background is better understood. It is this large-scale pattern too, I believe, that has the most to contribute to our understanding of the pattern of development of sociocultural systems that took place throughout the world in the postglacial period.

The Study Area

The study area falls within the northern, glaciated section of the Central Lowland physiographic province of North America, except for the Superior Upland in northeastern Minnesota (Figure 27.2). For the past 5,000 to 7,000 years, three plant biomes have trisected the region: open deciduous forest, northern coniferous forest, and prairie. During this period, the region was bordered by latitudinal transitions in biotic community related to a gradual reduction in solar radiation (Binford 2001). The lower boundary (at ca. 42.6° latitude) separated terrestrial plant harvesters in warmer, moister, more southern environments from terrestrial game hunters, who in turn were separated in the north (at ca. 49.5° latitude) from aquatic resource exploiters in resource-poor boreal forests. Following the retreat of the last (Wisconsin) continental glacier, the region experienced extreme climatic and vegetational

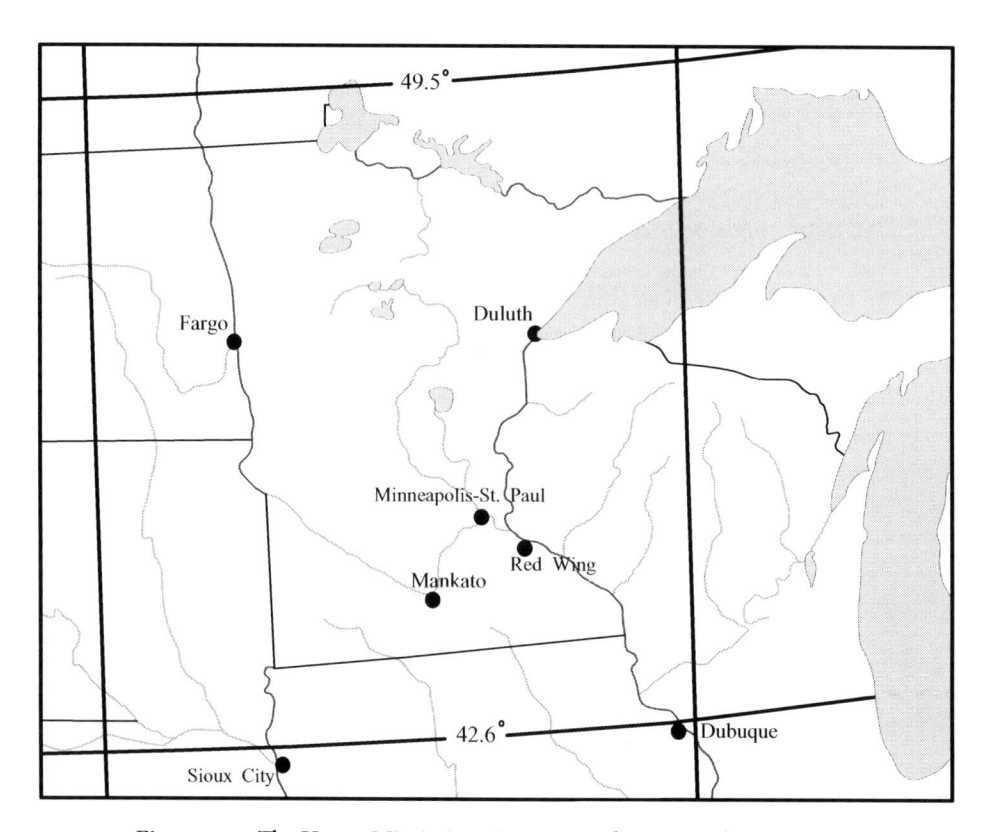

Figure 27.2 The Upper Mississippi River–Northeastern Plains Region.

dislocations, which are mentioned below. The region has a cool temperate climate, with cold, snowy winters and warm, humid summers.

Lifeways Through Time

The preliminary results of application of Binford's "frames of reference" to the study area's pre-Contact archaeological record are summarized here using nine types of human adaptation organized in a four-phase sequence (Gibbon and Anfinson 2008). It should be stressed that the types are tools for thinking about the results of subsistence resource intensification through time in the area, and as such they smooth over the complexity in detail that must once have existed. Other regions of prehistoric North America will have their own kinds and combinations of types, and tempos of change from one type to another.

Pioneer Foragers

Archaeological context. The archaeological record of the period (cal. 11200–10500 BC) consists of small numbers of isolated surface finds of fluted, leaf-shaped projectile points made of high-quality toolstone. Minnesota's sample—of 74 fluted points (8 Clovis-like, 17 Folsom, 12 Holcombe, 1 Cumberland, and 36 unassigned points, at least some of which are most likely Gainey), a spurred end scraper, and a fluted drill—is representative. Point styles from earliest to latest are thought to be Clovis, Gainey/Holcombe, Folsom, and Cumberland, with some overlap among styles. It should be stressed that the dynamic nature of the environment, which included massive flooding of large river valleys, did not favor the survival of early sites.

During the Late Glacial period, the region's rapidly changing land surface was dominated by postglacial lakes, meltwater rivers, remnants of glacial ice, open spruce parkland, and the lingering presence of the Laurentide continental glacier in the far north. Now-extinct animal species such as mastodon, mammoth, and giant beaver were present (to about 10900 BC), as were modern species such as white-tailed deer, beaver, moose, and black bear. The presence of white-tailed deer, rabbit, turtle, and other smaller animals at nearby mammoth and mastodon kill sites, such as Lange-Ferguson in western South Dakota and Kimmswick in eastern Missouri, lends inductive support to the notion that these hunter-gatherers were opportunistic foragers whose subsistence economy included small and large animals.

Human adaptations. Hunter-gatherers in the region at the time seem represented by a very small number of highly mobile Early Paleoindian families whose subsistence focus in this northern, cold weather, Late Glacial environment was hunting. Since they were the only hunter-gatherers in the region, they moved from one food patch to another in pursuit of large- and medium-sized terrestrial game animals in order to maintain their subsistence security. Their number remained too small and the amount of uninhabited area too large to attain the minimum population density required to form bounded territories. Given this free-wandering lifeway, their archaeological sites are scattered, small, artifact-poor, and generally nonaccumulative. In our research, we refer to this adaptation as Pioneer Forager.

The presence of a free-wandering lifeway during this period is supported by the predominance of single-find projectile points, use of high-quality toolstone from widely scattered quarries, a hunter's toolkit (as known more securely from other areas), the absence of long-term habitation sites, and possible association of a mastodon and Clovis point at the Boas site near the northeastern edge of the Driftless area in Wisconsin.

These early hunter-gatherers may represent warm weather foraging parties in the northern portion of their range, or colonizing parties responding to population growth in more resource-rich southern staging areas. Trends toward population growth and regionalization during the period are supported by the burgeoning presence of projectile points through time and their distribution (eight Clovis points are concentrated in the southern two-thirds of the region, but 17 later Folsom points have a southwestern concentration and 12 Holcombe points a northern concentration). There is no unequivocal evidence for the presence of an earlier adaptive type.

Coniferous Forest Game, Deciduous Forest Game, and Early Pedestrian Bison Hunters

Archaeological context. The second phase (cal 10500–3000 BC) in the sequence coincides with the region's Late Paleoindian (10500–7500 BC), Early Eastern Archaic (8500–5500 BC), and Middle Eastern Archaic/Early Plains Archaic (5500–3000 BC) archaeological record, which is also known mainly through the presence of projectile points. The points occur in a variety of unfluted lanceolate and notched forms. In Minnesota, at least 10 types of Late Paleoindian points have been identified, four transitional Paleoindian-Archaic types, four Early Archaic types, and 16 Middle Archaic types. Sites remain small and elusive, though there are more sites than earlier and many more may be buried a meter or more in alluvial settings. Poorer-quality toolstone was used widely for the first time, and chipped and ground stone adzes and axes become increasingly common in the forested western edge of the region.

This was a time of major climatic and vegetational change throughout the region. Deciduous forest dominated the southern portion early in the period (10500–7500 BC), while pine replaced the earlier spruce forest in the north by 9400 BC. Early Eastern Archaic points seem confined for the most part to the deciduous forest in the southeastern corner of the region, while partially contemporary Late Paleoindian points are widespread throughout all forests. By 8000 BC, tall-grass prairie began spreading eastward across Iowa and Minnesota in a time-transgressive manner. These severe vegetational dislocations were the result of the Atlantic climatic episode (Hypsithermal), during which warm and dry westerly winds blew across the region. Most sites in the expanding prairie are bison kill and processing stations, such as Smilden-Rostberg and Canning in eastern North Dakota, Granite Falls and Itasca in western Minnesota, and Cherokee in northwestern Iowa. After 3500 BC, the climate became cooler and wetter, and the prairie retreated, reaching its modern borders by about 3000 BC.

Human adaptations. The diversity of projectile point styles, focus on local toolstone, infrequent use of exotic stone, continued presence of a hunter's toolkit, and small, elusive sites provide inductive support for the model interpretation that small and mobile families of 12–21 people with a strong hunting focus now lived within food resource territories in which demographic packing was not yet a problem. Although these groups continued to position their residential sites in the landscape to facilitate the search for food on a daily-encounter basis, they now "mapped on" to the resources of a territory in an annual settlement-subsistence cycle. In contrast to the importance of well-made, tended facilities among terrestrial plant harvesters to the south, less-well-made weapons now become a feature of these northern hunters (Figure 27.3).

In our studies we designate the new lifeways of this phase as Coniferous Forest Game Hunter and Deciduous Forest Game Hunter (10500–3000 BC) for groups who focused on hunting terrestrial forest animals and Early Pedestrian Bison Hunter (9000–1500 BC) for groups who focused on hunting bison in the grasslands. As the

Figure 27.3 Kramer (upper row) and Turkey Tail points (lower row), with Minnesota points on the right.

prairie spread eastward, the early bison hunter lifeway spread eastward too, eclipsing forest hunters' lifeways except in the few remaining northern forests of the region. Because of the continuing focus on larger-game animals, ethnographic comparison suggests that males still did most of the hunting. As earlier, smaller animals, birds, fish, and plants were part of the diet. The increasing number of sites and artifacts indicates that the human population was growing, and by the end of the period some sites were regularly reoccupied during subsistence-settlement cycles, the region was becoming packed with daughter communities, and access to resources was becoming an issue.

Proto-Wild Rice Harvesters, Proto-Horticulturalists, and Late Pedestrian Bison Hunters

Archaeological context. The third phase (cal 3000 BC–AD 1000) in the sequence coincides with the region's Late Archaic (3000–800/500 BC) and Woodland (800/500 BC–AD 1000) archaeological record. Trends and events during this period include an increasing number and variety of sites; expansion in the number and variety of ground and polished stone artifacts such as adzes, axes, and grinding stones and slabs; a shift from the throwing stick (atlatl) to the bow and arrow (ca. AD 500); appearance of and refinement in pottery vessels (as early as 800–400 BC in some areas); use of native copper to make utilitarian artifacts such as spear points, celts, and harpoons (the Old Copper complex, 3800–1100 BC); and growing use of smaller animals, aquatic resources (fish, shellfish), waterfowl, wild plant foods (wild rice, tubers), and domesticated Eastern Woodland plants such as sunflower, goosefoot, and little barley (the Eastern Agricultural complex), though the trends varied throughout the region in intensity and timing (see also Pearsall, this volume). Regular base camps now occur around lakes and along rivers. Many of these sites are larger, show evidence of more regular occupation, and have more site furniture, such as roasting pits and sturdier houses, than earlier sites. Earthen burial mound clusters, some of which were used for centuries, appear by the end of the Archaic and are a hallmark of the Woodland tradition.

Culture histories of the Upper Mississippi River–Northeastern Plains region describe in detail the distribution and attributes of pottery and projectile point types, and the content of local archaeological cultures (Alex 2000; Benchley et al. 1997; Frison and Mainfort 1996; Gibbon and Anfinson 2008; Theler and Boszhardt 2003). These archaeological taxa group together by plant biome: the southeastern deciduous forest, the western tall-grass prairie, and the northern mixed conifer-hardwoods forest. In general, the region exhibits gradual, accumulative change through wetter and drier periods, and the impact of external cultural phenomena such as the Hopewell (AD 100–300) and Arvilla (AD 600–900) burial traditions.

Human adaptations. Many of the changes that occur in the archaeological record of this phase are accounted for in Binford (2001) by regional packing by small bands; a subsequent need to exploit second-order food resources (the broad-spectrum revolution) within smaller, spatially circumscribed territories in response to intensification pressures; decreasing residential mobility; increased investment in storage (a delayed-return tactic); and a growing need to stake claim to the resources of one's territory. These trends are reflected in the presence in the archaeological record of (1) an increasingly varied technology to take advantage of secondary food resources such as fish, wild rice, and Eastern Agricultural complex domesticates; (2) larger, more seasonally permanent base camps now positioned to take advantage of a diversity of resources; (3) long-term communal cemeteries that mark a group's right to a territory; (4) a wider variety of task-specific sites in new territories; (5) steady population increases (as seen in the rising number of sites); and (6) the first hints of social inequality (as seen in preferential burial treatment). These changes would have affected the organization of male and female labor, with men now engaged in less hunting and greater participation in a broader range of food resource activities.

Forced resource intensification was a time- and space-transgressive process, a process that accounts for the lag in appearance of new technologies and settlement-subsistence adaptations in some areas, such as into the Driftless area from areas to the south and into the western prairies from the Driftless area, though the pace of intensification seems to have been quicker to the north in the forested lakes area of central Minnesota. In our studies we designate this new lifeway Proto-Horticulturalist in the southeastern deciduous forest zone, Proto-Wild Rice Harvester for groups living in the northern forests, and Late Pedestrian Bison Hunter for groups in the grasslands that focused on hunting bison.

Horticulturalists and Intensive Wild Rice Harvesters

Archaeological context. Within a hundred-year period (AD 950–1050), a village farming lifeway appeared across the southern portion of the region (Silvernale along the Mississippi River in southeastern Minnesota, and Cambria, Great Oasis, and Mill Creek in the southwestern prairie area of the region). The presence of semipermanent and often fortified villages, new ceramic types, and new dependence on maize (corn) horticulture separate this lifeway from those that preceded it. All of these societies show some contact with more complex Middle Mississippian societies to the south. During the 13th century, these societies were replaced by bison-hunting Oneota horticulturalists across the southern portion of the region and by Northeastern Plains villagers in the Northeastern Plains. By about AD 1200, a parallel lifeway emerged suddenly in the forests of central Minnesota (the Psinomani archaeological culture) and gradually spread northward. Although still technically hunter-gatherers, these Native Americans now lived in semisedentary village clusters, harvested wild rice (the "corn of the north") more intensely, and made an entirely new type of ceramic vessel (Figure 27.4). Temperature and rainfall varied during this period from warm-moist (the Neo-Atlantic climatic episode of AD 800–1250), to warm-dry (the Pacific episode of AD 1250–1450), to warm-moist (AD 1450–1550), to cool-moist (the Neo-Boreal or Little Ice Age of AD 1550–1850).

Human adaptations. Many of the changes that occur in the archaeological record of this phase are accounted for in Binford (2001:314) by an emergent change

Figure 27.4 Pre-Emergence (bottom row) and Post-Emergence (top row) pottery vessels: northern Minnesota vessels on the left (upper, Sandy Lake; lower, Blackduck) and southern Minnesota vessels on the right (upper, Oneota; lower, Madison Cord Impressed).

that was brought on by increasing population size and intensification pressures, in which "very new properties abruptly appear that could not have been anticipated by projections from the characteristic behavior of the parent system." We interpret this change as a shift from forager societies at the small-band level to more settled, larger tribal societies dependent on domesticates (or an equivalent). But why did the shift occur when it did? One answer is that the warm-moist Neo-Atlantic climatic episode coupled with a new and hardy strain of maize led to development of village farming lifeways in portions of this cool temperate region. When warm-dry conditions returned during the Pacific period, the farming lifeway was replaced by more flexible bison-hunting Oneota maize horticulturalists. These climatic shifts certainly affected the lifeway of the people of the region, but a "changing climate" explanation does not account for the timing of the shift in the northern forests. Is there an explanation, then, that accounts for the emergence of both types of tribal societies?

In a review of the notion of tribe, Fried (1975) concludes that the tribal level of social organization is not an indigenous (evolutionary) development but rather a response to the presence of neighboring militaristic chiefdoms or states, which was the trigger for the emergent change. Thus, band-level societies in the southern portion of the study area who had experienced 4,000 years of gradual resource intensification shifted rapidly to a tribal level of organization in response to the emergence of a complex polity (Cahokia) to their south and, following the political collapse of Cahokia after AD 1250, northern band-level societies shifted as rapidly in interaction with spreading, possibly aggressive Oneota peoples at that time (see also Alt, Emerson, this volume). After their emergence, tribal-level societies persisted in the region to historic contact in the 17th century. In our studies we designate this new lifeway Horticulturalist in the southern portion of the study area and Intensive Wild Rice Harvester in the northern forests.

Pattern in the Past

Although application of Binford's methods to the study area is still in process, his approach shows how and why free-ranging groups of hunter-gatherers in the study region regularly responded to resource circumscription, became more socially complex through time, and eventually, in many instances, changed rapidly and dramatically into horticultural or complex hunter-gatherer groups. As reconstructed here, the pioneer foraging phase lasted 700 years, the phase of circumscribed but wide-ranging foraging 7,500 years, the phase of band-level resource intensification 4,000 years, and the phase of tribal societies 650 years (to Contact). Besides providing a pattern for comparison with other regions of the world, the proposed sequence of adaptive change and the duration of its phases constitutes a framework for research for archaeologists working in the region.

You might ask: In our post-September 11 world, isn't the study of the archaeology of the Upper Mississippi River-Northeastern Plains region a trivial pursuit? Aren't there more urgent tasks that need addressing, like global warming and terrorism? From my perspective, identifying and understanding long-term patterns in human development is one of these tasks. The pattern continues to unfold and will do so into the future—and many of the world's problems today are a consequence, I believe, of that unfolding pattern. This entry is a small contribution to the task.

REFERENCES

Alex, L. M. 2000. *Iowa's Archaeological Past*. University of Iowa Press, Iowa City.
Benchley, E. D., B. Nansel, C. A. Dobbs, S. M. Thurston Myster, and B. H. O'Connell. 1997. *Archeology and Bioarcheology of the Northern Woodlands*. Arkansas Archeological Survey Research Series 52. Arkansas Archeological Survey, Fayetteville.
Binford, L. R. 2001. *Constructing Frames of Reference: An Analytical Method for Archaeological Theory Building Using Hunter-Gatherer and Environmental Data Sets*. University of California Press, Berkeley.
Bodley, J. H. 2005. *Cultural Anthropology: Tribes, States, and the Global System*. 4th ed. McGraw-Hill, New York.
Fried, M. A. 1975. *The Notion of Tribe*. Benjamin Cummings, Menlo Park, CA.
Frison, G. C., and R. C. Mainfort (editors). 1996. *Archeological and Bioarcheological Resources of the Northern Plains*. Arkansas Archeological Survey Research Series 47. Arkansas Archeological Survey, Fayetteville.
Gibbon, G. E. (In press.) *Minnesota Archaeology: A Guide to the Prehistory of the Upper Mississippi River Region*. University of Minnesota Press, Minneapolis.
Sahlins, M. D. 1968. *Tribesmen*. Prentice-Hall, Englewood Cliffs, NJ.
———. 2004. *Stoneage Economics*. Routledge, New York.
Service, E. R. 1979. *The Hunters*. 2nd ed. Prentice-Hall, Englewood Cliffs, NJ.
Theler, J. L., and R. F. Boszhardt. 2003. *Twelve Millennia: Archaeology of the Upper Mississippi River Valley*. University of Iowa Press, Iowa City.
Wilber, K. 2000. *A Brief History of Everything*. Rev. ed. Shambhala, Boston.

CHAPTER 28

THE ARCHAEOLOGICAL IMPRINT OF ORAL TRADITIONS ON THE LANDSCAPE OF NORTHERN PLAINS HUNTER-GATHERERS

GERALD A. OETELAAR

On the Northern Plains of North America, archaeological models of settlement systems are generally based on the ecology and behavior of bison (Peck 2004). The annual subsistence round is often described in terms of the seasonal migrations of bison, from wintering grounds in the sheltered valleys of the foothills to summer pastures on the open grasslands. Even though the bison herds migrate across extensive tracts, the territories of the human groups are limited by the distribution of critical resources and by the prevailing mode of transportation (Vickers and Peck 2004). Bison herding behavior also accounts for seasonal patterns of human aggregation and dispersal, whereas topography, vegetation, and distance to fuel and water explain where people camp during their annual forays across the Northern Plains (Adams 1976; Brumley and Dau 1988). Although researchers now use GIS to develop sophisticated predictive models of site location, they still rely on the same suite of ecological variables to model human behavior (Friesen 1998).

Blackfoot elders have a very different perception of their traditional homeland, which extends from the North Saskatchewan River in the north to the Yellowstone River in the south and from the Rocky Mountains in the west to the Great Sand Hills in the east. The boundaries of this territory are not rigidly defined, although the Blackfoot and their neighbors use landmarks along well-established trails to delineate the approximate margins of their respective homelands. These landmarks include distinctive peaks near mountain passes on the west (Oetelaar and Oetelaar 2011), important fords across the rivers on the north and south, and prominent hills marking the location of trails along the eastern margin of the homeland (Figure 28.1). Pictographs, petroforms, cairns, medicine wheels, and tipi rings occur on or near these named places.

According to Blackfoot elders, the area so defined has been their traditional homeland since time immemorial, and the archaeological evidence tends to

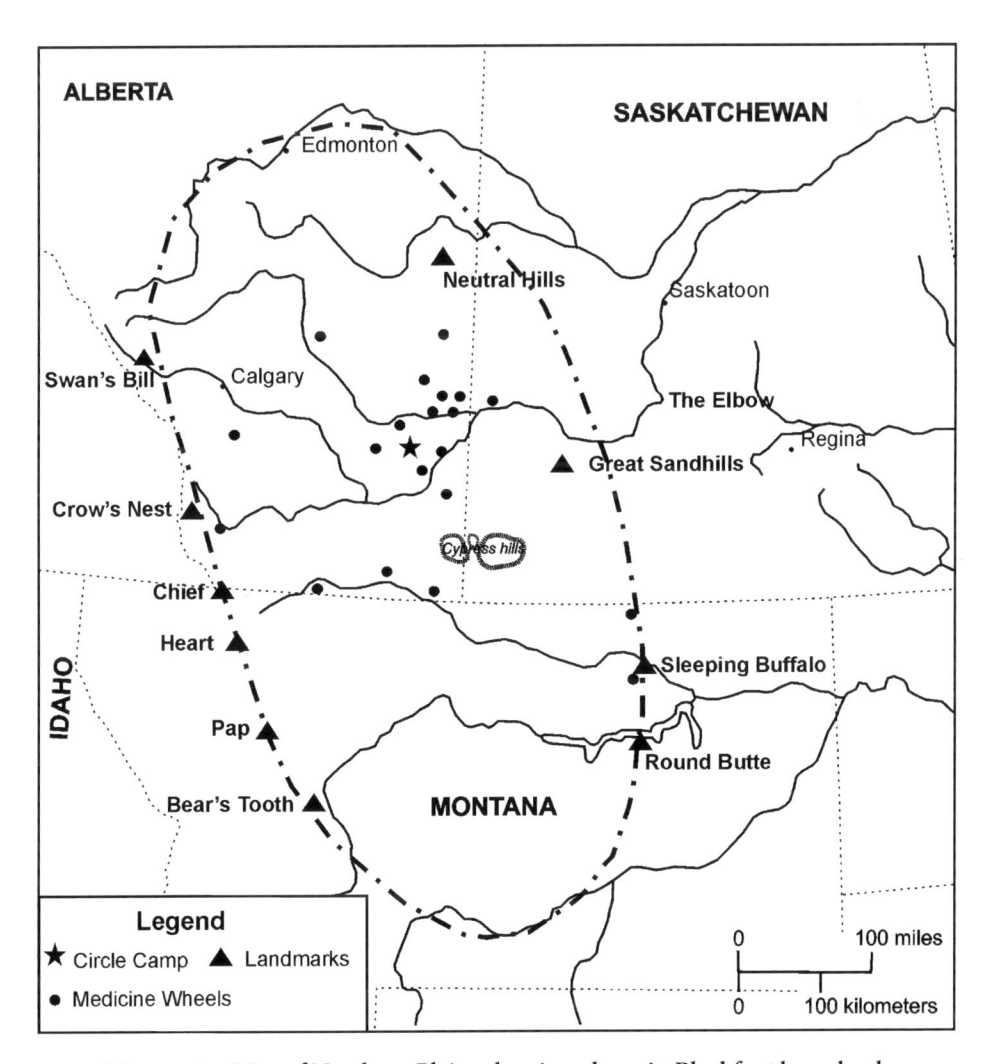

Figure 28.1 Map of Northern Plains showing places in Blackfoot homeland.

corroborate these claims of historical continuity (Vickers and Peck 2009). There is a general congruence between the extent of the Blackfoot homeland and the spatial distribution of diagnostic pottery and projectile point types (Peck and Ives 2001), of *iniskim* (Peck 2002), of Napi figures (Vickers 2008), of boulder monuments (Brumley 1988), and of distinctive rock art (Klassen 2003). Together, the distribution of these archaeological remains and the continuity evident in the material culture suggests a patterned use of the landscape extending over a millennium or more.

To the Blackfoot, the homeland is much more than a series of resource patches for humans and migrating bison herds. Instead, the Blackfoot view their homeland as a series of named locales linked by paths, movements, and narratives (Oetelaar and Meyer 2006; Oetelaar and Oetelaar 2006, 2011; Zedeño et al. 2006). The places are often outstanding natural features, river crossings, or resource patches perceived as focal points of spiritual energy. Myths and oral traditions explain how these landmarks were created by Napi, an ancestral being who left behind songs, sacred objects, and practices to commemorate his creative acts on earth (Oetelaar and Oetelaar 2011). Throughout the year, the Blackfoot follow in the footsteps of the ancestors and stop at the same places to perform activities and ceremonies in a prescribed order, while the associated landmarks serve as mnemonic devices that elicit the appropriate narratives. As such, the landscape is an archive or repository of traditional knowledge, and movement across the homeland becomes a journey through the history of the group.

This patterned movement across the landscape is sanctioned by a cosmology and is designed to fulfill obligations negotiated between the spirits and the Blackfoot people. The universe of the Blackfoot is divided into an upper world, a middle, and a lower. The middle world is home to the earth beings, including humans, four-legged animals, plants, rocks, and the earth itself (Blackfoot Gallery Committee 2001:9). The upper world is home to the sun, the moon, and morning star, as well as thunder and most of the birds. The lower world is inhabited by the water beings, as well as the beaver, otter, muskrat and certain waterfowl. In the long ago, the Blackfoot established sacred alliances with the spirits who control the availability of resources and the health of living communities (Bastien 2004). The alliances are maintained through rituals in which the Blackfoot communicate and negotiate directly with the spirits, often through intermediaries such as animals moving between the worlds. The rituals and negotiations with the spirits tend to occur at specific places on the landscape, where portals provide direct access to the upper or lower world. During the establishment of the sacred alliances, the spirits transferred medicine bundles to the Blackfoot people; along with prayers and offerings, they are used in rituals to maintain or restore the cosmic balance. Failure to perform these rituals or to observe the associated codes of ethical conduct toward the land, the resources, and the people will upset the spirits, who can withhold resources or cause illness within the community.

Efforts to maintain or reestablish balance in the universe involve the actions of individuals, communities, and larger social aggregates. Individuals can maintain the balance through their actions, offerings on the household altar, or vision quests. Households and communities participate in similar rituals during the opening of ceremonial bundles, the harvesting of resources, and important rites of passage. Finally, the larger social aggregates assemble once a year for the most important renewal ceremony of all, the sun dance. This ritual of eight to 10 days dedicated to the Sun involves several neighboring groups and is designed to guarantee future success in the acquisition of resources and to ensure the continued health of the community. Favored locations for the sun dance before the establishment of reserves include the confluence of the Red Deer and South Saskatchewan Rivers, the Cypress Hills, and the confluence of the Judith and Missouri Rivers (Oetelaar and Oetelaar 2006).

Since all of these places are found near the eastern margin of the Blackfoot homeland, participation in the sun dance required a scheduled movement from the sheltered river valleys bordering the Rocky Mountains to the open prairie. This journey took the Blackfoot people along well-established trails past familiar landmarks where they were able to renew their ties with the spirits, the ancestors, and neighboring groups; to repeat and transmit the rituals, songs and narratives stored in the archive; and to regenerate the land and its resources. Thus the sun dance and the associated pilgrimage of renewal was the prime motivation for the annual forays onto the plains, not the migratory habits of the bison.

Places, Narratives, and Movement

Landmarks within the Blackfoot homeland serve as navigational aids and as anchors for the oral traditions of the group. Distinctive mountain peaks along the western margin orient travelers approaching the Rocky Mountains from the east and identify passes through the mountains (Figure 28.2). Each named mountain peak is also situated near a lake and a spring, thus identifying these locations as places with access to all three worlds of the cosmos. Although the distinctive peaks are mentioned in several Blackfoot myths, Crow's Nest Mountain, the home of Raven, and Chief Mountain, the home of Thunder, figure prominently in the story of the Thunder Medicine bundle,[1] a narrative that clearly illustrates the intricate relationships among the places, the narratives, and the patterned movement of the Blackfoot. At a basic level, the story of Thunder and Raven explains the origin of winter and summer, the two seasons of the Blackfoot year, and identifies Raven as the master of winter and Thunder as the master of summer.

Blackfoot groups spend their winters in the sheltered valleys of the Foothills, where fuel is readily available. The greatest concentration of bison kill sites occurs in this portion of the Blackfoot homeland, a pattern archaeologists attribute to the unique topography, vegetation, and warm chinook winds. To the Blackfoot, the topography and vegetation were created for their benefit, whereas the chinook is

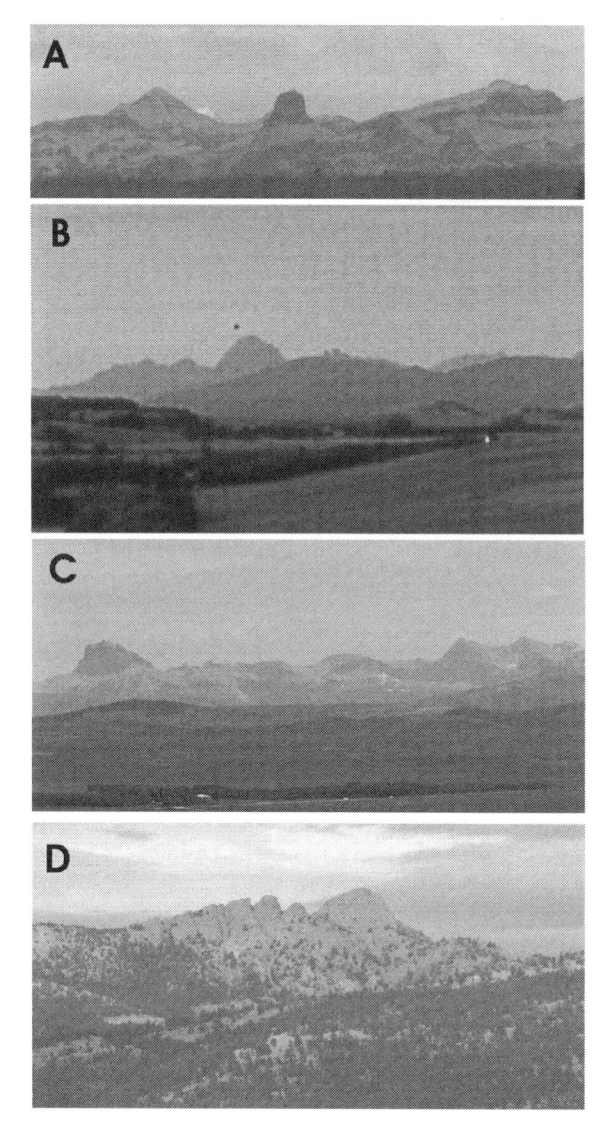

Figure 28.2 Photographs of (A) Swan's Bill, (B) Crow's Nest, (C) Chief, and (D) Bear's Tooth.

controlled by spirits (as indicated in a narrative about the Bear Who Stole the Chinook). At the same time, only certain places within the dissected terrain of the Foothills are appropriate for use as a bison jump or pound. The ideal kill site, to the archaeologists, included a gathering basin and associated drive lanes located upwind of a precipice concealed by a false horizon (e.g., Brink 2008). To the Blackfoot, the locations and uses of bison jumps or *pis'kuns* are identified in myths such as the women's and the men's *pis'kuns* of the First Marriage. The women's *pis'kun* is today known as the Old Women's Buffalo Jump (Forbis 1962), whereas the men's *pis'kun* is located along Jumping Pound Creek west of Calgary. In fact, each kill site in this portion of the homeland had a specific name and associated narrative.

Although small, the sample of excavated kill sites in the Foothills has produced evidence of repeated use, presumably reflecting investment in the drive lane complexes. To the Blackfoot people, specific *pis'kuns* were reused because they were related to significant events in the long ago and were thus maintained by assembling and burning the accumulating refuse, and by regularly burning the vegetation during the fall, winter, and early spring (Oetelaar and Oetelaar 2007). Therefore, the fescue grassland that attracted the bison to the Foothills during the winter was actually created and managed by the Blackfoot people and their ancestors, rather than being the product of a local climatic regime. Yet despite all of these preparations and intimate knowledge of bison behavior, the Blackfoot people still relied on the beaver bundle holder to call the buffalo to the *pis'kun* using the ceremony described in the myth of the Buffalo-Rock.

Operation of a successful bison drive involved the cooperation and coordination of a large number of people. To ensure timely participation by several groups in such communal ventures, the Blackfoot people maintained social ties with numerous households and communities scattered in the sheltered valleys of the Foothills. Throughout the winter, then, they visited relatives and friends, attended special occasions, and came together to hear the Napi stories. However, travel through the Foothills during the winter months can be dangerous because of sudden blizzards. Fortunately, Napi's encounter with a large boulder created a series of landmarks along the Old North Trail, the principal avenue of communication along the Foothills. In a prairie landscape blanketed with a sheet of white snow, the fragments (erratics) of this large boulder remain clearly visible as dark monoliths (Figure 28.3). To ensure safe passage through the area, Blackfoot travelers made offerings to these sacred rocks, as indicated by pictographs on the boulders and by the materials recovered from the base of these erratics (Brink 1981).

In addition to these basic survival strategies, the story of Thunder and Raven describes the transfer of the Thunder Medicine bundle with instructions to open the bundle at the first thunder of spring (Kehoe 2002; Zedeño 2008). This sound announces Thunder's return and advises the Blackfoot to begin their annual ritual cycle and movement toward the sacred sun dance ground (Reeves 1993:246). When opening the bundle, the Blackfoot people ask Thunder to protect them from lightning strikes as they travel across the open prairie and bring the rain that makes the grass and berries grow.

The Blood elder *Káinaikoăn* describes this journey as a systematic move from one named place to another, as the group traveled from Cut Bank Creek near the foot of Chief Mountain to the Cypress Hills and back (Uhlenbeck 1912:1–38). Although bison hunts are mentioned, *Káinaikoăn's* account focuses more on the collection and processing of various resources and the social relations of the people involved in these activities. As the Blackfoot moved along the path, the appearance of the landmark reminded the people of the place name. The place name, in turn, brought forth associated narratives, ceremonies, and rituals. This type of memory storage facilitated successful recollection and transmission of oral traditions but required regular visits to all of the named places.

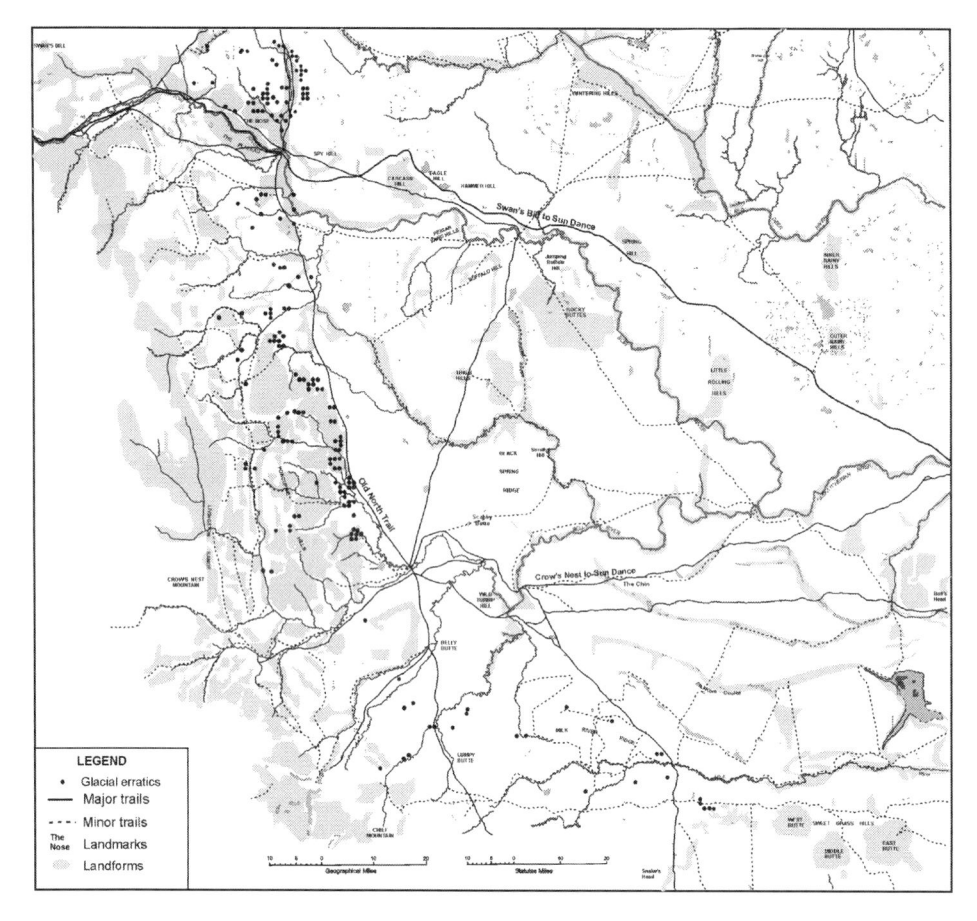

Figure 28.3 Map of Southern Alberta showing Old North Trail and trails to sun dance grounds.

Concentrations of tipi rings along the upper reaches of Cut Bank Creek (Kehoe 1960) and along the Marias in the vicinity of Medicine Rock Coulee identify the first two important stops on the journey. The third important stop along this trail was Battle Coulee, located in the vicinity of the Sweet Grass Hills, where the people camped for an extended period of time. These hills are known to the Blackfoot as *kutoyis*, or Sweet Pine Hills in reference to the alpine fir or sweet pine present on the slopes. The word *kutoyis* also refers to Blood-Clot or Smoking Star, the hero in one of the Blackfoot star myths, who rids the world of seven evil beings.

On a more practical level, the Blood-Clot story reminded people that it was now time to begin spiritual and secular preparations for the sun dance. Spiritual preparation involved fasting and ritual, while secular activities included collection of sweet pine and buffalo tongues. Sweet pine collected from the Sweet Grass Hills produced a sweeter, more concentrated aroma when burned as incense in the medicine lodge (McClintock 1968:524–525; Schwab 1994:66) while the buffalo tongues were gathered at this time for the Holy Women to cut into strips.

The archaeological evidence for these practices includes concentrations of tipi rings (Schwab 1994) and vision quest features near this landmark (Dormaar 2003; Dormaar and Reeves 1993), numerous bison kill sites along the Milk River (Keyser 1979), and pictographs in caves, on erratics and in the nearby coulees (Dormaar 2003).

The other named places along the trail between the Sweet Grass Hills and the Cypress Hills also have dense concentrations of tipi rings, from repeated visits by the Blackfoot people and their ancestors (Oetelaar and Oetelaar 2006). At one of these places, known as Manyberries, the Blackfoot people collected berries for the sun dance, following the procedure described in the myth of Old Man Sees Berries in the Water. While camped in the vicinity of this landmark, the people recounted stories and performed rituals but also managed the berry patch by removing dead twigs and unwanted shoots, pruning and coppicing the shoots and stems, and burying ripe berries as offerings (Oetelaar and Oetelaar 2007). To the Blackfoot people, then, the berry bushes were there because the ancestors came to these places, told stories, sang songs, and performed appropriate rituals while harvesting and drying the berries.

The ultimate destination of the journey was the sacred sun dance ground, a place where numerous groups, including those from adjoining homelands, came together to celebrate the Sun. The sun dance or *okan* involved establishing a circle camp, a formal arrangement of tipis in a large circle with an opening facing east. The Medicine Lodge, with its opening facing east as well, was erected in the center of the camp circle, following the Sun's instructions to Scarface. The tipi of the holy woman, where the sun dance or natoas bundle was kept and transferred as related in the story of the Woman Who Married Morning Star, was positioned between the Medicine Lodge and the western margin of the circle. Archaeological examples of camp circles are comparatively rare, but an encampment near the confluence of the Red Deer and South Saskatchewan Rivers includes more than 20 stone circles arranged in the form of a horseshoe with the opening facing northeast (Oetelaar and Oetelaar 2006). Although traces of the Medicine Lodge are missing, a medicine wheel located nearby may represent a monument designed to commemorate this important event.

Movement to and from the sun dance ground within the Blackfoot homeland involved a round trip of 800 kilometers following well-established trails (Figure 28.3), which, given the limitations of the dog travois (Henderson 1994), were located along the valley margins (Oetelaar and Meyer 2006; Oetelaar and Olson 2000). Using the dog and travois, a large group of people traveling 15 kilometers per day could cover this distance in 54 days, leaving 130 days to collect resources, meet friends, and conduct ceremonies (Oetelaar 2004). Placement of lodges along the valley margin was designed for convenience but also offered expansive views of the landscape, respite from annoying insects, and opportunities to communicate with the spirits who travel in the wind. Such patterned movement generated large camps near landmarks as well as smaller camps near favored stopping places every 15 kilometers or so (Lobb 2008; Moors 2007).

Conclusion

In short, the seasonal movement of the Blackfoot people was motivated by a desire to renew their ties with the land, the people, and the culture. This annual historic journey and ritual pilgrimage involved travel along well-established trails extending from the wintering grounds in the Foothills to the sun dance ground on the open prairie. The named places visited along the way served as navigational aids and repositories of traditional knowledge. These landmarks were created in the long ago by ancestral beings who left behind songs, sacred objects (Napi figures), and practices to commemorate their creative acts on earth. To retrieve and transmit the oral traditions stored in this archive, the Blackfoot had to visit these places regularly, leaving behind not only traces of their encampments but also their offerings. These practices are preserved in the archaeological record as concentrations of campsites (tipi rings), kill sites, vision quest structures, boulder monuments, petroforms, pictographs, petroglyphs, and offerings on or near these landmarks.

Acknowledgments

Many of the ideas presented in this paper derive from discussions with my mentors, Bruce and Deanna Starlight, Narcisse Blood, and Blair First Rider. I also owe a debt a gratitude to D. Joy Oetelaar who, as a historian, is vigilant in reviewing my use of historical sources. Finally, none of this research would have been possible without the generous support of the Social Sciences and Humanities Research Council (SSHRC) through its Major Collaborative Research Initiatives (MCRI) grant (412-1999-1000) and through its BOREAS grant (863-2006-0003). Of course, I alone am responsible for any errors or omissions.

Note

1. Myths are from Blackfoot Gallery Committee (2001), Grinnell (1962), McClintock (1968), and Wissler and Duvall (1995).

References

Adams, G. 1976. *Prehistoric Survey of the Lower Red Deer River, 1975*. Archaeological Survey of Alberta, Occasional Paper 3. Alberta Culture, Historical Resources Division, Edmonton.

Bastien, B. 2004. *Blackfoot Ways of Knowing: The Worldview of the Siksikaitsitapi.* University of Calgary Press, Calgary.

Blackfoot Gallery Committee (editor). 2001. *Nitsitapiisinni: The Story of the Blackfoot People.* Glenbow Museum, Calgary.

Brink, J. 1981. Rock Art Sites in Alberta: Retrospect and Prospect. In *Alberta Archaeology: Prospect and Retrospect*, edited by T. A. Moore, pp. 69–81. Archaeological Society of Alberta, Lethbridge.

———. 2008. *Imagining Head-Smashed-In: Aboriginal Buffalo Hunting on the Northern Plains.* AU Press, Edmonton.

Brumley, J. 1988. *Medicine Wheels on the Northern Plains: A Summary and Appraisal.* Archaeological Survey of Alberta, Manuscript Series 12. Alberta Culture and Multiculturalism, Edmonton.

———, and B. J. Dau. 1988. *Historical Resource Investigations Within the Forty Mile Coulee Reservoir.* Archaeological Survey of Alberta, Manuscript Series 13. Alberta Environment, Edmonton.

Dormaar, J. F. 2003. *Sweetgrass Hills: A Natural and Cultural History.* Lethbridge Historical Society, Lethbridge.

———, and B. O. K. Reeves. 1993. Vision Quest Sites in Southern Alberta and Northern Montana. In *Kunaitupii—Coming Together on Native Sacred Sites: Their Sacredness, Conservation, and Interpretation*, edited by B. O. K. Reeves and M. A. Kennedy, pp. 162–178. Archaeological Society of Alberta, Calgary.

Forbis, R. G. 1962. The Old Women's Buffalo Jump, Alberta. National Museum of Canada, Bulletin 180, *Contributions to Anthropology*, 1960, pt. 1, pp. 55–123. Department of Northern Affairs and National Resources, Ottawa.

Friesen, N. 1998. *Analysis of Archaeological Settlement Patterns in Grasslands National Park, Saskatchewan.* Master's thesis, University of Saskatchewan, Saskatoon.

Grinnell, G. B. 1962. *Blackfoot Lodge Tales: The Story of a Prairie People.* University of Nebraska, Lincoln.

Henderson, N. 1994. Replicating Dog Travois Travel on the Northern Plains. *Plains Anthropologist* 39:145–159.

Kehoe, A. B. 2002. Thunder's Pipe: The Blackfoot Ritual Year. *Cosmos* 18:19–33.

Kehoe, T. F. 1960. *Stone Tipi Rings in North-Central Montana and the Adjacent Portion of Alberta, Canada: Their Historical, Ethnological, and Archaeological Aspects.* Bureau of American Ethnology, Bulletin 173. Smithsonian Institution, Washington.

Keyser, J. D. 1979. Late Prehistoric Period Bison Procurement on the Milk River in North-Central Montana. *Archaeology in Montana*, vol. 20, no. 1.

Klassen, M. A. 2003. Spirit Images, Medicine Rocks: The Rock Art of Alberta. In *Archaeology in Alberta: A View from the New Millennium*, edited by J. W. Brink and J. F. Dormaar, pp. 154–186. Archaeological Society of Alberta, Medicine Hat.

Lobb, M. 2008. *In the Shadow of the Mountains and the Porcupine Hills: An Analysis of Prehistoric Land Use on the Pikani Reserve #147, Alberta.* Master's thesis, University of Calgary, Calgary.

McClintock, W. 1968. *The Old North Trail: Life, Legends and Religion of the Blackfeet Indians.* University of Nebraska Press, Lincoln. First published 1910 by Macmillan, London.

Moors, M. 2007. *Tipi Rings, Ceremonial Sites and the Siksikaitsitapi in Southern Alberta.* Master's thesis, University of Calgary, Calgary.

Oetelaar, G. A. 2004. Stone Circles, Social Organization and Special Places: Forbis' Skepticism Revisited. In *Archaeology on the Edge: New Perspectives from the Northern Plains*, edited by B. Kooyman and J. Kelley, pp. 125–155. University of Calgary Press, Calgary.

———, and D. Meyer. 2006. Movement and Native American Landscapes: A Comparative Approach. *Plains Anthropologist* 51(199):355–374.

Oetelaar G. A., and D. J. Oetelaar. 2006. People, Places and Paths: The Cypress Hills and the Nitsitapii Landscape of Southern Alberta. *Plains Anthropologist* 51(199):375–398.

———. 2007. The New Ecology and Landscape Archaeology: Incorporating the Anthropogenic Factor. *Canadian Journal of Archaeology* 31(3):65–92.

———. 2011. The Structured World of the Nitsitapii: The Landscape as Historical Archive Among Hunter-Gatherers of the Northern Plains. In *Structured Worlds: The Archaeology of Hunter-Gatherer Thought and Action*, edited by A. Cannon, pp. 69-94. Cambridge University Press, Cambridge.

Oetelaar, G. A., and C. Olson. 2000. Historic Trails and Precontact Landscapes: A Study of Land Use in the Calgary Area. In *The Entangled Past: Integrating History and Archaeology*, edited by M. Boyd, J. C. Erwin, and M. Hendrickson, pp. 312–318. Archaeological Association of the University of Calgary, Calgary.

Peck, T. R. 2002. Archaeologically Recovered Ammonites: Evidence for Long-Term Continuity in Nitsitapii Ritual. *Plains Anthropologist* 47(181):147–164.

———. 2004. *Bison Ethology and Native Settlement Patterns During the Old Women's Phase on the Northwestern Plains*. BAR International Series 1278. Archaeopress, Oxford.

———, and J. W. Ives. 2001. Late Side-Notched Projectile Points in the Northern Plains. *Plains Anthropologist* 46(176):163–193.

Reeves, B. O. K. 1993. Iniskim: A Sacred Nitsitapii Religious Tradition. In *Kunaitupii: Coming Together on Native Sacred Sites: Their Sacredness, Conservation, and Interpretation*, edited by B. O. K. Reeves and M. A. Kennedy, pp. 194–247. Archaeological Society of Alberta, Calgary.

Schwab, D. 1994. The Sweetgrass Hills: Cultural Landmarks on the Northwestern Plains. *Archaeology in Montana* 35(2):59–88.

Uhlenbeck, C. C. 1912. *A New Series of Blackfoot Texts from the Southern Peigans Blackfoot Reservation Teton County Montana, with the Help of Joseph Tatsey*. Johannes Muller, Amsterdam.

Vickers, J. R. 2008. Anthropomorphic Effigies of the Plains. *Plains Anthropologist* 53(206):199–221.

———, and T. R. Peck. 2004. Islands in a Sea of Grass: The Significance of Wood in Winter Campsite Selection on the Northwestern Plains. In *Archaeology on the Edge: New Perspectives from the Northern Plains*, edited by B. Kooyman and J. Kelley, pp. 95–124. University of Calgary Press, Calgary.

———. 2009. Identifying the Prehistoric Blackfoot: Approaches to Nitsitapii (Blackfoot) Culture History. In Mercury Series, Archaeology Paper 170, *Painting the Past with a Broad Brush: Papers in Honour of James Valliere Wright*, edited by D. L. Keenlyside and J.-L. Pilon, pp. 473–497. Canadian Museum of Civilization, Ottawa.

Wissler, C., and D. C. Duvall. 1995. *Mythology of the Blackfoot Indians*. With introduction by A. B. Kehoe. University of Nebraska Press, Lincoln.

Zedeño, M. N. 2008. Bundled Worlds: The Roles and Interactions of Complex Objects from the North American Plains. *Journal of Archaeological Method and Theory* 15:362–378.

———, K. Hollenback, and C. Grinnell. 2006. *From Path to Myth: Journeys and the Naturalization of Territorial Identity Along the Missouri River*, edited by J. E. Snead, C. L. Erickson, and J. A. Darling, pp. 106–132. University of Pennsylvania Museum of Archaeology and Anthropology, Philadelphia.

CHAPTER 29

SITUATING (PROTO) HISTORY ON THE NORTHWESTERN PLAINS AND ROCKY MOUNTAINS

LAURA L. SCHEIBER AND JUDSON BYRD FINLEY

The Northwestern Plains and adjacent areas are well known for a rich Paleoindian archaeological record, dating back more than 12.000 years. Holocene occupations are somewhat less recognized to those unfamiliar with the plains, although certainly buffalo jumps, tipi rings, and medicine wheels are part of a broader knowledge and lexicon about the archaeology of the continent. Inspired by a growing interest in colonial and frontier encounters and in bridging artificial divisions between prehistoric and historical archaeology as well as recent methodological innovations, plains and mountain archaeologists have begun turning their attention to study of the other side of the time spectrum, that is, the material record of Native lives in the 17th, 18th, and 19th centuries. This work compliments well-established programs of plains ethnohistory and also adds an important material aspect to an often-biased written record. The goals of this chapter are to problematize the relationship between the so-called prehistoric and historic eras on the Northwestern Plains and middle Rocky Mountains and to present two cases that exemplify recent research within a defined study area centered on the Bighorn Basin and Greater Yellowstone Ecosystem of northwestern Wyoming and south central Montana.

In part because of their somewhat inaccessible location within the middle of the continent, Native people of the western plains and mountains did not see permanent American settlement until late in the 19th century, almost 400 years after Spanish ships landed on the shores of Hispaniola. Townships in Wyoming and Montana were not founded until the early 1900s, long after places like Santa Fe, St. Louis, or even Denver. Twenty generations of nomadic residents in the short grass plains, high country plateaus, and mountain forests witnessed and participated in unprecedented change, much of it only distantly related to what was occurring outside the region. What this means is that archaeologists working in the western plains and mountains have access to an extended material data set that continues through the 19th century. This record is in some cases hundreds of years longer than in the rest of the country, before forced movement to reservations, missions, and ranching settlements. This time period is often referred to as the protohistoric, after the coming of French, British, and Spanish explorers but before everyday contact with American settlers. We contend that using this transitional shorthand between prehistory and history has important methodological and theoretical implications.

The western edge of the plains and the adjacent mountain corridors were a crossroads for numerous Native peoples during this dynamic time on the American frontier. Among these inhabitants were the Crow, Shoshone, Lakota, Cheyenne, Arapaho, Blackfoot, Assiniboine, Atsina, Kiowa, Comanche, Ute, and Plains Apache. European contact brought many changes as Native peoples became increasingly involved with the fur trade and were pushed and pulled into new territories. These changes are reflected in subsistence and settlement strategies, marriage patterns, trade negotiations, labor, and demography. Material inventories changed as well; firearms, equestrian tackle, metal pots and personal adornments, cotton and wool clothing, and glass beads were innovatively incorporated into native lifeways. Intermarriage among Native groups and between Native peoples and Europeans additionally led to new identities and group memberships.

Until recently, much of what we know archaeologically from this time period has come from burial contexts, especially as these burials were more actively sought by early collectors, hoping to find beadwork, old guns, axes, and knives. Most of these burials are single internments in rockshelters and small caves, but occasionally they are from cemeteries associated with European and American trading posts and forts. Analysis of human physical remains from these sites demonstrates a clear decline in average age at death after AD 1700. The average individual age during the Protohistoric/Historic (AD 1700–1900) was 25 years, compared to 33 years during the Late Prehistoric (AD 150–1700) and to 47 years during the Late Archaic (1050 BC–AD 450). More young people were dying, and very few adults survived to old age (Scheiber 2008). The Pitchfork burials (48PA42) represent an example from the recent past. In the first decade of the 19th century, the bodies of two young Crow men in their 20s were placed high in a rockshelter overlooking the Greybull River. They were buried with numerous European and Native-manufactured objects, including glass beads, dentalia shells, shell hair pipes, metal jewelry, buffalo robes, a wool coat, and a carved wooden bowl. From the high number of ectoparasites (lice) recovered from preserved hair, researchers concluded that these individuals were living away from their home for as long as a year prior to their death.

Additional archaeological data from this time period has come from the discovery of occasional campsites, as at River Bend (48NA202) or Medicine Lodge Creek (48BH499), of biographical style rock art sites such as No Water (48WA2066) or Joliet (24CB402), and of isolated vertical pole lodge structures in the mountains such as Paint Creek (48PA1085) or the Soapy Dale Peak Lodge (48HO107; Figure 29.1).

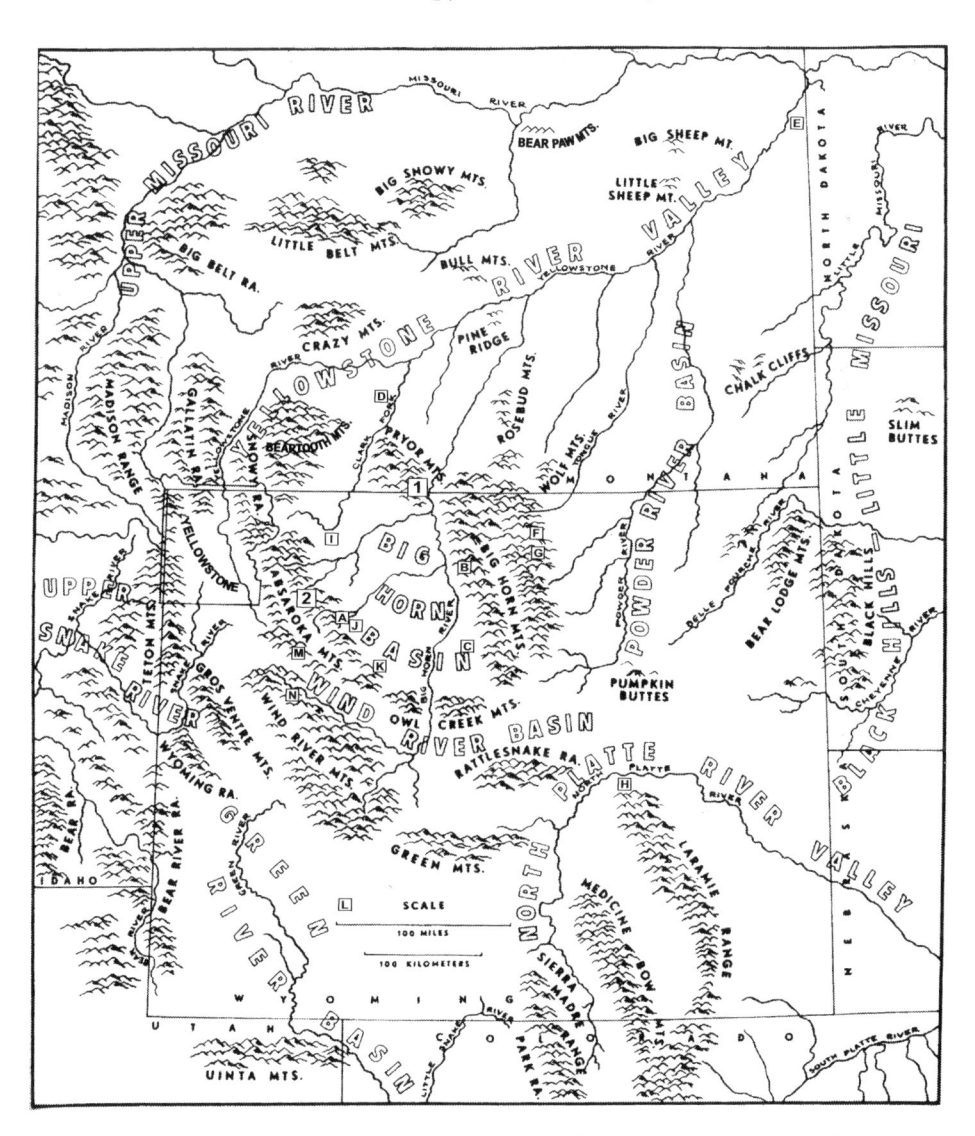

Figure 29.1 Map of the Northwestern Plains and Middle Rocky Mountains (base map from Frison 1991:5). (a) Pitchfork (48PA42), (b) Medicine Lodge Creek (48BH499), (c) No Water (48WA2066), (d) Joliet (24CB402), (e) Hagen (24DW2), (f) Big Goose (48SH313), (g) Piney Creek (48JO311), (h) River Bend (48NA202), (i) Paint Creek Lodge (48PA1085), (j) Soapy Dale Peak Lodge (48HO107), (k) Legend Rock (48HO4), (l) Eden Farson (48SW304), (m) Bull Elk Pass (48FR307) and Black Mountain (48FR494), (n) High Rise Village (48FR5891), (1) Bighorn Canyon, (2) Boulder Ridge.

Information from these sites however is not well-disseminated outside of a local context and word of mouth among regional archaeologists.

Crossing Divides

The western plains in Wyoming and Montana are located on the edge of the North American continental divide, and the metaphor of crossing divides in time and space is particularly salient in conceptualizing the recent past here. Archaeologists interested in the material record of recent Indian occupations straddle several culture areas, traditions, and frameworks for conceptualizing the past. The term *protohistoric* is often used as an intermediate period between prehistory and history, although definitions may emphasize material goods and encounters over indigenous culture change and continuity.

> The protohistoric is regarded as the transitional period between the initial receipt of European goods by the aboriginal inhabitants of a region which signals the end of the prehistoric, and the arrival of Europeans in the area which marks the beginning of the historic period [Ray 1978:26].

The end of the prehistoric on the western plains would therefore probably date to somewhere between 1600 and 1700 and is typically signified by access to and use of some European-manufactured goods. Demographic patterns and other factors suggest that disease epidemics affected sedentary farmers in the eastern plains along the Missouri river by the early 1600s. Although some Indian people in the far west may have had regular contact with European trappers and traders during this time, these encounters were probably uncommon. The spread of the horse across the plains beginning in the early 1700s is probably one of the most concrete changes that affected Plains cultures throughout the area. The spread of the horse may have been patchy, however, and conclusions about changing mobility may be oversimplified. Mobility, territory, and accessibility certainly changed, but to what extent and by whom remains to be explored. A variety of written accounts are available before sustained contact with European Americans in the wider region, although it is not until after the Louisiana Purchase and Lewis and Clark's Corps of Discovery in 1806 that we have any written documents of Native people living in the Greater Yellowstone area.

The start of the historic period is also problematic. On the western plains, history is set sometime during the 19th century, in the 100 years between Lewis and Clark's travels in 1806 and the massacre at Wounded Knee in 1890. The historic period is often subtly defined by and symbolically connected with cultural destruction, and dissociation from former ways of life, when mobile hunter-gatherers become ranchers and farmers on government-mandated reservations. Forced settlement or daily constraint on the mobility of hunter-gatherers is, then, what ultimately defines the historic. This is the decisive end to a protohistoric or transitional period, and most archaeologists have not been able to trace (or been interested in tracing) the material signature of reservation-period occupants. How do we cross this divide between prehistory and history and the legacy of prehistoric and historic archaeology? We have three main concerns with the appropriateness of designating a separate period (protohistory) from what comes before or after.

1. Is the protohistoric a date or a process? As archaeologists, we are not accustomed to measuring time in decades, and we often lack the fine-grained information to accurately refine our dates within the two or three centuries under investigation. However, we know from written records that considerable culture change occurred during this time, where decades do make a difference. The protohistoric is often defined by artifact presence—trade beads, cartridges, metal arrow heads—so that the definition becomes more about these objects than choices to incorporate these items into traditional material cultural repertoires.
2. How do we define these centuries without overreliance on artifact ratios (that is, marking time by the relative percentages of indigenous to introduced materials)? There is a tacit assumption that people uncritically chose European-manufactured objects soon after they became available. These artifacts become diagnostic index fossils, not hallmarks of change in the resulting interpretations. In fact, native people often chose to use a mixture of old and new materials following access to metal and glass objects. Matching material change to social change is thus difficult when artifact assemblages of the 1830s could be very similar to those from the 1530s, but originating from very different social, economic, and political contexts. This is complicated by the high mobility of plains peoples, which in many cases is not conducive to extensive discussion of cultural identity and similarity and difference between specific groups. In the absence of European trade goods, however, we may not be able to separate circa AD 1500 occupations from circa AD 1800 occupations, and thus in practice we may extend what we call (late) prehistoric sites all the way into the 19th century.
3. How does cultural identity become *visible* in archaeological contexts? Because of a fairly extensive ethnohistoric and ethnographic literature on the plains, we have a sense of the type and distribution of Native groups that may correspond with archaeological assemblages. Although we can rarely associate archaeological complexes with known descendant communities, after about AD 1700 these tribal identities can be explored in more detail.

Stemming from these concerns is the realization that the archaeology of this period of time on the Northwestern Plains and Rocky Mountains may differ from other areas of North America because of

1. The relative geographic isolation in the middle of the country
2. The unique physical surroundings in overlapping zones of transition among three primary research and cultural areas (Great Plains, Interior Plateau, and Great Basin), all having their own archaeological chronologies and taxonomies
3. The character of hunter-gatherers' mobility compared to settlements of farmers in much of the rest of the continent
4. The relative position of Native peoples vis-à-vis different kinds of European colonial settlements and outposts (with differing agendas and philosophies)
5. The late American settlement in this area
6. The extensive research by ethnohistorians and ethnographers characterizing the people and lifeways of the Great Plains that may inhibit or discourage pursuing other lines of evidence
7. The dominant historical narrative of the settling of the West

Two Case Studies

Two case studies involving the archaeology of recent nomadic hunter-gatherer occupants of the Northwestern Plains and Rocky Mountains exemplify relevant issues related to researching the material record of the 17th, 18th, and 19th centuries. Our conclusions are based on archaeological research focused on documenting Crow and Shoshone migration, residence, and landscape use in northern Wyoming and southern Montana, in the Bighorn Basin, and in the Greater Yellowstone area.

Tipi Rings, Domestic Space, and the Crow

According to oral histories, the Crow separated from the Hidatsa in the Middle Missouri region of present-day North Dakota during the 1500s and resettled on the western plains of Montana sometime between 1550 and 1650. A handful of archaeological sites document this journey, notably a single earthlodge at the Hagen site (24DW2) on the Montana–North Dakota border and bison processing campsites on the eastern slope of the Bighorn Mountains such as Big Goose (48SH313) and Piney Creek (48JO311). Identifying theses sites as Crow is primarily based on pottery that is stylistically similar to that found in the Middle Missouri area. By just 300 years later, during the Fort Laramie Treaty of 1851, the Crow leader Awé Kúalawaachish (Sits in the Middle of the Land) defined the Crow homeland, known as *Iichiia Shoopé*, as extending from the Black Hills in the southeast to the Wind River Mountains in the southwest, from the Beartooth Mountains in the southwest to the Bear Paw Mountains in the northeast. The Crow people lived within these four corners, represented symbolically and metaphorically by the four-pole foundation of the Crow tipi. The words *Iichiia Shoopé* literally mean the four base poles of the tipi.

Our first case study focuses on an extensive domestic tipi ring landscape numbering in the thousands at Bighorn Canyon National Recreation Area (Figure 29.2). Tipi rings, or stone circles, are one of the most common archaeological sites on the Northwestern Plains. Rocks that were often placed around the base of the tipi to hold it down remained in place when the camp was moved. They also preserve the footprint of the lodge, the conceptual and symbolic home of the Crow people. Archaeologists studying stone circle sites can address daily lives in a domestic context, use of space, social and economic organization, and ideology. Bighorn Canyon is located on the northern edge of the Bighorn Basin and is adjacent to the modern Crow Reservation. The Crow continue to tell many stories about the canyon area. Studying tipi rings at Bighorn Canyon is important for addressing Native-centered identity and migration in a domestic context.

Most of the data at stone circles sites can be retrieved from the surface, minimizing the potential impacts due to subsurface investigation. Limited test excavations target potentially datable buried hearths. A number of the dated rings at Bighorn Canyon were occupied during AD 1400–1600, which falls within the few centuries when the Crow probably arrived in the western country. The majority of Plains Indians construct their tipi from a three-pole tripod foundation, which leaves an oval footprint and an oval stone circle. However, the Crow, Blackfoot, and Shoshone all used four-pole foundations. Although we cannot definitively say the Bighorn Canyon campsites were left by Crow people, they are contemporaneous with the Crow migration, and the circular footprint is more likely from a four-pole lodge.

Figure 29.2 Stone circle at Two Eagle site, Bighorn Canyon (BICA 08–01-SC29; note possible doorway opening in lower center).

The Crow call events that happened in the past "the time when we used stones to weigh down our lodges." The word for this is *Biiaakashissihipee*. According to Crow tribal history, a boy named Big Metal or Uuwatisee was raised by bighorn sheep after he was abandoned by his stepfather in the mountains. He later returned to his people bringing metal and tipi stakes, and stakes replaced stones for holding down tipi covers. This pattern appears to hold true throughout the plains, and it is exceedingly rare to find rocks, not stakes, around the base of tipis in historic photographs. Campsites that date to the 18th or 19th centuries are thus quite difficult to identify. Some researchers have suggested that very large rings postdate the introduction of the horse, but this age-size correlation remains unresolved and is not supported by the evidence. Therefore the archaeological signatures of these campsites only loosely point to the time period of interest, after Crow migrations into the area. Although we could simply label these stone circle sites as prehistoric in age because of their lack of diagnostic historic artifacts, we think it is important to acknowledge changes to the social landscape of this time in the metaphorical context of domestic spaces.

Sheep Traps, Hunting Landscapes, and the Shoshone

As a comparison, the Shoshone people of Wyoming, Montana, and Idaho are essentially a Great Basin group, some of whom migrated east across the Rocky Mountains during the last thousand years. Considerable debate exists as to the duration of Shoshone occupation in the west, with arguments ranging from 5,000 years to 500 years ago (Nabokov and Loendorf 2004). The Shoshone world in the 17th through 19th centuries covered most of the mountains, plains, and basins of Wyoming, although the Snakes (as they were often called) expanded extensively throughout the plains as horse traders, raiders, and middlemen traveling as far south as the pueblos in New Mexico and as far north as Blackfoot country in Saskatchewan (Secoy 1953). By the late 1700s, military power shifted away from the Shoshone as their neighbors became mounted and armed, and they may have been intensifying resource procurement in and occupation of new places. During the 1930s, anthropologists such as Julian Steward recorded numerous Shoshone bands of the 19th century throughout Idaho, Wyoming, and parts of Utah and Nevada designated by primary food resource (sheep eaters, buffalo eaters, salmon eaters, pine nut eaters). These designations were fluid, with flexible group membership.

In Wyoming, the Shoshone are best known as being buffalo eaters in the interior basins and plains and sheep eaters in the mountains. The plains sites include well-known examples such as the Dinwoody style of rock art at Legend Rock (48HO4) and the Eden Farson antelope processing and campsite (48SW304). The mountain sites are characterized by a handful of high-elevation wooden sheep trap complexes that include cribbed log structures, drive lines, and catch pens (Figure 29.3). These sites, such as Bull Elk Pass (48FR307) and Black Mountain (48FR494), show evidence of bighorn sheep hunting and possibly of intensification of mountain

Figure 29.3 Sheep traps of the Absaroka Mountains: (a) Black Mountain sheep trap, wooden catch pen; (b) Bull Elk Pass sheep trap, wooden catch pen (note two v-shaped drive lines in upper right).

resources in the 19th century. Killing bighorn sheep is also metaphorically associated with hunting magic and rain shamanism among Numic-speaking (Shoshonean) groups living farther west (Whitley 1994).

Our second case study focuses on these hunting features and associated campsites in the Absaroka mountains on the western side of the Bighorn Basin in northwestern Wyoming. The antiquity of these sites is not clear. The state of wood preservation would indicate a fairly recent age, and a few dendrochronology dates place creation of the wooden drivelines and cribbed log features around 1800. It is possible, though, that wood from earlier visits decayed and disappeared. Very few associated artifacts (and no metal) have been found in or near the sheep traps. We cannot say for certain if the Mountain Shoshone used these sites prior to 1800 (although some evidence for this seems to exist at the High Rise Village sites in the Wind River Mountains). Undated stone drivelines in the vicinity suggest a possible older presence.

Recent forest fires have exposed a number of late period campsites that are associated with the sheep traps and that contain what have traditionally been considered diagnostic Shoshone pottery, projectile points, and other tools. These campsites show diverse activities associated with animal hunting, along with an intriguing mixture of materials: obsidian, Intermountain Ware ceramics, steatite, metal arrowheads, cans, and glass trade beads.

This case study concentrates on two sheep traps and at least six campsites at an area known as Boulder Ridge. These sites may have been occupied serially through time, with occupations ranging from 2,000 years ago to 100 years ago. Most were visited during the height of the Rocky Mountain fur trade, and we are interested in the extent to which these mountain people chose to participate in this phenomenon. The mountain sites appear to have been mostly abandoned by 1850, although with continued use into at least the 1920s. We are hesitant to draw a line between Indian and American use of the ridge, and we are considering the pathways and kinds of Indian access to traditional landscapes after 1870.

Making distinctions among prehistoric, protohistoric, and historic at the high-elevation sites is particularly challenging. In the absence of dated contexts and Euro-American-manufactured objects, we would likely call these assemblages prehistoric; if one or two beads, protohistoric; if hundreds of beads, late protohistoric or historic; and if 1920s trash, we may assume it was left by local ranchers, not Indians. Archaeologists can avoid these models of unidirectional change relating percentage of Euro-American objects to time by integrating other events related to movement and mobility (see Oetelaar, this volume), using obsidian sourcing, ceramics sourcing, activity area analysis, GIS-based landscape patterning, and other means of dating these sites (radiocarbon, obsidian hydration, and thermoluminescence). On the basis of these kinds of datasets, we think the Shoshone who occupied the hunting landscapes at Boulder Ridge and the region may have developed new identities as mountain people during the 19th century, related in part to their relationships with other Shoshone bands and to other plains residents (both foreign and familiar).

Conclusion

These case studies are unique examples in the archaeology of the recent past of the Northwestern Plains and Rocky Mountains because we are able, with some interpretive license, to isolate the cultural identity of the occupants of the sites. With nomadic peoples, this can be extremely difficult, and it certainly sets the research and time period apart from work done in other places with well-established community farming signatures.

These case studies share a focus on interpretation of the domestic spaces, landscapes, and daily lives of nomadic hunter-gatherers between about 1500 and 1900. Both look at migrations of Indian people from faraway places: former farmers moving east across the plains from the Missouri River and into the unglaciated Missouri Plateau of Montana, and Great Basin foragers crossing the mountains from Idaho and Utah, and coming into the high country surrounding the interior basins of Wyoming.

As archaeologists, we are interested in tracing why they moved, regionally and locally. We want to know what materials they brought with them and what items they adopted once they got there. We ask how they created social landscapes in their new homes. Only indirectly were these decisions related to European and American colonies on the coasts, as opposed to internal social dynamics. If we simply refer to these centuries as an initial reaction to European people and their material inventories, we take away Indian decision making during this time and do not acknowledge long-term indigenous histories. This is especially true given the many years of residence and resistance between introduction of horses from the south and growing entanglement in the French fur trade to the north in the 1700s, and arrival of American homesteaders in places like the Bighorn Basin in the 1890s. Archaeologists can provide narratives that transcend these artificial boundaries. At the same time, we acknowledge that this time is central to how identity is revealed, negotiated, and transformed among historic Plains Indian societies. Perhaps we as archaeologists want to designate a separate period because we want a time *before* as much as *after*, a time that is in fact neither.

We prefer to recenter Native history not just as influenced by the Americans or French or British or Spanish. What happened on the Northwestern Plains and Rocky Mountains between 1500 and 1900 occurred over the course of 20 generations before sustained European contact. Designating a separate period between prehistory and history continues to mark a contrast between the two. We feel that the terms *protohistoric* and *contact period* inhibit research on recent hunter-gatherers, and they should be abandoned or used with caution. Instead, we choose to present chronologies by calendric dates, whenever possible. This decision requires a different kind of training on the part of the archaeologist, combining strengths and knowledge of archaeology, historical archaeology, history, ethnohistory, and anthropology.

REFERENCES

Frison, G. C. 1991. *Prehistoric Hunters of the High Plains*. 2nd ed. Academic Press, New York.

Nabokov, P., and L. L. Loendorf. 2004. *Restoring a Presence: American Indians and Yellowstone National Park*. University of Oklahoma Press, Norman.

Ray, A. J. 1978. History and Archaeology of the Northern Fur Trade. *American Antiquity* 43(1):26–34.

Scheiber, L. L. 2008. Life and Death on the Northwestern Plains: Mortuary Practices and Cultural Transformations. In *Skeletal Biology and Bioarchaeology of the Northwestern Plains*, edited by G. W. Gill and R. Weathermon, pp. 22–41. University of Utah Press, Salt Lake City.

Secoy, F. R. 1953. *Changing Military Patterns on the Great Plains (17th Century Through Early 19th Century)*. Monographs of the American Ethnological Society 21. University of Washington Press, Seattle.

Whitley, D. S. 1994. By the Hunter, for the Gatherer: Art, Social Relations and Subsistence Change in the Prehistoric Great Basin. *World Archaeology* 25(3):356–373.

SUGGESTED READING

Adams, R. 2006. The Greater Yellowstone Ecosystem, Soapstone Bowls and the Mountain Shoshone. *World Archaeology* 38(3):528–546.

Banks, K. M., and J. S. Snortland. 1995. Every Picture Tells a Story: Historic Images, Tipi Camps, and Archaeology. *Plains Anthropologist* 40(152):125–144.

Davis, L. B. (editor). 1983. *Microcosm to Macrocosm: Advances in Tipi Ring Investigation and Interpretation*. Plains Anthropologist Memoir 19, vol. 28, no. 102, pt. 2.

Frison, G. C., C. A. Reher, and D. N. Walker. 1990. Prehistoric Mountain Sheep Hunting in the Central Rocky Mountains of North America. In *Hunters of the Recent Past*, edited by L. B. Davis and B. O. K. Reeves, pp. 208–240. Unwin-Hyman, London.

Lightfoot, K. G. 1995. Culture Contact Studies: Redefining the Relationship Between Prehistoric and Historical Archaeology. *American Antiquity* 60(2):199–217.

Scheiber, L. L., and M. D. Mitchell (editors). 2010. *Across a Great Divide: Change and Continuity in Native North America, 1400–1900*. University of Arizona Press, Tucson.

Sundstrom, L. 2002. Steel Awls for Stone Age Plainswomen: Rock Art, Religion, and the Hide Trade on the Northern Plains. *Plains Anthropologist* 47(181):99–119.

Wood, W. R. (editor). 1998 *Archaeology on the Great Plains*. University Press of Kansas, Lawrence.

CHAPTER 30

THE ORIGINS AND DEVELOPMENT OF FARMING VILLAGES IN THE NORTHERN GREAT PLAINS

MARK D. MITCHELL

THE emergence of villages—aggregated communities housing at least 100 people—marks a decisive transformation of the social landscape. People living in nucleated settlements structure their interactions with one another differently than people living in isolated homesteads or small hamlets. They mobilize labor differently, control access to social and material resources differently, and experience and exploit the environment differently. Each difference has consequences for gender roles, economic practices, household composition, the scope and character of supra-household social institutions, and the prevalence of collective violence. The Northern Plains is no exception: an account of the origins and development of aggregated communities there is crucial to a broader understanding of the social history of the region.

The First Villages

The earliest aggregated settlements in the Northern Plains belong to a culture-historical taxon known as the Initial variant of the Middle Missouri tradition (Winham and Calabrese 1998; Wood 2001). The Middle Missouri tradition was one expression of the widespread and long-lasting Plains Village pattern. Plains Village communities shared a set of basic economic and technological features, including a mixed farming and hunting economy, residence in substantial houses near arable land, extensive use of subterranean storage facilities, and production of distinctive stone and bone implements and ceramic containers. However, not all Plains Villagers lived in aggregated communities; Central Plains tradition households, for instance, built autonomous farmsteads.

Initial Middle Missouri sites straddle the Plains-Prairie border, from central South Dakota eastward into northwest Iowa (Figure 30.1). Archaeologists define several local phases for the Initial variant, but the most prominent differences exist between western communities located on the Missouri River and eastern communities located on major northern tributaries of the Missouri (Johnson 2007a; Henning and Toom 2003; Tiffany 2007b).

Initial Middle Missouri villages first appeared in the 11th century (Johnson 2007a; Tiffany 2007a). At one time archaeologists thought the eastern settlements, particularly those assigned to the Mill Creek culture, had been founded before those in the west. However, recent chronological assessments show that villages appeared in the east and west at about the same time (Johnson 2007a; Henning and Toom 2003; Tiffany 2007a). Radiocarbon dates suggest the Initial variant lasted roughly 300 years, from AD 1000 to 1300 (Johnson 2007a; Toom 1992b), but ceramic cross-dating (described in more detail later) narrows that range somewhat (Tiffany 2007a). Recent debate about the age and duration of the Initial variant turns partly on how it is defined. In this chapter, sites assigned to the Great Oasis complex are excluded because they exhibit a dispersed rather than aggregated community pattern (Tiffany and Alex 2001).

Initial Middle Missouri settlements were built on bluffs or terraces overlooking major streams, a location that provided ready access to timber and agricultural land as well as to upland bison habitat. Eastern Initial variant sites are generally smaller than their western contemporaries; on the Missouri River in central South Dakota, Initial variant sites encompass 3 hectares on average (Toom 1992a:table 3), but Mill Creek sites in northwest Iowa are seldom larger than about 0.4 hectare (Henning 2007). Many Initial variant communities anticipated warfare; roughly half of the known sites are fortified (Tiffany 1982). A shallow ditch, backed by a line of vertical posts, completely encircles some eastern settlements. In the west, villagers frequently built their settlements on high, defensible terraces, a location requiring only limited investment in defensive works. Initial Middle Missouri communities relocated frequently (Lensink 2005; Toom 1992a). Some settlements may have been occupied as long as 50 years, but most lasted

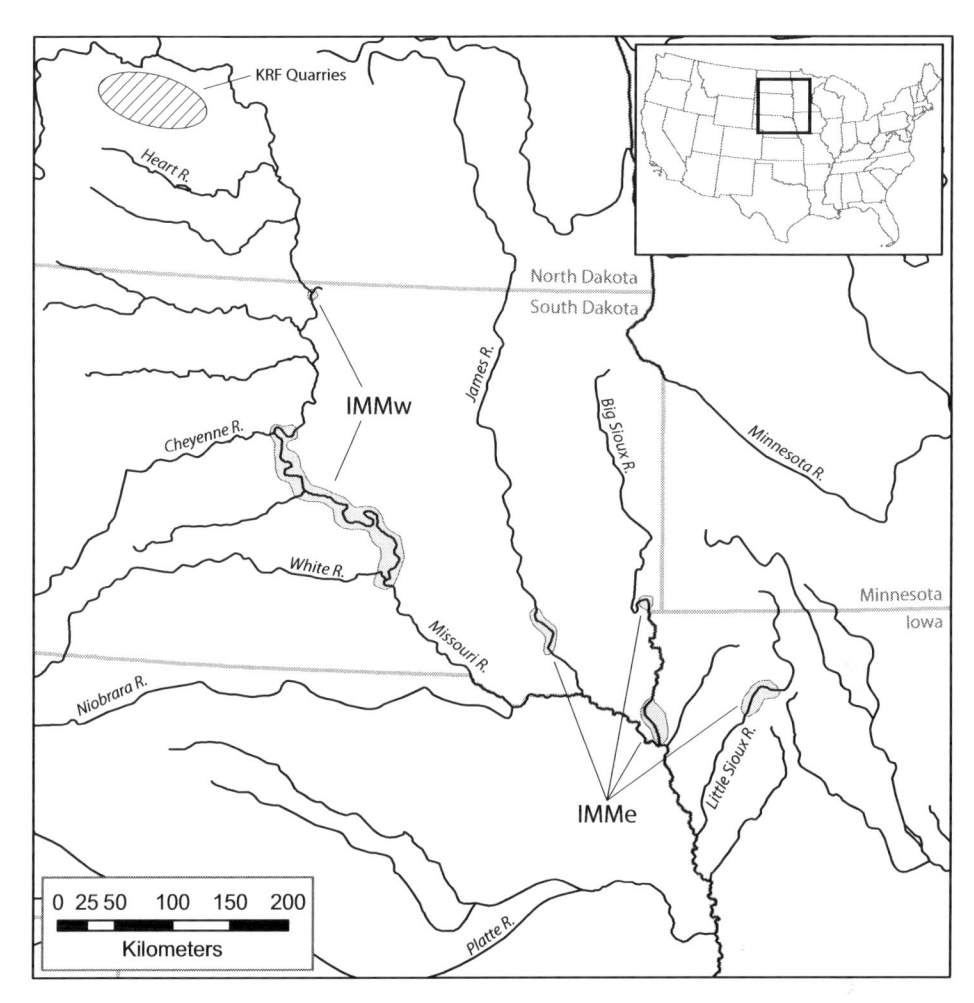

Figure 30.1 Map showing distribution of western (IMMw) and eastern (IMMe) Initial Middle Missouri villages on the Plains-Prairie border (location of the primary Knife River flint or KRF quarries is also shown).

just half that time. This short duration suggests that only a few communities were occupied concurrently in each locality, and therefore that the aggregate population was correspondingly small. About 250 people lived in each community (Toom 1992a).

Initial variant settlements were made up of a compact cluster of rectangular, semisubterranean, timber-frame houses (Figure 30.2). Most houses opened to the south or southwest and incorporated one or two hearths; storage pits lined the walls and filled the spaces between them. On average, excavated houses in the east enclose 50.7 square meters, while those in the west enclose 80.3 square meters each (Lensink and Tiffany 2005). However, house sizes vary significantly. The smallest western house, for instance, covers just 45 square meters, while the largest covers 177 square meters. This range suggests that several types of households may have been present (Tiffany 2007a), or that household status varied.

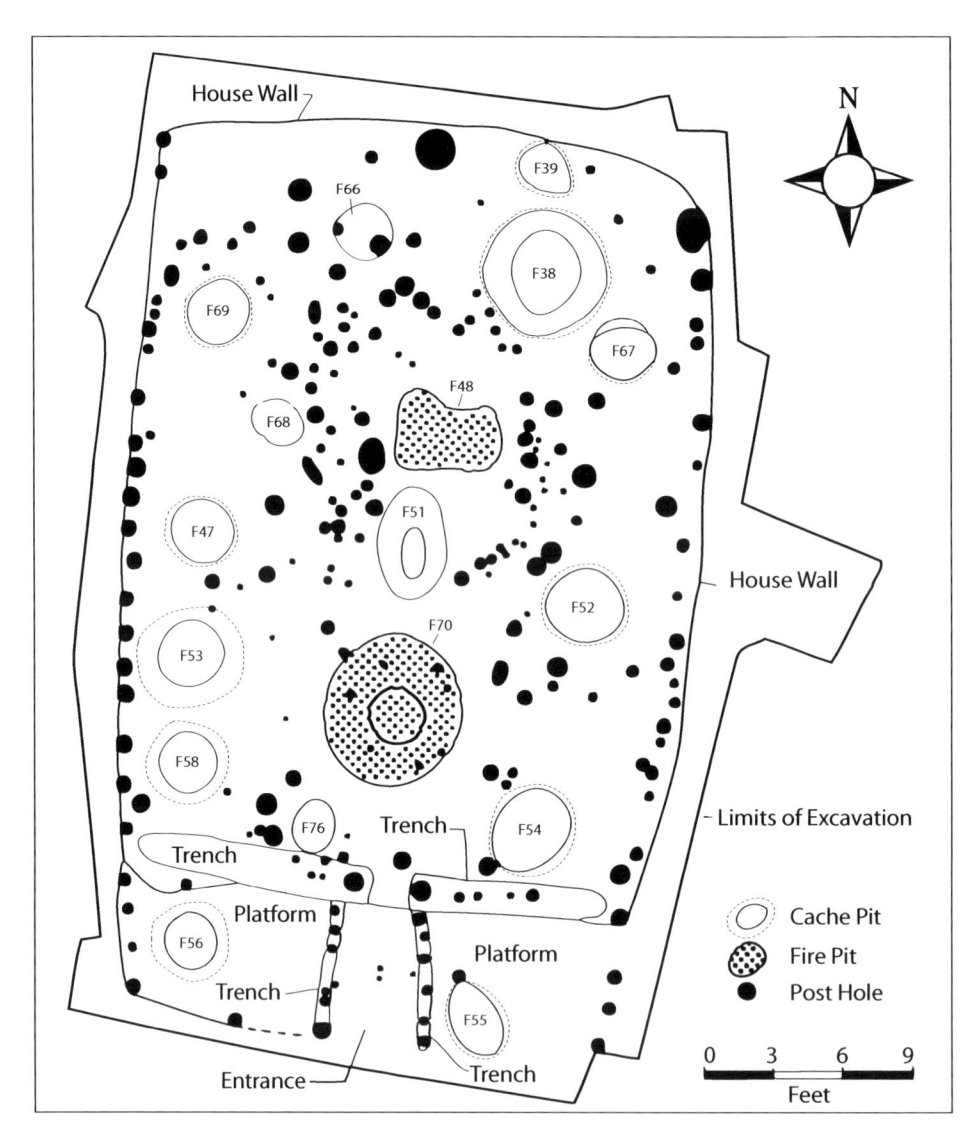

Figure 30.2 Plan view of an Initial Middle Missouri house from the Langdeau site (39LM209).

Initial Middle Missouri villagers pursued a flexible subsistence economy that combined intensive maize agriculture with large-scale bison hunting, supplemented by foraging and fishing. In addition to maize, the agricultural system incorporated beans and squash, as well as domesticated sunflowers, marshelder, and tobacco (Adair 2003; Nickel 2007). They also harvested—and perhaps cultivated—various weedy annuals and gathered a range of wild fleshy fruits. The relative emphasis placed on different subsistence activities likely varied both spatially and temporally.

Several lines of evidence indicate that the earliest villages were founded by local Late Woodland households. The local origin of aggregated settlements is most apparent in the east, where there are clear stylistic connections between Initial variant Mill Creek pottery and Late Woodland Great Oasis pottery. In the west, continuity with antecedent Late Woodland ceramic styles is less obvious, perhaps indicating that a number of local populations were involved (Johnson 2007a:168). In any case, the economic practices of Great Oasis and other Late Woodland communities clearly anticipated those of their village-dwelling neighbors and descendants (Tiffany and Alex 2001).

The most conspicuous difference between the villagers of the 1000s and their Late Woodland progenitors, apart from the types of settlements they built, is the former's deep involvement in long-distance exchange. Mill Creek villagers in particular have been called the "preeminent traders" of the day (Henning 2007:71), owing mostly to abundant evidence for their interactions with stratified Mississippian societies to the south and east, especially with the dominant Mississippian polity at Cahokia (Alt, this volume). Mississippian imports in eastern Initial variant assemblages include red-slipped and shell-tempered pots, earspools, chunkey stones (biconcave discoidals), whole and cut marine shells, marine shell beads and pendants, basal-notched projectile points, and Long-nosed God masquette earrings. The shell-tempered vessels, known as Ramey Incised and Powell Plain, likely were produced by specialist potters living near Cahokia (Pauketat 2004). Even more abundant, though, are locally made copies inspired by distinctive Mississippian forms, including seed jars; bowls; plates; high-rim water bottles; and pots with angular shoulders, anthropomorphic and zoomorphic effigy handles, and rolled rims. Both the imports and the copies bear ideologically charged imagery. In exchange, Mill Creek traders may have offered bison hides and meat (Tiffany 1991) as well as exotic commodities such as bird-wing fans (Fishel 1997).

Mississippian imports are less common on western Initial variant sites (Henning and Toom 2003:215). A few red-slipped vessels occur, but shell-tempered vessels seem to be absent (Tiffany 2007b). Still, marine shell beads and pendants are present in western assemblages, and potters there produced a variety of Mississippian-inspired forms, notably rolled-rim jars bearing Ramey-style decoration. Imported copper seems to have been more common in the west. However, the most abundant exotic material in western assemblages is Knife River flint, a high-quality toolstone quarried in present-day western North Dakota (Johnson 1984, 2007b). At the Sommers site, in the core area of western Initial variant settlement and some 375 kilometers from the primary flint quarries, more than 50 percent of the flaked stone assemblage consists of Knife River flint. A small portion of this may derive from local gravels, but Knife River flint is largely absent from later assemblages in the same area. Whether or how the Knife River flint procurement system was connected with the Mississippian exchange pursued by eastern Initial variant communities is not known.

The clear linkage between the appearance of aggregated communities and initiation of long-distance trade on the Plains-Prairie border has both chronological and processual implications. Current ceramic chronologies suggest that interaction began during Cahokia's Lohmann phase, between 1050 and 1100, but expanded significantly during the subsequent Stirling phase, between 1100 and 1200 (Lensink 2005; Tiffany

2003, 2007b; Tiffany and Alex 2001). At Cahokia, the late 1000s and early 1100s was a time of explosive population growth and fundamental political reorganization that scholars dub the "Big Bang" (Alt, this volume; Pauketat 2004). The correlation between Initial Middle Missouri aggregation and the advent of Mississippian trade strongly suggests that Cahokia's sudden growth was a critical catalyst for village formation. In fact, Initial variant aggregation was just one aspect of the widespread process of "Mississippianization" that affected many Late Woodland societies in the upper Mississippi River valley and adjacent areas in the 11th and 12th centuries (Emerson, this volume). Because this process was marked by styles that define the Stirling phase at Cahokia, it has been described as the "Stirling horizon" (Green 1997) or the "Stirling interaction sphere" (Tiffany 2003). However, not every community interacted exclusively with Cahokia, and the character of the interactions between Mississippian and non-Mississippian groups varied from place to place.

Exchange between Initial Middle Missouri communities and Cahokia likely was built on a system of alliances established through ceremonial adoptions between prominent men (Tiffany 1991). Mississippian–Initial Middle Missouri marriages may also have played a role. Initial variant traders used these relationships to acquire objects and materials signifying their connection to distant sources of power, which they in turn used to bolster their claims to local prestige and leadership.

To underwrite their participation in the trade network, leading households and lineages sought to produce or control surpluses of the region's two most important resources, maize and bison. This likely involved recruitment of related or allied households through public gift exchanges, as well as altered social relationships that gave men greater access to women's labor and allowed men to pass their accumulated wealth to male heirs (Lensink 2005). The result was a rapid coalescence of formerly autonomous households around successful traders, as well as intensification of maize production and bison hunting.

Many archaeologists rightly question whether staples supplied by Initial Middle Missouri traders would have been needed at Cahokia. In fact, it seems unlikely that Cahokians controlled the trade, which in any case may have been intermittent. But the question of Mississippian control is not at issue here. The emergence of compact farming communities should not be seen as a byproduct of an externally imposed regional system, but rather as material expression of the social relationships engendered by the local uses to which traders put the prestige goods they acquired through exchange. The initial impulse for village formation may have come from the sudden flourishing of Cahokia in the 1000s, but it was the consequent reordering of local Initial Middle Missouri social relationships and economic practices that kept aggregated settlements together. Indeed, aspects of the relationships and practices embodied in Initial variant communities were foreshadowed by a series of comparatively gradual ideological, economic, and material changes that took place among Late Woodland groups during the centuries before Cahokia's Big Bang (Benn and Green 2000:482).

The effects of Mississippianization were felt only dimly in the west, but there too aggregation seems to have been bound up with trade. Copper, marine shell, and copies of Mississippian ceramic forms may have served the same catalytic role that direct imports did in the east. However, the fact that Knife River flint likely functioned as a common commodity, rather than solely as a marker of status, suggests that other social processes were at work as well.

Village Expansion

In the early 13th century, Cahokia was in decline and the alliances that had stimulated formation of aggregated Initial Middle Missouri communities were breaking down. But village life did not end in the Northern Plains. Rather, the 1200s witnessed dramatic expansion of aggregated settlements in the Missouri River valley north of the Initial variant heartland, a region known as the Middle Missouri subarea (Figure 30.3). These 13th-century communities, which archaeologists assign to the Extended variant of the Middle Missouri tradition, likely appeared first in the northern half of the subarea. Extended variant communities were also present in the southern Middle Missouri during the 1200s, but it is not clear whether they coexisted with Initial Middle Missouri communities there (Johnson 2007a; Tiffany 2007a).

The Knife River flint procurement system operated by western Initial variant communities played an important role in development of the Extended variant (Ahler 2007; Johnson 2007b). In the 11th and 12th centuries, the efforts of Initial Middle Missouri traders to obtain this stone brought them into regular and intimate contact with Late Woodland bison hunters living near the quarries. The ensuing process of hunter-gatherer acculturation is best documented at Menoken Village, a fortified 12th-century community of at least 14 houses located east of the Missouri (Figure 30.3). The residents of this community were not farmers, but their stone, bone, and pottery technology combined the distinctive practices of their Late Woodland ancestors with those of their Plains Village business partners (Ahler 2007; Krause 2007). In the following century, this acculturation process gave rise to Extended variant communities that could trace their ancestry to both Late Woodland and Plains Village groups. However, the basic economic transformation accompanying this second phase of "neolithization" differed from that experienced by Late Woodland groups on the Plains-Prairie border in the 1000s: in the south, Late Woodland farmers added regular bison hunting to their economic system, but in the north Late Woodland hunters added maize farming (Ahler 2007).

With a mean population of just over 300, Extended variant communities were roughly the same size as their Initial variant predecessors (Mitchell 2011). However, Initial and Extended variant communities differed in several ways. At about 115 square meters on average, Extended variant houses are nearly 50 percent larger than western Initial variant houses and more than twice as large as eastern Initial variant houses. They also are more uniform in design and construction than Initial variant houses. Extended Middle Missouri communities exhibit evidence of

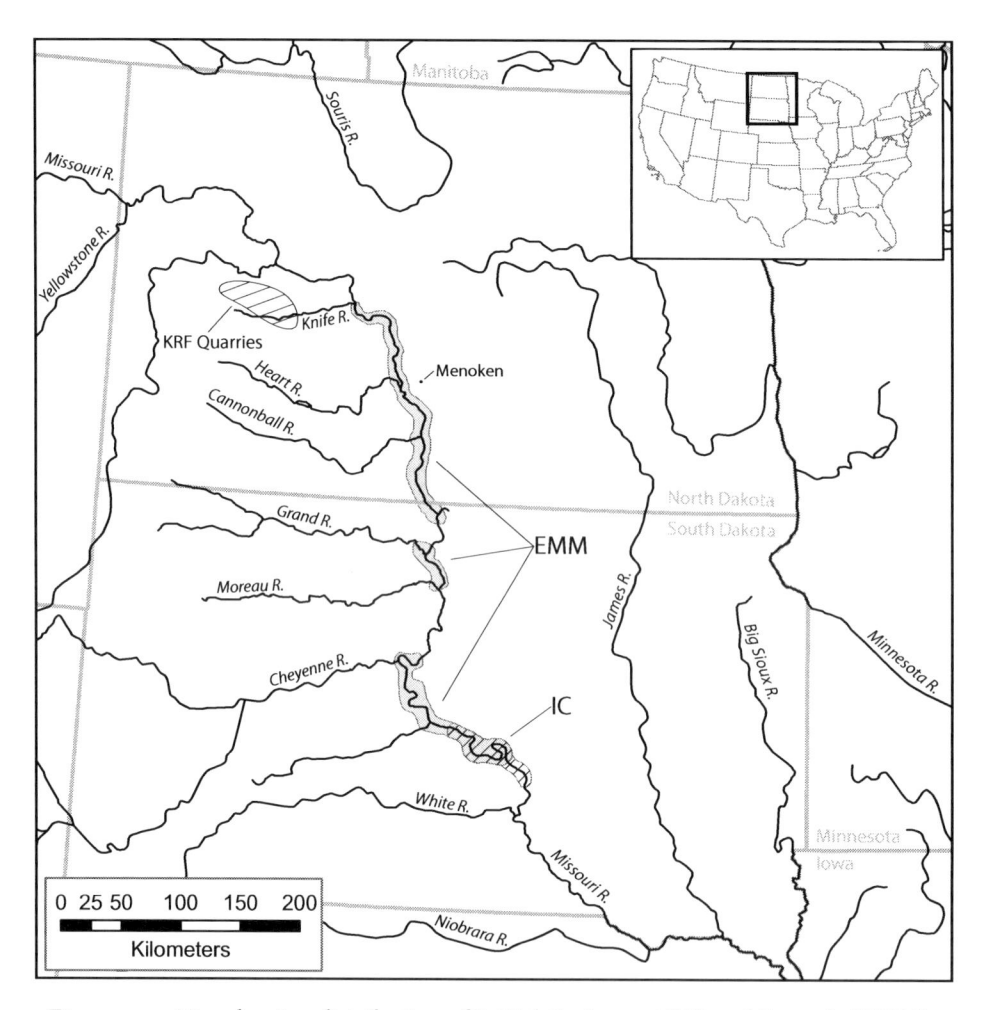

Figure 30.3 Map showing distribution of Initial Coalescent (IC) and Extended Middle Missouri (EMM) villages; location of Menoken Village (32BL2), a Late Woodland settlement; and area of the primary Knife River flint or KRF quarries.

advance planning, with houses often laid out in irregular rows or arcs around a large, continuously maintained interior plaza. Only a few Extended variant communities were fortified.

New Village Communities in the Northern Plains

About 1300, bearers of a distinct cultural tradition archaeologists call the Coalescent began building villages in the Middle Missouri subarea. Relatively little is known about these newcomers, whose communities are assigned to the Initial variant of the Coalescent tradition. Only a handful of Initial Coalescent villages were built, almost all of them confined to a relatively short stretch of the Missouri in southeast South Dakota (Figure 30.3). At one time, archaeologists thought they represented a migration of Central Plains tradition groups driven northward by drought. However, recent research suggests that the historical relationships between the Coalescent and Central Plains traditions are more complex than that (Johnson 1998, 2007a; Steinacher and Carlson 1998). In the early 1400s, Extended Coalescent communities, likely founded by the descendants of those first Initial Coalescent pioneers, began to appear throughout the southern Middle Missouri, from the eastern edge of the Plains in southeast South Dakota northward to the North Dakota border (Johnson 2007a).

Coalescent communities were organized differently from Middle Missouri tradition settlements (Krause 1999). Most were larger, and their constituent houses more widely spaced, resulting in much lower residential density. On average, the density of Initial Coalescent villages was just half that of contemporaneous Extended Middle Missouri villages (Johnson 1998; Mitchell 2011). Compared to compact Middle Missouri tradition settlements, Extended Coalescent communities consisted of scattered clusters or long lines of houses. The extremely short-lived occupation of many Extended Coalescent villages suggests they were even more transient than their Middle Missouri tradition contemporaries.

Coalescent villagers built large, timber-frame houses with extended entryways; their distinctive circular plan featured four massive center posts surrounding a large central hearth (Figure 30.4). Excavated Initial Coalescent houses average 59.7 square meters, while Extended Coalescent houses average 110.8 square meters (Johnson 1998). By the time Europeans arrived on the Missouri in the 18th century, all of the farming groups there had adopted a more-or-less-standardized successor to this Coalescent architectural style (Roper and Pauls 2005).

Village Consolidation

By the late 1700s, farming villages on the Missouri had coalesced into a handful of settlement clusters. This clustering was no doubt prompted in part by regional population declines brought on by European epidemic diseases. However, the timing and rate of settlement aggregation varied widely. In the northern half of the Middle Missouri, settlement clusters began forming long before the advent of Europeans in the Americas, but in the southern half significant clustering did not occur until the latter part of the 18th century (see also Noble, this volume).

Two processes were involved in forming what came to be the largest settlement cluster, centered on the confluence of the Heart and Missouri rivers in North Dakota (Mitchell 2011; Wood 1967). First, mean settlement size increased rapidly and dramatically, from just over 300 people in the 1200s and 1300s to nearly 900 in the

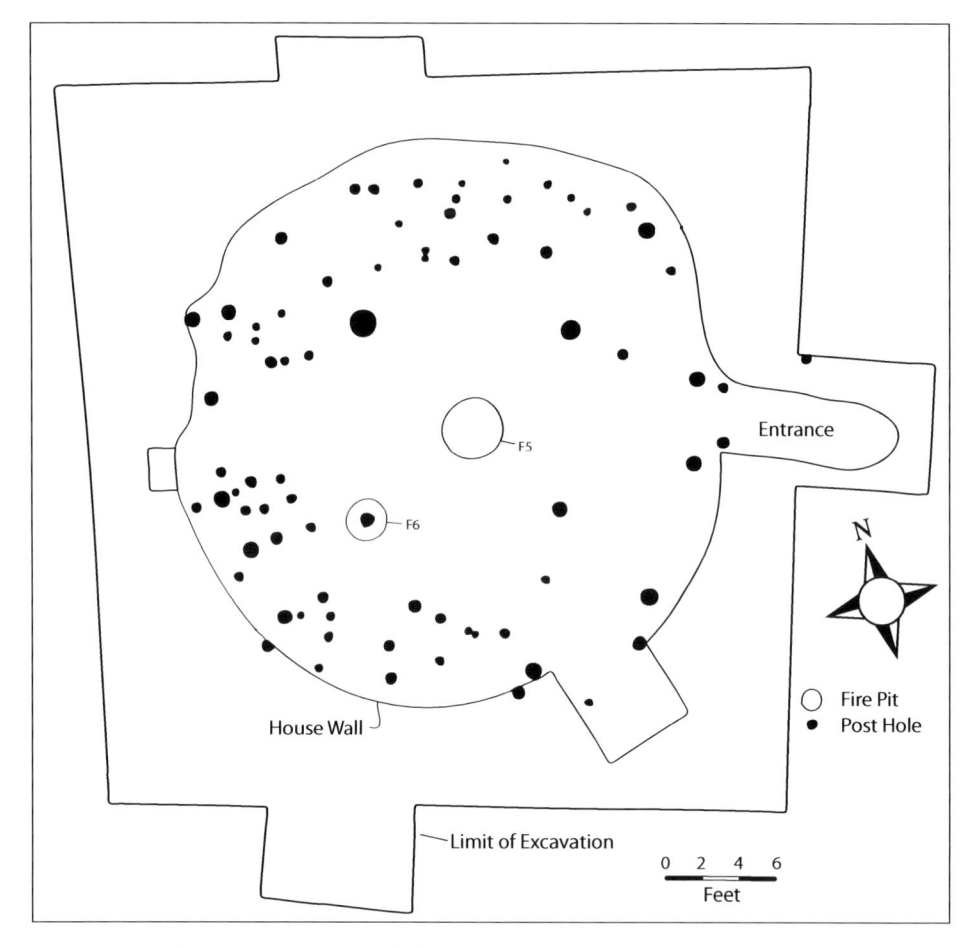

Figure 30.4 Plan view of an Extended Coalescent house from the La Roche site (39ST9).

1400s and 1500s. A few 16th-century towns sheltered more than 2,000 people. Second, the portion of the valley occupied by Middle Missouri tradition communities shrank significantly. In the 14th century, Extended variant settlements could be found throughout the subarea. After 1400, no Middle Missouri tradition communities were built below the mouth of the Cannonball River. In the 16th century, settlement further contracted to a roughly 40 kilometer stretch of the Missouri above and below the Heart. The outcome of these two processes was an unprecedented increase in population density; when fur traders visited in the middle of the 18th century, the Heart region cluster, made up of about six communities, was home to some 9,000 people.

Archaeologists used to attribute formation of this cluster to warfare. It does seem likely that Initial Coalescent and Extended Middle Missouri communities came into conflict in the southern Middle Missouri in the 1300s, but chronological data now show that Middle Missouri tradition settlement already had begun to shift northward before expansion of Extended Coalescent settlement in the 1400s

(Johnson 2007a). Moreover, there are abundant ceramic, architectural, and other data demonstrating substantial interaction between Coalescent and Middle Missouri tradition communities in the 1400s and 1500s (Mitchell 2011).

Instead, it now seems that consolidation of Middle Missouri settlement was prompted by both local and long-distance exchange, and especially by the emergence of household and community craft specialization and the resulting need for periodic markets (Mitchell 2011). Larger settlements maximized the utility of such economic differentiation, and shorter distances between settlements decreased the costs of transporting craft products and other items to market. Competition with other farming villages for meat, hides, and crafts offered by mobile groups may have amplified the process of village consolidation. In fact, a new round of forager-farmer interaction seems to have begun in the late 1300s and 1400s, as evidenced by the occurrence of acculturated ceramic assemblages in Montana, Alberta, Manitoba, and eastern North Dakota (Michlovic 2008), as well as by the northward movement of Knife River flint (Walde 2006) and perhaps maize (Boyd et al. 2006).

Conclusion

In the Northern Plains, the basic social and economic strategies embodied in village life proved remarkably resilient (Wood 1974). Elsewhere in North America, such as the northern Southwest, early villages came together and dissolved episodically. By contrast, on the Missouri, farmers lived exclusively in aggregated settlements of various sizes from the 1000s into the late 1800s. The durability of this community type was underwritten in part by the region's ecological diversity, which permitted a dynamic subsistence economy based on both bison hunting and maize agriculture (Toom 1992a). The mosaic of riparian and upland microenvironments surrounding Northern Plains villages allowed constituent households to tailor their subsistence practices to short- and long-term fluctuations in the productivity of particular resources and in the availability of labor.

Though a variety of social, ecological, and economic factors were involved, long-distance interaction was the catalyst that sparked formation of early villages in the Northern Plains. In the 11th and 12th centuries, interaction with Cahokia was crucial to the social construction of eastern Initial Middle Missouri villages. In the west, exchange with mobile bison hunters played an equivalent role. In both cases, trade drew households into aggregated settlements, which in turn produced a cascade of social changes that reinforced and sustained village life (Tiffany 2007a). In a very real sense, early villages in the Northern Plains were material manifestations of exchange.

Even after the decline of Cahokia and the end of the Knife River flint trade, though, exchange continued to play a key role in the history of villages in the Northern Plains. Continuing a pattern begun during Initial variant times, in the 1400s and 1500s farmers on the Missouri cultivated economic and social relationships with mobile hunting and gathering groups. Intervillage interaction expanded at the same time. Together, these relationships, along with local economic reorganization and intensification, led to formation of at least one major settlement cluster. The ensuing concentration of population further reinforced the farming villages' role as ports of trade. In the 17th and 18th centuries, European fur traders and their native clients appropriated elements of this system for their own purposes.

REFERENCES

Adair, M. J. 2003. Great Plains Paleoethnobotany. In *People and Plants in Ancient Eastern North America*, edited by P. E. Minnis, pp. 258–346. Smithsonian Books, Washington, DC.

Ahler, S. A. 2007. Origins of the Northern Expression of the Middle Missouri Tradition. In *Plains Village Archaeology: Bison Hunting Farmers in the Central and Northern Plains*, edited by S. A. Ahler and M. Kay, pp. 15–31. University of Utah Press, Salt Lake City.

Benn, D. W., and W. Green. 2000. Late Woodland Cultures in Iowa. In *Late Woodland Societies: Tradition and Transformation Across the Midcontinent*, edited by T. E. Emerson, D. L. McElrath, and A. C. Fortier, pp. 429–496. University of Nebraska Press, Lincoln.

Boyd, M., C. Surette, and B. A. Nicholson. 2006. Archaeobotanical Evidence of Prehistoric Maize (*Zea mays*) Consumption at the Northern Edge of the Great Plains. *Journal of Archaeological Science* 33(8):1129–1140.

Fishel, R. L. 1997. Medicine Birds and Mill Creek–Middle Mississippian Interaction: The Contents of Feature 8 at the Phipps Site (13CK21). *American Antiquity* 62(3):538–553.

Green, W. 1997. Middle Mississippian Peoples. *Wisconsin Archeologist* 78(1–2):203–222.

Henning, D. R. 2007. Continuity and Change in the Eastern Plains, A.D. 800–1700: An Examination of Exchange Patterns. In *Plains Village Archaeology: Bison Hunting Farmers in the Central and Northern Plains*, edited by S. A. Ahler and M. Kay, pp. 67–82. University of Utah Press, Salt Lake City.

———, and D. L. Toom. 2003. Cambria and the Initial Middle Missouri Variant Revisited. *Wisconsin Archaeologist* 84(1 & 2):197–217.

Johnson, C. M. 1984. Time, Space, and Cultural Tradition as Factors in Lithic Resource Exploitation in the Middle Missouri Subarea. *Plains Anthropologist* 29(106):289–302.

———. 1998. The Coalescent Tradition. In *Archaeology on the Great Plains*, edited by W. R. Wood, pp. 308–344. University Press of Kansas, Lawrence.

———. 2007a. *A Chronology of Middle Missouri Plains Village Sites*. Contributions to Anthropology 47. Smithsonian Institution, Washington, DC.

———. 2007b. Jones Village: An Initial Middle Missouri Frontier Settlement. In *Plains Village Archaeology: Bison Hunting Farmers in the Central and Northern Plains*, edited by S. A. Ahler and M. Kay, pp. 41–52. University of Utah Press, Salt Lake City.

Krause, R. A. 1999. Kinship, Tradition and Settlement Pattern: An Archaeology of Prehistoric Middle Missouri Community Life. In *Making Places in the Prehistoric World: Themes in Settlement Archaeology*, edited by J. Bruck and M. Goodman, pp. 129–144. University College London Press, London.

———. 2007. A Potter's Tale. In *Plains Village Archaeology: Bison Hunting Farmers in the Central and Northern Plains*, edited by S. A. Ahler and M. Kay, pp. 32–40. University of Utah Press, Salt Lake City.

Lensink, S. C. 2005. This Old Earthlodge Village: How Long Were Sites of the Middle Missouri Tradition Occupied? In *Plains Earthlodges: Ethnographic and Archaeological Perspectives*, edited by D. C. Roper and E. P. Pauls, pp. 132–156. University of Alabama Press, Tuscaloosa.

———, and J. A. Tiffany. 2005. Great Oasis in Time and Space. Report 22, *The Cowan Site: A Great Oasis Community in Northwest Iowa*, edited by S. C. Lensink and J. A. Tiffany, pp. 125–137. Office of the State Archaeologist, Iowa City, IA.

Michlovic, M. G. 2008. The Shea Phase of the Northeastern Plains Village Culture. In North Dakota Archaeology 7, *Papers in Northeastern Plains Prehistory*, edited by M. G. Michlovic and D. L. Toom, pp. 35–51. North Dakota Archaeological Association, Grand Forks.

Mitchell, M. D. 2011. *Continuity and Change in the Organization of Mandan Craft Production, 1400–1750*. Ph.D. dissertation, University of Colorado, Boulder.

Nickel, R. K. 2007. Cultigens and Cultural Traditions in the Middle Missouri. In *Plains Village Archaeology: Bison Hunting Farmers in the Central and Northern Plains*, edited by S. A. Ahler and M. Kay, pp. 126–136. University of Utah Press, Salt Lake City.

Pauketat, T. R. 2004. *Ancient Cahokia and the Mississippians*. Cambridge University Press, Cambridge.

Roper, D. C., and E. P. Pauls. 2005. What, Where, and When Is an Earthlodge? In *Plains Earthlodges: Ethnographic and Archaeological Perspectives*, edited by D. C. Roper and E. P. Pauls, pp. 1–31. University of Alabama Press, Tuscaloosa.

Steinacher, T. L., and G. F. Carlson. 1998. The Central Plains Tradition. In *Archaeology on the Great Plains*, edited by W. R. Wood, pp. 235–268. University Press of Kansas, Lawrence.

Tiffany, J. A. 1982. *Chan-Ya-Ta: A Mill Creek Village*. Report 15. Office of the State Archaeologist, University of Iowa, Iowa City.

———. 1991. Modeling Mill Creek–Mississippian Interaction. Monographs in World Archaeology 2, *New Perspectives on Cahokia: Views from the Periphery*, edited by J. B. Stoltman, pp. 319–348. Prehistory Press, Madison, WI.

———. 2003. Mississippian Connections with Mill Creek and Cambria. *Plains Anthropologist* 48(184):21–34.

———. 2007a. Examining the Origins of the Middle Missouri Tradition. In *Plains Village Archaeology: Bison Hunting Farmers in the Central and Northern Plains*, edited by Stanley A. Ahler and Marvin Kay, pp. 3–14. University of Utah Press, Salt Lake City.

———. 2007b. *The Swanson Site Reexamined: The Middle Missouri Tradition in Central South Dakota*. Special Publication 12. South Dakota Archaeological Society, Sioux Falls.

———, and L. M. Alex. 2001. Great Oasis Archaeology: New Perspectives from the DeCamp and West Des Moines Burial Sites in Central Iowa. Memoir 33, *Plains Anthropologist*, vol. 46, no. 178. Plains Anthropological Society, Lincoln, NE.

Toom, D. L. 1992a. Early Village Formation in the Middle Missouri Subarea of the Plains. Supplement, *Research in Economic Anthropology* 6:131–191.

———. 1992b. Radiocarbon Dating of the Western Initial Middle Missouri Variant: Some New Dates and a Critical Review of Old Dates. *Plains Anthropologist* 37(139):115–128.

Walde, D. 2006. Sedentism and Pre-contact Tribal Organization on the Northern Plains: Colonial Imposition or Indigenous Development? *World Archaeology* 38(2):291–310.

Winham, R. P., and F. A. Calabrese. 1998. The Middle Missouri Tradition. In *Archaeology on the Great Plains*, edited by W. R. Wood, pp. 269–307. University Press of Kansas, Lawrence.

Wood, W. R. 1967. An Interpretation of Mandan Culture History. Smithsonian Institution, Bureau of American Ethnology Bulletin No. 198, *River Basin Surveys Papers 39*. Government Printing Office, Washington, DC.

———. 1974. Northern Plains Village Cultures: Internal Stability and External Relationships. *Journal of Anthropological Research* 30(1):1–16.

———. 2001. Plains Village Tradition: Middle Missouri. In *Handbook of North American Indians*, vol. 13, *Plains*, edited by R. J. DeMallie, pp. 186–195. Smithsonian Institution, Washington, DC.

CHAPTER 31

PLANTING THE PLAINS: THE DEVELOPMENT AND EXTENT OF PLAINS VILLAGE AGRICULTURALISTS IN THE SOUTHERN AND CENTRAL PLAINS

RICHARD R. DRASS

NATIVE societies on the Plains are often viewed as focused on bison hunting, the pattern beginning in Paleoindian times with Folsom hunters and extending to historic tribes characterized as nomads on horseback following bison herds across great expanses of prairie. Although bison can be considered the principal game of the Plains, by about AD 1000 much of the southern and central Plains, including drier western prairies, was occupied by sedentary groups who depended on a mix of hunting, gathering, and horticulture, with corn, beans, squash, and other cultivated plants representing a significant part of their diet. Year-round settlements appear across the Plains at this time, ranging in size from farmsteads and hamlets of a few houses to villages of 200 or more people, with some villages fortified by the 16th century. Long-distance exchange networks allowed interaction with the Pueblos of the Southwest and the mound builder societies of the Southeast. Although the subsistence and settlement patterns changed dramatically in western areas just before the arrival of Europeans, the village pattern persisted for hundreds of years, extending into the 19th century in eastern Plains settings. This study reviews development of farming societies in the southern and central Plains and examines the factors that led to changes in lifestyles during the period between AD 1000 and 1800.

The Emergence of Early Plains Farmers and Village Life

The appearance of sedentary groups on the southern and central Plains is marked by adoption of plant cultivation, or more specifically by expansion of cultivation as an important subsistence activity. Around AD 1000, corn becomes a significant resource on the Plains, although native plants such as sunflower and marshelder are also grown for food. Squash, although not abundant at any villager sites, was probably an early cultigen on the Plains, and beans appear by AD 1200 (Adair 2006; Drass 2008). Wild plants were always important resources for Plains groups and continued to be extensively exploited after the arrival of corn and other crops. The beginnings of extensive gardening appear to result from influences that arrived from the Southwest or Southeast, or from both. The mechanics of adoption of horticulture in the Plains are still being studied, but it appears that in most cases migration of people from outside the Plains was not involved. Local groups probably adopted crops to supplement wild plants and the deer, bison, antelope, small game, and fish they hunted. A variety of factors, such as population increase and a climate favorable for corn, resulted in very rapid expansion of corn horticulture on the Plains.

The earliest horticulturalists settled in isolated farmsteads or small hamlets of a few houses along rivers and streams throughout the southern and central Plains. Plant cultivation and perhaps agricultural groups may have spread west from the Kansas City area in the central Plains, reaching the prairies of western Kansas by around AD 1100 (Roper 2006, 2007). Complexes in this area include such Central Plains tradition groups as the Upper Republican, Smoky Hill, Nebraska, Itskari, and Steed-Kisker phases (Figure 31.1; see Roper 2006; Scheiber 2006). Farther south, early farmsteads or hamlets appear in both the eastern and western prairies about the same time, between AD 1000 and 1100 (Drass 1997). By around AD 1200, sedentary groups were present in the far west on the High Plains of the Texas and Oklahoma panhandles. Sites in the southern Plains are defined as the Pomona, Bluff Creek, Pratt, and Henrietta complexes and the Odessa, Antelope Creek, Paoli, Custer, Turkey Creek, and Washita River phases (Brosowske and Bevitt 2006; Drass 1998; Roper 2006a).

Early Plains villagers placed homes in bottomland settings, where they had easy access to game and usable plants and where the most productive and easily tillable soils were found. These groups adapted to local environments that vary significantly across the Plains from east to west and north to south. In the moister eastern prairie

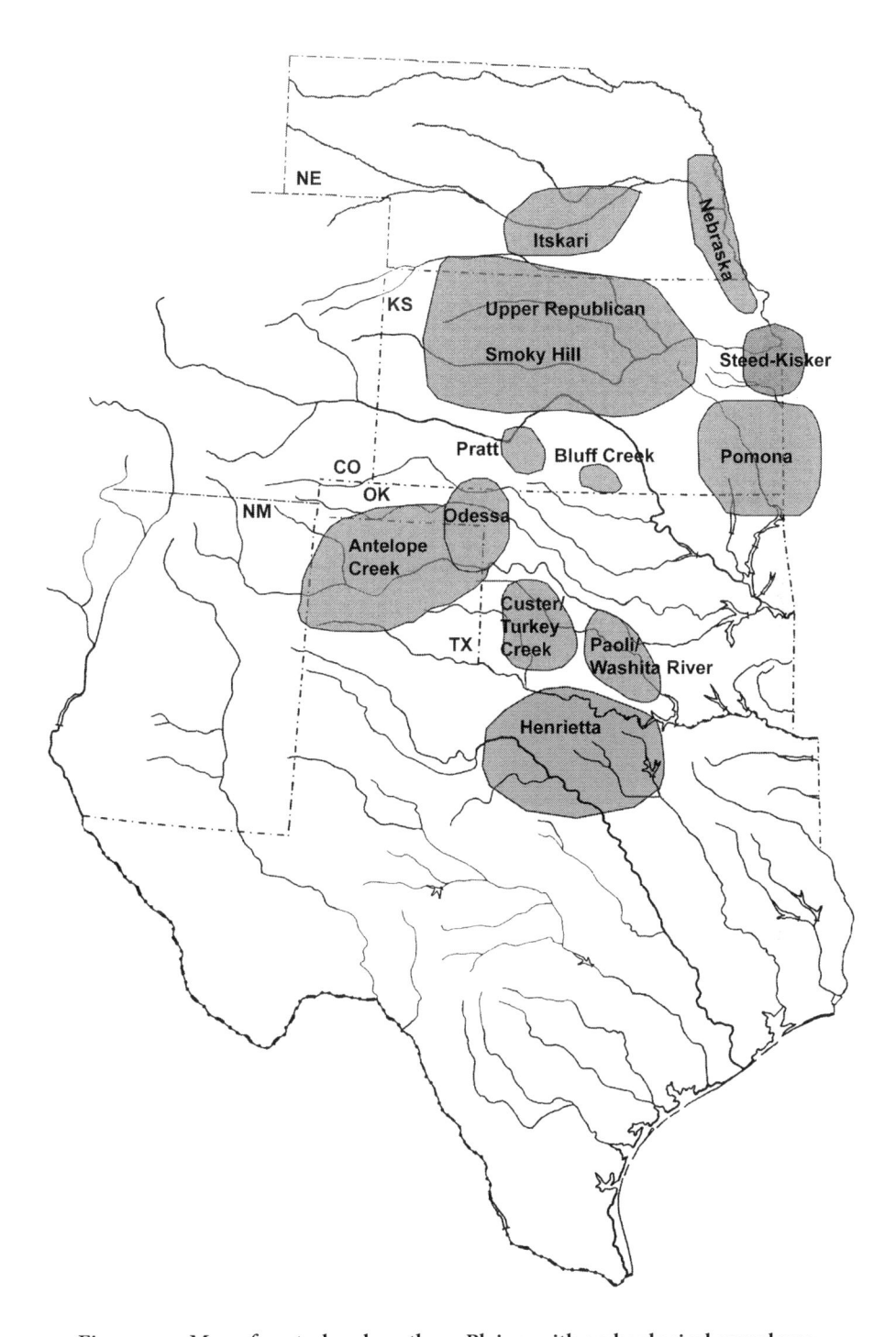

Figure 31.1 Map of central and southern Plains, with archeological complexes.

settings, corn production may have been more reliable, with higher yields compared to drier western short-grass prairie settings. Weedy plants such as lambs quarter and goosefoot were common in gardens and around houses, and they were exploited and may have been encouraged in all areas. Other wild plants included various species depending on local availability, but fruits such as grapes and plums as well as various grass seeds, nuts, and probably tubers such as prairie turnips were gathered by most villagers. The larger streams in the east could supply significant amounts of fish and other aquatic resources, but western groups had access to few aquatic animals and relied more on game. Deer were hunted by all groups; rabbits, rodents, birds, and other small animals supplemented the larger game. Turtles, especially box turtles, seem to have been regularly collected by most villagers, with some sites containing large numbers (see Haury 2008). Bison, however, was by far the most productive meat resource on the Plains and tended to be exploited as the primary meat source when available (Drass 1998; Graves 2008; Haury 2008). Few bison may have been present at eastern Plains sites before about AD 1250, but bison remains increase significantly at later sites in this area (Drass 1997). Bison may also have become more common at western villages after 1250.

The first permanent structures for these villagers were usually square or rectangular houses built with wall posts covered in grass and plastered with clay. Walls and roofs were supported with beams that crossed two to four central support posts surrounding a central hearth. Northern structures may have had earth covering over grass thatch on roofs (Blakeslee 2006; Roper and Pauls 2005), while most houses in the warmer southern Plains had simple grass-covered roofs. Extended entryways are common but not universal in the area. Interior posts suggest wall benches, door screens, and other internal features. Some houses may have had small earthen berms against walls or were built in areas dug a few centimeters into the ground.

In the short-grass prairies of the Texas and Oklahoma panhandles, generally west of the 100th meridian, houses include a variety of construction techniques. Pit houses have recently been documented (Boyd 2008; Brosowske 2005; Brosowske and Bevitt 2006). Many of them are circular or oval, 4 to 8 meters in diameter and dug about 1 to 1.5 meters deep with small vertical posts against the walls (Brosowske 2005). Central posts supported a roof that may have been earth-covered. A central hearth is present, and anteroom storage facilities occur inside some structures. Others are square or rectangular houses with central channels and sloping extended entryways; these may also have been earth-covered (Boyd 2004). Similar structures were built on the surface or dug only slightly below the ground; many have stone slab wall foundations and no earthen roofs. In addition, large contiguous-room stone foundation structures are present during the early village period (Lintz 1986). These varied house constructions may be in response to extremes of cold and hot weather, aggravated by high winds in the High Plains. Construction techniques may also reflect influences from the central Plains and Southwest regions.

Other features are found near houses, with the most common being cylindrical and bell-shaped storage pits. These pits are around 1 meter in diameter and about the same depth, although bell-shaped pits are usually slightly larger in diameter. Most were probably lined with grass or sometimes with clay or caliche plaster, but they were frequently filled with trash when abandoned. The pits may have functioned primarily for storing crops, and the volume has been used to estimate crop yields for villager sites (Nepstad-Thornberry et al. 2002).Other external features include hearths, arbors, and possibly racks for drying hides or for other activities.

Material culture is very similar across the Plains during this period, with stylistic variations in ceramics, use of a number of lithic materials, and some distinctions in tool designs characterizing different groups. Corner-notched arrow points are gradually replaced with triangular unnotched and side-notched forms. Cordmarked pots are common in most early assemblages, but plain, smoothed jars dominate later assemblages, except in the High Plains area where cordmarking remained the prevailing ceramic finish. Variations in rim form, handle design, lip shape, and decoration, along with a number of decorative techniques such as incising, punctuation, and appliqué increase over time at village sites (Figure 31.2). Distinctive stone tools include diamond-beveled knives that were probably used to butcher bison and other large game, small planoconvex end scrapers, celts (i.e., ungrooved axe heads), and flake and T-shaped drills. Stone pipes and pipe reamers are common at sites after about AD 1200. Tobacco seeds have been documented at villages that date to about this time, possibly indicating extensive cultivation of this plant for the first time in the Plains (Drass 2008). Preferred chert resources are exploited during this period, and certain materials are brought some distance to villages.

A variety of bone implements characterize the village period sites. Tools include items used in hide production, manufacture of arrow shafts, and sewing, but among the more common bone implements are digging tools typically made from bison and deer bone (Figure 31.3). Bison tibia digging stick tips, horn core hoes, and scapula hoes are common at all but the earliest eastern villages. By about AD 1250, they are common at all villages; the abundance of these digging tools is another piece of evidence for the importance of plant cultivation among central and southern Plains village societies. They remain valuable agricultural tools into the late 18th century, when metal implements replace them.

Other than isolated house sites, village layouts are not well defined. But increasing use of remote sensing has the promise of yielding more information on distribution of houses and other features within sites (e.g., Brosowske 2008; Cook and Dunbar 2008; Maki and Brosowske 2007). Early village settlement patterns suggest small sites are dispersed along rivers and permanent streams, with hunting camps and lithic acquisition sites nearby. Larger villages appear around AD 1200–1250; some of them have distinct cemetery areas nearby. Ossuaries are found near some central Plains villages (Roper 2006).These settlements remain in or near major stream valleys, although some villagers moved to higher settings for access to prairie resources, particularly bison, or for defensive purposes. Several villages in the High Plains are set on high isolated mesas. Village densities along the Washita River in central Oklahoma indicate settlements may have been within 2.4 kilometers of each other during the period AD 1250–1450 (Brooks 1987).

Figure 31.2 Plains villager pottery.

Corn, Bison, and Changing Plains Villager Lifestyles

The increase in village size and density of settlements after about AD 1250 suggests rising populations in the area until about AD 1450. A drying trend on this part of the Plains began about AD 1000 or 1100 (Drass 1997; Hall 1988). Rainfall, however, remained sufficient for growing corn although reliability of crops may have decreased after 1250

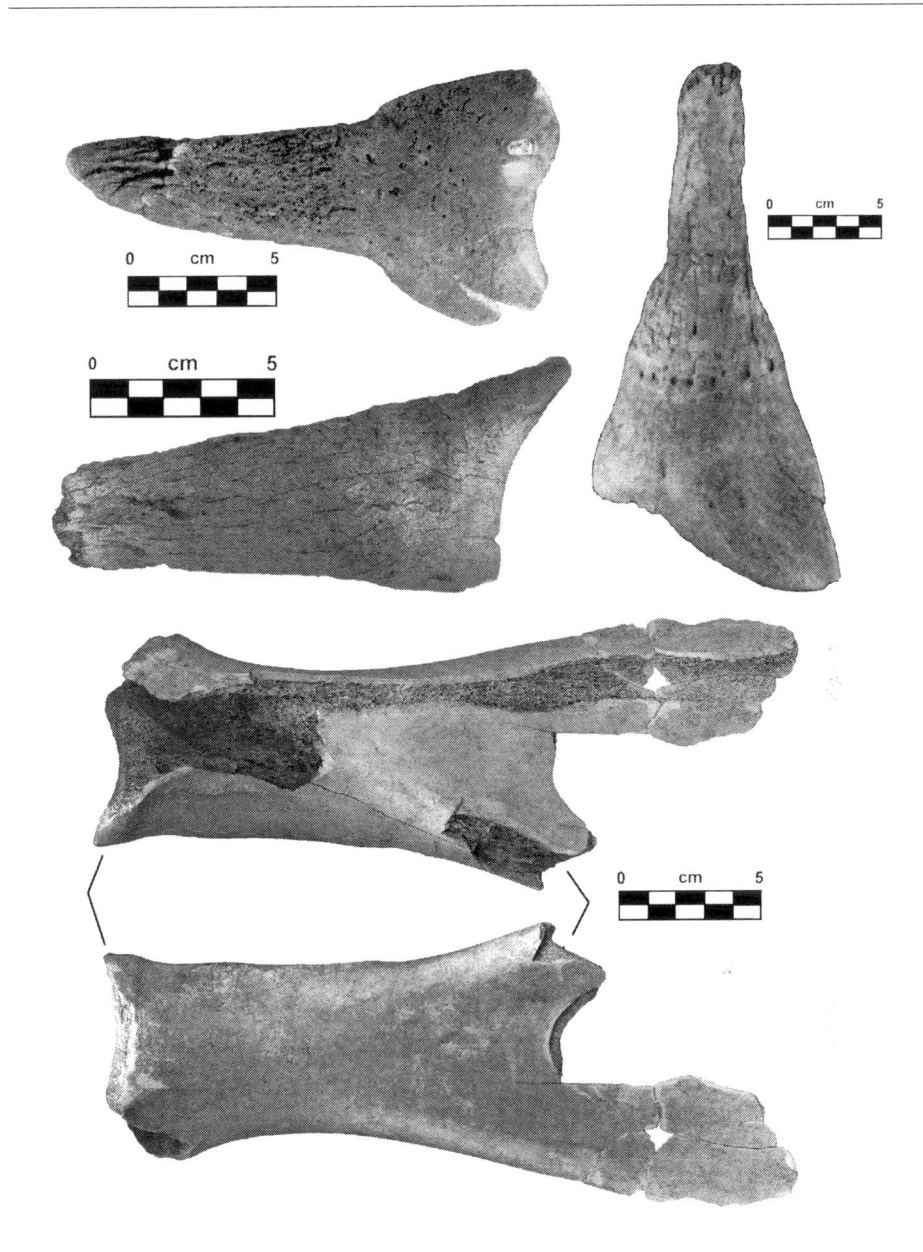

Figure 31.3 Bone digging tools from Plains sites.

in some areas. One response to an increasing population and drying conditions may have been intensification of high-yield agriculture, specifically corn production. By AD 1300, cultivation of native crops such as marshelder and possibly sunflower is reduced, with more specialization in corn production and probably associated productive crops such as beans and squash (Adair 2006; Drass 2008). At the same time, bison herds were growing in size and moving farther east (Drass 1997; Huebner 1991; Ricklis 1992); by the 16th or early 17th century, historic reports indicate bison herds in woodlands east of the Plains. Thus bison were readily available in areas where there previously had been few.

Southern and central Plains villagers could respond to periods of shortage by boosting returns of two important resources, corn and bison, at the same time. This dual exploitation pattern continues and intensifies significantly in eastern areas of the southern Plains after about AD 1400 or 1450. In parts of the central Plains, however, agricultural groups may have abandoned drier western areas and moved east to moister settings as early as AD 1300 (Roper 2006). Also, although bison hunting and corn agriculture were the major resources in many areas after 1250, local conditions had an impact on groups' relying on specific resources, and at various times settlements may have incorporated a broad-spectrum subsistence pattern that included a diversity of wild plants and small game in response to reductions in crop yields or the availability of bison.

During the same period, regional trade increases. Materials from the Southwest and Southeast appear at most sites, although generally in relatively small amounts until after AD 1450. Greater distribution of high-quality cherts from specific sources indicates that north-south trade within the Plains probably also grew (Roper 2006a). Trade may have functioned to expand contacts, allowing redistribution of resources during periods of local shortages. Rainfall and thus crop production, and to a degree bison herd distributions, are highly variable over time and over relatively short distances on the Plains. Villagers attempted to manipulate their environment to boost resource productivity. The primary tool was fire, which was used to clear prairies and fields and promote new grass growth, attracting bison herds closer to villages. Southern and central Plains groups, however, also expanded reciprocal trade networks as a means of alleviating risk from failed crops and other reductions in resources. The social mechanism for this may have been the Calumet ceremony, which seems to have developed in the area at this time (Blakeslee 1981). Calumet supplied a formalized method for individuals from diverse groups to interact, reduced the potential for conflict, and encouraged reciprocal gifts (Baugh 2008). Plains groups used migration and warfare as responses to population pressures and shortfalls in resources on the Plains, but long-distance exchange appears to have been used with greater frequency throughout the village period, including after the arrival of Europeans.

By the time Coronado arrived, portions of the Plains had been abandoned by villagers and settlement patterns had changed significantly in other areas. An abrupt change appears across the central and southern Plains around AD 1450, marking the Protohistoric period. Site densities decline dramatically indicating decreased populations. Groups also coalesce into larger extended communities or complex composite villages. Fortified villages are present as early as AD 1500, and sedentary groups disappear from western prairies. In the central Plains, ancestral Wichita groups are found in the village clusters of the Little River and Lower Walnut phases of the Great Bend aspect, and the Pawnee are represented by the Lower Loup phase. Farther south, Wheeler and Garza phase groups represent other Wichita subdivisions (Vehik 1994). In addition, the Dismal River aspect in the western prairies of the central Plains and the Tierra Blanca phase in the Texas panhandle represent the arrival of Apache groups in the region (Boyd 2001; Habicht-Mauche 1992; Scheiber 2006; Vehik 1994).

A drying climate less suitable for agriculture is often cited as the primary factor in the settlement changes at this time, but migrations and conflict, economic specialization, changing trade patterns, and other factors contributed to development of protohistoric and early historic adaptations (Vehik 1994, 2006). Corn cultivation continued in some western regions but was apparently much reduced (Adair 2006; Brosowske and Bevitt 2006). While agriculture became less reliable, bison herds expanded and groups in the High Plains and western prairies intensified bison hunting, often abandoning all agriculture. Trade with Puebloan and eastern Plains groups increased, probably to move corn and other agricultural commodities to western Plains tribes. The mobility needed to extensively exploit bison herds and the migration of new groups such as the Apache and later the Comanche and others into the area also resulted in greater potential for conflict. This likely influenced settlement patterns, with the more agricultural groups contracting to larger villages that could field more warriors and be fortified.

Eastern Plains villagers moved to clustered settlements and may have intensified a pattern of seasonal (fall-early winter) bison hunting with large communal hunts. Hunts by large village or multivillage groups afforded more protection and allowed groups to kill and process large amounts of bison. Coalescence apparently influenced social organization, with heightened complexity and more defined hierarchy (Vehik 2002). Trade relationships with distant groups that had developed during the early period were expanded, and the Calumet ceremony became widespread and possibly more formalized during this period. Corn agriculture may have further intensified at eastern villages to meet the needs of the expanding regional trade.

Protohistoric material culture was modified slightly, but overall it remained similar to early villager assemblages. Large scrapers for processing bison hides became common, and there was expanded use of the highest-quality lithics for tools. House construction abruptly changed to predominantly circular forms with earth lodges in the central Plains and beehive-shaped grass thatch houses appearing at Wichita sites in the southern Plains. Houses also were typically bigger at this time (Perkins et al. 2008; Roper 2006b), suggesting larger families or multifamily households. Pits remained important storage facilities but often became significantly larger.

Arrival of the Spanish and French onto the Plains in the 16th and 17th centuries did not result in any immediate or dramatic changes in Plains societies. In fact, direct contact was very irregular and intermittent before about 1700. Diseases may have had an impact on eastern villagers, further reducing populations, but there is little evidence for major changes before 1700. Horses arrive in numbers on the southern Plains by the early 17th century, but few trade goods or guns make it to this area of the Plains. Horses and to a degree guns transformed central and southern Plains groups by 1700 by increasing mobility and conflict and decreasing transport costs. Raiding for horses and slaves increased conflict with the Apache to the west and the Osage to the east. Around this time, Wichita groups appear to have coalesced into even larger fortified villages, possibly composed of multitribal or multiethnic groups (Baugh 2007; Perkins and Baugh 2008). Paired villages are present by the early 1700s if not earlier. In the early 18th century, trade with the French brings European goods in quantity, affecting local economics and some social structures.

The eastern villagers such as the Wichita and Pawnee, however, basically incorporated Europeans into their economy with only minor changes to native cultures. Bison hunting and hide processing are intensified to obtain trade goods, and European goods are adapted to traditional uses in native societies. Perhaps the major impact on Plains villager societies, which are now concentrated in the eastern Plains, comes from the greater mobility of native groups and expansion of hunting territories to obtain more hides and other resources for trade. Conflict swells, with mobile hunters in the west raiding villagers in the east. Villagers, however, also raided western groups to obtain horses and slaves, although it is likely that exchange networks were maintained with some groups. The Osage from the east also expanded westward onto the Plains, attempting to limit the access of villagers to European trade. By the early to mid-1700s, Plains villager economies have reoriented more toward the east and trade with French, English, and eventually American groups. There is still extensive trade with western Plains groups such as the Comanche to obtain bison robes, and especially horses, which could be used in the European trade. In exchange, the western tribes received corn and some European trade items. In the southern Plains, economic factors as well as pressure from the Osage eventually result in movement of northern Wichita villagers south into Texas, and they become middlemen in regional trade.

Conclusion

Like many areas of North America, the Plains proved to be amenable to prehistoric agriculture; central and southern Plains villager societies adapted native plants for cultivation and adopted crops and farming techniques from outside the region by about AD 1000. Sedentary farmsteads and hamlets rapidly expanded along rivers and streams across the Plains, including the drier western prairies, where variable rainfall could severely affect corn production. Climate changed during this period, and villagers responded by manipulating local settings to maintain or improve resource productivity. The villager period is marked by increasing agricultural activity through time, with a move toward specialization in corn production and less use of native crops. Subsistence in the area, however, was always closely linked with major game, particularly deer and bison, and bison hunting also intensified over time.

Villager groups occupied the eastern Plains into the historic period, moving toward larger and complex villages accompanied with social, economic, and political changes that began before the first Europeans arrived in the area. Growing conflict led to concentrations of villages or hamlets and construction of fortifications at villages. Expansion of long-distance trade networks allowed villagers to reduce the risk of periodic local crop failures by maintaining contact with people in diverse settings. In contrast, groups in the west reduced agricultural production around AD 1450 or abandoned farming altogether to intensively hunt bison and trade bison products with Pueblo groups in the Southwest or with eastern Plains farmers. The arrival of the horse in the southern Plains in the 17th century, which entailed better mobility and lower transportation costs, at a time when bison were abundant, allowed further intensification of bison hunting. The horse, however, also permitted more raiding and expansion of hunting territories, fueling conflict. The Calumet ceremony, recorded by some of the early European explorers in the Plains, may have been the primary social mechanism that allowed continued long-distance trade between various groups across the southern and central Plains.

Central and southern Plains villagers rapidly incorporated Europeans as part of their extensive trade network, adapting new materials and goods to native economies. For the Wichita, access to French traders in the late 17th century resulted in emphasis on trade to the east, whereas earlier the more extensive trade seems to have been toward the west. The villager economies and social and political systems are only briefly recorded in historic documents, and the archeological record is just beginning to reveal the intricacies of the trade system and types of changes that occurred over the 250-year period after extended European contact but before the tribes were subjugated to reservations.

REFERENCES

Adair, M. J. 2006. Plains Plants. In *Handbook of North American Indians*, vol. 3, *Environment, Origins, and Population*, edited by D. H. Ubelaker, pp. 365–374. Smithsonian Institution, Washington DC.

Baugh, T. G. 2007. Warfare Among the Kirikir'i·s: Archeology, Ethnography, and Ethnohistory. *The Kansas Anthropologist* 28:1–22.

———. 2008. The Anthropology of Trade and Exchange: An Essay on Kirikir'i·s and Southern Plains Political Economy. Memoir 40, Plains Anthropologist 53, *Land of Our Ancestors: Studies in Protohistoric and Historic Wichita Cultures*, edited by Timothy G. Baugh and Stephen M. Perkins, pp. 415–430. Plains Anthropological Society, Lincoln, NE.

Blakeslee, D. L. 1981. The Origin and Spread of the Calumet Ceremony. *American Antiquity* 46:759–768.

———. 2006. Middle Ceramic Period Earthlodges as the Product of Craft Traditions. In *Plains Earthlodges: Ethnographic and Archaeological Perspectives*, edited by D. C. Roper and E. P. Pauls, pp. 83–110. University of Alabama Press, Tuscaloosa.

Boyd, D. K. 2001. Querchos and Teyas: Protohistoric Hunters and Gatherers in the Texas Panhandle-Plains, A.D. 1540–1700. *Texas Archeological Society Bulletin* 72:5–22.

———. 2004. Hank's House 1: Anatomy of a Burned Pithouse. http://www.texasbeyondhistory.net/villagers/hank1/index.html.

———. 2008. Prehistoric Agriculture on the Canadian River of the Texas Panhandle: New Insights from West Pasture Sites on the M-Cross Ranch. In Advances in Ethnobotany, edited by D. Youngblood and P. Dering. *Plains Anthropologist* 205:33–57.

Brooks, R. L. 1987. *The Arthur Site: Settlement and Subsistence Structure at a Washita River Phase Village*. Studies in Oklahoma's Past 15. Oklahoma Archeological Survey, Norman.

Brosowske, S. 2005. *The Evolution of Exchange in Small-Scale Societies of the Southern High Plains*. Ph.D. dissertation, University of Oklahoma, Norman.

———. 2008. Archaeology in the Top of Texas: The 2008 and 2009 TAS Field Schools. *Texas Archeology* 52(1):6–10.

———, and C. T. Bevitt. 2006. Looking South: The Middle Ceramic Period in Southern Kansas and Beyond. In *Kansas Archaeology*, edited by R. J. Hoard and W. E. Banks, pp. 180–205. University Press of Kansas, Lawrence.

Cook, G., and J. Dunbar. 2008. Mapping an Eighteenth-Century Wichita Village Site. *In Land of Our Ancestors: Studies in Protohistoric and Historic Wichita Cultures*, edited by T. G. Baugh and S. M. Perkins, pp. 487–502. Memoir 40, *Plains Anthropologist* 53.

Drass, R. R. 1997. *Culture Change on the Eastern Margins of the Southern Plains*. Studies in Oklahoma's Past 19, Oklahoma Archeological Survey, University of Oklahoma; and Oklahoma Anthropological Society, Memoir 7, Norman.

———. 1998. The Southern Plains Villagers. In *Archaeology on the Great Plains*, edited by W. R. Wood, pp. 415–455. University Press of Kansas, Lawrence.

———. 2008. Corn, Beans, and Bison: Cultivated Plants and Changing Economies of the Late Prehistoric Villagers on the Plains of Oklahoma and Northwest Texas. Plains Anthropologist, vol. 53, no. 205, *Advances in Ethnobotany*, edited by D. Youngblood and P. Dering, pp. 7–31.

Graves, N. 2008. Protohistoric Bison Hunting in the Central Plains: A Study of Faunal Remains from the Crandall Site (14CR420). Memoir 40, Plains Anthropologist 53, *Land of Our Ancestors: Studies in Protohistoric and Historic Wichita Cultures*, edited by T. G. Baugh and S. M. Perkins, pp. 531–550. Plains Anthropological Society, Lincoln, NE.

Habicht-Mauche, J. A. 1992. Coronado's Querchos and Teyas in the Archaeological Record of the Texas Panhandle. *Plains Anthropologist* 37:247–259.

Hall, Stephen A. 1988. Environment and Archaeology of the Central Osage Plains. *Plains Anthropologist* 33:203–218.

Haury, C. E. 2008. Bison and Box Turtles: Faunal Remains from the Lower Walnut Settlement. Memoir 40, *Plains Anthropologist* 53, *Land of Our Ancestors: Studies in Protohistoric and Historic Wichita Cultures*, edited by T. G. Baugh and S. M. Perkins, pp. 503–530. Plains Anthropological Society, Lincoln, NE.

Huebner, J. A. 1991. Late Prehistoric Bison Populations in Central and Southern Texas. *Plains Anthropologist* 36:343–358.

Lintz, C. R. 1986. *Architecture and Community Variability Within the Antelope Creek Phase of the Texas Panhandle*. Studies in Oklahoma's Past 14, Oklahoma Archeological Survey, Norman.

Maki, D., and S. Brosowske. 2007. The 2008 Texas Archaeological Society (TAS) Field School: An Opportunity to Test Geophysical Anomalies on a Massive Scale. Paper presented at the 72nd Annual Meeting of the Society for American Archaeology, Austin, TX.

Nepstad-Thornberry, C., L. S. Cummings, and K. Puseman. 2002. A Model for Upper Republican Subsistence and Nutrition in the Medicine Creek Locality: A New Look at Extant Data. In *Medicine Creek: Seventy Years of Archaeological Investigations*, edited by D. C. Roper, pp. 197–211. University of Alabama Press, Tuscaloosa.

Perkins, S. M., and T. G. Baugh. 2008. Protohistory and the Wichita. Memoir 40, *Plains Anthropologist* 53, *Land of Our Ancestors: Studies in Protohistoric and Historic Wichita Cultures*, edited by T. G. Baugh and S. M. Perkins, pp. 381–394. Plains Anthropological Society, Lincoln, NE.

Perkins, S. M., S. C. Vehik, and R. R. Drass. 2008. The Hide Trade and Wichita Social Organization: An Assessment of Ethnological Hypotheses Concerning Polygyny. Memoir 40, *Plains Anthropologist* 53. *Land of Our Ancestors: Studies in Protohistoric and Historic Wichita Cultures*, edited by T. G. Baugh and S. M. Perkins, pp. 431–443, Plains Anthropological Society, Lincoln, NE.

Ricklis, R. A. 1992. The Spread of a Late Prehistoric Bison Hunting Complex: Evidence from the South-Central Coastal Prairie of Texas. *Plains Anthropologist* 37:262–273.

Roper, D. C. 2006a. The Central Plains Tradition. In *Kansas Archaeology*, edited by R. J. Hoard and W. E. Banks, pp. 105–132. University Press of Kansas, Lawrence.

———. 2006b. The Pawnee in Kansas: Ethnohistory and Archaeology. In *Kansas Archaeology*, edited by R. J. Hoard and W. E. Banks, pp. 233–247. University Press of Kansas, Lawrence.

———. 2007. The Origins and Expansion of the Central Plains Tradition. In *Plains Village Archaeology: Bison-Hunting Farmers in the Central and Northern Plains*, edited by S. A. Ahler and M. Kay, pp. 53–63. University of Utah Press, Salt Lake City.

———, and E. P. Pauls. 2005. What, Where, and When Is an Earthlodge? In *Plains Earthlodges: Ethnographic and Archaeological Perspectives*, edited by D. C. Roper and E. P. Pauls, pp. 1–31. University of Alabama Press, Tuscaloosa.

Scheiber, L. L. 2006. The Late Prehistoric on the High Plains of Western Kansas: High Plains Upper Republican and Dismal River. In *Kansas Archaeology*, edited by R. J. Hoard and W. E. Banks, pp. 151–164. University Press of Kansas, Lawrence.

Vehik, S. C. 1994. Cultural Continuity and Discontinuity in the Southern Prairies and Cross Timbers. In *Plains Indians, A.D. 500–1500*, edited by K. H. Schlesier, pp. 239–263. University of Oklahoma Press, Norman.

———. 2002. Conflict, Trade, and Political Development on the Southern High Plains. *American Antiquity* 67:37–64.

———. 2006. Wichita Ethnohistory. In *Kansas Archaeology*, edited by R. J. Hoard and W. E. Banks, pp. 206–218. University Press of Kansas, Lawrence.

CHAPTER 32

WOMEN ON THE EDGE: LOOKING AT PROTOHISTORIC PLAINS-PUEBLO INTERACTION FROM A FEMINIST PERSPECTIVE

JUDITH A. HABICHT-MAUCHE

SINCE the 1960s, feminist perspectives have increasingly come to permeate many aspects of anthropological and archaeological practice in North America. Feminist analysis does not embody a single theory or method but is a broad rubric that has fostered a robust and diverse set of critical analytic agendas (Collier and Yanagisako 1989). These approaches call on us to focus on the day-to-day experience of women's lives and how the strategies and choices of women actors have been both enabled and constrained by culturally and historically defined systems of power and inequality. These systems are embodied in various institutional and material aspects of daily life, among them organization of labor, structures of kinship, marriage and family life, and political strategies of prestige and alliance.

Archaeology, in particular, is useful for exploring how such systems come to be dynamically constituted under specific cultural and historical conditions. The protohistoric period (AD 1450 to 1700) was an especially dynamic and transformative moment for the native peoples living along the borderlands of the North

American Southwest and Southern Plains. On the western margins of the Southern Plains, this period was marked by the transition from generalized mixed hunting-gathering-farming economies to those based on more intensive hunting of bison and specialized production and exchange of bison products, especially tanned hides (see Drass, Mitchell, this volume). Archaeological and ethnohistoric data suggest that accumulation and distribution of processed bison hides played an expanding role in male prestige-building activities on the Southern Plains during this transitional period.

Because women in this system were the primary producers of men's wealth (in the form of processed bison hides), the exchange of women and control of women's labor may have become a central feature of men's competitive status-building efforts. One strategy open to some men to increase the output of women's labor in their households was to expand the practice of polygyny, negotiating marriages to multiple wives. Other strategies may have been to actively recruit nonlocal women's labor through raiding and captive taking, negotiation of cross-cultural marriage alliances, and patronage of refugee families. These interregional interactions, both cooperative and violent, were most intense between the nomadic bison hunters of the southern High Plains and the agricultural villages of the Eastern Pueblos.

In this chapter, I review evidence for the rising importance of bison hunting, bison hide processing, and interregional exchange along the western margins of the Southern Plains in the period after AD 1450. I also summarize ceramic evidence for the presence of nonlocal, especially Southwestern Pueblo, women living among various nomadic and seminomadic bison-hunting groups in what is now the Texas Panhandle and western Oklahoma. I also present tentative evidence for a shift in the status of Southern Plains women, as marked by their apparently diminished access to exotic raw materials and ornaments. I argue that, during the protohistoric period, restructuring of the gendered division of labor and context of production and exchange, in conjunction with the presence of nonlocal women as new social actors, disrupted local women's traditional social networks and arenas of social action and had a significant impact on the role and status of women on the Southern Plains.

PROTOHISTORIC PLAINS-PUEBLO INTERACTION

Documents dating from the time of Francisco Vázquez de Coronado's initial *entrada* in 1540 (Flint and Flint 2005) to the first successful colonization of the province of New Mexico by Juan de Oñate (Hammond and Rey 1953) at the turn of the 17th century provide us with the earliest recorded descriptions of the native peoples of the southern High Plains and their interactions, both friendly and violent, with the Pueblo villagers of the Rio Grande Valley. According to these accounts, the badlands and high flat plains of the Llano Estacado, which extended east of the Rio

Grande Valley and southern Rocky Mountains, were the domain of various groups of highly mobile, bison-hunting nomads who lived in portable hide tents that they carried from place to place on the backs of dogs. There are hints that some of these groups may also have practiced limited maize horticulture, but the primary focus of their economy appears to have been the hunting of bison and processing of bison products for exchange to agricultural village groups living along the borders of the Southern Plains. These accounts vividly describe the periodic trading visits of nomadic Plains bison hunters to eastern frontier pueblos such as Pecos, Taos, Picurís, and San Marcos. During the course of these visits, specialized, processed bison products such as dried meat, hides, and rendered fat were exchanged for the agricultural produce and craft specialties of the settled villagers, especially maize, ceramics, and cotton cloth.

Archaeological evidence from both the Southwest and Southern Plains mirrors the ethnohistoric accounts and testifies to the important economic and social ties that linked these two regions of southern North America in the centuries immediately preceding and following direct European contact. At Pecos, A. V. Kidder (1932) recovered a complex of materials that clearly indicated interaction with bison-hunting groups to the east. This material included a Plains-style toolkit notable for its association with the processing of bison hides and consisting of snub-nosed end scrapers, two- and four-edged beveled knives, and bison bone end scrapers. The presence of exotic lithic raw materials, such as Alibates agate from quarries along the Canadian River in Texas, also suggests contact and trade between the inhabitants of Pecos and nomadic peoples to the east. Other evidence of Plains-Pueblo exchange includes an increase in the amount of eastern freshwater shells recovered from Rio Grande Pueblo sites beginning in the 15th century.

In turn, numerous finds of southwestern materials and artifacts have been recovered from various archaeological contexts throughout the Southern Plains. Pueblo pottery, obsidian, turquoise, Pacific coast shells, and other materials of southwestern origin first occur in notable quantities on sites of the late prehistoric Antelope Creek phase, located along the Canadian River in the northern Texas Panhandle and dating to between AD 1200 and 1500. More extensive evidence of interregional contact and trade have been recovered from a series of archaeological complexes associated with the highly specialized bison-hunting groups who occupied the western margins of the Southern Plains during the protohistoric period (AD 1450–1700).

These groups have been identified archaeologically as the Wheeler Phase, centered on the mixed-grass prairies of western Oklahoma and the Tierra Blanca and Garza complexes located on high plains of the Texas Panhandle (see Figure 32.1). The Tierra Blanca complex most likely represents the intrusion of nomadic Athapaskan-speaking, proto-Apache groups onto the southern High Plains. Wheeler Phase and Garza Complex sites, on the other hand, most likely represent the ancestors of various groups who came to be known collectively in historic times as the Wichita. These western-most subgroups of the Wichita appear to have relied much less on agriculture and much more on intensive bison hunting than their linguistic relatives in the Arkansas River region of Oklahoma and Kansas. Scattered evidence

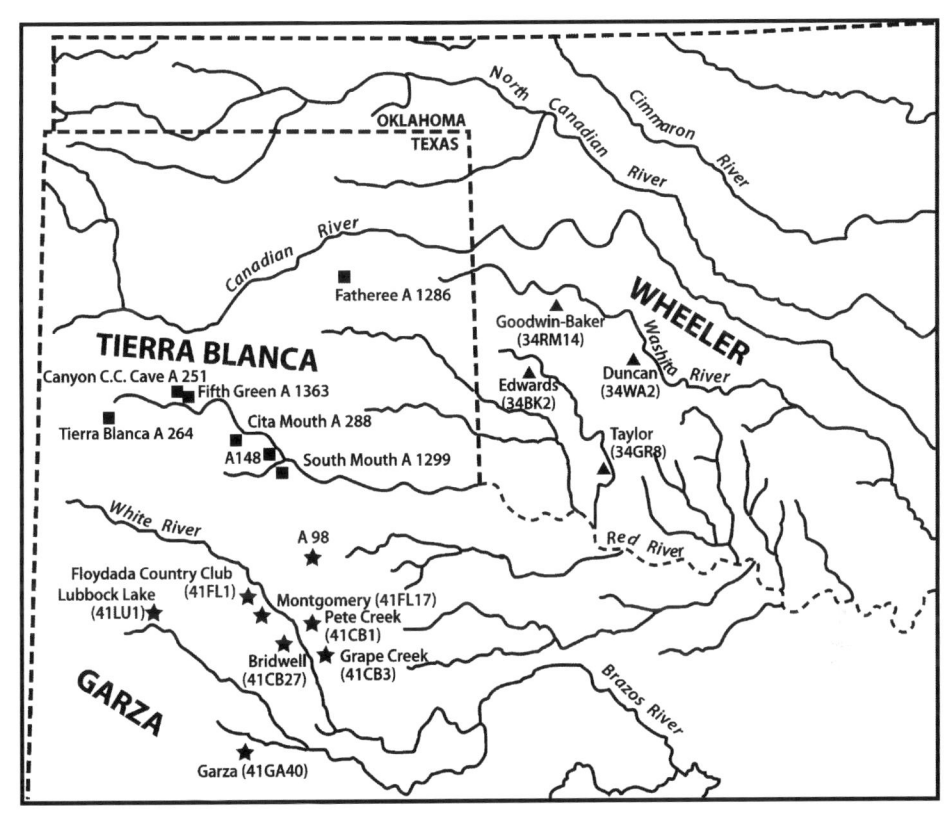

Figure 32.1 Location of protohistoric complexes on the Southern Plains discussed in this chapter.

of contact between more sedentary Plains Village groups and the Rio Grande Pueblos—in the form of small quantities of Rio Grande pottery, obsidian, shell jewelry and turquoise—has also been noted as far north and east as western and central Kansas, among what are also generally interpreted as ancestral Wichita villages (Wedel 1950, 1982). The variety, abundance and widespread distribution of southwestern trade goods on sites throughout the Southern Plains, and extending into the Central Plains, reflect a dramatic increase in the frequency and intensity of Plains-Pueblo interactions beginning around the middle of the fifteenth century.

Bison Hides, Women's Labor, and Men's Status

This heightened contact and interaction, particularly between the farming peoples of the Pueblo Southwest and nomadic and seminomadic bison hunters on the Southern Plains, appears to have coincided with a period of increasing environmental, demographic, and social instability in both areas. Katherine Spielmann (1982, 1991) suggested that trade in basic subsistence goods, such as exchange of maize for bison meat, may have intensified at this time as a way for people in both the Rio Grande Valley and the Southern Plains to create a buffer against the unpredictability of local hunting, foraging, and horticultural productivity. Alternatively, Timothy Baugh (1982, 1986) modeled interregional exchange between the Southwest and Southern Plains from a more political economic perspective that emphasized the existence of a large-scale division of labor between distinct regional populations. In the absence of any overarching political structure, he argued that the ties of economic dependency created by this division of labor bound these groups into a dynamic yet coherent interregional system. More recently, Susan Vehik (2002) has developed a more agent-based approach to understanding the intensification of regional and interregional trade during the protohistoric period, arguing that political leaders and competitors for political leadership on the Southern Plains may have exploited the social disruptions and demographic upheavals of these times to enhance their own individual power and prestige. Trade, in this context, would have given ambitious Southern Plains men the means to accrue the resources necessary to participate in competitive status-building activities.

Nonsubsistence items, such as personal ornaments and exotic lithic materials, probably would have played a more important role in such competitive and alliance-building transactions than basic subsistence items because of their greater potential for being converted into visible symbols of status and for being accumulated as objects of wealth. Well-made bison robes and tanned hides could also have served as important high-status items that circulated regularly through this system. Spanish accounts of various expeditions to the Southern Plains during the mid-16th and early-17th centuries would seem to support such an interpretation. These accounts record several instances where large quantities of dressed hides were presented as formal, diplomatic gifts to the Spanish by the male leaders of various nomadic bison-hunting groups encountered on the Southern Plains (Forbes 1994).

Bison dominate the faunal assemblages at most protohistoric sites along the western margins of the Southern Plains. Most of these bison bones are highly fractured, suggesting that they were systematically processed for marrow extraction and bone grease manufacture (cf. Boszhardt, this volume). Scattered postholes, interpreted as the remains of racks and scaffolds for drying meat and dressing hides, have also been identified at several Garza Complex and Wheeler Phase sites. Shallow pits surrounded by rocks may have been used for bone grease extraction, using an ethnographically recorded technique of stone boiling in hides. Tools that are associated specifically with hide processing activities, such as small snub-nosed end scrapers, two- and four-edged bevel knives, serrated metapodial fleshers, and a variety of bone awls, frequently occur on Southern Plains sites dated after AD 1450 (Creel 1991). At several of these sites, unifacially retouched scrapers outnumber every other formal tool category. Overall, these archaeological data appear to support documentary evidence for intensification of bison hunting and processing on the Southern Plains during the protohistoric period, associated with a sharper focus on the manufacture of exchangeable commodities such as dried meat, bone grease, pemmican, and dressed hides.

In particular, dressed hides—which are durable, storable, and easily transportable—may have shifted from being relatively mundane items produced primarily for domestic use during late prehistoric times to highly specialized commodities whose conspicuous consumption, distribution, and exchange came to mark individual wealth and status during the protohistoric period. Later accounts from the historic Plains fur and hide trade suggest that finely made bison robes and dressed hides were valued not only for their functional utility but for what their quantity and quality suggested about the competency and power of both hunter (man-husband) and processor (woman-wife).

Intensification of hide production for exchange would have entailed a major shift in the organization of labor, especially along gender lines, among the groups living on the western margin of the Southern Plains. During the late prehistoric period, women would have been principally responsible for gathering wild plants and for gardening. Among Plains Village groups, such as the late prehistoric Antelope Creek phase (AD 1250–1500) people of the Canadian River Valley, farming was primarily the arena of women who would have controlled distribution and use of agricultural products and other domestic items, both within their own households and through individual exchange. With the demise of Plains Village farming economies along the western margins of the Southern Plains, the focus of women's labor would have shifted from farming to hide production.

With this shift, women may have no longer controlled the products of their own labor to the degree that they had in the past. Feminist scholars note that women's status, cross-culturally, is determined less by how hard they work or the specific kind of tasks they perform, and more by the degree to which they are able to assert control over the fruits of their efforts (Collier 1988; Weist 1980). Dressed hides, though largely the product of women's labor, may have been more often co-opted by their male partners (husbands) and family members (brothers) for use in competitive exchanges and alliance-building activities. Thus men's power and status within Southern Plains society may have been more determined during the protohistoric period by their ability to control women's labor and appropriate the products of that labor.

Strategies for Increasing and Controlling Women's Labor

Another insight of recent feminist scholarship has been to show that within the context of domestic family households, lineages, and broader kin networks, the interests of men, their wives, and their wives' families may not always coincide (Collier and Yanagisako 1989). The shift from subsistence farming to commodity-based hide production among groups living on the western margins of the Southern Plains during the protohistoric period would have put women and men in these societies in a highly interdependent but potentially antagonistic relationship to one another. The most closely related modern descendant groups to the protohistoric occupants of the western Southern Plains are the Eastern Apache and the Wichita. Historic and ethnographic evidence suggests that, at least until the late 19th century, both of these groups were organized matrilineally, with economic production and social reproduction centered around a core group of related women. Marriages were negotiated between kin groups, with husbands generally going to live with and work for their wives' families. Thus a married man's interest in promoting his own status within such a context would inevitably be in conflict on some level with his social and economic obligations to his wife and her kin. In addition, he would have to compete with his wife's male kin, particularly her brothers, for control of the products of his wife's labor and her children's labor for use in competitive status-building activities.

This situation gives women a certain level of social power as they are able to play the interests of their husbands and brothers against one another to the best advantage of themselves and their children. However, within the context of protohistoric Southern Plains social dynamics, where women's labor was being converted into men's status through the medium of dressed hides, the most successful men would have been those who could increase the size of their domestic female workforce, while minimizing their social and economic obligations to those workers and their kin.

Processing hides was labor-intensive work, with each bison robe representing about 70 woman-hours of labor. This effort potentially conflicted with other economic and domestic tasks performed by Southern Plains women: foraging, farming, preparing food, making pottery, rearing children. These tasks were performed most efficiently when they could be divided among a group of women working together within the same domestic unit. Nineteenth-century accounts of the Plains fur and hide trade indicate that a single woman was capable of producing only about a dozen dressed hides per season, significantly fewer than the number of animals a man could kill even without the aid of horses or guns. However, these same accounts also suggest that the number of hides processed per woman per year could be nearly doubled if multiple women worked cooperatively within the same domestic group (Jablow 1950).

There were several ways Plains men could have improved their access to and control over women's labor. Two possible strategies, used by nomadic Plains men during the later-19th-century fur and hide trade, were intensification of the practice of polygyny and incorporation of captive women into domestic groups as "slaves" or lower-ranking "chore wives." Other practices that some men may have engaged in, which could have contributed to an increase in nonlocal women and their available labor on the protohistoric Southern Plains, are negotiation of interethnic marriage alliances and patronage of individuals or families who may have fled to the Plains as refugees, escaping the economic, social, and demographic upheavals brought by Spanish contact and colonialism in the Southwest (Habicht-Mauche 2008).

Historic documents suggest that the practice of polygyny grew significantly among nomadic Plains groups during the late 18th and 19th centuries in response to the market demands of the Euro-American hide trade (Albers and Medicine 1983). The 1880 U.S. census of the Cheyenne indicates that as many as 20–25 percent of households were polygynous (Moore 1991). And among the Wichita, combined data from documentary and archaeological sources suggest that both house sizes and the number of people within households were rising throughout the 18th century (Baugh and Perkins 2008), possibly indicative of increased polygyny in response to the hide trade and the need for more women's labor per household. Currently there is no archaeological or ethnohistoric evidence for the practice of polygyny among groups occupying the western margins of the Southern Plains during the earlier 16th and 17th centuries, but this practice was clearly a culturally acceptable strategy that could have been mobilized by ambitious men to enhance their status.

Another strategy for enlarging the pool of available female labor within domestic units would have been to recruit women laborers from outside the local group, through violent raiding and captive taking, by negotiating exogamous marriage alliances with trading partners, or by incorporating stray refugees into the domestic unit. Spanish documents from colonial New Mexico record that raids by bison-hunting nomads, as well as taking captives, especially women and children, was a common feature of frontier life along the Southwest-Southern Plains borderlands throughout the 17th, 18th, and 19th centuries. Accounts of the Coronado expedition suggest that violent raids on eastern frontier Pueblos, such as those in the Galisteo Basin, may have extended back to the early 16th century, predating Spanish contact. Spanish colonial records also note the presence of Pueblo refugees living among Plains nomadic groups. In at least one instance, these refugees' Pueblo kin asked Spanish colonial authorities for help in liberating and returning their relatives, who they claimed were being exploited for their labor by their Plains hosts (Brooks 2002). Marriages between Pueblo women and Plains men are not well documented in early historic records from New Mexico, and they would have been discouraged culturally by most Pueblo families, who generally favored village or ethnic endogamy. However, in the case of some poorer, low-ranking Pueblo families this strategy may have given them sustained access to Plains trade goods that could have been converted to food during times of economic instability. We should not dismiss this strategy as impossible just because it would not have been favored or the norm. As both practice and feminist critiques have taught us, there is often a difference between the structural rules that ethnologists traditionally describe as reflecting social reality and how social relationships are actually negotiated day-to-day.

Evidence for the presence of nonlocal women may be reflected in the diverse pottery types associated with protohistoric sites on the western margin of the Southern Plains. Although some of these sites, especially those on the High Plains of Texas, have produced little or no evidence of pottery, others have yielded a confusing and complex array of types associated with a broad range of Southwestern, Southern Plains, and Southeastern ceramic traditions.

Various analyses suggest that much of this nonlocal style pottery was imported to the Southern Plains from adjacent regions of North America. For example, petrographic studies clearly indicate that all of the Rio Grande-style glaze-painted pottery recovered from these sites was manufactured at Pueblo villages in New Mexico (Leonard 2006). Several other petrographic studies, however, have demonstrated that at least some of the exotic-style pottery recovered from protohistoric sites on the Southern Plains was produced locally (Habicht-Mauche 1988, 2000). These locally made, but exotic-style, pottery types reflect a variety of quite distinct technological traditions and regional styles. For example, analysis of Rio Grande-style "faint striated" utility ware recovered from sites associated with protohistoric complexes in the Texas Panhandle and western Oklahoma demonstrated that a significant proportion of this pottery was made using a variety of clays and tempers that are locally available in the immediate vicinity of these sites but that are clearly atypical of similar ceramic vessels known to have been produced by Pueblo potters in New Mexico. Examples of Caddo-style pottery, similar to contemporary types from north central and east Texas, have also been recovered from several Garza Complex sites. Petrographic analyses of several examples suggest that these Caddo-style pots were made from clays locally exposed along the edge of the Caprock escarpment of the Llano Estacado.

In sum, there is now substantial evidence that pottery reflecting a mix of Southwestern and Southeastern ceramic traditions was made locally at the Southern Plains during the protohistoric period, starting as early as the 16th century. Traditionally, Native American pottery was made and used by women, particularly in the context of domestic food preparation, storage, and service activities. These women usually learned to make pottery as young girls by watching and working with other women in their home village or within their local domestic group. Therefore the presence of locally made, exotic-style pottery within protohistoric assemblages on the Southern Plains offers strong evidence for the presence of women of nonlocal origin at these sites.

The Changing Role and Status of Women on the Southern Plains

As discussed previously, Pueblo women, and possibly other nonlocal women, came to be present on the protohistoric Southern Plains as the result of a variety of social and economic strategies that linked the peoples of the Southwest–Southern Plains–Southeast borderlands of North America during the 16th and 17th centuries. By integrating these women and their children into the domestic units under their control, ambitious Plains men were able to augment their access to women's labor and appropriate the products of that labor for their own status-building activities. In some instances, local women may have been able to use these practices to their advantage to enhance their own status by turning over the more mundane household tasks and daily drudgery to younger and lower-ranking women in the household. This freed elder women and senior wives to focus on the more detailed sewing and elaborate decorating of skins and clothing that added to their quality and value as exchange goods. A woman's skill and artistry in this arena commanded respect and added to her prestige (Albers and Medicine 1983).

However, in the long run the presence of these nonlocal women would have disrupted local women's traditional social networks and had a significant impact on their role and status in protohistoric Southern Plains society. With the demise of farming economies along the western margins of the Southern Plains, women were no longer the primary producers of subsistence goods. Instead they were workers who transformed the products of the hunt, obtained by men, into food (bison meat) and durable wealth (hides). Women may have continued to control distribution of meat and other food within their own households and through trade, but they probably had less control over distribution of dressed hides, which appear by the 16th century to have become central to the ritualized gift exchanges that defined men's status.

Traditionally men, in these matrilineal societies, would have sought to marry women from the most prosperous and high-ranking kin groups. A man's success and status was tied to that of his in-laws, to whom he owed his labor and support (Collier 1988). However, intensification of hide production for exchange, to acquire food as well as to negotiate status, changed the social calculus that defined the relative status of husbands and wives. As men engaged more and more in practices that allowed them to recruit women's labor from outside the residential group, the role and status of women as the core of social relations within the residential group would have diminished.

There is some tentative archaeological evidence to suggest that the status of women on the Southern Plains may have been declining during the 16th and 17th centuries. In comparison to their late prehistoric Plains Village counterparts, protohistoric Garza complex women appear to have had less access to exotic, high-status exchange goods, especially high-quality lithic material such as obsidian and personal ornaments such as turquoise jewelry and Pacific shell beads (Habicht-Mauche 2005). However, much more archaeological research at protohistoric Southern Plains sites will be required to fully understand the material ramifications of this social process.

In making this argument for the shifting status of women along the western margins of the Southern Plains during the protohistoric period, I do not intend to reinforce the ethnocentric 19th-century Euro-American stereotype of Plains women as submissive drudges. Throughout the protohistoric period, Southern Plains women certainly would have benefited from the labor they provided in support of the ambitious status-building activities of their menfolk, and in so doing gained a level of social power and prestige in their own right. Protohistoric nomadic groups on the Southern Plains probably retained significant vestiges of their matrilineal past, which continued to allow women to negotiate their interests and their children's against those of brothers and husbands. The experience of any particular woman probably varied according to her social connections, age, status, and personal history within the local group. Certainly the experience of local women would have been different from that of nonlocal women, and senior wives would have differed from junior wives or captives. Nevertheless, the arenas where social power and status could be negotiated within Southern Plains society were clearly shifting in favor of men throughout the protohistoric period, setting the stage for the social dynamics recorded in the historic era of the 18th- and 19th-century Plains fur and hide trade.

A generation of feminist scholarship in anthropology has forced us to abandon universalist models of male dominance in human societies. At the same time, the hope that we would find some idealized matriarchy among the non-Western or ancient peoples of the world has also proven to be a naïve chimera. Instead, feminist perspectives, especially in archaeology, have allowed us to explore how the day-to-day lives of men and women are shaped by the contingencies of culture and history. Such studies are particularly revealing at dynamic transitional moments, as in the case of the protohistoric period along the North American Southern Plains–Southwest Pueblo frontier, when indigenous peoples, both men and women, stood on the brink of being engulfed by Western colonialism and modern capitalism and yet still acted largely in the context of their own contested interests and values.

REFERENCES

Albers, P., and B. Medicine (editors). 1983. *The Hidden Half: Studies of Plains Indian Women*. University Press of America, Washington, DC.

Baugh, T. G. 1982. *Edwards I (34BK2): Southern Plains Adaptations in the Protohistoric Period*. Studies in Oklahoma's Past 8. Oklahoma Archaeological Survey, Norman.

———. 1986. Culture History and Protohistoric Societies in the Southern Plains. Memoir 21, *Plains Anthropologist* vol. 31, no. 114, pt. 2, In *Current Trends in Southern Plains Archaeology*, edited by T. G. Baugh, pp. 167–187. Plains Anthropological Society, Lincoln, NE.

———, and S. M. Perkins (editors). 2008. *Land of Our Ancestors: Studies in Protohistoric and Historic Wichita Cultures*. Memoir 40, *Plains Anthropologist*. Vol. 53, no. 208, pp. 375–594. Plains Anthropological Society, Lincoln, NE.

Brooks, J. F. 2002. *Captives and Cousins: Slavery, Kinship, and Community in the Southwest Borderlands*. University of North Carolina Press, Chapel Hill.

Collier, J. F. 1988. *Marriage and Inequality in Classless Societies*. Stanford University Press, Palo Alto, CA.

———, and S. J. Yanagisako. 1989. Theory in Anthropology Since Feminist Practice. *Critique of Anthropology* 9(2):27–37.

Creel, Darrell. 1991. Bison Hides in Late Prehistoric Exchange in the Southern Plains. *American Antiquity* 56:40–49.

Flint, R., and S. C. Flint (editors and translators). 2005. *Documents of the Coronado Expedition, 1539–1542: "They Were Not Familiar with His Majesty, nor Did They Wish to Be His Subjects."* Southern Methodist University Press, Dallas.

Forbes, J. D. 1994. *Apache, Navaho, and Spaniard*. 2nd ed. University of Oklahoma Press, Norman.

Habicht-Mauche, J. A. 1988. *An Analysis of Southwestern-Style Utility Ware Ceramics from the Southern Plains in the Context of Protohistoric Plains-Pueblo Interaction*. Ph.D. dissertation, Harvard University, Cambridge, MA.

———. 2000. Pottery, Food, Hides and Women: Labor, Production, and Exchange Across the Protohistoric Plains-Pueblo Frontier. In *The Archaeology of Regional Interaction in the Prehistoric Southwest*, edited by M. Hegmon, pp. 209–231. University Press of Colorado, Niwot.

———. 2005. The Shifting Role of Women and Women's Labor on the Protohistoric Southern High Plains. In *Gender and Hide Production*, edited by L. Frink and K. Weedman, pp. 37–55. AltaMira Press, Walnut Creek, CA.

———. 2008. Captive Wives? The Role and Status of Non-Local Women on the Protohistoric Southern High Plains. In *Invisible Citizens: Captives and Their Consequences*, edited by C. M. Cameron, pp. 181–204. University of Utah Press, Salt Lake City.

Hammond, G. P., and A. Rey (translators). 1953. *Don Juan de Onate, Colonizer of New Mexico, 1595–1628*. University of New Mexico Press, Albuquerque.

Jablow, J. 1950. *The Cheyenne in Plains Indian Trade Relations, 1795–1840*. University of Washington Press, Seattle.

Kidder, A. V. 1932. *The Artifacts of Pecos*. Yale University Press, New Haven, CT.

Leonard, K. 2006. Directionality and Exclusivity of Plains-Pueblo Exchange During the Protohistoric Period (A.D. 1450–1700). In *The Social Life of Pots: Glaze Wares and Cultural Transformation in the American Southwest, A.D. 1250–1680*, edited by J. A. Habicht-Mauche, S. L. Eckert, and D. L. Huntley, pp. 232–252. University of Arizona Press, Tucson.

Moore, J. H. 1991. The Developmental Cycle of Cheyenne Polygyny. *American Indian Quarterly* 15(3):311–328.

Spielmann, K. A. 1982. *Inter-Societal Food Acquisition Among Egalitarian Societies: An Ecological Study of Plains/Pueblo Interaction in the American Southwest*. Ph.D. dissertation. University of Michigan. University Microfilms, Ann Arbor, MI.

———, (editor). 1991. *Farmers, Hunters, and Colonists: Interaction Between the Southwest and the Southern Plains*. University of Arizona Press, Tucson.

Vehik, S. C. 2002. Conflict, Trade, and Political Development on the Southern Plains. *American Antiquity* 67(1):37–64.

Wedel, W. R. 1950. Notes on Plains-Southwestern Contacts in the Light of Archaeology. In *For the Dean: Essays in Anthropology in Honor of Byron Cummings*, edited by E. K. Reed and D. S. King, pp. 99–116. Hohokam Museum Association, Tucson, AZ.

———. 1982. Further Notes on Puebloan-Central Plains Contacts in Light of Archaeology. In Memoir No. 3, Oklahoma Anthropological Society, Contributions No. 1, *Pathways to Plains Prehistory: Anthropological Perspectives of Plains Natives and Their Pasts*, edited by D. G. Wycoff and J. L. Hofman, pp. 145–152. Cross Timbers Heritage Association, Duncan, Oklahoma.

Weist, K. M. 1980. Plains Indian Women: An Assessment. In *Anthropology on the Great Plains*, edited by W. R. Wood and M. Liberty, pp. 255–271. University of Nebraska Press, Lincoln.

CHAPTER 33

CAHOKIA INTERACTION AND ETHNOGENESIS IN THE NORTHERN MIDCONTINENT

THOMAS E. EMERSON

The period from AD 900 to 1500 represents one of tremendous change in the northern Midcontinent. Driven by conditions of political and social asymmetry, environmental and economic variation, and climate change, the natives in the fan-shaped region anchored at St. Louis and stretching northeast along the course of the Illinois River valley formed a network of interacting yet diverse groups (Figure 33.1). In this region the social, political, and population dynamics generated by North America's first city, Cahokia, reverberated through the northern midcontinent at a level not experienced again until the impact of European expansion in the 1600s. The region pivoted on the American Bottom, an expanse of Mississippi River floodplain between the modern communities of Alton and Chester, Illinois. Stretching linearly about 160 kilometers, the floodplain is rich in backwater lakes, sloughs, swamps, wet and dry prairies, and assorted woodlands—a prime habitat for hunters, fishers, and gatherers as well as later farming folks.

Located on the main water transportation route in the continental United States, the American Bottom is near the junction of the Missouri and Illinois rivers. These two major rivers link the region westward to the foothills of the Rocky Mountains, eastward to the Great Lakes and Atlantic, and south to the Gulf of Mexico. It is also the intersection of several physiographic zones, including the Ozark Plateau, the Prairie Peninsula, and the Mississippian Embayment. Yet despite these seemingly

CAHOKIA INTERACTION AND ETHNOGENESIS

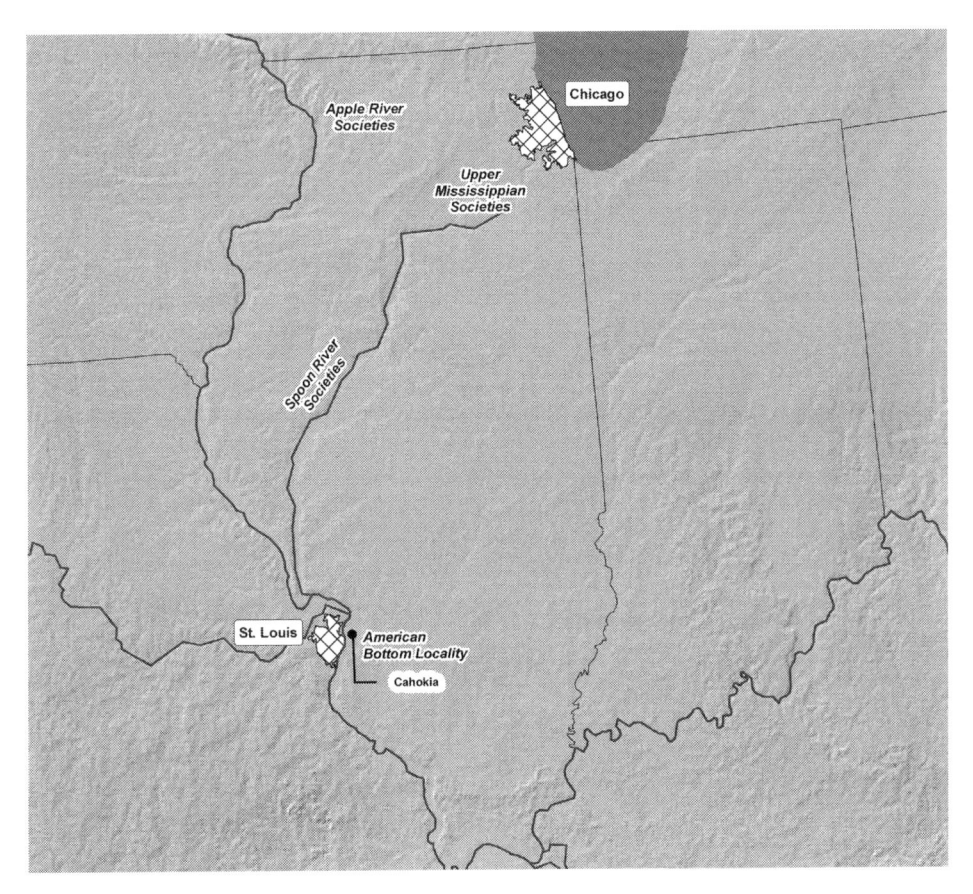

Figure 33.1 Distribution of regional Mississippian societies.

attractive attributes, native occupation of the American Bottom, unlike the Illinois valley to the north, remained intermittent until about AD 600, when populations quickly increased (Fortier et al. 2006).

At that time in the American Bottom, people known to archaeologists as the Patrick phase had adopted the bow and arrow and were making effective thin-walled cooking pots (Fortier and Jackson 2000). Patrick sites are ubiquitous across the landscape; the increase in population size, density, and territorially based mobility that they represent stands in marked contrast to earlier Woodland peoples. These people were probably swidden horticulturalists who grew native seed crops, not maize. Clusters of their houses and pits were scattered throughout the American Bottom, in both the floodplain and the adjacent uplands. These sites include small, subterranean, rectangular and keyhole structures as well as large, likely communal, single-post buildings with many surrounding deep storage pits and earth ovens. The small structures were only about 2 meters in size, large enough for sleeping and protection from severe weather but little else. As encountered archaeologically, they seldom contain living debris or hearths. The large structures, presumed to be for community activities, were found only in the long-term, densely used floodplain villages.

The regional ethnobotanical evidence is clear that in the ninth century most groups across the northern midcontinent below the northern climatic limit were familiar with maize cultivation and had incorporated it into their subsistence practices in varying degrees (Pearsall, this volume; Simon 2000). Although over the next few hundred years some groups in the Illinois River valley began to live in clustered, often riverside, settlements and were probably progressively dependent on agriculture, such instances were uncommon and primarily restricted to the central Illinois River valley. Most groups in the northern midcontinent continue a traditional, residentially mobile lifestyle from earlier times, living in small bands, perhaps cultivating some maize as a seasonal dietary supplement, and remaining widely dispersed across the landscape.

However, in the American Bottom the trends initiated in the Patrick phase accelerated after AD 900. Post-AD 900 Terminal Late Woodland villagers were sedentary farmers clustered into large villages including up to 100 or 150 houses, with evidence of internal social and political differentiation (Kelly 2000). For the first time we see the appearance of what becomes a later signature of the area: the village courtyard or square. Evidence for political organization is limited, but it is reasonable to suggest that these people were tribally organized, some groups likely expressing the emergent properties of petty chiefdoms (*sensu* Redmond 1998).

A characteristic of this period was the abandonment of much of the landscape and the appearance of large, nucleated, floodplain population centers. Many of the apparently multigenerational villages were concentrated in areas that access productive backwater and slackwater lakes, high floodplain ridges and broad alluvial slopes of prime agricultural land, and water and land transportation and communication routes. No doubt village packing around localities of prime resources created a highly volatile local human dynamic, but we have little evidence of active violence, and fortified villages were absent. Timothy Pauketat (1994) hypothesized that, by the early 11th century, these villages were organized into a series of small-scale collaborative chiefdoms, thus setting the stage for one of the major social and political transformations in pre-Columbian Eastern North America, the rise of Cahokia (see also Alt, this volume).

The mid-11th-century appearance of Cahokia was a societal shift on a scale previously unknown in native North America (Pauketat 2004). During the preceding Terminal Late Woodland period, people had begun to gather into population centers, they had become maize agriculturalists, they were experimenting with various new ceramic forms and technologies, and so forth; but they were still essentially small-scale, diverse, village farmers. The rise of Cahokia changed all that.

Whether the impetus for Cahokia was religious, political, or economic is unknown. What is clear archaeologically is material manifestation of an immense urge to unify the American Bottom societies. Initiation of intensive construction of mounded religious and political centers such as Cahokia itself was the product of unifying political and social choice, the coming together of a diverse set of peoples to build a new vision of society.

By the 12th century the central political-administrative complex of Cahokia covered more than 14.5 square kilometers (Pauketat 2004). It included three large ritual-political precincts of monuments, plazas, and elite populations stretching more than 11 kilometers east-west, including Cahokia on the western end, the East St. Louis precinct on the eastern shore of the Mississippi River, and the St. Louis precinct anchoring the western end on the Missouri bank of the Mississippi River. At its height in the mid-11th, 12th, and early 13th centuries, Cahokia's highly nucleated, urbanized population may have peaked at 10,000 to 15,000 individuals, with at least an equal number living in the many surrounding rural farmsteads and nodal villages, or clustered in the 14 contemporary single and multiple mound centers within 25 kilometers of Monks Mound, the large pyramid at the site's center (Emerson 2002; Pauketat and Lopinot 1997). Cahokia's local control may have extended to an area of 9,300 square kilometers in all or part of six modern Illinois and Missouri counties. The question of how far beyond the core area Cahokia's power, trade, military control, or interest reached is more difficult to define.

Cahokia's Midcontinental Impact

Examining the multiple scales and degrees of impact of Cahokia on the post-AD 1050 peoples of the northern midcontinent centering on the Illinois River valley is intriguing. Stretching from the northern American Bottom to the shores of Lake Michigan, the Illinois valley groups range from those within the immediate interaction sphere of Cahokia to those whose distance may have promoted varying levels of cordial or hostile relations, to those for whom Cahokia may have been a near-mythical distant southern land.

About 70 kilometers by river north of Cahokia lay the entrance to the mouth of the Illinois River, one of the Mississippi's major tributaries (Figure 33.1). It winds northeast about 440 kilometers to connect to the Des Plaines River, which continues another 240 kilometers into southern Wisconsin. But about 100 kilometers from this junction, near present-day Chicago, it is possible to leave the Des Plaines and follow Portage Creek to Mud Lake, cross the continental divide, and enter the Chicago River flowing into Lake Michigan. This corridor represents a major transportation and communication route from the Atlantic Ocean to the Great Lakes to the Mississippi River and ultimately the Gulf of Mexico. It is not surprising, then, that Cahokia's influence moved along this route into very different northern environments and societies.

The lower Illinois River valley immediately adjacent to Cahokia is a rich area of backwater lakes, broad and flat terraces, and adjacent wooded bluffs; it was a major location for the Middle Woodland and the subsequent Late Woodland fluorescence in the Midcontinent (see also Wilson, this volume). Yet only the Audrey site, a 3 hectare village, has several burial mounds and cemeteries, and a scattering of small household sites known to date to the Mississippian period. This apparently anomalous Mississippian void on the edge of a major population center like Cahokia has mystified researchers. Generally it is believed that the lower Illinois River valley served as a breadbasket for Cahokia. The lack of large towns in the valley but the presence of small households would support the view that individual Cahokian farm families expanded into the lower valley in the 12th century to exploit the readily available agricultural land and plentiful wild resources. The role of the Audrey village and the large burial sites was harder to explain but may represent the movement of larger colonial populations into the valley (Delaney-Rivera 2004).

The bioanthropological evidence suggests that the lower valley people are not replaced by Mississippian populations but rather become culturally Mississippian through time (Steadman 1998). This pattern would accommodate data that suggest the Jersey Bluff Woodland resident populations may coexist with Cahokian emigrants for as much as several centuries. Within the lower valley, researchers have also noted that early Cahokian populations cluster at the southern end while later ones cluster at the northern end of the valley. This differential distribution may reflect the early influence and power of Cahokia and the later importance of the northern Central Illinois River valley temple towns. The role of the lower valley as a buffer zone between the numerous temple towns of the Central Illinois River valley Spoon River and La Moine River cultures and central Cahokia has been considered. Such a model assumes a political and social relationship between Cahokia and the Central Illinois valley Mississippians that swung from cooperative to competitive at various points in their history. It is clear that it will take considerable focused research to resolve these issues (Conrad 1991; Emerson 1991).

Cahokian impacts were more apparent in the Central Illinois River valley (see also Wilson, this volume). Within this 210 kilometer stretch of river, we know of at least seven Mississippian towns, associated cemeteries, and hundreds of hamlets and farmsteads. Archaeological evidence indicates that about AD 1100 a small group of elite Cahokians and their retainers moved into this region (Conrad 1991). This in-migration is marked by the appearance of physically different people, new ritual styles, and distinctive ceramic, artifactual, and architectural forms in the existing Maple Mills and Bauer Branch Late Woodland communities. Within a generation or two, these people had created a unique "creole" blend of Cahokian and Late Woodland cultures in the central valley and two of its major tributaries, the Spoon and La Moine. Two cultural variants are known, each assuming the name of one of the tributaries, the Spoon and La Moine River cultures. The Spoon River Culture is the better studied of these two Mississippian variants (Figure 33.1).

The Spoon and La Moine culture towns in the central valley appear to represent large permanent settlements occupied by as many as several hundred people (Conrad 1991). Each town has at least one flat-topped platform mound. The Orendorf site mound served as the base for a mortuary structure, but others may have been platforms for houses of local leaders. Cemeteries and burial mounds lie adjacent to the town and may contain hundreds of graves. The houses of the villagers were typically laid out around a central square ground bordered by a number of large structures that served as residences for the local elites or as religious sanctuaries. By the late 1100s, most of these 4 to 8 hectare towns were fortified, with palisades sometimes including bastions.

The central towns were ringed by dozens of small hamlets and single farms (Conrad 1991, Harn 1994). Some interpretations see them as summer residences for town dwellers fanning out across the landscape to tend their dispersed fields, while others believe these were permanent homes for a large, scattered, rural Mississippian residential population. There is no doubt that the resources these people tapped were plentiful. Subsistence and skeletal studies have shown they were full-time maize farmers who also fully exploited the local fauna, avian, and aquatic resources.

By the 1200s, violence was an integral way of life among the petty chiefdoms in the central valley (Emerson 1999, 2007; Steadman 2008; Strezewski 2006; Wilson, this volume). This situation may have been exacerbated by the intrusion of northern Oneota peoples into the valley in the last half of the 13th century. At least five large villages from what is known as the Bold Counselor phase have been discovered (Esarey and Conrad 1998). The material evidence indicates vigorous interaction between the Oneota newcomers and the local Spoon River Culture residents, with houses having both local and Oneota ceramics on their floors. Despite indications of some peaceful interaction, evidence for the assertion of a high level of violence is present in the Norris Farm 36 cemetery, containing numerous individuals who died violent deaths, with some mutilated and scalped. Whether the conflict was ethnically driven between the Oneota and Spoon River residents or between local competing chiefdoms is unknown. What is certain is that by the mid-15th century virtually all of the temple towns in the central valley had been abandoned; the area was not reoccupied until the Illinois tribes moved into the region in during the next century or two.

North of the Big Bend in the Illinois River, the river changes dramatically. In the upper valley the drop is steep, resulting in a shallow, fairly straight channel through the Woodfordian Till Plain. The floodplain is narrow, with few sloughs, backwater lakes, or wetlands. The adjoining bluff lines were lightly wooded and immediately abut vast expanses of prairies. Though hardly a harsh environment, the upper river is considerably less endowed in those natural resources that make the central and lower valley so attractive to native populations. For many years, this less bountiful landscape was interpreted as the reason for the failure of full-fledged Mississippian populations to spread into this area.

The impact of the central valley chiefdoms resonated northward to affect Woodland groups beyond their immediate borders. After about AD 800, the upper valley was inhabited by Terminal Late Woodland groups who manufactured a distinctive collared ceramic ware, possessed the bow and arrow, practiced an incipient maize agriculture, lived in small family groups, and were widely dispersed across the landscape. The origins of these people, known locally as the Des Plaines Complex, seem to lie to the east in Indiana and Ohio (Emerson and Titelbaum 2000). They appeared to have been residentially mobile, although there are suggestions they may have gathered seasonally for social and mortuary ceremonies. However, we have found no villages comparable to those associated with the contemporaneous Maple Mills Late Woodland people in the central valley.

The Des Plaines Complex groups disappear from the upper valley during the 900s and are replaced by the Langford Phase, Upper Mississippian Tradition about AD 1100 (Emerson 1999; Figure 33.1). The evidence for this in situ cultural shift has been well documented and appears due to significant changes in Des Plaines Complex life styles caused by the impact of central valley chiefdoms' pattern of warfare. The Langford heartland stretches for about 80 kilometers from Starved Rock to the origin point of the Illinois River (Jeske 2000). Within this area were numerous large sedentary villages surrounded by small hamlets and specialized camps. New isotopic evidence confirms that these people are full-time agriculturalists who, like the contemporaneous Cahokians far to the south, gain most of their protein from maize (Emerson et al. 2005). They also actively exploit the available floral and faunal resources and often focus heavily on elk hunting and fishing. Each of these villages has at least one and sometimes several multigenerational burial mounds and associated cemeteries, resembling their central valley neighbors. Langford material culture appears little different from that associated with their Terminal Late Woodland progenitors. Ceramics do shift in vessel shape and design, although retaining an identical Late Woodland paste. The vessels become globular with short flared, straight, or everted rims and now carry Mississippian-derived symbols on their shoulders (Figure 33.2).

The transformation of local trans-egalitarian Terminal Late Woodland hunters and gatherer and incipient farmers into Langford Tradition tribally organized sedentary farmers is a dramatic materialization of the process of ethnogenesis or, as it is called locally, tribalization. Rather than being a result of new subsistence practices, population pressure, or technological changes, the emergence of what is recognized as "Langford" is a direct result of a dramatic shift in the local political and social environment. This shift is due to intrusion of the Mississippian chiefdoms into the central valley in the 11th century. Terminal Late Woodland and Spoon River Culture interaction through such mechanisms as exchange, feasting, ritual participation, and intermarriage, and especially raiding and warfare, produced a series of structural changes in nearby Late Woodland lifeways (Conrad 1991; Esarey 2000). They include intensification of maize agriculture, establishment of dense population

Figure 33.2 Langford Phase vessel (courtesy of Illinois State Archaeological Survey).

aggregates and decreased residential mobility, increased social and status differentiation as well as greater control of local leadership, elaboration of mound ceremonialism, accentuated boundedness and territorialism among various social groups, and more emulation and adoption of some Mississippian social and ideological concepts (Emerson 1999). The coincidental timing of the rise (ca. AD 1100s) and "fall" (ca. AD 1400s) of the Mississippian and Upper Mississippian cultural patterns further suggests that their mutual histories were in some way inescapably linked.

Historical Outgrowths

About a century after the emergence of the Langford Tradition in the upper valley, another group appeared, known to archaeologists as the Fisher Tradition (Brown and Sasso 2001; Emerson and Brown 1992; Jeske 2003). The sudden appearance and subsequent fate of the Fisher culture in northeastern Illinois is perplexing. Distinctive, shell-tempered, highly decorated Fisher ceramics began to appear at about AD 1200 in the upper valley, especially along the Kankakee River (Figure 33.3). Although low-density Fisher settlements reach down the Illinois River as far as the Big Bend, there are few large occupations known. Two large sites that have been investigated are the Fisher Mound and Village at the junction of the Des Plaines and Kankakee Rivers (excavated by the avocational archaeologist George Langford in the early 19th century) and the Hoxie Farm site in south Chicago, where recent work by the University of Illinois discovered a large fortified Late Fisher phase village.

Langford's extensive salvage of the Fisher site, in the face of large-scale gravel quarrying, explored a dozen burial mounds and cemeteries and many of the more than 50 pit house depressions, but the multicomponent nature of the occupation restricted the value of his work in defining the Fisher phase beyond identification of typical ceramic forms. More insightful has been the excavations conducted in a

Figure 33.3 Fisher Phase vessel (courtesy of Indiana Historical Society).

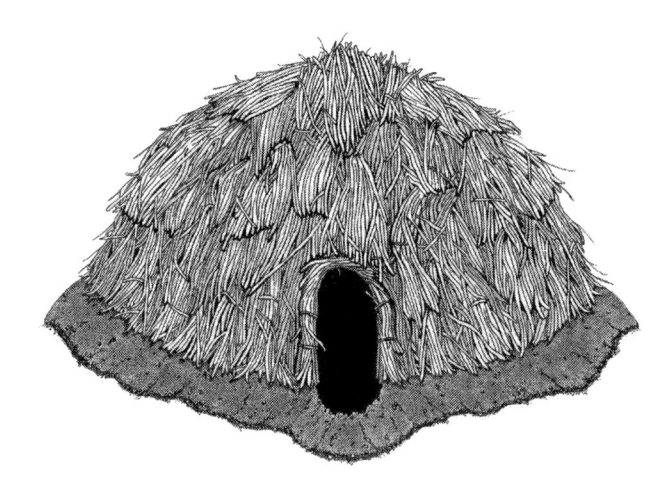

Figure 33.4 Reconstruction of Fisher Phase pit house (drawing by Val Vallese, courtesy of Illinois State Archaeological Survey).

portion of a fortified village occupied in the 14th century by Late Fisher phase groups. The massive village, surrounded by multiple ditches and banks and a sturdy palisade that may have contained several hundred deep semisubterranean oval structures (Figure 33.4), was probably occupied for less than a decade in a time of regional crisis. This fortified location abuts an open-air work area and multiple small cemeteries on the bank of the local creek, where more than 1,500 pits were encountered (Jackson and Emerson 2010).

Although the Fisher phase is still poorly understood, we know these people were farmers living in a few large, sometimes fortified, villages in a time of unstable political conditions and intergroup violence (Brown and Sasso 2001; Emerson and Brown 1992). Their house forms are unknown elsewhere in the Midwest. They used the local fauna extensively, and unlike their Langford neighbors they had access to bison scapula hoes. Whether they obtained the bison parts through trade or hunting small local herds is unknown. Fisher shell-tempered ceramics superficially resemble the grit-tempered, globular pots of the contemporaneous Langford phase people. On closer examination, however, one finds that Fisher vessels are more highly decorated and have a series of decorative attributes that hearken to groups in Indiana and extreme western Ohio. The Hoxie Farm village also included a small set of vessels indicating connections to the Caborn-Wellborn villagers near the mouth of the Wabash River. It is not unreasonable to see active connections by this group with their easterly neighbors.

By the 15th century, the material signatures of Fisher and Langford groups disappear from the archaeological record of northeastern Illinois (Brown and Sasso 2001; Emerson and Brown 1992). Some regional scholars believe the Fisher groups "evolved" into people represented by the Huber phase, a typical Oneota manifestation in the northern Midcontinent (Faulkner 1972). The Huber phase material culture resembles that of earlier Upper Mississippi groups, but a dramatic change in house form occurs with introduction of multifamily long houses (Figure 33.5). The Huber phase has alternately been viewed as disappearing just prior to French contact in the AD 1600s or as representing the folks who met the French. Depending on one's reading of the ethnohistoric records, the Huber phase may represent either Algonquian or Siouan speaking groups. The post–AD 1400 history of the people in this region is still very much a work in progress, and it is important to view the various archaeological scenarios as hypotheses to be tested rather than proven interpretations.

Conclusion

Tracing the material, social, religious, and political effect of Cahokia's interactions, influences, and inspirations up the Illinois River valley gives archaeologists an opportunity to view the actual dynamics during a brief slice of time in northern midcontinental prehistory (Emerson 1999). Seldom in the archaeological record are we able to examine multiscalar levels of interaction of demonstrably contemporaneous groups.

In this case, however, we are able to observe the absorption of the lower Illinois River valley into the inner sphere of Cahokian economic life; creation of a series of petty chiefdoms in the central valley that emulate Cahokia practices but in a distinctly local way; intrusion of a northern Oneota group into the central valley that disrupts the valley's political and social scene; the effect of Spoon and La Moine Rivers chiefly culture of raiding and warfare on the bordering Terminal Late Woodland hunters and gatherers, resulting in creation of a new Langford lifestyle; and intrusion of Fisher Tradition groups into the northeastern parts of the Langford people territory, perhaps setting off local hostilities.

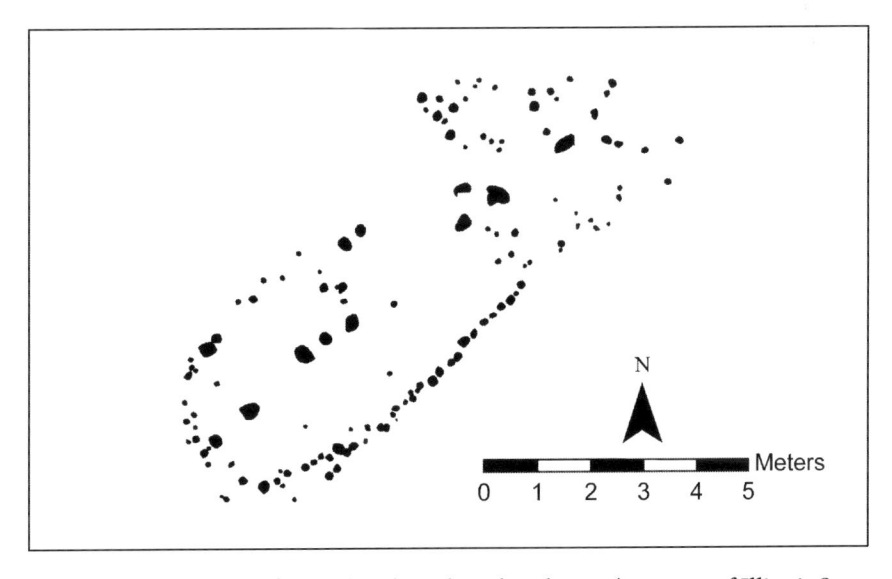

Figure 33.5 Plan map of partial Huber Phase longhouse (courtesy of Illinois State Archaeological Survey).

Investigation of social and political dynamics in the northern midcontinent is possible only because of a long tradition of investigating the complex histories of regional groups, including large datasets involving whole villages and associated settlement patterns, constant focus on habitation archaeology, and concern with everyday material culture and its contextual setting. This, combined with strict attention to relative and absolute chronologies, has let regional archaeologists truly bring the "histories" of these long-absent people to life.

REFERENCES

Brown, J. A., and R. F. Sasso. 2001. Prelude to History on the Eastern Prairies. In *Societies in Eclipse: Archaeology of the Eastern Woodlands, A.D. 1400–1700*, edited by D. S. Brose, C. W. Cowan, and R. C. Mainfort, Jr., pp. 205–228. Smithsonian Institution, Washington, DC.

Conrad, L. A. 1991. The Middle Mississippian Cultures of the Central Illinois River Valley. In *Cahokia and the Hinterlands: Middle Mississippian Cultures of the Midwest*, edited by T. E. Emerson and R. B. Lewis, pp. 164–182. University of Illinois Press, Urbana.

Delaney-Rivera, C. 2004. From Edge to Frontier: Early Mississippian Occupation of the Lower Illinois River Valley. *Southeastern Archaeology* 23:41–56.

Emerson, T. E. 1991. Some Perspectives on Cahokia and the Northern Mississippian Expansion. In *Cahokia and the Hinterlands: Middle Mississippian Cultures of the Midwest*, edited by T. E. Emerson and R. B. Lewis, pp. 221–236. University of Illinois, Urbana.

———. 1999. The Langford Tradition and the Process of Tribalization on the Middle Mississippian Borders. *Midcontinental Journal of Archaeology* 24:3–55.

———. 2002. An Introduction to Cahokia 2002: Diversity, Complexity and History. *Midcontinental Journal of Archaeology* 27(2):127–148.

———. 2007. Cahokia and the Evidence for Late Pre-Columbian Warfare in the North American Midcontinent. In *North American Indigenous Warfare and Ritual Violence*, edited by R. J. Chacon and R. G. Mendoza, pp. 127–148. University of Arizona Press, Tucson.

———, and J. A. Brown. 1992. The Late Prehistory and Protohistory of Illinois. In *Calumet and Fleur-de-Lys: Archaeology of Indian and French Contact in the Midcontinent*, edited by J. A. Walthall and T. E. Emerson, pp. 77–128. Smithsonian Institution, Washington, DC.

Emerson, T. E., K. M. Hedman, and M. L. Simon. 2005. Marginal Horticulturalists or Maize Agriculturalists? Archaeobotanical, Paleopathological, and Isotopic Evidence Relating to Langford Maize Consumption. *Midcontinental Journal of Archaeology* 30(1):67–118.

Emerson, T. E., and A. Titelbaum. 2000. The Des Plaines Complex and the Late Woodland Stage in Northern Illinois. In *Late Woodland Societies: Tradition and Transformation in the Midcontinent*, edited by T. E. Emerson, D. L. McElrath, and A. C. Fortier, pp. 413–428. University of Nebraska Press, Lincoln.

Esarey, D. 2000. The Late Woodland Maples Mills and Mossville Phase Sequence in the Central Illinois River Valley. In *Late Woodland Societies: Tradition and Transformation in the Midcontinent*, edited by T. Emerson, D. McElrath, and A. Fortier, pp. 387–410. University of Nebraska Press, Lincoln.

———, and L. A. Conrad. 1998. The Bold Counselor Phase of the Central Illinois River Valley: Oneota's Middle Mississippian Margins. *Wisconsin Archeologist* 79(2):38–61.

Faulkner, C. H. 1972. *The Late Prehistoric Occupation of Northwestern Indiana*. Indiana Historical Society, Prehistory Research Series 5, Indianapolis.

Fortier, A. C., T. E. Emerson, and D. L. McElrath. 2006. Calibrating and Reassessing American Bottom Culture History. *Southeastern Archaeology* 25(2):168–209.

Fortier, A. C., and D. K. Jackson. 2000. The Formation of a Late Woodland Heartland in the American Bottom, Illinois cal A.D. 650–900. In *Late Woodland Societies: Tradition and Transformation Across the Midcontinent*, edited by T. E. Emerson, D. L. McElrath, and A. C. Fortier, pp. 122–147. University of Nebraska Press, Lincoln.

Harn, A. D. 1994. *Variation in Mississippian Settlement Patterns: The Larson Settlement System in the Central Illinois River Valley*. Reports of Investigations. Illinois State Museum, Springfield.

Jackson, D. K., and T. E. Emerson (editors). 2010. *The Hoxie Farm Site Fortified Village: Late Fisher Phase Occupation in South Suburban Chicago*. Illinois State Archaeological Survey, Studies in Archaeology (in press).

Jeske, R. J. 2000. The Washington Irving Site: Langford Tradition Adaptation in Northern Illinois. In Illinois State Museum Scientific Papers 28, *Mounds, Modoc, and Mesoamerica: Papers in Honor of Melvin L. Fowler*, edited by S. R. Ahler, pp. 265–294. Illinois State Museum, Springfield.

———. 2003. Langford and Fisher Ceramic Traditions: Moiety, Ethnicity or Power Relations in the Upper Midwest? In *A Deep-Time Perspective: Studies in Symbols, Meaning, and the Archaeological Record: Papers in Honor of Robert L. Hall*, edited by J. D. Richards and M. L. Fowler. *Wisconsin Archeologist* 84(1–2):165–180.

Kelly, J. E. 2000. The Nature and Context of Emergent Mississippian Cultural Dynamics in the Greater American Bottom. In *Late Woodland Societies: Tradition and Transformation Across the Midcontinent*, edited by T. E. Emerson, D. L. McElrath, and A. C. Fortier, pp. 163–175. University of Nebraska Press, Lincoln.

Pauketat, T. R. 1994. *The Ascent of Chiefs: Cahokia and Mississippian Politics in Native North America*. The University of Alabama Press, Tuscaloosa.

———. 2004. *Ancient Cahokia and the Mississippians*. University of Cambridge Press, Cambridge, UK.

———, and N. H. Lopinot. 1997. Cahokian Population Dynamics. In *Cahokia: Domination and Ideology in the Mississippian World*, edited by T. R. Pauketat and T. E. Emerson, pp. 103–123. University of Nebraska Press, Lincoln.

Redmond, E. M. 1998. The Dynamics of Chieftaincy and the Development of Chiefdoms. In *Chiefdoms and Chieftaincy in the Americas*, edited by E. M. Redmond, pp. 1–17. University Press of Florida, Gainesville.

Simon, M. L. 2000. Regional Variations in Plant Use Strategies in the Midwest During the Late Woodland. In *Late Woodland Societies: Tradition and Transformation Across the Midcontinent*, edited by T. E. Emerson, D. L. McElrath, and A. C. Fortier, pp. 37–75. University of Nebraska Press, Lincoln.

Steadman, D. W. 1998. The Population Shuffle in the Central Illinois Valley: A Diachronic Model of Mississippian Biocultural Interactions. *World Archaeology* 30(2):306–326.

———. 2008. Warfare Related Trauma at Orendorf, a Middle Mississippian Site in West-Central Illinois. *American Journal of Physical Anthropology* 136:51–64.

Strezewski, M. 2006. Patterns of Interpersonal Violence at the Fisher Site. *Midcontinental Journal of Archaeology* 31(2):249–180.

CHAPTER 34

THE EFFIGY MOUND TO ONEOTA REVOLUTION IN THE UPPER MISSISSIPPI RIVER VALLEY

ROBERT F. BOSZHARDT

THE Upper Mississippi Valley (UMV) represents an environmental and cultural cross-road (Figure 34.1). Geographically, this region is dominated by the north-south corridor of the Mississippi River, which connects a northern glacial lakes region with the confluences of the Ohio and Missouri Rivers in the midcontinent and southward to the Gulf of Mexico. Biologically, the UMV is crossed by the northern edge of the Prairie Peninsula, with an associated resource rich-"tension zone" between mixed forests to the north and east and savannah/prairie to the south and west (Curtis 1959).

At this geographic and biological intersection lies a distinct topographic subregion called the "Driftless Area," which played a key role in the transition from Late Woodland horticulturalists to Oneota farmers. This unglaciated terrain covers much of southwestern Wisconsin, extending into Illinois, Iowa, and Minnesota. It is a dynamic landscape of deep valleys carved into sandstone and limestone formations. Bedrock exposures permitted ready access to local chert and silicified sandstones as well as caves and rockshelters. All local streams feed the Mississippi River, which during the Pleistocene cut across the Driftless Area during torrential glacial meltwater floods, creating a dramatic gorge.

The Driftless Area provided a mixed biotic province with prairie/savannah communities on upland ridge tops and sandy outwash terraces, deciduous forests on protected north and east facing slopes and in floodplains, and stands of pine at

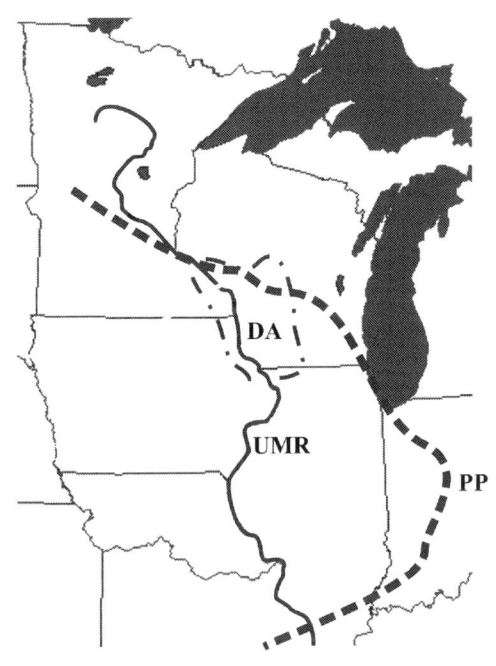

DA: Driftless Area
UMR: Upper Mississippi River
PP: Prairie Penninsula/"Tension Zone"

Figure 34.1 The Upper Mississippi River Valley and unglaciated Driftless Area, in relation to the eastern edge of the Prairie Peninsula and corresponding resource-rich, biological "tension zone."

protected sandstone outcrops and tamarack in bogs at the upper reaches of many valleys. During the late Holocene, the Driftless Area was an ideal habitat for white-tailed deer, elk, and bear. Bison occasionally ventured into this dissected landscape, but true herds were available only to the west. The floodplains, particularly the broad bottomlands of the Upper Mississippi, offered an incredible wealth of riparian beaver and muskrat along with fish, fresh water mussels, turtles, waterfowl, cattails, lotus, and wild rice from spring to fall. In this latitude, the Mississippi River freezes over every winter.

THE LATE WOODLAND EFFIGY MOUND CULTURE

There were nearly 3,000 effigy mounds in Wisconsin alone (Birmingham and Eisenberg 2000:109). The mounds ranged from recognizable animals such as humans and birds to less distinct "bears," "deer," "wolf," etc., and long-tailed "lizards," "panthers," or "turtles," as well as a variety of confounding forms (Figure 34.2). Some mounds

Figure 34.2 Photograph of bird-shaped effigy mound along the Lower Wisconsin River in the Driftless Area.

clearly represent birds of the sky, others land animals, and the long-tailed mounds likely represent water spirits or horned serpents of the mythological underworld (Birmingham and Eisenberg 2000). Others are uncertain.

The distribution of effigy mounds clearly conforms to the savannah region of southern Wisconsin, including all of the Driftless Area (Figure 34.3). Until recently, the Effigy Mound Culture was generally conceived of as a single entity. Since the 1990s archaeologists have discerned intraregional differences in mound forms, and they tend to correlate with geographical and material culture subdivisions. For example, long-tailed "panther" mounds are common in glaciated eastern Wisconsin but nearly absent from the unglaciated southwestern area. Likewise, within the Driftless Area "bear" mounds are common in the southern portion while long-tailed panthers occur to the north. Associated differences in ceramics, projectile point styles, and raw material preferences have been used to define phases that segregate these subregions (Boszhardt and Goetz 2000).

In the early 20th century, diagnostic artifacts were first recognized for the Effigy Mound Culture. In the 1920s and 1930s, Will C. McKern of the Milwaukee Public Museum associated cord-impressed, grit-tempered "Lake Michigan" ware with the effigy mounds. In the 1950s, as radiocarbon dates became available, the age of the mounds and habitation sites that also produced cord-impressed pottery was established from ca. AD 700–1100. The cord-impressed pottery was renamed Madison ware, and associated artifacts included unnotched Madison Triangular points that represent adoption of bow and arrow technology.

Since then, the chronological position of the Effigy Mound Culture has been clarified through additional and more precise radiocarbon dates, and a historical

Figure 34.3 Overlap of the distribution of effigy mounds in southern Wisconsin, including the entire Driftless Area.

sequence for the Late Woodland stage in southern Wisconsin has been developed (Stoltman and Christensen 2000). The sequence begins with an Initial period (ca. AD 500–700) followed by a Mature period (AD 700–1000) and terminating with a Final period (AD 1000–1200). It was during the Mature period that the majority of effigy mound construction occurred and Madison ware flourished. The Final period is marked by Mississippian influences and associated changes in ceramics such as the rapid spread of collared wares and a transition to shell tempering, as well as the end of effigy mound construction.

Subsistence remains from open-air and rockshelter sites reveal an economy that was focused on hunting and gathering. A seasonal round included warm-season congregations along lakes and rivers, where construction of effigy mounds served as a social bonding mechanism (Mallam 1976). During the fall and winter, as lacustrine and riverine resources began to freeze over, Effigy Mound families seem to have dispersed to protected interior settings, where the primary focus was hunting white-tailed deer to survive the winter. Excavated Driftless Area rockshelters contained ubiquitous Late Woodland occupations, with faunal assemblages dominated by bones of fall-winter killed deer, much of which had been crushed to extract marrow (Theler 1987; see also Habicht-Mauche, this volume).

Beginning around AD 950, effigy mounds were first constructed at interior Driftless Area locations. Because mounds could not have been constructed during winter when the ground is frozen, they indicate warm-season group activities at interior settings. Furthermore, subsistence remains from contemporary camps indicate year-round occupation of both interior and Mississippi River floodplain settings for the first time. These new subsistence and settlement practices reveal a breakdown of the traditional seasonal round; while the distribution of Effigy mound sites at this time suggests a "packing" of the landscape caused by increased population. Hunter-gatherer societies tend to adapt to packed landscape conditions by intensifying harvest of wetland resources and by turning to cultivation (Binford 2001; Theler and Boszhardt 2006). In the UMV, as effigy mound groups packed the landscape, there was a dramatic increase in fresh water mussel harvesting along the Mississippi floodplain, and corn was cultivated for the first time.

Social pressures associated with landscape packing appear to have resulted in further subdivisions within the Effigy Mound region. In the Driftless Area, there is clear evidence of formation of a territorial boundary along the Bad Axe River Valley, where 69 effigy mounds were recorded. In contrast, the comparable next valley to the north (Coon Creek) contained no recorded effigy mounds. The 69 mounds in the Bad Axe Valley marked the northern edge of the Eastman phase, which is also recognized on the basis of bird and bear mounds, Madison ware pottery, and both un-notched and side-notched arrow tips, nearly all of which were made of local chert. In contrast, the northern portion of the Driftless Area contains numerous long-tailed panther mounds, and contemporary habitations are recognized by a distinct pottery type called Angelo Punctated. In addition, the associated projectile points are nearly all un-notched triangular arrow tips made from silicified sandstone. The latter traits have been used to define the Lewis phase as a distinct effigy mound society from that of the Eastman phase (Boszhardt and Goetz 2000).

THE ONEOTA CULTURE

In the early 20th century, Ellison Orr and Charles Ruben Keyes explored archaeological sites in northeast Iowa. Within the Upper Iowa River (originally known as the Oneota River), they documented villages and burials that contained distinctive shell-tempered pottery for which Keyes (1927) coined the term *Oneota Culture*. Several sites produced Oneota pottery in direct association with French trade artifacts, and thus Oneota was recognized as a late prehistoric-protohistoric culture. By the late 20th century, the overall range of the Oneota Culture was recognized as extending from Lake Michigan to the Missouri River, and from the American Bottom—the stretch of floodplain opposite modern-day St. Louis, Missouri—to the northern edge of the Prairie Peninsula (Boszhardt 1998; Henning 1998). The Oneota sites found within this region tended to be clustered in distinct localities with broad unoccupied areas in between (Figure 34.4).

Although the generally late time frame for Oneota was established by several protohistoric sites, the chronological beginning of Oneota has been long debated. The debate was initiated with the onset of radiocarbon dating in the late 1950s. At that time, it was generally accepted that Oneota had emerged in response to northward influences from the Middle Mississippian center at Cahokia (see, e.g., Griffin 1960). Robert Hall's work (1962) at Carcajou Point in southeastern Wisconsin

Figure 34.4 Locations of various clustered Oneota village localities in the Upper Midwest. They were not all occupied at the same time, but vast areas in between were essentially unoccupied from ca. AD 1150 to 1650. AR = Apple River, BE = Blue Earth, BC = Bold Counselor, F = Fisher, H = Huber, K = Koshkonong, LAX = La Crosse, LSR = Little Sioux River, LW = Lake Winnebago, Me = Mero, Mo = Moingona, RW = Red Wing, SEI = Southeast Iowa, UIR = Upper Iowa River.

included the first reported C-14 dates for Oneota, and these were employed in his sequential model of Oneota horizons. By the late 1960s, the relatively few C-14 dates from Oneota sites included some that preceded AD 1000, suggesting Oneota emerged prior to northward expansion of Middle Mississippian influences (Gibbon 1969; Henning 1970; Overstreet 1981).

It was not until the 1990s, after several hundred radiocarbon dates became available for Oneota sites (including suites of 10–20 dates from key single-component sites), that the age of the earliest sites found clarity (Boszhardt et al. 1995). It now appears that the earliest verifiable Oneota manifestations occur in the Red Wing (Minnesota) and Apple River (Illinois) localities along the UMV. The early Oneota components in these localities are well dated to AD 1150–1250 and are referred to as the Silvernale/Link/Bartron and Bennett/Mills phase sequences, respectively. Thus the Oneota Culture appears to have begun around AD 1150 and continued nearly 550 years, before disappearing from the archaeological record in the early 1700s. During this five-and-a-half-century span, Oneota groups appear to have moved periodically, abandoning some localities in favor of others.

A number of historic tribes are thought to owe their ancestry to the Oneota, largely on the basis of the direct historical approach that connects protohistoric Oneota sites with tribes reported for the same areas: the Ioway, Oto, Ho-Chunk/Winnebago, Missouri, Ponca, perhaps some bands of the Eastern Dakota Sioux (e.g., Santee), and the Miami. Most of these tribes spoke dialects of Chiwere or

Dhegihan Siouan languages, but the archaeological manifestation does not appear to correlate exclusively with specific linguistic groups.

In many respects, the material culture of the Oneota is distinctive from preceding Late Woodland complexes. Oneota ceramic vessels are often cited as the most diagnostic artifact, and it is often possible to recognize an Oneota component on the basis of recovery of a single shell-tempered sherd. Oneota pots are nearly all shell-tempered and globular in form, but there are stylistic variations and they tend to shift in sync across widely spaced localities. Other Oneota artifacts include unnotched triangular arrow tips, and a relatively high frequency of end scrapers, sandstone abraders, celts, bison scapula hoes, manos, and metates. Sheet copper beads, pendants, and rings occur at many Oneota sites. Toward the protohistoric period, distinctive catlinite smoking pipes, engraved tablets, pendants, and beads became more common.

Oneota subsistence differed from that of Late Woodland cultures in two main realms. First, most Oneota groups practiced relatively intensive farming, growing corn, squash, tobacco, little barley and, after AD 1300, beans in extensive ridged field systems. Their summer agricultural activities were complemented by extensive harvesting of fish, mussels, beaver, waterfowl, crawfish, and wild rice. Second, the Oneota economy incorporated bison, a Plains-oriented resource almost entirely absent from UMV Late Woodland societies. Communal bison hunts may have happened seasonally, with Oneota groups walking hundreds of miles for this task.

Middle Mississippian and the Effigy Mound to Oneota Transition

On the basis of well over a century of research, it is clear that the Effigy Mound culture occupied much of southern Wisconsin and adjacent portions of the UMV from ca. AD 750–1050, and that this culture was replaced around AD 1150 by the Oneota. This rapid transformation witnessed the end of effigy mound construction, a shift from grit- to shell-tempered pottery, nucleation of settlements from widespread hamlets to villages within widely separate localities, and an economic change from hunter-gatherer horticulturalists to intensive farmers who also hunted bison. Why and how did this revolutionary cultural change occur, where and when it did?

One key component to answering this question is recognizing that Late Woodland societies, with the technological advantage of the bow and arrow, had reached a packing threshold (Theler and Boszhardt 2006). With population increases resulting in occupation of nearly every available landscape niche, the traditional seasonal round was fractured. No longer could groups congregate at lake and riverine settings during spring-summer and then disperse to the interior during fall-winter. Instead, for the first time groups occupied interior valleys like the Bad Axe, year round. Others were forced to stay along the frozen Mississippi River through the winter. The predictable responses to packing are increased reliance on wetland resources and horticulture; both were adopted by Driftless Area Effigy Mound peoples. Along the Mississippi River, numerous Effigy Mound shell middens attest to intensified harvest of fresh water mussels, presumably drying some to store for winter sustenance (Theler 1987). In the Bad Axe Valley, local fish were also taken and corn appears for the first time in both settings (Theler and Boszhardt 2006). This packed landscape created social tensions, and territorial boundaries were marked by effigy mounds. The boundary established at the Bad Axe Valley separated Eastman phase people in the south from Lewis phase people to the north.

At the same time this northern scenario was unfolding, a complex Middle Mississippian society was forming in the American Bottom region, centered on the site of Cahokia far to the south (see Alt, this volume). Beginning around AD 1050 in what Pauketat (1997) has termed the "Big Bang," there was a dramatic change in the American Bottom, including construction of platform mounds and other earth works at Cahokia (Alt, this volume). Around Cahokia, this period of rapid change in the American Bottom is referred to as the Lohmann phase, and it lasted only two generations, being followed by the Stirling phase, which may be distinguished by the decorated pottery type Ramey Incised (Alt, this volume).

Almost immediately, ca. AD 1050, Middle Mississippians (aka Cahokians) ventured up the Mississippi River to the Driftless Area and within a century had dramatically affected local Late Woodland societies (see also Emerson, this volume). The earliest evidence of American Bottom activity in the UMV is from the Fisher Mounds Site Complex in western Wisconsin at ca. AD 1050. This site is situated at the mouth of Coon Valley, which appears to have served as a no-man's land between Eastman and Lewis phase Effigy Mound peoples (Boszhardt and Goetz 2000). One area of the Fisher Mounds Complex produced red-slipped pottery, including vessels that were manufactured in the American Bottom, as well as Ste. Genevieve and Crescent Hills Burlington chert flake tools (Benden 2004, Stoltman et al. 2008).

At Trempealeau, Wisconsin, 50 miles upriver from Fisher Mounds, investigations have found nearly pure early Mississippian habitation areas immediately beneath a series of distinctive platform mounds (Green and Rodell 1994; Pauketat et al. 2010). Excavations at the Squier Garden, Pelkey, and Stull sites in 2010 and 2011 produced quantities of early Cahokian ceramics and exotic flint stone imported from the American Bottom region. The platform mounds imply a more substantial Mississippian presence than at Fisher Mounds, yet the Trempealeau occupation seems to have lasted only a decade or two. Nearby are the largest effigy mound complexes in the Lewis phase territory. Although the relationship between the indigenous Late Woodlanders and Mississippians is not yet clear, one basin pit at the Pelkey site contained both Cahokian and Lewis phase (Angelo Punctated) ceramic vessel fragments in direct association.

There is almost no other evidence for Lohmann phase contact in the UMV. However, with the onset of the Stirling phase, Middle Mississippian interaction to the north increased dramatically. A number of sites dating to ca. AD 1100 have produced Ramey Incised pottery in the northern hinterlands, including the famous fortified site of Aztalan in southeastern Wisconsin. Two contemporary palisaded villages (Hartley Fort and Fred Edwards) are known for the Eastman phase portion of the Driftless Area (McKusick 1973; Finney and Stoltman 1991).

Like Aztalan, these sites are in remote interior settings and produced imported Middle Mississippian vessels and local imitations, a variety of Late Woodland pottery (including Madison ware, Aztalan Collared, and other distinctive types), and hybrids of Late Woodland and Mississippian wares. The remote Gottschall Rockshelter, also in the Driftless Area, contains a pictograph composition of distinctive Mississippian iconography, such as forked eyes and tattooed humans with sunbursts on their foreheads and chains dangling below. No diagnostic Middle Mississippian pottery has been reported from Gottschall, but Aztalan Collared was recovered. In the Lewis phase territory to the north, the Iva site contained imported Ramey Incised and Powell Plain vessels, in direct association with a late variant of Angelo Punctated pottery, along with Aztalan Collared and evidence of a feasting episode (Boszhardt 2004). No Oneota artifacts have been found at any of these Final Late Woodland sites.

At the southern edge of the Driftless Area, along the lower Apple River, a complex of Mississippian sites spanned several centuries. The earliest (Lundy and John Chapman) are affiliated with the Bennett phase (AD 1050–1150) and include Ramey Incised pottery and rectangular houses (Emerson et. al 2007). Subsistence remains from these sites indicate cultivation of corn and harvesting of some bison. The nearby Mills site may have had a platform mound, but local components dating after AD 1150 contain more globular, shell-tempered vessels that mark the Mills phase. The latter are comparable to contemporary ceramics found at Red Wing, which is situated at the opposite end of the Driftless Area.

At Red Wing, there is a nominal Late Woodland presence, but by AD 1150 there were a number of large agricultural villages, many of which were associated with oval or conical mounds. The earliest villages at Red Wing produced globular-shaped vessels with rolled rims and shoulder motifs that clearly derive from Ramey Incised and are characteristic of the Silvernale phase. The Diamond Bluff site covered several hundred acres and contained hundreds of mounds. At the extreme southern tip of the Diamond Bluff terrace was a bird (sky) mound and at the northern end a long-tailed panther (underworld) mound. Excavation of the panther revealed a burial associated with a shell-tempered pot, indicating a Lewis phase effigy mound with a Mississippian-inspired vessel. Silvernale sites have also produced a few other Middle Mississippian artifacts such as tri-notched arrow tips and long-nose god masquettes. In addition, bison bones occur, among them scapulae hoes. By AD 1200, the rims of the shell-tempered, globular-shaped vessels at Red Wing (like those of the Mills phase at Apple River) became higher, a trend that continued through most Oneota complexes until European contact.

Conclusion

In the centuries before AD 1000, much of the Midwest was inhabited by Late Woodland peoples who were primarily horticulturalists and hunter gatherers, aided by adoption of bow and arrow technology (Gibbon, this volume). In the Driftless Area, Late Woodland groups constructed distinctive animal-shaped effigy mounds during this period. By the 11th century, it seems that regional population increases had packed the landscape, which restricted movement, affected settlement patterns, and forced changes in subsistence practices. As social tensions rose, boundaries were established. The Late Woodland world was in a tenuous state.

At precisely that moment, Cahokian emigrants ventured 600 kilometers up the Mississippi River to establish settlements at Fisher Mounds (in the no-man's land between the Eastman and Lewis phase territories) and Trempealeau (in the heart of the Lewis phase). Why they left Cahokia and came to the Driftless Area is a topic of ongoing research, but their effect on the Effigy Mound Culture was profound. By AD 1100, Cahokia had established a strong presence in the northern hinterlands at places such as Aztalan, Fred Edwards, and Hartley Fort. These villages were supported by the first intensive corn agriculture in the region, and all show extensive blending of Cahokian and Terminal Woodland material culture. All the villages were also protected by fortified walls and they were abandoned by ca. AD 1150, coinciding with the onset of the decline of Cahokia (Alt, this volume).

By AD 1150, the Effigy Mound Culture had ceased to exist, having been replaced by the Oneota Culture. There is no evidence that Effigy Mound peoples moved elsewhere or that Oneota people came from other regions. Thus it is almost certain that the Effigy Mound people, along with other Woodland-based groups in the Midwest, became Oneota. The earliest Oneota complexes developed along the UMV between ca. AD 1150–1200 at Red Wing and Apple River, situated at opposite ends of the Driftless Area. Although Oneota populations shifted to various locations over the next 500 years, their way of life dominated the Upper Midwest and UMV for the remainder of the pre-Contact past.

References

Benden, D. M. 2004. The Fisher Mounds Site Complex: Evidence for an Early Mississippian Presence in the Upper Mississippi Valley. *Minnesota Archaeologist* 63:7–24.

Binford, L. R. 2001. *Constructing Frames of Reference: An Analytical Method for Archaeological Theory Building Using Hunter-Gatherer and Environmental Data Sets*. University of California Press, Berkeley.

Birmingham, R. A., and L. E. Eisenberg. 2000. *Indian Mounds of Wisconsin*. University of Wisconsin Press, Madison.

Boszhardt, R. F. 1998. Oneota Horizons: A La Crosse Perspective. *Wisconsin Archeologist* 79:196–226.

———. 2004. The Late Woodland and Middle Mississippian Component at the Iva Site, La Crosse County, Wisconsin in the Driftless Area of the Upper Mississippi River Valley. *Minnesota Archaeologist* 63:1–26.

———, and N. Goetz. 2000. An Apparent Late Woodland Boundary in Western Wisconsin. *Midcontinental Journal of Archaeology* 25: 269–287.

Boszhardt, R. F., W. Holtz, and J. Nienow. 1995. A Compilation of Oneota Radiocarbon Dates as of 1995. Report 20, Office of the State Archaeologist, *Oneota Archaeology: Past, Present, and Future*, edited by W. Green, pp. 203–227. University of Iowa, Iowa City.

Curtis, J. T. 1959. *The Vegetation of Wisconsin: An Ordination of Plant Communities.* University of Wisconsin Press, Madison.

Emerson, T. E., P. G. Millhouse, and M. B. Schroeder. 2007. The Lundy Site and the Mississippian Presence in the Apple River Valley. *Wisconsin Archeologist* 88(2):1–123.

Finney, F. A., and J. B. Stoltman. 1991. The Fred Edwards Site: A Case of Stirling Phase Culture Contact in Southwestern Wisconsin. Monographs in World Archaeology 2, *New Perspectives on Cahokia: Views from the Periphery*, edited by J. B. Stoltman, pp. 229–252. Prehistory Press, Madison, WI.

Gibbon, G. E. 1969. The Walker-Hooper and Bornick Sites: Two Grand River Phase Oneota Sites in Central Wisconsin. Ph.D. dissertation, University of Wisconsin, Madison.

Green, W., and R. L. Rodell. 1994. The Mississippian Presence and Cahokia Interaction at Trempealeau, Wisconsin. *American Antiquity* 59:334–359.

Griffin, J. B. 1960. A Hypothesis for the Prehistory of the Winnebago. In *Culture in History*, edited by S. Diamond, pp. 809–865. Columbia University Press, New York.

Hall, R. L. 1962. *The Archaeology of Carcajou Point.* University of Wisconsin Press, Madison.

Henning, D. R. 1970. Development and Interrelationships of Oneota Culture in the Lower Missouri River Valley. *Missouri Archaeologist* 32.

———. 1998. Managing Oneota: A Reiteration and Testing of Contemporary Archaeological Taxonomy. *Wisconsin Archeologist* 79(2):9–29.

Keyes, C. R. 1927. Prehistoric Man in Iowa. *Palimpsest* 8:125–229.

Mallam, R. C. 1976. *The Iowa Effigy Mound Manifestation: An Interpretive Model.* Report 9, Office of the State Archaeologist. University of Iowa, Iowa City.

McKusick, M. 1973. *The Grant Oneota Village.* Report 4, Office of the State Archaeologist. University of Iowa, Iowa City.

Overstreet, D. F. 1981. Investigations at the Pipe Site (47-Fd-10) and Some Perspectives on Eastern Wisconsin Oneota Prehistory. *Wisconsin Archeologist* 63:365–525.

Pauketat, T. R. 1997. Cahokian Political Economy. In *Cahokia: Domination and Ideology in the Mississippian World*, edited by T. R. Pauketat and T. E. Emerson, pp. 30–51. University of Nebraska Press, Lincoln.

———, D. M. Benden, and R. F. Boszhardt. 2010. New Evidence of the Cahokian Occupation of Trempealeau. Poster presented at the 56th Midwest Archaeological Conference, Bloomington, IN.

Stoltman, J. B., D. M. Benden, and R. F. Boszhardt. 2008. Evidence in the Upper Mississippi Valley for Pre-Mississippian Cultural Interaction with the American Bottom. *American Antiquity* 73(2):317–336.

Stoltman, J. B., and G. W. Christiansen. 2000. The Late Woodland Stage in the Driftless Area of the Upper Mississippi Valley. In *Late Woodland Societies: Tradition and*

Transformation Across the Midcontinent, edited by T. E. Emerson, D. L. McElrath, and A. C. Fortier, pp. 497–524. University of Nebraska Press, Lincoln.

Theler, J. L. 1987. *Woodland Tradition Economic Strategies: Animal Resource Utilization in Southwestern Wisconsin and Northeastern Iowa*. Report 17, Office of the State Archaeologist. University of Iowa, Iowa City.

———, and R. Boszhardt. 2006. Collapse of Crucial Resources and Culture Change: A Model for the Woodland to Oneota Transition in the Upper Midwest. *American Antiquity* 71(3):433–472.

CHAPTER 35

POST-CONTACT CULTURAL DYNAMICS IN THE UPPER GREAT LAKES REGION

VERGIL E. NOBLE

EUROPEAN explorers, missionaries, and fur traders first encountered North American natives along the eastern seaboard of what would later become Canada and the United States. Long before face-to-face contact occurred in the interior reaches, the presence of those intruders was already being felt among aboriginal peoples of the upper Great Lakes region. As fur-bearing game in the East was steadily depleted in order to fuel the trade, native middlemen such as the Huron obtained pelts from more distant groups in exchange for items they had acquired from their European partners. Vast continental trading networks had developed thousands of years earlier, during the Archaic period, and exotic new commodities now flowed along those same routes (see Chapdelaine, Gibbon, Milner, this volume). European-manufactured goods, durable and unusual in appearance, were quickly integrated into the assemblage of native material culture, subtly foreshadowing the profound changes that would ultimately result in acculturation of interior North American peoples.

Colonization efforts along the Atlantic seaboard and the St. Lawrence River valley came to impose intense pressure on native populations, increasing competition and conflict among many aboriginal groups. This in turn would bring about dramatic changes in political organization, settlement patterns, and demographics. Kin groups coalesced into larger tribal entities. Those closely involved with the commerce began to settle in large villages around trading centers, which made them more susceptible to European control and vulnerable to their devastating infectious diseases. Some would be displaced from their homelands in the East and moved westward, where they subsequently came into conflict with other groups that they encountered. Widespread epidemics of smallpox and other exotic maladies would eventually affect many native populations, reducing their numbers and fragmenting their traditional social systems.

Throughout the first half of the 17th century, French explorers were to make occasional forays into the upper Great Lakes, establishing first contact with native peoples of the interior. Beginning with Samuel de Champlain's arrival at Lake Huron in 1615, the French pressed ever farther into the western Great Lakes of Michigan and Superior. Missionaries would later establish themselves among native peoples in the region during the second half of the 17th century, and by the close of that century several military installations had been founded on the once-distant inland sea. Their hold on the western lakes became even firmer in the opening decades of the 18th century with establishment of several important fur-trading posts, chiefly Ft. Michilimackinac at the Straits of Mackinac in 1715.

ARCHAEOLOGICAL RESEARCH

North American archaeologists began to take an abiding interest in the Contact period very early, during development of the modern discipline. It was logically reasoned that, by examining protohistoric sites, archaeologists might be able to bridge the unintelligible gap between late pre-Columbian native populations, identified only in terms of perceived cultural traditions reflected in the material culture, and the historic tribal groups that would later come into being. This was the case in every quarter of the continent, but it was especially true on the Great Plains of the United States and on both sides of the Canadian border in the Great Lakes region (Mason 1976). Indeed, the search for ethnic identity in the archaeological record remains an important research focus on Contact period sites.

Accordingly, in the 1930s archaeologists such as George I. Quimby began to study early historic material culture, particularly glass beads and ornaments of trade silver, in order to help establish artifact chronologies and temporal connections among sites of the upper Great Lakes. Quimby's landmark summation (1966) of 30 years' research on the subject, *Indian Culture and European Trade Goods*, remains in print and is still frequently cited by scholars of the fur trade more than 40 years after its initial publication. Meanwhile, in Canada archaeologists Kenneth Kidd, Wilfred Jury, and others would begin to undertake excavations at mission sites such as Sainte-Marie I on Georgian Bay of Lake Huron and the native villages they served.

European fortifications that had served the burgeoning fur trade of the 18th century, however, would quickly become the primary centers of archaeological attention, chiefly in support of efforts to reconstruct such sites for heritage tourism. Perhaps the earliest work of that sort in the upper Great Lakes was conducted by the Minnesota Historical Society, in the mid-1930s, at the Grand Portage trading depot on the north shore of Lake Superior. Michigan State University began excavations at

Fort Michilimackinac in 1959, under the direction of Moreau S. Maxwell, and various researchers have worked there every year since that time. By now, the archaeological sites of almost every other French or British fur-trade installation that once served the North American interior also have been investigated, to a lesser degree.

Although scholars have justifiably lamented diminished interest in historic Native American archaeology (e.g., Rubertone 2000), over the past 50 years important investigations have been carried out intermittently at sites of the upper Great Lakes. Indeed, fieldwork has resulted in acquisition of field data bearing on patterns of cultural change and continuity among indigenous peoples. This research holds great promise for improved understanding of the Contact period with respect to changes in lifeways that came about through protracted and intensifying interaction between natives and Europeans. Herein, I review a few representative field projects contributing to our perspective on the historical processes that played out in the Great Lakes region.

Village Sites

Among the major archaeological projects carried out in the upper Great Lakes are several investigations that center on places where Jesuit missions were established among native peoples during the 17th century. Although missionaries assigned to those remote localities were generally few in number, compared with personnel at later fur-trading installations, Jesuit fathers were actively committed to the conversion of natives and to the perceived "improvement" of their lives. Excavations at village sites associated with missions provide much useful information on the initial effects of direct contact between European and native populations.

In addition to those native occupations associated with early historic missions in the upper Great Lakes, a few other archaeological investigations have examined occupation sites elsewhere in the region. Such sites, contrasted with late pre-Contact settlements, offer clues to the extent and character of culture change in contexts where direct exposure to European influences was not as intensive.

Marquette Mission Site

The Marquette Mission site (20MK82), located in St. Ignace, Michigan, on the north side of the Straits of Mackinac joining lakes Huron and Michigan, includes the site of a native village occupied by the Tionontate (Petun) Huron during the latter decades of the 17th century. Driven by the Iroquois from their traditional homeland east of Lake Huron's Georgian Bay, and decimated by both warfare and disease, several bands of Huron relocated to lands at the western end of Lake Superior in what is now Wisconsin. Routed by Siouan peoples in the mid-1660s, the Tionontate eventually resettled near the mission founded by Fr. Jacques Marquette in 1671.

The native occupation associated with Marquette's St. Ignace mission has been the subject of numerous field studies since 1971 (Figure 35.1). Archaeological evidence derived from the Tionontate village supports the conclusion that important aspects of Huron culture persisted through the end of the 17th century in key areas, such as subsistence practices (particularly those related to fishing) and traditional settlement patterns. Villagers readily employed exotic materials from Europe, to be sure, but they also retained many traditional items of material culture and were not dependent on trade goods. In fact, there is considerable evidence indicating adaptation of European articles for traditional uses, for example, projectile points flaked from broken glass (Branstner 1992).

Comparing the Tionontate village assemblage with data derived from the nearby Juntunen site, a late prehistoric occupation on Bois Blanc Island, Fitting (1976:327) observes that "if the introduction of European trade goods had any effect at all on the subsistence base, it was to amplify the trends already present." It is also apparent from Fitting's comparative study, however, that materials recovered from the Marquette Mission site show growing emphasis on personal adornment, which is reflected both in expansion of native crafts and amassing of European-made decorative artifacts. He sees this noticeable shift in material culture patterning as indicating certain social and ceremonial changes brought on by circumstances of the fur trade.

Rock Island Site II

One of the most important Contact-period occupation sites yet to be studied in the upper Great Lakes is located on the sandy southwestern shore of Rock Island in northern Lake Michigan. Part of the archipelago extending north from Wisconsin's

Figure 35.1 Michigan State University excavations at the Marquette Mission site, 1986 (photo by Vergil Noble).

Door Peninsula toward Michigan's Upper Peninsula, Rock Island advantageously borders a passage connecting the waters of Green Bay to the rest of Lake Michigan.

Surviving documents of the 17th century make occasional reference to French visits at native villages on the many islands that dot northern Lake Michigan. The historic record, however, is often vague and imprecise. Therefore it is difficult to conclude with certainty which island or native group was meant in any particular account. Nevertheless, it is known that La Salle sailed his ill-fated ship, the *Griffin*, as far as Green Bay in 1679, shortly before it was lost in a storm, and it is very probable that he traded at Rock Island. A few years earlier, Fr. Marquette and his exploring partner, Louis Jolliet, may also have passed Rock Island as they entered Green Bay by canoe to ascend the Fox River to the Wisconsin River confluence and descend the Mississippi to the Gulf of Mexico in 1673.

Ronald J. Mason's initial archaeological survey (1986) of Rock Island State Park, carried out in 1969, disclosed three native sites on the island's south shore. Of those, Rock Island Site II (47DR128) contained substantial cultural remains relating to the early Historic period, and it would be subject to extensive study by field crews from Lawrence University over the next four summers. Excavations revealed that the site has multiple components, with strata representing four distinct early Historic period occupations (Figure 35.2).

Analyses of cultural material, coupled with study of relevant documentary sources, led investigators to conclude that the initial occupation occurred sometime between 1641 and 1651, and further, that the occupants represented a small band of Potawatomi. The second distinctive occupation period commenced immediately following the first and lasted only two years. During that time a defensive palisade

Figure 35.2 Rock Island Site II excavation unit profile showing occupation zone strata (photo courtesy of Ronald J. Mason, Lawrence University, used with permission).

apparently was constructed around the small village. Comparative analysis of the artifact assemblage, particularly potsherds found in this stratum, with others found elsewhere in the upper Great Lakes region suggests a Huron-Petun-Ottawa ethnicity for Period 2 occupants of Rock Island Site II.

The third Historic-period occupation at Rock Island Site II appears to have been longer in duration (ca. 1670–1730) but is again interpreted as Potawatomi owing to the presence of distinctive ceramic wares recovered from midden deposits. A final native encampment inferred from the archeological record was much later (ca. 1760–1770); from the material culture, it appears to have been associated with the Ottawa. Discovery of numerous exotic European goods in this occupation zone indicates that site inhabitants were then fully engaged in the fur trade.

It is worth noting that, although categorized here simply as a native village, Rock Island Site II also includes a small native cemetery, apparently associated with the final occupation period. Fourteen burials were examined by the excavators, who discerned interesting patterns in the data observed. Mason speculates that burials in the cemetery, which seems to have been used for a very short time, could be largely the result of an epidemic disease that swept through the population. He also notes that, although social stratification is not plainly demonstrable, differences in the furnishings of graves, particularly among the young, suggest that some families were better off than others and articulated the fact in lavish treatment of their dead.

Pre-Contact occupation of Rock Island extends back to the Middle Woodland period and perhaps even further. Indeed, the natural resources available seasonally here and elsewhere in the archipelago attracted native peoples fully a thousand years before Europeans came to the area. It is evident, however, that the strategic importance of this island grew, as did the fur trade, during the 17th and 18th centuries, and the forced movement of peoples throughout that period likely accounts for the various historic occupations evident at Rock Island Site II.

Mortuary Sites

It is well established that certain sociocultural patterns are reflected in treatment of the dead and manner of burial. Accordingly, analysis of archaeological evidence from mortuary contexts can provide an important perspective on the human past and the workings of culture. Two early Historic period burial localities, excavated in the 1960s, are worthy of discussion for the insights they offer on culture change among native peoples of the upper Great Lakes region. Then, as now, archaeological investigation of mortuary sites was rare and often conducted after inadvertent discovery. The two excavation projects considered here were both undertaken to salvage skeletal remains and associated funerary objects that otherwise would have been destroyed by construction activities. Human remains and grave furnishings have since been repatriated, but the restudy of statistical and other data compiled during their initial analysis has the potential to yield additional information on cultural processes during the Contact period.

Lasanen Site

The Lasanen site (20MA21) is situated within the city limits of St. Ignace, Michigan, on an ancient beach ridge overlooking the north shore of the Straits of Mackinac. Discovered in 1966, while excavation of a house foundation on private property was in progress, the landowner alerted staff members of the Mackinac Island State Park Commission that several human burials had been exposed by a bulldozer. Urgent salvage excavations were begun to recover skeletal remains and associated artifacts within the footprint of the building. Later that summer, faculty and students from Michigan State University undertook additional rescue excavations adjacent to the new house. Findings from the 1966 excavations were summarized in an edited monograph on the Lasanen site (Cleland 1971), but minor investigations subsequently carried out at the site in 1967 were not reported formally.

Initial investigation of the Lasanen site resulted in recovery of human remains and associated grave furnishings from 19 small burial pits. Many of those pits were lined with rock and had been dug into dense gravel to the underlying hard-pan marl, which was encountered at varying depths up to 1 meter beneath the ground surface. Many of the ossuary features, however, had been damaged by construction activities or disturbed by untrained individuals before they could be properly recorded by archaeologists. Data derived from the site therefore represent an incomplete sample of the cultural deposits at Lasanen.

Analysis indicates that most of the burial pits contained secondary burials of partial skeletons derived from one or more individuals; multiple interments in the same pit may represent family groups. Because of the small sample, and the frequent commingling of grave furnishings with bones from several individuals, it was difficult for researchers to draw any definitive conclusions relating to association of specific artifact types with particular individuals. It appears, however, that two age grades were culturally recognized for purposes of burial ceremonialism, with adults treated one way and children under 12 years of age treated another. There are also subtle indications of differential treatment by sex. Female interments tend to have more artifacts contributed to the graves, particularly articles of personal adornment, but males appear to have been buried with artifacts of greater rarity and value.

In comparing the burials at Lasanen with burials discovered at the late prehistoric Juntunen site, on Bois Blanc Island, Fitting (1976) points out that the number and variety of grave goods interred with the dead during the early Historic period is significantly higher. With nearly equal numbers of individuals represented in the two burial populations, statistics show that the dead at Lasanen have more than 130 times the number of grave furnishings on average than Juntunen, and that only four of the 55 late-prehistoric burials contained any associated grave furniture. Moreover, a staggering 99 percent of the Lasanen offerings are either of European manufacture or made by native hands employing European-derived technology. Those facts argue for a marked increase proportionately of one artifact class, items of adornment, in the native material cultural assemblage (Figure 35.3). The data also present a convincing case for the dramatic elaboration of traditional native ritual during the early Historic period.

Of particular interest, Charles E. Cleland (1971) observes that key characteristics of the Lasanen burials are entirely consistent with Antoine de La Mothe Cadillac's description of a Feast of the Dead ceremony he witnessed while serving as the French commandant at Fort de Buade in St. Ignace (1694–1697). This apparent association with the last such event recorded by Europeans is an opportunity for the site to elucidate changes in burial ceremonialism during the Historic period, as well as between historic and precontact times.

The St. Ignace event, as witnessed by Cadillac and represented by remains at Lasanen, differs in several important respects from the far more elaborate Feast of the Dead practiced in Huronia during the first half of the 17th century, and even from the later Algonquian variant (cf. Hickerson 1960). Accordingly, the Lasanen site, compared with places such as the major Huron ossuary (ca. 1624–1636), excavated at Ossossane in Ontario (Kidd 1953), can inform scholars about the evolution and ultimate decline of this ceremony, which was so important to upholding the fur

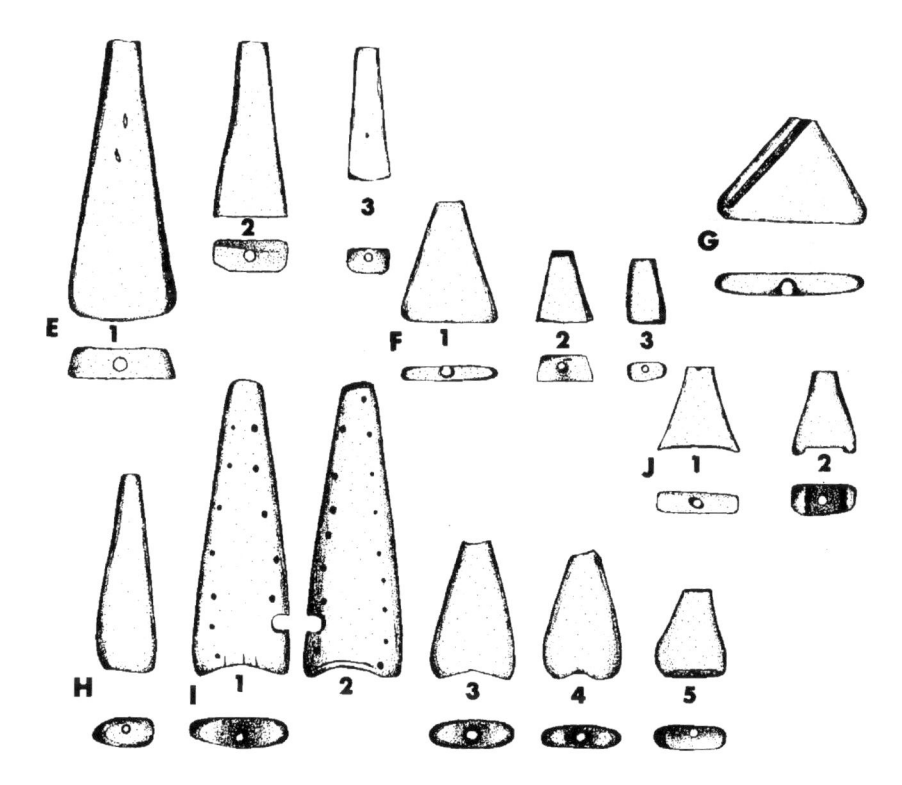

Figure 35.3 Carved catlinite articles of adornment from the Lasanen site (Cleland 1971:45, figure 27; illustration copyright The Michigan State University Museum, reproduced with permission).

trade through initiation and maintenance of reciprocal native alliances, as well as through ritual consumption of surplus trade goods.

Fletcher Site Cemetery

Located in Bay City, Michigan, the Fletcher site (20BY28) is a multicomponent locality on the west bank of the Saginaw River near its outlet on Lake Huron. Although occupation of the site area appears to extend as far back as the Early Woodland period, the primary focus of archaeological attention at Fletcher was an unmarked early Historic period cemetery used by Native Americans. First revealed in the summer of 1967 by earthmoving activities associated with dredging operations on the river, the exposed burials quickly attracted a legion of "treasure hunters" to the site. Soon thereafter, the first archaeological team arrived from Michigan State University to carry out emergency excavations within the affected area. Over the course of several field sessions continuing through 1970, nearly 100 burials eventually were recorded at the site. Data are incomplete for almost a third of them, however, owing to the damaging effects of disturbances prior to the arrival of archaeologists on the scene (Mainfort 1979).

The Fletcher cemetery is believed to have been used during the third quarter of the 18th century (ca. 1750–1765), and it is known from various historic records that northern Algonquian speakers were in the Saginaw Bay area during the 17th and 18th centuries. Indeed, a map of the area produced by the surveyor Thomas Hutchins in 1762 indicates the presence of "Ottawas and Cheapwas" in a village comprising 200 Indian warriors, at roughly the same locality as the Fletcher site. It is probable that the Fletcher graves derive from that native community, which may have had a total population of at least 800.

Mortuary practices defined by the burials in this native cemetery mirror the effects of prolonged and intensive participation in the fur trade. In contrast with the older burials found at Lasanen, interments for the most part are primary and singular; they exhibit evidence of containment in cedar coffins. More important, analysis of the grave furnishings shows there are notable disparities in distribution of wealth among individuals interred at Fletcher, and the spatial arrangement of graves also indicates status differences within the burial population (Figure 35.4).

Robert Mainfort (1985) interprets these data as indications of an emergent social structure radically different from earlier conditions in the region. Privileged burial locations, marked differences in the value of grave furniture among rows, and high-value artifacts interred with children, among other observations, are seen as clearly pointing to some degree of social ranking among group members—though not to the extent of that found in chiefdoms. The data do not argue for the existence of ascribed status; nor do they imply that the wealthy in this society had power and influence over others. The Fletcher site burials, however, offer vital insights as to the origins of social ranking among native groups in the upper Great Lakes and demonstrate the utility of mortuary data toward understanding human history.

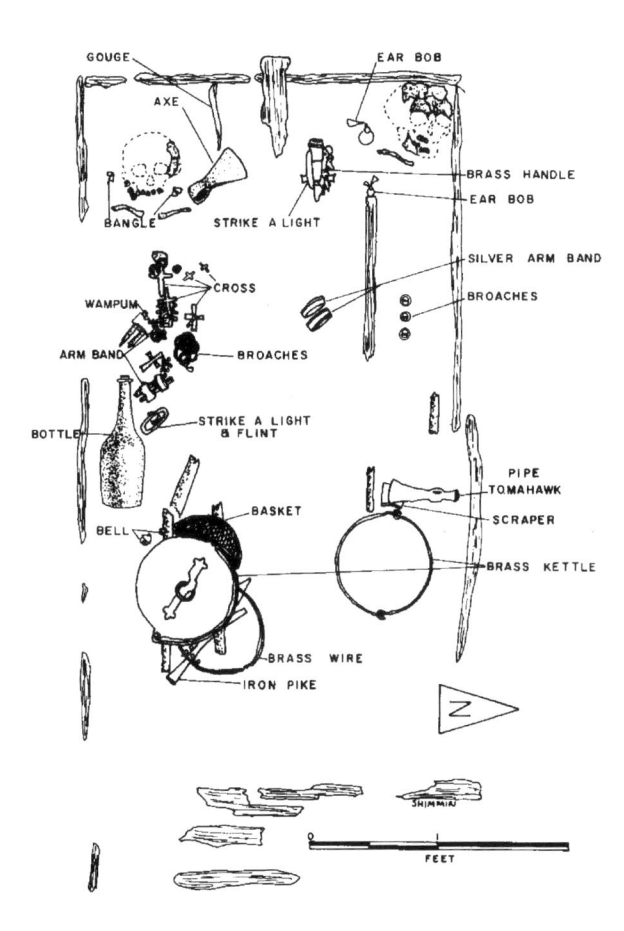

Figure 35.4 Burial 50, Fletcher site (Mainfort 1979:326, figure 8; illustration copyright The Michigan State University Museum, reproduced with permission).

Conclusion

Although many extremely useful eyewitness accounts pertaining to the Contact period survive, including the extensive *Jesuit Relations* (Thwaites 1896–1901), they furnish only limited and often inaccurate views of native life that may reflect misunderstandings and cultural biases. Further, contemporary European observers were entirely ignorant of the ancient ancestors of peoples they encountered, and they were not attempting to document or explain cultural changes occurring among the indigenous North American populations. Some accounts, however, do illuminate the varied means other than trade by which European material culture entered native society. Other documents, particularly trading manifests, underscore the magnitude of many goods that generally do not appear in the archaeological record (Anderson 1991), such as the European textiles and native basketry that figured prominently as articles of exchange.

Archaeological research provides a unique perspective on the native cultures that Europeans encountered in the upper Great Lakes and ultimately changed.

Though subject to its own imperfect database, archaeology can reveal much about the dynamic cultural processes at work during the early Historic period. Relatively few Contact period native sites have been excavated in the region, compared with the great number that must have existed, and far fewer native sites of the 19th century have been examined for comparison. Nevertheless, viewed in the light of existing data derived from contemporaneous sites in other regions, as well as data from prehistoric sites throughout the upper Great Lakes, even the handful of studies described here can offer important insights into the effects of European contact on native culture in North America. Reinvigorated commitment to this subject will doubtless shed even greater light on the questions only touched on here.

ACKNOWLEDGMENTS

Figure 35.2 is reproduced with the permission of Lawrence University. Figures 35.3 and 35.4 are reproduced with the permission of the Michigan State University Museum. I am grateful to William A. Lovis (Michigan State University) and Ronald J. Mason (Lawrence University) for provision of images from their respective institutions. I also thank Carol I. Mason (Lawrence University), who was extremely helpful in selecting transparencies to illustrate Rock Island Site II. Several points made in this chapter reflect insights I gained from a conversation with Charles E. Cleland (professor emeritus, Michigan State University), who kindly offered his views on the early Historic period after reading a draft.

REFERENCES

Anderson, D. L. 1991. Variability in Trade at Eighteenth-Century French Outposts. In *French Colonial Archaeology: The Illinois Country and The Western Great Lakes*, edited by J. A. Walthall, pp. 218–236. University of Illinois Press, Urbana.

Branstner, S. M. 1992. Tionontate Huron Occupation at the Marquette Mission. In *Calumet and Fleur-de-lys: Archaeology of Indian and French Contact in the Mid-Continent*, edited by J. A. Walthall and T. E. Emerson, pp. 177–201. Smithsonian Institution, Washington, DC.

Cleland, C. E. (editor). 1971. *The Lasanen Site: An Historic Burial Locality in Mackinac County, Michigan*. Publications of the Museum, Michigan State University, Anthropological Series, vol. 1, no. 1. Michigan State University, East Lansing.

Fitting, J. E. 1976. Patterns of Acculturation at the Straits of Mackinac. In *Cultural Change and Continuity: Essays in Honor of James Bennett Griffin*, edited by C. E. Cleland, pp. 321–334. Academic Press, New York.

Hickerson, H. 1960. The Feast of the Dead Among the Seventeenth Century Algonkians of the Upper Great Lakes. *American Anthropologist* 62(1):81–107.

Kidd, K. 1953. The Excavation and Identification of a Huron Ossuary. *American Antiquity* 18(4):359–379.

Mainfort, R. C., Jr. 1979. *Indian Social Dynamics in the Period of European Contact: Fletcher Site Cemetery, Bay County, Michigan.* Publications of the Museum, Michigan State University, Anthropological Series, vol. 1, no. 4. Michigan State University, East Lansing.

———. 1985. Wealth, Space, and Status in a Historic Indian Cemetery. *American Antiquity* 50(3):555–579.

Mason, R. J. 1976. Ethnicity and Archaeology in the Upper Great Lakes. In *Cultural Change and Continuity: Essays in Honor of James Bennett Griffin*, edited by C. E. Cleland, pp. 49–361. Academic Press, New York.

———. 1986. *Rock Island: Historical Indian Archaeology in the Northern Lake Michigan Basin.* MCJA Special Paper 6. Kent State University Press, Kent, OH.

Quimby, G. I. 1966. *Indian Culture and European Trade Goods: The Archaeology of the Historic Period in the Western Great Lakes Region.* University of Wisconsin Press, Madison.

Rubertone, P. E. 2000. The Historical Archaeology of Native Americans. *Annual Review of Anthropology* 29:425–446.

Thwaites, R. G. (editor). 1896–1901. *The Jesuit Relations and Allied Documents: Travels and Explorations of the Jesuit Missionaries in New France, 1610–1791.* 73 vols. Burrows Bros., Cleveland.

V. Midsouth and Southeast

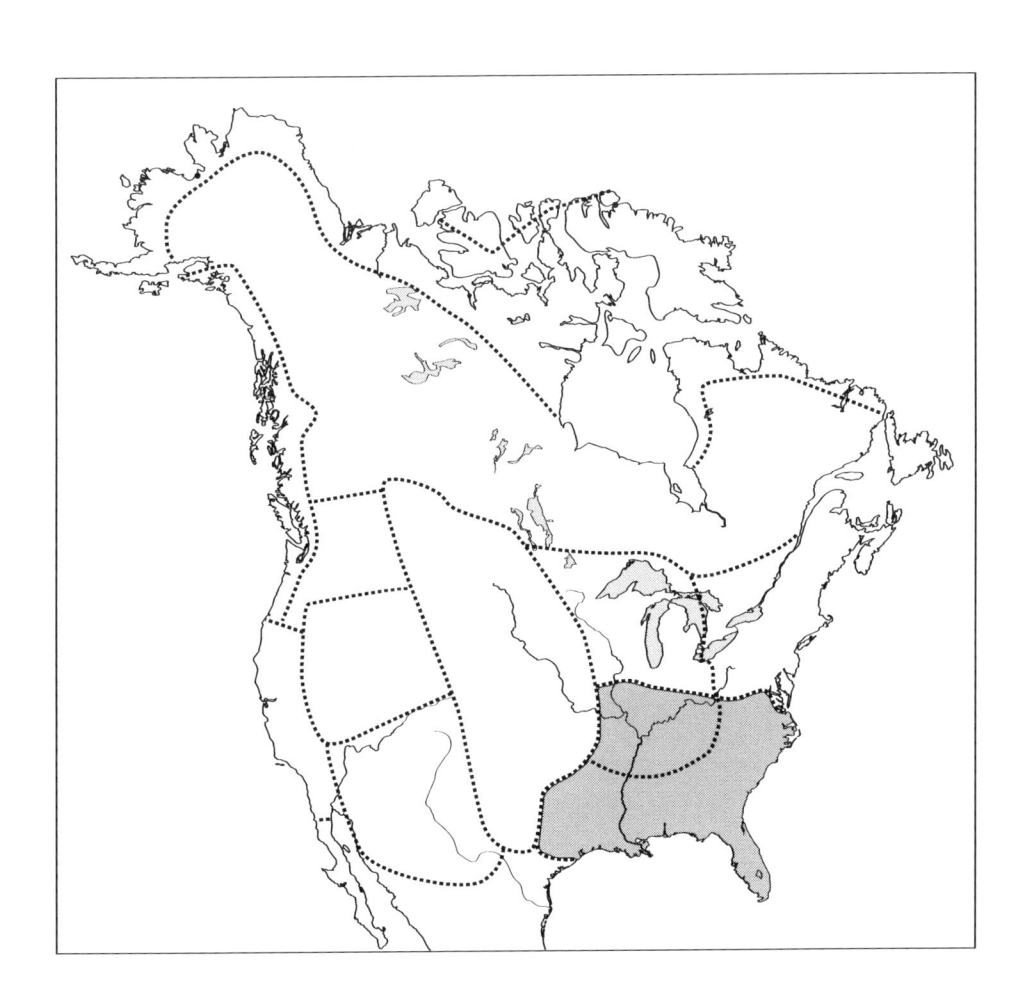

CHAPTER 36

MOUND-BUILDING SOCIETIES OF THE SOUTHERN MIDWEST AND SOUTHEAST

GEORGE R. MILNER

THE pre-Columbian period in the Midsouth and Southeast is often said to have encompassed two cultural florescences marked by many mounds and elaborate artifacts. There is some truth in such a statement, but reality was more complicated. Not all populations dating to these periods—Middle Woodland (ca. 200 BC to AD 400) and Mississippian (ca. AD 1050 to 1600)—built mounds, participated in exchanges of many fancy artifacts, or shared the same settlement patterns and subsistence practices. Mound construction was likewise not limited to these two intervals of time. Some earlier mounds, such as the largest at Poverty Point (Figure 36.1), were every bit as impressive as most of the later ones. What these two cultural florescences show—along with the achievements of earlier people during the Archaic period, which spanned many thousands of years and ended early in the first millennium BC—is that there was no simple linear progression in cultural development, however that might be measured (see also Gibbon, and Sassaman and Randall, this volume).

Figure 36.1 The largest mound at Poverty Point, Louisiana (photo by G. R. Milner).

MOUNDS AND EARTHWORKS

There is good evidence for mound building, presumably accompanied by a commensurately rich ceremonial life, as early as the middle of the fourth millennium BC at Watson Brake, Louisiana, where mounds and intervening ridges defined a large oval area (Saunders et al. 2005). Earthen (or shell) mounds, as well as a demarcation of open spaces partly or entirely surrounded by mounds or embankments, were associated with many societies from then onward. Their construction often represented continuity in existing practices, modified to meet local needs, but sometimes they appear to have been entirely independent developments.

From the historic period back to the late first millennium AD, many major settlements were arranged around open spaces flanked by special forms of architecture, typically including mounds but sometimes only large wooden buildings. Despite differences among these societies, including site layouts ranging from dispersed to closely spaced residential structures, there was some continuity across time and space in how plazas and associated mounds were used and what they signified. In fact, the mound and plaza arrangement is considered a hallmark of Mississippian societies, notably Cahokia in Illinois and Moundville in Alabama (Alt, Blitz, this volume; Fowler 1997; Knight and Steponaitis 1998), and it was present in some of their immediate predecessors. Early examples of mounds fronting plazas occur in the middle and lower Mississippi River valley, including its principal tributaries (Rees, this volume). One such site, which dates to the late first millennium AD, is Toltec on the Arkansas River; it has two plazas and several big mounds, plus a number of smaller ones (Rolingson 1998).

Many of the late prehistoric mounds were rectangular platforms for wooden buildings associated with leading members of these societies, or structures used for community-related functions, such as council houses. Highly ranked people elevated themselves, literally and figuratively, above their fellow community members by putting their houses on mounds. Charnel structures for the bones of important ancestors were also placed on these earthen platforms.

Middle Woodland earthworks built many hundreds of years earlier—most notably, impressive enclosures in southern Ohio, such as Newark and Fort Ancient (Connolly 1998; Lepper 1998)—also defined ritually and socially significant spaces (Charles, this volume). A number of these geometric and irregular earthworks, many enclosing up to about a dozen hectares and sometimes much more, encompassed wooden buildings littered with debris from making ceremonial objects and mounds that covered structures filled with human remains and many fine objects of great ritual significance. The enclosures were not defensive in nature; they were too large to be manned by local communities, and they were often pierced by numerous openings, as at Fort Ancient (Figure 36.2; Connolly 1998).

Large numbers of Middle Woodland mounds were built elsewhere in the Midwest and Southeast, although there were few earthen enclosures. Most mounds were for burial purposes. In Illinois, centrally located, log-lined crypts used on multiple occasions that often contained several individuals and fancy artifacts were common (Brown 1979). Situated around them were simpler graves that usually held single individuals with fewer and plainer objects. Log tombs have also been found elsewhere in the Eastern Woodlands, although their number and placement indicate different mound construction histories. For example, large Adena mounds in the middle Ohio River valley, many dating to the late first millennium BC (Early to Middle Woodland), often have multiple log tombs, along with less elaborate graves.

Figure 36.2 Part of the embankment surrounding a hilltop at Fort Ancient, Ohio (photo by G. R. Milner).

They were capped by layers of soil denoting periodic renewals of the burial areas (Milner and Jefferies 1987).

Adena people also built many small embankments, usually circles flanked internally by shallow ditches, that typically enclosed less than a hectare. The circles sometimes surrounded a mound, or as at Mt. Horeb in Kentucky (Webb 1941) the interior was walled off by closely spaced posts. Their connection with the larger and somewhat later Middle Woodland earthworks is unclear, although there was some continuity in the use of ritually significant places because they are often found together.

An even older site, Poverty Point in Louisiana, dating to the late second millennium BC, is one of the most remarkable earthen constructions in the Eastern Woodlands (Gibson 2000; Kidder 2002; Kidder, this volume). A massive mound is situated at the apex of nested and curved ridges that end at a steep slope overlooking a bayou. Additional mounds are also present at, or near, the site. Poverty Point's overall configuration is unique, and it has also yielded numerous small objects, including beads of various shapes, made from nonlocal materials. Other late Middle Archaic to Late Archaic mounds are distributed widely across the lower Mississippi Valley and Gulf Coast (Russo 1996, 2004). Also dotting the Gulf and south Atlantic coasts are irregular rings of shell that have been interpreted as either deliberate constructions or middens. Even if only debris heaps, they could be indicative of how social groups arranged themselves because the shell was presumably discarded reasonably close to where people lived. Little, if anything, connects the Archaic mounds to the later burial mounds so widely distributed across the Eastern Woodlands; in fact, the same has been said for Watson Brake and much later Poverty Point (Saunders et al 2005).

Purposeful Archaic mound building can be contrasted with extensive and deep middens consisting of shell and soil in coastal areas and some parts of the midcontinent, especially along the Tennessee, Ohio, and Green Rivers (ca. 4500 to 1000 BC). These debris-filled middens resulted from repeated or permanent occupation of resource-rich places. Over time, sites no doubt acquired significance as a group's traditional home, making them even more attractive to successive generations of people. In the midcontinent, many of the middens contain skeletons, as well as habitation-related features. The arrangement of graves, however, shows that burial occurred near camps rather than in formally organized and demarcated cemeteries maintained for lengthy periods of time (Milner and Jefferies 1998).

Regardless of whether the Archaic earth and shell mounds were purposeful constructions or debris heaps—there are unambiguous examples of both—they are indicative of what have been called complex hunter-gatherer social systems. These people lived semisedentary lives, settling for long periods in especially favorable places, and they resisted being pushed off their land, as shown by casualties from conflicts. Cooperative interactions established with neighboring groups resulted in exchanges of items of social or ritual significance, many of which ended up in graves. Occasionally places of special significance were identified by permanent markers in the form of deliberately constructed mounds.

Sociopolitical Organization

There is no direct link between a particular kind of archaeological indicator, such as big mounds or fancy objects, and a specific type of sociopolitical structure. For example, both Middle Woodland and Mississippian groups featured elaboration of ceremonial activities and much else that went with it, but archaeologists regard these societies as being quite different, often calling the earlier ones tribes and the later ones chiefdoms. The principal difference is the presence in Mississippian societies of formal leadership positions that were inherited according to fixed rules, backed by tradition, and featured some control over the group as a whole. In the earlier societies, certain individuals by virtue of their competence, charisma, age, or genealogical position enjoyed some influence over the affairs of other community members, but it was situationally limited to particular contexts.

One distinction between Middle Woodland and Mississippian societies is how people were treated during their lives as opposed to what happened after they died (Milner 2004). In both groups of societies, certain people received special attention in sometimes protracted funerary proceedings; but how they were treated relative to other community members during life was much different. In the Mississippian societies, people of importance often had large houses on mounds, and they possessed fancy objects that denoted their high social standing. No such consistent differences have been detected in Middle Woodland habitation sites. This does not mean all people of the same age and sex were treated the same, but that any special roles and positions of influence were restricted to specific situations. For example, some people buried with many fine artifacts in Ohio's mortuary-related structures were probably shamans recognized for their ability to negotiate between the real and supernatural worlds (Brown 2006; Case and Carr 2008).

The distribution of objects in Ohio's mortuary-related structures suggests that different segments of society, perhaps much like historic-period clans, were associated with various totemic animals (Case and Carr 2008). Social-group affiliation similarly cross-cut residential units such as villages in later Mississippian societies, but there was also a noticeable vertical ranking of at least some of those very same groups (Muller 1997). Positions of authority in Mississippian societies, despite relatively powerful leaders at places such as Cahokia, remained firmly embedded in a segmental social structure where different lineages were associated with certain rights and obligations. One indication of the importance of kin affiliation to even the highest-ranked people is the presence of mortuary facilities containing many people buried together alongside valued objects in mounds, such as those at major sites in the Cahokia area (Figure 36.3; Milner 1998).

Simply labeling societies, of course, does not get us very far; there was much diversity among the groups within whatever societal category one chooses to use. This issue has been discussed extensively in terms of Mississippian societies, which displayed considerable variation in population size, geographical extent, differentiation among settlements, social distance between individuals of high and low rank,

Figure 36.3 The largest mound in the United States is Monks Mound, at Cahokia, Illinois (photo by G. R. Milner).

a leader's capacity to influence subordinates, and the ability to mobilize labor for mound building and other major tasks. Terms such as *simple* and *complex*, denoting the number of decision-making levels above a local community, capture some of this variation (Anderson 1994). In simple chiefdoms, a chief who occupied the principal site (often marked by one or more mounds) exerted some control over people in neighboring and typically smaller settlements. This same pattern was repeated in complex chiefdoms, except the leader of one such group of sites dominated the others; subchiefs in turn presided over their own clusters of settlements. Thus a complex chiefdom was a spatially and socially segmented system readily divisible into structurally similar parts, with each district being politically quasi-autonomous and economically self-sufficient with regard to basic needs. These two kinds of chiefdoms are also idealized types, and variation on the general theme makes the overall picture of diverse and ever-changing relations among the residential and social groups making up these societies, including their distribution across the landscape, a good deal more complex (Beck 2003; Blitz 1999).

Perhaps the longest-running debate over the nature of Mississippian societies centers on Cahokia, the biggest prehistoric site in the United States (Alt, Emerson, this volume, Milner 1998; Muller 1997; Pauketat 2004). This site, with about 100 mounds spread across 10 square kilometers of Mississippi River bottomland, dominated sites distributed along 100 kilometers of the valley, and laterally into the surrounding uplands for at least several tens of kilometers (Milner 1998). The issue boils down to whether Cahokia was organized along lines similar to those of its Eastern Woodlands contemporaries, what emergent properties (if any) arose largely as a function of its size and the number of groups it encompassed, and whether those properties were sufficient to have made it structurally and functionally different from its Mississippian counterparts elsewhere. Nothing at this point indicates the underlying organizational principles were demonstrably different at Cahokia, but this should not be mistaken as saying that all Mississippian societies were the same; they most assuredly were not. Archaeologically distinctive outcomes within the Mississippian category resulted from diverse natural and social settings, cultural traditions, and historical trajectories, despite strong shared commonalities in their fundamental organizational structure.

Regardless of the specific nature of sociopolitical systems, individual populations were widely distributed across the best land, principally river valleys and coastlines. They were separated by uninhabited areas, which were often used as hunting territories. Over time, the distribution of people and regionally ascendant groups changed as individual populations expanded, contracted, and moved as part of a continual jostling for environmentally and socially advantageous positions. This pattern of occupation is best documented for the half millennium preceding direct European contact (Anderson 1991, 1994). Clusters of Mississippian settlements, for example, typically stretched only several tens of kilometers along rivers, although some of them, including Cahokia in the broad Mississippi River valley, were much larger (Hally 1993; Milner 1998).

Subsistence Practices

It is absolutely clear that the capacity to mobilize enough labor to build impressive mounds did not require an economic system based squarely on agriculture. Only relatively late in pre-Columbian times were mounds built by people who spent much of their time cultivating plants. But even then, not all mound-building peoples relied heavily on agriculture, such as those in the lower Mississippi River valley as late as the early first millennium AD (Fritz 2000).

In the midcontinent, the first evidence of domestication in several native plants—changes in seed size and other morphological characteristics—dates to somewhat more than 4,000 years ago (Fritz 2000; Smith 1989). These plants favor disturbed habitats, such as river banks, mudflats from receding floodwaters, and the organically enriched soils of repeatedly occupied camps. Charred seeds of cultigens first become common in archaeological samples from midcontinental sites that date back as far as ca. 2,000 years ago, during the Middle Woodland period (Milner 2004; Smith 1989). They signal the appearance of new subsistence strategies with a heavier emphasis on what people could grow in gardens. Maize, ultimately from Mesoamerica, made its appearance in the Eastern Woodlands early in the first millennium AD, but it did not become a major part of diets until ca. AD 800, earlier in some places than in others (Pearsall, this volume). Beans, also an introduced crop, were added to the mix as much as half a millennium later. Thus the road to agriculture was long, but it was by no means smooth. It was more steplike than gradual, with major shifts toward several native plants and maize being separated by many centuries.

It makes sense that the move to agriculture took place in a series of steps. Societies are forever changing, but there are occasionally times when further adjustments require a major transformation in multiple and diverse aspects of life. More intensive forms of food production, regardless of why they were adopted, can necessitate significant modifications in group mobility, residential group size, male-female relationships, seasonal scheduling of activities, and technology, including both tools and storage capacity. Changes in such integrated systems could result in steplike shifts when viewed from an archaeological perspective where a short unit of time can be several generations long.

Intergroup Interaction

The amount of intergroup exchange and the intensity of warfare varied over time, although there was no simple relationship between the two. For example, numerous nonlocal items were passed from one group to another during the Middle Woodland and Mississippian periods. Intergroup conflict, however, was much more common and severe among the Mississippian societies.

For the most part, items including those made from copper and marine shell moved long distances in "down-the-line" exchanges from one individual to the next. Many of these objects were highly prized for their symbolic content and as formal acknowledgment of various social transactions. The distribution of marine-shell beads among the hunter-gatherers who occupied middens along the Green River in Kentucky is consistent with relatively few people (perhaps those who were particularly charismatic or able) being the principal nodes through which these objects were passed from one group to another (Milner et al. 2009; see also Chapdelaine, this volume). This sort of movement of items, both shell ornaments and utilitarian stone hoes, even typified Mississippian times (Muller 1997). Many, but not all, of them were exchanged among the leading members of late prehistoric chiefdoms to mark their high rank and to seal various social and political arrangements, such as alliances, between neighboring societies.

A notable exception to the general pattern occurred during Middle Woodland times, when boundaries among groups were permeable enough to allow some individuals to travel safely across long distances (Case and Carr 2008). Two large hoards of Yellowstone obsidian at the Hopewell site in Ohio are examples of items that presumably moved in such a manner. Whatever happened to permit, and even encourage, a wide distribution of valued and symbolically significant objects among Middle Woodland societies took place within the context of unusually peaceful intergroup relations, as indicated by the near absence of skeletons showing signs of war-related trauma (Milner 1999).

Little is known about conflict among the earliest mobile hunter-gatherers to occupy the Eastern Woodlands because there are so few well-preserved skeletons. Later semisedentary hunter-gatherers who occupied the Archaic midden sites, however, occasionally fought one another, as shown by projectile points embedded in bones (Milner 1999). The likelihood of disputes erupting into outright violence varied over time and from one place to another, to judge from the irregular distribution of sites yielding skeletons with distinctive conflict-related trauma.

The Middle Woodland decline in hostilities is likely real—that is, not a result of poor sampling—because many skeletons have been examined. This peaceful situation was not destined to last, and intergroup relations took a marked turn for the worse in some places late in the first millennium AD (Milner 1999). From that point into historic times, many of the victims of violence died in ambushes, often far from the safety of their village. Fighting sometimes took a great toll on communities, as at Norris Farms in Illinois where at least one-third of the adults were killed in ambushes involving only a few individuals apiece. Such attacks were presumably punctuated by occasional massacres of situationally disadvantaged villagers. This is a common pattern among small-scale societies, and just such an event has been documented archaeologically at 14th-century Crow Creek in South Dakota (Willey and Emerson 1993).

Warfare peaked across the Midsouth and Southeast during the late 13th to 14th centuries, to judge from the number of Mississippian sites with defensive palisades (see also Wilson, this volume). Many objects of great ritual and social significance were also being exchanged at the time, despite hostile relations among many groups. This is consistent with leading members of neighboring societies increasing their efforts to forge alliances, settle differences, and establish peace. Objects marking those relationships would have been in demand in such circumstances and widely exchanged.

Conclusion

It is true there were more people in the late pre-Columbian period than there were many thousands of years earlier. Furthermore, societies were organized differently, groups were not as mobile, and more intensive subsistence practices were in place. Yet there was no orderly progression over time in the size of populations, how people distributed themselves across the land, or the ways food was acquired, settlements were configured, and societies were structured and interacted with one another. Accommodations to natural and social settings, resulting in a remarkably diverse array of historically contingent outcomes, were made within the context of existing technological capacities, economic systems, social organizations, intergroup relations, and worldviews. A shift over the past few decades from the use of a relatively few sites as exemplars of particular times and places to a fuller appreciation of the great diversity that existed among contemporaneous peoples throughout prehistory is one consequence of the vastly richer archaeological record that is now available, largely a result of heavily funded cultural resource management projects.

REFERENCES

Anderson, D. G. 1991. Examining Prehistoric Settlement Distribution in Eastern North America. *Archaeology of Eastern North America* 19:1–22.

———. 1994. *The Savannah River Chiefdoms*. University of Alabama Press, Tuscaloosa.

Beck, R. A., Jr. 2003. Consolidation and Hierarchy: Chiefdom Variability in the Mississippian Southeast. *American Antiquity* 68:641–661.

Blitz, J. H. 1999. Mississippian Chiefdoms and the Fission-Fusion Process. *American Antiquity* 64:577–592.

Brown, J. A. 1979. Charnel Houses and Mortuary Crypts: Disposal of the Dead in the Middle Woodland Period. In *Hopewell Archaeology: The Chillicothe Conference*, edited by D. S. Brose and N. Greber, pp. 211–219. Kent State University Press, Kent, OH.

———. 2006. The Shamanic Element I Hopewellian Period Ritual. In *Recreating Hopewell*, edited by D. K. Charles and J. E. Buikstra, pp. 475–488. University Press of Florida, Gainesville.

Case, D. T., and C. Carr. 2008. *The Scioto Hopewell and Their Neighbors*. Springer, New York.

Connolly, R. P. 1998. Architectural Grammar Rules at the Fort Ancient Hilltop Enclosure. In *Ancient Earthen Enclosures of the Eastern Woodlands*, edited by R. C. Mainfort, Jr., and L. P. Sullivan, pp. 85–113. University Press of Florida, Tallahassee.

Fowler, M. L. 1997. *The Cahokia Atlas*. Rev. ed. Illinois Transportation Archaeological Research Program, University of Illinois, Urbana.

Fritz, G. J. 2000. Native Farming Systems and Ecosystems in the Mississippi River Valley. In *Imperfect Balance: Landscape Transformations in the Precolumbian Americas*, edited by D. L. Lentz, pp. 225–249. Columbia University Press, New York.

Gibson, J. L. 2000. *The Ancient Mounds of Poverty Point: Place of Rings*. University Press of Florida, Gainesville.

Hally, D. J. 1993. The Territorial Size of Mississippian Chiefdoms. *Archaeology of Eastern North America: Papers in Honor of Stephen Williams*, edited by J. B. Stoltman, pp. 143–168. Archaeological Report 25. Mississippi Department of Archives and History, Jackson.

Kidder, T. R. 2002. Mapping Poverty Point. *American Antiquity* 67:89–101.

Knight, V. J., Jr., and V. P. Steponaitis. 1998. A New History of Moundville. In *Archaeology of the Moundville Chiefdom*, edited by V. J. Knight Jr., and V. P. Steponaitis, pp. 1–25. Smithsonian Institution, Washington, DC.

Lepper, B. T. 1998. The Archaeology of the Newark Earthworks. In *Ancient Earthen Enclosures of the Eastern Woodlands*, edited by R. C. Mainfort Jr., and L. P. Sullivan, pp. 114–134. University Press of Florida, Tallahassee.

Milner, G. R. 1998. *The Cahokia Chiefdom: The Archaeology of a Mississippian Society*. Smithsonian Institution Press, Washington, DC.

———. 1999. Warfare in Prehistoric and Early Historic Eastern North America. *Journal of Archaeological Research* 7:105–151.

———. 2004. *The Moundbuilders*. Thames and Hudson, London.

———, J. E. Buikstra, and M. D. Wiant. 2009. Archaic Burial Sites in the Midcontinent. In *Archaic Societies: Diversity and Complexity Across the Midcontinent*, edited by T. E. Emerson, D. McElrath, and A. C. Fortier, pp. 115–135. State University of New York Press, Albany.

———, and R. W. Jefferies. 1987. A Reevaluation of the WPA Excavation of the Robbins Mound in Boone County, Kentucky. In *Current Archaeological Research in Kentucky: Volume One*, edited by D. Pollack, pp. 33–42. Kentucky Heritage Council, Frankfort.

———. 1998. The Read Archaic Shell Midden in Kentucky. *Southeastern Archaeology* 17:119–132.
Muller, J. 1997. *Mississippian Political Economy*. Plenum, New York.
Pauketat, T. R. 2004. *Ancient Cahokia and the Mississippians*. Cambridge University Press, Cambridge, UK.
Rolingson, M. A. 1998. *Toltec Mounds and Plum Bayou Culture: Mound D Excavations*. Research Series 54. Arkansas Archeological Survey, Fayetteville.
Russo, M. 1996. Southeastern Archaic Mounds. In *Archaeology of the Mid-Holocene Southeast*, edited by K. E. Sassaman and D. G. Anderson, pp. 259–287. University Press of Florida, Gainesville.
———. 2004. Measuring Shell Rings for Social Inequality. In *Signs of Power*, edited by J. L. Gibson and P. J. Carr, pp. 26–70. University of Alabama Press, Tuscaloosa.
Saunders, J. W., R. D. Mandel, C. G. Sampson, C. M. Allen, E. T. Allen, D. A. Bush, J. K. Feathers, K. J. Gremillion, C. T. Hallmark, H. E. Jackson, J. K. Johnson, R. Jones, R. T. Saucier, G. L. Stringer, and M. F. Vidrine. 2005. Watson Brake, a Middle Archaic Mound Complex in Northeast Louisiana. *American Antiquity* 70:631–668.
Smith, B. D. 1989. Origins of Agriculture in Eastern North America. *Science* 246:1566–1571.
Webb, W. S. 1941. *Mt. Horeb Earthworks Site 1 and the Drake Mound Site 11, Fayette County Kentucky*. Reports of Anthropology and Archaeology, vol. 5, no. 2. University of Kentucky, Lexington.
Willey, P., and T. E. Emerson. 1993. The Osteology and Archaeology of the Crow Creek Massacre. *Plains Anthropologist* 38:227–269.

CHAPTER 37

REENVISIONING EASTERN WOODLANDS ARCHAIC ORIGINS

DALE L. MCELRATH AND THOMAS E. EMERSON

While we have readily admitted that successive waves of people or ideas could also penetrate to the New World, we have been slow to give up the idea that some pilgrim band of elephant hunters laid the foundation of aboriginal American culture.

—D. Byers (1959:235)

FOR more than 50 years, North American archaeologists have largely accepted a simple evolutionary relationship between late Pleistocene Paleoindian societies and early Holocene Archaic societies. The conventional scenario saw small bands of big-game hunters entering the New World and passing through an ice-free corridor to spread throughout interior North America and eventually reach the tip of South America, in just a few hundred years. These were presumed to be the ancestral population for all subsequent Holocene Archaic societies. With increasing acceptance of the radiocarbon dates at Monte Verde and Meadowcroft Rockshelter, along with additional recent evidence (e.g., Paisley Cave, Topper, and Gault), this paradigm is no longer viable (Bonnischen et al. 2005).

Instead, many scholars accept New World colonization by potentially much earlier coastal populations relying on maritime resources. How, or whether, these earlier migrations are related to the Clovis phenomenon is not known. In these scenarios, the Clovis people could actually represent the "Last Americans" to arrive in North America in late glacial times. Paleoindian specialists are just now beginning to acknowledge this new version of history and assess the impact on interpretations of Clovis culture. In particular, Clovis must now be considered in a historical context as interacting with earlier, and potentially much more complex, social systems. Paleoindian peoples, instead of being pioneers of an empty landscape, may be latecomers forced by crowded coastal populations into the as-yet-unexploited midcontinental grasslands. Archaic researchers also need to assess the potential relationship between the hypothesized Pleistocene coastal maritime groups and the Early Holocene Archaic. Perhaps such groups are ancestral to Eastern Woodlands Archaic peoples.

It is clear that Paleoindian studies have reached a crossroads, with a majority of Paleoindian scholars now questioning the "Clovis First" model (Bonnischen et. al. 2005). To be sure, there are still fierce defenders of the traditional view, but even the original architect of this paradigm seems circumspect in a recent article (Haynes 2005). This issue has significant implications for modeling Early Archaic societies, depending on whether they are presumed to be an outgrowth from a common Paleoindian ancestry or an as-yet-undefined pre-Clovis maritime culture (see Anderson, Waguespack, this volume).

Peopling the New World

The antiquity of human entry into the New World has been one of the longest-running and most contentious debates in North American archaeology, with little resolution in sight. Scientists in the early 20th century, led by the famed physical anthropologist Ales Hrdlicka, were convinced people entered the New World in very recent times, perhaps a few thousand years BC. It was not until the discovery of extinct megafauna and associated artifacts at Folsom and Clovis, New Mexico and the chronometric analysis of Vance Haynes (1964) that the entry date was pushed back to about 12000 BP. However, South America researchers have for some time now, accepted dates in the 20,000–30,000 year range and have theoretically divorced themselves from their North American colleagues (Gruhn 2005), the majority of whom, until recently, defamed any radiocarbon date that exceeded 12,000 years in age. Now that this Maginot Line has been crossed, it makes sense that much earlier dates should be entertained. Since seagoing vessels were necessary to colonize Australia (minimally 45000 BP and possibly 65000 BP) and Japan (minimally 30000 BP), and northern latitude cold-weather-adapted technologies were sufficiently well developed to enable occupation of major parts of eastern Siberia by 45000 BP, it would indeed be surprising if colonization of North America's west coast had not begun by at least 30000 BP, especially since Northeast Asia and North

America were joined for lengthy periods after 50,000 years ago. The possibility—in fact, the probability—of an early coastal entry into the New World appears strong.

We thought this was a moot point for those of us studying later time periods until recently, when we began to systematically examine the nature of the Archaic in the Midcontinent (Emerson et al. 2009). We were struck with the profound differences between Early Archaic and Paleoindian lifestyles (Koldehoff and Walthall 2009; McElrath, Fortier et al. 2009) that caused us to question whether the interior Eastern Woodlands Archaic actually derived from specialized Fluted Point traditions or from earlier maritime-adapted economies. Although we are open to a movement of people from East Asia to the New World on the order of 20,000–30,000 years ago, we are willing to use the conservative benchmark of 15,000–16,000 years ago, around which some consensus has developed, as sufficient for our purpose (see Waguespack, this volume). The point of this discussion is simply that if populations of maritime-oriented groups spread along the western coastal areas of the New World in pre-Clovis times, are not these groups more likely to have been the predecessors of the Archaic populations that were present in large numbers in the New World in early Holocene times?

Although several researchers have suggested a likely coastal entry into North America (Dixon 2000; Fladmark 1979), the most persistent proponent of a coastal entry is Jon Erlandson (see Erlandson and Braje, this volume). Erlandson envisions the existence of an almost continuous near-shore "kelp highway" that would have followed the Pacific Rim from Japan along the coast of Asia to the Bering Land Bridge and down the western coast of North America, an ecological avenue that would have been attractive to maritime-oriented populations (Erlandson et al. 2007). Dixon (2000) has suggested that having reached the Isthmus of Panama, early colonizers would have easily crossed it and expanded into the Caribbean to move north and south along the Gulf coastlines of both South and North America. Unlike the traditional view presented for Clovis, the earlier maritime hunter-fisher-gatherers would be far more populous, sedentary, and perhaps socially and technologically complex. If we accept the traditional view of Clovis people as highly mobile, small-scale, hunting-gathering groups, they would have had a very specialized economy and found themselves interacting with groups who were much more numerous and complex. This scenario might mean that Clovis groups were even more analogous to modern-day Kung bushmen than realized by those who favor this outdated analogy (see Emerson et. al. 2009), particularly in the sense that the latter also depended heavily on interactions with neighboring complex societies in order to satisfy many of their needs.

Coasting into America

Archaeologists have spent decades conceptualizing how small groups of grassland specialized big-game hunter-gatherers might have populated the New World, virtually ignoring the potential impact of maritime-oriented groups who might have colonized the coastal areas of the Americas (but see Surovell 2003). Instead of the high mobility that is usually posited for hunter-gatherer groups (despite strong evidence to the contrary in temperate areas; see Binford 1980), coastal occupation might have happened at a much slower rate, and it would almost certainly have involved sedentism or at least restricted home ranges. Use of coastal resources represents one of the most ancient specialized human adaptations, identified in South Africa at 150,000 years ago; Stringer (2000) speaks of humans "coasting out of Africa" at an early date, perhaps 100,000 years ago. Stringer has argued that this specialized adaptation enabled humans to spread out of Africa along the shorelines of Arabia and into southern Asia. Low water levels during the Late Pleistocene would have allowed them to colonize Indonesia, and as Stringer (2002) points out, coastal adaptation may have buffered them from dramatic changes in plant and animal ecology that inland areas underwent during the Pleistocene.

Whether "down the coast" movement was initiated as a result of natural population growth or in response to overexploitation of preferred resources such as intertidal mollusks is not known, but a combination of the two would seem reasonable. In any event, humans seemed to have invented watercraft at some point in their coastal ventures, making the trip to Australia perhaps as early as 60,000 years ago according to several archaeologists. In any event, at 45,000 years ago there is evidence in Siberia for human habitation. At this point it gets very complicated, not only from an evidentiary point of view but also because of several scholarly positions that have been staked out and vociferously defended. The race to defend a new "earliest" date just prior to 12,000 years ago has begun, but most of the evidence seems to allow a date in excess of 15,000 years. We favor an earlier date to account for people in the interior on the time scale indicated by Paisley Cave, Gault, or Meadowcroft Rockshelter (cf. Anderson, Waguespack, this volume). But regardless of whether one favors a date of 15,000 or much earlier, one point remains the same: these groups derive from populations that were adapted to coastal life for tens of thousands of years. Rather than being simple hunter-gatherers, they likely arrived in North America with a complex social and technological organization, regardless of whether they came at 30,000 or 15,000.

This may sound like a radical proposition, but it should be quite evident from existing concepts of how and why social complexity develops. Maritime economies in certain regions have long been recognized as potentially yielding the level of abundance that will support both sedentism and large population. Moseley (1975) argues that it formed the basis for development of prehistoric Andean civilizations and in North America alone it is credited with allowing development of chiefdoms along the Northwest Coast, California coast, and Gulf coast, often without the help of domesticated plants (cf. Maschner on North Pacific, Perry, Sassaman and Randall, this volume). However, because archaeologists have started the evolutionary clock with the arrival of big-game hunters and gatherers arriving at a very late date (i.e., 12000 BP), we have wrongly assumed that complexity perforce appears much later in the New World, after the big-game hunters had time to "settle in" and begin the slow evolutionary climb.

The Changing Face of Eastern Woodlands Archaic

In reviewing the history and development of the term *Archaic* (Emerson et al. 2009), we have noted several incongruencies between the data on this period and the position vis-à-vis an evolutionary outgrowth of Clovis Culture. The term was originally coined to describe assemblages with specific diagnostic tool types in the northeast; these assemblages lacked ceramics, and Eastern Woodlands archaeologists eventually extended the term to any aceramic site. Such assemblages were said to represent a hunting-fishing-collecting lifestyle that may have been contemporaneous with ceramic-bearing ones. The term as initially suggested was criticized by prominent regional archaeologists of the day because of the connotation that the cultures depositing the assemblages were primitive—a view, in their opinion, that did not apply to the sophisticated types and variety of tools recovered from many such sites.

The first national conference on the Archaic was published in a special issue of *American Antiquity* (Byers 1959). The most influential of these articles was Melvin Fowler's interpretation of the recent excavations at Modoc Rock Shelter, in southwestern Illinois. This key site contained a radiocarbon-dated sequence of deposits from Early Archaic through Late Archaic times (8000–2000 BC), and Fowler used it as the springboard to summarize what was known about the Archaic in the Midwest and Midsouth. Fowler's discussion of the Modoc sequence forms much of the basis for our understanding of the Archaic even today, and many of his tenets were adopted by the New Archaeologists. For example, his use of the concepts of ecology and adaptation to the environment, although seldom cited by New Archaeologists, were central to their interpretation of the Archaic less than two decades later.

In the 1950s, it was a reasonable proposition (given the in situ evolutionary bias of scholars) that Paleoindian groups gave rise to the generalized Archaic patterns archaeologists were investigating, at least in the interior western United States. At the First Archaic Conference, however, the Eastern Woodlands Archaic lost much of its identity. Early archaeologists saw fishing (either maritime or freshwater) as an essential element of the Eastern Woodlands Archaic lifestyle. Unfortunately, the idea that Archaic societies were supported by hunting-*fishing*-collecting economies was sacrificed in recognizing an affinity with cultures from the Great Plains to California. As Byers concluded, "In time, archaeologists began to realize the continent-wide distribution of remains of people who appear to have been hunters and gatherers" (Byers 1959:230). The Archaic had become a panregional North American stage of development (Willey and Phillips 1955); and the most common aspect of these diverse assemblages was that they represented the remains of "hunter-gatherers," a subject that would, in a few short years under the New Archaeology paradigm, be a focus for worldwide scrutiny (see Sassaman and Randall, this volume).

It is important to note that the relationship between the Paleoindian and Archaic cultures was still considered an open question at this First Archaic

Conference. Both Byers (1959) and Fowler (1959) argued that Paleoindian and Archaic populations were separate and distinct populations because of the long period during which the two lifestyles coexisted. Fowler argued that Archaic collectors formed a later migration from Siberia, while Byers argued that both traditions stemmed from earlier population crossing(s) of the Bering Land bridge.

If the relationship between Paleoindian and Archaic cultures remained an open question in 1959, the door began to close on this thinking in 1964, with publication of a pivotal review by C. Vance Haynes, Jr., of available radiocarbon dates from Fluted Point sites. Using recently gathered radiocarbon dates presented by geologists for the closing and opening of a corridor between main ice sheets in Canada/Alaska, and comparing them with the recent dates on Fluted Point sites in the western United States, Haynes argued convincingly that Clovis sites all postdated the opening of an ice-free corridor; thus he argued that Clovis represented the "First Americans."

This scenario was quickly adopted by mainstream scholars, and when James B. Griffin, the most influential Eastern Woodland archaeologist at the time, published his famous synthesis of Eastern Woodlands archaeology in *Science* he forthrightly proclaimed, "The major themes of the prehistoric Indian occupation of Eastern North America are those of gradual cultural development, or evolution . . . from small migratory bands of hunters to agricultural societies of tribes, towns, and temples" (Griffin 1967:175). Although he seemed to leave some wiggle room for people's entry into North America by suggesting that the ice-free corridor was never completely closed after 18000 BP, and initially implying that occupation in North America could date as early as 15000 BP, later in the article Griffin adopted a more empiricist attitude, suggesting that the only hard evidence for early occupation was the Fluted Point traditions dating at about 12000 BP; he described this culture as the "initial occupation," after which there were no major migrations. In retrospect, his thinking was based not only on the available "hard evidence" and influenced by Haynes's convincing assessment (1964) of current evidence but also on more global considerations of population expansions. Thus he pointed out that migration into North America should be of similar antiquity to the initial occupation of Australia; although he did not offer a date for this, he was clearly thinking of one after 20,000 years ago. (John Mulvaney had demonstrated in the early 1960s, from his work at Kenniff Cave, that people had arrived in Australia by at least 19,000 years ago; Murray 2007:488.) Modern researchers now recognize a conservative date for occupation of Australia at 45,000 years ago, while others push it back to 60,000 years (Stringer 2002).

Conceptually, little has changed in Eastern Woodlands Archaic studies since Griffin's summary, especially in terms of the major focus on cultural evolution from hunter-gatherers to horticulturalists. This was evident in the 1983 synthesis *Archaic Hunters and Gatherers in the American Midwest* (Phillips and Brown), as well as the most recent overview, *Archaic Societies: Diversity and Complexity Across the Midcontinent* (Emerson et al. 2009). In our review chapters, however, we noted conflicts between the neo-evolutionary paradigm and emerging data on the Archaic (see also

Sassaman and Randall, this volume). In particular, the early evidence for complexity hinges on mound construction in Middle Archaic times and emphasis on fishing as an economic base (Styles and McMillan 2009). It was also observed that the data no longer supported the concept of highly mobile Early Archaic hunters traversing the uplands (e.g., Brown and Vierra 1983). In fact, the new evidence recognizes significant large, long-term Early Archaic base camps in deeply buried contexts in major river trenches (McElrath et al. 2009).

THE DALTON CHALLENGE

Perhaps the most direct assault on the concept of a gradualist Paleo–Early Archaic transition comes from careful examination of the Dalton phenomenon in the Central Mississippi valley (Emerson et al. 2009; Koldehoff and Walthall 2009). Dalton Culture as recognized in the Central Mississippi valley includes two distinct diagnostic tool types: the Dalton point and the Dalton adze (Figure 37.1). The Dalton point is reminiscent of the Clovis shape in outline but is not fluted, and it is usually larger than most fluted point types. The Dalton adze is perhaps the earliest recognizable woodworking tool in this region; use-wear analysis has led researchers to suggest that it was employed primarily for woodworking, for example, in manufacturing dugout canoes (Yerkes and Gaertner 1997). It has become clear that many of the cached Dalton points were placed with the dead, and sites yielding large numbers of caches presumably represent large cemeteries (Morse 1997).

Although Dalton Culture has traditionally been viewed as the logical segue from Paleoindian to Early Archaic in the Southeast (Smith 1986; Anderson and Sassaman 1996), Koldehoff and Walthall (2009) have argued that the Central Mississippi

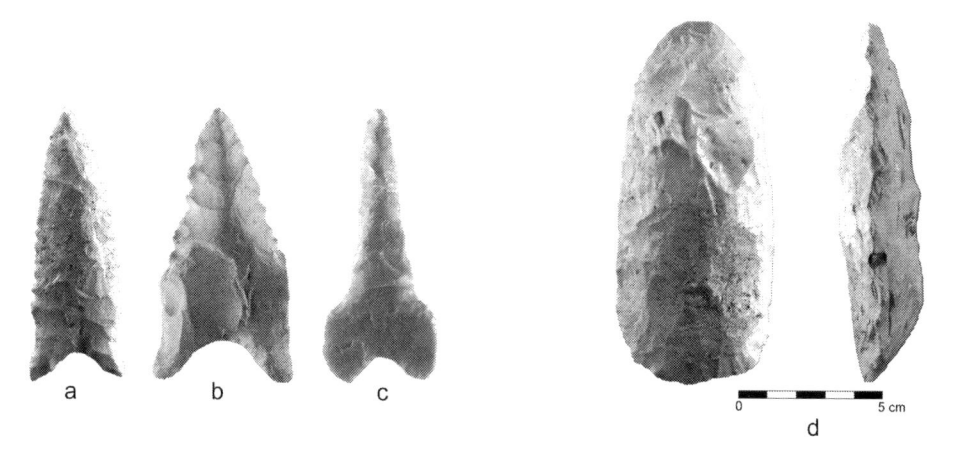

Figure 37.1 Dalton period diagnostics: (a–c) Dalton points showing resharpening sequence; (d) Dalton adze blade (dorsal and side views).

valley Dalton is a distinct phenomenon, separate from the various Dalton-like or Dalton-related cultures that occur in the greater southeast. Its northern extent is the American Bottom, where it is well represented.

John Walthall (1998) noted a major distinction between Dalton and Fluted Point sites: even though Dalton and Dalton-like materials are commonly reported from lower levels of rockshelters and cave sites throughout the southeast, Clovis points are never recovered from these contexts. Moreover, rather than constituting a logical sequence from Paleoindian to Archaic, Dalton appears to be a fully developed Archaic river-oriented culture (Emerson et al. 2009; Koldehoff and Walthall 2009). In particular, construction of dugout canoes and burial of individuals in large cemeteries show no connection with Clovis-related cultures. Previous examinations have focused on presumed technological similarities in lithic production between Clovis and Dalton cultures (Bradley 1997), but the experts disagree on the level of relatedness. It is important to point out that several generalized lanceolate point types contextually demonstrated as dating to Early and even Late Archaic times were originally thought to be later Paleoindian tools. Additionally, ambiguous dates for the ending of the late Paleoindian societies and the beginnings of Dalton Culture suggest a possible gap of several thousand years between the two, making it hard to argue for a convincing evolutionary continuity.

These considerations and others lead us to suggest that earlier Gulf Coast maritime societies constitute a more logical progenitor for Dalton Culture. Because Dalton people are river-oriented, canoe-based fishing groups, they are far removed from the grassland-oriented, highly mobile, specialized big-game hunters. A relationship has simply been assumed because Fluted Point Culture is designated as ancestral to all Archaic groups in North America. Given what we now know about earlier maritime populations, it would seem prudent to reassess the history of Early Archaic traditions in general, and Dalton in particular. If Dalton Culture derives from earlier non-Clovis coastal and riverine-related populations, then we would expect that such cultures were in part contemporaneous and may have interacted with Clovis and other Fluted Point cultures.

This new scenario of large populations prior to the arrival or indigenous development of Fluted Point grassland hunters has multiple implications for understanding both Fluted Point and Early Archaic traditions. In many ways, it may explain the more enigmatic elements of Fluted Point Culture. For example, having large preexisting breeding populations could have facilitated rapid spread of a specialized technology and potentially explain how Fluted Point technology became a phenomenon of two continents in two short centuries (Waters and Stafford 2007). Without endorsing any chosen path or mechanism for bringing Clovis to the New World, it would lend credence to a little-accepted idea that the most logical preexisting lithic tradition for Clovis rests in the Solutrean Traditions of Europe (Bradley and Stanford 2004). Importing a breeding-size population from Europe in a single historical event is a conceptually difficult undertaking, but introducing disoriented hunters, perhaps fairly regularly, to North America, is more in the realm of theoretical possibility. The time scale involved is more reasonable, and would provide enough time for this

Solutrean technology to incubate in the New World (the Solutrean ends about 5,000 years before Clovis is thought to begin), and having the skill and technology to dispatch large denizens in the continental interior might have been a welcome addition for the New World collecting and fishing folk.

Coastal groups often have access to durable media for cutting, piercing, and chopping from shell, bone, and ivory without the necessity of using chipped stone technology. Interior riverine folk may have adopted chipped stone technology from the resourceful newcomers to supplement the abundant variety of maritime natural raw elements that could be found along coastal waters but that would have been less available along interior waterways and lakes.

Conclusion

The stereotypical conditions whereby both continents are filled up by early specialized grassland hunters who are subsequently forced to turn to other economic pursuits as they expand into woodland environments no longer holds. The old "settling in" model is dead, as it should be. Unlike the highly mobile specialized hunter-gatherers whom archaeologists have modeled, the immigrating coastal groups presumably have fewer constraints on population growth or inhibitions against developing social mechanisms favoring inequality and complexity. Potential for frontier expansion without radically altering their preferred mode of subsistence would have occurred primarily in two directions, either down the coast or upriver to inland regions, with the latter refocusing on freshwater and terrestrial resources. Down-the-coast-migration for daughter communities that fission as a result of predictable social tensions would probably constitute the conservative approach to maintaining established lifestyles. This would have been available to frontier or near-frontier groups willing to leapfrog settled coastal areas. Inland migration would have happened early in the colonization episode, simply because as populations spread down the seaboard groups in earlier settled regions would find themselves further and further away from virgin coastal environs. Thus occupation of near-coastal interior North America would be, archaeologically at least, almost as ancient as the coastal areas.

Such Pleistocene-age coastal communities today would be submerged under several meters of water as the direct result of melting glaciers feeding the oceans; this is true not just for North America but for communities worldwide. This may seem like an expedient explanation for the lack of evidence to support this theory, but sufficient data are emerging that point in this direction. Aside from the evidence for pre-Clovis sites mentioned above, there is substantial evidence for sophisticated deep-water maritime fishing at an early period on the west coast (Rick et al. 2001); add to this the evidence for mass harvesting of fish in the Midcontinent (Styles and McMillan 2009) and a sophisticated level of watercraft construction in the southeast during Early Archaic times (Wheeler et al. 2003) and one begins to appreciate the antiquity involved in this economic pursuit. It is extremely unlikely that specialized mega-fauna hunters and gatherers new to the fishing lifestyle could have achieved such expertise during early Holocene times without a long tradition of maritime exploitation. From these observations, we need to rethink the ramifications of early fishing societies in the interior Eastern Woodlands vis-à-vis their specific relationship with Paleoindian hunter-gatherers and the ancient maritime coastal colonies that preceded them. We would have to conclude that the specialized large-game grassland hunters are most likely an adaptation to a crowded landscape where they expanded into the empty grasslands. Paleoindian culture represents an adaption to a sparsely populated and underused niche; it is a dead-end adaption, not the parent population of the Western Hemisphere. For this we must seek the oceanic maritime groups. Dalton Culture, as the founding Early Archaic culture in the Central Mississippi River valley, holds the key to many of the answers we seek.

REFERENCES

Anderson, D. G., and K. E. Sassaman. 1996. *The Paleoindian and Early Archaic Southeast*. University of Alabama Press, Tuscaloosa.

Binford, L. R. 1980. Willow Smoke and Dogs' Tails: Hunter-Gatherer Settlement Systems and Archaeological Site Formation. *American Antiquity* 45(1):4–20.

Bonnischen, R., B. T. Lepper, D. Stanford, and M. R. Waters (editors). 2005. *Paleoamerican Origins: Beyond Clovis*. Center for the Study of the First Americans, Texas A&M University, College Station.

Bradley, B. A. 1997. Flaked Stone Technology at the Sloan Site. In *Sloan: A Paleoindian Dalton Cemetery in Northeast Arkansas*, edited by D. F. Morse, pp. 53–57. Smithsonian Institution, Washington, DC.

———, and D. Stanford. 2004. The North Atlantic Ice-Edge Corridor: A Possible Palaeolithic Route to the New World. *World Archaeology* 36(4):459–476.

Brown, J. A., and R. K. Vierra. 1983. What Happened in the Middle Archaic? Introduction to an Ecological Approach to Koster Site Archaeology. In *Archaic Hunters and Gatherers in the American Midwest*, edited by J. L. Phillips and J. A. Brown, pp. 165–196. Academic Press, New York.

Byers, D. S. 1959. An Introduction to Five Papers on the Archaic Stage. *American Antiquity* 24(1):229–262.

Dixon, J. E. 2000. *Bones, Boats, and Bison: Archeology and the First Colonization of Western North America*. University of New Mexico Press, Albuquerque.

Emerson, T. E., D. L. McElrath, and A. C. Fortier (editors). 2009. *Archaic Societies: Diversity and Complexity Across the Midcontinent*. State University of New York Press, Albany.

Erlandson, J. M., M. H. Graham, B. J. Burque, D. Corbett, J. A. Estes, and R. S. Steneck. 2007. The Kelp Highway Hypothesis: Marine Ecology, the Coastal Migration Theory, and the Peopling of the Americas. *Journal of Island and Coastal Archaeology* 2(2):161–174.

Fladmark, K. R. 1979. Routes: Alternate Migration Corridors for Early Man in North America. *American Antiquity* 44(1):55–69.

Fowler, M. L. 1959. Modoc Rock Shelter: An Early Archaic Site in Southern Illinois. *American Antiquity* 24:257–270.

Griffin, J. B. 1967. Eastern North American Archaeology: A Summary. *Science* 156(3772):175–191.

Gruhn, R. 2005. The Ignored Continent: South America in Models of Earliest American Prehistory. In *Paleoamerican Origins: Beyond Clovis*, edited by R. Bonnischen, B. T. Lepper, D. Stanford, and M. R. Waters, pp. 199–208. Center for the Study of the First Americans, Texas A&M University, College Station.

Haynes, C. V. 1964. Fluted Projectile Points: Their Age and Dispersion. *Science* 145(3639):1408–1413.

———. 2005. Clovis, Pre-Clovis, Climate Change, and Extinctions. In *Paleoamerican Origins: Beyond Clovis*, edited by R. Bonnischen, B. T. Lepper, D. Stanford, and M. R. Waters, pp. 113–132. Center for the Study of the First Americans, Texas A&M University, College Station.

Koldehoff, B., and J. A. Walthall. 2009. Dalton and the Early Holocene Midcontinent: Setting the Stage. In *Archaic Societies of the Midcontinent*, edited by T. E. Emerson, D. L. McElrath, and A. C. Fortier, pp. 137–151. State University of New York, Albany.

McElrath, D. L., A. C. Fortier, B. Koldehoff, and T. E. Emerson. 2009. The American Bottom: An Archaic Cultural Crossroads. In *Archaic Societies: Diversity and Complexity Across the Midcontinent*, edited by T. E. Emerson, D. L. McElrath, and A. C. Fortier, pp. 317–375. State University of New York, Albany.

Morse, D. F. 1997. *Sloan: A Paleoindian Dalton Cemetery in Arkansas*. Smithsonian Institution, Washington, DC.

Moseley, M. 1975. *The Maritime Foundations of Andean Civilization*. Benjamin Cummings, Menlo Park, CA.

Murray, T. 2007. *Milestones in Archaeology: A Chronological Encyclopedia*. AVC-Clio, Santa Barbara, CA.

Phillips, J. L., and J. A. Brown (editors). 1983. *Archaic Hunters and Gatherers in the American Midwest*. Academic Press, New York.

Rick, T. C., J. M. Erlandson, and R. L. Vellanoweth. 2001. Paleocoastal Marine Fishing on the Pacific Coast of the Americas: Perspectives from Daisy Cave, California. *American Antiquity* 66(4):593–613.

Smith, B. D. 1986. The Archaeology of the Southeastern United States: From Dalton to de Soto, 10,500–500 B.P. In *Advances in World Archaeology* 5, edited by F. Wendorf and A. E. Close, pp. 1–92. Academic Press, New York.

Stringer, C. 2000. Coasting out of Africa. *Nature* 405:24–27.

———. 2002. Modern Human Origins: Progress and Prospects. *Philosophical Transactions: Biological Sciences* 357(1420):563–579.

Styles, B. W., and R. B. McMillan. 2009. Archaic Faunal Exploitation in the Prairie Peninsula and Surrounding Regions of the Midcontinent. In *Archaic Societies: Diversity and Complexity Across the Midcontinent*, edited by T. E. Emerson, D. L. McElrath, and A. C. Fortier, pp. 39–80. State University of New York, Albany.

Surovell, T. A. 2003. Simulating Coastal Migration in New World Colonization. *Current Anthropology* 44(4):581–591.

Walthall, J. A. 1998. Overwinter Strategy and Early Holocene Hunter-Gatherers in Temperate Forests. *Midcontinental Journal of Archaeology* 23(1):1–22.

Waters, M. R., and T. W. Stafford, Jr. 2007. Redefining the Age of Clovis: Implications for the Peopling of the Americas. *Science* 315(1122):1122–1126.

Wheeler, R. J., J. J. Miller, R. M. McGee, D. Ruhl, B. Swann, and M. Memory. 2003. Archaic Period Canoes from Newnans Lake, Florida. *American Antiquity* 68(3):533–552.

Willey, G. R., and P. Phillips. 1955. Method and Theory in American Archeology II: Historical Developmental Interpretation. *American Anthropologist* 57(4):723–819.

Yerkes, R., and L. M. Gaertner. 1997. Microwear Analysis of Dalton Artifacts. In *Sloan: A Paleoindian Dalton Cemetery in Arkansas*, edited by D. F. Morse, pp. 58–71. Smithsonian Institution, Washington, DC.

CHAPTER 38

POVERTY POINT

TRISTRAM R. KIDDER

Poverty Point is an archaeological site of the same name and a cultural pattern in the lower Mississippi Valley, roughly from Memphis, Tennessee, to the Gulf of Mexico. This culture is dated ca. 3600–3100 cal BP. Traditionally, Poverty Point is identified by use of fired clay cooking balls; diagnostic projectile point or knife forms; intensive consumption of lithic raw materials derived from great distances; microlithic tools; a lapidary industry emphasizing beads, gorgets, and plummets; and a hunter-gatherer subsistence pattern focused on extraction of floodplain resources, especially fish, deer, and nuts.

Poverty Point culture is best known at the Poverty Point site. The Poverty Point community encompasses an area of about 7.5 kilometers along the edge of Maçon Ridge, a Pleistocene terrace overlooking the alluvial floodplain of the Mississippi River. The community consists of a concentrated habitation zone centered on the ridges and mounds of Poverty Point, as well as more dispersed but still concentrated settlement localities surrounding the main settlement complex (Figure 38.1). The core of Poverty Point is composed of an area of roughly 200 ha and is dominated by six concentric ridges and five mounds (Figure 38.2). Two mounds located outside of the site core, Motley (on the north) and Lower Jackson (on the south), mark the boundaries of the community.

Numerous traits characterizing Poverty Point culture are widely distributed in the lower Mississippi Valley. Many sites are said to participate in this culture if they employ of one or more of the constellation of traits, most notably use of clay cooking balls or consumption of nonlocal lithic materials. As a consequence, *Poverty Point culture* is a term applied widely and with little discrimination. Because some sites, especially those physically close to Poverty Point, manifest many of the same material traits and characteristics that are seen at the type site, most researchers agree there is a core area where it is reasonable to assume these are members of a

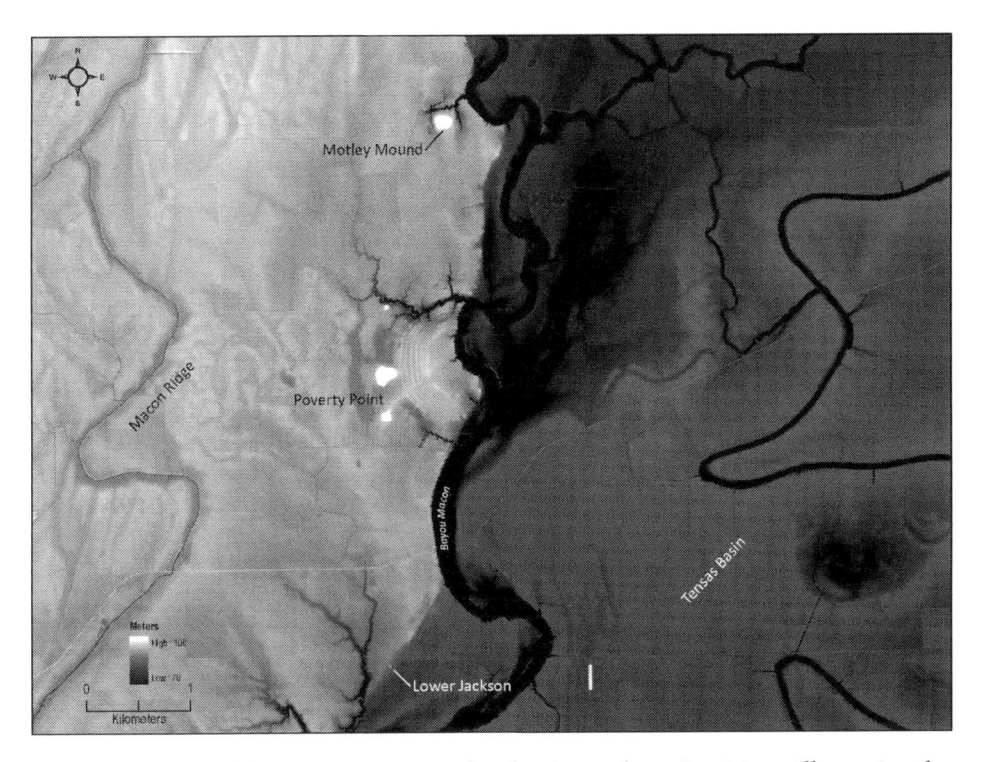

Figure 38.1 Map of the Poverty Point site locality in northeast Louisiana, illustrating the area from Lower Jackson Mound on the south to Motley on the north.

shared community. However, the notion of a geographically extensive Poverty Point culture is not tenable; not all contemporary communities share many of the settlement or material traits characteristic of the type community. Some traits (especially clay cooking balls) used to define Poverty Point culture have considerable temporal duration, making it unwise to use them as markers of participation in a shared social or political community.

The Poverty Point site is *sui generis*; understanding Poverty Point must take into account this singularity. Many characteristics of the cultural pattern at this time are also unique for their time, especially the presence of settlement hierarchies based on site size and the accumulation of long-distance exchange goods. Of course, to suggest Poverty Point is entirely unique is somewhat misleading. Poverty Point is a hunter-gatherer example of a global occurrence, the outsized central place with monument architecture that attracts people who generate novel cultural practices unlike those seen before (Alt, Lekson this volume). These sites usually appear early in cultural trajectories when population increase, technological improvements, and social innovation align to generate a regional cultural florescence. The hunter-gatherer-fisher lifestyle of the Poverty Point people is a point of departure for this unique occurrence. Because pursuit of subsistence is frequently seen as the causal force of change in hunter-gatherers, much else about these societies—especially elements assumed to generate change in agrarian societies, such as ritual, religion, social interactions, and charismatic personalities—is ignored or seen as inconsequential.

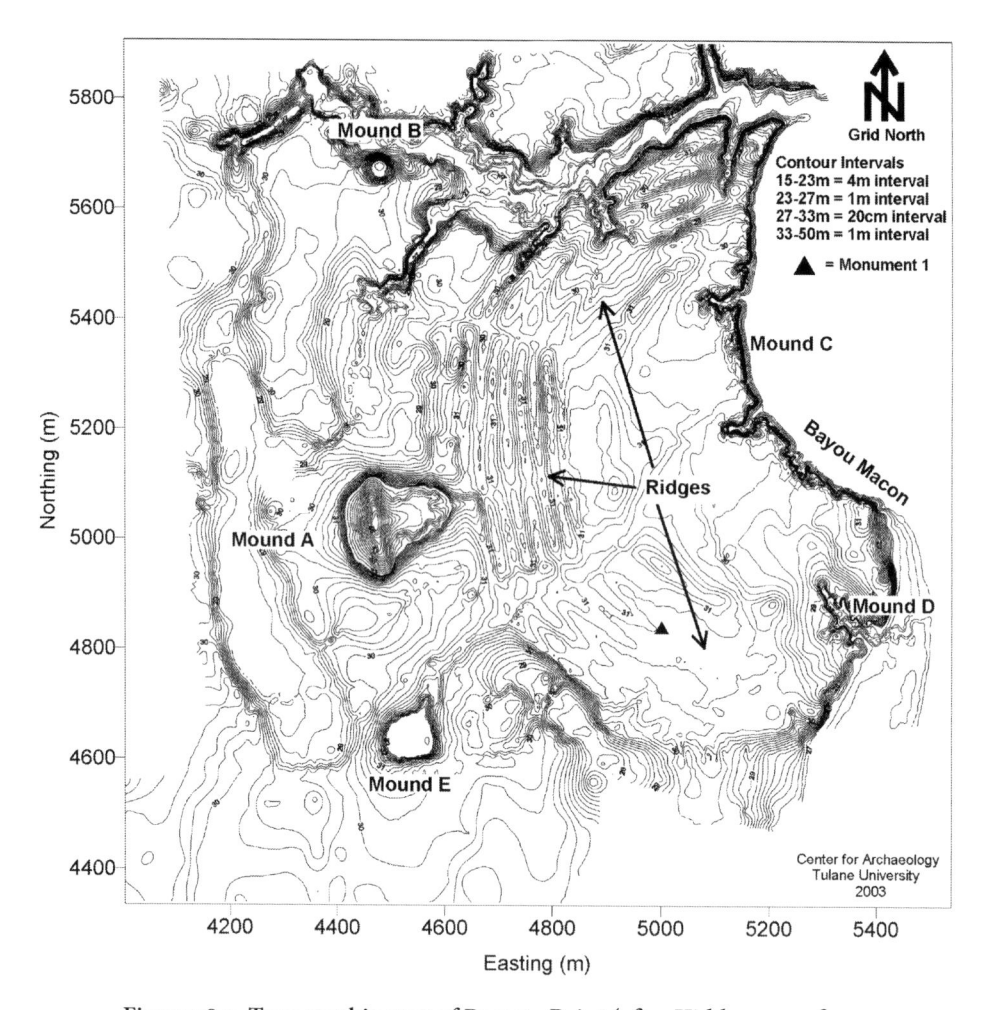

Figure 38.2 Topographic map of Poverty Point (after Kidder 2002: fig. 1; Ortmann 2003: fig. 1).

Scale

When discussing Poverty Point's uniqueness, the starting point is its spatial and architectural scale. The centerpiece of the monumental construction is Mound A (Figure 38.3). The mound is roughly T-shaped and 22 meters high at its apex, with the platform on the east standing 10 meters tall. East to west and north to south, the mound is about 210 meters at its longest. Computation of earth moving indicates it has a volume of 238,500 cubic meters. To put this into context, Mound A is the second largest earthwork in the East, exceeded only by Cahokia's Monks Mound. Similarly, if we look at total earth moved for mound construction, Poverty Point exceeds all sites, with the exception of Cahokia. Further, if we look at spatial extent, Poverty Point is more than twice as large as the next largest Poverty Point–age site

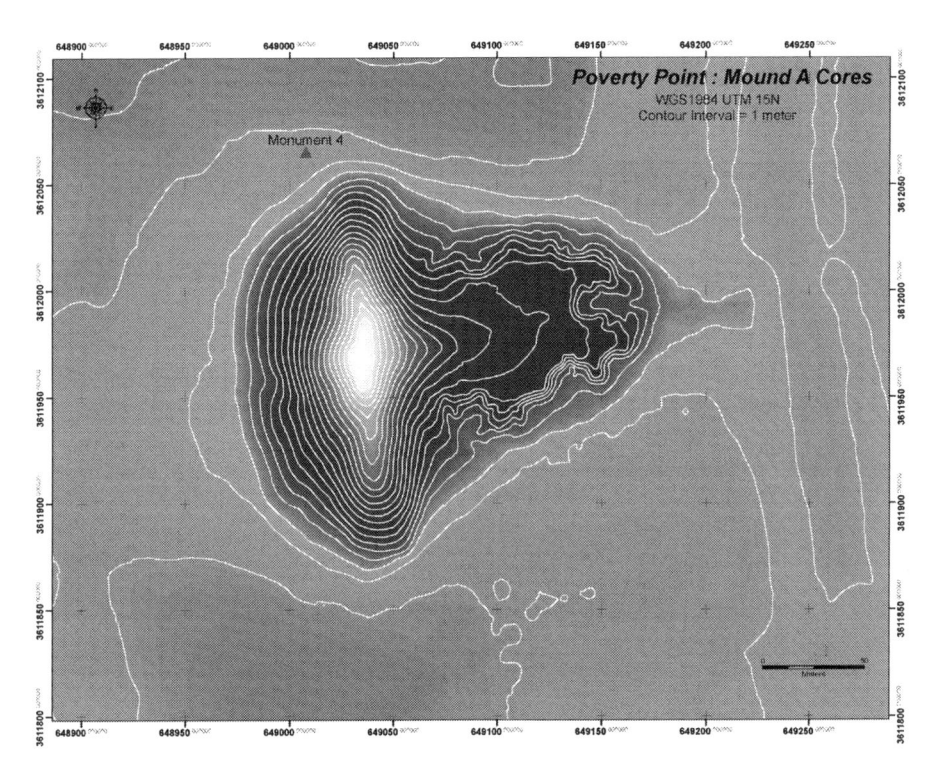

Figure 38.3 Topographic map of Poverty Point Mound A.

(Jaketown in west central Mississippi), more than 10 times larger than the next largest site, and at least 50 times larger than the average site of its time.

But spatial scale is not the only dimension of Poverty Point's singularity. Poverty Point is a stone-age site in an area where there is no stone. Despite this deficit, the site yields remarkable quantities of lithic materials. To acquire locally available chert, an inhabitant would have to travel in excess of 50 kilometers to the east or west. This is a two-day journey at a minimum, even accounting for use of waterways. Nevertheless, in almost every context at Poverty Point nonlocal chert—here defined to come from a distance in excess of 500 kilometers—predominates. Nonlocal chert is always more than 50 percent of the lithic assemblage and frequently rises to more than 75 percent. Moreover, the source areas for commonly used nonlocal lithics are frequently in excess of 1,000 kilometers distant. It is important to note that nonlocal stone is not represented by a few pieces or even a few hundred pieces. In many instances—e.g., Burlington, Cobden/Dongala, Wyandote/Harrison County gray, and novaculite, to name some of the most common chipped stone sources—the quantities found at Poverty Point are staggering. More than 70 metric tons of exotic stone is incorporated in the ridges. A single cache of steatite vessel fragments—thought to come from source areas in the southern Appalachian region—yielded 2,724 pieces representing 200–300 vessels.

Poverty Point people imported raw materials and objects that were incorporated into the functional domain—cutting tools, drills, axes, adzes, points, and the like. There was an emphasis on the mundane, but often lost in the vast quantities of functional stone is a plethora of nonutilitarian lapidary material shaped into goods that transcend functional use.

Organization and History

These issues of scale beget questions of how this society was organized. A persistent question is, What was the nature and organization of the social structure at Poverty Point and among contemporary groups composing the communities within Poverty Point's ambit? There is no obvious evidence of social inequality and political differentiation within Poverty Point or among its settlements. Even though the Poverty Point site is many times larger than nearby communities, there are no clear wealth differences between Poverty Point and outlying communities when measured by access to exotic raw materials. A perplexing aspect of this search for evidence of ranking is the lack of burials at Poverty Point; this absence is a real deficit, and not the product of acidic soil or lack of excavation.

Most contemporary analysts now conclude Poverty Point's social structure was corporate and egalitarian, adopting a model of hunter-gatherer behavior wherein resource sharing and status-suppressing behaviors inhibited formation of social or economic inequalities. Absent from this discussion is the possibility that ritual processes may have regulated behavior in ways that cloak archaeologically visible evidence of ranking or status differentiation while promoting age- or gender-based leadership positions. It is hard to imagine that political and social organization could be completely acephalous. Earth moving at the scale seen at Poverty Point, no matter how prolonged, required a relatively large labor pool and a sociopolitical system capable of orchestrating monument building while ensuring day-to-day subsistence needs.

The issue of social organization has focused on whether Poverty Point was a great town or a vacant ceremonial center. Some argue Poverty Point was a large community occupied year round by a substantial population. In this perspective, the site is a massively outsized equivalent of contemporary Late Archaic communities. Besides size, the other distinguishing factors are the earthworks. The mounds are considered to represent magical barriers to malign forces, while the ridges are loci of habitation, perhaps organized around kinship ideals. In a contrasting view, Poverty Point itself was a locus of infrequent (possibly seasonal) population aggregation by groups drawn to the site by trade fairs, which were opportunities to exchange resources and information, find mates, and socialize. The type site supported a small residential population but served largely as a vacant ceremonial center. The mounds were constructed over time as the cumulative outcome of a thousand-year process. These perspectives on Poverty Point social organization demonstrate the significance of understanding the temporal duration and population size of the site.

Most archaeologists working at Poverty Point argue the site has a short history, even though the radiocarbon data suggest a 600–800 year occupation span. Chronometric data, however, are difficult to use because of deficiencies in sample selection, laboratory problems, and lack of a consistent approach to analysis of radiocarbon dates. In the short-chronology, complex-society scenario, the site was occupied and its features constructed very rapidly, in spans ranging from several hundred years to as few as 40. The architecture is considered contemporary and the product of a plan executed by a population with local ancestry and clear ties to the Middle Archaic mound builders.

Recent research, however, suggests Poverty Point has a more complex chronology and history. There is now no evidence of direct continuity from the Middle Archaic mound builders who occupied northeast Louisiana in the period ca. 5600–4800 cal BP to the people who occupied Poverty Point. There is a hiatus in radiocarbon-dated or typologically recognized occupations ca. 4800–3600 cal BP. What happened in this interval, and what became of the Middle Archaic populations who once were so common, is at present unknown. Poverty Point's initial occupation at ca. 3600 cal BP was without local demographic precedent.

Poverty Point was first occupied ca. 3600 cal BP. The earliest secure date comes from atop the initial mound stage of Mound B. This mound was built as a sequential series of flat-topped stages, each used for a short duration before being covered by the next stage. It was located on a north-south axis that includes Mound E (which is at present undated but may be contemporary with, or earlier than, Mound B) and Lower Jackson Mound, a Middle Archaic structure dated ca. 5000 cal BP (Figure 38.1). This common axis suggests the people who built Mound B (and E?) strategically linked their founding monument with an ancestral landscape distant in both time and space.

When Mound B was erected, there was a sizable community at Poverty Point, but as yet there were no ridges or other mounds (except perhaps Mound E). This occupation dates ca. 3600–3400 cal BP. These first occupants had a fully formed Poverty Point material culture; however, there is likely a good deal more heterogeneity in the composition of the material assemblage than previously acknowledged.

The projectile point or knife styles and forms of the people who first settled Poverty Point are remarkably diverse and contrast with earlier and later settlements where only one or two styles are found at a given time. At Poverty Point there are dozens of point styles in settlement contexts, of which six types are most common. They have restricted but overlapping geographic distributions in the territories around Poverty Point. These data hint that the site's occupants were drawn from communities with differing technological practices and who had dissimilar ideas about form. This suggests the people who lived at and built Poverty Point came to the site from separate (but not necessarily far distant) regions, bringing with them diverse technologies and divergent views of society, kin, community, and cosmos.

Beginning ca. 3400 cal BP, the site was transformed. The initiation seems to be the abrupt termination of Mound B by construction of an earthen cap over the final flat-topped mound stage. First, the occupants gathered a number of hide and basket containers, filled them with dirt, and placed them on the summit of the final stage floor. Then the entire mound was covered with a mantle of dirt that entombed the mound stages; the mound was then abandoned, and the area was not used again.

At roughly the same time, the ridges were constructed. The ridges were built in a continuous process over a generation or two. In constructing the ridges, the site's inhabitants erased the existing community structure and the social relations embedded in that landscape, reconfiguring the settlement into a planned form distinct from what came before. The initial stages of Mound C are contemporary with construction of the ridges. These deposits form couplets of midden and clean fill; the couplets are distinctive for their color and texture. Then, after being used for some duration, the mound was capped ca. 3300–3200 cal B.P with a deposit of heterogeneous sediment containing abundant artifacts.

Mound A was built last. Prior to construction of the mound, the land surface consisted of a swamp 1–2 meters deep. The vegetation was burned off ca. 3342–3165 cal BP. Once burned, the swamp was instantly buried beneath a thin layer of gray-to-white pure silt. The rest of the mound was then immediately erected using multicolored soils.

Evidence that the mound was built rapidly comes from several sources. The initial stage was placed over submound deposits immediately after the vegetation was burned. Intact uncarbonized roots and other plant parts were sealed from oxidation and decomposition. The boundary between the underlying dark pre-mound deposit and the initial light-colored mound stage is sharp; there is no bioturbation evident in this initial stage or between these deposits. The main stage was loaded so quickly the underlying premound soils were extruded through the initial-stage deposit as the weight of the main mound squeezed the still-plastic swamp sediments upward. The main stage was constructed using loess-derived silt, which erodes readily; yet we do not have any indication of erosion or weathering-related displacement of soils. Rainfall in northeast Louisiana averages 11.35 centimeters per month. There have only been two months with no rainfall in the period monitored by the instrument record. Because there is no probability for two consecutive months without rain, we believe the mound had to be erected in a short period of time. If it had been constructed over a longer span or in multiple stages, we would have expected evidence of erosion, bioturbation, soil formation, or signs of a construction pause, none of which was found.

Rapid construction of Mound A provides a window for estimating the population necessary to create such an edifice. Previous attempts to reconstruct population size assumed construction was a gradual process (ranging from 40 to 1,000 years). Thus even though the earthmoving at Poverty Point is impressive in total volume, measured over many years the required population dwindles to a small number. Our data indicate a minimum labor force of 1,019 individuals was required, assuming the mound took 90 days to build. Given a ratio of three dependents for every laborer, we arrive at a minimum population of slightly more than 4,000 persons at Poverty Point for a roughly 90-day period. Such a large population is well in excess of any known hunter-gatherer population and suggests the labor catchment for construction of Mound A required workers drawn from communities over an area in excess of the estimated 1,800 square kilometer area of Poverty Point's direct cultural influence. Moreover, Mound A is only one of a number of earthworks at the site.

Although the ridges were likely surfaces on which people lived, the function of Mound A is unknown. There is no evidence on or within the mound of structures, features, or occupation surfaces, and no occupation debris associated with mound-top activities is found on the flanks of the mound or immediately around it. Mound A has always been understood as a ritual feature. It was first considered an effigy of a bird flying west, and later as a representation of earth-island, the cosmological center of creation. Our work emphasizes this ritual aspect of the mound and situates it in the Native American mythological tradition. The structured sequence of construction—burial of the wet, dark, premound swamp with light-colored sediments and rapid construction of the main stage over this—can be read as a recapitulation of the historical myth of Emergence or of Earth Diver. The temporal gap between historical myth and construction of Mound A renders a specific interpretation moot. We hypothesize the building of this earthwork represents an enactment of ritual where the builders covered the watery chaos of precreation and erected a monument symbolizing the triumph of creation over the forces of chaos. This narrative is also written in the entire site plan. Mound A is situated astride an axis that links the Middle Archaic Lower Jackson site—erected 1,500 years before Poverty Point's mounds were started—to Mound B, the earliest monument at Poverty Point. In placing Mound A on this axis, the builders were engaging an ancestral history and exploiting the authority of an even earlier origin story.

Discussion

Poverty Point itself is an anomaly, but it has a context that gives further credence to the notion that the site's functions and the activities of its inhabitants (or visitors) are unique in its time. Most consider Poverty Point the nucleus of regional developments. In many cases, centers develop first and are followed, in time, by developments in outlying regions. The history of Poverty Point seems backwards, however. Here the smaller mounds come first, with the biggest last; further, the earliest sites manifesting Poverty Point-like material characteristics are distant from Poverty Point. In contrast to a model that would have Poverty Point at the center of a web of culture radiating out from the center, the reverse seems true: Poverty Point is the center of a collapsing network that draws into itself through time. There is however, a wider context that should give us pause to think how we conceive Poverty Point, and indeed the history of eastern North America.

Prior to Poverty Point—or at least prior to ca. 4000 cal BP—Archaic peoples of the Southeast were loosely integrated by complex, overlapping, and geographically widespread networks of interactions, mediated by exchange of nonutilitarian ritual goods. Exchange networks in the Middle Archaic—notably the Benton Interaction sphere, bannerstone exchange along the eastern seaboard, bone pin trade across the southeast-midwest border, and the stone bead network in the western southeast—are common. Further evidence of emerging complexity and increasing emphasis on territorial persistence is evident in mound building. In parts of the southeast, notably Florida and the lower Mississippi Valley, mound building was relatively common, especially compared to Poverty Point times.

Mounds built during the Middle Archaic were generally of similar sizes, and some were built incrementally over multiple centuries (see also Lightfoot and Luby, this volume). Even though across the southeast we can detect emergence of central places on the landscape—some associated with earthworks and others with places where the dead were interred—in no case can we identify a singular node of social, political, or material interaction. In most every instance, these central places—e.g., Indian Knoll in Kentucky, Watson Brake in Louisiana, Hoor's Island in Florida, or Black Earth in Illinois, to name only a few—accumulated over time, and the markers of complexity emerge slowly and are rare. Some areas may have participated more fully in these exchange systems—e.g., the Green River—but this may be a reflection of demography and the accidents of history as much as economic or social power (see also Sassaman and Randall, this volume).

There is a shift in the dynamics of interaction in the period 4800–3600 cal BP. The networks of exchange that integrated the Archaic of the East disappear and are for a period hard to detect. In time, however, they are replaced by a new phenomenon focused on and exemplified at Poverty Point. At this time Poverty Point and related contemporary sites in the lower Mississippi Valley (e.g., Claiborne, Jaketown) are the only nodes of long-distance or rare trade goods exchange. Poverty Point is indisputably the singular center of raw material circulation; goods in large quantities flow in but nothing tangible flows out. There is no material signal of Poverty Point interaction at sites within the contemporary exchange catchment, which encompasses much of the southeast and midcontinent. Thus, however manifest, Poverty Point and its contemporary satellite centers enfold into themselves the role(s) once filled by the exchange networks that twined together earlier Archaic societies of the east.

Conclusion

Fully explaining Poverty Point is at present beyond our reach. We are beginning to contextualize the history through establishing a fine(r)-grain chronology at the type site and among contemporary settlements. Scholars in the field conceive Poverty Point in a framework defined by classical hunter-gatherer theory; this theory privileges the material and economic and has never embraced a notion that hunter-gatherers have a particularly complex worldview or ritual cosmology. Even Poverty Point, whose uniqueness is well known and widely acknowledged, has been seen as just a very big version of contemporary Late Archaic sites; its primary distinction is its magnitude. Exchange is argued to be the motivator for the site's size and the complexity of its material culture.

There is, however, more to Poverty Point than contemporary theory indicates. Perhaps the most crucial insight of recent work is recognizing the singularity of the site and its complicated history. Poverty Point is not just a bigger version of its contemporaries; in the context of its time it is entirely *sui generis*. Debates dichotomizing the site as a great town or vacant ceremonial center obscure nuances and variability of Poverty Point's social, political, and ritual organization and history. Our challenge is to overcome biases about what constitutes hunter-gatherer complexity. Complexity is almost always framed by economic or political considerations. In most models, hunter-gatherer complexity does not embed possibilities that these people had complex ritual practices, embarked on pilgrimages, constructed cults and cult centers, manifested cosmologies that transcended vast swaths of space, or had charismatic leaders. The populace living at Poverty Point and those living within the sphere of Poverty Point's influence may have done some or even all of these things. These people undoubtedly engaged in activities and behaviors far more complex and dynamic than anything we have conceived. The people who built and lived at Poverty Point surely did something out of the ordinary. Extraordinary sites require historically contextualized explanations to account for their differences. It is time we rethink Poverty Point and explore the exceptional possibilities of the site and its history.

REFERENCES

Kidder, T. R. 2002. Mapping Poverty Point. *American Antiquity* 67:89–101.

Ortmann, A. L. 2003. *Project 2/01: Results of 2001 and 2002 Field Seasons at Poverty Point*. Report on File, Louisiana Division of Archaeology, Baton Rouge.

Suggested Reading

Gibson, J. L. 2000. *Ancient Mounds of Poverty Point: Place of Rings*. University Press of Florida, Gainesville.

———. 2007. "Formed from the Earth of That Place": The Material Side of Community at Poverty Point. *American Antiquity* 72:509–523.

———, and P. J. Carr (editors). 2004 *Signs of Power: The Rise of Complexity in the Southeast*. University of Alabama Press, Tuscaloosa.

Jackson, H. E. 1991. The Trade Fair in Hunter-Gatherer Interaction: The Role of Intersocietal Trade in the Evolution of Poverty Point Culture. Occasional Papers 9, *Between Bands and States*, edited by S. A. Gregg, pp. 265–286. Center for Archaeological Investigations, Southern Illinois University, Carbondale.

Kidder, T.R. 2011. Transforming Hunter-Gatherer History at Poverty Point. In *Hunter-Gatherer Archaeology as Historical Process*, edited by K. E. Sassaman and D. H. Holley, Jr., pp. 95–119. University of Arizona Press, Tucson.

———, and K. E. Sassaman. 2009. The View from the Southeast. In *Archaic Societies: Diversity and Complexity Across the Midcontinent*, edited by T. Emerson, D. McElrath, and A. Fortier, pp. 667–694. State University of New York Press, Albany.

Webb, C. H. 1982. *The Poverty Point Culture*. 2nd ed., rev. Geoscience and Man 17. Geoscience Publications, Department of Geography and Anthropology, Louisiana State University, Baton Rouge.

CHAPTER 39

ORIGINS OF THE HOPEWELL PHENOMENON

DOUGLAS K. CHARLES

THE Hopewell phenomenon of the American Midwest is known for its geometric earthworks and burial mounds, importation and exchange of exotic materials, skilled crafting of objects, widely shared symbolism and design motifs, and elaborate funerary practices. The first decade of this century has produced a burst of scholarship reassessing our understanding of Hopewell and the Middle Woodland period (e.g., Applegate and Mainfort 2005; Byers 2004; Carr and Case 2005; Case and Carr 2008; Charles and Buikstra 2006; Charles et al. 2004; Connolly and Lepper 2004; Greber 2003; Seeman 2004; Van Gilder and Charles 2003). Abrams (2009) presents a comprehensive overview of the current state of Hopewell research, particularly in the northern region comprising the modern states of Illinois, Indiana, and Ohio (Figure 39.1). The material culture associated with the Hopewell phenomenon is generally recognized, but the social, economic, and political dynamics of Hopewell have yet to be definitively articulated.

Archaeologists approaching Hopewell from a processual, behavioral, selectionist, or postprocessual approach (e.g., Hegmon 2003; Hodder 2001) tend to focus on explanation or interpretation and introduce particular theoretical and methodological perspectives that shape their views of the phenomenon. What most analysts share, whatever their orientation, is a conception (or at least presentation) of Hopewell as a uniform and singular entity, in which any temporal and spatial variation in the manifestations of the phenomenon is largely ignored (save perhaps an Ohio–non-Ohio distinction). The phenomenon was undoubtedly more dynamic than these perspectives would suggest, and an understanding of Hopewell will entail appreciation of both the agency of the participants and the historical and environmental conditions within which they found themselves.

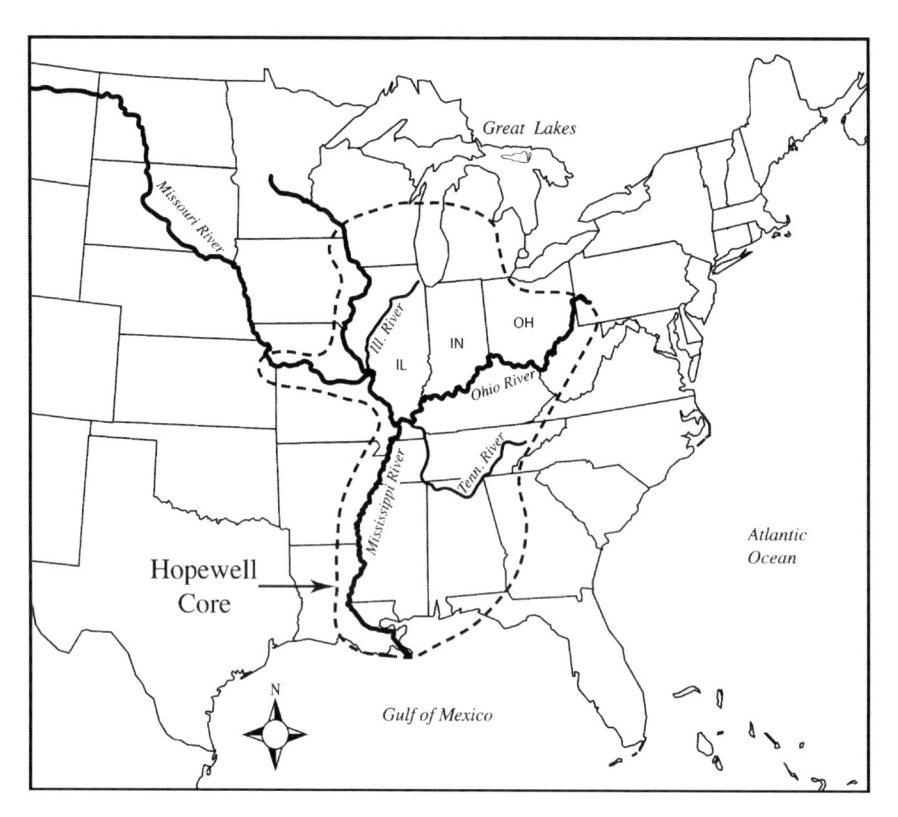

Figure 39.1 Core area of the Hopewell phenomenon, ca. 1800 BP.

Chronology and Geography of Hopewell

The chronological ranges assigned to Hopewell by archaeologists vary from 300 to 500 years, generally falling between 100 BC and AD 400, meaning the phenomenon lasted 12 to 25 generations, depending on the time span specified and whether generation length is set at 20 or 25 years. In any case, the material culture employed and its meanings and uses are likely to have varied substantially over that period. Greber (2005) has recently resurrected James Stoltman's point (1978) that in most areas the imprecision of our dates extends to a century or more, further complicating chronological reconstruction. Simply sorting out the published radiocarbon dates across the geographic range of the Hopewell phenomenon—calibrated or not, quality and nature of stratigraphic contexts, specifically Hopewell rather than Middle Woodland—will be a major task.

Geographically, the extent of just the core of Hopewell (Figure 39.1) covers well over a million square kilometers (or over 500,000 square miles), and this area doesn't encompass the sources of such materials as obsidian, copper, and mica that circulated through the Hopewellian world. Furthermore, the distribution of what we count as Hopewell participation, contact, or influence surely varied temporally. Figure 39.2

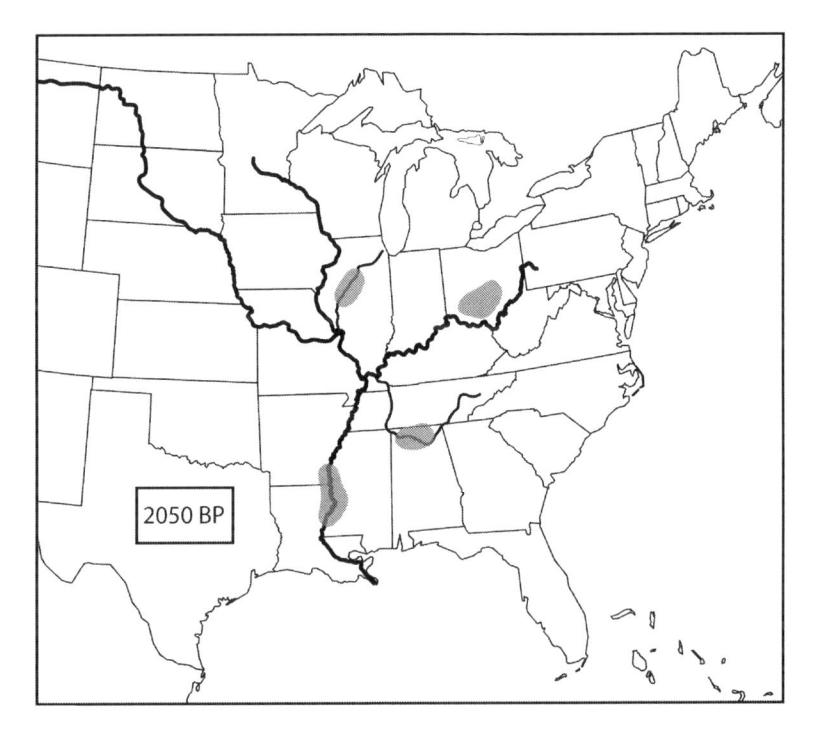

Figure 39.2 A–F Hypothetical expressions of Hopewell material practice at 100-year intervals.

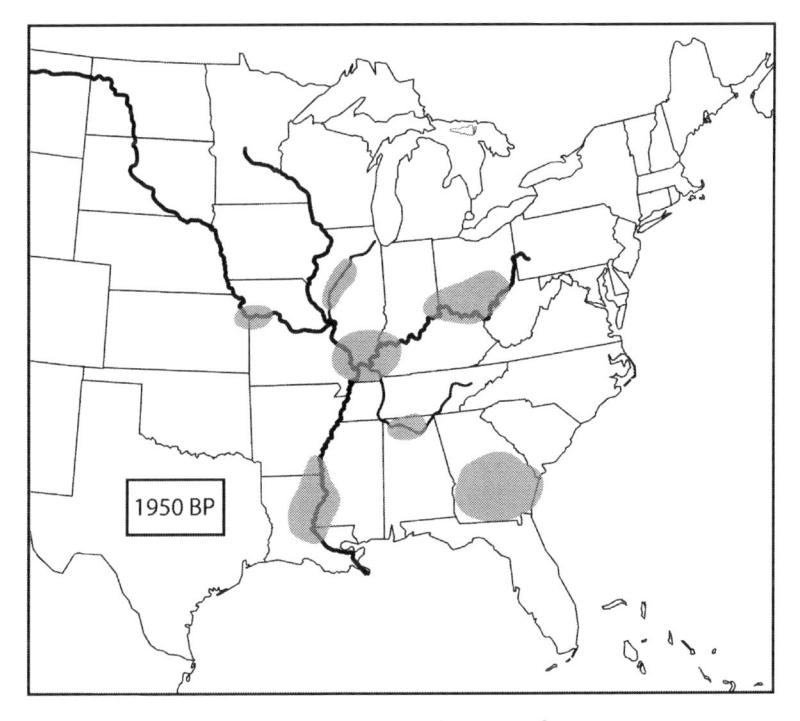

Figure 39.2 A–F (*continued*)

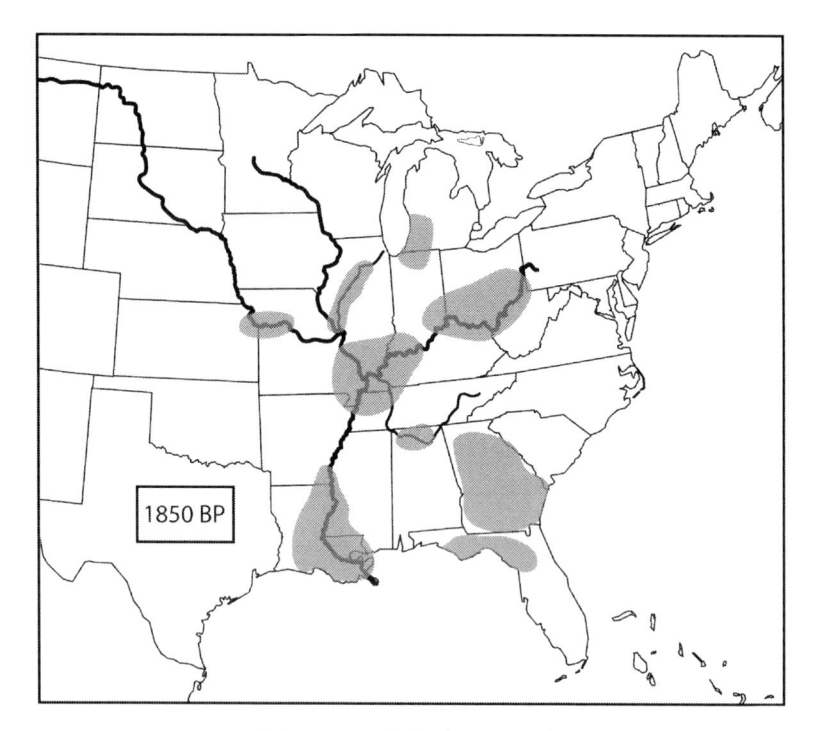

474   MIDSOUTH AND SOUTHEAST

1850 BP

Figure 39.2 A–F (*continued*)

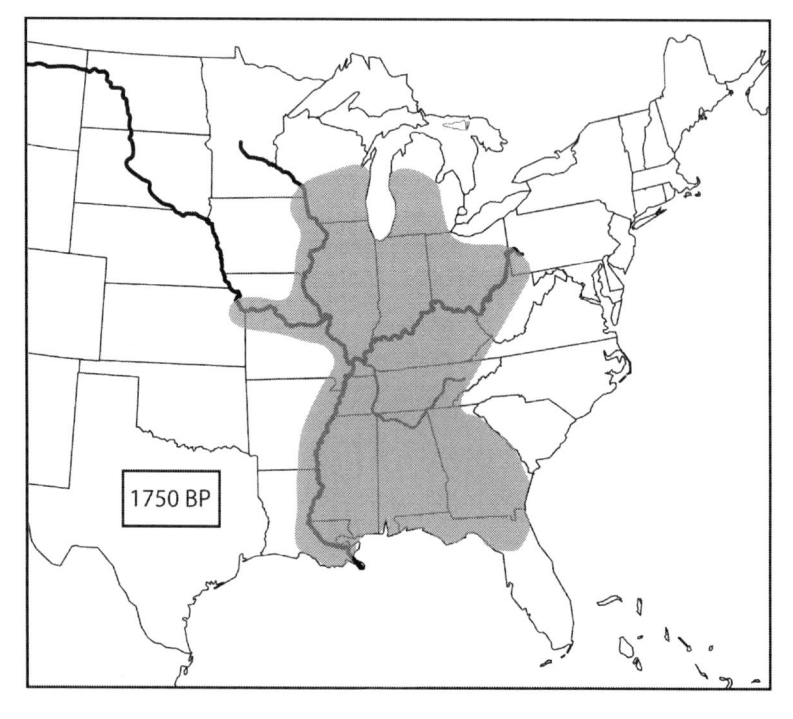

1750 BP

Figure 39.2 A–F (*continued*)

ORIGINS OF THE HOPEWELL PHENOMENON

Figure 39.2 A–F (*continued*)

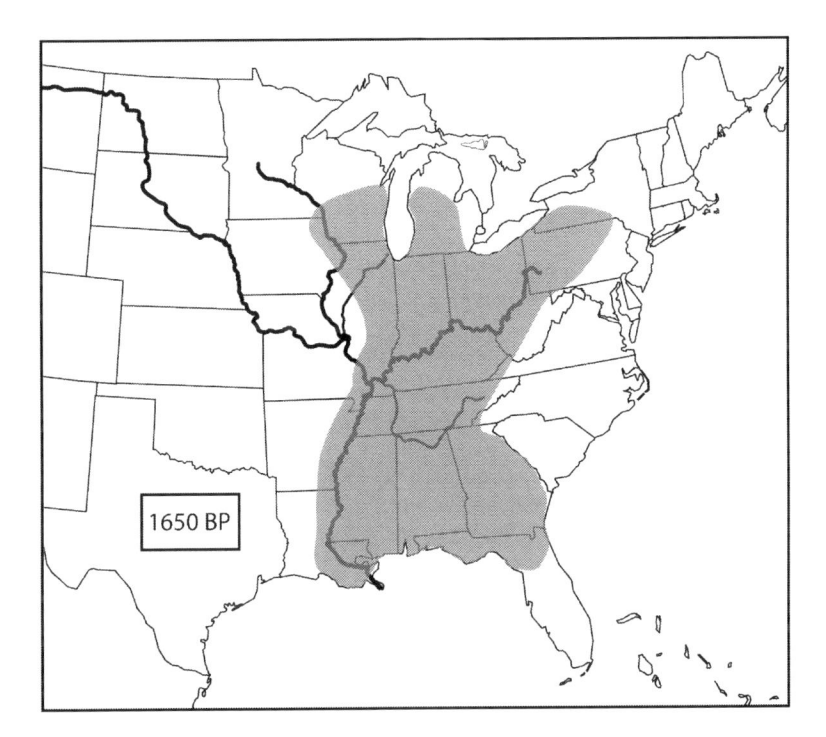

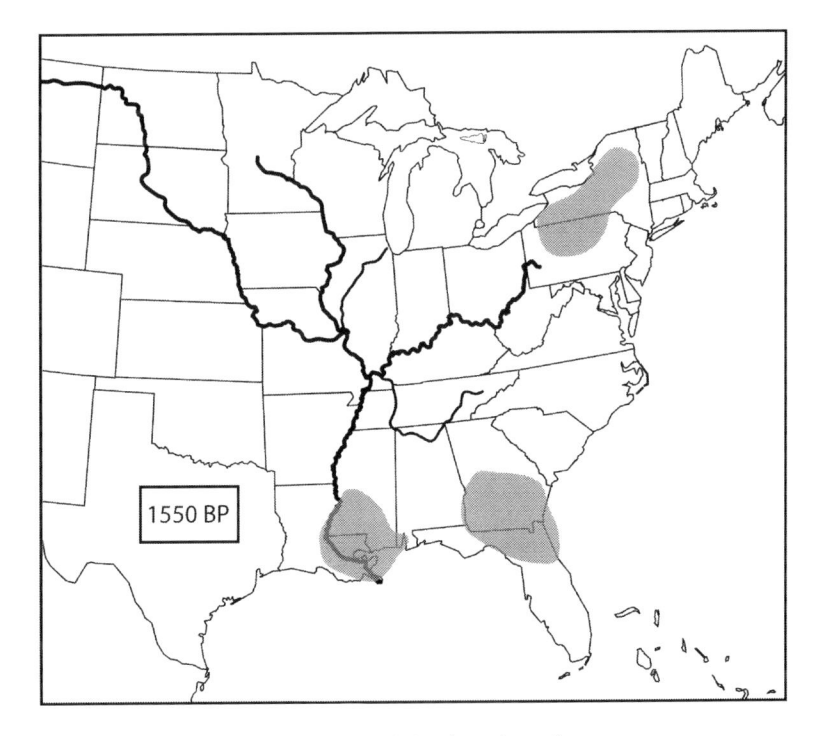

Figure 39.2 A–F (*continued*)

presents a hypothetical sequence, at 100-year intervals, of the area encompassed by the Hopewell phenomenon. At a finer scale, even the peak of Hopewell around AD 200–300 would have contained lacunae representing zones of minimal participation. Standard maps like Figure 39.1 portray only the general extent of Hopewell expression at a particular point in time, or more likely over a span of time. A single characterization of Hopewell is an inadequate expression of the dynamic chronological and geographic distributions of Hopewellian practice, and much additional research and sorting and compilation of existing data will be necessary before our descriptions approach the prehistoric reality.

The Hopewell Phenomenon as Practice

Robert Hall has argued that the Calumet ceremonialism of Plains tribes is historically related to elements of the Hopewell phenomenon:

> Calumet ceremonialism . . . functioned on an intertribal, political level to establish and maintain peaceful relationships between unrelated groups by creating fictions of kinship between the principals involved. It functioned in the area of economic adaptation by cushioning villages or bands against the dangers of crop failure or changes in the availability of game animals, doing so by establishing friendly patterns of exchange with neighbors upon whom one might fall back in time of need. And it functioned at the social level by providing means by which a capable and worthy person could rise in status through personal achievements. It is not difficult to imagine a similar network of relationships among Hopewell societies [Hall 1997:156–157].

Seen in this light, the Hopewell phenomenon arose through the practices of individuals and groups (Charles et al. 2004). Certainly those individuals buried in Hopewell mounds or cremated in Hopewell facilities were incorporated into Hopewell in death, whether or not they participated in life, but beyond that, individual participation is difficult to observe archaeologically. Collectivities of people were also engaged in the Hopewell phenomenon. Earthwork and burial sites created by these collectivities furnish the majority of the deposits of material culture through which Hopewell is known.

We may refer to at least some of these groups of people as communities. Over the last half century, *community* has been defined theoretically in terms of structural-functional, historical-developmental, ideational, and interactional models (Yaeger and Canuto 2000:2). These need not be mutually exclusive categories. In a comparison of southern Ohio, southern Indiana, and western Illinois, Ruby et al. (2005) have defined three hierarchical but linked categories of Hopewellian communities: residential, sustainable, and symbolic. *Residential communities* are groups of individuals and families who regularly live, work, and interact in physical proximity. *Sustainable communities* are associations of residential—or segments of residential—communities that are sufficiently large to foster routine networks for exchange of mates and food or other resources, negotiation of collections rights, etc. Sustainable communities have longer-term stability than is the case for smaller residential communities. *Symbolic communities* are based on voluntary or hereditary memberships manifested through shared symbolic and ritual forms; they may encompass or cross-cut residential and sustainable communities in various ways. Members of these several communities presumably engaged with the objects and symbolism we term Hopewell in quantitatively and qualitatively different ways. Hopewellian (or probably more accurately Middle Woodland) residential communities appear to have been predominantly small hamlets (Smith 1992). The Hopewellian earthwork and mound complexes probably indicate the existence of symbolic communities. The larger of the sites were potentially involved in sustainable community formation and maintenance, while the smaller sites may have connected lineages living in scattered hamlets.

The Hopewell Environment

The communities most engaged in the Hopewell phenomenon were located within the area indicated in Figure 39.1. But again, not all communities within this area participated equally, or at all. Furthermore, Hopewell "influence," for lack of a better term, extended beyond the area demarcated. We can, however, make more precise delineations. Braun (1987) argued that the Middle Woodland period was marked by the coalescence of populations into the major river valleys of the American Midwest. More precisely, it would seem that although the rivers were important, access to diverse soil-, rainfall-, and temperature-based ecozones was equally vital.

Figure 39.3 is based on EPA-designated Ohio and Indiana Level IV ecoregions (http://www.epa.gov/wed/pages/ecoregions/ohin_eco.htm) with an overlay of the Ohio Hopewell polities and associated earthwork sites as defined by Pacheco and Dancey (2006); see also Carr 2008:42–53). Sites are not concentrated in the Ohio River valley, but in eastern Ohio they are predominantly situated along secondary rivers transecting the boundary between the glaciated and unglaciated zones. The eastern Low Lime Drift Plain portion of the Erie/Ontario Drift Plain is largely characterized by a rolling landscape distinct from the unglaciated, stream-dissected Western Alleghany Plateau. In central and southwestern Ohio, sites cluster along the boundary between the Loamy, High Lime Till Plains and either the unglaciated zone or the Pre-Wisconsinan Drift Plains. The Till Plains are dominated by soils that developed from loamy, limy, glacial deposits and are typically better draining and more fertile than the soils of the Drift Plains.

There seems to be little evidence of occupation across the heavily dissected terrain of the south-central Interior Plateau of Indiana. The Mann site, more in line

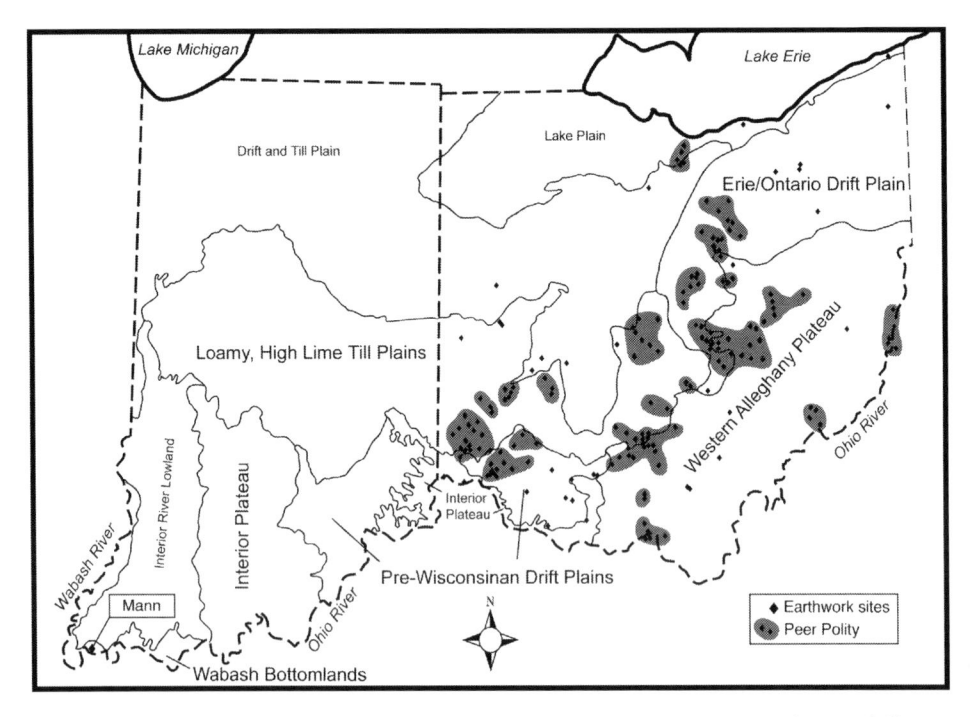

Figure 39.3 Distribution of Hopewell sites in Ohio and Indiana as they relate to different ecoregions.

with Braun's assertion, is located in the Wabash Bottomlands of the Ohio River valley, a region with a pronounced Mississippian-type biotic assemblage where, historically, significant numbers of waterfowl overwintered and where floodplains were seasonally inundated (Figure 39.3). Other important Hopewell manifestations are similarly found along the major rivers. For example, Trempealeau lies along the Mississippi River in the Driftless Area of southwestern Wisconsin, Havana originated along the Illinois River in the same Interior River Lowland (Level III) ecoregion that the Crab Orchard Tradition (including the Mann site) occupies, Marksville is focused on the Mississippi Alluvial Plain, and Copena is situated along the Tennessee valley where it dissects the southern margin of the Interior Plateau ecoregion. Highly productive and diverse combinations of floodplain and upland resources characterize these areas.

Significant spatial patterns appear at smaller scales as well. In the vicinity of the Paint Creek-Scioto River junction in southern Ohio, Early Woodland Adena (ca. 500 BC–AD 0) mound sites are widely scattered across the region, suggesting dispersed population. Hopewell mounds, on the other hand, are clearly concentrated in the river and stream valleys (Seeman and Branch 2006:figures 6.4 and Figure 6.5). In the lower Illinois valley, the earliest ceramics and burial mounds are in the north end of the valley, although there are a few habitation sites and mounds with early dates farther south (Charles 1992b; King et al. 2011). Looking just at the distribution of the major ceremonial complexes, one sees a clear north to south chronological trend moving down the valley from the Naples Russell-Elizabeth complex to Mound House, to Kamp, to Peisker. The Early and early Middle Woodland periods in the American Bottom of the Mississippi River valley are characterized by repeated incursions into a sparsely inhabited floodplain by small, transient populations from surrounding regions, including the Black Sand, Marion, Morton, Havana, and Crab Orchard phases (Farnsworth and Emerson 1986; Fortier 2001). Substantial Middle Woodland populations were not present until after 1900 BP, with the appearance of the Havana/Hopewell Holding phase (Fortier 2001; Fortier et al. 1989).

Origin (and End) of the Hopewell Phenomenon

The general presumption is that Hopewell was a development out of Early Woodland cultures. The most obvious connection is in Ohio between what has been termed Adena and Hopewell, although the geographic and chronological relationships of the two phenomena are not straightforward (Applegate and Mainfort 2005). Although there is cultural continuity from the Early into the Middle Woodland period, there is also a largely overlooked and potentially complicating scenario that bears scrutiny.

Kidder (2006) has compiled a large number of radiocarbon dates from archaeological sites in the lower Mississippi valley, southeastern Missouri, and the Upper Tennessee/Little Tennessee regions. In all three areas, there was a marked break between Late Archaic and Early Woodland dates corresponding to a major worldwide climatic episode ca. 3000–2600 BP. The proximate cause of this event was "a change in galactic cosmic ray intensity and solar irradiation possibly amplified by variations in the earth's geomagnetic field. Analysis of $\Delta^{14}C$ data indicates a notable decrease in solar radiation that is implicated in a massive reorganization of global and ocean circulation systems" (Kidder 2006:212). The result in Eastern North America was a period of cooler and wetter weather; "[a]ll or at least most of the Mississippi River basin was evidently affected and parts of the basin experienced floods of historically unprecedented size and duration" (Kidder 2006:216). Those cultures we identify as Archaic disappeared from the valleys at this time—including, in the lower Mississippi valley, the Poverty Point culture.

Fifteen years earlier, Hajic (1990) described this period of flooding in the lower Illinois River valley, and though there were indications of a large-scale climate episode, the high-resolution climate data available to Kidder did not yet exist. Ceramic and mortuary data from this region clearly demonstrate an occupational hiatus at this time, extending through most of the Early Woodland period (Farnsworth and Emerson 1986). Hajic (1990) noted that the lower Illinois channel stabilized by 2700 BP, and the natural levee and yazoo stream systems stabilized shortly thereafter.

Alluvial and colluvial fans stabilized and the yazoo system was largely in filled by 2100 BP. From this point forward, the river valley was more or less what we see today. Van Nest (1997, 2006) has more recently documented continued, if less intense, flooding through the Early Woodland into the Middle Woodland period. One may infer from the Illinois valley data that conditions conducive to permanent reoccupation of the floodplains did not follow immediately upon the end of the climate episode Kidder cites. In other words, the impact of the episode extended much longer in time, and the geographic correspondence of the core of Hopewell and the Eastern Woodland portion of the Mississippi drainage (Figure 39.1) is not coincidental.

Implicit in Hall's argument (1997) is the notion that Hopewellian and Plains Calumet ceremonialism were fundamentally social, economic, and political in nature (Charles et al. 2004). Put in Hall's terms, the question of Hopewell origins becomes, Why did individual status, subsistence buffering, and political alliance formation and maintenance suddenly become so important in the Mississippi River drainage beginning around 2100 BP? Archaic populations had abandoned the highly diverse and productive riverine ecozones nearly a millennium before, when these areas became unfit for occupation during an episode of global climate change. The answer to the question is that what we call Hopewell represents the period of intense socioeconomic and political activity that developed as previously widely dispersed residential communities converged on and actively reclaimed the again-inhabitable floodplains of the Mississippi River and its second- and third-order tributaries and forged new sustainable and symbolic communities. The chrono-geographic variation in expression of the Hopewell phenomenon reflects the variability across the region as different riverine systems attained their modern relative states of equilibrium.

Likewise, the end of Hopewell was not a collapse, but rather the diminishing and disappearance of ritual and exchange practices as the floodplain environments and demographic influx stabilized, again varying regionally. Tribal kinship networks were established, supplanting ritual as the primary medium for social and economic negotiation (Charles et al. 2004). Understanding the origins and subsequent history of the Hopewell phenomenon requires that both the practices of the participants and the conditions in which they found themselves be explored.

REFERENCES

Abrams, E. M. 2009. Hopewell Archaeology: A View from the Northern Woodlands. *Journal of Archaeological Research* 17:169–204.

Applegate, D., and R. C. Mainfort Jr. (editors). 2005. *Woodland Period Systematics in the Middle Ohio Valley*. University of Alabama Press, Tuscaloosa.

Braun, D. P. 1987. Coevolution of Sedentism, Pottery Technology, and Horticulture in the Central Midwest, 200 B.C.–A.D. 600. Center for Archaeological Investigations

Occasional Papers 7, *Emergent Horticultural Economies of the Eastern Woodlands*, edited by W. F. Keegan, pp. 153–181. Southern Illinois University, Carbondale.

Byers, A. M. 2004. *The Ohio Hopewell Episode: Paradigm Lost and Paradigm Gained*. University of Akron Press, Akron, OH.

Carr, C. 2008. Environmental Settings, Natural Symbols, and Subsistence. *The Scioto Hopewell and Their Neighbors: Bioarchaeological Documentation and Cultural Understanding*, edited by D. T. Case and C. Carr, pp. 41–100. Kluwer Academic/Plenum, New York.

———, and D. T. Case (editors). 2005. *Gathering Hopewell: Society, Ritual, and Ritual Interaction*. Kluwer Academic/Plenum, New York.

Case, D. T., and C. Carr (editors). 2008. *The Scioto Hopewell and Their Neighbors: Bioarchaeological Documentation and Cultural Understanding*. Kluwer Academic/Plenum, New York.

Charles, D. K. 1992. Woodland Demographic and Social Dynamics in the American Midwest: Analysis of a Burial Mound Survey. *World Archaeology* 24:175–197.

———, and J. E. Buikstra (editors). 2006. *Recreating Hopewell*. University Press of Florida, Gainesville.

———, J. Van Nest, and J. E. Buikstra. 2004. From the Earth: Minerals and Meaning in the Hopewellian World. In *Soil, Stones, and Symbols: Cultural Perceptions of the Mineral World*, edited by N. Boivin and M. A. Owoc, pp. 43–70. UCL Press, London.

Connolly, R. P., and B. T. Lepper (editors). 2004. *The Fort Ancient Earthworks: Prehistoric Lifeways of the Hopewell Culture in Southwestern Ohio*. Ohio Historical Society, Columbus.

Farnsworth, K. B., and T. E. Emerson (editors). 1986. *Early Woodland Archeology*, Kampsville Seminars in Archeology 2. Center for American Archeology, Kampsville, IL.

Fortier, A. C. 2001. A Tradition of Discontinuity: American Bottom Early and Middle Woodland Culture History Reexamined. In *The Archaeology of Traditions: Agency and History Before and After Columbus*, edited by T. R. Pauketat, pp. 174–194. University Press of Florida, Gainesville.

———, T. O. Maher, J. A. Williams, M. C. Meinkoth, K. E. Parker, and L. S. Kelly. 1989. *The Holding Site: A Hopewell Community in the American Bottom*. American Bottom Archaeology FAI-270 Site Reports 19. University of Illinois Press, Urbana.

Greber, N. B. 2003. Chronological Relationships Among Ohio Hopewell Sites: Few Dates and Much Complexity. In *Theory, Method, and Practice in Modern Archaeology*, edited by R. J. Jeske and D. K. Charles, pp. 88–113. Praeger, Westport, CT.

———. 2005. Adena and Hopewell in the Middle Ohio Valley: To Be or Not to Be? In *Woodland Period Systematics in the Middle Ohio Valley*, edited by D. Applegate and R. C. Mainfort Jr., pp. 19–39. University of Alabama Press, Tuscaloosa.

Hajic, E. R. 1990. *Late Pleistocene and Holocene Landscape Evolution, Depositional Subsystems, and Stratigraphy in the Lower Illinois River Valley*. Ph.D. dissertation, University of Illinois, Urbana.

Hall, R. L. 1997. *An Archaeology of the Soul: North American Indian Belief and Ritual*. University of Illinois Press, Urbana.

Hegmon, M. 2003. Setting Theoretical Egos Aside: Issues and Theory in North American Archaeology. *American Antiquity* 68:213–243.

Hodder, I. (editor). 2001. *Archaeological Theory Today*. Polity/Blackwell, Malden, MA.

Kidder, T. R. 2006. Climate Change and the Archaic to Woodland Transition (3000–2500 cal B. P.) in the Mississippi River Basin. *American Antiquity* 71:195–231.

King, J. L., J. E. Buikstra, and D. K. Charles. 2011. Time and Archaeological Traditions in the Lower Illinois Valley. *American Antiquity* 76:500–528.

Pacheco, P. J., and W. S. Dancey. 2006. Integrating Mortuary and Settlement Data on Ohio Hopewell Society. In *Recreating Hopewell*, edited by D. K. Charles and J. E. Buikstra, pp. 2–25. University Press of Florida, Gainesville.

Ruby, B. J., C. Carr, and D. K. Charles. 2005. Community Organizations in the Scioto, Mann and Havana Hopewellian Regions: A Comparative Perspective. In *Gathering Hopewell: Society, Ritual, And Ritual Interaction*, edited by C. Carr and D. T. Case, pp. 119–176. Kluwer Academic/Plenum, New York.

Seeman, M. F. 2004. Hopewell Art in Hopewell Places. In *Hero, Hawk and Open Hand: American Indian Art of the Ancient Midwest and South*, edited by R. V. Sharp, pp. 57–71. Art Institute of Chicago in association with Yale University Press, New Haven, CT.

———, and J. L. Branch. 2006. The Mounded Landscapes of Ohio: Hopewell Patterns and Placement. In *Recreating Hopewell*, edited by D. K. Charles and J. E. Buikstra, pp. 106–121. University Press of Florida, Gainesville.

Smith, B. D. 1992. Hopewellian Farmers of Eastern North America. In *Rivers of Change: Essays on Early Agriculture in Eastern North America*, edited by B. D. Smith, pp. 201–248. Smithsonian Institution, Washington, DC.

Stoltman, J. B. 1978. Temporal Models in Prehistory: An Example from Eastern North America. *Current Anthropology* 19:703–746.

Van Gilder, C., and D. K. Charles. 2003. Archaeology as Cultural Encounter: The Legacy of Hopewell. In *Theory, Method, and Practice in Modern Archaeology*, edited by R. J. Jeske and D. K. Charles, pp. 114–129. Praeger, Westport, CT.

Van Nest, J. 1997. *Late Quaternary Geology, Archeology, and Vegetation in West-Central Illinois: A Study in Geoarcheology*. Ph.D. dissertation, University of Iowa, Iowa City.

———. 2006. Rediscovering This Earth: Some Ethnogeological Aspects of the Illinois Valley Hopewell Mounds. In *Recreating Hopewell*, edited by D. K. Charles and J. E. Buikstra, pp. 403–426. University Press of Florida, Gainesville.

Yaeger, J., and M. A. Canuto. 2000. Introducing an Archaeology of Communities. In *The Archaeology of Communities: A New World Perspective*, edited by M. A. Canuto and J. Yaeger, pp. 1–15. Routledge, London.

CHAPTER 40

MONUMENTAL LANDSCAPE AND COMMUNITY IN THE SOUTHERN LOWER MISSISSIPPI VALLEY DURING THE LATE WOODLAND AND MISSISSIPPI PERIODS

MARK A. REES

Much of what is known today about ancient Native American cultures of the Lower Mississippi Valley (LMV) stems from studies of sites with earthen mounds, along with ceramic artifacts that have provided a major source of culture-historical information (e.g., Phillips 1970). Phillips et al. (1951:5–6) described the LMV in their landmark survey as extending more than 900 kilometers (559 miles), from the Ohio River to the Gulf of Mexico. This includes the area north of the Arkansas River, subsequently referred to as the Central Mississippi Valley. Northern and southern segments of the LMV have long been distinguished largely on the basis of ceramics, separated around the Arkansas Lowland. The focus here is on Native American communities of the southern LMV during the centuries following the Middle Woodland or Marksville period (AD 1–400), although the northern LMV and earlier periods are mentioned in comparative context (Figure 40.1).

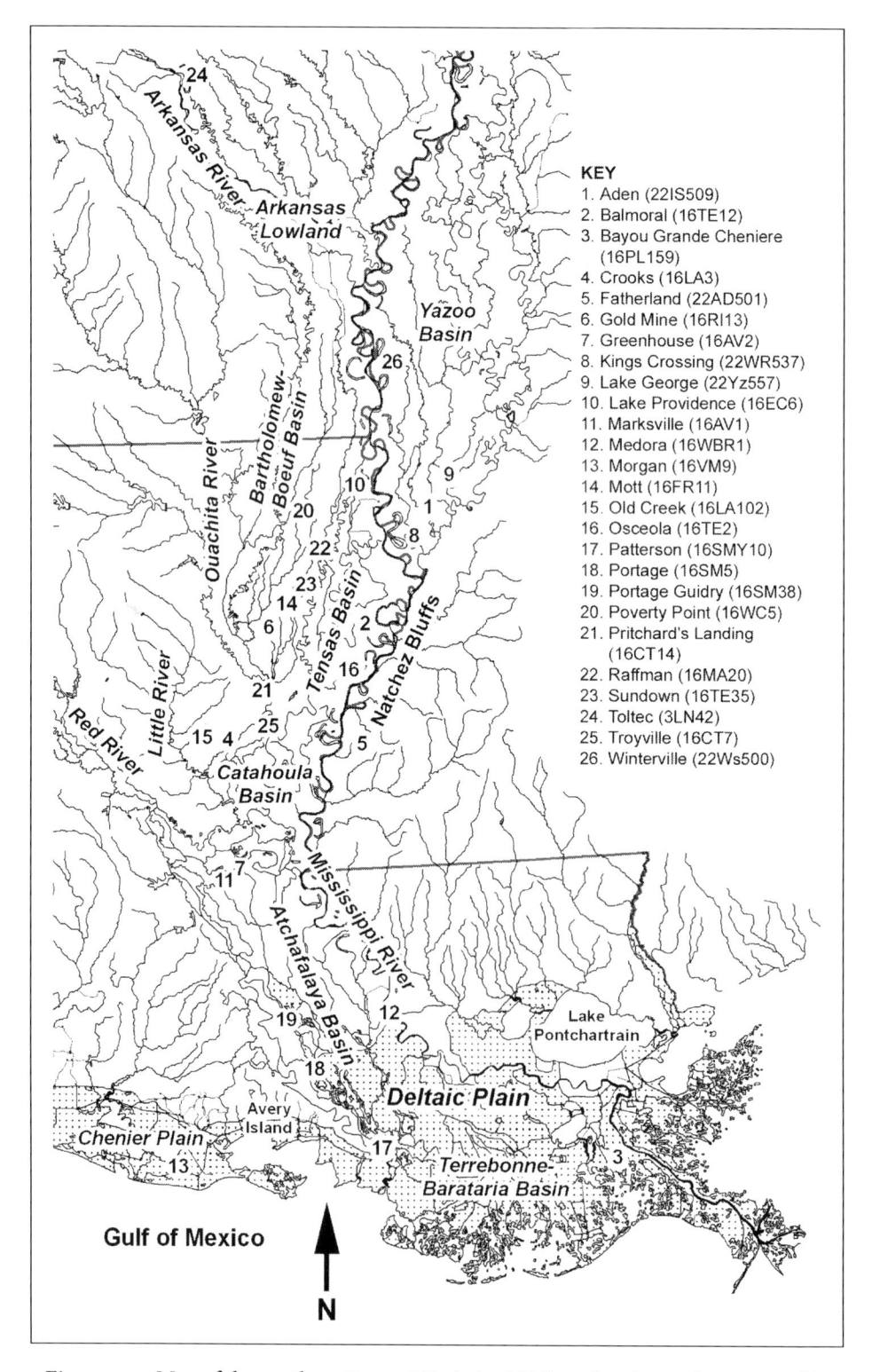

Figure 40.1 Map of the southern Lower Mississippi Valley, showing major geographic regions and sites mentioned in the text.

The complex geomorphology of the LMV is paralleled by its cultural diversity and extraordinary history, challenging conventional explanations for development of social inequality and complexity. Complex, nonstate societies described as chiefdoms appeared in the Mississippi Valley and southeastern United States with remarkable rapidity beginning in the 11th century AD, as evinced by distributions of nonlocal artifacts and well-crafted ornate objects, agricultural intensification, and construction of immense, flat-topped mounds that supported elite residences and mortuaries (Alt, this volume; Blitz, this volume). Production of monumental landscapes in the southern LMV, beginning as early as the Middle Archaic, proceeded independently of agriculture, craft specialization, and long-distance exchange, casting doubt on a direct or consistent correlation among economic intensification, social inequality, and complexity. Of particular interest in this regard is the relationship between monumental landscape and community during the Late Woodland (ca. AD 400–1200) and Mississippi (AD 1200–1700) periods. The former is subdivided into the Baytown (AD 400–700) and Coles Creek (AD 700–1200) periods. A series of cultures were identified in the southern LMV by the mid-20th century, including Troyville, Coles Creek, Plaquemine, and Mississippian.

In breaking into the homogeneity and similitude represented by these archaeological cultures, it is possible to recognize historical circumstances and processes of community and political culture. Instead of ceramics or portable artifacts, emphasis is placed on monumental landscapes as places of political engagement, experience, and meaning. *Monumental landscape* refers to earthen mounds, architecture, plazas, enclosures, and aspects of the built environment not just of seemingly impractical large size and elaboration but associated with representations of political ideology and complexity. Such landscapes were created and re-created by communities, and in some instances they represent a vision of community in built environment, broadcast throughout a region. Baytown and Coles Creek periods in the southern LMV can be understood in this light, not as a Late Woodland transition or Mississippian emergence but as alternative histories of complexity. Monumental alteration of landscape points toward consummate, local-level events that challenge gradualist perspectives of culture history and cultural evolution, in a region where variable inequalities were constituted by social heterogeneity and coercion, as well as hierarchy and compliance. A historical anthropology of the LMV can be advanced from this archaeology of monumental landscapes, where Native Americans reinvented traditions and initiated historical processes that shaped their communities and collective futures.

Commemorating Community and Place

Few features of landscape loom as large in southeastern archaeology as earthen mounds. Functionalist views of monumental landscape predominate, whether elevated platforms of chiefly residences, mortuary temples, plazas, embankments, ceremonial spaces, or enclosures (Milner, this volume). Monument making is associated worldwide with development of social complexity, from conspicuous consumption of labor and resources to displays of authority and prestige, political competition, consolidation, and central places of regional political economy. Both function and use are geared to interpretations of structure, and whether political, economic, or symbolic, monumental space is viewed taxonomically.

Late Woodland Troyville and Coles Creek mounds are consequently thought to have "replaced" previous Middle Woodland conical-burial and platform-ceremonial mounds. If Mississippian platform mounds were the logical, next-larger step in cultural development, complex societies of the Late Woodland seemed to explain, or be explained by, subsequent events. Yet the monumental architecture of Fatherland, Medora, Greenhouse, Troyville, Marksville, Poverty Point, and even earlier, Middle Archaic sites flout this typology, raising doubt as to whether inalienable, processual qualities of landscape should be viewed as typical culture traits and a direct or definitive measure of complexity (see Kidder, this volume). Categories such as Coles Creek mound site and ceremonial center signify equivalence and similitude, conflating cultural variation. Coles Creek communities did not evolve into Mississippian chiefdoms and must be understood on their own terms, as historical processes. Community suggests a sense of shared identity, values, and tradition stemming from the local level, although not confined to kinship and compliance. Viewing landscape as historically unique and meaningful—in terms of production of community, identity, and place—produces a different historical narrative.

As commemorative space, monumental landscape embodies collective memories of conflicted pasts. To monumentalize is to memorialize in grand, seemingly immovable fashion the rebirth or reinvention of tradition. The processes of monument making, commemoration, re-creation, and transformation of the built environment involve political-ritual performance and emphasize one or more interpretations of the past. Monumental landscapes comprise and promulgate, and are sometimes literally inscribed with, historical representations of a political-religious order, from the simultaneously ideological and material to the coercive. Monument making and commemorations of place were politicized, supracommunity practices, negotiations of local and regional political culture, in which ideological compliance and orthodoxy were visibly asserted, contested, and overturned. Community and identity are thus reimagined, re-created, affirmed, and resisted through landscape, from perception of intransient place and experience of materiality to creation of homeland, movement, colonization, and exile.

Monumental landscape in the LMV and greater Southeast was part of this historical process, involving cosmological referents, assertions of identity in creation of place, negotiation of inequalities and power relations, political consolidation, population movements, decentralization, and abandonment. This is evident at Cahokia in the American Bottom of the Mississippi Valley, where production of monumental landscapes on an unparalleled scale represented a transformation of community and engagement in Mississippian political culture, whether consensual, contested, or coerced (Alt, this volume). Comparable historical processes occurred later downriver in the Yazoo Basin at Lake George and Winterville, centuries earlier at Toltec in the Arkansas Lowland, and at Troyville, below the Ouachita-Tensas confluence, where monument making coincided with reinvention of identity and tradition. Coles Creek, Troyville, and earlier monument construction can be understood from this perspective. In contexts where food surpluses, control of production, acquisition, and display were minimal, constrained, or discouraged, people still invested symbolic capital in built environments, perception and production of social order and identity in landscape, and a sense of place (Cobb and Nassaney 2002:531).

Later southeastern mounds were earth icons of creation: birth and fertility, death and renewal. The oral histories of Muskogean tribes relate legends of migration and earth emergence, including mounds in and upon which the bones of ancestors were entombed. The Natchez Great Sun and earlier Mississippian chiefs resided on mound summits. With their deaths, the houses were demolished or burned and a new earthen mantle added, upon which the residence of their successor might have been built (Brown 2007:153; Neitzel 1965:64–85). The authority of venerated ancestors and lineages thus materialized in sacred landscapes through mortuary ceremonialism and commemorations, involving political ritual and feasting. Just as social distinctions and inequalities might be sanctioned or obscured, segregation of space was a form of coercive or symbolic violence in contested landscapes. Desecration of mortuary temples in warfare was not merely a random act of violence or affront to an adversary's status, but an effort to annihilate community at its place of origin.

Monumentalizing Community in the LMV

Previously referred to as a "very dull period, a cultural interregnum" (Phillips 1970:912) and a time of "gray" cultures (Williams and Brain 1983:404), the Late Woodland corresponds with major changes in the southern LMV, commencing with what Jon Gibson (1985:323) characterized as a time of "incipient urbanism" in the Ouachita basin. More recent studies have indicated population movements and growth; increased construction of monumental architecture, particularly platform mounds; intensification of foraging; and introduction of maize agriculture during the last two centuries of the Coles Creek period (Fritz and Kidder 1993; Kidder 2002). T. R. Kidder (2004b:552–553) thus describes the Late Woodland as a period of "dynamic change" in social organization, subsistence economies, settlement, technology, and political complexity, despite relatively plain ceramics and scarce evidence for long-distance exchange. To understand these changes it is necessary to look at the earlier transformation of community through landscape, as represented at the Troyville mound site.

Troyville culture of the Baytown period is distinguished from contemporaneous Baytown culture to the north by monumental architecture and the persistence of Marksville ceramic types (Kidder 2004b; Lee 2010). It has been regarded as a problematic subdivision of Marksville and Coles Creek (Belmont 1984), with similarities in ceramics at Coles Creek sites to the south and along the coast characterized as Troyville–Coles Creek culture (Ford 1951). Despite disagreements concerning the concept of Troyville culture, the Troyville site represents a conspicuous, defining moment in the inception of Coles Creek monumentality. Located at the confluence of the Ouachita, Tensas, and Little rivers in present-day Jonesville, Louisiana, Troyville had the largest and most impressive monumental architecture of the southern LMV during the Baytown period (Figure 40.2). Although well known from salvage excavations (Walker 1936), Troyville was practically obliterated by the 1930s and is still not well understood (Lee et al. 2010). The majority of communities in the southern LMV at this time were small, dispersed hamlets (Kidder 2004b:554). Far from a typical community, Troyville represented an unparalleled

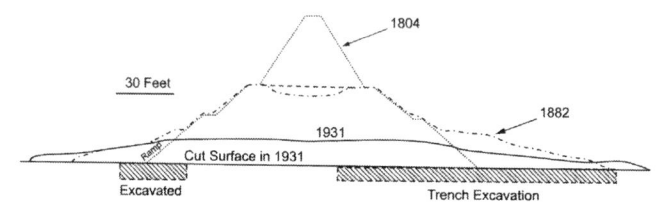

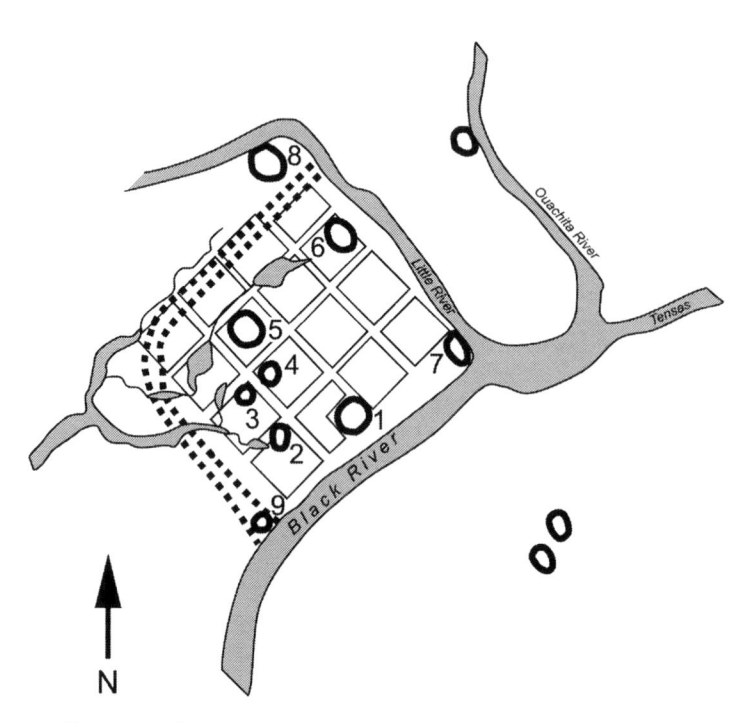

Figure 40.2 Plan view of the Troyville site (16CT7) and cross-section reconstruction of the Great Mound, based on Walker (1936:10–11, figures 3 and 4).

collaboration of people drawn together in monumental transformation of community and landscape.

The now-leveled Great Mound at Troyville is estimated to have been raised more than 24 meters (80 feet) above the alluvial valley, with two terraces and a cone-shaped or conical summit. Between eight and 12 additional mounds were arranged around a plaza and nearly all enclosed by an earthen embankment (Walker 1936:1-16). The mound arrangement and enclosure design were reminiscent of the Middle Woodland Marksville site, located 59 kilometers (36.7 miles) to the southwest (McGimsey 2003). As at Marksville, a combination of platform and conical mounds appear to have been built at Troyville. The embankment delineated a mound-and-plaza precinct oriented on the sunrise, as well as rivers that connected it with communities in the LMV. Alignments of mounds, embankment, and architecture may have been designed according to celestial movements, as seen later at Toltec in the Arkansas Lowland to the north (Rolingson 2002:54). Communal assemblies involving mortuary rituals and feasts are suggested by mass secondary interments, large ceramic vessels in mound contexts, and large fire pits at Troyville and sites such as Gold Mine and Old Creek (Belmont 1984; Kidder 1998).

Although Troyville bears similarities to the sacred landscape of earlier Middle Woodland sites, there are significant departures. The embankment at Troyville was to some extent occupied domestic space, rather than a purely ceremonial enclosure (Lee 2010:147–151). The size and design of the Great Mound further distinguishes Troyville. The fleeting image of a conical mound on the summit of a platform mound has long perplexed archaeologists, thought by some to have served as a signal or watch tower (Walker 1936:4-13). Conical mounds at Middle Woodland sites such as Marksville and Crooks contained mass burials of individuals with a wide range of elaborate grave offerings and nonlocal items, interpreted as evidence of connections with contemporaneous Hopewell culture in the Ohio Valley and mortuary ceremonialism with possible Tchula period (800 BC—AD 1) antecedents (Charles, this volume; Kidder 2002:72–79). As at Marksville and Crooks, Troyvillians constructed a conical mound over an earlier-stage platform that served as a mortuary facility or tomb (Walker 1936:20-31). At Troyville the underlying platform was not covered; instead it supported and elevated a conical mound. Unfortunately, little is known about the upper levels of the Great Mound at Troyville, but such symbolism would have resonated among people long accustomed to platform-mound mortuary ceremonialism. If Middle Woodland landscapes represent the communal-mortuary practices of segmentary societies, the creators of the Great Mound at Troyville accomplished a political-religious innovation sometime in the mid-17th century AD (Lee 2010:155). An ancient earth icon, integrating the sacred and secular in commemorating communal death and renewal, was recognized in a new and different way.

Evidence for an unprecedented disjuncture with Middle Woodland civic ceremonialism is scattered in places throughout the subsequent Coles Creek period. It may even explain a subsequent historical conjuncture: nearly synchronous commencement of a new form of mound-and-plaza construction in the LMV. Within a century following AD 700, while people were still living at Troyville, communities were constructing substructural platform mounds throughout the southern LMV, from the Lower Yazoo Basin to the Delta (Kidder 1998; Phillips 1970). Coles Creek, named for a small creek that joins the Mississippi north of Natchez, is known for its distinctively incised ceramics. Although conical mounds were still constructed, there was appreciable acceleration in the building and use of mounds as foundations for buildings, thought to have been elite residences and mortuary temples. Unlike earlier mound sites enclosed within embankments, Coles Creek monumental architecture commonly comprises between two and four mounds arranged around a central plaza (Kidder 1998:130; Williams and Brain 1983:405–407). This configuration is evident at Aden and Kings Crossing in the Lower Yazoo Basin, Balmoral and Sundown in the Tensas Basin, Patterson and Portage in the Atchafalaya Basin, and the Morgan site on the Chenier Plain (Figure 40.3). Numerous smaller sites without mounds, communities with single mounds, and much larger mound sites, such as Bayou Grande Cheniere, Greenhouse, Lake George, Mott, Osceola, Pritchard's Landing, and Raffman suggest the development of regional settlement hierarchies and associated complex polities or chiefdoms.

Kidder (1998, 2004a) argues for increased exclusivity in community planning during the Coles Creek period, as evident in progressively larger substructural mounds with inward-facing ramps, arranged around methodically designed plazas. This supports the argument for elite appropriation of civic-ceremonial space for residences, involving symbolic legitimation of authority integral to the ensuing evolution of chiefdoms. Yet in contrast to the contemporaneous emergent Mississippian, Coles Creek has seemed enigmatic in its lack of agricultural intensification and status differentiation in mortuary practices, incorporating few nonlocal craft goods despite constructing large ceremonial centers. One plausible explanation is a regional increase in political competition and conflict, as seen in aggregation of populations, adoption of the bow and arrow, proliferation of mound sites, and progressively larger monumental architecture. This might also account for the greater number of mound sites of comparable size and an apparent lack of a single, paramount center (see also Nassaney 2001:162–171).

The historical precedent for these changes lies not in Mesoamerica or Mississippian chiefdoms, but in the monumental transformation of community at Troyville. Platform mounds and embankments, formerly the domain of communal-mortuary ritual, became places for the living as well as the dead. Rather than civic space co-opted by an aspiring elite, thereby anticipating the development of chiefdoms, production and use of Coles Creek platform mounds suggests a more ancient disjuncture. Commemoration of ancestors in mortuary ritual may have been reinvented as an accolade for the living through association with corporate groups. The monumental landscape of Troyville hints at such a series of events, in which the political culture of communities was redefined in relation to warfare, alliances, and dispute resolution. In contrast to the public ceremonialism and cosmological referents of Middle Woodland landscapes, aggrandizement of corporate groups was associated with increased segregation of space, most notably in terms of platform mounds and plazas. Production of

MONUMENTAL LANDSCAPE AND COMMUNITY 491

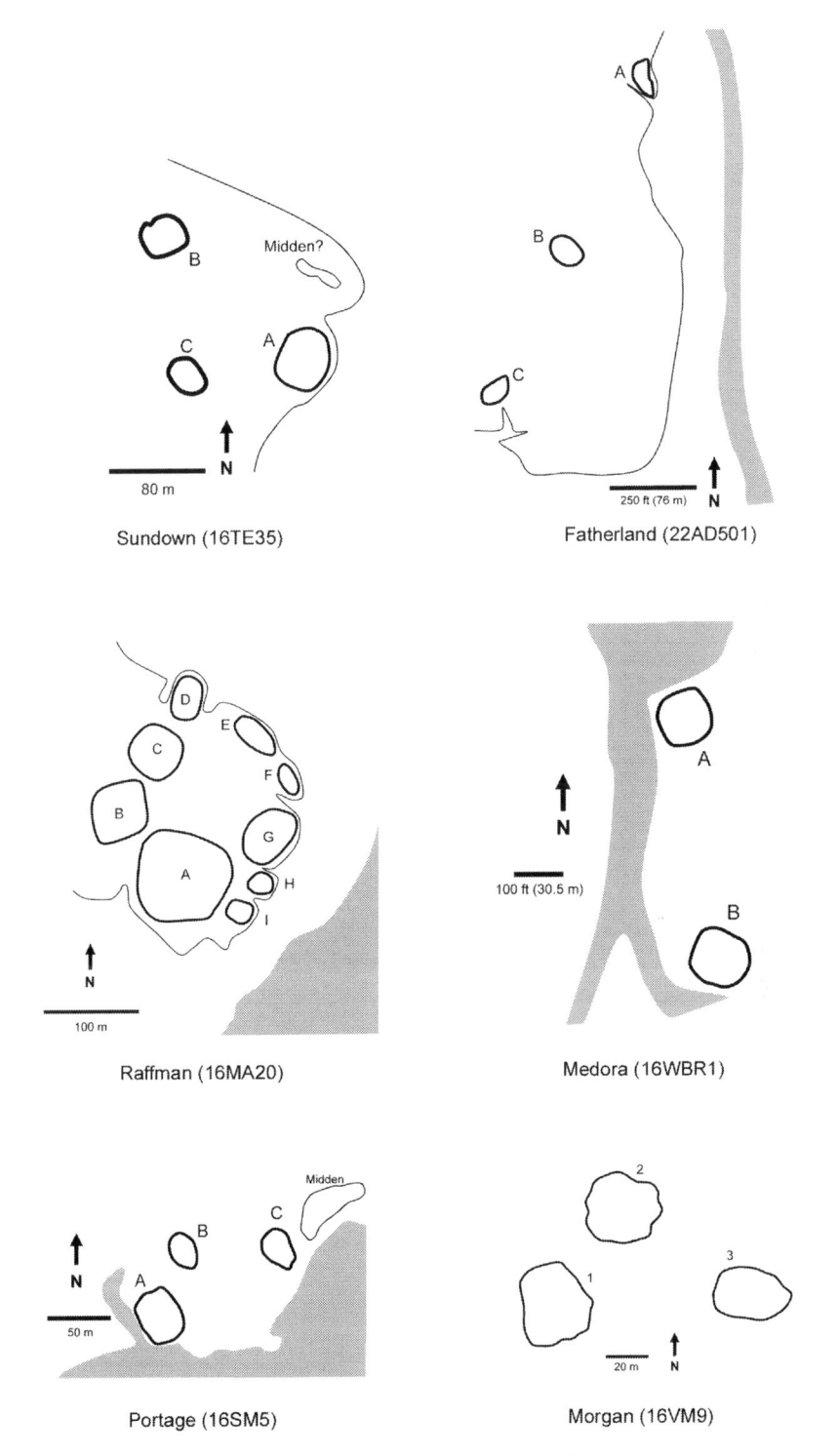

Figure 40.3 Plan views of selected mound sites in the southern LMV, ca. AD 700–1700: Fatherland (22AD501), Medora (16WBR1), Morgan (16VM9), Portage (16SM5), Raffman (16MA20), and Sundown (16TE35).

sacred, communal space by way of enclosures was abruptly discontinued. A realignment of social relations away from communalism and collectivity would have preceded institutionalized political hierarchies and hereditary chiefs (Knight 1990:6–7), yet entailed organization of complexity in terms of social heterogeneity. Such a monumental undertaking would have involved reinterpretations of identity and negotiations of political-religious authority across communities, with relatively negligible consequences for intensification of production or long-distance trade.

A further segregation of social relations is indicated in regional expansion and escalation of Coles Creek monumentality, while access to the political rituals and precincts of monumental landscapes became more restricted. This might be explained by a continued shift from community-integrating ceremonialism to more secular, kin-ordered alliances and dispute resolution in warfare, whether coordinated by ranked clans or lineages, as among Mississippian chiefdoms and the historic Natchez (Knight 1990:6–7). The new ceremonialism of platform mounds elevated both residences and mortuary temples, with subsequent interments rather than intentionally designed burial mounds. Adjacent plazas became gathering places for political-ritual performances, alliances, feasts, and related ceremonial events (Kidder 2002:85–86, 2004a). Such reinterpretation of monument making and community is suggested at Greenhouse in the Red River floodplain, below the Pleistocene terrace immediately northeast of Marksville (Figure 40.4). In contrast to the sacred enclosures and expansive, communal layout of Marksville, Greenhouse and other Coles Creek mound-and-plaza complexes represent the exigencies of community planning and more narrowly circumscribed residential space in contexts of increased regional competition and conflict.

The Late Woodland–Mississippian transition, dating at least two centuries later here than the northern LMV, bears the hallmarks of this earlier history. Similarities between Coles Creek and Plaquemine, especially in the Delta and along the coast, have been characterized as transitional Coles Creek (ca. AD 1000–1200). Plaquemine is alternatively described as a regional variant of Mississippian culture, a hybridization of Coles Creek and Mississippian, and indigenous development of Coles Creek (Rees and Livingood 2007). Like Coles Creek, Plaquemine communities are often compared with Mississippian polities and found lacking in the standard measurements of complexity and inequality: nonlocal artifacts, ornately crafted items interred as elite mortuary offerings, and pronounced settlement hierarchies (Williams and Brain 1983:413). Agricultural intensification, particularly maize, appears relatively late and is regionally variable. Yet monumental landscapes and historical accounts indicate substantial complexity during the Mississippi period.

The "Mississippianized Coles Creek" theory of Plaquemine origins is based on research at large mound sites in the Lower Yazoo Basin, particularly Lake George and Winterville, where contacts with Cahokia and other Mississippian communities upriver beginning around AD 1000 are thought to have produced Plaquemine culture (Williams and Brain 1983:409–414). Lake George and Winterville are hardly typical Plaquemine communities, however, with as many as 30 and 23 enormous

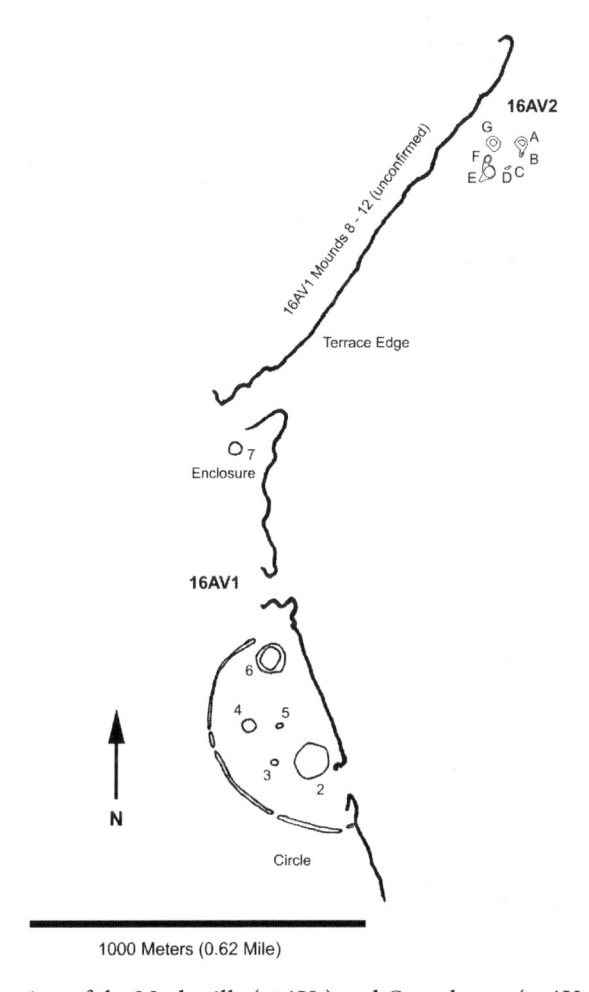

Figure 40.4 Plan view of the Marksville (16AV1) and Greenhouse (16AV2) sites, showing the relative placement and size of monumental landscape.

platform mounds, respectively, near the northern limits of Plaquemine site distribution. Recent research at Lake Providence has confirmed contacts between late Coles Creek communities in the upper Tensas Basin and Mississippians in the American Bottom, possibly through intermediaries in the Lower Yazoo Basin (Wells and Weinstein 2007:56–64). Mississippian material culture, such as shell-tempered ceramics, stone hoes, and triangular arrow points as well as nonlocal artifacts associated with the Southeastern Ceremonial Complex, is otherwise minimal and generally late in the Tensas Basin southward, supporting the argument for cultural continuity and localized, indigenous development of Plaquemine traditions (Kidder 1998). This is borne out by similarities in material culture and monumental landscapes among coastal variants of Coles Creek and Plaquemine, at mound sites such as Greenhouse, Portage Guidry, Morgan, and Medora, where the concept of Plaquemine was conceived (Ford 1951; Quimby 1951).

Limited Mississippianization in the southern LMV occurred in the form of localized adoption of nonlocal practices and material culture, and isolated yet influential movements of people, ideas, and trade goods in the context of preexisting communities. In contrast, Ian Brown (2007:154–159) argues for discontinuities between Coles Creek and Plaquemine architecture and mound construction at sites on the Natchez Bluffs, suggesting population movement and resettlement. People in the Delta traded and interacted with Mississippians along the coast as far east as Mobile Bay, to such an extent that it becomes difficult to distinguish archaeological cultures on the basis of ceramic types or the incidence of shell-tempering (Weinstein and Dumas 2008). During the last century and a half of the Mississippi period, one or more migrations of nonlocal Mississippians, possibly from the Lower Yazoo Basin to Avery Island, Louisiana, focused on salt production and trade (Brown 1999). Population movements in the southern LMV thus coincide with the beginning of recorded history and surely predate it by millennia.

Construction of monumental landscapes was curtailed with the demographic disruptions and disease epidemics following arrival of foreigners from overseas. Putting an end to the De Soto expedition in AD 1543, hundreds of warriors in flotillas of canoes forced the Spanish to retreat down the Mississippi. At least two large polities, likely ancestral to the Tunica and Natchez, were defending territories along the river. Use and reuse of mound precincts nonetheless continued into the 18th century, as seen at the Natchez Grand Village of Fatherland. The Great Sun resided in a large house on a platform mound at Fatherland. Across the plaza, a temple mound held the remains of venerated ancestors (Neitzel 1965:64–85). The Natchez commemorated the death of Tattooed Serpent, War Chief and brother of the Great Sun, with elaborate mortuary ritual, including human sacrifice and burial within the temple. Such palpable, symbolic violence both reinforced and was sanctioned by social distinctions and inequalities, with archaeological parallels centuries earlier in Mound 72 at Cahokia (Pauketat 2004:87–93). Yet as Brown (2007:148) has noted, Fatherland is a relatively small and unimpressive site, characteristically Plaquemine in terms of monumental landscape and material culture.

Warfare and political conflict among the Natchez, Tunica, and other historic tribes have likely precursors in Plaquemine and Coles Creek. In the context of factionalism and regional conflict, variable complexities and inequalities were organized around social heterogeneity, symbolic violence, and coercion. Conquest, compliance, and regional consolidation were constrained to some extent by local identity politics. Since Late Woodland times, the contradictions of heterogeneity and hierarchy played out on the local and regional levels, at increasingly exclusionary mound-and-plaza precincts. Decisive events occurred *during* culture periods, among communities at specific places such as Troyville. Mortuary ceremonialism and political-religious ritual were the venue for these historical disjunctures, reinventing tradition and transforming the monumental landscape. Power relations within and between communities transpired for the most part independently of economic intensification, hence the dearth of status differentiation in mortuary ceremonialism, paucity of nonlocal goods and craft specialization, and deferred or minimal agricultural production. Symbolic capital and authority were invested in social relations and people—the Great Sun and War Chief, ancestral lineages and corporate groups—and the lofty places where they lived and were entombed. An alternative Mississippian history lies in the ruins of Troyville and subsequent Coles Creek mound-and-plaza construction, where the landscape reflects a reorganization of community and reinterpretation of identity. Archaeologists are only just beginning to uncover this monumental history.

REFERENCES

Belmont, J. S. 1984. The Troyville Concept and the Gold Mine Site. *Louisiana Archaeology* 9(1982):65–98.

Brown, I. W. 1999. Salt Manufacture and Trade from the Perspective of Avery Island, Louisiana. *Midcontinental Journal of Archaeology* 24(2):113–151.

———. 2007. Plaquemine Culture in the Natchez Bluffs Region of Mississippi. In *Plaquemine Archaeology*, edited by M. A. Rees and P. C. Livingood, pp. 145–160. University of Alabama Press, Tuscaloosa.

Cobb, C. R., and M. S. Nassaney. 2002. Domesticating Self and Society in the Woodland Southeast. In *The Woodland Southeast*, edited by D. G. Anderson and R. C. Mainfort Jr., pp. 525–539. University of Alabama Press, Tuscaloosa.

Ford, J. A. 1951. *Greenhouse: A Troyville-Coles Creek Period Site in Avoyelles Parish, Louisiana*. Anthropological Papers of the American Museum of Natural History, vol. 44, pt. 1. American Museum of Natural History, New York.

Fritz, G. J., and T. R. Kidder. 1993. Recent Investigations into Prehistoric Agriculture in the Lower Mississippi Valley. *Southeastern Archaeology* 12(1):1–14.

Gibson, J. L. 1985. Ouachita Prehistory. *Louisiana Archaeology* 10(1983):319–335.

Kidder, T. R. 1998. Mississippi Period Mound Groups and Communities in the Lower Mississippi Valley. In *Mississippian Towns and Sacred Spaces: Searching for an Architectural Grammar*, edited by R. B. Lewis and C. Stout, pp. 123–150. University of Alabama Press, Tuscaloosa.

———. 2002. Woodland Period Archaeology of the Lower Mississippi Valley. In *The Woodland Southeast*, edited by D. G. Anderson and R. C. Mainfort Jr., pp. 66–90. University of Alabama Press, Tuscaloosa.

———. 2004a. Plazas as Architecture: An Example from the Raffman Site, Northeast Louisiana. *American Antiquity* 69(3):514–532.

———. 2004b. Prehistory of the Lower Mississippi Valley After 800 B.C. In *Handbook of North American Indians*, vol. 14, *Southeast*, edited by R. D. Fogelson, pp. 545–559. Smithsonian Institution Press, Washington, DC.

Knight, V. J., Jr. 1990. Social Organization and the Evolution of Hierarchy in Southeastern Chiefdoms. *Journal of Anthropological Research* 46(1):1–23.

Lee, A. L. 2010. Troyville and the Baytown Period. In *Archaeology of Louisiana*, edited by M. A. Rees, pp. 135–156. Louisiana State University Press, Baton Rouge.

Lee, A., J. Biddescombe, D. Bruner, D. Harlan, A. Montana, J. McKnight, C. Nolan, R. Smith, and J. Yakubik. 2010. *Archaeological Data Recovery and Monitoring at the Troyville Mounds Site (16CT7), Catahoula Parish, Louisiana*. Louisiana Department of Transportation and Development, Baton Rouge. Earth Search, New Orleans.

McGimsey, C. R. 2003. The Rings of Marksville. *Southeastern Archaeology* 22(1):47–62.

Nassaney, M. S. 2001. The Historical-Processual Development of Late Woodland Societies. In *The Archaeology of Traditions: Agency and History Before and After Columbus*, edited by T. R. Pauketat, pp. 157–173. University Press of Florida, Gainesville.

Neitzel, R. S. 1965. *Archeology of the Fatherland Site: The Grand Village of the Natchez.* Anthropological Papers of the American Museum of Natural History, vol. 51, pt. 1. American Museum of Natural History, New York.

Pauketat, T. R. 2004. *Ancient Cahokia and the Mississippians.* Cambridge University Press, Cambridge, UK.

Phillips, P. 1970. *Archaeological Survey in the Lower Yazoo Basin, Mississippi, 1949–1955.* Papers of the Peabody Museum of American Archaeology and Ethnology, vol. 60, pts. 1 and 2. Harvard University, Cambridge, MA.

———, J. A. Ford, and J. B. Griffin. 1951. *Archaeological Survey in the Lower Mississippi Alluvial Valley, 1940–1947.* Papers of the Peabody Museum of Archaeology and Ethnology, 25. Harvard University, Cambridge, MA.

Quimby, G. I. 1951. *The Medora Site, West Baton Rouge Parish, Louisiana.* Anthropological Series, vol. 24, no. 2. Field Museum of Natural History, Chicago.

Rees, M. A., and P. C. Livingood. 2007. Introduction and Historical Overview. In *Plaquemine Archaeology*, edited by M. A. Rees and P. C. Livingood, pp. 1–19. University of Alabama Press, Tuscaloosa.

Rolingson, M. A. 2002. Plum Bayou Culture of the Arkansas–White River Basin. In *The Woodland Southeast*, edited by D. G. Anderson and R. C. Mainfort, Jr., pp. 44–65. University of Alabama Press, Tuscaloosa.

Walker, W. M. 1936. *The Troyville Mounds, Catahoula Parish, Louisiana.* Bureau of American Ethnology, Bulletin No. 113. Smithsonian Institution, Washington, DC.

Weinstein, R. A., and A. A. Dumas. 2008. The Spread of Shell-Tempered Ceramics along the Northern Coast of the Gulf of Mexico. *Southeastern Archaeology* 27(2):202–221.

Wells, D. C., and R. A. Weinstein. 2007. Extraregional Contact and Cultural Interaction at the Coles Creek–Plaquemine Transition: Recent Data from the Lake Providence Mounds, East Carroll Parish, Louisiana. In *Plaquemine Archaeology*, edited by M. A. Rees and P. C. Livingood, pp. 38–65. University of Alabama Press, Tuscaloosa.

Williams, S., and J. P. Brain. 1983. *Excavations at the Lake George Site, Yazoo County, Mississippi, 1958–1960.* Papers of the Peabody Museum of Archaeology and Ethnology, 74. Harvard University, Cambridge, MA.

CHAPTER 41

MAKING MISSISSIPPIAN AT CAHOKIA

SUSAN M. ALT

UNDERSTANDING the Mississippian phenomenon is intimately tied to understanding Cahokia, the largest settlement at the heart of the most complex polity in ancient Native North America. Comprehending Cahokia, in turn, means understanding how diverse peoples can come together and create a greater community and polity through ritual and religion. It also means telling the story of how social and political projects can ultimately fail. Cahokia undeniably possessed a singular history, one that built on earlier Woodland period histories and events and continues to have an impact today.

The size of Cahokia and its monuments rivals the earliest cities of Mesoamerica and other parts of the world (Figure 41.1). Within its dozen square kilometer area are more than 120 earthen pyramids or mounds; the nearly 5 hectare base of the largest, Monks Mound, covers about four-fifths of the area of the Pyramid of the Sun at Teotihuacán in Mexico and just a little more than the Pyramid of Khufu in Egypt. The central core of Cahokia is largely preserved in the modern archaeological park located in Collinsville, Illinois, but during its heyday the central city complex actually sprawled into modern-day East St. Louis, Illinois, with a sister complex across the Mississippi River in St. Louis, Missouri (Emerson 2002; Pauketat 2004). Ongoing research in the immediate hinterlands may well be moving those boundaries ever farther out as new discoveries indicate that Cahokia emplaced settlements in key locales around the region (Alt 2006a). Even farther afield, recent excavations in the distant north have verified the existence of a short-term colony or mission at Trempealeau, Wisconsin, possibly one of a dozen or more sizeable Cahokian or Cahokianized settlements (Pauketat et al. 2010; Stoltman 2000).

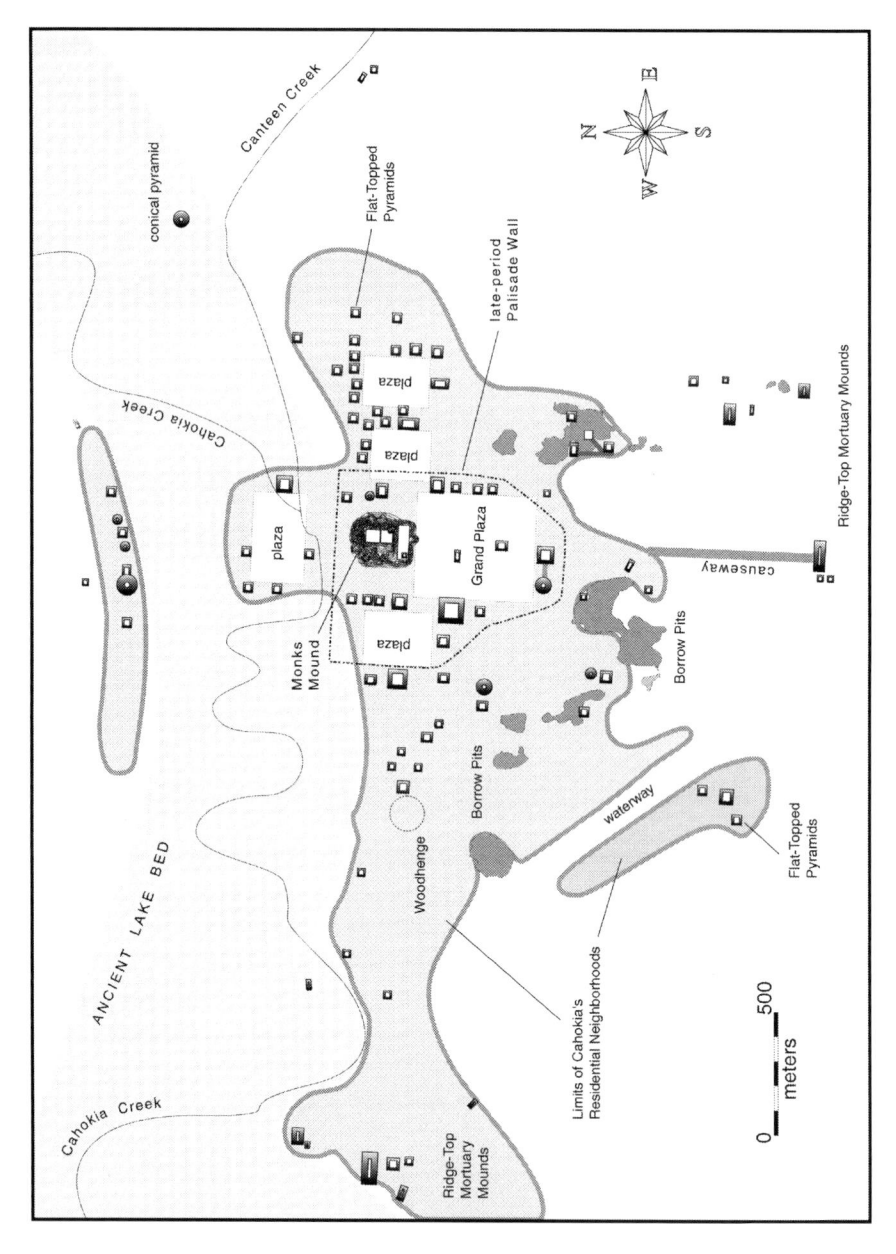

Figure 41.1 Plan view of the Cahokia site.

This new research complicates the Cahokia story and moves us further from the old position, common in the 1980s, that Cahokia was simply a large town at the center of a typical Mississippian chiefdom that, even though physically large, had little power over or effect on the histories of Midwestern and Southeastern people (Milner 1998; Muller 1997; Saitta 1994). However, as the story is currently being rewritten, Cahokia was in fact a very complex polity, one that does not fit typical expectations for chiefdoms (Alt 2010; Pauketat 2007). On the one hand, Cahokia witnessed a mix of immigrants, pilgrims, and local people who interacted in complicated ways, resulting in creation of new rites and organizations that instilled new senses of personal, communal, and political identity. On the other hand, Cahokia seems to have colonized or missionized the north (Figure 41.2). Locally, all of this played out as a novel economy of farmers in outlying areas who provisioned the administrators, specialists, artists, and traders in and around Cahokia proper. Presumably, it was the Cahokians who then authorized outposts in faraway locales, perhaps to facilitate import of nonlocal materials if not to spread their religious ideas.

Back to the Beginning

Before Cahokia, people in the Midwest lived in what archaeologists call Late Woodland cultures. The Late Woodland period in the Midwest (ca. AD 400–1050) is usually cast as a dark age made up of "good gray cultures" that followed the elaborate networks of the Middle Woodland (Hopewell) people, primarily in Ohio (but see Charles, Milner, Rees, this volume). There are few large villages or ceremonial centers and every indication of highly localized, if territorial, lifeways. Cultural objects

Years C.E.	Western Wisconsin	Greater Cahokia	Lower Ohio
1500	Large Oneota villages	Vacant	Caborn-Welborn palisaded villages
1400			
1300		Sand Prairie phase diminution	Mississippian centers depopulated
1200		Moorehead phase reorganization	Kincaid founded
1100	Stirling-horizon villages	Stirling phase monumentalism	Angel founded
1000	Cahokian missions	Cahokia's Big Bang	Migrations to Cahokia from Yankeetown villages
900	Effigy Mound Culture	Unpalisaded villages develop Maize intensified	

Figure 41.2 Chronology of Cahokia compared to the Lower Ohio and Western Wisconsin regions.

and artwork from the Late Woodland period lack the sophistication that marked the Middle Woodland period (ca. 100 BC–AD 400), and interregional interaction reached an all-time low. But then, the Late Woodland people had other concerns.

An increase in sedentism, organized violence, and fortified settlements marked the Late Woodland period in many parts of the Midwest. Given the small scale of most Late Woodland communities, warfare was seldom a large-scale affair. Most was probably small intervillage raids that stemmed from family feuds or territorial infringements (Milner 1999). Acts of warfare during this time were spotty, with some places such as the Illinois River valley (north of the Cahokia region) showing sporadic indications of arrowshot or clubbed individuals (Emerson 2007).

Other regions may have been characterized by far less intercommunity violence. In fact, there seems to have been one region that experienced little or none of it between the ninth through early 11th centuries AD, or the Terminal Late Woodland period. This was the region around the so-called American Bottom, the stretch of Mississippi River floodplain wherein later people built the city of Cahokia. The reasons for this apparent lack of violence are uncertain, but the absence of a threat of conflict might be the ultimate reason Cahokia was built where it was. At least a century before Cahokia's conversion from a very large Terminal Late Woodland village into a Native American city, immigrants were moving into the region. In some ways, it appears that Cahokia, the American Indian city, began with this influx of immigrants. Perhaps they sought the peace and prosperity that Late Woodland life in the American Bottom allowed.

By AD 1000, Cahokia had grown considerably, perhaps reaching a population of around 1,000 people. Only a few decades later, this population peaked at between 10,000 and 15,000 people (Pauketat and Lopinot 1997). The sudden growth of Cahokia, now generally called its Big Bang, took place around AD 1050 and saw more than just population growth. There were concurrent changes in community organization, architecture, technology, material culture, and ritual. These developments were so rapid, in fact, that some earlier investigators believed a new population of Mississippian people must have moved into Cahokia from someplace else (Perino 1959; Porter 1974).

Since then, this scenario has been modified several times, with data accumulated by the FAI 270 highway mitigation project in the 1970s being used to argue that most of the Mississippian changes of the 11th century had precedents in local traditions (Kelly 1990). Mississippian-period Cahokia was thus said by the 1980s to have been a product of internal change, initiated and carried out by American Bottom people presumably owing to external environmental, or in the 1990s political, causes (Emerson 2002; Milner 1998; Pauketat 1994; Pauketat and Emerson 1997).

This story held sway into the early 2000s but has recently been challenged on the basis of more than a decade of new excavations at the outlying sites mentioned earlier. As it turns out, immigrants did have a hand in what happened at Cahokia; they just weren't Mississippian to start with, and they did not come in and take over (Alt 2001, 2002, 2006a, 2006b).

Immigrants

It now appears that Cahokia's development hinged on immigration and at Cahokia proper this began decades before AD 1050. The possibility was first suggested by Robert Hall (1975), on the basis of his reading of the diversity of local and nonlocal pottery styles in the early phases of this great site. Others thought this diversity was evidence of trade, not immigration (Kelly 1991). However, most foreign-styled wares in these Terminal Late Woodland and early Mississippian contexts are not specialty vessels but well-worn cooking pots found in domestic deposits, sometimes concentrated near certain houses. Especially evident before AD 1050 are households who made cooking jars with the characteristics of Varney Red-Filmed pottery from southeastern Missouri.

Today, the best evidence of immigrants comes from a farming district, the Richland complex, a day's walk east of Cahokia in the uplands (Alt 2002; Pauketat 2003). Villages in that district, most of which date to the late 11th and early 12th centuries AD, were intimately associated with Cahokia. The people here, most of them farmers, used a distinctive style of garden-hoe blade (in three shapes) made in and imported from localities 150 kilometers to the south (Figure 41.3). They also possessed a few of the easily identified Cahokia-style projectile points, chunkey stones, and Ramey Incised vessels, all of which may have been made at or nearer to Cahokia proper (Figures 41.4, 41.5, 41.6).

All of these villages had unique characteristics that, in the aggregate, were odd for their time and place, seemingly out of step with the coeval pattern at Cahokia. One village, the Halliday site, was apparently home to people who made Varney Red-Filmed pottery and used a few foreign adzes from southeastern Missouri. The residents of another smaller village, the Knoebel site, had some Yankeetown pottery,

Figure 41.3 Cahokian hoe blade (photograph by S. Alt).

Figure 41.4 Cahokia-style notched projectile points from Pfeffer site, Richland complex, St. Clair County, Illinois (photograph by S. Alt).

Figure 41.5 Cahokia-style chunkey stone (photograph by S. Alt).

tools made from glacial cobbles, and Wyandotte chert from Indiana. At these and others, late-11th-century houses were built with single-set posts rather than Cahokia-style wall trenches. Some of these houses were rigidly organized around open courtyards, similar to the old Terminal Late Woodland custom at Cahokia. Others were associated with domestic refuse that included nonlocal cherts or chert tools and broken vessels made in foreign styles.

All of these discrepancies seem to indicate that the upland villages were founded by people who included immigrants from, among other places, the Varney and Yankeetown phases of southeastern Missouri and southwestern Indiana, respectively. These immigrants were not isolated from Cahokia. Rather, they seem to have been integral to the very fabric of Cahokian society, especially after AD 1050. At

Figure 41.6 Ramey Incised rim sherd showing variant of the Ramey scroll motif, Olszewski site (11S465), St. Clair County, Illinois (photograph by S. Alt).

that time, distributional evidence indicates the immigrants were provisioning Cahokia and, in return, were given access to the political and ritual life of the greater regional community.

More important, it seems that immigrants helped shape what would become the greatest pre-Columbian polity in North America; not incidentally, it helped launch a Mississippian civilization that then spread across eastern North America. The effect of the immigrants on local society and politics, likely unintentional and unexpected, was as a melting pot (in the New York sense). People from multiple locales, traditions, and histories were the primer for the changes that we know today as Cahokia.

Numerous studies and theories speak to the dynamics—variously called creolization, syncretism, or hybridity—engendered through the interactions of diverse people. But we need not view immigrants as the bearers of a new culture that was then superimposed over the local one (see Perino 1959 or Porter 1974). Rather, immigrants bring about cultural change simply by interacting with their new neighbors in everyday ways, even if they endeavor to fit in to their new environment. Such novel interactions happen in spaces where new rules, actions, and objects can be conceived, created, and acted on (following Bhabha 1994). Immigrants, that is, can spark a give-and-take that leads in turn to innovation, with all parties striving to find a place of mutual understanding.

Life at Cahokia

The new spaces of Cahokia were built with the aid of immigrants, pilgrims, and locals through massive public construction projects. Most obviously, these included public plazas, pyramidal earthen mounds, and oversized upright posts. Increasingly, it is apparent that construction of mounds, plazas, and posts was not a long, slow process but rapid and massive, coordinated in short bursts of communal effort (Alt et al. 2010; Collins and Chalfant 1993; Dalan et al. 2003; Pauketat 1993). Presumably, engaging in communal activities built community cohesiveness. Simply changing the material particulars and the spatiality of life through mounds, plazas, and other aspects of planned neighborhoods changed the meanings and practices attached to other material categories and thus reorder the particulars of day-to-day life (*sensu* Gosden 2005). There might have been unintended consequences as well (Joyce 2004; Pauketat 2000).

As it grew, Cahokia became a place of marked spaces and overt material signals. Marker posts declared sacred spaces and compounds, walls and screens blocked lines of sight, T-shaped buildings indicated the places of leaders, circular structures were sweat lodges and places of healing, huge buildings were places for public councils. Elaboration of place and the remarkable range of shapes, sizes, and configurations of buildings and open spaces, I suspect, was a function of Cahokia's diverse population. All of these spaces and architectural forms disciplined bodily movement and delimited access in ways and to a degree not found at any other pre-Columbian center in eastern North America. Presumably such discipline was necessary to coordinate the movements and labor of people.

The most elaborate rituals and constructions at Cahokia, with perhaps the greatest disciplinary effect, also happened in its earliest Mississippian phases. These were the elaborate mortuary rites of Mound 72 and at least a dozen other ridge-top mounds. Here were found elaborate burials of elites and sacrificial victims, presumably part of great staged, public mortuary events. At such times, select people (most often younger women) were ceremonially killed, probably in the service of religious ideals. One event involved the sacrifice of 53 women (Fowler et al. 1999). Another entailed the likely execution of three or four women with their young children, buried alongside the bones of long-dead ancestors (Alt and Pauketat 2007). Other finds, such as a possible bound woman in a post pit, were unearthed at the East St. Louis site (Hargrave 2007).

The burials in Mound 72 and the other ridge-top mounds offer a glimpse into development of the new Mississippian religion that was being constructed through mortuary performances (Emerson et al. 2008). Among the bodies in Mound 72, for instance, was a man buried on a bead-studded, falcon-shaped cape (Rose 1999). He was buried on top of another man, surrounded by other individuals, all suggesting to many a concern with dualities, such as upper-world and underworld, and ideas of adoption, captive taking, and resurrection (Hall 1997). In particular, the men of the shell-bead blanket may be impersonators of the mythic character Redhorn, or He-Who-Wears-Human-Heads-as-Earrings, and his brother, who together in various historic-era Plains and Midwestern accounts defeat giants and resurrect their father (Brown 2003). The character is also seen in cave paintings and is depicted on a Cahokia-style carved stone figurine (Diaz-Granados and Duncan 2000; Emerson 2003; Emerson et al. 2003; Salzer and Rajnovich 2000).

Conclusion

This narrative and possibly related ones of feminine and masculine persons or mythic characters appear in other carved Cahokian figures, feminine ones often associated with crops, serpents, and the baskets that held ancestral bones, and masculine ones showing culture heroes, warriors, shamans, and a chunkey player. Oddly, the feminine forms seldom left the region, while the masculine statuettes and smoking pipes that had been made at Cahokia were eventually taken away to places as far off as Oklahoma, Wisconsin, and Alabama (Alt and Pauketat 2007; Emerson 2007). The reasons for or effects of this distribution of Cahokian things (and narratives) is difficult to know. For instance, it may seem odd that, even though the American Bottom itself appeared generally peaceful, Cahokians did not depict themselves or their dealings with other people nonviolently. Certainly, the sacrificial burials in Mound 72 attest to a form of violence, albeit sanctioned.

By AD 1150, palisade walls with regularly spaced bastions had been constructed around the ceremonial core of Cahokia and East St Louis. The population was in decline at the center and the upland villages were abandoned. Mound building became less frequent and houses were built larger, perhaps to accommodate larger families or food stores increasingly held inside (Mehrer and Collins 1995). Meanwhile, access to exotic goods probably became less restricted, new kinds of ceremonial pots were made, and personal ornamentation seems to have been more common for more people. Although the signs of greater household size and access have been interpreted as a kind of economic climax (Trubitt 2000), population contraction and diminution of public works projects probably signal a failure of central control (see Figure 41.2). The decline of Cahokia had begun.

For reasons not well understood, Cahokia was largely depopulated by AD 1350, its people dispersed in ways that make them difficult to track. Where they went and who they became is uncertain. Perhaps more difficult to understand is why knowledge of Cahokia seems to have disappeared during this dispersal phase. The events at Cahokia provoked the spread of a new "Mississippian" way of thinking and being across the eastern United States, but the tale of the great city seems to have been lost in the intervening centuries. Perhaps this was a willful forgetting of a place that, even though it birthed an important way of life and a new religion, was also a place where powerful politics ultimately failed its people.

References

Alt, S. M. 2001. Cahokian Change and the Authority of Tradition. In *The Archaeology of Traditions: Agency and History Before and After Columbus*, edited by T. R. Pauketat, pp. 141–156. University Press of Florida, Gainesville.

———. 2002. Identities, Traditions, and Diversity in Cahokia's Uplands. *Midcontinental Journal of Archaeology* 27:217–236.

———. 2006a. *Cultural Pluralism and Complexity: Analyzing a Cahokian Ritual Outpost.* Ph.D. dissertation, University of Illinois, Urbana.

———. 2006b. The Power of Diversity: The Roles of Migration and Hybridity in Culture Change. Center for Archaeological Investigations, Occasional Paper 33, *Leadership and Polity in Mississippian Society*, edited by B. M. Butler and P. D. Welch, pp. 289–308. Southern Illinois University, Carbondale.

———. 2010. *Ancient Complexities: New Perspectives in Precolumbian North America.* University of Utah Press, Salt Lake City.

———, J. D. Kruchten, and T. R. Pauketat. 2010. The Construction and Use of Cahokia's Grand Plaza. *Journal of Field Archaeology* 35(2):131–146.

Alt, S. M., and T.,R. Pauketat. 2007. Sex and the Southern Cult. In *The Southeastern Ceremonial Complex*, edited by A. King, pp. 232–250. University of Alabama Press, Tuscaloosa.

Bhabha, H. K. 1994. *The Location of Culture.* Routledge, London.

Brown, J. B. 2003. The Cahokia Mound 72-Sub1 Burials as Collective Representation. *Wisconsin Archeologist* 84:81–97.

Collins, J. M., and M. L. Chalfant. 1993. A Second-Terrace Perspective on Monks Mound. *American Antiquity* 58:319–332.

Dalan, R. A., G. R. Holley, W. I. Woods, H. W. Watters Jr., and J. A. Koepke. 2003. *Envisioning Cahokia: A Landscape Perspective.* Northern Illinois University Press, DeKalb.

Diaz-Granados, C. M., and J. R. Duncan. 2000. *The Petroglyphs and Pictographs of Missouri.* University of Alabama Press, Tuscaloosa.

Emerson, T. E. 2002. An Introduction to Cahokia 2002: Diversity, Complexity, and History. *Midcontinental Journal of Archaeology* 27(2):127–148.

———. 2003. Materializing Cahokia Shamans. *Southeastern Archaeology* 22:135–154.

———. 2007. Cahokia and the Evidence for Late Pre-Columbian War in the North American Midcontinent. In *North American Indigenous Warfare and Ritual Violence*, edited by R. J. Chacon and R. G. Mendoza, pp. 129–148. University of Arizona Press, Tucson.

———, S. M. Alt, and T. R. Pauketat. 2008. Locating American Indian Religion at Cahokia and Beyond. Center for Archaeological Investigations, Occasional Paper 36, *Religion, Archaeology, and the Material World*, edited by L. Fogelin, pp. 216–236. Southern Illinois University, Carbondale.

Emerson, T. E., R. E. Hughes, M. R. Hynes, and S. U. Wisseman. 2003. The Sourcing and Interpretation of Cahokia-Style Figures in the Trans-Mississippi South and Southeast. *American Antiquity* 68:287–314.

Fowler, M. L., J. C. Rose, B. Vander Leest, and S. R. Ahler. 1999. *The Mound 72 Area: Dedicated and Sacred Space in Early Cahokia.* Illinois State Museum, Reports of Investigations 54. Illinois State Museum Society, Springfield.

Gosden, C. 2005. What Do Objects Want? *Journal of Archaeological Method and Theory* 12(3):193–211.

Hall, R. L. 1975. Chronology and Phases at Cahokia. In *Perspectives in Cahokia Archaeology*, edited by J. A. Brown, pp. 15–31. Illinois Archaeological Survey, Bulletin 10. University of Illinois, Urbana.

———. 1997. *An Archaeology of the Soul: Native American Indian Belief and Ritual.* University of Illinois Press, Urbana.

Hargrave, E. A. 2007. Human Remains. Illinois Transportation Archaeological Research Program, Transportation Archaeological Research Reports 22, *The Archaeology of the*

East St. Louis Mound Center, Part II: The Northside Excavations, edited by A. C. Fortier, pp. 77–83. University of Illinois, Urbana.

Joyce, R. A. 2004. Unintended Consequences? Monumentality as a Novel Experience in Formative Mesoamerica. *Journal of Archaeological Method and Theory* (11):5–29.

Kelly, J. E. 1990. The Emergence of Mississippian Culture in the American Bottom Region. In *The Mississippian Emergence*, edited by B. D. Smith, pp. 113–152. Smithsonian Institution, Washington, DC.

———. 1991. The Evidence for Prehistoric Exchange and Its Implications for the Development of Cahokia. In *New Perspectives on Cahokia: Views from the Periphery*, edited by J. B. Stoltman, pp. 65–92. Prehistory, Madison, WI.

Mehrer, M. W., and J. M. Collins. 1995. Household Archaeology at Cahokia and in Its Hinterlands. In *Mississippian Communities and Households*, edited by J. D. Rogers and B. D. Smith, pp. 32–57. University of Alabama Press, Tuscaloosa.

Milner, G. R. 1998. *The Cahokia Chiefdom: The Archaeology of a Mississippian Society*. Smithsonian Institution Press, Washington, DC.

———. 1999. Warfare in Prehistoric and Early Historic Eastern North America. *Journal of Archaeological Research* 7(2):105–151.

Muller, J. D. 1997. *Mississippian Political Economy*. Plenum Press, New York.

Pauketat, T. R. 1993. *Temples for Cahokia Lords: Preston Holder's 1955–1956 Excavations of Kunnemann Mound*. Memoirs of the University of Michigan Museum of Anthropology 26. University of Michigan, Ann Arbor.

———. 1994. *The Ascent of Chiefs: Cahokia and Mississippian Politics in Native North America*. University of Alabama Press, Tuscaloosa.

———. 2000. The Tragedy of the Commoners. In *Agency in Archaeology*, edited by M.-A. Dobres and J. Robb, pp. 113–129. Routledge, London.

———. 2003. Resettled Farmers and the Making of a Mississippian Polity. *American Antiquity* 68:39–66.

———. 2004. *Ancient Cahokia and the Mississippians*. Cambridge University Press, Cambridge, UK.

———. 2007. *Chiefdoms and Other Archaeological Delusions*. AltaMira, Walnut Creek, CA.

———, D. Benden, and R. F. Boszhardt. 2010. New Evidence of the Cahokian Occupation of Trempealeau. In *Midwest Archaeological Conference*, Bloomington, IN, October 21–24.

Pauketat, T. R., and T. E. Emerson (editors). 1997. *Cahokia: Domination and Ideology in the Mississippian World*. University of Nebraska Press, Lincoln.

Pauketat, T. R., and N. H. Lopinot. 1997. Cahokian Population Dynamics. In *Cahokia: Domination and Ideology in the Mississippian World*, edited by T. R. Pauketat and T. E. Emerson, pp. 103–123. University of Nebraska Press, Lincoln.

Perino, G. 1959. Recent Information from Cahokia and Its Satellites. *Central States Archaeological Journal* 6:130–138.

Porter, J. W. 1974. *Cahokia Archaeology as Viewed from the Mitchell Site: A Satellite Community at A.D. 1150–1200*. Ph.D. dissertation, University of Wisconsin, Madison.

Rose, J. C. 1999. Mortuary Data and Analysis. Illinois State Museum, Reports of Investigations 54, *The Mound 72 Area: Dedicated and Sacred Space in Early Cahokia*, edited by M. L. Fowler, J. C. Rose, B. Vander Leest, and S. R. Ahler, pp. 63–82. Illinois State Museum Society, Springfield.

Saitta, D. J. 1994. Agency, Class, and Archaeological Interpretation. *Journal of Anthropological Archaeology* 13(3):201–227.

Salzer, R. J., and G. Rajnovich. 2000. *The Gottschall Rockshelter: An Archaeological Mystery*. Prairie Smoke Press, St. Paul, MN.

Stoltman, J. B. 2000. A Reconsideration of the Cultural Processes Linking Cahokia to Its Northern Hinterlands During the Period A.D. 1000–1200. In *Mounds, Modoc, and Mesoamerica: Papers in Honor of Melvin L. Fowler*, edited by S. R. Ahler, pp. 439–467. Illinois State Museum Scientific Papers 28. Illinois State Museum, Springfield.

Trubitt, M. B. D. 2000. Mound Building and Prestige Goods Exchange: Changing Strategies in the Cahokia Chiefdom. *American Antiquity* 65:669–690.

CHAPTER 42

MISSISSIPPIAN IN THE DEEP SOUTH: COMMON THEMES IN VARIED HISTORIES

ADAM KING

In this chapter, I focus on illustrating three points regarding Mississippian societies of the Deep South—that is, people who grew corn, built platform mounds, and practiced social ranking. The first is that there is a great deal of variation in how Mississippian societies (from sometime after AD 1000 to the coming of Europeans) looked and operated in this region. The second point is that despite this variation there are a set of common elements out of which Mississippian societies emerged. Finally, the history of all Mississippian centers is marked by radical transformations that resulted in either abandonment or restructuring of those centers and their meaning. In illustrating these points, I use two archaeological examples: the Etowah River valley of northwestern Georgia and the middle Savannah River valley separating central South Carolina from central Georgia (Figure 42.1).

North American archaeologists have been enamored with the Mississippian period for a long time. Large mounds, elaborate art objects, and complex sites captured the imagination of archaeologists and antiquarians of the late 19th century, and that hold has not lessened since. Of course, the notion of exactly what *Mississippian* is has changed over this long time and continues to be a subject of discussion (see Anderson 1994; Pauketat 2007). Owing to its early-20th-century roots, Mississippian was first conceived of as a cultural designation defined largely by construction of earthen platform mounds and production of shell-tempered pottery. Its origins were understood to be in the Mississippi River valley, where these elements of material culture appear earliest in the archaeological record. As each new wave of theory swept across our discipline, ideas about Mississippian changed. It became a cultural adaptation focused on intensive corn agriculture, and a political formation based in ranked societies or chiefdoms. Then it was conceived of as historically contingent hegemonies developed in local regions. Coming full circle, Pauketat (2007) has now argued that we should think of Mississippian as a civilization whose origins are in the emergence of the great Mississippian site of Cahokia.

Following these theoretical trends, exploration of Mississippian has focused on inventorying material traits such as pottery types, reconstructing subsistence practices, and identifying political and social institutions and leadership strategies. In this chapter, I follow the line of reasoning that views social formations as being actively generated and regenerated through the efforts of people and interest groups attempting to craft identity and a sense of history. From this perspective, understanding Mississippian communities and social groups depends on understanding how those communities and social groups were formed and shaped by the continuing process of negotiation and accommodation.

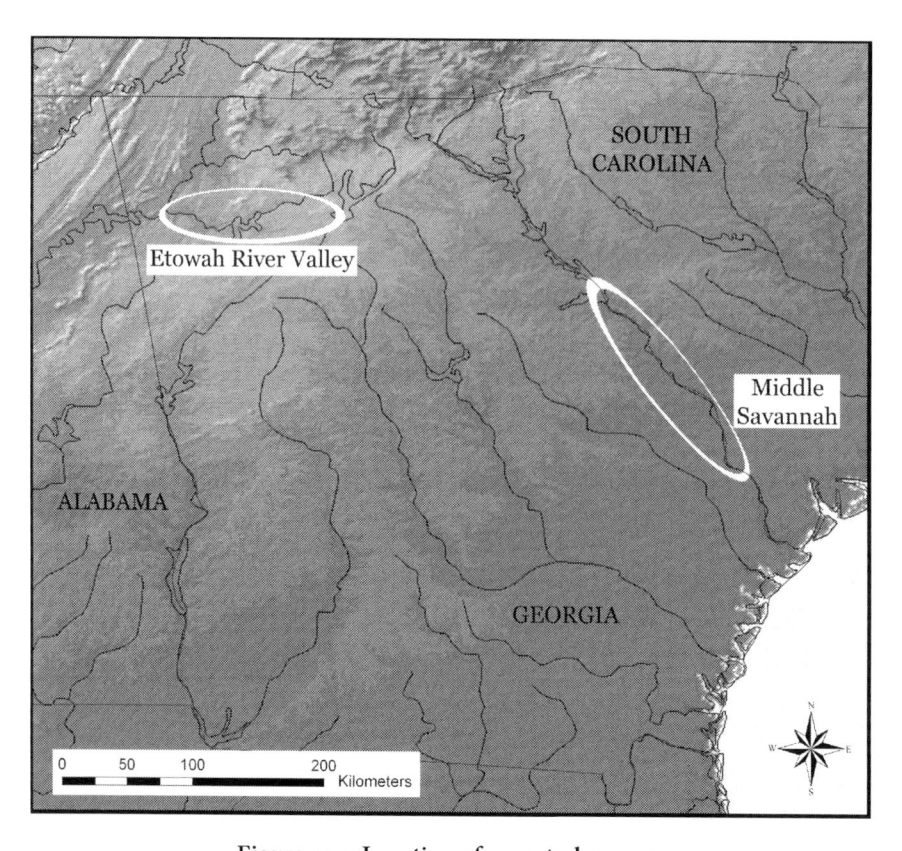

Figure 42.1 Location of case study areas.

Mississippian on the Middle Savannah River

The appearance of Mississippian communities in the middle Savannah River valley came somewhat later than in other parts of Deep South (Figure 42.2). In this area, pottery traditions and settlement patterns associated with the Late Woodland period persisted as late as AD 1200 (King and Stephenson 2003; Stephenson and King 2005). Around or shortly after AD 1000, when Mississippian towns were first established in other areas, the middle Savannah River valley was occupied by groups making two distinctly different pottery traditions: complicated stamped and cordmarked. The cordmarked pottery is associated with the Savannah I phase and connects to a widespread cordmaking tradition in the Coastal Plain of Georgia and South Carolina. Savannah I phases date from approximately AD 800 to 1200. Settlements were small and dispersed throughout the uplands, along major streams and the Savannah River. Although excavations have not been conducted to confirm this, Cabak et al. (1996) argued that these settlements represent dispersed households likely engaged in a mix of foraging and cultivation. This is based on the similarity in location and distribution of Savannah I sites to Early Woodland period sites, where excavation has confirmed the presence of permanent households (Sassaman 1993).

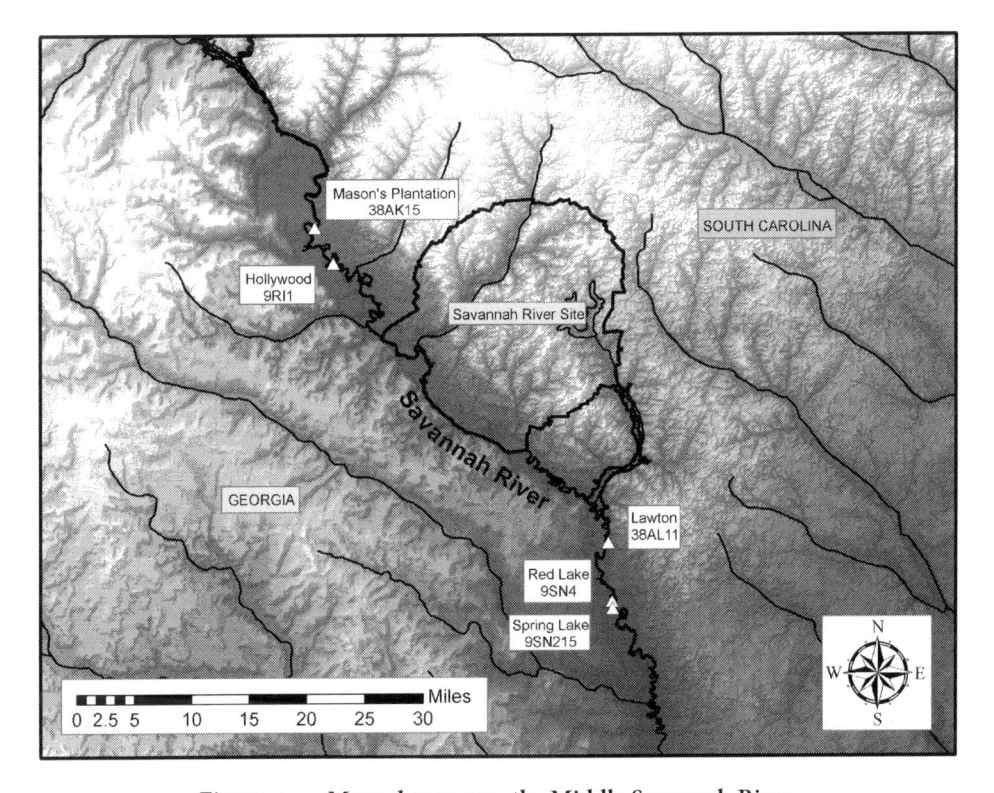

Figure 42.2 Mound towns on the Middle Savannah River.

The complicated stamped tradition is associated with the Sleepy Hollow phase in the middle Savannah valley (King and Stephenson 2003). The key characteristic of this phase is the presence of complicated stamped motifs and rim forms most closely associated with the Pisgah tradition of the Appalachian Summit of North Carolina (Dickens 1976). Sites associated with this phase appear as early as AD 900 and persist until approximately AD 1150. Pisgah tradition sites in the Appalachian summit are associated with classic Mississippian material culture markers, including platform mounds and burials with elaborately decorated objects made from nonlocal materials. In the middle Savannah valley, there are no mounds dating to the Sleepy Hollow phase; nor have any elaborately decorated nonlocal items been found. In fact, Sleepy Hollow phase settlement appears identical to that of the Savannah I phase, consisting of sites distributed across the uplands and along the Savannah River terraces, and presumed to represent permanent households.

By AD 1150, the situation changed on the middle Savannah (King and Stephenson 2003). Savannah I sites continue to appear, but the Sleepy Hollow phase gives way to the Lawton phase. In terms of settlement, the Lawton phase sites continue the pattern established earlier. In terms of pottery, the connections to the Appalachian Summit disappear, and now complicated stamped motifs resemble those made across the Piedmont and Ridge and Valley regions of Georgia and South Carolina. Pottery impressed with the cobs of shelled corn also appear during this phase, providing the first clear evidence for corn horticulture in the middle Savannah. Still, unlike other areas in the Deep South, no platform mounds, elaborate grave offerings, or compact communities were present.

Sometime around AD 1250, the middle Savannah Valley went through a fairly dramatic change. The ceramic assemblage diversity that had persisted for three centuries disappeared, as the only recognizable phase became Hollywood. The Hollywood phase pottery represents a regional variant of Savannah period assemblages found across Georgia and South Carolina. It has long been argued that the Savannah pottery tradition is a direct descendant of the earlier Etowah period complicated stamped pottery traditions associated with the Lawton phase and the like. During the Hollywood phase, sites with platform mounds appear both at the Fall Line (Hollywood and Masons Plantation) and further down river at the Lawton, Red Lake, and Spring Lake sites (Figure 42.3). Despite efforts to find chronological differences among the sites, evidence produced through archaeology indicates that all of these sites were built at the same time—during the Hollywood phase.

With the appearance of the mound towns, settlement in the middle Savannah valley changed markedly (King and Stephenson 2003; Stephenson and King 2005). This is evident in data from 35 years of systematic survey on the Savannah River Site, a Department of Energy facility located between the two clusters of Hollywood phase sites on the Savannah River. Those data show a precipitous decline in settlements in this zone between mound centers and a shift in the location of those settlements toward the newly established mound sites. It appears that the building of the mounds drew settlement toward them, creating a zone in between that was largely unoccupied.

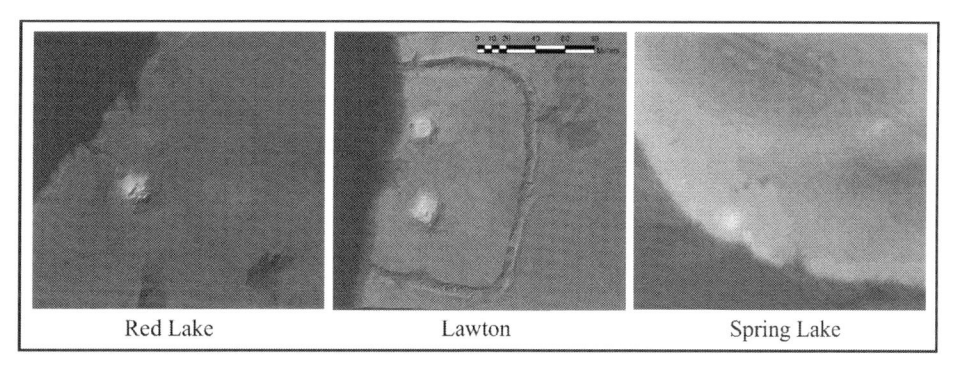

Figure 42.3 Plan maps of Lawton, Red Lake, and Spring Lake.

The data simply are not available to understand clearly how and why these changes happened. One explanation offered is based on a series of logical leaps using circumstantial evidence. While reexcavating and extending a looter's hole dug into the summit of the North Mound at Lawton, Stephenson and King (2004) encountered a premound building associated with cremated human remains. C. B. Moore excavated a trench through the same mound and recorded evidence for structures within the mound as well as the presence of cremated human remains. Outside of these few encounters with human remains, no graves have been found at any of the middle Savannah valley mound sites (Red Lake, Lawton, and Spring Lake). However, looters are reported to have found many burials as cremations interred inside pottery vessels on natural sand ridges in the river floodplain and terraces. Those vessels belong to phases dating from AD 1250 to 1450 and therefore overlap with the Hollywood phase.

It seems reasonably clear that establishment of the mound town correlates with a settlement shift to the vicinity of those towns. What drew people to settle near those mounds, and also to devote surplus labor to their building? In the middle Savannah valley, this is the key to establishment of Mississippian communities. Both Mississippian symbolism (Lankford 2007; Reilly 2007) and ethnographic information (see for example Hall 1997) make it clear that the path of souls after death and the mortuary ritual were important elements of eastern Native American beliefs. This may be most famously reflected in the transformation of the Moundville site in Alabama after AD 1200. At that time, Knight (1998) argues, much of the resident population left the site and it became a place reserved for rituals of death and burial; in essence, the site became a necropolis. The symbolism dominating Moundville art, especially expressed on engraved pottery, reflects this transformation in depicting imagery associated with death and the Path of Souls (Steponaitis and Knight 2004).

It is possible to interpret the structural remains beneath and within the North Mound at Lawton as mortuary processing facilities. They are associated with a small quantity of cremated human remains, which are found in much greater numbers at sand ridge sites along the Savannah River. The mound towns, like Lawton, may have been where the dead were prepared for their afterlife journey. If this is the case, creation of the mound towns and relocation of populations to their vicinity was facilitated by adopting an ideology focusing on access to the afterlife or path of souls. Although it may have privileged those who ran the rituals of death, this ideology represented a set of beliefs and practices that were adopted by whole social segments once living dispersed across a much wider area. With no evidence that coercion could have played a role in its adoption, we are left with a consensual process that likely involved negotiation among social segments and eventual accommodation of differing ideas.

The three towns established were relatively modest places, by Mississippian mound town standards. The Lawton site (38AL11) has two mounds flanking a small plaza and a well-defined ditch with embankment, all covering approximately 2 hectares. The Red Lake site (9Sn4) covers approximately 3 hectares and has three mounds flanking a small plaza (Dale 2007), while the nearby Spring Lake site (9Sn87) also covers about 2 hectares and has a single mound located adjacent to a small plaza (Wood 2009).

Despite arguments to the contrary, there is little reason to believe that these towns were anything but independent communities. Hally (1993) and Wood (2009) have both argued that the three middle Savannah mound towns constitute a single complex chiefdom—a social formation based on social ranking with a two- or three-tiered system of political administration. This inference is, in part, based on Hally's arguments (1993) about the spacing of mound towns and organization of Mississippian chiefdoms. Using patterning in the spacing, Hally has argued that single mounds separated from others by more than 20 kilometers were simple chiefdoms, while two or more mound towns within 20 kilometers of one another were primary and secondary capitals in a complex chiefdom.

The problem is that there is no clearly identifiable primary center in this set of mound towns in the middle Savannah valley, as predicted by models of complex chiefdoms (see Anderson 1994; Hally 1993). If the number of mounds is considered, then Red Lake might be the primary center. If the amount of labor invested is the key indicator (see Wood 2009), then Lawton should be the dominant center. Unfortunately, we really do not know enough about the sites to properly place them in an administrative hierarchy. The number of mounds or amount of labor invested is a poor proxy for place in an administrative hierarchy, which is assessed only by understanding how many kinds of functions each center served (Peebles and Kus 1977).

Blitz (1999) has argued that the three sites do not represent a simple or complex chiefdom but instead should be thought of differently. Using his Fission-Fusion model, he argues that the three sites must represent a collection of Mississippian social groups united in some type of confederacy where the hierarchical relationships implied by Hally's model are not present, or at least are not emphasized.

I suspect that Blitz may be closer to the actual relationship among those towns. The breaking apart or fusing together of individual social units or towns, however, may not have a lot to do with their creation or location. The key in this situation is the absence of hierarchy and centrality in the relationship among the towns. Here I follow Blitz and draw on descriptions of historic period Creek towns or *talwas* (Ethridge 2003; Wesson 2008). Towns consisted of a center and associated households that were dispersed up and down river valleys, sometimes up to several kilometers from the center. The settlements associated with one town were often located only a few kilometers from the settlements associated with another nearby town. Despite the fact that towns were located relatively close to one another, each had its own history and its own civic-ceremonial space. Clan membership, marriage, and alliances tied towns and their members together, and towns were often linked in mother-daughter relationships as the latter formed when they broke away from the former. Kinship and alliance can create or have hierarchy embedded within them, but in general Creek *talwas* were linked though politically independent.

This is likely a reasonable model for the situation in the middle Savannah valley. All the sites are roughly the same size and are structured in a similar fashion. They probably represent independent towns, each with its own sacred center. There were certainly links among the towns created by kinship and alliances, and some towns may have been acknowledged as older and therefore were due greater respect. There was no overarching political structure tying these towns together, and no single town was seen as dominating the others.

The rather abrupt appearance of mound towns in the middle Savannah is mirrored by their equally abrupt disappearance. By AD 1400 Red Lake, Lawton, and Spring Lake were all abandoned, and settlement had rebounded in the devoid areas throughout the Hollywood phase. It appears that with the demise of the mound towns, settlement distribution, and by extension the organization and structure of societies, returned to what it had been before AD 1200. As Hally (1996) has shown, it is not uncommon for Mississippian mound towns in the Deep South to become abandoned after only a single phase of occupation. As we see in the next example, if mound towns are not abandoned then they are transformed in ways that change their structure and likely meaning.

The Emergence of Mississippian on the Etowah River

In the Etowah River valley, the appearance of Mississippian society came about with establishment of the Etowah site as a community. This event is currently placed sometime around AD 1000 (King 2003). Before establishment of Etowah, the landscape of northern Georgia, northeastern Alabama, and southeastern Tennessee was dominated by a series of social groups, each with a distinct material culture and history. In northern Georgia, they are associated with the Woodstock phase (Cobb and Garrow 1995; Markin 2007), whose material culture is dominated by complicated stamped pottery, densely settled and often palisaded communities, and evidence for reliance on corn production. In eastern Tennessee, the groups involved are associated with Hamilton culture, characterized by settled communities, reliance on corn agriculture, and use of communal burial mounds (Schroedl 1998). To the west were groups associated with Coker Ford, Cane Creek, and Ellis phases of the Coosa drainage in Alabama (Little 1999). As with the Woodstock phase, sites of these phases show evidence of corn cultivation and a concern for, if not participation in, warfare as evidenced by fortifications and sites located in defensible settings.

Following Little's arguments (1999), one may assert that during the Late Woodland period this region was occupied by a series of geographically distinct population groupings. Each group had its own material culture, but the shared aspects of settlement and pottery manufacture suggest a degree of interaction among the groups. The presence of corn and other domesticates indicates reliance on gardening as an important subsistence practice. Cross-culturally, settings where distinct groups of horticulturalists occupy the landscape are often associated with a high incidence of small-scale but endemic warfare. That this was the case in northern Georgia is supported by the presence of fortifications and the importance of defense in settlement location. It is also suggested by the recent appearance of small, triangular projectile points in this region. As Blitz (1988) has argued, projectile points of this kind signal the appearance of bow and arrow technology, which had a dramatic impact on the conduct of warfare.

I have argued that the Etowah site emerged as an important center as a result of these social circumstances (King 2003). Some of the earliest cultural features at Etowah are a series of large pits, ranging from 3 to 10 meters in diameter and up to 4 meters deep, that were filled with large quantities of animal bone and broken pottery. I have suggested that they were borrow pits used as the source of fill for Etowah's Mound A (King 2003). The pits were filled with refuse quickly, leaving no time for walls to slump or sediments to accumulate at the bottom. The animal bone included in them shows few signs of carnivore gnawing, suggesting the refuse was buried quickly.

On the basis of this information, I have argued that the earliest mound construction at Etowah took place in conjunction with feasting (King 2003). Feasting and mound construction were parts of a rite of intensification that brought disparate groups together and cast them into common action. Given what we know about mounds, they were likely symbols of the earth, such that building and renewing them was a means of manipulating and renewing the earth (Knight 1989). Following this, I suggested that the emergence of Etowah was a product of a coalescence of those distinct Late Woodland groups. Their coming together effectively halted the intercommunity conflict. The reason for the coalescence was to renew the earth, thereby ensuring maturity of the crops and continuity of social groups.

The emergence of Mississippian at Etowah was created as distinct social groups came together under a unifying ideology that stopped intercommunity warfare, ensured maturation of crops, and created a new kind of community (Figure 42.4).

As evidence of this coalescence, Little (1999) cites mixing of various pottery tempering agents in the earliest Mississippian deposits at Etowah. Shell, limestone, and sand were dominant tempering agents in the various Late Woodland phases of the region, but all are found in the Early Mississippian deposits at Etowah. Recently, geophysical data generated by a gradiometer survey of Etowah has produced more circumstantial evidence of this coalescence. In those data, Walker (2009) identifies approximately 100 magnetic anomalies that closely match excavated examples of Mississippian period wall-trench structures. In northern Georgia, wall-trench architecture is found only in the period from about AD 1000 to 1200—the period when Etowah was founded. These anomalies cluster around a series of plazas, creating the appearance of a series of small villages within the larger Etowah community. This pattern of subcommunities is what might be expected if the Etowah community comprised distinct social segments.

This new community was the first of its kind in the Etowah River valley, and one of a very few to have developed throughout the region at this time (Figure 42.5). By AD 1100, two more Mississippian mound towns were established in the Etowah River valley, at the Wilbanks and Long Swamp sites. Like Etowah, they were small communities with modest mounds. It is unclear what their relationship was to Etowah, but it is likely they were daughter communities established by social segments that split from Etowah. Given this, these communities were probably connected by marriage ties, clan membership, and a shared history. As with the case on

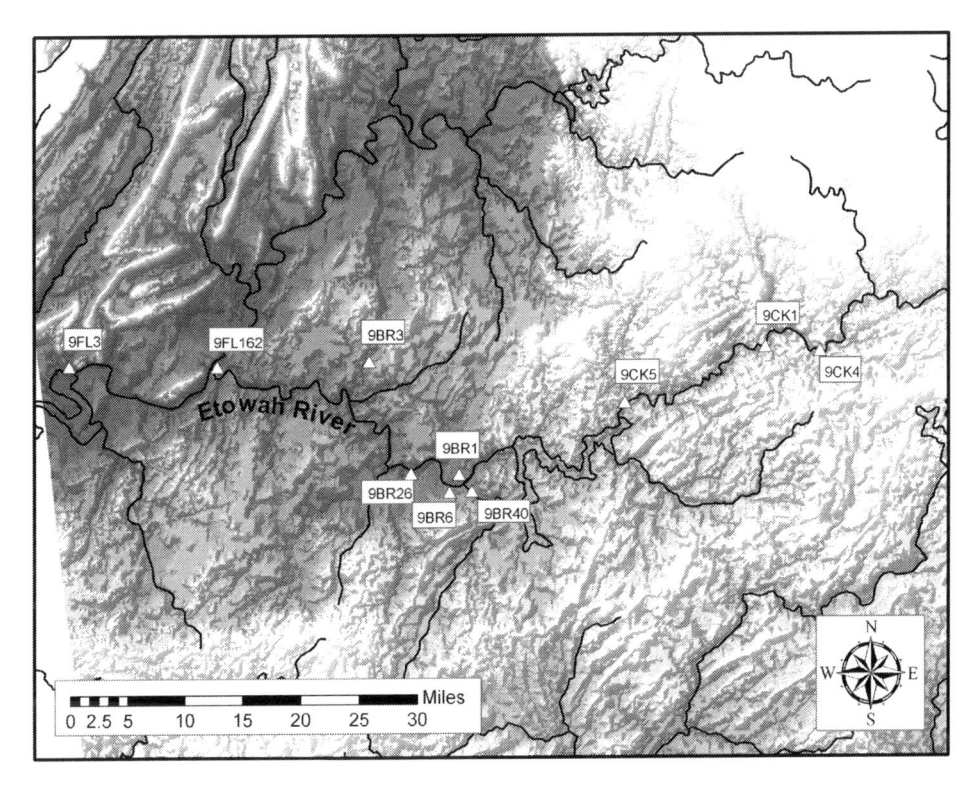

Figure 42.4 Mound towns in the Etowah River Valley from AD 1000 to 1350.

the middle Savannah valley, there is no compelling reason to suspect that any one town held sway over the others.

Sometime after AD 1200, Etowah, Wilbanks, and Long Swamp all were abandoned. The precise reasons are unclear, but it seems that this abandonment extended throughout the Etowah River valley. When people returned to Etowah and the other former mound towns, the landscape was dramatically reorganized. Instead of three similar mound towns, it quickly became clear that Etowah was the dominant center in the valley. The existing mounds at the site were significantly enlarged, and a third mound (Mound C) was initiated. In it the inhabitants of Etowah buried people and elaborate objects made using foreign materials and decorated with foreign art styles. With the return of people to Etowah came establishment of four new, but much smaller, mound towns a short distance from the site as well as reoccupation of Wilbanks and Long Swamp.

Then, within decades of the site's reoccupation, Etowah went through another transformation. The residential zone east of Mound A at the site was transformed into a large, clay-lined plaza and the entire site was surrounded by a palisade with a complex of ditches and borrows. Additionally, I have argued that the site's burial mound, Mound C, was transformed from a cemetery for honored dead into an *axis mundi* or sacred center (King 2009). In essence, the entire Etowah site became a sacred precinct after AD 1325 and the most impressive place in the entire river valley.

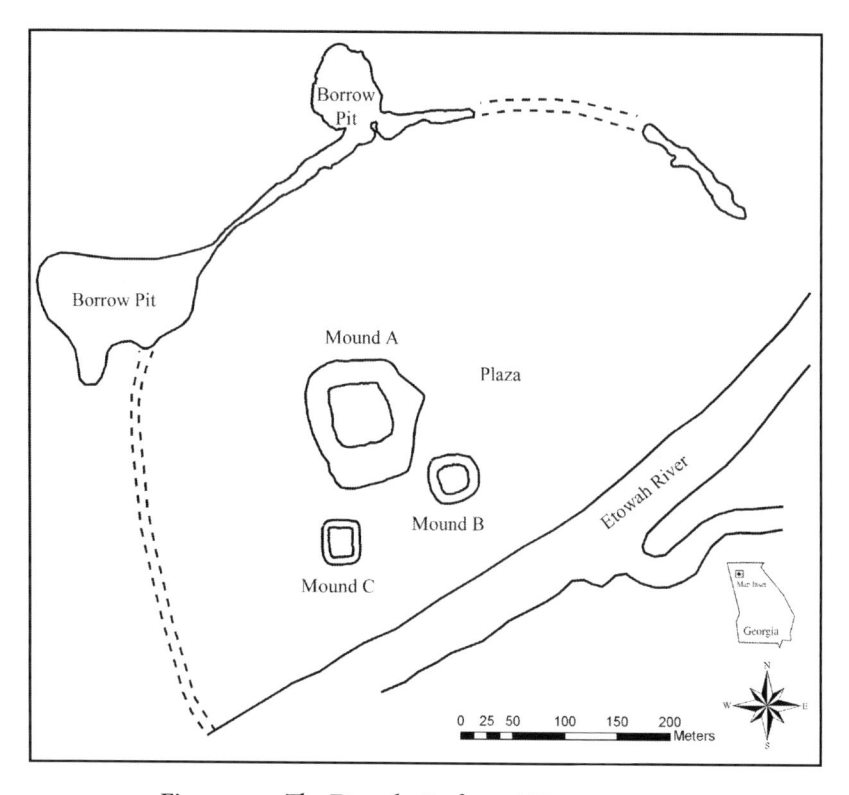

Figure 42.5 The Etowah site from AD 1000 to 1350.

Common Origins, Divergent Histories, Radical Transformations

The case studies I include in this chapter illustrate two points along a spectrum of things called Mississippian. The Etowah River valley is dominated by a single, large center—the Etowah site—whose history as an important place extends throughout the entire Mississippian period. At certain points in that history, creation of large monuments and manipulation of elaborately decorated and symbolically loaded items play an important role. Recognizable Mississippian material culture comes later to the middle Savannah River valley, where a series of small mound sites are built and abandoned all within a century. The mounds and associated communities are small, and there is no evidence that elaborate, symbolic objects were an important part of ritual or displays of status.

Despite these differences, their histories exhibit certain parallels that speak to important aspects of Mississippian societies in the Deep South. One of those parallels is the importance of cultural plurality and population movement in the development of Mississippian communities. This echoes Pauketat's argument (2007) that Mississippian was a social innovation created by population movement and the melding of traditions of distinctive social groups. In the Savannah River valley, this cultural plurality existed for a few centuries before Mississippian communities formed, but such formation involved population relocation and presumably aggregation of distinct social groups around the newly established mound towns. In the Etowah River valley, Mississippian was created as distinct social groups came together at Etowah in the common effort of world renewal. Cultural plurality is visible in the blending of pottery traditions and in the presence of distinctive subcommunities within the Etowah site.

Another similarity in the history of these two areas is that the relationships among the mound towns created were not dominated by political and social hierarchy. Instead, it appears that in both cases newly formed mound towns were largely independent. This, I suspect, was generally the norm in most regions throughout the Southeast where Mississippian communities emerged. Not until later in the history of various regions did political competition and dominance become a concern of power-seeking individuals and social segments.

The third commonality in these case studies is that within a few centuries of developing, the communities that were created experienced radical transformations. In the middle Savannah valley, this radical transformation took the form of abandonment of the mound towns and dispersal of populations, returning to settlement practices and organization of society found in previous centuries. In the Etowah River valley, the mound towns established were abandoned after two centuries; when people returned, the nature of mound centers and the relationship among them changed dramatically. Etowah was quickly transformed from a community into a fortified sacred precinct with massive monuments flanking grand plazas. At that same time, as many as five smaller communities emerged within a day's walk of Etowah, leaving the impression that the site had become a center dominating all others in the valley.

By referring to all late pre-Contact agricultural groups building earthen platform mounds as Mississippian, scholars often mask the great diversity in those societies. In the Deep South, as elsewhere in the Southeast and Midwest, there was a great deal of variation in the scale and organization of Mississippian period societies. Our understanding of that variability is furthered little if we limit our investigation to counting mounds, looking at the number and value of burial goods, and measuring site extent. Exploring development of Mississippian communities as a historical process, rather than fitting them into existing classification schemes, leaves room for variation in what we call Mississippian and provides a framework for recognizing it.

REFERENCES

Anderson, D. G. 1994. *The Savannah River Chiefdoms: Political Change in the Late Prehistoric Southeast*. University of Alabama Press, Tuscaloosa.

Blitz, J. 1988. Adoption of the Bow in Prehistoric North America. *North American Archaeologist* 9(2):123–145.

———. 1999. Mississippian Chiefdoms and the Fission-Fusion Process. *American Antiquity* 64(4):577–592.

Cabak, M. A., K. E. Sassaman, and J. C. Gillam. 1996. *Distributional Archaeology in the Aiken Plateau: Intensive Survey of E Area, Savannah River Site, Aiken County, South Carolina*. Savannah River Archaeological Research Papers 8. Occasional Papers of the Savannah River Archaeological Research Program, South Carolina Institute of Archaeology and Anthropology. University of South Carolina, Columbia.

Cobb, C., and P. Garrow. 1995. Woodstock Culture and the Question of Mississippian Emergence. *American Antiquity* 61:21–38.

Dale, E. K. 2007. The Red Lake Site (9SN4): *A Middle Mississippian Mound Town in the Central Savannah River Valley*. Master's thesis, University of South Carolina, Columbia.

Dickens, R. S. 1976. *Cherokee Prehistory: The Pisgah Phase in the Appalachian Summit Region*. University of Tennessee Press, Knoxville.

Ethridge, R. 2003. *Creek Country: The Creek Indians and Their World 1796–1816*. University of North Carolina Press, Chapel Hill.

Hall, R. L. 1997. *An Archaeology of the Soul: North American Indian Belief and Ritual*. University of Illinois Press, Urbana.

Hally, D. J. 1993. The Territorial Size of Mississippian Chiefdoms. In *Archaeology of Eastern North America: Papers in Honor of Stephen Williams*, edited by J. B. Stoltman, pp. 143–168. Archaeological Report 25. Mississippi Department of Archives and History, Jackson, MI.

———. 1996. Platform Mound Construction and the Instability of Mississippian Chiefdoms. In *Political Structure and Change in the Prehistoric Southeastern United States*, edited by J. F. Scarry, pp. 92–127. University Press of Florida, Gainesville.

King, A. 2003. *Etowah: The Political History of a Chiefdom Capital*. University of Alabama Press, Tuscaloosa.

———. 2009. Multiple Groups, Overlapping Symbols and the Creation of a Sacred Space at Etowah's Mound C. In *Mississippian Mortuary Studies: Beyond Hierarchy and the Representationist Perspective*, edited by L. P. Sullivan and R. C. Mainfort Jr., pp. 54–73. University Press of Florida, Gainesville.

———, and D. K. Stephenson. 2003. From Potsherds to Political Cycling: The Mississippian Occupation of the Middle Savannah Valley. Paper presented at the 60th Annual Meeting of the Southeastern Archaeological Conference, November. Charlotte, NC.

King, A., C. P. Walker, and F. K. Reilly III. 2008. Geophysical Research at Etowah: 2005–2008. Report submitted to the Georgia Department of Natural Resources, Atlanta.

Knight, V. J. 1989. Symbolism of Mississippian Mounds. In *Powhatan's Mantle: Indians in the Colonial Southeast*, edited by P. H. Wood, G. A. Waselkov, and M. T. Hatley, pp. 279–291. University of Nebraska Press, Lincoln.

———. 1998. Moundville as a Diagrammatic Ceremonial Center. In *Archaeology of the Moundville Chiefdom*, edited by V. J. Knight and V. P. Steponaitis, pp. 1–25. Smithsonian Institution, Washington, DC.

Lankford, G. E. 2007. The "Path of Souls": Some Death Imagery in the Southeastern Ceremonial Complex. In *Ancient Objects and Sacred Realms*, edited by F. K. Reilly III and J. F. Garber, pp. 174–212. University of Texas Press, Austin.

Little, K. J. 1999. The Role of Late Woodland Interactions in the Emergence of Etowah. *Southeastern Archaeology* 18(1):45–56.

Markin, J. 2007. *Woodstock: The Rise of Political Complexity in Northern Georgia*. Ph.D. dissertation, University of Georgia, Athens.

Pauketat, T. R. 2007. *Chiefdoms and Other Archaeological Delusions*. AltaMira Press, Lanham, MD.

Peebles, C. S., and S. Kus. 1977. Some Archaeological Correlates of Ranked Societies. *American Antiquity* 42:421–448.

Reilly, F. K. 2007. The Petaloid Motif: A Celestial Symbolic Locative in the Shell Art of Spiro. In *Sacred Objects, Ancient Realms: Interpretations of Mississippian Iconography*, edited by F. K. Reilly and J. Garber, pp. 39–55. University of Texas Press, Austin.

Sassaman, K. E. 1993. *Early Woodland Settlement in the Aiken Plateau: Archaeological Investigations at 38AK157, Savannah River Site, Aiken County, South Carolina*. Savannah River Archaeological Research Papers 3. Occasional Papers of the Savannah River Archaeological Research Program, South Carolina Institute of Archaeology and Anthropology, University of South Carolina, Columbia.

Schroedl, G. F. 1998. Mississippian Towns in the Eastern Tennessee Valley. In *Mississippian Towns and Sacred Spaces: Searching for an Architectural Grammar*, edited by R. B. Lewis and C. B. Stout, pp. 64–92. University of Alabama Press, Tuscaloosa.

———. 2005. *Woodland and Mississippian Period Settlement in the Middle Savannah River Valley*. Paper presented at the 70th Annual Meeting of the Society for American Archaeology, March, Salt Lake City.

Steponaitis, V. P., and V. J. Knight. 2004. Moundville Art in Historical and Social Context. In *Hero, Hawk, and Open Hand: American Indian Art of the Ancient Midwest and Southeast*, edited by R. V. Sharp, pp. 167–182. Yale University Press, New Haven, CT.

Walker, C. P. 2009. *Landscape Archaeo-Geophysics: A Study of Magnetometer Surveys from Etowah (9BR1), the George C. Davis Site (41CE14), and the Hill Farm Site (41BW169)*. Ph.D. dissertation, University of Texas, Austin.

Wesson, C. B. 2008. *Households and Hegemony: Early Creek Prestige Goods, Symbolic Capital and Social Power*. University of Nebraska Press, Lincoln.

Wood, M. J. 2009. *Mississippian Chiefdom Organization: A Case Study from the Savannah River Valley*. Ph.D. dissertation, University of Georgia, Athens.

CHAPTER 43

LIVING WITH WAR: THE IMPACT OF CHRONIC VIOLENCE IN THE MISSISSIPPIAN-PERIOD CENTRAL ILLINOIS RIVER VALLEY

GREGORY D. WILSON

The Central Illinois River Valley (CIRV) of west-central Illinois has a complex history of migration and culture contact that was strongly affected by violence (Conrad 1991; Esarey and Conrad 1998; Milner et al. 1991; Steadman 2001). Located on the northern periphery of the Mississippian cultural area, the CIRV has the potential to transform our understanding of the impact and outcomes of intergroup violence in middle-range societies (Figures 43.1 and 43.2). In this chapter, I argue that changing patterns of violence substantially altered the lives of those who lived in this region. To make my case I discuss archaeological patterns of violence from four different periods of the late Prehistoric era: the terminal late Woodland period (AD 700 to 1100), the early Mississippian period (AD 1100 to 1250), the middle Mississippian Period (AD 1250 to 1300), and the late Mississippian period (AD 1300 to 1440).

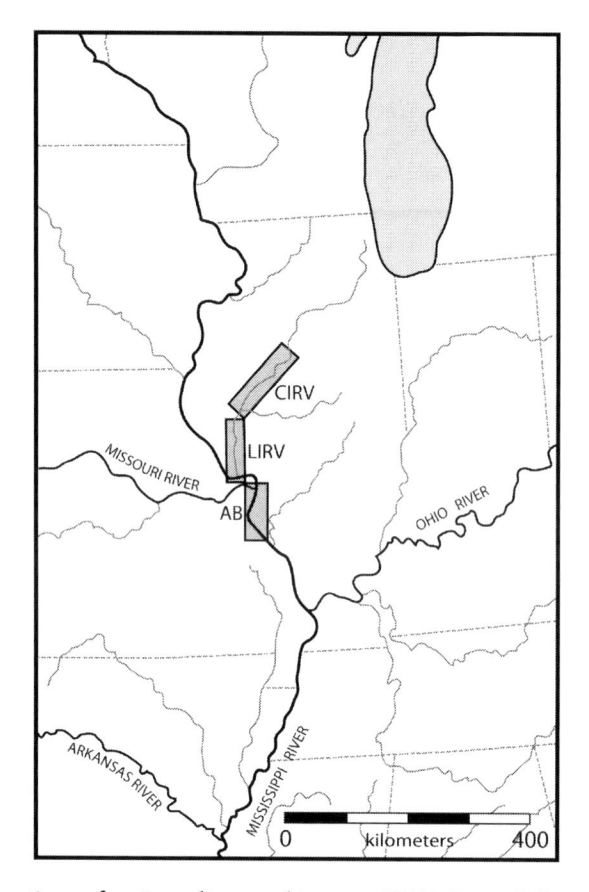

Figure 43.1 Locations of regions discussed in text: CIRV, Central Illinois River Valley; LIRV, Lower Illinois River Valley; AB, American Bottom.

LATE WOODLAND PERIOD

The Late Woodland period was an era of intensifying hostilities across much of eastern North America (Cobb and Garrow 1996; Little 1999; Milner 2007). Intergroup conflict ensued from adoption of a more sedentary way of life based on plant cultivation, associated population increases, and use of new military and hunting technologies such as the bow and arrow (Blitz 1988; Milner 1999:122, 2007). In settling into particular regional locales, Native American groups also began to forge localized cultural identities and traditions. These changes altered the scale and intensity of violence throughout much of eastern North America.

Such patterns of violence are well represented in both the lower and central portions of the Illinois Valley. Excavation of late Woodland burial mounds in the lower Valley has revealed cemetery groups with numerous incidences of violence-related skeletal trauma. A number of the individuals buried in the Koster, Pete Klunk, and Schild site mounds exhibit evidence of violent injury or death (Perino 1973a, 1973b, 1973c). Documented injuries include embedded arrow points, severed appendages, blunt force cranial trauma, and decapitation. In some cases injured

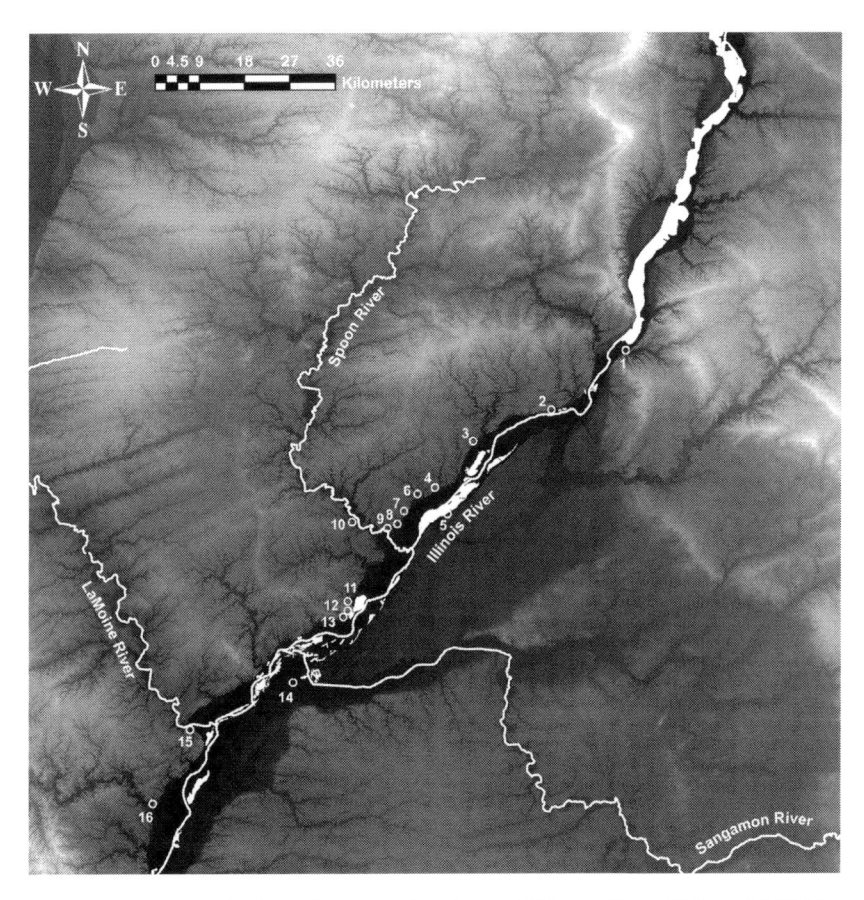

Figure 43.2 Locations of selected sites in the Central Illinois River Valley: (1) Hildemyer; (2) Kingston Lake; (3) Orendorf; (4) Gooden; (5) Liverpool Lake; (6) C. W. Cooper; (7) Norris Farms no. 36, Morton; (8) Dickson, Eveland, Myer Dickson; (9) Larson; (10) Buckeye Bend; (11) Emmons; (12) Fiedler; (13) Crable; (14) Lawrenz Gun Club; (15) Star Bridge; (16) Walsh.

individuals were buried together in groups, suggesting they died at the same time (Perino 1973a:146). Excavation of Late Woodland burial mounds at the Gooden site in the Central Valley has also revealed instances of violence-related skeletal trauma in the form of graves with multiple interments and individuals with embedded arrow points (Cole and Deuel 1937:191–198).

This osteological evidence of Late Woodland violence corresponds with the emergence of multiple localized settlement groups in different portions of the Mississippi and Illinois valleys and the intervening uplands of west-central Illinois. In the Central Illinois River Valley, there is evidence of two contemporaneous Late Woodland groups, represented by the Bauer Branch phase in the southern part of the region and the Mossville phase in the northern part of the region. These two groups are represented primarily by small and dispersed settlements in portions of the valley and western uplands (Esarey 2000:398; Green and Nolan 2000:362). However, the presence of village-sized settlements on natural levees and floodplain ridges indicates an emerging focus on the riverine environment of the CIRV (Esarey

2000:392). Antagonism or social avoidance among these groups is indicated by minimal intermixture of Mossville and Bauer Branch pottery types at representative sites (Green and Nolan 2000:368).

How did intergroup violence affect the lives of the Late Woodland occupants of the CIRV? The absence of village fortifications at this time indicates that hostilities were intermittent rather than chronic in duration. Moreover, the presence of Late Woodland sites in a variety of upland and floodplain settings displays no obvious preference for defensive settlement locations. Considered collectively, the settlement and skeletal data suggest that terminal Late Woodland hostilities in the region consisted of periodic, small-scale skirmishes punctuated by occasional larger confrontations. Dovetailing with settlement-subsistence trends of decreasing mobility, such hostilities likely contributed to development of larger social aggregates with spatially circumscribed social identities.

Early Mississippian Period

By AD 1050, early Mississippian groups in the American Bottom (178 river kilometers south of the CIRV) managed to transcend the divisive tribal politics of the Woodland era to found Cahokia, the largest and most complex Native American civilization in prehistoric North America (Figure 40.1; Alt, Emerson, this volume; Pauketat 2004). The emergence of political complexity in the American Bottom had a profound influence on neighboring groups. In several cases, this influence appears to have resulted from the northern movement of Cahokians into portions of the Upper Mississippi Valley, including the Central Illinois River Valley, the Apple River Valley of northwestern Illinois, the Aztalan area of southeastern Wisconsin, and the Red Wing area of Minnesota (Emerson 1991, this volume).

Small but influential groups of Cahokians appear to have emigrated to the CIRV around AD 1050. It is unclear whether the arrival of these Mississippian envoys was requested or if they relocated on their own accord, but the result was the Mississippianization of local Late Woodland groups (Conrad 1991; Harn 1991). An important aspect of the CIRV's Mississippianization was termination of Late Woodland-type hostilities in the region. Early Mississippian settlement patterns in the CIRV consist of small and widely distributed sites centered on nodal religious communities such as the Eveland and Kingston Lake sites, which do not appear to be fortified (Conrad 1991). From these patterns, it is tempting to conclude that a Cahokian presence in the CIRV brought an end to violence. But this was not the case. Among the Mississippian traditions that Cahokians brought with them to the CIRV was a new kind of violence involving public execution and elaborate mortuary ritualism. The excavation of Mound 72 at Cahokia uncovered multiple mass graves filled with executed women and men, the bodies of which were arranged so as to reference certain religious narratives (Brown 2006; Fowler et al. 1999). Among these executed individuals was a group of four men who had been beheaded and behanded. On the basis of isotopic analysis of bone chemistry, one surmises that at least some of these sacrificial victims were nonlocal in origin and may be raiding captives from afar (Alt 2008; Ambrose and Krigbaum 2003).

Similar mortuary interments of sacrificial victims have been identified in the CIRV at the Dickson Mounds Museum site (Conrad 1991, 1993). Bearing a striking resemblance to Mound 72 Cahokia, the Dickson Mounds Museum example consists of a burial pit with four beheaded adult men, with pots arranged in place of their heads (Conrad 1991). Thus peace in the Illinois Valley appears to have included some notable exceptions.

Such violent spectacles involving execution of nonlocal peoples likely changed the way that early Mississippian inhabitants in both the Illinois Valley and the American Bottom perceived violence and death. That is, contextualized within an emerging political and religious movement, such events may have fundamentally altered people's notions of group identity and membership, as well as their willingness to participate in increasingly ritually and politically structured violence. The religious and political integration of early Mississippian groups in the CIRV also had the potential to change the scale of violence in the region, thus setting the stage for larger-scale confrontations.

Middle and Late Mississippian Periods

The end of the 12th century brought important changes to midcontinental North America. Native American groups throughout much of the central and upper Mississippi Valley settled into compact villages protected by wooden palisade walls (Emerson 2007:135–137; Morse and Morse 1983). The escalation of violence indicated by construction of these fortifications is further revealed by evidence that a number of these villages were burned to the ground (Morse and Morse 1983; O'Brien 2001; Price and Griffin 1979). In some cases outlying farmsteads associated with fortified villages were also burned, possibly a result of being attacked.

Understanding why violence began to escalate at this time is complicated by a multiplicity of potential causal factors. The expanding populations of sedentary agricultural societies clearly played a role in intensifying Middle Mississippian hostilities (Larson 1972; Milner 2007:196). Prime agricultural land occupied and controlled by one Mississippian group would have restricted the mobility and expansion of others. Moreover, resource scarcity would have been magnified by creation of unoccupied buffer zones between hostile populations (Anderson 1994; Hally 1993; Milner 2007:196).

On the basis of the Middle Mississippian appearance of ritual weaponry and iconographic depictions of violence, one can posit that warring also appears to have become part of a widespread system by which warrior-age men, including the ruling elite, gained status and authority (Dye 2004; Knight 1986). This male-oriented aggrandizement strategy may have helped counterbalance the increasing power of female-oriented institutions of authority based on control of food production.

Middle Mississippian warfare appears to have been particularly intense in the CIRV in comparison to the American Bottom region to the south, where more highly populated and complexly organized settlements served to deter potential raiding parties (Wilson and Steadman 2007). Around AD 1200, the early Mississippian settlement pattern of dispersed communities was replaced by fortified and nucleated towns linked with smaller outlying settlements. Orendorf is the earliest and best-understood fortified village in the CIRV. The Middle Mississippian occupation of the site consisted of four sequentially rebuilt towns; at least three stages were protected by wooden palisade walls with regularly spaced bastions. Orendorf's final occupation, settlement D, consisted of a 5 hectare palisaded settlement with an estimated population of 400 to 500 inhabitants (Conrad 1991:133). Settlement D underwent two episodes of village expansion; each time the palisade wall was also expanded and rebuilt. This trend toward population amalgamation was likely inspired by intensifying hostilities in the region. Around AD 1250, the Orendorf site was the target of a large-scale direct assault resulting in complete incineration of the village. The presence of in situ whole artifacts on the floor of many of these burned structures suggests that village occupants had little time to evacuate before their homes were destroyed.

Successful assault on a fortified Mississippian settlement like Orendorf would have been no small feat for a war party. Orendorf's wooden palisade would have presented a major obstacle. Attackers would have been extremely vulnerable to projectile assault once they entered the 40–50 meter killing radius of an archer-manned bastion (see Keeley et al. 2007:70; Lafferty 1973). Scaling this wall while dodging arrow fire would have been equally precarious. Alternatively, with only stone celts as woodworking tools it would have been very difficult to dismantle portions of the wall to gain entrance (see Keener 1999 for discussion of Native American military tactics used against palisade walls). Even after Orendorf's defenses were breached, attackers would still have to confront the town's occupants in direct combat.

Estimating the size of the offensive force necessary to conquer a village like Orendorf is complicated, but a common military science ratio offered for such a scenario is three attackers to one defender.[1] If approximately half of Orendorf's estimated population of 400 were fit for combat, then a successful offensive on the community would have consisted of a minimum of 600 attackers. If only a quarter of Orendorf's occupants were combat ready, then perhaps as few as 300 attackers may have been sufficient to take the village. Two important insights derive from these estimations. First, an effective assault force would have had to be drawn from several Orendorf-sized settlements. Secondly, in a direct assault scenario there would have been the potential for the attacking group to suffer heavy casualties (Keeley et al. 2007; Milner 2007:188). Collectively these two factors indicate that a military campaign capable of successfully assaulting a fortified Mississippian village such as Orendorf would have required multivillage-level planning and a readiness to endure significant causalities.

The violent incineration of Orendorf was not the last large-scale attack of its kind in the CIRV. Archaeologists have determined that Middle Mississippian village sites such as Buckeye Bend and Star Bridge were also attacked and burned to the ground, judging from the presence of hundreds of burned buildings visible as blackened rectangular surface stains in modern agricultural fields (Conrad 1991). Surface survey and small-scale excavations have also identified extensive burning at other Middle Mississippian villages in the region (Conrad 1991; Morse et al. 1953).

Analysis of human skeletal remains yields another important line of information by which to assess the scale and intensity of hostilities in the CIRV at this time. Steadman's recent analysis of the Orendorf site skeletal population (2008) has revealed an adult trauma rate higher than reported for any other Mississippian site in the southeastern United States. Violence-related mortuary patterns include a mass grave with at least 15 interments and numerous other individuals with embedded arrow points, scalp marks, and blunt force cranial trauma.

The Crable phase marks the final chapter in the late Prehistory of the CIRV (Conrad 1991; Esarey and Conrad 1998). This era commenced around AD 1300, when an Oneota group known archaeologically as the Bold Counselor phase entered the CIRV from the northern midcontinent. It is unclear whether this emigration was intrusive or involved some kind of alliance of Oneota and local Mississippian groups.

There are several indications that intergroup violence may have been in flux at this time. First, there are important changes in distribution of settlements in the region; much of the regional populace appears to have consolidated into and around five primary villages along a 33 kilometer stretch of the western bluff of the Illinois Valley (Esarey and Conrad 1998). Very few sites dating to this period have been identified outside running distance of these main villages. The presence of incinerated domestic structures with intact floor assemblages at the Morton Village and Crable sites indicates these communities may have been subject to periodic attacks. The dense and well-defined middens at Crable phase sites (Esarey and Conrad 1998), however, indicate that some of these villages had longer occupation spans than earlier villages such as Buckeye Bend, Orendorf, and Star Bridges. The relative longevity of some villages after AD 1300 suggests that the large-scale assaults of the 1200s were less frequent, or at least less devastating. Perhaps the multivillage alliances that facilitated large attacks no longer existed. It is also possible that the objectives of violence shifted away from attacking fortified villages and toward ambushing individuals and small groups in the rural countryside.

The skeletal record also suggests that intergroup hostilities in the CIRV were changing throughout the 13th and 14th centuries. These changes are made visible through a brief comparison of the 13th century Mississippian cemetery at the Orendorf site and the early-14th Oneota cemetery at the Norris Farms number 36 site. Although the injuries displayed by victims of violence at Norris Farms number 36 are similar to those of earlier Middle Mississippian victims at the Orendorf site (Milner et al. 1991; Steadman 2008), there are indications that the violent confrontations involving the Norris Farms Oneota population were smaller in scale than those endured by the Orendorf Middle Mississippian population. For example, the Norris Farm number 36 cemetery lacks evidence of a mass grave such as the one from Orendorf (Steadman 2008). Milner et al. (1991) have also argued that many of the Norris Farms number 36 victims were killed in remote locations, while alone or in small groups, and were later found and brought back to their home village for burial (see also Santure et al. 1990). He bases this argument on the presence of individuals represented by varying levels of skeletal completeness, the prevalence of scavenger damage, and patterns of postmortem mutilation, all of which suggest that some time passed between an individual's death and burial (Milner et al. 1991). Lack of similar evidence at the Orendorf site is consistent with other indications that larger-scale assaults were more frequent in the 13th century than in 14th century CIRV.

How did the chronic violence of the 13th and 14th centuries have an impact on the lives of the regional inhabitants of the CIRV? On the basis of the frequency of skeletal lesions such as cribra orbitalia and porotic hyperostosis, Milner et al. (1991) have suggested that the threat of attack compromised the subsistence practices of the 13th century occupants of the Morton Village. In other words, it was no longer safe to leave the protective walls of the village to hunt, fish, gather, and farm.

Perhaps the most archaeologically visible change was the nucleation of regional inhabitants into compact, fortified villages. In addition to altering patterns of regional mobility and health, this move also entailed a steady increase in village size. For example, the early-13th-century Mississippian village at the Orendorf site was expanded twice, to ultimately cover 5 hectares. Larger fortified villages such as the 8 hectare Larson site were established later in the 13th century. This trend toward larger settlements was likely inspired by escalating violence in the region. As hostilities intensified, it became riskier to live outside the protective walls of a fortified village. Larger villages would have increased the number of potential attackers and defenders available to particular social groups.

Other important changes in community organization also took place as residential groups relocated within the spatial confines of fortified villages. Earthen monuments, ceremonial buildings, plazas, and other specialized ceremonial facilities once positioned at nodal communities were now closely juxtaposed with ordinary houses, storage pits, and other domestic features. These changes may have entailed more direct incorporation of certain ritual practices into everyday life, as now many ordinary domestic routines would have literally and figuratively been carried out in the shadow of mounds, ceremonial buildings, and other sacred spaces.

Over the long run, intergroup violence also appears to have influenced development of political complexity in the region. As Cahokia fragmented to the south in the late 13th century, there was an increase in the size and number of Mississippian settlements in the CIRV, especially in the vicinity of the confluence of the Spoon and Illinois Rivers. It was during this era that the Larson site mound and village were built, along with other nearby villages and farmsteads. This was also the period when much of the mound construction took place at the Dickson Mounds mortuary complex (Harn 1980:76). This Mississippian florescence, however, appears to have been cut short by intensification of hostilities in the region. The number of catastrophically burned and abandoned villages dating to the 13th century is grim testament to the scale and intensity of warfare during this era. The chaotic aftermath of these village assaults, large-scale population displacements, and loss of life appears to have substantially narrowed the opportunities for political aggrandizement in the region.

Exactly who the allies and enemy combatants were in these hostilities is unclear. By 1450, however, Native American groups had largely abandoned the Central Illinois River Valley as well as the American Bottom and the Ohio-Mississippi confluence area to the south (Cobb and Butler 2002). The ultimate fate of these people whose lives were so profoundly affected by violence is unknown.

NOTE

1. This estimate assumes that both attackers and defenders had similar weaponry.

REFERENCES

Alt, S. 2008. Unwilling Immigrants: Culture Change and the "Other" in Mississippian Societies. In *Invisible Citizens: Slavery in Ancient Pre-state Societies,* edited by C. M. Catherine, pp. 205–222. University of Utah Press, Salt Lake City.

Ambrose, S. H., and J. Krigbaum. 2003. Bone Chemistry and Bioarchaeology. *Journal of Anthropological Archaeology* 22:193–199.

Anderson, D. G. 1994. *The Savannah River Chiefdoms: Political Change in the Late Prehistoric Southeast.* University of Alabama Press, Tuscaloosa.

Blitz, J. 1988. Adoption of the Bow in Prehistoric North America. *North American Archaeologist* 9(2):123–145.

Brown, J. A. 2006. Where's the Power in Mound Building? An Eastern Woodlands Perspective. In Center for Archaeological Investigations Occasional Papers 33, *Leadership & Polity in Mississippian Society,* edited by B. M. Butler and P. D. Welch, pp. 197–213. Southern Illinois University, Carbondale.

Cobb, C. R, and B. M. Butler. 2002. The Vacant Quarter Revisited: Late Mississippian Abandonment of the Lower Ohio Valley. *American Antiquity* 67:625–641.

Cobb, C. R., and P. H. Garrow. 1996. Woodstock Culture and the Question of Mississippian Emergence. *American Antiquity* 61:21–37.

Cole, F.-C., and T. Deuel. 1937. *Rediscovering Illinois.* University of Chicago Press, Chicago.

Conrad, L. A. 1991. The Middle Mississippian Cultures of the Central Illinois Valley. In *Cahokia and the Hinterlands: Middle Mississippian Cultures of the Midwest,* edited by T. E. Emerson, pp. 119–156. University of Illinois Press, Urbana.

———. 1993. Two Elaborate Mississippian Graves from the Kingston Lake Site, Peoria County. *Illinois Archaeology* 5(1–2):297–314.

Dye, D. H. 2004. Art, Ritual, and Chiefly Warfare in the Mississippian World. In *Hero, Hawk, and Open Hand*, edited by R. V. Sharp, pp. 191–206. Yale University Press, New Haven, CT.

Emerson, T. E. 1991. Some Perspectives on Cahokia and the Northern Mississippian Expansion. In *Cahokia and the Hinterlands: Middle Mississippian Cultures of the Midwest*, edited by T. E. Emerson and R. B. Lewis, pp. 221–236. University of Illinois Press, Urbana.

———. 2007. Cahokia and the Evidence for Late Pre-Columbian War in the North American Midcontinent. In *North American Indigenous Warfare and Ritual Violence*, edited by R. J. Chacon and R. G. Mendoza, pp. 129–148. University of Arizona Press, Tucson.

Esarey, D. 2000. The Late Woodland Maples Mills and Mossville Phase Sequence in the Central Illinois River Valley. In *Late Woodland Societies: Tradition and Transformation Across the Midcontinent*, edited by T. E. Emerson, D. L. McElrath, and A. C. Fortier, pp. 387–412. University of Nebraska Press, Lincoln.

———, and L. A. Conrad. 1998. The Bold Counselor Phase of the Central Illinois River Valley: Oneota's Middle Mississippian Margin. *Wisconsin Archaeologist* 79(2):38–61.

Fowler, M. L., J. Rose, B. Vander Leest, and S. A. Ahler. 1999. *The Mound 72 Area: Dedicated and Sacred Space in Early Cahokia*. Illinois State Museum, Reports of Investigation 54. Illinois State Museum Society, Springfield.

Green, W., and D. J. Nolan. 2000. Late Woodland Peoples in West-Central Illinois. In *Late Woodland Societies: Tradition and Transformation Across the Midcontinent*, edited by T. E. Emerson, D. L. McElrath, and A. C. Fortier, pp. 345–386. University of Nebraska Press, Lincoln.

Hally, D. J. 1993. The Territorial Size of Mississippian Chiefdoms. In *Archaeology of Eastern North America: Papers in Honor of Stephen Williams*, edited by J. B. Stoltman, pp. 143–168. Mississippi Department of Archives and History, Jackson.

Harn, A. D. 1980. *The Prehistory of Dickson Mounds: The Dickson Excavation*. Dickson Mounds Museum Anthropological Studies 35. Illinois State Museum, Springfield.

———. 1991. The Eveland Site: Inroad to Spoon River Mississippian Society. In Monographs in World Archaeology 2, *New Perspectives on Cahokia: Views from the Periphery*, edited by J. B. Stoltman, pp. 129–153. Prehistory Press, Madison, WI.

Keeley, L. H., M. Fontana, and R. Quick. 2007. Baffles and Bastions: The Universal Features of Fortifications. *Journal of Archaeological Research* 15:55–95.

Keener, C. S. 1999. An Ethnohistorical Analysis of Iroquois Assault Tactics Used Against Fortified Settlements of the Northeast in the Seventeenth Century. *Ethnohistory* 46(4):777–807.

Knight, V. J., Jr. 1986. The Institutional Organization of Mississippian Religion. *American Antiquity* 51(4):675–687.

Lafferty, R. H., III. 1973. *An Analysis of Prehistoric Southeastern Fortifications*. Master's thesis, Southern Illinois University, Carbondale.

Larson, L. H., Jr. 1972. Functional Considerations of Warfare in the Southeast During the Mississippi Period. *American Antiquity* 37:383–392.

Little, K. J. 1999. The Role of Late Woodland Interactions in the Emergence of Etowah. *Southeastern Archaeology* 18(1):45–56.

Milner, G. R. 1999. Warfare in Prehistoric and Early Historic Eastern North America. *Journal of Archaeological Research* 7:105–151.

———. 2007. Warfare, Population, and Food Production in Prehistoric Eastern North America. In *North American Indigenous Warfare and Ritual Violence*, edited by R. J. Chacon and R. G. Mendza, pp. 182–201. University of Arizona Press, Tucson.

———, E. Anderson, and V. G. Smith. 1991. Warfare in Late Prehistoric West-Central Illinois. *American Antiquity* 56:581–603.

Morse, D. F., and P. A. Morse. 1983. *Archaeology of the Central Mississippi Valley*. Academic Press, New York.

Morse, D., G. Schoenbeck, and D. F. Morse. 1953. Fiedler Site. *Journal of the Illinois State Archaeological Society* 3(2):35–46.

O'Brien, M. J. (editor). 2001. *Mississippian Community Organization: The Powers Phase in Southeastern Missouri*. Kluwer Academic/Plenum, New York.

Pauketat, T. R. 2004. *Ancient Cahokia and the Mississippians*. Cambridge University Press, Cambridge, UK.

Perino, G. H. 1973a. The Koster Mounds, Greene County, Illinois. In Illinois Archaeological Survey Bulletin 9, *Late Woodland Site Archaeology in Illinois: 1*, pp. 141–210. University of Illinois Press, Urbana.

———. 1973b. The Late Woodland Component at the Pete Klunk Site, Calhoun County, Illinois. In Illinois Archaeological Survey Bulletin 9, *Late Woodland Site Archaeology in Illinois: 1*, pp. 58–89. University of Illinois Press, Urbana.

———. 1973c. The Late Woodland Component at the Schild Sites, Greene County, Illinois. In Illinois Archaeological Survey Bulletin 9, *Late Woodland Site Archaeology in Illinois: 1*, pp. 90–140. University of Illinois Press, Urbana.

Price, J. E., and J. B. Griffin. 1979. *The Snodgrass Site of the Powers Phase of Southeast Missouri*. Anthropological Papers 66. Museum of Anthropology, University of Michigan, Ann Arbor.

Santure, S. K., A. D. Harn, and D. Esarey. 1990. *Archaeological Investigations at the Morton Village and Norris Farms 36 Cemetery*. Reports of Investigations 45, Illinois State Museum, Springfield.

Steadman, D. W. 2001. Mississippians in Motion? A Population Genetic Analysis of Interregional Gene Flow in West-Central Illinois. *American Journal of Physical Anthropology* 114(1):61–73.

———. 2008. Warfare Related Trauma at Orendorf, a Middle Mississippian Site in West-Central Illinois. *American Journal of Physical Anthropology* 136:51–64.

Wilson, G. D., and D. W. Steadman. 2007. City Walls and Frontier Fortifications: Variation in Warfare Between the Middle Mississippian American Bottom and Central Illinois River Valley. Presented at the Southeastern Archaeological Conference, November, Knoxville, TN.

CHAPTER 44

MOUNDVILLE IN THE MISSISSIPPIAN WORLD

JOHN H. BLITZ

IN the 13th century AD, Moundville was one of the largest pre-Columbian settlements in the American Southeast. Spread over 325 acres were at least 29 earthen mounds arranged around an extensive open area or plaza, dozens of houses for a thousand or more people, and a surrounding wooden stockade more than a kilometer in length (Figure 44.1). Moundville was the central place of a regional territory with smaller, single-mound centers and a dispersed population living in nearby homesteads (Figure 44.2). These archaeological sites are found along the Black Warrior River in west-central Alabama, on the heavily forested Gulf Coastal Plain, a physiographic region with diverse flora and fauna, substantial rainfall, mild winters, and long hot summers. Moundville's location was well suited to the subsistence needs of farming and hunting populations: fish and turtles from the river, floodplain soils for slash-and-burn hoe cultivation of maize, nearby sources of stone for tools, and habitats for abundant plant and animal foods. In this chapter, Moundville's development from AD 1000–1600 is traced, from the poorly understood convergence of indigenous Woodland and foreign Mississippian cultural practices shared by the founding population to rapid establishment of a planned fortified town with massive earthen monuments, and later, conversion of the town into a depopulated place of cultic rituals and funerals for those who resided elsewhere. When the Spanish explorer Hernando De Soto arrived 300 years later, Moundville was abandoned.

Moundville's people participated in the late pre-Columbian cultural development known as Mississippian (AD 900 to European Contact). Mississippian communities built monumental earthen mounds in the form of flat-topped pyramids (see also Alt, King, Milner, this volume). Most archaeologists interpret these mound "centers" as places of social, political, and religious importance marking a

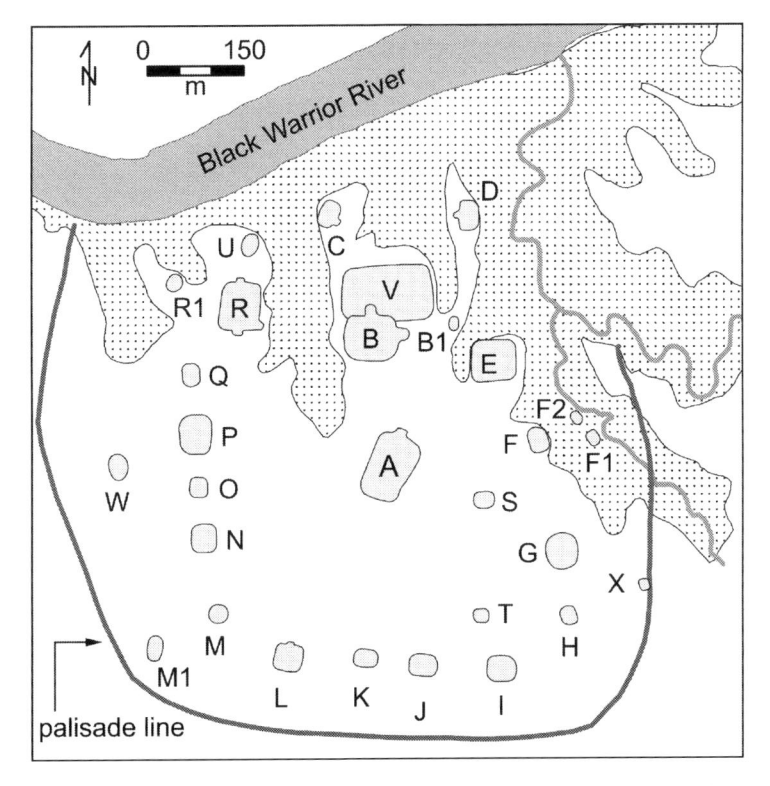

Figure 44.1 Schematic map of the Moundville site (copyright ©2009 by John H. Blitz).

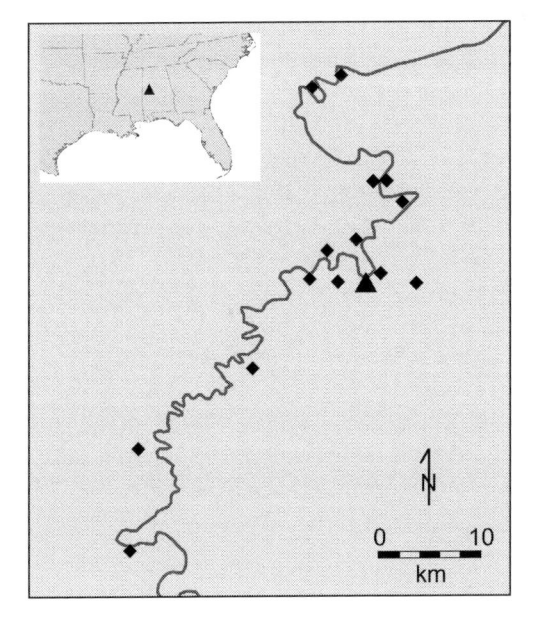

Figure 44.2 Location of Moundville (triangle) and single-mound sites in the Black Warrior River valley, Alabama (copyright ©2009 by John H. Blitz).

local or regional territory. Better chronologies and more extensive excavations have disclosed that the histories and uses of Mississippian mound centers, such as Moundville, were more variable and mutable through time than previously thought. Some centers were built, used, and abandoned over a short time span. Other centers had long, continuous occupation. Still other centers were used, abandoned for generations, and then reoccupied and reused once more. There were "vacant" ceremonial centers with few occupants or episodic use, centers with dense residential neighborhoods, and centers that were used in both ways at different points in time. As the needs, values, customs, and beliefs of Mississippian peoples changed through time, the manner in which Mississippian communities built, altered, refurbished, and used their mound centers changed as well. New ways of building houses, making and decorating pottery, and displaying evolving symbols of religious belief also accompanied these cultural changes.

With the theme of culture change in mind, we review Moundville's history as four sequential occupation periods: Moundville's Origins (AD 1020–1200), Moundville as a Fortified Town (AD 1200–1300), Moundville as a Ceremonial Center (AD 1300–1450), and Moundville's Decline (AD 1450–1600). Although culture change is continuous, the transitions between occupation periods were accompanied by significant shifts in values and practices. Life for Moundville's people differed in each period. Because extensive and detailed studies of Moundville are readily available, we focus on two aspects of culture change in Moundville's history evident in the material remains: social memory and collective identity. Anthropologists use the concept of social memory to refer to how communities and groups construct shared perceptions about "the way things were in the past" (Van Dyke and Alcock 2003:2). These shared perceptions about the past are used by communities, groups, and leaders to justify why people do things in certain ways in the present. Abstract ideas about perceptions and values must be represented with material things to make them "real" to people. Social memory is made real by building it into the landscape where people reside and act. Construction, spatial arrangement, and refurbishing of mounds, houses, plazas, and burial grounds at Mississippian centers are examples of how social memory was incorporated into the built environment. Shared needs, values, customs, and beliefs are also made real with material expressions of collective identity.

The term *collective identity* is used here to refer to the perception of unity, belonging, and uniqueness shared by members of social groups (Snow 2001). Expression of collective identity at the scale of community and society helps integrate groups with divergent or conflicting interests, and it permits individuals to feel they are a part of something larger than themselves. One way collective identity expresses community and group affiliation is through the forms, decorations, and styles of objects and how these objects are used. Common things such as houses, pottery, and dress, as well as the symbols rendered on valued ornaments and sacred items, may convey collective identity as these things are made, used, and displayed in daily activities or in emotional ritual performances. Differences in material expression of collective identity may mark the social boundaries among groups, communities, and societies. If the built environment was rearranged and reorganized and the old styles, forms, and symbols of material goods were replaced by new styles, forms, and symbols, archaeologists may infer that important cultural changes occurred that required materialization of new social memories and new collective identities.

Archaeology at Moundville

The archaeological site of Moundville is protected and open to the public as Moundville Archaeological Park, owned and administered by the University of Alabama. Extensively studied for decades, there is detailed knowledge of the site and its ancient inhabitants (Blitz 2008; Knight and Steponaitis 2006). Each generation of researchers asked their own questions about Moundville as evidence accumulated and interests changed with the concerns of the time. Nineteenth-century investigators wanted to know who built the mounds. The most popular theory of the time proposed that a vanished "Moundbuilder race," and not the Native Americans, had built Moundville and similar earthworks. Once Native American construction of the mounds was accepted, turn-of-the-century antiquarians such as C. B. Moore concentrated on artifacts as aesthetic art objects. From Moundville's mounds and graves, Moore obtained many remarkable artifacts: round and rectangular stone disks smeared with paint pigments and used as "palettes"; large stone smoking pipes in the form of humans and catlike monsters; stone bowls carved as serpent-bird effigies; badges and emblems of stone, copper, and shell; and dozens of glossy black pottery bottles engraved with elaborate abstract and representational motifs.

Later, modern excavation techniques were employed to answer questions of *when* and *where* about Moundville's culture history, accomplished by inventories of artifacts and architecture used to identify ancient "cultures" that could be mapped with spatial distributions and ordered into time periods. Depression-era work programs at Moundville excavated dozens of house remains, hundreds of burials, and thousands of artifacts in residential areas away from the mounds. Processual archaeology of the 1970s through 1980s, concerned with the *how* and *why* of culture change, identified Moundville as a rank society with inherited social status and a chiefdom form of sociopolitical organization. Data on subsistence, economy, social organization, and health were collected consistent with materialist theories of cultural evolution. Ceramic phases of changing pottery styles (Moundville I–IV phases) anchored to radiocarbon dates identified Moundville's occupation periods (Knight and Steponaitis 2006). Recent research asks questions about the economic and ideological sources of power, the meanings of ancient symbols, and the domestic and community practices that created a central place, maintained households, and established or altered social memory and collective identity (Wilson 2010).

Moundville's Origins (AD 1020–1200)

Inquiries into the origin of Moundville address an important research interest of North American archaeology: understanding the causal factors for institutionalization of social rank and the rise of complex society. The causes of rank and complexity are not limited to local environmental, subsistence, and demographic conditions. Interaction between populations may inject foreign ideas, products, or social groups into a region. Creation of social memory and formation of collective identity accompanied the rise and decline of rank and complexity at Moundville.

The Mississippian way of life was first established in the central Mississippi Valley between AD 800 and 1000, a time when populations increased, ranked social organization appeared, maize became a staple food, and extensive local and regional exchange networks developed (Kelly 2000). During this same time span, there were no Mississippian populations in west-central Alabama. Instead, the regional Late Woodland people continued to follow their way of life unaltered by the causal forces that had created Mississippian elsewhere (Jenkins 2003). Later, during the AD 1020–1140 interval, local archaeological phases referred to as Terminal Woodland began to undergo Mississippianization, that is, acquisition of Mississippian ideas, materials, and organizations from populations that already followed these new practices (Jenkins 2003). The Terminal Woodland phases differ substantially from the Mississippian Moundville I phase (AD 1120–1250) in settlement, subsistence, social organization, and material remains. The radiocarbon dates, however, suggest a temporal overlap in the phase time spans, allowing the possibility of interaction and cultural borrowing among groups with Woodland and Mississippian traditions. For example, Terminal Woodland sites have handled globular jars, some tempered with shell, a vessel form and production practice common to Mississippian societies outside the region; yet some of these pots retain the slightly pointed bases of the local Woodland pottery tradition (Jenkins 2003). A new form of domestic dwelling, a semisubterranean house with a sunken floor, was adopted even as the traditional Woodland house form continued to be built. Maize production increased but still remained a dietary supplement rather than a staple food. No Terminal Woodland settlement hierarchies, mound construction, or elaborate burials have been identified. For these reasons, Terminal Woodland is assumed to represent the material remains of egalitarian groups without significant political centralization or social ranking.

During the early Moundville I subphase (AD 1120–1200), sites in the Moundville region show the consequences of Mississippianization (Blitz 2008). There was a fusion of Woodland and Mississippian styles and forms in material goods (Jenkins 2003). Some people continued to build semisubterranean houses, while others adopted the distinctive wall-trench houses of Mississippian origin, and still others lived in "hybrid" houses that combined these building techniques. Mississippian shell-tempered pottery forms and decoration became dominant, but Woodland pottery continued to be made. In other words, it appears that for several generations local populations in west-central Alabama varied in the degree to which they retained the older indigenous Woodland traditions and adopted the new Mississippian practices, even among households at the same sites.

The common Mississippian settlement hierarchy of dispersed houses (often referred to as farmsteads) arranged around a mound center was established for the first time, evidence of accelerated investment in lands for maize production, increased political integration, and social ranking. Two small mounds, X and 1TU50 (located just beyond the mapped area in Figure 44.1), were built about 1 kilometer apart, the first to be erected at Moundville. Limited excavations reveal that the earthen platforms were constructed in stages; they contain evidence of buildings, marine-shell bead making, mica and other nonlocal stone, paint pigments, and food remains. If these two mounds are like the better-known examples built later, they served as central facilities where leaders hosted ritual and political activities for local households. Addition of multiple stages to platform mounds over a span of time greater than a single generation is interpreted as evidence that formal leadership roles and inherited social rank were initiated at this time.

Mississippianization appears to be a syncretistic cultural phenomenon created by the interaction of populations with different collective identities. It is now clear that all of the Mississippian materials and practices found in the Moundville region by AD 1120—shell-tempered pottery, semisubterranean houses, wall-trench houses, the farmstead-mound center organization, social ranking, and increased maize production—had been flourishing in the central Mississippi valley for more than 100 years. Construction of commemorative mounds signaled rearrangement of power and authority in the region and materialized new social memories on the landscape. But these observations alone do not tell us why local populations adopted the new way of life.

MOUNDVILLE AS A FORTIFIED TOWN (AD 1200–1300)

Around AD 1200, the community of dispersed households along the 1 kilometer length of high ground at the Moundville locale underwent a rapid transformation. An ambitious construction project was initiated as multiple mounds were built around the perimeter of a large central plaza, a log palisade with tower bastions was erected, and new residential areas occupied the space between plaza and palisade. Because current evidence indicates that mounds, plaza, residential areas, and palisade were established close in time (late Moundville I subphase, AD 1200–1250), it is probable that Moundville was a planned community (Knight and Steponaitis 2006). Given the presence of the palisade fortification, perhaps defense was a motivation for households to aggregate into a large town.

It is probable that the spatial arrangement of the community plan was not a local invention, however, but an attempt to emulate the cultural module of mound-plaza arrangements found at Mississippian centers located outside the region. A new collective identity was established. Production of the old Woodland pottery and house forms ceased, replaced by Mississippian pottery in a distinctive Moundville style and the ubiquitous Mississippian wall-trench house. Houses were no longer dispersed as they had been earlier but were now clustered tightly together in "residential groups" composed of five to 12 houses separated from other residential group-clusters by 50–100 meters of open space (Wilson 2008). The same range of house form, size, and arrangement as well as domestic artifact assemblages were replicated in all the residential clusters. Whereas earlier houses were abandoned after a few years, houses in the new residential groups were rebuilt again and again in the same spot, a clue that maintaining household location was important in the new community organization. The plaza was created by leveling and filling portions of the great open area enclosed by the mound arrangement, covering the locations of earlier houses. The two original platform mounds were abandoned, and in the case of Mound X the palisade line was constructed directly over it (Knight and Steponaitis 2006).

Perhaps families associated with the two old mounds established new mounds in the multiple-mound arrangement, or perhaps they were excluded from a place in the new order. Removal of old houses and abandonment of mounds represents a prehistoric example of the memory manipulation, or institutionalized forgetting, that often accompanies radical social change; the past was denied and erased by reconfiguring the social spaces where people lived. No doubt there were winners and losers as community labor was redirected, new households were founded in residential groups, a social hierarchy formed, and new values held sway. Conformity to the new material culture and community plan was deemed necessary and appropriate to reinforce a new collective identity. Rebuilding houses in the same location in residential groups illustrates the new concern with perpetuation of household social memory. These changes in social relations, organization, and values were accompanied by increased maize production and population aggregation, but they occurred without significant technological change.

Mound construction, use, and spatial arrangement perpetuated and reflected the new social order. These monumental platforms, oriented to the cardinal directions, are thought to be earth or world icons based on direct ethnographic analogy. Mound summits have remains of communal meeting places, mortuary facilities, ritual precincts, elite houses, storage facilities, or combinations of these features. Around the plaza periphery, larger mounds without burials alternate with smaller mounds that contain human remains. These mound pairs and one or more adjacent residential groups form a spatial unit thought to represent the corporate facilities of a kin group or similar social segment (Knight 2006; Wilson 2008). Periodically, addition of a new construction stage renewed the mound-world symbol at times of crisis for the affiliated corporate group; thus mound building reaffirmed group continuity and identity while potentially editing social memory (Pauketat and Alt 2003). The larger mounds B, R, V, and E, together with mounds C and D (where some of the most elaborate costumed burials were found by Moore), are thought to form a high-status precinct on the northern side of the site. Mounds on the southern side of the site are smaller. Mound A is centrally located in the plaza, apart from the plaza-periphery arrangement of the other mounds. In contrast to the smaller corporate-group mounds, mounds A and B are so massive and distinctive that it is assumed they were built with labor contributed by all social segments. Mound size and arrangement mirror Moundville's social hierarchy of ranked social segments (Knight 2006).

Moundville as a Ceremonial Center (AD 1300–1450)

During this interval, Moundville was transformed from a thriving town to a sparsely occupied ceremonial center (Knight and Steponaitis 2006). There is evidence that a large portion of the residential population left the site. Mound A and most mounds in the southern portion of the site were no longer used; the palisade was no longer maintained. Houses in residential groups were abandoned and not rebuilt, and in their place small cemeteries were established at the locations where the houses once stood (Wilson 2008). Most of the dated burials at Moundville are after AD 1300, and most of the dated house remains and middens in the residential groups are prior to that date (Knight and Steponaitis 2006). Some people remained at the site. Mound B and some of the larger northern mounds continued to be used. Some middens and house remains that date to this interval have been found further from the plaza than the abandoned residential groups, suggesting a reorganization of residential space. Still, it appears that much of the population left Moundville.

Where did the social segments go when they abandoned their mounds and residential groups and moved out? It was probably not far, for there was a proliferation of single-mound centers in the valley during this time. These single-mound sites have long been viewed as "administrative centers" subordinate to a capital at Moundville. However, the timing of their founding suggests loss of political power for Moundville's top-rank leaders as rival leaders and their followers left Moundville to establish their own centers nearby (Blitz 2008). For these rival social segments, construction of social memory by mound building was diverted from Moundville to their new estates. Other social memories were forged as people living elsewhere asserted their ancestral claims to Moundville by returning their dead for burial at the location of the abandoned residential groups (Wilson 2010). There is material evidence of new collective identities as well. House forms changed once again, this time from the old wall-trench structures to a new trend with single-set wall posts. Placed with the honored dead were pottery bottles and ornaments of copper, shell, and stone decorated with a new emphasis on representational art such as bones, skulls, scalps, cross-in-circle, falcons, winged serpents and other symbols thought to represent concerns with ancestors, war, and death (Knight and Steponaitis 2006).

Moundville's Decline (AD 1450–1600)

After AD 1400, the number of burials at Moundville decreased (Knight and Steponaitis 2006). The dead were no longer supplied with the highly symbolic copper, shell, and stone ornaments and ritual gear that symbolized the values that had been so important to Moundville's inhabitants over the previous century or more. Because these artifacts were displayed and used in cultic rituals and marked the social roles of those who organized and advocated the cults, a decline in production and use of this symbolism suggests loss of faith in the beliefs they represented and lessened authority on the part of the leaders associated with the old ideology. Some symbols continued to be engraved on pots, and some pendants and palettes continued to be made in the early part of this interval, but the social and political efficacy of the cultic practices was spent. Concurrently, mound construction ended at Moundville, and only four mounds show signs of summit activities (Knight and Steponaitis 2006).

As Moundville ceased to be an important place, six single-mound centers with affiliated homesteads continued to prosper elsewhere in the valley as the local unit of economic, political, and ritual organization. At least two of these single-mound centers have extensive cemeteries, an indication that burial at Moundville was no longer highly valued. Investment in social memory was now localized at the small centers, not at Moundville. These changes took place prior to the passage of De Soto's army through the Black Warrior River region in 1540. No place resembling Moundville is described in the ambiguous Spanish accounts. In the latter half of the 16th century, regional populations of the Moundville IV phase declined. The centuries-long role of mound building in construction of social memory ceased. Skeletal evidence from the small village sites indicate poor health and nutrition attributable to the impact of Old World diseases left in the wake of European contact. Moundville was abandoned.

Conclusion

No doubt the reader has deduced that archaeology at Moundville has been more successful at detecting the consequences of culture change than explaining why the changes occurred. Like their counterparts elsewhere in North America, archaeologists at Moundville have identified evidence for some potential causes of change—intensification and mobilization of food surpluses and labor, cultural interaction that introduced new products and ideas, religious beliefs that inspired devotion and validated rank or authority—but the complex sequences of cause and effect in culture change are difficult to confirm, even in societies that can be observed today. Nevertheless, we have reviewed the archaeological evidence at Moundville for two universal aspects of culture change: construction of social memory and formation of collective identity.

Each culture shift in the four occupation episodes at Moundville initiated, ended, or altered social memory and collective identity. Social memory and collective identity required intentional actions to implement and were made real to communities, groups, and individuals by material referents. The residues of these actions and materials left physical evidence that archaeologists have found, documented, and interpreted at Moundville and other Mississippian centers. The hard-won successes of past researchers hold considerable promise that more insights about Moundville's people and their place in the Mississippian world are forthcoming.

REFERENCES

Blitz, J. H. 2008. *Moundville*. University of Alabama Press, Tuscaloosa.

Jenkins, N. J. 2003. The Terminal Woodland/Mississippian Transition in West and Central Alabama. *Journal of Alabama Archaeology* 49(1–2):1–62.

Kelly, J. E. 2000. The Nature and Context of Emergent Mississippian Cultural Dynamics in the American Bottom. In *Late Woodland Societies: Tradition and Transformation Across the Midcontinent*, edited by T. E. Emerson, D. L. McElrath, and A. C. Fortier, pp. 163–178. University of Nebraska Press, Lincoln.

Knight, V. J., Jr. 2006. Moundville as a Diagrammatic Ceremonial Center. In *Archaeology of the Moundville Chiefdom*, edited by V. J. Knight Jr., and V. P. Steponaitis, pp. 44–62. Reprint. University of Alabama Press, Tuscaloosa. Originally published 1998 by Smithsonian Institution Press, Washington, DC.

———, and V. P. Steponaitis. 2006. A New History of Moundville. In *Archaeology of the Moundville Chiefdom*, edited by V. J. Knight Jr., and V. P. Steponaitis, pp. 1–25. Reprint. University of Alabama Press, Tuscaloosa. Originally published 1998 by Smithsonian Institution Press, Washington, DC.

Pauketat, T. R., and S. M. Alt. 2003. Mounds, Memory, and Contested Mississippian History. In *Archaeologies of Memory*, edited by R. Van Dyke and S. E. Alcock, pp. 151–179. Blackwell, Malden, MA.

Snow, D. 2001. Collective Identity and Expressive Forms. Center for the Study of Democracy Paper 01–07. http://escholarship.org/uc/item/2zn1t7bj.

Van Dyke, R., and S. E. Alcock. 2003. Archaeologies of Memory: An Introduction. In *Archaeologies of Memory*, edited by R. Van Dyke and S. E. Alcock, pp. 1–13. Blackwell, Malden, MA.

Wilson, G. D. 2008. *The Archaeology of Everyday Life at Early Moundville*. University of Alabama Press, Tuscaloosa.

———. 2010. Community, Identity, and Social Memory at Moundville. *American Antiquity* 75(1):3–18.

VI. Greater Southwest and Northern Mexico

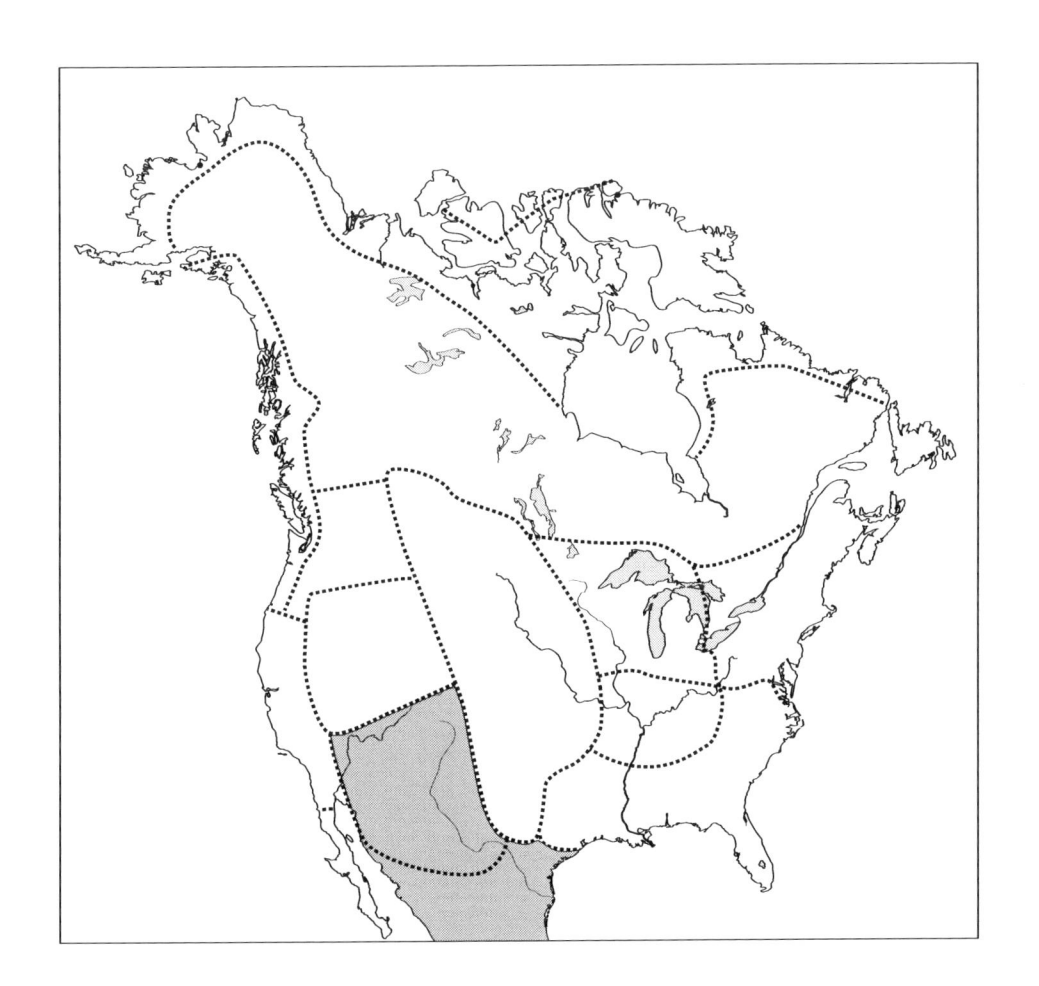

CHAPTER 45

THE ARCHAEOLOGY OF THE GREATER SOUTHWEST: MIGRATION, INEQUALITY, AND RELIGIOUS TRANSFORMATIONS

BARBARA J. MILLS

The Greater Southwest (Figure 45.1) is often considered a laboratory for archaeology because of the visibility and preservation of sites, fine-grained chronological control, and rich ethnographic record. The literature is voluminous, and there are literally hundreds if not thousands of archaeologists working in the area. Geographically defined as from Durango (Colorado) to Durango (Mexico) and Las Vegas (New Mexico) to Las Vegas (Nevada), there are many more archaeologists working in the United States, but research interests are shared by those working on both sides of the international border. In this chapter, I focus on a few key topics and refer the reader to longer works for more comprehensive overviews (especially Cordell 1997; Lekson 2009; Plog 1997). My goal is to point out a few major themes in current research to place contemporary work in context.

Because of the prevalence of independent dates in the Southwest and abundant decorated ceramics, chronological frameworks are well developed for most of the area; dating of sites can be as precise as 25–50 year increments. Independent dates are not uniformly available for the entire region and are particularly problematic for the southern Southwest and for sites older than the last two millennia. Nonetheless, the chronological data are the basis for relatively fine-grained historical trajectories and identification of many transitions that occurred roughly simultaneously across the entire Southwest.

Most current archaeological research in the Southwest focuses on prehistoric agriculturalists. Before discussing themes that relate to this wider body of research, two other periods of current research should be pointed out. One is of the earliest foragers in the Southwest, generally referred to as Clovis. Association of megafauna with Clovis hunters in southern New Mexico at about 11500 BP has been established for more than half a century (Haynes and Huckell 2007), and recent work in northern Mexico is extending knowledge of Clovis hunting practices to new places and even new species of prey (Holliday et al. 2009).

The other key period is the Early Agricultural, when corn and other domesticated crops are adopted. The relatively short period of time in which corn agriculture made its way into the Southwest has been used to support two models:

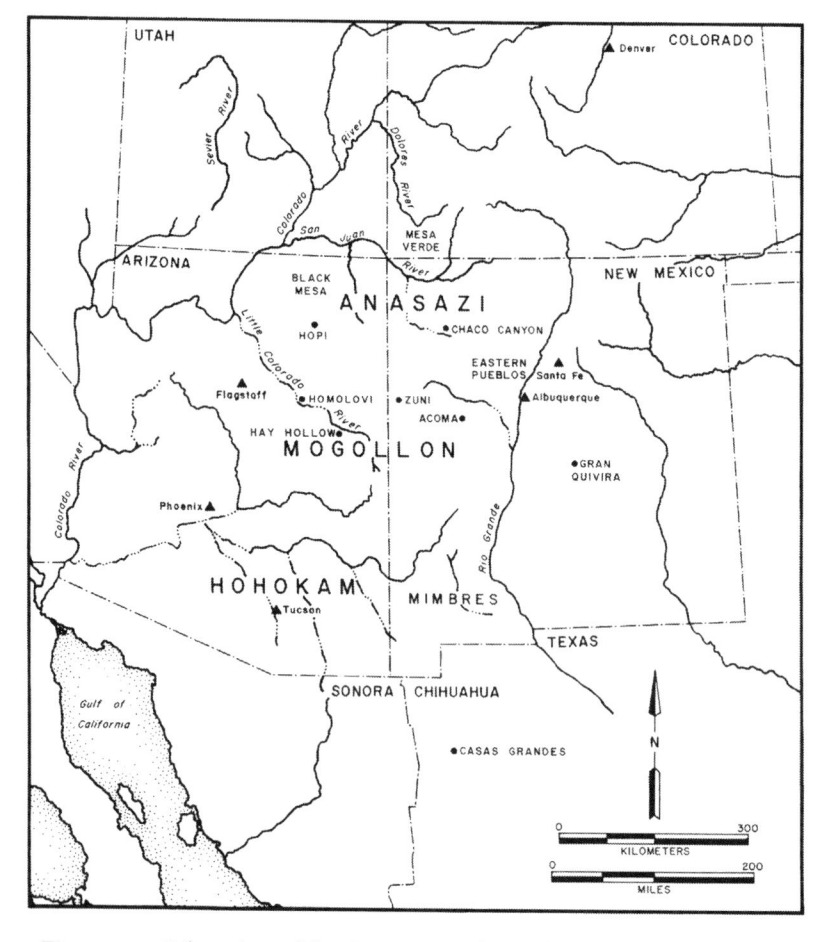

Figure 45.1 Select sites of the Greater Southwest (courtesy Crow Canyon Archaeological Center).

migration of agriculturalists, and diffusion of corn among foragers already living in the area (see Vierra 2005; Merrill et al. 2009). Whichever model is correct, the gap between domestication of corn in Mesoamerica and adoption by Southwest foragers continues to decrease. Corn was present in the southern Southwest by 2100 cal BC, if not earlier. Perhaps even more important, the temporal gap between village agriculturalists in Mesoamerica and those in the Southwest is also decreasing. The size and permanence of early Southwestern villages are debated, but having clusters of houses associated with abundant storage and investment in agricultural features in the second millennium BC implies organizational changes that were harbingers of later agriculturalists in the area (see Young, this volume).

Once agricultural villages were established, regional differentiation in architecture and other technologies becomes more pronounced. Much of this diversity is because of decreasing mobility and increasing territoriality. Yet the connectedness of the Southwest should never be underestimated; changes in one area are often related to changes in another. For heuristic purposes, I reintroduce the concept of "hinge points," which was presented by Cordell and Gumerman (1989), to refer to particular points in time when the trajectories of Southwestern societies seem to change in tandem (Table 45.1). Regionally specific chronologies are still useful, but they don't emphasize the connectedness of the regions to each other that these hinge points succinctly present. The connectedness of the Southwest—both within and with other regions (see Hall, Peregrine and Lekson, this volume)—is an important key theme in much current research. This is especially important in research that looks at topics such as migration, social inequalities (including conflict and violence), and religious transformations—topics that are at the forefront of current research in the Southwest.

Migration and Identity

Few other topics have crept into Southwestern archaeology so innocently, and then taken over so completely, as has the topic of migration. Migration is a central theme in much of the literature over the past 15 years or so (e.g., Cameron 1995; Clark 2001; Hill et al. 2004; Lyons 2003; Spielmann 1998). Earlier work on migration in the Southwest was present, especially the classic work of Emil Haury (1958), but the extent to which archaeologists are now talking, writing, and recognizing migration is fundamental to understanding interpretations of Southwest archaeology today.

Importantly, current discussion of migration is often paired with discussion of identity (e.g., Duff 2002; Neuzil 2008). Migration is also a critical part of the Native American Graves Protection and Repatriation Act (NAGPRA), making research that links the identities of those in the past to those in the present of contemporary social and political importance. Whether or not this research is conducted explicitly as part of NAGPRA, the topics of migration and identity often draw on ethnography

Table 45.1 Major Hinge Points in Southwestern Prehistory

Date (AD)	Descriptive Title	Significant Areal Changes
200/500	Initiation	• Plateau: Widespread occupation of pithouses, decreased mobility, increased territoriality, greater demands on labor over earlier (Archaic) period, and earliest suprahousehold ritual structures (great kivas). • Southern valleys: Beginning of the complex of traits that are recognized as Hohokam by AD 500 in the Phoenix and Tucson basins, including construction of clusters of pit structures surrounding large plazas with adjoining ceremonial structures.
770/800	Expansion	• Plateau: Transition to large, aggregated villages (Pueblo I period) with above-ground structures and evidence for a period of violence. Residential mobility still high, with frequent moves of settlements (and even entire valleys depopulated). Followed by expansion of dispersed populations into different areas of the Plateau (ca. AD 900) with diversification of agricultural strategies, increased storage, and apparent population increase. Exception is Chaco Canyon, which begins to differentiate itself from other areas with more persistent and larger settlements and probable in-migration from other areas of the Southwest. • Southern valleys: Ratcheting up of size and extent of canal systems in Hohokam area, spread of a new ideology into Hohokam area with clear ties to West Mexico, construction and use of large ball courts, beginning of community specialization in craft production, and cremation burials with nearby ritually destroyed items. Population increase and expansion of Hohokam into other valleys (such as the Tonto Basin) and evidence for wider network of exchange and interaction, including the Mimbres area.
1000/1050	Differentiation	• Plateau: Peak period of occupation in Chaco, followed by major period of construction of Chaco outlier great houses over large area of northwestern NM, southern CO, southeastern UT, and northeast AZ, but most other areas of Plateau continue pattern of small, dispersed sites. Great houses are focus of ritual for surrounding communities, and at least at Pueblo Bonito the residences of elite families and the focus of ritual for the surrounding region. • Southern valleys: In Hohokam area, a new iconography and greater diversity of ritual practices ranging from domestic to villagewide, large ball courts replaced with smaller ball courts and new type of capped mounds (with possible elite control), continued evidence for high degree of community specialization in craft production coupled with market exchange around ball courts. In Mimbres area, late transition to above-ground structures, greater interaction with Pueblo areas to the north, and beginning of Classic Mimbres iconography.

Table 45.1 (*continued*)

Date (AD)	Descriptive Title	Significant Areal Changes
1130/1150	Reorganization	• Plateau: Chaco Canyon largely depopulated, with commensurate increase in settlements in San Juan drainage (including Aztec), increased period of aggregation and violence, and a major drought. • Southern valleys: Beginning of Classic period in the Hohokam area with transition to above-ground structures surrounded by adobe compound walls, reduction in community specialization and overall exchange throughout the area. End of ball court system and decrease in Hohokam influence outside of Phoenix Basin, with increasing differentiation between regions. Platform mounds become the focus of a new ideological system, many villages and settlement systems reorganized as canal system expanded into new areas.
1275/1300	Aggregation	• Plateau: Large-scale depopulation of the Four Corners and out-migration to east and south, including the southern valleys, ratcheting up of settlement sizes in Puebloan areas still occupied (beginning of Pueblo IV period), and aggregation into fewer sites. • Southern valleys: Migration from Plateau into several southern valleys. Platform mounds elaborated and used for ritual as well as residence, and evidence of more restricted access to some rituals while others more widespread (e.g., Salado imagery by AD 1325). More variable stream flow data indicate many highs and lows that required massive rebuilding at some times and not enough water at others. Beginning of peak (Medio) period at Casas Grandes with diversity of ritual architecture (including many kinds not seen in other areas of the Southwest), differentiation of burials, and expansion of trade networks.
1400/1450	Depopulation/ Consolidation	• Plateau: Another period of migration and consolidation associated with prolonged period of unpredictable climate, which results in large areas of the Southwest being depopulated. Evidence of intertribal violence, deterioration of health, breakdown of trade routes, and restructuring of identities in areas still occupied, primarily the areas of historic Eastern and Western Pueblos. Possible early migration of Athapaskan speakers into area. • Southern valleys: End of Hohokam system following long period of declining health and population. Dispersion of population into smaller *rancheria* settlements. End of Medio period at Casas Grandes. Partial replacement of population with more mobile groups.
1539–1600	Exploration	• Earliest expeditions of Spanish into the Southwest, crossing both southern valleys and plateau. Earliest domesticated animals, plants, and introduction of European infectious diseases. Earliest tree-ring-dated Navajo site in San Juan area at 1541.

Source: modified from Cordell and Gumerman 1989:6, with some additions from Mills et al. 2006.

and oral history (e.g., Dongoske et al. 1997; Ferguson and Colwell-Chanthaphohn 2006; Ferguson and Lomaomvaya 1999).

The major issues surrounding migration research include many of the same questions asked by the earlier Southwestern archaeologists. Among them are the social scale of migrants, the distances moved, and especially the consequences of migration (Mills 2011). Late-13th-century migration from northeast Arizona to southeast Arizona has been known about since the 1950s. What is different from past interpretations is that there are now many more examples, suggesting it was not just a small population organized into a few households or suprahousehold groups who moved, but a large enough population displacement to regard most of the southern Southwest (especially the Phoenix, Tonto, San Pedro, Safford, and Aravaipa areas) as regions that contained people with multiple origins. People living in any one of these regions were living in a multiethnic community—much as they are today in terms of their diversity—and the migrations were on such a large scale as to be called diasporas (Mills 2011).

Another aspect of migration research is relating oral history and migration. More broadly, this is about the intersection of differing histories: oral, archaeological, and documentary. One of the best recent examples is the intersection of Zuni migration history and archaeology relating to depopulation of the Upper Little Colorado valley (Ferguson 2007). Concentration of Zuni place names from oral histories, the direction of movement from these histories, depopulation of settlements, and close tracking of material culture changes in the Zuni area during the 14th century all furnish mutual support for migration to the Zuni Pueblo or the "Middle Place."

Migration research in the Southwest is not without its critics. In fact, because of the strong surge in publications on the topic there is bound to be a diversity of opinions about particular migrations in particular areas. For example, in the Rio Grande area archaeologists are debating the extent of the Mesa Verde migrations in the late 13th century. Nonetheless, as Varien et al. (this volume) and Hill et al. (2004) point out, the demographic patterns across the northern Southwest are dramatic. There was extensive out-migration from the Four Corners in the 13th century and coalescence of populations closer to the historic pueblos (including those of the Rio Grande valley). Because of the large databases put together by these projects, the scope of migration, coalescence, and depopulation is more appreciated. Some of the debate centers on interpretation of continuities in technological and ritual traditions. Considerable new research is being conducted using the concepts of technological style and communities of practice to track migration (e.g., chapters in Habicht-Mauche et al. 2006; Hegmon et al. 2000; Neuzil 2008; Stark et al. 1998), and we can expect to see these interpretations refined and added to in the next decades.

Many of the other topics investigated by Southwestern archaeologists are tied to migration, among them social inequality, violence and conflict, and religious transformations. The idea that first-comers possess established ties to territories that must be negotiated by newcomers is common in the ethnographic literature on migration. Close correlation of periods of migration with many of the hinge points discussed earlier also suggests that migration histories are an important foundation of other changes in the Southwest.

Social Inequalities

Inequality can be based on a number of social dimensions, notably gender, age, status, and prestige—all of which create different forms of hierarchy and ways in which power is distributed. Prior to 1990, many Southwestern archaeologists recognized there are many sources of inequality, but most shied away from actually using the term *hierarchy*. Gregory Johnson's chapter (1989) in a volume titled *Dynamics of Southwestern Prehistory* (Cordell and Gumerman 1989), one of the most frequently cited articles about the Southwest in the 1990s, distinguished between sequential and simultaneous hierarchies. It should have opened the door to alternative ways of thinking about structured inequality but did not, precisely because Johnson tied it to traditional neoevolutionary typologies. Johnson's contribution sidestepped discussion of simultaneous hierarchies in the Southwest, relegating all variation in the area to sequential hierarchies. He justified this because it was clear to him that the Southwest could not sustain the surplus production required to support more "complex" forms of organization, such as the neoevolutionary categories of chiefdoms and states. Simultaneous hierarchies were present only in these more complex societies, which were not apparent (to him) in the Southwest.

This picture has changed considerably in the last 15 years as archaeologists grapple with (1) evidence that there were elites and hierarchical organizations in many areas of the Southwest, especially (but not necessarily limited to) the Chaco, Hohokam, and Casas Grandes areas; (2) alternative ways of thinking about the basis of power and authority, including theories of value along which prestige may be located; and (3) reevaluation of the ethnographic literature in light of alternative prestige structures that demonstrates they were not the egalitarian societies many archaeologists once thought (Lamphere 2000).

There is now widespread recognition that parts of the Southwest show contrasting ways of expressing differences in power. In a book of case studies addressing leadership in the prehispanic Southwest (Mills 2000), the authors all found evidence for pronounced changes in leadership in their respective areas. Ritual leadership, such as those individuals responsible for specific religious sodalities, was identified as one way in which prestige was structured. A particularly important commonality among the case studies was that they took diachronic perspectives on how leadership changed, grounding their discussion within longer-term events within each area. A salient feature was that many of the transformations in leadership occurred with migration into their respective areas.

Archaeologists in the Southwest now are much more comfortable with talking about elites and the presence of hierarchy. Nonetheless, there are many points of disagreement about how those hierarchies were structured for specific cases in the Southwest. For example, Lekson (2006:37) presents an interpretation in which Chaco was ruled by kings and queens and represents "one of the Pueblo world's few garden-variety chiefdoms or petty kingdoms or cacicazgos." He dichotomizes leadership as either "something political, permanent, and hierarchical or something ritual and ceremonial, spiritual, situational, and evanescent" (28) and rejects the possibility that Chaco was ruled by members of ritual hierarchies. Instead, he regards the archaeological evidence from Chaco as evidence for only political power, rather than for ritual power. Proof is in three "facts" about Chaco: "retainers" buried with two high-status burials, great houses, and the regional primacy of Chaco.

Lekson's three facts are not necessarily or exclusively based in political power. In counterpoint and in the same volume, Sebastian (2006) points out the logical problems with dichotomizing political and ritual power and marshals several cases to show how ritual may be the basis for a great deal of both hierarchy and political power. There is little doubt that ancient Chacoans were organized according to a number of alternative prestige structures (gender, descent, residence group, etc.), and that many if not all of them were ritual and political. Power at Chaco was manifested in numerous ways. As Sebastian and others (Lamphere 2000; Mills 2004) have pointed out with respect to the Southwest record, we should not assume that the basis for this power was exclusively economic. Alternative ways of looking at how prestige was valued in the past cannot avoid vast amounts of ceremonial production and consumption, especially at Pueblo Bonito (Neitzel 2003). This is not to say that these prestige structures had nothing to do with the economy. Rather, indigenous values were not exclusively based on economic motives.

To interpret ritual hierarchies at Chaco does not mean they were the same forms of ritual hierarchy found in historic and contemporary Pueblo society; there is more evidence to the contrary (see Fowles, this volume). Pueblo Bonito was unique within the Chaco world, as well as within the trajectory of Ancestral and Historic Pueblos. To be able to argue for the distinctiveness of Chaco requires employing new approaches to how value is assessed in the past and tying past practices to concepts such as meaning, memory, and materiality. These concepts have only begun to be embraced by Southwestern archaeologists (e.g., Mills and Walker 2008; Van Dyke 2004, 2007; Walker 2008), but there is much in the Southwestern material record suggesting that approaches such as these have a great deal to offer for understanding past societies in the region.

Every society has a number of alternative prestige structures; at Chaco it is increasingly clear there was at least one particularly hierarchical and powerful distinction that was based on both family relationships and ritual authority. This distinction is probably the same one that is materially evident in the two clusters of human remains within Pueblo Bonito, found within two of the oldest sections of the building (Akins 2003; Neitzel 2003). These clusters include both primary and secondary burials, and their distinctive morphology suggests family crypts (rather than sacrificing of retainers), many of whom shared common descent. Family members memorialized those who were buried in these crypts by placing objects of memory in them and redepositing parts of bodies with those previously interred as a form of ancestor veneration.

On the basis of these patterns, several authors (Heitman and Plog 2005; Mills 2008; Wills 2005) have argued that Chaco may be an example of a "house society," a form of segmentary organization in which people are linked over several generations through property ownership and residence (Gillespie and Joyce 2000). These groups are a prestige structure, creating hierarchies in terms of access to people and resources. They also are bound together by ritual practices that further perpetuation of the house.

The concept of house society has also been recently applied to the Hohokam area. Douglas Craig's work (2007) builds on the fact that Preclassic period Hohokam courtyard groups are reproduced over time within settlements. Later structures were built over earlier structures, creating palimpsests of "daisy chains." Craig's work at the Preclassic Grewe site demonstrated there were inequalities among households, and those in the longest-lived courtyard groups were, in fact, the largest. If recruitment of labor is considered to be one way in which hierarchies of power are created, then the residential groups represented by courtyard groups are good evidence for inequalities perpetuated over the life of the settlement. The Preclassic Hohokam house was transformed in the Classic period, when compounds and platform mound communities were occupied. Inequalities were even more pronounced during the Classic period in terms of spatial segregation and most likely access to resources.

Alternative prestige structures in Hohokam and Casas Grandes societies included differences in how ritual hierarchies were used as a basis for power. The diversity of ritual architecture found in these two areas represents varying organization of ritual activities (see chapters by Fish and Fish, and VanPool and VanPool, this volume). A degree of competition between the affiliated community members who directed construction of one kind of ritual structure over another was likely present. How these structures were related to residential groups is something archaeologists in both areas have not yet fully explored. There are indications that houses constructed closer to the plazas in sites such as Snaketown were larger and probably hosted more feasts than those more distant from the core district. Even in later Classic period Hohokam sites, residences closer to platform mounds have greater amounts of exotic materials than do those living in compounds furthest from the mounds, such as found in the Marana Community of the Tucson Basin.

Perhaps the best evidence for inequalities of status and power found in the Southwest is in the record for violence and conflict. Most of the evidence is in small-scale conflict, but there are exceptions. Iconographic depictions of decapitations are present in ceramics and rock art, including Classic Mimbres pottery dating to the AD 1000s and Pueblo IV period rock art dating especially to the 14th and 15th centuries (Schaafsma 2000). Iconographic depictions can be debated as being metaphorical, but there is nothing metaphorical in the evidence for trauma and other physical forms of violence on human remains. Lambert (2002) reviews much of the evidence from human remains in the Southwest, ranging from the Basketmaker II to the Pueblo IV period. Although most of the sites are in the northern Southwest (with spikes in the Basketmaker II, Pueblo I, and Pueblo III periods), Casas Grandes (or Paquimé) in northern Mexico stands out in having a significant number of human remains showing signatures of death through violent means. Although some of the specific cases and lines of evidence are still being debated, it is clear that conflict was part of the social landscape of the Southwest. This conflict reinforced inequality of power among villagers living in the Southwest over nearly two millennia.

Religious Transformations

A third important theme in current research in the Southwest centers on the archaeology of ritual and religion. There are several strands of research—none of which have been well integrated—but given the rich ethnographic record it is surprising that Southwest archaeologists have not taken a lead in more general studies of the archaeology of religion. The focus in the archaeology of the Southwest has predominantly been on introduction of new religious practices or cults (Adams 1991; Crown 1994), especially those that transcend individual areas. Such an approach is important in that the new forms of practice are usually seen as highly contrastive with what came before, and that they highlight connections across regions.

How to look at religion in the past has varied widely among Southwestern archaeologists. Previous approaches relied on religious iconography, especially rock art, painted ceramics, figurines, and kiva murals. The Southwest has a rich record of iconographic depictions, but more so in the northern Southwest and Casas Grandes (see VanPool and VanPool, this volume). Another tack has been through suprahousehold architecture, including ceremonial rooms, kivas, great kivas, plazas, ball courts, capped mounds, platform mounds, and effigy mounds. There are only a few areas of the Southwest in the post-AD 500 period that are without one or more of these forms of public or ceremonial architecture—evidence for nested sets of social and ritual practices. Yet what usually comes out of comparisons is their variability. Similarly, there is a high degree of variation in mortuary behavior, one of the most conservative yet significant aspects of religious ritual. A new group of approaches uses evidence from depositional practices, including the concepts of singularities, enriched deposits, structured deposits, and life history pathways (Adams and LaMotta 2006; Mills and Walker 2008). These approaches have opened up a new way to address materiality, meaning, and differences in ritual practice.

Despite their theoretical and methodological characteristics, most approaches to religious ritual in the Southwest have focused on transformation rather than on the sociality of religion at a particular point in time. Although many of these have been called the introduction of new cults, Southwest archaeologists should be sympathetic with Kelley Hays-Gilpin's statement that "rather than wholesale movements of particular ritual complexes we should expect changing constellations of features" (2006:76). As she also points out, archaeologists in the Southwest have mostly been looking at scales that are too large to understand how religious ritual changes when these changes most likely occur at the sodality level on the part of particular leaders. Changes in Southwestern religion were undoubtedly brought about by individuals, but there are periods when the changes were particularly sweeping and even abrupt. This is not to underplay the strong continuities in ritual practices evident across the Southwest, but that there were times and places when particularly dramatic changes were present.

The religious transformation of Southwestern societies may be especially relevant for understanding the Pueblo IV period, with its wide changes beginning in the late 13th century (see Fowles, this volume). And although environmental change is taken for granted by many Southwestern archaeologists, this period shows a sudden reversal in climatic predictability that may have been an especially important contributing factor. Jeffery Dean's important analysis (1996) shows that over a millennium of Southwestern history there was a fairly stable and predictable pattern of rainfall; but this pattern was disrupted by a particularly chaotic period from AD 1250 to 1450. During this time, there was no way to know where summer dominant rainfall would prevail as opposed to a bimodal pattern. Farmers (and their crops), adapted to the predictable pattern over hundreds of years, were faced with not knowing when and where rainfall would come. At the early end of this period is one of the largest migrations in the Southwestern trajectory (see Varien et al., this volume). In the mid-1300s, a regionwide transition occurred that in the north is called the Katsina religion (Adams 1991; or Kachina, as in Hall, this volume) and in the south is associated with the Salado ideology (Crown 1994). By the mid-1400s, a period of violence occurred, there was massive depopulation of many areas of the Southwest, and migrants ratcheted up aggregation in areas that created the footprint of most of the contemporary Puebloan villages (see Fowles, this volume). Chaotic environmental conditions likely contributed to the chaotic social conditions that are evident during this period.

What Is on the Horizon?

In this short chapter, it is difficult to include all of the directions that Southwest archaeology is taking. But it is worth mentioning a few additional themes. First is collaboration with descendant communities, which has always been important and is becoming even more so. Second, there has been an increase in use of ethnographic information by archaeologists, tempered by knowledge of the problems of using ethnographic analogy. These ethnographies are being used in new ways, especially for understanding issues of identity, religion, and cultural affiliation. Finally, there is a trend toward large-scale syntheses and compilation and analysis of regional-scale databases. All of these are themes that will take interpretations of the archaeology of the Southwest into new directions—and continue to make the region an ideal laboratory for archaeology.

REFERENCES

Adams, E. C. 1991. *The Origin and Development of the Pueblo Katsina Cult*. University of Arizona Press, Tucson.

———, and V. M. LaMotta. 2006. New Perspectives on an Ancient Religion: Katsina Ritual and the Archaeological Record. In *Religion in the Prehispanic Southwest*, edited by C. S. VanPool, T. L. VanPool, and D. A. Phillips Jr., pp. 53–66. AltaMira Press, Lanham, MD.

Akins, N. J. 2003. The Burials of Pueblo Bonito. In *Pueblo Bonito: Center of the Chacoan World*, edited by J. E. Neitzel, pp. 94–106. Smithsonian Institution Press, Washington, DC.

Cameron, C. M. 1995. Migration and the Movement of Southwestern Peoples. *Journal of Anthropological Archaeology* 14:104–124.

Clark, J. J. 2001. *Tracking Prehistoric Migrations: Pueblo Settlers Among the Tonto Basin Hohokam*. Anthropological Papers of the University of Arizona 65. University of Arizona Press, Tucson.

Cordell, L. S. 1997. *Archaeology of the Southwest*. 2nd ed. Academic Press, New York.

———, and G. J. Gumerman. 1989. Cultural Interaction in the Prehistoric Southwest. In *Dynamics of Southwest Prehistory*, edited by L. S. Cordell and G. J. Gumerman, pp. 1–17. Smithsonian Institution, Washington, DC.

Craig, D. B. 2007. Courtyard Groups and the Emergence of House Estates in Early Hohokam Society. In Center for Archaeological Investigations Occasional Paper 35, *The Durable House: House Society Models in Archaeology*, edited by R. A. Beck Jr., pp. 446–463. Southern Illinois University, Carbondale.

Crown, P. L. 1994. *Ceramics and Ideology: Salado Polychrome Pottery*. University of New Mexico Press, Albuquerque.

Dean, J. S. 1996. Demography, Environment, and Subsistence Stress. Santa Fe Institute Studies in the Sciences of Complexity Proceedings 24, *Evolving Complexity and Environmental Risk in the Prehistoric Southwest*, edited by J. A. Tainter and B. B. Tainter, pp. 25–56. Addison-Wesley, Reading, MA.

Dongoske, K. E., M. Yeatts, R. Anyon, and T. J. Ferguson. 1997. Archaeological Cultures and Cultural Affiliation: Hopi and Zuni Perspectives in the American Southwest. *American Antiquity* 62:600–608.

Duff, A. I. 2002. *Western Pueblo Identities: Regional Interaction, Migration, and Transformation*. University of Arizona Press, Tucson.

Ferguson, T. J. 2007. Zuni Traditional History and Cultural Geography. In *Zuni Origins: Toward a New Synthesis of Southwestern Archaeology*, edited by D. A. Gregory and D. R. Wilcox, pp. 377–403. University of Arizona Press, Tucson.

———, and C. Colwell-Chanthaphohn. 2006. *History Is in the Land: Multivocal Tribal Traditions in Arizona's San Pedro Valley*. University of Arizona Press, Tucson.

———, and M. Lomaomvaya. 1999. Hoopoq'yaqam niqw Wukoskyavi (Those Who Went to the Northeast and Tonto Basin): Hopi-Salado Cultural Affiliation Study. Hopi Cultural Preservation Office, Kiqötsmovi, AZ.

Gillespie, S. D., and R. A. Joyce (editors). 2000. *Beyond Kinship: Social and Material Reproduction in House Societies.* University of Pennsylvania Press, Philadelphia.

Habicht-Mauche, J. A., S. L. Eckert, and D. L. Huntley. 2006. *The Social Life of Pots: Glaze Wares and Cultural Dynamics in the Southwest, AD 1250–1680.* University of Arizona Press, Tucson.

Haury, E. W. 1958. Evidence at Point of Pines for a Prehistoric Migration from Northern Arizona. Social Science Bulletin 27, *Migrations in New World Culture History*, edited by R. H. Thompson, pp. 1–8. University of Arizona, Tucson.

Haynes, C. V., and B. B. Huckell (editors). 2007. *Murray Springs: A Clovis Site with Multiple Activity Areas in the San Pedro Valley, Arizona.* Anthropological Papers of the University of Arizona 71. University of Arizona Press, Tucson.

Hays-Gilpin, K. 2006. Icons and Ethnicity: Hopi Painted Pottery and Murals. In *Religion in the Prehispanic Southwest*, edited by C. S. VanPool, T. L. VanPool, and D. A. Phillips Jr., pp. 67–80. AltaMira Press, Lanham, MD.

Hegmon, M., M. C. Nelson, and M. J. Ennes. 2000. Corrugated Pottery, Technological Style, and Population Movement in the Mimbres Region of the American Southwest. *Journal of Anthropological Research* 56:217–240.

Heitman, C. H., and S. Plog. 2005. Kinship and the Dynamics of the House: Rediscovering Dualism in the Pueblo Past. In *A Catalyst for Ideas: Anthropological Archaeology and the Legacy of Douglas W. Schwartz*, edited by V. L. Scarborough, pp. 69–100. SAR Press, Santa Fe.

Hill, J. B., J. J. Clark, W. H. Doelle, and P. D. Lyons. 2004. Prehistoric Demography in the Southwest: Migration, Coalescence, and Hohokam Population Decline. *American Antiquity* 69:689–716.

Holliday, V. T., E. P. Gaines, and G. Sanchez-Miranda. 2009. *Geoarchaeology of El Fin del Mundo, a Clovis Site in Sonora, Mexico.* Paper presented at the Geological Society of the Americas Annual Meeting, October, Portland, OR.

Johnson, G. A. 1989. Dynamics of Southwestern Prehistory: Far Outside—Looking In. In *Dynamics of Southwest Prehistory*, edited by L. S. Cordell and G. J. Gumerman, pp. 371–389. Smithsonian Institution Press, Washington, DC.

Lambert, P. M. 2002. The Archaeology of War: A North American Perspective. *Journal of Archaeological Research* 10:207–241.

Lamphere, L. 2000. Gender Models in the Southwest: A Sociocultural Perspective. In *Women and Men in the Prehispanic Southwest: Labor, Power, & Prestige*, edited by P. L. Crown, pp. 379–401. SAR Press, Santa Fe.

Lekson, S. H. 2006. Chaco Matters: An Introduction. In *The Archaeology of Chaco Canyon: An Eleventh-Century Pueblo Regional Center*, edited by S. H. Lekson, pp. 3–44. SAR Press, Santa Fe.

———. 2009. *A History of the Ancient Southwest.* SAR Press, Santa Fe.

Lyons, P. D. 2003. *Ancestral Hopi Migrations.* Anthropological Papers of the University of Arizona 68. University of Arizona Press, Tucson.

Merrill, W. L., R. J. Hard, J. B. Mabry, G. J. Fritz, K. R. Adams, J. R. Roney, and A. C. MacWilliams. 2009. The Diffusion of Maize to the Southwestern United States and Its Impact. *PNAS* 106:21019–21026.

Mills, B. J. (editor). 2000. *Alternative Leadership Strategies in the Prehispanic Southwest.* University of Arizona Press, Tucson.

———. 2004. The Establishment and Defeat of Hierarchy: Inalienable Possessions and the History of Collective Prestige Structures in the Puebloan Southwest. *American Anthropologist* 106(2):238–251.

———. 2008. Remembering While Forgetting: Depositional Practice and Social Memory at Chaco. In *Memory Work: Archaeologies of Material Practices*, edited by B. J. Mills and W. H. Walker, pp. 81–108. School for Advanced Research Press, Santa Fe.

———. 2011. Themes and Models for Understanding Migration in the Southwest. In *Movement, Connectivity, and Landscape Change*, edited by M. C. Nelson and C. Strawhacker, pp. 345–359. University Press of Colorado, Boulder.

———, and W. H. Walker. 2008. Introduction: Memory, Materiality, and Depositional Practice. In *Memory Work: Archaeologies of Material Practices*, edited by B. J. Mills and W. H. Walker pp. 3–23. School for Advanced Research Press, Santa Fe.

Neitzel, J. E. 2003. Artifact Distributions at Pueblo Bonito. In *Pueblo Bonito: Center of the Chacoan World*, edited by J. E. Neitzel, pp. 107–126. Smithsonian Institution, Washington, DC.

Neuzil, A. I. 2008. *In the Aftermath of Migration: Renegotiating Ancient Identity in Southeastern Arizona*. Anthropological Papers of the University of Arizona 73. University of Arizona Press, Tucson.

Plog, S. 1997. *Ancient Peoples of the Southwest*. Thames and Hudson, London.

Schaafsma, P. 2000. *Warrior, Shield, and Star: Imagery and Ideology of Pueblo Warfare*. Western Edge Press, Santa Fe, NM.

Sebastian, L. 2006. The Chaco Synthesis. In *The Archaeology of Chaco Canyon: An Eleventh-Century Pueblo Regional Center*, edited by S. H. Lekson, pp. 393–422. SAR Press, Santa Fe.

Spielmann, K. A. (editor). 1998. *Migration and Community Reorganization: The Pueblo IV Period in the American Southwest*. Arizona State University Anthropological Research Papers 51. Arizona State University, Tempe.

Stark, M. T., M. D. Elson, and J. J. Clark. 1998. Social Boundaries and Technical Choices in Tonto Basin Prehistory. In *The Archaeology of Social Boundaries*, edited by M. T. Stark, pp. 208–231. Smithsonian Institution, Washington, DC.

Van Dyke, R. M. 2004. Memory, Meaning, and Masonry: The Late Bonito Chacoan Landscape. *American Antiquity* 69(3):413–431.

———. 2007. *The Chaco Experience: Landscape and Ideology at the Center Place*. School of Advanced Research Press, Santa Fe.

Vierra, B. J. (editor). 2005. *The Late Archaic Across the Borderlands: From Foraging to Farming*. University of Texas Press, Austin.

Walker, W. H. 2008. Practice and Nonhuman Social Actors: The Afterlife Histories of Witches and Dogs in the American Southwest. In *Memory Work: Archaeologies of Material Practices*, edited by B. J. Mills and W. H. Walker, pp. 137–158. SAR Press, Santa Fe.

Wills, W. H. 2005. Economic Competition and Agricultural Involution in the Precontact North American Southwest. In *A Catalyst for Ideas: Anthropological Archaeology and the Legacy of Douglas W. Schwartz*, edited by V. L. Scarborough, pp. 41–67. SAR Press, Santa Fe.

CHAPTER 46

DIVERSITY IN FIRST-MILLENNIUM AD SOUTHWESTERN FARMING COMMUNITIES

LISA YOUNG

COMMUNITIES are a vital component of human societies, both in the past and present. Communities create a sense of belonging and social identity among people who are not necessarily related to one another, yet membership is often fluid and dynamic (see also Rees, this volume). Because archaeologists cannot directly observe the social interactions that create this sense of shared identity, we have devised various approaches to study the organization of ancient communities using material remains (Yaeger and Canuto 2000). Analyses of public architecture and site layout are particularly useful for identifying differences in community organization (Kolb and Snead 1997). In this chapter, I examine variation in early farming communities in the American Southwest, a region with the longest continuously occupied villages in the United States.

In the Southwest, the concept of the community has been especially useful for examining the organization of aggregated settlements. For example, archaeologists used the phrase "Chacoan community" to describe the social, economic, and religious relationships between large sites with distinctive architectural features and surrounding smaller sites in northwest New Mexico and beyond (Marshall et al. 1979). By 1990, the concept of the community became so important that a regional biennial conference focused specifically on the dynamic nature of ancient communities in the Southwest (Wills and Leonard 1994).

Most of the research on southwestern communities, however, has focused on sites that postdate AD 1000 (Reed 2000), a time when regional differences were clearly visible in architecture and ceramic styles. To explore the origins of these regional traditions, archaeologists are currently investigating the organization of earlier communities, especially those inhabited between AD 200 and 900, a period when cultural diversity first emerged in this region (Young and Herr 2012).

Defining Southwestern Communities

Southwestern archaeologists often use Murdock's definition of community (1949), which emphasizes the interactions that occurred between people who live near each other (Wills and Leonard 1994). These types of communities are commonly called residential communities or *villages*. Studies of southwestern communities have largely focused on pueblos, a term first used by Spanish explorers in the 1500s to describe the apartment-style villages they encountered on their travels through Arizona and New Mexico. The boundaries of pueblo communities are easily defined because houses share walls, and are located near community spaces such as a plaza or special ceremonial structures. Archaeologists have also noted that pueblo sites often occurred in clusters (Adams and Duff 2004; Powers 1984) and that ancient people identified themselves as members in communities that extended beyond the boundaries of their own village. To use an example from a contemporary descendant community to illustrate this point: a Hopi person's identity is based on clan affiliation, membership in a religious organization, the village where an individual grew up, and the mesa associated with this village. As this example illustrates, an individual belongs to multiple communities and not all are defined by co-residence.

Although pueblo villages are often portrayed as the quintessential southwestern farming communities, pueblo-style architecture was not used during all times or in all places in the American Southwest. To understand the organization of communities in situations where connections between households and sites are not easily defined by masonry walls, southwestern archaeologists also examine structures that were built for large gatherings, often called "public architecture" (Wills and Leonard 1994). These buildings are differentiated from domestic houses on the basis of their size, layout, or unique features. Archaeologists assume that the events occurring within these structures included people from neighboring sites. For example, on the Colorado Plateau and the high mountainous regions of the Southwest, researchers have explored how great kivas (i.e., very large semisubterranean structures) were the focal point of gatherings involving dispersed households (Herr 2001). In the Sonoran Desert of southern Arizona, archaeologists have proposed that ball courts and later platform mounds (Elson 2007) were the venue for events that integrated individuals from multiple villages. In both areas, the presence of public architecture represented the desire to build a permanent facility for community gatherings. In turn, the construction of these structures linked community events to a specific location. Because of their size, great kivas and ball courts must have been built with the cooperation of many individuals. Consequently, the act of constructing these public structures reinforced community membership.

Archaeologists originally identified regional differences in public architecture during the 1930s. However, only recently have we begun to explore how these differences can be used to understand variation in the organization of early southwestern farming communities.

Origins of Diverse Southwestern Farming Communities

Corn was introduced into the southwestern United States from Mexico more than 4,000 years ago (see also Pearsall, this volume). However, villages or residential communities were not a regular part of the southwestern social landscape until more than 2,000 years later. Early farmers lived in pithouses that were built by digging into the ground to create the floor and part of the walls of the structure. The roof was then constructed over this pit. Early pithouse sites were usually small with fewer than five contemporaneous houses. Undecorated brownware pots became a regular part of a household's toolkit starting around AD 200. For the next couple of centuries, the material cultural of pithouse dwellers across the Southwest was relatively homogeneous.

Starting around AD 500, population increased throughout the Southwest (Dean et al. 1994), especially in the Sonoran Desert of southern Arizona and in the Four Corners region of the Colorado Plateau (Figure 46.1). Sites in areas of high population density often contained more than 10 contemporaneously occupied pithouses and are generally called "villages" by archaeologists. During this time, regional differences in house styles, site layout, and decorated pottery also developed.

These regional differences in material culture were the characteristics that early archaeologists used to identify archaeological culture areas (Kidder 1924). The original classificatory terminology used to describe regional variation in the Southwest was *Hohokam* to refer to groups in the Sonoran Desert of southern Arizona, *Mogollon* to refer to groups living in the mountainous regions of central Arizona and south-central New Mexico, and *Anasazi* to refer to groups on the Colorado Plateau. *Ancestral Pueblo* has largely replaced Anasazi in deference to descendant pueblo communities. I compare public architecture and the layout of pithouse sites in the Sonoran Desert and on the Colorado Plateau to illustrate differences in the organization of early farming communities.

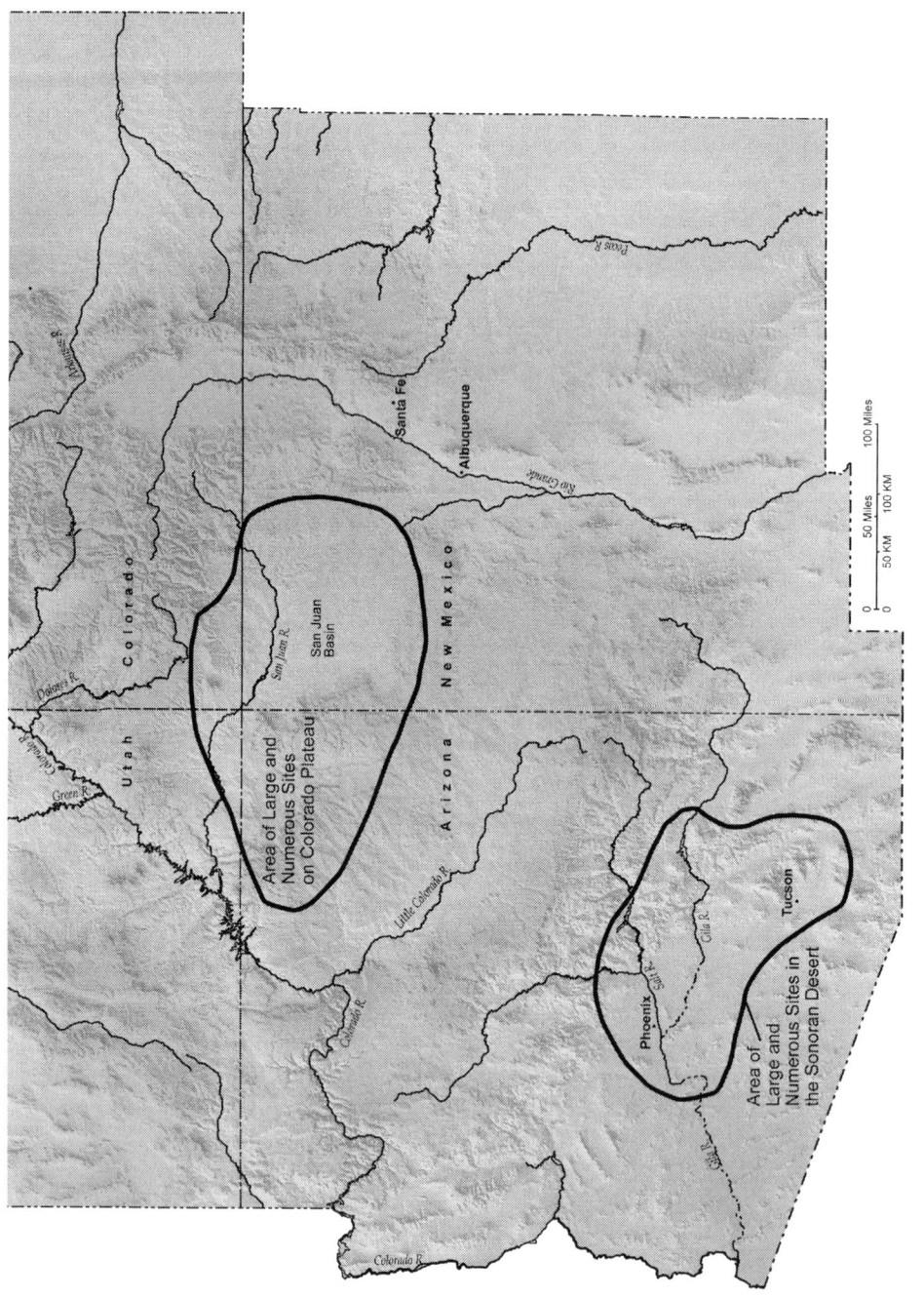

Figure 46.1 Map of Southwestern United States with areas where large and numerous sites were found dating to the ninth century AD (based on Dean et al. 1994:figure 4.14, 4,000 contour line).

Communities in the Sonoran Desert of Arizona

In the Sonoran Desert regions of southern Arizona, large pithouse settlements became common by AD 500. In locations with reliable resources, especially water, these villages were inhabited for more than five centuries (Craig and Henderson 2007). Formation of villages in this area was associated with expansion of irrigation systems along major rivers and their tributaries. The coordinated labor necessary to construct and maintain extensive irrigation canal systems and manage water resources may have provided the incentive for households to live together in larger communities (Wallace and Lindeman 2012).

At villages throughout this region, households were organized around a courtyard. These clusters of pithouses, called courtyard groups, typically included two to four contemporaneous pithouses with associated features that faced a small open space or courtyard (Figure 46.2). At the large sites, courtyard groups were built around a central plaza. The courtyard groups immediately surrounding the plaza often contained a larger-than-average pithouse, which has been interpreted as a leader's house (Wallace 2007). In situations where pithouses were rebuilt, households often chose to maintain the same courtyard layout as new houses replaced older ones (Craig and Henderson 2007). This persistence in courtyard organization may reflect the importance of family inheritance in these early villages. Burials and shrines found in plaza areas, in addition to figurines found in household trash, have

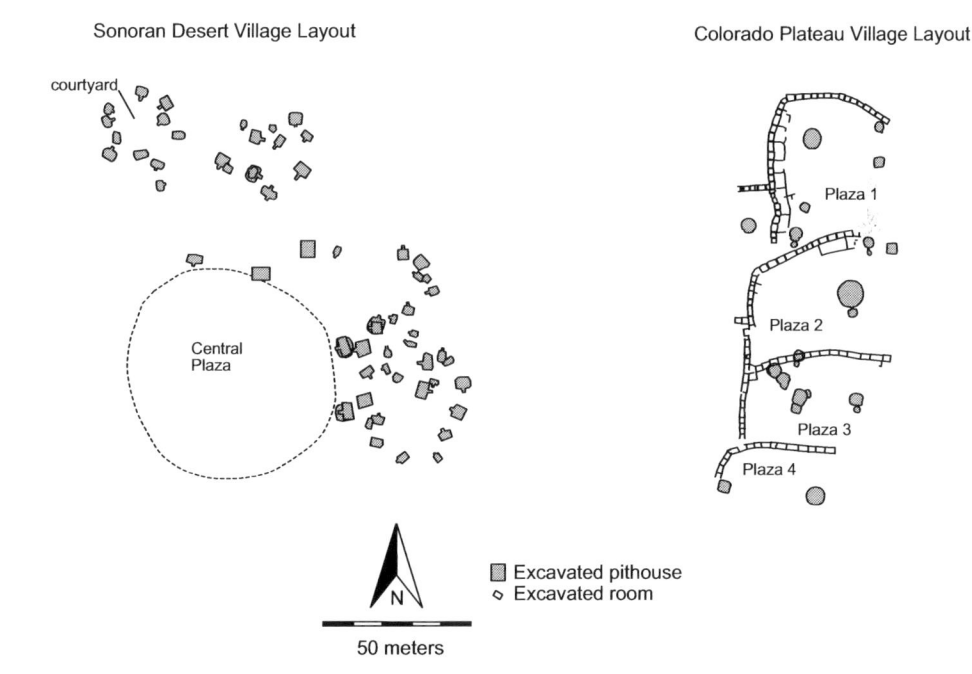

Figure 46.2 Comparison of village layout from the Sonoran Desert (Valencia Veija, AD 450–650) and the Colorado Plateau (Alkali Ridge Site 13, AD 760–790; redrawn from Fish and Fish 2007:figure 2.4; and Brew 1946:figure 27, only areas with extensive excavation are shown).

led archaeologists to suggest that ancestor veneration was an important part of the spiritual life of Sonoran Desert communities.

By AD 800, many of the largest villages in the Tucson and Phoenix basins added a ball court to the central plaza area (Elson 2007), with some villages building more than one. Communal cooking features have been found near the plazas, suggesting that feasting was an important component of events associated with the ball courts or plazas. Sites with ball courts were centrally located along irrigation canals and surrounded by smaller sites that did not have ball courts. Archaeologists propose that the activities involving ball courts brought people from these surrounding villages to the larger sites for intervillage community events.

Ball courts were constructed by digging into the ground to create a leveled and prepared oval surface (Figure 46.3). High earthen embankments with openings on opposite ends were then created on the sides of this central area. The interior walls of the earthen embankments were often plastered. The size of ball courts varied; small ones had at least 200 square meters of interior space, while others contained an inner area that was as much as three times larger. On the basis of general similarities in form to Mesoamerican ball courts, archaeologists have interpreted southern Arizona ball courts as the locus of sporting events, probably with religious overtones. Rubber balls were recovered from a few sites in this region. Figurines from ninth and 10th century AD sites often depict individuals wearing hats and clothing with padded upper arms, reminiscent of images of ball players from Mexico (Fish and Fish 2007). Ball courts continued to be an important feature of communities in the Sonoran Desert regions until they were replaced by platform mounds around AD 1050.

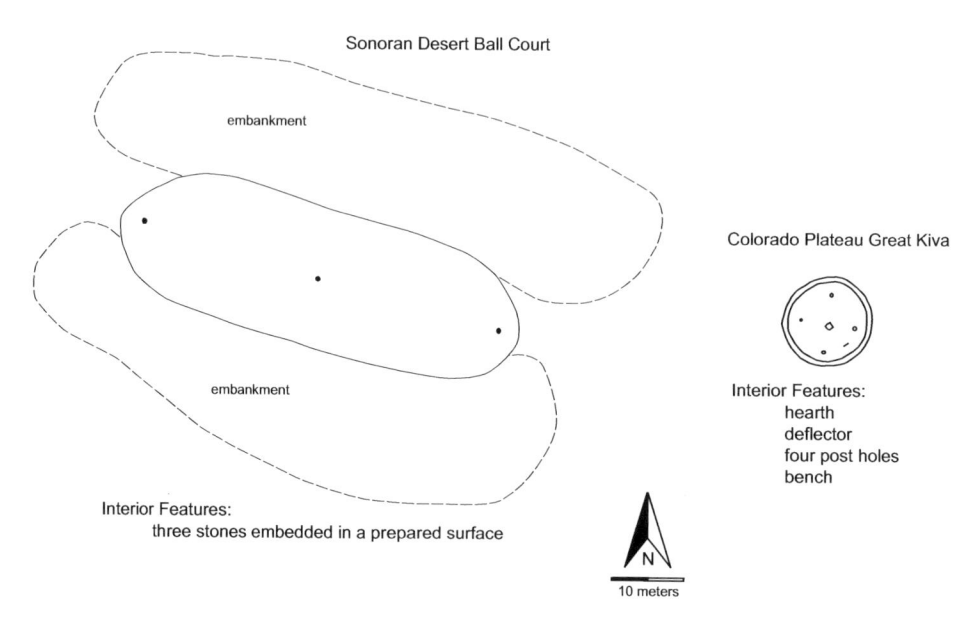

Figure 46.3 Comparison of the public architecture from the Sonoran Desert (Snaketown Ballcourt 1) and the Colorado Plateau (Shabik'eschee Village great kiva; redrawn from Gladwin 1937:figure 11 and Roberts 1929:figure 24).

Communities on the Colorado Plateau

In contrast to the Sonoran Desert, development of villages on the Colorado Plateau was later and more sporadic. Across this region, small pithouse sites with three to five contemporaneous households were the norm. Starting around AD 500, a few notable large sites that housed more than 20 contemporary households were built. These sites are located in or near the San Juan Basin, the focus of the later Chaco phenomenon (see Lekson, this volume). Between AD 750 and 880, the highest density of large sites occurred in areas north of the San Juan River (i.e., the Mesa Verde area). By this time, site layout was standardized across the Colorado Plateau. Sites consisted of pithouses and associated clusters of surface rooms located to the north or west of the pithouses. At larger villages, these pithouse groupings were clustered and the number of surface rooms per pithouse was large (Figure 46.2). Some of these clusters contained a very large pithouse, which has been interpreted as the homes of leaders (Wilshusen 2006).

In contrast to the Sonoran Desert pithouse communities, pithouse sites in the northern Southwest were not continuously inhabited for long periods of time. Large regional surveys identified periods when populations migrated in and out of specific areas of the Colorado Plateau. Movement on varying temporal and spatial scales continued to be important into the second millennium AD and is an essential part of contemporary pueblo origin stories (Naranjo 2008).

Starting around AD 500, pithouse dwellers in certain areas of the northern Southwest built large circular structures (more than 10 meters in diameter), called great kivas. Sites with great kivas were most commonly found in areas with high population densities, especially in the Four Corners region. The walls of great kivas were usually built with upright slabs, and many of these structures contained benches. Most were roofed, with an interior floor area of at least 80 square meters. To collect, shape, and place the stones for the walls and beams for the roofs, a group of people larger than the inhabitants of a single site was needed.

Archaeologists use the word *kiva* to describe semisubterranean ceremonial structures. The function of the earliest great kivas has been debated since the first example of this type of structure was excavated (Roberts 1929). We will probably never know the details of the events that occurred within great kivas, but examination of anthropomorphic images in the rock art and pottery from the eight century AD offers some interesting insights. A rock art panel in the Four Corners area depicted lines of people facing a large circle. Archaeologists have proposed that this image represents a procession or dance centered around a great kiva (Wilshusen 2006:22). Several figures in these panels carried staffs or wore headdresses. In addition, three bowls from this period depict individuals holding hands in a circle, also reminiscent of a dance. These images suggest that ceremonies involving processions or dances were an important component to community gatherings. Construction of great kivas indicates that communities wanted to create a permanent location for these events.

Comparing Community Organization

The differences in site layout and public architecture at pithouse sites in the Sonoran Desert and on the Colorado Plateau suggest that diverse organizational strategies began to emerge in southwestern communities by about AD 500. Sonoran Desert villages were stable residential communities where courtyards (and presumably farmland) were passed down between multiple generations (Craig and Henderson 2007). Within villages, households shared clearly definable public spaces in courtyards and plazas. Groups gathered for intervillage events in the plazas and ball courts of larger and more centrally located settlements. The earth embankments of ball courts could have easily accommodated hundreds of spectators, suggesting that community gatherings were large and activities were visible to onlookers.

Colorado Plateau households, in contrast, oriented their villages toward a cardinal direction, usually the south or east. Long-term occupation of sites was rare. Most villages did not have clearly defined shared spaces outside of structures, and sites with great kivas were widely scattered on the landscape. These kivas, especially the roofed ones, probably accommodated fewer than 200 adults. Activities inside these structures were visible only to people within them.

Conclusion

Archaeologists have long recognized that regional differences in material culture developed during the first millennium AD in the American Southwest. This comparison of public architecture and village layout indicates that these differences also reflect the diverse ways that early farming communities were organized.

This variation in pithouse community organization reflects differences in cultural identity and the role of community leaders. In the Sonoran Desert an individual's identity was based not only on associations with a courtyard group and a village but also with a cluster of villages that shared irrigation canals and gathered for events centered around a ball court (Fish and Fish 2007). Relatively short-term use of Colorado Plateau pithouse communities indicates that connections to specific villages or great kivas were more fluid and that group identity may have been created through movement and shared ceremonies. Comparison of size and layout of structures built for community gatherings also revealed differences in the types of activities held within them. Events within ball courts and plazas of Sonoran Desert communities were highly visible, while activities within great kivas were enclosed and restricted. In both areas, archaeologists have used the presence of large pithouses to argue for emergence of community leaders. The differences in public architecture suggest that the source of influence or power of leaders varied regionally. Leaders who hosted events in and around ball courts in southern Arizona needed to accommodate and feed the many people who attended these gatherings. In contrast, leaders who hosted events in great kivas may have depended on their knowledge of ceremonies and associated rituals to bring dispersed households together for community gatherings. At later period sites, the restrictive nature of great kivas has been interpreted as a reflection of control of esoteric and ceremonial knowledge as the basis for leadership (Crown and Judge 1991:303).

By AD 200, southwestern households lived in small pithouse sites, grew corn, and made brownware pottery. Within a few centuries, large villages with their own distinctive material culture and traditions had emerged on the Colorado Plateau and in the Sonoran Desert. Variation in site layout and public architecture indicates that the process of forming and maintaining communities took differing trajectories in these areas and was the foundation of cultural diversity in the American Southwest.

REFERENCES

Adams, E. C., and A. I. Duff. 2004. *The Protohistoic Pueblo World, A.D. 1275–1600*. University of Arizona Press, Tucson.

Brew, J. O. 1946. *Archaeology of Alkali Ridge, Southeastern Utah*. Papers of the Peabody Museum of American Archaeology and Ethnology, Harvard University.

Craig, D. B., and T. K. Henderson. 2007. Houses, Households, and Household Organization. In *The Hohokam Millennium*, edited by S. K. Fish and P. R. Fish, pp. 31–37. School of American Research Press, Santa Fe, NM.

Crown P. L., and W. J. Judge. 1991. Synthesis and Conclusions. In *Chaco and Hohokam: Prehistoric Regional Systems in the American Southwest*, edited by P. L. Crown and W. J. Judge, pp. 293–308. School of American Research Press, Santa Fe, NM.

Dean, J. S., W. H. Doelle, and J. D. Orcutt. 1994. Adaptive Stress: Environment and Demography. In *Themes in Southwest Prehistory*, edited by G. J. Gumerman, pp. 53–86. School of American Research Press, Santa Fe, NM.

Elson, M. D. 2007. Into the Earth and Up from the Sky: Hohokam Ritual Architecture. In *The Hohokam Millennium*, edited by S. K. Fish and P. R. Fish, pp. 49–56. School of American Research Press, Santa Fe, NM.

Fish, P. R., and S. K. Fish. 2007. Community, Territory, and Polity. In *The Hohokam Millennium*, edited by S. K. Fish and P. R. Fish, pp. 39–47. School of American Research Press, Santa Fe, NM.

Gladwin, H. S., E. W. Haury, E. B. Sayles, and N. Gladwin. 1937. *Excavations at Snaketown: Material Culture*. Medallion Papers 25. Gila Pueblo, Globe, AZ.

Herr, S. A. 2001. *Beyond Chaco: Great Kiva Communities on the Mogollon Rim Frontier*. Anthropological Papers of the University of Arizona 66. University of Arizona Press, Tucson.

Kidder, A. V. 1924. *An Introduction to the Study of Southwest Archaeology, with a Preliminary Account of the Excavations at Pecos*. Yale University Press, New Haven, CT.

Kolb, M. J., and J. E. Snead. 1997. It's a Small World After All: Comparative Analyses of Community Organization in Archaeology. *American Antiquity* 62(4):609–628.

Marshall, M. P., J. R. Stein, R. W. Loose, and J. E. Novotny. 1979. *Anasazi Communities of the San Juan Basin*. Public Service Company of New Mexico and New Mexico Historic Preservation Bureau, Albuquerque.

Murdock, G. P. 1949. *Social Structure*. Macmillan, New York.

Naranjo, T. 2008. Life as Movement: A Tewa View of Community and Identity. In *The Social Production of Communities: Structure, Agency, and Identity*, edited by M. D. Varien and J. M. Potter, pp. 251–262. AltaMira Press, Lanham, MD.

Powers, R. P. 1984, Outliers and Roads in the Chaco System. In *New Light on Chaco Canyon*, pp. 45–58. School of American Research Press, Santa Fe, NM.

Reed, P. F. 2000. Fundamental Issues in Basketmaker Archaeology. In *Foundations of Anasazi Culture: The Basketmaker-Pueblo Transition*, edited by P. F. Reed, pp. 3–16. University of Utah Press, Salt Lake City.

Roberts, F. H. H., Jr. 1929. *Shabik'eschee Village: A Late Basket Maker Site in the Chaco Canyon, New Mexico*. Bureau of American Ethnology, Bulletin 92. Smithsonian Institution, Washington, DC.

Wallace, H. 2007. Hohokam Beginnings. In *The Hohokam Millenium*, edited by S. K. Fish and P. R. Fish, pp. 13–21. School of American Research Press, Santa Fe, NM.

———, and M. Lindeman. 2012. Hohokam Village Formation in the Phoenix and Tucson Basins. In *Southwestern Pithouse Communities, AD 200–900*, edited by L. C. Young and S. A. Herr, pp. 34–44. University of Arizona Press, Tucson.

Wills, W. H., and R. D. Leonard. 1994. Preface. In *The Ancient Southwestern Community: Models and Methods for the Study of Prehistoric Social Organization*, edited by W. H. Wills and R. D. Leonard, pp. xiii–xvi. University of New Mexico Press, Albuquerque.

Wilshusen, R. H. 2006. The Genesis of Pueblos: Innovations Between 500 and 900 CE. In *The Mesa Verde World: Explorations in Ancestral Pueblo Archaeology*, edited by D. G. Nobel, pp. 19–28. School of American Research Press, Santa Fe, NM.

Yaeger, J., and M. A. Canuto. 2000. Introducing an Archaeology of Communities. In *The Archaeology of Communities: A New World Perspective*, edited by M. A. Canuto and J. Yaeger, pp. 1–15. Routledge, London.

Young, L. C., and S. A. Herr (editors). (2012). *Southwestern Pithouse Communities*, AD 200–900. University of Arizona Press, Tucson.

CHAPTER 47

HOHOKAM SOCIETY AND WATER MANAGEMENT

SUZANNE K. FISH AND PAUL R. FISH

In the southwestern United States, the Hohokam of southern Arizona are notable for the scale and diversity of their water management and for the deep sedentism and dense populations their agricultural productivity made possible. The Hohokam domain was centered near modern Phoenix in the hot, dry Sonoran Desert biome. Although the populous inhabitants of an extensively irrigated core area along the Salt and Gila rivers in the Phoenix Basin elaborated many hallmarks of Hohokam culture, local populations largely replicated these organizational and stylistic modes in outlying basins, where they combined more limited irrigation with other farming techniques.

Given that Hohokam sociopolitical organization never met the criteria for a state according to most scholars, Hohokam society embodies the unusual social correlates of large-scale, coordinated water management outside the confines of a comprehensive legal system, coercive governmental force, or bureaucracy. As an indication of the impressive scale of canal systems in the Phoenix Basin, major trunk lines totaled 600 kilometers, extended as much as 30 kilometers from river intakes, and watered an estimated 20,000 to 40,000 hectares (Figures 47.1 and 47.2). In the New World, such irrigation infrastructure was exceeded only in Andean empires. Maximum population estimates for the same Hohokam core area range from 25,000 to more than 100,000.

Notwithstanding the absence of state-level control over their massive canal networks, the Hohokam persisted as an archaeologically distinct tradition for 1,000 years, from approximately AD 500 until at least 1450. The worldwide rarity of ethnographic analogs for such an enduring but organizationally middle-range irrigation society presents a challenge for interpreting higher-order Hohokam political and social institutions (Hunt et al. 2005).

Figure 47.1 Hohokam mainline canals: (a) well-preserved canal segment at the northeastern edge of today's Phoenix metropolitan area (scale indicated by vehicle tracks in channel; photo by Helga Tiewes, courtesy of the Arizona State Museum, University of Arizona); (b) archaeologist Bruce Masse stands beside superimposed Salt River canal cross-sections near the site of Pueblo Grande in Phoenix, Arizona (adapted from Masse 1976:21–22).

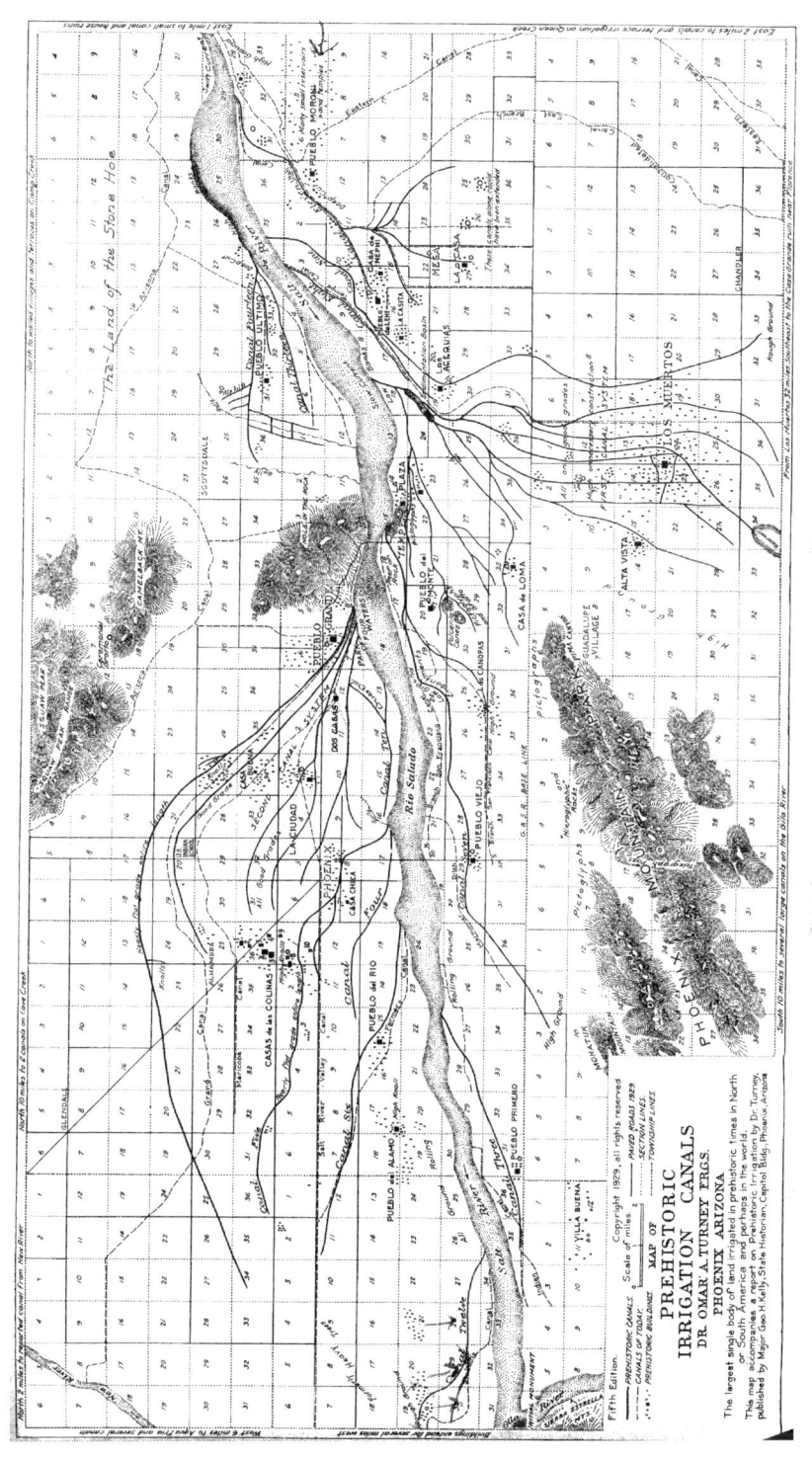

Figure 47.2 Omar Turney (1929), engineer for the city of Phoenix, compiled this map of major Hohokam sites and canal systems on the Salt River in the 1920s, on the basis of earlier records and remains still visible at the time.

Cultivators drew on a common repertoire of desert farming strategies throughout the Hohokam sequence. Members of this broad cultural tradition also came to share distinctive modes of material culture and settlement organization, as well as ideology underlying ritual and civic institutions and public architecture. A closer linkage in these aspects with Mesoamerican-related societies to the south set the Hohokam apart from other major archaeological traditions in the Southwest region (Figure 47.3). Covering a maximum extent of 50,000 square kilometers, comparable in size to the state of South Carolina, the Hohokam sphere encompassed groups that in all probability spoke multiple dialects or languages and claimed differing origins. Reflecting neither a singular ethnic identity nor a politically cohesive realm, Hohokam territory varied over time as local populations selectively incorporated dominant styles and ideology. For example, in peripheral sectors, Hohokam styles of pottery did not invariably coincide with the building of Hohokam modes of public architecture.

A transition in the organizational scale of society around AD 500 marks the beginning of what archaeologists designate as the Hohokam sequence, with widespread consolidation of styles in artifacts, architecture, and other material culture. Residents came together in more permanent settlements with well-built pithouses. In the largest villages, houses surrounded central plazas. Soon, Hohokam in the Phoenix Basin began to construct massive irrigation systems, which expanded near their topographic limits within a few hundred years. Red-on-buff pottery, a regionally distinctive hallmark of Hohokam affiliation, made its first appearance. Mesoamerican-inspired ball courts and ritual objects, such as figurines and censers, signaling participation in Hohokam ideology, reached their greatest regional extent between AD 700 and 1150 during the Preclassic period (Figure 47.4).

Figure 47.3 Large ceramic male and female figurines are part of a set dating to AD 750–900; pads on the upper arms resemble similar pads on West Mexican figurines that represent players in ball courts, who also wear turbans (photograph courtesy of David Doyel).

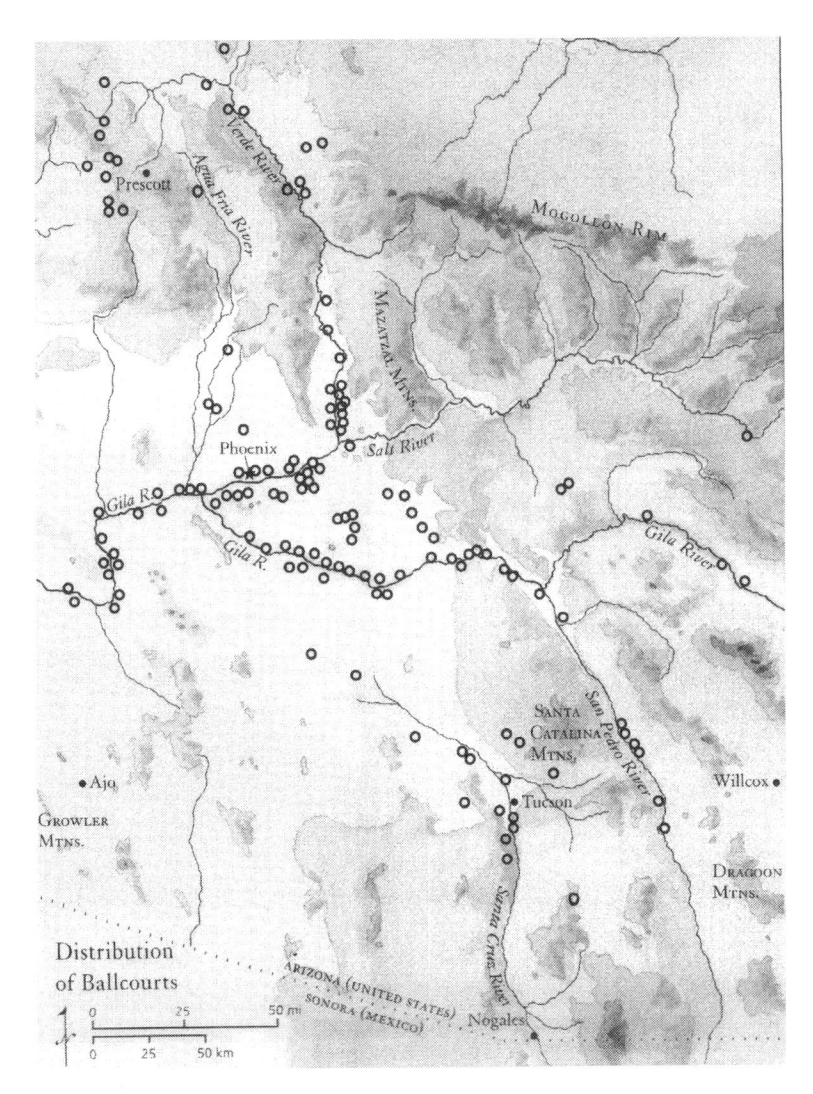

Figure 47.4 Map of Hohokam ball court and platform mound distributions in Arizona (adapted from maps by Molly O'Halloran, in Fish and Fish 2008b).

The transition to the Classic period after AD 1150 was a watershed in Hohokam development. Red-on-buff pottery produced in the Phoenix Basin ceased to circulate throughout, and the Hohokam joined a broad Southwestern trend toward polychrome types. Pithouses gave way to adobe rooms inside walled compounds. The Hohokam no longer built ball courts and instead erected earthen platform mounds that supported ritual buildings within walled precincts (Figure 47.4). Canal systems in the Phoenix Basin reached their greatest capacity in conjunction with intensification of nonirrigated agriculture, as residential densities increased in many of the largest centers and regional migrations added to population diversity. Sometime between AD 1400 and 1550, the Hohokam trajectory shifted significantly, and archaeologists lose sight of a coherent archaeological culture.

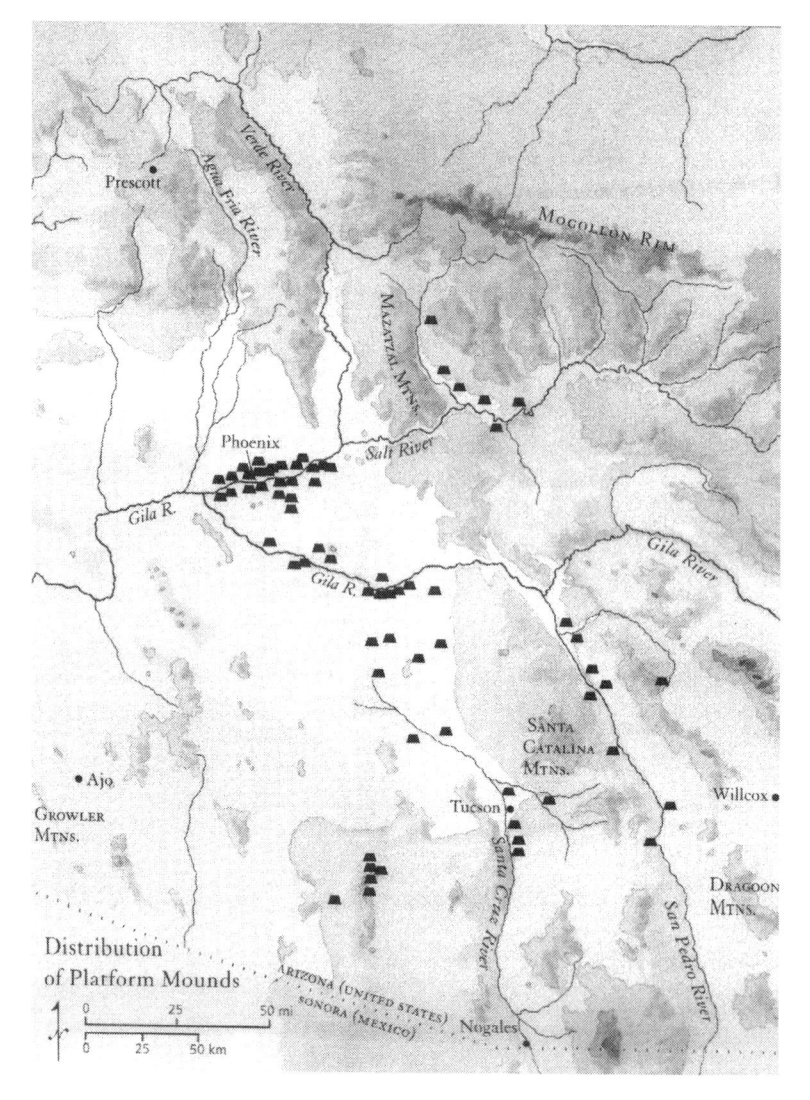

Figure 47.4 *(continued)*

ROOTS OF HOHOKAM WATER MANAGEMENT

The Hohokam are now known to have had local roots in many generations of preceramic and early ceramic farmers. Radiocarbon determinations on maize and squash indicate southern Arizona cultivation of Mexican domesticates by at least 4,200 years ago. Canals near Tucson, among the oldest dated instances in the New World, supplied fields by 1500 BC, 2,000 years prior to the Hohokam sequence. The earliest canals were 1 to 2 kilometers in length on the floodplains of the Santa Cruz River and its major tributaries (Doolittle and Mabry 2006). These networks would have required some level of communal management for construction, maintenance, and operation. Preceding cultivators also practiced floodwater farming from tributaries on alluvial fans and along mountain fronts, nonriverine settings that were basic elements of subsequent Hohokam settlement patterns.

The Hohokam tradition emerged from less differentiated occupations with plain ceramics across the Southwest. The earliest domestic pottery in southern Arizona appeared about AD 50. Central plazas, a hallmark of Hohokam settlement organization at larger villages, appeared by AD 500. At two major villages, Valencia Vieja (Wallace 2008) in the Tucson Basin and Snaketown (Haury 1976) in the Phoenix Basin, large central plazas contained burials and offertory caches; square structures of foremost size combining ritual and residential functions faced onto the plazas, with other residences behind them. Although information is limited about irrigation systems in the Phoenix Basin before the advent of decorated Hohokam pottery, an early main canal at Snaketown on the Gila River may have extended 5 kilometers. On the Salt River, a small canal has been dated prior to AD 50; by AD 500 canals of greater magnitude must have served substantial sites more than 7 kilometers away from the river.

Hohokam Developments of the Preclassic Period

Between AD 650 and 1150, in the Preclassic period, occupations containing Hohokam red-on-buff or brown pottery reached a maximum extent of 50,000 square kilometers surrounding the Phoenix Basin core. Although scholars agree that the highest population densities were in the Phoenix Basin, figures for any part of this territory during any period are difficult to derive. Remains of Hohokam earthen architecture have low surface visibility, typically precluding room count. Highest densities in the core coincide with modern mechanized agriculture and urban sprawl; settlements elsewhere were more dispersed. Although the largest villages with public architecture became increasingly aggregated through time, the most populous only occasionally exceeded 1,000 inhabitants. However, households in widespread farmsteads and small hamlets contributed to regionally high population.

In the foremost villages, Preclassic residents constructed ball courts at the edge of central plazas, according to the tenets of a widely shared ideology. These earthen-banked facilities in central sites served sets of smaller surrounding settlements. Ball courts drew in outlying populations for social and economic interchange during the ritual ballgames or other events associated with these features (Abbott et al. 2007).

Hohokam archaeologists use the term *community* for the characteristic territorial entities in Hohokam settlement patterns that consist of a central site with public architecture and an outlying set of affiliated settlements (Fish and Fish 2008a; Doyel and Fish 2000). Preclassic ball courts, corresponding to the central sites in their respective

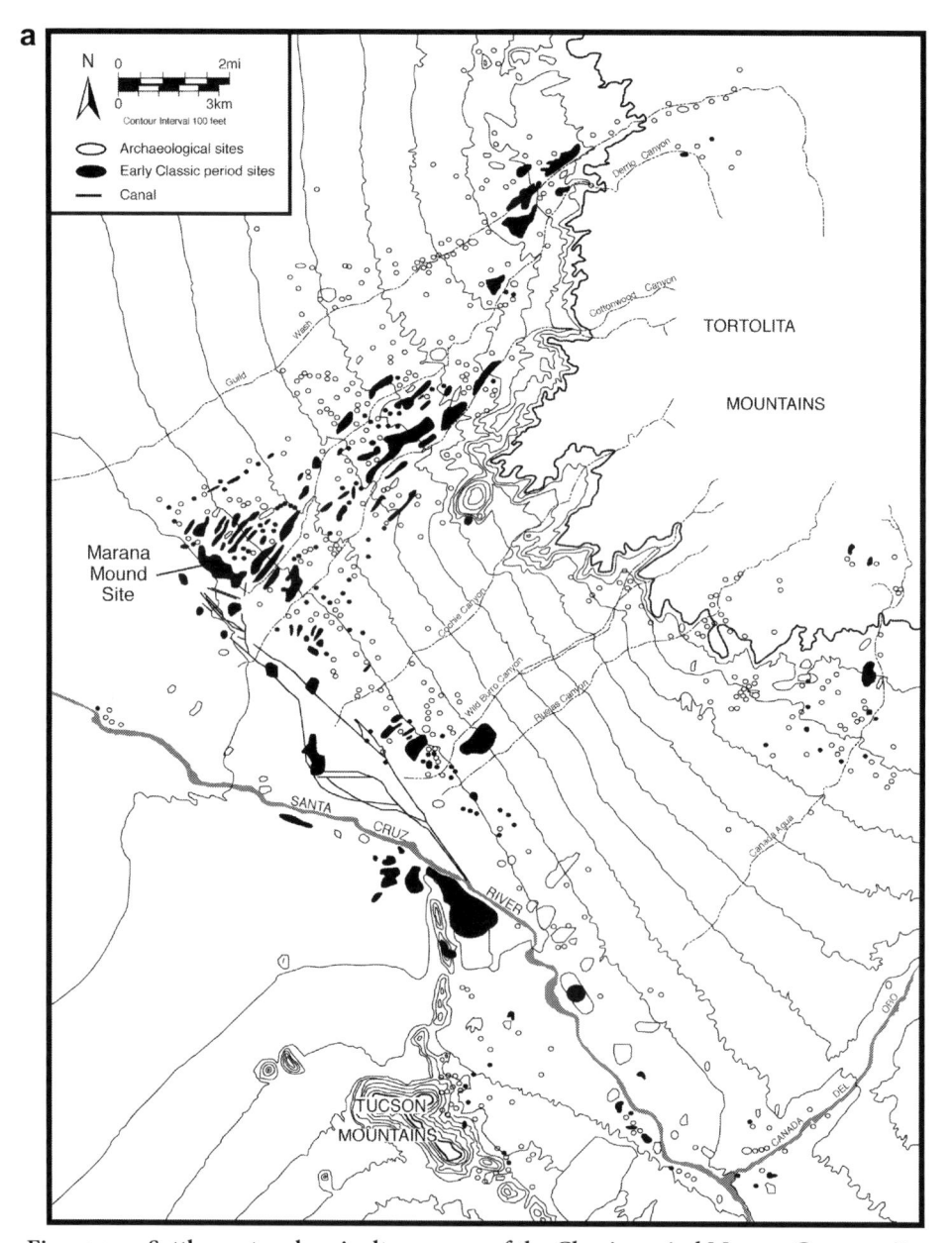

Figure 47.5 Settlement and agriculture zones of the Classic period Marana Community in the northern Tucson Basin: (a) arrangement of affiliated sites around the platform mound center in the 146 km² community; (b) basin cross-section showing zonation of settlement and diversified agriculture.

communities, tend to be concentrated in irrigable lands along rivers, as did Hohokam population generally (Figure 47.4). Nevertheless, the organizational and territorial configuration of such multisite communities was also replicated in other relatively populous basin areas, where opportunities for riverine irrigation were minor or absent and where inhabitants farmed primarily by other means (Figure 47.5).

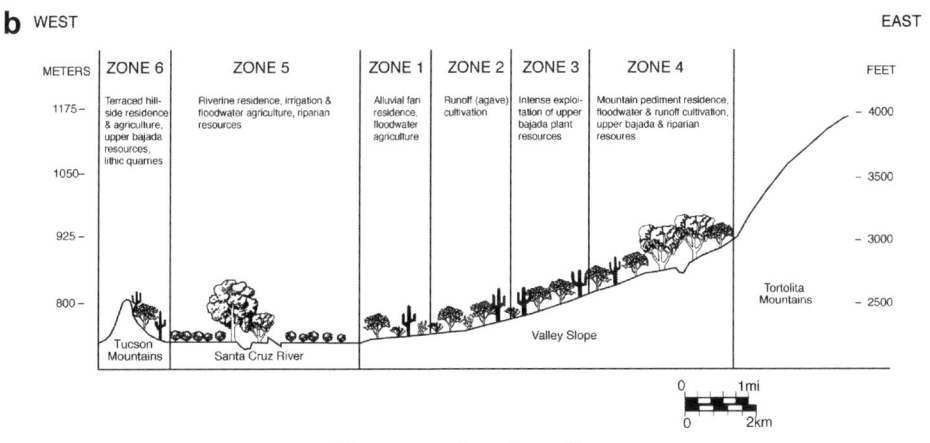

Figure 47.5 (*continued*)

Within Preclassic settlements, extended family households typically occupied sets of two to six pithouses opening onto a common courtyard. Residents of these "courtyard groups" shared burial areas, roasting pits, and other facilities. Archaeologists often attribute the larger size and greater continuity of some pithouse groups to the success of a prominent household head in attracting and maintaining the cooperation of other nuclear families. Rebuilt in place for up to 250 years in the larger riverine centers, the persistence of courtyard groups suggests their landholding role and their estatelike nature in perpetuating rights to the most productive irrigated land (Craig and Henderson 2008). Like multisite communities, courtyard groups were not exclusive to irrigated zones but also occurred where prolonged residence was based on alternative water sources.

Evidence for social inequality is not pronounced in the Preclassic period in terms of personal wealth, elevated role directly linked to public architecture, or management of expanded canal systems. In a recent study, however, a connection could be drawn between construction of a site's ball court and several nearby large, persistent courtyard groups with more costly pithouses. An adjacent cluster of communal roasting pits appears to have provisioned feasting at the time of ball court construction (Craig and Henderson 2008).

Ball court centers were spaced roughly 5 kilometers apart along the main lines of the Salt and Gila canal systems (Figure 47.4), strongly suggesting that they and their surrounding communities were integrally involved in organization and administration of these irrigation networks, which attained near-maximum length by the middle of the Preclassic period. Regular spacing may in part reflect optimal distances for day-to-day agricultural activities and internal communication. The more inclusive term *irrigation community* is applied to all the settlements along a canal system with a common intake, united by the requisites of overall coordination, construction, maintenance, and water allocation. Some networks extended more than 30 kilometers, defining overall irrigation communities that united one to six sequential ball court communities along their path (Figure 47.2). Leaders at these centers probably had a role in marshaling communal labor and decision making for both their own canal segments and systemwide undertakings (e.g. Crown 1987).

Hohokam archaeologists have advanced few specific models of how overall canal system management developed in concert with increasing scale, largely because available evidence provides few specific clues. Higher-order leaders cannot be unequivocally identified by truly lavish burials and residences, or distinctive insignia of power and privilege. A likely indicator of ritual or political preeminence among ball court centers and their leaders is the presence of the largest instances and multiple courts, but patterning in this regard is not clear. By the Classic period after AD 1150, the largest mound centers along a canal system were sometimes auspiciously positioned for controlling flow nearest canal intakes; in other cases, the largest centers were in a terminal position, where water rights would have needed most forceful assertion.

Hohokam Consolidation in the Classic Period

The transition to the Classic period after AD 1150 transformed all sectors of Hohokam society (Bayman 2001). Adobe rooms replaced pithouses. Especially at larger villages and central sites, sets of these adobe rooms were enclosed within tall compound walls. The more emphatically demarcated co-resident families of walled compounds often represented multiple households. The new domestic arrangements formalized the social and corporate identity of the compound group. Greater seclusion also afforded opportunities for unmonitored accumulation and storage. Likewise, compounds with enlarged membership facilitated economic diversification and specialization, wider external linkages, and enhanced leadership roles for compound heads, while heightening the potential for social inequality.

Trends toward centralization and social differentiation progressed throughout Classic times (Bayman 2001; Crown and Fish 1994; Fish and Fish 2000). Platform mounds, topped by adobe rooms, replaced ball courts at the center of multisite communities. Comparison of the distributions of Preclassic ball courts and Classic platform mounds shows geographic disjunctures and overall shrinkage in the extent of the later platform mounds (Figure 47.4), as populations distant from the Phoenix core opted in or out of definitive Hohokam institutions. Likewise, the predominance of Phoenix Basin red-painted pottery faded as polychrome ceramics became the common decorated type within and beyond Hohokam boundaries.

The Classic period witnessed organizational consolidation. Where local residents built both earlier and later versions of Hohokam public architecture, they replaced ball courts with fewer platform mounds. The communities surrounding platform mound centers, however, tended to encompass larger arrays of settlements, territory, and population. Density at the largest sites reached a high point for the Hohokam sequence. Increasing settlement hierarchy can also be measured by differential investment in public architecture. Very large ball courts and more than one court had indicated differentiation during Preclassic times, but platform mound complexes at one or a few large centers overshadowed all others in multiple basins toward the end of the Classic period.

Openness and accessibility were increasingly restricted in public as well as residential spheres. Unlike the approachable and inclusive settings of ball courts, platform mounds and buildings in the surrounding precinct were enclosed behind massive compound walls. Platform mounds were often centrally located within their sites but not always associated with well-defined plazas. Neither a majority of residents nor visitors to Classic centers could have participated in or even viewed mound activities. Inside the mound precincts, walls, corridors, and rooms further controlled access.

Although Phoenix Basin irrigation networks attained much of their ultimate extent by AD 900, they continued to expand internally and were increasingly conjoined into larger systems along the Salt and Gila Rivers just before and into the Classic period. The resulting configuration of irrigation communities, combined with fewer platform mound centers and larger associated territories, created the context for enacting higher-level control over distribution of water. Indeed, because heavy Classic period demand appears to have approached available river flow in the Phoenix Basin by this time (Howard 1993), allocation decisions would have encompassed far larger aggregates of population and territory. In the well-studied Tonto Basin to the east, similar processes of irrigation consolidation and more expansive community boundaries also prevailed.

As increasingly dense populations inhabited mound centers and their surrounding communities, in tandem with maximum extension of canals, farmers brought marginal land under cultivation. Techniques for capture and retention of rain-fed overland runoff had been employed in prior times, but their dramatic proliferation demonstrates the dynamic response of Hohokam farmers to demographic change and productive demands. Just prior to the Classic period, extensive arrays of stone agricultural features began to appear on dry slopes throughout the Hohokam domain (Figure 47.5).

"Rockpile" fields consisted of individual piles of cobbles and linear alignments. The rockpiles served as mulches to enhance moisture for planting placed in them and along the alignments, which functioned as contour terraces and check dams. These fields were located beyond the limits of irrigation in the Phoenix core. Plantings in such runoff-supplied fields emphasized drought-adapted crops, primarily the succulent agave, which yields food and fiber. The rockpile fields, stone grids, and similar arrays of agricultural features offer strong evidence for intensified and specialized agricultural production for the concentrated populations of later Hohokam times (Fish et al. 1992; Fish and Fish 2004).

A growing concentration of power, embodied by leaders, is evident in the more expansive multisite communities of the Classic period (Bayman 2001; Fish and Fish

2000). Rooms increased and were more complexly arranged in platform mound precincts over time; communal storage and food preparation facilities have been identified in many cases. Greater diversity is also apparent in mound types, including instances with pillars and towerlike forms with astronomically oriented features. Three of the largest mound centers in the Phoenix Basin came to overshadow others in prominence as measured by investment in public architecture, one each to the north and south of the Salt River and one along the Gila River. Rare occurrences such as adobe "thrones" and above-ground sarcophagi at these sites hint at the emergence of superordinate leaders. Perhaps more significant, a few men, women, and children were buried in later Classic mound precincts, which implies particular family lines had come to preside over the associated public affairs. Connections among hereditary leadership, management of canal systems, and intensified production in the Classic period are nevertheless conjectural. Multiple and even competing sources of leadership and political power may have been present in Hohokam society (Fish and Fish 2001). Canal system managers may have mingled with ritual specialists, political leaders, and heads of kin groups in the varied room clusters atop and surrounding the largest mounds.

The Final Transition

The Hohokam did not exist apart from larger regional trends. Major demographic shifts as well as concurrent consolidation of population and territory transformed the Southwest in late pre-Hispanic times. Continuing migrations within Puebloan territory and to the south largely emptied entire regional expanses that had been home to farming peoples. From a baseline at AD 1275, when migrations were already under way, distribution of agriculturalists showed dramatic changes by AD 1400. Equally significant is the correspondence between persistent, often aggregated settlement at AD 1400 and those places where gravity irrigation was still practiced in post-Contact times (Fish and Fish 1994). Many late-occupied areas of the Southwest centered on irrigable land that absorbed incoming northerners who were enfolded with local populations in consolidation processes.

On the basis of annual streamflow reconstructions derived from tree-ring data, a destructive series of floods have been retrodicted for the Salt and Gila Rivers between AD 1350 and 1420 (Graybill et al. 2006:114–116). Not only has the destruction of canal systems been attributed to such floods (which occurred at similar scales at earlier points in the Hohokam sequence) but also changes to rivers channel that eliminated advantageous positions for intake. Geomorphological investigations have as yet failed to disclose physical evidence of these events, however. Lower water levels in the Salt and Gila Rivers from AD 1450 to 1870, again derived from tree-ring data, have also been posited as major threats to the consolidated settlements of terminal Hohokam populations (Waters and Ravesloot 2001).

In keeping with sweeping rearrangements of regional population that accelerated toward the end of the Hohokam sequence, unsettled times are reflected in O'odham oral histories of conflict between the final leaders at late Classic period platform mound centers and other groups. The ultimate blow to the cultural configuration maintained by the Hohokam may well have been devastating and rapidly advancing Old World diseases, in conjunction with the emergence of mounted raiders who also acquired firearms and seriously disrupted neighboring agricultural societies.

Archaeologists lose sight of the Hohokam in the murky era between AD 1450 and the late 1600s, when Spaniards first described their homeland. Although some scenarios emphasize disastrous environmental forces as bringing an end to the remarkable Phoenix Basin canals, O'odham descendants resurrected Hohokam-scale gravity networks on the Gila River before 1850, as did later Phoenix pioneers along the Salt River. Arising from a long tradition of earlier farmers, Hohokam cultivators achieved a continuing cultural trajectory for a millennium. Their lifeways embodied centuries of solutions to the changing challenges faced by desert agriculturalists, a legacy carried forward until today by today's O'odham peoples.

REFERENCES

Abbott, D. E., A. E. Smith, and E. Gallaga. 2007. Ballcourts and Ceramics: The Case for Hohokam Marketplaces in the Arizona Desert. *American Antiquity* 50:48–66.

Bayman, J. M. 2001. The Hohokam of Southwest North America. *Journal of World Prehistory* 15:257–311.

Craig, D. B., and T. K. Henderson. 2008. Houses, Households, and Household Organization. In *The Hohokam Millennium*, edited by S. Fish and P. Fish, pp. 39–48. School of Advanced Research Press, Santa Fe, NM.

Crown, P. 1987. Classic Period Hohokam Settlement and Land Use in the Casa Grande Ruin Area, Arizona. *Journal of Field Archaeology* 14:147–162.

——, and S. K. Fish. 1996. Gender and Status in the Hohokam Pre-classic to Classic Transition. *American Anthropologist* 98:803–817.

Doolittle, W. F., and J. Mabry. 2006. Environmental Mosaics, Agricultural Diversity, and the Evolutionary Adoption of Maize in the American Southwest. In *Histories of Maize*, edited by J. Staller, R. Tykot, and B. Benz, pp. 109–121. Academic Press, San Diego.

Doyel, D. E., and S. K. Fish. 2000. Prehistoric Villages and Communities in the Arizona Desert. In *The Hohokam Village Revisited*, edited by D. E. Doyel, S. K. Fish, and P. R. Fish, pp. 1–36. American Association for the Advancement of Science, Glenwood Springs, CO.

Fish, S. K., and P. R. Fish. 1994. Prehistoric Desert Farmers of the Southwest. *Annual Review of Anthropology* 23:83–108.

——. 2000. The Institutional Contexts of Hohokam Complexity. In *Alternative Leadership Strategies in the Prehispanic Southwest*, edited by B. Mills, pp. 154–167. University of Arizona Press, Tucson.

―――. 2004. Unsuspected Magnitudes: Expanding the Scale of Hohokam Agriculture. In *The Archaeology of Global Change: The Impact of Humans on Their Environment*, edited by C. L. Redman, S. James, P. Fish, and J. D. Rogers, pp. 208–223. Smithsonian Institution Press, Washington, DC.

―――. 2008a. Community, Territory, and Polity. In *The Hohokam Millennium*, edited by S. Fish and P. Fish, pp. 39–48. School for Advanced Research Press, Santa Fe, NM.

――― (editors). 2008b. *The Hohokam Millennium*. School for Advanced Research Press, Santa Fe, NM.

―――, and J. H. Madsen. 1992. *The Marana Community in the Hohokam World*. Anthropological Papers of the University of Arizona 56. University of Arizona Press, Tucson.

Graybill, D. A., D. A. Gregory, G. S. Funkhouser, and F. L. Nials. 2006. Long-Term Streamflow Reconstructions, River Channel Morphology, and Aboriginal Irrigation Systems Along the Salt and Gila Rivers. In *Environmental Change and Human Adaptation in the Ancient American Southwest*, edited by D. E. Doyel and J. S. Dean, pp. 69–123. University of Utah Press, Salt Lake City.

Haury, E. W. 1976. *The Hohokam: Desert Farmers and Craftsmen*. University of Arizona Press, Tucson.

Howard, J. B. 1993. A Paleohydraulic Approach to Examining Agricultural Intensification in Hohokam Irrigation Systems. In *Economic Aspects of Water Management in the Prehispanic New World*, edited by V. Scarborough and B. Issac, pp. 231–322. Research in Economic Anthropology, Supplement 7. JAI Press, Greenwich.

Hunt, R. C., D. Guillet, D. Abbott, J. Bayman, P. Fish, S. Fish, K. Kintigh, and J. Neely. 2005. Plausible Ethnographic Analogies for the Social Organization of Hohokam Canal Irrigation. *American Antiquity* 70:433–456.

Masse, W. B. 1976. *The Hohokam Expressway Project: A Study of Prehistoric Irrigation in the Salt River Valley, Arizona*. Arizona State Museum, University of Arizona, Tucson.

Turney, O. A. 1929. *The Land of the Stone Hoe*. Arizona Republican Print Shop, Phoenix.

Wallace, H. D. 2008. Hohokam Beginnings. In *The Hohokam Millennium*, edited by S. Fish and P. Fish, pp.13–22. School for Advanced Research Press, Santa Fe.

Waters, M. R., and J. C. Ravesloot. 2001. Landscape Change and the Cultural Evolution of the Hohokam Along the Middle Gila River and Other River Valleys in South-Central Arizona. *American Antiquity* 66: 285–300.

CHAPTER 48

TERRACED LIVES: *CERROS DE TRINCHERAS* IN THE NORTHWEST/SOUTHWEST

BRIDGET M. ZAVALA

ARCHAEOLOGISTS and explorers alike have applied the term *cerro de trincheras* to pre-Hispanic sites built on hills, characterized by the presence of terraces or stone walls. Recent investigations reveal that these enigmatic sites represent one of the most long-lived architectural traditions in northwest Mexico and the Southwest United States (NW/SW). On hundreds of hills from Durango, Mexico, to southern Arizona, pre-Hispanic inhabitants built their homes on the slopes and summits of elevated landforms (generally isolated volcanic hills). In this chapter, I propose that better understanding of what I will call "hills with entrenchments" can be had by applying an embodied-landscape perspective focusing on the everyday experiences of the folks who made these elevated spaces home.

Until a decade ago, these sites were believed to be a relatively restricted phenomenon, both in time and space; archaeologists proffered simplistic functional explanations that revolved mainly around defense as well as agricultural and ritual or ceremonial interpretations. Notwithstanding, with the breath of cultural resource management (CRM) research on the U.S. side of the border and the growth of studies focused on northern Mexico, we now know that the site type includes a great deal of variation (temporal, spatial, cultural, internal, regional, etc.) that needs to be addressed by an approach that can account for the wide rage of contrasts within site type.

In general, these theoretical frameworks posit that the social landscape shapes and molds social practices (Giddens 1979). Furthermore, "space is not an empty dimension along which social groupings become structured, but has to be considered in terms of its involvement in the constitution of systems of interaction" (1986:368). Thus we can consider how living on *cerros de trincheras* both structures and is structured by the daily practices of the people who lived on these hills. Architecture and spatial distribution provide an entry point that, if used at varying scales, can help archaeologists comprehend the day-to-day lives of the pre-Hispanic inhabitants of these terraced village sites.

OVERVIEW

Before we go any further, we must consider what is meant by *cerro de trincheras*. The term has been applied to hills with stone walls or terraces without mortar (Sauer and Brand 1932:67). Archaeologists have recorded more than 300 *cerros* to date in the modern-day states of Arizona, New Mexico, Sonora, Chihuahua, and Durango (Figure 48.1), generally in the Basin and Range province. This type of site, also called fortified hills and fortresses by the archaeologists who have recorded them, crosscuts eight archaeological traditions: San Pedro Cochise, Hohokam, Trincheras, Rio Sonora, Mogollon, Casas Grandes, Loma San Gabriel, and Chalchihuites. The earliest hills with entrenchments were built more than 3,000 years ago as some of the first agricultural villages of the SW/NW (Roney and Hard 1998, 2001, 2002, 2004;

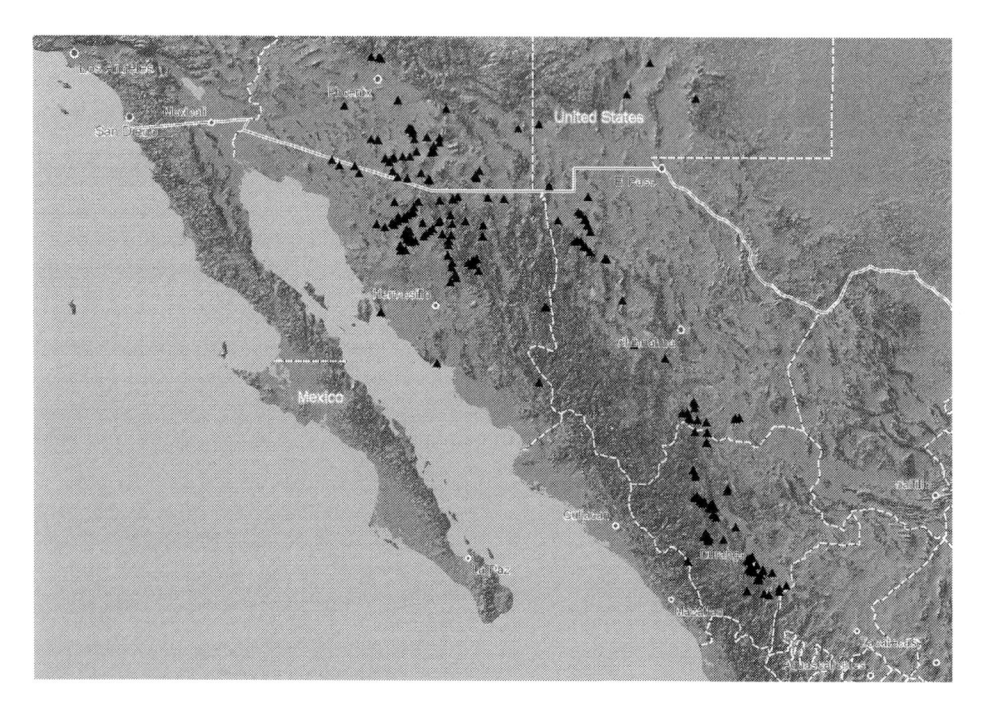

Figure 48.1 Distribution *of cerros de trincheras* in northwest Mexico and the U.S. Southwest.

Hard and Roney 1998), while others were late pre-Hispanic sites dating from 500 years ago and spanning a total of 2,500 years.

At *cerros de trincheras*, builders erected terraces by placing walls or berms on the sides of the generally isolated volcanic hills, filling the void with rubble and trash, and covering this with a layer of sediment, thus creating a flat living space on the slope of the hill. Although terraces are generally thought to be the defining feature, some *cerros* have only dry-masonry walls that define circular and quadrangular stone foundations, as well as larger communal features. The inhabitants of these places constructed walls to subdivide terraces, circumscribe certain areas of the site, or bisect the living areas of the hill. Movement from one terrace or area of the hill to another is often aided by stairs, ramps, and paths (Zavala 1998; Hartman and Hartman 1979). Archaeologists have frequently recorded rock art (Ferg 1979) and bedrock mortars at these sites, as well. The presence of abundant domestic material, including ceramic sherds, chipped stone, groundstone, worked marine shell, botanical material, and bone, makes it clear that these places served as habitation sites. It is important to note that though these components are often found at *cerros de trincheras*, they are not all necessarily present at all of these sites.

Interpretations of *cerros de trincheras* offered to date can generally be classified into three functional categories: defensive, agricultural, and religious or ceremonial. Most investigators dealing with them have explained these sites as defensible villages or refuge sites (McGee 1895; Downum et al. 1985; Sauer and Brand 1932; Hoover 1941; Bowen 1976; Stacy 1971). As Hoover (1941:231) said, "the hill sites . . . are so indicative of the defense motive that any other explanation seems absurd." Recent resurgence of interest in the role of warfare in the NW/SW has led several researchers to revisit the discussion of *cerros de trincheras* in this respect (Le Blanc 1999).

The strategic locations, interpretation of terraces and walls as fortifications (Fontana et al. 1959; Larson 1972; Wilcox 1979; Le Blanc 1999), and records of battles during historic times (Fish et al. 1992) have been used as evidence for the defensive hypothesis. Though it is true that the uphill location of the sites gives an edge for defense, it hardly explains an architectural pattern that cross-cuts eight archaeological traditions and 2,500 years.

As more and more data become available and investigators continue to document individual *cerro* particularities, as well as their role in specific regions, valleys, and time periods, some researchers have moved beyond functional interpretation to allow for a more dynamic view of these elevated sites that considers symbolic aspects of hill life (Amador Bech and Medina 2007, 2008; Zavala 2006; Wallace et al. 2007), the role of monumentality (O'Donovan 2000, 2004) and use of particular sectors by ritual specialists (Deleonardo 2005). For example, Paul and Suzanne Fish have been looking at the ritual nature of enclosures commonly found at the summit of these sites as places that "celebrate the spiritual qualities of these landforms, reify elevated spiritual status *vis-à-vis* lower basin settlements, ensure locational exclusivity in ritual practice, and enhance dramatic communication of calendrics or momentous ceremonial events" (Fish and Fish 2007:194).

Landscape Approaches in Archaeology

Archaeologists seeking to repopulate our versions of the past have turned to approaches like those forwarded by landscape studies. These supply an alternative conceptualization of the world that does not succumb to the strict dichotomy between the environment and the site but seeks to involve the surrounding landscape in the overall picture of the past, considering these realms as inexorably intertwined (Cosgrove 1995). Specifically, landscape studies consider space, according to Tilley, "as social productions, are always centered in relation to human agency and are amenable to reproduction or change because their constitution takes place as part of the day-to-day praxis or practical activity of individuals and groups in the world" (1994:10). Power and position represent integral aspects of all landscape studies; landscape signifies and often contains various meanings whose claims to truth are dealt with contextually (Cosgrove 1995). Meaning is linked to material culture through embodied experience: "Our bodily being-in-the-world provides the fundamental ground, or starting point, for our description of it" (Tilley 2004, 2). As Basso states: "Geographical landscapes are never culturally vacant . . . [but rather are] filled to brimming with past and present significance" (1996:143). Furthermore, "[p]lace . . . is a sensual experience, with the body, social identity, and shifting perceptions of society intersecting through daily, lived spatial experiences" (Van Dyke and Alcock 2003:6).

So how can we use this "way of seeing the world" (Cosgrove 1998:13) to better understand *cerros de trincheras*? The study of *cerros de trincheras* clearly demonstrates that sites and their inhabitants are never separate from the environment and vice versa. Tilley's words apply here: "The architecture of the stones resides in a fusion of their physical form and location or placement in the landscape, the sensual experience of these stones and the ideas and memories, histories and mythologies that became associated with them" (2004:35). This "fusion" is made visible through architecture and other material culture at *cerros* where builders chose to appropriate hills and make them the stage of their everyday lives; this demonstrates that the hills themselves are meaningful and serve, as landscape studies would hold, as "the medium for action that can not be divorced from the action itself" (Tilley 1994:10). Furthermore, these settings are integral in the process of social reproduction:

> Relations are always material and social at once, so that material culture is not an added extra in social life, but right at its heart. Once we start to look at the creation of social relations through the medium of material things, then objects become social agents in their own right and their formal properties and their combination into assemblages both become important. The durable nature of material things, especially once landscape is included, makes it difficult to ignore questions of history. People are socialized within material settings, so that the world is an important part of social reproduction, as one generation succeeds the next [Gosden 1999:120].

Thus landscape approaches can allow us to explore how "prehistoric social identities were created or sustained, reproduced or transformed through the agency of stones" (Tilley 2004:217).

Experiencing *Cerros De Trincheras*: The Public, the Private, and the Monumental

Turning from ideas to concrete examples, in the balance of this chapter I apply a landscape approach that explores different aspects of everyday life on *cerros de trincheras*. Methodologically speaking, accessing everyday lived experience of archaeological sites needs to involve analysis using multiple scales, incorporation of sensorial observations, and consideration of surroundings as an integral part of the activities and meanings the spaces hosted. In this section, I briefly present five examples—from Cerro de Trincheras in Sonora, Cerro Juanaqueña, hill sites in the Magdalena Valley during the Early Ceramic and El Cerro periods, and Cerro Buchunamichi—that bring to light aspects of privacy and monumentality, the interrelatedness of cerros as experienced through vision, and the significance of living on a hill itself.

The diverse inhabitants who dwelled on hilltops and hill sides in the NW/SW designed and experienced their space in their own way, in some cases building spaces for activities meant to include a wide audience while others were set apart from the public gaze. Some designs make it hard to find secluded areas, while others are quite private. One *trincheras* site where privacy is especially hard to come by is Cerro de Trincheras (Figure 48.2) in Trincheras, Sonora (occupied from AD 1250 to 1450), the largest terraced hill recorded in the region (Villalpando and McGuire 2009). Its 900 terraces or living platforms were largely sculpted into the northern face of the hill, covering an area of 1 square kilometer where rock foundations and *jacales* were erected with perishable superstructures. The layout made activities on the terraces accessible to the view of folks living on terraces above them, while these could see levels below, and so forth. In keeping with this pattern, the most public of their public spaces, La Cancha, is a rectangular structure measuring 51 meters by 13 meters. It is highly on display, at the very base of the hill, where folks from most of

Figure 48.2 The site of Cerro de Trincheras in Sonora, Mexico.

the terraced surface could witness the ritual activities held there. Yet not all areas of the hill were easily accessed or seen. At the crest of the hill, there are a series of structures, including low terraces and circular and rectangular rock foundations surrounding a spiral shaped structure like that of a bisected gastropod. In this area, activities were set apart from the prying gaze of everyday glances.

It would be easy to attribute the paucity of private space to the large number of terraces at Cerro de Trincheras, but there is something about the design of the layout in combination with the amphitheater-shaped northern face of the hill that creates the sense of varying degrees of visibility. Furthermore, this hill stands out from surrounding hills in the valley for its sheer size, making it the only hill in the neighborhood that could accommodate 900 terraces in the first place. We can appreciate the choices the builders made if we consider the contrast with another of the larger terraced hills in the NW/SW, such as Cerro Juanaqueña (Figure 48.3), located in northwestern Chihuahua. It is a terraced hill built during the late archaic (3,000 years before present) where pre-Hispanic builders placed more than 300 terraces on the slopes of this volcanic hill. Here terraces are set apart by groups, and the curvature of the hill is such that activities are generally visible only on the same terrace level. As on Cerro de Trincheras, the

Figure 48.3 The view from a terrace at Cerro Juanaqueña in Chihuahua, Mexico.

summit features are set apart from the rest of the site here by a perimeter wall fashioned by adjoining a series of terraces on the crest of the hill.

Here, what is important is that the hill is inexorably implicated in life at these locations. Furthermore, the visual links and the visual ruptures help to imbue the space with meanings that are lived. As Van Dyke and Alcock (2003:6) state, "Place, above all, is a sensual experience, with the body, social identity, and shifting perceptions of society intersecting through daily, lived spatial experiences." These experiences are highly variable from hill to hill, and among built and unbuilt areas at each location. The degree of privacy or lack thereof is crafted into the layout of the lived space, the experience of the place, and the surrounding landscape.

Now we redirect our gaze from a place on the valley floor to the hill itself. From this vantage point, several researchers have pointed out the monumental nature of *cerros de trincheras* emanating from appropriation of imposing landforms combined with the visual impact of the terraced slopes (McGuire and Elisa Villalpando C. 1998; Nelson 2002:230–233; O'Donovan 2002, 2004). As McGuire and Villalpando (1998:5) state in reference to the site of Cerro de Trincheras in Sonora: "By terracing the hill, the Trincheras folk transformed a prominent natural feature into a human creation that expresses their social organization and religious beliefs. They achieved a degree of monumentality and distinction for their town that never could have been achieved by stacking the same rock into a pueblo, or mound." Monumentality in this perspective serves as a "visible point of reference for memory on the landscape" (Joyce 2003:111). To be monumental, a place need not be large; "artefacts can be places and places may be artefacts, monuments can be landscapes and landscapes may be monuments" (Tilley 2004:217). Furthermore, *cerros de trincheras* builders were able to "make statements of relatedness among people, land and power" (Nelson 2007:234). Thus when the people chose to craft home or village or temple on an elevated location, they fused the "relationship between the place and its broader landscape, making the experience of each more vivid" (Thomas 2006:355).

That said, how does monumentality actually play out at these terraced hills? First, given the heterogeneity of the site type, the experience of monumentality differs from one hill to another. To illustrate this point, I present two examples from the Magdalena Valley, in Sonora during two contrasting periods, and one from the Rio Sonora Valley. These examples take into account the sight line up to the hill and then from the hill out to the surrounding valley as previously described (the examples presented here were modeled using digital elevation models or DEMs, at a scale of 1:50,000 meters from the Instituto Nacional de Estadística y Geografía (INEGI).

In the Magdalena Valley people lived on the valley floor as well as on the slopes of more than a dozen hills. Folks living above were looking down onto the sites on the valley floor, onto the slopes of other hills, and beyond. Despite the visual advantage that uphill life gives a settlement, it varies greatly. Fish and Fish (2007:170–171) identify six *cerros de trincheras* in the valley with Early Ceramic Period occupation (prior to 1300 AD) of the Trincheras Archaeological Tradition.

Figure 48.4 shows the topography and the areas that were visible from the *cerros* occupied during the Early Ceramic Period if an observer were placed on the summit

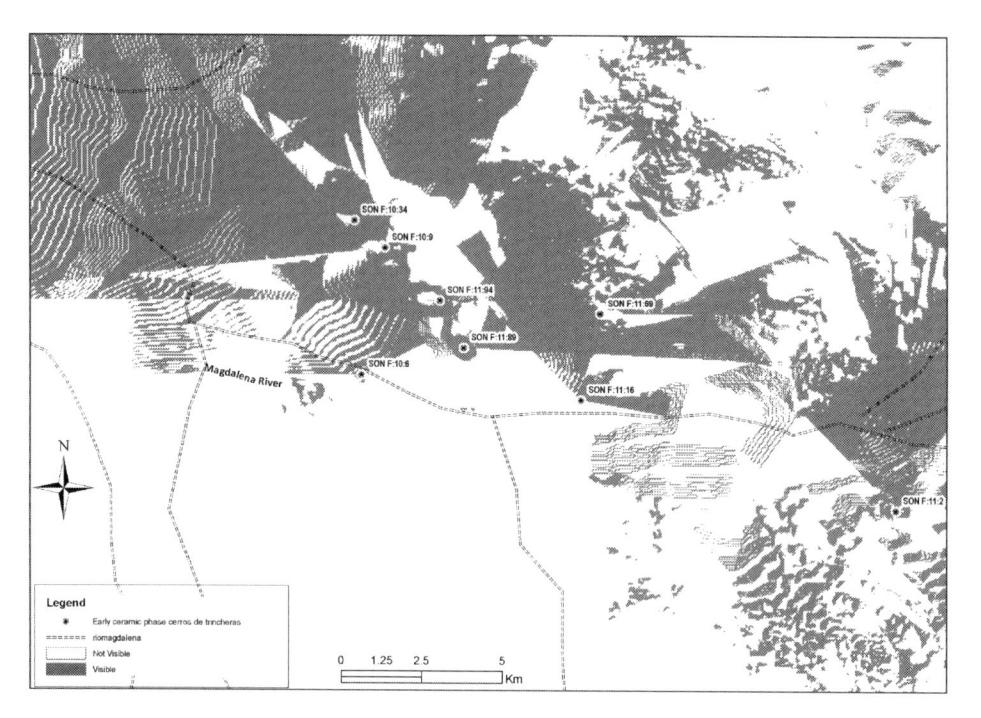

Figure 48.4 Visibility of and from *cerros de trincheras* in the Magdalena Valley, Sonora, during the early ceramic period.

of each of these sites. Here we can appreciate how places were built within visual range of one another, thus articulating and reinforcing social relationships in a way that cannot be duplicated on the valley floor. Yet if we compare this model with the illustration (Figure 48.5) of the areas visible during the subsequent El Cerro Period (1300–1450 AD), we realize the occupants of the 11 *cerros* in that valley not only saw each other but were able to exert visual control over almost all of the landscape surrounding the regional center of Cerro de Trincheras. This reflects a change in the priorities of the occupants of these terraced hill sites, in keeping with the unique hegemonic role this special place had in the region.

By contrast, the site Cerro Buchunamichi is a small terraced hill (120 meters by 120 meters, 0.2 hectare) located along the Río Sonora valley. Here the occupants built fewer than 10 narrow terraces and two summit structures (10 by 20 meters) accompanied by petroglyphs of geometric forms (three spirals and one figure eight). This low hill was originally reported by Sauer and Brand (1932:102) and reminds us that you "don't have to be a big imposing landform to be important" (Thomas 2006:357). As illustrated in Figure 48.6, this site is nestled in a narrow valley that impedes the view to and from the hill, and of it from other positions on the valley floor (in marked contrast to the previous examples). Furthermore, this is the only terraced hill in the area. The visual impact is minimal, but the importance of this place emerges from the highest point of this site, which has been crafted as an exceptional place (as are many of the summits of *cerros de trincheras*). When we consider these extraordinary summit places, we must remember that "from an

TERRACED LIVES 593

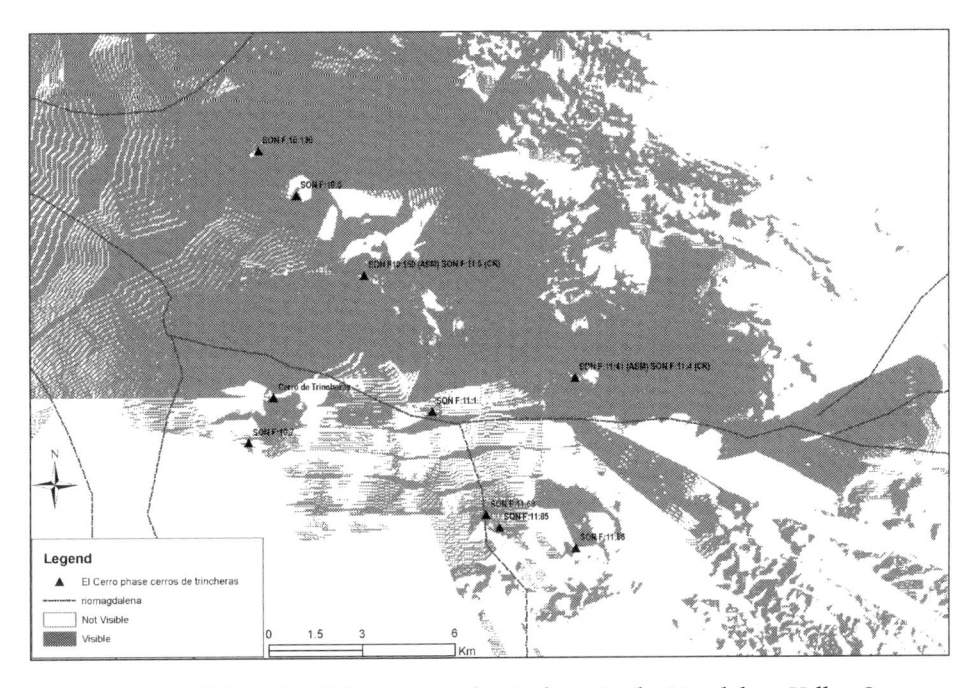

Figure 48.5 Visibility of and from *cerros de trincheras* in the Magdalena Valley, Sonora, during the El Cerro period.

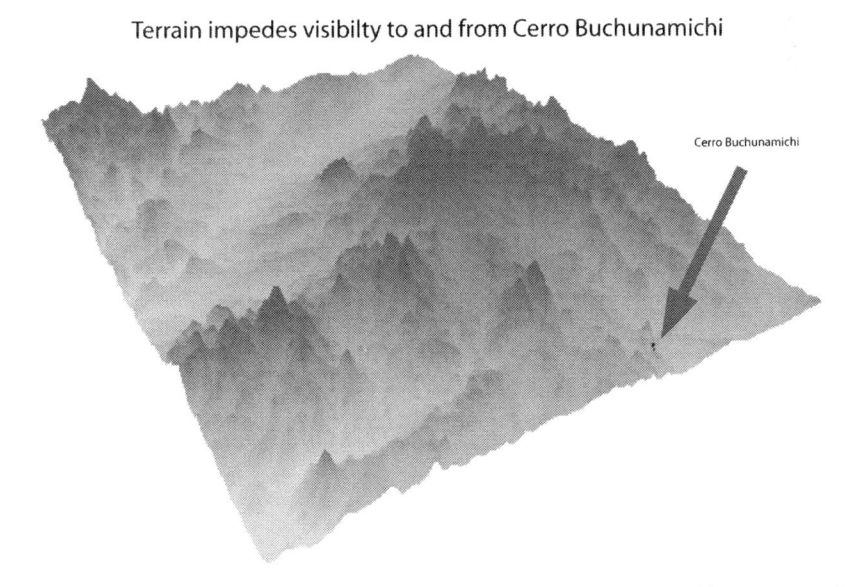

Figure 48.6 Location of Cerro Buchunamichi in the Rio Sonora Valley, Sonora; the terrain impedes the visibility to and from Cerro Buchunamichi.

embodied perspective we relate to place and landscape through ... relational coordinates of our body" (Tilley 2004:5). The result is that elevated places are usually "associated with light and air" and because they "lie up and above always tend to be privileged culturally and emotionally while places situated down below tend to be associated with darkness and death" (Tilley 2004:5).

Conclusion

Cerros de trincheras were places made by more than the movement of stones. The large number of *cerros* in the SW/NW and the longevity of the site type show that for folks in the past verticality was important. That is the quality that binds these elevated sites together. Otherwise, all sorts of aspects also make *cerros* unlike one another, differentiate sectors of the hills, and result in varied sensual experiences of the space. Our task now is to contextualize these similarities and differences in the past that were once brimming with significance, of which today only rock and hill remain.

References

Amador Bech, J., and A. Medina. 2007. Construcción Simbólica del Paisaje en los Cerros de Trincheras del Noroeste de Sonora. Paper presented at the 28th Mesa Redonda de la Sociedad Mexicana de Antropología a 70 años de su fundación, en homenaje para Alfonso Caso Derechos Humanos: Pueblos Indígenas, Cultura y Nación, Mexico City, Mexico.
———. 2008. Los Cerros de Trincheras en el Noroeste de Sonora, Una Mirada Desde la Arqueología de Paisaje. Paper presented at the 73rd Annual Meeting of the Society for American Archaeology, Vancouver, BC, Canada.
Basso, K. 1996. *Wisdom Sits in Places: Landscape and Language Among the Western Apache*. University of New Mexico Press, Albuquerque.
Bowen, T. 1976. *The Archaeology of the Central Coast of Sonora, Mexico*. Anthropological Papers of the University of Arizona 27. University of Arizona Press, Tucson.
Cosgrove, D. E. 1995. Landscape and Myths, Gods, and Humans. In *Landscape: Politics and Perspectives*, edited by B. Bender, pp. 281–305. Berg, Providence, RI.
———. 1998. *Social Formation and Symbolic Landscape*. University of Wisconsin Press, Madison.
Deleonardo, S. M. 2005. *A Voice Intended for the Spirits Themselves: Analysis of Excavations at El Mirador (The Lookout) of Cerro de Trincheras and Nearby Residential Area B7*. Master's thesis, State University of New York, Binghamton.
Downum, C. E., J. E. Douglas, and B. C. Douglas. 1985. Community Structure and Agricultural Strategies at Cerro Prieto (AZ AA:7:11). In *Proceedings of the 1983 Hohokam Symposium*, pt. 2, edited by A. E. Dittert and D. E. Dove, pp. 545–556. Arizona Archaeological Society, Phoenix.
Ferg, A. 1979. The Petroglyphs of Tumamoc Hill. *Kiva* 45(1–2):95–118.

Fish, S. K., and P. R. Fish. 2007. Regional Heartlands and Transregional Trends. In Amerind Studies in Archaeology, *Trincheras Sites in Time, Space, and Society*, edited by P. R. Fish, S. K. Fish, and M. E. Villalpando, pp. 165–194. University of Arizona Press, Tucson.

———, and J. H. Madsen. 1992. An Introduction to Time, Place and Research. Anthropological Papers of the University of Arizona 56. *The Marana Community in the Hohokam World*, edited by S. K. Fish, P. R. Fish, J. J. Field, and J. H. Madsen, pp. 1–10. University of Arizona Press, Tucson.

Fontana, B. I., J. C. Greenleaf, and D. D. Cassidy. 1959. A Fortified Arizona Mountain. *Kiva* 25(4):213–282.

Giddens, A. 1979. *Central Problems in Social Theory: Action, Structure, and Contradiction in Social Analysis*. University of California Press, Berkeley.

———. 1986. *The Constitution of Society: Outline of the Theory of Structuration*. University of California Press, Berkeley.

Gosden, C. 1999. *Anthropology and Archaeology: A Changing Relationship*. Routledge, London.

Hard, R. J., and J. R. Roney. 1998. A Massive Terraced Village Complex in Chihuahua, Mexico, 3000 Years Before Present. *Science* 279:1661–1664.

Hartman, G. H., and W. K. Hartman. 1979. Prehistoric Trail Systems and Related Features on the Slopes of Tumamoc Hill. *Kiva* 45(1–2):39–69.

Hoover, J. W. 1941. Cerros de Trincheras of the Arizona Papagueria. *Geographical Review* 31:228–239.

Joyce, R. A. 2003. Fragments of the Classic Maya Past. In *Archaeologies of Memory*, edited by R. Van Dyke and S. E. Alcock, pp. 104–125. Blackwell, Malden, MA.

Larson, S. M. 1972. The Tumamoc Hill Site Near Tucson, Arizona. *Kiva* 38(2):95–101.

Le Blanc, S. 1999. *Prehistoric Warfare in the American Southwest*. University of Utah Press, Salt Lake City.

McGee, W. J. 1895. The Beginning of Agriculture. *American Anthropologist* 8(4):350–375.

McGuire, R. H., and M. E. Villalpando. 1998. Cerro de Trincheras: A Prehispanic Terraced Town in Sonora, Mexico. *Archaeology in Tucson* 12(1):1–5.

Nelson, B. A. 2007. Crafting of Places: Mesoamerican Monumentality in Hilltop Sites. In *Trincheras Sites in Time, Space, and Society*, edited by P. R. Fish, S. K. Fish, and M. E. Villalpando C., pp. 229–246. University of Arizona Press, Tucson.

O'Donovan, M. 2000. Cerros de Trincheras and the Landscape. Paper presented at the 65th Annual Meeting of the Society for American Archaeology, April, Philadelphia.

———. 2002. New Perspectives on Site Function and Scale of Cerro de Trincheras, Sonora, Mexico: The 1991 Surface Survey. University of Arizona, Arizona State Museum, Tucson.

———. 2004. The Role of Cerro de Trincheras Sites in the Northwest Mexican and American Southwest Landscape. In *Surveying the Archaeology of Northwest Mexico*, pp. 27–45. University of Utah Press, Salt Lake City.

Roney, J. R., and R. J. Hard. 1998. A Note on the Temporal and Geographic Distribution of Cerros de Trincheras. Paper presented at the Arizona Archaeological Council, Fall Meeting and Symposium, October 23–24, Flagstaff.

———. 2001. Una Investigación Arqueológica de los Sitios con Trincheras del Arcaico Tardío en Chihuahua México. Las Investigaciones de Campo 1999. Report submitted to the Consejo de Arqueología INAH, Archivo Técnico, Mexico City, Mexico. Center for Archaeological Research, University of Texas, San Antonio.

———. 2002. Early Agriculture in Northwestern Chihuahua. In *Traditions, Transitions, and Technologies: Themes in Southwestern Archaeology*, edited by S. Schlanger, pp. 160–177. University of Colorado Press, Boulder.

———. 2004. A Review of Cerros de Trincheras in Northwestern Chihuahua. In *Surveying the Archaeology of Northwest Mexico*, edited by G. Newell and E. Gallaga, pp.127–147. University of Utah Press, Salt Lake City.

Sauer, C., and D. D. Brand. 1932. Prehistoric Settlements of Sonora with Special Reference to Cerros de Trincheras. In *University of California Publications in Geography* 5, pp. 67–149. University of California Press, Berkeley.

Stacy, V. K. P. 1971. *The Trincheras Problem: Prehistoric Utilization of Vertical Space in South Central Arizona*. Ph.D. dissertation, University of Arizona, Tucson.

Thomas, J. 2006. From Dwelling to Building. *Journal of Iberian Archaeology* 8: 349–359.

Tilley, C. 1994. *A Phenomenology of Landscape*. Berg, Oxford.

———. 2004. *The Materiality of Stone: Explorations in Landscape Phenomenology*. Berg, Oxford.

Van Dyke, R., and S. E. Alcock. 2003. Archaeologies of Memory: An Introduction. In *Archaeologies of Memory*, edited by R. Van Dyke and S. E. Alcock, pp.1–13. Blackwell, Malden, MA.

Villalpando C. E., and R. H. McGuire. 2009. *Entre Muros de Piedra: La Arqueología del Cerro de Trincheras*. Centro INAH Sonora, Hermosillo, Sonora, Mexico.

Wallace, H. D., P. R. Fish, and S. K. Fish. 2007. Tumamoc Hill and the Early Pioneer Period. In *Trincheras Sites in Time, Space, and Society*, edited by P. R. Fish, S. K. Fish, and M. E. Villalpando, pp. 53–95. Amerind Studies in Archaeology. University of Arizona Press, Tucson.

Wilcox, D. R. 1979. Warfare Implications of Dry-Laid Masonry Walls on Tumamoc Hill. *Kiva* 45(1–2):15–38.

Zavala, B. M. 1998. *Building Trincheras: An Analysis of Architectural Features at Cerro de Trincheras*. Master's thesis, State University of New York, Binghamton.

———. 2006. Exploring the Symbolic at Cerros de Trincheras. In *Religion in the Prehispanic Southwest*, edited by C. S. VanPool, T. L. VanPool, and D. A. Phillips, pp. 135–146. Rowman-Altamira, Lanham, MD.

CHAPTER 49

CHACO'S HINTERLANDS

STEPHEN H. LEKSON

CHACO Canyon was the center of an 11th-century region about the size of Ireland. (Recent summaries of Chaco archaeology include, among others, Lekson 2006b; Mathien 2005; Mills 2002; Reed 2004; Van Dyke 2008; and the very accessible Noble 2004.) The bleak sandstone canyon in the deserts of northwestern New Mexico seems a very unlikely place for such a center. Yet the importance of Chaco Canyon is unmistakably manifest in a dozen remarkably large sandstone masonry buildings called "Great Houses," enormously larger than any other buildings of Chaco's time. The largest Chaco Canyon Great Houses were huge, symmetrical, geometric structures covering acres of leveled land, with as many as 700 rooms stacked up five stories tall (Lekson 1984). Chaco Great Houses began about AD 850, reached a sort of critical mass around 1000, and then exploded in a century-long building boom, from AD 1020 to 1125, when the region reached its maximum extent. Then Great House construction stopped—at Chaco. The tradition continued elsewhere (as we shall see).

GREAT HOUSES

Great Houses at Chaco Canyon were not "pueblos"; that is, they were not independent Native farming towns like those at modern pueblos of Hopi, Zuni, Acoma, and the modern Native Rio Grande villages. During Chaco's era, farming families lived in small, single-family houses of six rooms and a pithouse. Many thousands of these tiny single-family houses were scattered across the Four Corners region. Great Houses were few in number: only a dozen huge Great Houses in or around Chaco Canyon, and perhaps 200 smaller but still impressive Great

Houses ("outliers") positioned strategically throughout the Four Corners, among the farming communities (Lekson 1991).

Chaco Great Houses were not Pueblo villages, communal, egalitarian, and ritually based. Great Houses were elite residences, like Mesoamerican palaces—or, rather, they were *intended to be* palaces (Lekson 2006b; Lekson et al. 2006; see also Bernardini 1999; Neitzel 2003; Windes 1984, 1987; but cf. Vivian 1990, the most important dissenter in this matter). They housed high-status families who were something like princes and kings—or they *tried* to be kings (Lekson 2009; see also Neitzel 2003). They built a city—or something *like* a city (Lekson et al. 2006)—from which they controlled a vast region—or *thought* they controlled a region (Lekson 1991; cf. Kantner and Kintigh 2006). Chaco, with several hundred elites and a thousand commoners, was trying to be a local version of a Postclassic Mesoamerican capital (Lekson 2009; Peregrine and Lekson, this volume). But they got it wrong: they built it in the wrong place, at the wrong time.

Chaco was culturally affiliated with modern Pueblos (and other Southwestern groups), but it was not a developmental stage of steady progress toward the lifeways and philosophies of modern Pueblo peoples. Chaco, instead, was an experiment in very "un-Pueblo" urbanism, hierarchical government, and regional polity (a fact perhaps first recognized by Gordon Vivian; Vivian and Mathews 1965). That experiment ended badly, and Chaco's way was ultimately rejected by Pueblo peoples. The Native groups who became Hopi, Zuni, and the other Pueblos reformulated and reinvented themselves after AD 1300, adopting practices that ensured nothing like Chaco would ever rise again. There are clear cultural affiliations between modern Pueblos and Chaco, but also dramatic and profound historical discontinuities. So profound, indeed, that projecting such modern Pueblo institutions as "kivas" and "katsinas" back across that divide—from modern Pueblos to ancient Chaco—is problematic, at best.

The central idea at Chaco was political power, perhaps cloaked or embedded in ritual. Ritual, like the poor, is always with us, ranging from the communal and community-building ceremonials of modern Pueblos to the chilling power plays of Red Square and Pyongyang. We don't know Chaco's rituals, but they probably edged (at least a bit) more toward the latter than the former (cf. Mills, this volume).

Pursuit of political power—Chaco's central idea—began as early as AD 500 ("Basketmaker III," 500 to 700) in exceptionally large pithouses at sites such as Shabik'eschee, also at Chaco Canyon (Lekson 2009). Big pithouses presumably housed elite families, knock-offs of earlier Hohokam Big Houses (Fish and Fish, this volume). Those early attempts failed; early Four Corners peoples didn't need or want kings. After those false starts, the specific form of Chaco Great Houses came into focus in the northern San Juan area (later, the Mesa Verde region) in the 700s and 800s ("Pueblo I") as "U"-shaped room blocks surrounding very elaborate, "oversized" pithouses (Wilshusen and Van Dyke 2006; Windes 2007). These "proto-Great Houses" were short-lived: typically built, used, and abandoned in a generation or two. "Proto-Great-Houses" bounced around the northern San Juan, eventually moving up the Chaco River, where they finally *took*; the Great Houses of Chaco Canyon were permanent, lasting centuries. "Proto-Great-Houses" evolved into massive, rigidly geometric, monumental structures that addressed esoteric cosmologies and, above all, symbolized power. Great Houses began as trophy homes. At Chaco, they became palaces.

Chaco Citified

Chaco was a city, different in conception and detail from Postclassic Mesoamerican or Mississippian cities, but modestly urban nevertheless (Lekson et al. 2006). The reader may recoil from terms like "urban" and "city" applied to a Southwestern site, and indeed, Chaco did not look like the crowded, busy, metropolitan sites—from Ur to the Big Apple—leading through the millennia to stormy, husky, brawling modern urbanism. Not all cities were like that; not all roads lead to or through Rome. There are many other, non-Western ways to build cities (e.g., Agnew et al. 1984; Doxiadis 1968; Fletcher 1995; Rapoport 1977; Smith 2003). Western (and many non-Western) cities are densely packed, but not all were. Chaco, like modern Sun Belt cities, had an advantage lacking for Manhattan: lots of space. Chaco was spacious—impressively so. Broad open areas separated major buildings, increasing visual drama. Intervisibility across space gave Chaco an openness that counters our preconceptions about urban density (Fletcher 1995:117). Intervisiblity over distance was (literally) a worldview inspired by the Plateau's vast vistas (Van Dyke 2008). Distance itself was not a barrier or impediment; distance *defined* Chaco and its region. Space was a key element of their political cosmology, political symbolism, and urban aesthetic. Chaco city planning followed different rules from Ur or Chicago.

What, then, is a city? Bruce Trigger offered a useful, cross-cultural definition: "The key defining feature of an urban center is that it performs specialized functions in relation to a broader hinterland" (Trigger 2003:120; see also Cowgill 2004:526–527; and Smith 2003). As we shall see, Chaco did that.

Chaco's Hinterlands

The Chacoan hinterland or "regional system" was one of three mega-polities that shaped Southwestern prehistory. The Hohokam region, defined by ball courts (Fish and Fish, this volume), rose a couple of centuries before Chaco; indeed, Chaco was in some ways a geopolitical reaction to the earlier, explosive Hohokam "Colonial Period," from AD 700 to 950. Chaco and its spin-offs dominated the Four Corners from 1000 to 1300. Thereafter, the center of gravity shifted south, to the great city of Paquimé and its Casas Grandes regional system, which flourished from 1250 to 1450 (Whalen and Minnis 2001). For more than seven centuries, Southwestern history—local or regional—was shaped by regional entities for which we find no parallels in modern ethnography.

Hohokam, Chaco, and Casas Grandes were culturally and historically distinct, and their "regional systems" operated in very different ways. But all three were remarkably comparable in geographic extent (Lekson 2009). Whatever they might have been, the Hohokam, Chaco, and Paquimé regions were approximately *the same size*. Chaco was a unique historical event, but the scale of its regional system was, for the Southwest, typical. And modest, by contemporary Mississippian and Mesoamerican standards (a theme to which we will return).

Chaco's region was defined by two hundred small Great Houses, called "outliers," scattered over most of the southern Colorado Plateau (Figure 49.1). "Outlier" suggests a center—which Chaco Canyon surely was—and "regional system" implies interconnection—which less surely was the case. But beyond those two stipulations, Chaco's "regional system" should be understood as a pleasantly vague and indefinite appellation, with loads of potential meanings. Some Great Houses, such as Chimney Rock in south-central Colorado, were probably Chacoan colonies or impositions, while many other "outliers" were local families mimicking ("emulating") Chacoan styles; still, both were part of the larger regional system.

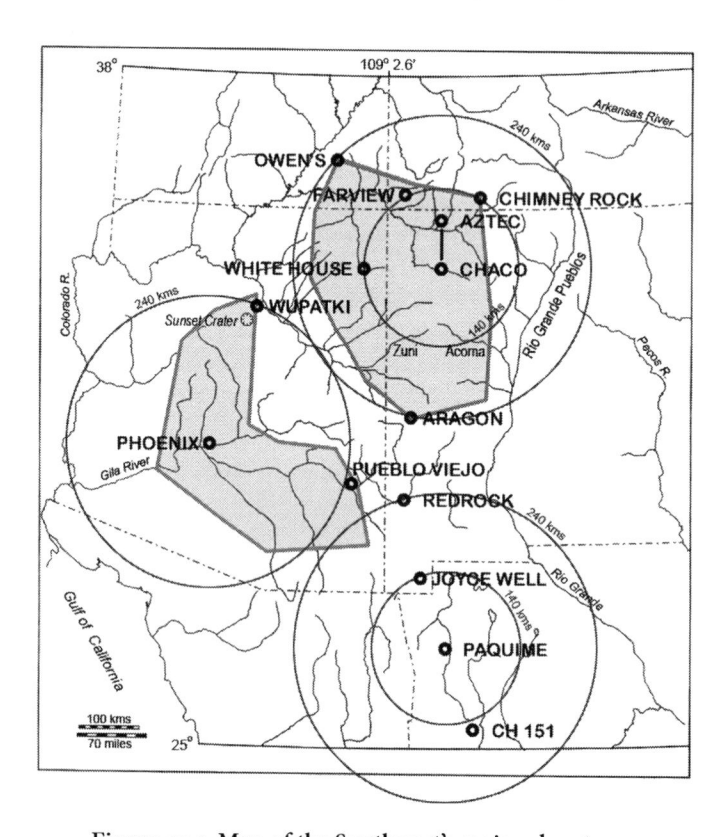

Figure 49.1 Map of the Southwest's regional systems.

Indeed, there has been much debate over the boundaries, the operations, and even the reality of the Chacoan regional system. Despite the fact that a number of Chaco-like sites at great distances from the canyon were well known by the 1930s, the political partitioning of archaeology in the Four Corners made it very difficult to map the Chaco region, when the effort began in the 1980s. In contrast, it was far easier to define the Hohokam regional system (Wilcox and Sternberg 1983). Not the fieldwork, which was arduous, but the acceptance of a regional system: Hohokam was neatly contained within southern Arizona and did not cross state lines. Consequently, Hohokam archaeology, well into the third quarter of the 20th century, was essentially the domain of a single institution and a single scholar of the Old School: Emil Haury, at the University of Arizona (Reid and Doyel 1986).

Not so in the Four Corners, quartered by four states and scores of personal research areas. Chaco was in New Mexico; this posed a problem for archaeologists based in Colorado, Arizona, and Utah. And within those larger political divisions, archaeologists trained in or heirs to New Archaeology typically thought of each valley—*their* valley—as a complete "natural laboratory," entire of itself. The Chaco regional system (whatever it was) completely overshot the research scales of 1970s Southwestern archaeology. The scale of the Chaco region was indeed prodigious and evoked understandable skepticism: it was *too big*.

How big is too big? How far is too far? What are realistic scales for Chaco, and for the ancient Southwest? We should shed modern preconceptions: our world is at once very small and very large. We think nothing of flying 4,000 miles to Paris, but we balk at walking four miles to a restaurant. A far better reference would be Chaco's Mississippian and Mesoamerican contemporaries. Both operated on scales far larger than any so far suggested for Chaco. Cahokia's engagement with sites 500 kilometers or more from the Mississippian city is a matter for research and debate: Aztalan in Wisconsin, Spiro in Oklahoma, and Macon Plateau in Georgia come to mind (Alt, this volume). And the obvious connections between the Postclassic capitals of Tula and Chichen Itza, more than 1,000 kilometers apart, are a chestnut of Mesoamerican archaeology—again, debated and researched (Smith and Berdan 2003). Southwestern archaeology, in contrast, often seems daunted by distances of only 50 or 60 kilometers—the distance, for example, from Aztec Ruins to Mesa Verde (Varien et al., this volume).

For Chaco, there was an inner core of undeniable "outliers" out to about 140–150 kilometers from Chaco—"undeniable" in that denial is simply, psychologically that. Out at 150 kilometers sat Chimney Rock ("the ultimate outlier"; Malville 2004), Farview (a classic Chaco "outlier" at Mesa Verde), and White House (ditto at Canyon de Chelly)—three archetypical "outlier" Great Houses. The farthest, most distant "outlier" candidates—sites such as Owen's Site at the head of Grand Gulch and Aragon in the Mogollon highlands—were an additional 100 kilometers out, that is, about 240–250 kilometers from Chaco (Figure 49.1). Those uttermost outliers are, in all important respects, identical to outlier Great Houses in the 150 kilometer inner core—local ceramics, of course, and local stone masonry, but the same buildings (Figure 49.2).

Figure 49.2 Pueblo del Arroyo, Chaco Canyon, New Mexico: major construction in the late 1070s and again in the early 1100s; the circular "triwall" attached to the rear of the building (front of this image) was perhaps the last major construction at the site either never completed or (more likely) constructed and later demolished (image by Dennis Holloway, http://www.dennisrhollowayarchitect.com/).

Thus the Chacoan regional system had an inner core area at about 150 kilometers, and an outer limit out around 250 kilometers. What mean these radii, when the sandals hit the road? Chacoan commerce was foot-driven, delivered by tumpline backpacks on porters. No carts, no horses, no boats, no rivers. How far and how much could people move, on their feet and on their backs?

Travel distances have obvious implications for economic interactions, for example in transporting bulk foodstuffs, such as maize. Kent Lightfoot (1979) suggested a 50 kilometer limit for "prehistoric food redistribution" at Chaco; beyond that limit, transport was uneconomical (the porter ate the portage). Lightfoot's 50 kilometer limit became a rule of thumb—and another nail in the coffin of "complex cultural ecosystems." This radius around Chaco gets you only the stinking deserts of the interior San Juan Basin, so Lightfoot's limit was cited as proof that Chaco's regional system was not economic, at least not in subsistence economy (e.g., Sebastian 1992:88). The 50 kilometer rule, however, is far too short. Robert Drennan (1984), looking at bulk food transport in Mesoamerica, set a much longer limit for regular commerce, an absolute (and extreme) maximum distance of 275 kilometers: "Ordinarily, we should expect transport of such staples to be restricted to substantially shorter distances" (1984:110). And more recently, Nancy Malville (who studies porters worldwide) concluded that "foot transport of food stuffs and durable goods would have been feasible in the pre-Hispanic American Southwest on a regular basis over distances of at least 100 to 150 km and on an occasional basis over much longer distances" (Malville 2001:230; see also Santley and Alexander 1992:44, who independently estimate an outer limit of 150 kilometers for Postclassic "trafficking in bulky goods"). We know that tens of thousands of very large beams were trafficked over those distances, to build Great Houses in treeless Chaco; it appears that foodstuff too moved within that inner core (Benson et al. 2003). Benson's "sourcing" of corn cobs and his analysis of Chaco's agricultural potential suggest that very little corn was grown in Chaco Canyon, yet a great deal of corn was consumed there. I think that the inner limit for regular bulk goods transportation of corn, for example, was on the order of Malville's 150 kilometer limit, while occasional movement of bulk goods might have reached Drennan's 275 kilometer limit. Certainly, Chacoan precious prestige goods—macaw feather artifacts, copper bells, shell insignia, and so forth—could easily reach out and touch someone at 250 kilometer, the empirical limit of outliers.

Beyond, Before, and After the Hinterlands

We can understand Chaco's drive to political power as a historical by-product of Mesoamerican civilizations. Mesoamerica had kings and cities for over a millennium before Chaco, and we can be sure that peoples of the Four Corners were well aware of both (Peregrine and Lekson, this volume). When environment or historical contingency or bald ambition suggested a change in regimes, the Mesoamerican model was the obvious gold standard. Chaco and other Southwestern polities "emulated" Mesoamerica, translated into local idioms and media, just as headmen in central Utah or the Mimbres Valley emulated Chaco: poorly, but recognizably.

The *fact* of Southwestern political systems should not alarm us. Chaco and its sister cities were unremarkable, local, pale reflections of the North American states and empires of their times. Given the contemporaries, it's remarkable that it took the Southwest so long to get around to political power. The answer probably is: the Four Corners deserts were a silly place to try to build a civilization.

Indeed, the more interesting question is, Why did this happen at Chaco? We can understand Phoenix and Paquimé, with their rich river valleys and canal irrigation. But why Chaco? Chaco has little to recommend it: no forests, little water, severely limited farmlands, no valuable local resources. Yet that was where the Pueblo people built their first city.

History and place were crucial. Chaco, because of its historical symbolism, legitimized the 11th-century political and urban experiment. Chaco defined a geomantic line of deep historical importance. It is an alarming fact that the largest and most interesting sites of the Four Corner's several eras were built on or very near a north-south meridian, which began at Chaco, bouncing back and forth, north to south, over seven centuries (Lekson 1999, 2009).

It began, apparently, at Chaco: from AD 500 to 700 (Basketmaker III), two huge pithouse villages marked Chaco as a remarkable place. Each site was 10 times larger than the next largest settlements of their time. Four Corners' pithouse settlements of that time averaged one or two houses; a few reached 20. Shabik'eschee and its sister site at Chaco each had more than a hundred pithouses, and each had a central, monumental structure we call (perhaps incorrectly) a Great Kiva—the earliest examples of a building type that continued through and beyond Chaco's times. In the following period, from 700 to 900 (Pueblo I), the largest and most complex settlement rose 130 kilometers in an empty valley more or less directly north of Chaco: the Ridges Basin/Blue Mesa complex just south of Durango, Colorado. Ridges Basin/Blue Mesa was by far the largest settlement of its times, and it centered on a complex of unique monumental structures—including an improbable tower!—at a location called "Sacred Ridge" (Potter and Chuipka 2007). Shabik'eschee and Ridges Basin/Blue Mesa were part of dynamic, shifting, short-term settlement systems, towns that came and went. The road to political power finally reached a permanent location to the south, back at Chaco, from 850 to 1125 (Pueblo II). And when Chaco ended, its political idea did not disappear but moved to a new location, at Aztec Ruins (1110 to 1280, Pueblo III; Figure 49.3), 90 kilometers to the north on the same meridian. Aztec recreated Chaco during the heyday of Mesa Verde (Varien et al., this volume). But Aztec could not perpetuate Chaco's successes, and the Pueblo experiment in political power ended with political and spiritual turmoil, violence, warfare, drought, and out-migration. This was the grim legacy rejected by the people who became the modern Pueblos, during the era from 1250 to 1450 (Pueblo IV). The great city of that era—blatantly Mesoamerican and spectacularly non-Puebloan—was Paquimé (1250–1450), built on Chaco's meridian, far to the south in Chihuahua. Chaco's political energy was perpetuated or recreated at Paquimé, but Pueblo people were content to stay behind, building new apolitical societies.

Chaco's hinterlands included most of the ancestral Pueblo world, from Hopi on the west to the Rio Grande on the east, and from the Rocky Mountains on the very edge of the Colorado Plateau to the south. Great Houses were built *almost* at Hopi and *almost* at the Rio Grande; the areas in the extreme east and west remained outside the regional system, exceptions that proved the rule. Neither area, however, can be understood in isolation from the great events of the Four Corners, and the supernova that was Chaco Canyon.

Archaeologists of an earlier age spoke of the "Pueblo II expansion," a vast penumbra of quasi-pueblolike architecture and pottery that, in the 11th and 12th centuries, reached west to Las Vegas, Nevada; north to Wyoming; east beyond the Rio Grande; and south into the Chihuahua deserts. Dynamics on that scale are uncomfortable for today's archaeology, and we do not often hear "Pueblo II expansion" these days. It has been nibbled away, undercut by dozens of local sequences and area prehistories. But the older archaeologists really saw something, and it is no coincidence that their Pueblo II expansion was contemporary with Chaco and its regional system. Chaco's hinterlands may have been within 250 kilometers of the canyon, but its effects and influences carried much farther in space and time. Chaco's history

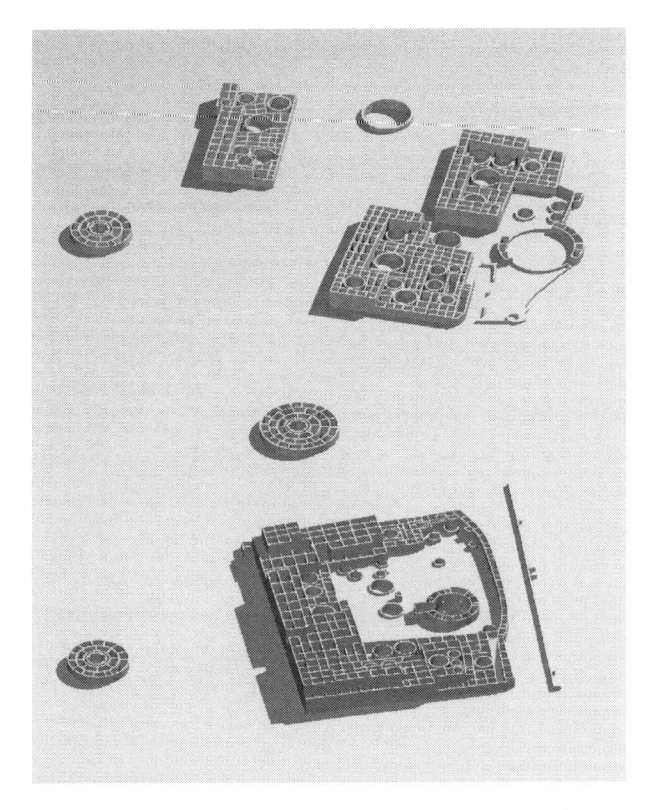

Figure 49.3 Aztec Ruins, Aztec, New Mexico: major construction beginning about 1110 continuing through 1280; the largest and most famous Chaco site excavated outside the canyon, Aztec Ruins—now widely recognized as a successor of Chaco—is approximately 80 km north of Chaco Canyon; East Ruin, in the foreground, was the largest single construction project ever undertaken by Chacoan builders; circular triwalls formed the architectural focus of Aztec Ruins, and similar structures, scattered throughout much of the Mesa Verde region, suggest that Aztec too had hinterlands (image by Dennis Holloway, http://www.dennisrhollowayarchitect.com/).

underwrote the Mesa Verde era of Pueblo III and shaped, in the breach, the subsequent (Pueblo IV) emergence of modern Pueblos.

REFERENCES

Agnew, J. A., J. Mercer, and D. E. Sopher (editors). 1984. *The City in Cultural Context*. Allen & Unwin, Boston.
Benson, L., L. Cordell, K. Vincent, H. Taylor, J. Stein, G. L. Farmer, and K. Futa. 2003. Ancient Maize from Chacoan Great Houses: Where Was It Grown? *Pennsylvania Museum of Archaeology and Anthropology* 100:13111–13115.
Bernardini, W. 1999. Reassessing the Scale of Social Action at Pueblo Bonito, Chaco Canyon, New Mexico. *Kiva* 64:447–470.

Cowgill, G. L. 2004. Origins and Development of Urbanism: Archaeological Perspectives. *Annual Review of Anthropology* 33:525–549.

Doxiadis, C. A. 1968. *Ekistics: An Introduction to the Science of Human Settlements*. Oxford University Press, New York.

Drennan, R. D. 1984. Long Distance Transport Costs in Pre-Hispanic Mesoamerica. *American Anthropologist* 86(1):105–112.

Fletcher, R. 1995. *The Limits of Settlement Growth: A Theoretical Outline*. New Studies in Archaeology. Cambridge University Press, Cambridge, UK.

Kantner, J. W. and K. W. Kintigh. 2006. The Chaco World. In *The Archaeology of Chaco Canyon: An Eleventh-Century Pueblo Regional Center*, edited by S. H. Lekson, pp. 153–188. School of American Research Press, Santa Fe, NM.

Lekson, S. H. 1984. *Great Pueblo Architecture of Chaco Canyon*. Publications in Archaeology 18B. National Park Service, Albuquerque, NM.

———. 1991. Settlement Patterns and the Chaco Region. In *Chaco and Hohokam*, edited by P. L. Crown and W. J. Judge, pp. 31–55. School of American Research Press, Santa Fe, NM.

———. 1999. *The Chaco Meridian: Centers of Political Power in the Ancient Southwest*. AltaMira Press, Walnut Creek, CA.

——— (editor). 2006a. *The Archaeology of Chaco Canyon*. SAR Press, Santa Fe, NM.

———. 2006b. Lords of the Great House. In *Palaces and Power in the Americas*, edited by J. Christie and P. Sarro, pp. 99–113. University of Texas Press, Austin.

———. 2009. *A History of the Ancient Southwest*. School of Advanced Research Press, Santa Fe, NM.

———, T. C. Windes, and P. J. McKenna. 2006. Architecture. In *The Archaeology of Chaco Canyon: An Eleventh-Century Pueblo Regional Center*, edited by S. H. Lekson, pp. 67–116. School of American Research Press, Santa Fe, NM.

Lightfoot, K. G. 1979. Food Redistribution Among Prehistoric Pueblo Groups. *Kiva* 44:319–330.

Malville, J. M. (editor). 2004. *Chimney Rock: The Ultimate Outlier*. Lexington Books, Lanham, MD.

Malville, N. J. 2001. Long-Distance Transport of Bulk Goods in the Pre-Hispanic American Southwest. *Journal of Anthropological Anthropology* 20:230–243.

Mathien, F. J. 2005. *Culture and Ecology of Chaco Canyon and the San Juan Basin*. Publications in Archaeology 18H. National Park Service, Santa Fe, NM.

Mills, B. J. 2002. Recent Research on Chaco: Changing Views on Economy, Ritual and Society. *Journal of Archaeological Research* 10(1):65–117.

Neitzel, J. E. (editor). 2003 *Pueblo Bonito: Center of the Chacoan World*. Smithsonian Books, Washington, DC.

Noble, D. G. (editor). 2004. *In Search of Chaco*. SAR Press, Santa Fe.

Potter, J. M., and J. Chuipka. 2007. Early Pueblo Communities and Cultural Diversity in the Durango Area: Preliminary Results from the Animas—La Plata Project. *Kiva* 72:407–430.

Rapoport, A. 1977. *Human Aspects of Urban Form: Towards a Man-Environment Approach to Urban Form and Design*. Pergamon Press, Oxford and New York.

Reed, P. F. 2004. *The Puebloan Society of Chaco Canyon*. Greenwood Press, Westport, CT.

Reid, J. J., and D. E. Doyel (editors). 1986. *Emil W. Haury's Prehistory of the Southwest*. University of Arizona Press, Tucson.

Santley, R. S., and R. T. Alexander. 1992. The Political Economy of Core-Periphery Systems. In *Resources, Power and Interregional Interaction*, edited by E. M. Schortman and P. A. Urban, pp. 23–49. Plenum Press, New York.

Sebastian, L. 1992. *The Chaco Anasazi: Sociopolitical Evolution in the Prehistoric Southwest.* Cambridge University Press, Cambridge, UK.

Smith, M. E., and F. F. Berdan (editors). 2003. *The Postclassic Mesoamerican World.* University of Utah Press, Salt Lake City.

Smith, M. I. (editor). 2003. *The Social Construction of Ancient Cities.* Smithsonian Books, Washington, DC.

Trigger, B. G. 2003. *Understanding Early Civilizations: A Comparative Study.* Cambridge University Press, Cambridge, UK.

Van Dyke, R. M. 2008. *The Chaco Experience: Landscape and Ideology at the Center Place.* SAR Press, Santa Fe, NM.

Vivian, G. R., and T. W. Mathews. 1965. *Kin Kletso: A Pueblo III Community in Chaco Canyon, New Mexico.* Technical Series 6(1). Southwest Parks and Monuments Association, Tucson, AZ.

Vivian, R. G. 1990. *The Chacoan Prehistory of the San Juan Basin.* Academic Press, San Diego, CA.

Whalen, M. E., and P. E. Minnis. 2001. *Casas Grandes and Its Hinterland: Prehistoric Regional Organization in Northwest Mexico.* University of Arizona Press, Tucson.

Wilcox, D. R., and C. Sternberg. 1983. Hohokam Ball Courts and Their Interpretation. *Arizona State Museum Archaeological Series* 160.

Wilshusen, R. H., and R. M. Van Dyke. 2006. Chaco's Beginnings. In *The Archaeology of Chaco Canyon: An Eleventh-Century Pueblo Regional Center*, edited by S. H. Lekson, pp. 211–260. School of American Research Press, Santa Fe, NM.

Windes, T. C. 1984. A New Look at Population in Chaco Canyon. Reports of the Chaco Center 8, *Recent Research on Chaco Prehistory*, edited by W. J. Judge and J. D. Schelberg, pp. 75–87. Division of Cultural Research, National Park Service, Albuquerque, NM.

——— (editor). 1987. *Investigations at the Pueblo Alto Complex, Chaco Canyon, New Mexico, 1975–79.* 2 vols. Publications in Archaeology 18F. National Park Service, Santa Fe., NM.

———. 2007. Gearing Up and Piling On: Early Great Houses in the Interior San Juan Basin. In *The Architecture of Chaco Canyon, New Mexico*, edited by S. H. Lekson, pp. 45–92. University of Utah Press, Salt Lake City.

CHAPTER 50

THE MESA VERDE REGION

MARK D. VARIEN, TIMOTHY A. KOHLER, AND SCOTT G. ORTMAN

The Mesa Verde region (MVR), located in the Four Corners area of the southwestern United States (Figure 50.1), contains one of the best-known and most intensively studied archaeological records of a Neolithic society found anywhere in the world. Among the characteristics that make the MVR ideal for archaeological research and public interpretation are an incredible number of highly visible sites, remarkable preservation, precise dating, short- and long-term reconstructions of temperature and precipitation, and a long history of research dating from 1874. In addition, although Pueblo people have not lived in the MVR since the late 13th century AD, the continued vibrancy of Pueblo communities in adjacent regions creates opportunities to combine archaeology, ethnography, language, and oral tradition to create a holistic account of Pueblo history. This summary synthesizes research by many individuals but focuses on the authors' recent study, the Village Ecodynamics Project (Kohler et al. 2007).

Maize was introduced to the Four Corners area about 4,000 years ago (see also Pearsall, this volume). A 1,500-year period of experimentation with maize followed before Mesa Verde Pueblo people became dependent on farming, and full expression of the Neolithic was not realized until about AD 600. The most intensive period of Pueblo occupation occurred between AD 600 and 1280, with population peaking in the mid-1200s, just a few decades before migration left the MVR entirely depopulated. Here we highlight the relationships among key elements of the Pueblo occupation of the MVR: introduction of domesticated food production, the causes and consequences of population growth, the effects of climate change, intensification of warfare, the degree of sedentism and frequency of population movement, formation of villages, and emergence of complex social and political organization.

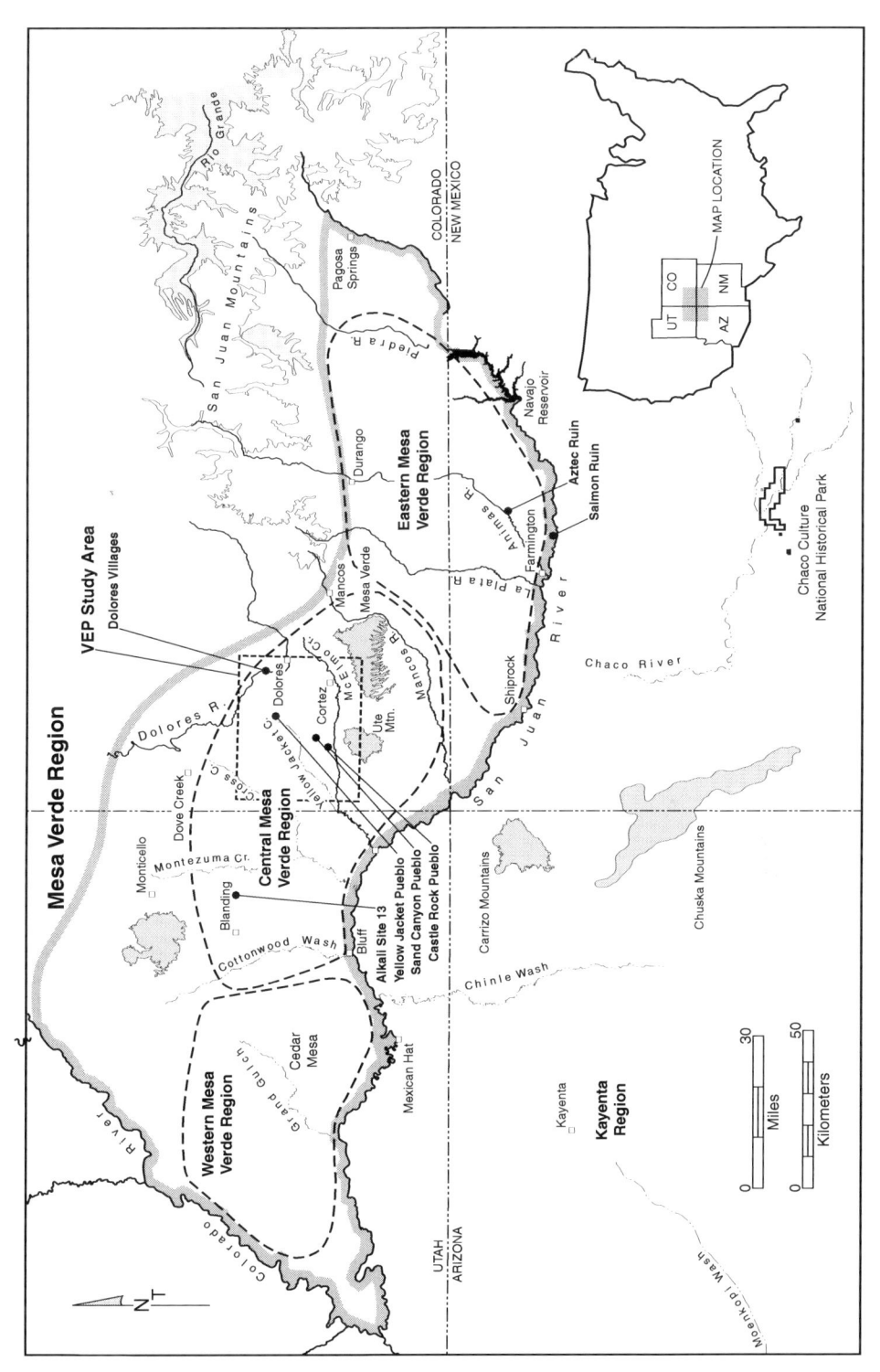

Figure 50.1 Map of the Mesa Verde region showing the western, central, and eastern subdivisions, the Village Ecodynamics Project study area, and key sites mentioned in the text (courtesy Crow Canyon Archaeological Center).

Introduction and Spread of Agriculture

Maize was domesticated in the Rio Balsas region of Mexico about 6,500 years ago, reached southern Arizona about 4,000 years ago, and then leapfrogged north, reaching the Four Corners by 1940 BC. Despite this rapid spread, the full transition to an agricultural lifeway in the MVR took about 1,500 years. Use of maize on the high-elevation Colorado Plateau required selection for varieties that could survive cooler temperatures and shorter growing seasons, and it required development of varieties that could be grown without irrigation. Analyses of settlement patterns, botanical remains, and human-bone isotopes indicate it wasn't until about 400 BC that Pueblo farmers became dependent on maize for the majority of their calories. Ancient DNA, dental characteristics, and artifacts suggest that these early farmers included at least two distinct groups: one consisted of people who migrated to the western MVR from southern Arizona, and the second consisted of local hunter-gatherers who adopted agriculture in the eastern MVR (Matson 2003).

Early dependency on maize farming did not in itself herald full development of the Neolithic in the MVR. This was instead accomplished through a series of innovations between 400 BC and AD 600, including enhancements to the nutritional value of maize, addition of cultivated beans and squash, development of maize varieties that could be grown without irrigation, introduction of the bow and arrow, and the appearance of well-fired pottery suitable for cooking. Together, these enabled unprecedented population growth, which in turn encouraged rapid sociopolitical and cultural change in the MVR.

Population Growth and the Neolithic Demographic Transition

The "Neolithic demographic transition" (NDT) designates the demographic changes that accompanied and made possible the spread of the Neolithic mode of production. NDT theory postulates that the Neolithic mode of production—which included a productive package of domesticates and tools—spread quickly and was accompanied by abrupt population increase. Population growth was based on increased fertility, likely due to decreased birth spacing that resulted from greater sedentism and a younger age of weaning, which in turn was prompted by the availability of new baby foods, perceived economic advantages to having more children, decreased costs of carrying infants, and the reduced need to resolve scheduling conflicts with women's labor. Eventually, population growth from higher fertility was offset by increased mortality, precipitated at least in part by disease transmission in aggregated settings. Together these transitions in fertility and mortality are called the NDT.

Bocquet-Appel (2002) first recognized the NDT in Europe and, with Naji, documented an NDT for North America; Kohler and others have examined this in detail for the Southwest United States. These studies use a paleodemographic indicator that tracks changes in crude birth rate (fertility) by measuring the proportion of the population between five and 19 years old. These values indicate that intrinsic growth increased markedly in the MVR around AD 600 and continued until about AD 1200. This demographic change did not occur with initial introduction of maize; rather it took place only after development of the full Neolithic package. Although it took longer to incubate, the NDT pattern eventually achieved in the MVR is similar to that documented for Europe (including the Near East), North America, and the greater U.S. Southwest. The Neolithic represents one of those few moments in human history—similar to today—when dramatic productive advances significantly raise regional carrying capacities and enable an unprecedented rate of culture change.

The NDT sets the backdrop for Pueblo occupation of the MVR, which we reconstruct using data from the Village Ecodynamics Project (VEP). VEP archaeologists assembled a database of about 9,000 sites from an 1,800 square kilometer area of southwestern Colorado. Ortman et al. (2007) used these data to estimate the population of each habitation site during 14 chronological phases between AD 600 and 1280. Varien et al. (2007) built on this analysis to reconstruct the population history of the region. Our paleodemographic reconstruction shows two cycles of occupation, each lasting about 300 years (Figure 50.2). Population density became much higher in the second cycle and peaked in the mid-1200s. The two cycles share many similarities: in-migration was involved in initiating each cycle, population density increased until the final phase, the proportion of population residing in villages rose throughout the cycle, and out-migration and population decline set in during the final phase. We calculated rates of population growth or decline for all periods and identified five periods when in-migration was likely, and two periods of probable out-migration. This demographic reconstruction suggests a more dynamic population history than was recognized previously, and it now seems likely that people from different areas and with a variety of backgrounds contributed to this history.

An Ever-Changing Environment

The environmental context for culture change in the MVR includes both annual and long-term variation. This environmental variability—largely reconstructed from analyses of tree rings and pollen cores—resulted in an ever-changing distribution of productive resources, including wild plants and animals and agricultural crops. Here we summarize the most recent and relevant studies that examine interaction between Pueblo people and their ever-changing environment.

Between 500 BC and AD 600, long-term climatic trends oscillated between wetter and drier conditions. The earliest farmers in the eastern MVR responded by

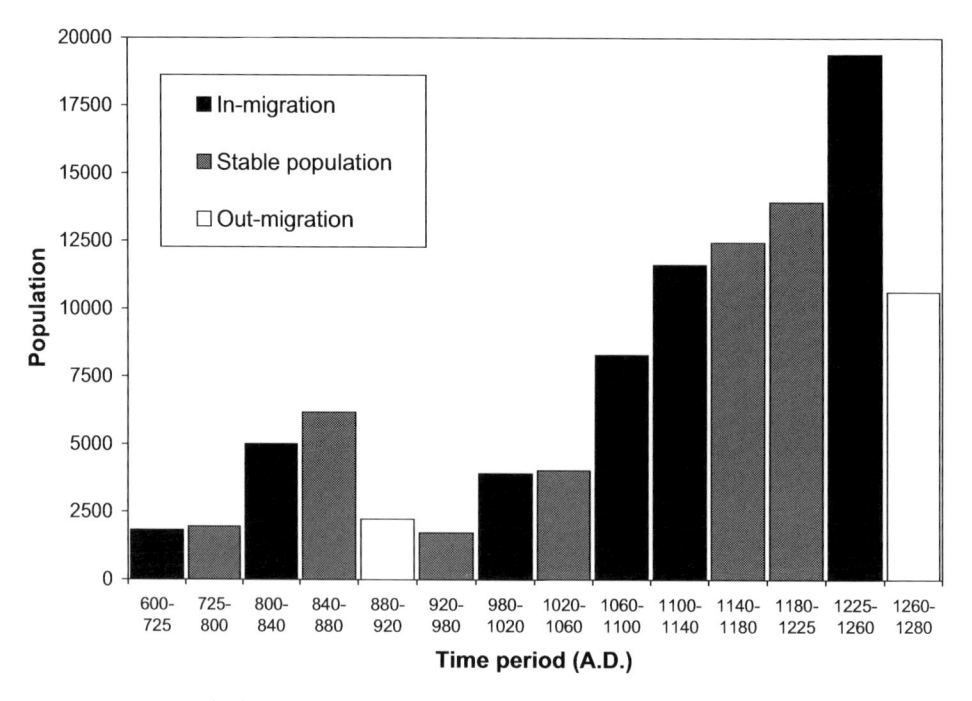

Figure 50.2 Graph showing population estimates from the Village Ecodynamics Project (courtesy Crow Canyon Archaeological Center).

moving to higher elevations during dry periods to take advantage of greater moisture in these areas. During wet periods these farmers moved to lower elevations to take advantage of the longer growing season there. The period from about 100 BC to AD 600 has also been identified as a cold episode, although temperatures increased slowly during this interval. The exception was warmer temperatures during the fourth century AD, when some Pueblo populations moved to more northern and higher locations.

The population growth in the MVR that began at about AD 600 corresponds to markedly warmer and wetter conditions that allowed farmers to expand into areas previously too risky for agriculture. Very cold conditions with dry winters began during the late 800s and persisted for most of the next century, coincident with the population decline in Figure 50.2. Favorable conditions returned in the 11th and 12th centuries AD, but toward the end of the 1100s a long-term trend of cooler temperatures and drier winters began that would have reduced agricultural yields, undoubtedly contributing to the break-up of farming societies across the northern Southwest and possibly to the downturn in intrinsic growth rates across the Pueblo World after AD 1200. Against this background of low-frequency change, Kohler and colleagues (2007) reconstructed annual variation in temperature and precipitation and its effect on maize production for the AD 600–1300 period in the VEP study area. Their results suggest periods of low productivity in the late 600s, the middle 700s, the late 800s and early 900s, around 1000, around 1100, about 1130–1150, the early 1200s, and the late 1200s.

Sedentism and Population Movement

Varien (1999) conducted a systematic analysis of household mobility and community persistence between AD 600 and 1280. He measured household residential movement on the basis of accumulation of cooking pottery at habitation sites. These data suggest that, during the seventh century, the average residential site was occupied for about eight years. Then, between about AD 725 and 1100, the length of residential site occupation increased to an average of 20 years, or one human generation. Finally, between AD 1100 and 1280 the average occupation span more than doubled to an interval greater than two human generations. These increases in occupation span are systematically related to changes in site structure, including greater investment in architecture, larger site size, appearance of formal storage areas, greater investment in labor and materials for both storage and habitation facilities, and more formal refuse disposal (Varien and Ortman 2005). Rising occupation span is also associated with changes in organization of activities. Architectural spaces became more specialized, permanent features were moved inside structures, and extramural areas were intensively maintained to accommodate multiple activities.

Ethnoarchaeological research indicates these changes are associated with agricultural intensification and the presence of cultivated fields immediately surrounding the residence. It appears that households claimed agricultural land when they constructed new houses, and residential movement was linked to land tenure. Varien argues that between AD 600 and 1100 a claim to land was valid only while the land was being used, but from AD 1100 to 1280 this changed to a system characterized by heritable property rights. The land tenure system, coupled with relatively low mobility, was a significant mechanism by which persistent economic and social inequality could accumulate across generations.

Varien (1999) also examined the persistence of communities typically composed of many sites. Using analyses of pottery, tree harvesting, and the mode of structure abandonment, he shows that communities persisted for a period much longer than the occupation span of individual farmsteads. During the early cycle, households moved every 20 years or less, but several communities lasted for as long as 200 years. During the later cycle, households moved at a frequency between one and three generations, but communities had histories lasting three centuries or more. Thus households negotiated their movement in a social landscape defined by a network of persistently occupied communities.

Population and Warfare

In a simple model for the relationship between population size and warfare in a closed system, Peter Turchin proposes that internal warfare increases with population size, with a temporal lag, until warfare eventually causes population to decline, after which warfare also declines. Sarah Cole developed an index for warfare by tabulating the incidence of skeletal trauma likely due to violence, which includes "parry" fractures to the ulna or radius, perimortem and antemortem cranial fractures, and archaeological contexts where human remains were disarticulated and modified culturally (Kuckelman 2002). The proportion of individuals with warfare-related trauma ranges from zero in some periods to almost 90 percent between AD 1140 and 1180.

Kohler combines these data with the VEP population history to examine how this model applies to the MVR (Kohler et al. 2009). During the first population cycle, warfare lagged behind population changes, as predicted by the model. However, between AD 1020 and 1180 more warfare preceded population increase, instead of following it. This suggests the MVR was not a closed system during this period. Higher-than-expected violence during the 11th and 12th centuries may reflect attempts by the Chaco polity, the primary regional center located south of the MVR, to expand into the MVR. Several independent lines of evidence are consistent with this interpretation; for example, escalating violence in the 1000s is suggested by stockades around some farmsteads.

By around 1200, after the mid-1100s collapse of the polity in Chaco Canyon, the expected relationship between population and warfare reemerged in the MVR, although the level of warfare at that time was lower relative to population size than in the first population cycle. However, females are underrepresented in 13th-century burial populations in the MVR, but overrepresented in contemporaneous populations from northwestern New Mexico. Some of the females found in the latter sites did not receive formal burial, had few accompanying grave goods, and exhibited a high incidence of skeletal trauma. Kohler and Turner (2006) interpret these data as suggesting successful raiding for women, who were removed as captives. Increased warfare characterizes the final period of Pueblo occupation in the MVR, between 1260 and 1280. There are several well-documented cases of warfare from this period that are associated with drought and subsistence stress (Kuckelman 2002). At Castle Rock Pueblo, warfare resulted in the massacre of most or all residents of this small village. A battle also appears to have ended the occupation of Sand Canyon Pueblo after much of the population had already left.

Formation of Villages

During most periods, Pueblo people in the MVR lived in small hamlets occupied by one or a few households. However, a number of sites large enough to situate nine or more households formed during each population cycle. Ortman (in Varien et al. 2007) estimated the proportion of households that lived in these villages through time, using block surveys in the VEP study area for which we have a 100 percent sample of both villages and smaller habitations. The proportion of households residing in villages generally increased throughout both occupation cycles and peaked during the final period of population decline at the end of each cycle, at about AD 900 and again around 1270. It appears population density was only one of the factors that encouraged growth and maintenance of villages.

The earliest villages formed in the late AD 700s. Their form and layout varied substantially from east to west, as exemplified by the differences between the Sacred Ridge site near Durango, Colorado, and Alkali Ridge Site 13 near Blanding, Utah. These differences suggest that at least two distinct ethnic groups created these settlements. A century later, villages in the Dolores River Valley exhibited similar differences in form, despite being created on opposing shores of a river in a single valley (Wilshusen and Ortman 1999). This cycle of village formation does not follow increases in warfare, so these first villages do not appear to have been primarily defensive in nature. Their appearance does correspond to periods of relatively high potential agricultural production; one factor supporting their growth was opportunities for exchange of maize between unrelated households. Early villages were often situated at relatively high elevations, which would have been ideal for hunting large game, especially mule deer. These early villages seem to have facilitated large-game hunting, which would have become ever more important as large game were depleted by overhunting. The faunal assemblages of these early villages do in fact have a high frequency of large game (see Driver 2002).

During the later demographic cycle, villages were initially centered on buildings that exhibit characteristics of the monumental buildings in Chaco Canyon. These larger buildings were typically located on mesa tops in highly visible settings and were surrounded by a cluster of smaller hamlets. These great-house-and-hamlet villages were constructed in the MVR between AD 1080 and 1140, but many continued to be occupied between AD 1140 and 1260. It is likely these villages have more to do with population administration, or even control, than with defense.

Many new villages were constructed during the 13th century, and they display new patterns in their setting, architecture, and layout that likely indicate important changes in social organization. These 13th-century villages moved to canyon settings—including placement of some in alcoves (Figure 50.3)—where they were built on or near springs (Ortman and Bradley 2002). Other innovations are bilateral layout; enclosing walls; towers; public architecture that includes multiwalled structures, plazas, and kivas; and clustering of public architecture in one section of the village. Some of these features—settings that restrict access, increased residential aggregation, towers, enclosing walls, and securing a spring—may be related to intensification of warfare during this period.

Figure 50.3 Photograph of Cliff Palace at Mesa Verde National Park (courtesy Crow Canyon Archaeological Center).

EMERGENCE OF SOCIAL AND POLITICAL COMPLEXITY

Social and political complexity increased over the course of the AD 600–1280 period, but reconstructing these developments remains a challenge. It is clear that the complexity that did develop was not continuous; instead, complexity increased during the two episodes of village formation. For example, several analysts have shown that large game were consumed more often in villages than in small settlements during all periods, and that communal feasting was also more common in larger settlements. These patterns suggest that although social power in the MVR may have been linked to control of ritual knowledge, as it is in historic Pueblo communities, it also had material, subsistence-related correlates (Figure 50.4).

The difference in complexity during the two demographic cycles derives in part from differences in population and their impact on local resources. During the first cycle, relatively low populations concentrated on a modified slash-and-burn agricultural system and hunting of large game, but during the second cycle relatively dense populations focused on more intensive agricultural systems, hunting of small game, and raising of turkeys for meat. The much larger population of the second cycle simultaneously reduced the net per capita energy gains from existing resources and depleted slowly renewable resources such as deer and forested lands.

Prior to the late AD 700s, we think MVR Pueblo societies were not characterized by persistent inequalities that accumulated across generations, even though

Figure 50.4 Photograph of Mesa Verde pottery (courtesy Crow Canyon Archaeological Center).

there were certainly specific individuals in every generation who distinguished themselves by their special talents and achievements. In the sparsely settled landscapes they inhabited, the main problem would have been developing peaceful relationships with neighbors in order to maintain access to resources and potential mates. The public architecture of this period, which includes great kivas and circular dance plazas, likely reflects social mechanisms that emerged for this purpose.

Early Pueblo villages formed adjacent to highland areas rich in large game when the MVR population grew large enough to depress local deer populations as a result of hunting; thus opportunities for organizing hunting expeditions to provision the population with meat may have been one of the factors behind the growth of these villages. Kohler and Reed's analysis (2011) of village locations between AD 780 and 920 indicates the entire settlement system was biased toward efficiency in large-game procurement by placing villages where deer could most easily be hunted.

Oversized pit structures appear in the late AD 700s; they are inferred to have been the homes of successful lineage heads who may also have been hunt leaders. This occurred about the same time that great kivas were incorporated into villages as well. Perhaps the great kiva ceremonies were orchestrated, directly or indirectly, by the most senior lineage or hunt leaders, creating a new level of leadership at the top of the sociopolitical hierarchy.

During the second cycle, a variety of evidence indicates that unprecedented social and political differentiation developed among and within villages. Rank-size analysis of settlements shows that one site, Yellow Jacket Pueblo, emerged as a primary center when Chaco influence penetrated the region (AD 1080–1140). After AD 1140, however, the settlement system developed into a network of villages lacking a primary center in which local polities competed with one another. The number and size of these local polities also increased from AD 1060 through at least 1260. By the mid-1200s, significant amounts of labor were being mobilized to build public architecture and maintain nondomestic storage space. Pottery and faunal analyses indicate that stored food was distributed at public feasts. Ritual was intensified, as evidenced by new forms of public architecture, especially multiwalled structures, which served as residences and as locations for exclusive ritual activities (Ortman and Bradley, in Varien and Wilshusen 2002). The presence of big houses that sponsored and controlled ritual activities suggests that distinct leaders were emerging in these villages. However, it is striking that this architectural evidence is not supported by mortuary evidence, which does not indicate individual aggrandizement. Thus social power may have been vested in groups rather than in individuals, or mortuary ceremonies might have been designed to mask rather than assert social differences. Finally, as noted earlier, warfare also intensified during the late 13th century, and this may have led to alliance formation.

During the second demographic cycle, the MVR appears to have reached a demographic and socioeconomic threshold at which it was difficult to maintain a settlement system of independent local communities. Our demographic reconstruction indicates that the population density of the mid-AD 1200s approached levels that preceded the emergence of regional polities and hereditary ranking in other parts of the world, such as Mesoamerica. The population density of the MVR was similar to that of the Valley of Mexico and the Valley of Oaxaca about 600–700 years after their initial colonization by farmers, and immediately prior to development of regional polities and ranked societies.

It is remarkable that in all three regions, population density reached similar levels about six centuries after their initial colonization by people who lived in year-round habitations, made pottery, and grew maize as a dietary staple. However, in the Mesa Verde case—instead of the emergence of hereditary ranking and regional polities—the settlement system disintegrated and the entire population moved to areas where new societies that reflect ethnographic Pueblo patterns were taking shape (Kohler et al. 2010). These new societies were organized very differently from MVR societies, and they may have been in part a response to the Pueblo experience in the MVR.

REFERENCES

Bocquet-Appel, J.-P. 2002. Paleoanthropological Traces of a Neolithic Demographic Transition. *Current Anthropology* 43:637–650.

Driver, J. C. 2002. Faunal Variation and Change in the Northern San Juan Region. In *Seeking the Center Place: Archaeology and Ancient Communities in the Mesa Verde Region*, edited by M. D. Varien and R. H. Wilshusen, pp 143–160. University of Utah Press, Salt Lake City.

Kohler, T. A., K. Bocinsky, S. Crabtree, and B. Ford. 2011. Exercising the Model: Settlement Efficiency and Changes in Locational Practice. In *Emergence and Collapse of Early*

Villages: Models of Central Mesa Verde Archaeology (draft title), edited by T. A. Kohler and M. D. Varien. University of California Press, Berkeley.

Kohler, T. A., S. Cole, and S. Ciupe. 2009. Population and Warfare: A Test of the Turchin Model in Pueblo Societies. In *Patterns and Process in Cultural Evolution*, edited by S. Shennan, pp. 277–296. University of California Press, Berkeley.

Kohler, T. A., C. D. Johnson, M. Varien, S. Ortman, R. Reynolds, Z. Kobti, J. Cowan, K. Kolm, S. Smith, and L. Yap. 2007. Settlement Ecodynamics in the Prehispanic Central Mesa Verde Region. In *The Model-Based Archaeology of Socionatural Systems*, edited by T. A. Kohler and S. van der Leeuw, pp. 61–104. SAR Press, Santa Fe, NM.

Kohler, T. A., and C. Reed. 2011. Explaining the Structure and Timing of Formation of Pueblo I Villages in the Northern U.S. Southwest. In *Sustainable Lifeways: Cultural Persistence in an Ever-Changing Environment*, edited by N. F. Miller, C. M. Moore, and K. Ryan, pp. 150–179. University of Pennsylvania Museum of Archaeology and Anthropology, Philadelphia.

Kohler, T. A., and K. K. Turner. 2006. Raiding for Women in the Prehispanic Northern Pueblo Southwest? A Pilot Examination. *Current Anthropology* 47:1035–1045.

Kohler, T. A., M. D. Varien, and A. Wright (editors). 2011. *Leaving Mesa Verde: Peril and Change in the Thirteenth-Century Southwest*. University of Arizona Press, Tucson.

Kuckelman, K. A. 2002. Thirteenth-Century Warfare in the Central Mesa Verde Region. In *Seeking the Center Place: Archaeology and Ancient Communities in the Mesa Verde Region*, edited by M. D. Varien and R. H. Wilshusen, pp 233–253. University of Utah Press, Salt Lake City.

Matson, R. G. 2003. The Spread of Maize Agriculture into the U.S. Southwest. In McDonald Institute Monographs, *Examining the Farming/Language Dispersal Hypothesis*, edited by P. Bellwood and C. Renfrew, pp. 341–356. University of Cambridge, Cambridge, UK.

Ortman S. G., and B. A. Bradley. 2002. Sand Canyon Pueblo: The Container in the Center. In *Seeking the Center Place: Archaeology and Ancient Communities in the Mesa Verde Region*, edited by M. D. Varien and R. H. Wilshusen, pp 41–78. University of Utah Press, Salt Lake City.

Ortman, S. G., M. D. Varien, and T. L. Gripp. 2007. Empirical Bayesian Methods for Archaeological Survey Data: An Application from the Mesa Verde Region. *American Antiquity* 72:241–272.

Varien, M. D. 1999. *Sedentism and Mobility in a Social Landscape*. University of Arizona Press, Tucson.

———, and S. G. Ortman. 2005. Accumulations Research in the Southwest United States: Middle-Range Theory for Big-Picture Problems. *World Archaeology* 37, *Archaeology of North America*, edited by M. Shott, pp. 132–155.

———, T. A. Kohler, D. G. Glowacki, and C. D. Johnson. 2007. Historical Ecology in the Mesa Verde Region: Results from the Village Project. *American Antiquity* 72:273–299.

Varien, M. D., and R. H. Wilshusen (editors). 2002. *Seeking the Center Place: Archaeology and Ancient Communities in the Mesa Verde Region*. University of Utah Press, Salt Lake City.

Wilshusen, R. H., and S. G. Ortman. 1999. Rethinking the Pueblo I Period in the San Juan Drainage: Aggregation, Migration, and Cultural Diversity. *Kiva* 64:369–400.

CHAPTER 51

WARFARE AND CONFLICT IN THE LATE PRE-COLUMBIAN PUEBLO WORLD

JAMES E. SNEAD

Archaeological research on warfare and conflict in the late Pre-Columbian American Southwest has from its inception been deeply structured by cultural and scholarly biases toward the Pueblo world, past and present. The origin and evolution of these preconceptions is complex, shaped by 19th- and 20th-century ideas about Native American society, contemporary political debate regarding assimilation and identity, and the widespread tendency among anthropologists and laypeople alike to project their fears and desires onto the mute stones of pueblo ruins. These prejudices are deeply ingrained and have ramifications in modern politics. Such obstacles, paradoxically, only emphasize the importance of the subject. If the Southwest is indeed a "laboratory for anthropology," in Don Fowler's phrase (2000), then developing means to study warfare and violence in such a charged context will offer guidance for addressing the subject in other, equally challenging environments, ultimately making a more valuable contribution to anthropological knowledge.

Frames of Reference

Early anthropologists working in the American Southwest had no difficulty imagining a violent Pre-Columbian past. Adolph Bandelier, for example, described new Pueblo villages as requiring locations that were "reasonably *safe from an enemy*"

(1892:32, emphasis in original). Such correlations were derived in part from history and ethnography, since some of the people with whom he spoke had fought battles themselves. Anthropological perceptions were inevitably colored by the nature of 19th-century warfare in the Southwest—conflict pitting Spanish/Mexican settlers and their Pueblo allies against Comanche, Apache, and Navajo raiders—and the scholarly literature of the era is replete with references to concerns over such predatory bands (for example, Hewett 1909:437). Thus when archaeologists began addressing the issue of warfare in the ancestral Pueblo context, they projected such large-scale struggles between Pueblo and Athapaskan cultures deep into the past (see Kidder 1924).

Ideas about Pueblo conflict changed dramatically in the 1930s, as the "culture and personality" school of cultural anthropology gained popularity. Depictions of Pueblo society structured around harmony and balance—what Ruth Benedict labeled "Apollonian culture"—gained considerable influence. It is not difficult to perceive intellectuals such as Benedict working in the long shadow of fascism, seeking relief in other cultures (Fowler 2000:340), but this required overlooking much information gathered by previous generations of scholars. Some interest in Pueblo warfare continued among archaeologists, but they largely acquiesced in establishing what Lawrence Keeley has described as a "pacified past" (1996).

This persisted for several decades, even while it became increasingly clear that Athapaskans had made a relatively late entry into the Southwest and thus a "clash of cultures" could not account for warfare deeper than a century or two into Pre-Columbian time; despite the revolution in archaeological thought that took place in the 1960s, archaeological attitudes toward warfare changed little (although see Woodbury 1959). The popularity of theoretical approaches such as cultural ecology created research frameworks declaring that "war was 'bad' and that environment was 'good'" (Haas and Creamer 1997:239), hindering exploration of the topic.

The iconoclastic spirit of the 1970s and 1980s, however, ultimately created conditions in which war reemerged as a research interest. This process was advanced by both expanding general interest in the topic of tribal warfare (see Redmond 1994) and an increasingly unavoidable array of empirical evidence for conflict in the southwestern context. Particularly influential in this regard was the work of Jonathan Haas and Winifred Creamer in the Kayenta region of northern Arizona. Their study of settlement patterns identified an array of features—defensive settlement locations, line-of-site community organization, burned sites—that implied persistent conflict during the 13th century AD (1993). This work was followed by two overviews of warfare in the Pre-Columbian Southwest as a whole, assembling information from diverse contexts and time periods to build a picture of intermittent but deadly conflict (Wilcox and Haas 1994; LeBlanc 1999). A final, influential study from the 1990s was Cristy and Jacqueline Turner's *Man Corn*, which argued that anthropophagy had been widespread in ancestral Pueblo society (1999).

These studies have been variably critiqued, but collectively they threw open the window for the subject of conflict and warfare in the ancestral Pueblo world. A series of detailed case studies followed (see Lambert 2002, and the studies in

Rice and LeBlanc 2001). Fieldwork in southwestern Colorado was particularly influential at this juncture, documenting severe episodes of conflict. One of them is the site of Cowboy Wash, where a small pithouse settlement dating to the AD 1150s was destroyed with some of its inhabitants killed and eaten. The other prominent case is Castle Rock Pueblo, a more substantial settlement than Cowboy Wash, built in the mid-AD 1200s, that shows evidence of a systematic attack and, again, significant, brutalized casualties among its inhabitants (see Kuckelman 2002). Both of these projects described systematic warfare against settled populations that resulted in localized devastation, casualties, and apparent anthropophagy.

This florescence of research on warfare has had several interesting and unexpected results. One, as argued by D. Wilcox and colleagues, is that concern for the "causes" of Pueblo warfare remains closely linked to environmental/adaptive issues such as resource stress, despite the availability of other theoretical models (Wilcox et al. 2006). In some circles a certain "orthodoxy" has set in, particularly regarding expectations of extreme violence, derived from the southwestern Colorado cases and the Turners' work on anthropophagy. Thus the question "How can it be warfare without evidence for casualties?" is raised. The converse—that apparent evidence for extreme violence or warfare in general has been misinterpreted—is also heard, both in scholarly venues (Darling 1999; Dongoske et al. 2000) and in the newspapers. The public nature of this controversy, coming at a time when Native voices are increasingly prominent in studies of the Pueblo past, has had a certain dampening effect on the study of controversial topics.

A few systematic, empirical studies of Pueblo conflict grounded in anthropological theory and Pueblo ethnography have been conducted (e.g., Schaafsma 2000), but on the whole further pursuit of this subject has stalled. A certain emotional toll is exacted by empirical study of conflict, which—combined with how the implications of ancient warfare play out in the modern political arena—discourages research. This is unfortunate, since increasing awareness of the centrality of conflict in the human past is becoming a significant archaeological contribution to anthropological knowledge. The legacy of the past 150 years is that information about warfare is available in the American Southwest, and that without discounting challenges it represents a critical opportunity to better understand it.

The discussion in this chapter pertains to evidence for warfare and conflict in one particular area of the Southwest, the northern Rio Grande region of New Mexico, from the 13th to the 16th centuries AD (roughly Pueblo III–Pueblo IV). This is the eastern Pueblo heartland, home of many thriving pueblo communities in the modern era with associated deep continuity of occupation and ethnographic tradition. It has also seen archaeological research since the 1880s, with a substantial body of empirical evidence. These data have not, however, been thoroughly examined in context (beyond LeBlanc 1999). Evidence for Pueblo warfare in the northern Rio Grande region is thus a useful opportunity both to evaluate the presence and nature of such processes and to critique how it is interpreted.

Patterns of Evidence

It is difficult to avoid a certain typological approach to empirical evidence for warfare. Several summaries of such characteristics exist (in particular, Wilcox and Haas 1994). Such "checklists" have their own problems, but at least they constitute a basis to begin the discussion. One of the most commonly cited patterns of archaeological evidence associated with warfare is *intentional destruction* of sites. In the southwestern context this typically means systematic or selective burning of pueblos, which—despite the fire-resistant properties of mud architecture—is regularly encountered in the archaeological record. The particular challenge is discerning accident from intent, and then different sorts of intention, not all of which necessarily reflect warfare.

In early years, burned sites were documented in the northern Rio Grande region by archaeologists such as A. V. Kidder, who identified destruction by fire at Forked Lightning Ruin and at an early occupation of Pecos Pueblo itself (1958:58); and Frank Hibben, whose 1930s excavations at Riana Ruin found both extensive burning and destruction of domestic assemblages (1937:49). Both of these episodes were attributed to warfare, although contemporary interpretations of the burned Arrowhead Ruin near Pecos implied a more planned process of abandonment (Holden 1955:113). Over the decades, systematic burning was identified at Pueblo Alamo, Pueblo Largo, Arroyo Hondo II, Manzanares, the Palisade Ruin, Wheeler, Pot Creek Pueblo, and most recently at LA4624 on the Pajarito Plateau (Allen 1973; Alexander 1971; Creamer 1993; Dutton 1953; Fowles 2004; Peckham 1981; Steen 1980). This is a measurable percentage of the larger sites excavated in the region, and it points to a widespread pattern.

Greater precision regarding such a pattern of burned sites, however, is challenging. The majority of these pueblos were destroyed between AD 1200 and 1350, and many were among the more sizable villages of this era. The few later sites burned—such as Wheeler at the end of the 1300s and Arroyo Hondo II circa 1420—were relatively small compared to the large pueblos of the day, none of which appear to have been destroyed by fire. There are also some local clusters of burned sites. Riana Ruin and Palisade Ruin, for instance, are two contemporary burned sites quite close to each other. Room assemblages associated with burned sites also differ; some, like Arrowhead, were relatively sparse, while excavation of sites such as Wheeler yielded smashed ceramic vessels and similar debris on the floors. Some interesting data exist regarding expectations for intentional burning: at Arroyo Hondo I, dating to the early 14th century, 6 out of 66 excavated ground floor rooms had burned, implying some sort of periodic accident, while 21 out of 50 ground floor rooms excavated in the second, late-14th-century component showed signs of burning, indicating a much more substantive event (Creamer 1993:13, 42).

The presence of *casualties* is another standard indicator of warfare, but one in which there is significantly limited evidence in the Northern Rio Grande. There are very few cases of human remains found in contexts that suggest violent death. One of these was "a partially charred skeleton" in a burned room at Riana Ruin (Hibben 1937:49). Suggestive but enigmatic are human remains found in kivas, in particular at Te'ewi, where excavations in the 1950s uncovered 24 bodies in a burned kiva (Wendorf 1953:93). The larger context of this find at Te'ewi remain obscure, and of the dozens of other kivas excavated in the region there has been only one other similar find, at Arroyo Hondo, where several bodies were found in a collapsed kiva (Palkovich 1980:21). Limited evidence for a broader catastrophe at these sites makes further interpretation difficult, and it is interesting to ponder the general absence of casualties in other excavated contexts, particularly at the burned sites.

Landscape organization is a third category of evidence for conflict. Pueblo architecture itself—with blank exterior walls, limited access to the interior, and flat rooftops that could serve as fighting platforms—is often thought of as a defensive adaptation. The larger-scale landscape context for these sites is also considered to reflect preparedness for war. The most widely cited is placing sites in defensive positions. The topography of the region does not offer opportunities for dramatic, pinnacle-topping redoubts as found elsewhere in the Southwest (Welch and Bostwick 2001), but there are a large number of examples of pueblos built on "high ground" of possible strategic significance. These include Tsiping, on a commanding mesa top at the northern limits of the region, and Tsankawi, built on a clearly defensible summit on the central Pajarito Plateau. Both are relatively substantial pueblos that would have housed hundreds of people. Several other significant sites—such as Pecos, Colina Verde, and Pueblo Largo—were built on locally prominent hills or ridgelines.

A pattern of defensive site location is not, however, ubiquitous in the northern Rio Grande. Many prominent sites—including Tyuonyi on the Pajarito Plateau and San Marcos in the Galisteo—were established in low-lying, distinctly nondefensive locations. As with burned sites, there appears to be a temporal or subregional element to this pattern, with most of the defensive sites founded relatively early in the sequence, and the large, less defensible sites built later. There are also few obvious defensive outposts on high ground near these sites; more typically, small hilltops near large pueblos are occupied by shrines. No systematic search has been made for "watchposts," however, and we have no reason to suspect that any formal facilities for sentries would have even been necessary.

One less commonly discussed aspect of a landscape organized for war is the presence or absence of smaller facilities such as field houses. Such outlying installations are commonly found in the southwestern landscape in the hinterlands of pueblo communities and are usually thought of as a farming strategy adopted when quality land was scarce close to the center. This distribution of population across the countryside has implications for conditions of war and peace as well, however. When the risk of conflict was high, people using field houses during the growing season would have been untenably exposed to raiding. Archaeological surveying in the northern Rio Grande has documented thousands of field houses, and there is evidence for relatively rapid establishment and disestablishment of such networks.

In general, field-house networks are scarcer in the 13th century than afterward (Snead 2008a), although they were present elsewhere in the Southwest in earlier times (for instance, Rohn 1977:99). Richard Lang (1977) notes that the large number of field houses associated with San Cristobal date largely to the 14th century but disappear afterward, a change he attributes to a shifting agricultural strategy but for which alternate interpretations may be sought. A similar absence of field houses is evident for the vicinity of Tsankawi; in contrast, field-house systems expand in other parts of the Pajarito Plateau during the 14th and 15th centuries (Powers and Orcutt 1999; Preucel 1990). There is not a simple regionwide correlation to be made here, but it may be possible to use existing information to sort through these apparently contrasting patterns and integrate them with other categories of evidence for or against conflict.

A final category of evidence for conflict is *iconography*. Use of symbols associated with war or conflict is often a proxy for the presence of the real thing. There are several important media for symbolism associated with ancestral Pueblo culture, in particular ceramics and petroglyphs or pictographs, and several systematic attempts to identify symbol "systems" have been made (for example, Adams 1991; Crown 1994; Schaafsma 1992). Polly Schaafsma has made a detailed study of petroglyphs in the northern Rio Grande in comparison to ethnographically documented imagery from historic Pueblo contexts, noting that the proliferation of shields, masks, and related imagery in petroglyphs from the early 14th century onward correlate with an increasingly pervasive ritual system focused on war (2000:156). Such iconography was not universally distributed in the northern Rio Grande—best known from southerly areas such as the Galisteo Basin and the southern Pajarito Plateau—but she makes a compelling case that in visual communication, at least, the ancestral Puebloans of the region were strongly focused on conflict as the Pre-Columbian era drew to a close.

Burnt Corn Pueblo

The empirical evidence for warfare discussed here is diverse and variably convincing. The overall picture may reveal the level of conflict differing with place and time, but patterns of data presented here have all been explained in ways that do not necessarily lead to war. The most compelling scenarios for warfare in the ancestral Pueblo world come when such evidence is tightly integrated, as in the example of Burnt Corn Pueblo.

Burnt Corn is a cluster of eight small structures and a 50-room plaza pueblo on a ridge in the western Galisteo Basin. It was established in the late 1200s and completely destroyed by fire sometime thereafter, probably no later than AD 1310 (Figure 51.1). Fieldwork at Burnt Corn and in the surrounding landscape, conducted over several years in the 2000s, has produced an interesting study of conflict 'on the ground' (Snead and Allen in press).

Figure 51.1 Views of Burnt Corn Pueblo in 2005: upper, pueblo in background (Petroglyph Hill in foreground); lower, adobe walls under excavation.

In addition to total destruction, other evidence from Burnt Corn points to something catastrophic taking place. The fire burned a considerable quantity of corn that had been drying on the roofs of the buildings, a considerable loss under any circumstances. The interiors of the rooms excavated, however, were quite clean, with minimal floor assemblages. No direct evidence for human casualties was found, although less than 5 percent of the estimated number of rooms at the site were examined. The implications are that the pueblo was "cleaned up" prior to demolition, although this does not appear to have minimized the severity of the incident, because once the pueblo burned the immediate vicinity was never put to use again, despite the presence of later field houses nearby.

The ridgetop location of Burnt Corn implies some concern with defensibility, and several contemporary farmstead-sized structures were closely clustered within eyesight of the pueblo itself. Beyond this range, there was little formal evidence for land use by the Burnt Corn population apart from shrine construction. Test excavations took place at two of the Burnt Corn farmsteads, one of which clearly burned. Additional excavations at a small site cluster 8 kilometers west, called the Lodestar Community, indicated that burning also terminated the late-13th-century occupation there. At the most substantively excavated structure, Lodestar North, broken vessels were found on the structure floor below the destruction layer.

The overall impression derived from Burnt Corn and vicinity in the early 14th century AD is of a perceived level of threat that culminated in widespread destruction. Whether or not this was "war," it certainly had dire implications for the population of these communities, who either dispersed or moved on to unknown destinations. Examination of data from other archaeological sites in the Galisteo Basin dating to the beginning of the 14th century—in particular, Manzanares, a large pueblo community in the eastern basin that is almost the precise contemporary of Burnt Corn—have identified evidence for destruction at these locations as well. Thus the picture, on multiple scales, is one of devastation, but not of homogeneity, since the "cleaned up" aspects of Burnt Corn pueblo were not universal. It is also interesting that subsequent inhabitants of the area, though they avoided Burnt Corn itself, were fairly well dispersed throughout the landscape, implying a very different perception of threat. What happened at Burnt Corn and in the neighborhood thus appears to be a product of very specific conditions and circumstances that will be better defined in future research.

Theoretical Significance

The empirical evidence from the northern Rio Grande between AD 1200 and 1550 presented here, along with the details of the Burnt Corn case study, suggest that warfare was a significant presence in ancestral Pueblo society during the period. In and of itself the assertion is significant; warfare has played only a small role in models of social processes in the region (for an exception, see Lekson 2002). Over the last 50 years, archaeologists have been concerned with environment and adaptation, explaining change through climatic trends, land-use practices, and labor strategies. People came together at various times to take advantage of the positive opportunities of collective action, and drifting apart when conditions were less optimal. It is now clear that such models, even if useful, have failed to evaluate the range of social factors that motivated human action. Conflict, in some cases leading to outright hostility and war, was as much a factor as cooperation, if not more so.

The current debate over warfare in the ancient Southwest emphasizes the ambiguity of empirical evidence as well as new looks at Pueblo ethnography; it has been argued that ritual practices in which buildings and even entire settlements could be "decommissioned" have been misinterpreted as signs of warfare. This discussion is an important sign of the increasing sophistication of our approaches. It can also, however, present a false choice, implying that ritual and warfare were distinct processes, and also that competitive conditions could be universally resolved by a set of social sanctions that may have involved violence but not war. There are, indeed, ways to envision culturally specific responses to competition in the Pueblo world (see Snead 2008b), but exclusion of warfare from these responses verges on denial.

Evidence from the archaeological record in the northern Rio Grande indicates that local people perceived the risk of conflict and in some cases suffered the brunt of its ultimate force. The Pueblo people who were met by Adolph Bandelier knew all about war (see Ellis 1955), and the archaeological record provides considerable reason to believe that this experience, in various forms, was of long duration. Our failure to include war and conflict in our efforts to understand ancestral Pueblo history looks increasingly like wishful thinking.

REFERENCES

Adams, E. C. 1991. *The Origin and Development of the Pueblo Katsina Cult*. University of Arizona Press, Tucson.

Alexander, R. K. 1971. LA 6869: The Wheeler Site. Laboratory of Anthropology Note 101, *Salvage Archaeology in the Galisteo Dam and Reservoir Area, New Mexico*, edited by D. W. Kayser and G. H. Ewing, pp. 34–94. Museum of New Mexico, Santa Fe, NM.

Allen, J. W. 1973. The Pueblo Alamo Project: Salvage at the Junction of U.S. 85 and U.S. 285 South of Santa Fe, New Mexico. *Museum of New Mexico, Research Section, Laboratory of Anthropology Notes* 86.

Bandelier, A. F. 1892. *Final Report of Investigations Among the Indians of the Southwestern United States, Carried on Mainly in the Years from 1880 to 1885*. Part 2. Papers of the Archaeological Institute of America, American Series, 4. J. Wilson and Son, Cambridge, MA.

Creamer, W. 1993. *The Architecture of Arroyo Hondo Pueblo, New Mexico*. School of American Research Press, Arroyo Hondo Archaeological Series 7. Santa Fe, NM.

Crown, P. L. 1994. *Ceramics and Ideology: Salado Polychrome Pottery*. University of New Mexico Press, Albuquerque.

Darling, J. A. 1999. Mass Inhumation and the Execution of Witches in the American Southwest. *American Anthropologist* 100:732–752.

Dongoske, K. E., D. L. Martin, and T. J. Ferguson. 2000. Critique of the Claim of Cannibalism at Cowboy Wash. *American Antiquity* 65:179–190.

Dutton, B. P. 1953. Galisteo Basin Again Scene of Archaeological Research. *El Palacio* 60(10):339–351.

Ellis, F. H. 1955. Patterns of Aggression and the War Cult in Southwestern Pueblos. *Southwestern Journal of Anthropology* 7(2):177–201.

Fowler, D. D. 2000. *A Laboratory for Anthropology: Science and Romanticism in the American Southwest, 1846–1930*. University of New Mexico Press, Albuquerque.

Fowles, S. M. 2004. *The Making of Made People: The Prehistoric Evolution of Hierocracy Among the Northern Tiwa of New Mexico*. Ph.D. dissertation, University of Michigan. University Microfilms, Ann Arbor, MI.

Haas, J., and W. Creamer. 1993. Stress and Warfare Among the Kayenta Anasazi of the Thirteenth Century A.D. *Fieldiana Anthropology*, n.s., no. 21.

———. 1997. Warfare Among the Pueblos: Myth, History, and Ethnology. *Ethnohistory* 44(2):235–261.

Hewett, E. L. 1909. The Excavations at Tyuonyi, New Mexico, in 1908. *American Anthropologist* 11(3):434–455.

Hibben, F. C. 1937. *Excavation of the Riana Ruin and Chama Valley Survey*. The University of New Mexico Bulletin, Anthropological Series, vol. 2, no. 1. University of New Mexico Press, Albuquerque.

Holden, J. 1955. A Preliminary Report on Arrowhead Ruin. *El Palacio* 62(4):102–119.

Keeley, L. H. 1996. *War Before Civilization*. Oxford University Press, New York.

Kidder, A. V. 1924. *An Introduction to the Study of Southwestern Archaeology*. Yale University Press, New Haven, CT.

———. 1958. *Pecos, New Mexico: Archaeological Notes*. Papers of the R. S. Peabody Foundation for Archaeology 5. Phillips Academy, the Foundation, Andover, MA.

Kuckelman, K. A. 2002. Thirteenth-Century Warfare in the Central Mesa Verde Region. In *Seeking the Center Place: Archaeology and Ancient Communities in the Mesa Verde Region*, edited by M. D. Varien and R. H. Wilshusen, pp. 233–253. University of Utah Press, Salt Lake City.

Lambert, P. M. 2002. The Archaeology of War: A North American Perspective. *Journal of Archaeological Research* 10(3):207–242.

Lang, R. W. 1977. *Archaeological Survey of the Upper San Cristobal Drainage, Galisteo Basin, Santa Fe County*. Unpublished manuscript on file, School of American Research, Santa Fe, NM.

LeBlanc, S. A. 1999. *Prehistoric Warfare in the American Southwest*. University of Utah Press, Salt Lake City.

Lekson, S. H. 2002. War in the Southwest, War in the World. *American Antiquity* 67(4):607–624.

Palkovich, A. M. 1980. *Pueblo Population and Society: The Arroyo Hondo Skeletal and Mortuary Remains*. Arroyo Hondo Archaeology Series 3. School of American Research Press, Santa Fe, NM.

Powers, R. P., and J. D. Orcutt. 1999. Summary and Conclusion. In Intermountain Cultural Resources Management, Professional Paper No. 57, *The Bandelier Archaeological Survey*, edited by R. P. Powers and J. D. Orcutt, pp. 551–589. Intermountain Region, National Park Service, Santa Fe, NM.

Preucel, R. W., Jr. 1990. *Seasonal Circulation and Dual Residence in the Pueblo Southwest: A Prehistoric Example from the Pajarito Plateau, New Mexico*. Garland, New York.

Redmond, E. 1994. *Tribal and Chiefly Warfare in South America*. Memoirs of the Museum of Anthropology of the University of Michigan 28. Ann Arbor.

Rice, G. E., and S. A. LeBlanc (editors). 2001. *Deadly Landscapes: Case Studies in Prehistoric Southwestern Warfare*. University of Utah Press, Salt Lake City.

Rohn, A. H. 1977. *Cultural Change and Continuity on Chapin Mesa*. Regents Press of Kansas, Lawrence.

Schaafsma, P. 1992. *Rock Art in New Mexico*. Museum of New Mexico Press, Santa Fe.

———. 2000. *Warrior, Shield and Star: Imagery and Ideology of Pueblo Warfare*. Western Edge Press, Santa Fe, NM.

Snead, J. E. 2008a. *Ancestral Landscapes of the Pueblo World*. University of Arizona Press, Tucson.

———. 2008b. War and Place: Landscapes of Conflict in Prehistory. *Journal of Conflict Archaeology* 4(1–2):147–158.

———, and M. W. Allen. In press. *Burnt Corn Pueblo: Conflict and Conflagration in the Galisteo Basin, AD 1250–1325*. Anthropological Papers of the University of Arizona.

Steen, C. R. 1980. LA 10607: The Manzanares Site. *Papers of the Archaeological Society of New Mexico 5, Collected Papers in Honor of Helen Greens Blumenschein*, edited by A. H. Schroeder, pp. 129–139. Albuquerque.

Turner, C. G., II, and J. A. Turner. 1999. *Man Corn: Cannibalism and Violence in the Prehistoric American Southwest*. University of Utah Press, Salt Lake City.

Welch, J. R., and T. W. Bostwick (editors). 2001. The Archaeology of Ancient Tactical Sites. *Arizona Archaeologist* 32.

Wendorf, F. 1953. Excavations at Te'ewi. Monographs of the School of American Research 17, *Salvage Archaeology in the Chama Valley, New Mexico*, assembled by F. Wendorf, pp. 34–93. Santa Fe, NM.

Wilcox, D. R., D. A. Gregory, J. B. Hill, and G. Funkhouser. 2006. The Changing Contexts of Warfare in the North American Southwest, A. D. 1200–1700. In The Archaeological Society of New Mexico 32, *Southwest Interludes: Papers in Honor of Charlotte J. and Theodore R. Frisbie*, edited by R. Wiseman, T. C. O'Laughlin, and C. Snow, pp. 203–232. Archaeological Society of New Mexico, Albuquerque.

Wilcox, D. R., and J. Haas. 1994. The Scream of the Butterfly: Competition and Conflict in the Prehistoric Southwest. In *Themes in Southwest Prehistory*, edited by G. J. Gumerman, pp. 211–238. School of American Research Press, Santa Fe.

Woodbury, R. 1959. A Reconsideration of Pueblo Warfare in the Southwestern United States. *Actas del XXXIII Congreso Internacional de Americanistas* 21:124–133. Editorial Lehmann, Costa Rica.

CHAPTER 52

THE PUEBLO VILLAGE IN AN AGE OF REFORMATION (AD 1300–1600)

SEVERIN FOWLES

IN his contribution to the present volume, Stephen Lekson reiterates what I take to be one of the most profound shifts in archaeological understandings of the Pueblo past. I am not referring to Lekson's interpretation of the Chaco Phenomenon per se, much though this regional system of the 11th and 12th centuries stands at the heart of a great many enduring debates within Southwestern archaeology. Rather, I am referring to the comments he makes—here almost in passing but elsewhere more vigorously (Lekson 2009; see also Kantner 2004:157–158)—regarding the post-Chaco period and the manner in which descendant Pueblo communities of the 13th and later centuries may have looked back on the undertakings of their ancestors in the San Juan basin. Consider this: Chaco, writes Lekson (this volume), "was an experiment in very 'un-Pueblo' urbanism, hierarchical government, and regional polity," an experiment that "ended badly" and "was ultimately rejected by Pueblo peoples."

This is a striking statement that demands unpacking. What does it mean to describe a period of Pueblo ancestry as "very un-Pueblo"? Clearly, the claim being made here is not simply that the Chaco Phenomenon was "pre-Pueblo," that it came before, and so cannot be fully equated with, the subsequent world of indigenous peoples known to us from colonial documents and 20th-century ethnographies. No, the claim is stronger than this, for it implies that what occurred in Chaco canyon— "urbanism, hierarchical government, and regional polity"—was somehow antithetical to the ethos of the contemporary Pueblos. In developing his position, Lekson echoes comments occasionally made by Pueblo individuals themselves. Rina Swentzell of Santa Clara Pueblo, for instance, writes of her first visit to Chaco this way:

> My response to the canyon was that some sensibility other than my Pueblo ancestors had worked on the Chaco great houses. There were the familiar elements ... but they were overlain by a strictness and precision of design and execution that was unfamiliar.... It was clear that the purpose of these great villages was not to restate their oneness with the earth but to show the power and specialness of humans. For me, they represented a desire to control [Swentzell 2004:50].

Chaco's un-Pueblo-ness, in this reading, springs from its apparently hubristic relationship to power, which would be quite out of place among the muted hierarchies and egalitarian ethos of the contemporary Pueblos. As an individual from Laguna Pueblo further suggested, Chacoan leaders of the 11th century, with "enormous amounts of power," appear to have been "causing changes that were never meant to happen" (as quoted in Lekson 2006:104). To call the Chaco Phenomenon "un-Puebloan," then, is to mark it as a historically situated period of transgression.

Needless to say, it is possible for some contemporary Pueblo individuals to call Chaco un-Puebloan only because they live in societies that have become "un-Chacoan" in certain key respects, begging the dual questions of when and how this change unfolded in the past. Hence, the second remarkable claim in Lekson's statement: that the pre-Columbian history of the northern Southwest is characterized not just by a gradual evolution of one era into another but by a widespread social movement involving conscious rejection of Chacoan organization—a dialectical swing, in other words, from hierarchical to egalitarian, from Chaco to anti-Chaco.

Archaeological theory has traditionally made little or no room for the possibility of this sort of historicized cultural rejection; nor has it offered meaningful commentary on why some premodern societies made the principled decision to walk away from hierarchy (but see Fowles 2002). Certainly there has been much discussion of archaeological sequences characterized by the "loss" of complexity, by "devolution," or by social "collapse" (Tainter 1988). Discussions of this sort have recently been extended to a popular audience through the writing of Jared Diamond (2005), who has specifically drawn on the end of Chaco as a key example of what he takes to be a human proclivity toward failed environmental adaptation. Critiques of Diamond's work, and of his interpretation of Chaco in particular, have been offered from within the discipline (McAnany and Yoffee 2009), but it remains the case that in their frequent use of the rhetoric of collapse archaeologists—no less than Diamond himself—implicitly stigmatize historical movements away from institutionalized inequality while at the same time valorizing elitism. (In discussing Chacoan "collapse," for instance, Tainter 1988:190 writes, "Chacoan society of the American Southwest may, like the Romans, have attempted too much of a good thing." It is this sense of Chaco as "a good thing" that is now being rethought.) What has been repeatedly missed is the special political and moral resonance of the term *rejection*.

Until about a decade ago, there were few alternatives within Southwest archaeology. Though not explicitly treating the post-Chaco period as a dark age, most did regard it as an evolutionary step backward. In the early 20th century, for instance, Roberts (1935:32) divided Pueblo prehistory into three grand periods: a pre-Chaco "Developmental Pueblo period" (AD 700–1000), a Chacoan "Great Pueblo period" (AD 1000–1300), and a post-Chaco "Regressive Pueblo period" (AD 1300–1700), the last of which denoted "the period in which there was a general recession from the preceding cultural peak" (also Kidder 1927:490). The terminology has since changed, of course, but the notion that a golden age of the Pueblos was over by the end of the 13th century has persisted.

In this sense, the recent shift in Southwestern discourse from "regression" to "rejection" is highly significant. Chaco has been recoded. Rather than a nostalgic golden age, Chaco is increasingly presented in darker terms as an oppressive and exploitative tradition, quasi-Mesoamerican in its approach to leadership, that was purposively abandoned (see Kantner 2004; Lekson 2009). And by extension, our image of post-Chaco communities is also being transformed. No longer a fallen people, they are beginning to look more like the product of a widespread populist revolt. Whether or not one agrees with this new reading of Pueblo prehistory (and there are many who do not), it is important to acknowledge what is at stake in the debate: namely, the most significant challenge to 19th-century notions of progress that Southwestern archaeologists have yet to produce.

In the remainder of the essay, I briefly summarize key developments in the post-Chaco archaeology of what is commonly referred to as the Pueblo IV period (AD 1300–1600) in the northern Southwest. My aim in this selective review is not to endorse a model of rejection over regression per se (sympathetic though I am to the former), but instead to offer up for consideration a third potentially unifying theme: reformation. The Pueblo IV period, I suggest, is best understood as an *age of reformation*, characterized by both a widespread social critique of the prior "theocratic" order of the Chacoan world as well as the institution of a reactionary and more aggressively egalitarian culture in which (1) the privileges of leadership were downplayed, (2) social uniformity and collectivism were emphasized, and (3) access to the spirits was, if not democratized, then at least drawn into communal experience far more than in the prior era. Herein lies the great relevance of the Pueblo IV period to anthropology generally, for in it we find what may be the best-documented countercultural tradition in world prehistory.

Politics in the Wake of the 13th Century

To speak of a Pueblo reformation implies much about what in fact was being reformed. For want of space, I must rely on Lekson's chapter in this volume as well as the large supporting literature making the case for a relatively high level of elitism during the Chacoan era (Kantner 2004; Lekson 2009; but see Mills, this volume). This was a period of time—locally referred to as the Pueblo II period (AD 900–1150)—when the northern Southwest appears to have been divided between a population of "commoners" living in modest vernacular roomblocks of 10–15 rooms and a smaller population of better-fed individuals who dwelt in much more formal multistory Great Houses and exerted a significant degree of influence over long-distance trade. The height of Chaco Canyon's regional presence was during the 11th and early 12th centuries, after which the center of gravity shifted north to the northern San Juan basin, where the Chaco tradition, broadly conceived, reorganized and continued in some form (though with increasing difficulty) into the early Pueblo III period (AD 1150–1300; Lekson and Cameron 1995; Van Dyke 2009).

The end of the 13th century properly marks the beginning of the period that concerns me here. Much has been written on the challenges confronted by ancestral Pueblo communities, during what Lipe (1995) refers to as the "turbulent 1200s." Intensification of intervillage violence is clearly apparent in the many burned structures, unburied bodies, and skeletal indications of traumatic death (see Snead, this volume). At Castle Rock Pueblo in southwest Colorado, for instance, 41 victims of coordinated violence were found beneath charred architectural remains (Kuckelman et al. 2002), and similarly sobering archaeological contexts dating to the 13th century have been encountered in many other parts of the northern Southwest (LeBlanc 1999). Such incidents undoubtedly were but one part of a broader era of political transformation linked to the end of the Chacoan tradition, and this appears to have been motivation enough for thousands of individuals to emigrate out of the Four Corners region. During the final quarter of the 13th century, a period of extended drought complicated matters further, although recent modeling suggests that agricultural potential was never so severely reduced as to be the sole cause of regional abandonment (Varien et al. 2007). Regardless, by AD 1325 the former nexus of the Pueblo world was strikingly empty (Figure 52.1).

Within Southwestern archaeology, it is traditional to discuss migration as a cultural process driven by "pushes" and "pulls" (e.g., Cameron 1993). In the case of the large-scale migrations of the 13th century, for instance, it is assumed that drought and endemic social instability in the Four Corners region pushed, while the low population density and well-watered river valleys of the neighboring Rio Grande region pulled. Such language, however, obscures a deeper reading of migration as a political act. As numerous incidents during the early colonial era demonstrate, Pueblo dissidence, particularly prior to the reservation system, was typically expressed through movement away from an area of conflict, which is to say that the Pueblos participated in the age-old strategy of voting with one's feet that prevailed in most parts of the world prior to the nation-state and the systematic commodification of land. The Spanish repeatedly encountered newly abandoned villages, particularly along the Rio Grande where groups dodged the colonial yoke by migrating west to the Hopi mesas or east to join the Apache on the Plains. Similar strategies were employed when internal conflict arose. Indigenous factionalism, for instance, appears to have prompted nearly constant streams of emigration as well as the occasional abandonment of whole villages (Schroeder 1968). Indeed, Pueblo oral history is replete with accounts of past villages that grew corrupt and had to be purified

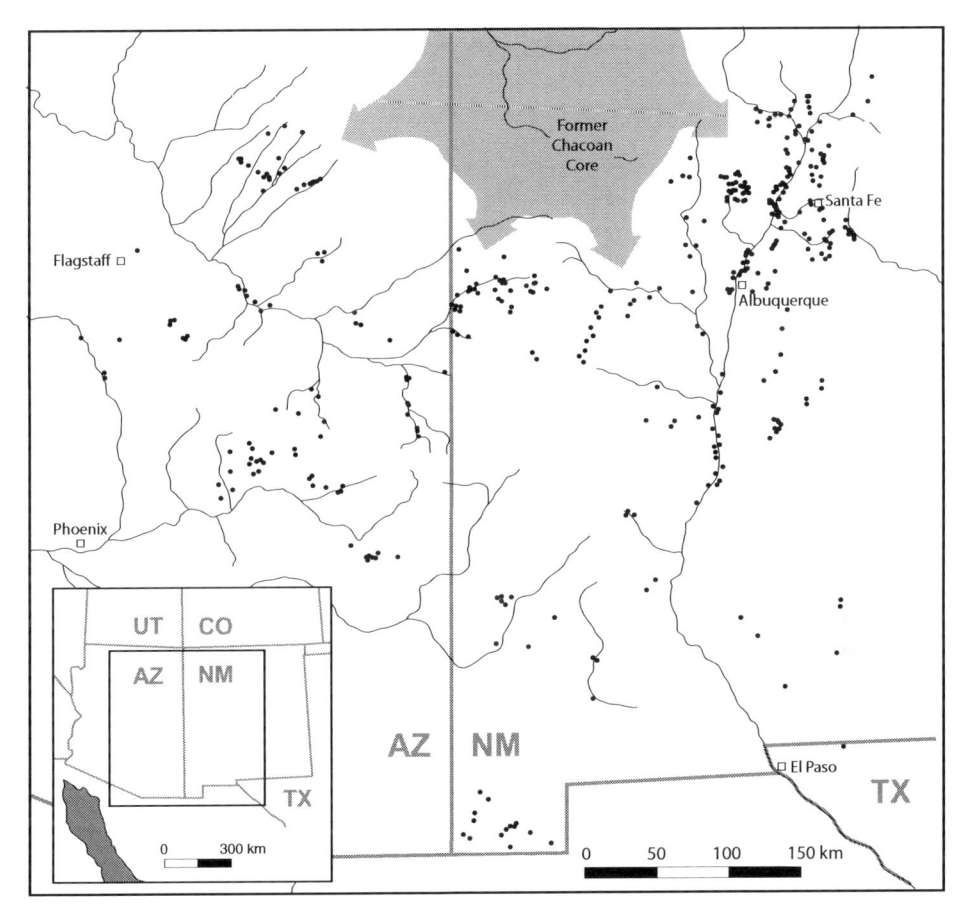

Figure 52.1 Map of the American Southwest showing Pueblo IV village sites having more than 50 rooms (after Adams and Duff 2004:figure 1.1).

through destruction and a collective movement away (Courlander 1971; Whiteley 1988). During the pre-reservation period, then, migration was less a response to external pushes and pulls than it was a species of Pueblo ethics, social critique, and political practice (Fowles 2010, 2011). The abandonment of Chaco Canyon in the 12th century and much of the greater sphere of former Chacoan influence at the close of the 13th century must be read in this light.

The point becomes clearer when we look to the postmigration villages themselves. A great deal of research has been devoted to tracing migration pathways following abandonment of the Four Corners region, and even though many details remain obscure there is little doubt that a significant percentage of the formerly Chacoan population relocated to the Rio Grande valley, the Zuni area, and the Hopi mesas—those regions, in other words, that continue to be the centers of Pueblo occupation today. Interactions between autochthonous and immigrant groups undoubtedly varied (Bernardini and Fowles 2010; Duff 1998). Nevertheless, the new villages established across the northern Southwest during the 14th and 15th centuries came to be characterized by a common settlement logic: nearly all were aggregated architectural masses with hundreds of rooms delimiting large enclosed or semienclosed plazas that were outfitted with a limited number of ritual facilities or kivas (Figure 52.2).

When the Pueblo IV village is compared with the Chacoan great house of old, the differences are striking. Whereas great houses were often built with excessive formality, employing fine masonry, iconic architectural details, and a greater number of roofing beams than were necessary, Pueblo IV villages employed far humbler and less expensive architectural styles. More important, the Pueblo IV village was truly a collectivist facility, designed to house the masses on a daily basis in uniformly modest domestic spaces that were largely indistinguishable one from the other. In contrast, the Chacoan great house—even if its doors were periodically opened to pilgrims—was the special residence of a small subset of the population. Perhaps Lekson (2006) goes too far when he refers to them as "palaces," but if we accept that there is a sense in which some great houses were at least palacelike, then we should also acknowledge that the villages built in the wake of the Chacoan era leaned in the direction of communes or kibbutzim.

Many Southwestern archaeologists, of course, would disagree with the last statement. For 30 years the relative level of hierarchical organization has been the most contentious Pueblo IV issue (for reviews see Cordell 1999; McGuire and Saitta 1996; Plog 1995). Here is not the place to revisit in detail the many arguments offered by those who see command-and-obey elites at the helm of 14th- and 15th-century communities. Suffice it to say that such arguments traditionally rely on the following evidence: (1) the impressive scale of Pueblo IV villages, which by the 15th century averaged well over 500 ground floor rooms; (2) clustering of villages into loose-knit regional polities or confederacies with thousands of individuals (Adams and Duff 2004); (3) architectural indications of defensive concerns (LeBlanc 1999) and increased regional trade, both of which would have required a relatively high level of group coordination; (4) evidence of increased feasting activity (Graves and Spielmann 2000; Potter 2000); and (5) ethnographic reports from descendant communities of hierarchical relations vis-à-vis access to rituals, sacred objects, and esoteric knowledge as well as the status that accompanies them (Potter and Perry 2000).

All but the last are circumstantial, and even the religious hierarchies recorded by ethnographers may be interpreted in very different ways. Pueblo priests certainly stood in positions of great respect and high status, for instance, but their lives were not ones of material privilege; nor did they have much coercive power over others. On the contrary, it was the priestly "elite" who, within indigenous ideologies, undertook the most taxing labor for the benefit of the community at large (Fowles 2010, 2012). Writing of Zuñi, Bunzel observed:

> The priesthoods are the branch of religious service that carries the greatest prestige and heaviest responsibilities. Because of the heavy responsibilities the office is avoided rather than sought, and considerable difficulty is experienced in recruiting the priesthoods. As one informant said, "They have to catch the men young to make them priests. For if they are old enough to realize all that is required of them, they will refuse" [Bunzel 1932:542].

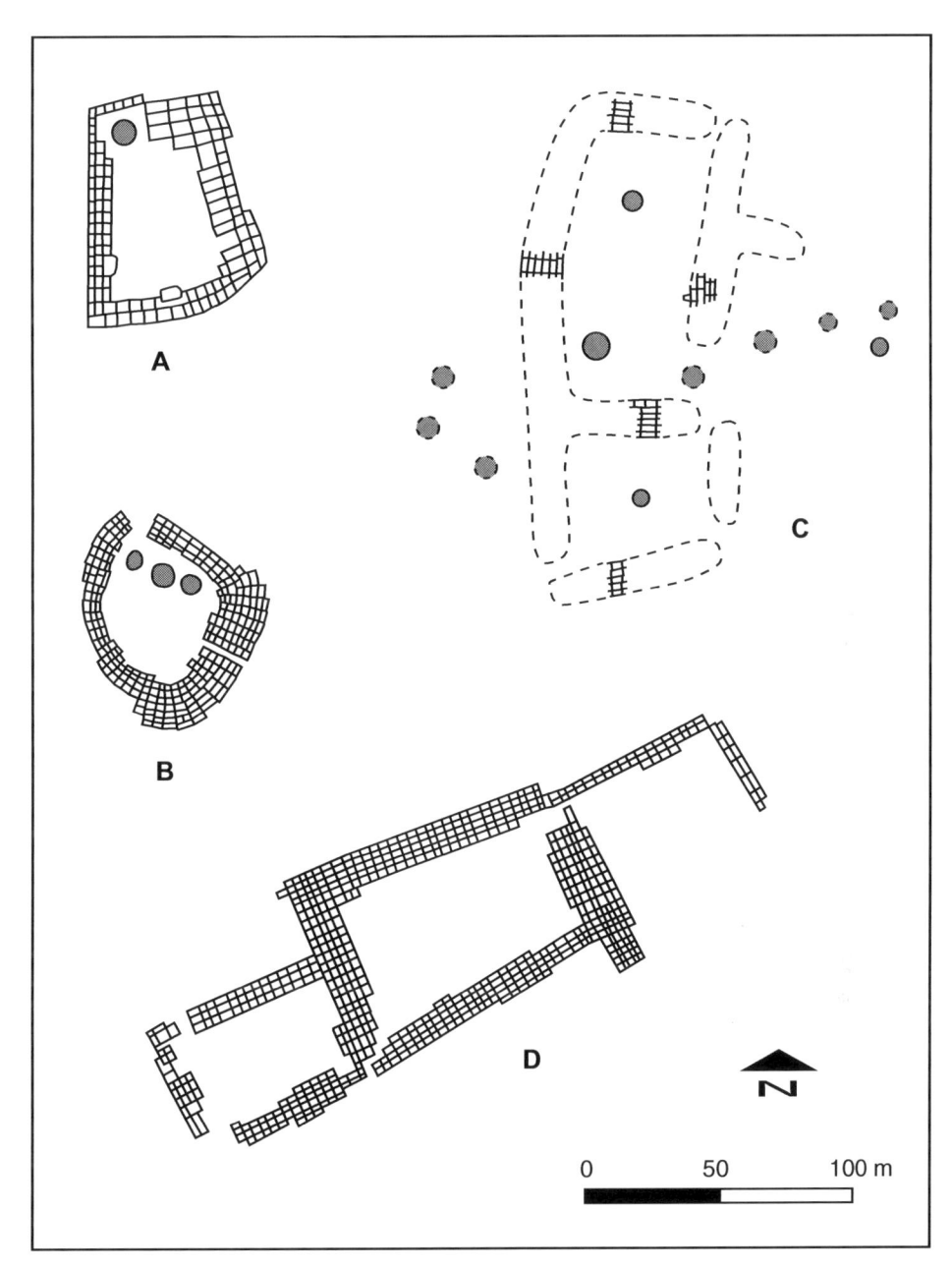

Figure 52.2 Examples of Pueblo IV villages from across the Southwest: A = Awatovi, B = Tyuonyi (LA 82), C = Te'ewi, D = Homol'ovi II (after Morgan 1994; Snead et al. 2004:figure 3.7; Wendorf 1953; and Adams 1991:figure 8.2, respectively).

If we are to refer to the ethnographic Pueblos as "hierarchical" or "stratified," then we must also acknowledge that the Pueblo conceptions of "hierarchy" and "stratification" are very different from those put forward in Western political discourse. The same can be said of Pueblo "elites" (for whom the old Mel Brooks line "It's good to be the king" would simply have had little or no traditional referent). There is a complicated question of cultural translation here that is too easily bypassed by those seeking to make the Pueblos appear "complex" in orthodox evolutionary terms.

Regardless, archaeological models of the internal structure of Pueblo IV villages have been strongly influenced by late-19th- and early-20th-century ethnographies, much to the dismay of those who bemoan the supposed "tyranny of the ethnographic record" in Southwest archaeology and stress the incompatibility of models drawn from recent Pueblo sociopolitical organizations that have been variously altered by the epidemics, violence, and colonial reorganization of the historic period. Such scholars claim that prior to the population decline of the 17th and 18th centuries, and especially prior to colonial efforts to ban warfare and curtail the power of indigenous leaders, far more stratified societies would have characterized the region (e.g., Lightfoot and Upham 1989; Wilcox 1981).

Although acknowledging the major social changes of the past five centuries, most Southwest archaeologists nevertheless find these arguments forced, rightly observing that—by the archaeological standards used elsewhere in the world—the late pre-Columbian period still exhibits remarkably little evidence of elitism. Settlement patterns do not support the conclusion that one village ever truly controlled any other village; craft specialization, even if present in many areas, does not appear to have been centrally managed; domestic spaces within villages were radically uniform and universally modest (nothing even close to an elite residence has been identified from the Pueblo IV period); and in those cases where individuals were buried with special ritual objects, there is little evidence that these presumed leaders had privileged access to food or other nonritual resources (see Spielmann 1994 for a review). In short, the archaeological record testifies that those inequalities that did exist were muted in their overt material expression. Bearing in mind, therefore, that "egalitarianism" is first and foremost an ideology—an ethos or asserted principle that need not be accompanied by a high level of on-the-ground social equality—there are indeed grounds for continued inquiry into the foundations and internal logic of the Pueblo IV "egalitarian tradition."

Perhaps the more important point, however, is that whether one refers to Pueblo IV society as egalitarian, heterarchical, corporate, ritually stratified, anarchist, or something else, it was *not* a "pristine" egalitarian (or heterarchical, or corporate, etc.) society. Far from it. Pueblo IV society must be understood as standing within history, as a widespread social response not only to changing environmental conditions (the standard *deus ex machina* causal variable in the Southwest) but also to the more overtly hierarchical and centralized societies that preceded it.

Spiritual Renaissance

Two great debates drive the study of Pueblo IV period villages. The first, touched on above, surrounds the question of political organization: archaeologists in the region want to know how "complex" communities were and what sort of power their leaders wielded. The second focuses on Pueblo IV ritual practice, specifically on the issue of how we are to understand the abundant iconographic and architectural evidence for a shift in Pueblo ceremonialism during the 14th century. To a certain extent, the former dominated research in the 1980s whereas the latter dominated research in the 1990s.[1] Needless to say, each implicates the other, and both continue to drive new work.

Published just as prehistoric religion was emerging as a major subject of inquiry within archaeology generally, Adams's landmark study (1991) into the origin and development of katsina ritual was well poised to have significant impact on Pueblo IV studies, as indeed it has. The katsina are powerful spirits within the Pueblo world who act as intermediaries between humans and the higher deities and so are the focus of much ritual, notably including dramatic masked dances open to the entire community. Anthropologists in the Southwest had debated the history and temporal depth of katsina ceremonialism since the 1930s, but it was not until Adams's research that ethnographic and archaeological evidence was drawn together into a coherent model of the tradition's Pueblo IV origins.

Adams's model is solidly functionalist. Katsina ritual, he suggests, spread across the northern Southwest during the 14th century as a means of integrating diverse communities of immigrants and autochthons in the aftermath of late-13th-century population dislocations and environmental hardship. The social work performed by katsina ritual, according to Adams, was impressive. Strong iconographic elements such as masks, stepped clouds, and lightning would have made the esoteric aspects of katsina belief widely accessible, establishing a common ritual idiom for multicultural and linguistically diverse postmigration communities. Villagewide katsina dramas would have enhanced group solidarity further, but more tangibly they would have also redistributed food, disciplined transgressors, and established codes of proper behavior. Moreover, universal participation in katsina societies (again, according to Adams) would have had important structural implications, cross-cutting kin groups and providing a rationale for consensus building and collective action.

That a new ritual order was established during the 14th century is undisputed. Whereas prior villages contained many small kivas, each presumably serving the ritual needs of an individual kin group, Pueblo IV villages contained fewer but more centrally located kivas that presumably served the community as a whole. Part and parcel of this shift toward a more collective pattern was the eventual disappearance of "great kivas"—formerly the key venue for large-scale ritual events—and their replacement by large enclosed plazas, which Adams (1991) has convincingly argued must be regarded as giant ceremonial structures designed as much for community-wide ritual as for village defense. Add to this a simultaneous shift from more abstract to highly iconic imagery in rock art, ceramics, and kiva murals, as well as increasingly elaborate networks of village shrines (Duwe 2011, Fowles 2009), and one indeed confronts what Ware and Blinman (2000:400) refer to as an "eruption of ritual organizational novelty," a dramatic new approach to materializing and hence accessing the spirit world.

Aspects of Adams's model have been both expanded and critiqued. Some emphasize that katsina were but one part—and in some regions a relatively small part—of a much larger set of beliefs and ritual sodalities spreading throughout the Pueblo IV Southwest (Crown 1994; Ware and Blinman 2000). Others draw attention to the connections between early katsina iconography and warfare, suggesting that katsina ritual may have been a vehicle for expression of disunity and competition no less than ecological fertility and social harmony (Plog and Solometo 1997). Still others argue that democratization of certain public rituals during the Pueblo IV period went hand-in-hand with development of other, more secretive rituals controlled by exclusive priesthoods (Potter and Perry 2000). Needless to say, there are many details for regional specialists to debate.

But let us not lose sight of the historicity of Pueblo IV ritual and the broader, evolutionary quandary it presents. How are we to understand the 14th-century shift not only toward aggregated villages but also toward an unprecedented intensity of ritual practice and iconography within the residential core of the community? And how are we to understand the apparent fact that this shift was embedded within a larger trajectory *away* from the "complexity" of the Chacoan era?

The orthodox answer to these questions used to go something like this: Chaco was an experiment in centralized leadership and labor extraction that proved ecologically unsustainable in the marginal Southwestern landscape. Environmental stress during the 12th and 13th centuries exposed this unsustainability, prompted Chacoan collapse, and led to a sharp increase in competition, violence, and widespread population dislocations. Ultimately, from the ashes arose the aggregated Pueblo IV village, which may have been gathered together for purposes of defense or to benefit from various economies of scale but was *held* together by a vibrant new set of ritual practices that largely obviated the need for a strong managerial elite. Distilled further, one could say that Pueblo prehistory, in this reading, came to look like a failed progression toward institutionalized inequality that was stymied by a marginal environment and was forced to seek an evolutionary compromise: religion as a "functional alternative to political power" (borrowing from Rappaport 1971:72).

I want to take for granted the many criticisms that might be—and, to a certain extent, have been—leveled against the environmental determinism, functionalism, and Enlightenment notions of progress tangled up in this account. The more damning indictment, I think, is the profound lack of fit with the Pueblos' own understanding of their past. Here is not the place to inquire into the nature of Pueblo historical consciousness, much though an inquiry of this sort is desperately needed (but see Ortman 2010). Suffice to it say that the Pueblos have their own grand narratives, many of which describe a hubristic past world of political and spiritual transgression that was corrected through establishment of new communities committed to social, ecological, and ritual balance. In a sense, where Western discourse tends to valorize complexity, Pueblo discourse valorizes a kind of social simplicity (Fowles 2010). And where Western archaeologists may read Pueblo religion in adaptationist terms as a functional alternative to political power, the Pueblos seem to regard their religious organization—with its communal rituals and prestigious but self-sacrificing priestly leaders—in historical terms as a *political* alternative to coercive and dangerously self-serving power. One might say, then, that the Pueblo IV village was the outgrowth not of cultural collapse but of a difficult era of religiopolitical reformation (or as Ortman 2010 puts it in his account of Tewa ethnogenesis, of "religious revolution").

Conclusion

In what is now a classic essay on egalitarianism, J. Woodburn (1982:431) began with the observation that "egalitarian," as a political notion, "carries with it echoes of revolution, of fervour for equality in opposition to elaborate structures of inequality." It is worth bearing in mind that the term references not only small-scale hunter-gatherers but also 18th-century French intellectuals and utopianists seeking to overcome hierarchy and violently uproot the *ancien régime*. Egalitarianism, in other words, need be neither "primitive" (i.e., evolutionarily prior to hierarchy and coercive power) nor peaceful; in fact, some political anthropologists have argued that it is more often just the opposite (Clastres 1989).

Archaeologists in the American Southwest have recently come to appreciate this fact. If three decades of inquiry into the "complexity" of Pueblo IV villages failed to produce widely satisfactory conclusions, this is perhaps because the issue will be meaningfully understood only once (1) Pueblo IV societies have been placed in their historical position and (2) Pueblo IV social agents have been granted a historical consciousness to guide their actions (see also Van Dyke 2009). This does not mean adopting a so-called direct historical approach in which one works backwards from the ethnographic present across the impacts of colonialism to reconstruct a pre-Columbian pattern. On the contrary, it means tracking Pueblo history *forward*, acknowledging at each step of the way that Pueblo communities were also tracking and responding to their history—not just in origin stories but in their political convictions as well.

Note

1. Stimulated by the impact of NAGPRA legislation, Pueblo IV research during the first decade of the 21st century has been dominated by questions of migration, identity, heritage, memory, ethnogenesis, and the relationship between archaeology and oral history (see Mills 2004). To its credit, perhaps, this work has been far less polemical and hence has not yet led to the sort of strong debate seen in previous decades.

REFERENCES

Adams, E. C. 1991. *The Origin and Development of the Pueblo Katsina Cult*. University of Arizona Press, Tucson.

———, and A. I. Duff. 2004. Settlement Clusters and the Pueblo IV Period. In *The Protohistoric Pueblo World, A.D. 1275–1600*, edited by E. C. Adams and A. I. Duff, pp. 3–16. University of Arizona Press, Tucson.

Bernardini, W., and S. Fowles. 2010. Becoming Hopi, Becoming Tiwa: Two Pueblo Histories of Movement. In *Changing Histories, Landscapes, and Perspectives: The 20th Anniversary Southwest Symposium*, edited by P. Nelson and C. Strawhacker. University of Colorado Press, Denver.

Bunzel, R. L. 1932. Introduction to Zuñi Ceremonialism. *Forty-Seventh Annual Report of the Bureau of American Ethnology 1929–1930*, pp. 467–544.

Cameron, C. M. 1993. Abandonment and Archaeological Interpretation. In *Abandonment of Settlements and Regions*, edited by C. M. Cameron and S. A. Tomka, pp. 3–7. Cambridge University Press, New York.

Clastres, P. 1989. *Society Against the State*. Zone Books, New York.

Cordell, L. 1999. How Were Precolumbian Southwestern Polities Organized? In *Great Towns and Regional Polities in the Prehistoric American Southwest and Southeast*, edited by J. E. Neitzel, pp. 81–94. Amerind Foundation, Dragoon, AZ.

Courlander, H. 1971. The Destruction of Palatkwapi. In *The Fourth World of the Hopis*, pp. 56–71. Crown Publishers, New York.

Crown, P. L. 1994. *Ceramics and Ideology: Salado Polychrome Pottery*. University of New Mexico Press, Albuquerque.

Diamond, J. 2005. *Collapse: How Societies Choose to Fail or Succeed*. Viking Press, New York.

Duff, A. 1998. The Process of Migration in the Late Prehistoric Southwest. Anthropological Research Papers 51, *Migration and Reorganization: The Pueblo IV Period in the American Southwest*, edited by K. Spielmann, pp. 31–52. Arizona State University, Tempe.

Duwe, S. 2011. *The Prehispanic Tewa World: Space, Time, and Becoming in the Pueblo Southwest*. Unpublished Ph.D. dissertation, University of Arizona, Tucson.

Fowles, S. 2002. Inequality and Egalitarian Rebellion: A Dialectic in Tonga History. In *The Archaeology of Tribal Society*, edited by W. Parkinson, pp. 74–96. International Monographs in Prehistory, Ann Arbor.

———. 2009. The Enshrined Pueblo: Villagescape and Cosmos in the Northern Rio Grande. *American Antiquity* 74(3):448–466.

———. 2010. A People's History of the American Southwest. In *Ancient Complexities: New Perspectives in Pre-Columbian North America*, edited by S. M. Alt. University of Utah Press, Provo.

———. 2011. Movement and the Unsettling of the Pueblos. In *Rethinking Anthropological Perspectives on Migration*, edited by G. Cabana and J. Clark. University of Florida Press, Gainesville.

———. 2012. On Torture in Societies Against the State. In *Violence and Civilization*, edited by R. Campbell. Joukowsky Institute, Brown University, Providence, RI.

Graves, W. M., and K. A. Spielmann. 2000. Leadership, Long-Distance Exchange, and Feasting in the Protohistoric Rio Grande. In *Alternative Leadership Strategies in the Prehispanic Southwest*, edited by B. J. Mills, pp. 45–59. University of Arizona Press, Tucson.

Kantner, J. 2004. *Ancient Puebloan Southwest*. Cambridge University Press, New York.

Kidder, A. V. 1927. Southwestern Archaeological Conference. *Science* 66(17):489–491.

Kuckelman, K. A., R. R. Lightfoot, and D. L. Martin. 2002. The Bioarchaeology and Taphonomy of Violence at Castle Rock and Sand Canyon Pueblos, Southwestern Colorado. *American Antiquity* 67(3):486–513.

LeBlanc, S. A. 1999. *Prehistoric Warfare in the American Southwest*. University of Utah Press, Salt Lake City.

Lekson, S. H. 2006. Lords of the Great House: Pueblo Bonito as a Palace. In *Palaces and Power in the Americas: From Peru to the Northwest Coast*, edited by J. J. Christie and P. J. Sarro, pp. 99–114. University of Texas Press, Austin.

———. 2009. *A History of the Ancient Southwest*. School for Advanced Research Press, Santa Fe, NM.

———, and C. M. Cameron. 1995. The Abandonment of Chaco Canyon, the Mesa Verde Migrations, and the Reorganization of the Pueblo World. *Journal of Anthropological Archaeology* 14:184–202.

Lightfoot, K. G., and S. Upham. 1989. Complex Societies in the Prehistoric American Southwest: A Consideration of the Controversy. In *The Sociopolitical Structure of Prehistoric Southwestern Societies*, edited by S. Upham, K. G. Lightfoot, and R. A. Jewett, pp. 3–32. Westview Press, Boulder, CO.

Lipe, W. D. 1995. The Depopulation of the Northern San Juan: Conditions in the Turbulent 1200s. *Journal of Anthropological Archaeology* 14:143–169.

McAnany, P. A., and N. Yoffee (editors). 2009. *Questioning Collapse: Human Resilience, Ecological Vulnerability, and the Aftermath of Empire*. Cambridge University Press, New York.

McGuire, R. H., and D. J. Saitta. 1996. Although They Have Petty Captains, They Obey Them Badly: The Dialectics of Prehispanic Western Pueblo Social Organization. *American Antiquity* 61:197–216.

Mills, B. J. (editor). 2004. *Identity, Feasting, and the Archaeology of the Greater Southwest*. University Press of Colorado, Boulder.

Morgan, W. N. 1994. *Ancient Architecture of the Southwest*. University of Texas Press, Austin.

Ortman, S. G. 2010. Genes, Language and Culture in Tewa Ethnogenesis, A.D. 1150–1400. Unpublished Ph.D. dissertation, Arizona State University, Tempe.

Plog, S. 1995. Equality and Hierarchy: Holistic Approaches to Understanding Social Dynamics in the Pueblo Southwest. In *Foundations of Social Inequality*, edited by T. D. Price and G. M. Feinman, pp. 189–206. Plenum Press, New York.

———, and J. Solometo. 1997. The Never-Changing and the Ever-Changing: The Evolution of Western Pueblo Ritual. *Cambridge Archaeological Journal* 7(2):161–182.

Potter, J. M. 2000. Pots, Parties, and Politics: Communal Feasting in the American Southwest. *American Antiquity* 65:471–492.

———, and E. M. Perry. 2000. Ritual as a Power Resource in the American Southwest. In *Alternative Leadership Strategies in the Prehispanic Southwest*, edited by B. J. Mills, pp. 60–78. University of Arizona Press, Tucson.

Rappaport, R. 1971. Ritual, Sanctity, and Cybernetics. *American Anthropologist* 73:59–76.

Roberts, F. H. H. 1935. A Survey of Southwestern Archaeology. *American Anthropologist* 37(1):1–35.

Schroeder, A. 1968. Shifting for Survival in the Spanish Southwest. *New Mexico Historical Review* 43:291–310.

Snead, J. E, W. Creamer, and T. Van Zandt. 2004. "Ruins of Our Forefathers": Large Sites and Site Clusters in the Northern Rio Grande. In *The Protohistoric Pueblo World, A. D. 1275–1600*, edited by E. C. Adams and A. I. Duff, pp. 26–34. University of Arizona Press, Tucson.

Spielmann, K. 1994. Clustered Confederacies: Sociopolitical Organization in the Protohistoric Rio Grande. In *The Ancient Southwest Community*, edited by W. H. Wills and R. D. Leonard, pp. 45–54. University of New Mexico Press, Albuquerque.

Swentzell, R. 2004. A Pueblo Woman's Perspective on Chaco Canyon. In *In Search of Chaco: New Approaches to an Archaeological Enigma*, edited by D. G. Noble, pp. 48–53. School of American Research, Santa Fe, NM.

Tainter, J. 1988. *The Collapse of Complex Societies*. Cambridge University Press, Cambridge, UK.

Van Dyke, R. M. 2009. Chaco Reloaded. *Journal of Social Archaeology* 9(2):220–248.

Varien, M. D., S. G. Ortman, T. A. Kohler, D. M. Glowacki, and C. D. Johnson. 2007. Historical Ecology in the Mesa Verde Region: Results from the Village Ecodynamics Project. *American Antiquity* 72(2):273–299.

Ware, J. A., and E. Blinman. 2000. Cultural Collapse and Reorganization: The Origin and Spread of Pueblo Ritual Sodalities. In *The Archaeology of Regional Interaction*, edited by M. Hegmon, pp. 381–409. University Press of Colorado, Boulder.

Wendorf, F. 1953. *Salvage Archaeology in the Chama Valley, New Mexico*. Monograph of the School of American Research 17. Santa Fe, NM.

Whiteley, P. 1988. *Deliberate Acts*. University of Arizona Press, Tucson.

Wilcox, D. R. 1981. Changing Perspectives on the Protohistoric Pueblos, A.D. 1450–1700. In *The Protohistoric Period in the North American Southwest, A.D. 1450–1700*, edited by D. R. Wilcox, pp. 378–409. Arizona State University Anthropological Research Paper 24. Tempe. AZ.

Woodburn, J. 1982. Egalitarian Societies. *Man.* 17(3):431–451.

CHAPTER 53

CASAS GRANDES PHENOMENON

CHRISTINE S. VANPOOL
AND TODD L. VANPOOL

BETWEEN AD 1200 and 1450, the Casas Grandes Phenomenon—a distinctive political and religious system—swept across northwestern Mexico, southeastern Arizona, southern New Mexico, and westernmost Texas (Figure 53.1). The hallmark of this phenomenon is its symbolic system, dominated by horned serpent and macaw imagery that is reflected on polychrome pottery and rock art and in architecture. Southwestern archaeologists generally agree that the Casas Grandes phenomenon reflects one of the most socially complex pre-Columbian cultural systems in the North American Southwest. The area is dominated by pueblolike communities built on river flood plains (Phillips 1989:382–383), but the defining characteristics are best illustrated at Paquimé (formally called Casas Grandes), the economic and political heart of the system (Bradley 2000; Di Peso 1974; Whalen and Minnis 2009).

PAQUIMÉ AS A REGIONAL CAPITAL

Situated on the west bank of the Río Casas Grandes in the modern town limits of Casas Grandes, Chihuahua, Mexico, Paquimé was excavated by C. Di Peso and E. Contreras in the 1950s as part of the Joint Casas Grandes Expedition (Di Peso 1974; Minnis and Whalen 2004). Multiple ceremonial platforms and I-shaped ball courts emphasized Paquimé's prominence and its social connections with

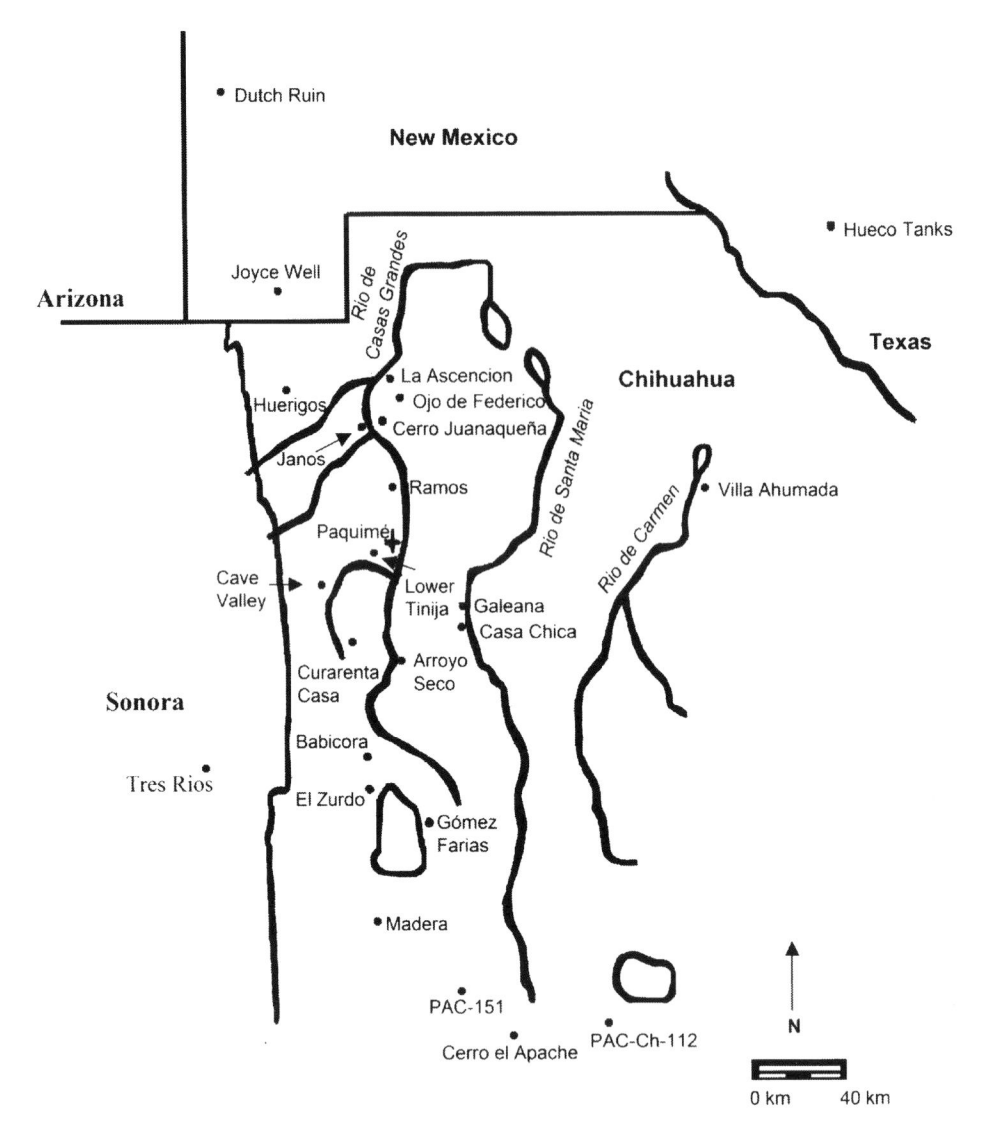

Figure 53.1 Map of the Casas Grandes region.

Mesoamerican people. Only about half the settlement was excavated, but it produced a greater number and variety of copper artifacts and ocean shell than any other settlement in the North American Southwest. Paquimé also had massive, overbuilt architecture; a planned layout; canals that funneled water through the city; three large reservoirs; a deep walk-in well; and store rooms that held utilitarian goods such as metates and exotica that included literally tons of ocean shell (Di Peso 1974). It had 576 deliberate human burials containing a range of burial goods attesting to substantial social differentiation (Rakita 2009; Ravesloot 1988). The settlement's inhabitants also raised, sacrificed, and ritually buried more than 300 scarlet macaws, which were typically killed by breaking the neck, and more than 500 turkeys, which were typically decapitated (Di Peso et al. 1974 vol. 8:289). There is no evidence that these birds were eaten.

Paquimé must have been seen and heard from miles around, thanks to birds squawking, craftsmen making goods, children playing, and the general hustle and bustle of urban life. Even after it was abandoned, Paquimé was still imposing. It was one of the first ruins in the North American Southwest noticed by Spanish explorers, perhaps as early as General Francisco de Ibarra's 1564–1565 exploration of Chihuahua. Baltazar de Obregón reported in 1584:

> This great city . . . contains buildings that seem to have been built by the ancient Romans. The view is magnificent. . . . There are many houses of great size, strength, and height. These houses are six or seven stories high, with towers and walls, which strengthen for protection and defense against its enemies, which without a doubt, tended to be at war with its inhabitants. The houses contain large and magnificent patios paved with enormous, beautiful stones. There are hand carved stones that supported the magnificent pillars made of heavy trunks brought from far away. The walls of the houses are stuccoed and painted in many shades and colors [quoted in Gamboa 2002:41].

Even after hundreds of years of additional weathering, looting, and excavation, Paquimé remains impressive. In 1998, the site was dedicated as a UNESCO World Heritage site.

During the 1300s, other large sites (albeit not as large as Paquimé) were built along major rivers, and smaller villages were built in various topographic settings from flood plains to cliff and rock shelters high in the Sierra Madre Occidental (Bagwell 2006; Cruz Antillón et al. 2004; Gamboa 2002; Kelley et al. 1999; MacWilliams 2001a, 2001b; Phillips 1989; Schaafsma and Riley 1999; Whalen and Minnis 2001). Casas Grandes polychromes with elaborate symbols, ball courts, and other architectural features indicate that these towns interacted with one another at some level (Whalen and Minnis 2001, 2009). Settlements near Paquimé, especially within 30 kilometers, reflect direct economic integration with the site's elites, but settlements as far away as the boot heel of New Mexico (about 140 kilometers to the northwest) reflect close symbolic and political integration too (Harmon 2005; Skibo et al. 2002).

Di Peso (1974:329) suggested the interconnected settlements could be divided hierarchically into three tiers: Paquimé, occupied by many thousands of people, was the first tier; large settlements occupied by an estimated 500 to 1,000 people, such as Galeana on the banks of Rio Santa Maria, were the second tier; and smaller settlements occupied by an estimated 100 to 500 people were the third tier (Figure 53.1). Even smaller homesteads were scattered across the area. These settlements were organized, according to Di Peso (1974), such that goods and services flowed from the smaller sites into the second-tiered sites and then into Paquimé. Di Peso's ideas have been supported by more recent research (e.g., Cruz Antillón et al. 2004).

Whalen and Minnis (2001) have further proposed that the regional system can be understood in terms of the distance of the settlements from Paquimé. They found that settlements within 30 kilometers tend to be organized into small settlement clusters dominated by larger "administrative" centers, that settlements between 30 and 60 kilometers tend to reflect only limited economic and political integration with each other or Paquimé, and that settlements outside this range tend to be small and economically independent. But Whalen and Minnis do not consider the relationship between Paquimé and the large second-tier "Animas phase" settlements in the boot heel of New Mexico. These settlements are more than 100 kilometers from Paquimé but appear to be tightly integrated with the settlement, as reflected by ball courts and ceramic symbolism, which is atypical of the "outer-zone" settlements in the areas Whalen and Minnis considered (Harmon 2005; VanPool et al. 2005).

Mesoamerican Influence at Paquimé

Paquimé specifically, and the Casas Grandes region in general, reflect the most direct influence of Mesoamerican cultures in the whole of the Southwest (Di Peso 1974; Kelley 2000; Riley 2008:29; T. L. VanPool et al. 2008). This influence is characterized by shared architectural traits such as platform effigy mounds and I-shaped ball courts, shared iconography and religious practices, trade goods such as West Mexican copper and ocean shell, burial traditions and human sacrifice, pottery effigy vessel morphology, and the religious significance of macaws (Bradley 2000; Di Peso 1974; Harmon 2005; Rakita 2009; Vargas 2001; VanPool and VanPool 2007). These traits demonstrate at least some level of cultural continuity with Mesoamerican groups, especially the Aztatlán trading tradition (Foster 1999; Kelley 2000; T. L. VanPool et al. 2008).

The Origins of the Casas Grandes Phenomenon

Although universally recognized as an important development in Southwestern prehistory, comparatively little is known about the Casas Grandes phenomenon because of the lack of intense research in northern Chihuahua, relative to other areas of the North American Southwest. One area where this is most directly reflected is in the understanding of the origins of the phenomenon. Four general ideas have been proposed:

- An intrusion of Mesoamerican traders looking for Southwestern goods such as turquoise: Di Peso (1974) proposed that Toltec traders established Paquimé sometime around AD 1100. Subsequent dating analysis indicates that Di Peso's dates were erroneously early, and that the Casas Grandes phenomenon postdated the Toltec empire (Bradley 2000), but the idea that Paquimé was founded either directly by Mesoamerican traders or by those who sought to participate in the Aztatlán Mesoamerican trading system continues to be proposed (Foster 1999; Kelley 2000).

- An intrusion of elites from the northern Southwest: Lekson (1999) has proposed that elites from the Chaco Canyon/Aztec political systems in northern New Mexico and southern Colorado traveled due south to establish a new political capital at Paquimé. He suggested they adopted Mesoamerican symbolism to legitimize themselves and sought to integrate indigenous people from northern Chihuahua and southern New Mexico.
- An outgrowth of the Classic Mimbres occupation of New Mexico: Kidder (1939), Sayles (1936), and C. S. VanPool et al. (2008) propose that the Casas Grandes phenomenon is in part derived from the preceding Classic Mimbres occupation, which ended around AD 1150, on the basis of demographic trends and symbolic and religious similarities.
- *In situ* development from the preceding Viejo period: Whalen and Minnis (2001, 2003) propose that the Casas Grandes Phenomenon was largely a continuation of trends present in the Viejo period (AD 900 to 1200) occupation of the Casas Grandes region, on the basis of settlement location and the presence of West Mexican exotica in late Viejo settlements.

These hypotheses are not mutually exclusive. For example, Lekson (1999) proposes the elites of the Casas Grandes phenomenon came from the Chaco/Aztec system but the "commoners" were attracted in large part from the Mimbres area. Likewise, the Casas Grandes system could be an outgrowth from the Viejo period and also reflect the spread of the Aztatlán trading system. Additional research is necessary to better understand which of these hypotheses are supported.

CASAS GRANDES SYMBOLISM AND RELIGION

As previously noted, the spread and extent of the Casas Grandes phenomenon is best reflected in the distribution of a distinctive symbolic system, especially as it is manifested on pottery. This symbolism reflects Mesoamerican themes such as the horned serpent, and it likely reflects an emphasis on tobacco shamanism focused on water control (VanPool and VanPool 2007; see also Hall, this volume).

Water Symbolism

The emphasis on water symbolism is reflected through the entire region but is especially exemplified at Paquimé, which we believe was metaphorically considered a "water city" (VanPool and VanPool 2007). The importance of water is reflected by its dominance in ritual contexts (Walker and MacGahee 2001). For example, the Walk-in Well at Paquimé was a hidden subterranean water source with extremely limited access, built in the heart of the village (Figure 53.2; Di Peso 1974:356; Di Peso et al. 1974 vol. 4:377). To reach the Walk-in Well, one had to step over a human skullcap embedded in the floor of the room with the hidden entrance and descend 19 stairs (Di Peso et al. 1974 vol. 4:372–381; Walker and MacGahee 2001). Valuable artifacts and "ceremonial paraphernalia," such as copper tinklers, animal bones, small stone and ceramic effigies, and beads of turquoise and shell (both commonly associated with water), were strewn down the stairs (Di Peso et al. 1974 vol. 4:356, 377–381). The bones included bison, red-tailed hawk, pronghorn, bobcat, various other animals, and isolated fragments of human bone. Animals such as bear and badger were reflected as ceramic effigies, several of which were broken at the neck and found without the associated pottery body (Di Peso et al. 1974 vol. 4:379). The animal bones, shell, "decapitated" effigy heads, and artifacts such as copper and green stones like turquoise are probably ritual offerings similar to the water offering given to springs and caves throughout Mesoamerica (Di Peso 1974; McNatt 1996: 85–86; Miller and Taube 1993:43). Such entrances into the underworld in turn represented the *axis mundi*, the center place of creation at which the upper world, the lower world, and the four corners of this world were united (Garber and Mathews 2004). We will expand on this point in the discussion of shamanism below.

The connection between Paquimé and water is also reflected directly throughout the city. Paquimé's farmers diverted water from a warm spring 3.61 kilometers northwest of the site and from the Río Casas Grandes into their village using a system of canals and drainages (Di Peso et al. 1974 vol. 5:830). The city also had two

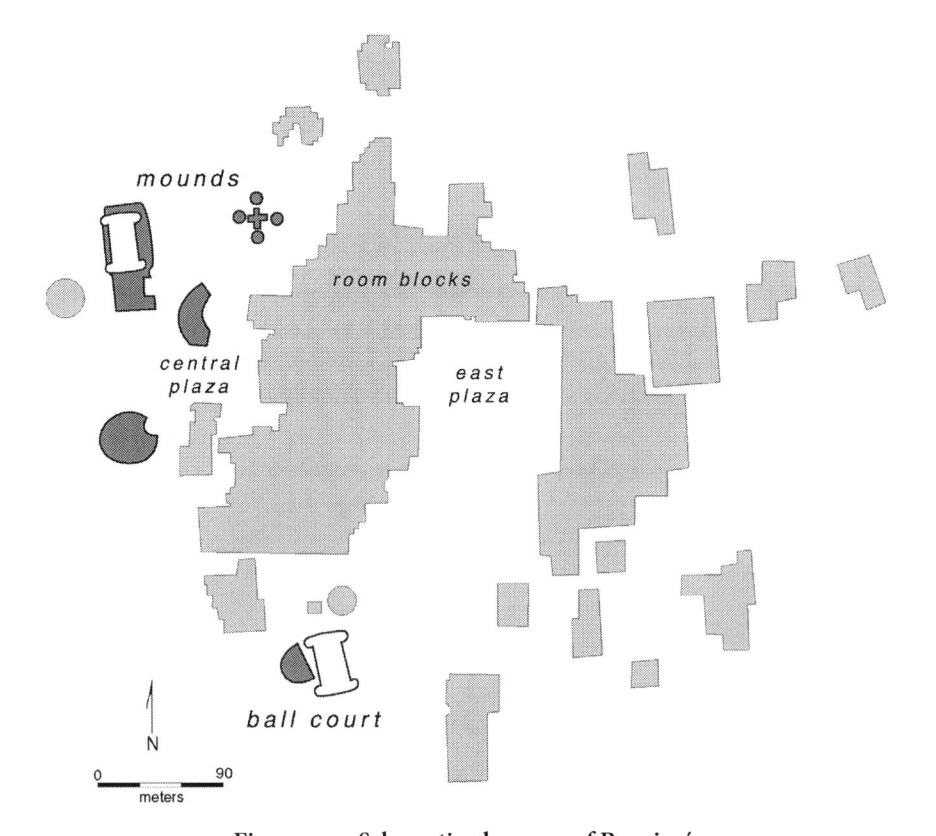

Figure 53.2 Schematic plan map of Paquimé.

reservoirs, one of which had an "offering" of a Playas Red jar wrapped in a necklace of turquoise, shell, and slate that contained several necklaces and a horn, possibly from a bison or a mountain sheep, buried in a small shaft covered by a rock slab at the center of its basin (Di Peso et al. 1974 vol. 5:836). Inclusion of marine shell and turquoise, which symbolized rain and water throughout the Americas, as part of the offering reinforces the significance of water (Miller and Taube 1993:174).

As was the case at the Walk-in Well, significant animals may have also been placed in the canals. Seventeen mud turtles (*Kinosternon sonoriense* and *Kinosternon* sp.) were found in the canals at Paquimé (Di Peso et al. 1974 vol. 8:250), despite the fact that the Chihuahuan desert is outside their typical natural range. Di Peso et al. (250) argued that these turtles were intentionally introduced from the mountains in Arizona, given that they are ordinarily found in woodlands at an elevation above 1,550 meters and are primarily aquatic animals that only occasionally take to dry land (generally after heavy rain). Although most of the turtles were found in the water system, four were found inside the room block, indicating their use by humans perhaps for food and for their carapaces (room 7–8; Di Peso et al. 250). Turtles symbolized water throughout the Americas, and Southwestern Pueblo groups continue to use turtle rattles, especially on the legs of some katsinas who stomp while dancing to make the rattles and their feet sound like rain and thunder (Miller and Taube 1993:174; Parsons 1996).

The presence of spiritual/mythic creatures, especially the horned serpent, in rock art near water sources also emphasizes the cosmological importance of water. The association between horned serpents and water is further reflected by the "Mound of the Serpent," a 113.30 meter-long platform mound at Paquimé shaped like a horned serpent. The mound runs along one edge of the site and likely helped divert water around the main ceremonial complex (Di Peso et al. 1974). Its tail turns to point directly at Arroyo de Los Monos, a spring with a dense concentration of rock art 15 kilometers away (Schaafsma 1998).

Horned/Plumed Serpents

Perhaps because of the association with water symbolism, horned serpents are the dominant design in Casas Grandes symbolism, represented in several forms. Complete horned or plumed serpents are quite rare but are instead depicted as serpents with undulating bodies, a forward-pointing horn, a backward pointing horn or plume, a checkered body, and a "finned" tail (Figure 53.3; Kidder 1916; VanPool and VanPool 2007). Far more common are simple "half-spade" motifs of the serpent's head, with a forward-pointing horn, eye, and mouth (Schaafsma 1998; VanPool and VanPool 2007). These are the most prevalent designs on the Casas Grandes polychromes. Given that these polychromes were found in every possible context (domestic, ritual, refuse), they were viewed by everyone one and were likely the central ethnic/religious marker of the Casas Grandes phenomenon (VanPool et al. 2006). Further, the religious importance of the horned serpent is reflected by the

Figure 53.3 Casas Grandes horned/plumed serpent.

previously mentioned Mound of the Serpent at Paquimé, which is associated with a ritually significant roomblock having a wall decorated with a carved horned or plumed serpent image (Di Peso et al. 1974 vol. 5:475–522; Walker 2002).

Six horned serpent designs have been identified on Classic Mimbres pottery, but this does not assume a dominant role in any Southwestern symbolic system until the Casas Grandes phenomenon (Schaafsma 1998; C. S. VanPool et al. 2008). The rise in importance of horned serpent imagery is consistent with evidence for Mesoamerican influence, in that the feather serpent became a patron deity for Mesoamerican traders after AD 600 and until European contact (Evans 2004:353; Ringle et al. 1998) and is central to the Aztatlán trading system (which was associated with a religious cult). Di Peso (1974:548–549) directly tied the horned serpent to Quetzalcoatl, the "Old Creator God" of the Aztecs and other Mesoamerican groups that had domain over water and irrigation (see also Schaafsma 1980:238). This association with water is also reflected in ethnographic and archaeological evidence from elsewhere in the North American Southwest (Parsons 1996; Stevenson 1985; Tedlock 1979). Many ethnographically studied groups in the U.S. Southwest (and Mesoamerica) believed that horned/plumed serpents live in water and control rain, snow, and the flow of water in springs and lakes (Crown 1994:166; Dutton 1963:49; Parsons 1996; Schaafsma 1980:238). Schaafsma (1998) documents the association of horned serpent rock art from throughout the Casas Grandes region near springs, which is consistent with the ethnographic association with water. On the basis of the context of the images and general New World ethnographic information, one can posit that the horned/plumed serpent was likely integral to water ceremonies taking place at the Mound of the Serpent.

Taube (2000) demonstrates that the serpents' "feathers" can actual be corn silk (see also Evans 2004:162) and proposes that feathered serpents throughout Mesoamerica and the Southwest had a rich metaphoric association with maize (161; Ringle et al. 1998; Taube 2000; see also Hays-Gilpin et al. 2004 and Schaafsma 1980, who also note a connection between the Southwestern feathered serpents and maize). A similar maize metaphor may have been associated with the Casas Grandes

Figure 53.4 Casas Grandes supernatural realm.

horned/plumed serpent, which is decorated with maize motifs, the most identifiable of which is its checkerboard collar of squares with dots (Figure 53.4; see Hays-Gilpin et al. 2004 and Taube 2000 for discussion of the linkage between the squares-with-dots motif and maize). Conceptualizing the horned/plumed serpent as a maize serpent fits well with Di Peso's proposal that it represents the "Old Creator God," or fertility deity, and was likely the patron deity of Casas Grandes religion, used by elites to negotiate with other Mesoamerican groups.

Macaws

Scarlet (red) and military (green) macaws were sacrificed and buried at Paquimé by the hundreds and were a common motif on pottery (Di Peso et al. 1974 vol. 8:274; VanPool and VanPool 2007:100–103). Among Mesoamerican groups, the green feathers of the Quetzal also symbolize water and maize and were associated with Quetzalcoatl, who was a rattlesnake with quetzal feathers (Ringle et al. 1998; Taube 2000). Perhaps the green feathers of the military macaws had a similar association, reflecting a link between macaws and horned serpents. They may have even been used as part of the feathered and horned serpent headdresses depicted throughout the Casas Grandes region (Riley 2005; Schaafsma 1998). From ethnographic analogy with historic pueblo groups, scarlet macaws may have also been associated with maize, as well as the sun (VanPool and VanPool 2007:100–101).

Shamanism and Smoking Males

The theme underlying the symbolic system seems to be the concept of shamanic transformation and what anthropologists call the classic shamanic journey (VanPool and VanPool 2007). Effigies depict smoking males who are decorated with a distinctive cross-shaped design (resembling a pound sign) and often with horned serpents. These same designs are represent on (and only on) individuals wearing horned serpent headdresses, individuals with horns growing out of their head, and anthropomorphic individuals with macaw heads who are shown interacting with supernatural creatures, including horned serpents (Figure 53.4). Di Peso (1974:308,

570) considered male smokers to be "medicine men" or "witch doctors," but recent research indicates that a similar symbolic pattern associated with tobacco shamanism is present among West Mexican groups (VanPool and VanPool 2007). Contextual information indicates that high-status burials were associated with the horned serpent imagery characteristic of these shamans. The House of the Walk-in Well was also associated with seven of the nine pipes discovered at Paquimé that are identical to those depicted on the male smoker effigies, suggesting it was a ritual area serving as a portal into the underworld through which the shaman traveled. Similar associations among water, caves, and shamanism are found throughout Mesoamerica, again emphasizing the connection between West Mexican cultures and the Casas Grandes phenomenon.

Leadership and Elites in the Casas Grandes World

The symbolic system, settlement pattern, and architecture emphasize the role of elites throughout the Casas Grandes phenomenon. The prominence of the horned serpents emphasizes the importance of the shamans, who could directly interact with them. Burial patterns, emphasis on large public architecture with private ritual spaces, and hording of goods all reflect a system in which elites sought to legitimize themselves and control the economic and religious/cosmological structure of the region (Harmon 2005; Rakita 2009; Ravesloot 1988; Whalen and Minnis 2009). A cosmology based on horned/plumed serpents and macaws, both of which are associated with water, maize, and leadership among Mesoamerican traders, was central to this effort. Using this cosmological system, the elites at Paquimé and perhaps throughout the region sought to tie themselves to a system of trade and prestige that spread from West Mexico upward toward the modern-day U.S. Southwest (Kelley 2000; Riley 2005; T. L. VanPool et al. 2008).

Conclusion

How or why the Casas Grandes system ended is uncertain. Di Peso (1974) proposes that the settlement was sacked and destroyed, this notion based on the presence of extensive burning and more than 80 individuals who did not receive formal burials. His idea is not supported by evidence for warfare throughout the region, although the 14th and 15th centuries certainly were characterized by conflict elsewhere in the Southwest (Rice and LeBlanc 2001). Regardless, sometime before AD 1450 the grand settlements throughout the Casas Grandes region were uniformly abandoned. When the Spanish arrived in the area about a century later, it was occupied by hunters and gatherers.

REFERENCES

Bagwell, E. A. 2006. Domestic Architectural Production in Northwest Mexico. Ph.D. dissertation, University of New Mexico, Albuquerque.

Bradley, R. J. 2000. Recent Advances in Chihuahuan Archaeology. In *Greater Mesoamerica: The Archaeology of West and Northwest Mexico*, edited by M. S. Foster and S. Gorenstein, pp. 221–239. University of Utah Press, Salt Lake City.

Crown, P. L. 1994. *Ceramics and Ideology: Salado Polychrome Pottery*. University of New Mexico Press, Albuquerque.

Cruz Antillón, R., R. D. Leonard, T. D. Maxwell, T. L. VanPool, M. J. Harmon, C. S. VanPool, D. A. Hyndman, and S. S. Brandwein. 2004. Galeana, Villa Ahumada, and Casa Chica: Diverse Sites in the Casas Grandes Region. In *Future Directions: The Archaeology of Northwest Mexico*, edited by G. E. Newell and E. Gallaga Murrieta, pp. 149–176. University of Utah Press, Salt Lake City.

Di Peso, C. C. 1974. *Casas Grandes: A Fallen Trading Center of the Gran Chichimeca*, vols. 1–3. Amerind Foundation, Dragoon, AZ; and Northland Press, Flagstaff, AZ.

———, J. B. Rinaldo, and G. J. Fenner (editors). 1974. *Casas Grandes: A Fallen Trading Center of the Gran Chichimeca. Dating and Architecture*, vols. 4–8. Amerind Foundation, Dragoon, AZ; and Northland Press, Flagstaff, AZ.

Dutton, B. P. 1963. *Sun Father's Way: The Kiva Murals of Kuaua, a Pueblo Ruin, Coronado State Monument, New Mexico*. University of New Mexico Press, Albuquerque.

Evans, S. T. 2004. *Ancient Mexico and Central America: Archaeology and Culture History*. Thames and Hudson, London and New York.

Foster, M. S. 1999. The Aztatlán Tradition of West and Northwest Mexico and Casas Grandes: Speculations on the Medio Period Florescence. In *The Casas Grandes World*, edited by C. F. Schaafsma and C. L. Riley, pp. 149–163. University of Utah Press, Salt Lake City.

Gamboa, E. 2002. Casas Grandes Culture. In *Talking Birds, Plumed Serpents, and Painted Women: The Ceramics of Casas Grandes*, edited by J. Stuhr, pp. 41–43. Tucson Museum of Art and Historic Block, Tucson, AZ.

Garber, J. F., and J. P. Mathews. 2004. Models of Cosmic Order: Physical Expression of Sacred Space Among the Ancient Maya. *Ancient Mesoamerica* 15:49–59.

Harmon, M. J. 2005. *Centralization, Cultural Transmission, and "the Game of Life and Death" Within Northern Mexico*. Ph.D. dissertation, University of New Mexico, Albuquerque.

Hays-Gilpin, K. A., L. D. Webster, and P. Schaafsma. 2004. The Iconography of Tie-Dye Textiles in the Ancient Americas. *Cosmos* 20:33–56.

Kelley, J. C. 2000. The Aztatlán Mercantile System: Mobile Traders and the Northwestern Expansion of Mesoamerican Civilization. In *Greater Mesoamerica: The Archaeology of West and Northwest Mexico*, edited by M. S. Foster and S. Gorenstein, pp. 137–154. University of Utah Press, Salt Lake City.

Kelley, J. H., J. D. Stewart, A. C. MacWilliams, and L. C. Neff. 1999. A West Central Chihuahuan Perspective on Chihuahuan Culture. In *The Casas Grandes World*, edited by C. F. Schaafsma and C. L. Riley, pp. 63–77. University of Utah Press, Salt Lake City.

Kidder, A. V. 1916. The Pottery of the Casas Grandes District, Chihuahua. In *Holmes Anniversary Volume; Anthropological Essays Presented to W. Henry Holmes in Honor of His Seventieth Birthday*, pp. 253–268. J. W. Bryan Press, Washington, DC.

———. 1939. Notes on the Archaeology of the Babicora District, Chihuahua. In *So Live the Works of Men*, edited by D. D. Brand and F. E. Harvey, pp. 221–230. University of New Mexico Press, Albuquerque.

Lekson, S. H. 1999. *The Chacoan Meridian: Centers of Political Power in the American Southwest*. AltaMira, Walnut Creek, CA.

MacWilliams, A. C. 2001a. *The Archaeology of Laguna Bustillos Basin, Chihuahua, Mexico*. Ph.D. dissertation, University of Arizona, Tucson.

———. 2001b. Beyond the Reach of Casas Grandes: Archaeology in Central Chihuahua. In *From Paquimé to Mata Ortiz: The Legacy of Ancient Casas Grandes*, edited by G. Johnson, pp. 55–64. San Diego Museum of Man, San Diego, CA.

McNatt, L. 1996. The Archaeology of Belize. *Journal of Cave and Karst Studies* 58(2):81–99.

Miller, M., and K. Taube. 1993. *An Illustrated Dictionary of the Gods and Symbols of Ancient Mexico and the Maya*. Thames and Hudson, New York.

Minnis, P. E., and M. E. Whalen. 2004. Chihuahuan Archaeology: An Introductory History. In *Surveying the Archaeology of Northwest Mexico*, edited by G. E. Newell and E. Gallaga, pp. 289–296. University of Utah Press, Salt Lake City.

Parsons, E. C. 1996 [1939]. *Pueblo Indian Religion*. 2 vols. Bison Books edition, University of Nebraska Press, Lincoln.

Phillips, D. A., Jr. 1989. Prehistory of Chihuahua and Sonora, Mexico. *Journal of World Prehistory* 3:373–401.

Rakita, G. F. M. 2009. *Ancestors and Elites: Emergent Complexity and Ritual Practices in the Casas Grandes Polity*. AltaMira Press, Lanham, MD.

Ravesloot, J. C. 1988. *Mortuary Practices and Social Differentiation at Casas Grandes, Chihuahua, Mexico*. University of Arizona Press, Tucson.

Rice, G. E., and S. A. LeBlanc (editors). 2001. *Deadly Landscapes: Case Studies in Prehistoric Southwestern Warfare*. University of Utah Press, Salt Lake City.

Riley, C. L. 2008. Aztlan: The Prehistoric Southwest as a Mexican Civilization. *El Palacio: Art, History and Culture of the Southwest* 113(4):26–31.

Ringle, W. M., T. Gallereta Negrón, and G. J. Bey III. 1998. The Return of Quetzalcoatl: Evidence for the Spread of a World Religion During the Epiclassic Period. *Ancient Mesoamerica* 9:183–232.

Sayles, E. B. 1936. *Some Southwestern Pottery Types, Series V*. Gila Pueblo Foundation, Globe, AZ.

Schaafsma, C. F., and C. L. Riley. 1999. The Casas Grandes World: Analysis and Conclusion. In *The Casas Grandes World*, edited by C. F. Schaafsma and C. L. Riley, pp. 237–249. University of Utah Press, Salt Lake City.

Schaafsma, P. 1980. *Indian Rock Art of the Southwest*. School of American Research Press, Santa Fe, NM; and University of New Mexico Press, Albuquerque.

———. 1998. The Paquimé Rock Art Style, Chihuahua, Mexico. In *Rock Art of the Chihuahuan Desert Borderlands*, edited by S. Smith-Savage and R. J. Mallouf, pp. 33–44. Sul Ross State University and Texas Park and Wildlife Department, Center for Big Bend Studies, Alpine, TX.

Skibo, J. M., E. B. McCluney, and W. H. Walker. 2002. *The Joyce Well Site: On the Frontier of the Casas Grandes World*. University of Utah Press, Salt Lake City.

Stevenson, M. C. 1985 [1904]. *The Zuni Indians: 23rd Annual Report, 1901–1902*. Bureau of American Ethnology. Rio Grande Press, Glorieta, NM.

Taube, K. 2000. Lightning Celts and Corn Fetishes: The Formative Olmec and the Development of Maize Symbolism in Mesoamerica and the American Southwest. In *Olmec Art and Archaeology in Mesoamerica*, edited by J. E. Clark and M. E. Pye, pp. 297–337. National Gallery of Art, Washington, DC; distributed by Yale University Press, New Haven, CT.

Tedlock, D. 1979. Zuni Religion and Worldview. In *Handbook of North American Indians*, vol. 9, *Southwest*, edited by A. Ortiz, pp. 499–508. Smithsonian Institution, Washington, DC.

VanPool, C. S., and T. L. VanPool. 2007. *Signs of the Casas Grandes Shamans*. University of Utah Press, Salt Lake City.

———, and M. Harmon. 2008. Plumed and Horned Serpents of the American Southwest. In *Touching the Past: Ritual, Religion, and the Trade of Casas Grandes*, edited by G. Nielsen-Grimm and P. Stavast, pp. 47–58. Museum of Peoples and Culture, Brigham Young University, Provo, UT.

VanPool, T. L., C. S. VanPool, and R. D. Leonard. 2005. The Casas Grandes Core and Periphery. In *Archaeology Between the Borders: Papers from the 13th Biennial Jornada Mogollon Conference*, edited by M. Thompson, J. Jurgena, and L. Jackson, pp. 25–35. El Paso Museum of Archaeology, El Paso, TX.

VanPool, T. L., C. S. VanPool, and D. A. Phillips, Jr. 2006. The Salado and Casas Grandes Phenomena: Evidence for a Religious Schism in the Greater Southwest. In *Religion in the Prehispanic Southwest*, edited by C. S. VanPool, T. L. VanPool, and D. A. Phillips, Jr., pp. 235–51. AltaMira Press, Lanham, MD.

———, G. F. M. Rakita, and R. D. Leonard. 2008. Birds, Bells, and Shells: The Long Reach of the Aztatlán Trading Tradition. In *Touching the Past: Traditions of Casas Grandes*, edited by G. Nielsen-Grimm, pp. 5–14. BYU University Press, Provo, UT.

VanPool, T. L., C. S. VanPool, G. F. M. Rakita, and R. D. Leonard. 2008. Birds, Bells, and Shells: The Long Reach of the Aztatlán Trading Tradition. In *Touching the Past: Ritual, Religion, and Trade of Casas Grandes*, edited by G. Nielsen-Grimm and P. Stavast, pp. 5–14. Museum of Peoples and Cultures, Brigham Young University, Provo, UT.

Vargas, V. D. 2001. Mesoamerican Copper Bells in the Pre-Hispanic Southwestern United States and Northwestern Mexico. In *The Road to Aztlan: Art from a Mythic Homeland*, edited by V. M. Fields and V. Zamudio-Taylor, pp. 196–211. Los Angeles County Museum of Art, Los Angeles; and University of New Mexico Press, Albuquerque.

Walker, W. H. 2002. Stratigraphy and Practical Reason. *American Anthropologist* 104:159–177.

———, and G. MacGahee. 2001. Animated Waters: The Ritualized Life History of Wells, Reservoirs, and Springs at Casas Grandes, Chihuahua. Paper presented at the 66th Annual Meeting of the Society for American Archaeology, April, New Orleans.

Whalen, M. E., and P. E. Minnis. 2001. *Casas Grandes and Its Hinterlands: Prehistoric Regional Organization in Northwest Mexico*. University of Arizona Press, Tucson.

———. 2003. The Local and the Distant in the Origin of Casas Grandes, Chihuahua, Mexico. *American Antiquity* 68:314–332.

———. 2009. *The Neighbors of Casas Grandes: Excavating Medio Period Communities of Northwest Chihuahua, Mexico*. University of Arizona Press, Tucson.

Index

abandonment, 176, 177, 180, 189, 400, 486, 509, 518, 519, 531, 540, 613, 623, 634, 635; Moundville, 542
Actor-Network-Theory, 23
adaptation: cultural, 113, 124; Desert Culture, 188; hunter-gatherer, 329
Adena, 439
agency, 271; gendered, 386
agency-based models, 230
agricultural tools: Plains, 377, *See* hoes
agriculture, 20, 74, 81, 203, 221, 224, 362, 379, 381, 382, 388, 400, 443, 444, 487, 516, 575, 577, 610; field, 73, 281; Hohokam, 581; maize, 79; monumentality before, 485; proto-, 203; Southwestern, 612, *See* Eastern Agricultural complex
Alaska, 135
Algonquian, 129, 285, 286, 293; Powhatan, 310
Algonquian cultural development, 314; dialects, 311; history: and Werowocomoco, 316; Tidewater, 314
Allouez, Claude, 64
altruism, 208
American Bottom, 398, 399, 417, 479, 486, 493, 500, 505, 526, 527, 531
Anangula Tradition, 138
ancestors, 490, 555, 566, 631
Ancestral Pueblo, 563
Anderson, Gary, 40
Antelope Creek phase, 391
anthropology: culture and personality school, 621; historical, 485
anthropophagy, 622
archaeology: American, 29; approaches, 471; feminist, 386, 396; historical, 42, 46, 310; indigenous, 12, 319; mission, 42; Paleoindian, 87; post-postmodern, 325; prehistoric vs. historical, 8; processual, 311; theory, 632
Archaic, 164, 264, 289; California, 217; history of concept, 452; Maritime, northeast, 252, *See* Poverty Point
architecture, 14, 42, 45, 67, 162, 220, 262, 298, 418, 438, 461, 465, 485, 486, 487, 489, 490, 494, 500, 517, 537, 549, 551, 555, 562, 563, 568, 569, 574, 577, 579, 580, 581, 582, 588, 604, 613, 615, 617, 618, 623, 624, 645, 646, 654; ceremonial, 556; circular, 381; field houses, 625; Hohokam earthen, 577; Midwestern, 406; monumental, 488; new forms of, 541; pithouses, 563; Plains, 360, 376;

public, 561, 562; public Hohokam, 574; rebuilding, 540; ritual, 555; supra-household, 556; wall trench, 305, 502, 538
Arctic, 113
Arctic Small Tool tradition, 117, 121, 122
Arnold, Jeanne, 230, 232
arrow points, 5, 166, 242, 356, 377, 493, 524, 525, 529, *See* projectile points
Arrow Sacrifice ceremony, 277
astronomers, 228
astronomy, 56, 67, 306; and settlement organization, 305
atlatl, 56, 59, 61, 332
axis mundi, 518, 650
Aztalan (Wisconsin), 418, 526, 601
Aztatlán Mesoamerican trading system, 648
Aztec (Mexico), 54, 55
Aztec Ruins (New Mexico), 601

ball court centers, 579
ball courts, 53, 66, 550, 556, 562, 563, 566, 568, 574, 575, 577, 580, 581, 599, 645, 647, 648; Hohokam, 566
ball game, 46, 53
Bandelier, Adolph, 43, 620
Bannon, John, 40
Baugh, Timothy, 390
beads, 45, 165, 166, 227, 348, 351, 356, 416, 423, 440, 460, 650, *See* shell beads
beadwork, 312, 348
Bear's Journey. *See* Missaukee Earthworks
Beringia, 89
Big Bang. *See* Cahokia
Bighorn Basin, 347
Binford, Lewis, 21, 312, 326; collector-forager model, 190; frames of reference, 327, 329
bison, 376; bone, 390; communal hunts, 416; hides and lithic tools, 381, 388, 391; tools, 377
bison hunting, 70, 362, 364, 365, 369, 373, 380, 381, 382, 383, 387, 388, 390
Black Warrior River, 534
Blackfoot, 337; homeland, 338
Blanton, Dennis, 315
Boas, Franz, 29
boats, 115, 117, 118, 119, 120, 121, 137, 142, 152, 154, 157, 162, 227, 602, *See* canoes
Bodley, John, 326
Bolton, Herbert, 39

bone tools, 126, 166, 242, 275, See bison
borderlands, 39
bow and arrow, 56, 129, 202, 227, 267, 332, 399, 403, 412, 416, 419, 490, 516, 524, 610
Brew, John Otis, 43
bundles, 9, 341
burial mounds, 217, 219, 289, 292, 301, 401, 402, 404, 405, 440, 471, 478, 492, 516, 524; Late Woodland, 525, See mounds
burial practices, 427, 430; Fort Ancient and Monongahela, 301; Hopewell, 476; Paquimé, 654
burials, 217; human and nonhuman, 214
Burnt Corn Pueblo, 625
Bushnell, Amy, 41

cache blades, 255
caches, 90, 101, 219, 454, 577
Cactus Hill, 92, 96
Cahokia, 56, 61, 67, 68, 289, 305, 334, 363, 364, 398, 417, 438, 441, 486, 497, 510, 526; city of, 500; decline of, 369; Monks Mound, 442, 462, 497; organization, 442; political-administrative complex, 400, See human sacrifice
calendrics, 587
California, 40, 42, 47, 54, 60, 69, 74, 75, 76, 78, 137, 150, 187, 199, 224; colonial, 236; mounded landscapes, 213; Native, 235; pilgrimage, 41
California Bight, 225
Californio identities, 236, 239
Calumet ceremonialism, 56, 476, 480
Cambria, 333
canoes, 165, 166, 227, 231, 264, 454, 455, 494, See boats
captives, 13, 393, 396, 527, 614, See warfare
Casas Grandes, 66, 553, 600; phenomenon, 645; regional system, 647, See Paquimé
catastrophic, 135, 138, 140, 531, 627
celestial alignments. See astronomy
celts, 332, 377, 416, 528
cemeteries, 101, 126, 127, 165, 213, 215, 217, 231, 255, 267, 301, 333, 348, 377, 401–406, 427, 430, 440, 454, 455, 518, 524, 529, 530, 541, 542
Central Illinois River valley, 402, 523, 531
ceramics: and social boundaries, 289; and women, 393; ceremonial, 505; Effigy Mound ware, 413; Great Lakes, 291; Hohokam, 577, 580; Middle Woodland, 257; Mimbres, 555; Moundville phases, 537; Moundville style, 540; Oneota, 403; Plains, 363, 377; shell-tempered, 299, 363, 405, 416, 418, 493, 509; stamped, 512; symbolism, 648; Woodland, 255, 266
ceremonial enclosures, 292
ceremonial monument centers, 292
ceremonialism, 492, See Midéwiwin; burial, 267; mortuary, 494
cerros de trincheras: described, 585, 587
Chaco, 553, 614; as postclassic capital, 598; Canyon, 66, 597; collapse, 632; Great Houses, 599, 634; phenomenon, 567, 602, 631; Pueblo Bonito, 554.
Champlain, Samuel de, 274
Channel Island Barbed points, 154
Channel Islands, 154, 213, 225
chert, 125, 126, 127, 164, 227, 232, 253, 255, 377, 410, 414, 417, 463, 502; Poverty Point, 463; Indiana, 502; Knife River flint, 363, 365, 369; Onondaga, 256; Ramah, 126; sources, 252
Chesapeake, 311
chiefdoms, 12, 14, 21, 44, 46, 228, 235, 334, 400, 403, 404, 407, 430, 441, 442, 444, 451, 485, 490, 492, 499, 510, 514, 554; as neoevolutionary category, 553; criticisms of, 19; emergence, 312; mission period, 45; Mississippian, 403, 486, 514; paramount, 46; Powhatan, 310, 311; simple or complex, 514; talwas, 515
chiefs: California, 227; hereditary, 44; Panamanian, 70
Chimney Rock, 600, 601
Chumash, 224
chunkey, 14, 53, 363, 501, 505, See ball game
city: Chaco, 599; historical reference to Casas Grandes, 647; Mississippian, 601; Paquimé, 649, See Cahokia, Chaco
Cleland, Charles, 429
climate change, 101, 135, 190, 191, 193, 398, 480, 608, 611
Clovis, 86, 97, 99, 330, 449, 548, See pre-Clovis; and other fluted points, 98; regional diversity, 91; technology, 156
Clovis First model, 153, 157, 449
Coalescent tradition, 367
Cole, Sarah, 614
colonization: Paleoindian, 94; pre-Paleoindian, 149, 448
Colony Ross, 238, 240
communities: Mississippian, 513, 536; symbolic, 477; Woodland, 500
community, 486; Cahokian, 504; defined, 476; Hohokam, 577; irrigation, 579; monumental transformation of, 489; reinforced by construction, 563; Southwestern, 561, 562
community patterns: SunWatch, 305
complex societies, 12
complexity, 175, 229, 486, 492, 640; cultural, 168; gradualist perspectives, 230; origins of, 168; political, economic, 162; social, Southwestern, 616, See chiefdoms, Keatley Creek
Contrary behavior, 58
copper, 416, 444, 603, 650; Jamestown, 318
corn agriculture. See maize, maize agriculture
Corn Mother, 61
corn, beans, and squash. See maize, beans, and squash
Coronado expedition, 65, 387, 393
cosmology, 12, 53, 226, 318, 338, 469, 599, 654; commonalities, 61

cosmos, 12, 24, 306, 339, 465; Blackfoot, 338; gendered, 340; SunWatch, 305
crafting: Hopewell, 471
Craig, Douglas, 555
cuisine: communal, 566
culinary practices. *See* practices, culinary
culinary traditions, 14, 73, *See* traditions
cultural diversity, 224, 225, 485, 562, 569
culture: archaeological, 30; as intersubjective understandings, 327; as symbols and information, 70; Hohokam, 575
culture core, 20; Numic, 188

Dalton, 101, 454
dance, 339, 341, 342, 343, 344, 567, 617, 639
Danger Cave, 193
De Soto, Hernando, 534
Dean, Jeffery, 557
Deep South, 511, 520
Deetz, James, 42
deities, 53, 56, 61, 275, 639, 652, 653
demography, 11, 142, 167, 225, 229, 232, 348, 468
Des Plaines Complex, 403
Di Peso, Charles, 645
Diamond, Jared, 632
DNA analysis, 126, 276, 610
Dog Soldiers, 54, 56
Dorset, 117, 122, 131; Paleoeskimos, 130
Drennan, Robert, 602
Driftless Area, 410

Eastern Agricultural complex, 332
ecological approaches: criticism of, 20
ecology: cultural, 188; evolutionary, 191; new ecologies, 22
Effigy Mound Culture, 412
egalitarianism, 641
Englehardt, Zephrin, 40
Erlandson, Jon, 232, 450
Etowah site, 515, 519
evolutionary change, 208
evolutionary models, 262; challenged, 263
evolutionary theory: Darwinian, 21
evolutionism: social, 187
exchange, 20, 23, 25, 44, 45, 46, 68, 125, 126, 127, 129, 130, 132, 168, 173, 179, 206, 224, 226, 229, 231, 232, 236, 292, 293, 311, 312, 314, 315, 316, 318, 363, 364, 369, 373, 380, 382, 387, 388, 390, 391, 395, 404, 422, 431, 444, 461, 464, 468, 471, 476, 477, 480, 485, 487, 538, 550, 551, 615; and bison products, 382; bison hides, 395; bison products, 363, 387; California, 226; Plains, 363; Plains-Pueblo, 387; Poverty Point, 463
execution, 526, *See* human sacrifice
explanations: criticism of functionalism, 585

farmers: Cahokian, 402; desert, 574; Late Woodland, Plains, 365; mobile, 269, 277, 332; Oneota, 410; Paquimé, 650
Feast of the Dead, 54, 429
feasting, 67, 130, 160, 168, 182, 208, 209, 218, 220, 221, 232, 314, 315, 404, 418, 487, 492, 516, 555, 566, 579, 616, 618, 636; communal, 489
feminist perspectives, 386
Fiedel, Stuart, 276
Fish, Paul, 587
Fish, Suzanne, 587
Fission-Fusion model, 514
Five Nations Confederacy, 273
Fletcher site, 430
flint. *See* chert
fluted traditions, 193, *See* Clovis, Folsom
Folsom, 87, 92
foragers, 190; Ice Age, 137; pioneer, 329; sedentary, 175; strategies, 175, 185, *See* Great Basin
foraging strategies, 194
foraging theory, 191, 192
Ford, James, 44
Fort Ancient, 297, 439
fortifications, 167, 275, 292, 316, 516, 527, 529, 539; Mississippian, 402, *See* warfare
Four Corners, 563, 603, 608
Fowler, Don, 620
Francis, John, 41
Fraser Villages, 179
Fremont phenomenon, 194, 196
Fried, Morton, 326

game: gambling, 226, *See* ball courts, chunkey
gender, 100, 227, 237, 240, 359, 391, 464, 553, 554, *See* labor
Gibson, Jon, 487
Great Basin, 76, 185, 199, 200, *See* Shoshone
Great Houses. *See* Chaco
Great Lake effect, 290
Great Lakes, 249, 275, 285, 424
Great Oasis, 333, 360
Griffin, James, 453
Guest, Francis, 40
Guzman, Nuno de, 65

Hackel, Stephen, 40
Hall, Robert, 414, 476, 501
harpoon hunting, 119, 165, 332
Hart, John, 276
Haudenosaunee. *See* Iroquoian
Haury, Emil, 549, 601
Haynes, Vance, 449, 453
Hays-Gilpin, Kelley, 557
Hearne, Samuel, 69
Heizer, Robert, 188
heterarchical, 638
Hewett, Edgar Lee, 43

Hibben, Frank, 623
hinge points, 549
historic period: problems of definition, 350, 356
history: as adaptation, criticized, 124; as practice; borderlands, 40; Eastern Subarctic, 132; in place, 25; longue duree, 327; migration, 552; Mississippian, 510; monumental, 495; Powhatan, 318; Pueblo, 608; scientific, questioned, 31; singular, Cahokia, 497; tribal, 354, *See* hunter-gatherer, practice theory
Hodge, Frederick, 43
hoes, 377, 406, 416, 418, 444, 493
Hohokam, 553, 563, 571, 600
Holocene, 201, 287
Hopewell phenomenon, 471, 476
Hopewell site, 444
Hopewellian Complex: southern Michigan, 289
horned serpent, 645, 649, 651
horticultural. *See* agriculture
house forms: Petal, 301, *See* architecture
house society, 555
Huasteca, 68
Hudson's Bay Company, 69
human sacrifice, 56, 61, 277, 504. *See* execution
Hume, Ivor Noel, 46
hunter-gatherer, 19, 212; Archaic in the Northeast, 253; complex, 142, 160, 179; packing, 414; movement and identity, 344; theoretically considered, 19, *See* adaptations; famers, mobile
hunter-gatherer-fisher societies, 224
Huron, 130, 273, 424
hybridity, 503

Ibarra, Francisco de, 647
identities. *See* landscape, theoretically considered
identity: Chumash, 232; collective, 536; visibility, 351
ideology, 67, 185, 295, 353, 485, 514, 516, 542, 550, 557, 574, 577, 638
immigrants: historical effects of, 503
interaction sphere. *See* Hopewell phenomenon; Meadowood
Inuit, 135
Iroquoians, 130, 259, 273, 285; archaeological visibility, 276; cultural pattern, 275; disappearance, 259
Iroquois Confederacy, 274
irrigation. *See* labor
isotopes, 268, 277

Jackson, Helen Hunt, 41
Jamestown, 310
Jennings, Jesse, 188
Jesuit Relations, 431
Johnson, Gregory, 553
Juanillo Revolt of 1597, 46

Jury, Wilfred, 423

Kachina, 56, *See* katsina
katsina, 639, 640; Paquimé, 651
Keatley Creek, 177; complexity, 180
Kehoe, Alice, 33
kelp highway, 152
Kennewick Man, 31
Kessell, John, 40
Keyes, Charles, 414
Kidd, Kenneth, 423
Kidder, Alfred, 43, 388, 623
Kidder, T. R., 487
kill sites, 339
kivas, 567, 568, 598; Great, 604
Knife River flint. *See* chert
Kodiak Archipelago, 135
Kroeber, Alfred, 29, 187

La Florida, 44
labor, 23, 44, 99, 168, 175, 190, 191, 193, 195, 202, 205, 206, 227, 236, 237, 240, 241, 242, 243, 275, 292, 333, 348, 359, 364, 369, 387, 390, 391, 392, 393, 394, 395, 442, 443, 464, 466, 467, 486, 504, 513, 514, 540, 541, 543, 550, 555, 565, 580, 610, 613, 618, 628, 636, 640; and women's status, 395; forced, 238; gendered, 239, 241, 386, 392; Hohokam canals, 571; women's, 391
Lake Michigan, 287
Lake Ontario, 249
Lake Superior, 287, 423
landscape: colonial, 241; embodied, 585, 594; functionalist views, 485; monumental, 485, 487, 495; mounded, 212; sacred, 487, 489, 518; theoretically considered, 588; tipi ring, 353; violence, 624; Werowocomoco, 316; Woodland, 489
Langford, George, 405
Lanoraie site, 258
Lasanen site, 428
leaders, 44, 46, 65, 68, 227, 311, 318, 390, 402, 441, 469, 504, 536, 538, 541, 542, 557, 567, 568, 569, 580, 581, 582, 583, 617, 618, 638, 639, 641; hereditary, 228; Hohokam, 580
leadership, 20, 208, 224, 305, 319, 364, 390, 405, 464, 510, 538, 553, 554, 569, 580, 582, 617, 633, 640, 654; Algonquian, 318; Chacoan, 632; Crow, 352; early forms of, 568; Hohokam, 582; indigenous, 311; Mississippian, 441, 487; Paquimé, 654; Puebloan, 638; questions concerning Chaco, 554; ritual, 553; small-scale, 208
Lekson, Stephen, 631
Lightfoot, Kent, 8, 42, 602
Lillooet phenomenon, 176
lineages, 46, 82, 140, 160, 280, 303, 305, 315, 364, 391, 441, 477, 487, 492, 495

lithic technology, 241, 242, 289
Lower Mississippi Valley, 483
Lowie, Robert, 29

macaws, 646
Macon Plateau, 601
Madisonville horizon, 300
Mainfort, Robert, 430
maize, 45, 52, 66, 73, 79, 83, 268, 277, 290, 333, 362, 416, 443, 509, 654; and bison, 364; and relationship to Iroquoian history, 278; appearance in Michigan, 289; Chacoan, 603; Coles Creek period, 487; cooking, 81; early Southwest, 549; introduction, 81; introduction into Southwest, 563; Mesa Verde, 608; Oneota farmers, 334
maize agriculture, 56, 269, 276, 290, 299, 369, 380, 381, 403, 404, 419, 510, 516, 534, 548; as new technology, 267
maize, beans, and squash, 66, 281, 373, See squash
Malville, Nancy, 602
Mann site, 477
Maritime Tradition, 255
marriage, 135, 160, 228, 232, 243, 303, 348, 386, 387, 393, 515, 517; interethnic, 392; Plains-Mississippian, 364
marriage alliances, 135, 232, 387, 393
Mason, Ronald, 426
matrilineal, 275, 276, 392, 395
McKern classification system, 29
McKern, Will, 412
Meadowcroft, 92, 96, 448, 451
Meadowood, 127, 255
Medieval Climatic Anomaly, 204, 231, 232
memory, 536, 554
Mesa Verde, 552, 601, 608
Mesoamerica, 52, 497; indigenous knowledge of, 65
Mesoamerican symbolism, 649
Michigan, 424
Middle Missouri tradition, 360, See traditions
Middlesex funerary complex, 255
Midéwiwin, 293
migration, 13, 20, 31, 89, 94, 126, 141, 149, 151, 152, 154, 157, 158, 194, 195, 251, 255, 275, 276, 315, 352, 353, 367, 374, 380, 381, 402, 453, 456, 487, 523, 549, 550, 551, 552, 553, 608, 611, 634, 635, 641; Athapaskan, 621; Cahokian, 501; coastal, 156, 456; Crow, 353; Mesa Verde, 552; Na-Dene, 150; out of Chaco, 604; Puebloan, 611; Puebloan-Hohokam, 582; Southwest, 549, 552, See immigrants
migration hypothesis, 276
Mill Creek, 333, 360
Milwaukee Public Museum, 412
Minnesota, 328
Minthorn, Armand, 31
Missaukee Earthworks, 293, 295

Mission Santa Catalina de Guale, 41, 44, 45
missions: Cahokian, 499; Franciscan, 237; Jesuit, 424
Mississippi River: travelled by natives, 64
Mississippian, 305, 333, 417, 497, 505, 509, 538; emergence of, 516; empire, 277; related to Fort Ancient and Monongahela, 299
Mississippianization, 364, 492, 494, 526, 538
Missouri River, 360
Modoc Rock Shelter, 452
Mogollon, 563
Mojave Desert, 205
Monacans, 311
Monongahela, 297
Monte Verde, 153, 448
monumentality, 68, 488, 492, 587, 589, 591; boulder, 338
Moore, C. B., 537
mortuary practices, 45, 289, 314, 315, 489, 490, See burial practices
mound building, 437, 438, 540; Archaic, 440; as cultural narrative, 467; Poverty Point, 466
mounds, 212; California compared to Woodlands, 219; Coles Creek and Troyville, 486; effigy, 411, 556; platform, 486, 509, 538, 556, 562, 580; platform ceremonialism, 492; platform, Hohokam, 555; shell, 220, 221; Troyville, 489
Mound 72 at Cahokia, 62, 494, 504, 505, 506, 507, 526, 527, 532
Moundville, 438, 534; art, 513; chronology, 536
movement: forced, 348; human and nonhuman, 12; religious, 527; theoretically considered, 339

narratives: archaeological, 242; movements, 338
National Historic Preservation Act, 32
Native American Graves Protection and Repatriation Act, 549, See repatriation
Nelson, Nels, 43
Neoevolutionary models, 21, See evolutionism
Neolithic demographic transition, 610
Neutral Confederacy, 273
New Archaeology, 452, 537, 601
New England, 263
New York, 249
Newark earthworks, 439
Northwest Coast, 137, 150, 160, 173
Norton Tradition, 140
Numic spread, 194
nut processing, 76

Obregón, Baltazar de, 647
obsidian, 164, 173, 201, 202, 205, 206, 226, 241, 242, 356, 388, 389, 395, 444, 472
Oetelaar, Gerald, 24
oikoumene: defined, 64
Old Copper complex, 332
Oneota, 333, 403, 414

Orendorf, 528
organization: ritual, 228
Orr, Ellison, 414
ossuaries, 278, 315, 316, 377, 428, 429, See burial practices
outliers: Chaco, 600
Owens Valley, 199
Ozette, 166

Pacific Period, 164
Paisley Caves, 150, 451
palaces: critically considered, 636, See Chaco, Great Houses
Paleo-Arctic tradition, 115
Paleoeskimos, 126, 128
Paleoethnobotany, 74
Paleoindian, 82, 137, 250, 347, 448; belief systems, 103
Paleolithic, 3, 91, 115, 157
Paquimé, 53, 66, 600, 645, See Casas Grandes
Path of Souls, 54, 513
Pawnees, 56, 57, 61, 382
pax (Cahokiana, Chaco, Hopewelliana, etc.), 13
Peck 2-2 site, 298, 303
Pecos, 69, 388, 623
Pendergast, James, 258
Phoenix Basin, 571
pilgrimage, 339, 344, See California
pipes, 348, 377, 416, 505, 537, 654
Pithouse period, 175
pithouses. See architecture
place making, 12, 24; and narratives, 339; monuments, 486
Plains Village tradition, 83, See villages
Plateau region, 173
plazas, 45, 52, 67, 298–307, 366, 401, 438, 485, 489, 490, 492, 494, 495, 503, 504, 514, 517–519, 530, 534, 536, 540, 541, 550, 555, 556, 565, 566, 568, 574, 577, 581, 615, 617, 625, 636, 639; burials and shrines in, 565; Hohokam courtyard groups, 555
plurality, 519
Pocahontas, 310
polygyny, 392
population, 225; Cahokia, 401; dense, 571; movement, 519, 613; Great Lakes, 277; nonliterate societies, 203; pressure, 193; relationships to intensification, 230; trends, 175, 379, 610
portals, 338
Postclassic world, 67
postcolonial theory, 41
posts (or poles): marker, 54, 504
potlatch, 168
Potomac Creek site, 316
Potter, Stephen, 314
pottery: as metaphor for cultural entity, 286, See ceramics

Poverty Point, 12, 25, 219, 437, 440, 460, 465, 479
Powell, John Wesley, 187
power, 21, 22, 43, 44, 46, 47, 54, 56, 68, 70, 166, 168, 228, 229, 230, 231, 232, 311, 318, 327, 354, 364, 386, 390, 391, 395, 396, 401, 402, 430, 468, 486, 499, 519, 528, 537, 539, 541, 553, 554, 555, 556, 568, 580, 581, 582, 591, 598, 599, 603, 604, 616, 618, 632, 636, 638, 640, 641; political, 604; social, 327, 392
Powhatan, 310
Powhatan's Mantle, 312
practice theory, 23
practices: community, 486; culinary, 242, 266; domestic, 240; Iroquoian, 275; lithic production, 241; Mississippian, 534; new Mississippian, 538; ritual, 555; theoretically considered, 585
Pre-Clovis, 150, 153
presidios, 237
prestige goods, 12, 314, 315, 364, 603
priests, 318; Jesuit, 275; Pueblo, 636
procession, 567
production: cultural, 236
projectile points, 331; at Poverty Point, 465; Cahokia-style, 501; Desert Series, 202; Madison, 412; metal, 351; Midwestern, 412; northeast, 252; triangular, 493, See arrowheads
protohistoric, 350; Plains, 388
Pueblo IV, 633, 638
Pueblo reformation, 633
Pueblo society, 554

Quetzalcoatl, 653
Quimby, George, 423

rainfall: Southwest, 557
Ramey Incised jars, 363, 418, 501
Ramsden, Peter, 277
Rancho Petaluma, 236, 238, 239, 240
ranchos, 237
Randall, Asa, 9
Ranked societies, 168, See chiefdoms
ranking, 441, 464, 509, 539, 618; Moundville, 538
Rank-size analysis, 617
Red Paint People, 69
Red Wing, 415, 418, 419, 526
Reese River, 189
religion, 15, 19, 47, 239, 461, 497, 504, 505, 556, 557, 558, 640; Casas Grandes, 653; compared to politics, 640; Puebloan, 636, 639; Southwestern, 556, 557
repatriation, 33, 271
ritual: activities, 555, 590, 618; practice, 292, 556, 587, 639, 640
rituals, 52, 66, 67, 227, 304, 338, 339, 341, 343, 489, 492, 504, 513, 514, 534, 542, 551, 569, 598, 636, 640, 641

INDEX

Roanoke colony, 318
rock art, 228, 337, 625, 639; Gottschall, 418; Puebloan, 555
Rountree, Helen, 314

Sagard, Gabriel, 275
Sahlins, Marshall, 326
Salado ideology, 557
Sampson, Don, 32
Sandos, James, 40
Sassaman, Kenneth, 9
Savannah River valley, 511
scalping, 277
scrapers, 89, 91, 93, 242, 252, 377, 381, 388, 390, 416
seed collecting, 77, 103
seeds: starchy, 265, 288, 362, 374, 376, 443
September 11th, 335
Service, Elman, 326
settlement: organization, 67, 574, 577; patterns, 201, 204, 205, 206, 312, 373, 377, 380, 381, 408, 419, 422, 425, 437, 511, 526, 577, 610, 621
Shabik'eshchee, 604
shamans, 226, 228, 441, 505, 653, 654; and horned serpents, 654
shell beads, 173, 202, 206, 226, 231, 363, 395, 444; currency, 224, *See* beads, beadwork
shell middens, 229
shell mounds, 25, *See* mounds
Shoshone, 354, 356
Siouan languages, 416, *See* Monacans
Smith, John, 311
Snaketown, 577
Snow, Dean, 276
soapstone: cooking technology, 266
Society for American Archaeology, 32
Solutrean Traditions of Europe, 455
Sonoran Desert, 565
Southeastern Ceremonial Complex, 493
Southwest: defined, 547
specialization, 167, 224, 225, 227, 230, 232, 262, 369, 379, 381, 382, 485, 494, 550, 551, 580, 638
Spelman, Henry, 311
Spielmann, Katherine, 390
Spiro, 69, 601
squash, 66, 73, 74, 79, 80, 81, 82, 83, 269, 270, 297, 362, 379, 416, 576, 610, *See* maize, beans, and squash
St. Lawrenc: river, 422; valley, 249, 274
Steward, Julian, 20, 186
Stoltman, James, 472
storage, 14, 20, 73, 74, 76, 78, 80, 81, 166, 168, 175, 176, 179, 190, 207, 226, 229, 230, 231, 266, 293, 300, 301, 304, 305, 314, 332, 341, 360, 361, 376, 381, 394, 399, 444, 530, 540, 549, 550, 580, 582, 613, 618
Strachey, William, 311
structuration. *See* practice theory
styles: artistic, 165; hybridized, 419
Sun Dance, 57, 343

SunWatch village, 298, 305
Susquehanna tradition, 126
sweat baths and lodges, 53, 278, 504

Taylor, Walter, 21
technologies: as part of culture cores, 188
Teotihuacan, 61
territorialism, 291
Thomas, David Hurst, 189
Thule, 117, 121, 131; and Inuit descendants, 123
tipi rings, 337, 342, 343, 344, 347, 353
tobacco, 79, 80, 82, 362, 377, 416, 649, 654
Toltec (Arkansas), 438
traditions: Aleutian, 140; archaeological, 115, 117; as performed, 240; burial, 166; Central Plains, 367; ceramic, 269; Chaco, 634; Coalescent, 367; egalitarian, critically considered, 638; Hohokam, 577; Late Woodland, 485; melding of, 519; Middle Woodland, 478; Middle Missouri, 360; Plateau, 175; pre-Clovis, 150; regional, 139; Woodland, 267
travel: boats, 231; long distance, 65, *See* boats, canoes
tribalization, 404
Trigger, Bruce, 599
trincheras. *See* cerro de trincheras
Troyville, 488, 489
Turner, E. Randolph, 312
turquoise, 388

Uniformitarianism, 19
Upper Mississippi Valley, 410
Uto-Aztecan, 186

Vallejo, Mariano, 238
valuables, 12, 44, 46, 168, 387, 390, 430, *See* prestige goods
Vehik, Susan, 390
villages: circular, 303; "closing", 208; complex, multilineal, 279; early Southwestern, 615; Plains, 359, 374
violence, 14, 177, 229, 231, 359, 400, 403, 406, 445, 487, 494, 500, 505, 523, 524, 525, 526, 527, 529–531, 549, 550–552, 555, 557, 604, 614, 620, 622, 628, 634, 638, 640, *See* warfare
vision quest, 343
visuality, 589
Vivian, Gordon, 598

Walk-in Well. *See* Paquimé
Walthall, John, 455
warfare, 13, 14, 135, 140, 141, 162, 167, 168, 229, 230, 267, 269, 271, 275, 282, 360, 368, 380, 404, 407, 424, 444, 487, 490, 492, 494, 500, 516, 523, 528, 531, 555, 587, 604, 608, 613–615, 618,

620–623, 625, 627, 628, 638, 640; Orendorf; as opposed to violence, 628; assault tactics, 528; captive taking, 504; evidence, 444; evidence of, 525, 529, 556, 623; gendered patterns, 614; gendered roles, 528; Paquimé, 654; raiding, 387, 445, 500, 621; Southwestern, 613, 620; theoretically considered, 627; tribal, 621
Warren, William, 286
water symbolism: Paquimé, 649
Watson Brake, 438
weaponry: ritual, 527, *See* projectile points, arrow points

Weber, David, 40
weroances, 318, *See* leadership
Werowocomoco, 310, 316
Werowocomoco Research Group, 319
Wilber, Ken, 326
wild rice, 82, 332, 333, 411, 416
Wissler, Clark, 187
women: Plains, 387, *See* gender
Wonderley, Anthony, 281
Woodland Period, 255, 288, 471
Worth, John, 41
Wounded Knee, 350

Printed in Poland
by Amazon Fulfillment
Poland Sp. z o.o., Wrocław